WEDNESDAY 26 AUGUST 2015 NUMBER 61334
PUBLISHED BY AUTHORITY | ESTABLISHED 1665
WWW.THEGAZETTE.CO.UK

Supplement No. 1
of Tuesday 25 August 2015

List of Statutory Publications 2014

Contents

Preliminary Information	2
UK Legislation	4
Public general acts	4
Public general acts - explanatory notes	5
Local acts	6
Measures of the General Synod	7
Other statutory publications	7
Statutory Instruments, by subject heading	7
Statutory Instruments, by number	205
Subsidiary Numbers	236
Scottish Legislation	241
Acts of the Scottish Parliament	241
Acts of the Scottish Parliament - Explanatory notes	242
Other Scottish statutory publications	None listed
Scottish Statutory Instruments, by subject heading	242
Scottish Statutory Instruments, by number	268

Northern Ireland Legislation	272
Acts of the Northern Ireland Assembly	272
Acts of the Northern Ireland Assembly - explanatory notes	272
Other Northern Ireland statutory publications	273
Statutory Rules of Northern Ireland, by subject heading	273
Statutory Rules of Northern Ireland, by number	293
Welsh Assembly Legislation	296
Measures of the National Assembly for Wales	296
Acts of the National Assembly for Wales	296
Acts of the National Assembly for Wales - Explanatory notes	296
Alphabetical Index	298

Preface

Content and Layout

This list contains details of the statutory publications and accompanying explanatory documents published during the year. It is arranged in three main sections that group the primary and delegated legislation of the United Kingdom, England & Wales, Scotland and Northern Ireland (Statutory Instruments made by the National Assembly for Wales are included within the UK section). Within each section the publications are listed in the same order:

Acts and their Explanatory Notes;

Statutory Instruments or Statutory Rules, arranged under subject headings. Each entry includes, where available or appropriate: the enabling power; the date when the instrument was issued, made and laid and comes into force; a short note of any effect; territorial extent and classification; a note of the relevant EU legislation; pagination; ISBN and price;

A numerical listing of the instruments, with their subject heading. This list also includes any subsidiary numbers in the series: C for commencement orders; L for instruments relating to court fees or procedure in England and Wales; NI for Orders in Council relating only to Northern Ireland; S for instruments relating only to Scotland; W for instruments made by the National Assembly for Wales;

There is a single alphabetical, subject index.

Unpublished Statutory Instruments

Although the majority of Statutory Instruments are formally published, some SIs of limited, local application are not printed but are available online at legislation.gov.uk and are listed in this publication.

Access to Documents

The full text of all legislation and delegated legislation (Statutory Instruments) is available from the The National Archives website, www.legislation.gov.uk on the day of publication. The website contains a complete dataset from 1988 for Acts and 1987 for Statutory Instruments and partial datasets for earlier years.

The full text of the general statutory instruments and statutory rules are also published in the respective annual editions of: Statutory Instruments, Scottish Statutory Instruments, Statutory Instruments made by the National Assembly for Wales and Statutory Rules of Northern Ireland.

Copies of legislation and published delegated legislation can be purchased from the addresses on the back cover.

Copies of non-print instruments unobtainable from The Stationery Office may be obtained from:

The National Archives, Kew, Richmond, Surrey, TW9 4DU (from 1922 onwards – except for the years 1942, 1950, 1951 and up to SI no. 940 of 1952). Please quote repository reference TS37

British Library, Official Publications and Social Sciences Service, 96 Euston Road, London, NW1 2DB (as before, up to 1980)

Belfast Statutory Publications Office, Castle Buildings, Stormont, Belfast, BT4 3SR (non-print Statutory Rules)

Standing Orders

Standing orders can be set up to ensure the receipt of all statutory publications in a particular subject area, without the need to continually scan lists of new publications or place individual orders. The subject categories used can be either broad or very specific. For more information please contact the TSO Standing Orders department on 0870 600 5522, or fax: 0870 600 5533.

Copyright

Legislation from official sources is reproducible freely under waiver of copyright. Full details of which can be found at:
http://www.nationalarchives.gov.uk/doc/open-government-licence/

Most other TSO publications are Crown or Parliamentary copyright. Information about the licensing arrangements for Crown and Parliamentary copyright can be found on The National Archives' website at
http://www.nationalarchives.gov.uk/doc/open-government-licence/.

To find out more about licensing please contact:

Information Policy Team

The National Archives

Kew, Richmond, Surrey

TW9 4DU

psi@nationalarchives.gsi.gov.uk

List of Abbreviations

accord.	accordance
art(s).	article(s)
c.	chapter
C.	Commencement
CI.	Channel Islands
E.	England
EC	European Commission
EU	European Union
G.	Guernsey
GB.	Great Britain
GLA	Greater London Authority
IOM	Isle of Man
J.	Jersey
L.	Legal: fees or procedure in courts in E. & W.
NI.	Northern Ireland
para(s).	paragraph(s)
reg(s).	regulation(s)
s(s).	section(s)
S.	Scotland
sch(s).	schedule(s)
SI.	Statutory instrument(s)
SR.	Statutory rule(s) of Northern Ireland
SR & O.	Statutory rules and orders
SSI	Scottish Statutory Instrument
UK.	United Kingdom
W.	Wales

UK LEGISLATION

Acts

Public General Acts 2013

Crime and Courts Act 2013 (correction slip): Chapter 22. - 1 sheet: 30 cm. - Correction slip (to ISBN 9780105422136) dated March 2014. - Free

Financial Services (Banking Reform) Act 2013 (correction slip): Chapter 33. - 1 sheet: 30 cm. - Correction slip (to ISBN 9780105433132) dated March 2014. - Free

Public General Acts 2014

Anti-Social Behaviour, Crime and Policing Act 2014: Chapter 12. - ix, 232p.: 30 cm. - Royal assent, 13 March 2014. An Act to make provision about anti-social behaviour, crime and disorder, including provision about recovery of possession of dwelling-houses; to make provision amending the Dangerous Dogs Act 1991, the Police Act 1997, Schedules 7 and 8 to the Terrorism Act 2000, the Extradition Act 2003 and Part 3 of the Police Reform and Social Responsibility Act 2011; to make provision about firearms, about sexual harm and violence and about forced marriage; to make provision about the police, the Independent Police Complaints Commission and the Serious Fraud Office; to make provision about invalid travel documents; to make provision about criminal justice and court fees. Explanatory notes to assist in the understanding of the Act are available separately (ISBN 9780105612148). With correction slip dated August 2014. - 978-0-10-541214-4 £28.75

Care Act 2014: Chapter 23. - vii, 157p.: 30 cm. - Royal assent, 14 May 2014. An Act make provision to reform the law relating to care and support for adults and the law relating to support for carers; to make provision about safeguarding adults from abuse or neglect; to make provision about care standards; to establish and make provision about Health Education England; to establish and make provision about the Health Research Authority; to make provision about integrating care and support with health services. Explanatory notes to assist in the understanding of the Act are available separately (ISBN 9780105623144). - 978-0-10-542314-0 £23.25

Childcare Payments Act 2014: Chapter 28. - [iii], 47p.: 30 cm. - Royal Assent, 17 December 2014. An Act to make provision with the making of payments to persons towards the costs of childcare; and to restrict the availability of an exemption from income tax in respect of the provision for an employee of childcare, or vouchers for obtaining childcare, under a scheme operated by or on behalf of the employer. Explanatory notes to assist in the understanding of the Act are available separately (ISBN 9780105628149). - 978-0-10-542814-5 £9.75

Children and Families Act 2014: Chapter 6. - vii, 241p.: 30 cm. - Royal assent, 13 March 2014. An Act to make provision about children, families, and people with special educational needs or disabilities; to make provision about the right to request flexible working. Explanatory notes to assist in the understanding of the Act are available separately (ISBN 9780105606147). - 978-0-10-540614-3 £28.75

Citizenship (Armed Forces) Act 2014: Chapter 8. - [8]p.: 30 cm. - Royal assent, 13 March 2014. An Act to make provision in connection with applications for naturalisation as a British citizen made by members or former members of the armed forces. Explanatory notes to assist in the understanding of the Act will be available separately. - 978-0-10-540814-7 £4.00

Co-operative and Community Benefit Societies Act 2014: Chapter 14. - viii, 123p.: 30 cm. - Royal assent, 14 May 2014. An Act to consolidate certain enactments relating to co-operative societies, community benefit societies and other societies registered or treated as registered under the Industrial and Provident Societies Act 1965, with amendments to give effect to recommendations of the Law Commission and the Scottish Law Commission. Explanatory notes to assist in the understanding of the Act will be available separately. - 978-0-10-541414-8 £20.75

Data Retention and Investigatory Powers Act 2014: Chapter 27. - [2], 8, [1]p.: 30 cm. - Royal assent, 17 July 2014. An Act to make provision, in consequence of a declaration of invalidity made by the Court of Justice of the European Union in relation to Directive 2006/24/EC, about the retention of certain communications data; to amend the grounds for issuing interception warrants, or granting or giving certain authorisations or notices, under Part 1 of the Regulation of Investigatory Powers Act 2000; to make provision about the extra-territorial application of that Part and about the meaning of 'telecommunications service' for the purposes of that Act; to make provision about additional reports by the Interception of Communications Commissioner; to make provision about a review of the operation and regulation of investigatory powers. Explanatory notes to assist in the understanding of the Act are available separately (ISBN 97801056271). - 978-0-10-542714-8 £6.00

Deep Sea Mining Act 2014: Chapter 15. - [2], 9p.: 30 cm. - Royal assent, 14 May 2014. An Act to make provision about deep sea mining. Explanatory notes to assist in the understanding of the Act are available separately (ISBN 9780105615149). - 978-0-10-541514-5 £6.00

Defence Reform Act 2014: Chapter 20. - iii, 54p.: 30 cm. - Royal assent, 14 May 2014. An Act to make provision in connection with any arrangements that may be made by the Secretary of State with respect to the provision to the Secretary of State of defence procurement services; to make provision relating to defence procurement contracts awarded, or amended, otherwise than as the result of a competitive process; to make provision in relation to the reserve forces of the Crown. Explanatory notes to assist in the understanding of the Act are available separately (ISBN 9780105620143). - 978-0-10-542014-9 £10.00

European Union (Approvals) Act 2014: Chapter 3. - [8]p.: 30 cm. - Royal assent, 30th January 2014. An Act to make provision approving for the purposes of section 8 of the European Union Act 2011 certain draft decisions under Article 352 of the Treaty on the Functioning of the European Union. Explanatory notes to assist in the understanding of the Act will be available separately. - 978-0-10-540314-2 £4.00

Finance Act 2014: Chapter 26. - xv, 646p.: 30 cm. - Royal assent, 17 July 2014. An Act to grant certain duties, to alter other duties, and to amend the law relating to the National Debt and the Public Revenue, and to make further provision in connection with finance. Explanatory notes to the Act are available separately (ISBN 9780105626145). - 978-0-10-542614-1 £57.75

Gambling (Licensing and Advertising) Act 2014: Chapter 17. - [2], 4p.: 30 cm. - Royal assent, 14 May 2014. An Act to make provision about the licensing and advertising of gambling. Explanatory notes to assist in the understanding of the Act are available separately (ISBN 9780105617143). - 978-0-10-541714-9 £6.00

House of Lords Reform Act 2014 : Chapter 24. - [1], 4p.: 30 cm. - Royal assent, 14 May 2014. An Act to make provision for resignation from the House of Lords; and to make provision for the expulsion of Members of the House of Lords in specified circumstances. Explanatory notes to assist in the understanding of the Act are available separately (ISBN 9780105624141). - 978-0-10-542414-7 £6.00

Immigration Act 2014: Chapter 22. - v, 129p.: 30 cm. - Royal assent, 14th May 2014. An Act make provision about immigration law; to limit, or otherwise make provision about, access to services, facilities and employment by reference to immigration status; to make provision about marriage and civil partnership involving certain foreign nationals. Explanatory notes to assist in the understanding of the Act are available separately (ISBN 9780105622147). - 978-0-10-542214-3 £20.75

Inheritance and Trustees' Powers Act 2014: Chapter 16. - [2], 14p.: 30 cm. - Royal assent, 14 May 2014. An Act to make further provision about the distribution of estates of deceased persons and to amend the law relating to the powers of trustees. Explanatory notes to assist in the understanding of the Act are available separately (ISBN 9780105616146). - 978-0-10-541614-2 £6.00

Intellectual Property Act 2014: Chapter 18. - ii, 25p.: 30 cm. - Royal assent, 14 May 2014. An Act to make provision about intellectual property. Explanatory notes to assist in the understanding of the Act are available separately (ISBN 9780105618140). - 978-0-10-541814-6 £6.00

PUBLIC GENERAL ACTS - EXPLANATORY NOTES 2014

International Development (Gender Equality) Act 2014: Chapter 9. - [8]p.: 30 cm. - Royal assent, 13 March 2014. An Act to promote gender equality in the provision by the Government of development assistance and humanitarian assistance to countries outside the United Kingdom. Explanatory notes to assist in the understanding of the Act are available separately (ISBN 9780105609148). - 978-0-10-540914-4 £4.00

Leasehold Reform (Amendment) Act 2014: Chapter 10. - [8]p.: 30 cm. - Royal assent, 13 March 2014. An Act to amend the Leasehold Reform, Housing and Urban Development Act 1993 in relation to the permitted signatories of notices. Explanatory notes to assist in the understanding of the Act are available separately (ISBN 9780105610144). - 978-0-10-541014-0 £4.00

Local Audit and Accountability Act 2014: Chapter 2. - iii, 113p.: 30 cm. - Royal assent, 30 January 2014. An Act to make provision for and in connection with the abolition of the Audit Commission for Local Authorities and the National Health Service in England; to make provision about the accounts of local and certain other public authorities and the auditing of those accounts; to make provision about the appointment, functions and regulation of local auditors; to make provision about data matching; to make provision about examinations by the Comptroller and Auditor General relating to English local and other public authorities; to make provision about the publication of information by smaller authorities; to make provision about compliance with codes of practice on local authority publicity; to make provision about access to meetings and documents of local government bodies; to make provision about council tax referendums; to make provision about polls consequent on parish meetings. Explanatory notes to assist in the understanding of the Act are available separately (ISBN 9780105602149). - 978-0-10-540214-5 £18.50

Mesothelioma Act 2014: Chapter 1. - ii, 16p.: 30 cm. - Royal assent, 30 January 2014. An Act to establish a Diffuse Mesothelioma Payment Scheme and make related provision; and to make provision about the resolution of certain insurance disputes. Explanatory notes to assist in the understanding of the Act will be available separately. - 978-0-10-540114-8 £5.75

National Insurance Contributions Act 2014: Chapter 7. - [1], ii, 24p.: 30 cm. - Royal assent, 13 March 2014. An Act to make provision in relation to national insurance contributions. Explanatory notes to assist in the understanding of the Act is available separately (ISBN 9780105607144). - 978-0-10-540714-0 £5.75

Northern Ireland (Miscellaneous Provisions) Act 2014: Chapter 13. - [1], ii, 22p.: 30 cm. - Royal assent, 13 March 2014. An Act to make provision about donations, loans and related transactions for political purposes in connection with Northern Ireland; to amend the Northern Ireland Assembly Disqualification Act 1975 and the Northern Ireland Act 1998; to make provision about the registration of electors and the administration of elections in Northern Ireland; and to make miscellaneous amendments in the law relating to Northern Ireland. Explanatory notes to assist in the understanding of the Act are available separately (ISBN 9780105613145). - 978-0-10-541314-1 £5.75

Offender Rehabilitation Act 2014: Chapter 11. - ii, 45p.: 30 cm. - Royal assent, 13 March 2014. An Act to make provision about the release, and supervision after release, of offenders; to make provision about the extension period for extended sentence prisoners; to make provision about community orders and suspended sentence orders. Explanatory notes to assist in the understanding of the Act are available separately (ISBN 9780105611141). - 978-0-10-541114-7 £9.75

Pensions Act 2014: Chapter 19. - iv, 117p.: 30 cm. - Royal assent, 14 May 2014. An Act to make provision about pensions and about benefits payable to people in connection with bereavement. Explanatory notes to assist in the understanding of the Act are available separately (ISBN 9780105619147). - 978-0-10-541914-3 £19.00

Supply and Appropriation Act 2014: Chapter 5. - ii, 88, [4]p.: 30 cm. - Royal assent, 13 March 2014. An Act to authorise the use of resources for the years ending with 31 March 2008, 31 March 2009, 31 March 2010, 31 March 2011, 31 March 2012, 31 March 2013, 31 March 2014 and 31 March 2015; to authorise the issue of sums out of the Consolidated Fund for the years ending with 31 March 2013, 31 March 2014 and 31 March 2015; and to appropriate the supply authorised by this Act for the years ending with 31 March 2008, 31 March 2009, 31 March 2010, 31 March 2011, 31 March 2012, 31 March 2013 and 31 March 2014. - 978-0-10-540514-6 £15.50

Supply and Appropriation (Main Estimates) Act 2014: Chapter 25. - [1], 77p.: 30 cm. - Royal assent, 17 July 2014. An Act to authorise the use of resources for the year ending with 31 March 2015; to authorise both the issue of sums out of the Consolidated Fund and the application of income for that year; and to appropriate the supply authorised for that year by this Act and by the Supply and Appropriation (Anticipation and Adjustments) Act 2014. - 978-0-10-542514-4 £14.25

Taxation of Pensions Act 2014: Chapter 30. - [ii], 78p.: 30 cm. - Royal Assent, 17 December 2014. An Act to make provision in connection with the taxation of pensions. Explanatory notes to assist in the understanding of the Act are available separately (ISBN 9780105630142). - 978-0-10-543014-8 £9.75

Transparency of Lobbying, Non-Party Campaigning and Trade Union Administration Act 2014: Chapter 4. - iii, 67p.: 30 cm. - Royal assent, 30 January 2014. An Act to make provision for establishing and maintaining a register of persons carrying on the business of consultant lobbying and to require those persons to be entered in the register; to make provision about expenditure and donations for political purposes; to make provision about the Electoral Commission's functions with respect to compliance with requirements imposed by or by virtue of enactments; to make provision relating to a trade union's duty to maintain a register of members under section 24 of the Trade Union and Labour Relations (Consolidation) Act 1992. Explanatory notes to assist in the understanding of the Act are available separately (ISBN 9780105604143)- 978-0-10-540414-9 £13.75

Wales Act 2014: Chapter 29. - [ii], 39p.: 30 cm. - Royal assent, 17 December 2014. An Act to make provision about elections to and membership of the National Assembly for Wales; to make provision about the Welsh Assembly Government; to make provision about the setting by the Assembly of rates of income tax to be paid by Welsh taxpayers and about the devolution of taxation powers to the Assembly; to make related amendments to Part 4A of the Scotland Act 1998; to make provision about borrowing by the Welsh Ministers; to make miscellaneous amendments in the law relating to Wales. Explanatory notes to assist in the understanding of the Act are available separately (ISBN 9780105629146). - 978-0-10-542914-2 £9.75

Water Act 2014: Chapter 21. - v, 248p.: 30 cm. - Royal assent, 14 May 2014. An Act to make provision about the water industry; about compensation for modification of licences to abstract water; about main river maps; about records of waterworks; for the regulation of the water environment; about the provision of flood insurance for household premises; about internal drainage boards; about Regional Flood and Coastal Committees. Explanatory notes to assist in the understanding of the Act are available separately (ISBN 9780105621140). - 978-0-10-542114-6 £29.75

Public General Acts - Explanatory Notes 2013

Energy Act 2013: Chapter 32: explanatory notes. - 106p.: 30 cm. - These notes refer to the Energy Act 2013 (c. 32) (ISBN 9780105432135) which received Royal assent on 18 December 2013. - 978-0-10-563213-9 £16.00

Financial Services (Banking Reform) Act 2013: Chapter 33: explanatory notes. - 61p.: 30 cm. - These notes refer to the Financial Services (Banking Reform) Act 2013 (c. 33) (ISBN 9780105433132) which received Royal assent on 18 December 2013. - 978-0-10-563313-6 £10.75

Public General Acts - Explanatory Notes 2014

Anti-Social Behaviour, Crime and Policing Act 2014: Chapter 12: explanatory notes. - 111p.: 30 cm. - These notes refer to the Anti-Social Behaviour, Crime and Policing Act 2014 (c. 12) (ISBN 9780105412144) which received Royal assent on 13 March 2014. - 978-0-10-561214-8 £16.00

Care Act 2014: Chapter 23: explanatory notes. - 108p.: 30 cm. - These notes refer to the Care Act 2014 (c. 23) (ISBN 9780105423140) which received Royal assent on 14 May 2014. - 978-0-10-562314-4 £16.50

Childcare Payments Act 2014: Chapter 28: explanatory notes. - [41]p.: 30 cm. - These notes refer to the Childcare Payments Act 2014 (c.28) (ISBN 9780105428145) which received Royal Assent on 17 December 2014. - 978-0-10-562814-9 £9.75

Children and Families Act 2014: Chapter 6: explanatory notes. - 125p.: 30 cm. - These notes refer to the Children and Families Act 2014 (c. 6) (ISBN 9780105406143) which received Royal assent on 13 March 2014. - 978-0-10-560614-7 £18.50

Data Retention and Investigatory Powers Act 2014: Chapter 27: explanatory notes. - 11p.: 30 cm. - These notes refer to the Data Retention and Investigatory Powers Act 2014 (c. 27) (ISBN 9780105427148) which received Royal assent on 17 July 2014. - 978-0-10-562714-2 £6.00

Deep Sea Mining Act 2014: Chapter 15: explanatory notes. - [8]p.: 30 cm. - These notes refer to the Deep Sea Mining Act 2014 (c. 15) (ISBN 9780105415145) which received Royal assent on 14 May 2014. - 978-0-10-561514-9 £6.00

Defence Reform Act 2014: Chapter 20: explanatory notes. - 32p.: 30 cm. - These notes refer to the Defence Reform Act 2014 (c. 20) (ISBN 9780105420149) which received Royal assent on 14 May 2014. - 978-0-10-562014-3 £10.00

Gambling (Licensing and Advertising) Act 2014: Chapter 17: explanatory notes. - [12]p.: 30 cm. - These notes refer to the Gambling (Licensing and Advertising) Act 2014 (c. 17) (ISBN 9780105417149) which received Royal assent on 14 May 2014. - 978-0-10-561714-3 £6.00

House of Lords Reform Act 2014 : Chapter 24: explanatory notes. - [12]p.: 30 cm. - These notes refer to the House of Lords Reform Act 2014 (c. 24) (ISBN 9780105424147) which received Royal assent on 14 May 2014. - 978-0-10-562414-1 £6.00

Immigration Act 2014: Chapter 22: explanatory notes. - 60p.: 30 cm. - These notes refer to the Immigration Act 2014 (c. 22) (ISBN 9780105422143) which received Royal assent on 14 May 2014. - 978-0-10-562214-7 £11.00

Inheritance and Trustees' Powers Act 2014: Chapter 16: explanatory notes. - 18, [1]p.: 30 cm. - These notes refer to the Intellectual Inheritance and Trustees' Powers Act 2014 (c. 16) (ISBN 9780105416142) which received Royal assent on 14 May 2014. - 978-0-10-561614-6 £5.75

Intellectual Property Act 2014: Chapter 18: explanatory notes. - 20p.: 30 cm. - These notes refer to the Intellectual Property Act 2014 (c. 18) (ISBN 9780105418146) which received Royal assent on 14 May 2014. - 978-0-10-561814-0 £6.00

International Development (Gender Equality) Act 2014: Chapter 9: explanatory notes. - [8]p.: 30 cm. - These notes refer to the International Development (Gender Equality) Act 2014 (c. 9) (ISBN 9780105409144) which received Royal assent on 13 March 2014. - 978-0-10-560914-8 £4.00

Leasehold Reform (Amendment) Act 2014: Chapter 10: explanatory notes. - [8]p.: 30 cm. - These notes refer to the Leasehold Reform (Amendment) Act 2014 (c. 10) (ISBN 9780105410140) which received Royal assent on 13 March 2014. - 978-0-10-561014-4 £4.00

Local Audit and Accountability Act 2014: Chapter 2: explanatory notes. - 36p.: 30 cm. - These notes refer to the Local Audit and Accountability Act 2014 (c. 2) (ISBN 9780105402145) which received Royal assent on 30 January 2014. - 978-0-10-560214-9 £9.75

National Insurance Contributions Act 2014: Chapter 7: explanatory notes. - 22p.: 30 cm. - These notes refer to the National Insurance Contributions Act 2014 (c. 7) (ISBN 9780105407140) which received Royal assent on 13 March 2014. - 978-0-10-560714-4 £6.00

Northern Ireland (Miscellaneous Provisions) Act 2014: Chapter 13: explanatory notes. - 23p.: 30 cm. - These notes refer to the Northern Ireland (Miscellaneous Provisions) Act 2014 (c. 13) (ISBN 9780105413141) which received Royal assent on 13 March 2014. - 978-0-10-561314-5 £5.75

Offender Rehabilitation Act 2014: Chapter 11: explanatory notes. - 28p.: 30 cm. - These notes refer to the Offender Rehabilitation Act 2014 (c. 11) (ISBN 9780105411147) which received Royal assent on 13 March 2014. - 978-0-10-561114-1 £5.75

Pensions Act 2014: Chapter 19: explanatory notes. - 35p.: 30 cm. - These notes refer to the Intellectual Pensions Act 2014 (c. 19) (ISBN 9780105419143) which received Royal assent on 14 May 2014. - 978-0-10-561914-7 £10.00

Taxation of Pensions Act 2014: Chapter 30: explanatory notes. - [42]p.: 30 cm. - These notes refer to the Taxation of Pensions Act 2014 (c.30) (ISBN 9780105630142) which received Royal Assent on 17 December 2014. - 978-0-10-563014-2 £9.75

Transparency of Lobbying, Non-Party Campaigning and Trade Union Administration Act 2014: Chapter 4: explanatory notes. - 30p.: 30 cm. - These notes refer to the Transparency of Lobbying, Non-Party Campaigning and Trade Union Administration Act 2014 (c. 4) (ISBN 9780105404149) which received Royal assent on 30 January 2014. - 978-0-10-560414-3 £9.75

Wales Act 2014: Chapter 29: explanatory notes. - [32]p.: 30 cm. - These notes refer to the Wales Act 2014 (c.29) (ISBN 9780105629146) which received Royal Assent on 17 December 2014. - 978-0-10-562914-6 £9.75

Water Act 2014: Chapter 21: explanatory notes. - 67p.: 30 cm. - These notes refer to the Water Act 2014 (c. 21) (ISBN 9780105421146) which received Royal assent on 14 May 2014. - 978-0-10-562114-0 £11.00

Local Acts 2013

City of London (Various Powers) Act 2013: Chapter vii. - [2], 12p.: 30 cm. - Royal assent, 18 December 2013. An Act to amend the provision for the control of street trading in the City of London; to make provision relating to City walkways; and for related purposes. - This is a corrected version of that issued on 3 January 2014 (same ISBN): page 1 numbering of sub-paragraph (5) was incorrect. It is being issued free of charge to all known recipients of the original. - 978-0-10-545728-2 £5.75

Humber Bridge Act 2013: Chapter vi. - [2], 14p.: 30 cm. - Royal assent, 18 December 2013. An Act to amend the constitution of the Humber Bridge Board and to confer new borrowing and other powers on it; to make new provision for the recovery of any deficit of the Board from local authorities in the area; to confer new powers for the setting and revision of tolls and to make other provision for and in connection with the operation of the bridge; and for connected purposes. - 978-0-10-545718-3 £5.75

London Local Authorities and Transport for London Act 2013: Chapter v. - [1], ii, 15p.: 30 cm. - Royal assent, 18 December 2013. An Act to confer powers upon local authorities in London and upon Transport for London; and for related purposes. This is a corrected reprint replacing the original (published 03.01.2014) and an earlier reprint issued 17.02.2014. - 978-0-10-545738-1 £5.75

Local Acts 2014

Buckinghamshire County Council (Filming on Highways) Act 2014: Chapter ii. - [8]p.: 30 cm. - Royal assent, 17 December 2014. Buckinghamshire County Council (Filming on Highways) Act 2014. An Act to confer powers on Buckinghamshire County Council in relation to filming on highways. - Corrected reprint. Please note this Act was originally published on 22nd December 2014, but did not appear in the Daily List. - 978-0-10-545798-5 £4.25

Hertfordshire County Council (Filming on Highways) Act 2014: Chapter i. - [8]p.: 30 cm. - Royal assent, 30 January 2014. Hertfordshire County Council (Filming on Highways) Act 2014. An Act to confer powers on Hertfordshire County Council in relation to filming on highways. - Corrected reprint. Please note this Act was originally published on 14th February 2014, this corrected reprint is being issued free of charge to all known recipients of that Act. - 978-0-10-545748-0 £4.25

MEASURES OF THE GENERAL SYNOD

Measures of the General Synod 2014

1   Church of England (Miscellaneous Provisions) Measure 2014 - ii, 29p.: 30 cm. - Royal Assent, 14 May 2014. A Measure passed by the General Synod of the Church of England to amend section 67 of the Ecclesiastical Commissioners Act 1840; to amend section 25 of the Burial Act 1857; to amend section 5 of the Episcopal Endowments and Stipends Measure 1943; to amend the Church Commissioners Measure 1947; to amend the Parochial Church Councils (Powers) Measure 1956; to amend the Clergy Pensions Measure 1961; to amend sections 2 and 3 of the Ecclesiastical Jurisdiction Measure 1963; to amend section 3 of the Faculty Jurisdiction Measure 1964; to amend the Overseas and Other Clergy (Ministry and Ordination) Measure 1967; to amend the Synodical Government Measure 1969; to amend the Endowments and Glebe Measure 1976; to amend the Incumbents (Vacation of Benefices) Measure 1977; to amend the Patronage (Benefices) Measure 1986; to amend the Care of Churches and Ecclesiastical Jurisdiction Measure 1991; to amend the Cathedrals Measure 1999; to confer power on chancellors to determine fees; to extend the powers of the General Cemetery Company; to make provision for Christ Church, Oxford; to make provision for the tenure of office of vicars general and surrogates; to amend the Dioceses Pastoral and Mission Measure 2007; to make minor and consequential amendments to other enactments. - 978-0-10-545788-6 £10.00

2   Bishops and Priests (Consecration and Ordination of Women) Measure 2014 - [4], 3p.: 30 cm. - A Measure passed by the General Synod of the Church of England to make provision for the consecration of women as bishops and for the continuation of provision for the ordination of women as priests; to repeal the Priests (Ordination of Women) Measure 1993. The Priest (Ordination of Women) Measure 1993 is repealed & the Equality Act 2010 amended. - 978-0-10-855731-6 £3.00

Other statutory publications

Her Majesty's Stationery Office.

Chronological table of the statutes [1235-2013]. - 3v. (xiii, 3058p.): hdbk: 25 cm. - 3 vols. not sold separately. Part 1: Covering the acts of the Parliaments of England, Great Britain and the United Kingdom from 1235 to the end of 1968; Part 2: Covering the acts of the Parliaments of the United Kingdom from 1969 to the end of 1992; Part 3: Covering the Acts of the Parliaments of the United Kingdom from 1993 to the end of 2013, the acts of the Parliaments of Scotland from 1424 to 1707, the acts of the Scottish Parliament from 1999 to the end of 2013, the acts of the National Assembly for Wales passed from 2012 to 2013, the Measures of the National Assembly for Wales from 2008 to 2011 and the Church Assembly measures and General Synod measures from 1920 to the end of 2013. - 978-0-11-840547-8 £430.75 per set

Statutory Instruments

Arranged by Subject Headings

Acquisition of land, England

The Home Loss Payments (Prescribed Amounts) (England) Regulations 2014 No. 2014/1966. - Enabling power: Land Compensation Act 1973, s. 30 (5). - Issued: 30.07.2014. Made: 23.07.2014. Laid: 28.07.2014. Coming into force: 01.10.2014. Effect: S.I. 2008/1598 revoked with savings. Territorial extent & classification: E. General. - 2p.: 30 cm. - 978-0-11-111927-3 £4.25

Aggregates levy

The Aggregates Levy (Registration and Miscellaneous Provisions) (Amendment) Regulations 2014 No. 2014/836. - Enabling power: Finance Act 2001, ss. 24 (4), 45 (5). - Issued: 02.04.2014. Made: 27.03.2014. Laid: 28.03.2014. Coming into force: 01.04.2014. Effect: S.I. 2001/4027 amended. Territorial extent & classification: E/W/S/NI. General. - 2p.: 30 cm. - 978-0-11-111291-5 £4.00

The Revenue and Customs (Amendment of Appeal Provisions for Out of Time Reviews) Order 2014 No. 2014/1264. - Enabling power: Finance Act 2008, s. 124 (1) (2) (6) (7) (b). - Issued: 21.05.2014. Made: 14.05.2014. Coming into force: In accord. with art. 1 (2). Effect: 1994 c.9, c.23; 1996 c.8; 2000 c.17; 2001 c.9; 2003 c.14; S.I. 2003/3102; 2007/1509, 2157, 3298 amended. Territorial extent & classification: E/W/S/NI. General. - Supersedes draft SI (ISBN 9780111112991) issued 03/04/14. - 8p.: 30 cm. - 978-0-11-111499-5 £6.00

Agricultural employment, England

The Enterprise and Regulatory Reform Act 2013 (Commencement No. 4 and Saving Provision) (Amendment) Order 2014 No. 2014/824 (C.33). - Enabling power: Enterprise and Regulatory Reform Act 2013, s. 103 (3) (4). Bringing into operation various provisions of the 2013 Act on 31.03.2014, 30.09.2014, in accord. with art. 2. - Issued: 01.04.2014. Made: 26.03.2014. Effect: S.I. 2013/2979 (C.122) amended. Territorial extent & classification: E. General. - 4p.: 30 cm. - 978-0-11-111282-3 £4.00

The Enterprise and Regulatory Reform Act 2013 (Commencement No. 7 and Amendment) Order 2014 No. 2014/2481. - Enabling power: Enterprise and Regulatory Reform Act 2013, ss. 100, 103 (3) (4). Bringing into operation various provisions of the 2013 Act on 15.09.2014, 31.12.2014, in accord. with art. 2 & 3A. - Issued: 23.09.2014. Made: 14.09.2014. Effect: S.I. 2013/1455 (C.55), 2979 (C.122) amended. Territorial extent & classification: E. General. - 4p.: 30 cm. - 978-0-11-112092-7 £4.25

Agriculture

The Agriculture (Miscellaneous Revocations) Regulations 2014 No. 2014/1902. - Enabling power: European Communities Act 1972, s. 2 (2). - Issued: 23.07.2014. Made: 15.07.2014. Laid: 21.07.2014. Coming into force: 20.08.2014. Effect: S.I. 1973/1642; 1977/1304; 1980/124, 1394; 1988/1001, 1267; 1989/576, 1823; 1992/695; 1995/184 & S.R. 1992/190 revoked. Territorial extent & classification: E/W/S/NI. General. - 2p.: 30 cm. - 978-0-11-111867-2 £4.25

The Common Agricultural Policy (Competent Authority and Coordinating Body) Regulations 2014 No. 2014/3260. - Enabling power: European Communities Act 1972, s. 2 (2). - Issued: 16.12.2014. Made: 08.12.2014. Laid: 11.12.2014. Coming into force: 01.01.2015. Effect: S.I. 2001/3020 revoked. Territorial extent & classification: E/W/S/NI. General. - 4.: 30 cm. - 978-0-11-112523-6 £4.25

The Common Agricultural Policy (Control and Enforcement, Cross-Compliance, Scrutiny of Transactions and Appeals) Regulations 2014 No. 2014/3263. - Enabling power: European Communities Act 1972, s. 2 (2), sch. 2 para. 1A & Finance Act 1973, s. 56 (1). - Issued: 17.12.2014. Made: 09.12.2014. Laid: 11.12.2014. Coming into force: 01.15.2015. Effect: 27 SIs, revoked. Territorial extent & classification: E/W/S/NI. General. - 44p.: 30 cm. - 978-0-11-112526-7 £10.00

The Public Bodies (Abolition of Food from Britain) Order 2014 No. 2014/1924. - Enabling power: Public Bodies Act 2011, ss. 1 (1), 6 (1) (5), 24 (1), 35 (2). - Issued: 25.07.2014. Made: 17.07.2014. Coming into force: 18.07.2014 & 19.07.2014, in accord. with art. 1. Effect: 1967 c.13, 22; 1975 c.24, 25; 1986 c.49; 2000 c.36; 2002 asp 11; 2006 c.16; 2011 c.24 partially repealed & 1983 c.3 repealed & S.I. 1991/1997; 1993/1572; 1999/1319, 1747; 2001/1294; 2002/794; 2002/2812 (C.86), 2843; 2003/1326; 2008/948 partially revoked & S.I. 1983/366 (C.13); 1986/1596 (C.57) 1998/879 (C.19) revoked. Territorial extent & classification: E/W/S/NI. General. - Supersedes draft S.I. (ISBN 9780111114599) issued 09.05.2014. - 8p.: 30 cm. - 978-0-11-111897-9 £4.25

The Scotland Act 1998 (Modification of Functions) Order 2014 No. 2014/2753 (S.3). - Enabling power: Scotland Act 1998, ss. 106, 112 (1). - Issued: 20.10.2014. Made: 13.10.2014. Laid: 15.10.2014. Coming into force: 01.03.2015. Effect: None. Territorial extent & classification: E/W/S/NI. General. - 4p.: 30 cm. - 978-0-11-112184-9 £4.25

The Seeds and Vegetable Plant Material (Nomenclature Changes) Regulations 2014 No. 2014/487. - Enabling power: Plant Varieties and Seeds Act 1964, ss. 16 (1) (1A) & European Communities Act 1972, s. 2 (2). - Issued: 11.03.2014. Made: 04.03.2014. Laid: 06.03.2014. Coming into force: 31.03.2014. Effect: S.I. 1995/2652; 2001/3510; 2011/463 amended. Territorial extent and classification: E/W/S/NI. General. - EC note: These regulations implement Commission Implementing Directive 2013/45/EU amending Council Directives 2002/55/EC and 2008/72/EC and Commission Directive 2009/145/EC. - 4p.: 30 cm. - 978-0-11-111091-1 £4.00

Agriculture, England

The Common Agricultural Policy Basic Payment and Support Schemes (England) Regulations 2014 No. 2014/3259. - Enabling power: European Communities Act 1972, s. 2 (2). - Issued: 16.12.2014. Made: 08.12.2014. Laid: 11.12.2014. Coming into force: 01.01.2015. Effect: S.I. 2010/540 revoked with saving & S.I. 2009/1771; 2013/3027 revoked. Territorial extent & classification: E. General. - 8p.: 30 cm. - 978-0-11-112522-9 £6.00

The Official Feed and Food Controls (England) and the Food Safety and Hygiene (England) (Amendment) Regulations 2014 No. 2014/2748. - Enabling power: European Communities Act 1972, s. 2 (2), sch. 2, para. 1A. - Issued: 20.10.2014. Made: 13.10.2014. Laid: 17.10.2014. Coming into force: 11.11.2014. Effect: S.I. 2009/3255; 2013/2996 amended. Territorial extent & classification: E. General- EC note: These Regulations provide for the enforcement of Commission Reg (EU) no. 704/2014 on certification requirements for imports into Union of sprouts and seeds intended for the production of sprouts. These Regs also provide for the enforcement of Commission Reg (EU) no. 579/2014 granting derogation from certain provisions of Annex II to Reg (EC) no. 852/2004. These Regs also provide for the enforcement of Commission Reg (EU) no. 218/2014. - 4p.: 30 cm. - 978-0-11-112181-8 £4.25

The Uplands Transitional Payment Regulations 2014 No. 2014/112. - Enabling power: European Communities Act 1972, s. 2 (2). - Issued: 29.01.2014. Made: 21.01.2014. Laid: 24.01.2014. Coming into force: 14.02.2014. Effect: S.I. 2009/138 revoked. Territorial extent & classification: E. General. - EC note: These Regulations partially implement Council Regulation (EC) no. 1698/2005 on support for rural development by the European Agricultural Fund for Rural Development (EAFRD) and Council Regulation (EC) no. 1257/1999 on support for rural development from the European Agricultural Guidance and Guarantee Fund (EAGGF), in so far as those Council Regulations relate to less favoured areas. - 12p.: 30 cm. - 978-0-11-110874-1 £5.75

Agriculture, Wales

The Agricultural Subsidies and Grants Schemes (Appeals) (Wales) (Amendment) Regulations 2014 No. 2014/2894 (W.295). - Enabling power: European Communities Act 1972, s. 2 (2), sch. 2, para. 1A. - Issued: 14.11.2014. Made: 04.11.2014. Laid before the National Assembly for Wales: 07.11.2014. Coming into force: 01.12.2014. Effect: S.I. 2006/3342 (W.303) amended. Territorial extent & classification: W. General. - In English and Welsh. Welsh title: Rheoliadau Cynlluniau Cymorthdaliadau a Grantiau Amaethyddol (Apelau) (Cymru) (Diwygio) 2014. - 8p.: 30 cm. - 978-0-348-11014-2 £4.25

The Common Agricultural Policy Basic Payment Scheme (Provisional Payment Region Classification) (Wales) (Amendment) Regulations 2014 No. 2014/2367 (W.230). - Enabling power: European Communities Act 1972, s. 2 (2), sch. 2, para. 1A. - Issued: 29.09.2014. Made: 05.09.2014. Laid before the National Assembly for Wales: 05.09.2014. Coming into force: 26.09.2014. Effect: S.I. 2014/1835 (W.189) amended. Territorial extent & classification: W. General. - With correction slip dated January 2015. - In English and Welsh. Welsh title: Rheoliadau Cynllun Taliad Sylfaenol y Polisi Amaethyddol Cyffredin (Dosbarthiad Rhanbarthau Talu Dros Dro) (Cymru) (Diwygio) 2014. - 8p.: 30 cm. - 978-0-348-10991-7 £4.25

The Common Agricultural Policy Basic Payment Scheme (Provisional Payment Region Classification) (Wales) Regulations 2014 No. 2014/1835 (W.189). - Enabling power: European Communities Act 1972, s. 2 (2), sch. 2, para. 1A. - Issued: 25.07.2014. Made: 11.07.2014. Laid before the National Assembly for Wales: 14.07.2014. Coming into force: 04.08.2014. Effect: None. Territorial extent & classification: W. General. - EC note: These Regulations make provision, in relation to Wales, for the administration of Council Regulation (EC) No 1307/2013, in relation to direct payments to farmers under support schemes of the Common Agricultural Policy. - In English and Welsh. Welsh title: Rheoliadau Cynllun Taliad Sylfaenol y Polisi Amaethyddol Cyffredin (Dosbarthiad Rhanbarthau Talu Dros Dro) (Cymru) 2014. - 8p.: 30 cm. - 978-0-348-10974-0 £6.00

The Common Agricultural Policy (Integrated Administration and Control System and Enforcement and Cross Compliance) (Wales) Regulations 2014 No. 2014/3223 (W.328). - Enabling power: European Communities Act 1972, s. 2 (2), sch. 2, para. 1A. - Issued: 18.12.2014. Made: 08.12.2014. Laid before the National Assembly for Wales: 10.12.2014. Coming into force: 01.01.2015. Effect: S.I. 2004/3280 (W.284); 2005/3367 (W.264); 2006/2831 (W.252), 3343 (W.304); 2007/970 (W.87); 2009/3270 (W.287); 2010/38 (W.11), 1892 (W.185); 2011/2941 (W.317); 2012/3093 (W.311); 2014/371 (W.39) revoked. Territorial extent & classification: W. General. - In English and Welsh. Welsh title: Rheoliadau'r Polisi Amaethyddol Cyffredin (System Integredig Gweinyddu a Rheoli a Gorfodi a Thrawsgydymffurfio) (Cymru) 2014. - 32p.: 30 cm. - 978-0-348-11030-2 £6.00

The Common Agricultural Policy Single Payment and Support Schemes (Cross Compliance) (Wales) (Amendment) Regulations 2014 No. 2014/371 (W.39). - Enabling power: European Communities Act 1972, s. 2 (2). - Issued: 03.03.2014. Made: 18.02.2014. Laid before the National Assembly for Wales: 20.02.2014. Coming into force: 21.02.2014. Effect: S.I. 2004/3280 (W.284) amended. Territorial extent & classification: W. General. - Revoked by WSI 2014/3223 (W.328) (ISBN 9780348110302). - In English and Welsh. Welsh title: Rheoliadau Cynllun Taliad Sengl a Chynlluniau Cymorth y Polisi Amaethyddol Cyffredin (Trawsgydymffurfio) (Cymru) (Diwygio) 2014. - 8p.: 30 cm. - 978-0-348-10891-0 £4.00

The Official Feed and Food Controls (Wales) (Amendment) Regulations 2014 No. 2014/2714 (W.271). - Enabling power: European Communities Act 1972, s. 2 (2), sch. 2, para. 1A. - Issued: 21.10.2014. Made: 08.10.2014. Laid before the National Assembly for Wales: 10.10.2014. Coming into force: 06.11.2014. Effect: S.I. 2009/3376 (W.298) amended. Territorial extent & classification: W. General. - In English and Welsh. Welsh title: Rheoliadau Rheolaethau Swyddogol ar Fwyd Anifeiliaid a Bwyd (Cymru) (Diwygio) 2014. - [8]p.: 30 cm. - 978-0-348-11001-2 £4.25

The Rural Development Programmes (Wales) Regulations 2014 No. 2014/3222 (W.327). - Enabling power: European Communities Act 1972, s. 2 (2), sch. 2, para. 1A. - Issued: 16.12.2014. Made: 08.12.2014. Laid before the National Assembly for Wales: 09.12.2014. Coming into force: 01.01.2015. Effect: None. Territorial extent & classification: W. General. - In English and Welsh. Welsh title: Rheoliadau Rhaglenni Datblygu Gwledig (Cymru) 2014. - 20p.: 30 cm. - 978-0-348-11029-6 £6.00

Animals: Animal health

The Diseases of Swine Regulations 2014 No. 2014/1894. - Enabling power: European Communities Act 1972, s. 2 (2). - Issued: 23.07.2014. Made: 16.07.2014. Laid before Parliament and the National Assembly of Wales: 18.07.2014. Coming into force: 14.08.2014. Effect: S.I. 1980/146; 2003/2329, 2456 (W.239), 2913, 3273 (W.323); 2009/1372 (W.135), 1580 (W.156); S.S.I. 2003/426, 586; 2009/173 revoked. Territorial extent & classification: E/W/S. General. - EC note: Implements provisions for the control of: (i) swine vesicular disease contained Directive 92/119/EEC; (ii) classical swine fever contained in Council Directive 2001/89/EC; (iii) African swine fever contained in Council Directive 2002/60/EC. - 38p.: 30 cm. - 978-0-11-111859-7 £10.00

The Non-Commercial Movement of Pet Animals (Amendment) Order 2014 No. 2014/3158. - Enabling power: European Communities Act 1972, s. 2 (2), sch. 2, para. 1A. - Issued: 03.12.2014. Made: 27.11.2014. Laid before Parliament: 28.11.2014. Coming into force: 29.12.2014. Effect: S.I. 1974/2211; 2011/1197, 2379 (W.252), 2883; S.S.I. 2012/177 amended. Territorial extent & classification: E/W/S. General. - EC note: This instruments amends the 2011 Order to update the enforcement provisions and import requirements for pet animals entering Great Britain as a result of Regulation (EU) no. 576/2013 on the non-commercial movement of pet animals and repealing Regulation (EC) no. 998/2003. - 12p.: 30 cm. - 978-0-11-112422-2 £6.00

Animals, England: Animal health

The Sheep and Goats (Records, Identification and Movement) (England) (Amendment) Order 2014 No. 2014/331. - Enabling power: Animal Health Act 1981, ss. 1, 8 (1). - Issued: 20.02.2014. Made: 13.02.2014. Coming into force: In accord. with art. 1. Effect: S.I. 2009/3219 amended. Territorial extent & classification: E. General. - 8p.: 30 cm. - 978-0-11-110984-7 £4.00

The Tuberculosis (Deer and Camelid) (England) Order 2014 No. 2014/2337. - Enabling power: Animal Health Act 1981, ss. 1, 7 (1), 8 (1), 15 (4), 25, 34 (7) (a), 83 (2). - Issued: 09.09.2014. Made: 21.08.2014. Coming into force: 01.10.2014. Effect: S.I. 1989/878; 1993/2010 revoked. Territorial extent & classification: E. General. - 12p.: 30 cm. - 978-0-11-112018-7 £6.00

The Tuberculosis (Deer and Camelid) Slaughter and Compensation (England) Order 2014 No. 2014/2338. - Enabling power: Animal Health Act 1981, ss. 32 (2) (3). - Issued: 09.09.2014. Made: 01.09.2014. Laid: 03.09.2014. Coming into force: 01.10.2014. Effect: S.I. 1989/1316 revoked. Territorial extent & classification: E. General. - 4p.: 30 cm. - 978-0-11-112017-0 £4.25

The Tuberculosis (England) (Amendment) Order 2014 No. 2014/714. - Enabling power: Animal Health Act 1981, ss. 1, 8 (1), 15 (4), 25, 83 (2). - Issued: 24.03.2014. Made: 18.03.2014. Coming into force: 06.04.2014 except for art. 2 (8) which comes into force 30.06.2014. Effect: S.I. 2007/740 amended. Territorial extent & classification: E. General. - Revoked by SI 2014/2383 (ISBN 9780111120422). - 4p.: 30 cm. - 978-0-11-111246-5 £4.00

The Tuberculosis (England) Order 2014 No. 2014/2383. - Enabling power: Animal Health Act 1981, ss. 1, 7 (1), 8 (1), 15 (4), 25, 87 (2), 88 (2). - Issued: 12.09.2014. Made: 02.09.2014. Coming into force: 01.10.2014. Effect: S.I. 2007/740; SI 2012/1391; SI 2014/714 revoked. Territorial extent & classification: E. General. - 16p.: 30 cm. - 978-0-11-112042-2 £6.00

Animals, England: Prevention of cruelty

The Welfare of Animals at the Time of Killing Regulations 2014 No. 2014/1240. - Enabling power: European Communities Act 1972, sch. 2, para. 1A. - Issued: 21.05.2014. Made: 10.04.2014. Laid: 16.05.2014. Coming into force: 20.05.2014. Effect: 1968 c.27; 1974 c.3; 1986 c.14; S.I. 2009/1574; 2013/2216 amended & S.I. 1995/731; 1999/400; 2000/656 revoked in relation to England & S.I. 2000/3352; 2001/3830; 2003/3272; 2006/1200; 2007/402; 2012/501 revoked. Territorial extent & classification: E. General. - Revoked by SI 2014/1258 (ISBN 9780111115015). - 48p.: 30 cm. - 978-0-11-111500-8 £10.00

The Welfare of Wild Animals at Time of Killing (Revocation) Regulations 2014 No. 2014/1258. - Enabling power: European Communities Act 1972, sch. 2, para. 1A. - Issued: 21.05.2014. Made: 15.05.2014. Coming into force: 19.05.2014. Effect: S.I. 2014/1240 revoked. Territorial extent & classification: E. General. - 2p.: 30 cm. - 978-0-11-111501-5 £4.25

Animals, Wales

The Animal Welfare (Breeding of Dogs) (Wales) Regulations 2014 No. 2014/3266 (W.333). - Enabling power: Animal Welfare Act 2006, sch. 1, parts 1 and 3, ss. 13 (2), (7) (8) (e) (10). - Issued: 23.12.2014. Made: 10.12.2014. Laid before the National Assembly for Wales:-. Coming into force: 30.04.2015. Effect: 1973 c.60; 1994 c.19; 1975 c.50; 1976 c.38; 1981 c.37 amended. Territorial extent & classification: W. General. - In English and Welsh. Welsh title: Rheoliadau Lles Anifeiliaid (Bridio Cwn) (Cymru) 2014. - [20]p.: 30 cm. - 978-0-348-11031-9 £6.00

Animals, Wales: Animal health

The Animal By-Products (Enforcement) (Wales) Regulations 2014 No. 2014/517 (W.60). - Enabling power: European Communities Act 1972, s. 2 (2), sch. 2, para. 1A. - Issued: 20.03.2014. Made: 05.03.2014. Laid before the National Assembly for Wales: 07.03.2014. Coming into force: 28.03.2014. Effect: S.I. 2006/179 (W.30), 180 (W.31), 3309 (W.299), 3310 (W.300); 2007/842 (W.74), 3544; W.S.I. 2008/3154 (W.282); S.I. 2010/675; W.S.I. 2010/900 (W.93) amended & S.I. 1995/614 revoked in relation to Wales & S.I. 2002/1472 (W.146); 2003/1849 (W.199); 2003/2754 (W.265); W.S.I. 2011/2377 (W.250) revoked. Territorial extent & classification: W. General. - EC note: These Regulations continue to enforce, in Wales, Regulation 1069/2009 laying down health rules as regards animal by-products and derived products not intended for human consumption and repealing Regulation 1774/2002. They also continue to enforce, in Wales, Regulation 142/2011 implementing Regulation 1069/2009 and implementing Council Directive 97/78/EC as regards certain samples and items exempt from veterinary checks at the border. - In English and Welsh. Welsh title: Rheoliadau Sgil-gynhyrchion Anifeiliaid (Gorfodi) (Cymru) 2014. - 40p.: 30 cm. - 978-0-348-10916-0 £9.75

The Tuberculosis (Miscellaneous Amendments) (Wales) Order 2014 No. 2014/632 (W.72). - Enabling power: Animal Health Act 1981, ss. 1, 8 (1), 15 (4), 25, 83 (2). - Issued: 04.04.2014. Made: 12.03.2014. Laid before the National Assembly for Wales: 14.03.2014. Coming into force: 06.04.2014. Effect: S.I. 2010/1379 (W.122); 2011/692 (W.104) amended. Territorial extent & classification: W. General. - In English and Welsh. Welsh title: Gorchymyn Twbercwlosis (Diwygiadau Amrywiol) (Cymru) 2014. - 12p.: 30 cm. - 978-0-348-10927-6 £5.75

Animals, Wales: Prevention of cruelty

The Welfare of Animals at the Time of Killing (Consequential Amendments) (Wales) Regulations 2014 No. 2014/2124 (W.208). - Enabling power: European Communities Act 1972, s. 2 (2). - Issued: 18.08.2014. Made: 06.08.2014. Laid before the National Assembly for Wales: 08.08.2014. Coming into force: 05.09.2014. Effect: 1968 c.27; 1974 c.3; 1986 c.14; S.I. 2013/2216 amended. Territorial extent & classification: W. General. - In English and Welsh. Welsh title: Rheoliadau Lles Anifeiliaid Adeg eu Lladd (Diwygiadau Canlyniadol) (Cymru) 2014. - 4p.: 30 cm. - 978-0-348-10985-6 £4.25

The Welfare of Animals at the Time of Killing (Wales) Regulations 2014 No. 2014/951 (W.92). - Enabling power: European Communities Act 1972, sch. 2, para. 1A. - Issued: 22.04.2014. Made: 08.04.2014. Laid before the National Assembly for Wales: 10.04.2014. Coming into force: 20.05.2014. Effect: S.I. 2009/1557 (W.152) amended & S.I. 1995/731; 1999/400; 2000/656; 2007/2461 (W.208) revoked in relation to Wales. Territorial extent & classification: W. General. - EC note: The Regulations make provision in Wales for the administration and enforcement of Council Regulation(EC) No 1099/2009 of 24 September 2009 on the protection of animals at the time of killing. - In English and Welsh. Welsh title: Rheoliadau Lles Anifeiliaid Adeg eu Lladd (Cymru) 2014. - 68p.: 30 cm. - 978-0-348-10937-5 £11.00

Annual tax on enveloped dwellings

The Annual Tax on Enveloped Dwellings (Indexation of Annual Chargeable Amounts) Order 2014 No. 2014/854. - Enabling power: Finance Act 2013, ss. 101 (5). - Issued: 03.04.2014. Made: 26.03.2014. Effect: None. Territorial extent & classification: E/W/S/NI. General. - 4p.: 30 cm. - 978-0-11-111305-9 £4.00

The Taxes (Definition of Charity) (Relevant Territories) (Amendment) Regulations 2014 No. 2014/1807. - Enabling power: Finance Act 2010, sch. 6, para. 2 (3) (b). - Issued: 15.07.2014. Made: 09.07.2014. Laid: 10.07.2014. Coming into force: 31.07.2014. Effect: S.I. 2010/1904 amended. Territorial extent & classification: E/W/S/NI. General. - 4p.: 30 cm. - 978-0-11-111781-1 £4.25

Architects

The Architects Act 1997 (Amendments etc) Order 2014 No. 2014/4. - Enabling power: European Communities Act 1972, s. 2 (2) & Architects Act 1997, sch. 1, para. 24. - Issued: 14.01.2014. Made: 07.01.2014. Laid: 13.01.2014. Coming into force: 10.02.2014. Effect: 1997 c.22 amended & S.I. 2008/1331 partially revoked. Territorial extent & classification: E/W/S/NI. General. - EC note: Implements Decision 2/2011 of the EU Swiss Joint Committee. - 4p.: 30 cm. - 978-0-11-110805-5 £4.00

Arms and ammunition

The Anti-social Behaviour, Crime and Policing Act 2014 (Commencement No. 2, Transitional and Transitory Provisions) Order 2014 No. 2014/949 (C.43). - Enabling power: Anti-social Behaviour, Crime and Policing Act 2014, s. 185 (1) (7). Bringing into operation various provisions of the 2014 Act on 13.05.2014, 01.06.2014, 16.06.2014, 14.07.2014, in accord. with arts. 2 to 6. - Issued: 14.04.2014. Made: 08.04.2014. Effect: None. Territorial extent & classification: E/W/S/NI. General. - 8p.: 30 cm. - 978-0-11-111401-8 £6.00

The Firearms (Amendment) Rules 2014 No. 2014/1239. - Enabling power: Firearms Act 1968, ss. 26A, 26B, 27 (2), 53. - Issued: 20.05.2014. Made: 10.05.2014. Coming into force: 20.05.2014. Effect: S.I. 1998/1941 amended. Territorial extent & classification: E/W/S. General. - 24p.: 30 cm. - 978-0-11-111491-9 £6.00

Arms and ammunition, England and Wales

The Anti-social Behaviour, Crime and Policing Act 2014 (Consequential Amendments) Order 2014 No. 2014/2522. - Enabling power: Anti-social Behaviour, Crime and Policing Act 2014, s. 181 (2). - Issued: 24.09.2014. Made: 18.09.2014. Coming into force: In accord. with art. 1. Effect: 1968 c.27 amended. Territorial extent & classification: E/W/S. General. - Supersedes draft SI (ISBN 9780111117514) issued 08/07/14 - 2p.: 30 cm. - 978-0-11-112096-5 £4.25

Arms and ammunition, Scotland

The Anti-social Behaviour, Crime and Policing Act 2014 (Consequential Amendments) Order 2014 No. 2014/2522. - Enabling power: Anti-social Behaviour, Crime and Policing Act 2014, s. 181 (2). - Issued: 24.09.2014. Made: 18.09.2014. Coming into force: In accord. with art. 1. Effect: 1968 c.27 amended. Territorial extent & classification: E/W/S. General. - Supersedes draft SI (ISBN 9780111117514) issued 08/07/14 - 2p.: 30 cm. - 978-0-11-112096-5 £4.25

Atomic energy and radioactive substances

The Nuclear Industries Security (Amendment) and Nuclear Security (Prescribed Material) Regulations 2014 No. 2014/526. - Enabling power: Anti-terrorism, Crime and Security Act 2001, s. 77. - Issued: 12.03.2014. Made: 06.03.2014. Laid: 10.03.2014. Coming into force: 31.03.2014. Effect: S.I. 2003/403 amended. Territorial extent & classification: E/W/S/NI. General. - This Statutory Instrument has been printed to correct errors in S.I. 2013/190 (9780111534090) and is being issued free of charge to all known recipients of that Statutory Instrument. - 4p.: 30 cm. - 978-0-11-111124-6 £4.00

Auditors

The Local Audit (Delegation of Functions) and Statutory Audit (Delegation of Functions) Order 2014 No. 2014/2009. - Enabling power: Companies Act 2006, ss. 1252, 1253, sch. 13, paras 7 (3), 11 (2) (3) (a). - Issued: 04.08.2014. Made: 29.07.2014. Coming into force: In accord. with art. 1. Effect: S.I. 2012/1741 amended. Territorial extent & classification: E/W except for art. 10 which extends to the UK. General. - Supersedes draft S.I. (ISBN 9780111116609) issued 19.06.2014. - 8p.: 30 cm. - 978-0-11-111935-8 £4.25

Banks and banking

The Banking Act 2009 (Mandatory Compensation Arrangements Following Bail-in) Regulations 2014 No. 2014/3330. - Enabling power: Banking Act 2009, ss. 60A (1) to (4), 259 (1) & European Communities Act 1972, s. 2 (2). - Issued: 29.12.2014. Made: 17.12.2014. Coming into force: 01.01.2015. Effect: None. Territorial extent & classification: E/W/S/NI. General. - Supersedes draft SI (ISBN 9780111123706) issued 27/11/14. - 8p.: 30 cm. - 978-0-11-112642-4 £6.00

The Banking Act 2009 (Restriction of Special Bail-in Provision, etc.) Order 2014 No. 2014/3350. - Enabling power: Banking Act 2009, ss. 47 (2) (4), 48 (2) (3) (4), 48P (3) (5) (6), 259 (1). - Issued: 29.12.2014. Made: 17.12.2014. Coming into force: 01.01.2015. Effect: None. Territorial extent & classification: E/W/S/NI. General. - Supersedes draft SI (ISBN 9780111123683) issued 27/11/14. - 8p.: 30 cm. - 978-0-11-112641-7 £6.00

The Bank Recovery and Resolution Order 2014 No. 2014/3329. - Enabling power: European Communities Act 1972, s. 2 (2). - Issued: 09.01.2015. Made: 17.12.2014. Coming into force: 01.01.2015. Effect: 2000 c.8; 2009 c.1 & S.I. 2009/319, 322; 2014/1831 amended. Territorial extent & classification: E/W/S/NI. General. - Supersedes draft S.I. (ISBN 9780111123782) issued 28/11/14. - 88p.: 30 cm. - 978-0-11-112654-7 £16.00

The Banks and Building Societies (Depositor Preference and Priorities) Order 2014 No. 2014/3486. - Enabling power: European Communities Act 1972, s. 2 (2) & Building Societies Act 1986, s. 90B (1) (5). - Issued: 09.01.2015. Made: 17.12.2014. Coming into force: 01.01.2015. Effect: 1985 c.66; 1986 c.45, c.53; 1996 c.52; 2008 c.17; 2010 asp 17; S.I. 1989/2405 (NI. 19); 1994/2421; S.R. 1995/225 amended. Territorial extent & classification: E/W/S/NI. General. - Supersedes draft S.I. (ISBN 9780111123676) issued 27/11/14. - 24p.: 30 cm. - 978-0-11-112652-3 £6.00

The Financial Services Act 2012 (Commencement No. 6) Order 2014 No. 2014/3323 (C.156). - Enabling power: Financial Services Act 2012, s. 122 (3) (4). Bringing various provisions of the 2012 Act into operation on 01.01.2015. - Issued: 23.12.2014. Made: 17.12.2014. Effect: None. Territorial extent & classification: E/W/S/NI. General. - 4p.: 30 cm. - 978-0-11-112615-8 £4.25

The Financial Services and Markets Act 2000 (Excluded Activities and Prohibitions) Order 2014 No. 2014/2080. - Enabling power: Financial Services and Markets Act 2000, ss. 142D, 142E, 142F. - Issued: 11.08.2014. Made: 23.07.2014. Coming into force: In accord. with art. 1 (2) (3). Effect: None. Territorial extent & classification: E/W/S/NI. General. - Supersedes draft S.I. (ISBN 9780111117101) issued 01.07.2014. - 24p.: 30 cm. - 978-0-11-111961-7 £6.00

The Financial Services and Markets Act 2000 (Ring-fenced Bodies and Core Activities) Order 2014 No. 2014/1960. - Enabling power: Financial Services and Markets Act 2000, ss. 142A (2) (b), 142B (2), 142F, 428 (3). - Issued: 11.08.2014. Made: 23.07.2014. Coming into force: 01.01.2015. Effect: None. Territorial extent & classification: E/W/S/NI. General. - Supersedes draft SI (ISBN 9780111117118) issued 01.07.2014. - 12p.: 30 cm. - 978-0-11-111921-1 £6.00

The Financial Services (Banking Reform) Act 2013 (Commencement No. 7) Order 2014 No. 2014/3160 (C.138). - Enabling power: Financial Services (Banking Reform) Act 2013, s. 148 (5). Bringing into operation various provisions of this Act on 31.12.2014, in accord. with art. 2. - Issued: 04.12.2014. Made: 26.11.2014. Effect: None. Territorial extent & classification: E/W/S/NI. General. - 4p.: 30 cm. - 978-0-11-112423-9 £4.25

Betting, gaming and lotteries

The Categories of Gaming Machine (Amendment) Regulations 2014 No. 2014/45. - Enabling power: Gambling Act 2005, ss. 236, 355 (1). - Issued: 20.01.2014. Made: 14.01.2014. Coming into force: 15.01.2014 in accord. with reg. 1. Effect: S.I. 2007/2158 amended. Territorial extent & classification: E/W/S. General. - Supersedes draft S.I. (ISBN 9780111104781) issued 17.10.2013- 2p.: 30 cm. - 978-0-11-110842-0 £4.00

The Courts and Tribunals Fees (Miscellaneous Amendments) Order 2014 No. 2014/590 (L.6). - Enabling power: Courts Act 2003, s. 92 & Insolvency Act 1986, ss. 414, 415 & Tribunals, Courts and Enforcement Act 2007, s. 42, 49 (3) & Constitutional Reform Act 2005, s. 52 & Mental Capacity Act 2005. s. 54 & Gender Recognition Act 2004, s. 7 (2). - Issued: 19.03.2014. Made: 11.03.2014. Laid: 13.03.2104. Coming into force: 06.04.2014. Effect: S.I. 2004/3120; 2006/758; 2007/1745; 2008/1052, 1053, 1054; 2009/213, 1114; 2010/42; 2011/2344; 2013/1179, 1893 amended. Territorial extent & classification: E/W. General. - 16p.: 30 cm. - 978-0-11-111194-9 £5.75

The Gambling (Licensing and Advertising) Act 2014 (Commencement No.1) (Amendment and Consequential Amendments) Order 2014 No. 2014/2646 (C.117). - Enabling power: Gambling (Licensing and Advertising) Act 2014, s. 6 (5) (6). Bringing various provisions of the 2014 Act into operation on 01.10.2014. - Issued: 06.10.2014. Made: 29.09.2014. Coming into force: in accord. with art. 2. Effect: S.I. 2014/2444 (C.107) amended. Territorial extent & classification: E/W/S. General. - 2p.: 30 cm. - 978-0-11-112116-0 £4.25

The Gambling (Licensing and Advertising) Act 2014 (Commencement No.1) Order 2014 No. 2014/2444 (C.107). - Enabling power: Gambling (Licensing and Advertising) Act 2014, s. 6 (5). Bringing various provisions of the 2014 Act into operation on 01.10.2014. - Issued: 18.09.2014. Made: 10.09.2014. Coming into force: in accord. with art. 2. Effect: None. Territorial extent & classification: E/W/S. General. - 2p.: 30 cm. - 978-0-11-112078-1 £4.25

The Gambling (Licensing and Advertising) Act 2014 (Transitional Provisions) (Amendment) (No.2) Order 2014 No. 2014/2665. - Enabling power: Gambling (Licensing and Advertising) Act 2014, s. 1 (4) (6) (7). - Issued: 08.10.2014. Made: 01.10.2014. Laid: 02.10.2014. Coming into force: 23.10.2014. Effect: S.I. 2014/1641 amended. Territorial extent & classification: E/W/S. General. - 2p.: 30 cm. - 978-0-11-112123-8 £4.25

The Gambling (Licensing and Advertising) Act 2014 (Transitional Provisions) (Amendment) Order 2014 No. 2014/1675. - Enabling power: Gambling (Licensing and Advertising) Act 2014, s. 1 (4) (6) (7). - Issued: 03.07.2014. Made: 26.06.2014. Laid: 27.06.2014. Coming into force: 16.07.2014. Effect: S.I. 2014/1641 amended. Territorial extent & classification: E/W/S. General. - This Statutory Instrument has been made in consequence of a defect in S.I. 2014/1641 (ISBN 9780111117071) and is being issued free of charge to all known recipients. - 2p.: 30 cm. - 978-0-11-111729-3 £4.25

The Olympic Lotteries (Payments out of the Olympic Lottery Distribution Fund) Regulations 2014 No. 2014/1510. - Enabling power: Horserace Betting and Olympic Lottery Act 2004, ss. 26 (2) (c) (4) (a), 36 (2) (a). - Issued: 13.06.2014. Made: 05.06.2014. Laid: 10.06.2014. Coming into force: 22.07.2014. Effect: None. Territorial extent & classification: E/W/S/NI. General. - 2p.: 30 cm. - 978-0-11-111634-0 £4.25

Betting, gaming and lotteries, England and Wales

The Gambling (Licensing and Advertising) Act 2014 (Transitional Provisions) Order 2014 No. 2014/1641. - Enabling power: Gambling (Licensing and Advertising) Act 2014, s. 1 (4) (6) (7). - Issued: 01.07.2014. Made: 23.06.2014. Laid: 25.06.2014. Coming into force: 16.07.2014. Effect: None. Territorial extent & classification: E/W/S. General. - A defect in this SI has been corrected by SI 2014/1675 (ISBN 9780111117293) which is being issued free of charge to all known recipients of 2014/1641. - 8p.: 30 cm. - 978-0-11-111707-1 £4.25

Betting, gaming and lotteries, Scotland

The Gambling (Licensing and Advertising) Act 2014 (Transitional Provisions) Order 2014 No. 2014/1641. - Enabling power: Gambling (Licensing and Advertising) Act 2014, s. 1 (4) (6) (7). - Issued: 01.07.2014. Made: 23.06.2014. Laid: 25.06.2014. Coming into force: 16.07.2014. Effect: None. Territorial extent & classification: E/W/S. General. - A defect in this SI has been corrected by SI 2014/1675 (ISBN 9780111117293) which is being issued free of charge to all known recipients of 2014/1641. - 8p.: 30 cm. - 978-0-11-111707-1 £4.25

British nationality

The British Nationality (General) (Amendment) Regulations 2014 No. 2014/1465. - Enabling power: British Nationality Act 1981, s. 41 (1) (ba) (1A). - Issued: 12.06.2014. Made: 05.06.2014. Laid: 10.06.2014. Coming into force: 01.07.2014. Effect: S.I. 2003/548 amended. Territorial extent & classification: E/W/S/NI/Islands/British Overseas Territories. General. - 2p.: 30 cm. - 978-0-11-111616-6 £4.25

Broadcasting

The Audiovisual Media Services Regulations 2014 No. 2014/2916. - Enabling power: European Communities Act 1972, s. 2 (2). - Issued: 11.11.2014. Made: 04.11.2014. Laid: 06.11.2014. Coming into force: 01.12.2014. Effect: 2003 c.21 amended. Territorial extent & classification: E/W/S/NI. General. - 4p.: 30 cm. - 978-0-11-112295-2 £4.25

The Broadcasting (Independent Productions) (Amendment) Order 2014 No. 2014/3137. - Enabling power: Communications Act 2003, ss. 277 (2) (b), 309 (2) (b), sch. 12, paras. 1 (2) (b), 7 (2) (b). - Issued: 02.12.2014. Made: 24.11.2014. Coming into force: 25.11.2014 in accord. with art. 1. Effect: S.I. 1991/1408 amended. Territorial extent & classification: E/W/S/NI. General. - Supersedes draft S.I. (ISBN 9780111118825) issued 24.07.2014. - 2p.: 30 cm. - 978-0-11-112411-6 £4.25

The Television Broadcasting Regulations 2014 No. 2014/1184. - Enabling power: European Communications Act 1972, s. 2 (2). - Issued: 13.05.2014. Made: 01.05.2014. Laid: 07.05.2014. Coming into force: 31.05.2014. Effect: 1996 c.55 amended/partially repealed. Territorial extent & classification: E/W/S/NI. General. - 2p.: 30 cm. - 978-0-11-111464-3 £4.25

Building and buildings, England and Wales

The Building (Amendment) Regulations 2014 No. 2014/2362. - Enabling power: Building Act 1984, ss. 1, 3, 34, sch. 1 paras. 1, 2, 4, 4A, 7, 8 (1), 10. - Issued: 10.09.2014. Made: 04.09.2014. Laid: 08.09.2014. Coming into force: 01.10.2014. Effect: S.I. 2010/2214 amended. Territorial extent & classification: E/W. General. - 2p.: 30 cm. - 978-0-11-112024-8 £4.25

The Building Regulations & c. (Amendment) Regulations 2014 No. 2014/579. - Enabling power: Building Act 1984, ss. 1, 3, 34, sch. 1, paras 1, 2, 4, 4A, 7, 8 (1), 10. - Issued: 17.03.2014. Made: 10.03.2014. Laid: 13.03.2014. Coming into force: 06.04.2014. Effect: S.I. 2010/2214, 2215 amended. Territorial extent & classification: E/W. General. - 8p.: 30 cm. - 978-0-11-111182-6 £5.75

The Energy Performance of Buildings (England and Wales) (Amendment) Regulations 2014 No. 2014/880. - Enabling power: European Communities Act 1972, s. 2 (2). - Issued: 04.04.2014. Made: 31.03.2014. Laid: 02.04.2014. Coming into force: 06.04.2014. Effect: S.I. 2012/3118 amended. Territorial extent & classification: E/W. General. - 4p.: 30 cm. - 978-0-11-111338-7 £4.25

Building and buildings, Wales

The Building (Amendment) (Wales) Regulations 2014 No. 2014/110 (W.10). - Enabling power: Building Act 1984, ss. 1, 34, sch. 1, paras 1, 4, 7, 10. - Issued: 30.01.2014. Made: 21.01.2014. Laid before the National Assembly for Wales: 23.01.2014. Coming into force: 31.07.2014. Effect: S.I. 2010/2214, 2215 amended. Territorial extent & classification: W. General. - In English and Welsh. Welsh title: Rheoliadau Adeiladu (Diwygio) (Cymru) 2014. - 12p.: 30 cm. - 978-0-348-10861-3 £5.75

The Building (Approved Inspectors etc.) (Amendment) (Wales) Regulations 2014 No. 2014/58 (W.5). - Enabling power: Building Act 1984, ss. 1, 16 (9), 17 (1) (6), 47 (1) (2) (5), 49 (5), 50 (1) (4) (6), 51 (1) (2), 51A (2) (3) (6), sch. 1, paras 2, 4, 4A, 10. - Issued: 24.01.2014. Made: 14.01.2014. Laid before the National Assembly for Wales: 16.01.2014. Coming into force: 10.02.2014. Effect: S.I. 2010/2215 amended in relation to Wales. Territorial extent & classification: W. General. - In English and Welsh. Welsh title: Rheoliadau Adeiladu (Arolygwyr Cymeradwy etc.) (Diwygio) (Cymru) 2014. - 8p.: 30 cm. - 978-0-348-10856-9 £5.75

Building societies

The Banks and Building Societies (Depositor Preference and Priorities) Order 2014 No. 2014/3486. - Enabling power: European Communities Act 1972, s. 2 (2) & Building Societies Act 1986, s. 90B (1) (5). - Issued: 09.01.2015. Made: 17.12.2014. Coming into force: 01.01.2015. Effect: 1985 c.66; 1986 c.45, c.53; 1996 c.52; 2008 c.17; 2010 asp 17; S.I. 1989/2405 (NI. 19); 1994/2421; S.R. 1995/225 amended. Territorial extent & classification: E/W/S/NI. General. - Supersedes draft S.I. (ISBN 9780111123676) issued 27/11/14. - 24p.: 30 cm. - 978-0-11-112652-3 £6.00

The Building Societies (Accounts and Related Provisions) (Amendment) Regulations 2014 No. 2014/48. - Enabling power: Building Societies Act 1986, s. 74 (1) (2) (3) (4). - Issued: 22.01.2014. Made: 14.01.2014. Laid: 16.01.2014. Coming into force: In accord. with art. 1(2). Effect: S.I. 1998/504 amended. Territorial extent & classification: E/W/S/NI. General. - 2p.: 30 cm. - 978-0-11-110844-4 £4.00

The Building Societies (Bail-in) Order 2014 No. 2014/3344. - Enabling power: European Communities Act 1972, s. 2 (2) & Financial Services (Banking Reform) Act 2013, ss. 17 (2) to (4), 142 (3). - Issued: 24.12.2014. Made: 18.12.2014. Laid: 19.12.2014. Coming into force: 10.01.2015. Effect: 1986 c.53; 2009 c.1 & S.I. 2009/805; 2014/3330 amended. Territorial extent & classification: E/W/S/NI. General. - 16p.: 30 cm. - 978-0-11-112633-2 £6.00

The Building Societies (Funding) and Mutual Societies (Transfers) Act 2007 (Commencement No. 2) Order 2014 No. 2014/2796 (C.124). - Enabling power: Building Societies (Funding) and Mutual Societies (Transfers) Act 2007, s. 6 (2). Bringing into operation various provisions of the 2007 Act on 20.11.2014. - Issued: 23.10.2014. Made: 16.10.2014. Effect: None. Territorial extent & classification: E/W/S/NI. General. - 2p.: 30 cm. - 978-0-11-112198-6 £4.25

Business names

The Company, Limited Liability Partnership and Business Names (Sensitive Words and Expressions) Regulations 2014 No. 2014/3140. - Enabling power: Companies Act 2006, ss. 55 (1), 56 (1) (b), 1194 (1), 1195 (1) (b), 1292 (1). - Issued: 03.12.2014. Made: 26.11.2014. Laid: 27.11.2014. Coming into force: 31.01.2015. Effect: S.I. 2009/2615 revoked. Territorial extent & classification: E/W/S/NI. General. - For approval by resolution of each House of Parliament within twenty-eight days. - 12p.: 30 cm. - 978-0-11-112414-7 £6.00

Capital gains tax

The Double Taxation Relief and International Tax Enforcement (Belgium) Order 2014 No. 2014/1875. - Enabling power: Taxation (International and Other Provisions) Act 2010, s. 2 & Finance Act 2006, s. 173 (1) to (3). - Issued: 23.07.2014. Made: 16.07.2014. Effect: None. Territorial extent & classification: E/W/S/NI. General. - Supersedes draft SI (ISBN 9780111116272) issued 13/06/14. - 8p.: 30 cm. - 978-0-11-111837-5 £4.25

The Double Taxation Relief and International Tax Enforcement (Canada) Order 2014 No. 2014/3274. - Enabling power: Taxation (International and Other Provisions) Act 2010, s. 2 & Finance Act 2006, s. 173 (1) to (3). - Issued: 17.12.2014. Made: 10.12.2014. Coming into force: 10.12.2014. Effect: 1980/709 amended. Territorial extent & classification: E/W/S/NI. General. - Supersedes draft S.I. (ISBN 9780111121801) issued 20/10/14. - 20p.: 30 cm. - 978-0-11-112537-3 £6.00

The Double Taxation Relief and International Tax Enforcement (Iceland) Order 2014 No. 2014/1879. - Enabling power: Taxation (International and Other Provisions) Act 2010, s. 2 & Finance Act 2006, s. 173 (1) to (3). - Issued: 23.07.2014. Made: 16.07.2014. Effect: None. Territorial extent & classification: E/W/S/NI. General. - Supersedes draft SI (ISBN 9780111116296) issued 13/06/14. - 24p.: 30 cm. - 978-0-11-111841-2 £6.00

The Double Taxation Relief and International Tax Enforcement (Japan) Order 2014 No. 2014/1881. - Enabling power: Taxation (International and Other Provisions) Act 2010, s. 2 & Finance Act 2006, s. 173 (1) to (3). - Issued: 23.07.2014. Made: 16.07.2014. Effect: None. Territorial extent & classification: E/W/S/NI. General. - Supersedes draft SI (ISBN 9780111116289) issued 23/07/14. - 20p.: 30 cm. - 978-0-11-111843-6 £6.00

The Double Taxation Relief and International Tax Enforcement (Tajikistan) Order 2014 No. 2014/3275. - Enabling power: Taxation (International and Other Provisions) Act 2010, s. 2 & Finance Act 2006, s. 173 (1) to (3). - Issued: 17.12.2014. Made: 10.12.2014. Effect: None. Territorial extent & classification: E/W/S/NI. General. - Supersedes draft S.I. (ISBN 9780111121726) issued 17/10/14. - 24p.: 30 cm. - 978-0-11-112538-0 £6.00

The Double Taxation Relief and International Tax Enforcement (Zambia) Order 2014 No. 2014/1876. - Enabling power: Taxation (International and Other Provisions) Act 2010, s. 2 & Finance Act 2006, s. 173 (1) to (3). - Issued: 23.07.2014. Made: 16.07.2014. Effect: None. Territorial extent & classification: E/W/S/NI. General. - Supersedes draft SI (ISBN 9780111116302) issued 13/06/14. - 24p.: 30 cm. - 978-0-11-111838-2 £6.00

The Double Taxation Relief (Federal Republic of Germany) Order 2014 No. 2014/1874. - Enabling power: Taxation (International and Other Provisions) Act 2010, s. 2. - Issued: 23.07.2014. Made: 16.07.2014. Effect: None. Territorial extent & classification: E/W/S/NI. General. - Supersedes draft SI (ISBN 9780111116241) issued 13/06/14. - 8p.: 30 cm. - 978-0-11-111836-8 £6.00

The Finance Act 2014, Schedule 37, Paragraph 22 (Commencement) Order 2014 No. 2014/2461 (C.110). - Enabling power: Finance Act 2014, sch. 37 para. 22 (2). Bringing into operation various provisions of this Act on 01.10.2014 in accord. with art. 2. - Issued: 19.09.2014. Made: 12.09.2014. Effect: 2014 c.26 amended. Territorial extent & classification: E/W/S/NI. General. - 4p.: 30 cm. - 978-0-11-112087-3 £4.25

The Individual Savings Account (Amendment No. 2) Regulations 2014 No. 2014/1450. - Enabling power: Taxation of Chargeable Gains Act 1992, s. 151 (1) (2) & Income Tax (Trading and Other Income) Act 2005, ss. 694 (1) (3) (5), 695 (1) (2), 699, 701 (1) (2) (3) (5). - Issued: 10.06.2014. Made: 04.06.2014. Laid: 05.06.2014. Coming into force: 01.07.2014. Effect: S.I. 1998/1870 amended. Territorial extent & classification: E/W/S/NI. General. - 8p.: 30 cm. - 978-0-11-111596-1 £4.25

The Individual Savings Account (Amendment) Regulations 2014 No. 2014/654. - Enabling power: Income Tax (Trading and Other Income) Act 2005, ss. 694, 695, 695A (2) (c), 696, 701 (1) (4) (5) & Taxation of Chargeable Gains Act 1992, s. 151 (1) (2). - Issued: 20.03.2014. Made: 14.03.2014. Laid: 14.03.2014. Coming into force: 06.04.2014. Effect: S.I. 1998/1870 amended. Territorial extent & classification: E/W/S/NI. General. - 8p.: 30 cm. - 978-0-11-111228-1 £4.00

The International Tax Enforcement (Anguilla) Order 2014 No. 2014/1357. - Enabling power: Finance Act 2006, s. 173 (1) to (3). - Issued: 03.06.2014. Made: 27.05.2014. Coming into force: 03.06.2014. Effect: None. Territorial extent & classification: E/W/S/NI. General. - Supersedes draft SI (ISBN 9780111110539) issued 06.03.14. - 8p.: 30 cm. - 978-0-11-111529-9 £6.00

The International Tax Enforcement (British Virgin Islands) Order 2014 No. 2014/1359. - Enabling power: Finance Act 2006, s. 173 (1) to (3). - Issued: 03.06.2014. Made: 27.05.2014. Coming into force: 03.06.2014. Effect: None. Territorial extent & classification: E/W/S/NI. General. - Supersedes draft SI (ISBN 9780111110546) issued 06.03.14. - 8p.: 30 cm. - 978-0-11-111531-2 £6.00

The International Tax Enforcement (Turks and Caicos Islands) Order 2014 No. 2014/1360. - Enabling power: Finance Act 2006, s. 173 (1) to (3). - Issued: 03.06.2014. Made: 27.05.2014. Coming into force: 03.06.2014. Effect: None. Territorial extent & classification: E/W/S/NI. General. - Supersedes draft SI (ISBN 9780111110560) issued 06.03.14. - 8p.: 30 cm. - 978-0-11-111532-9 £6.00

The Lloyd's Underwriters (Conversion of Partnerships to Underwriting through Successor Companies) (Tax) Regulations 2014 No. 2014/3133. - Enabling power: Finance Act 1993, s. 182 (1) (b). - Issued: 02.12.2014. Made: 26.11.2014. Laid: 27.11.2014. Coming into force: 19.12.2014. Effect: 1993 c.34 amended. Territorial extent & classification: E/W/S/NI. General. - 8p.: 30 cm. - 978-0-11-112405-5 £6.00

The Offshore Funds (Tax) (Amendment) Regulations 2014 No. 2014/1931. - Enabling power: Taxation (International and Other Provisions) Act 2010, s. 354. - Issued: 28.07.2014. Made: 21.07.2014. Laid: 22.07.2014. Coming into force: 12.08.2014. Effect: S.I. 2009/3001 amended. Territorial extent & classification: E/W/S/NI. General. - 2p.: 30 cm. - 978-0-11-111903-7 £4.25

The Taxation of Chargeable Gains (Gilt-edged Securities) Order 2014 No. 2014/1120. - Enabling power: Taxation of Chargeable Gains Act 1992, sch. 9, para. 1. - Issued: 06.05.2014. Made: 28.04.2014. Coming into force: 06.05.2014. Effect: None. Territorial extent & classification: E/W/S/NI. General. - 2p.: 30 cm. - 978-0-11-111445-2 £4.25

The Taxes (Definition of Charity) (Relevant Territories) (Amendment) Regulations 2014 No. 2014/1807. - Enabling power: Finance Act 2010, sch. 6, para. 2 (3) (b). - Issued: 15.07.2014. Made: 09.07.2014. Laid: 10.07.2014. Coming into force: 31.07.2014. Effect: S.I. 2010/1904 amended. Territorial extent & classification: E/W/S/NI. General. - 4p.: 30 cm. - 978-0-11-111781-1 £4.25

The Unauthorised Unit Trusts (Tax) (Amendment) Regulations 2014 No. 2014/585. - Enabling power: Finance Act 2013, s. 217. - Issued: 18.03.2014. Made: 12.03.2014. Laid: 13.03.2014. Coming into force: 06.04.2014. Effect: S.I. 2013/2819 amended. Territorial extent & classification: E/W/S/NI. General. - 4p.: 30 cm. - 978-0-11-111189-5 £4.00

Channel Tunnel

The Channel Tunnel (International Arrangements) (Amendment) Order 2014 No. 2014/1814. - Enabling power: Channel Tunnel Act 1987, s. 11. - Issued: 15.07.2014. Made: 08.07.2014. Laid: 14.07.2014. Coming into force: 05.08.2014. Effect: S.I. 1993/1813 amended. Territorial extent & classification: E/W/S/NI. General. - 4p.: 30 cm. - 978-0-11-111786-6 £4.25

Charities

The Taxes (Definition of Charity) (Relevant Territories) (Amendment) Regulations 2014 No. 2014/1807. - Enabling power: Finance Act 2010, sch. 6, para. 2 (3) (b). - Issued: 15.07.2014. Made: 09.07.2014. Laid: 10.07.2014. Coming into force: 31.07.2014. Effect: S.I. 2010/1904 amended. Territorial extent & classification: E/W/S/NI. General. - 4p.: 30 cm. - 978-0-11-111781-1 £4.25

Charities, England and Wales

The Charities (Exception from Registration) (Amendment) Regulations 2014 No. 2014/242. - Enabling power: Charities Act 2011, ss. 30 (2) (c). - Issued: 14.02.2014. Made: 05.02.2014. Laid: 13.02.2014. Coming into force: 31.03.2014. Effect: S.I. 1996/180 amended & 2012/1734 revoked. Territorial extent & classification: E/W. General. - 2p.: 30 cm. - 978-0-11-110942-7 £4.00

Children and young persons

The Child Poverty Act 2010 (Persistent Poverty Target) Regulations 2014 No. 2014/3232. - Enabling power: Child Poverty Act 2010, s. 6 (3). - Issued: 11.12.2014. Made: 05.12.2014. Coming into force: 31.12.2014. Effect: None. Territorial extent & classification: E/W/S/NI. General. - Supersedes draft S.I. (ISBN 9780111121870) issued 21.10.2014. - 2p.: 30 cm. - 978-0-11-112487-1 £4.25

The Children and Families Act 2014 (Commencement No. 2) (Amendment) Order 2014 No. 2014/1134 (C.47). - Enabling power: Children and Families Act 2014, s. 139 (6) (7). Bringing into operation various provisions of the 2014 Act on 01.05.2014. - Issued: 07.05.2014. Made: 30.04.2014. Effect: S.I. 2014/889 (C.38) amended. Territorial extent & classification: E/W/S. General. - 2p.: 30 cm. - 978-0-11-111452-0 £4.25

The Children and Families Act 2014 (Commencement No. 2) Order 2014 No. 2014/889 (C.38). - Enabling power: Children and Families Act 2014, s. 139 (6) (7). Bringing into operation various provisions of the 2014 Act on 01.04.2014, 22.04.2014, 13.05.2014, 25.07.2014, 01.09.2014 in accord. with arts 3 to 7. - Issued: 07.04.2014. Made: 31.03.2014. Effect: None. Territorial extent & classification: E/W/S. General. - 4p.: 30 cm. - 978-0-11-111354-7 £4.25

The Children and Families Act 2014 (Commencement No. 4) Order 2014 No. 2014/2609 (C.114). - Enabling power: Children and Families Act 2014, s. 139 (6). Bringing into operation various provisions of the 2014 Act on 01.10.2014. - Issued: 02.10.2014. Made: 26.09.2014. Effect: None. Territorial extent & classification: E/W/S. General. - 4p.: 30 cm. - 978-0-11-112111-5 £4.25

The Children and Families Act 2014 (Commencement No. 5 and Transitional Provision) Order 2014 No. 2014/2749 (C.120). - Enabling power: Children and Families Act 2014, s. 137 (1), 139 (6). Bringing into operation various provisions of the 2014 Act on 22.10.2014, in accord. with art 3. - Issued: 20.10.2014. Made: 13.10.2014. Effect: None. Territorial extent & classification: E/W/S. General. - 4p.: 30 cm. - 978-0-11-112182-5 £4.25

The Children's Hearings (Scotland) Act 2011 (Consequential Provisions) Order 2014 No. 2014/2747. - Enabling power: Scotland Act 1998, ss. 104, 112 (1), 113 (2) (5). - Issued: 20.10.2014. Made: 13.10.2014. Laid: 15.10.2014. Coming into force: 06.11.2014. Effect: 2000/413, 414, 415, 419 amended. Territorial extent & classification: E/W/S/NI. General. - 4p.: 30 cm. - 978-0-11-112179-5 £4.25

Children and young persons, England

The Adoption and Care Planning (Miscellaneous Amendments) Regulations 2014 No. 2014/1556. - Enabling power: Adoption and Children Act 2002, ss. 9 (1) (a), 140 (7) (8) & Children Act 1989, ss. 22C (11), 31A (3), 34 (8) (za), 104 (4), sch. 2, para. 12E. - Issued: 18.06.2014. Made: 09.06.2014. Laid: 18.06.2014. Coming into force: 25.07.2014. Effect: S.I. 2005/389; 2010/959 amended. Territorial extent & classification: E. General. - 4p.: 30 cm. - 978-0-11-111653-1 £4.25

The Adoption and Children Act Register Regulations 2014 No. 2014/1492. - Enabling power: Adoption and Children Act 2002, ss. 125 (1) (1A) (4), 128 (1) (2) (5), 129 (2A) (3), 140 (7) (8). - Issued: 19.06.2014. Made: 09.06.2014. Laid: 18.06.2014. Coming into force: 25.07.2014. Effect: S.I. 2005/389 amended. Territorial extent & classification: E. General. - 8p.: 30 cm. - 978-0-11-111657-9 £6.00

The Adoption and Children Act Register (Search and Inspection) (Pilot) Regulations 2014 No. 2014/1957. - Enabling power: Adoption and Children Act 2002, ss. 128A (1) to (4), 140 (7) (8). - Issued: 29.07.2014. Made: 23.07.2014. Coming into force: 25.07.2014, in accord. with reg. 1. Effect: None. Territorial extent & classification: E. General. - Supersedes draft S.I. (ISBN 9780111116418) issued 16.06.2014. - 8p.: 30 cm. - 978-0-11-111918-1 £4.25

The Adoption Information and Intermediary Services (Pre-Commencement Adoptions) (Amendment) Regulations 2014 No. 2014/2696. - Enabling power: Adoption and Children Act 2002, ss. 9 (1), 98 (1) (1A) (2) (3), 140 (7) (8). - Issued: 13.10.2014. Made: 02.10.2014. Laid: 09.10.2014. Coming into force: 31.10.2014. Effect: S.I. 2005/890 amended. Territorial extent & classification: E. General. - 8p.: 30 cm. - 978-0-11-112134-4 £4.25

The Adoption Support Services (Amendment) Regulations 2014 No. 2014/1563. - Enabling power: Adoption and Children Act 2002, s. 4B, 140 (7) (8). - Issued: 19.06.2014. Made: 09.06.2014. Laid: 18.06.2014. Coming into force: 25.07.2014. Effect: S.I. 2005/691 amended. Territorial extent & classification: E. General. - 4p.: 30 cm. - 978-0-11-111662-3 £4.25

The Care Planning and Care Leavers (Amendment) Regulations 2014 No. 2014/1917. - Enabling power: Children Act 1989, ss. 22C (11), 23E (1B) (1C) (2), 26 (1) (2), 31A (3), 104 (4), sch. 2, para. 19B (7). - Issued: 25.07.2014. Made: 17.07.2014. Laid: 22.07.2014. Coming into force: 18.08.2014. Effect: S.I. 2010/959, 2571 amended. Territorial extent & classification: E. General. - 4p.: 30 cm. - 978-0-11-111891-7 £4.25

The Childcare (Childminder Agencies) (Cancellation etc) Regulations 2014 No. 2014/1922. - Enabling power: Childcare Act 2006, ss. 69A, 69B (4), 104 (2). - Issued: 13.08.2014. Made: 06.08.2014. Laid: 11.08.2014. Coming into force: 01.09.2014. Effect: None. Territorial extent & classification: E. General. - 8p.: 30 cm. - 978-0-11-111974-7 £6.00

The Childcare (Childminder Agencies) (Miscellaneous Amendments) Regulations 2014 No. 2014/1921. - Enabling power: Childcare Act 2006, ss. 12 (2), 35 (2) (c), 36 (2) (c), 37A (3), 54 (2) (c), 55 (2) (c), 56A (3), 59, 65A (5), 67, 69 (1), 75, 76A, 83 (1) (2), 84 (1) (3), 90 (2), 104 (2). - Issued: 13.08.2014. Made: 06.08.2014. Laid: 11.08.2014. Coming into force: 01.09.2014. Effect: S.I. 2007/722, 3490; 2008/976, 1804; 2009/1547 amended. Territorial extent & classification: E. General. - 8p.: 30 cm. - 978-0-11-111975-4 £6.00

The Childcare (Childminder Agencies) (Registration, Inspection and Supply and Disclosure of Information) Regulations 2014 No. 2014/1920. - Enabling power: Childcare Act 2006, ss. 51A (2) (a) (c) (3) (b) (5), 51B (2), 51D (4), 61A (2) (a) (c) (3) (b) (5), 61B (2), 61E (4), 83A (1) (2), 84A (1) (3), 89, 92 (3), 104 (2). - Issued: 13.08.2014. Made: 06.08.2014. Laid: 11.08.2014. Coming into force: 01.09.2014. Effect: None. Territorial extent & classification: E. General. - 16p.: 30 cm. - 978-0-11-111973-0 £6.00

The Childcare (Learning and Development Requirements and Exemptions from Registration) (Amendment) Order 2014 No. 2014/913. - Enabling power: Childcare Act 2006, ss. 33 (2) (3), 34 (3) (4), 39 (1) (a), 42 (1) (2), 44 (1) to (4), 52 (2) (3), 53 (3) (4), 104 (2). - Issued: 10.04.2014. Made: 03.04.2014. Laid: 08.04.2014. Coming into force: 01.09.2014. Effect: S.I. 2007/1772 amended. Territorial extent & classification: E. General. - 4p.: 30 cm. - 978-0-11-111376-9 £4.25

The Childcare Providers (Information, Advice and Training) Regulations 2014 No. 2014/2319. - Enabling power: Childcare Act 2006, ss. 13 (1), 104 (2). - Issued: 05.09.2014. Made: 28.08.2014. Laid: 03.09.2014. Coming into force: 24.09.2014. Effect: S.I. 2007/1797 revoked. Territorial extent & classification: E. General. - 4p.: 30 cm. - 978-0-11-112005-7 £4.25

The Childcare (Provision of Information About Young Children) (England) (Amendment) Regulations 2014 No. 2014/3197. - Enabling power: Childcare Act 2006, ss. 99 (1) (2) (b), 104 (2). - Issued: 08.12.2014. Made: 28.11.2014. Laid: 04.12.2014. Coming into force: 01.01.2015. Effect: S.I. 2009/1554 amended. Territorial extent & classification: E. General. - 4p.: 30 cm. - 978-0-11-112449-9 £4.25

The Childcare (Welfare and Registration Requirements) (Amendment) Regulations 2014 No. 2014/912. - Enabling power: Childcare Act 2006, ss. 35, 36, 39 (1) (b), 43 (1) (3), 44 (1) to (4), 54, 55, 59, 67, 104 (2). - Issued: 10.04.2014. Made: 03.04.2014. Laid: 08.04.2014. Coming into force: 01.09.2014. Effect: S.I. 2008/974, 975; 2012/938 amended. Territorial extent & classification: E. General. - 12p.: 30 cm. - 978-0-11-111375-2 £6.00

The Children and Young Persons Act 2008 (Relevant Care Functions) (England) Regulations 2014 No. 2014/2407. - Enabling power: Children and Young Persons Act 2008, ss. 1 (6) (7), 40 (12). - Issued: 15.09.2014. Made: 09.09.2014. Coming into force: 10.09.2014. Effect: None. Territorial extent & classification: E. General. - Supersedes draft S.I. (ISBN 9780111116920) issued 27.06.2014. - 2p.: 30 cm. - 978-0-11-112059-0 £4.25

The Children (Performances and Activities) (England) Regulations 2014 No. 2014/3309. - Enabling power: Children and Young Persons Act 1933, ss. 25 (2) (8) & Children and Young Persons Act 1963, ss. 37 (3) (4) (5) (6), 39 (3) (5). - Issued: 19.12.2014. Made: 15.12.2014. Laid: 17.12.2014. Coming into force: 06.02.2015. Effect: S.I. 1968/1728; 1998/1678; 2000/10, 2384 revoked in respect of England. Territorial extent & classification: E. General. - 16p.: 30 cm. - 978-0-11-112576-2 £6.00

Her Majesty's Chief Inspector of Education, Children's Services and Skills (Fees and Frequency of Inspections) (Children's Homes etc.) (Amendment) Regulations 2014 No. 2014/670. - Enabling power: Children Act 1989, ss. 87D (2), 104 (4) (a) & Care Standards Act 2000, ss. 16 (3), 118 (5) (6) & Education and Inspections Act 2006, ss. 155 (1) (2), 181 (2). - Issued: 25.03.2014. Made: 25.02.2014. Laid: 17.03.2014. Coming into force: 01.04.2014. Effect: S.I. 2007/694 amended. Territorial extent & classification: E. General. - This Statutory Instrument has been published in substitution of S.I. 2014/410 (ISBN 9780111110287) to replace the incorrect version of that Statutory Instrument which was published in error. It is being issued free of charge to all known recipients of that Statutory Instrument. Revoked by SI 2015/551 (ISBN 9780111132265). - 4p.: 30 cm. - 978-0-11-111235-9 £4.00

The Inspectors of Education, Children's Services and Skills (No. 2) Order 2014 No. 2014/498. - Enabling power: Education and Inspections Act 2006, s. 114 (1). - Issued: 11.03.2014. Made: 05.03.2014. Coming into force: 06.03.2014. Effect: None. Territorial extent & classification: E. General. - 2p.: 30 cm. - 978-0-11-111102-4 £4.00

The Inspectors of Education, Children's Services and Skills (No. 3) Order 2014 No. 2014/1103. - Enabling power: Education and Inspections Act 2006, s. 114 (1). - Issued: 02.05.2014. Made: 28.04.2014. Coming into force: 29.04.2014. Effect: None. Territorial extent & classification: E. General. - 2p.: 30 cm. - 978-0-11-111436-0 £4.25

The Inspectors of Education, Children's Services and Skills (No. 4) Order 2014 No. 2014/1354. - Enabling power: Education and Inspections Act 2006, s. 114 (1). - Issued: 03.06.2014. Made: 27.05.2014. Coming into force: 28.05.2014. Effect: None. Territorial extent & classification: E. General. - 2p.: 30 cm. - 978-0-11-111526-8 £4.25

The Inspectors of Education, Children's Services and Skills (No. 5) Order 2014 No. 2014/1560. - Enabling power: Education and Inspections Act 2006, s. 114 (1). - Issued: 19.06.2014. Made: 12.06.2014. Coming into force: 13.06.2014. Effect: None. Territorial extent & classification: E. General. - 2p.: 30 cm. - 978-0-11-111656-2 £4.25

The Inspectors of Education, Children's Services and Skills (No. 6) Order 2014 No. 2014/1877. - Enabling power: Education and Inspections Act 2006, s. 114 (1). - Issued: 23.07.2014. Made: 16.07.2014. Coming into force: 17.07.2014. Effect: None. Territorial extent & classification: E. General. - 2p.: 30 cm. - 978-0-11-111839-9 £4.25

The Inspectors of Education, Children's Services and Skills (No. 7) Order 2014 No. 2014/2921. - Enabling power: Education and Inspections Act 2006, s. 114 (1). - Issued: 12.11.2014. Made: 05.11.2014. Coming into force: 06.11.2014. Effect: None. Territorial extent & classification: E. General. - 2p.: 30 cm. - 978-0-11-112300-3 £4.25

The Inspectors of Education, Children's Services and Skills Order 2014 No. 2014/261. - Enabling power: Education and Inspections Act 2006, s. 114 (1). - Issued: 18.02.2014. Made: 11.02.2014. Coming into force: 12.02.2014. Effect: None. Territorial extent & classification: E. General. - 2p.: 30 cm. - 978-0-11-110965-6 £4.00

The Local Authority (Duty to Secure Early Years Provision Free of Charge) (Amendment) Regulations 2014 No. 2014/1705. - Enabling power: Childcare Act 2006 ss. 7, 104 (2). - Issued: 07.07.2014. Made: 27.06.2014. Laid: 03.07.2014. Coming into force: 01.09.2014. Effect: S.I. 2013/3193 amended. Territorial extent & classification: E. General. - 2p.: 30 cm. - 978-0-11-111740-8 £4.25

The Local Authority (Duty to Secure Early Years Provision Free of Charge) Regulations 2014 No. 2014/2147. - Enabling power: Childcare Act 2006 ss. 7, 7A, 9A, 104 (2). - Issued: 18.08.2014. Made: 11.08.2014. Laid: 14.08.2014. Coming into force: 08.09.2014. Effect: S.I. 2013/3193; 2014/1705 revoked. Territorial extent & classification: E. General. - 8p.: 30 cm. - 978-0-11-111988-4 £6.00

Children and young persons, England and Wales

The Adoption and Children Act 2002 (Commencement No. 12) Order 2014 No. 2014/1961 (C.90). - Enabling power: Adoption and Children Act 2002, s. 148 (1). Bringing into operation various provisions of the 2002 Act on 25.07.2014, in accord. with art. 2. - Issued: 29.07.2014. Made: 22.07.2014. Effect: None. Territorial extent & classification: E/W. General- 12p.: 30 cm. - 978-0-11-111922-8 £6.00

The Disclosure and Barring Service (Core Functions) (Amendment) Order 2014 No. 2014/238. - Enabling power: Protection of Freedoms Act 2012, sch. 8, para. 8 (1) (d). - Issued: 13.02.2014. Made: 05.02.2014. Laid: 13.02.2014. Coming into force: 10.03.2014. Effect: S.I. 2012/2522 amended. Territorial extent & classification: E/W. General. - 4p.: 30 cm. - 978-0-11-110938-0 £4.00

The Protection of Freedoms Act 2012 (Commencement No. 3) (Amendment) Order 2014 No. 2014/831 (C.35). - Enabling power: Protection of Freedoms Act 2012, ss. 116 (1). Bringing into operation various provisions of the 2012 Act on 31.12.2014. - Issued: 01.04.2014. Made: 24.03.2014. Coming into force: 31.03.2014. Effect: S.I. 2012/2234 C.89 amended. Territorial extent & classification: E/W/NI. General. - 2p.: 30 cm. - 978-0-11-111286-1 £4.00

Children and young persons, Northern Ireland

The Protection of Freedoms Act 2012 (Commencement No. 3) (Amendment) Order 2014 No. 2014/831 (C.35). - Enabling power: Protection of Freedoms Act 2012, ss. 116 (1). Bringing into operation various provisions of the 2012 Act on 31.12.2014. - Issued: 01.04.2014. Made: 24.03.2014. Coming into force: 31.03.2014. Effect: S.I. 2012/2234 C.89 amended. Territorial extent & classification: E/W/NI. General. - 2p.: 30 cm. - 978-0-11-111286-1 £4.00

Children and young persons, Wales

The Adoption Agencies (Wales) (Amendment) Regulations 2014 No. 2014/567 (W.68). - Enabling power: Adoption and Children Act 2002, ss. 9 (1) (a), 140 (7) (8), 142 (4) (5). - Issued: 26.03.2014. Made: 10.03.2014. Laid before the National Assembly for Wales: 11.03.2014. Coming into force: 01.04.2014. Effect: S.I. 2005/1313 (W.95) amended. Territorial extent & classification: W. General. - In English and Welsh. Welsh title: Rheoliadau Asiantaethau Mabwysiadu (Cymru) (Diwygio) 2014. - 8p.: 30 cm. - 978-0-348-10925-2 £5.75

The Children and Families (Wales) Measure 2010 (Commencement No. 8) Order 2014 No. 2014/373 (W.41). - Enabling power: Children and Families (Wales) Measure 2010, ss. 74 (2), 75 (3). Bringing into operation various provisions of the 2010 Measure on 28.02.2014. - Issued: 03.03.2014. Made: 18.02.2014. Effect: None. Territorial extent & classification: W. General. - In English and Welsh. Welsh title: Gorchymyn Mesur Plant a Theuluoedd (Cymru) 2010 (Cychwyn Rhif 8) 2014. - 8p.: 30 cm. - 978-0-348-10892-7 £5.75

The Children and Families (Wales) Measure 2010 (Commencement No. 9) Order 2014 No. 2014/1606 (W.164) (C.64). - Enabling power: Children and Families (Wales) Measure 2010, s. 75 (3). Bringing into operation various provisions of the 2010 Measure on 30.06.2014, 01.07.2014, in accord. with art. 2. - Issued: 26.06.2014. Made: 11.06.2014. Effect: None. Territorial extent & classification: W. General. - In English and Welsh. Welsh title: Gorchymyn Mesur Plant a Theuluoedd (Cymru) 2010 (Cychwyn Rhif 9) 2014. - 8p.: 30 cm. - 978-0-348-10955-9 £6.00

The Representations Procedure (Wales) Regulations 2014 No. 2014/1795 (W.188). - Enabling power: Children Act 1989, ss. 24D (1A), 24D (2), 26(3A) (3B) (3C) (4A) (5) (5A) (6), 26A (3), 104 (4),104A. sch. 7, para. 6. - Issued: 25.07.2014. Made: 07.07.2014. Laid before the National Assembly for Wales: 09.07.2014. Coming into force: 01.08.2014. Effect: W.S.I. 2007/1357 (W.128) amended & W.S.I. 2005/3365 (W.262) revoked with saving. Territorial extent & classification: W. General. - In English and Welsh. Welsh title: Rheoliadau Gweithdrefn Sylwadau (Cymru) 2014. - 20p.: 30 cm. - 978-0-348-10973-3 £6.00

The Social Services Complaints Procedure (Wales) Regulations 2014 No. 2014/1794 (W.187). - Enabling power: Health and Social Care (Community Health and Standards) Act 2003, ss. 114 (3) (4) (5) (b) (c), 115 (1) (2) (4) (5) (6), 195 (1) (b). - Issued: 23.07.2014. Made: 07.07.2014. Laid before the National Assembly for Wales: 09.07.2014. Coming into force: 01.08.2014. Effect: S.I. 2007/1357 (W.128); 2011/964 (W.138) amended & S.I. 2005/3366 (W.263) revoked with saving. Territorial extent & classification: W. General. - In English and Welsh. Welsh title: Rheoliadau Gweithdrefn Gwynion y Gwasanaethau Cymdeithasol (Cymru) 2014. - 20p.: 30 cm. - 978-0-348-10970-2 £6.00

Child trust funds

The Child Trust Funds (Amendment No. 2) Regulations 2014 No. 2014/1453. - Enabling power: Child Trust Funds Act 2004, ss. 3 (3) (5), 5 (4), 7, 12 (2), 13, 15, 28 (1) (3). - Issued: 11.06.2014. Made: 04.06.2014. Laid: 05.06.2014. Coming into force: 01.07.2014. Effect: S.I. 2004/1450 amended. Territorial extent & classification: E/W/S/NI. General. - 2p.: 30 cm. - 978-0-11-111600-5 £4.25

The Child Trust Funds (Amendment) Regulations 2014 No. 2014/649. - Enabling power: Child Trust Funds Act 2004, ss. 3 (1) to (3) (4) (d) (5), 12 (2), 28 (1) (3). - Issued: 20.03.2014. Made: 14.03.2014. Laid: 14.03.2014. Coming into force: 06.04.2014. Effect: S.I. 2004/1450 amended. Territorial extent & classification: E/W/S/NI. General. - 4p.: 30 cm. - 978-0-11-111225-0 £4.00

Cinema and films

The Films Co-Production Agreements (Amendment) Order 2014 No. 2014/1561. - Enabling power: Films Act 1985, sch. 1, para. 4 (5). - Issued: 19.06.2014. Made: 12.06.2014. Coming into force: 11.07.2014. Effect: S.I. 1985/960 amended & S.I. 2011/236 revoked. Territorial extent & classification: E/W/S/NI. General. - 4p.: 30 cm. - 978-0-11-111658-6 £4.25

Civil aviation

The Air Navigation (Amendment) (No. 2) Order 2014 No. 2014/1888. - Enabling power: Civil Aviation Act 1982, ss. 60 (1) (2) (b) (3) (h) (3) (n) (3) (q) (4). - Issued: 23.07.2014. Made: 16.07.2014. Laid: 23.07.2014. Coming into force: 16.08.2014. Effect: S.I. 2009/3015 amended. Territorial extent & classification: E/W/S/NI. General. - With correction slip dated January 2015. - 4p.: 30 cm. - 978-0-11-111850-4 £4.25

The Air Navigation (Amendment) (No. 3) Order 2014 No. 2014/2920. - Enabling power: Civil Aviation Act 1982, ss. 60 (1) (2) (3) (c) (h) (n), 102. - Issued: 12.11.2014. Made: 05.11.2014. Laid: 12.11.2014. Coming into force: 10.12.2014. Effect: S.I. 2009/3015 amended & S.I. 2011/2261 revoked. Territorial extent & classification: E/W/S/NI. General. - 4p.: 30 cm. - 978-0-11-112299-0 £4.25

The Air Navigation (Amendment) (No. 4) Order 2014 No. 2014/3302. - Enabling power: Civil Aviation Act 1982, ss. 60 (1) (2) (b) (3) (c) (e) (f) (g) (h) (m) (n) (4), 61 (1) (a), 102. - Issued: 17.12.2014. Made: 10.12.2014. Laid: 17.12.2014. Coming into force: 10.01.2015. Effect: 1961 c.64; 1979 c.2; 1982 c.16; 1984 c.27; S.I. 1991/1325; 2006/601; 2009/3015 amended. Territorial extent & classification: E/W/S/NI. General. - 28p.: 30 cm. - 978-0-11-112567-0 £6.00

The Air Navigation (Amendment) Order 2014 No. 2014/508. - Enabling power: Civil Aviation Act 1982, ss. 60 (1) (2) (3) (e) (f) (n) (q) (4), 61 (1) (a). - Issued: 12.03.2014. Made: 05.03.2014. Laid: 12.03.2014. Coming into force: 06.04.2014. Effect: S.I. 2009/3015 amended. Territorial extent & classification: E/W/S/NI. General. - 8p.: 30 cm. - 978-0-11-111112-3 £4.00

The Air Navigation (Jersey) Order 2008 (Revocation) Order 2014 No. 2014/2713. - Enabling power: Civil Aviation Act 1982, ss. 60, 61 (1) (2), 77, 101 & Civil Aviation Act 1982, s. 102 (1) (2), sch. 13 & Airports Act 1986 Act, s. 35. - Issued: 15.10.2014. Made: 08.10.2014. Coming into force: in accord. with art. 1. Effect: S.I. 2008/2562 revoked with savings. Territorial extent & classification: Jersey. General. - 2p.: 30 cm. - 978-0-11-112150-4 £4.25

The Air Navigation (Overseas Territories) (Amendment) (No. 2) Order 2014 No. 2014/3281. - Enabling power: Civil Aviation Act 1949, ss. 8 (2) (3). - Issued: 17.12.2014. Made: 10.12.2014. Laid: 17.12.2014. Coming into force: In accord. with art. 1. Effect: S.I. 2013/2870 amended. Territorial extent & classification: UK Overseas Territories with the exception of British Antarctic Territory and Gibraltar. General. - 4p.: 30 cm. - 978-0-11-112542-7 £4.25

The Air Navigation (Overseas Territories) (Amendment) Order 2014 No. 2014/2925. - Enabling power: Civil Aviation Act 1949, ss. 8 (1) (a) (2) (c) (f) (g) (h) (n) (3). - Issued: 12.11.2014. Made: 05.11.2014. Laid: 12.11.2014. Coming into force: In accord. with art. 1. Effect: S.I. 2013/2870 amended. Territorial extent & classification: UK Overseas Territories with the exception of British Antarctic Territory and Gibraltar. General. - 8p.: 30 cm. - 978-0-11-112305-8 £4.25

The Air Navigation (Overseas Territories) (Environmental Standards) Order 2014 No. 2014/2926. - Enabling power: Civil Aviation Act 1949, s. 8 (1) (2) (p) & Civil Aviation Act 1982, s. 108 (1). - Issued: 12.11.2014. Made: 05.11.2014. Laid: 12.11.2014. Coming into force: 03.12.2014. Effect: None. Territorial extent & classification: All the British Overseas Territories except Gibraltar. General. - 12p.: 30 cm. - 978-0-11-112306-5 £6.00

The Air Navigation (Restriction of Flying) (Abingdon Air and Country Show) Regulations 2014 No. 2014/215. - Enabling power: S.I. 2009/3015, art. 161. - Issued: 06.02.2014. Made: 03.02.2014. Coming into force: 03.05.2014. Effect: None. Territorial extent & classification: E. Local. - Available at http://www.legislation.gov.uk/uksi/2014/215/contents/made Non-print

The Air Navigation (Restriction of Flying) (Ascot) (Amendment) Regulations 2014 No. 2014/1939. - Enabling power: S.I. 2009/3015, art. 161. - Issued: 23.07.2014. Made: 14.07.2014. Coming into force: 14.08.2014. Effect: S.I. 2014/1558 amended. Territorial extent & classification: E. Local. - Available at http://www.legislation.gov.uk/uksi/2014/1939/contents/made Non-print

The Air Navigation (Restriction of Flying) (Ascot) Regulations 2014 No. 2014/1558. - Enabling power: S.I. 2009/3015, art. 161. - Issued: 16.06.2014. Made: 12.06.2014. Coming into force: 14.08.2014. Effect: None. Territorial extent & classification: E. Local. - Available at http://www.legislation.gov.uk/uksi/2014/1558/contents/made Non-print

CIVIL AVIATION

The Air Navigation (Restriction of Flying) (Auchterarder) (Amendment) Regulations 2014 No. 2014/1938. - Enabling power: S.I. 2009/3015, art. 161. - Issued: 23.07.2014. Made: 14.07.2014. Coming into force: 24.09.2014. Effect: S.I. 2014/1657 amended. Territorial extent & classification: E. Local. - Available at http://www.legislation.gov.uk/uksi/2014/1938/contents/made Non-print

The Air Navigation (Restriction of Flying) (Auchterarder) Regulations 2014 No. 2014/1657. - Enabling power: S.I. 2009/3015, art. 161. - Issued: 27.06.2014. Made: 24.06.2014. Coming into force: 24.09.2014. Effect: None. Territorial extent & classification: E. Local. - Available at http://www.legislation.gov.uk/uksi/2014/1657/contents/made Non-print

The Air Navigation (Restriction of Flying) (Balado) Regulations 2014 No. 2014/1141. - Enabling power: S.I. 2009/3015, art. 161. - Issued: 06.05.2014. Made: 28.04.2014. Coming into force: 10.07.2014. Effect: None. Territorial extent & classification: E. Local. - Available at http://www.legislation.gov.uk/uksi/2014/1141/contents/made Non-print

The Air Navigation (Restriction of Flying) (Bournemouth) Regulations 2014 No. 2014/1281. - Enabling power: S.I. 2009/3015, art. 161. - Issued: 20.05.2014. Made: 15.05.2014. Coming into force: 28.08.2014. Effect: None. Territorial extent & classification: E. Local. - Available at http://www.legislation.gov.uk/uksi/2014/1281/contents/made Non-print

The Air Navigation (Restriction of Flying) (Bristol Channel) Regulations 2014 No. 2014/2392. - Enabling power: Air Navigation Order 2009, art. 161. - Issued: 08.09.2014. Made: 22.08.2014. Coming into force: 05.09.2014. Effect: None. Territorial extent & classification: E. Local. - Available at http://www.legislation.gov.uk/uksi/2014/2392/contents/made Non-print

The Air Navigation (Restriction of Flying) (Cheltenham Festival) Regulations 2014 No. 2014/139. - Enabling power: S.I. 2009/3015, art. 161. - Issued: 27.01.2014. Made: 22.01.2014. Coming into force: 11.03.2014. Effect: None. Territorial extent & classification: E. Local. - Available at http://www.legislation.gov.uk/uksi/2014/139/contents/made Non-print

The Air Navigation (Restriction of Flying) (Cholmondeley Castle) Regulations 2014 No. 2014/272. - Enabling power: S.I. 2009/3015, art. 161. - Issued: 10.02.2014. Made: 05.02.2014. Coming into force: 13.06.2014. Effect: None. Territorial extent & classification: E. Local. - Available at http://www.legislation.gov.uk/uksi/2014/272/contents/made Non-print

The Air Navigation (Restriction of Flying) (Dunsfold) Regulations 2014 No. 2014/1579. - Enabling power: S.I. 2009/3015, art. 161. - Issued: 17.06.2014. Made: 10.06.2014. Coming into force: 23.08.2014. Effect: None. Territorial extent & classification: E. Local. - Available at http://www.legislation.gov.uk/uksi/2014/1579/contents/made Non-print

The Air Navigation (Restriction of Flying) (Duxford Aerodrome) (No. 2) Regulations 2014 No. 2014/1235. - Enabling power: S.I. 2009/3015, art. 161. - Issued: 15.05.2014. Made: 13.05.2014. Coming into force: 23.05.2014. Effect: None. Territorial extent & classification: E. Local. - Available at http://www.legislation.gov.uk/uksi/2014/1235/contents/made Non-print

The Air Navigation (Restriction of Flying) (Duxford Aerodrome) Regulations 2014 No. 2014/88. - Enabling power: S.I. 2009/3015, art. 161. - Issued: 21.01.2014. Made: 16.01.2014. Coming into force: 24.05.2014. Effect: None. Territorial extent & classification: E. Local. - Available at http://www.legislation.gov.uk/uksi/2014/88/contents/made Non-print

The Air Navigation (Restriction of Flying) (Eastbourne) Regulations 2014 No. 2014/1278. - Enabling power: S.I. 2009/3015, art. 161. - Issued: 20.05.2014. Made: 15.05.2014. Coming into force: 14.08.2014. Effect: None. Territorial extent & classification: E. Local. - Available at http://www.legislation.gov.uk/uksi/2014/1278/contents/made Non-print

The Air Navigation (Restriction of Flying) (Farnborough Air Show) (Amendment) Regulations 2014 No. 2014/1973. - Enabling power: S.I. 2009/3015, art. 161. - Issued: 23.07.2014. Made: 11.07.2014. Coming into force: 13.07.2014. Effect: S.I. 2014/700 amended. Territorial extent & classification: E. Local. - Available at http://www.legislation.gov.uk/uksi/2014/1973/contents/made Non-print

The Air Navigation (Restriction of Flying) (Farnborough Air Show) Regulations 2014 No. 2014/700. - Enabling power: S.I. 2009/3015, art. 161. - Issued: 13.03.2014. Made: 27.02.2014. Coming into force: 07.07.2014. Effect: None. Territorial extent & classification: E. Local. - Available at http://www.legislation.gov.uk/uksi/2014/700/contents/made Non-print

The Air Navigation (Restriction of Flying) (Folkestone) Regulations 2014 No. 2014/273. - Enabling power: S.I. 2009/3015, art. 161. - Issued: 10.02.2014. Made: 05.02.2014. Coming into force: 07.06.2014. Effect: None. Territorial extent & classification: E. Local. - Available at http://www.legislation.gov.uk/uksi/2014/273/contents/made Non-print

The Air Navigation (Restriction of Flying) (Giro d'Italia Stage 1) (Amendment) Regulations 2014 No. 2014/1191. - Enabling power: S.I. 2009/3015, art. 161. - Issued: 12.05.2014. Made: 02.05.2014. Coming into force: 09.05.2014. Effect: S.I. 2014/1144 amended. Territorial extent & classification: E. Local. - Available at http://www.legislation.gov.uk/uksi/2014/1191/contents/made Non-print

The Air Navigation (Restriction of Flying) (Giro d'Italia Stage 1) Regulations 2014 No. 2014/1144. - Enabling power: S.I. 2009/3015, art. 161. - Issued: 06.05.2014. Made: 28.04.2013. Coming into force: 09.05.2014. Effect: None. Territorial extent & classification: E. Local. - Available at http://www.legislation.gov.uk/uksi/2014/1144/contents/made Non-print

The Air Navigation (Restriction of Flying) (Giro d'Italia Stage 2) (Amendment) Regulations 2014 No. 2014/1192. - Enabling power: S.I. 2009/3015, art. 161. - Issued: 12.05.2014. Made: 02.05.2013. Coming into force: 10.05.2014. Effect: S.I. 2014/1143 amended. Territorial extent & classification: E. Local. - Available at http://www.legislation.gov.uk/uksi/2014/1192/contents/made Non-print

The Air Navigation (Restriction of Flying) (Giro d'Italia Stage 2) Regulations 2014 No. 2014/1143. - Enabling power: S.I. 2009/3015, art. 161. - Issued: 06.05.2014. Made: 28.04.2013. Coming into force: 10.05.2014. Effect: None. Territorial extent & classification: E. Local. - Available at http://www.legislation.gov.uk/uksi/2014/1143/contents/made Non-print

The Air Navigation (Restriction of Flying) (Giro d'Italia Stage 3) Regulations 2014 No. 2014/1193. - Enabling power: S.I. 2009/3015, art. 161. - Issued: 12.05.2014. Made: 02.05.2013. Coming into force: 11.05.2014. Effect: None. Territorial extent & classification: E. Local. - Available at http://www.legislation.gov.uk/uksi/2014/1193/contents/made Non-print

The Air Navigation (Restriction of Flying) (Glasgow 2014 Commonwealth Games, Cycle Time Trial Event, Muirhead, North Lanarkshire Prohibited Zone) Regulations 2014 No. 2014/439. - Enabling power: S.I. 2009/3015, art. 161. - Issued: 03.04.2014. Made: 26.03.2014. Coming into force: 01.05.2014. Effect: None. Territorial extent & classification: E. General. - 4p.: 30 cm. - 978-0-11-111310-3 £4.00

The Air Navigation (Restriction of Flying) (Glasgow 2014 Commonwealth Games, Diving Event, Edinburgh) Regulations 2014 No. 2014/849. - Enabling power: S.I. 2009/3015, art. 161. - Issued: 04.04.2014. Made: 26.03.2014. Coming into force: 30.07.2014. Effect: None. Territorial extent & classification: E. General. - 4p.: 30 cm. - 978-0-11-111319-6 £4.00

The Air Navigation (Restriction of Flying) (Glasgow 2014 Commonwealth Games, Glasgow Prohibited Zone EGP502) Regulations 2014 No. 2014/437. - Enabling power: S.I. 2009/3015, art. 161. - Issued: 03.04.2014. Made: 26.03.2014. Coming into force: 01.05.2014. Effect: None. Territorial extent & classification: E. General. - 4p.: 30 cm. - 978-0-11-111311-0 £4.00

The Air Navigation (Restriction of Flying) (Glasgow 2014 Commonwealth Games, Glasgow Restricted Zone EGR503) Regulations 2014 No. 2014/848. - Enabling power: S.I. 2009/3015, art. 161. - Issued: 04.04.2014. Made: 26.03.2014. Coming into force: 01.05.2014. Effect: None. Territorial extent & classification: E. General. - 8p.: 30 cm. - 978-0-11-111318-9 £4.00

The Air Navigation (Restriction of Flying) (Glasgow 2014 Commonwealth Games, Shooting Event, Barry Buddon, Angus) Regulations 2014 No. 2014/850. - Enabling power: S.I. 2009/3015, art. 161. - Issued: 04.04.2014. Made: 26.03.2014. Coming into force: 25.07.2014. Effect: None. Territorial extent & classification: E. General. - 4p.: 30 cm. - 978-0-11-111321-9 £4.00

CIVIL AVIATION

The Air Navigation (Restriction of Flying) (Glasgow 2014 Commonwealth Games, Triathlon Event, Strathclyde Country Park, North Lanarkshire Prohibited Zone) Regulations 2014 No. 2014/438. - Enabling power: S.I. 2009/3015, art. 161. - Issued: 03.04.2014. Made: 26.03.2014. Coming into force: 01.05.2014. Effect: None. Territorial extent & classification: E. General. - 4p.: 30 cm. - 978-0-11-111309-7 £4.00

The Air Navigation (Restriction of Flying) (Glastonbury Festival) Regulations 2014 No. 2014/141. - Enabling power: S.I. 2009/3015, art. 161. - Issued: 28.01.2014. Made: 23.01.2014. Coming into force: 23.06.2014. Effect: None. Territorial extent & classification: E. Local. - Available at http://www.legislation.gov.uk/uksi/2014/141/contents/made Non-print

The Air Navigation (Restriction of Flying) (Her Majesty The Queen's Birthday Flypast) Regulations 2014 No. 2014/216. - Enabling power: S.I. 2009/3015, art. 161. - Issued: 06.02.2014. Made: 03.02.2014. Coming into force: 10.06.2014. Effect: None. Territorial extent & classification: E. Local. - Available at http://www.legislation.gov.uk/uksi/2014/216/contents/made Non-print

The Air Navigation (Restriction of Flying) (Hylands Park) Regulations 2014 No. 2014/1140. - Enabling power: S.I. 2009/3015, art. 161. - Issued: 06.05.2014. Made: 29.04.2014. Coming into force: 15.08.2014. Effect: None. Territorial extent & classification: E. Local. - Available at http://www.legislation.gov.uk/uksi/2014/1140/contents/made Non-print

The Air Navigation (Restriction of Flying) (Jet Formation Display Team, County Londonderry) Regulations 2014 No. 2014/1555. - Enabling power: S.I. 2009/3015, art. 161. - Issued: 16.06.2014. Made: 10.06.2014. Coming into force: 29.08.2014. Effect: None. Territorial extent & classification: E. Local. - Available at http://www.legislation.gov.uk/uksi/2014/1555/contents/made Non-print

The Air Navigation (Restriction of Flying) (Jet Formation Display Teams) (No. 2) Regulations 2014 No. 2014/746. - Enabling power: S.I. 2009/3015, art. 161. - Issued: 19.03.2014. Made: 11.0.2014. Coming into force: 19.03.2014. Effect: None. Territorial extent & classification: E. Local. - Available at http://www.legislation.gov.uk/uksi/2014/746/contents/made Non-print

The Air Navigation (Restriction of Flying) (Jet Formation Display Teams) (No. 3) Regulations 2014 No. 2014/809. - Enabling power: S.I. 2009/3015, art. 161. - Issued: 26.03.2014. Made: 24.03.2014. Coming into force: 31.05.2014. Effect: None. Territorial extent & classification: E. Local. - Available at http://www.legislation.gov.uk/uksi/2014/809/contents/made Non-print

The Air Navigation (Restriction of Flying) (Jet Formation Display Teams) (No. 4) (Amendment) Regulations 2014 No. 2014/2389. - Enabling power: Air Navigation Order 2009, art. 161. - Issued: 08.09.2014. Made: 22.08.2014. Coming into force: 23.08.2014. Effect: None. Territorial extent & classification: E. Local. - Available at http://www.legislation.gov.uk/uksi/2014/2389/contents/made Non-print

The Air Navigation (Restriction of Flying) (Jet Formation Display Teams) (No. 4) Regulations 2014 No. 2014/1528. - Enabling power: S.I. 2009/3015, art. 161. - Issued: 10.06.2014. Made: 05.06.2014. Coming into force: 08.08.2014. Effect: None. Territorial extent & classification: E. Local. - Available at http://www.legislation.gov.uk/uksi/2014/1528/contents/made Non-print

The Air Navigation (Restriction of Flying) (Jet Formation Display Teams) Regulations 2014 No. 2014/214. - Enabling power: S.I. 2009/3015, art. 161. - Issued: 06.02.2014. Made: 03.02.2014. Coming into force: 12.03.2014. Effect: None. Territorial extent & classification: E. Local. - Available at http://www.legislation.gov.uk/uksi/2014/214/contents/made Non-print

The Air Navigation (Restriction of Flying) (Jim Clark Rally) Regulations 2014 No. 2014/1002. - Enabling power: S.I. 2009/3015, art. 161. - Issued: 15.04.2014. Made: 10.04.2014. Coming into force: 30.05.2014. Effect: None. Territorial extent & classification: E. Local. - Available at http://www.legislation.gov.uk/uksi/2014/1002/contents/made Non-print

The Air Navigation (Restriction of Flying) (Newport) (Amendment) Regulations 2014 No. 2014/2206. - Enabling power: S.I. 2009/3015, art. 161. - Issued: 08.09.2014. Made: 13.08.2014. Coming into force: 03.09.2014. Effect: S.I. 2014/1840 amended. Territorial extent & classification: E. Local. - Available at http://www.legislation.gov.uk/uksi/2014/2206/contents/made Non-print

The Air Navigation (Restriction of Flying) (Newport) Regulations 2014 No. 2014/1840. - Enabling power: S.I. 2009/3015, art. 161. - Issued: 08.09.2014. Made: 08.07.2014. Coming into force: 03.09.2014. Effect: None. Territorial extent & classification: E. Local. - Available at http://www.legislation.gov.uk/uksi/2014/1840/contents/made Non-print

The Air Navigation (Restriction of Flying) (Northampton Sywell) (No. 2) Regulations 2014 No. 2014/274. - Enabling power: S.I. 2009/3015, art. 161. - Issued: 10.02.2014. Made: 05.02.2014. Coming into force: 17.08.2014. Effect: None. Territorial extent & classification: E. Local. - Available at http://www.legislation.gov.uk/uksi/2014/274/contents/made Non-print

The Air Navigation (Restriction of Flying) (Northampton Sywell) (No. 3) Regulations 2014 No. 2014/318. - Enabling power: S.I. 2009/3015, art. 161. - Issued: 17.02.2014. Made: 13.02.2014. Coming into force: 29.08.2014. Effect: None. Territorial extent & classification: E. Local. - Available at http://www.legislation.gov.uk/uksi/2014/318/contents/made Non-print

The Air Navigation (Restriction of Flying) (Northampton Sywell) Regulations 2014 No. 2014/140. - Enabling power: S.I. 2009/3015, art. 161. - Issued: 27.01.2014. Made: 22.01.2014. Coming into force: 30.05.2014. Effect: None. Territorial extent & classification: E. Local. - Available at http://www.legislation.gov.uk/uksi/2014/140/contents/made Non-print

The Air Navigation (Restriction of Flying) (Northern Ireland International Air Show) Regulations 2014 No. 2014/1578. - Enabling power: S.I. 2009/3015, art. 161. - Issued: 17.06.2014. Made: 10.06.2014. Coming into force: 06.09.2014. Effect: None. Territorial extent & classification: E. Local. - Available at http://www.legislation.gov.uk/uksi/2014/1578/contents/made Non-print

The Air Navigation (Restriction of Flying) (Overton) Regulations 2014 No. 2014/1580. - Enabling power: S.I. 2014/1580, art. 161. - Issued: 17.06.2014. Made: 10.05.2014. Coming into force: 22.08.2014. Effect: None. Territorial extent & classification: E. Local. - Available at http://www.legislation.gov.uk/uksi/2014/1580/contents/made Non-print

The Air Navigation (Restriction of Flying) (Pembrey) Regulations 2014 No. 2014/2393. - Enabling power: Air Navigation Order 2009, art. 161. - Issued: 08.09.2014. Made: 22.08.2014. Coming into force: 03.09.2014. Effect: None. Territorial extent & classification: E. Local. - Available at http://www.legislation.gov.uk/uksi/2014/2393/contents/made Non-print

The Air Navigation (Restriction of Flying) (RAF Fairford, Gloucestershire) (Amendment) Regulations 2014 No. 2014/2450. - Enabling power: Air Navigation Order 2009, art. 161. - Issued: 15.09.2014. Made: 04.09.2014. Coming into force: 05.09.2014. Effect: S.I. 2014/2391 amended. Territorial extent & classification: E. General. - Available at http://www.legislation.gov.uk/uksi/2014/2450/contents/made Non-print

The Air Navigation (Restriction of Flying) (RAF Fairford, Gloucestershire) Regulations 2014 No. 2014/2391. - Enabling power: Air Navigation Order 2009, art. 161. - Issued: 08.09.2014. Made: 29.08.2014. Coming into force: 03.09.2014. Effect: None. Territorial extent & classification: E. Local. - Available at http://www.legislation.gov.uk/uksi/2014/2391/contents/made Non-print

The Air Navigation (Restriction of Flying) (Remembrance Sunday) Regulations 2014 No. 2014/2520. - Issued: 22.09.2014. Made: 18.09.2014. Coming into force: 09.11.2014. Effect: None. Territorial extent & classification: E. Local. - Available at http://www.legislation.gov.uk/uksi/2014/2520/contents/made Non-print

CIVIL AVIATION

The Air Navigation (Restriction of Flying) (Rendcomb Aerodrome) Regulations 2014 No. 2014/1194. - Enabling power: S.I. 2009/3015, art. 161. - Issued: 12.05.2014. Made: 02.05.2013. Coming into force: 11.05.2014. Effect: None. Territorial extent & classification: E. Local. - Available at http://www.legislation.gov.uk/uksi/2014/1194/contents/made Non-print

The Air Navigation (Restriction of Flying) (RNAS Culdrose) Regulations 2014 No. 2014/1008. - Enabling power: S.I. 2009/3015, art. 161. - Issued: 15.04.2014. Made: 10.04.2014. Coming into force: 31.07.2014. Effect: None. Territorial extent & classification: E. Local. - Available at http://www.legislation.gov.uk/uksi/2014/1008/contents/made Non-print

The Air Navigation (Restriction of Flying) (RNAS Yeovilton) Regulations 2014 No. 2014/1007. - Enabling power: S.I. 2009/3015, art. 161. - Issued: 15.04.2014. Made: 10.04.2014. Coming into force: 25.07.2014. Effect: None. Territorial extent & classification: E. Local. - Available at http://www.legislation.gov.uk/uksi/2014/1007/contents/made Non-print

The Air Navigation (Restriction of Flying) (Royal Air Force Cosford) Regulations 2014 No. 2014/783. - Enabling power: S.I. 2009/3015, art. 161. - Issued: 24.03.2014. Made: 18.03.2014. Coming into force: 07.06.2014. Effect: None. Territorial extent & classification: E. Local. - Available at http://www.legislation.gov.uk/uksi/2014/783/contents/made Non-print

The Air Navigation (Restriction of Flying) (Royal Air Force Topcliffe) Regulations 2014 No. 2014/1142. - Enabling power: S.I. 2009/3015, art. 161. - Issued: 06.05.2014. Made: 28.04.2014. Coming into force: 11.05.2014. Effect: None. Territorial extent & classification: E. Local. - Available at http://www.legislation.gov.uk/uksi/2014/1142/contents/made Non-print

The Air Navigation (Restriction of Flying) (Royal Air Force Waddington) Regulations 2014 No. 2014/1005. - Enabling power: S.I. 2009/3015, art. 161. - Issued: 15.04.2014. Made: 10.04.2014. Coming into force: 03.07.2014. Effect: None. Territorial extent & classification: E. Local. - Available at http://www.legislation.gov.uk/uksi/2014/1005/contents/made Non-print

The Air Navigation (Restriction of Flying) (Royal International Air Tattoo RAF Fairford) Regulations 2014 No. 2014/275. - Enabling power: S.I. 2009/3015, art. 161. - Issued: 13.02.2014. Made: 10.02.2014. Coming into force: 09.07.2014. Effect: None. Territorial extent & classification: E. Local. - Available at http://www.legislation.gov.uk/uksi/2014/275/contents/made Non-print

The Air Navigation (Restriction of Flying) (Salthouse, Norfolk) (Amendment No. 2) Regulations 2014 No. 2014/28. - Enabling power: S.I. 2009/3015, art. 161. - Issued: 14.01.2014. Made: 09.01.2014, at 17.55 hours. Coming into force: with immediate effect. Effect: S.I. 2014/13 amended. Territorial extent & classification: E. Local. - Revoked by SI 2014/36 (non-print). - Available at http://www.legislation.gov.uk/uksi/2014/28/contents/made Non-print

The Air Navigation (Restriction of Flying) (Salthouse, Norfolk) (Amendment) Regulations 2014 No. 2014/14. - Enabling power: S.I. 2009/3015, art. 161. - Issued: 13.01.2014. Made: 08.01.2014 at 16.00 hours. Coming into force: With immediate effect. Effect: S.I. 2014/13 amended. Territorial extent & classification: E. Local. - Revoked by SI 2014/36 (non-print). - Available at http://www.legislation.gov.uk/uksi/2014/14/contents/made Non-print

The Air Navigation (Restriction of Flying) (Salthouse, Norfolk) Regulations 2014 No. 2014/13. - Enabling power: S.I. 2009/3015, art. 161. - Issued: 13.01.2014. Made: 07.01.2014 at 20.29 hours. Coming into force: With immediate effect. Effect: None. Territorial extent & classification: E. Local. - Revoked by SI 2014/36 (non-print). - Available at http://www.legislation.gov.uk/uksi/2014/13/contents/made Non-print

The Air Navigation (Restriction of Flying) (Salthouse, Norfolk) (Revocation) Regulations 2014 No. 2014/36. - Enabling power: S.I. 2009/3015, art. 161. - Issued: 15.01.2014. Made: 10.01.2014, at 15.00 hours. Coming into force: with immediate effect. Effect: S.I. 2014/13, 14, 28 revoked. Territorial extent & classification: E. Local. - Available at http://www.legislation.gov.uk/uksi/2014/36/contents/made Non-print

The Air Navigation (Restriction of Flying) (Shoreham-by-Sea) Regulations 2014 No. 2014/1495. - Enabling power: S.I. 2009/3015, art. 161. - Issued: 10.06.2014. Made: 05.06.2014. Coming into force: 30.08.2014. Effect: None. Territorial extent & classification: E. Local. - Available at http://www.legislation.gov.uk/uksi/2014/1495/contents/made Non-print

The Air Navigation (Restriction of Flying) (Silverstone and Turweston) Regulations 2014 No. 2014/142. - Enabling power: S.I. 2009/3015, art. 161. - Issued: 28.01.2014. Made: 23.01.2014. Coming into force: 05.07.2014. Effect: None. Territorial extent & classification: E. Local. - Available at http://www.legislation.gov.uk/uksi/2014/142/contents/made Non-print

The Air Navigation (Restriction of Flying) (Southport) Regulations 2014 No. 2014/1577. - Enabling power: S.I. 2009/3015, art. 161. - Issued: 18.06.2014. Made: 10.06.2014. Coming into force: 20.09.2014. Effect: None. Territorial extent & classification: E. Local. - Available at http://www.legislation.gov.uk/uksi/2014/1577/contents/made Non-print

The Air Navigation (Restriction of Flying) (State Opening of Parliament) Regulations 2014 No. 2014/1003. - Enabling power: S.I. 2009/3015, art. 161. - Issued: 15.04.2014. Made: 10.04.2014. Coming into force: 04.06.2014. Effect: None. Territorial extent & classification: E. Local. - Available at http://www.legislation.gov.uk/uksi/2014/1003/contents/made Non-print

The Air Navigation (Restriction of Flying) (Stirling) Regulations 2014 No. 2014/1196. - Enabling power: S.I. 2009/3015, art. 161. - Issued: 12.05.2014. Made: 07.05.2013. Coming into force: 28.06.2014. Effect: None. Territorial extent & classification: E. Local. - Available at http://www.legislation.gov.uk/uksi/2014/1196/contents/made Non-print

The Air Navigation (Restriction of Flying) (Stonehenge No.2) Regulations 2014 No. 2014/2486. - Issued: 19.09.2014. Made: 05.09.2014, at 15.00 hrs. Coming into force: 05.09.2014. Effect: None. Territorial extent & classification: E. Local. - Available at http://www.legislation.gov.uk/uksi/2014/2486/contents/made Non-print

The Air Navigation (Restriction of Flying) (Stonehenge) Regulations 2014 No. 2014/89. - Enabling power: S.I. 2009/3015, art. 161. - Issued: 21.01.2014. Made: 16.01.2014. Coming into force: 20.06.2014. Effect: None. Territorial extent & classification: E. Local. - Available at http://www.legislation.gov.uk/uksi/2014/89/contents/made Non-print

The Air Navigation (Restriction of Flying) (Sunderland) Regulations 2014 No. 2014/1006. - Enabling power: S.I. 2009/3015, art. 161. - Issued: 15.04.2014. Made: 10.04.2014. Coming into force: 25.07.2014. Effect: None. Territorial extent & classification: E. Local. - Available at http://www.legislation.gov.uk/uksi/2014/1006/contents/made Non-print

The Air Navigation (Restriction of Flying) (Tour de France Stage 1) Regulations 2014 No. 2014/944. - Enabling power: S.I. 2009/3015, art. 161. - Issued: 04.04.2014. Made: 01.04.2014. Coming into force: 05.07.2014. Effect: None. Territorial extent & classification: E. Local. - Available at http://www.legislation.gov.uk/uksi/2014/944/contents/made Non-print

The Air Navigation (Restriction of Flying) (Tour de France Stage 2) Regulations 2014 No. 2014/943. - Enabling power: S.I. 2009/3015, art. 161. - Issued: 04.04.2014. Made: 01.04.2014. Coming into force: 06.07.2014. Effect: None. Territorial extent & classification: E. Local. - Available at http://www.legislation.gov.uk/uksi/2014/943/contents/made Non-print

The Air Navigation (Restriction of Flying) (Tour de France Stage 3) Regulations 2014 No. 2014/1070. - Enabling power: S.I. 2009/3015, art. 161. - Issued: 25.04.2014. Made: 10.04.2014. Coming into force: 07.07.2014. Effect: None. Territorial extent & classification: E. Local. - Available at http://www.legislation.gov.uk/uksi/2014/1070/contents/made Non-print

The Air Navigation (Restriction of Flying) (Trooping the Colour) Regulations 2014 No. 2014/945. - Enabling power: S.I. 2009/3015, art. 161. - Issued: 04.04.2014. Made: 31.03.2014. Coming into force: 14.06.2014. Effect: None. Territorial extent & classification: E. Local. - Available at http://www.legislation.gov.uk/uksi/2014/945/contents/made Non-print

The Air Navigation (Restriction of Flying) (Wales Rally GB) Regulations 2014 No. 2014/2669. - Enabling power: S.I. 2009/3015, art. 161. - Issued: 03.10.2014. Made: 01.10.2014. Coming into force: 14.11.2014. Effect: None. Territorial extent & classification: W. Local. - Available at http://www.legislation.gov.uk/uksi/2014/2669/contents/made Non-print

The Air Navigation (Restriction of Flying) (Watnall) Regulations 2014 No. 2014/1802. - Enabling power: S.I. 2009/3015, art. 161. - Issued: 10.07.2014. Made: 14.06.2014, at 16.58 hrs. Coming into force: with immediate effect. Effect: None. Territorial extent & classification: E. Local. - Available at http://www.legislation.gov.uk/uksi/2014/1802/contents/made Non-print

The Air Navigation (Restriction of Flying) (Watnall) (Revocation) Regulations 2014 No. 2014/1817. - Enabling power: S.I. 2009/3015, art. 161. - Issued: 11.07.2014. Made: 14.06.2014, at 22.09 hrs. Coming into force: with immediate effect. Effect: S.I. 2014/1802 revoked. Territorial extent & classification: E. Local. - Available at http://www.legislation.gov.uk/uksi/2014/1817/contents/made Non-print

The Air Navigation (Restriction of Flying) (Weston Park) Regulations 2014 No. 2014/1304. - Enabling power: S.I. 2009/3015, art. 161. - Issued: 23.05.2014. Made: 19.05.2014. Coming into force: 15.08.2014. Effect: None. Territorial extent & classification: E. Local. - Available at http://www.legislation.gov.uk/uksi/2014/1304/contents/made Non-print

The Air Navigation (Restriction of Flying) (Wimbledon) Regulations 2014 No. 2014/90. - Enabling power: S.I. 2009/3015, art. 161. - Issued: 21.01.2014. Made: 16.01.2014. Coming into force: 23.06.2014. Effect: None. Territorial extent & classification: E. Local. - Available at http://www.legislation.gov.uk/uksi/2014/90/contents/made Non-print

The Civil Aviation (Access to Air Travel for Disabled Persons and Persons with Reduced Mobility) Regulations 2014 No. 2014/2833. - Enabling power: European Communities Act 1972, s. 2 (2). - Issued: 27.10.2014. Made: 16.10.2014. Laid: 27.10.2014. Coming into force: 01.12.2014. Effect: S.I. 2007/1895 revoked. Territorial extent & classification: E/W/S/NI. General. - 12p.: 30 cm. - 978-0-11-112218-1 £6.00

The Civil Aviation Act 2012 (Commencement No. 2) Order 2014 No. 2014/262 (C.12). - Enabling power: Civil Aviation Act 2012, s. 110 (1) (6) (a). Bringing into operation various provisions of the 2012 Act on 11.03.2014 & 01.04.2014. - Issued: 18.02.2014. Made: 10.02.2014. Effect: None. Territorial extent & classification: E/W/S/NI. General. - 2p.: 30 cm. - 978-0-11-110966-3 £4.00

The Civil Aviation (Miscellaneous Revocations) Regulations 2014 No. 2014/3225. - Enabling power: European Communities Act 1972, s. 2 (2). - Issued: 11.12.2014. Made: 03.12.2014. Laid: 11.12.2014. Coming into force: 05.01.2015. Effect: S.I. 1992/2673; 1994/1733; 1997/2329 revoked. Territorial extent & classification: E/W/S/NI. General. - EC note: These Regulations revoked S.I. 1992/2673 & 1994/1733 which ensured compliance with that much of EC Directive 91/670 as concerned the application of art. 5 of that Directive in Northern Ireland. This Directive was repealed by Regulation (EC) 216/2008. They also revoke S.I 1997/2329 which ensured compliance with Directive 93/65/EEC. This Directive was repealed by Regulation (EC) 552/2004. - 2p.: 30 cm. - 978-0-11-112482-6 £4.25

The Heathrow and Gatwick Airports - London Noise Insulation Grants (Revocations) Scheme 2014 No. 2014/3233. - Enabling power: Civil Aviation Act 1982, s. 79. - Issued: 12.12.2014. Made: 03.12.2014. Laid: 11.12.2014. Coming into force: 05.01.2015. Effect: S.I. 1989/247, 248 revoked. Territorial extent & classification: E/W/S/NI. General. - 2p.: 30 cm. - 978-0-11-112488-8 £4.25

Civil partnership

The Civil Partnership (Registration Abroad and Certificates) (Amendment) Order 2014 No. 2014/1107. - Enabling power: Civil Partnership Act 2004, ss. 241, 244. - Issued: 06.05.2014. Made: 28.04.2014. Laid: 06.05.2014. Coming into force: 03.06.2014. Effect: S.I. 2005/2761 amended. Territorial extent & classification: E/W/S/NI. General. - 2p.: 30 cm. - 978-0-11-111439-1 £4.25

The Marriage and Civil Partnership (Scotland) Act 2014 and Civil Partnership Act 2004 (Consequential Provisions and Modifications) Order 2014 No. 2014/3229. - Enabling power: Scotland Act 1998, ss. 104, 112 (1), 113 (2) to (5) (7) & Civil Partnership Act 2004, s. 259 (1). - Issued: 11.12.2014. Made: 04.12.2014. Coming into force: in accord. with art. 1 (2). Effect: 58 SIs & 22 Acts amended. Territorial extent & classification: E/W/S/NI. General. - Supersedes draft S.I. (ISBN 9780111122402) issued 31.10.2014. - 56p.: 30 cm. - 978-0-11-112483-3 £10.00

The Marriage (Same Sex Couples) Act 2013 and Marriage and Civil Partnership (Scotland) Act 2014 (Consequential Provisions) Order 2014 No. 2014/3061. - Enabling power: Marriage (Same Sex Couples) Act 2013, ss. 17 (2) (3) & Civil Partnership Act 2004, s. 259 (1) (4) & Scotland Act 1998, ss. 104, 112 (1), 113 (2) to (5). - Issued: 21.11.2014. Made: 17.11.2014. Laid before the Scottish Parliament: 18.11.2014. Coming into force: In accord. with art 1 (2) (3). Effect: S.I. 1952/1869; 1959/406; 1968/2049; 1975/556; 1979/643; 1986/1442; 1987/257, 2088; 1988/2256; 1995/300; 2001/2283 (W.172); 2005/438, 1513 (W.117), 3176; 2012/687 & 7 Church Measures amended. Territorial extent & classification: E/W/S. General. - 32p.: 30 cm. - 978-0-11-112343-0 £6.00

The Marriage (Same Sex Couples) Act 2013 (Consequential and Contrary Provisions and Scotland) and Marriage and Civil Partnership (Scotland) Act 2014 (Consequential Provisions) Order 2014 No. 2014/3168. - Enabling power: Marriage (Same Sex Couples) Act 2013, ss. 17 (1) to (3), 18 (4) (10), sch. 2 para. 1, sch. 4 para. 27 (3) (b) & Civil Partnership Act 2004, s. 259 (1) (3) & Scotland Act 1998, ss. 104, 112 (1), 113 (2) to (3) (5). - Issued: 04.12.2014. Made: 27.11.2014. Coming into force: In accord. with art 1 (2) (3). Effect: 1837 c.26; 1911 c.6; 1949 c.76; 1957 c.58; 1964 c.75; 1973 c.18, 45; 1975 c.60; 1976 c.31; 1981 c.45; 1992 c.4, c.5; 2007 c.18; Reserve Forces Non Regular Permanent Staff (Pension and Attributable Benefits Schemes) Regulations 2011 [not an SI] amended & S.I. 2014/560 partially revoked. Territorial extent & classification: S. General. - Supersedes draft S.S.I. (ISBN 9780111121900) issued 21.10.2014. - 16p.: 30 cm. - 978-0-11-112429-1 £6.00

The Marriage (Same Sex Couples) Act 2013 (Consequential and Contrary Provisions and Scotland) Order 2014 No. 2014/560. - Enabling power: Marriage (Same Sex Couples) Act 2013, ss. 17 (2) (3), 18 (10), sch. 2, para. 1 (1), sch. 4, 27 (3) (a) (b) & Civil Partnership Act 2004, s. 259 (1) (3) & Human Fertilisation and Embryology Act 2008, s. 64 (1) (2)- Issued: 13.03.2014. Made: 06.03.2014. Coming into force: In accord. with art. 1 (2) (3). Effect: 37 Acts & 18 SIs/WSIs amended. Territorial extent & classification: E/W/S/NI. General. - Supersedes draft S.I. (ISBN 9780111108727) issued 28.01.2014. Partially revoked by S.I. 2014/3168 (ISBN 9780111124291) in re to S. - 28p.: 30 cm. - 978-0-11-111158-1 £5.75

The Marriage (Same Sex Couples) Act 2013 (Consequential Provisions) Order 2014 No. 2014/107. - Enabling power: Marriage (Same Sex Couples) Act 2013, ss. 17 (2) (3), 18 (10) & Civil Partnership Act 2004, s. 259 (1) (4)- Issued: 28.01.2014. Made: 20.01.2014. Laid: 23.01.2014. Coming into force: 13.03.2014. Effect: 82 SIs/WSIs amended. Territorial extent & classification: E/W/S. General. - Partially revoked by SI 2015/601 (ISBN 9780111132661) in re to E/W. - 28p.: 30 cm. - 978-0-11-110869-7 £5.75

Civil partnership, England and Wales

The Registration of Civil Partnerships (Fees) Order 2014 No. 2014/1789. - Enabling power: Civil Partnership Act 2004, ss. 34 (1), 258 (2). - Issued: 14.07.2014. Made: 07.07.2014. Laid: 10.07.2014. Coming into force: 01.09.2014. Effect: S.I. 2005/1996, 3167; 2010/440; 2012/2761 revoked. Territorial extent & classification: E/W. General. - 4p.: 30 cm. - 978-0-11-111775-0 £4.25

Civil proceedings

The Crime and Courts Act 2013 (County Court and Family Court: Consequential Provision) Order 2014 No. 2014/1773. - Enabling power: Crime and Courts Act 2013, s. 59. - Issued: 10.07.2014. Made: 03.07.2014. Coming into force: 04.07.2014 in accord. with art. 1. Effect: 1984 c.28 & 1999, c.22 & S.I. 1991/1184 (L.12) amended. Territorial extent & classification: E/W. General. - 4p.: 30 cm. - 978-0-11-111762-0 £4.25

Clean air, England

The Clean Air (Miscellaneous Provisions) (England) Regulations 2014 No. 2014/3318. - Enabling power: Clean Air Act 1993, ss. 1 (3), 7 (1), 14 (7), 36 (6), 37 (3), 38 (1) (3) (a) to (d) (4), 63 (1). - Issued: 22.12.2014. Made: 15.12.2014. Laid: 17.12.2014. Coming into force: 07.01.2015. Effect: S.I. 1958/878; 1969/411, 1262; 1977/17, 18, 19 revoked. Territorial extent & classification: E. General. - 12p.: 30 cm. - 978-0-11-112601-1 £6.00

The Smoke Control Areas (Authorised Fuels) (England) (No. 2) Regulations 2014 No. 2014/2366. - Enabling power: Clean Air Act 1993, s. 20 (6). - Issued: 10.09.2014. Made: 02.09.2014. Laid: 05.09.2014. Coming into force: 01.10.2014. Effect: S.I. 2014/491 revoked. Territorial extent & classification: E. General. - 20p.: 30 cm. - 978-0-11-112027-9 £6.00

The Smoke Control Areas (Authorised Fuels) (England) Regulations 2014 No. 2014/491. - Enabling power: Clean Air Act 1993, s. 20 (6). - Issued: 12.03.2014. Made: 05.03.2014. Laid: 06.03.2014. Coming into force: 06.04.2014. Effect: S.I. 2013/2111 revoked. Territorial extent & classification: E. General. - Revoked by SI 2014/2383 (ISBN 9780111120279). - 16p.: 30 cm. - 978-0-11-111098-0 £5.75

The Smoke Control Areas (Exempted Fireplaces) (England) (No. 2) Order 2014 No. 2014/2404. - Enabling power: Clean Air Act 1993, s. 21. - Issued: 15.09.2014. Made: 02.09.2014. Laid: 09.09.2014. Coming into force: 01.10.2014. Effect: S.I. 2014/504 revoked. Territorial extent & classification: E. General. - Revoked by SI 2015/307 (ISBN 9780111129975). - 132p.: 30 cm. - 978-0-11-112056-9 £20.75

The Smoke Control Areas (Exempted Fireplaces) (England) Order 2014 No. 2014/504. - Enabling power: Clean Air Act 1993, s. 21. - Issued: 12.03.2014. Made: 05.03.2014. Laid: 06.03.2014. Coming into force: 06.04.2014. Effect: S.I. 2013/2112; 3026 revoked. Territorial extent & classification: E. General. - Revoked by SI 2014/2404 (ISBN 9780111120569). - 120p.: 30 cm. - 978-0-11-111108-6 £18.50

Clean air, Wales

The Smoke Control Areas (Authorised Fuels) (Wales) (Amendment) Regulations 2014 No. 2014/684 (W.74). - Enabling power: Clean Air Act 1993, s. 20 (6). - Issued: 02.04.2014. Made: 12.03.2014. Laid before the National Assembly for Wales: 18.03.2014. Coming into force: 11.04.2014. Effect: S.I. 2008/3100 (W.274); 2009/3225 (W.279); 2011/2909 (W.313); 2013/562 (W.65) revoked. Territorial extent & classification: W. General. - In English and Welsh. Welsh title: Rheoliadau Ardaloedd Rheoli Mwg (Tanwyddau Awdurdodedig) (Cymru) 2014. - 28p.: 30 cm. - 978-0-348-10930-6 £6.00

The Smoke Control Areas (Exempted Fireplaces) (Wales) Order 2014 No. 2014/694 (W.75). - Enabling power: Clean Air Act 1993, s. 21. - Issued: 04.04.2014. Made: 12.03.2014. Laid before the National Assembly for Wales: 18.03.2014. Coming into force: 11.04.2014. Effect: W.S.I. 2013/561 (W.64) revoked. Territorial extent & classification: W. General. - In English and Welsh. Welsh title: Gorchymyn Ardaloedd Rheoli Mwg (Lleoedd Tân Esempt) (Cymru) 2014. - 268p.: 30 cm. - 978-0-348-10929-0 £32.75

Climate change

The CRC Energy Efficiency Scheme (Amendment) Order 2014 No. 2014/502. - Enabling power: Climate Change Act 2008, ss. 44 (1), 46 (3), 90 (3) (a), sch. 2, sch. 3, para. 9. - Issued: 12.03.2014. Made: 05.03.2014. Laid before Parliament, Scottish Parliament, the National Assembly for Wales & the Northern Ireland Assembly: 10.03.2014. Coming into force: 01.04.2014. Effect: S.I. 2013/1119 amended. Territorial extent & classification: E/W/S/NI. General. - 8p.: 30 cm. - 978-0-11-111106-2 £4.00

The Greenhouse Gas Emissions Trading Scheme (Amendment) and National Emissions Inventory (Amendment) Regulations 2014 No. 2014/3075. - Enabling power: Finance Act 1973, s. 56 (1) (2) & European Communities Act 1972, s. 2 (2). - Issued: 24.11.2014. Made: 11.11.2014. Laid: 20.11.2014. Coming into force: 01.02.2014. Effect: S.I. 2005/2903 amended. Territorial extent & classification: E/W/S/NI. General. - 8p.: 30 cm. - 978-0-11-112356-0 £6.00

The Greenhouse Gas Emissions Trading Scheme (Amendment) Regulations 2014 No. 2014/3125. - Enabling power: Pollution Prevention and Control Act 1999, s. 2, 7 (9), sch.1, & European Communities Act 1972, s. 2 (2). - Issued: 01.12.2014. Made: 20.11.2014. Laid: 26.11.2014. Coming into force: 22.12.2014. Effect: S.I. 2012/3038 amended. Territorial extent & classification: E/W/S/NI. General. - EC note: These Regulations implement Regulation No 421/2014 amending Directive 2003/87/EC establishing a scheme for greenhouse gas allowance trading with the Community. Directive 2003/87/EC is currently implemented in the UK by the Greenhouse Gas Emissions Trading Scheme Regulations 2012 (the 2012 Regulations. The 2012 Regulations require aircraft operators which are administered by the UK to monitor and report their aviation emissions each calendar year and then to surrender sufficient emissions trading allowances to cover those emissions. These Regulations amend the 2012 Regulations. - 16p.: 30 cm. - 978-0-11-112401-7 £6.00

Climate change: Emissions trading

The CRC Energy Efficiency Scheme (Allocation of Allowances for Payment) (Amendment) (No. 2) Regulations 2014 No. 2014/3262. - Enabling power: Finance Act 2008, s. 21 (1) (2) (3). - Issued: 16.12.2014. Made: 10.12.2014. Laid: 11.12.2014. Coming into force: 01.04.2015. Effect: S.I. 2013/3103 amended. Territorial extent & classification: E/W/S/NI. General. - 4p.: 30 cm. - 978-0-11-112525-0 £4.25

The CRC Energy Efficiency Scheme (Allocation of Allowances for Payment) (Amendment) Regulations 2014 No. 2014/495. - Enabling power: Finance Act 2008, s. 21 (1) (2). - Issued: 11.03.2014. Made: 05.03.2014. Laid: 06.03.2014. Coming into force: 01.04.2014. Effect: S.I. 2013/3103 amended. Territorial extent & classification: E/W/S/NI. General. - This Statutory Instrument has been made in consequence of a defect in S.I. 2013/3103 and is being issued free of charge to all known recipients of that Statutory Instrument. - 2p.: 30 cm. - 978-0-11-111099-7 £4.00

Climate change levy

The Climate Change Agreements (Administration) (Amendment) Regulations 2014 No. 2014/2872. - Enabling power: Finance Act 2000, sch. 6, paras 52D, 146. - Issued: 04.11.2014. Made: 29.10.2014. Laid: 30.10.2014. Coming into force: 28.11.2014. Effect: S.I. 2012/1976 amended. Territorial extent & classification: E/W/S/NI. General. - 2p.: 30 cm. - 978-0-11-112260-0 £4.25

The Climate Change Agreements (Eligible Facilities) (Amendments) Regulations 2014 No. 2014/1318. - Enabling power: Finance Act 2000, sch. 6, paras 50 (3) (4), 146. - Issued: 29.05.2014. Made: 21.05.2014. Laid: 27.05.2014. Coming into force: 01.07.2014. Effect: S.I. 2012/2999 amended. Territorial extent & classification: E/W/S/NI. General. - 2p.: 30 cm. - 978-0-11-111519-0 £4.25

The Climate Change Levy (Fuel Use and Recycling Processes) (Amendment) Regulations 2014 No. 2014/844. - Enabling power: Finance Act 2000, sch. 6, paras 18 (2) (3). - Issued: 02.04.2014. Made: 26.03.2014. Coming into force: 01.04.2014. Effect: S.I. 2005/1715 amended. Territorial extent & classification: E/W/S/NI. General. - Supersedes draft SI (ISBN 9780111109519) issued 17/02/14. - 2p.: 30 cm. - 978-0-11-111297-7 £4.00

The Revenue and Customs (Amendment of Appeal Provisions for Out of Time Reviews) Order 2014 No. 2014/1264. - Enabling power: Finance Act 2008, s. 124 (1) (2) (6) (7) (b). - Issued: 21.05.2014. Made: 14.05.2014. Coming into force: In accord. with art. 1 (2). Effect: 1994 c.9, c.23; 1996 c.8; 2000 c.17; 2001 c.9; 2003 c.14; S.I. 2003/3102; 2007/1509, 2157, 3298 amended. Territorial extent & classification: E/W/S/NI. General. - Supersedes draft SI (ISBN 9780111112991) issued 03/04/14. - 8p.: 30 cm. - 978-0-11-111499-5 £6.00

Coal industry

The Coal Industry Act 1994 (Commencement No. 8 and Transitional Provision) Order 2014 No. 2014/888 (C.37). - Enabling power: Coal Industry Act 1994, ss. 68 (4) (5) (b). Bringing into force various provisions of the 1994 Act on 28.04.2014, in accord. with art 2. - Issued: 07.04.2014. Made: 31.03.2014. Laid: 02.04.2014. Coming into force: 28.04.2014. Effect: None. Territorial extent & classification: E/W/S/NI. General. - 2p.: 30 cm. - 978-0-11-111353-0 £4.25

The Coal Industry Act 1994 (Superannuation Scheme Winding Up) (Revocations and Savings) Regulations 2014 No. 2014/1986. - Enabling power: Coal Industry Nationalisation Act 1946, s. 37. - Issued: 31.07.2014. Made: 25.07.2014. Laid: 28.07.2014. Coming into force: 01.09.2014. Effect: S.I. 1949/17; 1951/393, 2010; 1952/2018; 1953/845; 1954/155, 970; 1955/281, 1345; 1956/248; 1957/156 revoked. Territorial extent & classification: E/W/S/NI. General. - 4p.: 30 cm. - 978-0-11-111932-7 £4.25

Commons, England

The Commons Act 2006 (Commencement No. 7, Transitional and Savings Provisions) (England) Order 2014 No. 2014/3026 (C.128). - Enabling power: Commons Act 2006, ss. 56 (1), 59 (1). Bringing into operation various provisions of the 2006 Act on 12.11.2014, 15.12.2014 in accord. with art. 3. - Issued: 19.11.2011. Made: 11.11.2011. Effect: None. Territorial extent & classification: E. General. - 4p.: 30 cm. - 978-0-11-112331-7 £4.25

The Commons Registration (England) Regulations 2014 No. 2014/3038. - Enabling power: Commons Act 2006, ss. 3 (5), 8 (1), 11 (5) (6), 14, 17 (3), 20, 21, 24 (1) to (2A) (3) (6) to (9), 59 (1), sch. 1, para. 1, sch. 2, paras 2 to 10, sch. 3, paras 2, 4, 5, 8 (3). - Issued: 20.11.2014. Made: 12.11.2014. Laid: 14.11.2014. Coming into force: 15.12.2014. Effect: S.I. 2007/457, 2585 cease to have effect in relation to the registration areas of Cumbria County Council and North Yorkshire County Council & S.I. 2008/1961; 2009/2018 revoked. Territorial extent & classification: E. General. - 84p.: 30 cm. - 978-0-11-112334-8 £14.25

The Commons (Town and Village Greens) (Trigger and Terminating Events) Order 2014 No. 2014/257. - Enabling power: Commons Act 2006, ss. 15C (5) (a) (7), 59 (1). - Issued: 18.02.2014. Made: 11.02.2014. Coming into force: 12.02.2014. Effect: 2006 c.26 amended. Territorial extent & classification: E. General. - Supersedes draft (ISBN 9780111106730) issued 10.12.2013. - 8p.: 30 cm. - 978-0-11-110958-8 £4.00

Commons, Wales

The Commons (Severance of Rights) (Wales) Order 2014 No. 2014/219 (W.29). - Enabling power: Commons Act 2006, ss. 9 (2) (7), 59 (1), 61 (1), sch. 1, paras 2 (1) (4). - Issued: 11.02.2014. Made: 04.02.2014. Laid before the National Assembly for Wales: 06.02.2014. Coming into force: 01.03.2014. Effect: S.I. 2007/583 (W.55) revoked. Territorial extent & classification: W. General. - In English & Welsh. Welsh title: Gorchymyn Tiroedd Comin (Hollti Hawliau) (Cymru) 2014. - 8p.: 30 cm. - 978-0-348-10886-6 £4.00

Community benefit societies

The Co-operative and Community Benefit Societies and Credit Unions Act 2010 (Commencement No. 2) Order 2014 No. 2014/183 (C.6). - Enabling power: Co-operative and Community Benefit Societies and Credit Unions Act 2010, s. 8 (2). Bringing into operation various provisions of the 2010 Act on 06.04.2014, 01.08.2014, in accord. with arts 2, 3. - Issued: 05.02.2014. Made: 30.01.2014. Effect: None. Territorial extent & classification: E/W/S/NI. General. - 2p.: 30 cm. - 978-0-11-110907-6 £4.00

The Co-operative and Community Benefit Societies and Credit Unions Act 2010 (Consequential Amendments) Regulations 2014 No. 2014/1815. - Enabling power: Co-operative and Community Benefit Societies and Credit Unions Act 2010, s. 6. - Issued: 15.07.2014. Made: 08.07.2014. Coming into force: 01.080.2014 in accord. with reg. 1. Effect: S.I. 1969/1037; 1990/2024; 1995/849, 1945 (S.142), 2801; 1996/1667; 1999/1549; 2001/544, 1062, 1744, 2617; 2004/353, 1450; 2005/590, 1529, 1788, 1986, 2415, 2531; 2008/565, 788, 1911; 2009/779, 1085, 1385, 2971; 2010/5; 2012/922, 1290, 1464, 1821, 2421; 2014/229 amended. Territorial extent & classification: E/W/S. General. - Supersedes draft S.I. (ISBN 9780111114865) issued 19.05.2014. - 12p.: 30 cm. - 978-0-11-111787-3 £6.00

The Co-operative and Community Benefit Societies and Credit Unions (Arrangements, Reconstructions and Administration) (Amendment) Order 2014 No. 2014/1822. - Enabling power: Co-operative and Community Benefit Societies and Credit Unions Act 2014, s. 118. - Issued: 16.07.2014. Made: 09.07.2014. Laid: 11.07.2014. Coming into force: 01.08.2014. Effect: S.I. 2014/229 amended. Territorial extent & classification: E/W/S. General. - 8p.: 30 cm. - 978-0-11-111793-4 £6.00

The Co-operative and Community Benefit Societies and Credit Unions (Investigations) Regulations 2014 No. 2014/574. - Enabling power: Co-operative and Community Benefit Societies and Credit Unions Act 2010, ss. 4 (1) (2) (a) (3) (7), 6, 7. - Issued: 17.03.2014. Made: 10.03.2014. Coming into force: 06.04.2014. Effect: 1965 c.12; 1979 c.34; 1985 c.6; 1986 c.46 modified & S.I. 2006/264 amended. Territorial extent & classification: E/W/S/NI. General. - Supersedes draft SI (ISBN 9780111108857) issued 30/01/14- 8p.: 30 cm. - 978-0-11-111173-4 £5.75

Community infrastructure levy, England and Wales

The Community Infrastructure Levy (Amendment) Regulations 2014 No. 2014/385. - Enabling power: Planning Act 2008, ss. 205 (1), 208 (8), 209 (5) (6), 211 (2) (4) to (6) (7B), 215 (3), 217 (1) to (4), 218 (2) to (6), 220 (1) to (3), 222 (1), 223 (1) (2). - Issued: 28.02.2014. Made: 23.02.2014. Coming into force: 24.02.2014 in accord. with reg. 1. Effect: S.I. 2010/948 amended. Territorial extent & classification: E/W. General. - Supersedes draft S.I. (ISBN 9780111108543) issued 23.01.2014. - 28p.: 30 cm. - 978-0-11-111016-4 £5.75

Companies

The Community Interest Company (Amendment) Regulations 2014 No. 2014/2483. - Enabling power: Companies (Audit, Investigations and Community Enterprise) Act 2004, ss. 30 (1) (2), 34 (3) (b), 62 (2). - Issued: 23.09.2014. Made: 14.09.2014. Coming into force: 01.10.2014. Effect: 2005/1788 amended. Territorial extent & classification: E/W/S/NI. General. - Supersedes draft S.I. (ISBN 9780111117200) issued on 02.07.2014. - 4p.: 30 cm. - 978-0-11-112093-4 £4.25

The Companies Act 2006 (Interconnection of Registers) Order 2014 No. 2014/1557. - Enabling power: European Communities Act 1972, s. 2 (2), sch. 2, para. 1A. - Issued: 18.06.2014. Made: 11.06.2014. Laid: 16.06.2014. Coming into force: 07.07.2014. Effect: 2006 c.46 amended. Territorial extent & classification: E/W/S/NI. General. - 4p.: 30 cm. - 978-0-11-111654-8 £4.25

The Companies (Striking Off) (Electronic Communications) Order 2014 No. 2014/1602. - Enabling power: Electronic Communications Act 2000, s. 8. - Issued: 24.06.2014. Made: 11.06.2014. Laid: 19.06.2014. Coming into force: 11.07.2014. Effect: 2006 c.46; S.I. 2009/1804 amended. Territorial extent & classification: E/W/S/NI. General. - 4p.: 30 cm. - 978-0-11-111671-5 £4.25

The Company, Limited Liability Partnership and Business Names (Sensitive Words and Expressions) Regulations 2014 No. 2014/3140. - Enabling power: Companies Act 2006, ss. 55 (1), 56 (1) (b), 1194 (1), 1195 (1) (b), 1292 (1). - Issued: 03.12.2014. Made: 26.11.2014. Laid: 27.11.2014. Coming into force: 31.01.2015. Effect: S.I. 2009/2615 revoked. Territorial extent & classification: E/W/S/NI. General. - For approval by resolution of each House of Parliament within twenty-eight days. - 12p.: 30 cm. - 978-0-11-112414-7 £6.00

European Economic Interest Grouping and European Public Limited-Liability Company (Amendment) Regulations 2014 No. 2014/2382. - Enabling power: European Communities Act 1972, s. 2 (2). - Issued: 15.09.2014. Made: 05.09.2014. Laid: 09.09.2014. Coming into force: 01.10.2014. Effect: S.I. 1989/638; 2004/2326; 2009/1803 amended. Territorial extent & classification: E/W/S/NI. General. - With correction slip dated December 2014. - 20p.: 30 cm. - 978-0-11-112041-5 £6.00

The Local Audit (Delegation of Functions) and Statutory Audit (Delegation of Functions) Order 2014 No. 2014/2009. - Enabling power: Companies Act 2006, ss. 1252, 1253, sch. 13, paras 7 (3), 11 (2) (3) (a). - Issued: 04.08.2014. Made: 29.07.2014. Coming into force: In accord. with art. 1. Effect: S.I. 2012/1741 amended. Territorial extent & classification: E/W except for art. 10 which extends to the UK. General. - Supersedes draft S.I. (ISBN 9780111116609) issued 19.06.2014. - 8p.: 30 cm. - 978-0-11-111935-8 £4.25

The Reports on Payments to Governments Regulations 2014 No. 2014/3209. - Enabling power: European Communities Act 1972, s. 2 (2) & Limited Liability Partnerships Act 2000, ss. 15, 17 & Companies Act 2006, ss. 468, 1069, 1105. - Issued: 10.12.2014. Made: 28.11.2014. Coming into force: 01.12.2014. Effect: None. Territorial extent & classification: E/W/S/NI. General. - Supersedes draft SI (ISBN 9780111122235) issued 28/10/14 - 16p.: 30 cm. - 978-0-11-112460-4 £6.00

Compensation

The Home Loss Payments (Prescribed Amounts) (England) Regulations 2014 No. 2014/1966. - Enabling power: Land Compensation Act 1973, s. 30 (5). - Issued: 30.07.2014. Made: 23.07.2014. Laid: 28.07.2014. Coming into force: 01.10.2014. Effect: S.I. 2008/1598 revoked with savings. Territorial extent & classification: E. General. - 2p.: 30 cm. - 978-0-11-111927-3 £4.25

Competition

The CMA Registers of Undertakings and Orders (Available Hours) Order 2014 No. 2014/558. - Enabling power: Enterprise Act 2002, ss. 91 (6), 166 (6). - Issued: 13.03.2014. Made: 06.03.2014. Coming into force: 01.04.2014. Effect: S.I. 2003/1373 revoked. Territorial extent & classification: E/W/S/NI. General. - 2p.: 30 cm. - 978-0-11-111156-7 £4.00

The Competition Act 1998 (Competition and Markets Authority's Rules) Order 2014 No. 2014/458. - Enabling power: Competition Act 1998, ss. 51 (5) (6), 71 (3), 75A (3) (4). - Issued: 07.03.2014. Made: 27.02.2014. Laid: 03.03.2014. Coming into force: 01.04.2014. Effect: S.I. 2004/2751 revoked. Territorial extent & classification: E/W/S/NI. General. - With correction slip dated December 2014. - 12p.: 30 cm. - 978-0-11-111067-6 £5.75

The Competition Act 1998 (Concurrency) Regulations 2014 No. 2014/536. - Enabling power: Competition Act 1998, ss. 54 (4) (5) to (6B), 71. - Issued: 13.03.2014. Made: 06.03.2014. Laid: 10.03.2014. Coming into force: 01.04.2014. Effect: S.I. 2004/1077 revoked. Territorial extent & classification: E/W/S/NI. General. - 8p.: 30 cm. - 978-0-11-111138-3 £5.75

The Competition and Markets Authority (Penalties) Order 2014 No. 2014/559. - Enabling power: Enterprise Act 2002, ss. 111 (4) (6), 124 (2) (b), 174D (4) (5) & Competition Act 1998, s. 40A (3). - Issued: 14.03.2014. Made: 06.03.2014. Laid: 10.03.2014. Coming into force: 01.04.2014. Effect: S.I. 2003/1371; 2007/461 revoked. Territorial extent & classification: E/W/S/NI. General. - 8p.: 30 cm. - 978-0-11-111157-4 £4.00

The Designation of the Competition and Markets Authority as a National Competition Authority Regulations 2014 No. 2014/537. - Enabling power: European Communities Act 1972, s. 2 (2) (a). - Issued: 13.03.2014. Made: 06.03.2014. Laid: 10.03.2014. Coming into force: 01.04.2014. Effect: None. Territorial extent & classification: E/W/S/NI. General. - 2p.: 30 cm. - 978-0-11-111139-0 £4.00

The Enterprise Act 2002 (Merger Fees and Determination of Turnover) (Amendment) Order 2014 No. 2014/534. - Enabling power: Enterprise Act 2002, ss. 121, 124 (2). - Issued: 13.03.2014. Made: 06.03.2014. Laid: 10.03.2014. Coming into force: 01.04.2014. Effect: S.I. 2003/1370 amended. Territorial extent & classification: E/W/S/NI. General. - 8p.: 30 cm. - 978-0-11-111136-9 £5.75

The Enterprise Act 2002 (Mergers) (Interim Measures: Financial Penalties) (Determination of Control and Turnover) Order 2014 No. 2014/533. - Enabling power: Enterprise Act 2002, ss. 94A (3) (4) (5), 124 (2). - Issued: 13.03.2014. Made: 06.03.2014. Laid: 10.03.2014. Coming into force: 01.04.2014. Effect: None. Territorial extent & classification: E/W/S/NI. General. - 8p.: 30 cm. - 978-0-11-111133-8 £5.75

The Enterprise Act 2002 (Part 9 Restrictions on Disclosure of Information) (Amendment) Order 2014 No. 2014/2807. - Enabling power: Enterprise Act 2002, s. 241 (6). - Issued: 23.10.2014. Made: 16.10.2014. Laid: 21.10.2014. Coming into force: 17.11.2014. Effect: 2002 c.40 amended. Territorial extent & classification: E/W/S/NI. General. - 2p.: 30 cm. - 978-0-11-112199-3 £4.25

The Enterprise Act 2002 (Protection of Legitimate Interests) (Amendment) Order 2014 No. 2014/891. - Enabling power: Enterprise Act 2002, ss. 68, 124 (2) (4). - Issued: 07.04.2014. Made: 31.03.2014. Coming into force: 01.04.2014. Effect: S.I. 2003/1592 amended. Territorial extent & classification: E/W/S/NI. General. - Supersedes draft SI (ISBN 9780111110690) issued 07.03.2014. - 12p.: 30 cm. - 978-0-11-111356-1 £6.00

The Enterprise and Regulatory Reform Act 2013 (Commencement No. 6, Transitional Provisions and Savings) Order 2014 No. 2014/416 (C.17). - Enabling power: Enterprise and Regulatory Reform Act 2013, ss. 100, 103 (3). Bringing into operation various provisions of the 2013 Act on 01.04.2014 & 06.04.2014, in ac cord. with arts 2, 3. - Issued: 10.03.2014. Made: 03.03.2014. Effect: None. Territorial extent & classification: E/W/S/NI. General. - 16p.: 30 cm. - 978-0-11-111081-2 £5.75

The Enterprise and Regulatory Reform Act 2013 (Competition) (Consequential, Transitional and Saving Provisions) (No. 2) Order 2014 No. 2014/549. - Enabling power: Enterprise and Regulatory Reform Act 2013, s. 99 (1) (2) (3). - Issued: 14.03.2014. Made: 06.03.2014. Laid: 10.03.2014. Coming into force: 01.04.2014. Effect: 56 instruments amended. Territorial extent & classification: E/W/S/NI. General. - 24p.: 30 cm. - 978-0-11-111151-2 £5.75

The Enterprise and Regulatory Reform Act 2013 (Competition) (Consequential, Transitional and Saving Provisions) Order 2014 No. 2014/892. - Enabling power: Enterprise and Regulatory Reform Act 2013, s. 99 (1) (2) (3). - Issued: 07.04.2014. Made: 31.03.2014. Coming into force: 01.04.2014. Effect: 50 Acts; 9 Orders; 1 Welsh Measure amended. Territorial extent & classification: E/W/S/NI. General. - Supersedes draft SI (ISBN 9780111110683) issued 07/03/14. - 64p.: 30 cm. - 978-0-11-111357-8 £11.00

The Financial Services (Banking Reform) Act 2013 (Commencement No. 4) Order 2014 No. 2014/823 (C.32). - Enabling power: Financial Services (Banking Reform) Act 2013, s. 148 (5). Bringing into operation various provisions of this Act on 01.04.2014 in accord. with art. 2. - Issued: 01.04.2014. Made: 25.03.2014. Effect: None. Territorial extent & classification: E/W/S/NI. General. - 4p.: 30 cm. - 978-0-11-111281-6 £4.00

The Financial Services (Banking Reform) Act 2013 (Commencement No. 6) Order 2014 No. 2014/2458 (C.109). - Enabling power: Financial Services (Banking Reform) Act 2013, s. 148 (5). Bringing into operation various provisions of this Act on 01.11.2014, in accord. with art. 2. - Issued: 19.09.2014. Made: 12.09.2014. Effect: None. Territorial extent & classification: E/W/S/NI. General. - 4p.: 30 cm. - 978-0-11-112084-2 £4.25

Constitutional law

The Children's Hearings (Scotland) Act 2011 (Consequential Provisions) Order 2014 No. 2014/2747. - Enabling power: Scotland Act 1998, ss. 104, 112 (1), 113 (2) (5). - Issued: 20.10.2014. Made: 13.10.2014. Laid: 15.10.2014. Coming into force: 06.11.2014. Effect: 2000/413, 414, 415, 419 amended. Territorial extent & classification: E/W/S/NI. General. - 4p.: 30 cm. - 978-0-11-112179-5 £4.25

The Marriage and Civil Partnership (Scotland) Act 2014 and Civil Partnership Act 2004 (Consequential Provisions and Modifications) Order 2014 No. 2014/3229. - Enabling power: Scotland Act 1998, ss. 104, 112 (1), 113 (2) to (5) (7) & Civil Partnership Act 2004, s. 259 (1). - Issued: 11.12.2014. Made: 04.12.2014. Coming into force: in accord. with art. 1 (2). Effect: 58 SIs & 22 Acts amended. Territorial extent & classification: E/W/S/NI. General. - Supersedes draft S.I. (ISBN 9780111122402) issued 31.10.2014. - 56p.: 30 cm. - 978-0-11-112483-3 £10.00

The National Assembly for Wales (Remuneration) Measure 2010 (Disqualification from Remuneration Board) Order 2014 No. 2014/1004 (W.93). - Enabling power: National Assembly for Wales (Remuneration) Measure 2010, s. 5 (2) (3). - Issued: 17.04.2014. Made: 11.04.2014. Coming into force: 12.04.2014, in accord. with art. 1. Effect: 2010 nawm 4 amended. Territorial extent & classification: W. General. - In English & Welsh. Welsh title: Gorchymyn Mesur Cynulliad Cenedlaethol Cymru (Taliadau) 2010 (Anghymhwyso o'r BwrddTaliadau) 2014. - 4p.: 30 cm. - 978-0-348-10936-8 £4.25

The Revenue Scotland and Tax Powers Act 2014 (Consequential Provisions and Modifications) Order 2014 No. 2014/3294. - Enabling power: Scotland Act 1998, ss. 104, 112 (1), 113 (2) (4) (5),114 (1). - Issued: 18.12.2014. Made: 11.12.2014. Coming into force: in accord. with art. 1 (2). Effect: None. Territorial extent & classification: E/W/S/NI. General. - Supersedes draft S.I. (ISBN 9780111121276) issued 15/10/14. - 8p.: 30 cm. - 978-0-11-112563-2 £4.25

The Scotland Act 1998 (Agency Arrangements) (Specification) Order 2014 No. 2014/1892. - Enabling power: Scotland Act 1998, ss. 93 (3), 113 (3). - Issued: 23.07.2014. Made: 16.07.2014. Laid before Parliament and Scottish Parliament: 23.07.2014. Coming into force: 03.11.2014. Effect: None. Territorial extent & classification: E/W/S. General. - 4p.: 30 cm. - 978-0-11-111854-2 £4.25

The Scotland Act 1998 (Modification of Functions) Order 2014 No. 2014/2753 (S.3). - Enabling power: Scotland Act 1998, ss. 106, 112 (1). - Issued: 20.10.2014. Made: 13.10.2014. Laid: 15.10.2014. Coming into force: 01.03.2015. Effect: None. Territorial extent & classification: E/W/S/NI. General. - 4p.: 30 cm. - 978-0-11-112184-9 £4.25

The Scotland Act 1998 (Modification of Schedule 5) Order 2014 No. 2014/1559. - Enabling power: Scotland Act 1998, s. 30 (2). - Issued: 19.06.2014. Made: 12.06.2014. Coming into force: 13.06.2014. in accord. with art. 1 (2). Effect: 1998 c.46 modified. Territorial extent & classification: UK. General. - Supersedes draft SI (ISBN 9780111111918) issued 18.03.2014. - 4p.: 30 cm. - 978-0-11-111655-5 £4.25

The Scotland Act 1998 (Transfer of Functions to the Scottish Ministers etc.) Order 2014 No. 2014/2918. - Enabling power: Scotland Act 1998, ss. 63 (1), 113 (3) (4) (5), 124 (2). - Issued: 12.11.2014. Made: 05.11.2014. Laid:-. Coming into force: 06.11.2014. Effect: None. Territorial extent & classification: E/W/S/NI. General. - Supersedes draft SI (ISBN 9780111117415) issued 07/07/14. - 4p.: 30 cm. - 978-0-11-112297-6 £4.25

The Scotland Act 2012 (Commencement No. 4) Order 2014 No. 2014/3250 (C.147). - Enabling power: Scotland Act 2012, s. 44 (4). Bringing into operation various provisions of the 2012 Act on 12.12.2014, in accord. with art. 2. - Issued: 16.12.2014. Made: 08.12.2014. Effect: None. Territorial extent & classification: E/W/S/NI. General. - 2p.: 30 cm. - 978-0-11-112515-1 £4.25

The Scottish Parliament (Constituencies and Regions) Order 2014 No. 2014/501 (S.1). - Enabling power: Scotland Act 1998, s. 113, sch. 1, para. 6 (1) (5). - Issued: 12.03.2014. Made: 05.03.2014. Coming into force: In accord. with art. 1 (2) (3). Effect: S.I. 2010/2691 revoked. Territorial extent & classification: E/W/S/NI. General. - 8p., map: 30 cm. - 978-0-11-111105-5 £5.75

The Social Care (Self-directed Support) (Scotland) Act 2013 (Consequential Modifications and Savings) Order 2014 No. 2014/513. - Enabling power: Scotland Act 1998, ss. 104, 112 (1), 113 (2) (4) (5). - Issued: 11.03.2014. Made: 04.03.2014. Laid: 06.03.2014. Coming into force: 01.04.2014. Effect: S.I. 1987/1967, 1973; 1991/2887; 1992/1815; 1996/207, 2890; 2002/1792, 2006; 2004/3120; 2006/213, 214, 758; 2007/1745; 2008/794, 1052, 1053, 1054; 2009/1114, 2131; 2010/42; 2011/2344; 2012/2885; 2013/1179, 1893, 3029 (W.301), 3035 (W.303) amended. Territorial extent & classification: UK. General. - This SI was affected by a defect in SI 2013/2302 which has been corrected by SI 2014/1834 (L.27) (ISBN 9780111118122) which is being issued free of charge to all known recipients of SI 2013/2302 and SI 2014/513. - 12p.: 30 cm. - 978-0-11-111117-8 £5.75

Consultant lobbying

The Transparency of Lobbying, Non-Party Campaigning and Trade Union Administration Act 2014 (Commencement and Transitional Provision No. 1) Order 2014 No. 2014/1236 (C.49). - Enabling power: Transparency of Lobbying, Non-Party Campaigning and Trade Union Administration Act 2014, s. 45 (1) (2). Bringing into operation various provisions of the 2014 Act on 23.05.2014, 01.07.2014, in accord. with art 2. - Issued: 19.05.2014. Made: 11.05.2014. Effect: None. Territorial extent & classification: E/W/S/NI. General. - 2p.: 30 cm. - 978-0-11-111488-9 £4.25

Consumer credit

The Consumer Credit Act 1974 (Green Deal) (Amendment) Order 2014 No. 2014/436. - Enabling power: Energy Act 2011, s.30. - Issued: 05.03.2014. Made: 27.02.2014. Coming into force: 28.02.2014 in accord. with art. 1 (2). Effect: 1974 c.39 amended. Territorial extent & classification: E/W/S/NI. General. - Supersedes draft S.I. (ISBN 9780111108130) issued 14.01.2014. - 12p.: 30 cm. - 978-0-11-111047-8 £5.75

The Consumer Credit (Information Requirements and Duration of Licences and Charges) (Amendment) Regulations 2014 No. 2014/2369. - Enabling power: Consumer Credit Act 1974, ss. 77A (2), 182 (2) (a) (b), 189 (1). - Issued: 10.09.2014. Made: 04.09.2014. Laid: 05.09.2014. Coming into force: 26.09.2014. Effect: S.I. 2007/1167 amended. Territorial extent & classification: E/W/S/NI. General. - 8p.: 30 cm. - 978-0-11-112028-6 £6.00

Consumer protection

The Aerosol Dispensers (Amendment) Regulations 2014 No. 2014/1130. - Enabling power: Consumer Protection Act 1987, s. 11. - Issued: 07.05.2014. Made: 28.04.2014. Laid: 01.05.2014. Coming into force: 19.06.2014. Effect: S.I. 2009/2824 amended. Territorial extent & classification: E/W/S/NI. General. - EC note: These Regulations implement Commission Directive 2013/10/EU as amended by the Corrigendum to that Directive- 4p.: 30 cm. - 978-0-11-111450-6 £4.25

The Consumer Protection (Amendment) Regulations 2014 No. 2014/870. - Enabling power: European Communities Act 1972, s. 2 (2). - Issued: 04.04.2014. Made: 31.03.2014. Coming into force: In accord. with reg. 1. Effect: 1967 c.7, c.14; 1973 c.52; 1985 c.73; S.I. 2008/1277; 2013/3134 amended. Territorial extent & classification: E/W/S/NI. General. - 16p.: 30 cm. - 978-0-11-111324-0 £5.75

The Enterprise Act 2002 (Part 8 EU Infringements) Order 2014 No. 2014/2908. - Enabling power: Enterprise Act 2002, ss. 210 (9), 212 (3). - Issued: 10.11.2014. Made: 03.11.2014. Laid: 05.11.2014. Coming into force: 27.11.2014. Effect: S.I. 2013/3168 revoked. Territorial extent & classification: E/W/S/NI. General. - This Statutory Instrument has been made in consequence of a defect in S.I. 2013/3168 (ISBN 9780111107355) and is being issued free of charge to all known recipients of that Statutory Instrument. - 4p.: 30 cm. - 978-0-11-112291-4 £4.25

The Enterprise Act 2002 (Part 9 Restrictions on Disclosure of Information) (Amendment) Order 2014 No. 2014/2807. - Enabling power: Enterprise Act 2002, s. 241 (6). - Issued: 23.10.2014. Made: 16.10.2014. Laid: 21.10.2014. Coming into force: 17.11.2014. Effect: 2002 c.40 amended. Territorial extent & classification: E/W/S/NI. General. - 2p.: 30 cm. - 978-0-11-112199-3 £4.25

The Gas and Electricity Regulated Providers (Redress Scheme) (Amendment) Order 2014 No. 2014/2378. - Enabling power: Consumers, Estate Agents and Redress Act 2007, s. 47 (1) to (3). - Issued: 12.09.2014. Made: 01.07.2014. Laid: 08.09.2014. Coming into force: 08.08.2014. Effect: None. Territorial extent & classification: E/W/S. General. - 2p.: 30 cm. - 978-0-11-112037-8 £4.25

The REACH Enforcement (Amendment) Regulations 2014 No. 2014/2882. - Enabling power: European Communities Act 1972, s. 2 (2). - Issued: 05.11.2014. Made: 25.10.2014. Laid: 31.10.2014. Coming into force: 01.12.2014. Effect: S.I. 2008/2852 amended. Territorial extent & classification: E/W/S/NI. General. - EC note: These Regulations provide for the enforcement of Regulation (EC) 1907/2006, as corrected, concerning the Registration, Evaluation, Authorisation and Restriction of Chemicals (REACH). - 4p.: 30 cm. - 978-0-11-112268-6 £4.25

Consumer protection, England and Wales

The Compensation (Claims Management Services) (Amendment) Regulations 2014 No. 2014/3239. - Enabling power: Compensation Act 2006, ss. 9, 15 (1) (b), sch., paras 1, 2, 8, 9, 10, 11, 13, 14, 16. - Issued: 12.12.2014. Made: 08.12.2014. Coming into force: In accord. with reg. 1. Effect: S.I. 2006/3322 amended. Territorial extent & classification: E/W. General. - Supersedes draft S.I. (ISBN 9780111118566) issued 23/07/14. - 8p.: 30 cm. - 978-0-11-112496-3 £6.00

The Financial Services (Banking Reform) Act 2013 (Commencement No. 2) Order 2014 No. 2014/772 (C.28). - Enabling power: Financial Services (Banking Reform) Act 2013, s. 148 (3). Bringing into operation various provisions of this Act on 21.03.2014 in accord. with art. 2. - Issued: 26.03.2014. Made: 20.03.2014. Effect: None. Territorial extent & classification: E/W. General. - 2p.: 30 cm. - 978-0-11-111254-0 £4.00

Contracting out, England

The Contracting Out (Local Authorities Social Services Functions) (England) Order 2014 No. 2014/829. - Enabling power: Deregulation and Contracting Out Act 1994, ss. 70 (2) (4), 77 (1). - Issued: 01.04.2014. Made: 26.03.2014. Coming into force: 01.04.2014. Effect: 1970 c.42 modified & S.I. 2011/1568 revoked. Territorial extent & classification: E. General. - Supersedes draft SI (ISBN 9780111109632) issued 18/02/14; Partially revoked by SI 2015/643 (ISBN 9780111132999). - 8p.: 30 cm. - 978-0-11-111284-7 £5.75

Contracting out, Wales

The Local Authorities (Contracting Out of Tax Billing, Collection and Enforcement Functions) (Amendment) (Wales) Order 2014 No. 2014/856. - Enabling power: Deregulation and Contracting Out Act 1994, ss. 69 (4), 70 (2) (4), 77 (1) (c). - Issued: 03.04.2014. Made: 27.03.2014. Coming into force: 28.03.2014, in accord. with art. 1 (1). Effect: S.I. 1996/1880 amended in relation to Wales. Territorial extent & classification: W. General. - Supersedes draft (ISBN 9780111110065) issued 27.02.2014. - 4p.: 30 cm. - 978-0-11-111308-0 £4.00

Co-operative societies

The Co-operative and Community Benefit Societies and Credit Unions Act 2010 (Commencement No. 2) Order 2014 No. 2014/183 (C.6). - Enabling power: Co-operative and Community Benefit Societies and Credit Unions Act 2010, s. 8 (2). Bringing into operation various provisions of the 2010 Act on 06.04.2014, 01.08.2014, in accord. with arts 2, 3. - Issued: 05.02.2014. Made: 30.01.2014. Effect: None. Territorial extent & classification: E/W/S/NI. General. - 2p.: 30 cm. - 978-0-11-110907-6 £4.00

The Co-operative and Community Benefit Societies and Credit Unions Act 2010 (Consequential Amendments) Regulations 2014 No. 2014/1815. - Enabling power: Co-operative and Community Benefit Societies and Credit Unions Act 2010, s. 6. - Issued: 15.07.2014. Made: 08.07.2014. Coming into force: 01.080.2014 in accord. with reg. 1. Effect: S.I. 1969/1037; 1990/2024; 1995/849, 1945 (S.142), 2801; 1996/1667; 1999/1549; 2001/544, 1062, 1744, 2617; 2004/353, 1450; 2005/590, 1529, 1788, 1986, 2415, 2531; 2008/565, 788, 1911; 2009/779, 1085, 1385, 2971; 2010/5; 2012/922, 1290, 1464, 1821, 2421; 2014/229 amended. Territorial extent & classification: E/W/S. General. - Supersedes draft S.I. (ISBN 9780111114865) issued 19.05.2014. - 12p.: 30 cm. - 978-0-11-111787-3 £6.00

The Co-operative and Community Benefit Societies and Credit Unions (Arrangements, Reconstructions and Administration) (Amendment) Order 2014 No. 2014/1822. - Enabling power: Co-operative and Community Benefit Societies and Credit Unions Act 2014, s. 118. - Issued: 16.07.2014. Made: 09.07.2014. Laid: 11.07.2014. Coming into force: 01.08.2014. Effect: S.I. 2014/229 amended. Territorial extent & classification: E/W/S. General. - 8p.: 30 cm. - 978-0-11-111793-4 £6.00

The Co-operative and Community Benefit Societies and Credit Unions (Investigations) Regulations 2014 No. 2014/574. - Enabling power: Co-operative and Community Benefit Societies and Credit Unions Act 2010, ss. 4 (1) (2) (a) (3) (7), 6, 7. - Issued: 17.03.2014. Made: 10.03.2014. Coming into force: 06.04.2014. Effect: 1965 c.12; 1979 c.34; 1985 c.6; 1986 c.46 modified & S.I. 2006/264 amended. Territorial extent & classification: E/W/S/NI. General. - Supersedes draft SI (ISBN 9780111108857) issued 30/01/14- 8p.: 30 cm. - 978-0-11-111173-4 £5.75

Copyright

The Copyright and Duration of Rights in Performances (Amendment) Regulations 2014 No. 2014/434. - Enabling power: European Communities Act 1972, s. 2 (2) & Enterprise and Regulatory Reform Act 2013, s. 78. - Issued: 05.03.2014. Made: 26.02.2014. Laid: 28.02.2014. Coming into force: 06.04.2014. Effect: 1988 c.48 amended. Territorial extent & classification: E/W/S/NI. General. - This Statutory Instrument has been printed to correct an error in S.I. 2013/1782 (ISBN 9780111101865) and is being issued free of charge to all known recipients of that Statutory Instrument. - 2p.: 30 cm. - 978-0-11-111045-4 £4.00

The Copyright and Rights in Performances (Certain Permitted Uses of Orphan Works) Regulations 2014 No. 2014/2861. - Enabling power: European Communities Act 1972, s. 2 (2). - Issued: 03.11.2014. Made: 27.10.14. Coming into force: 29.10.2014. Effect: 1988 c.48 amended. Territorial extent & classification: E/W/S/NI. General. - Supersedes draft S.I. (ISBN 9780111117682) issued 11.07.2014. - 8p.: 30 cm. - 978-0-11-112247-1 £6.00

The Copyright and Rights in Performances (Disability) Regulations 2014 No. 2014/1384. - Enabling power: European Communities Act 1972, s. 2 (2). - Issued: 06.06.2014. Made: 19.05.2014. Coming into force: 01.06.2014 at 00.01, in accord. with reg. 1. Effect: 1988 c.48 amended/partially repealed & S.I. 2003/2498; 2006/18 partially revoked & 2002 c.33 repealed. Territorial extent & classification: E/W/S/NI. General. - Supersedes draft SI (ISBN 9780111112694) issued 28/03/14- 12p.: 30 cm. - 978-0-11-111565-7 £6.00

The Copyright and Rights in Performances (Extended Collective Licensing) Regulations 2014 No. 2014/2588. - Enabling power: Copyright, Designs and Patents Act 1988, ss. 116B to 116D. - Issued: 30.09.2014. Made: 11.09.2014. Coming into force: 01.10.2014. Effect: None. Territorial extent & classification: E/W/S/NI. General. - Supersedes draft S.I. (ISBN 9780111116890) issued 27/06/14. - 16p.: 30 cm. - 978-0-11-112106-1 £6.00

The Copyright and Rights in Performances (Licensing of Orphan Works) Regulations 2014 No. 2014/2863. - Enabling power: Copyright, Designs and Patents Act 1988, s. 116A, C, D, sch. 2A paras 1A. C, D. - Issued: 03.11.2014. Made: 27.10.2014. Coming into force: 29.10.2014. Effect: None. Territorial extent & classification: E/W/S/NI. General. - Supersedes draft S.I. (ISBN 978011117644) issued 10.07.2014. - 8p.: 30 cm. - 978-0-11-112249-5 £6.00

The Copyright and Rights in Performances (Personal Copies for Private Use) Regulations 2014 No. 2014/2361. - Enabling power: European Communities Act 1972, s. 2 (2). - Issued: 10.09.2014. Made: 26.08.14. Coming into force: 01.10.2014. Effect: 1988 c.48 amended. Territorial extent & classification: E/W/S/NI. General. - Supersedes draft SI (ISBN 9780111116036) issued 10.06.2014. - 8p.: 30 cm. - 978-0-11-112023-1 £6.00

The Copyright and Rights in Performances (Quotation and Parody) Regulations 2014 No. 2014/2356. - Enabling power: European Communities Act 1972, s. 2 (2). - Issued: 10.09.2014. Made: 26.08.2014. Coming into force: 01.10.2014. Effect: 1988 c.48 amended. Territorial extent & classification: E/W/S/NI. General. - Supersedes draft SI (ISBN 928011116029) issued 10.06.2014. - 4p.: 30 cm. - 978-0-11-112022-4 £4.25

The Copyright and Rights in Performances (Research, Education, Libraries and Archives) Regulations 2014 No. 2014/1372. - Enabling power: European Communities Act 1972, s. 2 (2). - Issued: 04.06.2014. Made: 19.05.2014. Coming into force: In accord. with reg. 1. Effect: 1988 c.48; 1990 c.42; 2010 c.24; S.I. 1989/1067 amended & 1988 c.48 partially repealed & S.I. 2003/2498 partially revoked. Territorial extent & classification: E/W/S/NI. General. - Supersedes draft SI (ISBN 9780111112755) issued 31/03/14. - 20p.: 30 cm. - 978-0-11-111544-2 £6.00

The Copyright (Public Administration) Regulations 2014 No. 2014/1385. - Enabling power: European Communities Act 1972, s. 2 (2). - Issued: 06.06.2014. Made: 19.05.2014. Coming into force: 01.06.2014. Effect: 1977 c.37 partially repealed & S.I. 2011/2059 revoked. Territorial extent & classification: E/W/S/NI. General. - Supersedes draft SI (ISBN 9780111112731) issued 31.03.2014. - 4p.: 30 cm. - 978-0-11-111566-4 £4.25

The Copyright (Regulation of Relevant Licensing Bodies) Regulations 2014 No. 2014/898. - Enabling power: Copyright, Designs and Patents Act 1998, sch. A1, para. 7 (4). - Issued: 08.04.2014. Made: 01.04.2014. Laid: -Coming into force: 06.04.2014. Effect: None. Territorial extent & classification: E/W/S/NI. General. - Supersedes draft S.I. (ISBN 9780111110485) issued 06.03.2014. - 12p.: 30 cm. - 978-0-11-111363-9 £6.00

Coroners, England

The Coroners and Justice Act 2009 (Alteration of Coroner Areas) Order 2014 No. 2014/3157. - Enabling power: Coroners and Justice Act 2009, sch. 2, para. 2. - Issued: 03.12.2014. Made: 26.11.2014. Laid: 28.11.2014. Coming into force: 01.01.2015. Effect: None. Territorial extent & classification: E. General. - 2p.: 30 cm. - 978-0-11-112421-5 £4.25

Corporation tax

The Business Premises Renovation Allowances (Amendment) Regulations 2014 No. 2014/1687. - Enabling power: Capital Allowances Act 2001, ss. 360B (5), 360C (2) (a) (3), 360D (4). - Issued: 04.07.2014. Made: 30.06.2014. Laid: 01.07.2014. Coming into force: 22.07.2014. Effect: S.I. 2007/945 amended. Territorial extent & classification: E/W/S/NI. General. - 4p.: 30 cm. - 978-0-11-111738-5 £4.25

CORPORATION TAX

The Capital Allowances (Designated Assisted Areas) Order 2014 No. 2014/3183. - Enabling power: Capital Allowances Act 2001, s. 45K (2) (a) (3) (4). - Issued: 05.12.2014. Made: 01.12.2014. Laid: 02.12.2014. Coming into force: 23.12.2014. Effect: None. Territorial extent & classification: E/W/S/NI. General. - 4p.: 30 cm. - 978-0-11-112433-8 £4.25

The Capital Allowances (Energy-saving Plant and Machinery) (Amendment) Order 2014 No. 2014/1868. - Enabling power: Capital Allowances Act 2001, ss. 45A (3) (4). - Issued: 23.07.2014. Made: 16.07.2014. Laid: 17.07.2014. Coming into force: 07.08.2014. Effect: S.I. 2001/2541 amended. Territorial extent & classification: E/W/S/NI. General. - 2p.: 30 cm. - 978-0-11-111832-0 £4.25

The Capital Allowances (Environmentally Beneficial Plant and Machinery) (Amendment) Order 2014 No. 2014/1869. - Enabling power: Capital Allowances Act 2001, s. 45H (3) to (5). - Issued: 22.07.2014. Made: 16.07.2014. Laid: 17.07.2014. Coming into force: 07.08.2014. Effect: S.I. 2003/2076 amended. Territorial extent & classification: E/W/S/NI. General. - 2p.: 30 cm. - 978-0-11-111833-7 £4.25

The Changes in Accounting Standards (Loan Relationships and Derivative Contracts) Regulations 2014 No. 2014/3325. - Enabling power: Corporation Tax Act 2009, s. 465A. - Issued: 24.12.2014. Made: 17.12.2014. Coming into force: 31.12.2014. Effect: S.I. 2002/1970; 2004/3256, 3271 amended. Territorial extent & classification: E/W/S/NI. General. - Supersedes draft SI (ISBN 9780111123355) issued 21/11/14. - 4p.: 30 cm. - 978-0-11-112617-2 £4.25

The Community Amateur Sports Clubs (Exemptions) Order 2014 No. 2014/3327. - Enabling power: Corporation Tax Act 2010, ss. 662 (5A), 663 (5A). - Issued: 24.12.2014. Made: 17.12.2014. Laid: 18.12.2014. Coming into force: 01.04.2015. Effect: 2010 c.4 amended. Territorial extent & classification: E/W/S/NI. General. - 2p.: 30 cm. - 978-0-11-112619-6 £4.25

The Corporation Tax (Instalment Payments) (Amendment) Regulations 2014 No. 2014/2409. - Enabling power: Taxes Management Act 1970, s. 59E (1). - Issued: 15.09.2014. Made: 09.09.2014. Laid: 10.09.2014. Coming into force: 01.10.2014. Effect: S.I. 1998/3175 amended. Territorial extent & classification: E/W/S/NI. General. - 2p.: 30 cm. - 978-0-11-112060-6 £4.25

The Cultural Test (Video Games) Regulations 2014 No. 2014/1958. - Enabling power: Corporation Tax Act 2009, ss. 1217CB, 1217CC (7). - Issued: 29.07.2014. Made: 22.07.2014. Laid: 24.07.2014. Coming into force: 19.08.2014. Effect: None. Territorial extent & classification: E/W/S/NI. General. - 8p.: 30 cm. - 978-0-11-111919-8 £6.00

The Double Taxation Relief and International Tax Enforcement (Belgium) Order 2014 No. 2014/1875. - Enabling power: Taxation (International and Other Provisions) Act 2010, s. 2 & Finance Act 2006, s. 173 (1) to (3). - Issued: 23.07.2014. Made: 16.07.2014. Effect: None. Territorial extent & classification: E/W/S/NI. General. - Supersedes draft SI (ISBN 9780111116272) issued 13/06/14. - 8p.: 30 cm. - 978-0-11-111837-5 £4.25

The Double Taxation Relief and International Tax Enforcement (Canada) Order 2014 No. 2014/3274. - Enabling power: Taxation (International and Other Provisions) Act 2010, s. 2 & Finance Act 2006, s. 173 (1) to (3). - Issued: 17.12.2014. Made: 10.12.2014. Coming into force: 10.12.2014. Effect: 1980/709 amended. Territorial extent & classification: E/W/S/NI. - Supersedes draft S.I. (ISBN 9780111121801) issued 20/10/14. - 20p.: 30 cm. - 978-0-11-112537-3 £6.00

The Double Taxation Relief and International Tax Enforcement (Iceland) Order 2014 No. 2014/1879. - Enabling power: Taxation (International and Other Provisions) Act 2010, s. 2 & Finance Act 2006, s. 173 (1) to (3). - Issued: 23.07.2014. Made: 16.07.2014. Effect: None. Territorial extent & classification: E/W/S/NI. General. - Supersedes draft SI (ISBN 9780111116296) issued 13/06/14. - 24p.: 30 cm. - 978-0-11-111841-2 £6.00

The Double Taxation Relief and International Tax Enforcement (Japan) Order 2014 No. 2014/1881. - Enabling power: Taxation (International and Other Provisions) Act 2010, s. 2 & Finance Act 2006, s. 173 (1) to (3). - Issued: 23.07.2014. Made: 16.07.2014. Effect: None. Territorial extent & classification: E/W/S/NI. General. - Supersedes draft SI (ISBN 9780111116289) issued 23/07/14. - 20p.: 30 cm. - 978-0-11-111843-6 £6.00

The Double Taxation Relief and International Tax Enforcement (Tajikistan) Order 2014 No. 2014/3275. - Enabling power: Taxation (International and Other Provisions) Act 2010, s. 2 & Finance Act 2006, s. 173 (1) to (3). - Issued: 17.12.2014. Made: 10.12.2014. Effect: None. Territorial extent & classification: E/W/S/NI. General. - Supersedes draft S.I. (ISBN 9780111121726) issued 17/10/14. - 24p.: 30 cm. - 978-0-11-112538-0 £6.00

The Double Taxation Relief and International Tax Enforcement (Zambia) Order 2014 No. 2014/1876. - Enabling power: Taxation (International and Other Provisions) Act 2010, s. 2 & Finance Act 2006, s. 173 (1) to (3). - Issued: 23.07.2014. Made: 16.07.2014. Effect: None. Territorial extent & classification: E/W/S/NI. General. - Supersedes draft SI (ISBN 9780111116302) issued 13/06/14. - 24p.: 30 cm. - 978-0-11-111838-2 £6.00

The Double Taxation Relief (Federal Republic of Germany) Order 2014 No. 2014/1874. - Enabling power: Taxation (International and Other Provisions) Act 2010, s. 2. - Issued: 23.07.2014. Made: 16.07.2014. Effect: None. Territorial extent & classification: E/W/S/NI. General. - Supersedes draft SI (ISBN 9780111116241) issued 13/06/14. - 8p.: 30 cm. - 978-0-11-111836-8 £6.00

The Finance Act 2013, Schedules 17 and 18 (Tax Relief for Video Games Development) (Appointed Day) Order 2014 No. 2014/1962 (C.91). - Enabling power: Finance Act 2013, sch. 17, paras. 2, 3, sch. 18, para. 22. Bringing into operation various provisions of the 2013 Act on 01.04.2014. - Issued: 29.07.2014. Made: 22.07.2014. Effect: None. Territorial extent & classification: E/W/S/NI. General. - 2p.: 30 cm. - 978-0-11-111923-5 £4.25

The Finance Act 2014, Schedule 4 (Tax Relief for Theatrical Production) (Appointed Day) Order 2014 No. 2014/2228 (C.98). - Enabling power: Finance Act 2014, sch. 4, para. 16 (2). Bringing into operation various provisions of the 2014 Act on 22.08.2014. - Issued: 29.08.2014. Made: 22.08.2014. Effect: None. Territorial extent & classification: E/W/S/NI. General. - 2p.: 30 cm. - 978-0-11-111995-2 £4.25

The Finance Act 2014, Section 32 (Film Tax Relief) (Appointed Day) Order 2014 No. 2014/2880 (C.126). - Enabling power: Finance Act 2014, s. 32 (4) (6). Bringing into operation various provisions of the 2014 Act on 01.04.2014, in accord. with art. 2. - Issued: 05.11.2014. Made: 29.10.2014. Effect: 2014 c.26 amended. Territorial extent & classification: E/W/S/NI. General. - 2p.: 30 cm. - 978-0-11-112266-2 £4.25

The International Tax Enforcement (Anguilla) Order 2014 No. 2014/1357. - Enabling power: Finance Act 2006, s. 173 (1) to (3). - Issued: 03.06.2014. Made: 27.05.2014. Coming into force: 03.06.2014. Effect: None. Territorial extent & classification: E/W/S/NI. General. - Supersedes draft SI (ISBN 9780111110539) issued 06.03.14. - 8p.: 30 cm. - 978-0-11-111529-9 £6.00

The International Tax Enforcement (British Virgin Islands) Order 2014 No. 2014/1359. - Enabling power: Finance Act 2006, s. 173 (1) to (3). - Issued: 03.06.2014. Made: 27.05.2014. Coming into force: 03.06.2014. Effect: None. Territorial extent & classification: E/W/S/NI. General. - Supersedes draft SI (ISBN 9780111110546) issued 06.03.14. - 8p.: 30 cm. - 978-0-11-111531-2 £6.00

The International Tax Enforcement (Turks and Caicos Islands) Order 2014 No. 2014/1360. - Enabling power: Finance Act 2006, s. 173 (1) to (3). - Issued: 03.06.2014. Made: 27.05.2014. Coming into force: 03.06.2014. Effect: None. Territorial extent & classification: E/W/S/NI. General. - Supersedes draft SI (ISBN 9780111110560) issued 06.03.14. - 8p.: 30 cm. - 978-0-11-111532-9 £6.00

The Investment Transactions (Tax) Regulations 2014 No. 2014/685. - Enabling power: Finance (No. 2) Act 2005, ss. 17 (3), 18 & Corporation Tax Act 2010, s. 622A & Taxation (International and Other Provisions) Act 2010, s. 354 & Finance Act 2013, s. 217. - Issued: 21.03.2014. Made: 17.03.2014. Laid: 18.03.2014. Coming into force: 08.04.2014. Effect: S.I. 2006/964; 2009/3001; 2011/2999; 2013/2819 amended. Territorial extent & classification: E/W/S/NI. General. - 8p.: 30 cm. - 978-0-11-111237-3 £4.00

The Loan Relationships and Derivative Contracts (Change of Accounting Practice) (Amendment) Regulations 2014 No. 2014/3187. - Enabling power: Corporation Tax Act 2009, ss. 319, 598. - Issued: 05.12.2014. Made: 01.12.2014. Laid: 02.12.2014. Coming into force: 31.12.2014. Effect: S.I. 2004/3271 amended. Territorial extent & classification: E/W/S/NI. General. - 4p.: 30 cm. - 978-0-11-112437-6 £4.25

The Loan Relationships and Derivative Contracts (Disregard and Bringing into Account of Profits and Losses) (Amendment) Regulations 2014 No. 2014/3188. - Enabling power: Corporation Tax Act 2009, ss. 310, 328 (4) (7), 598 (1) (a) (4), 606 (4) (7). - Issued: 05.12.2014. Made: 01.12.2014. Laid: 02.12.2014. Coming into force: 31.12.2014. Effect: S.I. 2004/3256 amended. Territorial extent & classification: E/W/S/NI. General. - 8p.: 30 cm. - 978-0-11-112438-3 £6.00

The Offshore Funds (Tax) (Amendment) Regulations 2014 No. 2014/1931. - Enabling power: Taxation (International and Other Provisions) Act 2010, s. 354. - Issued: 28.07.2014. Made: 21.07.2014. Laid: 22.07.2014. Coming into force: 12.08.2014. Effect: S.I. 2009/3001 amended. Territorial extent & classification: E/W/S/NI. General. - 2p.: 30 cm. - 978-0-11-111903-7 £4.25

The Real Estate Investment Trust (Amendments to the Corporation Tax Act 2010 and Consequential Amendments) Regulations 2014 No. 2014/518. - Enabling power: Finance (No. 2) Act 2005, ss. 17 (3) (a) (b), 18 (1) & Corporation Tax Act 2010, ss. 528 (4B), 544 (6). - Issued: 12.03.2014. Made: 06.03.2014. Laid: 07.03.2014. Coming into force: 01.04.2014. Effect: 2010 c.4; S.I. 2006/964 amended. Territorial extent & classification: E/W/S/NI. General. - 4p.: 30 cm. - 978-0-11-111120-8 £4.00

The Taxation (International and Other Provisions) Act 2010 (Amendment to Section 371RE) (Controlled Foreign Companies) Regulations 2014 No. 2014/3237. - Enabling power: Taxation (International and Other Provisions) Act 2010, ss. 371RF (1) (2). - Issued: 15.12.2014. Made: 08.12.2014. Laid: 09.12.2014. Coming into force: 31.12.2014. Effect: 2010 c.8 amended. Territorial extent & classification: E/W/S/NI. General. - 2p.: 30 cm. - 978-0-11-112494-9 £4.25

The Taxation of Chargeable Gains (Gilt-edged Securities) Order 2014 No. 2014/1120. - Enabling power: Taxation of Chargeable Gains Act 1992, sch. 9, para. 1. - Issued: 06.05.2014. Made: 28.04.2014. Coming into force: 06.05.2014. Effect: None. Territorial extent & classification: E/W/S/NI. General. - 2p.: 30 cm. - 978-0-11-111445-2 £4.25

The Taxes (Definition of Charity) (Relevant Territories) (Amendment) Regulations 2014 No. 2014/1807. - Enabling power: Finance Act 2010, sch. 6, para. 2 (3) (b). - Issued: 15.07.2014. Made: 09.07.2014. Laid: 10.07.2014. Coming into force: 31.07.2014. Effect: S.I. 2010/1904 amended. Territorial extent & classification: E/W/S/NI. General. - 4p.: 30 cm. - 978-0-11-111781-1 £4.25

The Unauthorised Unit Trusts (Tax) (Amendment) Regulations 2014 No. 2014/585. - Enabling power: Finance Act 2013, s. 217. - Issued: 18.03.2014. Made: 12.03.2014. Laid: 13.03.2014. Coming into force: 06.04.2014. Effect: S.I. 2013/2819 amended. Territorial extent & classification: E/W/S/NI. General. - 4p.: 30 cm. - 978-0-11-111189-5 £4.00

Council tax, England

The Billing Authorities (Anticipation of Precepts) (Amendment) (England) Regulations 2014 No. 2014/35. - Enabling power: Local Government Finance Act 1992, ss. 41 (2A). 113 (1). - Issued: 20.01.2014. Made: 13.01.2014. Laid: 20.01.2014. Coming into force: 13.02.2014. Effect: S.I. 1992/3239 amended. Territorial extent & classification: E. General. - 2p.: 30 cm. - 978-0-11-110831-4 £4.00

The Council Tax Reduction Schemes (Prescribed Requirements) (England) (Amendment) (No. 2) Regulations 2014 No. 2014/3312. - Enabling power: Local Government Finance Act 1992, s. 113 (1) (2), sch. 1A, paras 2. - Issued: 22.12.2014. Made: 16.12.2014. Laid: 18.12.2014. Coming into force: 12.01.2015. Effect: S.I. 2012/2885 amended. Territorial extent & classification: E. General. - 8p.: 30 cm. - 978-0-11-112589-2 £6.00

The Council Tax Reduction Schemes (Prescribed Requirements) (England) (Amendment) Regulations 2014 No. 2014/448. - Enabling power: Local Government Finance Act 1992, s. 113 (1), sch. 1A, paras 2. - Issued: 06.03.2014. Made: 27.02.2014. Laid: 05.03.2014. Coming into force: 28.03.2014. Effect: S.I. 2012/2885 amended. Territorial extent & classification: E. General. - This Statutory Instrument has been made in consequence of defects in S.I. 2013/3181 (ISBN 9780111107454) and is being issued free of charge to all known recipients of that Statutory Instrument. - 2p.: 30 cm. - 978-0-11-111058-4 £4.00

The Local Authorities (Conduct of Referendums) (Council Tax Increases) (England) (Amendment) Regulations 2014 No. 2014/231. - Enabling power: Local Audit and Accountability Act 2014, s. 46. - Issued: 12.02.2014. Made: 06.02.2014. Laid: 12.02.2014. Coming into force: 10.03.2014. Effect: S.I. 2012/444 amended. Territorial extent & classification: E. General. - 2p.: 30 cm. - 978-0-11-110934-2 £4.00

The Localism Act 2011 (Consequential Amendments) Order 2014 No. 2014/389. - Enabling power: Localism Act 2011, s. 235 (2) (3), 236 (1). - Issued: 03.03.2014. Made: 24.02.2014. Coming into force: In accord. with art. 1 (2). Effect: 1992 c.14; 1999 c.29 amended. Territorial extent & classification: E/W. General. - Supersedes draft S.I. (ISBN 9780111107997) issued 09.01.2014. - 4p.: 30 cm. - 978-0-11-111019-5 £4.00

Council tax, Wales

The Council Tax (Administration and Enforcement) (Amendment) (Wales) Regulations 2014 No. 2014/129 (W.17). - Enabling power: Local Government Finance Act 1992, s. 113 (1) (2), sch. 2, paras 1 (1), 2 (2) (4) (a) (j), 4, 5, 8 to 10. - Issued: 31.01.2014. Made: 22.01.2014. Laid before the National Assembly for Wales: 24.01.2014. Coming into force: 14.02.2014. Effect: S.I. 1992/613 amended in relation to Wales. Territorial extent & classification: W. General. - 8p.: 30 cm. - 978-0-348-10862-0 £4.00

The Council Tax (Chargeable Dwellings) (Amendment) (Wales) Order 2014 No. 2014/2653 (W.261). - Enabling power: Local Government Finance Act 1992, ss. 3 (5) (b), 113 (1). - Issued: 09.10.2014. Made: 24.09.2014. Laid before the National Assembly for Wales: 01.10.2014. Coming into force: 22.10.2014. Effect: S.I. 1992/549 amended. Territorial extent & classification: W. General. - In English and Welsh: Welsh title: Gorchymyn y Dreth Gyngor (Anheddau Trethadwy) (Diwygio) (Cymru) 2014. - 4p.: 30 cm. - 978-0-348-10994-8 £4.25

The Council Tax (Demand Notices) (Wales) (Amendment) Regulations 2014 No. 2014/122 (W.12). - Enabling power: Local Government Finance Act 1992, s. 113 (1) (2), sch. 2, paras 1 (1), 2 (4) (e). - Issued: 04.02.2014. Made: 22.01.2014. Laid before the National Assembly for Wales: 24.01.2014. Coming into force: 14.02.2014. Effect: S.I. 1993/255 amended in relation to Wales. Territorial extent & classification: W. General. - 8p.: 30 cm. - 978-0-348-10884-2 £4.00

The Council Tax Reduction Schemes (Miscellaneous Amendments) (Wales) Regulations 2014 No. 2014/825 (W.83). - Enabling power: Local Government Finance Act 1992, s. 13A (4), 14A, 14B, 14C, 14D, 113 (1) (2), sch. 1B, para. 6. - Issued: 03.04.2014. Made: 25.03.2014. Coming into force: 26.03.2014 in accord. with reg. 1. Effect: W.S.I. 2013/588 (W.67), 3029 (W.301), 3035 (W.303) amended. Territorial extent & classification: W. General. - 8p.: 30 cm. - 978-0-348-10931-3 £4.25

The Council Tax Reduction Schemes (Prescribed Requirements and Default Scheme) (Wales) (Amendment) Regulations 2014 No. 2014/66 (W.6). - Enabling power: Local Government Finance Act 1992, s. 13A (4), sch. 1B, para. 6. - Issued: 22.01.2014. Made: 14.01.2013. Coming into force: 15.01.2014 in accord. with reg. 1 (2). Effect: S.I. 2013/3029 (W.301), 3035 (W.303) amended. Territorial extent & classification: W. General. - In English and Welsh. Welsh title: Rheoliadau Cynlluniau Gostyngiadau'r Dreth Gyngor (Gofynion Rhagnodedig a'r Cynllun Diofyn) (Cymru) (Diwygio) 2014. - 16p.: 30 cm. - 978-0-348-10855-2 £5.75

Countryside, England

The Access to the Countryside (Coastal Margin) (Cumbria) Order 2014 No. 2014/851. - Enabling power: Countryside and Rights of Way Act 2000, s. 3A (10). - Issued: 02.04.2014. Made: 24.03.2014. Coming into force: 02.04.2014. Effect: None. Territorial extent & classification: E. General. - 2p.: 30 cm. - 978-0-11-111302-8 £4.00

The Access to the Countryside (Coastal Margin) (Durham, Hartlepool and Sunderland) Order 2014 No. 2014/846. - Enabling power: Countryside and Rights of Way Act 2000, s. 3A (10). - Issued: 02.04.2014. Made: 24.03.2014. Coming into force: 02.04.2014. Effect: None. Territorial extent & classification: E. General. - 2p.: 30 cm. - 978-0-11-111300-4 £4.00

The Access to the Countryside (Coastal Margin) (Sea Palling to Weybourne) Order 2014 No. 2014/3128. - Enabling power: Countryside and Rights of Way Act 2000, s. 3A (10). - Issued: 02.12.2014. Made: 23.11.2014. Coming into force: 23.11.2014. Effect: None. Territorial extent & classification: E. General. - 2p.: 30 cm. - 978-0-11-112404-8 £4.25

COUNTY COURTS, ENGLAND AND WALES

The English Coast (Isle of Wight) Order 2014 No. 2014/1940. - Enabling power: Marine and Coastal Access Act 2009, s. 300 (2) (b) (5). - Issued: 28.07.2014. Made: 14.07.2014. Laid: 24.07.2014. Coming into force: 01.10.2014. Effect: None. Territorial extent & classification: E. General. - 2p.: 30 cm. - 978-0-11-111909-9 £4.25

The National Park Authorities (England) (Amendment) Order 2014 No. 2014/571. - Enabling power: Environment Act 1995, ss. 63 (1) (5), sch. 7, paras 1 (2) (3) , 2 (1) (2). - Issued: 14.03.2014. Made: 08.03.2014. Laid: 13.03.2014. Coming into force: 05.05.2014. Effect: S.I. 1996/1243 amended. Territorial extent & classification: E. General. - 4p.: 30 cm. - 978-0-11-111167-3 £4.00

County court, England and Wales

The Civil Procedure (Amendment No. 4) Rules 2014 No. 2014/867 (L.16). - Enabling power: Civil Procedure Act 1997, s. 2. - Issued: 04.04.2014. Made: 28.03.2014. Laid: 01.04.2014. Coming into force: 22.04.2014. Effect: S.I. 1998/3132 amended. Territorial extent & classification: E/W. General. - 8p.: 30 cm. - 978-0-11-111322-6 £5.75

The Civil Procedure (Amendment No. 5) Rules 2014 No. 2014/1233 (L.24). - Enabling power: Civil Procedure Act 1997, s. 2. - Issued: 19.05.2014. Made: 13.05.2014. Laid: 15.05.2014. Coming into force: 05.06.2014. Effect: S.I. 1998/3132; 2014/407, 867 amended. Territorial extent & classification: E/W. General. - 4p.: 30 cm. - 978-0-11-111485-8 £4.25

The Civil Procedure (Amendment No. 6) Rules 2014 No. 2014/2044 (L.28). - Enabling power: Civil Procedure Act 1997, s. 2 & Presumption of Death Act 1997, s. 9 (1) (2). - Issued: 07.08.2014. Made: 29.07.2014. Laid: 01.08.2014. Coming into force: 01.10.2014. Effect: S.I. 1998/3132 amended. Territorial extent & classification: E/W. General. - 12p.: 30 cm. - 978-0-11-111945-7 £6.00

The Civil Procedure (Amendment No. 7) Rules 2014 No. 2014/2948 (L.32). - Enabling power: Civil Procedure Act 1997, s. 2. - Issued: 17.11.2014. Made: 10.11.2014. Laid: 12.11.2014. Coming into force: 10.01.2015. Effect: S.I. 1998/3132 amended. Territorial extent & classification: E/W. General. - 8p.: 30 cm. - 978-0-11-112322-5 £6.00

The Civil Procedure (Amendment No. 8) Rules 2014 No. 2014/3299 (L.36). - Enabling power: Civil Procedure Act 1997, s. 2. - Issued: 23.12.2014. Made: 16.12.2014. Laid: 18.12.2014. Coming into force: In accord. with rule 2. Effect: S.I. 1998/3132 amended. Territorial extent & classification: E/W. General. - 32p.: 30 cm. - 978-0-11-112608-0 £6.00

The Civil Proceedings Fees (Amendment No. 2) Order 2014 No. 2014/1834 (L.27). - Enabling power: Courts Act 2003, s. 92 & Insolvency Act 1986, ss. 414, 415. - Issued: 17.07.2014. Made: 10.07.2014. Laid: 14.07.2014. Coming into force: 04.08.2014. Effect: S.I. 2008/1053 (L.5) amended. Territorial extent & classification: E/W. General. - This Statutory Instrument has been made in consequence of a defect in S.I. 2013/2302 (ISBN 9780111103944) and is being issued free of charge to all known purchasers of that Statutory Instrument and of S.I. 2014/513 (ISBN 9780111111178) which was also affected by the defect. A defect in this SI (1834) has been corrected by SI 2014/2059 (L.29) (ISBN 9780111118122) which is being issued free of charge to all known recipients of 1834. - 4p.: 30 cm. - 978-0-11-111812-2 £4.25

The Civil Proceedings Fees (Amendment No. 3) Order 2014 No. 2014/2059 (L.29). - Enabling power: Courts Act 2003, s. 92. - Issued: 07.08.2014. Made: 01.08.2014. Laid: 01.08.2014. Coming into force: 04.08.2014. Effect: S.I. 2008/1053 (L.5) amended. Territorial extent & classification: E/W. General. - This Statutory Instrument has been made in consequence of a defect in S.I. 2014/1834 (ISBN 9780111118122) and is being issued free of charge to all known recipients of that Statutory Instrument. - 2p.: 30 cm. - 978-0-11-111952-5 £4.25

The Civil Proceedings Fees (Amendment) Order 2014 No. 2014/874 (L.17). - Enabling power: Courts Act 2003, s. 92 & Insolvency Act 1986, ss. 414, 415. - Issued: 04.04.2014. Made: 27.03.2014. Laid: 01.04.2014. Coming into force: 22.04.2014. Effect: S.I. 2008/1053 (L.5) amended. Territorial extent & classification: E/W. General. - 12p.: 30 cm. - 978-0-11-111326-4 £6.00

The County Court Remedies Regulations 2014 No. 2014/982 (L.22). - Enabling power: County Courts Act 1984, s. 38 (3) (4) (5). - Issued: 16.04.2014. Made: 09.04.2014. Coming into force: In accord. with reg. 1. Effect: S.I. 1991/1222 revoked. Territorial extent & classification: E/W. General. - Supersedes draft SI (ISBN 9780111111536) issued 14/03/14. - 4p.: 30 cm. - 978-0-11-111411-7 £4.25

The Crime and Courts Act 2013 (Commencement No. 10 and Transitional Provision) Order 2014 No. 2014/954 (C.44). - Enabling power: Crime and Courts Act 2013, s. 61 (3). Bringing into operation various provisions of the 2013 Act on 22.04.2014. - Issued: 15.04.2014. Made: 09.04.2014. Effect: None. Territorial extent & classification: E/W. General. - 4p.: 30 cm. - 978-0-11-111406-3 £4.25

The Crime and Courts Act 2013 (Consequential, Transitional and Saving Provisions) Order 2014 No. 2014/820. - Enabling power: Crime and Courts Act 2013, ss. 59, 60. - Issued: 03.04.2014. Made: 27.03.2014. Coming into force: 22.04.2014. Effect: S.I. 1983/713 revoked with saving. Territorial extent & classification: E/W/S/NI. General. - 4p.: 30 cm. - 978-0-11-111314-1 £4.00

The Crime and Courts Act 2013 (County Court and Family Court: Consequential Provision) Order 2014 No. 2014/1773. - Enabling power: Crime and Courts Act 2013, s. 59. - Issued: 10.07.2014. Made: 03.07.2014. Coming into force: 04.07.2014 in accord. with art. 1. Effect: 1984 c.28 & 1999, c.22 & S.I. 1991/1184 (L.12) amended. Territorial extent & classification: E/W. General. - 4p.: 30 cm. - 978-0-11-111762-0 £4.25

The High Court and County Courts Jurisdiction (Amendment) Order 2014 No. 2014/821 (L.12). - Enabling power: Courts and Legal Services Act 1990, ss. 1, 120. - Issued: 10.04.2014. Made: 04.04.2014. Laid: 07.04.2014. Coming into force: 22.04.2014. Effect: S.I. 1991/724 amended. Territorial extent & classification: E/W. General. - 4p.: 30 cm. - 978-0-11-111383-7 £4.25

The London Insolvency District (County Court at Central London) Order 2014 No. 2014/818. - Enabling power: Insolvency Act 1986, s. 374. - Issued: 07.04.2014. Made: 31.03.2014. Laid: 01.04.2014. Coming into force: 22.04.2014. Effect: S.I. 2011/761 revoked. Territorial extent & classification: E/W. General. - 2p.: 30 cm. - 978-0-11-111345-5 £4.25

County courts, England and Wales

The Civil Procedure (Amendment No. 2) Rules 2014 No. 2014/482 (L.2). - Enabling power: Civil Procedure Act 1997, s. 2. - Issued: 10.03.2014. Made: 04.03.2014. Laid: 06.03.2014. Coming into force: 06.04.2014. Effect: S.I. 1998/3132 amended. Territorial extent & classification: E/W. General. - 8p.: 30 cm. - 978-0-11-111084-3 £4.00

The Civil Procedure (Amendment No. 3) Rules 2014 No. 2014/610 (L.10). - Enabling power: Civil Procedure Act 1997, s. 2. - Issued: 19.03.2014. Made: 12.03.2014. Laid: 14.03.2014. Coming into force: 06.04.2014. Effect: S.I. 1998/3132 amended. Territorial extent & classification: E/W. General. - With correction slip dated October 2014. - 4p.: 30 cm. - 978-0-11-111212-0 £4.00

The Civil Procedure (Amendment) Rules 2014 No. 2014/407 (L.1). - Enabling power: Civil Procedure Act 1997, s. 2. - Issued: 03.03.2014. Made: 24.02.2014. Laid: 27.02.2014. Coming into force: In accord. with rule 2. Effect: S.I. 1998/3132 amended. Territorial extent & classification: E/W. General. - 60p.: 30 cm. - 978-0-11-111026-3 £9.75

The County Court Jurisdiction Order 2014 No. 2014/503 (L.3). - Enabling power: County Courts Act 1984, s. 145. - Issued: 12.03.2014. Made: 05.03.2014. Coming into force: In accord. with art. 1. Effect: S.I. 1981/1123 revoked with savings. Territorial extent & classification: E/W. General. - Supersedes draft SI (ISBN 9780111107560) issued 23/12/13. - 4p.: 30 cm. - 978-0-11-111107-9 £4.00

The Courts and Tribunals Fees (Miscellaneous Amendments) Order 2014 No. 2014/590 (L.6). - Enabling power: Courts Act 2003, s. 92 & Insolvency Act 1986, ss. 414, 415 & Tribunals, Courts and Enforcement Act 2007, s. 42, 49 (3) & Constitutional Reform Act 2005, s. 52 & Mental Capacity Act 2005. s. 54 & Gender Recognition Act 2004, s. 7 (2). - Issued: 19.03.2014. Made: 11.03.2014. Laid: 13.03.2104. Coming into force: 06.04.2014. Effect: S.I. 2004/3120; 2006/758; 2007/1745; 2008/1052, 1053, 1054; 2009/213, 1114; 2010/42; 2011/2344; 2013/1179, 1893 amended. Territorial extent & classification: E/W. General. - 16p.: 30 cm. - 978-0-11-111194-9 £5.75

The Family Procedure (Amendment) Rules 2014 No. 2014/524 (L.5). - Enabling power: Courts Act 2003, ss. 75, 76. - Issued: 13.03.2014. Made: 06.03.2014. Laid: 10.03.2014. Coming into force: 13.03.2014. Effect: S.I. 2010/2955 amended. Territorial extent & classification: E/W. General. - 4p.: 30 cm. - 978-0-11-111122-2 £4.00

Credit unions

The Co-operative and Community Benefit Societies and Credit Unions Act 2010 (Commencement No. 2) Order 2014 No. 2014/183 (C.6). - Enabling power: Co-operative and Community Benefit Societies and Credit Unions Act 2010, s. 8 (2). Bringing into operation various provisions of the 2010 Act on 06.04.2014, 01.08.2014, in accord. with arts 2, 3. - Issued: 05.02.2014. Made: 30.01.2014. Effect: None. Territorial extent & classification: E/W/S/NI. General. - 2p.: 30 cm. - 978-0-11-110907-6 £4.00

The Co-operative and Community Benefit Societies and Credit Unions Act 2010 (Consequential Amendments) Regulations 2014 No. 2014/1815. - Enabling power: Co-operative and Community Benefit Societies and Credit Unions Act 2010, s. 6. - Issued: 15.07.2014. Made: 08.07.2014. Coming into force: 01.080.2014 in accord. with reg. 1. Effect: S.I. 1969/1037; 1990/2024; 1995/849, 1945 (S.142), 2801; 1996/1667; 1999/1549; 2001/544, 1062, 1744, 2617; 2004/353, 1450; 2005/590, 1529, 1788, 1986, 2415, 2531; 2008/565, 788, 1911; 2009/779, 1085, 1385, 2971; 2010/5; 2012/922, 1290, 1464, 1821, 2421; 2014/229 amended. Territorial extent & classification: E/W/S. General. - Supersedes draft S.I. (ISBN 9780111114865) issued 19.05.2014. - 12p.: 30 cm. - 978-0-11-111787-3 £6.00

The Co-operative and Community Benefit Societies and Credit Unions (Arrangements, Reconstructions and Administration) (Amendment) Order 2014 No. 2014/1822. - Enabling power: Co-operative and Community Benefit Societies and Credit Unions Act 2014, s. 118. - Issued: 16.07.2014. Made: 09.07.2014. Laid: 11.07.2014. Coming into force: 01.08.2014. Effect: S.I. 2014/229 amended. Territorial extent & classification: E/W/S. General. - 8p.: 30 cm. - 978-0-11-111793-4 £6.00

The Co-operative and Community Benefit Societies and Credit Unions (Investigations) Regulations 2014 No. 2014/574. - Enabling power: Co-operative and Community Benefit Societies and Credit Unions Act 2010, ss. 4 (1) (2) (a) (3) (7), 6, 7. - Issued: 17.03.2014. Made: 10.03.2014. Coming into force: 06.04.2014. Effect: 1965 c.12; 1979 c.34; 1985 c.6; 1986 c.46 modified & S.I. 2006/264 amended. Territorial extent & classification: E/W/S/NI. General. - Supersedes draft SI (ISBN 9780111108857) issued 30/01/14- 8p.: 30 cm. - 978-0-11-111173-4 £5.75

The Industrial and Provident Societies and Credit Unions (Arrangements, Reconstructions and Administration) Order 2014 No. 2014/229. - Enabling power: Enterprise Act 2002, s. 255 (1) (a) (4) (5). - Issued: 12.02.2014. Made: 04.02.2014. Laid: 07.02.2014. Coming into force: 06.04.2014. Effect: 1965 c.12; 1986 c.45; 2000 c.8; 2006 c.46; S.I. 1986/1915 (S.139), 1925; 2005/590; 2010/3023 applied with modifications. Territorial extent & classification: E/W/S/CI. General. - 36p.: 30 cm. - 978-0-11-110932-8 £9.75

The Industrial and Provident Societies and Credit Unions (Electronic Communications) Order 2014 No. 2014/184. - Enabling power: Electronic Communications Act 2000, ss. 8, 9. - Issued: 06.02.2014. Made: 30.01.2014. Laid: 03.02.2014. Coming into force: 06.04.2014. Effect: 1965 c.12 amended. Territorial extent & classification: E/W/S/CI. General. - 2p.: 30 cm. - 978-0-11-110908-3 £4.00

Criminal law

The Central African Republic (European Union Financial Sanctions) Regulations 2014 No. 2014/587. - Enabling power: European Communities Act 1972, s. 2 (2). - Issued: 18.03.2014. Made: 12.03.2014. Laid: 13.03.2014. Coming into force: 14.03.2014. Effect: None. Territorial extent & classification: E/W/S/NI. General. - EC note: These Regulations make provision relating to the enforcement of Council Regulation (EU) no. 224/2014 concerning restrictive measures in view of the situation in the Central African Republic. - 12p.: 30 cm. - 978-0-11-111190-1 £5.75

The Crime and Courts Act 2013 (Commencement No. 8) Order 2014 No. 2014/258 (C.11). - Enabling power: Crime and Courts Act 2013, s. 61 (2). Bringing into operation various provisions of the 2013 Act on 24.02.2014. - Issued: 17.02.2014. Made: 11.02.2014. Effect: None. Territorial extent & classification: E/W/S/NI. General. - 4p.: 30 cm. - 978-0-11-110961-8 £4.00

The Crime (International Co-operation) Act 2003 (Commencement No. 6) Order 2014 No. 2014/3192 (C.142). - Enabling power: Crime (International Co-operation) Act 2003, s. 94. Bringing into operation various provisions of the 2003 Act on 03.12.2014. - Issued: 08.12.2014. Made: 02.12.2014. Effect: None. Territorial extent & classification: E/W/S/NI. General. - 2p.: 30 cm. - 978-0-11-112445-1 £4.25

The Criminal Justice and Data Protection (Protocol No. 36) (Amendment) Regulations 2014 No. 2014/3191. - Enabling power: European Communities Act 1972, s. 2 (2). - Issued: 08.12.2014. Made: 02.12.2014. Laid: 02.12.2014. Coming into force: 03.12.2014. Effect: S.I. 2014/3141 amended. Territorial extent & classification: E/W/S/NI. General. - This S.I. amends the Criminal Justice and Data Protection (Protocol No. 36) Regulations 2014, S.I. 2014/3141 (ISBN 9780111124420) and is being issued free of charge to all known recipients of that S.I. EC: These Regulations are made immediately after, come into force simultaneously with, and make minor amendments to, the Criminal Justice and Data Protection (Protocol No. 36) Regulations 2014. - 4p.: 30 cm. - 978-0-11-112441-3 £4.25

The Criminal Justice and Data Protection (Protocol No. 36) Regulations 2014 No. 2014/3141. - Enabling power: European Communities Act 1972, s. 2 (2). - Issued: 08.12.2014. Made: 02.12.2014. Coming into force: In accord. with reg. 1. Effect: None. Territorial extent & classification: E/W/S/NI. General. - Supersedes draft S.I. (ISBN 9780111122723) issued 06.11.2014. - 92p.: 30 cm. - 978-0-11-112442-0 £16.00

The Enterprise Act 2002 (Publishing of Relevant Information under section 188A) Order 2014 No. 2014/535. - Enabling power: Enterprise Act 2002, s. 188A (1) (c). - Issued: 13.03.2014. Made: 06.03.2014. Laid: 10.03.2014. Coming into force: 01.04.2014. Effect: None. Territorial extent & classification: E/W/S/NI. General. - 2p.: 30 cm. - 978-0-11-111137-6 £4.00

The Fixed Penalty (Amendment) Order 2014 No. 2014/259. - Enabling power: Road Traffic Offenders Act 1988, s. 53. - Issued: 18.02.2014. Made: 10.02.2014. Laid: 18.02.2014. Coming into force: 01.04.2014. Effect: S.I. 2000/2792 amended Territorial extent & classification: E/W/S. General. - 2p.: 30 cm. - 978-0-11-110962-5 £4.00

The Iran (European Union Financial Sanctions) (Amendment) Regulations 2014 No. 2014/105. - Enabling power: European Communities Act 1972, s. 2 (2). - Issued: 28.01.2014. Made: 21.01.2014, at 12.45 pm. Laid: 21.01.2014, at 3.30 pm. Coming into force: 21.01.2014, at 4.30 pm. Effect: S.I. 2012/925 amended. Territorial extent & classification: E/W/S/NI. General. - EC note: These Regs amend the 2012 regulations (SI 2012/925 ISBN 9780111522882) which made provision relating to the enforcement of Council Reg (EU) 267/2012 concerning restrictive measures against Iran and repealing Reg no. 961/2010. The amending Regulation introduces revised financial institutions concerning the prohibitions on both transfers of funds between EU credit and financial institutions and Iranian credit and financial institutions, and transfers of funds to Iranian persons, entities and bodies. - 2.: 30 cm. - 978-0-11-110865-9 £4.00

The South Sudan (European Union Financial Sanctions) Regulations 2014 No. 2014/1827. - Enabling power: European Communities Act 1972, s. 2 (2), sch. 2, para. 1A. - Issued: 17.07.2014. Made: 11.07.2014, at 1.30 pm. Laid: 11.07.2014, at 2.30 pm. Coming into force: 11.07.2014, at 3.30 pm. Effect: None. Territorial extent & classification: E/W/S/NI. General. - EC note: These regs make provision relating to the enforcement of Council Regulation 748/2014 concerning restrictive measures in respect of the situation in South Sudan. - 12p.: 30 cm. - 978-0-11-111803-0 £6.00

The Sudan (European Union Financial Sanctions) Regulations 2014 No. 2014/1826. - Enabling power: European Communities Act 1972, s. 2 (2), sch. 2, para. 1A. - Issued: 17.07.2014. Made: 11.07.2014, at 1.30 pm. Laid: 11.07.2014, at 2.30 pm. Coming into force: 11.07.2014, at 3.30 pm. Effect: S.I. 2012/1507 revoked. Territorial extent & classification: E/W/S/NI. General. - EC note: These Regulations make provision relating to the enforcement of Council Regulation 747/2014 concerning restrictive measures in view of the situation in Sudan and repealing Regulations no. 131/2004 and no. 1184/2005. - 12p.: 30 cm. - 978-0-11-111802-3 £6.00

The Ukraine (European Union Financial Sanctions) (Amendment) Regulations 2014 No. 2014/507. - Enabling power: European Communities Act 1972, s. 2 (2). - Issued: 12.03.2014. Made: 06.03.2014, at 11.00 am. Laid: 06.03.2014, at 2.30 pm. Coming into force: 06.03.2014, at 3.30 pm. Effect: None. Territorial extent & classification: E/W/S/NI. General. - 12p.: 30 cm. - 978-0-11-111111-6 £5.75

The Ukraine (European Union Financial Sanctions) (No.2) Regulations 2014 No. 2014/693. - Enabling power: European Communities Act 1972, s. 2 (2), sch. 2, para. 1A. - Issued: 24.03.2013. Made: 18.03.2014 at 11.00 am. Laid: 18.03.2014 at 2.30 pm. Coming into force: 18.03.2014 at 3.30pm. Effect: None. Territorial extent & classification: E/W/S/NI. General. - These regulations make provision relating to the enforcement of Council Regulation (EU) no 269/2014. - 12p.: 30 cm. - 978-0-11-111239-7 £5.75

The Ukraine (European Union Financial Sanctions) (No.3) (Amendment No.2) Regulations 2014 No. 2014/3230. - Enabling power: European Communities Act 1972, s. 2 (2). - Issued: 12.12.2014. Made: 08.12.2014 at 11.30 am. Laid: .08.12.2014 at 3.30 pm. Coming into force: 08.12.2014 at 4.30 pm. Effect: S.I. 2014/2054 amended. Territorial extent & classification: E/W/S/NI. General. - 4p.: 30 cm. - 978-0-11-112485-7 £4.25

The Ukraine (European Union Financial Sanctions) (No.3) (Amendment) Regulations 2014 No. 2014/2445. - Enabling power: European Communities Act 1972, s. 2 (2). - Issued: 18.09.2014. Made: 12.09.2014. Laid: 15.09.2014 at 11.30 am. Coming into force: 15.09.2014 at 1.00 pm. Effect: S.I. 2014/2054 amended. Territorial extent & classification: E/W/S/NI. General. - 4p.: 30 cm. - 978-0-11-112079-8 £4.25

The Ukraine (European Union Financial Sanctions) (No.3) Regulations 2014 No. 2014/2054. - Enabling power: European Communities Act 1972, s. 2 (2), sch. 2, para. 1A. - Issued: 07.08.2014. Made: 01.08.2014 at 10.30 am. Laid: 01.08.2014 at 2.00 pm. Coming into force: 01.08.2014 at 3.00 pm. Effect: None. Territorial extent & classification: E/W/S/NI. General. - These regulations make provision relating to the enforcement of Council Regulation (EU) no 833/2014. - These regs make provision relating to the enforcement of Council Regulation (EU) no. 833/2014 concerning restrictive measures in view of Russia's actions destabilising the situation in Ukraine. - 12p.: 30 cm. - 978-0-11-111950-1 £6.00

The Yemen (European Union Financial Sanctions) Regulations 2014 No. 2014/3349. - Enabling power: European Communities Act 1972, s. 2 (2), sch. 2, para. 1A. - Issued: 29.12.2014. Made: 19.12.2014, at 10.30 am. Laid: 19.12.2014, at 12.15 pm. Coming into force: 19.12.2014, at 2.00 pm. Effect: None. Territorial extent & classification: E/W/S/NI. General. - 12p.: 30 cm. - 978-0-11-112639-4 £6.00

The Zimbabwe (Financial Sanctions) (Amendment) Regulations 2013 No. 2014/383. - Enabling power: European Communities Act 1972, s. 2 (2), sch. 2, para. 1A. - Issued: 28.02.2014. Made: 24.02.2014. Laid: 24.02.2014. Coming into force: 25.02.2014. Effect: S.I. 2009/847 amended/partially revoked & S.I. 2013/795 revoked. Territorial extent & classification: E/W/S/NI. General. - 4p.: 30 cm. - 978-0-11-111013-3 £4.00

Criminal law, England and Wales

The Anti-social Behaviour, Crime and Policing Act 2014 (Commencement No. 2, Transitional and Transitory Provisions) Order 2014 No. 2014/949 (C.43). - Enabling power: Anti-social Behaviour, Crime and Policing Act 2014, s. 185 (1) (7). Bringing into operation various provisions of the 2014 Act on 13.05.2014, 01.06.2014, 16.06.2014, 14.07.2014, in accord. with arts. 2 to 6. - Issued: 14.04.2014. Made: 08.04.2014. Effect: None. Territorial extent & classification: E/W/S/NI. General. - 8p.: 30 cm. - 978-0-11-111401-8 £6.00

The Anti-social Behaviour, Crime and Policing Act 2014 (Commencement No. 3) Order 2014 No. 2014/1226 (C.48). - Enabling power: Anti-social Behaviour, Crime and Policing Act 2014, s. 185 (5). Bringing into operation various provisions of the 2014 Act on 02.06.2014 in accord. with art. 2. - Issued: 16.05.2014. Made: 11.05.2014. Effect: None. Territorial extent & classification: E/W/S/NI. General. - 4p.: 30 cm. - 978-0-11-111478-0 £4.25

The Anti-social Behaviour, Crime and Policing Act 2014 (Commencement No. 5) Order 2014 No. 2014/2125 (C.96). - Enabling power: Anti-social Behaviour, Crime and Policing Act 2014, s. 185 (1). Bringing into operation various provisions of the 2014 Act on 01.09.2014. - Issued: 14.08.2014. Made: 07.08.2014. Effect: None. Territorial extent & classification: E/W/S/NI. General. - 8p.: 30 cm. - 978-0-11-111977-8 £4.25

The Costs in Criminal Cases (Legal Costs) (Exceptions) Regulations 2014 No. 2014/130. - Enabling power: Prosecution of Offences Act 1985, ss. 16A (6), 29 (2). - Issued: 30.01.2014. Made: 23.01.2014. Coming into force: 27.01.2014. Effect: 1985 c.23 amended. Territorial extent & classification: E/W. General. - Supersedes draft SI (ISBN 9780111106303) issued 28/11/13. - 2p.: 30 cm. - 978-0-11-110883-3 £4.00

The Crime and Courts Act 2013 (Commencement No. 1) (England and Wales) Order 2014 No. 2014/3268 (C.150). - Enabling power: Crime and Courts Act 2013, s. 61 (2). Bringing into operation various provisions of the 2013 Act on 02.03.2015. - Issued: 16.12.2014. Made: 08.12.2014. Effect: None. Territorial extent & classification: E/W. General. - 4p.: 30 cm. - 978-0-11-112531-1 £4.25

The Criminal Justice Act 1988 (Reviews of Sentencing) (Amendment) Order 2014 No. 2014/1651. - Enabling power: Criminal Justice Act 1988, s. 35 (4). - Issued: 01.07.2014. Made: 23.06.2014. Laid: 26.06.2014. Coming into force: 21.07.2014. Effect: S.I. 2006/1116 amended. Territorial extent & classification: E/W. General. - 2p.: 30 cm. - 978-0-11-111713-2 £4.25

The Criminal Justice Act 2003 (Alcohol Abstinence and Monitoring Requirement) (Prescription of Arrangement for Monitoring) Order 2014 No. 2014/1787. - Enabling power: Criminal Justice Act 2003, ss. 212A (6) (7), 330 (3) (b). - Issued: 11.07.2014. Made: 07.07.2014. Laid: 08.07.2014. Coming into force: 31.07.2014. Effect: None. Territorial extent & classification: E/W. General. - 2p.: 30 cm. - 978-0-11-111770-5 £4.25

The Criminal Justice Act 2003 (Commencement No. 32) Order 2014 No. 2014/633 (C.26). - Enabling power: Criminal Justice Act 2003, s. 336 (3) (4). Bringing into operation various provisions of the 2003 Act 01.04.2014 in accord. with art. 2. - Issued: 19.03.2014. Made: 13.03.2014. Effect: None. Territorial extent & classification: E/W. General. - 8p.: 30 cm. - 978-0-11-111222-9 £5.75

The Criminal Justice Act 2003 (Surcharge) (Amendment) Order 2014 No. 2014/2120. - Enabling power: Criminal Justice Act 2003, ss. 161A (2), 161B, 330 (4). - Issued: 13.08.2014. Made: 06.08.2014. Laid: 08.08.2014. Coming into force: 01.09.2014. Effect: S.I. 2012/1696 amended. Territorial extent & classification: E/W. General. - 2p.: 30 cm. - 978-0-11-111976-1 £4.25

The Criminal Justice and Police Act 2001 (Amendment) Order 2014 No. 2014/1365. - Enabling power: Criminal Justice and Police Act 2001, s. 1 (2). - Issued: 06.06.2014. Made: 27.05.2014. Coming into force: In accord. with art. 1 (2). Effect: 2001 c.16 amended. Territorial extent & classification: E/W. General. - 2p.: 30 cm. - 978-0-11-111560-2 £4.25

The Criminal Justice (Electronic Monitoring) (Responsible Person) (No. 2) Order 2014 No. 2014/669. - Enabling power: Bail Act 1976, s 3AC (2) & Criminal Justice Act 2003, ss. 215 (3), 253 (5), 330 (3) (a) & Criminal Justice and Immigration Act 2008, sch. 1, para. 26 (5). - Issued: 20.03.2014. Made: 13.03.2014. Coming into force: 23.03.2014 at 7.00 a.m. Effect: S.I. 2005/963; 2008/2713, 2768; 2009/2950; 2014/163 revoked. Territorial extent & classification: E/W. General. - 4p.: 30 cm. - 978-0-11-111233-5 £4.00

The Criminal Justice (Electronic Monitoring) (Responsible Person) Order 2014 No. 2014/163. - Enabling power: Bail Act 1976, s 3AC (2) & Criminal Justice Act 2003, ss. 215 (3), 253 (5), 330 (3) (a) & Criminal Justice and Immigration Act 2008, s. 147 (2) (b), sch. 1, para. 26 (5). - Issued: 04.02.2014. Made: 28.01.2014. Coming into force: 01.02.2014 at 7.00 a.m. Effect: S.I. 2005/963; 2008/2713, 2768; 2009/2950 amended. Territorial extent & classification: E/W. General. - Revoked by SI 2014/669 (ISBN 9780111112335). - 4p.: 30 cm. - 978-0-11-110896-3 £4.00

The Criminal Justice (European Protection Order) (England and Wales) Regulations 2014 No. 2014/3300. - Enabling power: European Communities Act 1972, s. 2 (2). - Issued: 23.12.2014. Made: 15.12.2014. Laid: 18.12.2014. Coming into force: 11.01.2015. Effect: None. Territorial extent & classification: E/W. General. - EC note: These Regulations transpose, for England and Wales, Directive 2011/99/EU of the European Parliament and of the Council of 13th December 2011 on the European Protection. - 12p.: 30 cm. - 978-0-11-112607-3 £6.00

The Legal Aid, Sentencing and Punishment of Offenders Act 2012 (Alcohol Abstinence and Monitoring Requirements) Piloting Order 2014 No. 2014/1777 (C.77). - Enabling power: Legal Aid, Sentencing and Punishment of Offenders Act 2012, s. 77 (1) (4) (8). Bringing into operation various provisions of the 2012 Act on 31.07.2014. - Issued: 11.07.2014. Made: 07.07.2014. Effect: None. Territorial extent & classification: E/W. General. - 4p.: 30 cm. - 978-0-11-111769-9 £4.25

The Legal Aid, Sentencing and Punishment of Offenders Act 2012 (Commencement No. 10) Order 2014 No. 2014/1291 (C.53). - Enabling power: Legal Aid, Sentencing and Punishment of Offenders Act 2012, s. 151 (1). Bringing into operation various provisions of the 2012 Act on 28.05.2014. - Issued: 27.05.2014. Made: 19.05.2014. Effect: None. Territorial extent & classification: E/W. General. - 4p.: 30 cm. - 978-0-11-111512-1 £4.25

The Offender Rehabilitation Act 2014 (Commencement No. 1) Order 2014 No. 2014/1287 (C.52). - Enabling power: Offender Rehabilitation Act 2014, s. 22 (1). Bringing into operation various provisions of the 2014 Act on 01.06.2014 in accord. with art. 2. - Issued: 23.05.2014. Made: 19.05.2014. Effect: None. Territorial extent & classification: E/W/S/NI. General. - 2p.: 30 cm. - 978-0-11-111510-7 £4.25

The Penalties for Disorderly Behaviour (Amount of Penalty) (Amendment) Order 2014 No. 2014/1383. - Enabling power: Criminal Justice and Police Act 2001, s. 3 (1). - Issued: 06.06.2014. Made: 27.05.2014. Laid: 03.06.2014. Coming into force: 24.06.2014. Effect: S.I. 2002/1837 amended. Territorial extent & classification: E/W. General. - 2p.: 30 cm. - 978-0-11-111558-9 £4.25

The Prosecution of Offences Act 1985 (Specified Proceedings) (Amendment) Order 2014 No. 2014/1229. - Enabling power: Prosecution of Offences Act 1985, s. 3 (3). - Issued: 16.05.2014. Made: 12.05.2014. Laid: 13.05.2014. Coming into force: 09.06.2014. Effect: S.I. 1999/904 amended. Territorial extent & classification: E/W. General. - 2p.: 30 cm. - 978-0-11-111480-3 £4.25

The Recovery of Costs (Remand to Youth Detention Accommodation) (Amendment) (No. 2) Regulations 2014 No. 2014/981. - Enabling power: Legal Aid, Sentencing and Punishment of Offenders Act 2012, s. 103 (2) (a) (6). - Issued: 16.04.2014. Made: 10.04.2014. Laid: 14.04.2014. Coming into force: 20.05.2014. Effect: S.I. 2013/507 amended. Territorial extent & classification: E/W. General. - 2p.: 30 cm. - 978-0-11-111410-0 £4.25

The Recovery of Costs (Remand to Youth Detention Accommodation) (Amendment) (No. 3) Regulations 2014 No. 2014/2931. - Enabling power: Legal Aid, Sentencing and Punishment of Offenders Act 2012, s. 103 (2) (a) (6). - Issued: 13.11.2014. Made: 06.11.2014. Laid: 10.11.2014. Coming into force: 01.12.2014. Effect: S.I. 2013/507 amended. Territorial extent & classification: E/W. General. - 2p.: 30 cm. - 978-0-11-112310-2 £4.25

The Recovery of Costs (Remand to Youth Detention Accommodation) (Amendment) Regulations 2014 No. 2014/562. - Enabling power: Legal Aid, Sentencing and Punishment of Offenders Act 2012, s. 103 (2) (a) (6). - Issued: 13.03.2014. Made: 05.03.2014. Laid: 11.03.2014. Coming into force: 01.04.2014. Effect: S.I. 2013/507 amended. Territorial extent & classification: E/W. General. - 2p.: 30 cm. - 978-0-11-111160-4 £4.00

The Serious Organised Crime and Police Act 2005 (Designated Sites under Section 128) (Amendment) (No. 2) Order 2014 No. 2014/2263. - Enabling power: Serious Organised Crime and Police Act 2005, s. 128 (2). - Issued: 02.09.2014. Made: 26.08.2014. Laid: 29.08.2014. Coming into force: 19.09.2014. Effect: S.I. 2007/930 amended. Territorial extent & classification: E/W. General. - 4p., map: 30 cm. - 978-0-11-112001-9 £4.25

The Serious Organised Crime and Police Act 2005 (Designated Sites under Section 128) (Amendment) Order 2014 No. 2014/411. - Enabling power: Serious Organised Crime and Police Act 2005, s. 128 (2). - Issued: 03.03.2014. Made: 25.02.2014. Laid: 27.02.2014. Coming into force: 26.03.2014. Effect: S.I. 2007/930 amended. Territorial extent & classification: E/W. General. - 2p.: 30 cm. - 978-0-11-111029-4 £4.00

Customs

The Export Control (Amendment) (No. 2) Order 2014 No. 2014/1069. - Enabling power: Export Control Act 2002, ss. 1, 2, 4, 5, 7. - Issued: 30.04.2014. Made: 17.04.2014. Laid: 25.04.2014. Coming into force: 17.05.2014. Effect: S.I. 2008/3231 amended. Territorial extent & classification: E/W/S/NI. General. - 28p.: 30 cm. - 978-0-11-111428-5 £6.00

The Export Control (Amendment) Order 2014 No. 2014/702. - Enabling power: Export Control Act 2002, ss. 1, 4, 5, 7. - Issued: 24.03.2014. Made: 18.03.2014. Laid: 19.03.2014. Coming into force: 09.04.2014. Effect: S.I. 2008/3231 amended. Territorial extent & classification: E/W/S/NI. General. - 8p.: 30 cm. - 978-0-11-111241-0 £4.00

The Export Control (Russia, Crimea and Sevastopol Sanctions) (Amendment) Order 2014 No. 2014/2932. - Enabling power: European Communities Act 1972, s. 2 (2) & Export Control Act 2002, ss. 1, 2, 3, 4, 5, 7. - Issued: 13.11.2014. Made: 05.11.2014. Laid: 07.11.2014. Coming into force: 29.11.2014. Effect: S.I. 2014/2357 amended. Territorial extent & classification: E/W/S/NI. General. - EC note: This Order makes provision for the enforcement of certain trade restrictions against Russia specified in Council Regulation (EU) no. 960/2014, which amends Council Regulation (EU) no. 833/2014 concerning restrictive measures in view of Russia's actions destabilising the situation in the Ukraine. - 4p.: 30 cm. - 978-0-11-112312-6 £4.25

The Export Control (Russia, Crimea and Sevastopol Sanctions) Order 2014 No. 2014/2357. - Enabling power: European Communities Act 1972, ss. 2 (2) & Export Control Act 2002, s. 1, 2, 3, 4, 5. - Issued: 09.09.2014. Made: 02.09.2014. Laid: 05.09.2014. Coming into force: 26.09.2014. Effect: S.I. 2008/3231 amended. Territorial extent & classification: E/W/S/NI. General. - EC note: This Order makes provision for the enforcement of certain trade restrictions against Russia specified in Council Regulation (EU) no. 833/2014. It also provides for the enforcement of trade and investment restrictions in response of the illegal annexation of Crimea and Sevastopol specified in Council Regulation (EU) no. 692/2014 as amended by Council Regulation (EU) no. 825/2014. - 8p.: 30 cm. - 978-0-11-112019-4 £6.00

The Export Control (Sudan, South Sudan and Central African Republic Sanctions) Regulations 2014 No. 2014/3258. - Enabling power: European Communities Act 1972, s. 2 (2). - Issued: 16.12.2014. Made: 09.12.2014. Laid: 10.12.2014. Coming into force: 31.12.2014. Effect: S.I. 2011/2925 revoked with saving. Territorial extent & classification: E/W/S/NI. General. - EC note: These regs make provision for the enforcement of certain trade restrictions against Sudan specified in Council Regulation (EC) no. 747/2014, no. 1184/2005 and no. 748/2014 and against the Central African Republic specified in no. 224/2014. - 8p.: 30 cm. - 978-0-11-112521-2 £6.00

The Export Control (Syria Sanctions) (Amendment) Order 2014 No. 2014/1896. - Enabling power: European Communities Act 1972, s. 2 (2), sch. 2, para. 1A. - Issued: 23.07.2014. Made: 16.07.2014. Laid: 18.07.2014. Coming into force: 08.08.2014. Effect: S.I. 2013/2012 amended. Territorial extent & classification: E/W/S/NI. General. - EC note: This Order makes provision for the enforcement of certain trade sanctions relating to Syrian cultural property specified in Council Regulation (EU) no. 1332/2013 which amends Council Regulation (EU) no. 36/2012 concerning restrictive measures in view of the situation in Syria. - 4p.: 30 cm. - 978-0-11-111860-3 £4.25

The Forest Law Enforcement, Governance and Trade (Amendment) (Fees) Regulations 2014 No. 2014/2339. - Enabling power: Finance Act 1973, s. 56 (1)- Issued: 09.09.2014. Made: 01.09.2014. Laid: 03.09.2014. Coming into force: 01.10.2014. Effect: S.I. 2012/178 amended. Territorial extent & classification: E/W/S/NI. General. - EC note: These Regulations amend the Forest Law Enforcement, Governance and Trade Regulations 2012 (S.I. 2012/178) which enforce Council Regulation (EC) No. 2173/2005 on the establishment of a FLEGT licensing scheme for imports of timber into the European Community and Commission Regulation (EC) No. 1024/2008 laying down detailed measures for the implementation of Council Regulation (EC) No. 2173/2005. - 2p.: 30 cm. - 978-0-11-112012-5 £4.25

The Transfrontier Shipment of Waste (Amendment) Regulations 2014 No. 2014/861. - Enabling power: European Communities Act 1972, s. 2 (2). - Issued: 03.04.2014. Made: 26.03.2014. Laid: 03.04.2014. Coming into force: 01.05.2014. Effect: S.I. 2007/1711 amended & partially revoked. Territorial extent & classification: E/W/S/NI. General. - 16p.: 30 cm. - 978-0-11-111317-2 £5.75

Customs and excise

The Revenue and Customs (Amendment of Appeal Provisions for Out of Time Reviews) Order 2014 No. 2014/1264. - Enabling power: Finance Act 2008, s. 124 (1) (2) (6) (7) (b). - Issued: 21.05.2014. Made: 14.05.2014. Coming into force: In accord. with art. 1 (2). Effect: 1994 c.9, c.23; 1996 c.8; 2000 c.17; 2001 c.9; 2003 c.14; S.I. 2003/3102; 2007/1509, 2157, 3298 amended. Territorial extent & classification: E/W/S/NI. General. - Supersedes draft SI (ISBN 9780111112991) issued 03/04/14. - 8p.: 30 cm. - 978-0-11-111499-5 £6.00

Dangerous drugs

The Misuse of Drugs Act 1971 (Amendment) (No. 2) Order 2014 No. 2014/3271. - Enabling power: Misuse of Drugs Act 1971, s. 2 (2). - Issued: 17.12.2014. Made: 10.12.2014. Coming into force: In accord. with art. 1. Effect: 1971 c.38 amended. Territorial extent & classification: E/W/S/NI. General. - Supersedes draft S.I. (ISBN 9780111123034) issued 12/11/14. - 2p.: 30 cm. - 978-0-11-112534-2 £4.25

The Misuse of Drugs Act 1971 (Amendment) Order 2014 No. 2014/1352. - Enabling power: Misuse of Drugs Act 1971, s. 2 (2) (3). - Issued: 03.06.2014. Made: 27.05.2014. Coming into force: In accord. with art. 1. Effect: 1971 c.38 amended. Territorial extent & classification: E/W/S/NI. General. - Supersedes draft S.I. (ISBN 9780111105504) issued 05.11.2013. - 2p.: 30 cm. - 978-0-11-111524-4 £4.25

The Misuse of Drugs Act 1971 (Ketamine etc.) (Amendment) Order 2014 No. 2014/1106. - Enabling power: Misuse of Drugs Act 1971, s. 2 (2). - Issued: 06.05.2014. Made: 28.04.2014. Coming into force: 10.06.2014. Effect: 1971 c.38 amended. Territorial extent & classification: E/W/S/NI. General. - 4p.: 30 cm. - 978-0-11-111438-4 £4.25

The Misuse of Drugs (Amendment) (England, Wales and Scotland) Regulations 2014 No. 2014/1377. - Enabling power: Misuse of Drugs Act 1971, ss. 7, 10, 22, 31. - Issued: 05.06.2014. Made: 27.05.2014. Laid: 03.06.2014. Coming into force: 24.06.2014. Effect: S.I. 2001/3998 amended. Territorial extent & classification: E/W/S. General. - 2p.: 30 cm. - 978-0-11-111556-5 £4.25

The Misuse of Drugs (Amendment No. 2) (England, Wales and Scotland) Regulations 2014 No. 2014/2081. - Enabling power: Misuse of Drugs Act 1971, ss. 22, 31. - Issued: 11.08.2014. Made: 03.08.2014. Laid: 08.8.2014. Coming into force: 05.09.2014. Effect: S.I. 2001/3998 amended. Territorial extent & classification: E/W/S. General. - 2p.: 30 cm. - 978-0-11-111962-4 £4.25

The Misuse of Drugs (Amendment No. 3) (England, Wales and Scotland) Regulations 2014 No. 2014/3277. - Enabling power: Misuse of Drugs Act 1971, ss. 7, 10, 22, 31. - Issued: 17.12.2014. Made: 11.12.2014. Laid: 17.12.2014. Coming into force: 07.01.2015. Effect: S.I. 2001/3998 amended. Territorial extent & classification: E/W/S. General. - 4p.: 30 cm. - 978-0-11-112549-6 £4.25

The Misuse of Drugs and Misuse of Drugs (Safe Custody) (Amendment) (England, Wales and Scotland) Regulations 2014 No. 2014/1275. - Enabling power: Misuse of Drugs Act 1971, ss. 7, 10, 22, 31. - Issued: 22.05.2014. Made: 16.05.2014. Laid: 20.05.2014. Coming into force: 10.06.2014. Effect: S.I. 1973/798; 2001/3998 amended. Territorial extent & classification: E/W/S. General. - 4p.: 30 cm. - 978-0-11-111504-6 £4.25

The Misuse of Drugs (Designation) (Amendment) (England, Wales and Scotland) Order 2014 No. 2014/1274. - Enabling power: Misuse of Drugs Act 1971, s. 7 (4). - Issued: 22.05.2014. Made: 16.05.2014. Laid: 20.05.2014. Coming into force: 10.06.2014. Effect: S.I. 2001/3997 amended. Territorial extent & classification: E/W/S. General. - 2p.: 30 cm. - 978-0-11-111503-9 £4.25

The Misuse of Drugs (Designation) (Amendment) (No. 3) (England, Wales and Scotland) Order 2014 No. 2014/3276. - Enabling power: Misuse of Drugs Act 1971, s. 7 (4). - Issued: 17.12.2014. Made: 11.12.2014. Laid: 17.12.2014. Coming into force: 07.01.2015. Effect: S.I. 2001/3997 amended. Territorial extent & classification: E/W/S. General. - 2p.: 30 cm. - 978-0-11-112548-9 £4.25

Dangerous drugs, England and Wales

The Misuse of Drugs (Designation) (Amendment No. 2) (England, Wales and Scotland) Order 2014 No. 2014/1376. - Enabling power: Misuse of Drugs Act 1971, s. 7 (4). - Issued: 05.06.2014. Made: 27.05.2014. Laid: 03.06.2014. Coming into force: 24.06.2014. Effect: S.I. 2001/3997 amended. Territorial extent & classification: E/W/S. General. - 2p.: 30 cm. - 978-0-11-111555-8 £4.25

Dangerous drugs, Scotland

The Misuse of Drugs (Designation) (Amendment No. 2) (England, Wales and Scotland) Order 2014 No. 2014/1376. - Enabling power: Misuse of Drugs Act 1971, s. 7 (4). - Issued: 05.06.2014. Made: 27.05.2014. Laid: 03.06.2014. Coming into force: 24.06.2014. Effect: S.I. 2001/3997 amended. Territorial extent & classification: E/W/S. General. - 2p.: 30 cm. - 978-0-11-111555-8 £4.25

Data protection

The Criminal Justice and Data Protection (Protocol No. 36) (Amendment) Regulations 2014 No. 2014/3191. - Enabling power: European Communities Act 1972, s. 2 (2). - Issued: 08.12.2014. Made: 02.12.2014. Laid: 02.12.2014. Coming into force: 03.12.2014. Effect: S.I. 2014/3141 amended. Territorial extent & classification: E/W/S/NI. General. - This S.I. amends the Criminal Justice and Data Protection (Protocol No. 36) Regulations 2014, S.I. 2014/3141 (ISBN 9780111124420) and is being issued free of charge to all known recipients of that S.I. EC: These Regulations are made immediately after, come into force simultaneously with, and make minor amendments to, the Criminal Justice and Data Protection (Protocol No. 36) Regulations 2014. - 4p.: 30 cm. - 978-0-11-112441-3 £4.25

The Criminal Justice and Data Protection (Protocol No. 36) Regulations 2014 No. 2014/3141. - Enabling power: European Communities Act 1972, s. 2 (2). - Issued: 08.12.2014. Made: 02.12.2014. Coming into force: In accord. with reg. 1. Effect: None. Territorial extent & classification: E/W/S/NI. General. - Supersedes draft S.I. (ISBN 9780111122723) issued 06.11.2014. - 92p.: 30 cm. - 978-0-11-112442-0 £16.00

The Data Protection (Assessment Notices) (Designation of National Health Service Bodies) Order 2014 No. 2014/3282. - Enabling power: Data Protection Act 1998, s. 41A (2) (b). - Issued: 17.12.2014. Made: 10.12.2014. Laid: 15.12.2014. Coming into force: 01.02.2015. Effect: None. Territorial extent & classification: E/W/S/NI. General. - 4p.: 30 cm. - 978-0-11-112543-4 £4.25

Defence

The Anti-social Behaviour, Crime and Policing Act 2014 (Commencement No. 2, Transitional and Transitory Provisions) Order 2014 No. 2014/949 (C.43). - Enabling power: Anti-social Behaviour, Crime and Policing Act 2014, s. 185 (1) (7). Bringing into operation various provisions of the 2014 Act on 13.05.2014, 01.06.2014, 16.06.2014, 14.07.2014, in accord. with arts. 2 to 6. - Issued: 14.04.2014. Made: 08.04.2014. Effect: None. Territorial extent & classification: E/W/S/NI. General. - 8p.: 30 cm. - 978-0-11-111401-8 £6.00

The Armed Forces Act 2011 (Commencement No. 5) Order 2014 No. 2014/1444 (C.54). - Enabling power: Armed Forces Act 2011, s. 32 (3). Bringing into operation various provisions of the 2011 Act on 04.06.2014. - Issued: 10.06.2014. Made: 01.06.2014. Effect: None. Territorial extent & classification: E/W/S/NI. General. - 2p.: 30 cm. - 978-0-11-111588-6 £4.25

The Armed Forces Act (Continuation) Order 2014 No. 2014/1882. - Enabling power: Armed Forces Act 2006, s. 382 (2). - Issued: 23.07.2014. Made: 16.07.2014. Effect: The Armed Forces Act 2006 shall, instead of expiring at the end of 02.11.2014, continue in force until 02.11.2015. Territorial extent & classification: E/W/S/NI/IoM/British Overseas Territories. General. - Supersedes draft SI (ISBN 9780111114742) issued 15/07/14. - 2p.: 30 cm. - 978-0-11-111844-3 £4.25

The Armed Forces (Powers of Stop and Search, Search, Seizure and Retention) (Amendment) Order 2014 No. 2014/934. - Enabling power: Armed Forces Act 2006, ss. 74, 92. - Issued: 11.04.2014. Made: 06.04.2014. Laid: 09.04.2014. Coming into force: 13.05.2014. Effect: S.I. 2009/2056 amended. Territorial extent & classification: E/W/S/NI/IoM. General. - 2p.: 30 cm. - 978-0-11-111394-3 £4.25

The Armed Forces (Terms of Service) (Amendment) Regulations 2014 No. 2014/3068. - Enabling power: Armed Forces Act 2006, ss. 328 (5), 329 (1) (2). - Issued: 24.11.2014. Made: 14.11.2014. Laid: 20.11.2014. Coming into force: 01.04.2015. Effect: S.I. 2006/2917, 2918; 2007/650, 3382 amended. Territorial extent & classification: E/W/S/NI/IoM/British Overseas Territories. General. - 8p.: 30 cm. - 978-0-11-112347-8 £6.00

The Defence Reform Act 2014 (Commencement No. 1) Order 2014 No. 2014/1751 (C.75). - Enabling power: Defence Reform Act 2014, s. 50 (1) (2). Bringing into operation various provisions for the 2014 Act on 14.07.2014, in accord. with arts 3, 4. - Issued: 09.07.2014. Made: 30.06.2014. Effect: None. Territorial extent & classification: E/W/S/NI/IoM/British Overseas Territories. General. - 2p.: 30 cm. - 978-0-11-111756-9 £4.25

The Defence Reform Act 2014 (Commencement No. 2) Order 2014 No. 2014/2370 (C.101). - Enabling power: Defence Reform Act 2014, s. 50 (1) (2). Bringing into operation various provisions of the 2014 Act on 05.09.2014, 01.10.2014. - Issued: 11.09.2014. Made: 03.09.2014. Effect: None. Territorial extent & classification: E/W/S/NI. General. - 2p.: 30 cm. - 978-0-11-112029-3 £4.25

The Defence Reform Act 2014 (Commencement No. 3) Order 2014 No. 2014/3162 (C.139). - Enabling power: Defence Reform Act 2014, s. 50 (1) (2). Bringing into operation various provisions of the 2014 Act on 05.12.2014. - Issued: 03.12.2014. Made: 27.11.2014. Effect: None. Territorial extent & classification: E/W/S/NI. General. - 2p.: 30 cm. - 978-0-11-112426-0 £4.25

The Offender Rehabilitation Act 2014 (Commencement No. 1) Order 2014 No. 2014/1287 (C.52). - Enabling power: Offender Rehabilitation Act 2014, s. 22 (1). Bringing into operation various provisions of the 2014 Act on 01.06.2014 in accord. with art. 2. - Issued: 23.05.2014. Made: 19.05.2014. Effect: None. Territorial extent & classification: E/W/S/NI. General. - 2p.: 30 cm. - 978-0-11-111510-7 £4.25

The RAF Barford St John Byelaws No. 2014/862. - Enabling power: Military Lands Act 1892, s. 14 (1). - Issued: 07.04.2014. Made: 19.03.2014. Coming into force: 19.07.2014. Effect: None. Territorial extent & classification: E/W/S/NI. General. - 16p., col. maps (folded): 30 cm. - 978-0-11-111320-2 £8.25

The RAF Croughton Byelaws 2014 No. 2014/855. - Enabling power: Military Lands Act 1892, s. 14 (1). - Issued: 04.04.2014. Made: 19.03.2014. Coming into force: 19.07.2014. Effect: None. Territorial extent & classification: E/W/S/NI. General. - 12p., col. maps (folded): 30 cm. - 978-0-11-111306-6 £8.25

The Reserve Forces (Payments to Employers and Partners) Regulations 2014 No. 2014/2410. - Enabling power: Reserve Forces Act 1996, s. 84A. - Issued: 16.09.2014. Made: 08.09.2014. Laid: 10.09.2014. Coming into force: 01.10.2014. Effect: None. Territorial extent & classification: E/W/S/NI. General. - 12p.: 30 cm. - 978-0-11-112061-3 £6.00

Designs

The Community Design (Amendment) Regulations 2014 No. 2014/2400. - Enabling power: European Communities Act 1972, s. 2 (2). - Issued: 15.09.2014. Made: 06.09.2014. Laid: 09.09.2014. Coming into force: 01.10.2014. Effect: S.I. 2005/2339 amended. Territorial extent & classification: E/W/S/NI. General. - 4p.: 30 cm. - 978-0-11-112052-1 £4.25

The Registered Designs (Amendment) Rules 2014 No. 2014/2405. - Enabling power: Registered Designs Act 1949, s. 36. - Issued: 15.09.2014. Made: 06.09.2014. Laid: 09.09.2014. Coming into force: 01.10.2014. Effect: S.I. 2006/1975 amended. Territorial extent & classification: E/W/S/NI. General. - 2p.: 30 cm. - 978-0-11-112057-6 £4.25

Devolution, Scotland

The Children's Hearings (Scotland) Act 2011 (Consequential Provisions) Order 2014 No. 2014/2747. - Enabling power: Scotland Act 1998, ss. 104, 112 (1), 113 (2) (5). - Issued: 20.10.2014. Made: 13.10.2014. Laid: 15.10.2014. Coming into force: 06.11.2014. Effect: 2000/413, 414, 415, 419 amended. Territorial extent & classification: E/W/S/NI. General. - 4p.: 30 cm. - 978-0-11-112179-5 £4.25

The Marriage and Civil Partnership (Scotland) Act 2014 and Civil Partnership Act 2004 (Consequential Provisions and Modifications) Order 2014 No. 2014/3229. - Enabling power: Scotland Act 1998, ss. 104, 112 (1), 113 (2) to (5) (7) & Civil Partnership Act 2004, s. 259 (1). - Issued: 11.12.2014. Made: 04.12.2014. Coming into force: in accord. with art. 1 (2). Effect: 58 SIs & 22 Acts amended. Territorial extent & classification: E/W/S/NI. General. - Supersedes draft S.I. (ISBN 9780111122402) issued 31.10.2014. - 56p.: 30 cm. - 978-0-11-112483-3 £10.00

The Marriage (Same Sex Couples) Act 2013 and Marriage and Civil Partnership (Scotland) Act 2014 (Consequential Provisions) Order 2014 No. 2014/3061. - Enabling power: Marriage (Same Sex Couples) Act 2013, ss. 17 (2) (3) & Civil Partnership Act 2004, s. 259 (1) (4) & Scotland Act 1998, ss. 104, 112 (1), 113 (2) to (5). - Issued: 21.11.2014. Made: 17.11.2014. Laid before the Scottish Parliament: 18.11.2014. Coming into force: In accord. with art 1 (2) (3). Effect: S.I. 1952/1869; 1959/406; 1968/2049; 1975/556; 1979/643; 1986/1442; 1987/257, 2088; 1988/2256; 1995/300; 2001/2283 (W.172); 2005/438, 1513 (W.117), 3176; 2012/687 & 7 Church Measures amended. Territorial extent & classification: E/W/S. General. - 32p.: 30 cm. - 978-0-11-112343-0 £6.00

The Marriage (Same Sex Couples) Act 2013 (Consequential and Contrary Provisions and Scotland) and Marriage and Civil Partnership (Scotland) Act 2014 (Consequential Provisions) Order 2014 No. 2014/3168. - Enabling power: Marriage (Same Sex Couples) Act 2013, ss. 17 (1) to (3), 18 (4) (10), sch. 2 para. 1, sch. 4 para. 27 (3) (b) & Civil Partnership Act 2004, s. 259 (1) (3) & Scotland Act 1998, ss. 104, 112 (1), 113 (2) to (3) (5). - Issued: 04.12.2014. Made: 27.11.2014. Coming into force: in accord. with art 1 (2) (3). Effect: 1837 c.26; 1911 c.6; 1949 c.76; 1957 c.58; 1964 c.75; 1973 c.18, 45; 1975 c.60; 1976 c.31; 1981 c.45; 1992 c.4, c.5; 2007 c.18; Reserve Forces Non Regular Permanent Staff (Pension and Attributable Benefits Schemes) Regulations 2011 [not an SI] amended & S.I. 2014/560 partially revoked. Territorial extent & classification: S. General. - Supersedes draft S.S.I. (ISBN 9780111121900) issued 21.10.2014. - 16p.: 30 cm. - 978-0-11-112429-1 £6.00

The Revenue Scotland and Tax Powers Act 2014 (Consequential Provisions and Modifications) Order 2014 No. 2014/3294. - Enabling power: Scotland Act 1998, ss. 104, 112 (1), 113 (2) (4) (5),114 (1). - Issued: 18.12.2014. Made: 11.12.2014. Coming into force: in accord. with art. 1 (2). Effect: None. Territorial extent & classification: E/W/S/NI. General. - Supersedes draft S.I. (ISBN 9780111121276) issued 15/10/14. - 8p.: 30 cm. - 978-0-11-112563-2 £4.25

The Scotland Act 1998 (Agency Arrangements) (Specification) Order 2014 No. 2014/1892. - Enabling power: Scotland Act 1998, ss. 93 (3), 113 (3). - Issued: 23.07.2014. Made: 16.07.2014. Laid before Parliament and Scottish Parliament: 23.07.2014. Coming into force: 03.11.2014. Effect: None. Territorial extent & classification: E/W/S. General. - 4p.: 30 cm. - 978-0-11-111854-2 £4.25

The Scotland Act 1998 (Modification of Functions) Order 2014 No. 2014/2753 (S.3). - Enabling power: Scotland Act 1998, ss. 106, 112 (1). - Issued: 20.10.2014. Made: 13.10.2014. Laid: 15.10.2014. Coming into force: 01.03.2015. Effect: None. Territorial extent & classification: E/W/S/NI. General. - 4p.: 30 cm. - 978-0-11-112184-9 £4.25

The Scotland Act 1998 (Modification of Schedule 5) Order 2014 No. 2014/1559. - Enabling power: Scotland Act 1998, s. 30 (2). - Issued: 19.06.2014. Made: 12.06.2014. Coming into force: 13.06.2014. in accord. with art. 1 (2). Effect: 1998 c.46 modified. Territorial extent & classification: UK. General. - Supersedes draft SI (ISBN 9780111111918) issued 18.03.2014. - 4p.: 30 cm. - 978-0-11-111655-5 £4.25

The Scotland Act 1998 (Transfer of Functions to the Scottish Ministers etc.) Order 2014 No. 2014/2918. - Enabling power: Scotland Act 1998, ss. 63 (1), 113 (3) (4) (5), 124 (2). - Issued: 12.11.2014. Made: 05.11.2014. Laid:-. Coming into force: 06.11.2014. Effect: None. Territorial extent & classification: E/W/S/NI. General. - Supersedes draft SI (ISBN 9780111117415) issued 07/07/14. - 4p.: 30 cm. - 978-0-11-112297-6 £4.25

The Scotland Act 2012 (Commencement No. 4) Order 2014 No. 2014/3250 (C.147). - Enabling power: Scotland Act 2012, s. 44 (4). Bringing into operation various provisions of the 2012 Act on 12.12.2014, in accord. with art. 2. - Issued: 16.12.2014. Made: 08.12.2014. Effect: None. Territorial extent & classification: E/W/S/NI. General. - 2p.: 30 cm. - 978-0-11-112515-1 £4.25

The Scottish Parliament (Constituencies and Regions) Order 2014 No. 2014/501 (S.1). - Enabling power: Scotland Act 1998, s. 113, sch. 1, para. 6 (1) (5). - Issued: 12.03.2014. Made: 05.03.2014. Coming into force: In accord. with art. 1 (2) (3). Effect: S.I. 2010/2691 revoked. Territorial extent & classification: E/W/S/NI. General. - 8p., map: 30 cm. - 978-0-11-111105-5 £5.75

The Social Care (Self-directed Support) (Scotland) Act 2013 (Consequential Modifications and Savings) Order 2014 No. 2014/513. - Enabling power: Scotland Act 1998, ss. 104, 112 (1), 113 (2) (4) (5). - Issued: 11.03.2014. Made: 04.03.2014. Laid: 06.03.2014. Coming into force: 01.04.2014. Effect: S.I. 1987/1967, 1973; 1991/2887; 1992/1815; 1996/207, 2890; 2002/1792, 2006; 2004/3120; 2006/213, 214, 758; 2007/1745; 2008/794, 1052, 1053, 1054; 2009/1114, 2131; 2010/42; 2011/2344; 2012/2885; 2013/1179, 1893, 3029 (W.301), 3035 (W.303) amended. Territorial extent & classification: UK. General. - This SI was affected by a defect in SI 2013/2302 which has been corrected by SI 2014/1834 (L.27) (ISBN 9780111118122) which is being issued free of charge to all known recipients of SI 2013/2302 and SI 2014/513. - 12p.: 30 cm. - 978-0-11-111117-8 £5.75

Diplomatic Service

The Consular Fees (Amendment) Order 2014 No. 2014/509. - Enabling power: Consular Fees Act 1980, s. 1 (1) (4A) (4B). - Issued: 12.03.2014. Made: 05.03.2014. Coming into force: 07.04.2014. Effect: S.I. 2012/798 amended. Territorial extent & classification: E/W/S/NI. General. - 2p.: 30 cm. - 978-0-11-111113-0 £4.00

Disabled persons

The Civil Aviation (Access to Air Travel for Disabled Persons and Persons with Reduced Mobility) Regulations 2014 No. 2014/2833. - Enabling power: European Communities Act 1972, s. 2 (2). - Issued: 27.10.2014. Made: 16.10.2014. Laid: 27.10.2014. Coming into force: 01.12.2014. Effect: S.I. 2007/1895 revoked. Territorial extent & classification: E/W/S/NI. General. - 12p.: 30 cm. - 978-0-11-112218-1 £6.00

The Rail Vehicle Accessibility (Non-Interoperable Rail System) (Blackpool Tramway) Exemption Order 2014 No. 2014/2660. - Enabling power: Equality Act 2010, ss. 183 (1) (2) (4) (a) (5), 207 (1) (4). - Issued: 10.10.2014. Made: 29.09.2014. Laid: 10.10.2014. Coming into force: 01.11.2014. Effect: None. Territorial extent & classification: E/W/S. General. - 4p.: 30 cm. - 978-0-11-112122-1 £4.25

The Railways and Rail Vehicles (Revocations and Consequential Amendments) Order 2014 No. 2014/3244. - Enabling power: Equality Act 2010, s. 184 (1) (2) (3) & S.I. 2008/2975, reg. 2 (1) (3) (c). - Issued: 15.12.2014. Made: 08.12.2014. Laid: 12.12.2014. Coming into force: 05.01.2015. Effect: S.I. 2001/3592 amended & S.I. 1994/2229; 1997/1531; 1999/2932; 2001/218, 1768; 2005/395 revoked. Territorial extent & classification: E/W/S. General. - 4p.: 30 cm. - 978-0-11-112506-9 £4.25

Disclosure of information

The Enterprise Act 2002 (Part 9 Restrictions on Disclosure of Information) (Amendment) Order 2014 No. 2014/2807. - Enabling power: Enterprise Act 2002, s. 241 (6). - Issued: 23.10.2014. Made: 16.10.2014. Laid: 21.10.2014. Coming into force: 17.11.2014. Effect: 2002 c.40 amended. Territorial extent & classification: E/W/S/NI. General. - 2p.: 30 cm. - 978-0-11-112199-3 £4.25

Disclosure of information, England and Wales

The Serious Crime Act 2007 (Specified Anti-Fraud Organisations) Order 2014 No. 2014/1608. - Enabling power: Serious Crime Act 2007, s, 68 (8). - Issued: 25.06.2014. Made: 18.06.2014. Laid: 25.06.2014. Coming into force: 21.07.2014. Effect: None. Territorial extent & classification: E/W. General. - 2p.: 30 cm. - 978-0-11-111681-4 £4.25

Dogs

The Anti-social Behaviour, Crime and Policing Act 2014 (Commencement No. 2, Transitional and Transitory Provisions) Order 2014 No. 2014/949 (C.43). - Enabling power: Anti-social Behaviour, Crime and Policing Act 2014, s. 185 (1) (7). Bringing into operation various provisions of the 2014 Act on 13.05.2014, 01.06.2014, 16.06.2014, 14.07.2014, in accord. with arts. 2 to 6. - Issued: 14.04.2014. Made: 08.04.2014. Effect: None. Territorial extent & classification: E/W/S/NI. General. - 8p.: 30 cm. - 978-0-11-111401-8 £6.00

Dogs, England and Wales

The Anti-social Behaviour, Crime and Policing Act 2014 (Commencement No. 2, Transitional and Transitory Provisions) Order 2014 No. 2014/949 (C.43). - Enabling power: Anti-social Behaviour, Crime and Policing Act 2014, s. 185 (1) (7). Bringing into operation various provisions of the 2014 Act on 13.05.2014, 01.06.2014, 16.06.2014, 14.07.2014, in accord. with arts. 2 to 6. - Issued: 14.04.2014. Made: 08.04.2014. Effect: None. Territorial extent & classification: E/W/S/NI. General. - 8p.: 30 cm. - 978-0-11-111401-8 £6.00

Ecclesiastical law, England

The Church of England (Miscellaneous Provisions) Measure 2014 (Appointed Day No. 1) Order 2014 No. 2014/1369. - Enabling power: Church of England (Miscellaneous Provisions) Measure 2014, s. 21 (2). Bringing various provisions of the 2014 Measure into force on 19.05.2014. - Issued: 04.06.2014. Made: 19.05.2014. Effect: None. Territorial extent & classification: E. General. - 2p.: 30 cm. - 978-0-11-111543-5 £4.25

The Church of England (Miscellaneous Provisions) Measure 2014 (Appointed Day No. 2 and Transitional and Saving Provisions) Order 2014 No. 2014/2077. - Enabling power: Church of England (Miscellaneous Provisions) Measure 2014, s. 21 (2). Bringing various provisions of the 2014 Measure into operation 30.07.2014 & 01.01.2015, in accord. with art. 2. - Issued: 08.08.2014. Made: 30.07.2014. Laid before Parliament: 06.08.2014. Effect: None. Territorial extent & classification: E. General. - 4p.: 30 cm. - 978-0-11-111960-0 £4.25

The Church Representation Rules (Amendment) Resolution 2014 No. 2014/2113. - Enabling power: Synodical Government Measure 1969 no. 2, s. 7 (1). - Issued: 12.08.2014. Made (passed by the General Synod): 15.07.2014. Laid before Parliament: 07.08.2014. Coming into force: In accord. with para. 1. Effect: Measure 1969 no 2 amended. Territorial extent & classification: E. General. - 4p.: 30 cm. - 978-0-11-111969-3 £4.25

The Ecclesiastical Judges, Legal Officers and Others (Fees) Order 2014 No. 2014/2072. - Enabling power: Ecclesiastical Fees Measure 1986, s. 6 (1) (1A) (2). - Issued: 08.08.2014. Made 11.07.2014. Laid: 06.08.2014. Coming into force: 01.01.2015. Effect: S.I. 2013/1922 revoked. Territorial extent & classification: E. General. - 12p.: 30 cm. - 978-0-11-111959-4 £6.00

The Ecclesiastical Offices (Terms of Service) (Amendment) Regulations 2014 No. 2014/2083. - Enabling power: Ecclesiastical Offices (Terms of Service) Measure 2009 no. 1, s. 2. - Issued: 08.08.2014. Made (sealed by the Archbishops' Council): 04.08.2014. Laid: 06.08.2014. Coming into force: 30.11.2014. Effect: S.I. 2009/2108 amended. Territorial extent & classification: E. General. - 4p.: 30 cm. - 978-0-11-111963-1 £4.25

The Legal Officers (Annual Fees) (Amendment) Order 2014 No. 2014/896. - Enabling power: Ecclesiastical Fees Measure 1986, s. 5 (1) (2). - Issued: 08.04.2014. Made: 11.02.2014. Laid: 04.04.2014. Coming into force: 20.04.2014. Effect: S.I. 2013/1918 amended. Territorial extent & classification: E. General. - 4p.: 30 cm. - 978-0-11-111361-5 £4.25

The Legal Officers (Annual Fees) Order 2014 No. 2014/895. - Enabling power: Ecclesiastical Fees Measure 1986, s. 5 (1) (2). - Issued: 23.10.2014. Made: 11.02.2014. Laid: 04.04.2014. Coming into force: 01.01.2015. Effect: S.I. 2013/1918 revoked. Territorial extent & classification: E. General. - This Statutory Instrument has been printed in substitution of the SI of same number (and ISBN) issued 08.04.2014, and is being issued free of charge to all known recipients of that Statutory Instrument. - 12p.: 30 cm. - 978-0-11-111360-8 £6.00

EDUCATION

The Parochial Fees and Scheduled Matters Amending Order 2014 No. 2014/813. - Enabling power: Ecclesiastical Fees Measure 1986, ss. 1 (1) (2) (3) (6), 2. - Issued: 31.03.2014. Made: 20.03.2014. Laid before Parliament: 27.03.2014. Coming into force: 01.01.2015. Effect: Ecclesiastical Fees Measure 1986 (1986 no. 2) amended. Territorial extent & classification: E. General. - 8p.: 30 cm. - 978-0-11-111276-2 £5.75

The Payments to the Churches Conservation Trust Order 2014 No. 2014/2252. - Enabling power: Mission and Pastoral Measure 2011, s. 65. - Issued: 01.09.2014. Made (Sealed by the Church Commissioners): 12.06.2014. Approved by the General Synod: 13.07.2014. Laid before Parliament: 28.08.2014. Coming into force: 01.04.2015. Effect: None. Territorial extent & classification: E. General. - 4p.: 30 cm. - 978-0-11-111997-6 £4.25

Education

The Education (Student Loans) (Repayment) (Amendment) Regulations 2014 No. 2014/651. - Enabling power: Teaching and Higher Education Act 1998, ss. 22, 42. - Issued: 20.03.2014. Made: 13.03.2014. Laid before Parliament and the National Assembly for Wales: 14.03.2014. Coming into force: 06.04.2014. Effect: S.I. 2009/470 amended. Territorial extent & classification: E/W/S/NI. General. - With correction slip dated October 2014. - 8p.: 30 cm. - 978-0-11-111227-4 £5.75

Education, England

The Children and Families Act 2014 (Transitional and Saving Provisions) (No. 2) Order 2014 No. 2014/2270. - Enabling power: Children and Families Act 2014, s. 137 (1). - Issued: 03.09.2014. Made: 26.08.2014. Coming into force: 01.09.2014. Effect: None. Territorial extent & classification: E. General. - 20p.: 30 cm. - 978-0-11-112003-3 £6.00

The Designation of Rural Primary Schools (England) Order 2014 No. 2014/2650. - Enabling power: Education and Inspections Act 2006, s. 15 (7) (b). - Issued: 06.10.2014. Made: 29.09.2014. Coming into force: 01.10.2014. Effect: S.I. 2013/2655 revoked. Territorial extent & classification: E. General. - 2p.: 30 cm. - 978-0-11-112117-7 £4.25

The Designation of Schools Having a Religious Character (Independent Schools) (England) (No. 2) Order 2014 No. 2014/2342. - Enabling power: School Standards and Framework Act 1998, s. 69 (3). - Issued: 08.09.2014. Made: 01.09.2014. Coming into force: 01.09.2014. Effect: S.I. 2003/3284; 2009/510 partially revoked. Territorial extent & classification: E. General. - Partially revoked by S.I. 2014/3361 (ISBN 9780111126486). - 4p.: 30 cm. - 978-0-11-112016-3 £4.25

The Designation of Schools Having a Religious Character (Independent Schools) (England) (No. 2) Order 2014 No. 2014/2320. - Enabling power: School Standards and Framework Act 1998, s. 69 (3). - Issued: 05.09.2014. Made: 01.09.2014. Effect: S.I. 2003/3284; 2009/510 partially revoked. Territorial extent & classification: E. General. - 4p.: 30 cm. - 978-0-11-112006-4 £4.25

The Designation of Schools Having a Religious Character (Independent Schools) (England) (No. 3) Order 2014 No. 2014/3361. - Enabling power: School Standards and Framework Act 1998, s. 69 (3). - Issued: 30.12.2014. Made: 22.12.2014. Effect: S.I. 2004/577; 2012/3174; 2014/2342 partially revoked. Territorial extent & classification: E. General. - 4p.: 30 cm. - 978-0-11-112648-6 £4.25

The Designation of Schools Having a Religious Character (Independent Schools) (England) Order 2014 No. 2014/1024. - Enabling power: School Standards and Framework Act 1998, s. 69 (3). - Issued: 23.04.2014. Made: 14.04.2014. Effect: S.I. 2012/3174 partially revoked. Territorial extent & classification: E. General. - 4p.: 30 cm. - 978-0-11-111416-2 £4.25

The Diocese of Bath and Wells (Educational Endowments) (Newbridge St. John's Church of England Infants' School) Order 2014 No. 2014/2006. - Enabling power: Education Act 1996, ss. 554, 556. - Issued: 30.07.2014. Made: 24.07.2014. Coming into force: 31.07.2014. Effect: None. Territorial extent & classification: E. Local. - Available at http://www.legislation.gov.uk/uksi/2014/2006/contents/made Non-print

The Diocese of Bradford (Educational Endowments) (St Augustine's Church of England Community School) Order 2014 No. 2014/2295. - Enabling power: Education Act 1996, ss. 554, 556 & Reverter of Sites Act 1987, s. 5. - Issued: 29.08.2014. Made: 27.08.2014. Coming into force: 01.09.2014. Effect: None. Territorial extent & classification: E. Local. - Available at http://www.legislation.gov.uk/uksi/2014/2295/contents/made Non-print

The Diocese of Lichfield (Educational Endowments) (Brereton National School) Order 2014 No. 2014/2719. - Enabling power: Education Act 1996, ss. 554, 556. - Issued: 10.10.2014. Made: 07.10.2014. Coming into force: 14.10.2014. Effect: None. Territorial extent & classification: E. Local. - Available at http://www.legislation.gov.uk/uksi/2014/2719/contents/made Non-print

The Diocese of Lichfield (Educational Endowments) (St. John's Infant School) Order 2014 No. 2014/3246. - Enabling power: Education Act 1996, ss. 554, 556. - Issued: 05.12.2014. Made: 02.12.2014. Coming into force: 12.12.2014. Effect: None. Territorial extent & classification: E. Local. Available at http://www.legislation.gov.uk/uksi/2014/3246/contents/made Non-print

The Diocese of Lichfield (Educational Endowments) (St. John's Junior School) Order 2014 No. 2014/3247. - Enabling power: Education Act 1996, ss. 554, 556. - Issued: 05.12.2014. Made: 02.12.2014. Coming into force: 12.12.2014. Effect: None. Territorial extent & classification: E. Local. Available at http://www.legislation.gov.uk/uksi/2014/3247/contents/made Non-print

The Diocese of Lichfield (Educational Endowments) (Wall Church of England School) Order 2014 No. 2014/2631. - Enabling power: Education Act 1996, ss. 554, 556. - Issued: 30.09.2014. Made: 25.09.2014. Coming into force: 01.10.2014. Effect: None. Territorial extent & classification: E. Local. - The order extinguishes the rights of any beneficiary under the trust which has arisen under the Reverter of Sites Act 1987, s. 1. Available at http://www.legislation.gov.uk/uksi/2014/3247/contents/made Non-print

The Diocese of Manchester (Educational Endowments) (The Former Scot Lane End Church of England Primary School) Order 2014 No. 2014/699. - Enabling power: Education Act 1996, ss. 554, 556. - Issued: 12.03.2014. Made: 06.03.2014. Coming into force: 01.04.2014. Effect: None. Territorial extent & classification: E. Local. - Available at http://www.legislation.gov.uk/uksi/2014/699/contents/made Non-print

The Diocese of York (Educational Endowments) (Ellerton Priory Church of England School) (Amendment) Order 2014 No. 2014/942. - Enabling power: Education Act 1996, ss. 554, 556. - Issued: 07.04.2014. Made: 03.04.2014. Coming into force: 07.04.2014. Effect: None. Territorial extent & classification: E. Local. - Available at http://www.legislation.gov.uk/uksi/2014/942/contents/made Non-print

The Education and Inspections Act 2006 (Commencement No. 8) Order 2014 No. 2014/2380 (C.104). - Enabling power: Education and Inspections Act 2006, s. 188 (3). Bringing into operation various provisions of the 2006 Act on 08.09.2014. - Issued: 10.09.2014. Made: 02.09.2014. Effect: None. Territorial extent & classification: E. General. - 8p.: 30 cm. - 978-0-11-112039-2 £6.00

The Education and Skills Act 2008 (Commencement No. 10 and Transitory Provisions) Order 2014 No. 2014/2379 (C.103). - Enabling power: Education and Skills Act 2008, s. 173 (4) (8). Bringing into operation various provisions fo the 2008 Act on 08.09.2014. - Issued: 10.09.2014. Made: 02.09.2014. Effect: None. Territorial extent & classification: E. General. - 8p.: 30 cm. - 978-0-11-112038-5 £4.25

The Education and Skills Act 2008 (Commencement No. 11 and Saving and Transitory Provisions) Order 2014 No. 2014/3364 (C.158). - Enabling power: Education and Skills Act 2008, s. 173 (4) (8). Bringing into operation various provisions of the 2008 Act on 05.01.2015. - Issued: 31.12.2014. Made: 22.12.2014. Effect: None. Territorial extent & classification: E. General. - 8p.: 30 cm. - 978-0-11-112650-8 £6.00

The Education (Grants etc) (Dance and Drama) (England) (Revocation) Regulations 2014 No. 2014/80. - Enabling power: Education Act 1996, s. 485. - Issued: 23.01.2014. Made: 13.01.2014. Laid: 20.01.2014. Coming into force: 12.02.2014. Effect: S.I. 2005/2114; 2007/464; 2012/956 partially revoked & S.I. 2001/2857; 2002/2064; 2005/677, 3436 revoked. Territorial extent & classification: E. General. - 4p.: 30 cm. - 978-0-11-110853-6 £4.00

The Education (Independent School Standards) (England) (Amendment) Regulations 2014 No. 2014/2374. - Enabling power: Education Act 2002, ss. 157 (1), 210 (7). - Issued: 10.09.2014. Made: 04.09.2014. Laid: 08.09.2014. Coming into force: 29.09.2014. Effect: S.I. 2010/1997 amended. Territorial extent & classification: E. General. - 4p.: 30 cm. - 978-0-11-112033-0 £4.25

The Education (Independent School Standards) Regulations 2014 No. 2014/3283. - Enabling power: Education and Skills Act 2008, ss. 94 (1) (2), 166 (6). - Issued: 17.12.2014. Made: 11.12.2014. Laid: 15.12.2014. Coming into force: 05.01.2015. Effect: None. Territorial extent & classification: E. General. - 20p.: 30 cm. - 978-0-11-112544-1 £6.00

The Education (National Curriculum) (Attainment Targets and Programmes of Study) (England) (Amendment) (No. 2) Order 2014 No. 2014/1941. - Enabling power: Education Act 2002, ss. 87 (3) (a) (b) (5), 210 (7). - Issued: 28.07.2014. Made: 21.07.2014. Laid: 23.07.2014. Coming into force: In accord. with art. 1. Effect: S.I. 2013/2232 amended & S.I. 2014/1867 revoked. Territorial extent & classification: E. General. - 4p.: 30 cm. - 978-0-11-111913-6 £4.25

The Education (National Curriculum) (Attainment Targets and Programmes of Study) (England) (Amendment) (No. 3) Order 2014 No. 2014/3285. - Enabling power: Education Act 2002, ss 87 (3) (b) (5), 210 (7). - Issued: 17.12.2014. Made: 10.12.2014. Laid: 15.12.2014. Coming into force: In accord. with art. 1. Effect: S.I. 2013/2232 amended. Territorial extent & classification: E. General. - 4p.: 30 cm. - 978-0-11-112546-5 £4.25

The Education (National Curriculum) (Attainment Targets and Programmes of Study) (England) (Amendment) Order 2014 No. 2014/1867. - Enabling power: Education Act 2002, ss. 87 (3) (a) (b) (5), 210 (7). - Issued: 22.07.2014. Made: 08.07.2014. Laid: 16.07.2014. Coming into force: In accord. with art. 1. Effect: S.I. 2013/2232 amended (01.09.2014). Territorial extent & classification: E. General. - Revoked by SI 2014/1941 (ISBN 9780111119136). - 4p.: 30 cm. - 978-0-11-111831-3 £4.25

The Education (Prescribed Courses of Higher Education) (Information Requirements) (England) Regulations 2014 No. 2014/2179. - Enabling power: Further and Higher Education Act 1992, s. 79 (c). - Issued: 21.08.2014. Made: 14.08.2014. Laid: 18.08.2014. Coming into force: 08.09.2014. Effect: None. Territorial application & classification: E. General. - Revoked by SI 2015/225 (ISBN 9780111129654). - 60p.: 30 cm. - 978-0-11-111992-1 £10.00

The Education (Provision of Full-Time Education for Excluded Pupils) (England) (Amendment) Regulations 2014 No. 2014/3216. - Enabling power: Education Act 1996, ss. 19 (3B), 569 (4) & Education and Inspections Act 2006, ss. 100 (2), 181 (2). - Issued: 11.12.2014. Made: 03.12.2014. Laid: 05.12.2014. Coming into force: 05.01.2015. Effect: S.I. 2007/1870 amended. Territorial extent & classification: E. General. - 2p.: 30 cm. - 978-0-11-112468-0 £4.25

The Education (School Teachers' Qualifications) (England) (Amendment) Regulations 2014 No. 2014/2697. - Enabling power: Education Act 2002, ss. 132 (1) (2), 145 (1), 210 (7). - Issued: 13.10.2014. Made: 05.10.2014. Laid: 08.10.2014. Coming into force: 01.11.2014. Effect: S.I. 2003/1662 amended. Territorial extent & classification: E. General. - 2p.: 30 cm. - 978-0-11-112135-1 £4.25

The Education (Student Support) (Amendment) Regulations 2014 No. 2014/2765. - Enabling power: Teaching and Higher Education Act 1998, ss. 22, 42 (6). - Issued: 21.10.2014. Made: 14.10.2014. Laid: 16.10.2014. Coming into force: In accord. with reg. 1. Effect: S.I. 2011/1986 amended. Territorial extent & classification: E. General. - 16p.: 30 cm. - 978-0-11-112189-4 £6.00

The Further and Higher Education (Student Support) (Amendment) Regulations 2014 No. 2014/1766. - Enabling power: Teaching and Higher Education Act 1998, ss. 22, 42 (6). - Issued: 10.07.2014. Made: 01.07.2014. Laid: 07.07.2014. Coming into force: 01.08.2014. Effect: S.I. 2011/1986; 2012/1818 amended. Territorial extent & classification: E. General. - 8p.: 30 cm. - 978-0-11-111757-6 £4.25

The Further Education Loans (Amendment) Regulations 2014 No. 2014/290. - Enabling power: Teaching and Higher Education Act 1998, ss. 22, 42 (6). - Issued: 18.02.2014. Made: 11.02.2014. Laid: 13.02.2014. Coming into force: 07.03.2014. Effect: S.I. 2012/1818 amended. Territorial extent & classification: E. General. - 2p.: 30 cm. - 978-0-11-110979-3 £4.00

The Independent Educational Provision in England (Prohibition on Participation in Management) Regulations 2014 No. 2014/1977. - Enabling power: Education and Skills Act 2008, ss. 128 (2) (3) (4) (5), 129 (2), 141 (1) (2). - Issued: 30.07.2014. Made: 22.07.2014. Laid: 25.07.2014. Coming into force: 01.09.2014. Effect: None. Territorial extent & classification: E. General. - 8p.: 30 cm. - 978-0-11-111930-3 £6.00

The Independent Inspectorates (Education and Boarding Accommodation) Regulations 2014 No. 2014/2158. - Enabling power: Children Act 1989, s. 87A (4A) & Education and Skills Act 2008, s. 106 (4). - Issued: 18.08.2014. Made: 11.08.2014. Laid: 14.08.2014. Coming into force: 08.09.2014. Effect: None. Territorial extent & classification: E. General. - 4p.: 30 cm. - 978-0-11-111989-1 £4.25

The Inspectors of Education, Children's Services and Skills (No. 2) Order 2014 No. 2014/498. - Enabling power: Education and Inspections Act 2006, s. 114 (1). - Issued: 11.03.2014. Made: 05.03.2014. Coming into force: 06.03.2014. Effect: None. Territorial extent & classification: E. General. - 2p.: 30 cm. - 978-0-11-111102-4 £4.00

The Inspectors of Education, Children's Services and Skills (No. 3) Order 2014 No. 2014/1103. - Enabling power: Education and Inspections Act 2006, s. 114 (1). - Issued: 02.05.2014. Made: 28.04.2014. Coming into force: 29.04.2014. Effect: None. Territorial extent & classification: E. General. - 2p.: 30 cm. - 978-0-11-111436-0 £4.25

The Inspectors of Education, Children's Services and Skills (No. 4) Order 2014 No. 2014/1354. - Enabling power: Education and Inspections Act 2006, s. 114 (1). - Issued: 03.06.2014. Made: 27.05.2014. Coming into force: 28.05.2014. Effect: None. Territorial extent & classification: E. General. - 2p.: 30 cm. - 978-0-11-111526-8 £4.25

The Inspectors of Education, Children's Services and Skills (No. 5) Order 2014 No. 2014/1560. - Enabling power: Education and Inspections Act 2006, s. 114 (1). - Issued: 19.06.2014. Made: 12.06.2014. Coming into force: 13.06.2014. Effect: None. Territorial extent & classification: E. General. - 2p.: 30 cm. - 978-0-11-111656-2 £4.25

The Inspectors of Education, Children's Services and Skills (No. 6) Order 2014 No. 2014/1877. - Enabling power: Education and Inspections Act 2006, s. 114 (1). - Issued: 23.07.2014. Made: 16.07.2014. Coming into force: 17.07.2014. Effect: None. Territorial extent & classification: E. General. - 2p.: 30 cm. - 978-0-11-111839-9 £4.25

The Inspectors of Education, Children's Services and Skills (No. 7) Order 2014 No. 2014/2921. - Enabling power: Education and Inspections Act 2006, s. 114 (1). - Issued: 12.11.2014. Made: 05.11.2014. Coming into force: 06.11.2014. Effect: None. Territorial extent & classification: E. General. - 2p.: 30 cm. - 978-0-11-112300-3 £4.25

The Inspectors of Education, Children's Services and Skills Order 2014 No. 2014/261. - Enabling power: Education and Inspections Act 2006, s. 114 (1). - Issued: 18.02.2014. Made: 11.02.2014. Coming into force: 12.02.2014. Effect: None. Territorial extent & classification: E. General. - 2p.: 30 cm. - 978-0-11-110965-6 £4.00

The National Curriculum (Exceptions for First, Second, Third and Fourth Key Stages) (England) (Amendment) (No. 2) Regulations 2014 No. 2014/3286. - Enabling power: Education Act 2002, s. 91. - Issued: 17.12.2014. Made: 10.12.2014. Laid: 15.12.2014. Coming into force: 01.09.2015. Effect: S.I. 2013/1487 amended. Territorial extent & classification: E. General. - 2p.: 30 cm. - 978-0-11-112547-2 £4.25

The National Curriculum (Exceptions for First, Second, Third and Fourth Key Stages) (England) (Amendment) Regulations 2014 No. 2014/1866. - Enabling power: Education Act 2002, s. 91. - Issued: 22.07.2014. Made: 08.07.2014. Laid: 16.07.2014. Coming into force: 01.09.2014. Effect: S.I. 2013/1487 amended. Territorial extent & classification: E. General. - 2p.: 30 cm. - 978-0-11-111830-6 £4.25

The Plymouth College of Art (Transfer to the Higher Education Sector) Order 2014 No. 2014/1507. - Enabling power: Education Reform Act 1988, s. 122A. - Issued: 13.06.2014. Made: 09.06.2014. Laid: 10.06.2014. Coming into force: 04.07.2014. Effect: None. Territorial extent & classification: E. General. - 2p.: 30 cm. - 978-0-11-111631-9 £4.25

The Prospects College of Advanced Technology (Government) Order 2014 No. 2014/2068. - Enabling power: Further and Higher Education Act 1992, ss. 20 (2), 21 (1), sch. 4. - Issued: 08.08.2014. Made: 27.07.2014. Laid: 05.08.2014. Coming into force: 31.08.2014. Effect: None. Territorial extent & classification: E. General. - 20p.: 30 cm. - 978-0-11-111955-6 £6.00

EDUCATION, ENGLAND AND WALES

The Prospects College of Advanced Technology (Incorporation) Order 2014 No. 2014/2067. - Enabling power: Further and Higher Education Act 1992, ss. 16 (1) (b) (5), 17 (2) (b). - Issued: 08.08.2014. Made: 27.07.2014. Laid: 05.08.2014. Coming into force: 31.08.2014. Effect: None. Territorial extent & classification: E. General. - 2p.: 30 cm. - 978-0-11-111954-9 £4.25

The Requirements for School Food Regulations 2014 No. 2014/1603. - Enabling power: School Standards and Framework Act 1998, ss. 114A, 138 (7). - Issued: 24.06.2014. Made: 16.06.2014. Laid: 20.06.2014. Coming into force: 01.01.2015. Effect: S.I. 2007/2359 revoked. Territorial extent & classification: E. General. - 12p.: 30 cm. - 978-0-11-111672-2 £6.00

The School Admissions (Admission Arrangements and Co-ordination of Admission Arrangements) (England) (Amendment) Regulations 2014 No. 2014/2886. - Enabling power: School Standards and Framework Act 1998, ss. 88C, 88E, 88F, 88H, 88K, 88M, 92, 100, 102, 138 (7). - Issued: 05.11.2014. Made: 30.10.2014. Laid: 03.11.2014. Coming into force: 19.12.2014. Effect: S.I. 2012/8 amended. Territorial extent & classification: E. General. - 8p.: 30 cm. - 978-0-11-112270-9 £4.25

The School Admissions Code (Appointed Day) Order 2014 No. 2014/3321. - Enabling power: School Standards and Framework Act 1998, s. 85 (5). The day appointed for the coming into force of the School Admissions Code is 19th December 2014. - Issued: 22.12.2014. Made: 16.12.2014. Effect: None. Territorial extent & classification: E. General. - 2p.: 30 cm. - 978-0-11-112606-6 £4.25

The School and Early Years Finance (England) Regulations 2014 No. 2014/3352. - Enabling power: School Standards and Framework Act 1998, ss. 45A, 45AA, 47, 47ZA, 47A (4) (4B), 48 (1) (2), 49 (2) (2A), 138 (7), sch. 14, para. 2B & Education Act 2002, s. 24 (3). - Issued: 30.12.2014. Made: 18.12.2014. Laid: 22.12.2014. Coming into force: 12.01.2015. Effect: S.I. 2012/2261 amended & S.I. 2012/2991 revoked (01.04.2015). Territorial extent & classification: E. General. - 28p.: 30 cm. - 978-0-11-112646-2 £10.00

The School Companies (Amendment) Regulations 2014 No. 2014/2923. - Enabling power: Education Act 2002, ss. 12, 210 (7). - Issued: 12.11.2014. Made: 05.11.2014. Laid: 07.11.2014. Coming into force: 01.12.2014. Effect: S.I. 2002/2978 amended. Territorial extent & classification: E. General. - 2p.: 30 cm. - 978-0-11-112302-7 £4.25

The School Governance (Constitution and Federations) (England) (Amendment) (No. 2) Regulations 2014 No. 2014/1959. - Enabling power: Education Act 2002, ss. 19 (1A) (3) (4A) (8), 20 (2) (3) (4), 21 (3), 24, 25, 34 (5), 35 (4) (5), 36 (4) (5), 210 (7). - Issued: 29.07.2014. Made: 22.07.2014. Laid: 25.07.2014. Coming into force: 31.08.2014. Effect: S.I. 2014/1257 amended. Territorial extent & classification: E. General. - 2p.: 30 cm. - 978-0-11-111920-4 £4.25

The School Governance (Constitution and Federations) (England) (Amendment) Regulations 2014 No. 2014/1257. - Enabling power: Education Act 2002, ss. 19 (1A) (2) (3) (4A) (8), 20 (2) (3) (4), 21 (3), 24, 25, 34 (5), 35 (4) (5), 36 (4) (5), 210 (7). - Issued: 21.05.2014. Made: 14.05.2014. Laid: 19.05.2014. Coming into force: 01.09.2014, for regs 1, 4, 5, 6; 01.09.2015, for remainder. Effect: S.I. 2012/1034, 1035; 2013/1624 amended & S.I. 2007/957 [after amending] , 960 revoked to the extent that those regs remain in force. Territorial extent & classification: E. General. - 8p.: 30 cm. - 978-0-11-111495-7 £6.00

The School Staffing (England) (Amendment) Regulations 2014 No. 2014/798. - Enabling power: Education Act 2002, ss. 35 (4), 36 (4). - Issued: 27.03.2014. Made: 19.03.2014. Laid: 26.03.2014. Coming into force: 01.09.2014. Effect: S.I. 2009/2680 amended. Territorial extent & classification: E. General. - 2p.: 30 cm. - 978-0-11-111267-0 £4.00

The Special Educational Needs and Disability Regulations 2014 No. 2014/1530. - Enabling power: Children and Families Act 2014, ss. 30 (8) (9), 34 (6), 36 (11), 37 (4), 41 (5), 44 (7), 45 (5), 46 (2), 47 (1) (2), 51 (4), 56 (1), 67 (3), 69 (3) (a), 80 (1). - Issued: 16.06.2014. Made: 04.06.2014. Laid: 11.06.2014. Coming into force: 01.09.2014. Effect: None. Territorial extent & classification: E. General. - 36p.: 30 cm. - 978-0-11-111642-5 £10.00

The Special Educational Needs (Code of Practice) (Appointed Day) Order 2014 No. 2014/2254. - Enabling power: Children and Families Act 2014, s. 78 (6). - Issued: 01.09.2014. Made: 22.08.2014. Coming into force: 01.09.2014. Effect: None. Territorial extent & classification: E. General. - 2p.: 30 cm. - 978-0-11-111998-3 £4.25

The Special Educational Needs (Consequential Amendments to Subordinate Legislation) Order 2014 No. 2014/2103. - Enabling power: Children and Families Act 2014, s. 136 (1) (2). - Issued: 12.08.2014. Made: 05.08.2014. Laid: 08.08.2014. Coming into force: 01.09.2014. Effect: 46 S.I.s amended. Territorial extent & classification: E. General. - 16p.: 30 cm. - 978-0-11-111967-9 £6.00

The Special Educational Needs (Direct Payments) (Pilot Scheme) (Extension and Amendment) Order 2014 No. 2014/166. - Enabling power: Education Act 1996, ss. 532B (1), 532C (1), 568 (5). - Issued: 04.02.2014. Made: 28.01.2014. Coming into force: 29.01.2014. Effect: S.I. 2012/206 amended. Territorial extent & classification: E. General. - 2p.: 30 cm. - 978-0-11-110901-4 £4.00

The Special Educational Needs (Miscellaneous Amendments) Regulations 2014 No. 2014/2096. - Enabling power: Children and Families Act 2014, ss. 44 (7), 49 (3). - Issued: 12.08.2014. Made: 05.08.2014. Laid: 08.08.2014. Coming into force: 01.09.2014. Effect: S.I. 2014/1530, 1652 amended. Territorial extent & classification: E. General. - 4p.: 30 cm. - 978-0-11-111965-5 £4.25

The Special Educational Needs (Personal Budgets) Regulations 2014 No. 2014/1652. - Enabling power: Children and Families Act 2014, s. 49 (3) (4). - Issued: 01.07.2014. Made: 24.06.2014. Coming into force: 01.09.2014. Effect: None. Territorial extent & classification: E. General. - 12p.: 30 cm. - 978-0-11-111714-9 £6.00

The Teachers' Disciplinary (Amendment) (England) Regulations 2014 No. 2014/1685. - Enabling power: Education Act 2002, s. 210 (7), sch. 11A- Issued: 04.07.2014. Made: 26.06.2014. Laid: 01.07.2014. Coming into force: 01.09.2014. Effect: S.I. 2012/560 amended. Territorial extent & classification: E. General. - 2p.: 30 cm. - 978-0-11-111736-1 £4.25

Education, England and Wales

The Education (School Teachers' Prescribed Qualifications, etc) (Amendment) Order 2014 No. 2014/1063. - Enabling power: Education Act 2002, ss. 122 (5), 210 (7). - Issued: 25.04.2014. Made: 16.04.2014. Laid: 23.04.2014. Coming into force: 01.09.2014. Effect: S.I. 2003/1709 amended. Territorial extent & classification: E/W. General. - 2p.: 30 cm. - 978-0-11-111424-7 £4.25

The School Teachers' Pay and Conditions Order 2014 No. 2014/2045. - Enabling power: Education Act 2002, ss. 122 (1), 123, 124. - Issued: 13.08.2014. Made: 04.08.2014. Coming into force: 01.09.2014. Effect: S.I. 2013/1932 revoked. Territorial extent & classification: E/W. General. - 4p.: 30 cm. - 978-0-11-111970-9 £4.25

The Teachers' Pensions (Amendment) Regulations 2014 No. 2014/424. - Enabling power: Superannuation Act 1972, ss. 9, 12, sch. 3. - Issued: 04.03.2014. Made: 25.02.2014. Laid: 04.03.2014. Coming into force: 01.04.2014. Effect: S.I. 2010/990 amended. Territorial extent & classification: E/W. General. - 8p.: 30 cm. - 978-0-11-111040-9 £5.75

The Teachers' Pension Scheme (Amendment) Regulations 2014 No. 2014/2652. - Enabling power: Public Service Pensions Act 2013, ss. 1 (1) (2) (d) (3) (4), 2, 3 (1) (2) (3) (a) (c) (4), 4 (1) (3), 5 (1), 7 (1), 8 (1) (a) (2) (a), 11 (1) (a) (2), 12 (1), (2), (3), (6), (7), 18 (1) (2) (4) (b) (5) to (9), 37 (c), sch. 1, para. 4, sch. 2, para. 4 (a), sch. 3, sch. 5, para. 18, sch. 7, paras. 1 (2) (ii), 2 (2) (ii), 5. - Issued: 06.10.2014. Made: 29.09.2014. Laid: 03.10.2014. Coming into force: 01.04.2015. Effect: None. Territorial extent & classification: E/W. General. - 12p.: 30 cm. - 978-0-11-112119-1 £6.00

The Teachers' Pension Scheme Regulations 2014 No. 2014/512. - Enabling power: Public Service Pensions Act 2013, ss. 1 (1) (2) (d) (3) (4), 2, 3 (1) (2) (3) (a) (c) (4), 4 (1) (3), 5 (1) (2) (4), 7 (1) (4), 8 (1) (a) (2) (a), 14, 18 (1) (2) (4) (b) (5) to (9), 37 (c), sch. 1, para. 4, sch. 2, para. 4 (a), sch. 3, sch. 5, para. 18, sch. 6, para. 6, sch. 7, paras. 1 (2) (ii), 2 (2) (ii), 5. - Issued: 12.03.2014. Made: 05.03.2014. Laid: 07.03.2014. Coming into force: In accord, with with reg. 1 (2). Effect: None. Territorial extent & classification: E/W. General. - 120p.: 30 cm. - 978-0-11-111116-1 £18.50

The Teachers' Pensions (Miscellaneous Amendments) (No. 2) Regulations 2014 No. 2014/2651. - Enabling power: Superannuation Act 1972, ss. 9, 12, sch. 3. - Issued: 06.10.2014. Made: 29.09.2014. Laid: 03.10.2014. Coming into force: 01.04.2015. Effect: S.I. 2010/990 amended. Territorial extent & classification: E/W. General. - 24p.: 30 cm. - 978-0-11-112118-4 £6.00

Education, Wales

The Cancellation of Student Loans for Living Costs Liability (Wales) Regulations 2014 No. 2014/1314 (W.134). - Enabling power: Teaching and Higher Education Act 1998, ss. 22, 42 (6). - Issued: 02.06.2014. Made: 21.05.2014. Laid before the National Assembly for Wales: 22.05.2014. Coming into force: 01.08.2014. Effect: None. Territorial extent & classification: W. General. - In English and Welsh. Welsh title: Rheoliadau Dileu Atebolrwydd dros Fenthyciadau i Fyfyrwyr at Gostau Byw (Cymru) 2014. - 8p.: 30 cm. - 978-0-348-10948-1 £6.00

The Designation of Schools Having a Religious Character (Wales) Order 2014 No. 2014/3261 (W.332). - Enabling power: School Standards and Framework Act 1998, ss. 69 (3) (4), 138 (7). - Issued: 30.12.2014. Made: 09.12.2014. Coming into force: 15.12.2014. Effect: S.I. 2007/972 (W.88) revoked. Territorial extent & classification: W. General. - In English and Welsh. Welsh language title: Gorchymyn Dynodi Ysgolion Sydd â Chymeriad Crefyddol (Cymru) 2014. - 24p.: 30 cm. - 978-0-348-11036-4 £6.00

The Diocese of Bangor (Educational Endowments) (Llangristiolus Church in Wales School) (Wales) Order 2014 No. 2014/1836 (W.190). - Enabling power: Education Act 1996, ss. 554, 556 (2) & Reverter of Sites Act 1987, s. 5. - Issued: 22.07.2014. Made: 09.07.2014. Coming into force: 31.07.2014. Effect: None. Territorial extent & classification: W. General. - In English and Welsh. Welsh language title: Gorchymyn Esgobaeth Bangor (Gwaddolion Addysgol) (Ysgol yr Eglwys yng Nghymru Llangristiolus) (Cymru) 2014. - 8p.: 30 cm. - 978-0-348-10969-6 £6.00

The Diocese of St Davids (Educational Endowments) (Abernant Church in Wales School) (Wales) Order 2014 No. 2014/2238 (W.220). - Enabling power: Education Act 1996, ss. 554, 556 & Reverter of Sites Act 1987, s. 5. - Issued: 02.09.2014. Made: 20.08.2014. Coming into force: 01.10.2014. Effect: None. Territorial extent & classification: W. Local. - Available at http://www.legislation.gov.uk/wsi/2014/2238/contents/made. - In English and Welsh. Welsh title: Gorchymyn Esgobaeth Tyddewi (Gwaddolion Addysgol) (Ysgol yr Eglwys yng Nghymru Aber-nant) (Cymru) 2014 Non-print

The Diocese of St Davids (Educational Endowments) (Llangennech Church in Wales School) (Wales) Order 2014 No. 2014/2235 (W.217). - Enabling power: Education Act 1996, ss. 554, 556 & Reverter of Sites Act 1987, s. 5. - Issued: 02.09.2014. Made: 20.08.2014. Coming into force: 01.10.2014. Effect: None. Territorial extent & classification: W. Local. - Available at http://www.legislation.gov.uk/wsi/2014/2235/contents/made. - In English and Welsh. Welsh title: Gorchymyn Esgobaeth Tyddewi (Gwaddolion Addysgol) (Ysgol yr Eglwys yng Nghymru Llangennech) (Cymru) 2014 Non-print

The Diocese of St Davids (Educational Endowments) (Llangynllo Church in Wales School) (Wales) Order 2014 No. 2014/2237 (W.219). - Enabling power: Education Act 1996, ss. 554, 556 & Reverter of Sites Act 1987, s. 5. - Issued: 02.09.2014. Made: 20.08.2014. Coming into force: 01.10.2014. Effect: None. Territorial extent & classification: W. Local. - Available at http://www.legislation.gov.uk/wsi/2014/2237/contents/made. - In English and Welsh. Welsh title: Gorchymyn Esgobaeth Tyddewi (Gwaddolion Addysgol) (Ysgol yr Eglwys yng Nghymru Llangynllo) (Cymru) 2014 Non-print

The Diocese of St Davids (Educational Endowments) (Spittal Church in Wales School) (Wales) Order 2014 No. 2014/2236 (W.218). - Enabling power: Education Act 1996, ss. 554, 556 & Reverter of Sites Act 1987, s. 5. - Issued: 02.09.2014. Made: 20.08.2014. Coming into force: 01.10.2014. Effect: None. Territorial extent & classification: W. Local. - Available at http://www.legislation.gov.uk/wsi/2014/2236/contents/made. - In English and Welsh. Welsh title: Gorchymyn Esgobaeth Tyddewi (Gwaddolion Addysgol) (Ysgol yr Eglwys yng Nghymru Spittal) (Cymru) 2014 Non-print

The Dissolution of Further Education Corporations (Publication of Proposals and Prescribed Bodies) (Wales) Regulations 2014 No. 2014/2126 (W.209). - Enabling power: Further and Higher Education Act 1992, ss. 27 (2) to (4), 27B (1), 89 (4). - Issued: 18.08.2014. Made: 06.08.2014. Laid before the National Assembly for Wales: 08.08.2014. Coming into force: 01.09.2014. Effect: None. Territorial extent & classification: W. General. - In English and Welsh. Welsh title: Rheoliadau Diddymu Corfforaethau Addysg Bellach (Cyhoeddi Cynigion a Chyrff Rhagnodedig) (Cymru) 2014. - 8p.: 30 cm. - 978-0-348-10984-9 £4.25

The Education (Amendments Relating to the Inspection of Education and Training) (Wales) Regulations 2014 No. 2014/1212 (W.128). - Enabling power: School Standards and Framework Act 1998, ss. 122 (1), 138 (7) (8), sch. 26, para. 6B (1) (a) & Learning and Skills Act 2002, ss. 77 (2) (9), 80 (4), 150, 152 & Education Act 2005, ss. 28(1) (8), 39 (2) (a), 42 (2) (a), 50 (4) (8), 55 (4), 56 (3), 57 (9) (10), 120 (2), sch. 4, para. (6) (b), sch. 6, paras 2 (1), 3 (1) - Issued: 16.05.2014. Made: 08.05.2014. Laid before the National Assembly for Wales: 12.05.2014. Coming into force: 01.09.2014. Effect: S.I. 1999/1441; 2001/2501 (W.204); 2006/1714 (W.176), 3103 (W.286) amended. Territorial extent & classification: W. General. - In English and Welsh. Welsh title: Rheoliadau Addysg (Diwygiadau sy'n Ymwneud ag Arolygu Addysg a Hyfforddiant) (Cymru) 2014. - 8p.: 30 cm. - 978-0-348-10943-6 £6.00

The Education (Consultation on School Term Dates) (Wales) Order 2014 No. 2014/1462 (W.143). - Enabling power: Education Act 2002, ss. 32B, 210. - Issued: 12.06.2014. Made: 04.06.2014. Laid before the National Assembly for Wales: 06.06.2014. Coming into force: 02.09.2014. Effect: None. Territorial extent & classification: W. General. - In English and Welsh. Welsh title: Rheoliadau Addysg (Ymgynhori ar Ddyddiadau Tymhorau Ysgol) (Cymru) 2014. - 8p.: 30 cm. - 978-0-348-10950-4 £6.00

The Education (European Institutions) and Student Support (Wales) (Revocation) Regulations 2014 No. 2014/1895 (W.194). - Enabling power: Teaching and Higher Education Act 1998, ss. 22, 42 (6), 43 (1). - Issued: 25.07.2014. Made: 16.07.2014. Laid before the National Assembly for Wales: 18.07.2014. Coming into force: 31.08.2014. Effect: W.S.I. 2013/765 (W.91) revoked. Territorial extent & classification: W. General. - In English and Welsh. Welsh title: Rheoliadau Addysg (Sefydliadau Ewropeaidd) a Chymorth i Fyfyrwyr (Cymru) (Dirymu) 2014. - 4p.: 30 cm. - 978-0-348-10977-1 £4.25

The Education (European University Institute) (Wales) Regulations 2014 No. 2014/3037 (W.303). - Enabling power: Teaching and Higher Education Act 1998, ss. 22, 42 (6), 43 (1). - Issued: 25.11.2014. Made: 12.11.2014. Laid before the National Assembly for Wales: 14.11.2014. Coming into force: 05.12.2014. Effect: W.S.I. 2009/3359 (W.295); 2010/1797 (W.173) revoked. Territorial extent & classification: W. General. - In English and Welsh. Welsh title: Rheoliadau Addysg (Athrofa Brifysgol Ewropeaidd) (Cymru) 2014. - 48p.: 30 cm. - 978-0-348-11016-6 £10.00

The Education (Inspectors of Education and Training in Wales) Order 2014 No. 2014/2922. - Enabling power: Education Act 2005, s. 19 (2). - Issued: 12.11.2014. Made: 05.11.2014. Coming into force: 06.11.2014. Effect: None. Territorial extent & classification: W. General. - 2p.: 30 cm. - 978-0-11-112301-0 £4.25

The Education (Local Curriculum for Pupils in Key Stage 4) (Wales) (Amendment) Regulations 2014 No. 2014/42 (W4). - Enabling power: Education Act 2002, ss. 116A (5), 116D (2), 210. - Issued: 28.01.2014. Made: 13.01.2014. Laid before the National Assembly for Wales: 15.01.2014. Coming into force: 05.02.2014. Effect: S.I 2009/3256 (W.284) amended. Territorial extent & classification: W. General. - This Statutory Instrument has been printed in substitution of the SI of same number and ISBN (issued 22.01.2014) and is being issued free of charge to all known recipients of that Statutory Instrument. - In English and Welsh. Welsh title: Rheoliadau Addysg (Cwricwlwm Lleol ar gyfer Disgyblion yng Nghyfnod Allweddol 4) (Cymru) (Diwygio) 2014. - 4p.: 30 cm. - 978-0-348-10853-8 £4.00

The Education (National Curriculum) (Foundation Phase) (Wales) Order 2014 No. 2014/1996 (W.198). - Enabling power: Education Act 2002, ss. 108 (2), 210. - Issued: 08.08.2014. Made: 23.07.2014. Laid before the National Assembly for Wales: 28.07.2014. Coming into force: 01.09.2014. Effect: W.S.I. 2008/1732 (W.169) revoked. Territorial extent & classification: W. General. - In English and Welsh. Welsh title: Gorchymyn Addysg (Y Cwricwlwm Cenedlaethol) (Y Cyfnod Sylfaen) (Cymru) 2014. - 4p.: 30 cm. - 978-0-348-10978-8 £4.25

The Education (Notification of School Term Dates) (Wales) Regulations 2014 No. 2014/1249 (W.130). - Enabling power: Education Act 2002, ss. 32A, 210. - Issued: 22.05.2014. Made: 12.05.2014. Laid before the National Assembly for Wales: 15.05.2014. Coming into force: 15.07.2014. Effect: None. Territorial extent & classification: W. General. - In English and Welsh. Welsh title: Rheoliadau Addysg (Hysbysu am Ddyddiadau Tymhorau Ysgol) (Cymru) 2014. - 8p.: 30 cm. - 978-0-348-10946-7 £4.25

EDUCATION, WALES

The Education (Pupil Referral Units) (Management Committees etc.) (Wales) Regulations 2014 No. 2014/2709 (W.270). - Enabling power: Education Act 1996, s. 569 (4) (5), sch. 1, paras 3, 6 (2), 15. - Issued: 27.10.2014. Made: 07.10.2014. Laid before the National Assembly for Wales: 09.10.2014. Coming into force: 31.10.2014, except for regs 22, 23, 23.02.2015. Effect: None. Territorial extent & classification: W. General. - In English and Welsh. Welsh title: Rheoliadau Addysg (Unedau Cyfeirio Disgyblion) (Pwyllgorau Rheoli etc.) (Cymru) 2014. - 28p.: 30 cm. - 978-0-348-10999-3 £6.00

The Education (School Development Plans) (Wales) Regulations 2014 No. 2014/2677 (W.265). - Enabling power: Education Act 1996, ss. 537, 569 (4) (5), sch. 1 para. 3 & Education Act 1997, ss. 19, 54 (3) (4) & Education Act 2002. ss. 21 (3), 30 (1) (2) , 131, 210. - Issued: 30.10.2014. Made: 01.10.2014. Laid before the National Assembly for Wales: 06.10.2014. Coming into force: 27.10.2014. Effect: 2007/1069 (W.109), 2011/1939 (W.207), 2940 (W.316) amended. Territorial extent & classification: W. General. - This S.I. has been printed in substitution of the S.I. of the same number & ISBN issued 27.10.2014, and is being issued free of charge to all known recipients of that S.I. - In English and Welsh. Welsh title: Rheoliadau Addysg (Cynlluniau Datblygu Ygsolion) (Cymru) 2014. - 12p.: 30 cm. - 978-0-348-11012-8 £6.00

The Education (Small Schools) (Wales) Order 2014 No. 2014/1133 (W.112). - Enabling power: Education (Wales) Measure 2011, ss. 15, 32. - Issued: 19.05.2014. Made: 29.04.2014. Laid before the National Assembly for Wales: 30.04.2014. Coming into force: 22.05.2014. Effect: None. Territorial extent & classification: W. General. - In English and Welsh. Welsh title: Gorchymyn Addysg (Ysgolion Bach) (Cymru) 2014. - 4p.: 30 cm. - 978-0-348-10945-0 £4.25

The Education (Student Support) (Wales) (Amendment) Regulations 2014 No. 2014/1712 (W.172). - Enabling power: Teaching and Higher Education Act 1998, ss. 22, 42 (6). - Issued: 16.07.2014. Made: 01.07.2014. Laid before the National Assembly for Wales: 04.07.2104. Coming into force: 25.07.2014. Effect: W.S.I. 2013/3177 (W.316) amended. Territorial extent & classification: W. General. - In English and Welsh. Welsh title: Rheoliadau Addysg (Cymorth i Fyfyrwyr) (Cymru) (Diwygio) 2014. - 8p.: 30 cm. - 978-0-348-10962-7 £4.25

The Education (Wales) Act 2014 (Commencement No. 1) Order 2014 No. 2014/1605 (W.163) (C.63). - Enabling power: Education (Wales) Act 2014 , s. 50 (4). Bringing into operation various provisions of the 2014 Act on 14.07.2014 & 01.09.2014, in accord. with art. 2. - Issued: 26.06.2014. Made: 17.06.2014. Effect: None. Territorial extent & classification: W. General. - In English and Welsh. Welsh title: Gorchymyn Deddf Addysg (Cymru) 2014 (Cychwyn Rhif 1) 2014. - 4p.: 30 cm. - 978-0-348-10956-6 £4.25

The Education (Wales) Act 2014 (Commencement No. 2) Order 2014 No. 2014/2162 (W.211) (C.97). - Enabling power: Education (Wales) Act 2014 , s. 50 (4). Bringing into operation various provisions of the 2014 Act on 18.08.2014 in accord. with art. 2. - Issued: 22.08.2014. Made: 07.08.2014. Effect: None. Territorial extent & classification: W. General. - In English and Welsh. Welsh title: Gorchymyn Deddf Addysg (Cymru) 2014 (Cychwyn Rhif 2) 2014. - 4p.: 30 cm. - 978-0-348-10986-3 £4.25

The Education (Wales) Measure 2009 (Pilot) (Revocation) Regulations 2014 No. 2014/3267 (W.334). - Enabling power: Education (Wales) Measure 2009, ss. 17 (1) (2), 24 (2). - Issued: 22.12.2014. Made: 11.12.2014. Laid before the National Assembly for Wales: 15.12.2014. Coming into force: 05.01.2015. Effect: None. Territorial extent & classification: W. General. - In English and Welsh. Welsh title: Rheoliadau Mesur Addysg (Cymru) 2009 (Treialu) (Dirymu) 2014. - 4p.: 30 cm. - 978-0-348-11032-6 £4.25

The Education (Wales) Measure 2011 (Commencement No. 3) Order 2014 No. 2014/1066 (W.105) (C.46). - Enabling power: Education (Wales) Measure 2011, s. 33. Bringing into operation various provisions of the 2011 Measure on 28.04.2014. - Issued: 25.04.2014. Made: 16.04.2014. Effect: None. Territorial extent & classification: W. General. - In English and Welsh. Welsh title: Gorchymyn Mesur Addysg (Cymru) 2011 (Cychwyn Rhif 2) 2014. - 2p.: 30 cm. - 978-0-348-10938-2 £4.25

The Education Workforce Council (Membership and Appointment) (Wales) Regulations 2014 No. 2014/2365 (W.229). - Enabling power: Education (Wales) Act 2014, s. 2 (2), 47 (1), sch. 1, paras 4, 9 (2), 12. - Issued: 22.09.2014. Made: 03.09.2014. Laid before the National Assembly for Wales: 05.09.2014. Coming into force: 29.09.2014, except as provided for in reg. 1 (1). Effect: S.I. 1999/1619, 3185; 2003/389 (W.51); 2007/812 (W.69); 2009/1352 (W.128); 2012/169 (W.28) revoked (01.04.2015). Territorial extent & classification: W. General. - In English and Welsh. Welsh title: Rheoliadau Cyngor y Gweithlu Addysg (Aelodaeth a Phenodi) (Cymru) 2014. - 12p.: 30 cm. - 978-0-348-10989-4 £6.00

The Federation of Maintained Schools (Wales) Regulations 2014 No. 2014/1132 (W.111). - Enabling power: Education Act 2002, ss. 19 (2) (3) (8), 20 (2) (3) (4A), 34 (5), 35 (4) (5), 36 (4) (5), 210 (7), 214 & Education (Wales) Measure 2011, ss. 6, 10, 11, 12, 13, 14, 18, 32. - Issued: 20.05.2014. Made: 29.04.2014. Laid before the National Assembly for Wales: 30.04.2014. Coming into force: 22.05.2014. Effect: 1998 c.31; S.I. 2005/3200 (W.236); 2006/873 (W.81) modified & W.S.I. 2012/2655 (W.287); 2013/2124 (W.207), 2127 (W.208) amended & W.S.I. 2010/638 (W.64) partially revoked. Territorial extent & classification: W. General. - In English and Welsh. Welsh title: Rheoliadau Ffedereiddio Ysgolion a Gynhelir (Cymru) 2014. - 104p.: 30 cm. - 978-0-348-10944-3 £16.50

The Further and Higher Education (Governance and Information) (Wales) Act 2014 (Commencement) Order 2014 No. 2014/1706 (W.171)(C.72). - Enabling power: Further and Higher Education (Governance and Information) (Wales) Act 2014, s. 11 (2) (3). Bringing into force various provisions of the 2014 Act on 01.08.2014, 01.09.2014, in accord. with arts 2 & 3. - Issued: 10.07.2014. Made: 01.07.2014. Effect: None. Territorial extent & classification: W. General. - In English and Welsh. Welsh title: Gorchymyn Deddf Addysg Bellach ac Uwch (Llywodraethu a Gwybodaeth) (Cymru) 2014(Cychwyn) 2014. - 4p.: 30 cm. - 978-0-348-10960-3 £4.25

The Government of Maintained Schools (Training Requirements for Governors) (Wales) (Amendment) Regulations 2014 No. 2014/2225 (W.214). - Enabling power: Education Act 2002, ss. 19, 210 & Education (Wales) Measure 2011, ss. 22 (3) (4), 32. - Issued: 01.09.2014. Made: 20.08.2014. Laid before the National Assembly for Wales: 22.08.2014. Coming into force: 19.09.2014. Effect: S.I. 2013/2124 (W.207) amended. Territorial extent & classification: W. General. - In English and Welsh. Welsh title: Rheoliadau Llywodraethu Ysgolion a Gynhelir Gofynion Hyfforddi ar gyfer Llywodraethwyr) (Cymru) (Diwygio) 2014. - 4p.: 30 cm. - 978-0-348-10987-0 £4.25

The Head Teacher's Report to Parents and Adult Pupils (Wales) (Amendment) Regulations 2014 No. 2014/1998 (W.199). - Enabling power: Education Act 1996; ss. 408, 569 (4) (5). - Issued: 08.08.2014. Made: 23.07.2014. Laid before the National Assembly for Wales: 28.07.2014. Coming into force: 01.09.2014. Effect: W.S.I. 2011/1943 (W.210) amended. Territorial extent & classification: W. General. - In English and Welsh. Welsh language title: Rheoliadau Adroddiad Pennaeth i Rieni a Disgyblion sy'n Oedolion (Cymru) (Diwygio) 2014. - 8p.: 30 cm. - 978-0-348-10979-5 £6.00

The Higher Education Funding Council for Wales (Supplementary Functions) Order 2014 No. 2014/1464 (W.145). - Enabling power: Further and Higher Education Act 1992, ss. 69 (5), 89 (4). - Issued: 13.06.2014. Made: 05.06.2014. Laid before the National Assembly for Wales: 09.06.2014. Coming into force: 31.08.2014. Effect: None. Territorial extent & classification: W. General. - In English and Welsh. Welsh title: Gorchymyn Cyngor Cyllido Addysg Uwch Cymru (Swyddogaethau Atodol) 2014. - 4p.: 30 cm. - 978-0-348-10953-5 £4.25

The National Curriculum (Assessment Arrangements for the Foundation Phase and the Second and Third Key Stages) (Wales) Order 2014 No. 2014/1999 (W.200). - Enabling power: Education Act 2002, ss. 108 (2) (b) (iii) (3) (c), 210. - Issued: 08.08.2014. Made: 23.07.2014. Laid before the National Assembly for Wales: 28.07.2014. Coming into force: 01.09.2014. Effect: None. Territorial extent & classification: W. General. - In English and Welsh. Welsh title: Gorchymyn y Cwricwlwm Cenedlaethol (Trefniadau Asesu ar gyfer y Cyfnod Sylfaen a'r Ail Gyfnod Allweddol a'r Trydydd Cyfnod Allweddol) (Cymru) 2014. - 4p.: 30 cm. - 978-0-348-10980-1 £4.25

The School Standards and Organisation (Wales) Act 2013 (Commencement No. 4 and Savings Provisions) Order 2014 No. 2014/178 (W.26) (C.5). - Enabling power: School Standards and Organisation (Wales) Act 2013, ss. 97, 100. Bringing into operation various provisions of this Act on 20.02.2014, in accord. with art 2- Issued: 06.02.2014. Made: 29.01.2014. Effect: None. Territorial extent & classification: W. General. - In English and Welsh. Welsh title: Gorchymyn Deddf Safonau a Threfniadaeth Ysgolion (Cymru) 2013 (Cychwyn Rhif 4 a Darpariaethau Arbed) 2014. - 8p.: 30 cm. - 978-0-348-10885-9 £4.00

The Staffing of Maintained Schools (Wales) (Amendment) Regulations 2014 No. 2014/1609 (W.165). - Enabling power: Education Act 1996, s. 569 (4) (5), sch. 1, para. 3 & Education Act 2002, ss. 19 (3), 21 (3), 34 (5), 35 (4) (5), 36 (4) (5), 210 (7) & Education (Wales) Measure 2011, ss. 18, 32. - Issued: 09.07.2014. Made: 18.06.2014. Laid before the National Assembly for Wales: 20.06.2014. Coming into force: 16.07.2014. Effect: S.I. 2006/873 (W.81) amended. Territorial extent & classification: W. General. - In English and Welsh. Welsh title: Rheoliadau Staffio Ysgolion a Gynhelir (Cymru) (Diwygio) 2014. - 16p.: 30 cm. - 978-0-348-10957-3 £6.00

The Student Fees (Amounts) (Wales) (Amendment) Regulations 2014 No. 2014/2071 (W.206). - Enabling power: Higher Education Act 2004, ss. 28 (6), 47 (5). - Issued: 04.09.2014. Made: 23.07.2014. Laid before the National Assembly for Wales: 04.08.2014. Coming into force: 31.08.2014. Effect: WSI. 2011/885 (W .129) amended. Territorial extent & classification: W. General. - In English and Welsh. Welsh title: Rheoliadau Ffioedd Myfyrwyr (Symiau) (Cymru) (Diwygio) 2014. - 8p.: 30 cm. - 978-0-348-10988-7 £4.25

Electoral Commission

The Electoral Commission (Limit on Public Awareness Expenditure) Order 2014 No. 2014/510. - Enabling power: Political Parties, Elections and Referendums Act 2000, ss. 13 (6), 156 (5) (b). - Issued: 12.03.2014. Made: 27.02.2014. Laid: 07.03.2014. Coming into force: 01.04.2014. Effect: S.I. 2002/505 revoked. Territorial extent & classification: UK. General. - 2p.: 30 cm. - 978-0-11-111114-7 £4.00

Electricity

The Contracts for Difference (Allocation) Regulations 2014 No. 2014/2011. - Enabling power: Energy Act 2013, ss. 6 (1), 10, 12 (1) to (3), 13 (2) (3) (8), 19. - Issued: 06.08.2014. Made: 31.07.2014. Coming into force: 01.08.2014 in accord. with reg. 1. Effect: None. Territorial extent & classification: E/W/S/NI. General. - Supersedes draft SI (ISBN 9780111117316) issued 03/07/14. - 40p.: 30 cm. - 978-0-11-111943-3 £10.00

The Contracts for Difference (Counterparty Designation) Order 2014 No. 2014/1709. - Enabling power: Energy Act 2013, s. 7. - Issued: 08.07.2014. Made: 01.07.2014. Coming into force: 01.08.2014. Effect: None. Territorial extent & classification: E/W/S/NI. General. - 2p.: 30 cm. - 978-0-11-111747-7 £4.25

The Contracts for Difference (Definition of Eligible Generator) Regulations 2014 No. 2014/2010. - Enabling power: Energy Act 2013, ss. 6 (1), 10 (3). - Issued: 06.08.2014. Made: 31.07.2014. Coming into force: 01.08.2014, in accord. with reg. 1. Effect: None. Territorial extent & classification: E/W/S/NI. - Supersedes draft (ISBN 9780111116807) issued 25.06.2014. - 8p.: 30 cm. - 978-0-11-111949-5 £6.00

The Contracts for Difference (Electricity Supplier Obligations) Regulations 2014 No. 2014/2014. - Enabling power: Energy Act 2013, ss. 6 (1) (5) (6), 9 (1) (2) (4) to (8) (10), 17, 18 (1) (2) (4), 19, 21 (1) (3), 22 (1), sch. 2, para. 16 (2). - Issued: 06.08.2014. Made: 31.07.2014. Coming into force: 01.08.2014 in accord. with reg. 1. Effect: None. Territorial extent & classification: E/W/S/NI. General. - Supersedes draft SI (ISBN 9780111116784) issued 25/06/14. - 40p.: 30 cm. - 978-0-11-111948-8 £10.00

The Contracts for Difference (Standard Terms) Regulations 2014 No. 2014/2012. - Enabling power: Energy Act 2013, ss. 6 (1), 11 (3), 14, 15 (2) (4), 16 (b), 19 (1) (2). - Issued: 06.08.2014. Made: 31.07.2014. Coming into force: 01.08.2014 in accord. with reg. 1. Effect: None. Territorial extent & classification: E/W/S. General. - Supersedes draft SI (ISBN 9780111116838) issued 25/06/14. - 12p.: 30 cm. - 978-0-11-111946-4 £6.00

The Electricity Act 1989 (Exemption from the Requirement for an Interconnector Licence) (Amendment) Order 2014 No. 2014/2587. - Enabling power: Electricity Act 1989, s. 5 (1) (8). - Issued: 29.09.2014. Made: 22.09.2014. Laid: 25.09.2014. Coming into force: 20.10.2014. Effect: S.I. 2006/2002 amended. Territorial extent & classification: E/W/S. General. - 2p.: 30 cm. - 978-0-11-112105-4 £4.25

The Electricity and Gas Appeals (Designation and Exclusion) Order 2014 No. 2014/1293. - Enabling power: Energy Act 2004, s. 173 (2) (b) (d) (7). - Issued: 27.05.2014. Made: 19.05.2014. Laid: 27.05.2014. Coming into force: 18.06.2014. Effect: S.I. 2005/1646; 2009/648; 2013/2429 revoked with savings. Territorial extent & classification: E/W/S. General. - 8p.: 30 cm. - 978-0-11-111513-8 £6.00

The Electricity and Gas (Billing) Regulations 2014 No. 2014/1648. - Enabling power: European Communities Act 1972, s. 2 (2). - Issued: 01.07.2014. Made: 24.06.2014. Laid: 26.06.2014. Coming into force: 17.07.2014. Effect: 1986 c.44; 1989 c.29 amended. Territorial extent & classification: E/W/S. General. - EC note: The modifications give effect to provisions on billing and billing information for gas and electricity consumption in articles 10 and 11 of and annex VII to Directive 2012/27/EU on energy efficiency. - 4p.: 30 cm. - 978-0-11-111709-5 £4.25

The Electricity and Gas (Energy Companies Obligation) (Amendment) (No. 2) Order 2014 No. 2014/3231. - Enabling power: Gas Act 1986, ss. 33BC, 33BD & Electricity Act 1989, ss. 41A, 41B & Utilities Act 2000, s. 103. - Issued: 11.12.2014. Made: 04.12.2014. Coming into force: 05.12.2014 in accord. with art. 1. Effect: S.I. 2012/3018 amended. Territorial extent & classification: E/W/S. General. - Supersedes draft S.I. (ISBN 9780111118962) issued 25.07.2014. - 16p.: 30 cm. - 978-0-11-112486-4 £6.00

The Electricity and Gas (Energy Companies Obligation) (Amendment) Order 2014 No. 2014/1131. - Enabling power: Gas Act 1986, ss. 33BC, 33BD & Electricity Act 1989, ss. 41A, 41B. - Issued: 07.05.2014. Made: 30.04.2014. Coming into force: 01.05.2014, in accord. with art. 1. Effect: S.I. 2012/3018 amended. Territorial extent & classification: E/W/S. General. - Supersedes draft SI (ISBN 9780111109229) issued 10.02.2014. - 8p.: 30 cm. - 978-0-11-111451-3 £4.25

The Electricity and Gas (Energy Companies Obligation) (Determination of Savings) (Amendment) Order 2014 No. 2014/2897. - Enabling power: Gas Act 1986, ss. 33BC, 33BD & Electricity Act 1989, ss. 41A, 41B. - Issued: 07.11.2014. Made: 03.11.2014. Laid: 05.11.2014. Coming into force: 01.12.2014. Effect: S.I. 2012/3018 amended. Territorial extent & classification: E/W/S. General. - Supersedes draft SI (ISBN 9780111109229) issued 10.02.2014. - 4p.: 30 cm. - 978-0-11-112287-7 £4.25

The Electricity and Gas (Energy Company Obligation) Order 2014 No. 2014/3219. - Enabling power: Gas Act 1986, ss. 33BC, 33BD & Electricity Act 1989, ss. 41A, 41B & Utilities Act 2000, ss. 103, 103A & European Communities Act 1972, s. 2 (2). - Issued: 10.12.2014. Made: 04.12.2014. Coming into force: In accord. with art. 1. Effect: None. Territorial extent & classification: E/W/S. General. - Supersedes draft S.I. (ISBN 9780111124758) issued 29/10/14. - 32p.: 30 cm. - 978-0-11-112475-8 £6.00

The Electricity and Gas (Internal Markets) Regulations 2014 No. 2014/3332. - Enabling power: European Communities Act 1972, s. 2 (2). - Issued: 29.12.2014. Made: 17.12.2014. Laid: 22.12.2014. Coming into force: 14.01.2015. Effect: 1986 c.44; 1989 c.29; S.I. 2011/2704 amended. Territorial extent & classification: E/W/S. General. - 4p.: 30 cm. - 978-0-11-112640-0 £4.25

The Electricity and Gas (Ownership Unbundling) Regulations 2014 No. 2014/3333. - Enabling power: European Communities Act 1972, s. 2 (2). - Issued: 29.12.2014. Made: 17.12.2014. Laid: 22.12.2014. Coming into force: 15.01.2015. Effect: S.I. 2011/2704 amended. Territorial extent & classification: E/W/S. General. - 4p.: 30 cm. - 978-0-11-112638-7 £4.25

The Electricity Capacity Regulations 2014 No. 2014/2043. - Enabling power: Energy Act 2013, ss. 27 to 33, 34 (3) to (6), 36, 38 (a), 40 (1), 63. - Issued: 06.08.2014. Made: 31.07.2014. Coming into force: In accord. with reg. 1. Effect: 1989 c.29 partially repealed (01.01.2015). Territorial extent & classification: E/W/S. General. - Supersedes draft SI (ISBN 9780111116852) issued 25/06/14. - 68p.: 30 cm. - 978-0-11-111944-0 £11.00

ELECTRICITY, ENGLAND AND WALES

The Electricity Capacity (Supplier Payment etc.) Regulations 2014 No. 2014/3354. - Enabling power: Energy Act 2013, ss. 27, 28, 30 to 33, 36, 40 (1). - Issued: 30.12.2014. Made: 17.12.2014. Coming into force: In accord. with reg. 1. Effect: S.I. 2014/2043 amended. Territorial extent & classification: E/W/S. General. - Supersedes draft SI (ISBN 9780111123119) issued 13/11/14 - 28p.: 30 cm. - 978-0-11-112647-9 £6.00

The Electricity (Exemption from the Requirement for a Generation Licence) (Berry Burn) Order 2014 No. 2014/94. - Enabling power: Electricity Act 1989, s. 5. - Issued: 24.01.2014. Made: 20.01.2014. Laid: 22.01.2014. Coming into force: 19.02.2014. Effect: None. Territorial extent & classification: E/W/S. General. - 2p.: 30 cm. - 978-0-11-110862-8 £4.00

The Electricity Market Reform (General) Regulations 2014 No. 2014/2013. - Enabling power: Energy Act 2013, ss. 6 (1), 12 (3), 16, 19, 63. - Issued: 06.08.2014. Made: 31.07.2014. Coming into force: 01.08.2014, in accord. with reg. 1. Effect: None. Territorial extent & classification: E/W/S/NI. General. - Supersedes draft (ISBN 9780111116791) issued 25.06.2014. - 12p.: 30 cm. - 978-0-11-111947-1 £6.00

The Feed-in Tariffs (Amendment) (No. 2) Order 2014 No. 2014/2865. - Enabling power: Energy Act 2008, ss. 43 (3) (a), 104 (2). - Issued: 03.10.2014. Made: 27.10.2014. Laid: 29.10.2014. Coming into force: 01.01.2015. Effect: S.I. 2012/2782 amended. Territorial extent & classification: E/W/S. General. - 4p.: 30 cm. - 978-0-11-112252-5 £4.25

The Feed-in Tariffs (Amendment) Order 2014 No. 2014/1601. - Enabling power: Energy Act 2008, ss. 43 (3) (a), 104 (2). - Issued: 24.06.2014. Made: 11.06.2014. Laid: 20.06.2014. Coming into force: 14.07.2014. Effect: S.I. 2012/2782 amended. Territorial extent & classification: E/W/S. General. - 2p.: 30 cm. - 978-0-11-111670-8 £4.25

The Gas and Electricity Regulated Providers (Redress Scheme) (Amendment) Order 2014 No. 2014/2378. - Enabling power: Consumers, Estate Agents and Redress Act 2007, s. 47 (1) to (3). - Issued: 12.09.2014. Made: 01.07.2014. Laid: 08.09.2014. Coming into force: 08.08.2014. Effect: None. Territorial extent & classification: E/W/S. General. - 2p.: 30 cm. - 978-0-11-112037-8 £4.25

The Power Purchase Agreement Scheme Regulations 2014 No. 2014/2511. - Enabling power: Energy Act 2013, s. 51 (1) to (5). - Issued: 24.09.2014. Made: 17.09.2014. Laid: 19.09.2014. Coming into force: In accord. with reg 1 (2) (3). Effect: None. Territorial extent & classification: E/W/S. General- 24p.: 30 cm. - 978-0-11-112095-8 £6.00

The Renewables Obligation Closure Order 2014 No. 2014/2388. - Enabling power: Electricity Act 1989, ss. 32K, 32LA. - Issued: 12.09.2014. Made: 08.09.2014. Coming into force: 09.09.2014 in accord. with art. 1. Effect: None. Territorial extent & classification: E/W/S. General. - Supersedes draft S.I. (ISBN 9780111117262) issued 02.07.2014. - 12p.: 30 cm. - 978-0-11-112047-7 £6.00

The Warm Home Discount (Amendment) Regulations 2014 No. 2014/695. - Enabling power: Energy Act 2010, ss. 9, 31 (5) (6). - Issued: 24.03.2014. Made: 13.03.2014. Coming into force: 14.03.2014, in accord. with reg. 1. Effect: S.I. 2011/1033 amended. Territorial extent & classification: E/W/S. General. - Supersedes draft S.I. (ISBN 9780111108482) issued 22.01.2014. - 2p.: 30 cm. - 978-0-11-111240-3 £4.00

Electricity, England and Wales

The Renewables Obligation (Amendment) Order 2014 No. 2014/893. - Enabling power: Electricity Act 1989, ss. 32 (1) (2), 32A (1) (2) (f) (g), 32C, 32J (3), 32K (1) (3), 32M (1). - Issued: 07.04.2014. Made: 31.03.2014. Coming into force: 01.04.2014. Effect: S.I. 2009/785 amended. Territorial extent & classification: E/W. General. - Supersedes draft SI (ISBN 9780111109311) issued 12/03/14. - 24p.: 30 cm. - 978-0-11-111358-5 £6.00

Electronic communications

The Audiovisual Media Services Regulations 2014 No. 2014/2916. - Enabling power: European Communities Act 1972, s. 2 (2). - Issued: 11.11.2014. Made: 04.11.2014. Laid: 06.11.2014. Coming into force: 01.12.2014. Effect: 2003 c.21 amended. Territorial extent & classification: E/W/S/NI. General. - 4p.: 30 cm. - 978-0-11-112295-2 £4.25

The Communications Act 2003 (Disclosure of Information) Order 2014 No. 2014/1825. - Enabling power: Communications Act 2003, s. 393 (3) (i) (4) (c). - Issued: 17.07.2014. Made: 09.07.2014. Coming into force: 10.07.2014 in accord. with art. 1. Effect: None. Territorial extent & classification: E/W/S/NI. General. - Supersedes draft SI (ISBN 9780111112953) issued 02.04.14. - 4p.: 30 cm. - 978-0-11-111799-6 £4.25

The Data Retention Regulations 2014 No. 2014/2042. - Enabling power: Data Retention and Investigatory Powers Act 2014, ss. 1 (3) (4) (5) (7), 2 (3) (4). - Issued: 06.08.2014. Made: 30.07.2014. Coming into force: In accord. with reg. 1 (2). Effect: None. Territorial extent & classification: E/W/S/NI. General. - 12p.: 30 cm. - 978-0-11-111942-6 £6.00

The Mobile Roaming (European Communities) (Amendment) Regulations 2014 No. 2014/2715. - Enabling power: European Communities Act 1972, s. 2 (2). - Issued: 15.10.2014. Made: 07.10.2014. Laid: 10.10.2014. Coming into force: 01.11.2013. Effect: S.I. 2007/1933 amended. Territorial extent & classification: E/W/S/NI. General. - 4p.: 30 cm. - 978-0-11-112151-1 £4.25

The Wireless Telegraphy (Exemption and Amendment) (Amendment) Regulations 2014 No. 2014/1484. - Enabling power: Wireless Telegraphy Act 2006, s. 8 (3). - Issued: 12.06.2014. Made: 06.06.2014. Coming into force: 27.06.2014. Effect: S.I. 2010/2512 amended. Territorial extent & classification: E/W/S/NI. General. - 4p.: 30 cm. - 978-0-11-111617-3 £4.25

The Wireless Telegraphy (Licence Charges) (Amendment) Regulations 2014 No. 2014/1295. - Enabling power: Wireless Telegraphy Act 2006, ss. 12, 13 (2), 122 (7). - Issued: 28.05.2014. Made: 21.05.2014. Coming into force: 01.06.2014. Effect: S.I. 2011/1128 amended. Territorial extent & classification: E/W/S/NI. General. - 4p.: 30 cm. - 978-0-11-111515-2 £4.25

The Wireless Telegraphy (Limitation on Number of Licences) Order 2014 No. 2014/774. - Enabling power: Wireless Telegraphy Act 2006, s. 29 (1) to (3). - Issued: 25.03.2014. Made: 19.03.2014. Coming into force: 09.04.2014. Effect: S.I. 2003/1902; 2006/2786 revoked. Territorial extent & classification: E/W/S/NI. General. - 32p.: 30 cm. - 978-0-11-111252-6 £5.75

The Wireless Telegraphy (Mobile Communication Services on Aircraft) (Exemption) Regulations 2014 No. 2014/953. - Enabling power: Wireless Telegraphy Act 2006, s. 8 (3). - Issued: 15.04.2014. Made: 09.04.2014. Coming into force: 30.04.2014. Effect: S.I. 2008/2427 revoked. Territorial extent & classification: E/W/S/NI. General. - EC note: These Regulations give effect to EU obligations of the UK contained in the Commission Decision 2013/654/EU of 12th November 2013 to include additional access technologies and frequency bands for mobile communications services on aircraft. - 8p.: 30 cm. - 978-0-11-111404-9 £6.00

Employment

The Scotland Act 1998 (Agency Arrangements) (Specification) Order 2014 No. 2014/1892. - Enabling power: Scotland Act 1998, ss. 93 (1), 113 (3). - Issued: 23.07.2014. Made: 16.07.2014. Laid before Parliament and Scottish Parliament: 23.07.2014. Coming into force: 03.11.2014. Effect: None. Territorial extent & classification: E/W/S. General. - 4p.: 30 cm. - 978-0-11-111854-2 £4.25

Employment agencies, etc.

The Conduct of Employment Agencies and Employment Businesses (Amendment) Regulations 2014 No. 2014/3351. - Enabling power: Employment Agencies Act 1973, ss. 5 (1), 12 (3). - Issued: 22.12.2014. Made: 15.12.2014. Coming into force: In accord. with reg. 1. Effect: S.I. 2003/3319 amended. Territorial extent & classification: E/W/S. General. - Supersedes draft S.I. (ISBN 97801111232560) issued 17/11/14. - 4p.: 30 cm. - 978-0-11-112644-8 £4.25

Employment and training

The Industrial Training Levy (Engineering Construction Industry Training Board) Order 2014 No. 2014/791. - Enabling power: Industrial Training Act 1982, ss. 11 (2) (2D), 12 (3) (4). - Issued: 27.03.2014. Made: 20.03.2014. Coming into force: 21.03.2014. Effect: None. Territorial extent & classification: E/W/S. General. - Supersedes draft SI (ISBN 9780111108345) issued 17.01.2014. - 8p.: 30 cm. - 978-0-11-111262-5 £5.75

Employment tribunals

The Employment Tribunals (Constitution and Rules of Procedure) (Amendment) (No. 2) Regulations 2014 No. 2014/611. - Enabling power: Employment Tribunals Act 1996, s. 71 (1) (30 (j), 41 (4). - Issued: 19.03.2014. Made: 12.03.2014. Laid: 14.03.2014. Coming into force: 06.04.2014. Effect: S.I. 2013/1237 amended. Territorial extent & classification: E/W/S. General. - 2p.: 30 cm. - 978-0-11-111213-7 £4.00

The Employment Tribunals (Constitution and Rules of Procedure) (Amendment) (No. 3) Regulations 2014 No. 2014/787. - Enabling power: Employment Tribunals Act 1996, ss. 7, 41 (4). - Issued: 26.03.2014. Made: 19.03.2014. Laid: 21.03.2014. Coming into force: 05.04.2014. Effect: S.I. 2014/271 amended. Territorial extent & classification: E/W/S. General. - This Statutory Instrument has been made in consequence of defects in S.I. 2014/271(ISBN 9780111109762) and is being issued free of charge to all known recipients of that Statutory Instrument. - 2p.: 30 cm. - 978-0-11-111257-1 £4.00

The Employment Tribunals (Constitution and Rules of Procedure) (Amendment) Regulations 2014 No. 2014/271. - Enabling power: Employment Tribunals Act 1996, ss. 7, 41 (4). - Issued: 18.02.2014. Made: 11.02.2014. Laid: 13.02.2014. Coming into force: 06.04.2014. Effect: S.I. 2013/1237 amended. Territorial extent & classification: E/W/S. General. - Defects in this SI have been corrected by SI 2014/787 (ISBN 9780111112571) which is being issued free of charge to all known recipients of 2014/271. - 4p.: 30 cm. - 978-0-11-110976-2 £4.00

The Employment Tribunals (Early Conciliation: Exemptions and Rules of Procedure) (Amendment) Regulations 2014 No. 2014/847. - Enabling power: Employment Tribunals Act 1996, ss. 18A (1) (11), 41 (4). - Issued: 03.04.2014. Made: 27.03.2014. Laid: 28.03.2014. Coming into force: 20.04.2014. Effect: S.I. 2014/254 amended. Territorial extent & classification: E/W/S. General. - 2p.: 30 cm. - 978-0-11-111301-1 £4.00

The Employment Tribunals (Early Conciliation: Exemptions and Rules of Procedure) Regulations 2014 No. 2014/254. - Enabling power: Employment Tribunals Act 1996, ss. 18A (7) (11) (12), 41 (4). - Issued: 18.02.2014. Made: 11.02.2014. Laid: 13.02.2014. Coming into force: 06.03.2014 for reg. 4; 06.04.2014 for all other purposes. Effect: None. Territorial extent & classification: E/W/S. General. - With correction slip dated December 2014. - 8p.: 30 cm. - 978-0-11-110977-9 £4.00

The Energy Act 2013 (Improvement and Prohibition Notices Appeals) Regulations 2014 No. 2014/468. - Enabling power: Energy Act 2013, s. 113, sch. 8, para. 6. - Issued: 10.03.2014. Made: 03.03.2014. Laid: 10.03.2014. Coming into force: 01.04.2014. Effect: S.I. 2013/1237, 1893 amended. Territorial extent & classification: E/W/S/NI. General. - 4p.: 30 cm. - 978-0-11-111089-8 £4.00

Energy

The Domestic Renewable Heat Incentive Scheme Regulations 2014 No. 2014/928. - Enabling power: Energy Act 2008, ss. 100 (1) (2), 104 (2). - Issued: 25.04.2014. Made: 08.04.2014. Coming into force: 09.04.2014, in accord. with reg. 1. Effect: S.I. 2011/2860 amended. Territorial extent & classification: E/W/S, General. - Supersedes draft SI (ISBN 9780111111192) issued 11.03.2014. - 60p.: 30 cm. - 978-0-11-111425-4 £10.00

The Energy Act 2004 (Commencement No. 11) Order 2014 No. 2014/1460 (C.58). - Enabling power: Energy Act 2004, s. 198 (2). Bringing into operation various provisions of the 2004 Act on 10.06.2014, in accord. with art. 2. - Issued: 11.06.2014. Made: 04.06.2014. Effect: None. Territorial extent & classification: E/W/S. General. - 4p.: 30 cm. - 978-0-11-111612-8 £4.25

The Energy Act 2004 (Designation of Publicly Owned Companies) (Revocation) Order 2014 No. 2014/1391. - Enabling power: Energy Act 2004, s. 39 (3) (b) (4). - Issued: 09.06.2014. Made: 02.06.2014. Laid: 05.06.2014. Coming into force: 30.06.2014. Effect: S.I. 2007/3479 revoked. Territorial extent & classification: E/W/S/NI. General. - 2p.: 30 cm. - 978-0-11-111564-0 £4.25

The Energy Act 2008 (Commencement No. 6) Order 2014 No. 2014/1461 (C.59). - Enabling power: Energy Act 2008, s. 110 (2) (3). Bringing into operation various provisions of the 2008 Act on 10.06.2014, in accord. with reg. 2. - Issued: 11.06.2014. Made: 04.06.2014. Effect: None. Territorial extent & classification: E/W/S/NI. General. - 4p.: 30 cm. - 978-0-11-111613-5 £4.25

The Energy Act 2013 (Commencement No. 1) Order 2014 No. 2014/251 (C.9). - Enabling power: Energy Act 2013, s. 156 (1) (4). Bringing into operation various provisions of the 2013 Act on 18.02.2014; 10.03.2014; 01.04.2014. - Issued: 14.02.2014. Made: 10.02.2014. Effect: None. Territorial extent & classification: E/W/S. General. - 2p.: 30 cm. - 978-0-11-110944-1 £4.00

The Energy Act 2013 (Office for Nuclear Regulation) (Consequential Amendments, Transitional Provisions and Savings) Order 2014 No. 2014/469. - Enabling power: Energy Act 2013, ss. 113, 114, 116. - Issued: 13.03.2014. Made: 03.03.2014. Laid: 10.03.2014. Coming into force: 01.04.2014. Effect: 14 Acts & 67 Statutory instruments amended & S.I. 1974/2056; 2003/403; 2005/1654; 2006/557, 2815; 2011/1885 partially revoked & S.I. 2002/2533 revoked. Territorial extent & classification: E/W/S/NI. General. - Partially revoked by SI 2015/595 (9780111134399) in relation to E & partially revoked by SI 2015/462 (ISBN 9780111131541) in re to E/W/S. - 88p.: 30 cm. - 978-0-11-111130-7 £15.50

The Energy Efficiency (Building Renovation and Reporting) Regulations 2014 No. 2014/952. - Enabling power: European Communities Act 1972, s. 2 (2), sch. 2, para. 1A (1). - Issued: 15.04.2014. Made: 08.04.2014. Laid: 09.04.2014. Coming into force: In accord. with reg. 1. Effect: None. Territorial extent & classification: E/W/S/NI. General. - EC note: These regs transpose art. 4 & 24 of Directive 2012/27/EU on energy efficiency, amending Directives 2009/125/EC and 2010/30/EU and repealing Directives 2004/8/EC and 2006/32/EC. - 4p.: 30 cm. - 978-0-11-111403-2 £4.25

The Energy Efficiency (Encouragement, Assessment and Information) Regulations 2014 No. 2014/1403. - Enabling power: European Communities Act 1972, s. 2 (2), sch. 2, para. 1A (1). - Issued: 09.06.2014. Made: 02.06.2014. Laid before Parliament: 05.06.2014. Coming into force: 26.06.2014. Effect: S.I. 2007/292; 2013/3220; 2014/952 amended. Territorial extent & classification: E/W/S/NI. General. - 12p.: 30 cm. - 978-0-11-111571-8 £6.00

The Energy Savings Opportunity Scheme Regulations 2014 No. 2014/1643. - Enabling power: European Communities Act 1972, s. 2 (2). - Issued: 01.07.2014. Made: 24.06.2014. Laid: 26.06.2014. Coming into force: 17.07.2014. Effect: None. Territorial extent & classification: E/W/S/NI. General. - EC note: Implement art. 8 (4) (5) (6) of Directive 2012/27/EU on energy efficiency. - 34p.: 30 cm. - 978-0-11-111708-8 £10.00

The Heat Network (Metering and Billing) Regulations 2014 No. 2014/3120. - Enabling power: European Communities Act 1972, s. 2 (2). - Issued: 01.12.2014. Made: 20.11.2014. Laid: 26.11.2014. Coming into force: In accord. with reg. 1. Effect: None Territorial extent & classification: E/W/S/NI. General. - These Regs implement arts 9 (1) (3), 10, 11 of Directive 2012/27/EU on energy efficiency amending Directives 2009/125/EC and 2010/30/EU. - 20p.: 30 cm. - 978-0-11-112398-0 £6.00

The Renewable Heat Incentive Scheme (Amendment) Regulations 2014 No. 2014/1413. - Enabling power: Energy Act 2008, ss. 100, 104. - Issued: 09.06.2014. Made: 27.05.2014. Coming into force: 28.05.2014 in accord. with reg. 1. Effect: S.I. 2011/2860 amended. Territorial extent & classification: E. General. - Supersedes draft SI (ISBN 9780111113936) issued 11.04.14. - 36p.: 30 cm. - 978-0-11-111572-5 £10.00

Energy conservation

The Ecodesign for Energy-Related Products and Energy Information (Amendment) Regulations 2014 No. 2014/1290. - Enabling power: European Communities Act 1972, s. 2 (2). - Issued: 28.05.2014. Made: 19.05.2014. Laid: 27.05.2014. Coming into force: 01.07.2014. Effect: S.I. 2010/2617; 2011/1524 amended. Territorial extent & classification: UK. General. - EC note: These Regulations partially implement Commission Regulations nos. 617/2013, 666/2013, 801/2013, 813/2013, 814/2013 and 66/2014 and Commission Delegated Regulations (EU) nos. 665/2013, 811/2013, 812/2013, and 65/2014. - 4p.: 30 cm. - 978-0-11-111511-4 £4.25

The Green Deal (Qualifying Energy Improvements) (Amendment) Order 2014 No. 2014/2020. - Enabling power: Energy Act 2011, s. 1 (4) (b). - Issued: 04.08.2014. Made: 29.07.2014. Coming into force: 30.07.2014, in accord. with art. 1. Effect: S.I. 2012/2105 amended. Territorial extent & classification: E/W/S. General. - Supersedes draft (ISBN 9780111116517) published 17.06.2014. - 2p.: 30 cm. - 978-0-11-111936-5 £4.25

Energy, England

The Fuel Poverty (England) Regulations 2014 No. 2014/3220. - Enabling power: Warm Homes and Energy Conservation Act 2000, s. 1A. - Issued: 10.12.2014. Made: 04.12.2014. Coming into force: In accord. with reg. 1. Effect: None. Territorial extent & classification: E. General. - Supersedes draft S.I. (ISBN 9780111122198) issued 28/10/14. - 2p.: 30 cm. - 978-0-11-112476-5 £4.25

Enforcement, England and Wales

The Crime and Courts Act 2013 (Commencement No. 9) Order 2014 No. 2014/830 (C.34). - Enabling power: Crime and Courts Act 2013, s. 61 (3). Bringing into operation various provisions of the 2013 Act on 06.04.2014. - Issued: 01.04.2014. Made: 24.03.2014. Effect: None. Territorial extent & classification: E/W. General. - 4p.: 30 cm. - 978-0-11-111285-4 £4.00

Enforcement, England and Wales: Commercial rent arrears recovery

The Certification of Enforcement Agents Regulations 2014 No. 2014/421. - Enabling power: Tribunals, Courts and Enforcement Act 2007. ss. 64, 90. - Issued: 04.03.2014. Made: 25.02.2014. Laid: 28.02.2014. Coming into force: 06.04.2014. Effect: None. Territorial extent & classification: E/W. General. - With correction slip dated October 2014. - 32p.: 30 cm. - 978-0-11-111037-9 £9.75

The Taking Control of Goods (Fees) Regulations 2014 No. 2014/1. - Enabling power: Tribunals, Courts and Enforcement Act 2007, s. 90, sch. 12. paras 13 (3), 42. 50 (4) (7), 62. - Issued: 10.01.2014. Made: 04.01.2014. Laid: 09.01.2014. Coming into force: 06.04.2014. Effect: None. Territorial extent & classification: E/W. General. - 12p.: 30 cm. - 978-0-11-110801-7 £5.75

The Tribunals, Courts and Enforcement Act 2007 (Consequential, Transitional and Saving Provision) Order 2014 No. 2014/600. - Enabling power: Tribunals, Courts and Enforcement Act 2007, s. 145 & Law of Distress Amendment Act 1888, s. 8. - Issued: 19.03.2014. Made: 12.03.2014. Laid: 14.03.2014. Coming into force: In accord. with reg. 2. Effect: 9 SIs amended & 5 SIs revoked in relation to E/W & 5 SIs revoked in part & 14 SIs revoked. Territorial extent & classification: E/W. General. - With correction slip dated October 2014. - 20p.: 30 cm. - 978-0-11-111200-7 £5.75

Enforcement, England and Wales: Taking control of goods

The Certification of Enforcement Agents Regulations 2014 No. 2014/421. - Enabling power: Tribunals, Courts and Enforcement Act 2007. ss. 64, 90. - Issued: 04.03.2014. Made: 25.02.2014. Laid: 28.02.2014. Coming into force: 06.04.2014. Effect: None. Territorial extent & classification: E/W. General. - With correction slip dated October 2014. - 32p.: 30 cm. - 978-0-11-111037-9 £9.75

The Taking Control of Goods (Fees) Regulations 2014 No. 2014/1. - Enabling power: Tribunals, Courts and Enforcement Act 2007, s. 90, sch. 12. paras 13 (3), 42. 50 (4) (7), 62. - Issued: 10.01.2014. Made: 04.01.2014. Laid: 09.01.2014. Coming into force: 06.04.2014. Effect: None. Territorial extent & classification: E/W. General. - 12p.: 30 cm. - 978-0-11-110801-7 £5.75

The Tribunals, Courts and Enforcement Act 2007 (Consequential, Transitional and Saving Provision) Order 2014 No. 2014/600. - Enabling power: Tribunals, Courts and Enforcement Act 2007, s. 145 & Law of Distress Amendment Act 1888, s. 8. - Issued: 19.03.2014. Made: 12.03.2014. Laid: 14.03.2014. Coming into force: In accord. with reg. 2. Effect: 9 SIs amended & 5 SIs revoked in relation to E/W & 5 SIs revoked in part & 14 SIs revoked. Territorial extent & classification: E/W. General. - With correction slip dated October 2014. - 20p.: 30 cm. - 978-0-11-111200-7 £5.75

Environmental protection

The Marine Licensing (Application Fees) (Amendment) Regulations 2014 No. 2014/950. - Enabling power: Marine and Coastal Access Act 2009, ss. 67 (2) (3), 316 (1) (b). - Issued: 15.04.2014. Made: 08.04.2014. Laid: 10.04.2014. Coming into force: 01.05.2014. Effect: S.I. 2014/615 amended. Territorial extent & classification: E/W/S/NI. General. - This Statutory Instrument has been made in consequence of defects in SI 2014/615 (ISBN 9780111112175) and is being issued free of charge to all known recipients of that Statutory Instrument. - 2p.: 30 cm. - 978-0-11-111402-5 £4.25

The Marine Licensing (Application Fees) Regulations 2014 No. 2014/615. - Enabling power: Marine and Coastal Access Act 2009, ss. 67 (2) (3), 316 (1) (b). - Issued: 19.03.2014. Made: 13.03.2014. Laid: 14.03.2014. Coming into force: 06.04.2014. Effect: S.I. 2011/564 revoked with savings. Territorial extent & classification: E/W/S/NI. General. - Defects in this SI have been corrected by SI 2014/950 (ISBN 9780111114025) which is being sent free of charge to all known recipients of 2014/615. - 8p.: 30 cm. - 978-0-11-111217-5 £5.75

The Non-Road Mobile Machinery (Emission of Gaseous and Particulate Pollutants) (Amendment) Regulations 2014 No. 2014/1309. - Enabling power: European Communities Act 1972, s. 2 (2). - Issued: 29.05.2014. Made: 20.05.2014. Laid: 28.05.2014. Coming into force: 24.06.2014. Effect: S.I. 1999/1053 amended. Territorial extent & classification: E/W/S/NI. General. - EC note: These regs amend the 1999 Regulations so as to implement the amendments made by Directive 2012/46/EU. - 4p.: 30 cm. - 978-0-11-111516-9 £4.25

The Producer Responsibility Obligations (Packaging Waste) (Amendment) Regulations 2014 No. 2014/2890. - Enabling power: Environment Act 1995, ss. 93, 94. - Issued: 06.11.2014. Made: 29.10.2014. Laid: 03.11.2014. Coming into force: 24.11.2014. Effect: S.I. 2007/871 amended. Territorial extent & classification: E/W/S. General. - 2p.: 30 cm. - 978-0-11-112282-2 £4.25

The REACH Enforcement (Amendment) Regulations 2014 No. 2014/2882. - Enabling power: European Communities Act 1972, s. 2 (2). - Issued: 05.11.2014. Made: 25.10.2014. Laid: 31.10.2014. Coming into force: 01.12.2014. Effect: S.I. 2008/2852 amended. Territorial extent & classification: E/W/S/NI. General. - EC note: These Regulations provide for the enforcement of Regulation (EC) 1907/2006, as corrected, concerning the Registration, Evaluation, Authorisation and Restriction of Chemicals (REACH). - 4p.: 30 cm. - 978-0-11-112268-6 £4.25

The Transfrontier Shipment of Waste (Amendment) Regulations 2014 No. 2014/861. - Enabling power: European Communities Act 1972, s. 2 (2). - Issued: 03.04.2014. Made: 26.03.2014. Laid: 03.04.2014. Coming into force: 01.05.2014. Effect: S.I. 2007/1711 amended & partially revoked. Territorial extent & classification: E/W/S/NI. General. - 16p.: 30 cm. - 978-0-11-111317-2 £5.75

The Waste Electrical and Electronic Equipment and Restriction of the Use of Certain Hazardous Substances in Electrical and Electronic Equipment (Amendment) Regulations 2014 No. 2014/1771. - Enabling power: European Communities Act 1972, s. 2 (2). - Issued: 10.07.2014. Made: 02.07.2014. Laid: 04.07.2014. Coming into force: 25.07.2014. Effect: S.I. 2012/3032; 2013/3113 amended. Territorial extent & classification: E/W/S/NI. General. - This Statutory Instrument has been printed to correct errors in S.I. 2013/3113 (ISBN 9780111106921) and is being issued free of charge to all known recipients of that Statutory Instrument. EC note: These Regulations amend the regulations implementing Council Directive 2012/19/EU on waste electrical and electronic equipment. - 8p.: 30 cm. - 978-0-11-111760-6 £6.00

Environmental protection, England

The Environmental Permitting (England and Wales) (Amendment) (England) Regulations 2014 No. 2014/2852. - Enabling power: Pollution Prevention and Control Act 1999, ss. 2, 7 (9). sch. 1. - Issued: 30.10.2014. Made: 23.10.2014. Laid: 27.10.2014. Coming into force: 01.01.2014. Effect: S.I. 2010/675 amended. Territorial extent & classification: E/W. General. - 8p.: 30 cm. - 978-0-11-112238-9 £6.00

Environmental protection, England and Wales

The Anti-social Behaviour, Crime and Policing Act 2014 (Commencement No. 7, Saving and Transitional Provisions) (Amendment) Order 2014 No. 2014/2754 (C.121). - Enabling power: Anti-social Behaviour, Crime and Policing Act 2014, s. 185 (1) (7). - Issued: 20.10.2014. Made: 14.10.2014. Coming into force: 20.10.2014. Effect: S.I. 2014/2590 (C.113) amended. Territorial extent & classification: E/W. General. - This Statutory Instrument corrects errors in SI. 2014/2590 (C.113) which was made on 24th September 2014 and published on 29th September 2014 (ISBN 9780111121078). It is being issued free of charge to all known recipients of that Statutory Instrument. - 4p.: 30 cm. - 978-0-11-112185-6 £4.25

The Anti-social Behaviour, Crime and Policing Act 2014 (Commencement No. 7, Saving and Transitional Provisions) Order 2014 No. 2014/2590 (C.113). - Enabling power: Anti-social Behaviour, Crime and Policing Act 2014, s. 185 (1) (7). Bringing into operation various provisions of the 2014 Act on 20.10.2014, in accord. with art. 2. - Issued: 01.10.2014. Made: 24.09.2014. Effect: None. Territorial extent & classification: E/W. General. - 8p.: 30 cm. - 978-0-11-112107-8 £6.00

The Anti-social Behaviour, Crime and Policing Act 2014 (Publication of Public Spaces Protection Orders) Regulations 2014 No. 2014/2591. - Enabling power: Anti-social Behaviour, Crime and Policing Act 2014, ss. 59 (8), 60 (3) (b), 61 (5) (6). - Issued: 01.10.2014. Made: 24.09.2014. Laid: 26.09.2014. Coming into force: 20.10.2014, in accord. with art. 1. Effect: None. Territorial extent & classification: E/W. General. - 2p.: 30 cm. - 978-0-11-112108-5 £4.25

The Environmental Permitting (England and Wales) (Amendment) Regulations 2014 No. 2014/255. - Enabling power: Pollution Prevention and Control Act 1999, s. 2, sch. 1. - Issued: 17.02.2014. Made: 10.02.2014. Laid before Parliament and the National Assembly for Wales: 11.02.2014. Coming into force: In accord. with reg. 1 (2) and (3). Effect: S.I. 2010/675; WSI 2013/755 (W.90) amended. Territorial extent & classification: E/W. General. - This Statutory Instrument has been partly made in consequence of defects in S.I. 2013/390 (ISBN 9780111535035) and is being issued free of charge to all known recipients of that Statutory Instrument. - 16p.: 30 cm. - 978-0-11-110949-6 £5.75

The Sulphur Content of Liquid Fuels (England and Wales) (Amendment) Regulations 2014 No. 2014/1975. - Enabling power: European Communities Act 1972, s. 2 (2). - Issued: 30.07.2014. Made: 21.07.2014. Laid before Parliament & the National assembly for Wales: 25.07.2014. Coming into force: 29.08.2014. Effect: S.I 2007/79 amended. Territorial extent & classification: E/W. General. - These Regulations implement matters concerning heavy fuel oil and gas oil (except marine fuel) in Council Directive 1999/32/EC relating to a reduction in the sulphur content of certain liquid fuels. - 8p.: 30 cm. - 978-0-11-111928-0 £6.00

The Waste (England and Wales) (Amendment) Regulations 2014 No. 2014/656. - Enabling power: European Communities Act 1972, s. 2 (2) & Control of Pollution (Amendment) Act 1989, ss. 5 (3) (b) (4) (b), 8 (2) & Pollution Prevention and Control Act 1999, s. 2, sch. 1. - Issued: 20.03.2014. Made: 14.03.2014. Laid: 14.03.2014. Coming into force: 06.04.2014. Effect: S.I. 2011/988 amended. Territorial extent & classification: E/W. General. - EC note: Transpose, for England and Wales, Directive 2008/98/EC on waste. - 8p.: 30 cm. - 978-0-11-111229-8 £4.00

Equality

The Enterprise and Regulatory Reform Act 2013 (Commencement No. 6, Transitional Provisions and Savings) Order 2014 No. 2014/416 (C.17). - Enabling power: Enterprise and Regulatory Reform Act 2013, ss. 100, 103 (3). Bringing into operation various provisions of the 2013 Act on 01.04.2014 & 06.04.2014, in ac cord. with arts 2, 3. - Issued: 10.03.2014. Made: 03.03.2014. Effect: None. Territorial extent & classification: E/W/S/NI. General. - 16p.: 30 cm. - 978-0-11-111081-2 £5.75

The Equality Act 2010 (Equal Pay Audits) Regulations 2014 No. 2014/2559. - Enabling power: Equality Act 2010, ss. 139A, 207 (1). - Issued: 26.09.2014. Made: 22.09.2014. Coming into force: 01.10.2014. Effect: None. Territorial extent & classification: E/W/S. General. - Supersedes draft (ISBN 978011117330) issued on 04.07.2014. - 12p.: 30 cm. - 978-0-11-112103-0 £6.00

Equal opportunities and human rights

The Equality Act 2006 (Dissolution of the Disability Committee) Order 2014 No. 2014/406. - Enabling power: Equality Act 2006, s. 39 (2) (c). - Issued: 03.03.2014. Made: 23.02.2014. Laid: 26.02.2014. Coming into force: 01.04.2014. Effect: 2006 c.3 partially repealed. Territorial extent & classification: E/W/S. General. - 2p.: 30 cm. - 978-0-11-111025-6 £4.00

European Communities, Wales

The Structural Funds (Welsh Ministers) Regulations 2014 No. 2014/92. - Enabling power: European Communities Act 1972, s. 2 (2). - Issued: 24.01.2014. Made: 17.01.2014. Laid: 21.01.2014. Coming into force: 11.02.2014. Effect: None. Territorial extent & classification: W. General. - 4p.: 30 cm. - 978-0-11-110859-8 £4.00

European Union

The European Communities (Designation) (No. 2) Order 2014 No. 2014/1890. - Enabling power: European Communities Act 1972, s. 2 (2) & Government of Wales Act 2006, s. 59 (1). - Issued: 23.07.2014. Made: 16.07.2014. Laid: 23.07.2014. Coming into force: 18.08.2014. Effect: S.I. 2001/3495 partially revoked. Territorial extent & classification: E/W/S/NI. General. - 4p.: 30 cm. - 978-0-11-111852-8 £4.25

The European Communities (Designation) (No. 3) Order 2014 No. 2014/2705. - Enabling power: European Communities Act 1972, s. 2 (2). - Issued: 15.10.2014. Made: 08.10.2014. Laid: 15.10.2014. Coming into force: 10.11.2014. Effect: S.I. 1991/755, S.I. 1999/654 partially revoked accord. to arts 6 & 7. Territorial extent & classification: E/W/S/NI. General. - 4p.: 30 cm. - 978-0-11-112143-6 £4.25

The European Communities (Designation) Order 2014 No. 2014/1362. - Enabling power: European Communities Act 1972, s. 2 (2). - Issued: 03.06.2014. Made: 27.05.2014. Laid: 03.06.2014. Coming into force: 26.06.2014. Effect: S.I. 1992/2870; 1998/2793; 2001/961, 3495; 2003/1888; 2004/3328; 2008/1792; 2009/3214 partially revoked & S.I. 2008/3117 revoked. Territorial extent & classification: E/W/S/NI. General. - 4p.: 30 cm. - 978-0-11-111534-3 £4.25

The European Union (Definition of Treaties) (Columbia and Peru Trade Agreement) Order 2014 No. 2014/266. - Enabling power: European Communities Act 1972, s. 1 (3). - Issued: 18.02.2014. Made: 11.02.2014. Coming into force: In accord with art. 2. Effect: None. Territorial extent & classification: E/W/S/NI. General. - Supersedes draft S.I. (ISBN 9780111104927) issued 23.10.2013. - 2p.: 30 cm. - 978-0-11-110970-0 £4.00

The European Union (Definition of Treaties) (Convention on International Interests in Mobile Equipment and Protocol thereto on matters specific to Aircraft Equipment) Order 2014 No. 2014/1885. - Enabling power: European Communities Act 1972, s. 1 (3). - Issued: 23.07.2014. Made: 16.07.2014. Coming into force: In accord. with art. 1. Effect: None. Territorial extent & classification: E/W/S/NI. General. - Supersedes draft SI (ISBN 9780111113233) issued 04/04/14. - 2p.: 30 cm. - 978-0-11-111847-4 £4.25

The European Union (Definition of Treaties) (Partnership and Cooperation Agreement) (Iraq) Order 2014 No. 2014/1883. - Enabling power: European Communities Act 1972, s. 1 (3). - Issued: 23.07.2014. Made: 16.07.2014. Coming into force: In accord with art. 2. Effect: None. Territorial extent & classification: E/W/S/NI. General. - Supersedes draft SI (ISBN 9780111116142) issued 23/07/14 - 2p.: 30 cm. - 978-0-11-111845-0 £4.25

The European Union (Definition of Treaties) (Partnership and Cooperation Agreement) (Mongolia) Order 2014 No. 2014/1889. - Enabling power: European Communities Act 1972, s. 1 (3). - Issued: 23.07.2014. Made: 16.07.2014. Coming into force: In accord with art. 2. Effect: None. Territorial extent & classification: E/W/S/NI. General. - Supersedes draft SI (ISBN 9780111116050) issued 23/07/14. - 2p.: 30 cm. - 978-0-11-111851-1 £4.25

The European Union (Definition of Treaties) (Partnership and Cooperation Agreement) (Philippines) Order 2014 No. 2014/1884. - Enabling power: European Communities Act 1972, s. 1 (3). - Issued: 23.07.2014. Made: 16.07.2014. Coming into force: In accord with art. 2. Effect: None. Territorial extent & classification: E/W/S/NI. General. - Supersedes draft SI (ISBN 9780111116098) issued 11/06/14. - 2p.: 30 cm. - 978-0-11-111846-7 £4.25

The European Union (Definition of Treaties) (Partnership and Cooperation Agreement) (Vietnam) Order 2014 No. 2014/1886. - Enabling power: European Communities Act 1972, s. 1 (3). - Issued: 23.07.2014. Made: 16.07.2014. Coming into force: In accord with art. 2. Effect: None. Territorial extent & classification: E/W/S/NI. General. - Supersedes draft SI (ISBN 9780111116104) issued 11/06/14- 2p.: 30 cm. - 978-0-11-111848-1 £4.25

Excise

The Biofuels and Other Fuel Substitutes (Payment of Excise Duties etc.) (Amendment) Regulations 2014 No. 2014/471. - Enabling power: Customs and Excise Management Act 1979, ss. 93 (1) (a) (b) (c) (2) (a) (c) (3), 118A (1) (2) & Hydrocarbon Oil Duties Act 1979, ss. 21 (1) (a) (2), sch. 3, para. 3. - Issued: 11.03.2014. Made: 04.03.2014. Laid: 06.03.2014. Coming into force: 01.04.2014. Effect: S.I. 2004/2065 amended. Territorial extent & classification: E/W/S/NI. General. - 2p.: 30 cm. - 978-0-11-111092-8 £4.00

The Finance Act 2009, Sections 101 and 102 (Remote Gambling Taxes) (Appointed Day) Order 2014 No. 2014/3324 (C.157). - Enabling power: Finance Act 2009, s. 104 (3) (4). Bringing into operation various provisions of the 2009 Act on 01.01.2015, in accord. with art. 3. - Issued: 23.12.2014. Made: 17.12.2014. Effect: None. Territorial extent & classification: E/W/S/NI. General. - 2p.: 30 cm. - 978-0-11-112616-5 £4.25

The Gaming Duty (Amendment) Regulations 2014 No. 2014/1930. - Enabling power: Finance Act 1997, ss. 12 (4). - Issued: 28.07.2014. Made: 21.07.2014. Laid: 22.07.2014. Coming into force: 01.10.2014. Effect: S.I. 1997/2196 amended & S.I. 2012/1897 revoked. Territorial extent & classification: E/W/S/NI. General. - 4p.: 30 cm. - 978-0-11-111902-0 £4.25

The General Betting, Pool Betting and Remote Gaming Duties (Registration, Records and Agents) Regulations 2014 No. 2014/2257. - Enabling power: Finance Act 2014, s. 163 (3), 164 (3) (6), 164 (7), 168, 189, 194 (1). - Issued: 02.09.2014. Made: 27.08.2014. Laid: 28.08.2014. Coming into force: 18.09.2014. Effect: None. Territorial extent & classification: E/W/S/NI. General. - 8p. : 30 cm. - 978-0-11-111999-0 £4.25

The General Betting, Pool Betting and Remote Gaming Duties (Returns, Payments, Information and Records) Regulations 2014 No. 2014/2912. - Enabling power: Finance Act 2014, ss. 164 (5) (6), 166, 167, 168, 189, 194 (1). - Issued: 11.11.2014. Made: 04.11.2014. Laid: 06.11.2014. Coming into force: 01.12.2014. Effect: S.I. 2014/2257 amended. Territorial extent & classification: E/W/S/NI. General. - 4p. : 30 cm. - 978-0-11-112293-8 £4.25

The Hydrocarbon Oil Duties (Reliefs for Electricity Generation) (Amendments for Carbon Price Support) Regulations 2014 No. 2014/713. - Enabling power: Hydrocarbon Oil Duties Act 1979, s. 20AA (1) (a) (2). - Issued: 25.03.2014. Made: 18.03.2014. Laid: 19.03.2014. Coming into force: 01.05.2014. Effect: S.I. 2005/3320 amended. Territorial extent & classification: UK. General. - 4p.: 30 cm. - 978-0-11-111245-8 £4.00

The Machine Games Duty (Types of Machine) Order 2014 No. 2014/47. - Enabling power: Finance Act 2012, sch. 24, para. 5 (4). - Issued: 20.01.2014. Made: 14.01.2014. Laid: 15.01.2014. Coming into force: 06.02.2014. Effect: 2012 c.14 amended. Territorial extent & classification: E/W/S/NI. General. - 2p.: 30 cm. - 978-0-11-110843-7 £4.00

The Other Fuel Substitutes (Rates of Excise Duty etc.) (Amendment) Order 2014 No. 2014/470. - Enabling power: Hydrocarbon Oil Duties Act 1979, ss. 6A (3) (5) (9). - Issued: 10.03.2014. Made: 04.03.2014. Laid: 06.03.2014. Coming into force: 01.04.2014. Effect: S.I. 1995/2716 amended. Territorial extent & classification: E/W/S/NI. General. - 2p.: 30 cm. - 978-0-11-111080-5 £4.00

Extradition

The Anti-social Behaviour, Crime and Policing Act 2014 (Commencement No. 4 and Transitional Provisions) Order 2014 No. 2014/1916 (C.87). - Enabling power: Anti-social Behaviour, Crime and Policing Act 2014, s. 185 (1) (7). Bringing into operation various provisions of the 2014 Act on 21.07.2014, 31.07.2014, and 01.04.2015. - Issued: 25.07.2014. Made: 18.07.2014. Effect: None. Territorial extent & classification: E/W/S/NI. General. - 8p.: 30 cm. - 978-0-11-111888-7 £4.25

Extradition, England and Wales

The Anti-social Behaviour, Crime and Policing Act 2014 (Commencement No. 6) Order 2014 No. 2014/2454 (C.108). - Enabling power: Anti-social Behaviour, Crime and Policing Act 2014, s. 185 (1). Bringing into operation various provisions of the 2014 Act on 01.10.2014, in accord. with art. 2. - Issued: 19.09.2014. Made: 10.09.2014. Effect: None. Territorial extent & classification: E/W. General. - 8p.: 30 cm. - 978-0-11-112081-1 £4.25

Family court, England and Wales

The Access to Justice Act 1999 (Destination of Appeals) (Family Proceedings) Order 2014 No. 2014/602 (L.7). - Enabling power: Access to Justice Act 1999, s. 56 (1) (3). - Issued: 19.03.2014. Made: 12.03.2014. Coming into force: In accord. with rule 1. Effect: S.I. 2011/1044 amended. Territorial extent & classification: E/W. General. - 4p.: 30 cm. - 978-0-11-111202-1 £4.00

The Crime and Courts Act 2013 (County Court and Family Court: Consequential Provision) Order 2014 No. 2014/1773. - Enabling power: Crime and Courts Act 2013, s. 59. - Issued: 10.07.2014. Made: 03.07.2014. Coming into force: 04.07.2014 in accord. with art. 1. Effect: 1984 c.28 & 1999, c.22 & S.I. 1991/1184 (L.12) amended. Territorial extent & classification: E/W. General. - 4p.: 30 cm. - 978-0-11-111762-0 £4.25

The Crime and Courts Act 2013 (Family Court: Consequential Provision) (No.2) Order 2014 No. 2014/879. - Enabling power: Crime and Courts Act 2013, ss. 58 (12) (c), 59. - Issued: 07.04.2014. Made: 31.03.2014. Laid: 01.04.2014. Coming into force: 22.04.2014. Effect: 35 SIs/SSIs amended & 3 SIs partially revoked & 12 SIs revoked. Territorial extent & classification: E/W. General. - 8p.: 30 cm. - With correction slip dated December 2014. - 978-0-11-111335-6 £6.00

The Crime and Courts Act 2013 (Family Court: Consequential Provision) Order 2014 No. 2014/605 (L.9). - Enabling power: Crime and Courts Act 2013, ss. 58 (12) (c), 59. - Issued: 19.03.2014. Made: 12.03.2014. Coming into force: In accord. with art. 1. Effect: 1970 c.31; 1971 c.32; 1972 c.18; 1974 c.47; 1978 c.22; 1979 c.53; 1982 c.53; 1985 c.61; 1990 c.41; 1992 c.12; 1995 c.18; 2007 c.15, c.29; 2012 c.10 amended. Territorial extent & classification: E/W. General. - Supersedes draft SI (ISBN 9780111108871) issued 30/01/14- 8p.: 30 cm. - 978-0-11-111208-3 £4.00

The Crime and Courts Act 2013 (Family Court: Transitional and Saving Provision) Order 2014 No. 2014/956. - Enabling power: Crime and Courts Act 2013, s. 60. - Issued: 15.04.2014. Made: 09.04.2014. Coming into force: 22.04.2014. Effect: None. Territorial extent & classification: E/W. General. - 4p.: 30 cm. - 978-0-11-111408-7 £4.25

The Family Court (Composition and Distribution of Business) (Amendment) Rules 2014 No. 2014/3297 (L.35). - Enabling power: Matrimonial and Family Proceedings Act 1984, ss. 31D (1) (3). - Issued: 24.12.2014. Made: 15.12.2014. Laid: 18.12.2014. Coming into force: 11.01.2015. Effect: None. Territorial extent & classification: E/W. General. - 4p.: 30 cm. - 978-0-11-112624-0 £4.25

The Family Court (Composition and Distribution of Business) Rules 2014 No. 2014/840 (L.13). - Enabling power: Matrimonial and Family Proceedings Act 1984, ss. 31D (1) (2) (3) (5) (a). - Issued: 04.04.2014. Made: 31.03.2014. Laid: 01.04.2014. Coming into force: 22.04.2014. Effect: None. Territorial extent & classification: E/W. General. - 16p.: 30 cm. - 978-0-11-111329-5 £6.00

The Family Court (Constitution of Committees: Family Panels) Rules 2014 No. 2014/842. - Enabling power: Courts Act 2003, s. 19 (1) (2). - Issued: 07.04.2014. Made: 21.03.2014. Laid: 01.04.2014. Coming into force: 22.04.2014. Effect: None. Territorial extent & classification: E/W. General. - 4p.: 30 cm. - 978-0-11-111330-1 £4.25

The Family Court (Contempt of Court) (Powers) Regulations 2014 No. 2014/833. - Enabling power: Matrimonial and Family Proceedings Act 1984, s. 31H (1). - Issued: 01.04.2014. Made: 26.03.2014. Laid: 28.03.2014. Coming into force: 22.04.2014. Effect: None. Territorial extent & classification: E/W. General. - 4p.: 30 cm. - 978-0-11-111288-5 £4.00

The Family Court Warrants (Specification of Orders) Order 2014 No. 2014/832. - Enabling power: Magistrates' Courts Act 1980, s. 125A (3). - Issued: 01.04.2014. Made: 26.03.2014. Laid: 28.03.2014. Coming into force: 22.04.2014. Effect: None. Territorial extent & classification: E/W. General. - 2p.: 30 cm. - 978-0-11-111287-8 £4.00

The Family Procedure (Amendment No. 2) Rules 2014 No. 2014/667 (L.11). - Enabling power: Courts Act 2003, ss. 75, 76 & Access to Justice Act 1999, s. 54 (1). - Issued: 20.03.2014. Made: 13.03.2014. Laid: 18.03.2014. Coming into force: 22.04.2014. Effect: S.I. 2010/2955 amended. Territorial extent & classification: E/W. General. - 28p.: 30 cm. - With correction slip dated December 2014. - 978-0-11-111231-1 £5.75

The Family Procedure (Amendment No. 3) Rules 2014 No. 2014/843 (L.15). - Enabling power: Courts Act 2003, ss. 75, 76 & Children and Families Act 2014, s. 10. - Issued: 09.04.2014. Made: 31.03.2014. Laid: 01.04.2014. Coming into force: 22.04.2014. Effect: S.I. 2010/2955 amended. Territorial extent & classification: E/W/S/NI. General. - With correction slip dated October 2014. - 20p.: 30 cm. - 978-0-11-111325-7 £6.00

The Family Procedure (Amendment No. 4) Rules 2014 No. 2014/3296 (L.34). - Enabling power: Courts Act 2003, ss. 75, 76. - Issued: 23.12.2014. Made: 15.12.2014. Laid: 18.12.2014. Coming into force: In accord. with rule 1. Effect: S.I. 2010/2955 amended. Territorial extent & classification: E/W/S/NI. General. - 12p.: 30 cm. - 978-0-11-112611-0 £6.00

The Justices' Clerks and Assistants (Amendment) Rules 2014 No. 2014/841 (L.14). - Enabling power: Matrimonial and Family Proceedings Act 1984, ss. 31O (1), 31P (1). - Issued: 07.04.2014. Made: 31.03.2014. Laid: 01.04.2014. Coming into force: 22.04.2014, in accord. with rule 1. Effect: S.I. 2014/603 amended. Territorial extent & classification: E/W. General. - 8p.: 30 cm. - 978-0-11-111332-5 £6.00

The Justices' Clerks and Assistants Rules 2014 No. 2014/603 (L.8). - Enabling power: Matrimonial and Family Proceedings Act 1984, ss. 31O (1), 31P (1). - Issued: 19.03.2014. Made: 12.03.2014. Coming into force: In accord. with rule 1. Effect: None. Territorial extent & classification: E/W. General. - Supersedes draft SI (ISBN 9780111108888) issued 19/03/14- 8p.: 30 cm. - 978-0-11-111203-8 £5.75

Family law: Child support

The Child Maintenance and Other Payments Act 2008 (Commencement No. 13) Order 2014 No. 2014/576 (C.24). - Enabling power: Child Maintenance and Other Payments Act 2008, s. 62 (3). Bringing into operation various provisions of the 2008 Act on 09.03.2014, in accord. with art. 2. - Issued: 17.03.2014. Made: 08.03.2014. Effect: None. Territorial extent & classification: E/W/S. General. - 8p.: 30 cm. - 978-0-11-111176-5 £4.00

The Child Maintenance and Other Payments Act 2008 (Commencement No. 14 and Transitional Provisions) and the Welfare Reform Act 2012 (Commencement No. 18 and Transitional and Savings Provisions) Order 2014 No. 2014/1635 (C.65). - Enabling power: Child Maintenance and Other Payments Act 2008 s. 62 (3) (4) & Welfare Reform Act 2012, s. 150 (3) (4) (c). Bringing into operation various provisions of the 2008 & 2012 Acts on 30.06.2014. - Issued: 30.06.2014. Made: 24.06.2014. Effect: S.I. 2012/3042; 2013/1860 amended. Territorial extent & classification: E/W/S. General. - 16p.: 30 cm. - 978-0-11-111704-0 £6.00

The Child Support (Consequential and Miscellaneous Amendments) (No. 2) Regulations 2014 No. 2014/1621. - Enabling power: Child Support Act 1991, ss. 43A, 51 (1), 52 (4). - Issued: 27.06.2014. Made: 23.06.2014. Laid: 23.06.2014. Coming into force: In accord. with reg 1. Effect: S.I. 2009/3151 modified & S.I. 2014/1386 varied. Territorial extent & classification: E/W/S. General. - This Statutory Instrument has been printed to correct errors in S.I. 2014/1386 (ISBN 9780111115572) and is being issued free of charge to all known recipients of that Statutory Instrument. - 4p.: 30 cm. - 978-0-11-111696-8 £4.25

The Child Support (Consequential and Miscellaneous Amendments) Regulations 2014 No. 2014/1386. - Enabling power: Child Support Act 1991, ss. 16 (1), 28E (5), 29 (2) (3), 32 (1) (2) (n), 34 (1), 42, 43A, 51 (1) (2) (a) (i), 52 (4), 54 (1), sch. 1, para. 11 & Child Maintenance and Other Payments Act 2008, s. 55 (3) (4), sch. 5, paras 2, 5. - Issued: 06.06.2014. Made: 31.05.2014. Laid: 06.06.2014. Coming into force: In accord. with reg 1. Effect: S.I. 1992/1815, 1989; 1996/2907; 2001/155; 2009/3151; 2012/2677; 2014/614 amended. Territorial extent & classification: E/W/S. General. - Errors in this SI have been corrected by SI 2014/1621 (ISBN 9780111116968) which is being sent free of charge to all known recipients of 2014/1386. - 12p.: 30 cm. - 978-0-11-111557-2 £6.00

The Child Support (Ending Liability in Existing Cases and Transition to New Calculation Rules) Regulations 2014 No. 2014/614. - Enabling power: Child Maintenance and Other Payments Act 2008, ss. 6 (2) (g), 55 (3) (4), sch. 5. paras 2, 3, 5, 6, 7. - Issued: 19.03.2014. Made: 12.03.2014. Coming into force: In accord. with reg. 1 (1). Effect: None. Territorial extent & classification: E/W/S. General. - Supersedes draft S.I. (ISBN 9780111106396) issued 02.12.2013. - 8p.: 30 cm. - 978-0-11-111216-8 £4.00

The Child Support Fees Regulations 2014 No. 2014/612. - Enabling power: Social Administration Act 1992, ss. 5 (1) (p), 189 (4) & Child Support Act 1991, ss. 43 (1), 51 (1) (2) (a) & Child Maintenance and Other Payments Act 2008, ss. 6 (1) to (4), 55 (3) (4). - Issued: 19.03.2014. Made: 12.03.2014. Coming into force: In accord. with reg. 1 (3) (4) (5). Effect: S.I. 1987/1968; 2013/380 amended. Territorial extent & classification: E/W/S. General. - Supersedes draft SI (ISBN 9780111106365) issued 02/12/13- 12p.: 30 cm. - 978-0-11-111214-4 £5.75

The Child Support (Northern Ireland Reciprocal Arrangements) Amendment Regulations 2014 No. 2014/1423. - Enabling power: Northern Ireland Act 1998, s. 87 (4) (9). - Issued: 09.06.2014. Made: 03.06.2014. Laid: 09.06.2014. Coming into force: 30.06.2014. Effect: S.I. 1993/584 amended. Territorial extent & classification: E/W/S. General. - 8p.: 30 cm. - 978-0-11-111582-4 £6.00

The Child Support, Pensions and Social Security Act 2000 (Commencement No. 15) Order 2014 No. 2014/1263 (C.51). - Enabling power: Child Support, Pensions and Social Security Act 2000, s. 86 (2). Bringing into operation various provisions of the 2000 Act on 16.05.2014 in accord. with art 2. - Issued: 21.05.2014. Made: 15.05.2014. Effect: None. Territorial extent & classification: E/W/S. General. - 8p.: 30 cm. - 978-0-11-111498-8 £4.25

Family law, England and Wales

The Anti-social Behaviour, Crime and Policing Act 2014 (Commencement No. 2, Transitional and Transitory Provisions) Order 2014 No. 2014/949 (C.43). - Enabling power: Anti-social Behaviour, Crime and Policing Act 2014, s. 185 (1) (7). Bringing into operation various provisions of the 2014 Act on 13.05.2014, 01.06.2014, 16.06.2014, 14.07.2014, in accord. with arts. 2 to 6. - Issued: 14.04.2014. Made: 08.04.2014. Effect: None. Territorial extent & classification: E/W/S/NI. General. - 8p.: 30 cm. - 978-0-11-111401-8 £6.00

The Marriage (Same Sex Couples) (Jurisdiction and Recognition of Judgments) Regulations 2014 No. 2014/543. - Enabling power: Domicile and Matrimonial Proceedings Act 1973, sch. A1, para. 5. - Issued: 12.03.2014. Made: 06.03.2014. Coming into force: 13.03.2014. Effect: None. Territorial extent & classification: E/W. General. - Supersedes draft S.I. (ISBN 9780111108703) issued 28.01.2014. - 4p.: 30 cm. - 978-0-11-111145-1 £4.00

Family proceedings

The Children and Families Act 2014 (Commencement No. 1) Order 2014 No. 2014/793 (C.30). - Enabling power: Children, Schools and Families Act 2014, s. 139 (3). Bringing into operation various provisions of the 2014 Act on 22.04.2014. - Issued: 27.03.2014. Made: 20.03.2014. Effect: None. Territorial extent & classification: E/W/S. General. - 2p.: 30 cm. - 978-0-11-111264-9 £4.00

The Children and Families Act 2014 (Commencement No. 2) (Amendment) Order 2014 No. 2014/1134 (C.47). - Enabling power: Children and Families Act 2014, s. 139 (6) (7). Bringing into operation various provisions of the 2014 Act on 01.05.2014. - Issued: 07.05.2014. Made: 30.04.2014. Effect: S.I. 2014/889 (C.38) amended. Territorial extent & classification: E/W/S. General. - 2p.: 30 cm. - 978-0-11-111452-0 £4.25

The Children and Families Act 2014 (Commencement No. 2) Order 2014 No. 2014/889 (C.38). - Enabling power: Children and Families Act 2014, s. 139 (6) (7). Bringing into operation various provisions of the 2014 Act on 01.04.2014, 22.04.2014, 13.05.2014, 25.07.2014, 01.09.2014 in accord. with arts 3 to 7. - Issued: 07.04.2014. Made: 31.03.2014. Effect: None. Territorial extent & classification: E/W/S. General. - 4p.: 30 cm. - 978-0-11-111354-7 £4.25

FAMILY PROCEEDINGS, ENGLAND AND WALES

The Children and Families Act 2014 (Commencement No. 5 and Transitional Provision) Order 2014 No. 2014/2749 (C.120). - Enabling power: Children and Families Act 2014, s. 137 (1), 139 (6). Bringing into operation various provisions of the 2014 Act on 22.10.2014, in accord. with art 3. - Issued: 20.10.2014. Made: 13.10.2014. Effect: None. Territorial extent & classification: E/W/S. General. - 4p.: 30 cm. - 978-0-11-112182-5 £4.25

The Children and Families Act 2014 (Transitional Provisions) Order 2014 No. 2014/1042. - Enabling power: Children and Families Act 2014, s. 137 (1). - Issued: 24.04.2014. Made: 15.04.2014. Coming into force: 22.04.2014. Effect: None. Territorial extent & classification: E/W/S. General. - 4p.: 30 cm. - 978-0-11-111419-3 £4.25

The Crime and Courts Act 2013 (Commencement No. 10 and Transitional Provision) Order 2014 No. 2014/954 (C.44). - Enabling power: Crime and Courts Act 2013, s. 61 (3). Bringing into operation various provisions of the 2013 Act on 22.04.2014. - Issued: 15.04.2014. Made: 09.04.2014. Effect: None. Territorial extent & classification: E/W. General. - 4p.: 30 cm. - 978-0-11-111406-3 £4.25

The Crime and Courts Act 2013 (County Court and Family Court: Consequential Provision) Order 2014 No. 2014/1773. - Enabling power: Crime and Courts Act 2013, s. 59. - Issued: 10.07.2014. Made: 03.07.2014. Coming into force: 04.07.2014 in accord. with art. 1. Effect: 1984 c.28 & 1999, c.22 & S.I. 1991/1184 (L.12) amended. Territorial extent & classification: E/W. General. - 4p.: 30 cm. - 978-0-11-111762-0 £4.25

The Crime and Courts Act 2013 (Family Court: Consequential Provision) (No.2) Order 2014 No. 2014/879. - Enabling power: Crime and Courts Act 2013, ss. 58 (12) (c), 59. - Issued: 07.04.2014. Made: 31.03.2014. Laid: 01.04.2014. Coming into force: 22.04.2014. Effect: 35 SIs/SSIs amended & 3 SIs partially revoked & 12 SIs revoked. Territorial extent & classification: E/W. General. - 8p.: 30 cm. - With correction slip dated December 2014. - 978-0-11-111335-6 £6.00

The Crime and Courts Act 2013 (Family Court: Consequential Provision) Order 2014 No. 2014/605 (L.9). - Enabling power: Crime and Courts Act 2013, ss. 58 (12) (c), 59. - Issued: 19.03.2014. Made: 12.03.2014. Coming into force: In accord. with art. 1. Effect: 1970 c.31; 1971 c.32; 1972 c.18; 1974 c.47; 1978 c.22; 1979 c.53; 1982 c.53; 1985 c.61; 1990 c.41; 1992 c.12; 1995 c.18; 2007 c.15, c.29; 2012 c.10 amended. Territorial extent & classification: E/W. General. - Supersedes draft SI (ISBN 9780111108871) issued 30/01/14- 8p.: 30 cm. - 978-0-11-111208-3 £4.00

Family proceedings, England and Wales

The Access to Justice Act 1999 (Destination of Appeals) (Family Proceedings) Order 2014 No. 2014/602 (L.7). - Enabling power: Access to Justice Act 1999, s. 56 (1) (3). - Issued: 19.03.2014. Made: 12.03.2014. Coming into force: In accord. with rule 1. Effect: S.I. 2011/1044 amended. Territorial extent & classification: E/W. General. - 4p.: 30 cm. - 978-0-11-111202-1 £4.00

The Child Arrangements Order (Consequential Amendments to Subordinate Legislation) Order 2014 No. 2014/852. - Enabling power: Children and Families Act 2014, s. 136. - Issued: 03.04.2014. Made: 27.03.2014. Laid: 31.03.2014. Coming into force: 22.04.2014. Effect: S.I. 1987/1967, 2024; 1991/893; 1992/2977; 1996/207, 2890; 2001/2743; 2002/3236; 2005/389, 1313, 3061; 2006/213; 2007/307, 310; 2008/794; 2009/1107; 2010/959, 2571; 2011/582, 712; 2012/10; 2013/1141, 2094, 3029, 3035 amended. Territorial extent & classification: E/W. General. - 8p.: 30 cm. - 978-0-11-111303-5 £5.75

The Courts and Tribunals Fees (Miscellaneous Amendments) Order 2014 No. 2014/590 (L.6). - Enabling power: Courts Act 2003, s. 92 & Insolvency Act 1986, ss. 414, 415 & Tribunals, Courts and Enforcement Act 2007, s. 42, 49 (3) & Constitutional Reform Act 2005, s. 52 & Mental Capacity Act 2005. s. 54 & Gender Recognition Act 2004, s. 7 (2). - Issued: 19.03.2014. Made: 11.03.2014. Laid: 13.03.2104. Coming into force: 06.04.2014. Effect: S.I. 2004/3120; 2006/758; 2007/1745; 2008/1052, 1053, 1054; 2009/213, 1114; 2010/42; 2011/2344; 2013/1179, 1893 amended. Territorial extent & classification: E/W. General. - 16p.: 30 cm. - 978-0-11-111194-9 £5.75

The Family Court (Composition and Distribution of Business) (Amendment) Rules 2014 No. 2014/3297 (L.35). - Enabling power: Matrimonial and Family Proceedings Act 1984, ss. 31D (1) (3). - Issued: 24.12.2014. Made: 15.12.2014. Laid: 18.12.2014. Coming into force: 11.01.2015. Effect: None. Territorial extent & classification: E/W. General. - 4p.: 30 cm. - 978-0-11-112624-0 £4.25

The Family Court (Composition and Distribution of Business) Rules 2014 No. 2014/840 (L.13). - Enabling power: Matrimonial and Family Proceedings Act 1984, ss. 31D (1) (2) (3) (5) (a). - Issued: 04.04.2014. Made: 31.03.2014. Laid: 01.04.2014. Coming into force: 22.04.2014. Effect: None. Territorial extent & classification: E/W. General. - 16p.: 30 cm. - 978-0-11-111329-5 £6.00

The Family Court (Contempt of Court) (Powers) Regulations 2014 No. 2014/833. - Enabling power: Matrimonial and Family Proceedings Act 1984, s. 31H (1). - Issued: 01.04.2014. Made: 26.03.2014. Laid: 28.03.2014. Coming into force: 22.04.2014. Effect: None. Territorial extent & classification: E/W. General. - 4p.: 30 cm. - 978-0-11-111288-5 £4.00

The Family Court Warrants (Specification of Orders) Order 2014 No. 2014/832. - Enabling power: Magistrates' Courts Act 1980, s. 125A (3). - Issued: 01.04.2014. Made: 26.03.2014. Laid: 28.03.2014. Coming into force: 22.04.2014. Effect: None. Territorial extent & classification: E/W. General. - 2p.: 30 cm. - 978-0-11-111287-8 £4.00

The Family Procedure (Amendment No. 2) Rules 2014 No. 2014/667 (L.11). - Enabling power: Courts Act 2003, ss. 75, 76 & Access to Justice Act 1999, s. 54 (1). - Issued: 20.03.2014. Made: 13.03.2014. Laid: 18.03.2014. Coming into force: 22.04.2014. Effect: S.I. 2010/2955 amended. Territorial extent & classification: E/W. General. - 28p.: 30 cm. - With correction slip dated December 2014. - 978-0-11-111231-1 £5.75

The Family Procedure (Amendment No. 3) Rules 2014 No. 2014/843 (L.15). - Enabling power: Courts Act 2003, ss. 75, 76 & Children and Families Act 2014, s. 10. - Issued: 09.04.2014. Made: 31.03.2014. Laid: 01.04.2014. Coming into force: 22.04.2014. Effect: S.I. 2010/2955 amended. Territorial extent & classification: E/W/S/NI. General. - With correction slip dated October 2014. - 20p.: 30 cm. - 978-0-11-111325-7 £6.00

The Family Procedure (Amendment No. 4) Rules 2014 No. 2014/3296 (L.34). - Enabling power: Courts Act 2003, ss. 75, 76. - Issued: 23.12.2014. Made: 15.12.2014. Laid: 18.12.2014. Coming into force: In accord. with rule 1. Effect: S.I. 2010/2955 amended. Territorial extent & classification: E/W/S/NI. General. - 12p.: 30 cm. - 978-0-11-112611-0 £6.00

The Family Procedure (Amendment) Rules 2014 No. 2014/524 (L.5). - Enabling power: Courts Act 2003, ss. 75, 76. - Issued: 13.03.2014. Made: 06.03.2014. Laid: 10.03.2014. Coming into force: 13.03.2014. Effect: S.I. 2010/2955 amended. Territorial extent & classification: E/W. General. - 4p.: 30 cm. - 978-0-11-111122-2 £4.00

The Family Proceedings Fees (Amendment) Order 2014 No. 2014/877 (L.20). - Enabling power: Courts Act 2003, ss. 92, 108 (6). - Issued: 07.04.2014. Made: 27.03.2014. Laid: 01.04.2014. Coming into force: 22.04.2014. Effect: S.I. 2008/1054 (L.6) amended. Territorial extent & classification: E/W. General. - 12p.: 30 cm. - 978-0-11-111331-8 £6.00

Family provision

The Inheritance and Trustees' Powers Act 2014 (Commencement) Order 2014 No. 2014/2039 (C.93). - Enabling power: Inheritance and Trustees' Powers Act 2014, s. 12 (2). Bringing into operation various provisions of the 2014 Act on 01.10.2014, in accord. with art. 2. - Issued: 05.08.2014. Made: 25.07.2014. Effect: None. Territorial extent & classification: E/W/S/NI. General. - 4p.: 30 cm. - 978-0-11-111940-2 £4.25

Fees and charges

The Kimberley Process (Fees) Regulations 2014 No. 2014/1684. - Enabling power: Finance Act 1973, s. 56 (1) (2). - Issued: 04.07.2014. Made: 30.06.2014. Laid: 01.07.2014. Coming into force: 22.07.2014. Effect: S.I. 2004/686 revoked. Territorial extent & classification: E/W/S/NI. General. - EC note: These Regs. prescribe fees to be paid to the Foreign and Commonwealth Office in connection with the issue of certificates by the Department in pursuance of the Community obligations of the UK under Council Reg (EC) 2368/2002, implementing the Kimberley Process certification scheme for the international trade in rough diamonds. - 2p.: 30 cm. - 978-0-11-111735-4 £4.25

FINANCIAL SERVICES AND MARKETS

The Measuring Instruments (EEC Requirements) (Fees) (Amendment) Regulations 2014 No. 2014/568. - Enabling power: Finance Act 1973, s. 56 (1) (2). - Issued: 14.03.2014. Made: 07.03.2014. Laid: 11.03.2014. Coming into force: 06.04.2014. Effect: S.I. 2004/1300 amended. Territorial extent & classification: E/W/S/NI. General. - 4p.: 30 cm. - 978-0-11-111163-5 £4.00

Financial services

The Revenue and Customs (Amendment of Appeal Provisions for Out of Time Reviews) Order 2014 No. 2014/1264. - Enabling power: Finance Act 2008, s. 124 (1) (2) (6) (7) (b). - Issued: 21.05.2014. Made: 14.05.2014. Coming into force: In accord. with art. 1 (2). Effect: 1994 c.9, c.23; 1996 c.8; 2000 c.17; 2001 c.9; 2003 c.14; S.I. 2003/3102; 2007/1509, 2157, 3298 amended. Territorial extent & classification: E/W/S/NI. General. - Supersedes draft SI (ISBN 9780111112991) issued 03/04/14. - 8p.: 30 cm. - 978-0-11-111499-5 £6.00

Financial services and markets

The Alternative Investment Fund Managers (Amendment) Order 2014 No. 2014/1313. - Enabling power: European Communities Act 1972, s. 2 (2) & Financial Services and Markets Act 2000, ss. 22 (1), 409 (1) (a) (b), 428 (3), sch. 2, para. 25. - Issued: 29.05.2014. Made: 21.05.2014. Laid: 23.05.2014. Coming into force: 31.05.2014. Effect: S.I. 2014/1292 amended. Territorial extent & classification: E/W/S/NI. General. - 2p.: 30 cm. - 978-0-11-111518-3 £4.25

The Alternative Investment Fund Managers Regulations 2014 No. 2014/1292. - Enabling power: European Communities Act 1972, s. 2 (2) & Financial Services and Markets Act 2000, ss. 22 (1), 409 (1) (a) (b), 428 (3), sch. 2, para. 25. - Issued: 29.05.2014. Made: 08.05.2014. Coming into force: In accord. with art. 1. Effect: 2000 c.8; S.I. 2001/544, 3084; 2013/1773, 1797 amended. Territorial extent & classification: E/W/S/NI. General. - This Order makes amendments to the United Kingdom's implementation of Directive 2001/161/EU of the European Parliament and the Council on Alternative Investment Fund Managers. - 12p.: 30 cm. - 978-0-11-111517-6 £6.00

The Banking Act 2009 (Banking Group Companies) Order 2014 No. 2014/1831. - Enabling power: Banking Act 2009, ss. 47, 81D (1), 259 (1). - Issued: 29.07.2014. Made: 09.07.2014. Coming into force: 01.08.2014. Effect: S.I. 2009/322 amended. Territorial extent & classification: E/W/S/NI. General. - Supersedes draft S.I. (ISBN 9780111115893) issued 10.06.2014. - 8p.: 30 cm. - 978-0-11-111809-2 £4.25

The Banking Act 2009 (Exclusion of Investment Firms of a Specified Description) Order 2014 No. 2014/1832. - Enabling power: Banking Act 2009, s. 258A (2) (b). - Issued: 29.07.2014. Made: 09.07.2014. Coming into force: 01.08.2014. Effect: None. Territorial extent & classification: E/W/S/NI. General. - Supersedes draft SI (ISBN 9780111115879) issued 10.06.2014. - 2p.: 30 cm. - 978-0-11-111810-8 £4.25

The Banking Act 2009 (Restriction of Partial Property Transfers) (Recognised Central Counterparties) Order 2014 No. 2014/1828. - Enabling power: Banking Act 2009, ss. 47, 48, 259 (1). - Issued: 18.07.2014. Made: 09.07.2014. Coming into force: 01.08.2014. Effect: S.I. 2009/322 amended. Territorial extent & classification: E/W/S/NI. General. - Supersedes draft (ISBN 9780111116234) issued 13.06.2014. - 12p.: 30 cm. - 978-0-11-111804-7 £6.00

The Banking Act 2009 (Third Party Compensation Arrangements for Partial Property Transfers) (Amendment) Regulations 2014 No. 2014/1830. - Enabling power: Banking Act 2009, s. 60. - Issued: 29.07.2014. Made: 09.07.2014. Coming into force: 01.08.2014. Effect: S.I. 2009/319 amended. Territorial extent & classification: E/W/S/NI. General. - Supersedes draft S.I (ISBN 9780111115909) issued 10.06.2014. - 2p.: 30 cm. - 978-0-11-111808-5 £4.25

The Bank Recovery and Resolution (No. 2) Order 2014 No. 2014/3348. - Enabling power: European Communities Act 1972, s. 2 (2) & Financial Services and markets Act 2000, s. 192B (4) & Banking Act 2009, s. 230. - Issued: 29.12.2014. Made: 18.12.2014. Laid: 19.12.2014. Coming into force: In accord. with art. 1 (2) (3). Effect: 2013 c.33; S.I. 1999/2979; 2001/2188; 2003/3226; 2004/1045; 2013/419, 3115 amended & 2006 c.46 modified. Territorial extent & classification: E/W/S/NI. General. - EC note: This Order is one of the instruments which implements Directive 2014/59/EU establishing a framework for the recovery and resolution of credit institutions and investment firms. - 128p.: 30 cm. - 978-0-11-112637-0 £19.00

The Bank Recovery and Resolution Order 2014 No. 2014/3329. - Enabling power: European Communities Act 1972, s. 2 (2). - Issued: 09.01.2015. Made: 17.12.2014. Coming into force: 01.01.2015. Effect: 2000 c.8; 2009 c.1 & S.I. 2009/319, 322; 2014/1831 amended. Territorial extent & classification: E/W/S/NI. General. - Supersedes draft S.I. (ISBN 9780111123782) issued 28/11/14. - 88p.: 30 cm. - 978-0-11-112654-7 £16.00

The Building Societies (Bail-in) Order 2014 No. 2014/3344. - Enabling power: European Communities Act 1972, s. 2 (2) & Financial Services (Banking Reform) Act 2013, ss. 17 (2) to (4), 142 (3). - Issued: 24.12.2014. Made: 18.12.2014. Laid: 19.12.2014. Coming into force: 10.01.2015. Effect: 1986 c.53; 2009 c.1 & 2009/805; 2014/3330 amended. Territorial extent & classification: E/W/S/NI. General. - 16p.: 30 cm. - 978-0-11-112633-2 £6.00

The Capital Requirements (Capital Buffers and Macro-prudential Measures) Regulations 2014 No. 2014/894. - Enabling power: European Communities Act 1972, s. 2 (2). - Issued: 08.04.2014. Made: 01.04.2014. Laid: 03.04.2014. Coming into force: In accord. with reg. 1. Effect: 1998 c.11 amended. Territorial extent & classification: E/W/S/NI. General. - 16p.: 30 cm. - 978-0-11-111359-2 £6.00

The Central Securities Depositories Regulations 2014 No. 2014/2879. - Enabling power: European Communities Act 1972, s. 2 (2). - Issued: 04.11.2014. Made: 29.10.2014. Laid: 30.10.2014. Coming into force: 21.11.2014. Effect: S.I. 2000 c.8; 2001/2188; 2013/418, 419 amended. Territorial extent & classification: E/W/S/NI. General. - 12p.: 30 cm. - 978-0-11-112265-5 £6.00

The Financial Services Act 2012 (Commencement No. 4) Order 2014 No. 2014/1447 (C.55). - Enabling power: Financial Services Act 2012, s. 122 (3) (4). Bringing various provisions of the 2012 Act into operation on 05.06.2014. - Issued: 10.06.2014. Made: 04.06.2014. Effect: None. Territorial extent & classification: E/W/S/NI. General. - 4p.: 30 cm. - 978-0-11-111593-0 £4.25

The Financial Services Act 2012 (Commencement No. 5) Order 2014 No. 2014/1847 (C.84). - Enabling power: Financial Services Act 2012, s. 122 (3) (4). Bringing various provisions of the 2012 Act into operation on 01.08.2014. - Issued: 22.07.2014. Made: 14.07.2014. Effect: None. Territorial extent & classification: E/W/S/NI. General. - 4p.: 30 cm. - 978-0-11-111820-7 £4.25

The Financial Services Act 2012 (Consequential Amendments) Order 2014 No. 2014/2371. - Enabling power: Financial Services Act 2012, ss. 115 (2), 118. - Issued: 11.09.2014. Made: 04.09.2014. Laid: 08.09.2014. Coming into force: 30.09.2014. Effect: SI 2003/1417 amended. Territorial extent & classification: E/W/S/NI. General. - 2p.: 30 cm. - 978-0-11-112030-9 £4.25

The Financial Services Act 2012 (Relevant Functions in relation to Complaints Scheme) Order 2014 No. 2014/1195. - Enabling power: Financial Services Act 2012, s. 85 (2) (b). - Issued: 14.05.2014. Made: 08.05.2014. Laid: 09.05.2014. Coming into force: 01.06.2014. Effect: None. Territorial extent & classification: E/W/S/NI. General. - 2p.: 30 cm. - 978-0-11-111470-4 £4.25

The Financial Services and Markets Act 2000 (Appointed Representatives) (Amendment) Regulations 2014 No. 2014/206. - Enabling power: Financial Services and Markets Act 2000, s. 39(1) (1C) (1E). - Issued: 10.02.2014. Made: 03.02.2014. Laid: 05.02.2014. Coming into force: 01.04.2014. Effect: S.I. 2001/1217 amended. Territorial extent & classification: E/W/S/NI. General. - 4p.: 30 cm. - 978-0-11-110920-5 £4.00

The Financial Services and Markets Act 2000 (Carrying on Regulated Activities by Way of Business) (Amendment) Order 2014 No. 2014/3340. - Enabling power: Financial Services and Markets Act 2000, s. 429 (1). - Issued: 24.12.2014. Made: 17.12.2014. Coming into force: 31.12.2014. Effect: S.I. 2001/1177 amended. Territorial extent & classification: E/W/S/NI. General. - Supersedes draft SI (ISBN 9780111123485) issued 24/11/14. For approval by resolution of each House of Parliament. - 2p.: 30 cm. - 978-0-11-112629-5 £4.25

The Financial Services and Markets Act 2000 (Consumer Credit) (Designated Activities) Order 2014 No. 2014/334. - Enabling power: Financial Services and Markets Act 2000, ss. 23 (1B), 428 (3). - Issued: 21.02.2014. Made: 13.02.2014. Coming into force: 01.04.2014. Effect: None. Territorial extent & classification: E/W/S/NI. General. - Supersedes draft S.I. (ISBN 9780111108352) issued 20.01.2014. - 4p.: 30 cm. - 978-0-11-110986-1 £4.00

FINANCIAL SERVICES AND MARKETS

The Financial Services and Markets Act 2000 (Consumer Credit) (Miscellaneous Provisions) (No. 2) Order 2014 No. 2014/506. - Enabling power: European Communities Act 1972, s. 2 (2) & Financial Services and Markets Act 2000, ss. 38, 426 (1). - Issued: 11.03.2014. Made: 05.03.2014. Laid: 07.03.2014. Coming into force: In accord. with art. 1. Effect: S.I. 2001/1201; 2005/1529; 2007/2157; 2013/1881; 2014/366 amended. Territorial extent & classification: E/W/S/NI. General. - 8p.: 30 cm. - 978-0-11-111110-9 £5.75

The Financial Services and Markets Act 2000 (Consumer Credit) (Miscellaneous Provisions) Order 2014 No. 2014/208. - Enabling power: European Communities Act 1972, s. 2 (2) & Financial Services and Markets Act 2000, s. 426 (1). - Issued: 10.02.2014. Made: 03.02.2014. Laid: 05.02.2014. Coming into force: In accord. with art. 1. Effect: S.I. 2004/2095; 2005/1529; 2010/1013; 2013/1881 amended. Territorial extent & classification: E/W/S/NI. General. - 12p.: 30 cm. - 978-0-11-110921-2 £5.75

The Financial Services and Markets Act 2000 (Consumer Credit) (Transitional Provisions) (No. 2) Order 2014 No. 2014/835. - Enabling power: Financial Services and Markets Act 2000, s. 426 (1). - Issued: 02.04.2014. Made: 27.03.2014. Laid: 27.03.2014. Coming into force: 01.04.2014. Effect: S.I. 2013/1881 amended. Territorial extent & classification: E/W/S/NI. General. - 2p.: 30 cm. - 978-0-11-111290-8 £4.00

The Financial Services and Markets Act 2000 (Consumer Credit) (Transitional Provisions) (No. 3) Order 2014 No. 2014/1446. - Enabling power: Financial Services and Markets Act 2000, s. 426 (1). - Issued: 10.06.2014. Made: 04.06.2014. Laid: 05.06.2014. Coming into force: 27.06.2014. Effect: S.I. 2013/1881 amended. Territorial extent & classification: E/W/S/NI. General. - 2p.: 30 cm. - 978-0-11-111592-3 £4.25

The Financial Services and Markets Act 2000 (Consumer Credit) (Transitional Provisions) (No. 4) Order 2014 No. 2014/2632. - Enabling power: Financial Services and Markets Act 2000, s. 426 (1). - Issued: 03.10.2014. Made: 26.09.2014. Laid: 30.09.2014. Coming into force: 21.10.2014. Effect: S.I. 2013/1881 amended. Territorial extent & classification: E/W/S/NI. General. - 2p.: 30 cm. - 978-0-11-112113-9 £4.25

The Financial Services and Markets Act 2000 (Consumer Credit) (Transitional Provisions) Order 2014 No. 2014/376. - Enabling power: Financial Services and Markets Act 2000, s. 426 (1). - Issued: 27.02.2014. Made: 19.02.2014. Laid: 24.02.2014. Coming into force: 01.04.2014. Effect: S.I. 2013/1881 amended. Territorial extent & classification: E/W/S/NI. General. - 4p.: 30 cm. - 978-0-11-111007-2 £4.00

The Financial Services and Markets Act 2000 (Disclosure of Confidential Information) (Amendment) Regulations 2014 No. 2014/883. - Enabling power: Financial Services and Markets Act 2000, ss. 349 (1) (b) (2) (3), 428 (3). - Issued: 07.04.2014. Made: 01.04.2014. Laid: 02.04.2014. Coming into force: 28.04.2014. Effect: S.I. 2001/2188 amended. Territorial extent & classification: E/W/S/NI. General. - 2p.: 30 cm. - 978-0-11-111344-8 £4.25

The Financial Services and Markets Act 2000 (Market Abuse) Regulations 2014 No. 2014/3081. - Enabling power: European Communities Act 1972, s. 2 (2). - Issued: 25.11.2014. Made: 19.11.2014. Laid: 20.11.2014. Coming into force: 15.12.2014. Effect: 2008 c.8 amended. Territorial extent & classification: E/W/S/NI. General. - 4p.: 30 cm. - 978-0-11-112362-1 £4.25

The Financial Services and Markets Act 2000 (Over the Counter Derivatives, Central Counterparties and Trade Repositories) (Amendment) Regulations 2014 No. 2014/905. - Enabling power: European Communities Act 1972, s. 2 (2). - Issued: 09.04.2014. Made: 02.04.2014. Laid: 04.04.2014. Coming into force: 01.05.2014. Effect: S.I. 2013/504 amended. Territorial extent & classification: E/W/S/NI. General. - EC note: Relates to implementation of certain articles Reg (EU) 648/2012; Commission Delegated Regulation (EU) no. 149/2013. - 4p.: 30 cm. - 978-0-11-111369-1 £4.25

The Financial Services and Markets Act 2000 (Regulated Activities) (Amendment) (No. 2) Order 2014 No. 2014/1448. - Enabling power: Financial Services and Markets Act 2000, ss. 22 (1) (5), sch. 2, para. 25. - Issued: 10.06.2014. Made: 04.06.2014. Laid: 05.06.2014. Coming into force: 27.06.2014. Effect: S.I. 2001/544 amended. Territorial extent & classification: E/W/S/NI. General. - 2p.: 30 cm. - 978-0-11-111594-7 £4.25

The Financial Services and Markets Act 2000 (Regulated Activities) (Amendment) (No. 3) Order 2014 No. 2014/1740. - Enabling power: Financial Services and Markets Act 2000, ss. 22 (1) (5), sch. 2, para. 25. - Issued: 10.07.2014. Made: 03.07.2014. Laid: 04.07.2014. Coming into force: 28.07.2014. Effect: S.I. 2001/544 amended. Territorial extent & classification: E/W/S/NI. General. - 2p.: 30 cm. - 978-0-11-111755-2 £4.25

The Financial Services and Markets Act 2000 (Regulated Activities) (Amendment) Order 2014 No. 2014/366. - Enabling power: Financial Services and Markets Act 2000, ss. 22 (1) (5), 428 (3), sch. 2, para. 25. - Issued: 25.02.2014. Made: 13.02.2014. Laid: 14.02.2014. Coming into force: In accord. with art. 1. Effect: 1974 c.39; 2000 c.8; S.I. 1983/1561; 2000/290; 2001/544, 1201, 1217; 2005/1529; 2007/1167; 2009/209, 774; 2010/1014; 2011/99; 2013/1881 amended. Territorial extent & classification: E/W/S/NI. General. - 32p.: 30 cm. - 978-0-11-110994-6 £5.75

The Financial Services and Markets Act 2000 (Regulated Activities) (Green Deal) (Amendment) Order 2014 No. 2014/1850. - Enabling power: Energy Act 2011, s. 30. - Issued: 21.07.2014. Made: 14.07.2014. Coming into force: 15.07.2014 in accord. with art. 1. Effect: S.I. 2001/544 amended. Territorial extent & classification: E/W/S. General. - Supersedes draft SI (ISBN 9780111115862) issued 10/06/14. - 8p.: 30 cm. - 978-0-11-111824-5 £6.00

The Financial Services and Markets Act 2000 (Transparency) Regulations 2014 No. 2014/1261. - Enabling power: European Communities Act 1972, s. 2 (2). - Issued: 21.05.2014. Made: 14.05.2014. Laid: 16.05.2014. Coming into force: 06.06.2014. Effect: 2000 c.8 modified. Territorial extent & classification: E/W/S/NI. General. - Revoked by SI 2014/3293 (ISBN 9780111125595). - 2p.: 30 cm. - 978-0-11-111496-4 £4.25

The Financial Services (Banking Reform) Act 2013 (Commencement No. 1) Order 2014 No. 2014/377 (C.14). - Enabling power: Financial Services (Banking Reform) Act 2013, s. 148 (5) (6). Bringing into operation various provisions of this Act on 01.03.2014, 01.04.2014 & 01.06.2014 in accord. with art. 2. - Issued: 27.02.2014. Made: 19.02.2014. Effect: None. Territorial extent & classification: E/W/S/NI. General. - 4p.: 30 cm. - 978-0-11-111008-9 £4.00

The Financial Services (Banking Reform) Act 2013 (Commencement No. 4) Order 2014 No. 2014/823 (C.32). - Enabling power: Financial Services (Banking Reform) Act 2013, s. 148 (5). Bringing into operation various provisions of this Act on 01.04.2014 in accord. with art. 2. - Issued: 01.04.2014. Made: 25.03.2014. Effect: None. Territorial extent & classification: E/W/S/NI. General. - 4p.: 30 cm. - 978-0-11-111281-6 £4.00

The Financial Services (Banking Reform) Act 2013 (Commencement No. 5) Order 2014 No. 2014/1819 (C.80). - Enabling power: Financial Services (Banking Reform) Act 2013, s. 148 (5) (6). Bringing into operation various provisions of this Act on 25.07.2014 in accord. with art. 2. - Issued: 13.08.2014. Made: 09.07.2014. Effect: None. Territorial extent & classification: E/W/S/NI. General. - 4p.: 30 cm. - 978-0-11-111790-3 £4.25

The Financial Services (Banking Reform) Act 2013 (Commencement No. 6) Order 2014 No. 2014/2458 (C.109). - Enabling power: Financial Services (Banking Reform) Act 2013, s. 148 (5). Bringing into operation various provisions of this Act on 01.11.2014, in accord. with art. 2. - Issued: 19.09.2014. Made: 12.09.2014. Effect: None. Territorial extent & classification: E/W/S/NI. General. - 4p.: 30 cm. - 978-0-11-112084-2 £4.25

The Financial Services (Banking Reform) Act 2013 (Disclosure of Confidential Information) Regulations 2014 No. 2014/882. - Enabling power: Financial Services (Banking Reform) Act 2013, ss. 92, 142 (3). - Issued: 07.04.2014. Made: 01.04.2014. Laid: 02.04.2014. Coming into force: 28.04.2014. Effect: None. Territorial extent & classification: E/W/S/NI. General. - 8p.: 30 cm. - 978-0-11-111343-1 £4.25

The Financial Services (Banking Reform) Act 2013 (Transitional Provision) Order 2014 No. 2014/378. - Enabling power: Financial Services (Banking Reform) Act 2013, s. 146 (1). - Issued: 27.02.2014. Made: 19.02.2014. Laid: 24.02.2014. Coming into force: 01.04.2014. Effect: None. Territorial extent & classification: E/W/S/NI. General. - 2p.: 30 cm. - 978-0-11-111009-6 £4.00

The Immigration Act 2014 (Bank Accounts) (Amendment) Order 2014 No. 2014/3074. - Enabling power: Immigration Act 2014, ss. 43 (1) (2). - Issued: 25.11.2014. Made: 19.11.2014. Coming into force: 12.12.2014. Effect: 2014 c.22 amended. Territorial extent & classification: E/W/S/NI. General. - Supersedes draft S.I. (ISBN 9780111119129) issued 28.07.2014. - 2p.: 30 cm. - 978-0-11-112364-5 £4.25

The Immigration Act 2014 (Bank Accounts) (Prohibition on Opening Current Accounts for Disqualified Persons) Order 2014 No. 2014/3086. - Enabling power: Immigration Act 2014, s. 40 (7). - Issued: 25.11.2014. Made: 19.11.2014. Coming into force: 12.12.2014. Effect: None. Territorial extent & classification: E/W/S/NI. General. - Supersedes draft S.I. (ISBN 9780111119112) issued 28.07.2014. - 4p.: 30 cm. - 978-0-11-112365-2 £4.25

The Immigration Act 2014 (Bank Accounts) Regulations 2014 No. 2014/3085. - Enabling power: Immigration Act 2014, s. 41. - Issued: 25.11.2014. Made: 19.11.2014. Coming into force: 12.12.2014. Effect: 2000 c.8 modified. Territorial extent & classification: E/W/S/NI. General. - Supersedes draft S.I. (ISBN 9780111119105) issued 29.07.2014. - 16p.: 30 cm. - 978-0-11-112363-8 £6.00

The Payments to Governments and Miscellaneous Provisions Regulations 2014 No. 2014/3293. - Enabling power: European Communities Act 1972, s. 2 (2). - Issued: 22.12.2014. Made: 12.12.2014. Laid: 15.12.2014. Coming into force: In accord. with reg. 1 (2). Effect: S.I. 2014/1261 revoked. Territorial extent & classification: E/W/S/NI. General. - 4p.: 30 cm. - 978-0-11-112559-5 £4.25

Fire and rescue services, England

The Fire and Rescue Authorities (National Framework) (England) (Revision) Order 2014 No. 2014/3317. - Enabling power: Fire and Rescue Services Act 2004, s. 21 (6). - Issued: 22.12.2014. Made: 16.12.2014. Laid: 18.12.2014. Coming into force: 12.01.2015. Effect: None. Territorial extent and classification: E. General. - 2p.: 30 cm. - 978-0-11-112599-1 £4.25

The Firefighters' Compensation Scheme (England) (Amendment) Order 2014 No. 2014/447. - Enabling power: Fire and Rescue Services Act 2004, ss. 34, 60. - Issued: 07.03.2014. Made: 28.02.2014. Laid: 06.03.2014. Coming into force: 01.04.2014. Effect: S.I. 2006/1811 amended. Territorial extent & classification: E. General. - 8p.: 30 cm. - 978-0-11-111074-4 £5.75

The Firefighters' Pension Scheme (Amendment) (England) Order 2014 No. 2014/446. - Enabling power: Fire Services Act 1947, s. 26 (1) to (5)- Issued: 07.03.2014. Made: 28.02.2014. Laid: 06.03.2014. Coming into force: 01.04.2014. Effect: S.I. 1992/129 amended in relation to England. Territorial extent & classification: E. General. - 4p.: 30 cm. - 978-0-11-111071-3 £4.00

The Firefighters' Pension Scheme (Amendment) (No. 2) (England) Order 2013 (correction slip) No. 2013/1392 Cor.. - 1 sheet.: 30 cm. Correction slip (to ISBN 9780111539941) dated December 2014. - Free

The Firefighters' Pension Scheme (England) (Amendment) (No. 2) Order 2013 (correction slip) No. 2013/1393 Cor.. - 1 sheet.: 30 cm. Correction slip (to ISBN 9780111539934) dated December 2014. - Free

The Firefighters' Pension Scheme (England) (Amendment) Order 2014 No. 2014/445. - Enabling power: Fire and Rescue Services Act 2004, ss. 34, 60. - Issued: 07.03.2014. Made: 28.02.2014. Laid: 06.03.2014. Coming into force: 01.04.2014. Effect: S.I. 2006/3432 amended. Territorial extent & classification: E. General. - 36p.: 30 cm. - 978-0-11-111072-0 £9.75

Fire and rescue services, Wales

The Firefighters' Compensation Scheme (Wales) (Amendment) Order 2014 No. 2014/3256 (W.331). - Enabling power: Fire and Rescue Services Act 2004, ss. 34, 60, 62. - Issued: 30.12.2014. Made: 08.12.2014. Laid before the National Assembly for Wales: 10.12.2014. Coming into force: 31.12.2014. Effect: S.I. 2007/1073 (W.111) amended. Territorial extent & classification: W. General. - In English and Welsh. Welsh title: Gorchymyn Cynllun Digolledu'r Diffoddwyr Tân (Cymru) (Diwygio) 2014. - 16p.: 30 cm. - 978-0-348-11034-0 £6.00

The Firefighters' Pension Scheme (Wales) (Amendment) Order 2014 No. 2014/3254 (W.330). - Enabling power: Fire and Rescue Services Act 2004, ss. 34, 60, 62. - Issued: 26.01.2015. Made: 08.12.2014. Laid before the National Assembly for Wales: 10.12.2014. Coming into force: 31.12.2014. Effect: S.I. 2007/1072 (W.110) amended. Territorial extent & classification: W. General. - In English and Welsh. Welsh title: Gorchymyn Cynllun Pensiwn y Diffoddwyr Tân (Cymru) (Diwygio) 2014. - 68p.: 30 cm. - 978-0-348-11039-5 £11.00

The Firefighters' Pension (Wales) Scheme (Amendment) Order 2014 No. 2014/3242 (W.329). - Enabling power: Fire Services Act 1947, s. 26(1) to (5) & Superannuation Act 1972, s. 12. - Issued: 26.01.2015. Made: 08.12.2015. Laid: 10.12.2015. Coming into force: 31.12.2015. Effect: S.I. 1992/129 amended. Territorial extent & classification: W. General. - In English and Welsh. Welsh language title: Gorchymyn Cynllun Pensiwn y Dynion Tân (Cymru) (Diwygio) 2014. - 40p.: 30 cm. - 978-0-348-11038-8 £10.00

The Firefighters' Pension (Wales) Scheme (Contributions) (Amendment) Order 2014 No. 2014/523 (W.64). - Enabling power: Fire and Rescue Services Act 2004, ss. 34, 60, 62. - Issued: 25.03.2014. Made: 04.03.2014. Laid before the National Assembly for Wales: 07.03.2014. Coming into force: 01.04.2014. Effect: S.I. 2007/1072 (W.110) amended. Territorial extent & classification: W. General. - In English and Welsh. Welsh title: Gorchymyn Cynllun Pensiwn y Dynion Tân (Cymru) (Cyfraniadau) (Diwygio) 2014. - 4p.: 30 cm. - 978-0-348-10919-1 £4.00

The Firefighters' Pension (Wales) Scheme (Contributions) (Amendment) Order 2014 No. 2014/522 (W.63). - Enabling power: Fire Services Act 1947, s. 26 (1). - Issued: 26.03.2015. Made: 04.03.2014. Laid before the National Assembly for Wales: 07.03.2014. Coming into force: 01.04.2014. Effect: S.I. 1992/129 amended in relation to Wales. Territorial extent & classification: W. General. - In English and Welsh. Welsh title: Gorchymyn Cynllun Pensiwn y Dynion Tân (Cymru) (Cyfraniadau) (Diwygio) 2014. - 4p.: 30 cm. - 978-0-348-10924-5 £4.00

Food

The Fish Labelling (Amendment) Regulations 2014 No. 2014/3104. - Enabling power: Food Safety Act 1990, ss. 6 (4), 16 (1), 17 (2), 26 (3), 48 (1) & European Communities Act 1972, sch. 2, para. 1A. - Issued: 28.11.2014. Made: 21.11.2014. Laid: 24.11.2014. Coming into force: 13.12.2014. Effect: S.I. 2013/1768 amended. Territorial extent & classification: E/W/S/NI. General. - 4p.: 30 cm. - 978-0-11-112385-0 £4.25

The Olive Oil (Marketing Standards) Regulations 2014 No. 2014/195. - Enabling power: European Communities Act 1972, s. 2 (2). - Issued: 06.02.2014. Made: 30.01.2014. Laid: 05.02.2014. Coming into force: In accord. with reg. 1. Effect: S.I. 1987/1783; 1992/2590; 1998/2410; 1999/1513; 2002/2761; 2004/2661; 2006/3367; S.R. 1987/431; 1988/383; 2008/189 revoked. Territorial extent & classification: E/W/S/NI. General. - 16p.: 30 cm. - 978-0-11-110913-7 £5.75

Food, England

The Food Information Regulations 2014 No. 2014/1855. - Enabling power: European Communities Act 1972, s. 2 (2), sch. 2, para. 1A & Food Safety Act 1990, ss. 6 (4), 16 (1), 17, 18, 26, 45, 48 (1), sch. 1, para. 1, 4 (b) & School Standards and Framework Act 1998, ss. 114A, 138 (7). - Issued: 21.07.2014. Made: 14.07.2014. Laid: 15.07.2014. Coming into force: In accord. with reg. 1 (5) to (8). Effect: 19 SIs amended & 24 SIs partially revoked & 17 revoked. Territorial extent & classification: E. General. - EC note: These Regulations implement in England Commission Directive 2008/100/EC amending Council Directive 90/496/EEC on nutrition labelling for foodstuffs as regards recommended daily allowances, energy conversion factors and definitions. Superseded by corrective reprint issued 22.08.2014 (ISBN 9780111540428). - 40p.: 30 cm. - 978-0-11-111825-2 £10.00

The Food Information Regulations 2014 No. 2014/1855. - Enabling power: European Communities Act 1972, s. 2 (2), sch. 2, para. 1A & Food Safety Act 1990, ss. 6 (4), 16 (1), 17, 18, 26, 45, 48 (1), sch. 1, para. 1, 4 (b) & School Standards and Framework Act 1998, ss. 114A, 138 (7). - Issued: 22.08.2014. Made: 14.07.2014. Laid: 15.07.2014. Coming into force: In accord. with reg. 1 (5) to (8). Effect: 19 SIs amended & 24 SIs partially revoked & 17 revoked. Territorial extent & classification: E. General. - EC note: These Regulations implement in England Commission Directive 2008/100/EC amending Council Directive 90/496/EEC on nutrition labelling for foodstuffs as regards recommended daily allowances, energy conversion factors and definitions. Supersedes SI of same title (ISBN 9780111118252) issued 21.07.2014. - 40p.: 30 cm. - 978-0-11-154042-8 £10.00

The Food Safety and Hygiene (England) (Amendment) Regulations 2014 No. 2014/2885. - Enabling power: European Communities Act 1972, s. 2 (2). - Issued: 07.11.2014. Made: 29.10.2014. Laid: 07.11.2014. Coming into force: 13.12.2014. Effect: S.I. 2013/2996 amended. Territorial extent & classification: E. General. - 4p.: 30 cm. - 978-0-11-112269-3 £4.25

The Official Feed and Food Controls (England) and the Food Safety and Hygiene (England) (Amendment) Regulations 2014 No. 2014/2748. - Enabling power: European Communities Act 1972, s. 2 (2), sch. 2, para. 1A. - Issued: 20.10.2014. Made: 13.10.2014. Laid: 17.10.2014. Coming into force: 11.11.2014. Effect: S.I. 2009/3255; 2013/2996 amended. Territorial extent & classification: E. General- EC note: These Regulations provide for the enforcement of Commission Reg (EU) no. 704/2014 on certification requirements for imports into Union of sprouts and seeds intended for the production of sprouts. These Regs also provide for the enforcement of Commission Reg (EU) no. 579/2014 granting derogation from certain provisions of Annex II to Reg (EC) no. 852/2004. These Regs also provide for the enforcement of Commission Reg (EU) no. 218/2014. - 4p.: 30 cm. - 978-0-11-112181-8 £4.25

The Products Containing Meat etc. (England) Regulations 2014 No. 2014/3001. - Enabling power: Food Safety Act 1990, ss. 6 (4), 16 (1) (a) (e), 26 (1) (a), 48 (1) & School Standards and Framework Act 1998, ss. 114A, 138 (7) (8). - Issued: 19.11.2014. Made: 12.11.2014. Laid: 13.11.2014. Coming into force: 13.12.2014. Effect: S.I. 2007/2359; 2014/1603 amended & S.I. 2009/3238; 2012/1809 partially revoked & 2003/2075; 2008/517 revoked. Territorial extent & classification: E. General. - 20p.: 30 cm. - 978-0-11-112329-4 £6.00

Food, Wales

The Fish Labelling (Wales) (Amendment) Regulations 2014 No. 2014/3079 (W.304). - Enabling power: Food Safety Act 1990, ss. 16 (1), 17 (2), 26 (1) (a) (3), 48 (1) & European Communities Act 1972, sch. 2, para 1A. - Issued: 28.11.2014. Made: 19.11.2014. Laid before the National Assembly for Wales: 20.11.2014. Coming into force: 13.12.2014. Effect: S.I. 2013/2139 (W.209) amended. Territorial extent & classification: W. General. - EC note: These Regulations amend the Fish Labelling (Wales) Regulations 2013 (the 2013 Regulations) in order to enforce the consumer information requirements of Chapter IV of Regulation (EU) No 1379/2013 on the common organisation of the markets in fishery and aquaculture products as read with Council Regulation (EC) No 1224/2009. It removes references to, and the definitions of, Council Regulation (EC) No 104/2000 and Commission Implementing Regulation (EC) No 2065/2001 which have been repealed by Regulation (EU) No 1379/2013 and Commission Implementing Regulation (EU) no 1420/2013. - In English and Welsh. Welsh language title: Rheoliadau Labelu Pysgod (Cymru) (Diwygio) 2014. - 8p.: 30 cm. - 978-0-348-11018-0 £6.00

The Food Hygiene Rating (Wales) Act 2013 (Commencement No. 2) Order 2014 No. 2014/3089 (W.310) (C.132). - Enabling power: Food Hygiene Rating (Wales) Act 2013, s. 27 (2). Bringing various provisions of the 2013 Act into operation on 28.11.2014. - Issued: 01.12.2014. Made: 18.11.2014. Effect: None. Territorial extent & classification: W. General. - In English and Welsh. Welsh title: Gorchymyn Deddf Sgorio Hylendid Bwyd (Cymru) 2013 (Cychwyn Rhif 2) 2014. - 4p.: 30 cm. - 978-0-348-11022-7 £4.25

The Food Hygiene (Wales) (Amendment) (No. 2) Regulations 2014 No. 2014/3080 (W.305). - Enabling power: European Communities Act 1972, s. 2 (2), sch. 2, para. 1A & Food Safety Act 1990, ss. 16 (1) (e), 48 (1). - Issued: 28.11.2014. Made: 19.11.2014. Laid before the National Assembly for Wales: 20.11.2014. Coming into force: 13.12.2014. Effect: S.I. 2006/31 (W.5) amended. Territorial extent & classification: W. General. - EC note: These Regulations, which apply to Wales, amend the Food Hygiene (Wales) Regulations 2006 (S.I. 2006/31 (W.5)), as already amended) (the 2006 Regulations). They make provision about raw milk, and are therefore related to the requirements provided for by Section IX of Annex III to Regulation (EC) No 853/2004 laying down specific hygiene rules for food of animal origin. - In English and Welsh. Welsh title: Rheoliadau Hylendid Bwyd (Cymru) (Diwygio) (Rhif 2) 2014. - 8p.: 30 cm. - 978-0-348-11019-7 £6.00

The Food Hygiene (Wales) (Amendment) Regulations 2014 No. 2014/1858 (W.192). - Enabling power: European Communities Act 1972, s. 2 (2), sch. 2, para. 1A. - Issued: 28.07.2014. Made: 14.07.2014. Laid before the National Assembly for Wales: 16.07.2014. Coming into force: 08.08.2014. Effect: S.I. 2006/31 (W.5) amended. Territorial extent & classification: W. General. - In English and Welsh. Welsh title: Rheoliadau Hylendid Bwyd (Cymru) (Diwygio) 2014. - 4p.: 30 cm. - 978-0-348-10976-4 £4.25

The Food Information (Wales) Regulations 2014 No. 2014/2303 (W.227). - Enabling power: European Communities Act 1972, s. 2 (2), sch. 2 para. 1A & Food Safety Act 1990, ss. 6 (4), 16 (1), 17, 18, 26, 45, 48 (1), sch. 1 paras 1, 4 (b) & ss. Healthy Eating in Schools (Wales) Measure 2009. - Issued: 26.09.2014. Made: 28.08.2014. Laid before the National Assembly for Wales: 29.08.2014. Coming into force: -: in accord. with reg. 1 (3) to (6). Effect: 17 SIs partially revoked, & 17 SIs revoked. Territorial extent & classification: W. General. - EC note: These Regulations make provision to enforce in Wales certain provisions of Regulation (EU) No 1169/2011 of the European Parliament and of the Council on the provision of food information to consumers, amending Regulations (EC) No 1924/2006 and (EC) No 1925/2006 of the European Parliament and of the Council, and repealing Commission Directive 87/250/EEC, Council Directive 1999/10/EC, Directive 2000/13/EC of the European Parliament and of the Commission Directives 2002/67/EC and 2008/5/EC and Commission Regulation (EC) No 608/2004. - In English and Welsh. Welsh language title: Rheoliadau Gwybodaeth am Fwyd (Cymru) 2014. - 64p.: 30 cm. - 978-0-348-10992-4 £11.00

The Food with Added Phytosterols or Phytostanols (Labelling) (Wales) (Amendment) Regulations 2014 No. 2014/440 (W.49). - Enabling power: Food Safety Act 1990, ss. 16 (1) (e) (f), 17, 26 (1) (3), 48 (1). - Issued: 10.03.2014. Made: 24.02.2014. Laid before the National Assembly for Wales: 28.02.2014. Coming into force: 21.03.2014. Effect: S.I. 2005/1224 (W.82) amended. Territorial extent & classification: W. General. - In English and Welsh. Welsh title: Rheoliadau Bwyd â Ffytosterolau neu Ffytostanolau Ychwanegol (Labelu) (Cymru) (Diwygio) 2014. - 4p.: 30 cm. - 978-0-348-10897-2 £4.00

The Infant Formula and Follow-on Formula (Wales) (Amendment) Regulations 2014 No. 2014/123 (W.13). - Enabling power: European Communities Act 1972, s. 2 (2) & Food Safety Act 1990, ss. 16 (1) (e), 17 (1), 48 (1). - Issued: 04.02.2014. Made: 22.01.2014. Laid before the National Assembly for Wales: 24.01.2014. Coming into force: 28.02.2014. Effect: S.I. 2007/3573 (W.316) amended. Territorial extent & classification: W. General. - These Regulations amend SI 2007/3573 (W.316) in order to implement Commission Directive 2013/46/EU in Wales. - In English and Welsh. Welsh title: Rheoliadau Fformiwla Fabanod a Fformiwla Ddilynol (Cymru) (Diwygio) 2014. - 4p.: 30 cm. - 978-0-348-10863-7 £4.00

The Official Feed and Food Controls (Wales) (Amendment) Regulations 2014 No. 2014/2714 (W.271). - Enabling power: European Communities Act 1972, s. 2 (2), sch. 2, para. 1A. - Issued: 21.10.2014. Made: 08.10.2014. Laid before the National Assembly for Wales: 10.10.2014. Coming into force: 06.11.2014. Effect: S.I. 2009/3376 (W.298) amended. Territorial extent & classification: W. General. - In English and Welsh. Welsh title: Rheoliadau Rheolaethau Swyddogol ar Fwyd Anifeiliaid a Bwyd (Cymru) (Diwygio) 2014. - [8]p.: 30 cm. - 978-0-348-11001-2 £4.25

The Products Containing Meat etc. (Wales) Regulations 2014 No. 2014/3087 (W.308). - Enabling power: 2009 nawm 3, ss. 4 (1) (2) (3) (8), 10 & Food Safety Act 1990, ss. 6 (4), 16 (1) (a) (e), 26 (1) (a), 48 (1). - Issued: 02.12.2014. Made: 18.11.2014. Laid before the National Assembly for Wales: 20.11.2014. Coming into force: -: 13.12.2014. Effect: W.S.I. 2013/1984 (W.194) amended & W.S.I. 2004/1396 (W.141); 2008/713 (W.74) revoked. Territorial extent & classification: W. General. - EC note:- In English and Welsh. Welsh language title: Rheoliadau Cynhyrchion sy'n Cynnwys Cig etc. (Cymru) 2014. - 24p.: 30 cm. - 978-0-348-11021-0 £6.00

The Transfer of Functions (Food) (Wales) Regulations 2014 No. 2014/1102 (W.110). - Enabling power: Food Safety Act 1990, ss. 6 (4), 16 (1) (e) (f), 17 (1) (2), 26 (1) (a) (3), 48 (1). - Issued: 08.05.2014. Made: 25.04.2014. Laid before the National Assembly for Wales: 29.04.2014. Coming into force: 23.05.2014. Effect: S.I. 2000/1866 (W.125); 2007/1040 (W.100), 2611 (W.222), 3573 (W.316) amended. Territorial extent & classification: W. General. - In English and Welsh. Welsh title: Rheoliadau Trosglwyddo Swyddogaethau (Bwyd) (Cymru) 2014. - 4p.: 30 cm. - 978-0-348-10939-9 £4.25

Friendly societies

The Building Societies (Funding) and Mutual Societies (Transfers) Act 2007 (Commencement No. 2) Order 2014 No. 2014/2796 (C.124). - Enabling power: Building Societies (Funding) and Mutual Societies (Transfers) Act 2007, s. 6 (2). Bringing into operation various provisions of the 2007 Act on 20.11.2014. - Issued: 23.10.2014. Made: 16.10.2014. Effect: None. Territorial extent & classification: E/W/S/NI. General. - 2p.: 30 cm. - 978-0-11-112198-6 £4.25

Fuel and electricity control

The Fuel and Electricity (Heating) (Control) (Revocations) Order 2014 No. 2014/1509. - Enabling power: Energy Act 1976, s. 17 (2). - Issued: 16.06.2014. Made: 06.06.2014. Laid: 10.06.2014. Coming into force: 09.07.2014. Effect: S.I. 1974/2160; 1980/1013 revoked. Territorial extent & classification: E/W/S. General. - 2p.: 30 cm. - 978-0-11-111633-3 £4.25

Gas

The Electricity and Gas Appeals (Designation and Exclusion) Order 2014 No. 2014/1293. - Enabling power: Energy Act 2004, s. 173 (2) (b) (d) (7). - Issued: 27.05.2014. Made: 19.05.2014. Laid: 27.05.2014. Coming into force: 18.06.2014. Effect: S.I. 2005/1646; 2009/648; 2013/2429 revoked with savings. Territorial extent & classification: E/W/S. General. - 8p.: 30 cm. - 978-0-11-111513-8 £6.00

The Electricity and Gas (Billing) Regulations 2014 No. 2014/1648. - Enabling power: European Communities Act 1972, s. 2 (2). - Issued: 01.07.2014. Made: 24.06.2014. Laid: 26.06.2014. Coming into force: 17.07.2014. Effect: 1986 c.44; 1989 c.29 amended. Territorial extent & classification: E/W/S. General. - EC note: The modifications give effect to provisions on billing and billing information for gas and electricity consumption in articles 10 and 11 of and annex VII to Directive 2012/27/EU on energy efficiency. - 4p.: 30 cm. - 978-0-11-111709-5 £4.25

The Electricity and Gas (Energy Companies Obligation) (Amendment) (No. 2) Order 2014 No. 2014/3231. - Enabling power: Gas Act 1986, ss. 33BC, 33BD & Electricity Act 1989, ss. 41A, 41B & Utilities Act 2000, s. 103. - Issued: 11.12.2014. Made: 04.12.2014. Coming into force: 05.12.2014 in accord. with art. 1. Effect: S.I. 2012/3018 amended. Territorial extent & classification: E/W/S. General. - Supersedes draft S.I. (ISBN 9780111118962) issued 25.07.2014. - 16p.: 30 cm. - 978-0-11-112486-4 £6.00

The Electricity and Gas (Energy Companies Obligation) (Amendment) Order 2014 No. 2014/1131. - Enabling power: Gas Act 1986, ss. 33BC, 33BD & Electricity Act 1989, ss. 41A, 41B. - Issued: 07.05.2014. Made: 30.04.2014. Coming into force: 01.05.2014, in accord. with art. 1. Effect: S.I. 2012/3018 amended. Territorial extent & classification: E/W/S. General. - Supersedes draft SI (ISBN 9780111109229) issued 10.02.2014. - 8p.: 30 cm. - 978-0-11-111451-3 £4.25

The Electricity and Gas (Energy Companies Obligation) (Determination of Savings) (Amendment) Order 2014 No. 2014/2897. - Enabling power: Gas Act 1986, ss. 33BC, 33BD & Electricity Act 1989, ss. 41A, 41B. - Issued: 07.11.2014. Made: 03.11.2014. Laid: 05.11.2014. Coming into force: 01.12.2014. Effect: S.I. 2012/3018 amended. Territorial extent & classification: E/W/S. General. - Supersedes draft SI (ISBN 9780111109229) issued 10.02.2014. - 4p.: 30 cm. - 978-0-11-112287-7 £4.25

The Electricity and Gas (Energy Company Obligation) Order 2014 No. 2014/3219. - Enabling power: Gas Act 1986, ss. 33BC, 33BD & Electricity Act 1989, ss. 41A, 41B & Utilities Act 2000, ss. 103, 103A & European Communities Act 1972, s. 2 (2). - Issued: 10.12.2014. Made: 04.12.2014. Coming into force: In accord. with art. 1. Effect: None. Territorial extent & classification: E/W/S. General. - Supersedes draft S.I. (ISBN 9780111124758) issued 29/10/14. - 32p.: 30 cm. - 978-0-11-112475-8 £6.00

The Electricity and Gas (Internal Markets) Regulations 2014 No. 2014/3332. - Enabling power: European Communities Act 1972, s. 2 (2). - Issued: 29.12.2014. Made: 17.12.2014. Laid: 22.12.2014. Coming into force: 14.01.2015. Effect: 1986 c.44; 1989 c.29; S.I. 2011/2704 amended. Territorial extent & classification: E/W/S. General. - 4p.: 30 cm. - 978-0-11-112640-0 £4.25

The Electricity and Gas (Ownership Unbundling) Regulations 2014 No. 2014/3333. - Enabling power: European Communities Act 1972, s. 2 (2). - Issued: 29.12.2014. Made: 17.12.2014. Laid: 22.12.2014. Coming into force: 15.01.2015. Effect: S.I. 2011/2704 amended. Territorial extent & classification: E/W/S. General. - 4p.: 30 cm. - 978-0-11-112638-7 £4.25

The Gas Act 1986 (Exemptions) (Revocations) Order 2014 No. 2014/528. - Enabling power: Gas Act 1986, s. 6A & Gas Act 1995, s. 6A. - Issued: 12.03.2014. Made: 06.03.2014. Laid: 10.03.2014. Coming into force: 06.04.2014. Effect: S.I. 1996/449, 471, 1354, 2795; 1997/2427; 1998/1779; 1999/2639, 3026, 3089; 2000/3206 revoked. Territorial extent & classification: E/W/S. General. - 2p.: 30 cm. - 978-0-11-111126-0 £4.00

The Gas and Electricity Regulated Providers (Redress Scheme) (Amendment) Order 2014 No. 2014/2378. - Enabling power: Consumers, Estate Agents and Redress Act 2007, s. 47 (1) to (3). - Issued: 12.09.2014. Made: 01.07.2014. Laid: 08.09.2014. Coming into force: 08.08.2014. Effect: None. Territorial extent & classification: E/W/S. General. - 2p.: 30 cm. - 978-0-11-112037-8 £4.25

The Gas Transit (EEC Requirements) (Revocation and Saving) Regulations 2014 No. 2014/529. - Enabling power: European Communities Act 1972, s. 2 (2). - Issued: 12.03.2014. Made: 06.03.2014. Laid: 10.03.2014. Coming into force: 06.04.2014. Effect: S.I. 1992/1190 revoked with savings. Territorial extent & classification: E/W/S. General. - 4p.: 30 cm. - 978-0-11-111127-7 £4.00

The Public Gas Transporter Pipe-line Works (Environmental Impact Assessment) (Amendment) (England) Regulations 2014 No. 2014/557. - Enabling power: European Communities Act 1972, s. 2 (2). - Issued: 14.03.2014. Made: 06.03.2014. Laid: 10.03.2014. Coming into force: 06.04.2014. Effect: S.I. 1999/1672 amended. Territorial extent & classification: E/W/S. General. - 4p.: 30 cm. - 978-0-11-111155-0 £4.00

The Warm Home Discount (Amendment) Regulations 2014 No. 2014/695. - Enabling power: Energy Act 2010, ss. 9, 31 (5) (6). - Issued: 24.03.2014. Made: 13.03.2014. Coming into force: 14.03.2014, in accord. with reg. 1. Effect: S.I. 2011/1033 amended. Territorial extent & classification: E/W/S. General. - Supersedes draft S.I. (ISBN 9780111108482) issued 22.01.2014. - 2p.: 30 cm. - 978-0-11-111240-3 £4.00

Gender recognition

The Courts and Tribunals Fees (Miscellaneous Amendments) Order 2014 No. 2014/590 (L.6). - Enabling power: Courts Act 2003, s. 92 & Insolvency Act 1986, ss. 414, 415 & Tribunals, Courts and Enforcement Act 2007, s. 42, 49 (3) & Constitutional Reform Act 2005, s. 52 & Mental Capacity Act 2005. s. 54 & Gender Recognition Act 2004, s. 7 (2). - Issued: 19.03.2014. Made: 11.03.2014. Laid: 13.03.2104. Coming into force: 06.04.2014. Effect: S.I. 2004/3120; 2006/758; 2007/1745; 2008/1052, 1053, 1054; 2009/213, 1114; 2010/42; 2011/2344; 2013/1179, 1893 amended. Territorial extent & classification: E/W. General. - 16p.: 30 cm. - 978-0-11-111194-9 £5.75

Government resources and accounts

The Government Resources and Accounts Act 2000 (Estimates and Accounts) Order 2014 No. 2014/3314. - Enabling power: Government Resources and Accounts Act 2000, s. 4A (3) (4). - Issued: 22.12.2014. Made: 16.12.2014. Laid: 17.12.2014. Coming into force: 31.01.2015. Effect: S.I. 2014/531 amended. Territorial extent & classification: E/W/S/NI. General. - 8p.: 30 cm. - 978-0-11-112596-0 £6.00

The Government Resources and Accounts Act 2000 (Estimates and Accounts) Order 2014 No. 2014/531. - Enabling power: Government Resources and Accounts Act 2000, s. 4A (3) (4). - Issued: 14.03.2014. Made: 06.03.2014. Laid: 10.03.2014. Coming into force: 01.04.2014. Effect: None. Territorial extent & classification: E/W/S/NI. General. - 16p.: 30 cm. - 978-0-11-111129-1 £5.75

The Whole of Government Accounts (Designation of Bodies) Order 2014 No. 2014/2234. - Enabling power: Government Resources and Accounts Act 2000, s. 10 (1). - Issued: 29.08.2014. Made: 22.08.2014. Laid: 27.08.2014. Coming into force: 22.09.2014. Effect: None. Territorial extent & classification: E/W/S/NI. General. - 136p.: 30 cm. - 978-0-11-111996-9 £20.75

Government trading funds

The Buying Agency Trading Fund (Amendment) Order 2014 No. 2014/561. - Enabling power: Government Trading Funds Act 1973, ss. 1 (1) (7), 6 (1). - Issued: 13.03.2014. Made: 06.03.2014. Laid: 11.03.2014. Coming into force: 01.04.2014. Effect: S.I. 1991/875 amended & S.I. 2011/2208 revoked. Territorial extent & classification: E/W/S/NI. General. - 2p.: 30 cm. - 978-0-11-111159-8 £4.00

The Medicines and Healthcare Products Regulatory Agency Trading Fund (Appropriation of Additional Assets and Liabilities) Order 2014 No. 2014/432. - Enabling power: Government Trading Funds Act 1973, ss. 1, 2 (2) (4) (7), 6 (1). - Issued: 05.03.2014. Made: 25.02.2014. Laid: 03.03.2014. Coming into force: 24.03.2014. Effect: None. Territorial extent & classification: E/W/S/NI. General. - 4p.: 30 cm. - 978-0-11-111043-0 £4.00

Harbours, docks, piers and ferries

The Able Marine Energy Park Development Consent Order 2014 No. 2014/2935. - Enabling power: Planning Act 2008, ss. 114, 115, 120, 122, sch. 5. pt. 1, paras 1 to 3, 10 to 17, 24, 26, 30A to 32, 32B to 34, 36, 37. - Issued: 11.11.2014. Made: 13.01.2014. Laid: 10.02.2014. Coming into force: 29.10.2014. Effect: None. Territorial extent & classification: E. Local. - 96p., col. map: 30 cm. - 978-0-11-112315-7 £22.50

The Associated British Ports (Fisher Fleet Quay) Harbour Revision Order 2014 No. 2014/2933. - Enabling power: Harbours Act 1964, ss. 14 (1) (2A) (3). - Issued: 13.11.2014. Made: 05.11.2014. Laid: 11.11.2014. Coming into force: 03.12.2014. Effect: None. Territorial extent & classification: E. Local. - 8p.: 30 cm. - 978-0-11-112313-3 £6.00

The Dover Harbour Revision Order 2014 No. 2014/2720. - Enabling power: Harbours Act 1964, s. 14 (1) (3). - Issued: 17.10.2014. Made: 09.10.2014. Laid: 14.10.2014. Coming into force: 05.11.2014. Effect: None. Territorial extent & classification: E. Local. - 8p.: 30 cm. - 978-0-11-112167-2 £4.25

The Lymington Harbour Revision Order 2014 No. 2014/1076. - Enabling power: Harbours Act 1964, s. 14 (1) (3). - Issued: 01.05.2014. Made: 24.04.2014. Laid: 01.05.2014. Coming into force: 23.05.2014. Effect: 1951 c.xxv amended & S.I. 2002/2586 amended & partially revoked. Territorial extent & classification: E. Local. - 16p.: 30 cm. - 978-0-11-111429-2 £6.00

The Lymington Harbour (Works) Revision Order 2014 No. 2014/17. - Enabling power: Harbours Act 1964, s. 14 (1) (3). - Issued: 15.01.2014. Made: 08.01.2014. Laid: 14.01.2014. Coming into force: 05.02.2014. Effect: None. Territorial extent & classification: E. Local. - 8p.: 30 cm. - 978-0-11-110815-4 £5.75

The Portsmouth Harbour (Abolition of Portsmouth and Gosport Joint Board) Revision Order 2014 No. 2014/1277. - Enabling power: Harbours Act 1964, s. 14 (2) (a). - Issued: 23.05.2014. Made: 16.05.2014. Laid: 23.05.2014. Coming into force: 16.06.2014. Effect: 1919 c.cxxii; 1920 c.lxviii partially repealed & 1809 c.cxc; 1812 c.lxxviii repealed. Territorial extent & classification: E. Local. - 4p.: 30 cm. - 978-0-11-111508-4 £4.25

Health and safety

The Acetylene Safety (England and Wales and Scotland) Regulations 2014 No. 2014/1639. - Enabling power: Health and Safety at Work etc. Act 1974, ss. 15 (1) (2) (3) (a) (c) (4) (a) (5) (9), 43 (2) (4) (5) (6), 80 (1), 82 (3) (a), sch. 3, paras. 1 (1) (2) (3) (5), 2 (1), 3, 4, 9, 12. - Issued: 01.07.2014. Made: 23.06.2014. Laid: 01.07.2014. Coming into force: 01.10.2014. Effect: S.I. 1998/494; 2009/1348; 2012/1652 amended & 1875 c.17; 2008 c.13, c.20 partially repealed & S.I. 1984/510; 2012/1652 partially revoked & S.R.& O. 1898/248; 1905/1128; 1919/809; 1937/54; 1947/805; S.I. 1978/1723, 1979/1378 revoked. Territorial extent & classification: E/W/S/NI. General. - 16p.: 30 cm. - 978-0-11-111712-5 £6.00

The Control of Explosives Precursors Regulations 2014 No. 2014/1942. - Enabling power: European Communities Act 1972, s. 2 (2), sch. 2, para 1A. - Issued: 28.07.2014. Made: 18.07.2014. Laid: 24.07.2014. Coming into force: 02.09.2014. Effect: S.I. 1975/1023; 1982/217, 218; 2013/50 amended. Territorial extent & classification: E/W/S. General. - EC note: These Regulations make provision to implement Regulation (EU) no. 98/2013 on the marketing and use of explosives precursors in England, Wales & Scotland. - 12p.: 30 cm. - 978-0-11-111914-3 £6.00

The Explosives Regulations 2014 No. 2014/1638. - Enabling power: European Communities Act 1972, s. 2 (2) & Health and Safety at Work etc. Act 1974, ss. 15 (1) (2) (3) (a) (c) (4) (b) (5) (6) (b) (9), 18 (2) (za) (a), 43 (2) (4) (5) (6), 80 (1), 82 (3) (a), sch. 3, paras. 1 (1) (2) (3) (4), 2, 3, 4, 5, 6 (1), 7, 12, 15 (1), 16, 18, 20. - Issued: 02.07.2014. Made: 23.06.2014. Laid: 01.07.2014. Coming into force: In accord. with reg. 1. Effect: 1875 c.17 (38 & 39 Vict.); 1930 c.clviii; 1951 c.58; 1979 c.2; 1979 c.58; 1990 c.43; 2003 c.22; 2013 c.32; S.I. 1969/1263; 1974/1885; 1975/1023; 1979/72; 1987/37; 1992/656; 1993/208; 1993/323; 1998/494; 1999/1736, 2024; 2008/2852; 2009/693, 1348; 2010/2214; 2011/1885; 2012/1652; 2013/1471; S.S.I. 2004/406; 2013/50 amended/repealed & 1951 c.58 repealed & S.I. 1974/1885; 1998/494; 2009/693; 2011/1885; 2014/469 partially revoked & S.R. & O. 1924/1129; 1926/823; S.I. 1974/2166; 1991/1531; 1993/2714; 1996/890; 2005/1082; 2007/2598; 2013/449 revoked. Territorial extent & classification: E/W/S. General. - EC note: These Regulations implement as regards Great Britain, Council Directive 93/15/EEC on the harmonization of the provisions relating to the pacing on the market and supervision of explosives for civil uses and Commission Directive 2008/43/EC. - Partially revoked by S.I. 2014/3248 (ISBN 9780111125106). - 112p.: 30 cm. - 978-0-11-111724-8 £16.50

The Genetically Modified Organisms (Contained Use) Regulations 2014 No. 2014/1663. - Enabling power: European Communities Act 1972, s. 2 (2) & Health and Safety At Work etc. Act 1974, ss. 15 (1) (2) (3) (b) (5) (b), 52 (2) (3), 82 (3) (a), sch. 3, paras. 1 (1) (b) (c) (2) (4) (5), 3, 4 (1), 5, 6, 8 (2), 9, 11, 13 (1) (3), 14, 15 (1), 16, 17. - Issued: 02.07.2014. Made: 23.06.2014. Laid: 30.06.2014. Coming into force: 01.10.2014. Effect: 1994 c.37 modified & S.I. 2012/1652 amended & S.I. 2000/283; 2002/63; 2005/2466; 2010/2840 revoked. Territorial extent & classification: E/W/S. General. - EC note: These Regs implement provisions of Directive 2009/41/EC which lays down measures for the contained use of genetically modified micro-organisms with a view to protecting human health and the environment. - 40p.: 30 cm. - 978-0-11-111722-4 £10.00

The Health and Safety (Miscellaneous Repeals and Revocations) Regulations 2014 No. 2014/486. - Enabling power: Health and Safety at Work etc. Act 1974, ss. 15 (1) (3) (a), 82 (3). - Issued: 10.03.2014. Made: 04.03.2014. Laid: 10.03.2014. Coming into force: 06.04.2014. Effect: 1961 c.34; 1963 c.41 partially repealed & S.I. 1938/610; 1948/707; 1974/1943; 1975/1011, 1012; 1976/2004, 2005 revoked. Territorial extent & classification: E/W/S. General. - 4p.: 30 cm. - 978-0-11-111088-1 £4.00

The Heavy Fuel Oil (Amendment) Regulations 2014 No. 2014/162. - Enabling power: European Communities Act 1972, s. 2 (2) & Health and Safety at Work etc. Act 1974, s. 15 (1) (2), sch. 3, para. 1 (1((b) & Planning (Hazardous Substances) Act 1990, ss. 5, 40. - Issued: 03.02.2014. Made: 28.01.2014. Laid: 30.01.2014. Coming into force: 20.02.2014. Effect: S.I. 1992/656; 1999/743 amended. Territorial extent & classification: E/W/S. General. - 4p.: 30 cm. - 978-0-11-110895-6 £4.00

The Mines Regulations 2014 No. 2014/3248. - Enabling power: Health and Safety at Work etc. Act 1974, ss. 15 (1) (2) (3) (a) (4) (a) (5) (8), 18 (2) (za) (a), 80 (1), 82 (3) (a), sch. 3 paras 1 (1) (2), 3, 6 (1), 8, 9, 10, 11, 13 (1) (3), 14, 16, 18 (a), 20, 21 (a) (b). - Issued: 16.12.2014. Made: 08.12.2014. Laid: 16.12.2014. Coming into force: 06.04.2015. Effect: 7 Acts partially repealed; 6 SIs partially revoked, 17 SIs revoked. Territorial extent & classification: E/W/S. General. - 44p.: 30 cm. - 978-0-11-112510-6 £10.00

The Petroleum (Consolidation) Regulations 2014 No. 2014/1637. - Enabling power: Health and Safety at Work etc. Act 1974, ss. 15 (1) (2) (3) (a) (c) (4) (6) (b) (8), 18 (2) (a), 43 (2) (4), 80 (1), 82 (3) (a), sch. 3, paras 1 (1) (2) (3) (4), 3 (1), 4, 9 12, 15 (1). - Issued: 30.06.2014. Made: 23.06.2014. Laid: 30.06.2014. Coming into force: 01.10.2014. Effect: 3 Acts repealed; 1 Act part repealed; 4 Acts amended; 9 SIs revoked; 4 SIs partially revoked & 5 SIs amended. Territorial extent & classification: E/W/S. General. - 20p.: 30 cm. - 978-0-11-111706-4 £6.00

The REACH Enforcement (Amendment) Regulations 2014 No. 2014/2882. - Enabling power: European Communities Act 1972, s. 2 (2). - Issued: 05.11.2014. Made: 25.10.2014. Laid: 31.10.2014. Coming into force: 01.12.2014. Effect: S.I. 2008/2852 amended. Territorial extent & classification: E/W/S/NI. General. - EC note: These Regulations provide for the enforcement of Regulation (EC) 1907/2006, as corrected, concerning the Registration, Evaluation, Authorisation and Restriction of Chemicals (REACH). - 4p.: 30 cm. - 978-0-11-112268-6 £4.25

Health care and associated professions

The Health and Social Care Act 2008 (Commencement No. 19) Order 2014 No. 2014/3251 (C.148). - Enabling power: Health and Social Care Act 2008, s. 170 (3) (4). Bringing into operation various provisions of the 2008 Act on 15.01.2015 in accord with art. 2. - Issued: 15.12.2014. Made: 08.12.2014. Effect: None. Territorial extent & classification: E. General. - 8p.: 30 cm. - 978-0-11-112516-8 £6.00

The Health Care and Associated Professions (Indemnity Arrangements) Order 2014 No. 2014/1887. - Enabling power: Health Act 1999, ss. 60, 62 (4) (4A). - Issued: 23.07.2014. Made: 16.07.2014. Coming into force: In accord. with art. 1 (2) (3). Effect: 1983 c.54; 1984 c.24; 1989 c.44; 1993 c.21; 1994 c.17 & S.I. 2002/253, 254; 2003/1572; 2004/291, 478, 627, 1767; 2005/3361, 3373; 2006/489, 490; 2008/1185; 2010/231, 1617 & S.S.I 2004/115, 116 & S.R. 1993/326; 2004/140 amended. Territorial extent & classification: E/W/S/NI. General. - Supersedes draft SI (ISBN 9780111114483) issued 23/07/14. - 32p.: 30 cm. - 978-0-11-111849-8 £6.00

The Health Professions Council (Registration and Fees) (Amendment) Rules 2013 Order of Council 2014 No. 2014/532. - Enabling power: S.I. 2002/254, arts. 7 (1) (2), 41 (2). - Issued: 13.03.2014. Made: 05.03.2014. Laid before Parliament & the Scottish Parliament: 10.03.2014. Coming into force: 01.04.2014. Effect: S.I. 2003/1572 amended. Territorial extent & classification: E/W/S/NI. General. - 4p.: 30 cm. - 978-0-11-111132-1 £4.00

Health care and associated professions: Dentists

The Dentists Act 1984 (Medical Authorities) (No. 2) Order 2014 No. 2014/1981. - Enabling power: S.I. 2009/1182, art. 7 (4) (b). - Issued: 31.07.2014. Made: 14.07.2014. Coming into force: 15.07.2014. Effect: None. Territorial extent & classification: E/W/S/NI. General. - 2p.: 30 cm. - 978-0-11-111931-0 £4.25

The Dentists Act 1984 (Medical Authorities) Order 2014 No. 2014/936. - Enabling power: S.I. 2009/1182, art. 7 (4) (b). - Issued: 14.04.2014. Made: 01.04.2014. Coming into force: 02.04.2014. Effect: None. Territorial extent & classification: E/W/S/NI. General. - 2p.: 30 cm. - 978-0-11-111395-0 £4.25

Health care and associated professions: Doctors

The General Medical Council (Fitness to Practise) (Amendment) Rules Order of Council 2014 No. 2014/1270. - Enabling power: Medical Act 1983, s. 35CC (1), sch. 4, paras 1 (1) (2) (2A), 5A (1) (2) (3) (3A), 5C (1). - Issued: 22.05.2014. Made: 13.05.2014. Laid: 21.05.2014. Coming into force: 25.06.2014. Effect: S.I. 2004/2608 amended. Territorial extent & classification: E/W/S/NI. General. - 8p: 30 cm. - 978-0-11-111502-2 £6.00

The General Medical Council (Licence to Practise and Revalidation) (Amendment) Regulations Order of Council 2014 No. 2014/1273. - Enabling power: Medical Act 1983, ss. 29A (2) to (4), 29B (1) (1A) (1B) (2D) (3), 29E (1) to (2A), 29J (2E) (3). - Issued: 22.05.2014. Made: 13.05.2014. Laid: 21.05.2014. Coming into force: 25.06.2014. Effect: S.I. 2012/2685 amended. Territorial extent & classification: E/W/S/NI. General. - 4p.: 30 cm. - 978-0-11-111507-7 £4.25

The General Medical Council (Restoration following Administrative Erasure) (Amendment) Regulations Order of Council 2014 No. 2014/1276. - Enabling power: Medical Act 1983, s. 31. - Issued: 22.05.2014. Made: 13.05.2014. Coming into force: 25.06.2014. Effect: S.I. 2004/2612 amended. Territorial extent & classification: E/W/S/NI. General. - 4p: 30 cm. - 978-0-11-111505-3 £4.25

The General Medical Council (Voluntary Erasure and Restoration following Voluntary Erasure) (Amendment) Regulations Order of Council 2014 No. 2014/1272. - Enabling power: Medical Act 1983, s. 31A. - Issued: 22.05.2014. Made: 13.05.2014. Laid: 21.05.2014. Coming into force: 25.06.2014. Effect: S.I. 2004/2609 amended. Territorial extent & classification: E/W/S/NI. General. - 4p: 30 cm. - 978-0-11-111506-0 £4.25

The Medical Act 1983 (Amendment) (Knowledge of English) Order 2014 No. 2014/1101. - Enabling power: Health Act 1999, ss. 60, 62 (4), sch. 3. - Issued: 02.05.2014. Made: 28.04.2014. Coming into force: 29.04.2014 in accord. with art. 1(1). Effect: 1983 c.54 amended. Territorial extent & classification: E/W/S/NI. General. - Supersedes draft S.I. (ISBN 9780111108932) issued 04.02.2014. - 8p.: 30 cm. - 978-0-11-111435-3 £6.00

Health care and associated professions: Nurses and midwives

The Nursing and Midwifery (Amendment) Order 2014 No. 2014/3272. - Enabling power: Health Act 1999, ss. 60, 62 (4), sch. 3. - Issued: 17.12.2014. Made: 10.12.2014. Coming into force: in accord. with art. 1. Effect: S.I. 2002/253 amended. Territorial extent & classification: E/W/S/NI. General. - Supersedes draft S.I. (ISBN 9780111121337) issued 13/10/14. - 8p.: 30 cm. - 978-0-11-112535-9 £4.25

The Nursing and Midwifery Council (Fees) (Amendment) Rules Order of Council 2014 No. 2014/3139. - Enabling power: S.I. 2002/253, arts 7 (1) (2), 33 (7) (a), 47 (2). - Issued: 02.12.2014. Made: 26.11.2014. Laid: 01.12.2014. Coming into force: 01.02.2015. Effect: S.I. 2004/1654 amended. Territorial extent & classification: E/W/S/NI. General. - 4p.: 30 cm. - 978-0-11-112413-0 £4.25

Healthcare and associated professions: Osteopaths

The General Osteopathic Council (Application for Registration and Fees) (Amendment) Rules Order of Council 2014 No. 2014/598. - Enabling power: Osteopaths Act 1993, ss. 6 (2) (4), 35 (2). - Issued: 18.03.2014. Made: 05.03.2014. Coming into force: 01.05.2014. Effect: S.I. 2000/1038 amended. Territorial extent & classification: E/W/S/NI. General. - 4p.: 30 cm. - 978-0-11-111198-7 £4.00

Health services, England

The Health Research Authority (Transfer of Staff, Property and Liabilities) and Care Act 2014 (Consequential Amendments) Order 2014 No. 2014/3090. - Enabling power: Care Act 2014, ss. 109 (4), 118, 125 (8). - Issued: 12.12.2014. Made: 18.11.2014. Coming into force: 01.01.2015. Effect: S.I. 1990/2024; 1995/2800; 1996/251; 1999/873, 874; 2011/2260 amended & S.I. 2012/1108, 1109 revoked. Territorial extent & classification: E. General. - This S.I. has been printed in substitution of the S.I. of the same number and ISBN issued 25.11.2014 and is being issued free of charge to all known recipients of that S.I. Partially revoked by SI 2015/559 (ISBN 9780111132296). - 8p.: 30 cm. - 978-0-11-112369-0 £4.25

Highways

The Heavy Goods Vehicles (Charging for the Use of Certain Infrastructure on the Trans-European Road Network) (Amendment) Regulations 2014 No. 2014/2437. - Enabling power: European Communities Act 1972, s. 2 (2). - Issued: 17.09.2014. Made: 11.09.2014. Laid: 12.09.2014. Coming into force: 07.10.2014. Effect: S.I. 2009/1914 amended. Territorial extent & classification: E/W/S/NI. General. - EC note: These Regulations amend S.I. 2009/1914 to implement the provisions of Directive 2011/76/EU amending Directive 1999/62/EC on the charging of the heavy goods vehicles to the use of certain road transport infrastructures. - 12p.: 30 cm. - 978-0-11-112071-2 £6.00

Highways, England

The A1 Motorway (Scotch Corner to Barton Connecting Roads) Scheme 2014 No. 2014/2127. - Enabling power: Highways Act 1980, ss. 16, 17, 19. - Issued: 14.08.2014. Made: 21.07.2014. Coming into force: 15.09.2014. Effect: None. Territorial extent & classification: E. Local. - 4p.: 30 cm. - 978-0-11-111984-6 £4.25

The A5 Trunk Road (A5-M1 Link Dunstable Northern Bypass) (Detrunking) Order 2014 No. 2014/1918. - Enabling power: Highways Act 1980, s. 10. - Issued: 25.07.2014. Made: 09.07.2014. Coming into force: 24.07.2014. Effect: None. Territorial extent & classification: E. Local. - 4p.: 30 cm. - 978-0-11-111892-4 £4.25

HIGHWAYS, ENGLAND

The A5 Trunk Road (A5 - M1 Link Dunstable Northern Bypass) Order 2014 No. 2014/1837. - Enabling power: Highways Act 1980, ss. 10, 41. - Issued: 17.07.2014. Made: 09.06.2014. Coming into force: 24.07.2014. Effect: None. Territorial extent & classification: E. Local. - 4p.: 30 cm. - 978-0-11-111814-6 £4.25

The A6 (M) Motorway (Stockport North-South Bypass) and Connecting Roads Scheme 1989 (Revocation) Order 2014 No. 2014/1043. - Enabling power: Highways Act 1980, s. 10. - Issued: 24.04.2014. Made: 08.04.2014. Coming into force: 30.04.2014. Effect: The A6 (M) Motorway (Stockport North-South Bypass) and Connecting Roads Scheme 1989 is revoked. Territorial extent & classification: E. Local. - 2p.: 30 cm. - 978-0-11-111420-9 £4.25

The A6 Trunk Road (Hazel Grove Diversion) Order 1989 (Revocation) Order 2014 No. 2014/1045. - Enabling power: Highways Act 1980, s. 10. - Issued: 24.04.2014. Made: 08.04.2014. Coming into force: 30.04.2014. Effect: The A6 Trunk Road (Hazel Grove Diversion) Order 1989 is revoked. Territorial extent & classification: E. Local. - 2p.: 30 cm. - 978-0-11-111422-3 £4.25

The A34 Trunk Road (Chilton Interchange) Slip Roads Order 2014 No. 2014/3027. - Enabling power: Highways Act 1980, ss. 10, 41. - Issued: 19.11.2014. Made: 27.10.2014. Coming into force: 17.12.2014. Effect: None. Territorial extent & classification: E. Local. - 2p.: 30 cm. - 978-0-11-112333-1 £4.25

The A38 Trunk Road (Plymouth Parkway Slip Roads) (Trunking and Detrunking) Order 2014 No. 2014/2141. - Enabling power: Highways Act 1980, ss. 10, 12. - Issued: 15.08.2014. Made: 18.07.2014. Coming into force: 22.08.2014. Effect: None. Territorial extent & classification: E. Local. - 8p., col. maps: 30 cm. - 978-0-11-111987-7 £8.50

The A47 Trunk Road (Postwick Interchange Slip Roads) Order 2014 No. 2014/3343. - Enabling power: Highways Act 1980, ss. 10, 41. - Issued: 24.12.2014. Made: 17.03.2014. Coming into force: 24.03.2014. Effect: None. Territorial extent & classification: E. Local. - 8p.: 30 cm. - 978-0-11-112632-5 £4.25

The A66 Trunk Road (Scotch Corner Junction to Violet Grange Farm) Order 2014 No. 2014/2130. - Enabling power: Highways Act 1980, ss. 10, 41. - Issued: 15.08.2014. Made: 21.07.2014. Coming into force: 15.09.2014. Effect: None. Territorial extent & classification: E. Local. - 2p.: 30 cm. - 978-0-11-111986-0 £4.25

The A138 (Replacement Chelmer Viaduct) (Trunking) Order 2014 No. 2014/2657. - Enabling power: Highways Act 1980, ss. 10, 41, 106. - Issued: 07.10.2014. Made: 26.09.2014. Coming into force: 03.10.2014. Effect: None. Territorial extent & classification: E. Local. - 2p.: 30 cm. - 978-0-11-112120-7 £4.25

The A523 Trunk Road (Hazel Grove Diversion Order) 1990 (Revocation) Order 2014 No. 2014/1044. - Enabling power: Highways Act 1980, s. 10. - Issued: 24.04.2014. Made: 08.04.2014. Coming into force: 30.04.2014. Effect: The A523 Trunk Road (Hazel Grove Diversion Order) 1990 revoked. Territorial extent & classification: E. Local. - 2p.: 30 cm. - 978-0-11-111421-6 £4.25

The Clifton Suspension Bridge (Revision of Tolls) Order 2014 No. 2014/926. - Enabling power: Transport Charges &c. (Miscellaneous Provisions Act 1954, s. 6. - Issued: 02.04.2014. Made: 24.03.2014. Coming into force: 31.03.2014. Effect: S.I. 2006/3375 revoked. Territorial extent & classification: E. Local. - Available at http://www.legislation.gov.uk/uksi/2014/926/contents/made Non-print

The Lincolnshire County Council (River Witham Bridge) Scheme 2013 Confirmation Instrument 2014 No. 2014/1871. - Enabling power: Highways Act 1980, s. 106 (3). - Issued: 22.07.2014. Made: 08.07.2014. Coming into force: In accord. with art. 1. Effect: None. Territorial extent & classification: E. Local. - With correction slip dated December 2014. - 8p., col. plan: 30 cm. - 978-0-11-111835-1 £5.25

The M1 Motorway (A5 - M1 Link Dunstable Northern Bypass Connecting Roads) Scheme 2014 No. 2014/1857. - Enabling power: Highways Act 1980, ss. 16, 17, 19. - Issued: 21.07.2014. Made: 09.07.2014. Coming into force: 24.07.2014. Effect: None. Territorial extent & classification: E. Local. - 4p.: 30 cm. - 978-0-11-111826-9 £4.25

The M11 Motorway (Junction 14 Connecting Road) Scheme 2014 No. 2014/3007. - Enabling power: Highways Act 1980, ss. 16, 17, 19. - Issued: 19.11.2014. Made: 10.11.2014. Coming into force: 17.11.2014. Effect: None. Territorial extent & classification: E. Local. - 2p.: 30 cm. - 978-0-11-112330-0 £4.25

The M40 Motorway (Junction 12 Improvements) Scheme 2014 No. 2014/3295. - Enabling power: Highways Act 1980, ss. 16, 17, 19. - Issued: 19.12.2014. Made: 15.09.2014. Coming into force: 25.09.2014. Effect: None. Territorial extent & classification: E. Local. - 4p.: 30 cm. - 978-0-11-112564-9 £4.25

The Reading Borough Council (River Thames Reading Pedestrian/Cycle Bridge) Scheme 2013 Confirmation Instrument 2014 No. 2014/1666. - Enabling power: Highways Act 1980, s. 106 (3). - Issued: 02.07.2014. Made: 24.06.2014. Coming into force: In accord. with art. 1. Effect: None. Territorial extent & classification: E. Local. - 8p., plans (some col.): 30 cm. - 978-0-11-111727-9 £8.50

The Severn Bridges Tolls Order 2014 No. 2014/3313. - Enabling power: Severn Bridges Act 1992, s. 9 (1) (2) (b) (3) (b) (4) (6). - Issued: 22.12.2014. Made: 15.12.2014. Coming into force: 01.01.2015. Effect: S.I. 2013/3246 revoked. Territorial extent & classification: E. Local. - 2p.: 30 cm. - 978-0-11-112594-6 £4.25

The Traffic Management (Bracknell Forest Borough Council) Permit Scheme Order 2014 No. 2014/2462. - Enabling power: Traffic Management Act 2004, ss. 34 (4) (5), 39 (2). - Issued: 19.09.2014. Made: 11.09.2014. Coming into force: 05.11.2014. Effect: None. Territorial extent & classification: E. General. - 60p.: 30 cm. - 978-0-11-112088-0 £10.00

The Traffic Management (Cheshire East Borough Council) Permit Scheme Order 2014 No. 2014/2460. - Enabling power: Traffic Management Act 2004, ss. 34 (4) (5), 39 (2). - Issued: 19.09.2014. Made: 11.09.2014. Coming into force: 03.11.2014. Effect: None. Territorial extent & classification: E. General. - 92p.: 30 cm. - 978-0-11-112086-6 £16.00

The Traffic Management (Cheshire West and Chester Borough Council) Permit Scheme Order 2014 No. 2014/3106. - Enabling power: Traffic Management Act 2004, ss. 34 (4) (5), 39 (2). - Issued: 28.11.2014. Made: 18.11.20144. Coming into force: 02.02.2015. Effect: None. Territorial extent & classification: E. General. - 44p.: 30 cm. - 978-0-11-112387-4 £10.00

The Traffic Management (Coventry City Council) Permit Scheme Order 2014 No. 2014/3311. - Enabling power: Traffic Management Act 2004, ss. 34 (4) (5), 39 (2). - Issued: 22.12.2014. Made: 08.12.2014. Coming into force: 16.03.2015. Effect: None. Territorial extent & classification: E. General. - 88p.: 30 cm. - 978-0-11-112584-7 £16.00

The Traffic Management (Norfolk County Council) Permit Scheme Order 2014 No. 2014/941. - Enabling power: Traffic Management Act 2004, ss. 34 (2). - Issued: 14.04.2014. Made: 31.03.2014. Coming into force: 06.05.2014. Effect: None. Territorial extent & classification: E. General. - 116p.: 30 cm. - 978-0-11-111398-1 £19.00

The Traffic Management (North Tyneside Council) Permit Scheme Order 2014 No. 2014/3109. - Enabling power: Traffic Management Act 2004, ss. 34 (4) (5), 39 (2). - Issued: 28.11.2014. Made: 18.11.2014. Coming into force: 09.02.2015. Effect: None. Territorial extent & classification: E. General. - 64p.: 30 cm. - 978-0-11-112391-1 £11.00

The Traffic Management (Sefton Metropolitan Borough Council) Permit Scheme Order 2014 No. 2014/3107. - Enabling power: Traffic Management Act 2004, ss. 34 (4) (5), 39 (2). - Issued: 28.11.2014. Made: 18.11.2014. Coming into force: 02.02.2015. Effect: None. Territorial extent & classification: E. General. - 56p.: 30 cm. - 978-0-11-112388-1 £10.00

The Traffic Management (Shropshire Council) Permit Scheme Order 2014 No. 2014/466. - Enabling power: Traffic Management Act 2004, ss. 34 (4) (5), 39 (2). - Issued: 07.03.2014. Made: 27.02.2014. Coming into force: 01.04.2014. Effect: None. Territorial extent & classification: E. General. - 102p., tables: 30 cm. - 978-0-11-111076-8 £16.00

The Traffic Management (Slough Borough Council) Permit Scheme Order 2014 No. 2014/3112. - Enabling power: Traffic Management Act 2004, ss. 34 (4) (5), 39 (2). - Issued: 28.11.2014. Made: 18.11.2014. Coming into force: 04.03.2015. Effect: None. Territorial extent & classification: E. General. - 60p.: 30 cm. - 978-0-11-112393-5 £10.00

The Traffic Management (Warrington Borough Council) Permit Scheme Order 2014 No. 2014/3108. - Enabling power: Traffic Management Act 2004, ss. 34 (4) (5), 39 (2). - Issued: 28.11.2014. Made: 18.11.2014. Coming into force: 02.02.2015. Effect: None. Territorial extent & classification: E. General. - 40p.: 30 cm. - 978-0-11-112390-4 £10.00

The Traffic Management (Warwickshire County Council) Permit Scheme Order 2014 No. 2014/3310. - Enabling power: Traffic Management Act 2004, ss. 34 (4) (5), 39 (2). - Issued: 22.12.2014. Made: 08.12.2014. Coming into force: 16.03.2015. Effect: None. Territorial extent & classification: E. General. - 88p.: 30 cm. - 978-0-11-112583-0 £16.00

The Traffic Management (West Berkshire Council) Permit Scheme Order 2014 No. 2014/3110. - Enabling power: Traffic Management Act 2004, ss. 34 (4) (5), 39 (2). - Issued: 28.11.2014. Made: 18.11.2014. Coming into force: 01.03.2015. Effect: None. Territorial extent & classification: E. General. - 60p.: 30 cm. - 978-0-11-112392-8 £10.00

The Traffic Management (Wokingham Borough Council) Permit Scheme Order 2014 No. 2014/3105. - Enabling power: Traffic Management Act 2004, ss. 34 (4) (5), 39 (2). - Issued: 28.11.2014. Made: 18.11.20144. Coming into force: 19.01.2015. Effect: None. Territorial extent & classification: E. General. - 60p.: 30 cm. - 978-0-11-112386-7 £10.00

The Walsall Metropolitan Borough Council (York's Bridge Replacement Scheme) Bridge Scheme 2014 Confirmation Instrument 2014 No. 2014/1799. - Enabling power: Highways Act 1980, s. 106 (3). - Issued: 14.07.2014. Made: 04.07.2014. Coming into force: In accord. with art. 1. Effect: None. Territorial extent & classification: E. Local. - 8p., 3 col. plans: 30 cm. - 978-0-11-111777-4 £8.50

Highways, England: Special roads

The M40 Motorway (Junction 10 Improvements) (Connecting Roads) Scheme 2014 No. 2014/2899. - Enabling power: Highways Act 1980, ss. 16, 17, 19. - Issued: 07.11.2014. Made: 31.07.2014. Coming into force: 20.09.2014. Effect: None. Territorial extent & classification: E. Local. - 4p.: 30 cm. - 978-0-11-112289-1 £4.25

Highways, England: Trunk roads

The A21 Trunk Road (Tonbridge Bypass to Pembury Bypass Dualling) (Detrunking) Order 1996 (Revocation) Order 2014 No. 2014/1337. - Enabling power: Highways Act 1980, ss. 10, 12, 41. - Issued: 28.05.2014. Made: 23.05.2014. Coming into force: 27.05.2014. Effect: S.I. 1996/808 revoked. Territorial extent & classification: E. Local. - Available at http://www.legislation.gov.uk/uksi/2014/1337/contents/made Non-print

The A21 Trunk Road (Tonbridge Bypass to Pembury Bypass Dualling) Order 1996 (Revocation) Order 2014 No. 2014/1330. - Enabling power: Highways Act 1980, ss. 10, 41. - Issued: 28.05.2014. Made: 23.05.2014. Coming into force: 27.05.2014. Effect: S.I. 1996/802 revoked. Territorial extent & classification: E. Local. - Available at http://www.legislation.gov.uk/uksi/2014/1330/contents/made Non-print

The A21 Trunk Road (Tonbridge Bypass to Pembury Bypass Dualling Side Roads) Order 1996 (Revocation) Order 2014 No. 2014/1329. - Enabling power: Highways Act 1980, ss. 12, 14, 41, 125, 326 (2). - Issued: 28.05.2014. Made: 23.05.2014. Coming into force: 27.05.2014. Effect: The A21 Trunk Road (Tonbridge Bypass to Pembury Bypass Dualling Side Roads) Order 1996 (Unnumbered) revoked. Territorial extent & classification: E. Local. - Available at http://www.legislation.gov.uk/uksi/2014/1329/contents/made Non-print

The A21 Trunk Road (Tonbridge Bypass to Pembury Bypass Dualling Slip Roads) Order 1996 (Revocation) Order 2014 No. 2014/1328. - Enabling power: Highways Act 1980, ss. 10, 41. - Issued: 02.07.2014. Made: 23.05.2014. Coming into force: 27.05.2014. Effect: S.I. 1996/807 revoked. Territorial extent & classification: E. Local. - Available at http://www.legislation.gov.uk/uksi/2014/1328/contents/made Non-print

The A21 Trunk Road (Tonbridge to Pembury Dualling) (Detrunking) Order 2014 No. 2014/1431. - Enabling power: Highways Act 1980, ss. 10, 12. - Issued: 04.06.2014. Made: 23.05.2014. Coming into force: 27.05.2014. Effect: None. Territorial extent & classification: E. Local. - Available at http://www.legislation.gov.uk/uksi/2014/1431/contents/made Non-print

The A21 Trunk Road (Tonbridge to Pembury Dualling) Order 2014 No. 2014/1331. - Enabling power: Highways Act 1980, ss. 10, 41. - Issued: 28.05.2014. Made: 23.05.2014. Coming into force: 27.05.2014. Effect: None. Territorial extent & classification: E. Local. - Available at http://www.legislation.gov.uk/uksi/2014/1331/contents/made Non-print

Highways, England and Wales

The Dartford - Thurrock Crossing (Amendment) Regulations 2014 No. 2014/2949. - Enabling power: Dartford - Thurrock Crossing Act 1988, ss. 25 (1) (2), 44. - Issued: 17.11.2014. Made: 10.11.2014. Laid: 12.11.2014. Coming into force: 05.12.2014. Effect: S.I. 1998/1908 amended. Territorial extent & classification: E/W. General. - 8p.: 30 cm. - 978-0-11-112324-9 £4.25

Highways, Wales

The Active Travel (Wales) Act 2013 (Commencement) Order 2014 No. 2014/2589 (W.256) (C.112). - Enabling power: Active Travel (Wales) Act 2013, s. 14 (1). Bringing into operation various provisions of the 2013 Act on 25.09.2014, in accord. with art. 2. - Issued: 29.10.2014. Made: 24.09.2014. Effect: None. Territorial extent & classification: W. General. - This Statutory Instrument has been printed in substitution of the SI of the same, title, number and ISBN (issued 17.10.2014) and is being issued free of charge to all known recipients of that Statutory Instrument. - In English and Welsh. Welsh title: Gorchymyn Deddf Teithio Llesol (Cymru) 2013 (Cychwyn) 2014. - 2p.: 30 cm. - 978-0-348-11003-6 £4.25

The Neath to Abergavenny Trunk Road (A465) (Abergavenny to Hirwaun Dualling and Slip Roads) and East of Abercynon to East of Dowlais Trunk Road (A4060), Cardiff to Glan Conwy Trunk Road (A470) (Connecting Roads) Order 1999, (Gilwern to Brynmawr) (Amendment) Order 2014 No. 2014/2716 (W.272). - Enabling power: Highways Act 1980, s. 10. - Issued: 14.10.2014. Made: 06.10.2014. Coming into force: 16.10.2014. Effect: S.I. 1999/2720 (W.9) amended. Territorial extent & classification: W. Local. - Welsh title: Gorchymyn Cefnffordd Castell-nedd - Y Fenni (A465) (Deuoli o'r Fenni i Hirwaun a'r Ffyrdd Ymuno ac Ymadael) a Chefnffordd Man i'r Dwyrain o Abercynon - Man i'r Dwyrain o Ddowlais (A4060), Cefnffordd Caerdydd - Glanconwy (A470) (Ffyrdd Cysylltu) 1999, (Gilwern i Fryn-mawr) (Diwygio) 2014. - Available at http://www.legislation.gov.uk/uksi/2014/2716/contents/made Non-print

Housing

The Rent Officers (Housing Benefit and Universal Credit Functions) (Local Housing Allowance Amendments) Order 2014 No. 2014/3126. - Enabling power: Housing Act 1996, s. 122 (1) (6). - Issued: 01.12.2014. Made: 24.11.2014. Laid: 01.12.2014. Coming into force: 08.01.2015. Effect: S.I. 1997/1984, 1995; 2013/382 amended. Territorial extent & classification: E/W/S. General. - 16p.: 30 cm. - 978-0-11-112402-4 £6.00

Housing, England

The Absolute Ground for Possession for Anti-social Behaviour (Review Procedure) (England) Regulations 2014 No. 2014/2554. - Enabling power: Housing Act 1985, s. 85ZA (7). - Issued: 26.09.2014. Made: 22.09.2014. Laid: 25.09.2014. Coming into force: 20.10.2014. Effect: None. Territorial extent & classification: E. General. - 4p.: 30 cm. - 978-0-11-112099-6 £4.25

The Allocation of Housing and Homelessness (Eligibility) (England) (Amendment) Regulations 2014 No. 2014/435. - Enabling power: Housing Act 1996, ss. 160ZA (2) (4), 172 (4), 185 (2) (3), 215 (2). - Issued: 05.03.2014. Made: 27.02.2014. Laid: 05.03.2014. Coming into force: 31.03.2014. Effect: S.I. 2006/1294 amended. Territorial extent & classification: E. General. - 4p.: 30 cm. - 978-0-11-111046-1 £4.00

The Anti-social Behaviour, Crime and Policing Act 2014 (Commencement No. 6) Order 2014 No. 2014/2454 (C.108). - Enabling power: Anti-social Behaviour, Crime and Policing Act 2014, s. 185 (1). Bringing into operation various provisions of the 2014 Act on 01.10.2014, in accord. with art. 2. - Issued: 19.09.2014. Made: 10.09.2014. Effect: None. Territorial extent & classification: E/W. General. - 8p.: 30 cm. - 978-0-11-112081-1 £4.25

The Housing Renewal Grants (Amendment) (England) Regulations 2014 No. 2014/1829. - Enabling power: Housing Grants, Construction and Regeneration Act 1996, ss. 3 (3), 30, 146 (1) (2). - Issued: 17.07.2014. Made: 10.07.2014. Laid: 16.07.2014. Coming into force: 13.08.2014. Effect: S.I. 1996/2890 amended. Territorial extent & classification: E. General. - 2p.: 30 cm. - 978-0-11-111806-1 £4.25

HOUSING, ENGLAND AND WALES

The Housing (Right to Buy) (Limit on Discount) (England) (Amendment) Order 2014 No. 2014/1865. - Enabling power: Housing Act 1985, s. 131. - Issued: 22.07.2014. Made: 15.07.2014. Laid: 18.07.2014. Coming into force: 20.07.2014. Effect: S.I. 2014/1378 amended. Territorial extent & classification: E. General. - This Statutory Instrument has been made in consequence of a defect in S.I. 2014/1378 (ISBN 9780111115510) and is being issued free of charge to all known recipients of that Statutory Instrument. - 2p.: 30 cm. - 978-0-11-111829-0 £4.25

The Housing (Right to Buy) (Limit on Discount) (England) Order 2014 No. 2014/1378. - Enabling power: Housing Act 1985, s. 131. - Issued: 05.06.2014. Made: 29.05.2014. Laid: 05.06.2014. Coming into force: 21.07.2014. Effect: S.I. 2012/734 partially revoked & S.I. 2013/677 revoked, with savings, in so far as it relates to dwelling houses within London authorities. Territorial extent & classification: E. General. - A defect in t his SI has been corrected by SI 2014/1865 (ISBN 9780111118290) which is being issued free of charge to all known recipients of SI 2014/1378. - 4p.: 30 cm. - 978-0-11-111551-0 £4.25

The Housing (Right to Buy) (Maximum Percentage Discount) (England) Order 2014 No. 2014/1915. - Enabling power: Housing Act 1985, ss. 129 (2A) (2B). - Issued: 25.07.2014. Made: 20.07.2014. Coming into force: 21.07.2014 in accord. with art. 1. Effect: None. Territorial extent & classification: E. General. - Supersedes draft S.I. (ISBN 9780111115534) issued 05.06.2014. - 4p.: 30 cm. - 978-0-11-111887-0 £4.25

The Prevention of Social Housing Fraud (Power to Require Information) (England) Regulations 2014 No. 2014/899. - Enabling power: Prevention of Social Housing Fraud Act 2013, ss. 7, 8, 9 (2) (b) (c). - Issued: 09.04.2014. Made: 03.04.2014. Coming into force: 04.04.2014 in accord. with reg. 1 (1). Effect: None. Territorial extent & classification: E. General. - Supersedes draft S.I. (ISBN 9780111110058) issued 27.02.2014. - 8p.: 30 cm. - 978-0-11-111364-6 £4.25

The Redress Schemes for Lettings Agency Work and Property Management Work (Requirement to Belong to a Scheme etc) (England) Order 2014 No. 2014/2359. - Enabling power: Enterprise and Regulatory Reform Act 2013, ss. 83 (1) (5) (9) (b), 84 (1) (7) (b), 85 (1) (a) (2) (a) (3) (4), 88 (1). - Issued: 09.09.2014. Made: 03.09.2014. Coming into force: In accord. with art. 1. Effect: None. Territorial extent & classification: E. General. - Supersedes draft SI (ISBN 9780111116821) issued 25/06/14 - 8p.: 30 cm. - 978-0-11-112021-7 £6.00

The Housing (Right to Buy) (Prescribed Forms) (Amendment) (England) Regulations 2014 No. 2014/1797. - Enabling power: Housing Act 1985, s. 176 (1) (5). - Issued: 14.07.2014. Made: 08.07.2014. Laid: 10.07.2014. Coming into force: 04.08.2014. Effect: S.I. 1986/2194 amended in relation to England. Territorial extent & classification: E. General. - 16p.: 30 cm. - 978-0-11-111773-6 £6.00

Housing, England and Wales

The Anti-social Behaviour, Crime and Policing Act 2014 (Commencement No. 2, Transitional and Transitory Provisions) Order 2014 No. 2014/949 (C.43). - Enabling power: Anti-social Behaviour, Crime and Policing Act 2014, s. 185 (1) (7). Bringing into operation various provisions of the 2014 Act on 13.05.2014, 01.06.2014, 16.06.2014, 14.07.2014, in accord. with arts. 2 to 6. - Issued: 14.04.2014. Made: 08.04.2014. Effect: None. Territorial extent & classification: E/W/S/NI. General. - 8p.: 30 cm. - 978-0-11-111401-8 £6.00

The Anti-social Behaviour, Crime and Policing Act 2014 (Commencement No. 7, Saving and Transitional Provisions) (Amendment) Order 2014 No. 2014/2754 (C.121). - Enabling power: Anti-social Behaviour, Crime and Policing Act 2014, s. 185 (1) (7). - Issued: 20.10.2014. Made: 14.10.2014. Coming into force: 20.10.2014. Effect: S.I. 2014/2590 (C.113) amended. Territorial extent & classification: E/W. General. - This Statutory Instrument corrects errors in SI. 2014/2590 (C.113) which was made on 24th September 2014 and published on 29th September 2014 (ISBN 9780111121078). It is being issued free of charge to all known recipients of that Statutory Instrument. - 4p.: 30 cm. - 978-0-11-112185-6 £4.25

The Anti-social Behaviour, Crime and Policing Act 2014 (Commencement No. 7, Saving and Transitional Provisions) Order 2014 No. 2014/2590 (C.113). - Enabling power: Anti-social Behaviour, Crime and Policing Act 2014, s. 185 (1) (7). Bringing into operation various provisions of the 2014 Act on 20.10.2014, in accord. with art. 2. - Issued: 01.10.2014. Made: 24.09.2014. Effect: None. Territorial extent & classification: E/W. General. - 8p.: 30 cm. - 978-0-11-112107-8 £6.00

Housing, Wales

The Allocation of Housing and Homelessness (Eligibility) (Wales) Regulations 2014 No. 2014/2603 (W.257). - Enabling power: Housing Act 1996, ss. 160A (3) (5), 172 (4), 185 (2) (3), 215 (2). - Issued: 16.10.2014. Made: 24.09.2014. Laid before the National Assembly for Wales: 01.10.2014. Coming into force: 31.10.2014. Effect: S.I. 2006/2645 (W.226), 2646 (W.227); 2009/393 (W.42) revoked & S.I. 2003/239 (W.36) partially revoked. Territorial extent & classification: W. General. - In English and Welsh. Welsh title: Rheoliadau Dyrannu Tai a Digartrefedd (Cymhwystra) (Cymru) 2014. - 12p.: 30 cm. - 978-0-348-10996-2 £6.00

The Anti-social Behaviour, Crime and Policing Act 2014 (Commencement No. 1 and Transitory Provisions) (Wales) Order 2014 No. 2014/1241 (W.129) (C.50). - Enabling power: Anti-social Behaviour, Crime and Policing Act 2014, s. 185 (3) (8). Bringing into operation various provisions of the 2014 Act on 13.05.2014, in accord. with art. 2. - Issued: 21.05.2014. Made: 13.05.2014. Effect: None. Territorial extent & classification: W. General. - In English and Welsh. Welsh title: Gorchymyn Deddf Ymddygiad Gwrthgymdeithasol, Troseddu a Phlismona 2014 (Cychwyn Rhif 1 a Darpariaethau Darfodol) (Cymru) 2014. - 4p.: 30 cm. - 978-0-348-10947-4 £4.25

The Anti-social Behaviour, Crime and Policing Act 2014 (Commencement No. 2 and Transitory Provisions) (Wales) Order 2014 No. 2014/2830 (W.286) (C.130). - Enabling power: Anti-social Behaviour, Crime and Policing Act 2014, s. 185 (3) (8). Bringing into operation various provisions of the 2014 Act on 21.10.2014, in accord. with art. 2. - Issued: 27.10.2014. Made: 20.10.2014. Effect: None. Territorial extent & classification: W. General. - In English and Welsh. Welsh title: Gorchymyn Deddf Ymddygiad Gwrthgymdeithasol, Troseddu a Phlismona 2014 (Cychwyn Rhif 2 a Darpariaethau Darfodol) (Cymru) 2014. - 8p.: 30 cm. - 978-0-348-11013-5 £6.00

The Housing (Wales) Act 2014 (Commencement No. 1) Order 2014 No. 2014/3127 (W.316)(C.136). - Enabling power: Housing (Wales) Act 2014, s. 145 (3). Bringing into operation various provisions of the 2014 Act on 01.12.2014, in accord. with art. 2. - Issued: 04.12.2014. Made: 24.11.2014. Effect: None. Territorial extent & classification: W. General. - In English and Welsh. Welsh title: Gorchymyn Deddf Tai (Cymru) 2014 (Cychwyn Rhif 1) 2014. - 8p.: 30 cm. - 978-0-348-11024-1 £6.00

The Prevention of Social Housing Fraud (Detection of Fraud) (Wales) Regulations 2014 No. 2014/826 (W.84). - Enabling power: Prevention of Social Housing Fraud Act 2013, ss. 7, 8. - Issued: 03.04.2014. Made: 25.03.2014. Coming into force: 28.03.2014. Effect: None. Territorial extent & classification: W. General. - In English and Welsh. Welsh language title: Rheoliadau Atal Twyll Tai Cymdeithasol (Darganfod Twyll) (Cymru) 2014. - 8p.: 30 cm. - 978-0-348-10932-0 £6.00

The Residential Property Tribunal Procedures and Fees (Wales) (Amendment No. 2) Regulations 2014 No. 2014/2553 (W.247). - Enabling power: Housing Act 2004, s. 250 (2), sch. 13. - Issued: 22.10.2014. Made: 17.10.2014. Coming into force: 01.10.2014. Effect: S.I 2012/531 (W.83) amended. Territorial extent & classification: W. General. - In English and Welsh. Welsh title: Rheoliadau Gweithdrefnau a Ffioedd Tribiwnlys Eiddo Preswyl (Cymru) (Diwygio Rhif 2) 2014. - 16p.: 30 cm. - 978-0-348-11007-4 £6.00

The Secure Tenancies (Absolute Ground for Possession for Anti-social Behaviour) (Review Procedure) (Wales) Regulations 2014 No. 2014/3278 (W.335). - Enabling power: Housing Act 1985, s. 85ZA (8). - Issued: 23.12.2014. Made: 09.12.2014. Laid before the National Assembly for Wales: 12.12.2014. Coming into force: 12.01.2015. Effect: None. Territorial extent & classification: W. General. - In English and Welsh. Welsh title: Rheoliadau Tenantiaethau Diogel (Sail Absoliwt ar gyfer Meddiannu am Ymddygiad Gwrthgymdeithasol) (Y Weithdrefn Adolygu) (Cymru) 2014. - 8p.: 30 cm. - 978-0-348-11033-3 £6.00

Human fertilisation and embryology

The Human Fertilisation and Embryology (Quality and Safety) Regulations 2014 No. 2014/2884. - Enabling power: European Communities Act 1972, s. 2 (2). - Issued: 07.11.2014. Made: 29.10.2014. Laid: 07.11.2014. Coming into force: 15.12.2014. Effect: 1990 c.37 amended. Territorial extent & classification: E/W/S/NI/Gibraltar. General. - 2p.: 30 cm. - 978-0-11-112276-1 £4.25

The Marriage (Same Sex Couples) Act 2013 (Consequential and Contrary Provisions and Scotland) Order 2014 No. 2014/560. - Enabling power: Marriage (Same Sex Couples) Act 2013, ss. 17 (2) (3), 18 (10), sch. 2, para. 1 (1), sch. 4, 27 (3) (a) (b) & Civil Partnership Act 2004, s. 259 (1) (3) & Human Fertilisation and Embryology Act 2008, s. 64 (1) (2)- Issued: 13.03.2014. Made: 06.03.2014. Coming into force: In accord. with art. 1 (2) (3). Effect: 37 Acts & 18 SIs/WSIs amended. Territorial extent & classification: E/W/S/NI. General. - Supersedes draft S.I. (ISBN 9780111108727) issued 28.01.2014. Partially revoked by S.I. 2014/3168 (ISBN 9780111124291) in re to S. - 28p.: 30 cm. - 978-0-11-111158-1 £5.75

Human tissue

The Human Tissue (Quality and Safety for Human Application) (Amendment) Regulations 2014 No. 2014/2883. - Enabling power: European Communities Act 1972, s. 2 (2). - Issued: 07.11.2014. Made: 29.10.2014. Laid: -07.11.2014. Coming into force: 15.12.2014. Effect: S.I. 2007/1523 amended. Territorial extent & classification: E/W/S/NI. General. - EC note: These Regulations amend SI 2007/1523 in order to transpose Commission Directive 2012/39/EU as regards certain technical requirements for the testing of human tissues and cells. - 2p.: 30 cm. - 978-0-11-112275-4 £4.25

The Quality and Safety of Organs Intended for Transplantation (Amendment) Regulations 2014 No. 2014/1459. - Enabling power: European Communities Act 1972, s. 2 (2). - Issued: 12.06.2014. Made: 04.06.2014. Laid: 12.06.2014. Coming into force: 14.07.2014. Effect: 2004 c.30; S.I. 2006/1260; 2012/1501 amended. Territorial extent & classification: E/W/S/NI. General. - 4p.: 30 cm. - 978-0-11-111611-1 £4.25

Immigration

The Accession of Croatia (Immigration and Worker Authorisation) (Amendment) Regulations 2014 No. 2014/530. - Enabling power: European Union (Croatian Accession and Irish Protocol) Act 2013, s. 4 (1) (2) (3) (9). - Issued: 14.03.2014. Made: 04.03.2014. Laid: 13.03.2014. Coming into force: 06.04.2014. Effect: S.I. 2013/1460 amended. Territorial extent & classification: UK. General. - 4p.: 30 cm. - 978-0-11-111128-4 £4.00

The Borders, Citizenship and Immigration Act 2009 (Commencement No. 3) Order 2014 No. 2014/2634 (C.116). - Enabling power: Borders, Citizenship and Immigration Act 2009, s. 58 (2) (3) (b). Bringing into operation various provisions of the 2009 Act on 27.10.2014. - Issued: 03.10.2014. Made: 28.09.2014. Effect: None. Territorial extent & classification: E/W/S/NI. General. - 2p.: 30 cm. - 978-0-11-112114-6 £4.25

The Channel Tunnel (Miscellaneous Provisions) (Amendment) Order 2014 No. 2014/409. - Enabling power: Channel Tunnel Act 1987, s. 11. - Issued: 03.03.2014. Made: 25.02.2014. Laid: 27.02.2014. Coming into force: In accord. with art. 1. Effect: S.I. 1994/1405 amended. Territorial extent & classification: E/W/S/NI. General. - 8p.: 30 cm. - 978-0-11-111027-0 £5.75

The Immigration Act 2014 (Bank Accounts) (Amendment) Order 2014 No. 2014/3074. - Enabling power: Immigration Act 2014, ss. 43 (1) (2). - Issued: 25.11.2014. Made: 19.11.2014. Coming into force: 12.12.2014. Effect: 2014 c.22 amended. Territorial extent & classification: E/W/S/NI. General. - Supersedes draft S.I. (ISBN 9780111119129) issued 28.07.2014. - 2p.: 30 cm. - 978-0-11-112364-5 £4.25

The Immigration Act 2014 (Bank Accounts) (Prohibition on Opening Current Accounts for Disqualified Persons) Order 2014 No. 2014/3086. - Enabling power: Immigration Act 2014, s. 40 (7). - Issued: 25.11.2014. Made: 19.11.2014. Coming into force: 12.12.2014. Effect: None. Territorial extent & classification: E/W/S/NI. General. - Supersedes draft S.I. (ISBN 9780111119112) issued 28.07.2014. - 4p.: 30 cm. - 978-0-11-112365-2 £4.25

The Immigration Act 2014 (Bank Accounts) Regulations 2014 No. 2014/3085. - Enabling power: Immigration Act 2014, s. 41. - Issued: 25.11.2014. Made: 19.11.2014. Coming into force: 12.12.2014. Effect: 2000 c.8 modified. Territorial extent & classification: E/W/S/NI. General. - Supersedes draft S.I. (ISBN 9780111119105) issued 29.07.2014. - 16p.: 30 cm. - 978-0-11-112363-8 £6.00

The Immigration Act 2014 (Commencement No. 1, Transitory and Saving Provisions) Order 2014 No. 2014/1820 (C.81). - Enabling power: Immigration Act 2014, ss. 73 (1), 75 (3). Bringing into operation various provisions of the 2014 Act on 14.07.2014; 28.07.2014 in accord. with arts 2, 3. - Issued: 16.07.2014. Made: 07.07.2014. Effect: None. Territorial extent & classification: E/W/S/NI. General. - With correction slip dated October 2014. - 4p.: 30 cm. - 978-0-11-111791-0 £4.25

The Immigration Act 2014 (Commencement No. 2) Order 2014 No. 2014/1943 (C.89). - Enabling power: Immigration Act 2014, s. 75 (3). Bringing into operation various provisions of the 2014 Act on 12.12.2014 in accord. with art. 2. - Issued: 28.07.2014. Made: 22.07.2014. Effect: None. Territorial extent & classification: E/W/S/NI. General. - 2p.: 30 cm. - 978-0-11-111915-0 £4.25

The Immigration Act 2014 (Commencement No. 3, Transitional and Saving Provisions) Order 2014 No. 2014/2771 (C.122). - Enabling power: Immigration Act 2014, ss. 35 (3), 73 (1), 75 (3). Bringing into operation various provisions of the 2014 Act on 20.10.2014, 17.011.2014, 01.12.2014 in accord. with arts 2 to 6. - Issued: 22.10.2014. Made: 15.10.2014. Effect: None. Territorial extent & classification: E/W/S/NI. General. - 12p.: 30 cm. - 978-0-11-112196-2 £6.00

The Immigration Act 2014 (Specified Anti-fraud Organisation) Order 2014 No. 2014/1798. - Enabling power: Immigration Act 2014, s. 40 (4). - Issued: 14.07.2014. Made: 08.07.2014. Laid: 11.07.2014. Coming into force: 02.08.2014. Effect: None. Territorial extent & classification: E/W/S/NI. General. - 2p.: 30 cm. - 978-0-11-111774-3 £4.25

The Immigration Act 2014 (Transitional and Saving Provisions) Order 2014 No. 2014/2928. - Enabling power: Immigration Act 2014, s. 73 (1). - Issued: 13.11.2014. Made: 06.11.2014. Coming into force: 10.11.2014. Effect: None. Territorial extent & classification: E/W/S/NI. General. - This Statutory Instrument has been made in consequence of defects in SI 2014/2771 (ISBN 9780111121962) and is being issued free of charge to all known recipients of that Statutory Instrument. - 4p.: 30 cm. - 978-0-11-112308-9 £4.25

The Immigration and Nationality (Cost Recovery Fees) (Amendment) Regulations 2014 No. 2014/2398. - Enabling power: Immigration, Asylum and Nationality Act 2006, ss. 51 (3), 52 (1) (3) (6). - Issued: 12.09.2014. Made: 04.09.2014. Laid: 10.09.2014. Coming into force: 01.10.2014. Effect: S.I. 2014/581 amended. Territorial extent & classification: E/W/S/NI. General. - 8p.: 30 cm. - 978-0-11-112050-7 £4.25

The Immigration and Nationality (Cost Recovery Fees) Regulations 2014 No. 2014/581. - Enabling power: Immigration, Asylum and Nationality Act 2006, ss. 51 (3), 52 (1) (3) (6). - Issued: 17.03.2014. Made: 11.03.2014. Laid: 13.03.2014. Coming into force: 06.04.2014. Effect: S.I. 2013/617 revoked. Territorial extent & classification: E/W/S/NI. General. - 20p.: 30 cm. - 978-0-11-111185-7 £5.75

The Immigration and Nationality (Fees) (Amendment) Order 2014 No. 2014/205. - Enabling power: Immigration, Asylum and Nationality Act 2006, ss. 51 (1) (2), 52 (1) (3). - Issued: 07.02.2014. Made: 03.02.2014. Coming into force: 04.02.2014 in accord. with art. 1. Effect: S.I. 2011/445 amended. Territorial extent & classification: E/W/S/NI. General. - 4p.: 30 cm. - 978-0-11-110919-9 £4.00

The Immigration and Nationality (Fees) (Consequential Amendments) Order 2014 No. 2014/2038. - Enabling power: Immigration Act 2014 s. 73 (2) (3). - Issued: 05.08.2014. Made: 29.07.2014. Laid: 31.07.2014. Coming into force: 01.09.2014. Effect: S.I. 2011/445 amended. Territorial extent & classification: E/W/S/NI. General. - 4p.: 30 cm. - 978-0-11-111939-6 £4.25

The Immigration and Nationality (Fees) Regulations 2014 No. 2014/922. - Enabling power: Immigration, Asylum and Nationality Act 2006, ss. 51 (3), 52 (1) (3) (6). - Issued: 10.04.2014. Made: 02.04.2014. Coming into force: 06.04.2014. Effect: S.I. 2013/749 amended. Territorial extent & classification: E/W/S/NI/CI. General. - 24p.: 30 cm. - 978-0-11-111379-0 £6.00

The Immigration (Control of Entry through Republic of Ireland) (Amendment) Order 2014 No. 2014/2475. - Enabling power: Immigration Act 1971, ss. 9 (2) (6), 32 (1). - Issued: 22.09.2014. Made: 14.09.2014. Laid: 17.09.2014. Coming into force: 12.10.2014. Effect: S.I. 1972/1610 amended. Territorial extent & classification: E/W/S/NI. General. - 4p.: 30 cm. - 978-0-11-112090-3 £4.25

The Immigration (Designation of Travel Bans) (Amendment) Order 2014 No. 2014/1849. - Enabling power: Immigration Act 1971, s. 8B (5). - Issued: 21.07.2014. Made: 14.07.2014. Laid: 16.07.2014. Coming into force: 21.07.2014. Effect: S.I. 2000/2724 amended & S.I. 2012/1663, 2058, 3010; 2013/678, 1745 revoked. Territorial extent & classification: E/W/S/NI. General. - Revoked by SI 2015/388 (ISBN 9780111130759). - 12p.: 30 cm. - 978-0-11-111822-1 £6.00

The Immigration (Employment of Adults Subject to Immigration Control) (Maximum Penalty) (Amendment) Order 2014 No. 2014/1262. - Enabling power: Immigration, Asylum and Nationality Act 2006, ss. 15 (2), 20 (1) (c). - Issued: 21.05.2014. Made: 15.05.2014. Coming into force: In accord. with art. 1 (2). Effect: S.I. 2008/132 amended. Territorial extent & classification: E/W/S/NI. General. - Supersedes draft SI (ISBN 9780111110102) issued 27/02/14. - 2p.: 30 cm. - 978-0-11-111497-1 £4.25

The Immigration (European Economic Area) (Amendment) (No. 2) Regulations 2014 No. 2014/1976. - Enabling power: European Communities Act 1972, s. 2 (2). - Issued: 30.07.2014. Made: 23.07.2014. Laid: 25.07.2014. Coming into force: 28.07.2014. Effect: S.I. 2006/1003 amended. Territorial extent & classification: E/W/S/NI. General. - 8p.: 30 cm. - 978-0-11-111929-7 £6.00

The Immigration (European Economic Area) (Amendment) (No. 3) Regulations 2014 No. 2014/2761. - Enabling power: European Communities Act 1972, s. 2 (2). - Issued: 21.10.2014. Made: 14.10.2014. Laid: 17.10.2014. Coming into force: 10.11.2014. Effect: S.I. 2006/1003 amended. Territorial extent & classification: E/W/S/NI. General. - 2p.: 30 cm. - 978-0-11-112186-3 £4.25

The Immigration (European Economic Area) (Amendment) Regulations 2014 No. 2014/1451. - Enabling power: European Communities Act 1972, s. 2 (2). - Issued: 10.06.2014. Made: 04.06.2014. Laid: 06.06.2014. Coming into force: 01.07.2014. Effect: S.I. 2006/1003 amended. Territorial extent & classification: E/W/S/NI. General. - 4p.: 30 cm. - 978-0-11-111597-8 £4.25

The Immigration (Notices) (Amendment) Regulations 2014 No. 2014/2768. - Enabling power: Nationality, Immigration and Asylum Act 2002, ss. 105, 112 (3). - Issued: 22.10.2014. Made: 15.10.2014. Laid: 16.10.2014. Coming into force: 06.11.2014. Effect: S.I. 2003/658 amended. Territorial extent & classification: E/W/S/NI. General. - 4p.: 30 cm. - 978-0-11-112195-5 £4.25

The Immigration (Passenger Transit Visa) (Amendment) Order 2014 No. 2014/1513. - Enabling power: Immigration and Asylum Act 1999, s. 41. - Issued: 13.06.2014. Made: 05.06.2014. Laid: 12.06.2014. Coming into force: 03.07.2014. Effect: S.I. 2003/1185 amended. Territorial extent & classification: E/W/S/NI. General. - Revoked by S.I. 2014/2702 (ISBN 9780111121405). - 2p.: 30 cm. - 978-0-11-111637-1 £4.25

The Immigration (Passenger Transit Visa) Order 2014 No. 2014/2702. - Enabling power: Immigration and Asylum Act 1999, s. 41. - Issued: 16.10.2014. Made: 08.10.2014. Laid: 16.10.2014. Coming into force: 01.12.2014. Effect: S.I. 2003/1185, 2628; 2004/1304; 2005/492; 2006/493; 2009/198, 1229, 1233; 2011/1553; 2012/116, 771; 2014/1513 revoked. Territorial extent & classification: E/W/S/NI. General. - 8p.: 30 cm. - 978-0-11-112140-5 £6.00

The Immigration (Removal of Family Members) Regulations 2014 No. 2014/2816. - Enabling power: Immigration and Asylum Act 1999, s. 10 (10) (b). - Issued: 24.10.2014. Made: 20.10.2014. Laid: 22.10.2014. Coming into force: 14.11.2014. Effect: None. Territorial extent & classification: E/W/S/NI. General. - 4p.: 30 cm. - 978-0-11-112203-7 £4.25

The Immigration (Residential Accommodation) (Prescribed Cases) Order 2014 No. 2014/2873. - Enabling power: Immigration Act 2014, ss. 37 (6) (a) (7). - Issued: 04.11.2014. Made: 28.10.2014. Laid: 30.10.2014. Coming into force: 01.12.2014. Effect: None. Territorial extent & classification: E/W/S/NI. General. - 4p.: 30 cm. - 978-0-11-112262-4 £4.25

The Immigration (Residential Accommodation) (Prescribed Requirements and Codes of Practice) Order 2014 No. 2014/2874. - Enabling power: Immigration Act 2014, ss. 24 (2) (4) (7) (8), 26 (2) (4) (7) (8), 29 (3) (6), 32 (6), 33 (5), 34 (1), 37 (1). - Issued: 04.11.2014. Made: 28.10.2014. Laid: 30.10.2014. Coming into force: 01.12.2014. Effect: None. Territorial extent & classification: E/W/S/NI. General. - 8p.: 30 cm. - 978-0-11-112263-1 £6.00

The Immigration (Restrictions on Employment) (Codes of Practice and Amendment) Order 2014 No. 2014/1183. - Enabling power: Immigration, Asylum and Nationality Act 2006, ss. 15 (3) (7), 19 (2), 20 (1), 23 (3), 25 (d). - Issued: 13.05.2014. Made: 06.05.2014. Laid: 08.05.2014. Coming into force: 16.05.2014. Effect: S.I. 2007/3290 amended. Territorial extent & classification: E/W/S/NI/CI. General. - 8p.: 30 cm. - 978-0-11-111463-6 £4.25

The Immigration Services Commissioner (Application Fee) (Amendment) Order 2014 No. 2014/2847. - Enabling power: Immigration and Asylum Act 1999, sch. 6, para. 5 (1). - Issued: 29.10.2014. Made: 23.10.2014. Laid: 27.10.2014. Coming into force: 17.11.2014. Effect: S.I. 2011/1366 amended. Territorial extent & classification: E/W/S/NI. General. - 2p.: 30 cm. - 978-0-11-112228-0 £4.25

Income tax

The Business Premises Renovation Allowances (Amendment) Regulations 2014 No. 2014/1687. - Enabling power: Capital Allowances Act 2001, ss. 360B (5), 360C (2) (a) (3), 360D (4). - Issued: 04.07.2014. Made: 30.06.2014. Laid: 01.07.2014. Coming into force: 22.07.2014. Effect: S.I. 2007/945 amended. Territorial extent & classification: E/W/S/NI. General. - 4p.: 30 cm. - 978-0-11-111738-5 £4.25

The Capital Allowances (Energy-saving Plant and Machinery) (Amendment) Order 2014 No. 2014/1868. - Enabling power: Capital Allowances Act 2001, ss. 45A (3) (4). - Issued: 23.07.2014. Made: 16.07.2014. Laid: 17.07.2014. Coming into force: 07.08.2014. Effect: S.I. 2001/2541 amended. Territorial extent & classification: E/W/S/NI. General. - 2p.: 30 cm. - 978-0-11-111832-0 £4.25

The Capital Allowances (Environmentally Beneficial Plant and Machinery) (Amendment) Order 2014 No. 2014/1869. - Enabling power: Capital Allowances Act 2001, s. 45H (3) to (5). - Issued: 22.07.2014. Made: 16.07.2014. Laid: 17.07.2014. Coming into force: 07.08.2014. Effect: S.I. 2003/2076 amended. Territorial extent & classification: E/W/S/NI. General. - 2p.: 30 cm. - 978-0-11-111833-7 £4.25

The Charitable Deductions (Approved Schemes) (Amendment) Regulations 2014 No. 2014/584. - Enabling power: Income Tax (Earnings and Pensions) Ac t 2003, s. 715. - Issued: 18.03.2014. Made: 12.03.2014. Laid: 13.03.2014. Coming into force: 06.04.2014. Effect: S.I. 1986/2211 amended. Territorial extent & classification: E/W/S/NI. General. - 4p.: 30 cm. - 978-0-11-111188-8 £4.00

The Double Taxation Relief and International Tax Enforcement (Belgium) Order 2014 No. 2014/1875. - Enabling power: Taxation (International and Other Provisions) Act 2010, s. 2 & Finance Act 2006, s. 173 (1) to (3). - Issued: 23.07.2014. Made: 16.07.2014. Effect: None. Territorial extent & classification: E/W/S/NI. General. - Supersedes draft SI (ISBN 9780111116272) issued 13/06/14. - 8p.: 30 cm. - 978-0-11-111837-5 £4.25

The Double Taxation Relief and International Tax Enforcement (Canada) Order 2014 No. 2014/3274. - Enabling power: Taxation (International and Other Provisions) Act 2010, s. 2 & Finance Act 2006, s. 173 (1) to (3). - Issued: 17.12.2014. Made: 10.12.2014. Coming into force: 10.12.2014. Effect: 1980/709 amended. Territorial extent & classification: E/W/S/NI. - Supersedes draft S.I. (ISBN 9780111121801) issued 20/10/14. - 20p.: 30 cm. - 978-0-11-112537-3 £6.00

The Double Taxation Relief and International Tax Enforcement (Iceland) Order 2014 No. 2014/1879. - Enabling power: Taxation (International and Other Provisions) Act 2010, s. 2 & Finance Act 2006, s. 173 (1) to (3). - Issued: 23.07.2014. Made: 16.07.2014. Effect: None. Territorial extent & classification: E/W/S/NI. General. - Supersedes draft SI (ISBN 9780111116296) issued 13/06/14. - 24p.: 30 cm. - 978-0-11-111841-2 £6.00

The Double Taxation Relief and International Tax Enforcement (Japan) Order 2014 No. 2014/1881. - Enabling power: Taxation (International and Other Provisions) Act 2010, s. 2 & Finance Act 2006, s. 173 (1) to (3). - Issued: 23.07.2014. Made: 16.07.2014. Effect: None. Territorial extent & classification: E/W/S/NI. General. - Supersedes draft SI (ISBN 9780111116289) issued 23/07/14. - 20p.: 30 cm. - 978-0-11-111843-6 £6.00

INCOME TAX

The Double Taxation Relief and International Tax Enforcement (Tajikistan) Order 2014 No. 2014/3275. - Enabling power: Taxation (International and Other Provisions) Act 2010, s. 2 & Finance Act 2006, s. 173 (1) to (3). - Issued: 17.12.2014. Made: 10.12.2014. Effect: None. Territorial extent & classification: E/W/S/NI. General. - Supersedes draft S.I. (ISBN 9780111121726) issued 17/10/14. - 24p.: 30 cm. - 978-0-11-112538-0 £6.00

The Double Taxation Relief and International Tax Enforcement (Zambia) Order 2014 No. 2014/1876. - Enabling power: Taxation (International and Other Provisions) Act 2010, s. 173 (1) to (3). - Issued: 23.07.2014. Made: 16.07.2014. Effect: None. Territorial extent & classification: E/W/S/NI. General. - Supersedes draft SI (ISBN 9780111116302) issued 13/06/14. - 24p.: 30 cm. - 978-0-11-111838-2 £6.00

The Double Taxation Relief (Federal Republic of Germany) Order 2014 No. 2014/1874. - Enabling power: Taxation (International and Other Provisions) Act 2010, s. 2. - Issued: 23.07.2014. Made: 16.07.2014. Effect: None. Territorial extent & classification: E/W/S/NI. General. - Supersedes draft SI (ISBN 9780111116241) issued 13/06/14. - 8p.: 30 cm. - 978-0-11-111836-8 £6.00

The Enactment of Extra-Statutory Concessions Order 2014 No. 2014/211. - Enabling power: Finance Act 2008, s. 160. - Issued: 10.02.2014. Made: 04.02.2014. Coming into force: 05.02.2014 in accord. with art. 1. Effect: 2003 c.1 amended. Territorial extent & classification: E/W/S/NI. General. - Supersedes draft S.I. (ISBN 9780111108000) issued 10.01.2014. - 8p.: 30 cm. - 978-0-11-110924-3 £5.75

The Finance Act 2009, Schedule 55 (Penalties for failure to make returns) (Appointed Days and Consequential Provision) Order 2014 No. 2014/2395 (C.105). - Enabling power: Finance Act 2009, ss. 106 (2) to (6). - Bringing into operation various provisions of the 2009 Act on 11.09.2014, 06.10.2014, 06.03.2015 in accordance with art. 2. - Issued: 16.09.2014. Made: 10.09.2014. Laid: -Effect: S.I. 2003/2682 amended. Territorial extent & classification: E/W/S/NI. General. - 4p.: 30 cm. - 978-0-11-112068-2 £4.25

The Finance Act 2009, Sections 101 and 102 (Interest on Late Payments and Repayments), Appointed Days and Consequential Provisions Order 2014 No. 2014/992 (C.45). - Enabling power: Finance Act 2009, s. 104 (3) (4) (5) (6) (7). Bringing into operation various provisions of the 2009 Act on 06.05.2014, in accord. with art. 3. - Issued: 17.04.2014. Made: 10.04.2014. Laid: 14.04.2014. Coming into force: 06.05.2014. Effect: 1970 c.9; 1992 c.5, 8; 2005 c.5; S.I. 2001/1004; 2003/2682; 2005/2045 amended. Territorial extent & classification: E/W/S/NI. General. - 8p.: 30 cm. - 978-0-11-111412-4 £4.25

The Finance Act 2009, Sections 101 and 102 (Interest on Late Payments and Repayments) (Consequential Amendments) Order 2014 No. 2014/1283. - Enabling power: Finance Act 2009, s. 104 (5) (6) (7). - Issued: 23.05.2014. Made: 16.05.2014. Laid: 19.05.2014. Coming into force: 20.05.2014. Effect: 1992 c.4, c.5, c.7, c.8; 2005 c.5; 2009 c.4 amended. Territorial extent & classification: E/W/S/NI. General. - 4p.: 30 cm. - 978-0-11-111509-1 £4.25

The Finance Act 2014, Schedule 37, Paragraph 22 (Commencement) Order 2014 No. 2014/2461 (C.110). - Enabling power: Finance Act 2014, sch. 37 para. 22 (2). Bringing into operation various provisions of this Act on 01.10.2014 in accord. with art. 2. - Issued: 19.09.2014. Made: 12.09.2014. Effect: 2014 c.26 amended. Territorial extent & classification: E/W/S/NI. General. - 4p.: 30 cm. - 978-0-11-112087-3 £4.25

The Finance Act 2014, Section 12 (Appointed Day) Order 2014 No. 2014/3226 (C.144). - Enabling power: Finance Act 2014, s. 12 (4). Bringing into operation various provisions of the 2014 Act on 01.01.2015, in accordance with art. 2. - Issued: 15.12.2014. Made: 09.12.2014. Laid: -Effect: None. Territorial extent & classification: E/W/S/NI. General. - 2p.: 30 cm. - 978-0-11-112509-0 £4.25

The Income and Corporation Taxes (Electronic Communications) (Amendment) Regulations 2014 No. 2014/489. - Enabling power: Finance Act 1999, s. 132. - Issued: 11.03.2014. Made: 04.03.2014. Laid: 06.03.2014. Coming into force: 27.03.2014. Effect: S.I. 2003/282 amended. Territorial extent & classification: E/W/S/NI. General. - 4p.: 30 cm. - 978-0-11-111094-2 £4.00

The Income Tax (Earnings and Pensions) Act 2003 (Amendment to SAYE Option Schemes Contributions Limit) Order 2014 No. 2014/402. - Enabling power: Income Tax (Earnings and Pensions) Act 2003, sch. 3, para. 25 (4). - Issued: 03.03.2014. Made: 25.02.2014. Laid: 26.02.2014. Coming into force: 19.03.2014. Effect: 2003 c.1 amended. Territorial extent & classification: E/W/S/NI. General. - 2p.: 30 cm. - 978-0-11-111023-2 £4.00

The Income Tax (Earnings and Pensions) Act 2003 (Section 684(3A)) Order 2014 No. 2014/2438. - Enabling power: Income Tax (Earnings and Pensions) Act 2003, s, 684(3B). - Issued: 17.09.2014. Made: 11.09.2014. Laid: 12.09.2014. Coming into force: 03.10.2014. Effect: 2003 c.1 amended. Territorial extent & classification: E/W/S/NI. General. - 2p.: 30 cm. - 978-0-11-112074-3 £4.25

The Income Tax (Indexation) Order 2014 No. 2014/3273. - Enabling power: Income Tax Act 2007, ss. 57 (6). - Issued: 17.12.2014. Made: 10.12.2014. Coming into force: 10.12.2014. Effect: None. Territorial extent & classification: E/W/S/NI. General. - 2p.: 30 cm. - 978-0-11-112536-6 £4.25

The Income Tax (Pay As You Earn) (Amendment No. 2) Regulations 2014 No. 2014/1017. - Enabling power: Income Tax (Earnings and Pensions) Act 2003, s. 684 (1) (2). - Issued: 22.04.2014. Made: 14.04.2014. Laid: 15.04.2014. Coming into force: 06.05.2014. Effect: S.I. 2003/2682 amended. Territorial extent & classification: E/W/S/NI. General. - 4p.: 30 cm. - 978-0-11-111415-5 £4.25

The Income Tax (Pay As You Earn) (Amendment No. 3) Regulations 2014 No. 2014/2396. - Enabling power: Income Tax (Earnings and Pensions) Act 2003, s. 684 (1) (2) & Finance Act 2009, sch. 55 paras 6C (5) (7) (8) (a) (9) (11). - Issued: 17.09.2014. Made: 11.09.2014, 11.15 am. Laid: 12.09.2014. Coming into force: 06.10.2014. Effect: S.I. 2003/2682 amended. Territorial extent & classification: E/W/S/NI. General. - 4p.: 30 cm. - 978-0-11-112072-9 £4.25

The Income Tax (Pay As You Earn) (Amendment No. 4) Regulations 2014 No. 2014/2689. - Enabling power: Income Tax (Earnings and Pensions) Act 2003, s. 684 (1) (2)- Issued: 13.10.2014. Made: 06.10.2014. Laid: 08.10.2014. Coming into force: in accord. with reg. 1. Effect: S.I. 2003/2682 amended. Territorial extent & classification: E/W/S/NI. General. - 4p.: 30 cm. - 978-0-11-112131-3 £4.25

The Income Tax (Pay As You Earn) (Amendment) Regulations 2014 No. 2014/474. - Enabling power: Provisional Collection of Taxes Act 1968, s. 1 (1) (2). - Issued: 07.04.2014. Made: 01.04.2014. Laid: 02.04.2014. Coming into force: 06.04.2014. Effect: S.I. 2003/2682 amended. Territorial extent & classification: E/W/S/NI. General. - 8p.: 30 cm. - 978-0-11-111341-7 £4.25

The Income Tax (Pay as You Earn) and the Income Tax (Construction Industry Scheme) (Amendment) Regulations 2014 No. 2014/472. - Enabling power: Taxes Management Act 1970, s. 113 (1) & Finance Act 1999, s. 133 & Finance Act 2002, s. 136 & Income Tax (Earnings and Pensions) Act 2003, s. 684 (1) (2) & Finance Act 2004, s. 73 & Finance Act 2009, sch. 56, para. 6 (8A) (a) (8B). - Issued: 19.03.2014. Made: 12.03.2014. Laid: 13.03.2014. Coming into force: In accord. with reg. 1 (2) (3). Effect: S.I. 2003/2682; 2005/2045 amended. Territorial extent & classification: E/W/S/NI. General- 8p.: 30 cm. - 978-0-11-111207-6 £5.75

The Income Tax (Professional Fees) Order 2014 No. 2014/859. - Enabling power: Income Tax (Earnings and Pensions) Act 2003, s. 343 (3) (4). - Issued: 03.04.2014. Made: 28.03.2014. Coming into force: 06.04.2014. Effect: 2003 c.1 amended. Territorial extent & classification: E/W/S/NI. General. - 2p.: 30 cm. - 978-0-11-111315-8 £4.00

The Income Tax (Recommended Medical Treatment) Regulations 2014 No. 2014/3227. - Enabling power: Income Tax (Earnings and Pensions) Act 2003, s. 320C (3) (c) (4) (7). - Issued: 15.12.2014. Made: 09.12.2014. Laid: 10.12.2014. Coming into force: 01.01.2015. Effect: 2003 c.1 amended. Territorial extent & classification: E/W/S/NI. General. - 2p.: 30 cm. - 978-0-11-112513-7 £4.25

The Income Tax (Removal of Ordinary Residence) Order 2014 No. 2014/3062. - Enabling power: Finance Act 2013, s. 219 (4) (5) (b). - Issued: 24.11.2014. Made: 17.11.2014. Laid: 18.11.2014. Coming into force: 06.04.2014. Effect: 2005 c.5 amended. Territorial extent & classification: E/W/S/NI. General. - 2p.: 30 cm. - 978-0-11-112344-7 £4.25

The Individual Savings Account (Amendment No. 2) Regulations 2014 No. 2014/1450. - Enabling power: Taxation of Chargeable Gains Act 1992, s. 151 (1) (2) & Income Tax (Trading and Other Income) Act 2005, ss. 694 (1) (3) (5), 695 (1) (2), 699, 701 (1) (2) (3) (5). - Issued: 10.06.2014. Made: 04.06.2014. Laid: 05.06.2014. Coming into force: 01.07.2014. Effect: S.I. 1998/1870 amended. Territorial extent & classification: E/W/S/NI. General. - 8p.: 30 cm. - 978-0-11-111596-1 £4.25

The Individual Savings Account (Amendment) Regulations 2014 No. 2014/654. - Enabling power: Income Tax (Trading and Other Income) Act 2005, ss. 694, 695, 695A (2) (c), 696, 701 (1) (4) (5) & Taxation of Chargeable Gains Act 1992, s. 151 (1) (2). - Issued: 20.03.2014. Made: 14.03.2014. Laid: 14.03.2014. Coming into force: 06.04.2014. Effect: S.I. 1998/1870 amended. Territorial extent & classification: E/W/S/NI. General. - 8p.: 30 cm. - 978-0-11-111228-1 £4.00

The International Tax Enforcement (Anguilla) Order 2014 No. 2014/1357. - Enabling power: Finance Act 2006, s. 173 (1) to (3). - Issued: 03.06.2014. Made: 27.05.2014. Coming into force: 03.06.2014. Effect: None. Territorial extent & classification: E/W/S/NI. General. - Supersedes draft SI (ISBN 9780111110539) issued 06.03.14. - 8p.: 30 cm. - 978-0-11-111529-9 £6.00

The International Tax Enforcement (British Virgin Islands) Order 2014 No. 2014/1359. - Enabling power: Finance Act 2006, s. 173 (1) to (3). - Issued: 03.06.2014. Made: 27.05.2014. Coming into force: 03.06.2014. Effect: None. Territorial extent & classification: E/W/S/NI. General. - Supersedes draft SI (ISBN 9780111110546) issued 06.03.14. - 8p.: 30 cm. - 978-0-11-111531-2 £6.00

The International Tax Enforcement (Turks and Caicos Islands) Order 2014 No. 2014/1360. - Enabling power: Finance Act 2006, s. 173 (1) to (3). - Issued: 03.06.2014. Made: 27.05.2014. Coming into force: 03.06.2014. Effect: None. Territorial extent & classification: E/W/S/NI. General. - Supersedes draft SI (ISBN 9780111110560) issued 06.03.14. - 8p.: 30 cm. - 978-0-11-111532-9 £6.00

The Investment Transactions (Tax) Regulations 2014 No. 2014/685. - Enabling power: Finance (No. 2) Act 2005, ss. 17 (3), 18 & Corporation Tax Act 2010, s. 622A & Taxation (International and Other Provisions) Act 2010, s. 354 & Finance Act 2013, s. 217. - Issued: 21.03.2014. Made: 17.03.2014. Laid: 18.03.2014. Coming into force: 08.04.2014. Effect: S.I. 2006/964; 2009/3001; 2011/2999; 2013/2819 amended. Territorial extent & classification: E/W/S/NI. General. - 8p.: 30 cm. - 978-0-11-111237-3 £4.00

The Offshore Funds (Tax) (Amendment) Regulations 2014 No. 2014/1931. - Enabling power: Taxation (International and Other Provisions) Act 2010, s. 354. - Issued: 28.07.2014. Made: 21.07.2014. Laid: 22.07.2014. Coming into force: 12.08.2014. Effect: S.I. 2009/3001 amended. Territorial extent & classification: E/W/S/NI. General. - 2p.: 30 cm. - 978-0-11-111903-7 £4.25

The Registered Pension Schemes (Accounting and Assessment) (Amendment) Regulations 2014 No. 2014/1928. - Enabling power: Finance Act 2004, s. 255. - Issued: 28.07.2014. Made: 21.07.2014. Laid: 22.07.2014. Coming into force: 01.09.2014. Effect: S.I. 2005/3454 amended. Territorial extent & classification: E/W/S/NI. General. - 4p.: 30 cm. - 978-0-11-111900-6 £4.25

The Registered Pension Schemes and Relieved Non-UK Pension Schemes (Lifetime Allowance Transitional Protection) (Individual Protection 2014 Notification) Regulations 2014 No. 2014/1842. - Enabling power: Finance Act 2004, s. 251 (1) & Finance Act 2014, sch. 6, paras 8, 9 (1). - Issued: 28.07.2014. Made: 21.07.2014 at 15.47 pm. Laid: 22.07.2014. Coming into force: 18.08.2014. Effect: None. Territorial extent & classification: E/W/S/NI. General. - 8p.: 30 cm. - 978-0-11-111907-5 £4.25

The Registered Pension Schemes (Provision of Information) (Amendment) Regulations 2014 No. 2014/1843. - Enabling power: Finance Act 2004, ss. 251, 282 (A1). - Issued: 28.07.2014. Made: 21.07.2014 at 15.48 pm. Laid: 22.07.2014. Coming into force: 18.08.2014. Effect: S.I. 2006/567 amended. Territorial extent & classification: E/W/S/NI. General. - 4p.: 30 cm. - 978-0-11-111905-1 £4.25

The Registered Pension Schemes (Transfer of Sums and Assets) (Amendment) Regulations 2014 No. 2014/1449. - Enabling power: Finance Act 2004, ss. 169 (1B), 282 (A1). - Issued: 10.06.2014. Made: 04.06.2014. Laid: 06.06.2014. Coming into force: 01.07.2014. Effect: S.I. 2006/499 amended. Territorial extent & classification: E/W/S/NI. General. - 2p.: 30 cm. - 978-0-11-111595-4 £4.25

The Taxes (Definition of Charity) (Relevant Territories) (Amendment) Regulations 2014 No. 2014/1807. - Enabling power: Finance Act 2010, sch. 6, para. 2 (3) (b). - Issued: 15.07.2014. Made: 09.07.2014. Laid: 10.07.2014. Coming into force: 31.07.2014. Effect: S.I. 2010/1904 amended. Territorial extent & classification: E/W/S/NI. General. - 4p.: 30 cm. - 978-0-11-111781-1 £4.25

The Taxes (Interest Rate) (Amendment) Regulations 2014 No. 2014/496. - Enabling power: Finance Act 1989, s. 178 (1) (2) (s) & Income Tax (Earnings and Pensions) Act 2003, s. 181 (2). - Issued: 11.03.2014. Made: 05.03.2014. Laid: 06.03.2014. Coming into force: 06.04.2014. Effect: S.I. 1989/1297 amended. Territorial extent & classification: E/W/S/NI. General. - 2p.: 30 cm. - 978-0-11-111100-0 £4.00

The Tax Relief for Social Investments (Accreditation of Social Impact Contractor) Regulations 2014 No. 2014/3066. - Enabling power: Income Tax Act 2007, ss. 257JE, 257JF. - Issued: 24.11.2014. Made: 17.11.2014. Laid: 18.11.2014. Coming into force: 10.12.2014. Effect: None. Territorial extent & classification: E/W/S/NI. General. - 8p.: 30 cm. - 978-0-11-112345-4 £4.25

The Unauthorised Unit Trusts (Tax) (Amendment) Regulations 2014 No. 2014/585. - Enabling power: Finance Act 2013, s. 217. - Issued: 18.03.2014. Made: 12.03.2014. Laid: 13.03.2014. Coming into force: 06.04.2014. Effect: S.I. 2013/2819 amended. Territorial extent & classification: E/W/S/NI. General. - 4p.: 30 cm. - 978-0-11-111189-5 £4.00

The Van Benefit and Car and Van Fuel Benefit Order 2014 No. 2014/2896. - Enabling power: Income Tax (Earnings and Pensions) Act 2003, s. 170 (1A) (2) (5) (6). - Issued: 05.12.2014. Made: 01.12.2014. Laid: 02.12.2014. Coming into force: 31.12.2014. Effect: 2003 c.1 amended. Territorial extent & classification: E/W/S/NI. General. - 2p.: 30 cm. - 978-0-11-112435-2 £4.25

The Venture Capital Trust (Amendment) Regulations 2014 No. 2014/1929. - Enabling power: Income Tax Act 2007, ss. 272 (2) (3), 284. - Issued: 28.07.2014. Made: 21.07.2014. Laid: 22.07.2014. Coming into force: 12.08.2014. Effect: S.I. 1995/1979 amended. Territorial extent & classification: E/W/S/NI. General. - 4p.: 30 cm. - 978-0-11-111901-3 £4.25

Industrial and provident societies

The Building Societies (Funding) and Mutual Societies (Transfers) Act 2007 (Commencement No. 2) Order 2014 No. 2014/2796 (C.124). - Enabling power: Building Societies (Funding) and Mutual Societies (Transfers) Act 2007, s. 6 (2). Bringing into operation various provisions of the 2007 Act on 20.11.2014. - Issued: 23.10.2014. Made: 16.10.2014. Effect: None. Territorial extent & classification: E/W/S/NI. General. - 2p.: 30 cm. - 978-0-11-112198-6 £4.25

The Industrial and Provident Societies and Credit Unions (Arrangements, Reconstructions and Administration) Order 2014 No. 2014/229. - Enabling power: Enterprise Act 2002, s. 255 (1) (a) (4) (5). - Issued: 12.02.2014. Made: 04.02.2014. Laid: 07.02.2014. Coming into force: 06.04.2014. Effect: 1965 c.12; 1986 c.45; 2000 c.8; 2006 c.46; S.I. 1986/1915 (S.139), 1925; 2005/590; 2010/3023 applied with modifications. Territorial extent & classification: E/W/S/CI. General. - 36p.: 30 cm. - 978-0-11-110932-8 £9.75

The Industrial and Provident Societies and Credit Unions (Electronic Communications) Order 2014 No. 2014/184. - Enabling power: Electronic Communications Act 2000, ss. 8, 9. - Issued: 06.02.2014. Made: 30.01.2014. Laid: 03.02.2014. Coming into force: 06.04.2014. Effect: 1965 c.12 amended. Territorial extent & classification: E/W/S/CI. General. - 2p.: 30 cm. - 978-0-11-110908-3 £4.00

The Industrial and Provident Societies (Increase in Shareholding Limit) Order 2014 No. 2014/210. - Enabling power: Industrial and Provident Societies Act 1975, s. 2 (1) (2) (3). - Issued: 11.02.2014. Made: 04.02.2014. Laid: 07.02.2014. Coming into force: 06.04.2014. Effect: S.I. 1981/395; 1994/341 revoked. Territorial extent & classification: E/W/S/NI. General. - 4p.: 30 cm. - 978-0-11-110928-1 £4.00

Industrial development

The Assisted Areas Order 2014 No. 2014/1508. - Enabling power: Industrial Development Act 1982, s. 1 (1) (3) (4) (7). - Issued: 13.06.2014. Made: 05.06.2014. Laid: 10.06.2014. Coming into force: 01.07.2014. Effect: S.I. 2007/107 revoked. Territorial extent & classification: E/W/S. General. - 52p.: 30 cm. - 978-0-11-111632-6 £10.00

Infrastructure planning

The Able Marine Energy Park Development Consent Order 2014 No. 2014/2935. - Enabling power: Planning Act 2008, ss. 114, 115, 120, 122, sch. 5. pt. 1, paras 1 to 3, 10 to 17, 24, 26, 30A to 32, 32B to 34, 36, 37. - Issued: 11.11.2014. Made: 13.01.2014. Laid: 10.02.2014. Coming into force: 29.10.2014. Effect: None. Territorial extent & classification: E. Local. - 96p., col. map: 30 cm. - 978-0-11-112315-7 £22.50

The Clocaenog Forest Wind Farm Order 2014 No. 2014/2441. - Enabling power: Planning Act 2008, ss. 114, 115, 120. - Issued: 17.09.2014. Made: 11.09.2014. Coming into force: 02.10.2014. Effect: None. Territorial extent & classification: E/W. General. - 50p.: 30 cm. - 978-0-11-112077-4 £10.00

The East Anglia ONE Offshore Wind Farm Order 2014 No. 2014/1599. - Enabling power: Planning Act 2008, ss. 114, 115, 120, 149A. - Issued: 27.06.2014. Made: 16.06.2014. Coming into force: 07.07.2014. Effect: None. Territorial extent & classification: E/W. General. - 132p.: 30 cm. - 978-0-11-111694-4 £20.75

The Hornsea One Offshore Wind Farm Order 2014 No. 2014/3331. - Enabling power: Planning Act 2008, ss. 114, 115, 120, 149A. - Issued: 23.12.2014. Made: 10.12.2014. Coming into force: 31.12.2014. Effect: None. Territorial extent & classification: E/W. General. - 162p.: 30 cm. - 978-0-11-112621-9 £23.25

The Infrastructure Planning (Applications: Prescribed Forms and Procedure) (Amendment) Regulations 2014 No. 2014/2381. - Enabling power: Planning Act 2008, ss. 37 (3), 232 (3). - Issued: 11.09.2014. Made: 04.09.2014. Laid: 09.09.2014. Coming into force: 01.10.2014. Effect: SI 2009/2264 amended. Territorial extent & classification: E/W. General. - 2p.: 30 cm. - 978-0-11-112040-8 £4.25

The National Grid (North London Reinforcement Project) Order 2014 No. 2014/1052. - Enabling power: Planning Act 2008, ss. 114, 115, 120. - Issued: 24.04.2014. Made: 16.04.2014. Coming into force: 07.05.2014. Effect: None. Territorial extent & classification: E. Local. - 68p.: 30 cm. - 978-0-11-111423-0 £11.00

The Rampion Offshore Wind Farm Order 2014 No. 2014/1873. - Enabling power: Planning Act 2008, ss. 114, 115, 120, 149A. - Issued: 24.07.2014. Made: 16.07.2014. Coming into force: 06.08.2014. Effect: None. Territorial extent & classification: E/W. General. - 124p.: 30 cm. - 978-0-11-111873-3 £19.00

The South Hook Combined Heat and Power Plant Order 2014 No. 2014/2846. - Enabling power: Planning Act 2008, ss. 114, 115, 120. - Issued: 29.10.2014. Made: 22.10.2014. Coming into force: 23.10.2014. Effect: None. Territorial extent & classification: E/W/S/NI. General. - 24p.: 30 cm. - 978-0-11-112227-5 £6.00

The Thames Water Utilities Limited (Thames Tideway Tunnel) Order 2014 No. 2014/2384. - Enabling power: Planning Act 2008, ss. 103, 114, 115, 120, 122, 123. Issued: 12.09.2014. Made: 03.09.2014. Coming into force: 24.09.2014. Effect: 1981 c.66, c.67 modified. Territorial extent & classification: E/W. Local. - 340p.: 30 cm. - 978-0-11-112043-9 £39.25

The Walney Extension Offshore Wind Farm Order 2014 No. 2014/2950. - Enabling power: Planning Act 2008, ss. 114, 115, 120, 149A. - Issued: 17.11.2014. Made: 07.11.2014. Coming into force: 28.11.2014. Effect: None. Territorial extent & classification: E. Local. - 108p.: 30 cm. - 978-0-11-112326-3 £16.50

The Willington C Gas Pipeline Order 2014 No. 2014/3328. - Enabling power: Planning Act 2008, ss. 114, 120. - Issued: 22.12.2014. Made: 16.12.2014. Coming into force: 07.01.2015. Effect: 1981 c.66 amended. Territorial extent & classification: E. Local. - 68p.: 30 cm. - 978-0-11-112620-2 £11.00

Infrastructure planning, England

The A556 (Knutsford to Bowdon Improvement) Development Consent Order 2014 No. 2014/2269. - Enabling power: Planning Act 2008, ss. 114, 115, 120, 122, sch. 5, paras. 1 to 3, 10 to 17, 19, 26, 36, 37. - Issued: 03.09.2014. Made: 28.08.2014. Coming into force: 18.09.2014. Effect: None. Territorial extent & classification: E. General. - 76p.: 30 cm. - 978-0-11-112004-0 £14.25

The Burbo Bank Extension Offshore Wind Farm (Correction) Order 2014 No. 2014/3301. - Enabling power: Planning Act 2008, s. 119, sch. 4. - Issued: 17.12.2014. Made: 10.12.2014. Coming into force: 11.12.2014. Effect: None. Territorial extent & classification: E. Local. - 4p.: 30 cm. - 978-0-11-112566-3 £4.25

The Burbo Bank Extension Offshore Wind Farm Order 2014 No. 2014/2594. - Enabling power: Planning Act 2008, ss. 114, 115, 120, 149A. - Issued: 01.10.2014. Made: 25.09.2014. Coming into force: 26.09.2014. Effect: None. Territorial extent & classification: E. Local. - 40p.: 30 cm. - 978-0-11-112109-2 £10.00

The Central Bedfordshire Council (Woodside Link Houghton Regis) Development Consent Order 2014 No. 2014/2637. - Enabling power: Planning Act 2008, ss. 114, 115, 120, 122, sch. 5, paras 1 to 3, 8, 10 to 17, 24, 26, 33, 36, 37. - Issued: 07.10.2014. Made: 30.09.2014. Coming into force: 21.10.2014. Effect: None. Territorial extent & classification: E. General. - 63p.: 30 cm. - 978-0-11-112121-4 £11.00

The Daventry International Rail Freight Interchange Alteration Order 2014 No. 2014/1796. - Enabling power: Planning Act 2008. ss. 114, 115, 120, 122, sch. 5, pt 1, paras 1 to 3, 10 to 18, 33, 34, 36, 37. - Issued: 14.07.2014. Made: 03.07.2014. Coming into force: 24.07.2014. Effect: None. Territorial extent & classification: E. Local. - 44p.: 30 cm. - 978-0-11-111772-9 £10.00

The Network Rail (Norton Bridge Area Improvements) Order 2014 No. 2014/909. - Enabling power: Planning Act 2008, ss. 114, 115, 120, 122, sch. 5, part 1, para. 1 to 3, 10 to 17, 24, 26, 36, 37. - Issued: 09.04.2014. Made: 31.03.2014. Coming into force: 21.04.2014. Effect: None. Territorial extent & classification: E. General. - 68p.: 30 cm. - With correction slip dated December 2014. - 978-0-11-111373-8 £11.00

Infrastructure planning, England and Wales

The North Killingholme (Generating Station) Order 2014 No. 2014/2434. - Enabling power: Planning Act 2008, ss. 114, 115, 120, 149A. - Issued: 17.09.2014. Made: 11.09.2014. Coming into force: 02.10.2014. Effect: None. Territorial extent & classification: E/W. General. - 72p.: 30 cm. - 978-0-11-112069-9 £11.00

Inheritance tax

The Inheritance Tax (Delivery of Accounts) (Excepted Estates) (Amendment) Regulations 2014 No. 2014/488. - Enabling power: Inheritance Tax Act 1984, s. 256 (1) (3). - Issued: 11.03.2014. Made: 04.03.2014. Laid: 06.03.2014. Coming into force: 01.04.2014. Effect: S.I. 2004/2543 amended. Territorial extent & classification: E/W/S/NI. General. - 4p.: 30 cm. - 978-0-11-111093-5 £4.00

The International Tax Enforcement (Anguilla) Order 2014 No. 2014/1357. - Enabling power: Finance Act 2006, s. 173 (1) to (3). - Issued: 03.06.2014. Made: 27.05.2014. Coming into force: 03.06.2014. Effect: None. Territorial extent & classification: E/W/S/NI. General. - Supersedes draft SI (ISBN 9780111110539) issued 06.03.14. - 8p.: 30 cm. - 978-0-11-111529-9 £6.00

The International Tax Enforcement (British Virgin Islands) Order 2014 No. 2014/1359. - Enabling power: Finance Act 2006, s. 173 (1) to (3). - Issued: 03.06.2014. Made: 27.05.2014. Coming into force: 03.06.2014. Effect: None. Territorial extent & classification: E/W/S/NI. General. - Supersedes draft SI (ISBN 9780111110546) issued 06.03.14. - 8p.: 30 cm. - 978-0-11-111531-2 £6.00

The International Tax Enforcement (Turks and Caicos Islands) Order 2014 No. 2014/1360. - Enabling power: Finance Act 2006, s. 173 (1) to (3). - Issued: 03.06.2014. Made: 27.05.2014. Coming into force: 03.06.2014. Effect: None. Territorial extent & classification: E/W/S/NI. General. - Supersedes draft SI (ISBN 9780111110560) issued 06.03.14. - 8p.: 30 cm. - 978-0-11-111532-9 £6.00

The Taxes (Definition of Charity) (Relevant Territories) (Amendment) Regulations 2014 No. 2014/1807. - Enabling power: Finance Act 2010, sch. 6, para. 2 (3) (b). - Issued: 15.07.2014. Made: 09.07.2014. Laid: 10.07.2014. Coming into force: 31.07.2014. Effect: S.I. 2010/1904 amended. Territorial extent & classification: E/W/S/NI. General. - 4p.: 30 cm. - 978-0-11-111781-1 £4.25

Insolvency, England and Wales

The Insolvency (Commencement of Proceedings) and Insolvency Rules 1986 (Amendment) Rules 2014 No. 2014/817. - Enabling power: Insolvency Act 1986, ss. 411, 412. - Issued: 07.04.2014. Made: 01.04.2014. Laid: 01.04.2014. Coming into force: 22.04.2014. Effect: S.I. 1986/1925 amended. Territorial extent & classification: E/W. General. - 16p.: 30 cm. - 978-0-11-111339-4 £6.00

Insolvency, England and Wales: Fees

The Insolvency Proceedings (Fees) (Amendment) Order 2014 No. 2014/583. - Enabling power: Insolvency Act 1986, ss. 414, 415. - Issued: 18.03.2014. Made: 11.03.2014. Laid: 12.03.2014. Coming into force: 06.04.2014. Effect: S.I. 2004/593 amended. Territorial extent & classification: E/W. General. - 4p.: 30 cm. - 978-0-11-111187-1 £4.00

Insurance

The Water Act 2014 (Commencement No. 2 and Transitional Provisions) Order 2014 No. 2014/3320 (C.155). - Enabling power: Water Act 2014, ss. 91 (1), 94 (3) (6). Bringing into operation various provisions of the 2014 Act on 01.01.2015, in accord. with arts 2, 4. - Issued: 22.12.2014. Made: 15.12.2014. Effect: None. Territorial extent & classification: E/W. General. - 4p.: 30 cm. - 978-0-11-112605-9 £4.25

Insurance premium tax

The Insurance Premium Tax (Non-taxable Insurance Contracts) Order 2014 No. 2014/2856. - Enabling power: Finance Act 1994, s. 71. - Issued: 25.11.2014. Made: 27.10.2014. Laid: 27.10.2014. Coming into force: 01.12.2014. Effect: 1994 c.9 amended. Territorial extent & classification: E/W/S/NI. General. - Approved by the House of Commons. Supersedes pre-approved version (ISBN 9780111122426) issued 31.10.2014. - 4p.: 30 cm. - 978-0-11-154044-2 £4.25

The Insurance Premium Tax (Non-taxable Insurance Contracts) Order 2014 No. 2014/2856. - Enabling power: Finance Act 1994, s. 71. - Issued: 31.10.2014. Made: 27.10.2014. Laid: 27.10.2014. Coming into force: 01.12.2014. Effect: 1994 c.9 amended. Territorial extent & classification: E/W/S/NI. General. - Superseded by approved version (ISBN 9780111540442) issued 25.11.2014. - 4p.: 30 cm. - 978-0-11-112242-6 £4.25

The Revenue and Customs (Amendment of Appeal Provisions for Out of Time Reviews) Order 2014 No. 2014/1264. - Enabling power: Finance Act 2008, s. 124 (1) (2) (6) (7) (b). - Issued: 21.05.2014. Made: 14.05.2014. Coming into force: In accord. with art. 1 (2). Effect: 1994 c.9, c.23; 1996 c.8; 2000 c.17; 2001 c.9; 2003 c.14; S.I. 2003/3102; 2007/1509, 2157, 3298 amended. Territorial extent & classification: E/W/S/NI. General. - Supersedes draft SI (ISBN 9780111112991) issued 03/04/14. - 8p.: 30 cm. - 978-0-11-111499-5 £6.00

Intellectual property

The Intellectual Property Act 2014 (Amendment) Regulations 2014 No. 2014/2329. - Enabling power: European Communities Act 1972, s. 2 (2). - Issued: 05.09.2014. Made: 28.08.2014. Laid: 03.09.2014. Coming into force: 29.09.2014. Effect: 2014 c.18 amended. Territorial extent & classification: E/W/S/NI. General. - This statutory instrument corrects errors in the Intellectual Property Act 2014 (ISBN 9780105418146). - 2p.: 30 cm. - 978-0-11-112009-5 £4.25

The Intellectual Property Act 2014 (Commencement No.1) Order 2014 No. 2014/1715 (C.74). - Enabling power: Intellectual Property Act 2014, s. 24 (1) (2). Bringing into operation various provisions of the 2014 Act on 15.07.2014, in accord. with art. 3. - Issued: 09.07.2014. Made: 02.07.2014. Effect: None. Territorial extent & classification: E/W/S/NI. General. - 2p.: 30 cm. - 978-0-11-111752-1 £4.25

The Intellectual Property Act 2014 (Commencement No. 2) Order 2014 No. 2014/2069 (C.94). - Enabling power: Intellectual Property Act 2014, s. 24 (1) (2). Bringing into operation various provisions of the 2014 Act on 01.08.2014, in accord. with art. 2. - Issued: 08.08.2014. Made: 31.07.2014. Effect: None. Territorial extent & classification: E/W/S/NI. General. - 2p.: 30 cm. - 978-0-11-111956-3 £4.25

The Intellectual Property Act 2014 (Commencement No. 3 and Transitional Provisions) Order 2014 No. 2014/2330 (C.100). - Enabling power: Intellectual Property Act 2014, ss. 23 (1) (b), 24 (1) (2). - Issued: 05.09.2014. Made: 28.08.2014. Coming into force: 01.10.2014. Effect: None. Territorial extent & classification: E/W/S/NI. General. - 8p.: 30 cm. - 978-0-11-112010-1 £4.25

International Criminal Court

The International Criminal Court Act 2001 (Jersey) Order 2014 No. 2014/2706. - Enabling power: International Criminal Court Act 2001, s. 79 (3). - Issued: 15.10.2014. Made: 08.10.2014. Coming into force: in accord. with art. 1. Effect: 2001 c.17 modified as specified in the Schedule. Territorial extent & classification: Bailiwick of Jersey. General. - 4p.: 30 cm. - 978-0-11-112144-3 £4.25

International development

The African Development Bank (Thirteenth Replenishment of the African Development Fund) Order 2014 No. 2014/2456. - Enabling power: International Development Act 2002, s. 11. - Issued: 19.09.2014. Made: 08.09.2014. Laid: -Coming into force: 09.09.2014, in accord. with art. 1. Effect: None. Territorial extent & classification: E/W/S/NI. General. - 4p.: 30 cm. - 978-0-11-112082-8 £4.25

The African Development Fund (Multilateral Debt Relief Initiative) (Amendment) Order 2014 No. 2014/2457. - Enabling power: International Development Act 2002, s. 11. - Issued: 19.09.2014. Made: 08.09.2014. Coming into force: 09.09.2014, in accord. with art. 1. Effect: S.I. 2006/2321 amended. Territorial extent & classification: E/W/S/NI. General. - Supersedes draft S.I. (ISBN 9780111116401) issued on 16.06.2014. - 2p.: 30 cm. - 978-0-11-112083-5 £4.25

The Crown Agents Holding and Realisation Board (Dissolution) Order 2009 No. 2014/1366. - Enabling power: Crown Agents Act 1979, sch. 5, para. 24 (2). - Issued: 04.06.2014. Made: 17.07.2009. Coming into force: 18.07.2009 in accord. with art. 1. Effect: None. Territorial extent & classification: E/W/S/NI. General. - 2p.: 30 cm. - 978-0-11-111540-4 £4.25

The International Development Association (Multilateral Debt Relief Initiative) (Amendment) Order 2014 No. 2014/3056. - Enabling power: International Development Act 2002, s. 11. - Issued: 21.11.2014. Made: 11.11.2014. Coming into force: In accord. with art. 1. Effect: S.I. 2006/2323 amended. Territorial extent & classification: E/W/S/NI. General. - Supersedes draft SI (ISBN 9780111116494) issued 17/06/14. - 2p.: 30 cm. - 978-0-11-112338-6 £4.25

The International Development Association (Seventeenth Replenishment) Order 2014 No. 2014/3055. - Enabling power: International Development Act 2002, s. 11. - Issued: 21.11.2014. Made: 11.11.2014. Coming into force: In accord. with art. 1. Effect: None. Territorial extent & classification: E/W/S/NI. General. - 4p.: 30 cm. - 978-0-11-112337-9 £4.25

International immunities and privileges

The African Legal Support Facility (Legal Capacities) Order 2014 No. 2014/1891. - Enabling power: International Organisations Act 1968, s. 1 (2). - Issued: 23.07.2014. Made: 16.07.2014. Coming into force: In accord. with art. 1. Effect: None. Territorial extent & classification: E/W/S/NI. General. - Supersedes draft SI (ISBN 9780111114278) issued 23/07/14. - 2p.: 30 cm. - 978-0-11-111853-5 £4.25

Investigatory powers

The Driving Standards Agency and the Vehicle and Operator Services Agency (Merger) (Consequential Amendments) Order 2014 No. 2014/467. - Enabling power: Regulation of Investigatory Powers Act 2000, ss. 30 (1) (3) (6), 46 (4), 78 (5) & Proceeds of Crime Act 2002, ss. 453 (1) (2), 459 (1) (2). - Issued: 07.03.2014. Made: 03.03.2014. Laid: 06.03.2014. Coming into force: 01.04.2014. Effect: S.I. 2007/934; 2009/975; 2010/521 amended. Territorial extent & classification: E/W/S/NI. General. - Incorrect price printed on document. - 8p.: 30 cm. - 978-0-11-111077-5 £4.00

The Regulation of Investigatory Powers (Covert Human Intelligence Sources: Code of Practice) Order 2014 No. 2014/3119. - Enabling power: Regulation of Investigatory Powers Act 2000, s. 71 (5). - Issued: 28.11.2014. Made: 19.11.2014. Coming into force: 10.12.2014. Effect: None. Territorial extent & classification: E/W/S/NI. General. - Supersedes draft S.I. (ISBN 9780111118580) issued 23.07.2014. - 2p.: 30 cm. - 978-0-11-112397-3 £4.25

The Regulation of Investigatory Powers (Covert Surveillance and Property Interference: Code of Practice) Order 2014 No. 2014/3103. - Enabling power: Regulation of Investigatory Powers Act 2000, s. 71 (5). - Issued: 26.11.2014. Made: 19.11.2014. Coming into force: 10.12.2014. Effect: None. Territorial extent & classification: E/W/S/NI. General. - Supersedes draft S.I. (ISBN 9780111118573) issued 23.07.2014. - 2p.: 30 cm. - 978-0-11-112384-3 £4.25

Judgments

The Civil Jurisdiction and Judgments (Amendment) Regulations 2014 No. 2014/2947. - Enabling power: European Communities Act 1972, s. 2 (2). - Issued: 17.11.2014. Made: 10.11.2014. Laid: 12.11.2014. Coming into force: 10.01.2015. Effect: 1982 c.27, c.37; 1989 c.40, & S.I. 1990/1504 (NI 10); 1991/724; 1999/2979; 2001/3928, 3929; 2007 (asp 6); 2013 c.26 amended. Territorial extent & classification: E/W/S/NI. General. - 12p.: 30 cm. - 978-0-11-112321-8 £6.00

Judgments, England and Wales

The Civil Jurisdiction and Judgments (Protection Measures) Regulations 2014 No. 2014/3298. - Enabling power: European Communities Act 1972, s. 2 (2). - Issued: 23.12.2014. Made: 15.12.2014. Laid: 18.12.2014. Coming into force: In accord. with reg. 1. Effect: S.I. 1981/1675 (NI.26) amended. Territorial extent & classification: E/W/NI. General. - 4p.: 30 cm. - 978-0-11-112609-7 £4.25

The Marriage (Same Sex Couples) (Jurisdiction and Recognition of Judgments) Regulations 2014 No. 2014/543. - Enabling power: Domicile and Matrimonial Proceedings Act 1973, sch. A1, para. 5. - Issued: 12.03.2014. Made: 06.03.2014. Coming into force: 13.03.2014. Effect: None. Territorial extent & classification: E/W. General. - Supersedes draft S.I. (ISBN 9780111108703) issued 28.01.2014. - 4p.: 30 cm. - 978-0-11-111145-1 £4.00

Judgments, Northern Ireland

The Civil Jurisdiction and Judgments (Protection Measures) Regulations 2014 No. 2014/3298. - Enabling power: European Communities Act 1972, s. 2 (2). - Issued: 23.12.2014. Made: 15.12.2014. Laid: 18.12.2014. Coming into force: In accord. with reg. 1. Effect: S.I. 1981/1675 (NI.26) amended. Territorial extent & classification: E/W/NI. General. - 4p.: 30 cm. - 978-0-11-112609-7 £4.25

Judicial appointments and discipline

The Judicial Appointments and Discipline (Addition of Office) Order 2014 No. 2014/2040. - Enabling power: Constitutional Reform Act 2005, s. 85 (3). - Issued: 06.08.2014. Made: 25.07.2014. Laid: 31.07.2014. Coming into force: 01.10.2014. Effect: 2005 c.4 amended. Territorial extent & classification: E/W/S/NI. General. - 2p.: 30 cm. - 978-0-11-111941-9 £4.25

The Judicial Discipline (Prescribed Procedures) Regulations 2014 No. 2014/1919. - Enabling power: Constitutional Reform Act 2005, ss. 115, 116, 117, 120, 121 & Coroners and Justice Act 2009, sch. 3, para. 14. - Issued: 25.07.2014. Made: 17.07.2013. Laid: 22.07.2014. Coming into force: 18.08.2014. Effect: S.I. 2013/1674 revoked. Territorial extent & classification: E/W/S/NI. General. - This Statutory Instrument has been made in consequence of defects in S.I. 2013/1674 (ISBN 9780111101117) and is being issued free of charge to all known recipients of that Statutory Instrument. Revoked by SI 2001/1966 (ISBN 9780111119273). - 12p.: 30 cm. - 978-0-11-111893-1 £6.00

Judicial appointments and discipline, England and Wales

The Judicial Appointments (Amendment) Order 2014 No. 2014/2898. - Enabling power: Tribunals, Courts and Enforcement Act 2007, s. 51 (1). - Issued: 07.11.2014. Made: 03.11.2014. Coming into force: In accord. with art. 1. Effect: S.I. 2008/2995 amended. Territorial extent & classification: E/W. General. - Supersedes draft SI (ISBN 9780111117590) issued 10/07/14 - 2p.: 30 cm. - 978-0-11-112288-4 £4.25

Justices of the Peace, England and Wales

The Local Justice Areas (No. 2) Order 2013 (correction slip) No. 2013/1878 Cor.. - Correction slip (to ISBN 9780111102381) dated December 2014. - 1 sheet: 30 cm. Free

The Local Justice Areas (No. 2) Order 2014 No. 2014/1899. - Enabling power: Courts Act 2003, ss. 8 (4), 108 (6). - Issued: 24.07.2014. Made: 17.07.2014. Laid: 18.07.2014. Coming into force: In accord. with art. 1. Effect: S.I. 2005/554 amended. Territorial extent & classification: E/W. General. - 4p.: 30 cm. - 978-0-11-111864-1 £4.25

The Local Justice Areas (No. 3) Order 2014 No. 2014/2867. - Enabling power: Courts Act 2003, ss. 8 (4), 108 (6). - Issued: 03.11.2014. Made: 25.10.2014. Laid: 29.10.2014. Coming into force: In accord. with art. 1. Effect: S.I. 2005/554 amended. Territorial extent & classification: E/W. General. - 4p.: 30 cm. - 978-0-11-112254-9 £4.25

The Local Justice Areas Order 2014 No. 2014/322. - Enabling power: Courts Act 2003, ss. 8 (4), 108 (6). - Issued: 20.02.2014. Made: 13.02.2014. Laid: 17.02.2014. Coming into force: In accord. with art. 1. Effect: S.I. 2005/554 amended. Territorial extent & classification: E/W. General. - 4p.: 30 cm. - 978-0-11-110981-6 £4.00

Land drainage, England

The Vale of Pickering Internal Drainage Board Order 2014 No. 2014/1030. - Enabling power: Land Drainage Act 1991, s. 3 (5) (7). - Issued: 24.04.2014. Made: 29.01.2014. Coming into force: In accord with art. 1. Effect: None. Territorial extent & classification: E. Local. - 4p.: 30 cm. - 978-0-11-111418-6 £4.25

Land drainage, England and Wales

The Lower Wye and River Lugg Internal Drainage Districts (Alteration of Boundaries) Order 2014 No. 2014/3194. - Enabling power: Land Drainage Act 1991, s. 3 (5). - Issued: 05.12.2014. Made: 26.11.2014. Coming into force: In accord with art. 1. Effect: None. Territorial extent & classification: E/W. General. - 4p.: 30 cm. - 978-0-11-112446-8 £4.25

Landfill tax

The Landfill Tax (Amendment) Regulations 2014 No. 2014/707. - Enabling power: Finance Act 1996, ss. 51 (1), 53 (1), 53 (4). - Issued: 24.03.2014. Made: 18.03.2014. Laid: 19.03.2014. Coming into force: 01.04.2014. Effect: S.I. 1996/1527 amended. Territorial extent & classification: E/W/S/NI. General. - 2p.: 30 cm. - 978-0-11-111244-1 £4.00

The Revenue and Customs (Amendment of Appeal Provisions for Out of Time Reviews) Order 2014 No. 2014/1264. - Enabling power: Finance Act 2008, s. 124 (1) (2) (6) (7) (b). - Issued: 21.05.2014. Made: 14.05.2014. Coming into force: In accord. with art. 1 (2). Effect: 1994 c.9, c.23; 1996 c.8; 2000 c.17; 2001 c.9; 2003 c.14; S.I. 2003/3102; 2007/1509, 2157, 3298 amended. Territorial extent & classification: E/W/S/NI. General. - Supersedes draft SI (ISBN 9780111112991) issued 03/04/14. - 8p.: 30 cm. - 978-0-11-111499-5 £6.00

Landlord and tenant, England

The Agricultural Holdings (Units of Production) (England) Order 2014 No. 2014/2712. - Enabling power: Agricultural Holdings Act 1986, sch. 6, para. 4. - Issued: 15.10.2014. Made: 05.10.2014. Laid: 10.10.2014. Coming into force: 07.11.2014. Effect: S.I. 2013/2607 revoked. Territorial extent & classification: E. General. - 8p.: 30 cm. - 978-0-11-112149-8 £4.25

The Enterprise and Regulatory Reform Act 2013 (Commencement No. 4 and Saving Provision) (Amendment) Order 2014 No. 2014/824 (C.33). - Enabling power: Enterprise and Regulatory Reform Act 2013, s. 103 (3) (4). Bringing into operation various provisions of the 2013 Act on 31.03.2014, 30.09.2014, in accord. with art. 2. - Issued: 01.04.2014. Made: 26.03.2014. Effect: S.I. 2013/2979 (C.122) amended. Territorial extent & classification: E. General. - 4p.: 30 cm. - 978-0-11-111282-3 £4.00

The Enterprise and Regulatory Reform Act 2013 (Commencement No. 7 and Amendment) Order 2014 No. 2014/2481. - Enabling power: Enterprise and Regulatory Reform Act 2013, ss. 100, 103 (3) (4). Bringing into operation various provisions of the 2013 Act on 15.09.2014, 31.12.2014, in accord. with art. 2 & 3A. - Issued: 23.09.2014. Made: 14.09.2014. Effect: S.I. 2013/1455 (C.55), 2979 (C.122) amended. Territorial extent & classification: E. General. - 4p.: 30 cm. - 978-0-11-112092-7 £4.25

Landlord and tenant, England and Wales

The Public Bodies (Abolition of the Committee on Agricultural Valuation) Order 2014 No. 2014/1068. - Enabling power: Public Bodies Act 2011, ss. 1 (1), 6 (1) (5), 35 (2). - Issued: 29.04.2014. Made: 22.04.2014. Coming into force: In accord. with art. 1. Effect: 1986 c.5; 2000 c.36; 2011 c.24 partially repealed. Territorial extent & classification: E/W. General. - Supersedes draft S.I. 2014 (ISBN 9780111109359) issued 14.02.2014. - 4p.: 30 cm. - 978-0-11-111426-1 £4.00

Landlord and tenant, Wales

The Agricultural Holdings (Units of Production) (Wales) Order 2014 No. 2014/41 (W.3). - Enabling power: Agricultural Holdings Act 1986, sch. 6, para. 4. - Issued: 29.01.2014. Made: 15.01.2014. Laid before the National Assembly for Wales: 16.01.2014. Coming into force: 14.02.2014. Effect: W.S.I. 2012/3022 (W.306) revoked. Territorial extent & classification: W. General. - Revoked by SI 2015/1020 (W.73) (ISBN 9780348110777). - In English and Welsh: Welsh title: Gorchymyn Daliadau Amaethyddol (Unedau Cynhyrchu) (Cymru) 2014. - 12p.: 30 cm. - 978-0-348-10858-3 £5.75

The Assured Tenancies and Agricultural Occupancies (Forms) (Amendment) (Wales) (No. 2) Regulations 2014 No. 2014/910 (W.89). - Enabling power: Housing Act 1988, ss. 13 (2), 45 (5). - Issued: 17.04.2014. Made: 02.04.2014. Coming into force: 04.04.2014. Effect: S.I. 1997/194 amended. Territorial extent & classification: W. General. - In English and Welsh: Welsh title: Rheoliadau Tenantiaethau Sicr a Meddianaethau Amaethyddol Sicr (Ffurflenni) (Diwygio) (Cymru) (Rhif 2) 2014. - 4p.: 30 cm. - 978-0-348-10935-1 £4.25

The Assured Tenancies and Agricultural Occupancies (Forms) (Amendment) (Wales) Regulations 2014 No. 2014/374 (W.42). - Enabling power: Housing Act 1988, ss. 13 (2), 45 (5). - Issued: 13.03.2014. Made: 20.02.2014. Coming into force: 21.02.2014. Effect: S.I. 1997/194 amended. Territorial extent & classification: W. General. - This Statutory Instrument has ben printed in substitution of the SI of the same number and ISBN (issued 10.03.2014) and is being issued free of charge to all known recipients of that Statutory Instrument. - In English and Welsh: Welsh title: Rheoliadau Tenantiaethau Sicr a Meddianaethau Amaethyddol Sicr (Ffurflenni) (Diwygio) (Cymru) 2014. - 4p.: 30 cm. - 978-0-348-10896-5 £4.00

The Leasehold Valuation Tribunals (Fees) (Wales) (Amendment) Regulations 2014 No. 2014/287 (W.36). - Enabling power: Commonhold and Leasehold Reform Act 2002, sch. 12, paras 1, 9. - Issued: 19.02.2014. Made: 11.02.2014. Laid before the National Assembly for Wales: 13.02.2014. Coming into force: 10.03.2014. Effect: S.I. 2004/683 (W.71) amended. Territorial extent & classification: W. General. - In English and Welsh: Welsh title: Rheoliadau Tribiwnlysoedd Prisio Lesddaliadau (Ffioedd) (Cymru) (Diwygio) 2014. - 4p.: 30 cm. - 978-0-348-10888-0 £4.00

The Rent Book (Forms of Notice) (Amendment) (Wales) Regulations 2014 No. 2014/493 (W.59). - Enabling power: Landlord and Tenant Act 1985, s. 5. - Issued: 12.03.2014. Made: 04.03.2014. Laid before the National Assembly for Wales: 06.03.2014. Coming into force: 31.03.2014. Effect: S.I. 1982/1474 amended in relation to Wales. Territorial extent & classification: W. General. - In English and Welsh: Welsh title: Rheoliadau'r Llyfr Rhent (Ffurflenni Hysbysu) (Diwygio) (Cymru) 2014. - 4p.: 30 cm. - 978-0-348-10902-3 £4.00

The Residential Property Tribunal Procedures and Fees (Wales) (Amendment) Regulations 2014 No. 2014/286 (W.35). - Enabling power: Housing Act 2004, s. 250 (2) (a), sch. 13. - Issued: 21.02.2014. Made: 11.02.2014. Laid before the National Assembly for Wales: 13.02.2014. Coming into force: 10.03.2014. Effect: W.S.I. 2012/531 (W.83) amended. Territorial extent & classification: W. General. - In English and Welsh. Welsh title: Rheoliadau Gweithdrefnau a Ffioedd Tribiwnlys Eiddo Preswyl (Cymru) (Diwygio) 2014. - 4p.: 30 cm. - 978-0-348-10889-7 £4.00

Legal aid and advice, England and Wales

The Civil Legal Aid (Financial Resources and Payment for Services) (Amendment) (No. 2) Regulations 2014 No. 2014/2701. - Enabling power: Legal Aid, Sentencing and Punishment of Offenders Act 2012, ss. 21 (2), 41 (1) (a) (b) (3) (c). - Issued: 14.10.2014. Made: 07.10.2014. Laid: 13.10.2014. Coming into force: 03.11.2013. Effect: S.I. 2013/480 amended. Territorial extent & classification: E/W. General. - 4p.: 30 cm. - 978-0-11-112139-9 £4.25

The Civil Legal Aid (Financial Resources and Payment for Services) (Amendment) Regulations 2014 No. 2014/812. - Enabling power: Legal Aid, Sentencing and Punishment of Offenders Act 2012, ss. 21 (2) (b), 41 (1) (a) (b) (2) (b) (3) (c). - Issued: 31.03.2014. Made: 24.03.2014. Laid: 27.03.2014. Coming into force: 22.04.2014. Effect: S.I. 2013/480 amended. Territorial extent & classification: E/W. General. - 4p.: 30 cm. - 978-0-11-111274-8 £4.00

The Civil Legal Aid (Merits Criteria) (Amendment) Regulations 2014 No. 2014/131. - Enabling power: Legal Aid, Sentencing and Punishment of Offenders Act 2012, ss. 11 (1) (b), 41 (1) (a) (b) (2) (b) (3) (c), sch. 3, para. 3 (2). - Issued: 30.01.2014. Made: 23.01.2014. Coming into force: 27.01.2014. Effect: S.I. 2013/104 amended. Territorial extent & classification: E/W. General. - 8p.: 30 cm. - 978-0-11-110884-0 £4.00

The Civil Legal Aid (Procedure) (Amendment) Regulations 2014 No. 2014/814. - Enabling power: Legal Aid, Sentencing and Punishment of Offenders Act 2012, ss. 12 (2) to (4), 41 (1) (a) (b) (3) (b) (c). - Issued: 31.03.2014. Made: 24.03.2014. Laid: 27.03.2014. Coming into force: 22.04.2014. Effect: S.I. 2012/3098 amended. Territorial extent & classification: E/W. General. - 8p.: 30 cm. - 978-0-11-111277-9 £4.00

The Civil Legal Aid (Procedure, Remuneration and Statutory Charge) (Amendment) Regulations 2014 No. 2014/1824. - Enabling power: Legal Aid, Sentencing and Punishment of Offenders Act 2012, ss. 2 (3), 12 (2) (3), 25 (3), 41 (3) (b). - Issued: 17.07.2014. Made: 05.07.2014. Laid: 11.07.2014. Coming into force: 01.08.2014. Effect: S.I. 2012/3098; 2013/422, 503 amended. Territorial extent & classification: E/W. General. - 4p.: 30 cm. - 978-0-11-111796-5 £4.25

The Civil Legal Aid (Remuneration) (Amendment) (No. 2) Regulations 2014 No. 2014/586. - Enabling power: Legal Aid, Sentencing and Punishment of Offenders Act 2012, ss. 2 (3), 41 (1) to (3). - Issued: 19.03.2014. Made: 12.03.2014. Laid: 14.03.2014. Coming into force: 22.04.2014. Effect: S.I. 2013/422 amended. Territorial extent & classification: E/W. General. - 12p.: 30 cm. - 978-0-11-111204-5 £5.75

The Civil Legal Aid (Remuneration) (Amendment) (No. 4) Regulations 2014 No. 2014/1389. - Enabling power: Legal Aid, Sentencing and Punishment of Offenders Act 2012, ss. 2 (3), 41 (1) (2) (3). - Issued: 06.06.2014. Made: 29.05.2014. Laid: 03.06.2014. Coming into force: 31.07.2014. Effect: S.I. 2013/422 amended. Territorial extent & classification: E/W. General. - 4p.: 30 cm. - 978-0-11-111562-6 £4.25

The Civil Legal Aid (Remuneration) (Amendment) Regulations 2014 No. 2014/7. - Enabling power: Legal Aid, Sentencing and Punishment of Offenders Act 2012, ss. 2 (3), 41 (1) (a) (b) (3) (b). - Issued: 14.01.2014. Made: 08.01.2014. Laid: 09.01.2014. Coming into force: 01.02.2014. Effect: S.I. 2013/422 amended. Territorial extent & classification: E/W. General. - 2p.: 30 cm. - 978-0-11-110809-3 £4.00

The Community Legal Service (Funding) (Counsel in Family Proceedings) (Amendment) Order 2014 No. 2014/2864. - Enabling power: Access to Justice Act 1999, s. 6 (4). - Issued: 03.11.2014. Made: 25.10.2014. Laid: 30.10.2014. Coming into force: 24.11.2014. Effect: S.I. 2001/1077 amended. Territorial extent & classification: E/W. General. - 4p.: 30 cm. - 978-0-11-112251-8 £4.25

The Criminal Legal Aid (Remuneration) (Amendment) (No.2) Regulations 2014 No. 2014/2422. - Enabling power: Legal Aid, Sentencing and Punishment of Offenders Act 2012, ss. 2 (3), 41 (1) to (3). - Issued: 16.09.2014. Made: 09.09.2014. Laid: 11.09.2014. Coming into force: 02.10.2014. Effect: S.I. 2013/435 amended. Territorial extent & classification: E/W. General. - 8p.: 30 cm. - 978-0-11-112066-8 £4.25

The Criminal Legal Aid (Remuneration) (Amendment) Regulations 2014 No. 2014/415. - Enabling power: Legal Aid, Sentencing and Punishment of Offenders Act 2012, ss. 2 (3), 41 (1) to (3). - Issued: 04.03.2014. Made: 26.02.2014. Laid: 27.02.2014. Coming into force: 20.03.2014. Effect: S.I. 2013/435 amended. Territorial extent & classification: E/W. General. - 32p.: 30 cm. - 978-0-11-111033-1 £9.75

The Legal Aid (Information about Financial Resources) (Amendment) Regulations 2014 No. 2014/901. - Enabling power: Legal Aid, Sentencing and Punishment of Offenders Act 2012, s. 22 (8). - Issued: 09.04.2014. Made: 01.04.2014. Coming into force: 02.04.2014 in accord. with reg. 1. Effect: S.I. 2013/628 amended. Territorial extent & classification: E/W. General. - Supersedes draft S.I. (ISBN 9780111108574) issued 23.01.2014. - 2p.: 30 cm. - 978-0-11-111366-0 £4.25

The Legal Aid, Sentencing and Punishment of Offenders Act 2012 (Amendment of Schedule 1) (Advocacy Exceptions) Order 2014 No. 2014/3305. - Enabling power: Legal Aid, Sentencing and Punishment of Offenders Act 2012, ss. 9 (2) (a), 41 (1) (b) (2) (a). - Issued: 19.12.2014. Made: 15.12.2014. Coming into force: in accord. with art. 1. Effect: 2012 c.10 amended. Territorial extent & classification: E/W. General. - This Order supersedes the defective draft S.I. (ISBN 9780111116210) issued 13/06/14 and is being issued free of charge to all known recipients of that draft SI. - 4p.: 30 cm. - 978-0-11-112569-4 £4.25

The Legal Aid, Sentencing and Punishment of Offenders Act 2012 (Community Care) Regulations 2014 No. 2014/1562. - Enabling power: Legal Aid, Sentencing and Punishment of Offenders Act 2012, s. 41 (1) (3) (c), sch. 1, part 1, para. 6 (3). - Issued: 19.06.2014. Made: 10.06.2014. Laid: 16.06.2014. Coming into force: 07.07.2014. Effect: None. Territorial extent & classification: E/W. General. - 4p.: 30 cm. - 978-0-11-111659-3 £4.25

Legal Services Commission, England and Wales

The Community Legal Service (Funding) (Amendment) Order 2014 No. 2014/1818. - Enabling power: Access to Justice Act 1999, ss. 6 (4), 25 (8) (8A). - Issued: 16.07.2014. Made: 08.07.2014. Laid: 10.07.2014. Coming into force: 31.07.2014. Effect: S.I. 2007/2441 amended. Territorial extent & classification: E/W. General. - 8p.: 30 cm. - 978-0-11-111789-7 £6.00

Legal services, England and Wales

The Financial Services (Banking Reform) Act 2013 (Commencement No. 2) Order 2014 No. 2014/772 (C.28). - Enabling power: Financial Services (Banking Reform) Act 2013, s. 148 (3). Bringing into operation various provisions of this Act on 21.03.2014 in accord. with art. 2. - Issued: 26.03.2014. Made: 20.03.2014. Effect: None. Territorial extent & classification: E/W. General. - 2p.: 30 cm. - 978-0-11-111254-0 £4.00

The Financial Services (Banking Reform) Act 2013 (Commencement No. 3) Order 2014 No. 2014/785 (C.29). - Enabling power: Financial Services (Banking Reform) Act 2013, s. 148 (4). Bringing into operation various provisions of this Act on 21.03.2014 in accord. with art. 2. - Issued: 27.03.2014. Made: 20.03.2014. Effect: None. Territorial extent & classification: E/W. General. - 2p.: 30 cm. - 978-0-11-111255-7 £4.00

The Legal Services Act 2007 (Appeals from Licensing Authority Decisions) (Chartered Institute of Patent Attorneys and Institute of Trade Mark Attorneys) Order 2014 No. 2014/1897. - Enabling power: Legal Services Act 2007, ss. 80 (1) (b) (4) (5), 204 (3) (4). - Issued: 23.07.2014. Made: 17.07.2014. Coming into force: In accord. with art. 2. Effect: 2007 c.29 modified. Territorial extent & classification: E/W. General. - Supersedes draft (ISBN 9780111116074) issued 11.06.2014. - 4p.: 30 cm. - 978-0-11-111862-7 £4.25

The Legal Services Act 2007 (Appeals from Licensing Authority Decisions) (Institute of Chartered Accountants in England and Wales) Order 2014 No. 2014/1898. - Enabling power: Legal Services Act 2007, ss. 80 (1) (b) (4), 204 (3) (4). - Issued: 23.07.2014. Made: 17.07.2014. Coming into force: 18.07.2014, in accord. with art. 2. Effect: 2007 c.29 modified. Territorial extent & classification: E/W. General. - Supersedes draft (ISBN 978011116081) issued 11.06.2014. - 4p.: 30 cm. - 978-0-11-111863-4 £4.25

The Legal Services Act 2007 (Approved Regulator) (No.2) Order 2014 No. 2014/2937. - Enabling power: Legal Services Act 2007, s. 206 (5). - Issued: 14.11.2014. Made: 06.11.2014. Coming into force: in accord. with art. 1. Effect: None. Territorial extent & classification: E/W. General. - 2p.: 30 cm. - 978-0-11-112318-8 £4.25

The Legal Services Act 2007 (Approved Regulator) Order 2014 No. 2014/1872. - Enabling power: Legal Services Act 2007, s. 206 (5). - Issued: 23.07.2014. Made: 17.07.2014. Coming into force: 18.07.2014, in accord. with art. 1. Effect: None. Territorial extent & classification: E/W. General. - Supersedes draft (ISBN 9780111116630) issued 20.06.2014. - 2p.: 30 cm. - 978-0-11-111861-0 £4.25

The Legal Services Act 2007 (Chartered Institute of Legal Executives) (Modification of Functions) Order 2014 No. 2014/3234. - Enabling power: Legal Services Act 2007, ss. 64 (2) (3) (4), 69 (1) (4) (5), 204 (3). - Issued: 12.12.2014. Made: 08.12.2014. Coming into force: 09.12.2014 in accord. with art. 1 (1). Effect: None. Territorial extent & classification: E/W. General. - Supersedes draft S.I. (ISBN 9780111121597) issued 15/10/14. - 4p.: 30 cm. - 978-0-11-112490-1 £4.25

The Legal Services Act 2007 (Claims Management Complaints) (Fees) Regulations 2014 No. 2014/3316. - Enabling power: Legal Services Act 2007, ss. 174A (3) (5), 204 (3) (b) (e). - Issued: 22.12.2014. Made: 15.12.2014. Coming into force: 28.01.2015. Effect: None. Territorial extent & classification: E/W. General. - Supersedes draft S.I. (ISBN 9780111122815) issued 05/11/14. - 8p.: 30 cm. - 978-0-11-112598-4 £6.00

The Legal Services Act 2007 (Commencement No. 12, Supplementary and Transitory Provision) Order 2014 No. 2014/3307 (C.152). - Enabling power: Legal Services Act 2007, ss. 208 (2) (4), 211 (2). Bringing into operation various provisions of the 2007 Act on 20.01.2015, 28.01.2015, in accord. with art. 2. - Issued: 22.12.2014. Made: 15.12.2014. Laid: 17.12.2014. Coming into force: 20.01.2015. Effect: None. Territorial extent & classification: E/W. General. - 8p.: 30 cm. - 978-0-11-112573-1 £6.00

The Legal Services Act 2007 (Levy) (No. 2) (Amendment) Rules 2014 No. 2014/1185. - Enabling power: Legal Services Act 2007, ss. 173, 174, 204 (2) (3) (4) (b). - Issued: 13.05.2014. Made: 30.04.2014. Laid: 09.05.2014. Coming into force: 02.07.2014. Effect: S.I. 2010/2911 amended. Territorial extent & classification: E/W. General. - 4p.: 30 cm. - 978-0-11-111465-0 £4.25

The Legal Services Act 2007 (Licensing Authority) (No. 2) Order 2014 No. 2014/3077. - Enabling power: Legal Services Act 2007, sch. 10, para. 15 (1) (a). - Issued: 25.11.2014. Made: 17.11.2014. Laid: 20.11.2014. Coming into force: 01.01.2015. Effect: None. Territorial extent & classification: E/W. General. - 2p.: 30 cm. - 978-0-11-112358-4 £4.25

The Legal Services Act 2007 (Licensing Authority) Order 2014 No. 2014/1925. - Enabling power: Legal Services Act 2007, sch. 10, para. 15 (1) (a). - Issued: 25.07.2014. Made: 21.07.2014. Laid: 22.07.2014. Coming into force: 14.08.2014. Effect: None. Territorial extent & classification: E/W. General. - 2p.: 30 cm. - 978-0-11-111898-6 £4.25

The Legal Services Act 2007 (the Chartered Institute of Patent Attorneys and the Institute of Trade Mark Attorneys) (Modification of Functions) Order 2014 No. 2014/3238. - Enabling power: Legal Services Act 2007, ss. 64 (2), 69 (1) (4) (6), 204 (3). - Issued: 15.12.2014. Made: 08.12.2014. Coming into force: in accord. with art. 2. Effect: None. Territorial extent & classification: E/W. General. - Supersedes draft S.I. (ISBN 9780111122020) issued 24/10/14. - 32p.: 30 cm. - 978-0-11-112495-6 £6.00

The Legal Services Act 2007 (The Institute of Chartered Accountants in England and Wales) (Modification of Functions) Order 2014 No. 2014/3236. - Enabling power: Legal Services Act 2007, ss. 64 (2) (3), 69 (1) (4), 204 (3). - Issued: 12.12.2014. Made: 08.12.2014. Coming into force: in accord. with art. 1 (2). Effect: None. Territorial extent & classification: E/W. General. - Supersedes draft S.I. (ISBN 9780111121610) issued 15/10/14. - 4p.: 30 cm. - 978-0-11-112493-2 £4.25

The Referral Fees (Regulators and Regulated Persons) Regulations 2014 No. 2014/3235. - Enabling power: Legal Aid, Sentencing and Punishment of Offenders Act 2012, s. 59 (1). - Issued: 12.12.2014. Made: 08.12.2014. Coming into force: In accord. with reg. 1. Effect: None. Territorial extent & classification: E/W. General. - Supersedes draft S.I. (ISBN 9780111121580) issued 15/10/14. - 2p.: 30 cm. - 978-0-11-112492-5 £4.25

Libraries

The Digital Economy Act 2010 (Appointed Day No. 4) Order 2014 No. 2014/1659 (C.68). - Enabling power: Digital Economy Act 2010, s. 47 (3). Bringing into operation various provisions of the 2010 Act on 30.06.2014, in accord. with art. 2. - Issued: 02.07.2014. Made: 25.06.2014. Effect: None. Territorial extent & classification: E/W/S/NI. General. - 2p.: 30 cm. - 978-0-11-111715-6 £4.25

The Public Lending Right Scheme 1982 (Commencement of Variation and Amendment) Order 2014 No. 2014/1945. - Enabling power: Public Lending Right Act 1979, s. 3 (7). - Issued: 29.07.2014. Made: 22.07.2014. Laid: 23.07.2014. Coming into force: 13.08.2014. Effect: S.I. 2014/1457 amended. Territorial extent & classification: E/W/S/NI. General. - This Statutory Instrument has been printed to correct errors in SI 2014/1457 (ISBN 9780111116067) and is being issued free of charge to all known recipients of that Statutory Instrument. - 4p.: 30 cm. - 978-0-11-111916-7 £4.25

The Public Lending Right Scheme 1982 (Commencement of Variations) Order 2014 No. 2014/1457. - Enabling power: Public Lending Right Act 1979, s. 3 (7). - Issued: 11.06.2014. Made: 03.06.2014. Laid: 05.06.2014. Coming into force: 01.07.2014. Effect: None. Territorial extent & classification: E/W/S/NI. General. - Corrected by SI 2014/1945 (ISBN 9780111119167) which is being issued free of charge to all known recipients of SI 2014/1457. - 4p.: 30 cm. - 978-0-11-111606-7 £4.25

Licences and licensing, England

The Licensing Act 2003 (FIFA World Cup Licensing Hours) Order 2014 No. 2014/1294. - Enabling power: Licensing Act 2003, ss. 172 (1) (3), 197 (2). - Issued: 27.05.2014. Made: 20.05.2014. Coming into force: 12.06.2014. Effect: None. Territorial extent & classification: E. General. - Supersedes draft S.I. (ISBN 9780111113370) issued 07.04.2014. - 4p.: 30 cm. - 978-0-11-111514-5 £4.25

Licences and licensing, England and Wales

The Legislative Reform (Entertainment Licensing) Order 2014 No. 2014/3253. - Enabling power: Legislative and Regulatory Reform Act 2006, s. 1. - Issued: 16.12.2014. Made: 01.12.2014. Coming into force: 06.04.2015. Effect: 2003 c.17 amended. Territorial extent & classification: E/W. General. - Supersedes draft SI (ISBN 9780111117675) issued 11/14/14 - 8p.: 30 cm. - 978-0-11-112518-2 £6.00

The Licensing Act 2003 (Hearings) (Amendment) Regulations 2014 No. 2014/2341. - Enabling power: Licensing Act 2003, ss. 183, 193, 197 (2). - Issued: 08.09.2014. Made: 01.09.2014. Laid: 05.09.2014. Coming into force: 01.10.2014. Effect: S.I. 2005/44 amended. Territorial extent & classification: E/W. General. - 2p.: 30 cm. - 978-0-11-112015-6 £4.25

The Licensing Act 2003 (Mandatory Conditions) Order 2014 No. 2014/1252. - Enabling power: Licensing Act 2003, ss. 19A, 73B, 197 (2). - Issued: 20.05.2014. Made: 14.05.2014. Coming into force: In accord. with art. 1. Effect: None. Territorial extent & classification: E/W. General. - Supersedes draft SI (ISBN 9780111113998) issued 14/04/14. - 4p.: 30 cm. - 978-0-11-111493-3 £4.25

The Licensing Act 2003 (Mandatory Licensing Conditions) (Amendment) Order 2014 No. 2014/2440. - Enabling power: Licensing Act 2003, ss. 19A, 73B, 197 (2). - Issued: 17.09.2014. Made: 11.09.2014. Coming into force: 01.10.2014. Effect: S.I. 2010/860 amended. Territorial extent & classification: E/W. General. - Supersedes draft S.I. (ISBN 978011116906) issued 27.06.2014. - 4p.: 30 cm. - 978-0-11-112076-7 £4.25

The Licensing Act 2003 (Permitted Temporary Activities) (Notices) (Amendment) Regulations 2014 No. 2014/2417. - Enabling power: Licensing Act 2003, ss. 100 (4) (5), 193, 197 (2). - Issued: 16.09.2014. Made: 09.09.2014. Laid: 10.09.2014. Coming into force: 01.10.2014. Effect: S.I. 2005/2918, amended. Territorial extent & classification: E/W. General. - 16p.: 30 cm. - 978-0-11-112063-7 £6.00

The Licensing Act 2003 (Personal Licences) (Amendment) Regulations 2014 No. 2014/3284. - Enabling power: Licensing Act 2003, ss. 133 (1) (2), 193, 197 (2). - Issued: 17.12.2014. Made: 10.12.2014. Laid: 15.12.2014. Coming into force: 05.01.2015. Effect: S.I. 2005/41 amended. Territorial extent & classification: E/W. General. - 4p.: 30 cm. - 978-0-11-112545-8 £4.25

Licences and licensing, Wales

The Licensing Act 2003 (Permitted Temporary Activities) (Notices and Fees) (Wales) Regulations 2014 No. 2014/1371. - Enabling power: Licensing Act 2003, ss. 100 (4) (5) (7), 193, 197 (2). - Issued: 05.06.2014. Made: 29.05.2014. Laid: 30.05.2014. Coming into force: 31.05.2014. Effect: S.I. 2005/79, 2918 amended. Territorial extent & classification: W. General. - 16p.: 30 cm. - 978-0-11-111545-9 £6.00

Licensing (marine)

The Marine Licensing (Application Fees) (Amendment) Regulations 2014 No. 2014/950. - Enabling power: Marine and Coastal Access Act 2009, ss. 67 (2) (3), 316 (1) (b). - Issued: 15.04.2014. Made: 08.04.2014. Laid: 10.04.2014. Coming into force: 01.05.2014. Effect: S.I. 2014/615 amended. Territorial extent & classification: E/W/S/NI. General. - This Statutory Instrument has been made in consequence of defects in SI 2014/615 (ISBN 9780111112175) and is being issued free of charge to all known recipients of that Statutory Instrument. - 2p.: 30 cm. - 978-0-11-111402-5 £4.25

The Marine Licensing (Application Fees) Regulations 2014 No. 2014/615. - Enabling power: Marine and Coastal Access Act 2009, ss. 67 (2) (3), 316 (1) (b). - Issued: 19.03.2014. Made: 13.03.2014. Laid: 14.03.2014. Coming into force: 06.04.2014. Effect: S.I. 2011/564 revoked with savings. Territorial extent & classification: E/W/S/NI. General. - Defects in this SI have been corrected by SI 2014/950 (ISBN 9780111114025) which is being sent free of charge to all known recipients of 2014/615. - 8p.: 30 cm. - 978-0-11-111217-5 £5.75

Limited liability partnerships

The Company, Limited Liability Partnership and Business Names (Sensitive Words and Expressions) Regulations 2014 No. 2014/3140. - Enabling power: Companies Act 2006, ss. 55 (1), 56 (1) (b), 1194 (1), 1195 (1) (b), 1292 (1). - Issued: 03.12.2014. Made: 26.11.2014. Laid: 27.11.2014. Coming into force: 31.01.2015. Effect: S.I. 2009/2615 revoked. Territorial extent & classification: E/W/S/NI. General. - For approval by resolution of each House of Parliament within twenty-eight days. - 12p.: 30 cm. - 978-0-11-112414-7 £6.00

Local government, England

The Aylesbury Vale (Electoral Changes) Order 2014 No. 2014/3334. - Enabling power: Local Democracy, Economic Development and Construction Act 2009, s. 59 (1). - Issued: 24.12.2014. Made: 16.12.2014. Coming into force: In accord. with art. 1 (2). Effect: None. Territorial extent & classification: E. General. - Supersedes draft SI (ISBN 9780111122136) issued 27/10/14. - 8p.: 30 cm. - 978-0-11-112622-6 £4.25

The Barnsley, Doncaster, Rotherham and Sheffield Combined Authority Order 2014 No. 2014/863. - Enabling power: Local Transport Act 2008, ss. 84, 91, 93 & Local Democracy, Economic Development and Construction Act 2009, ss. 103 to 105, 114 to 116. - Issued: 04.04.2014. Made: 31.03.2014. Coming into force: In accord with art. 1. Effect: None. Territorial extent & classification: E. General. - Supersedes draft SI (ISBN 9780111111314) issued 12.03.2014. - 12p.: 30 cm. - 978-0-11-111340-0 £6.00

The Bolsover (Electoral Changes) Order 2014 No. 2014/2562. - Enabling power: Local Government and Public Involvement in Health Act 2007, s. 92 (3). - Issued: 25.09.2014. Made: 14.07.2014. Coming into force: in accord. with art. 1 (2) (3). Effect: None. Territorial extent & classification: E. Local. - Available at http://www.legislation.gov.uk/uksi/2014/2562/contents/made Non-print

The Braintree (Electoral Changes) Order 2014 No. 2014/3335. - Enabling power: Local Democracy, Economic Development and Construction Act 2009, s. 59 (1). - Issued: 24.12.2014. Made: 16.12.2014. Coming into force: In accord. with art. 1 (2). Effect: None. Territorial extent & classification: E. General. - Supersedes draft SI (ISBN 9780111122105) issued 27/10/14. - 4p.: 30 cm. - 978-0-11-112623-3 £4.25

The Breckland (Electoral Changes) Order 2014 No. 2014/3290. - Enabling power: Local Democracy, Economic Development and Construction Act 2009, s. 59 (1). - Issued: 17.12.2014. Made: 02.12.2014. Coming into force: In accord. with art. 1 (2). Effect: None. Territorial extent & classification: E. General. - Supersedes draft SI (ISBN 9780011121740) issued 20/10/14. - 4p.: 30 cm. - 978-0-11-112555-7 £4.25

The Bromsgrove (Electoral Changes) Order 2014 No. 2014/18. - Enabling power: Local Democracy, Economic Development and Construction Act 2009, s. 59 (1). - Issued: 16.01.2014. Made: 08.01.2014. Coming into force: In accord. with art. 1 (2). Effect: None. Territorial extent & classification: E. Local. - Supersedes draft S.I. (ISBN 9780111105177) issued 04.11.2013. - 8p.: 30 cm. - 978-0-11-110817-8 £4.00

LOCAL GOVERNMENT, ENGLAND

The Business Improvement Districts (England) (Amendment) Regulations 2014 No. 2014/3199. - Enabling power: Local Government Act 2003, ss. 42, 55 (1) (2) (e), 123 (1) (a). - Issued: 09.12.2014. Made: 01.12.2014. Laid: 04.12.2014. Coming into force: 27.12.2014. Effect: S.I. 2004/2443 amended. Territorial extent & classification: E. General. - 2p.: 30 cm. - 978-0-11-112451-2 £4.25

The Business Improvement Districts (Property Owners) (England) Regulations 2014 No. 2014/3204. - Enabling power: Local Government and Housing Act 1989, ss. 150 (1) (2) (3) & Business Rate Supplements Act 2009, s. 29 (3), sch. 2, paras 2 (7), 5 (5) to (8), 7 (2) (3), 8, 10. - Issued: 09.12.2014. Made: 01.12.2014. Coming into force: In accord. with reg. 1. Effect: None. Territorial extent & classification: E. General. - Supersedes draft S.I. (ISBN 9780111122006) issued 24/10/14. - 40p.: 30 cm. - 978-0-11-112453-6 £10.00

The Business Rate Supplements Act 2009 (Commencement No. 2) (England) Order 2014 No. 2014/1860 (C.85). - Enabling power: Business Rate Supplements Act 2009, s. 32 (2). Bringing into operation various provisions of the 2009 Act on 16.07.2014. - Issued: 22.07.2014. Made: 15.07.2014. Effect: None. Territorial extent & classification: E. General. - 2p.: 30 cm. - 978-0-11-111827-6 £4.25

The Business Rate Supplements Act 2009 (Commencement No. 3) (England) Order 2014 No. 2014/3200 (C.143). - Enabling power: Business Rate Supplements Act 2009, s. 32 (2). Bringing into operation various provisions of the 2009 Act on 02.12.2014. - Issued: 09.12.2014. Made: 01.12.2014. Effect: None. Territorial extent & classification: E. General. - 2p.: 30 cm. - 978-0-11-112452-9 £4.25

The Canterbury (Electoral Changes) Order 2014 No. 2014/3336. - Enabling power: Local Democracy, Economic Development and Construction Act 2009, s. 59 (1). - Issued: 24.12.2014. Made: 16.12.2014. Coming into force: In accord. with art. 1 (2). Effect: None. Territorial extent & classification: E. General. - Supersedes draft SI (ISBN 9780111122112) issued 27/10/14. - 4p.: 30 cm. - 978-0-11-112625-7 £4.25

The Combined Authorities (Consequential Amendments) Order 2014 No. 2014/866. - Enabling power: Local Democracy, Economic Development and Construction Act 2009, ss. 114 to 116. - Issued: 04.04.2014. Made: 31.03.2014. Coming into force: 01.04.2014, in accord. with art. 1. Effect: 1968 c.73 amended. Territorial extent & classification: E. General. - Supersedes draft SI (ISBN 9780111111352) issued 12/03/14. - 4p.: 30 cm. - 978-0-11-111348-6 £4.25

The Corby (Electoral Changes) Order 2014 No. 2014/3287. - Enabling power: Local Democracy, Economic Development and Construction Act 2009, s. 59 (1). - Issued: 17.12.2014. Made: 02.12.2014. Coming into force: In accord. with art. 1 (2). Effect: None. Territorial extent & classification: E. General. - Supersedes draft SI (ISBN 9780111121757) issued 20/10/14. - 4p.: 30 cm. - 978-0-11-112551-9 £4.25

The Darlington (Electoral Changes) Order 2014 No. 2014/3338. - Enabling power: Local Democracy, Economic Development and Construction Act 2009, s. 59 (1). - Issued: 24.12.2014. Made: 16.12.2014. Coming into force: In accord. with art. 1 (2). Effect: None. Territorial extent & classification: E. General. - Supersedes draft SI (ISBN 9780111122129) issued 27/10/14. - 4p.: 30 cm. - 978-0-11-112627-1 £4.25

The Durham, Gateshead, Newcastle Upon Tyne, North Tyneside, Northumberland, South Tyneside and Sunderland Combined Authority Order 2014 No. 2014/1012. - Enabling power: Local Transport Act 2008, ss. 84, 91, 93 & Local Democracy, Economic Development and Construction Act 2009, ss. 103 to 105, 114 to 116. - Issued: 22.04.2014. Made: 14.04.2014. Coming into force: In accord. with art. 1. Effect: 1989 ch.42; S.I. 2013/2356 amended. Territorial extent & classification: E. General. - Supersedes draft SI (ISBN 9780111111819) issued 17.03.2014. - 12p.: 30 cm. - 978-0-11-111413-1 £6.00

The East Dorset (Electoral Changes) Order 2014 No. 2014/456. - Enabling power: Local Democracy, Economic Development and Construction Act 2009, s. 59 (1). - Issued: 06.03.2014. Made: 27.02.2014. Coming into force: In accord. with art. 1 (2). Effect: None. Territorial extent & classification: E. General. - Supersedes draft S.I. (ISBN 9780111106945) issued 20.12.2013. - 4p.: 30 cm. - 978-0-11-111064-5 £4.00

The East Lindsey (Electoral Changes) Order 2014 No. 2014/1189. - Enabling power: Local Democracy, Economic Development and Construction Act 2009, s. 59 (1). - Issued: 14.05.2014. Made: 07.05.2014. Coming into force: In accord. with art. 1 (2). Effect: None. Territorial extent & classification: E. Local. - Supersedes draft S.I. (ISBN 9780111110218) issued 03.03.2014. - 8p.: 30 cm. - 978-0-11-111468-1 £4.25

The Fenland (Electoral Changes) Order 2014 No. 2014/27. - Enabling power: Local Democracy, Economic Development and Construction Act 2009, s. 59 (1). - Issued: 16.01.2014. Made: 08.01.2014. Coming into force: In accord. with art. 1 (2). Effect: None. Territorial extent & classification: E. Local. - Supersedes draft S.I. (ISBN 9780111105276) issued 11.11.2013. - 8p.: 30 cm. - 978-0-11-110826-0 £4.00

The Gedling (Electoral Changes) Order 2014 No. 2014/19. - Enabling power: Local Democracy, Economic Development and Construction Act 2009, s. 59 (1). - Issued: 16.01.2014. Made: 08.01.2014. Coming into force: In accord. with art. 1 (2). Effect: None. Territorial extent & classification: E. Local. - Supersedes draft S.I. (ISBN 9780111105214) issued 11.11.2013. - 4p.: 30 cm. - 978-0-11-110818-5 £4.00

The Halton, Knowsley, Liverpool, St Helens, Sefton and Wirral Combined Authority Order 2014 No. 2014/865. - Enabling power: Local Transport Act 2008, ss. 84, 91, 93 & Local Democracy, Economic Development and Construction Act 2009, ss. 103 to 105, 114 to 116. - Issued: 04.04.2014. Made: 31.03.2014. Coming into force: In accord. with art. 1. Effect: None. Territorial extent & classification: E. General. - Supersedes draft SI (ISBN 9780111111345) issued 12/03/14. - 12p.: 30 cm. - 978-0-11-111347-9 £6.00

The Hambleton (Electoral Changes) Order 2014 No. 2014/21. - Enabling power: Local Democracy, Economic Development and Construction Act 2009, s. 59 (1). - Issued: 16.01.2014. Made: 08.01.2014. Coming into force: In accord. with art. 1 (2). Effect: None. Territorial extent & classification: E. Local. - Supersedes draft S.I. (ISBN 9780111104941) issued 08.11.2013. - 4p.: 30 cm. - 978-0-11-110820-8 £4.00

The Harrogate Stray Act 1985 (Tour de France) Order 2014 No. 2014/1190. - Enabling power: Localism Act 2011, s. 5 (1) (4) (5) (b) (6). - Issued: 14.05.2014. Made: 08.05.2014. Coming into force: In accord. with art. 1. Effect: None. Territorial extent & classification: E. Local. - Supersedes draft S.I. (ISBN 9780111110515) issued 05/03/2014. - 4p., map: 30 cm. - 978-0-11-111469-8 £4.25

The Herefordshire (Electoral Changes) Order 2014 No. 2014/20. - Enabling power: Local Democracy, Economic Development and Construction Act 2009, s. 59 (1). - Issued: 16.01.2014. Made: 08.01.2014. Coming into force: In accord. with art. 1 (2). Effect: None. Territorial extent & classification: E. Local. - Supersedes draft S.I. (ISBN 9780111104958) issued 08.11.2013. - 8p.: 30 cm. - 978-0-11-110819-2 £5.75

The Horsham (Electoral Changes) Order 2014 No. 2014/1335. - Enabling power: Local Government and Public Involvement in Health Act 2007, s. 92 (3). - Issued: 27.05.2014. Made: 20.05.2014. Coming into force: In accord. with art. 1 (2) (3). Effect: None. Territorial extent & classification: E. Local. - Available at http://www.legislation.gov.uk/uksi/2014/1335/contents/made
Non-print

The Kensington and Chelsea (Electoral Changes) Order 2014 No. 2014/25. - Enabling power: Local Democracy, Economic Development and Construction Act 2009, s. 59 (1). - Issued: 16.01.2014. Made: 09.01.2014. Coming into force: In accord. with art. 1 (2). Effect: None. Territorial extent & classification: E. Local. - Supersedes draft S.I. (ISBN 9780111105696) issued 13.11.2013. - 4p.: 30 cm. - 978-0-11-110824-6 £4.00

The Lancaster (Electoral Changes) Order 2014 No. 2014/455. - Enabling power: Local Democracy, Economic Development and Construction Act 2009, s. 59 (1). - Issued: 06.03.2014. Made: 27.02.2014. Coming into force: In accord. with art. 1 (2). Effect: None. Territorial extent & classification: E. General. - Supersedes draft S.I. (ISBN 9780111106952) issued 20.12.2013. - 8p.: 30 cm. - 978-0-11-111063-8 £4.00

The Leicester (Electoral Changes) Order 2014 No. 2014/3339. - Enabling power: Local Democracy, Economic Development and Construction Act 2009, s. 59 (1). - Issued: 24.12.2014. Made: 16.12.2014. Coming into force: In accord. with art. 1 (2). Effect: None. Territorial extent & classification: E. General. - Supersedes draft SI (ISBN 9780111122563) issued 03/11/14. - 4p.: 30 cm. - 978-0-11-112628-8 £4.25

The Local Audit and Accountability Act 2014 (Commencement No. 1) Order 2014 No. 2014/900 (C.39). - Enabling power: Local Audit and Accountability Act 2014, s. 49 (1) (5). Bringing into operation various provisions of the 2011 Act on 04.04.2014. - Issued: 09.04.2014. Made: 03.04.2014. Effect: None. Territorial extent & classification: E. General. - 4p.: 30 cm. - 978-0-11-111365-3 £4.25

LOCAL GOVERNMENT, ENGLAND

The Local Audit and Accountability Act 2014 (Commencement No. 2) Order 2014 No. 2014/940 (C.42). - Enabling power: Local Audit and Accountability Act 2011, s. 49 (1) (5). Bringing into operation various provisions of the 2014 Act on 09.04.2014, in accord. with art. 2. - Issued: 14.04.2014. Made: 08.04.2014. Effect: None. Territorial extent & classification: E. General. - 4p.: 30 cm. - 978-0-11-111397-4 £4.25

The Local Authorities (Capital Finance and Accounting) (England) (Amendment) Regulations 2014 No. 2014/1375. - Enabling power: Local Government Act 2003, ss. 21 (1), 123 (1). - Issued: 05.06.2014. Made: 28.05.2014. Laid: 04.06.2014. Coming into force: 30.06.2014. Effect: S.I. 2003/3146 amended. Territorial extent & classification: E. General. - 4p.: 30 cm. - 978-0-11-111548-0 £4.25

The Local Authorities (Conduct of Referendums) (Council Tax Increases) (England) (Amendment No. 2) Regulations 2014 No. 2014/925. - Enabling power: Local Government Finance Act 1992, ss. 52ZQ, 113. - Issued: 10.04.2014. Made: 03.04.2014. Coming into force: 04.04.2014 in accord. with reg. 1. Effect: S.I. 2012/444 amended. Territorial extent & classification: E. General. - Supersedes draft S.I. (ISBN 9780111110027) issued 26.02.2014. - 28p.: 30 cm. - 978-0-11-111382-0 £6.00

The Local Authorities (Conduct of Referendums) (England) (Amendment) Regulations 2014 No. 2014/924. - Enabling power: Local Government Act 2000, ss. 9MG, 105. - Issued: 10.04.2014. Made: 03.04.2014. Coming into force: In accord. with reg. 1. Effect: S.I. 2012/323 amended. Territorial extent & classification: E. General- Supersedes draft S.I. (ISBN 9780111110669) issued 06.03.2014. - 28p.: 30 cm. - 978-0-11-111381-3 £6.00

The Local Authorities (Elected Mayors) (Elections, Terms of Office and Casual Vacancies) (England) (Amendment) Regulations 2014 No. 2014/2172. - Enabling power: Local Government Act 2000, ss. 9HB, 105 (2). - Issued: 19.08.2014. Made: 13.08.2014. Laid: 14.08.2014. Coming into force: 05.09.2014. Effect: S.I. 2012/336 amended. Territorial extent & classification: E. General. - 4p.: 30 cm. - 978-0-11-111991-4 £4.25

The Local Authorities (Goods and Services) (Public Bodies) (England) Order 2014 No. 2014/1197. - Enabling power: Local Authorities (Goods and Services) Act 1970, s. 1 (5) (6). - Issued: 14.05.2014. Made: 07.05.2014. Laid: 09.05.2014. Coming into force: 01.06.2014. Effect: None. Territorial extent & classification: E. General. - 4p.: 30 cm. - 978-0-11-111471-1 £4.25

The Local Authorities (Standing Orders) (England) (Amendment) Regulations 2014 No. 2014/165. - Enabling power: Local Government and Housing Act 1989, ss. 8, 20, 190. - Issued: 04.02.2014. Made: 29.01.2014. Laid: 31.01.2014. Coming into force: 25.02.2014. Effect: S.I. 2001/3384 amended. Territorial extent & classification: E. General. - 4p.: 30 cm. - 978-0-11-110897-0 £4.00

The Local Government (Transparency Requirements) (England) Regulations 2014 No. 2014/2680. - Enabling power: Local Government, Planning and Land Act 1980, s. 3 (1) (2) (3) (4). - Issued: 10.10.2014. Made: 03.10.2014. Laid: 09.10.2014. Coming into force: 31.10.2014. Effect: None. Territorial extent & classification: E. General. - Revoked by SI 2015/480 (ISBN 9780111131787). - 4p.: 30 cm. - 978-0-11-112128-3 £4.25

The Local Government (Transparency) (Descriptions of Information) (England) Order 2014 No. 2014/2060. - Enabling power: Local Government, Planning and Land Act 1980, s. 3 (6). - Issued: 07.08.2014. Made: 20.06.2014. Laid: 24.06.2014. Coming into force: In accord. with art. 1. Effect: None. Territorial extent & classification: E. General. - Supersedes draft S.I. (ISBN 9780111116951) issued 27.06.14 - 2p.: 30 cm. - 978-0-11-111953-2 £4.25

The Middlesbrough (Electoral Changes) Order 2014 No. 2014/1188. - Enabling power: Local Democracy, Economic Development and Construction Act 2009, s. 59 (1). - Issued: 14.05.2014. Made: 07.05.2014. Coming into force: In accord. with art. 1 (2). Effect: None. Territorial extent & classification: E. Local. - Supersedes draft S.I. (ISBN 9780111110188) issued 03.03.2014. - 4p.: 30 cm. - 978-0-11-111467-4 £4.25

The Milton Keynes (Electoral Changes) Order 2014 No. 2014/22. - Enabling power: Local Democracy, Economic Development and Construction Act 2009, s. 59 (1). - Issued: 16.01.2014. Made: 08.01.2014. Coming into force: In accord. with art. 1 (2). Effect: None. Territorial extent & classification: E. Local. - Supersedes draft S.I. (ISBN 9780111105184) issued 04.11.2013. - 8p.: 30 cm. - 978-0-11-110821-5 £5.75

The Newark & Sherwood (Electoral Changes) Order 2014 No. 2014/1907. - Enabling power: Local Democracy, Economic Development and Construction Act 2009, s. 59 (1). - Issued: 24.07.2014. Made: 15.07.2014. Coming into force: In accord. with art. 1 (2). Effect: None. Territorial extent & classification: E. General. - Supersedes draft SI (ISBN 9780111115398) issued 04/06/14. - 8p.: 30 cm. - 978-0-11-111876-4 £6.00

The North Dorset (Electoral Changes) Order 2014 No. 2014/1906. - Enabling power: Local Democracy, Economic Development and Construction Act 2009, s. 59 (1). - Issued: 24.07.2014. Made: 15.07.2014. Coming into force: In accord. with art. 1 (2). Effect: None. Territorial extent & classification: E. General. - Supersedes draft SI (ISBN 9780111115473) issued 09.06.14. - 8p.: 30 cm. - 978-0-11-111875-7 £4.25

The North Somerset (Electoral Changes) Order 2014 No. 2014/3291. - Enabling power: Local Democracy, Economic Development and Construction Act 2009, s. 59 (1). - Issued: 17.12.2014. Made: 02.12.2014. Coming into force: in accord. with art. 1 (2). Effect: None. Territorial extent & classification: E. General. - Supersedes draft SI (ISBN 9780111121771) issued 20/10/14. - 8p.: 30 cm. - 978-0-11-112557-1 £6.00

The North West Leicestershire (Electoral Changes) Order 2014 No. 2014/3060. - Enabling power: Local Democracy, Economic Development and Construction Act 2009, s. 59 (1). - Issued: 21.11.2014. Made: 05.11.2014. Coming into force: In accord. with art. 1 (2). Effect: None. Territorial extent & classification: E. General. - Supersedes draft SI (ISBN 9780111118184) issued 21/07/14 - 8p.: 30 cm. - 978-0-11-112342-3 £6.00

The Openness of Local Government Bodies Regulations 2014 No. 2014/2095. - Enabling power: Local Audit and Accountability Act 2014, ss. 40, 43 (2). - Issued: 11.08.2014. Made: 05.08.2014. Coming into force: 06.08.2014 in accord. with reg. 1. Effect: 1960 c.67; 1972 c.70; S.I. 2012/2089 amended. Territorial extent & classification: E. General. - Supersedes draft S.I. (ISBN 9780111113554) issued 07.04.2014. - 8p.: 30 cm. - 978-0-11-111964-8 £6.00

The Selby (Electoral Changes) Order 2014 No. 2014/1911. - Enabling power: Local Government, Economic Development and Construction Act 2009, s. 59 (1). - Issued: 24.07.2014. Made: 14.07.2014. Coming into force: In accord. with art. 1 (2). Effect: None. Territorial extent & classification: E. Local. - Supersedes draft SI (ISBN 9780111114766) issued 16/05/14. - 4p.: 30 cm. - 978-0-11-111880-1 £4.25

The Sevenoaks (Electoral Changes) Order 2014 No. 2014/1308. - Enabling power: Local Government and Public Involvement in Health Act 2007, s. 92 (3). - Issued: 23.05.2014. Made: 20.05.2014. Coming into force: In accord. with art. 2. Effect: None. Territorial extent & classification: E. Local. - Available at http://www.legislation.gov.uk/uksi/2014/1308/contents/made Non-print

The Shepway (Electoral Changes) Order 2014 No. 2014/1908. - Enabling power: Local Democracy, Economic Development and Construction Act 2009, s. 59 (1). - Issued: 24.07.2014. Made: 14.07.2014. Coming into force: In accord. with art. 1 (2). Effect: None. Territorial extent & classification: E. Local. - Supersedes draft SI (ISBN 9780111114773) issued 24/07/14. - 4p.: 30 cm. - 978-0-11-111877-1 £4.25

The South Hams (Electoral Changes) Order 2014 No. 2014/3059. - Enabling power: Local Democracy, Economic Development and Construction Act 2009, s. 59 (1). - Issued: 21.11.2014. Made: 05.11.2014. Coming into force: In accord. with art. 1 (2). Effect: None. Territorial extent & classification: E. General. - Supersedes draft SI (ISBN 9780111118177) issued 21/07/14 - 4p.: 30 cm. - 978-0-11-112341-6 £4.25

The South Kesteven (Electoral Changes) Order 2014 No. 2014/3058. - Enabling power: Local Democracy, Economic Development and Construction Act 2009, s. 59 (1). - Issued: 21.11.2014. Made: 05.11.2014. Coming into force: In accord. with art. 1 (2). Effect: None. Territorial extent & classification: E. General. - Supersedes draft SI (ISBN 9780111118191) issued 23/07/14. - 8p.: 30 cm. - 978-0-11-112340-9 £4.25

The South Oxfordshire (Electoral Changes) Order 2014 No. 2014/23. - Enabling power: Local Democracy, Economic Development and Construction Act 2009, s. 59 (1). - Issued: 16.01.2014. Made: 08.01.2014. Coming into force: In accord. with art. 1 (2). Effect: None. Territorial extent & classification: E. Local. - Supersedes draft S.I. (ISBN 9780111105252) issued 11.11.2013. - 4p.: 30 cm. - 978-0-11-110822-2 £4.00

The South Ribble (Electoral Changes) Order 2014 No. 2014/3288. - Enabling power: Local Democracy, Economic Development and Construction Act 2009, s. 59 (1). - Issued: 17.12.2014. Made: 02.12.2014. Coming into force: In accord. with art. 1 (2). Effect: None. Territorial extent & classification: E. General. - Supersedes draft SI (ISBN 9780111121382) issued 17/10/14. - 8p.: 30 cm. - 978-0-11-112552-6 £4.25

The Stratford-on-Avon (Electoral Changes) Order 2014 No. 2014/3057. - Enabling power: Local Democracy, Economic Development and Construction Act 2009, s. 59 (1). - Issued: 21.11.2014. Made: 05.11.2014. Coming into force: In accord. with art. 1 (2). Effect: None. Territorial extent & classification: E. General. - Supersedes draft SI (ISBN 9780111118160) issued 21/07/14- 8p.: 30 cm. - 978-0-11-112339-3 £6.00

The Suffolk Coastal (Electoral Changes) Order 2014 No. 2014/3341. - Enabling power: Local Democracy, Economic Development and Construction Act 2009, s. 59 (1). - Issued: 24.12.2014. Made: 16.12.2014. Coming into force: In accord. with art. 1 (2). Effect: None. Territorial extent & classification: E. General. - Supersedes draft SI (ISBN 9780111122099) issued 27/10/14. - 8p.: 30 cm. - 978-0-11-112630-1 £4.25

The Telford & Wrekin (Electoral Changes) Order 2014 No. 2014/1910. - Enabling power: Local Democracy, Economic Development and Construction Act 2009, s. 59 (1). - Issued: 24.07.2014. Made: 14.07.2014. Coming into force: In accord. with art. 1 (2) (3). Effect: None. Territorial extent & classification: E. Local. - Supersedes draft SI (ISBN 9780111114759) issued 16/05/14. - 12p.: 30 cm. - 978-0-11-111879-5 £6.00

The Three Rivers (Electoral Changes) Order 2014 No. 2014/243. - Enabling power: Local Democracy, Economic Development and Construction Act 2009, s. 59 (1). - Issued: 13.02.2014. Made: 05.02.2014. Coming into force: In accord. with art. 1 (2) (3). Effect: None. Territorial extent & classification: E. General. - Supersedes draft S.I. (ISBN 9780111106549) issued 06.12.2013. - 8p.: 30 cm. - 978-0-11-110943-4 £4.00

The Uttlesford (Electoral Changes) Order 2014 No. 2014/1334. - Enabling power: Local Democracy, Economic Development and Construction Act 2009, s. 59 (1). - Issued: 29.05.2014. Made: 20.05.2014. Coming into force: In accord. with art. 1 (2). Effect: None. Territorial extent & classification: E. General. - Supersedes draft SI (ISBN 9780111110362) issued 10/03/14- 4p.: 30 cm. - 978-0-11-111523-7 £4.25

The Vale of White Horse (Electoral Changes) Order 2014 No. 2014/24. - Enabling power: Local Democracy, Economic Development and Construction Act 2009, s. 59 (1). - Issued: 16.01.2014. Made: 08.01.2014. Coming into force: In accord. with art. 1 (2). Effect: None. Territorial extent & classification: E. Local. - Supersedes draft S.I. (ISBN 9780111105269) issued 11.11.2013. - 8p.: 30 cm. - 978-0-11-110823-9 £4.00

The Warwick (Electoral Changes) Order 2014 No. 2014/26. - Enabling power: Local Democracy, Economic Development and Construction Act 2009, s. 59 (1). - Issued: 16.01.2014. Made: 08.01.2014. Coming into force: In accord. with art. 1 (2). Effect: None. Territorial extent & classification: E. Local. - Supersedes draft S.I. (ISBN 9780111105283) issued 05.11.2013. - 8p.: 30 cm. - 978-0-11-110825-3 £4.00

The Wellingborough (Electoral Changes) Order 2014 No. 2014/1909. - Enabling power: Local Democracy, Economic Development and Construction Act 2009, s. 59 (1). - Issued: 24.07.2014. Made: 15.07.2014. Coming into force: In accord. with art. 1 (2). Effect: None. Territorial extent & classification: E. General. - Supersedes draft SI (ISBN 9780111115374) issued 09/06/14. - 4p.: 30 cm. - 978-0-11-111878-8 £4.25

The West Yorkshire Combined Authority Order 2014 No. 2014/864. - Enabling power: Transport Act 1985, s. 85 & Local Transport Act 2008, ss. 84, 91, 93 & Local Democracy, Economic Development and Construction Act 2009, ss. 103 to 105, 114 to 116. - Issued: 07.04.2014. Made: 31.03.2014. Coming into force: In accord. with art. 1. Effect: None. Territorial extent & classification: E. General. - Supersedes draft SI (ISBN 9780111111420) issued 14/03/14. - 12p.: 30 cm. - 978-0-11-111346-2 £6.00

The Wyre (Electoral Changes) Order 2014 No. 2014/1187. - Enabling power: Local Democracy, Economic Development and Construction Act 2009, s. 59 (1). - Issued: 14.05.2014. Made: 07.05.2014. Coming into force: In accord. with art. 1 (2). Effect: None. Territorial extent & classification: E. Local. - Supersedes draft S.I. (ISBN 9780111110201) issued 03.03.2014. - 4p.: 30 cm. - 978-0-11-111466-7 £4.25

The York (Electoral Changes) Order 2014 No. 2014/3289. - Enabling power: Local Democracy, Economic Development and Construction Act 2009, s. 59 (1). - Issued: 17.12.2014. Made: 02.12.2014. Coming into force: In accord. with art. 1 (2). Effect: None. Territorial extent & classification: E. General. - Supersedes draft SI (ISBN 9780111121764) issued 17/10/14. - 4p.: 30 cm. - 978-0-11-112554-0 £4.25

Local government, England and Wales

The Legislative Reform (Payments by Parish Councils, Community Councils and Charter Trustees) Order 2014 No. 2014/580. - Enabling power: Legislative and Regulatory Reform Act 2006, s. 1. - Issued: 17.03.2014. Made: 11.03.2014. Coming into force: In accord. with art. 1(c). Effect: 1972 c.70; S.I. 1996/263 amended. Territorial extent & classification: E/W. General. - Supersedes draft SI (ISBN 9780111105825) issued 12/11/2013. - 4p.: 30 cm. - 978-0-11-111184-0 £4.00

The Local Audit and Accountability Act 2014 (Commencement No. 3) Order 2014 No. 2014/1596 (C.62). - Enabling power: Local Audit and Accountability Act 2014 s. 49 (1) (5). Bringing into operation various provisions of the 2014 Act on 18.06.2014, in accord. with art. 2. - Issued: 23.06.2014. Made: 17.06.2014. Effect: None. Territorial extent & classification: E/W. General. - 4p.: 30 cm. - 978-0-11-111668-5 £4.25

The Local Audit and Accountability Act 2014 (Commencement No. 4) Order 2014 No. 2014/3319 (C.154). - Enabling power: Local Audit and Accountability Act 2014 s. 49 (1) (5). Bringing into operation various provisions of the 2014 Act on 16.12.2014, in accord. with art. 2. - Issued: 22.12.2014. Made: 15.12.2014. Effect: None. Territorial extent & classification: E/W. General. - 4p.: 30 cm. - 978-0-11-112604-2 £4.25

The Local Audit (Auditor Panel Independence) Regulations 2014 No. 2014/2845. - Enabling power: Local Audit and Accountability Act 2014, s. 46, sch. 4, para. 2 (9). - Issued: 28.10.2014. Made: 22.10.2014. Coming into force: In accord. with reg. 1. Effect: 2014 c.2 amended. Territorial extent & classification: E/W. General. - Supersedes draft S.I. (ISBN 9780111117439) issued 07.07.2014. - 4p.: 30 cm. - 978-0-11-112226-6 £4.25

The Local Audit (Auditor Panel) Regulations 2014 No. 2014/3224. - Enabling power: Local Audit and Accountability Act 2014, s. 10 (8), sch. 4, paras 4, 5 (1) (b). - Issued: 11.12.2014. Made: 05.12.2014. Laid: 10.12.2014. Coming into force: 01.04.2015. Effect: None. Territorial extent & classification: E/W. General. - 8p.: 30 cm. - 978-0-11-112481-9 £4.25

The Local Audit (Auditor Resignation and Removal) Regulations 2014 No. 2014/1710. - Enabling power: Local Audit and Accountability Act 2014, ss. 16, 43 (2). - Issued: 08.07.2014. Made: 02.07.2014. Laid: 04.07.2014. Coming into force: 01.04.2015. Effect: None. Territorial extent & classification: E/W. General. - 8p.: 30 cm. - 978-0-11-111748-4 £6.00

The Local Audit (Delegation of Functions) and Statutory Audit (Delegation of Functions) Order 2014 No. 2014/2009. - Enabling power: Companies Act 2006, ss. 1252, 1253, sch. 13, paras 7 (3), 11 (2) (3) (a). - Issued: 04.08.2014. Made: 29.07.2014. Coming into force: In accord. with art. 1. Effect: S.I. 2012/1741 amended. Territorial extent & classification: E/W except for art. 10 which extends to the UK. General. - Supersedes draft S.I. (ISBN 9780111116609) issued 19.06.2014. - 8p.: 30 cm. - 978-0-11-111935-8 £4.25

The Local Audit (Liability Limitation Agreements) Regulations 2014 No. 2014/1628. - Enabling power: Local Audit and Accountability Act 2014, s. 14. - Issued: 30.06.2014. Made: 23.06.2014. Laid: 27.06.2014. Coming into force: 01.04.2015. Effect: None. Territorial extent & classification: E/W. General. - 2p.: 30 cm. - 978-0-11-111702-6 £4.25

The Local Audit (Professional Qualifications and Major Local Audit) Regulations 2014 No. 2014/1627. - Enabling power: Companies Act 2006, ss. 1219, 1292 (1), sch. 10, para. 13. - Issued: 30.06.2014. Made: 23.06.2014. Laid: 27.06.2014. Coming into force: 31.07.2014. Effect: None. Territorial extent & classification: E/W. General. - 8p.: 30 cm. - 978-0-11-111701-9 £6.00

The Local Authorities (Mayoral Elections) (England and Wales) (Amendment) Regulations 2014 No. 2014/370. - Enabling power: Local Government Act 2000, ss. 9HE, 44, 105. - Issued: 25.02.2014. Made: 13.02.2014. Coming into force: In accord. with reg. 1 (2). Effect: S.I. 2007/1024 amended & S.I. 2012/2059 revoked. Territorial extent & classification: E/W. General. - Supersedes draft SI (ISBN 9780111107683) issued 24.12.2013. - 42p.: 30 cm. - 978-0-11-110995-3 £9.75

The Public Interest Reports and Recommendations (Modification of Consideration Procedure) Regulations 2014 No. 2014/1629. - Enabling power: Local Audit and Accountability Act 2014, sch, 7, para. 5 (10). - Issued: 30.06.2014. Made: 23.06.2014. Laid: 27.06.2014. Coming into force: 01.04.2015. Effect: 2014 c.2 modified. Territorial extent & classification: E/W. General. - 2p.: 30 cm. - 978-0-11-111703-3 £4.25

Local government, Wales

The Accounts and Audit (Wales) Regulations 2014 No. 2014/3362 (W.337). - Enabling power: Local Government Act 2000, ss. 13, 105, 106 & Local Government Act 2003, ss. 21 (1) (2) (b) (5), 23 (2) (3), 24, 123 & Public Audit (Wales) Act 2004, ss. 39, 58. - Issued: 12.01.2015. Made: 22.12.2014. Laid before the National Assembly for Wales: 23.12.2014. Coming into force: 31.03.2015. Effect: S.I. 2007/399 (W.45) amended & S.I. 2005/368 (W.34), 2007/388 (W.39), 2010/683 (W.66), 2013/217 (W.29) revoked. Territorial extent & classification: W. General. - In English and Welsh. Welsh title: Rheoliadau Cyfrifon ac Archwilio (Cymru) 2014. - 27p.: 30 cm. - 978-0-348-11037-1 £6.00

The Local Authorities (Capital Finance and Accounting) (Wales) (Amendment) Regulations 2014 No. 2014/481 (W.58). - Enabling power: Local Government Act 2003, ss. 11 (1), 21 (1), 24, 123 (1). - Issued: 13.03.2014. Made: 27.02.2014. Laid before the National Assembly for Wales: 05.03.2014. Coming into force: 31.03.2014. Effect: S.I. 2003/3239 (W.319) amended. Territorial extent & classification: W. General. - This Statutory Instrument has been printed in substitution of the same number (and ISBN) issued 10.03.2014 and is being issued free of charge to all known recipients of that Statutory Instrument. - In English and Welsh. Welsh title: Rheoliadau Awdurdodau Lleol (Cyllid Cyfalaf a Chyfrifyddu) (Cymru) (Diwygio) 2014. - 8p.: 30 cm. - 978-0-348-10899-6 £5.75

The Local Authorities (Standing Orders) (Wales) (Amendment) Regulations 2014 No. 2014/1514 (W.155). - Enabling power: Local Government and Housing Act 1989, ss. 8, 20, 190. - Issued: 17.06.2014. Made: 09.06.2014. Laid before the National Assembly for Wales: 10.06.2014. Coming into force: 01.07.2014. Effect: S.I. 2006/1275 (W.121) amended. Territorial extent & classification: W. General. - In English and Welsh. Welsh title: Rheoliadau Awdurdodau Lleol (Rheolau Sefydlog) (Cymru) (Diwygio) 2014. - 12p.: 30 cm. - 978-0-348-10954-2 £6.00

The Local Authority Elections (Wales) Order 2014 No. 2014/3033 (W.302). - Enabling power: Local Government Act 2000, ss. 87, 105 (2) (3), 106 (1). - Issued: 10.12.2014. Made: 12.11.2014. Laid before the National Assembly for Wales: 14.11.2014. Coming into force: 09.12.2014. Effect: S.I. 2012/686 (W.94) revoked. Territorial extent & classification: W. General. - In English and Welsh. Welsh title: Gorchymyn Etholiadau Awdurdodau Lleol (Cymru) 2014. - 4p.: 30 cm. - 978-0-348-11027-2 £4.25

The Local Government Byelaws (Fixed Penalties) (Wales) Regulations 2014 No. 2014/2717 (W.273). - Enabling power: Local Government Byelaws (Wales) Act 2012, s. 13 (3) (4). - Issued: 22.10.2014. Made: 09.10.2014. Laid before the National Assembly for Wales: 13.10.2014. Coming into force: 07.11.2014. Effect: None. Territorial extent & classification: W. General. - In English and Welsh. Welsh title: Rheoliadau Is-ddeddfau Llywodraeth Leol (Cosbau Penodedig) (Cymru) 2014. - 4p.: 30 cm. - 978-0-348-10998-6 £4.25

The Local Government Byelaws (Wales) Act 2012 (Amendment) Order 2014 No. 2014/3111 (W.311). - Enabling power: Local Government Byelaws (Wales) Act 2012, ss. 9, 16. - Issued: 01.12.2014. Made: 18.11.2014. Coming into force: 19.11.2014. Effect: 2012 anaw 2 amended. Territorial extent & classification: W. General. - In English and Welsh. Welsh title: Gorchymyn Deddf Is-ddeddfau Llywodraeth Leol (Cymru) 2012 (Diwygio) 2014. - 8p.: 30 cm. - 978-0-348-11020-3 £6.00

The Local Government Byelaws (Wales) Act 2012 (Commencement No. 1) Order 2014 No. 2014/2121 (W.207) (C.95). - Enabling power: Local Government Byelaws (Wales) Act 2012, s. 22 (2). Bringing various provisions of the 2012 Act into operation on 15.08.2014. - Issued: 15.08.2014. Made: 24.07.2014. Effect: None. Territorial extent & classification: W. General. - In English and Welsh. Welsh title: Gorchymyn Deddf Is-ddeddfau Llywodraeth Leol (Cymru) 2012 (Cychwyn Rhif 1) 2014. - 4p.: 30 cm. - 978-0-348-10983-2 £4.25

The Local Government (Committees and Political Groups) (Amendment) (Wales) Regulations 2014 No. 2014/476 (W.56). - Enabling power: Local Government and Housing Act 1989, sch. 1, para. 1. - Issued: 28.03.2014. Made: 27.02.2014. Laid before the National Assembly for Wales: 05.03.2014. Coming into force: 01.05.2014. Effect: S.I. 1990/1553 amended in relation to Wales. Territorial extent & classification: W. General. - In English and Welsh. Welsh title: Rheoliadau Llywodraeth Leol (Pwyllgorau a Grwpiau Gwleidyddol) (Diwygio) (Cymru) 2014. - 8p.: 30 cm. - 978-0-348-10928-3 £4.00

The Local Government (Democracy) (Wales) Act 2013 (Commencement No. 1) Order 2014 No. 2014/380 (W.45) (C.15). - Enabling power: Local Government (Democracy) (Wales) Act 2013, s. 75 (3). Bringing various provisions of the 2013 Act into operation on 01.04.2014. - Issued: 12.03.2014. Made: 20.02.2014. Effect: None. Territorial extent & classification: W. General. - In English and Welsh. Welsh title: Gorchymyn Deddf Llywodraeth Leol (Democratiaeth) (Cymru) 2013 (Cychwyn Rhif 1) 2014. - 4p.: 30 cm. - 978-0-348-10901-6 £4.00

The Local Government (Wales) Measure 2009 (Amendment) Order 2014 No. 2014/1713 (W.173). - Enabling power: Local Government (Wales) Measure 2009, s. 38 (2). - Issued: 10.07.2014. Made: 01.07.2014. Coming into force: 02.07.2014, in accord. with art 1 (2). Effect: 2009 nawm 2 amended. Territorial extent & classification: W. General. - In English and Welsh. Welsh title: Gorchymyn Mesur Llywodraeth Leol (Cymru) 2009 (Diwygio) 2014. - 4p.: 30 cm. - 978-0-348-10959-7 £4.25

The Local Government (Wales) Measure 2011 (Commencement No. 3) Order 2014 No. 2014/453 (W.51) (C.20). - Enabling power: Local Government (Wales) Measure 2011 (nawm 4), s. 178 (3). Bringing various provisions of the 2011 Measure into operation on 28.02.2014. - Issued: 13.03.2014. Made: 27.02.2014. Effect: None. Territorial extent & classification: W. General. - In English and Welsh. Welsh title: Gorchymyn Mesur Llywodraeth Leol (Cymru) 2011 (Cychwyn Rhif 3) 2014. - 8p.: 30 cm. - 978-0-348-10914-6 £5.75

The Valuation Tribunal for Wales (Wales) (Amendment) Regulations 2014 No. 2014/554 (W.66). - Enabling power: Local Government Finance Act 1988, ss. 140 (4), 143 (1) (2), sch. 11, paras 1, 8. - Issued: 26.03.2014. Made: 07.03.2014. Laid before the National Assembly for Wales: 10.03.2014. Coming into force: 31.03.2014. Effect: WSI. 2010/713 (W.69) amended. Territorial extent & classification: W. General. - In English and Welsh: Welsh title: Rheoliadau Tribiwnlys Prisio Cymru (Cymru) (Diwygio) 2014. - 8p.: 30 cm. - 978-0-348-10921-4 £4.00

London government

The Greater London Authority (Consolidated Council Tax Requirement Procedure) Regulations 2014 No. 2014/3308. - Enabling power: Greater London Authority Act 1999, sch. 6, para. 10. - Issued: 19.12.2014. Made: 15.12.2014. Laid: 18.12.2014. Coming into force: 12.01.2015. Effect: 1999 c.29 amended. Territorial extent & classification: E. General. - 2p.: 30 cm. - 978-0-11-112575-5 £4.25

The Localism Act 2011 (Consequential Amendments) Order 2014 No. 2014/389. - Enabling power: Localism Act 2011, s. 235 (2) (3), 236 (1). - Issued: 03.03.2014. Made: 24.02.2014. Coming into force: In accord. with art. 1 (2). Effect: 1992 c.14; 1999 c.29 amended. Territorial extent & classification: E/W. General. - Supersedes draft S.I. (ISBN 9780111107997) issued 09.01.2014. - 4p.: 30 cm. - 978-0-11-111019-5 £4.00

Magistrates' courts, England and Wales

The Courts and Tribunals Fees (Miscellaneous Amendments) Order 2014 No. 2014/590 (L.6). - Enabling power: Courts Act 2003, s. 92 & Insolvency Act 1986, ss. 414, 415 & Tribunals, Courts and Enforcement Act 2007, s. 42, 49 (3) & Constitutional Reform Act 2005, s. 52 & Mental Capacity Act 2005. s. 54 & Gender Recognition Act 2004, s. 7 (2). - Issued: 19.03.2014. Made: 11.03.2014. Laid: 13.03.2104. Coming into force: 06.04.2014. Effect: S.I. 2004/3120; 2006/758; 2007/1745; 2008/1052, 1053, 1054; 2009/213, 1114; 2010/42; 2011/2344; 2013/1179, 1893 amended. Territorial extent & classification: E/W. General. - 16p.: 30 cm. - 978-0-11-111194-9 £5.75

The Crime and Courts Act 2013 (Commencement No. 10 and Transitional Provision) Order 2014 No. 2014/954 (C.44). - Enabling power: Crime and Courts Act 2013, s. 61 (3). Bringing into operation various provisions of the 2013 Act on 22.04.2014. - Issued: 15.04.2014. Made: 09.04.2014. Effect: None. Territorial extent & classification: E/W. General. - 4p.: 30 cm. - 978-0-11-111406-3 £4.25

The Criminal Procedure Rules 2014 No. 2014/1610 (L.26). - Enabling power: Bail Act 1976, s. 5B (9) & Criminal Law Act 1977, s. 48 & Senior Courts Act 1981, ss. 19, 52, 66, 67, 73 (2), 74 (2) (3) (4), 87 (4) & Criminal Evidence Act 1984, s. 81 Road Traffic Offenders Act 1988 s. 12 (1) & Criminal Procedure and Investigations Act 1996, ss. 19, 20 (3) & Powers of Criminal Courts (Sentencing) Act 2000, s. 155 (7) & Terrorism Act 2000, sch. 5, para. 10, sch. 6, para. 4, sch. 6A para. 5 & Proceeds of Crime Act 2002, ss. 91, 351 (2), 362 (2), 369 92), 375 (1) & Courts Act 2003, s. 69 & Criminal Justice Act 2003, ss. 30 (1), 132 (4), 132 (4), 174 (4) & Extradition Act 2003, ss. 36A, 36B (3), 118A (4), 118B (3)- Issued: 25.06.2014. Made: 11.06.2014. Laid: 25.06.2014. Coming into force: 06.10.2014. Effect: S.I. 2013/1554 revoked. Territorial extent and classification: E/W. General. - 392p.: 30 cm. - 978-0-11-111684-5 £39.25

The Family Procedure (Amendment) Rules 2014 No. 2014/524 (L.5). - Enabling power: Courts Act 2003, ss. 75, 76. - Issued: 13.03.2014. Made: 06.03.2014. Laid: 10.03.2014. Coming into force: 13.03.2014. Effect: S.I. 2010/2955 amended. Territorial extent & classification: E/W. General. - 4p.: 30 cm. - 978-0-11-111122-2 £4.00

The Magistrates' Courts Fees (Amendment) Order 2014 No. 2014/875 (L.18). - Enabling power: Courts Act 2003, ss. 92, 108 (6). - Issued: 04.04.2014. Made: 27.03.2014. Laid: 01.04.2014. Coming into force: 22.04.2014. Effect: S.I. 2008/1052 amended. Territorial extent & classification: E/W. General. - 4p.: 30 cm. - 978-0-11-111327-1 £4.25

Marine pollution

The Marine Licensing (Application Fees) (Amendment) Regulations 2014 No. 2014/950. - Enabling power: Marine and Coastal Access Act 2009, ss. 67 (2) (3), 316 (1) (b). - Issued: 15.04.2014. Made: 08.04.2014. Laid: 10.04.2014. Coming into force: 01.05.2014. Effect: S.I. 2014/615 amended. Territorial extent & classification: E/W/S/NI. General. - This Statutory Instrument has been made in consequence of defects in SI 2014/615 (ISBN 9780111112175) and is being issued free of charge to all known recipients of that Statutory Instrument. - 2p.: 30 cm. - 978-0-11-111402-5 £4.25

The Marine Licensing (Application Fees) Regulations 2014 No. 2014/615. - Enabling power: Marine and Coastal Access Act 2009, ss. 67 (2) (3), 316 (1) (b). - Issued: 19.03.2014. Made: 13.03.2014. Laid: 14.03.2014. Coming into force: 06.04.2014. Effect: S.I. 2011/564 revoked with savings. Territorial extent & classification: E/W/S/NI. General. - Defects in this SI have been corrected by SI 2014/950 (ISBN 9780111114025) which is being sent free of charge to all known recipients of 2014/615. - 8p.: 30 cm. - 978-0-11-111217-5 £5.75

The Merchant Shipping (Prevention of Pollution) (Limits) Regulations 2014 No. 2014/3306. - Enabling power: European Communities Act 1972, s. 2 (2) & Merchant Shipping Act 1995, ss. 85, 86, 128 (5) (6) & S.I. 1983/1106, art. 3 & S.I. 1987/470, art. 3 & S.I. 1987/2567, art. 2 & S.I. 1990/2595, art. 3 & S.I. 1996/282, art. 2 & S.I.2006/1248, arts. 2, 3 & S.I. 2006/2950, arts 3, 4, 5. - Issued: 19.12.2014. Made: 11.12.2014. Laid: 17.12.2012. Coming into force: 28.01.2015. Effect: S.I. 1998/2498; 1196/2154, 3010; 1998/1056; 2004/2110; 2008/2924, 3257; 2009/2796; 2010/1228 amended. Territorial extent & classification: E/W/S/NI. General. - 12p.: 30 cm. - 978-0-11-112570-0 £6.00

Marriage

The Consular Marriages and Marriages under Foreign Law (No. 2) Order 2014 No. 2014/3265. - Enabling power: Marriage (Same Sex Couples Act) 2013, s. 13 (1), sch. 6, paras 1, 2, 7, 13, 14. - Issued: 17.12.2014. Made: 10.12.2014. Coming into force: in accord with art. 1. Effect: 2014/1110 revoked. Territorial extent & classification: E/W/S/NI. General. - This S.I. has been printed to correct defects in S.I. 2014/1110 (ISBN 978011114414) and is being issued free of charge to all known recipients of that S.I. - 12p.: 30 cm. - 978-0-11-112530-4 £6.00

The Consular Marriages and Marriages under Foreign Law Order 2014 No. 2014/1110. - Enabling power: Marriage (Same Sex Couples Act) 2013, s. 13 (1), sch. 6, paras 1, 2, 7, 13, 14. - Issued: 06.05.2014. Made: 28.04.2014. Coming into force: 03.06.2014. Effect: 1906 c.40 partially repealed & 2006 asp 2; S.I. 2012/798 amended & S.I. 1970/1539; 1990/598; 2013/2875 revoked. Territorial extent & classification: E/W/S/NI. General. - Supersedes draft SI (ISBN 9780111108758) issued 29/01/14; Revoked by SI 2014/3184 (ISBN 9780111124345). - 8p.: 30 cm. - 978-0-11-111441-4 £6.00

The Marriage and Civil Partnership (Scotland) Act 2014 and Civil Partnership Act 2004 (Consequential Provisions and Modifications) Order 2014 No. 2014/3229. - Enabling power: Scotland Act 1998, ss. 104, 112 (1), 113 (2) to (5) (7) & Civil Partnership Act 2004, s. 259 (1). - Issued: 11.12.2014. Made: 04.12.2014. Coming into force: in accord. with art. 1 (2). Effect: 58 SIs & 22 Acts amended. Territorial extent & classification: E/W/S/NI. General. - Supersedes draft S.I. (ISBN 9780111122402) issued 31.10.2014. - 56p.: 30 cm. - 978-0-11-112483-3 £10.00

The Marriage (Same Sex Couples) Act 2013 and Marriage and Civil Partnership (Scotland) Act 2014 (Consequential Provisions) Order 2014 No. 2014/3061. - Enabling power: Marriage (Same Sex Couples) Act 2013, ss. 17 (2) (3) & Civil Partnership Act 2004, s. 259 (1) (4) & Scotland Act 1998, ss. 104, 112 (1), 113 (2) to (5). - Issued: 21.11.2014. Made: 17.11.2014. Laid before the Scottish Parliament: 18.11.2014. Coming into force: In accord. with art 1 (2) (3). Effect: S.I. 1952/1869; 1959/406; 1968/2049; 1975/556; 1979/643; 1986/1442; 1987/257, 2088; 1988/2256; 1995/300; 2001/2283 (W.172); 2005/438, 1513 (W.117), 3176; 2012/687 & 7 Church Measures amended. Territorial extent & classification: E/W/S. General. - 32p.: 30 cm. - 978-0-11-112343-0 £6.00

The Marriage (Same Sex Couples) Act 2013 (Commencement No. 2 and Transitional Provision) Order 2014 No. 2014/93 (C.3). - Enabling power: Marriage (Same Sex Couples) Act 2013, ss. 18 (4), 21 (3). Bringing into operation various provisions of the 2013 Act on 21.01.2014, 13.03.2014, 03.06.2014, in accord. with arts 2, 3, 5. - Issued: 24.01.2014. Made: 15.01.2014. Effect: None. Territorial extent & classification: E/W/S/NI. General. - 4p.: 30 cm. - 978-0-11-110861-1 £4.00

The Marriage (Same Sex Couples) Act 2013 (Commencement No. 3) Order 2014 No. 2014/1662 (C.70). - Enabling power: Marriage (Same Sex Couples) Act 2013, s. 21 (3). Bringing into operation various provisions of the 2013 Act on 30.06.2014, in accord. with arts 2, 3. - Issued: 02.07.2014. Made: 26.06.2014. Effect: None. Territorial extent & classification: E/W/S/NI. General. - 4p.: 30 cm. - 978-0-11-111718-7 £4.25

The Marriage (Same Sex Couples) Act 2013 (Commencement No. 4) Order 2014 No. 2014/3169 (C.140). - Enabling power: Marriage (Same Sex Couples) Act 2013, s. 21 (3). Bringing into operation various provisions of the 2013 Act on 10.12.2014, in accord. with art 2. - Issued: 04.12.2014. Made: 27.11.2014. Effect: None. Territorial extent & classification: E/W/S/NI. General. - 4p.: 30 cm. - 978-0-11-112430-7 £4.25

The Marriage (Same Sex Couples) Act 2013 (Consequential and Contrary Provisions and Scotland) and Marriage and Civil Partnership (Scotland) Act 2014 (Consequential Provisions) Order 2014 No. 2014/3168. - Enabling power: Marriage (Same Sex Couples) Act 2013, ss. 17 (1) to (3), 18 (4) (10), sch. 2 para. 1, sch. 4 para. 27 (3) (b) & Civil Partnership Act 2004, s. 259 (1) (3) & Scotland Act 1998, ss. 104, 112 (1), 113 (2) to (3) (5). - Issued: 04.12.2014. Made: 27.11.2014. Coming into force: In accord. with art 1 (2) (3). Effect: 1837 c.26; 1911 c.6; 1949 c.76; 1957 c.58; 1964 c.75; 1973 c.18, 45; 1975 c.60; 1976 c.31; 1981 c.45; 1992 c.4, c.5; 2007 c.18; Reserve Forces Non Regular Permanent Staff (Pension and Attributable Benefits Schemes) Regulations 2011 [not an SI] amended & S.I. 2014/560 partially revoked. Territorial extent & classification: S. General. - Supersedes draft S.S.I. (ISBN 9780111121900) issued 21.10.2014. - 16p.: 30 cm. - 978-0-11-112429-1 £6.00

The Marriage (Same Sex Couples) Act 2013 (Consequential and Contrary Provisions and Scotland) Order 2014 No. 2014/560. - Enabling power: Marriage (Same Sex Couples) Act 2013, ss. 17 (2) (3), 18 (10), sch. 2, para. 1 (1), sch. 4, 27 (3) (a) (b) & Civil Partnership Act 2004, s. 259 (1) (3) & Human Fertilisation and Embryology Act 2008, s. 64 (1) (2)- Issued: 13.03.2014. Made: 06.03.2014. Coming into force: In accord. with art. 1 (2) (3). Effect: 37 Acts & 18 SIs/WSIs amended. Territorial extent & classification: E/W/S/NI. General. - Supersedes draft S.I. (ISBN 9780111108727) issued 28.01.2014. Partially revoked by S.I. 2014/3168 (ISBN 9780111124291) in re to S. - 28p.: 30 cm. - 978-0-11-111158-1 £5.75

The Marriage (Same Sex Couples) Act 2013 (Consequential Provisions) Order 2014 No. 2014/107. - Enabling power: Marriage (Same Sex Couples) Act 2013, ss. 17 (2) (3), 18 (10) & Civil Partnership Act 2004, s. 259 (1) (4)- Issued: 28.01.2014. Made: 20.01.2014. Laid: 23.01.2014. Coming into force: 13.03.2014. Effect: 82 SIs/WSIs amended. Territorial extent & classification: E/W/S. General. - Partially revoked by SI 2015/601 (ISBN 9780111132661) in re to E/W. - 28p.: 30 cm. - 978-0-11-110869-7 £5.75

The Overseas Marriage (Armed Forces) Order 2014 No. 2014/1108. - Enabling power: Marriage (Same Sex Couples) Act 2013, sch. 6, paras. 8, 9, 14. - Issued: 06.05.2014. Made: 28.04.2014. Coming into force: 03.06.2014. Effect: None. Territorial extent & classification: E/W/S. General. - Supersedes draft SI (ISBN 9780111108802) issued 30/01/14. - 8p.: 30 cm. - 978-0-11-111440-7 £4.25

Medicines

The Human Medicines (Amendment) (No. 2) Regulations 2014 No. 2014/1878. - Enabling power: European Communities Act 1972, s. 2 (2) (5). - Issued: 23.07.2014. Made: 16.07.2014. Laid: 18.07.2014. Coming into force: In accord. with reg. 1. Effect: S.I. 2012/1916 amended. Territorial extent & classification: E/W/S/NI. General. - 12p.: 30 cm. - 978-0-11-111840-5 £6.00

The Human Medicines (Amendment) Regulations 2014 No. 2014/490. - Enabling power: European Communities Act 1972, s. 2 (2) (5). - Issued: 10.03.2014. Made: 04.03.2014. Laid: 10.03.2014. Coming into force: 31.03.2014. Effect: S.I. 2012/1916 amended. Territorial extent & classification: E/W/S/NI. General. - 8p.: 30 cm. - 978-0-11-111095-9 £5.75

The Veterinary Medicines (Amendment) Regulations 2014 No. 2014/599. - Enabling power: European Communities Act 1972, s. 2 (2) & Finance Act 1973, s. 56 (1). - Issued: 19.03.2014. Made: 11.03.2014. Laid: 14.03.2014. Coming into force: 14.04.2014. Effect: S. I. 2013/2033 amended. Territorial extent & classification: E/W/S/NI. General. - 4p.: 30 cm. - 978-0-11-111199-4 £4.00

Mental capacity, England and Wales

The Courts and Tribunals Fees (Miscellaneous Amendments) Order 2014 No. 2014/590 (L.6). - Enabling power: Courts Act 2003, s. 92 & Insolvency Act 1986, ss. 414, 415 & Tribunals, Courts and Enforcement Act 2007, s. 42, 49 (3) & Constitutional Reform Act 2005, s. 52 & Mental Capacity Act 2005. s. 54 & Gender Recognition Act 2004, s. 7 (2). - Issued: 19.03.2014. Made: 11.03.2014. Laid: 13.03.2104. Coming into force: 06.04.2014. Effect: S.I. 2004/3120; 2006/758; 2007/1745; 2008/1052, 1053, 1054; 2009/213, 1114; 2010/42; 2011/2344; 2013/1179, 1893 amended. Territorial extent & classification: E/W. General. - 16p.: 30 cm. - 978-0-11-111194-9 £5.75

Mental health, England

The Care and Support and After-care (Choice of Accommodation) Regulations 2014 No. 2014/2670. - Enabling power: Mental Health Act 1983, ss. 117A (1) (2) (4) & Care Act 2014, ss. 30 (1) (2), 125 (7) (8). - Issued: 31.10.2014. Made: 22.10.2014. Laid: 30.10.2014. Coming into force: in accord with reg. 1 (2). Effect: None. Territorial extent & classification: E. General. - 8p.: 30 cm. - 978-0-11-112243-3 £6.00

The National Health Service Commissioning Board and Clinical Commissioning Groups (Responsibilities and Standing Rules) (Amendment) Regulations 2014 No. 2014/91. - Enabling power: National Health Service Act 2006, ss. 3B (1), 272 (7) (8). - Issued: 24.01.2014. Made: 18.01.2014. Laid: 23.01.2014. Coming into force: 17.02.2014. Effect: S.I. 2012/2996 amended. Territorial extent & classification: E. General. - 2p.: 30 cm. - 978-0-11-110858-1 £4.00

Merchant shipping

The Carriage of Passengers and their Luggage by Sea (Interim Provisions) (Notice) (Revocation) Order 2014 No. 2014/1438. - Enabling power: Merchant Shipping Act 1995, sch. 6, Part II, par. 11. - Issued: 09.06.2014. Made: 01.06.2014. Laid: 06.06.2014. Coming into force: 30.06.2014. Effect: S.I. 1980/1125 revoked. Territorial extent & classification: E/W/S/NI. General. - 2p.: 30 cm. - 978-0-11-111585-5 £4.25

The Limitation of Liability for Maritime Claims (Parties to Convention) Order 1986 and the Carriage of Passengers and their Luggage by Sea (Parties to Convention) Order 1987 (Revocation) Order 2014 No. 2014/1355. - Enabling power: Merchant Shipping Act 1995, sch. 6, part II, para. 10, sch. 7, part II, para. 13. - Issued: 03.06.2014. Made: 27.05.2014. Coming into force: 28.05.2014. Effect: S.I. 1986/2224; 1987/931 revoked. Territorial extent & classification: E/W/S/NI. General. - 2p.: 30 cm. - 978-0-11-111527-5 £4.25

The Maritime Security (Jersey) Order 2014 No. 2014/265. - Enabling power: Aviation and Maritime Security Act 1990, s. 51 (1) & Merchant Shipping and Maritime Security Act 1997, s. 30 (3). - Issued: 18.02.2014. Made: 11.02.2014. Coming into force: In accord. with art. 1. Effect: 1990 c.31 partly extended to Jersey subject to exceptions, adaptations & modifications & S.I. 1996/2881 revoked (on the seventh day after the day on which it is registered by the Royal Court of Jersey). Territorial extent & classification: E/W/S/NI. General. - 24p.: 30 cm. - 978-0-11-110969-4 £5.75

The Merchant Shipping (Convention Relating to the Carriage of Passengers and their Luggage by Sea) Order 2014 No. 2014/1361. - Enabling power: Merchant Shipping Act 1995, ss. 183 (4) (6), 184 (1) (3). - Issued: 03.06.2014. Made: 27.05.2014. Coming into force: 28.05.2014 in accord. with art. 1 (1). Effect: 1995 c.21 amended & S.I. 1980/1092 revoked. Territorial extent & classification: E/W/S/NI. General. - Supersedes draft SI (ISBN 9780111112502) issued 25.04.14. - 20p.: 30 cm. - 978-0-11-111533-6 £6.00

The Merchant Shipping (Light Dues) (Amendment) Regulations 2014 No. 2014/527. - Enabling power: Merchant Shipping Act 1995, s. 205 (5). - Issued: 12.03.2014. Made: 06.03.2014. Laid: 10.03.2014. Coming into force: 01.04.2014. Effect: S.I. 1997/562 amended. Territorial extent & classification: E/W/S/NI. General. - 2p.: 30 cm. - 978-0-11-111125-3 £4.00

The Merchant Shipping (Maritime Labour Convention) (Consequential and Minor Amendments) 2014 No. 2014/1614. - Enabling power: European Communities Act 1972, s. 2 (2) & Merchant Shipping Act 1995, ss. 25 to 27, 32, 36, 47, 73 (3), 77, 78, 85. - Issued: 16.07.2014. Made: 09.07.2014. Laid: 15.07.2014. Coming into force: 07.08.2014. Effect: 1995 c.21; 1996 c.18; S.I. 1972/1698, 1700; 1979/97; 1989/102; 1991/2144; 1996/1921 (N.I. 18); 1997/1508; 1998/2771; 2002/2125; 2010/737; 2013/1785 amended & S.I. 1981/1076; 1995/1803 revoked. Territorial extent & classification: E/W/S/NI. General. - 12p.: 30 cm. - 978-0-11-111798-9 £6.00

The Merchant Shipping (Maritime Labour Convention) (Health and Safety) (Amendment) Regulations 2014 No. 2014/1616. - Enabling power: European Communities Act 1972, s. 2 (2) & Merchant Shipping Act 1995, ss. 85 (1) (a) (b) (3) (5) (7), 86 (1). - Issued: 15.09.2014. Made: 08.09.2014. Laid: 15.09.2014. Coming into force: 13.10.2014. Effect: SI 1997/2962 amended. Territorial extent & classification: E/W/S/NI. General. - 16p.: 30 cm. - 978-0-11-112048-4 £6.00

The Merchant Shipping (Maritime Labour Convention) (Hours of Work) (Amendment) Regulations 2014 No. 2014/308. - Enabling power: Merchant Shipping Act 1995, ss. 85 (1) (a) (b) (3) (5) (7), 86 (1) & European Communities Act 1972, s. 2 (2). - Issued: 19.02.2014. Made: 13.02.2014. Laid: 19.02.2014. Coming into force: 17.03.2014. Effect: 1996 c.17, c.18; S.I. 1996/1919 (N.I. 16), 1921 (N.I. 18); 1998/1833; S.R. 1998/386; S.I. 2002/2125 amended. Territorial extent & classification: E/W/S/NI. General. - 16p.: 30 cm. - 978-0-11-110980-9 £5.75

The Merchant Shipping (Maritime Labour Convention) (Minimum Requirements for Seafarers etc.) Regulations 2014 No. 2014/1613. - Enabling power: Merchant Shipping Act 1995, ss. 85 (1) (a) (b) (3) (5) to (7), 86 (1) (2) & European Communities Act 1972, s. 2 (2). - Issued: 17.07.2014. Made: 09.07.2014. Laid: 15.07.2014. Coming into force: 07.08.2014. Effect: None. Territorial extent & classification: E/W/S/NI. General. - EC note: Implements corresponding parts of the Agreement set out in annex to Council Directive 2009/13/EC and clauses 6 and 11 of Agreement to Council Directive 1999/63/EC. - 36p.: 30 cm. - 978-0-11-111800-9 £10.00

The Merchant Shipping (Prevention of Air Pollution from Ships) and Motor Fuel (Composition and Content) (Amendment) Regulations 2014 No. 2014/3076. - Enabling power: European Communities Act 1972, s. 2 (2) & S.I. 2006/1248, arts 2, 3 & S.I. 1996/282, s. 128 (5) (6). - Issued: 24.11.2014. Made: 17.11.2014. Laid: 24.11.2014. Coming into force: 16.12.2014. Effect: S.I. 1999/3107; 2008/2924 amended. Territorial extent & classification: E/W/S/NI. General. - 8p.: 30 cm. - 978-0-11-112357-7 £6.00

The Prevention of Oil Pollution (Convention Countries) (Revocation) Order 2014 No. 2014/499. - Enabling power: Merchant Shipping Act 1995, s. 147 (3). - Issued: 12.03.2014. Made: 05.03.2014. Laid: 12.03.2014. Coming into force: 07.04.2014. Effect: S.I. 1981/612 revoked. Territorial extent & classification: E/W/S/NI. General. - 2p.: 30 cm. - 978-0-11-111103-1 £4.00

Merchant shipping: Maritime security

The Port Security (Port of Bramble Island Dock, Felixstowe, Harwich, Harwich International, Ipswich and Mistley Quay) Designation Order 2014 No. 2014/604. - Enabling power: European Communities Act 1972, s. 2 (2). - Issued: 21.03.2014. Made: 11.03.2014. Laid: 21.03.2014. Coming into force: 14.04.2014. Effect: None. Territorial extent & classification: E/W/S/NI. General. - EC note: This Order is one of a series to implement Directive 2005/65/EC on enhancing port security at individual ports across the UK. The Directive was transposed in relation to the UK as a whole by the Port Security Regulations 2009 (S.I. 2009/2048). - 20p., col. plans: 30 cm. - 978-0-11-111205-2 £8.25

The Port Security (Port of Londonderry) Designation Order 2014 No. 2014/1811. - Enabling power: European Communities Act 1972, s. 2 (2). - Issued: 17 .07.2014. Made: 06.07.2014. Laid: 17.07.2014. Coming into force: 11.08.2014. Effect: None. Territorial extent & classification: E/W/S/NI. General. - EC note: This Order is one of a series to implement Directive 2005/65/EC on enhancing port security at individual ports across the UK. The Directive was transposed in relation to the UK as a whole by the Port Security Regulations 2009 (S.I. 2009/2048). - 8p., 3 maps: 30 cm. - 978-0-11-111783-5 £6.00

The Port Security (Port of London) Designation Order 2014 No. 2014/577. - Enabling power: European Communities Act 1972, s. 2 (2). - Issued: 31 .03.2014. Made: 05.03.2014. Laid: 17.03.2014. Coming into force: 10.04.2014. Effect: None. Territorial extent & classification: E/W/S/NI. General. - EC note: This Order is one of a series to implement Directive 2005/65/EC on enhancing port security at individual ports across the UK. The Directive was transposed in relation to the UK as a whole by the Port Security Regulations 2009 (S.I. 2009/2048). This Statutory Instrument has been printed in substitution of the SI of same number and ISBN (issued 17.03.2014) and is being issued free of charge to all known recipients of that Statutory Instrument. - 72p., col. plans: 30 cm. - 978-0-11-111179-6 £19.75

The Port Security (Port of Medway) Designation Order 2014 No. 2014/82. - Enabling power: European Communities Act 1972, s. 2 (2). - Issued: 23.01.2014. Made: 17.01.2014. Laid: 22.01.2014. Coming into force: 17.02.2014. Effect: None. Territorial extent & classification: E/W/S/NI. General. - EC note: This Order is one of a series to implement Directive 2005/65/EC on enhancing port security at individual ports across the UK. The Directive was transposed in relation to the UK as a whole by the Port Security Regulations 2009 (S.I. 2009/2048). - 20p., col. maps: 30 cm. - 978-0-11-110856-7 £8.25

The Port Security (Port of Plymouth) Designation Order 2014 No. 2014/8. - Enabling power: European Communities Act 1972, s. 2 (2). - Issued: 14.01.2014. Made: 08.01.2014. Laid: 14.01.2014. Coming into force: 14.02.2014. Effect: None. Territorial extent & classification: E/W/S/NI. General. - EC note: This Order is one of a series to implement Directive 2005/65/EC on enhancing port security at individual ports across the UK. The Directive was transposed in relation to the UK as a whole by the Port Security Regulations 2009 (S.I. 2009/2048). - 16p., col. maps: 30 cm. - 978-0-11-110810-9 £8.25

The Port Security (Port of Rosyth) Designation Order 2014 No. 2014/2007. - Enabling power: European Communities Act 1972, s. 2 (2). - Issued: 06.08.2014. Made: 24.07.2014. Laid: 30.07.2014. Coming into force: 30.08.2014. Effect: None. Territorial extent & classification: E/W/S/NI. General. - EC note: This Order is one of a series to implement Directive 2005/65/EC on enhancing port security at individual ports across the UK. The Directive was transposed in relation to the UK as a whole by the Port Security Regulations 2009 (S.I. 2009/2048). - 8p., col. map: 30 cm. - 978-0-11-111934-1 £8.50

Merchant shipping: Safety

The Merchant Shipping (International Safety Management (ISM) Code) Regulations 2014 No. 2014/1512. - Enabling power: European Communities Act 1972, s. 2 (2) & Merchant Shipping Act 1995, ss. 85 (1) (3) (5) to (7), 86 (1) (b) & S.I. 1998/1500. - Issued: 13.06.2014. Made: 07.06.2014. Laid: 12.06.2014. Coming into force: 18.07.2014. Effect: S.I. 2001/3209 amended. Territorial extent & classification: E/W/S/NI. General. - 12p.: 30 cm. - 978-0-11-111636-4 £6.00

The Merchant Shipping (Maritime Labour Convention) (Recruitment and Placement) Regulations 2014 No. 2014/1615. - Enabling power: European Communities Act 1972, s. 2 (2). - Issued: 16.07.2014. Made: 09.07.2014. Laid: 15.07.2014. Coming into force: 07.08.2014. Effect: None. Territorial extent & classification: E/W/S/NI. General. - 8p.: 30 cm. - 978-0-11-111794-1 £6.00

Ministers of the Crown

The Transfer of Functions (Chequers and Dorneywood Estates) Order 2014 No. 2014/2708. - Enabling power: Ministers of the Crown Act 1975, s. 1. - Issued: 15.10.2014. Made: 08.10.2014. Laid: 15.10.2014. Coming into force: 05.11.2014. Effect: 7 & 8 Geo 5 c.55 amended. Territorial extent & classification: E/W/S/NI. General. - 4p.: 30 cm. - 978-0-11-112146-7 £4.25

The Transfer of Functions (Elections) Order 2014 No. 2014/268. - Enabling power: Ministers of the Crown Act 1975, s. 1. - Issued: 18.02.2014. Made: 11.02.2014. Laid: 18.02.2014. Coming into force: 11.03.2014. Effect: 2011 c.13 amended. Territorial extent & classification: E/W. General. - 4p.: 30 cm. - 978-0-11-110972-4 £4.00

The Transfer of Functions (Royal Mail Pension Plan) Order 2014 No. 2014/500. - Enabling power: Ministers of the Crown Act 1975, s. 1. - Issued: 12.03.2014. Made: 05.03.2014. Laid: 12.03.2014. Coming into force: 02.04.2014. Effect: 2011 c.5 amended. Territorial extent & classification: E/W/S/NI. General. - 4p.: 30 cm. - 978-0-11-111104-8 £4.00

Mobile homes, England

The Mobile Homes Act 2013 (Commencement and Saving Provision) (England) Order 2014 No. 2014/816. - Enabling power: Mobile Homes Act 2013, s. 15 (2) (4). Bringing into operation various provisions of the 2013 Act on 01.04.2104. - Issued: 01.04.2014. Made: 25.03.2014. Effect: None. Territorial extent & classification: E. General. - 4p.: 30 cm. - 978-0-11-111279-3 £4.00

The Mobile Homes (Site Licensing) (England) Regulations 2014 No. 2014/442. - Enabling power: Caravan Sites and Control of Development Act 1960, s. 3 (5A) to (5D), 10 (1B) to (1F) & Mobile Homes Act 1983, sch. 1, pt. 1, ch. 2, paras 7B (7), 7C (1), 8B (7), 8C (1). - Issued: 05.03.2014. Made: 27.02.2014. Laid: 05.03.2014. Coming into force: 01.04.2014. Effect: S.I. 2013/981 amended. Territorial extent & classification: E. General. - 8p.: 30 cm. - 978-0-11-111049-2 £4.00

The Mobile Homes (Site Rules) (England) (Amendment) Regulations 2014 No. 2014/3073. - Enabling power: Mobile Homes Act 1983, ss. 2C (9), 2D (6) (7). - Issued: 24.11.2014. Made: 18.11.2014. Laid: 20.11.2014. Coming into force: 19.12.2014. Effect: S.I. 2014/5 amended. Territorial extent & classification: E. General. - 2p.: 30 cm. - 978-0-11-112351-5 £4.25

The Mobile Homes (Site Rules) (England) Regulations 2014 No. 2014/5. - Enabling power: Mobile Homes Act 1983, ss. 1 (2) (e) (9) (a), 2C (3) (6) (7), 2D, sch. 1, pt. 1, chp. 2, paras. 7B (7), 7C, 8B (7), 8C. - Issued: 13.01.2014. Made: 06.01.2014. Laid: 13.01.2014. Coming into force: 04.02.2014. Effect: S.I. 2011/1006; 2013/981 amended. Territorial extent & classification: E. General. - 16p.: 30 cm. - 978-0-11-110806-2 £5.75

Mobile homes, Wales

The Mobile Homes (Pitch Fees) (Prescribed Form) (Wales) Regulations 2014 No. 2014/1760 (W.175). - Enabling power: Mobile Homes (Wales) Act 2013, sch. 2, part 1, chapter 2, para. 23. - Issued: 18.07.2014. Made: 02.07.2014. Laid before the National Assembly for Wales: 04.07.2014. Coming into force: 01.10.2014. Effect: None. Territorial extent & classification: W. General. - In English and Welsh. Welsh title: Rheoliadau Cartrefi Symudol (Ffioedd am Leinau) (Ffurf Ragnodedig) (Cymru) 2014. - 24p.: 30 cm. - 978-0-348-10966-5 £6.00

The Mobile Homes (Selling and Gifting) (Wales) Regulations 2014 No. 2014/1763 (W.178). - Enabling power: Mobile Homes (Wales) Act 2013, ss. 52 (3) (8), 63 (1) (8) (9), sch. 2, part 1, ch. 1, paras 9 (4) (6), 10 (5) (7) (8) (10), 11 (2) (4), 12 (2) (5), 13 (5) (7) (9). - Issued: 25.07.2014. Made: 02.07.2014. Laid before the National Assembly for Wales: 04.07.2014. Coming into force: 01.10.2014. Effect: None. Territorial extent & classification: W. General. - In English and Welsh. Welsh title: Rheoliadau Cartrefi Symudol (Gwerthu a Rhoi yn Anrheg) (Cymru) 2014. - 40p.: 30 cm. - 978-0-348-10972-6 £10.00

The Mobile Homes (Site Rules) (Wales) Regulations 2014 No. 2014/1764 (W.179). - Enabling power: Mobile Homes (Wales) Act 2013, ss. 52, 63 (1) (6) (8) (9). - Issued: 07.08.2014. Made: 02.07.2014. Laid before the National Assembly for Wales: 04.07.2014. Coming into force: 01.10.2014. Effect: None. Territorial extent & classification: W. General. - In English and Welsh. Welsh title: Rheoliadau Cartrefi Symudol (Rheolau Safle) (Cymru) 2014. - 28p.: 30 cm. - 978-0-348-10981-8 £6.00

The Mobile Homes (Wales) Act 2013 (Commencement, Transitional and Saving Provisions) Order 2014 No. 2014/11 (W.1)(C.1). - Enabling power: Mobile Homes (Wales) Act 2013, ss. 58 (3) (b), 63 (1), 63 (9), 64 (2) (3). Bringing into force various provisions of the 2013 Act on 07.01.2014, 01.10.2014. - Issued: 13.01.2014. Made: 06.01.2014. Effect: None. Territorial extent & classification: W. General. - In English and Welsh. Welsh title: Gorchymyn Deddf Cartrefi Symudol (Cymru) 2013 (Cychwyn, Darpariaethau Trosiannol ac Arbed) 2014. - 4p.: 30 cm. - 978-0-348-10852-1 £4.00

The Mobile Homes (Written Statement) (Wales) Regulations 2014 No. 2014/1762 (W.177). - Enabling power: Mobile Homes (Wales) Act 2013, s. 49 (1) (e). - Issued: 18.07.2014. Made: 02.07.2014. Laid before the National Assembly for Wales: 04.07.2014. Coming into force: 01.10.2014. Effect: S.I. 2012/2675 (W.289) revoked. Territorial extent & classification: W. General. - In English and Welsh. Welsh title: Rheoliadau Cartrefi Symudol (Datganiad Ysgrifenedig) (Cymru) 2014. - 12p.: 30 cm. - 978-0-348-10967-2 £6.00

National assistance services, England

The National Assistance (Sums for Personal Requirements) Amendment (England) Regulations 2014 No. 2014/582. - Enabling power: National Assistance Act 1948, s. 22 (4). - Issued: 18.03.2014. Made: 11.03.2014. Laid: 14.03.2014. Coming into force: 07.04.2014. Effect: S.I. 2003/628 amended. Territorial extent & classification: E. General. - 2p.: 30 cm. - 978-0-11-111186-4 £4.00

National Crime Agency

The Crime and Courts Act 2013 (Application and Modification of Certain Enactments) Order 2014 No. 2014/1704. - Enabling power: Crime and Courts Act 2013, sch. 5, paras 27 (1) (b), 27 (2), 29, sch. 8, para. 7 (1) (b). - Issued: 07.07.2014. Made: 30.06.2014. Laid: 03.07.2014. Coming into force: 04.08.2014. Effect: 1971 c.77; 1984 c.60; 1999 c.33; 2003 c.38; S.I. 2013/1813 modified & S.I. 2006/987 revoked. Territorial extent & classification: E/W/S/NI. General. - 8p.: 30 cm. - 978-0-11-111739-2 £6.00

National debt

The Government Alternative Finance Arrangements Regulations 2014 No. 2014/1327. - Enabling power: Finance Act 2008, s. 157, sch. 46, paras. 3, 5, 6, 7, 9, 10, 11, 12. - Issued: 30.05.2014. Made: 22.05.2014. Laid: 23.05.2014. Coming into force: 16.06.2014. Effect: 1968 c.13 modified. Territorial extent & classification: E/W/S/NI. General. - 4p.: 30 cm. - 978-0-11-111520-6 £4.25

The National Savings Stock Register (Amendment) Regulations 2014 No. 2014/3214. - Enabling power: National Debt Act 1972, s. 3. - Issued: 11.12.2014. Made: 04.12.2014. Laid: 05.12.2014. Coming into force: 26.12.2014. Effect: S.I. 1976/2012 amended. Territorial extent & classification: E/W/S/NI. General. - Revoked by SI 2015/624 (ISBN 9780111133217). - 2p.: 30 cm. - 978-0-11-112464-2 £4.25

The Premium Savings Bonds (Maximum Holdings) (Amendment) Regulations 2014 No. 2014/1182. - Enabling power: National Debt Act 1972, s. 11. - Issued: 12.05.2014. Made: 06.05.2014. Laid: 07.05.2014. Coming into force: 01.06.2014. Effect: S.I. 1972/765 amended. Territorial extent & classification: E/W/S/NI. General. - Revoked by SI 2015/624 (ISBN 9780111133217). - 2p.: 30 cm. - 978-0-11-111462-9 £4.25

National Health Service, England

The Barnet and Chase Farm Hospitals National Health Service Trust (Dissolution) Order 2014 No. 2014/1597. - Enabling power: National Health Service Act 2006, ss. 25 (1), 272 (7), 273 (1), sch. 4, para. 28. - Issued: 23.06.2014. Made: 17.06.2014. Coming into force: 01.07.2014. Effect: S.I. 1999/892 revoked. Territorial extent & classification: E. General. - 2p.: 30 cm. - 978-0-11-111669-2 £4.25

The Barnet, Enfield and Haringey Mental Health National Health Service Trust (Establishment) Amendment Order 2014 No. 2014/1903. - Enabling power: National Health Service Act 2006, ss. 25 (1), 272 (7), 273 (1). - Issued: 23.07.2014. Made: 17.07.2014. Coming into force: 01.08.2014. Effect: S.I. 2001/1330 amended. Territorial extent & classification: E. General. - 2p.: 30 cm. - 978-0-11-111868-9 £4.25

The Care Act 2014 (Commencement No.3) Order 2014 No. 2014/3186 (C.141). - Enabling power: Care Act 2014, ss. 127 (1). Bringing into operation various provisions of the 2014 Act on 01.04.2015, in accord. with art 2. - Issued: 10.12.2014. Made: 03.12.2014. Effect: None. Territorial extent & classification: E. General. - 4p.: 30 cm. - 978-0-11-112472-7 £4.25

The Care and Support (Discharge of Hospital Patients) Regulations 2014 No. 2014/2823. - Enabling power: Care Act 2014, s. 125 (7), sch. 3 paras 2 (5) (b), 4 (6), 6, 8. - Issued: 24.10.2014. Made: 06.10.2014. Laid: 24.10.2014. Coming into force: in accord with reg. 1 (1). Effect: None. Territorial extent & classification: E. General. - 8p.: 30 cm. - 978-0-11-112206-8 £6.00

The Care Quality Commission (Reviews and Performance Assessments) Regulations 2014 No. 2014/1788. - Enabling power: Health and Social Care Act 2008, ss. 46 (1) (2), 161 (4). - Issued: 14.07.2014. Made: 07.07.2014. Laid: 11.07.2014. Coming into force: 01.10.2014. Effect: None. Territorial extent & classification: E. General. - 4p.: 30 cm. - 978-0-11-111771-2 £4.25

The Coventry and Warwickshire Partnership National Health Service Trust (Establishment) Amendment Order 2014 No. 2014/360. - Enabling power: National Health Service Act 2006, ss. 25 (1), 272 (7) (8), 273 (1). - Issued: 24.02.2014. Made: 17.02.2014. Coming into force: 10.03.2014. Effect: S.I. 2006/2524 amended. Territorial extent & classification: E. General. - 4p.: 30 cm. - 978-0-11-110992-2 £4.00

The Gloucestershire Care Services National Health Service Trust (Establishment) Amendment Order 2014 No. 2014/358. - Enabling power: National Health Service Act 2006, ss. 25 (1), 272 (7) (8), 273 (1). - Issued: 24.02.2014. Made: 17.02.2014. Coming into force: 10.03.2014. Effect: S.I. 2013/531 amended. Territorial extent & classification: E. General. - 2p.: 30 cm. - 978-0-11-110990-8 £4.00

The Gloucestershire Care Services National Health Service Trust (Originating Capital) Order 2014 No. 2014/792. - Enabling power: National Health Service Act 2006, s. 27, sch. 5, para. 1 (1). - Issued: 27.03.2014. Made: 20.03.2014. Coming into force: 31.03.2014. Effect: None. Territorial extent & classification: E. General. - 2p.: 30 cm. - 978-0-11-111263-2 £4.00

The Health and Social Care Act 2008 (Regulated Activities) Regulations 2014 No. 2014/2936. - Enabling power: Health and Social Care Act 2008, ss. 8, 20 (1) to (5A), 35, 86 (2) (4), 87 (1) (2), 161 (3) (4). - Issued: 13.11.2014. Made: 06.11.2014. Coming into force: In accord. with reg. 1. Effect: None. Territorial extent & classification: E. General. - 32p.: 30 cm. - 978-0-11-112316-4 £10.00

The Health and Social Care Act 2012 (Commencement No. 7 and Transitory Provision) Order 2014 No. 2014/39 (C.2). - Enabling power: Health and Social Care Act 2012, ss. 304 (10), 306. Bringing into operation various provisions of the 2012 Act on 01.03.2014; 01.04.2014 in accord. with art. 2. - Issued: 17.01.2014. Made: 09.01.2014. Coming into force: -Effect: None. Territorial extent & classification: E. General. - 8p.: 30 cm. - 978-0-11-110836-9 £5.75

The Health and Social Care Act 2012 (Commencement No. 8) Order 2014 No. 2014/1454 (C.57). - Enabling power: Health and Social Care Act 2012, s. 306. Bringing into operation various provisions of the 2012 Act on 09.06.2014 in accord. with art. 2. - Issued: 10.06.2014. Made: 04.06.2014. Coming into force: -Effect: None. Territorial extent & classification: E. General. - 8p.: 30 cm. - 978-0-11-111601-2 £6.00

NATIONAL HEALTH SERVICE, ENGLAND

The Health Education England Regulations 2014 No. 2014/3215. - Enabling power: Care Act 2014, ss. 104 (3) (b) (4) (13) (a), 105 (1), 125 (8), sch. 5, para. 2 (1) (2), sch. 6, para. 2 (8). - Issued: 10.12.2014. Made: 03.12.2014. Laid: 10.12.2014. Coming into force: 01.04.2015. Effect: S.I. 2012/2996 amended. Territorial extent & classification: E. General. - 4p.: 30 cm. - 978-0-11-112466-6 £4.25

The Health Education England (Transfer of Staff, Property and Liabilities) Order 2014 No. 2014/3218. - Enabling power: Care Act 2014, ss. 96 (4), 118, 125 (8). - Issued: 10.12.2014. Made: 03.12.2014. Coming into force: 01.04.2015. Effect: None. Territorial extent & classification: E. General. - 4p.: 30 cm. - 978-0-11-112470-3 £4.25

The Healthy Start Vitamins (Charging) Regulations 2014 No. 2014/3099. - Enabling power: National Health Service Act 2006, ss. 187, 272 (7) (8). - Issued: 26.11.2014. Made: 18.11.2014. Laid: 26.11.2014. Coming into force: 05.01.2015. Effect: S.I. 1976/516 shall cease to apply to England. Territorial extent & classification: E. General. - 4p.: 30 cm. - 978-0-11-112375-1 £4.25

The King's College Hospital NHS Foundation Trust (Transfer of Trust Property) Order 2014 No. 2014/1387. - Enabling power: National Health Service Act 2006, ss. 213, 217 (2), 272 (7) (8). - Issued: 09.06.2014. Made: 02.06.2014. Laid: 09.06.2014. Coming into force: 07.07.2014. Effect: None. Territorial extent & classification: E. General. - 4p.: 30 cm. - 978-0-11-111561-9 £4.25

The Legislative Reform (Clinical Commissioning Groups) Order 2014 No. 2014/2436. - Enabling power: Legislative and Regulatory Reform Act 2006, s. 1. - Issued: 17.09.2014. Made: 10.09.2014. Laid: -Coming into force: 01.10.2014. Effect: 2006 c.41 amended. Territorial extent & classification: E/W/S/NI. General. - Supersedes draft S.I. (ISBN 9780111111789) issued 17.03.2014. - 4p.: 30 cm. - 978-0-11-112070-5 £4.25

The London Ambulance Service National Health Service Trust (Establishment) Amendment Order 2014 No. 2014/1904. - Enabling power: National Health Service Act 2006, ss. 25 (1), 272 (7) (8), 273 (1). - Issued: 23.07.2014. Made: 17.07.2014. Coming into force: 01.08.2014. Effect: S.I. 1996/90 amended & partially revoked. Territorial extent & classification: E. General. - 2p.: 30 cm. - 978-0-11-111869-6 £4.25

The London North West Healthcare National Health Service Trust (Establishment) and the Ealing Hospital National Health Service Trust and the North West London Hospitals National Health Service Trust (Dissolution) Order 2014 No. 2014/2524. - Enabling power: National Health Service Act 2006, ss. 25 (1), 272 (7) (8), sch. 4, paras 5, 7, 28. - Issued: 25.09.2014. Made: 18.09.2014. Coming into force: 24.09.2014. Effect: None. Territorial extent & classification: E. General. - 4p.: 30 cm. - 978-0-11-112098-9 £4.25

The Mid Staffordshire NHS Foundation Trust (Dissolution and Transfer) Order 2014 No. 2014/2849. - Enabling power: National Health Service Act 2006, ss. 65LA (3), 272 (7). - Issued: 29.10.2014. Made: 22.10.2014. Laid: 24.10.2014. Coming into force: 01.11.2014. Effect: None. Territorial extent & classification: E. General. - 4p.: 30 cm. - 978-0-11-112231-0 £4.25

The National Health Service (Charges, Payments and Remission of Charges) (Uprating, Miscellaneous Amendments and Transitional Provision) Regulations 2014 No. 2014/545. - Enabling power: National Health Service Act 2006, ss. 115 (1) (2), 116 (2), 172 (1), 176 (1) (2), 178 (1), 1749 (3), 180 (1) to (5), 182, 183, 272 (7) (8). - Issued: 12.03.2014. Made: 05.03.2014. Laid: 11.03.2014. Coming into force: 01.04.2014. Effect: S.I. 2000/620; 2003/2382; 2005/3477; 2008/1186; 2013/461 amended. Territorial extent & classification: E. General. - Partially revoked by SI 2015/570 (ISBN 9780111132388). - 4p.: 30 cm. - 978-0-11-111147-5 £4.00

The National Health Service (Charges to Overseas Visitors) Amendment Regulations 2014 No. 2014/1534. - Enabling power: National Health Service Act 2006, ss. 175, 272 (7). - Issued: 17.06.2014. Made: 10.06.2014. Laid: 16.06.2014. Coming into force: 07.07.2014. Effect: S.I. 2011/1556 amended. Territorial extent & classification: E. General. - Revoked by S.I. 2015/238 (ISBN 9780111129807). - 2p.: 30 cm. - 978-0-11-111647-0 £4.25

The National Health Service (Clinical Negligence Scheme)(Amendment) Regulations 2014 No. 2014/933. - Enabling power: National Health Service Act 2006, ss. 71, 272 (7) (8). - Issued: 11.04.2014. Made: 03.04.2014. Laid: 09.04.2014. Coming into force: 01.05.2014. Effect: S.I. 1996/251 amended (in relation to England). Territorial extent & classification: E. General. - Revoked by SI 2015/559 (ISBN 9780111132296). - 4p.: 30 cm. - 978-0-11-111391-2 £4.25

The National Health Service Commissioning Board and Clinical Commissioning Groups (Responsibilities and Standing Rules) (Amendment) (No. 2) Regulations 2014 No. 2014/452. - Enabling power: National Health Service Act 2006, ss. 3B (1), 272 (7) (8). - Issued: 06.03.2014. Made: 27.02.2014. Laid: 06.03.2014. Coming into force: 01.04.2014. Effect: S.I. 2012/2996 amended. Territorial extent & classification: E. General. - 2p.: 30 cm. - 978-0-11-111062-1 £4.00

The National Health Service Commissioning Board and Clinical Commissioning Groups (Responsibilities and Standing Rules) (Amendment) (No. 3) Regulations 2014 No. 2014/1611. - Enabling power: National Health Service Act 2006, ss. 6E (1) (2) (3), 272 (7) (8). - Issued: 26.06.2014. Made: 19.06.2014. Laid: 26.06.2014. Coming into force: 01.10.2014. Effect: S.I. 2012/2996 amended. Territorial extent & classification: E. General. - 4p.: 30 cm. - 978-0-11-111686-9 £4.25

The National Health Service Commissioning Board and Clinical Commissioning Groups (Responsibilities and Standing Rules) (Amendment) Regulations 2014 No. 2014/91. - Enabling power: National Health Service Act 2006, ss. 3B (1), 272 (7) (8). - Issued: 24.01.2014. Made: 18.01.2014. Laid: 23.01.2014. Coming into force: 17.02.2014. Effect: S.I. 2012/2996 amended. Territorial extent & classification: E. General. - 2p.: 30 cm. - 978-0-11-110858-1 £4.00

The National Health Service (Exemptions from Charges, Payments and Remission of Charges) Amendment and Transitional Provisions Regulations 2014 No. 2014/2667. - Enabling power: National Health Service Act 2006, ss. 115 (1) (2), 116, 180, 181, 182, 183, 184, 272 (7) (8) (a). - Issued: 08.10.2014. Made: 01.10.2014. Laid: 08.10.2014. Coming into force: 01.11.2014. Effect: S.I. 2013/2382; 2008/1186; 2013/461 amended. Territorial extent & classification: E. General. - 4p.: 30 cm. - 978-0-11-112124-5 £4.25

The National Health Service (General Medical Services Contracts and Personal Medical Services Agreements) (Amendment No.2) Regulations 2014 No. 2014/2721. - Enabling power: National Health Service Act 2006, ss. 84 (3) (c), 89 (1) (2) (a), 94 (1), 272 (7) (8). - Issued: 17.10.2014. Made: 13.10.2014. Laid: 17.10.2014. Coming into force: in accord. with reg. 1 (2). Effect: S.I. 2004/291, 627 amended. Territorial extent & classification: E. General. - 4p.: 30 cm. - 978-0-11-112169-6 £4.25

The National Health Service (General Medical Services Contracts and Personal Medical Services Agreements) Amendment Regulations 2014 No. 2014/465. - Enabling power: National Health Service Act 2006, ss. 85, 89 (1) (2) (a) (c) (d) (3) (a) (4) (b) (6), 94 (1) (3) (c) (f) (8) (a) (9), 272 (7) (8). - Issued: 07.03.2014. Made: 03.03.2014. Laid: 06.03.2014. Coming into force: 01.04.2014. Effect: S.I. 2004/291, 627 amended. Territorial extent & classification: E. General. - 16p.: 30 cm. - 978-0-11-111075-1 £5.75

The National Health Service (General Medical Services Contracts) (Prescription of Drugs etc.) (Amendment) Regulations 2014 No. 2014/1625. - Enabling power: National Health Service Act 2006, ss. 88, 272 (7) (8). - Issued: 27.06.2014. Made: 23.06.2014. Laid: 25.06.2014. Coming into force: 01.08.2014. Effect: S.I. 2004/629 amended. Territorial extent & classification: E. General. - 2p.: 30 cm. - 978-0-11-111699-9 £4.25

The National Health Service (Liabilities to Third Parties Scheme) (Amendment) Regulations 2014 No. 2014/931. - Enabling power: National Health Service Act 2006, ss. 71, 272 (7) (8). - Issued: 11.04.2014. Made: 03.04.2014. Laid: 09.04.2014. Coming into force: 01.05.2014. Effect: S.I. 1999/873 amended. Territorial extent & classification: E. General. - 4p.: 30 cm. - 978-0-11-111389-9 £4.25

The National Health Service (Mandate Requirements) Regulations 2014 No. 2014/3487. - Enabling power: National Health Service Act 2006, ss. 13A (9), 272 (7) (8). - Issued: 09.01.2015. Made: 16.12.2014. Laid: 09.01.2015. Coming into force: 01.04.2015. Effect: None. Territorial extent & classification: E. General. - 2p.: 30 cm. - 978-0-11-112653-0 £4.25

The National Health Service (Pharmaceutical and Local Pharmaceutical Services) (Amendment and Transitional Provision) Regulations 2014 No. 2014/417. - Enabling power: National Health Service Act 2006, ss. 126, 129, 272 (7) (8), sch. 12, para. 3 (3) (h). - Issued: 04.03.2014. Made: 25.02.2014. Laid: 04.03.2014. Coming into force: 01.04.2014. Effect: S.I. 2013/349 amended. Territorial extent & classification: E. General. - This Statutory Instrument has been made, in part, as a consequence of defects in SI 2013/349 (ISBN 9780111534982) and is being issued free of charge to all known recipients of that Statutory Instrument. - 12p.: 30 cm. - 978-0-11-111034-8 £5.75

The National Health Service (Primary Dental Services) (Miscellaneous Amendments) Regulations 2014 No. 2014/443. - Enabling power: National Health Service Act 2006, ss. 104 (1) (2), 109 (1) (3), 169 (3), 272 (7) (8), 273 (4). - Issued: 05.03.2014. Made: 26.02.2014. Laid: 05.03.2014. Coming into force: 01.04.2014. Effect: S.I. 2005/3361, 3373, 3477; 2010/76 amended. Territorial extent & classification: E. General. - This Statutory Instrument has been made, in part, as a consequence of defects in S.I. 2013/364 (ISBN 9780111535196) and is being issued free of charge to all known recipients of that Statutory Instrument. This is additional to defects corrected by S.I. 2013/711 (ISBN 9780111537787). - 4p.: 30 cm. - 978-0-11-111050-8 £4.00

The National Health Service (Primary Ophthalmic Services and Optical Payments) (Miscellaneous Amendments) Regulations 2014 No. 2014/418. - Enabling power: National Health Service Act 2006, ss. 115 (3), 116, 121 (1) (2), 179 (3), 180 (1) (2), 181 (1) (2), 182, 188 (1), 272 (7) (8). - Issued: 04.03.2014. Made: 26.02.2014. Laid: 04.03.2014. Coming into force: 01.04.2014. Effect: S.I. 2008/1185, 1186; 2013/461 amended. Territorial extent & classification: E. General. - 4p.: 30 cm. - 978-0-11-111035-5 £4.00

The National Health Service (Property Expenses Scheme) (Amendment) Regulations 2014 No. 2014/932. - Enabling power: National Health Service Act 2006, ss. 71, 272 (7). - Issued: 11.04.2014. Made: 03.04.2014. Laid: 09.04.2014. Coming into force: 01.05.2014. Effect: S.I. 1999/874 amended. Territorial extent & classification: E. General. - 4p.: 30 cm. - 978-0-11-111390-5 £4.25

The National Health Service Trusts (Membership and Procedure) (Amendment) Order 2014 No. 2014/784. - Enabling power: National Health Service Act 2006, ss. 25 (4), 272 (7), sch. 4, para. 4 (1) (a). - Issued: 26.03.2014. Made: 19.03.2014. Laid: 21.03.2014. Coming into force: 14.04.2014. Effect: S.I. 1990/2024 amended. Territorial extent & classification: E. General. - 4p.: 30 cm. - 978-0-11-111253-3 £4.00

The National Health Service Trusts (Trust Funds: Appointment of Trustees) (Amendment) Order 2014 No. 2014/1905. - Enabling power: National Health Service Act 2006, ss. 272 (7) (8), 273 (1), sch. 4, para. 10. - Issued: 23.07.2014. Made: 17.07.2014. Coming into force: 31.07.2014. Effect: S.I. 2000/212 amended. Territorial extent & classification: E. General. - 2p.: 30 cm. - 978-0-11-111870-2 £4.25

The NHS Bodies (Transfer of Trust Property) Order 2014 No. 2014/230. - Enabling power: National Health Service Act 2006, ss. 213, 217 (2), 272 (7) (8). - Issued: 12.02.2014. Made: 29.01.2014. Laid: 07.02.2014. Coming into force: 03.03.2014. Effect: None. Territorial extent & classification: E. General. - 4p.: 30 cm. - 978-0-11-110933-5 £4.00

The NHS Business Services Authority (Awdurdod Gwasanaethau Busnes y GIG) (Transfer of Staff to the National Health Service Commissioning Board) Regulations 2014 No. 2014/413. - Enabling power: National Health Service Act 2006, ss. 28 (8), 272 (7) (8), sch. 6, para. 3 (8). - Issued: 04.03.2014. Made: 25.02.2014. Laid: 04.03.2014. Coming into force: 01.04.2014. Effect: None. Territorial extent & classification: E. General. - 4p.: 30 cm. - 978-0-11-111031-7 £4.00

The NHS Direct National Health Service Trust (Dissolution) Order 2014 No. 2014/588. - Enabling power: National Health Service Act 2006, ss. 25 (1), 272 (7), 273 (1), sch. 4, para. 28. - Issued: 18.03.2014. Made: 12.03.2014. Coming into force: 01.04.2014. Effect: S.I. 2007/478 revoked. Territorial extent & classification: E. General. - 2p.: 30 cm. - 978-0-11-111192-5 £4.00

The North Staffordshire Hospital Centre National Health Service Trust (Change of Name) (Establishment) Amendment Order 2014 No. 2014/2844. - Enabling power: National Health Service Act 2006, ss. 25 (1), 272 (7) (8), 273 (1). - Issued: 29.10.2014. Made: 22.10.2014. Coming into force: 02.11.2014. Effect: S.I. 1992/2559 amended. Territorial extent & classification: E. General. - 4p.: 30 cm. - 978-0-11-112233-4 £4.25

The Oxford Health NHS Foundation Trust (Transfer of Trust Property) Order 2014 No. 2014/1390. - Enabling power: National Health Service Act 2006, ss. 213, 217 (2), 272 (7) (8). - Issued: 09.06.2014. Made: 02.06.2014. Laid: 09.06.2014. Coming into force: 14.07.2014. Effect: None. Territorial extent & classification: E. General. - 2p.: 30 cm. - 978-0-11-111563-3 £4.25

The Pathfinder National Health Service Trust (Establishment) (Amendment) Order 2014 No. 2014/2459. - Enabling power: National Health Service Act 2006, ss. 25 (1), 272 (7) (8), 273 (1), sch. 4, para. 5 (2). - Issued: 19.09.2014. Made: 15.09.2014. Coming into force: 01.10.2014. Effect: S.I. 1994/3178 amended. Territorial extent & classification: E. General. - 4p.: 30 cm. - 978-0-11-112085-9 £4.25

The St George's Healthcare National Health Service Trust (Transfer of Trust Property) Order 2014 No. 2014/196. - Enabling power: National Health Service Act 2006, ss. 217 (2), 272 (7) (8), sch. 4, para. 10 (3). - Issued: 06.02.2014. Made: 29.01.2014. Coming into force: 03.03.2014. Effect: None. Territorial extent & classification: E. General. - 2p.: 30 cm. - 978-0-11-110915-1 £4.00

National Health Service, England and Wales

The Care Act 2014 (Commencement No.1) Order 2014 No. 2014/1714 (C.73). - Enabling power: Care Act 2014, s. 127 (1) (5). Bringing into operation various provisions of the 2014 Act on 07.07.2014, 15.07.2014, 01.10.2014, in accord. with arts 2, 3, 4. - Issued: 08.07.2014. Made: 02.07.2014. Effect: None. Territorial extent & classification: E/W. General. - 4p.: 30 cm. - 978-0-11-111750-7 £4.25

The Care Act 2014 (Commencement No.2) Order 2014 No. 2014/2473 (C.111). - Enabling power: Care Act 2014, ss. 124 (1) (2), 127 (1) (5). Bringing into operation various provisions of the 2014 Act on 01.10.2014, 01.01.2015 in accord. with arts 2, 3, 4, 5, 6. - Issued: 22.09.2014. Made: 12.09.2014. Effect: None. Territorial extent & classification: E/W. General. - 8p.: 30 cm. - 978-0-11-112089-7 £6.00

The National Health Service Pension Scheme, Additional Voluntary Contributions, Compensation for Premature Retirement and Injury Benefits (Amendment) Regulations 2014 No. 2014/78. - Enabling power: Superannuation Act 1972, ss. 10 (1) to (3A), 12 (2), 24 (1) (3) (4), sch. 3. - Issued: 23.01.2014. Made: 15.01.2014. Laid: 23.01.2014. Coming into force: 20.02.2014 for regs 1 (3), 9, 10; 13.03.2014 for remainder. Effect: S.I. 1995/300, 866; 2000/619; 2002/1311; 2008/653 amended. Territorial extent & classification: E/W. General. - 12p.: 30 cm. - 978-0-11-110851-2 £5.75

The National Health Service Pension Scheme (Amendment No.2) Regulations 2014 No. 2014/1607. - Enabling power: Superannuation Act 1972, ss. 10 (1) (2), 12 (1) (2) (4), sch. 3. - Issued: 24.06.2014. Made: 16.06.2014. Laid: 24.06.2014. Coming into force: 21.07.2014. Effect: S.I. 1995/300; 2008/653 amended. Territorial extent & classification: E/W. General. - 8p.: 30 cm. - 978-0-11-111676-0 £6.00

The National Health Service Pension Scheme (Amendment) Regulations 2014 No. 2014/570. - Enabling power: Superannuation Act 1972, ss. 10 (1) (2), 12 (1) (2) (4), sch. 3. - Issued: 17.03.2014. Made: 04.03.2014. Laid: 11.03.2014. Coming into force: 01.04.2014. Effect: S.I. 1995/300; 2008/653 amended. Territorial extent & classification: E/W. General. - 60p.: 30 cm. - 978-0-11-111166-6 £9.75

The Personal Injuries (NHS Charges) (Amounts) Amendment Regulations 2013 No. 2014/204. - Enabling power: Health and Social Care (Community Health and Standards) Act 2003, ss. 153 (2) (5), 195 (1) (2). - Issued: 10.02.2014. Made: 03.02.2014. Laid: 10.02.2013. Coming into force: 01.04.2013. Effect: S.I. 2007/115 amended (with saving). Territorial extent & classification: E/W. General. - Revoked by SI 2015/295 (ISBN 9780111129913). - 2p.: 30 cm. - 978-0-11-110918-2 £4.00

National Health Service, Wales

The Children and Families (Wales) Measure 2010 (Commencement No. 8) Order 2014 No. 2014/373 (W.41). - Enabling power: Children and Families (Wales) Measure 2010, ss. 74 (2), 75 (3). Bringing into operation various provisions of the 2010 Measure on 28.02.2014. - Issued: 03.03.2014. Made: 18.02.2014. Effect: None. Territorial extent & classification: W. General. - In English and Welsh. Welsh title: Gorchymyn Mesur Plant a Theuluoedd (Cymru) 2010 (Cychwyn Rhif 8) 2014. - 8p.: 30 cm. - 978-0-348-10892-7 £5.75

The Emergency Ambulance Services Committee (Wales) Regulations 2014 No. 2014/566 (W.67). - Enabling power: National Health Service (Wales) Act 2006, ss. 11, 12 (3), 13 (2) (c) (4) (c) , 203 (9) (10), sch. 2, para. 4. - Issued: 25.03.2014. Made: 10.03.2014. Laid before the National Assembly for Wales: 11.03.2014. Coming into force: 01.04.2014. Effect: None. Territorial extent & classification: W. General. - In English and Welsh. Welsh title: Rheoliadau'r Pwyllgor Gwasanaethau Ambiwlans Brys (Cymru) 2014. - 12p.: 30 cm. - 978-0-348-10920-7 £5.75

The National Health Service (Charges to Overseas Visitors) (Amendment) (Wales) Regulations 2014 No. 2014/1622 (W.166). - Enabling power: National Health Service (Wales) Act 2006, ss. 124, 203 (9) (10). - Issued: 30.06.2014. Made: 20.06.2014. Laid before the National Assembly for Wales: 24.06.2014. Coming into force: 19.070.2014. Effect: S.I. 1989/306 amended. Territorial extent & classification: W. General. - In English and Welsh. Welsh title: Rheoliadau'r Gwasanaeth Iechyd Gwladol (Ffioedd Ymwelwyr Tramor) (Diwygio) (Cymru) 2014. - 8p.: 30 cm. - 978-0-348-10958-0 £4.25

The National Health Service (Dental Charges) (Wales) (Amendment) Regulations 2014 No. 2014/461 (W.54). - Enabling power: National Health Service (Wales) Act 2006, ss. 125, 203 (9) (10). - Issued: 12.03.2014. Made: 01.03.2014. Laid before the National Assembly for Wales: 07.03.2014. Coming into force: 01.04.2014. Effect: S.I. 2006/491 (W.60) amended & WSI 2013/544 (W.57) revoked. Territorial extent & classification: W. General. - Revoked by WSI 2015/512 (W.44) (ISBN 9780348110524). - In English and Welsh: Rheoliadau'r Gwasanaeth Iechyd Gwladol (Ffioedd Deintyddol) (Cymru) (Diwygio) 2014. - 4p.: 30 cm. - 978-0-348-10913-9 £4.00

The National Health Service (General Medical Services Contracts) (Prescription of Drugs Etc.) (Wales) (Amendment) Regulations 2014 No. 2014/109 (W.9). - Enabling power: National Health Service (Wales) Act 2006, ss. 46 (2), 203 (9) (10). - Issued: 28.01.2014. Made: 20.01.2014. Laid before the National Assembly for Wales: 23.01.2014. Coming into force: 14.02.2014. Effect: S.I. 2004/1022 (W.119) amended. Territorial extent & classification: W. General. - In English and Welsh. Welsh title: Rheoliadau'r Gwasanaeth Iechyd Gwladol (Contractau Gwasanaethau Meddygol Cyffredinol) (Rhagnodi Cyffuriau Etc.) (Cymru) (Diwygio) 2014. - 8p.: 30 cm. - 978-0-348-10857-6 £4.00

National Health Service (Optical Charges and Payments) (Amendment) (Wales) Regulations 2014 No. 2014/462 (W.55). - Enabling power: National Health Service (Wales) Act 2006, ss. 128, 129, 130, 203 (9) (10). - Issued: 11.03.2014. Made: 01.03.2014. Laid before the National Assembly for Wales: 04.03.2014. Coming into force: 01.04.2014. Effect: S.I. 1997/818 amended. Territorial extent & classification: W. General. - In English and Welsh. Welsh title: Rheoliadau'r Gwasanaeth Iechyd Gwladol (Ffioedd a Thaliadau Optegol) (Diwygio) (Cymru) 2014. - 8p.: 30 cm. - 978-0-348-10898-9 £4.00

National Health Service (Optical Charges and Payments) (Amendment) (Wales) Regulations (No. 2) 2014 No. 2014/2015 (W.202). - Enabling power: National Health Service (Wales) Act 2006, ss. 71, 76 (9), 128, 129, 203 (9) (10). - Issued: 11.08.2014. Made: 28.07.2014. Laid before the National Assembly for Wales: 29.07.2014. Coming into force: 19.08.2014. Effect: S.I. 1997/818 amended. Territorial extent & classification: W. General. - In English and Welsh. Welsh title: Rheoliadau'r Gwasanaeth Iechyd Gwladol (Ffioedd a Thaliadau Optegol) (Diwygio) (Cymru) (Rhif 2) 2014. - 4p.: 30 cm. - 978-0-348-10982-5 £4.25

The National Health Service (Physiotherapist, Podiatrist or Chiropodist Independent Prescribers) (Miscellaneous Amendments) (Wales) Regulations 2014 No. 2014/2291 (W.226). - Enabling power: National Health Service (Wales) Act 2006, ss. 47, 80, 83, 86, 203 (9) (10) & Climate Change Act 2008, ss. 77, 90, sch. 6 para. 3. - Issued: 27.10.2014. Made: 27.08.2014. Laid before the National Assembly for Wales: 29.08.2014. Coming into force: 24.09.2014. Effect: S.I. 2004/478 (W.48), 2010/2880 (W.238), 2013/898 (W.102) amended. Territorial extent & classification: W. General. - In English and Welsh. Welsh title: Rheoliadau'r Gwasanaeth Iechyd Gwladol (Ffisiotheraphyddion-ragnodwyr, Podiatryddion-ragnodwyr neu Giropodyddion-ragnodwyr Annibynnol)) (Diwygiadau Amrywiol) (Cymru) 2014. - 8p.: 30 cm. - 978-0-348-10995-5 £6.00

The National Health Service (Travelling Expenses and Remission of Charges) (Wales) (Amendment) Regulations 2014 No. 2014/1099 (W.109). - Enabling power: National Health Service (Wales) Act 2006, ss. 130, 131, 132, 203 (9) (10). - Issued: 09.05.2014. Made: 26.04.2014. Laid before the National Assembly for Wales: 29.04.2014. Coming into force: 20.05.2014. Effect: S.I. 2007/1104 (W.116) amended. Territorial extent & classification: W. General. - In English and Welsh. Welsh title: Rheoliadau'r Gwasanaeth Iechyd Gwladol (Treuliau Teithio a Pheidio â Chodi Tâl) (Cymru) (Diwygio) 2014. - 4p.: 30 cm. - 978-0-348-10940-5 £4.25

The National Health Service (Welfare Reform Consequential Amendments) (Wales) Regulations 2014 No. 2014/460 (W.53). - Enabling power: National Health Service (Wales) Act 2006, ss. 71, 128, 129, 130, 131, 203 (9) (10). - Issued: 11.03.2014. Made: 01.03.2014. Laid before the National Assembly for Wales: 04.03.2014. Coming into force: 01.04.2014. Effect: S.I. 1986/975; 1997/818; 2007/1104 (W.116) amended. Territorial extent & classification: W. General. - In English and Welsh. Welsh title: Rheoliadau'r Gwasanaeth Iechyd Gwladol (Diwygiadau Canlyniadol Diwygio Lles) (Cymru) 2014. - 4p.: 30 cm. - 978-0-348-10900-9 £4.00

The The National Health Service (General Dental Services Contracts and Personal Dental Services Agreements) (Wales) (Amendment) Regulations 2014 No. 2014/872 (W.86). - Enabling power: National Health Service (Wales) Act 2006, ss. 61, 66, 203 (9) (10). - Issued: 15.04.2014. Made: 31.03.2014. Laid before the National Assembly for Wales: 01.04.2014. Coming into force: 01.05.2014. Effect: S.I. 2006/489 (W.58); 490 (W.59) amended. Territorial extent & classification: W. General. - In English and Welsh. Rheoliadau'r Gwasanaeth Iechyd Gwladol (Contractau Gwasanaethau Deintyddol Cyffredinol a Chytundebau Gwasanaethau Deintyddol Personol) (Cymru) (Diwygio) 2014. - 4p.: 30 cm. - 978-0-348-10934-4 £4.25

Nationality

The Immigration and Nationality (Cost Recovery Fees) (Amendment) Regulations 2014 No. 2014/2398. - Enabling power: Immigration, Asylum and Nationality Act 2006, ss. 51 (3), 52 (1) (3) (6). - Issued: 12.09.2014. Made: 04.09.2014. Laid: 10.09.2014. Coming into force: 01.10.2014. Effect: S.I. 2014/581 amended. Territorial extent & classification: E/W/S/NI. General. - 8p.: 30 cm. - 978-0-11-112050-7 £4.25

The Immigration and Nationality (Cost Recovery Fees) Regulations 2014 No. 2014/581. - Enabling power: Immigration, Asylum and Nationality Act 2006, ss. 51 (3), 52 (1) (3) (6). - Issued: 17.03.2014. Made: 11.03.2014. Laid: 13.03.2014. Coming into force: 06.04.2014. Effect: S.I. 2013/617 revoked. Territorial extent & classification: E/W/S/NI. General. - 20p.: 30 cm. - 978-0-11-111185-7 £5.75

The Immigration and Nationality (Fees) Regulations 2014 No. 2014/922. - Enabling power: Immigration, Asylum and Nationality Act 2006, ss. 51 (3), 52 (1) (3) (6). - Issued: 10.04.2014. Made: 02.04.2014. Coming into force: 06.04.2014. Effect: S.I. 2013/749 amended. Territorial extent & classification: E/W/S/NI/CI. General. - 24p.: 30 cm. - 978-0-11-111379-0 £6.00

Nature conservation, Wales

The Marine and Coastal Access Act 2009 (Commencement and Consequential Provisions) (Wales) Order 2014 No. 2014/3088 (W.309) (C.131). - Enabling power: Marine and Coastal Access Act 2009, ss. 316 (1) (b) (2), 324 (3) (4) (5) (6) (a) (b). Bringing into force various provisions of the 2009 Act on 12.12.2014. - Issued: 01.12.2014. Made: 18.11.2014. Coming into force: 12.12.2014. Effect: S.I. 1986/143 revoked in relation to Wales. Territorial extent & classification: W. General. - In English and Welsh. Welsh title: Gorchymyn Deddf y Môr a Mynediad i'r Arfordir 2009 (Cychwyn a Darpariaethau Canlyniadol) (Cymru) 2014. - 8p.: 30 cm. - 978-0-348-11023-4 £6.00

Northern Ireland

The District Electoral Areas (Northern Ireland) Order 2014 No. 2014/270. - Enabling power: Northern Ireland Act 1998, s. 84 (1) (3). - Issued: 18.02.2014. Made: 11.02.2014. Coming into force: In accord. with art. 1 (2) (3). Effect: S.I. 1993/226 revoked (12.02.2014). Territorial extent & classification: NI. General. - Supersedes draft S.I. (ISBN 9780111107546) issued 23.12.2013. - 12p.: 30 cm. - 978-0-11-110974-8 £5.75

The Electoral Registration and Administration Act 2013 (Commencement No. 1) (Northern Ireland) Order 2014 No. 2014/2439 (C.106). - Enabling power: Electoral Administration Act 2013, ss. 25 (1), 27 (1) (4). Bringing into operation various provisions of the 2013 Act, so far as they extend to Northern Ireland, on 15.09.2014, in accord. with art. 2. - Issued: 17.09.2014. Made: 11.09.2014. Effect: None. Territorial extent & classification: NI. General. - 4p.: 30 cm. - 978-0-11-112075-0 £4.25

The Northern Ireland Assembly (Elections) (Amendment) Order 2014 No. 2014/1804. - Enabling power: Northern Ireland Act 1998, ss. 34 (4) (6). - Issued: 17.07.2014. Made: 09.07.2014. Coming into force: 15.09.2014. Effect: S.I. 2001/2599 amended. Territorial extent & classification: NI. General. - 4p.: 30 cm. - 978-0-11-111805-4 £4.25

The Northern Ireland (Miscellaneous Provisions) Act 2014 (Commencement No. 1) No. 2014/2613 (C.115). - Enabling power: Northern Ireland (Miscellaneous Provisions) Act 2014. Bringing into operation various provisions of the 2013 Act, so far as they extend to Northern Ireland, on 27.09.2014, in accord. with art. 2. - Issued: 02.10.2014. Made: 26.09.2014. Effect: None. Territorial extent & classification: NI. General. - 2p.: 30 cm. - 978-0-11-112112-2 £4.25

Offshore installations

The Offshore Installations (Safety Zones) (No. 2) Order 2014 No. 2014/2260. - Enabling power: Petroleum Act 1987, ss. 22, 24 (2A). - Issued: 02.09.2014. Made: 26.08.2014. Coming into force: In accord. with art. 1(2). Effect: None. Territorial extent & classification: E/W/S. General. - 4p.: 30 cm. - 978-0-11-112000-2 £4.25

The Offshore Installations (Safety Zones) (No. 3) Order 2014 No. 2014/3212. - Enabling power: Petroleum Act 1987, s. 22 (1) (2). - Issued: 11.12.2014. Made: 02.12.2014. Coming into force: 25.12.2014. Effect: None. Territorial extent & classification: E/W/S. General. - 2p.: 30 cm. - 978-0-11-112462-8 £4.25

The Offshore Installations (Safety Zones) Order 2014 No. 2014/1253. - Enabling power: Petroleum Act 1987, s. 22. - Issued: 20.05.2014. Made: 14.05.2014. Coming into force: In accord. with art. 1(2). Effect: None. Territorial extent & classification: E/W/S. General. - 4p.: 30 cm. - 978-0-11-111494-0 £4.25

Olympic games and paralympic games

The Olympic Delivery Authority (Dissolution) Order 2014 No. 2014/3184. - Enabling power: London Olympic Games and Paralympic Games Act 2006, s. 9 (1) (2). - Issued: 05.12.2014. Made: 01.12.2014. Coming into force: in accord. with art. 1. Effect: 1958 c.51; 1967 c.13; 1972 c.11; 1975 c.24, c.25; 1999 c.29; 2000 c.36; 2006 c.12; 2011 c.15; 2011 c.20, c.22 amended & S.I. 2008/1890; 2011/2260 amended & S.I. 2011/1656 revoked. Territorial extent & classification: E/W/S/NI. General. - Supersedes draft S.I. (ISBN 9780111121566) issued 16.10.2014. - 8p.: 30 cm. - 978-0-11-112434-5 £4.25

Overseas territories

The Central African Republic (Sanctions) (Overseas Territories) Order 2014 No. 2014/1368. - Enabling power: United Nations Act 1946, s. 1 & St Helena Act 1833, s. 112 & British Settlements Acts 1887 and 1945. - Issued: 04.06.2014. Made: 27.05.2014. Laid: 03.06.2014. Coming into force: 24.06.2014. Effect: None. Territorial extent & classification: Anguilla; British Antarctic Territory; British Indian Ocean Territory; Cayman Islands; Falkland Islands; Montserrat; Pitcairn, Henderson, Ducie and Oeno Islands; St Helena, Ascension and Tristan da Cunha; South Georgia and the South Sandwich Islands; the Sovereign Base areas of Akrotiri and Dhekelia in the Island of Cyprus; Turks and Caicos Islands; Virgin Islands. General. - EC note: This Order gives effect in specified Overseas Territories to sanctions imposed on the Central African Republic UN Security Council resolutions 2127 (2013) and 2134 (2014) and reflects the implementation of these sanctions by the European Union in Council Decisions 2013/798/CFSP and 2014/125/CFSP. This SI replaces SI 2014/1363 which was never published. - 16p.: 30 cm. - 978-0-11-111542-8 £6.00

The Russia, Crimea and Sevastopol (Sanctions) (Overseas Territories) (Amendment) Order 2014 No. 2014/2919. - Enabling power: Saint Helena Act 1833, s. 112 & British Settlements Act 1887 & 1945. - Issued: 12.11.2014. Made: 05.11.2014. Laid: 12.11.2014. Coming into force: 13.11.2014. Effect: S.I. 2014/2710 amended. Territorial extent & classification: Anguilla, British Antarctic Territory, British Indian Ocean Territory, Cayman Is., Falkland Is., Montserrat, Pitcairn, Henderson, Ducie & Oeno Is., St Helena, Ascension & Tristan da Cunha, South Georgia & the South Sandwich Is., the Sovereign Base Areas of Akrotiri & Dhekelia (Cyprus), Turks & Caicos Is., Virgin Is. General. - 2p.: 30 cm. - 978-0-11-112298-3 £4.25

The Russia, Crimea and Sevastopol (Sanctions) (Overseas Territories) Order 2014 No. 2014/2710. - Enabling power: Saint Helena Act 1833, s. 112 & British Settlements Act 1887 & 1945. - Issued: 15.10.2014. Made: 08.10.2014. Laid: 15.10.2014. Coming into force: 16.10.2014. Effect: None. Territorial extent & classification: Anguilla, British Antarctic Territory, British Indian Ocean Territory, Cayman Is., Falkland Is., Montserrat, Pitcairn, Henderson, Ducie & Oeno Is., St Helena, Ascension & Tristan da Cunha, South Georgia & the South Sandwich Is., the Sovereign Base Areas of Akrotiri & Dhekelia (Cyprus), Turks & Caicos Is., Virgin Is. General. - 20p.: 30 cm. - 978-0-11-112147-4 £6.00

The South Sudan (Sanctions) (Overseas Territories) Order 2014 No. 2014/2703. - Enabling power: Saint Helena Act 1833, s. 112 & British Settlements Acts 1887 & 1945. - Issued: 15.10.2014. Made: 08.10.2014. Laid: 15.10.2014. Coming into force: 05.11.2014. Effect: None. Territorial extent & classification: Anguilla, British Antarctic Territory, British Indian Ocean Territory, Cayman Is., Falkland Is., Montserrat, Pitcairn, Henderson, Ducie & Oeno Is., St Helena, Ascension & Tristan da Cunha, South Georgia & the South Sandwich Is., the Sovereign Base Areas of Akrotiri & Dhekelia (Cyprus), Turks & Caicos Is., Virgin Is. General. - 16p.: 30 cm. - 978-0-11-112141-2 £6.00

The Sudan (Sanctions) (Overseas Territories) Order 2014 No. 2014/2707. - Enabling power: United Nations Act 1946, s. 1 & Saint Helena Act 1833, s. 112 & British Settlements Acts 1887 & 1945. - Issued: 15.10.2014. Made: 08.10.2014. Laid: 15.10.2014. Coming into force: 05.11.2014. Effect: S.I. 2004/1980, 2005/1258, 2012/361 revoked. Territorial extent & classification: Anguilla, British Antarctic Territory, British Indian Ocean Territory, Cayman Is., Falkland Is., Montserrat, Pitcairn, Henderson, Ducie & Oeno Is., St Helena, Ascension & Tristan da Cunha, South Georgia & the South Sandwich Is., the Sovereign Base Areas of Akrotiri & Dhekelia (Cyprus), Turks & Caicos Is., Virgin Is. General. - 16p.: 30 cm. - 978-0-11-112145-0 £6.00

The Syria (Restrictive Measures) (Overseas Territories) (Amendment) Order 2014 No. 2014/269. - Enabling power: Saint Helena Act 1833, s. 112 & British Settlements Acts 1887, 1945. - Issued: 18.02.2014. Made: 11.02.2014. Laid: 18.02.2014. Coming into force: 11.03.2014. Effect: S.I. 2012/1755 amended. Territorial extent & classification: Anguilla, British Antarctic Territory, British Indian Ocean Territory, Cayman Islands, Falkland Islands, Montserrat, Pitcairn, Henderson, Ducie and Oeno Islands, St. Helena, Ascension & Tristan da Cunha, South Georgia and South Sandwich Islands, The Sovereign Base Areas of Akrotiri and Dhekelia in the Island of Cyprus, Turks and Caicos Islands, Virgin Islands. General. - EC note: Give effect to changes adopted in Council Decision 2013/255 CFSP as amended by 2013/760/CFSP. - 8p.: 30 cm. - 978-0-11-110973-1 £5.75

The Ukraine (Sanctions) (Overseas Territories) (No. 2) Order 2014 No. 2014/1100. - Enabling power: St Helena Act 1833, s. 112 & British Settlements Acts 1887 and 1945. - Issued: 02.05.2014. Made: 28.04.2014. Laid: 29.04.2014. Coming into force: 30.04.2014. Effect: S.I. 2014/497 revoked. Territorial extent & classification: Anguilla; British Antarctic Territory; British Indian Ocean Territory; Cayman Islands; Falkland Islands; Montserrat; Pitcairn, Henderson, Ducie and Oeno Islands; St. Helena and Dependencies; South Georgia and South Sandwich Islands; the Sovereign Base Areas of Akrotiri and Dhekelia in the Island of Cyprus; Turks and Caicos Islands; Virgin Islands. General. - 12p.: 30 cm. - 978-0-11-111434-6 £6.00

The Ukraine (Sanctions) (Overseas Territories) (No. 3) Order 2014 No. 2014/1098. - Enabling power: St Helena Act 1833, s. 112 & British Settlements Acts 1887 and 1945. - Issued: 02.05.2014. Made: 28.04.2014. Laid: 29.04.2014. Coming into force: 30.04.2014. Effect: None. Territorial extent & classification: Anguilla; British Antarctic Territory; British Indian Ocean Territory; Cayman Islands; Falkland Islands; Montserrat; Pitcairn, Henderson, Ducie and Oeno Islands; St. Helena and Dependencies; South Georgia and South Sandwich Islands; the Sovereign Base Areas of Akrotiri and Dhekelia in the Island of Cyprus; Turks and Caicos Islands; Virgin Islands. General. - 12p.: 30 cm. - 978-0-11-111433-9 £6.00

The Ukraine (Sanctions) (Overseas Territories) Order 2014 No. 2014/497. - Enabling power: St Helena Act 1833, s. 112 & British Settlements Acts 1887 and 1945. - Issued: 12.03.2014. Made: 05.03.2014. Laid: 06.03.2014. Coming into force: 07.03.2014. Effect: None. Territorial extent & classification: Anguilla, British Antarctic Territory, British Indian Ocean Territory, Cayman Islands, Falkland Islands, Montserrat, Pitcairn, Henderson, Ducie and Oeno Islands, St. Helena and Dependencies, South Georgia and South Sandwich Islands, The Sovereign Base Areas of Akrotiri and Dhekelia in the Island of Cyprus, Turks and Caicos Islands, Virgin Islands. General. - 16p.: 30 cm. - 978-0-11-111101-7 £5.75

Partnership

The Reports on Payments to Governments Regulations 2014 No. 2014/3209. - Enabling power: European Communities Act 1972, s. 2 (2) & Limited Liability Partnerships Act 2000, ss. 15, 17 & Companies Act 2006, ss. 468, 1069, 1105. - Issued: 10.12.2014. Made: 28.11.2014. Coming into force: 01.12.2014. Effect: None. Territorial extent & classification: E/W/S/NI. General. - Supersedes draft SI (ISBN 9780111122235) issued 28/10/14 - 16p.: 30 cm. - 978-0-11-112460-4 £6.00

Patents

The Legislative Reform (Patents) Order 2014 No. 2014/1997. - Enabling power: Legislative and Regulatory Reform Act 2006, s. 1. - Issued: 01.08.2014. Made: 25.07.2014. Coming into force: 01.10.2014. Effect: 1977 c.37 amended. Territorial extent & classification: E/W/S/NI. General. - Supersedes draft S.I. (ISBN 9780111114537) issued 08.05.2014. - 4p.: 30 cm. - 978-0-11-111933-4 £4.25

The Patents (Amendment) (No. 2) Rules 2014 No. 2014/2401. - Enabling power: Patents Act 1977, ss. 25 (3) (5), 32, 74A, 77 (5A), 123. - Issued: 15.09.2014. Made: 08.09.2014. Laid: 09.09.2014. Coming into force: 01.10.2014. Effect: S.I. 2007/3291 amended. Territorial extent & classification: E/W/S/NI/IoM. General. - 4p.: 30 cm. - 978-0-11-112053-8 £4.25

The Patents (Amendment) Rules 2014 No. 2014/578. - Enabling power: Patents Act 1977, s. 123. - Issued: 17.03.2014. Made: 08.03.2014. Laid: 12.03.2014. Coming into force: 06.04.2014. Effect: S.I. 2007/3291 amended. Territorial extent & classification: E/W/S/NI. General. - This Statutory Instrument has been printed to correct errors in SI 2007/3291 (ISBN 9780110789989) and is being issued free of charge to all known recipients of that Statutory Instrument. - 4p.: 30 cm. - 978-0-11-111180-2 £4.00

The Patents (Supplementary Protection Certificates) Regulations 2014 No. 2014/2411. - Enabling power: European Communities Act 1972, s. 2 (2), sch. 2, para. 1A. - Issued: 15.09.2014. Made: 08.09.2014. Laid: 10.09.2014. Coming into force: 01.10.2014. Effect: 1977 c.37 amended. Territorial extent & classification: E/W/S/NI. General. - These Regulations amend the references in section 128B (2) of, and paragraph 7 (a) of Schedule 4A to, the Patents Act 1977 ("the Act") to Council Regulation (EEC) No 1768/92 of 18th June 1992 concerning the creation of a supplementary protection certificate for medicinal products. - 4p.: 30 cm. - 978-0-11-112062-0 £4.25

Payment scheme

The Diffuse Mesothelioma Payment Scheme (Amendment) Regulations 2014 No. 2014/917. - Enabling power: Mesothelioma Act 2014, s. 1. - Issued: 11.04.2014. Made: 07.04.2014. Laid: 07.04.2014. Coming into force: 01.04.2014. Effect: S.I. 2014/916 amended. Territorial extent & classification: E/W/S/NI. General. - 4p.: 30 cm. - 978-0-11-111392-9 £4.25

The Diffuse Mesothelioma Payment Scheme (Levy) Regulations 2014 No. 2014/2904. - Enabling power: Mesothelioma Act 2014, ss. 13, 17 (4). - Issued: 10.11.2014. Made: 03.11.2014. Laid: 07.11.2014. Coming into force: 28.11.2014. Effect: None. Territorial extent & classification: E/W/S/NI. General. - 4p.: 30 cm. - 978-0-11-112290-7 £4.25

The Diffuse Mesothelioma Payment Scheme Regulations 2014 No. 2014/916. - Enabling power: Mesothelioma Act 2014, ss. 1, 17 (4). - Issued: 11.04.2014. Made: 05.04.2014. Coming into force: In accord. with reg. 2. Effect: None. Territorial extent & classification: E/W/S/NI. General. - 20p.: 30 cm. - 978-0-11-111386-8 £6.00

The Mesothelioma Act 2014 (Commencement No. 1) Order 2014 No. 2014/459 (C.21). - Enabling power: Mesothelioma Act 2014, s. 19 (1). Bringing into force various provisions of the Act on 04.03.2014, 31.03.2014 & 01.09.2014. - Issued: 07.03.2014. Made: 03.03.2014. Effect: None. Territorial extent & classification: E/W/S/NI. General. - 2p.: 30 cm. - 978-0-11-111070-6 £4.00

Pensions

The Armed Forces and Reserve Forces (Compensation Scheme) (Amendment) Order 2014 No. 2014/412. - Enabling power: Armed Forces (Pensions and Compensation) Act 2004, s. 1 (2). - Issued: 04.03.2014. Made: 23.02.2014. Laid: 27.02.2014. Coming into force: 07.04.2014. Effect: S.I. 2011/517 amended. Territorial extent & classification: E/W/S/NI. General. - 8p.: 30 cm. - 978-0-11-111030-0 £4.00

The Armed Forces Early Departure Payments Scheme Regulations 2014 No. 2014/2328. - Enabling power: Public Service Act 2013, s. 1 (1). - Issued: 05.09.2014. Made: 31.08.2014. Laid: 04.09.2014. Coming into force: 01.04.2015 Effect: None. Territorial extent & classification: E/W/S/NI. General. - 12p.: 30 cm. - 978-0-11-112008-8 £6.00

The Armed Forces Pension Regulations 2014 No. 2014/2336. - Enabling power: Public Service Pensions Act 2013, ss. 1 (1), 2 (h) (3) (4), 2, 3 (1) (2) (3) (a) (c), (4), 4 (1) to (3) (5), 5 (1) to (6) (8), 7 (1) (2) (a) (4), 11 (1) (2), 12 (1) to (3) (6) (7), 13 (1) to (3), 14, 18 (1) (2) (4) (b) (5) to (9), 25, 37 para (c), sch. 1, para. 1, 2 para. 1, sch. 3, sch. 5, para. 1, 6 para. 1, sch. 7 paras 1 (2), 2 (2). - Issued: 08.09.2014. Made: 31.08.2014. Laid: 04.09.2014. Coming into force: 01.04.2015. Effect: None. Territorial extent & classification: E/W/S/NI. General. - 68p.: 30 cm. - 978-0-11-112011-8 £11.00

The Armed Forces Pension Scheme and Armed Forces Early Departure Payments Scheme (Amendment) Order 2014 No. 2014/2958. - Enabling power: Armed Forces (Pensions and Compensation) Act 2004, ss. 1 (1), 10 (2). - Issued: 17.11.2014. Made: 08.11.2014. Laid: 13.11.2014. Coming into force: 17.12.2014. Effect: S.I. 2005/437, 438 amended. Territorial extent & classification: E/W/S/NI. General. - With correction slip dated November 2014. - 4p.: 30 cm. - 978-0-11-112327-0 £4.25

The Automatic Enrolment (Earnings Trigger and Qualifying Earnings Band) Order 2014 No. 2014/623. - Enabling power: Pensions Act 2008, ss. 3 (1) (c), 5 (1) (c), 13 (1) (a) (b). - Issued: 19.03.2014. Made: 12.03.2014. Coming into force: 06.04.2014. Effect: 2008 c.30 amended & S.I. 2013/667 partially revoked. Territorial extent & classification: E/W/S. General. - Partially revoked by SI 2015/468 (ISBN 9780111131602). - 4p.: 30 cm. - 978-0-11-111219-9 £4.00

The Financial Assistance Scheme (Qualifying Pension Scheme Amendments) Regulations 2014 No. 2014/837. - Enabling power: Pensions Act 2004, ss. 286, 315 (2), 318 (1). - Issued: 02.04.2014. Made: 27.03.2014. Coming into force: 28.03.2014 in accord. with reg. 1. Effect: S.I. 2005/1986 amended. Territorial extent & classification: E/W/S/NI. General. - Supersedes draft SI (ISBN 9780111108987) issued 05/02/14. - 2p.: 30 cm. - 978-0-11-111292-2 £4.00

The Guaranteed Minimum Pensions Increase Order 2014 No. 2014/515. - Enabling power: Pension Schemes Act 1993, s. 109 (2). - Issued: 17.03.2014. Made: 10.03.2014. Coming into force: 06.04.2014. Effect: None. Territorial extent & classification: E/W/S. General. - Supersedes draft SI (ISBN 9780111108772) issued 29/01/14. - 2p.: 30 cm. - 978-0-11-111172-7 £4.00

The Judicial Pensions (Contributions) (Amendment) Regulations 2013 No. 2014/483. - Enabling power: District Judges (Magistrates' Courts) Pensions Act (Northern Ireland) 1960, s. 8A (1) (6) (7) & Judicial Pensions Act 1981, s. 33ZA (1) (6) (7) & Judicial Pensions and Retirement Act 1993, ss. 9A (1), 29. - Issued: 10.03.2014. Made: 04.03.2014. Laid: 06.03.2014. Coming into force: 01.04.2014. Effect: S.I. 2012/516 amended. Territorial extent & classification: E/W/S/NI. General. - 2p.: 30 cm. - 978-0-11-111085-0 £4.00

The Judicial Pensions (Widows', Widowers' and Children's Benefits) (Amendment) Regulations 2014 No. 2014/288. - Enabling power: Judicial Pensions Act 1981, s. 23. - Issued: 19.02.2014. Made: 11.02.2014. Laid: 13.02.2014. Coming into force: 13.03.2014. Effect: S.I. 1987/375; 1991/2731 amended. Territorial extent & classification: E/W. General. - 2p.: 30 cm. - With correction slip dated December 2014. - 978-0-11-110978-6 £4.00

The Naval, Military and Air Forces Etc. (Disablement and Death) Service Pensions (Amendment) Order 2014 No. 2014/505. - Enabling power: Social Security (Miscellaneous Provisions) Act 1977, ss. 12 (1), 24 (3). - Issued: 12.03.2014. Made: 05.03.2014. Laid: 12.03.2014. Coming into force: 07.04.2014. Effect: S.I. 2006/606 amended. Territorial extent & classification: E/W/S/NI. General. - 12p.: 30 cm. - 978-0-11-111109-3 £5.75

The Occupational and Personal Pension Schemes (Automatic Enrolment) (Amendment) Regulations 2014 No. 2014/715. - Enabling power: Pension Schemes Act 2008, ss. 16 (3) (c), 28 (2) (b), 99, 144 (4). - Issued: 24.03.2014. Made: 18.03.2014. Coming into force: 01.04.2014. Effect: S.I. 2010/772 amended. Territorial extent & classification: E/W/S. General. - Supersedes draft S.I. (ISBN 9780111108918) issued 03.02.2014. - 4p.: 30 cm. - 978-0-11-111247-2 £4.00

The Occupational Pension Schemes (Miscellaneous Amendments) Regulations 2014 No. 2014/540. - Enabling power: Pension Schemes Act 1993, ss. 19 (4) (c), 182 (2) & Pensions Act 1995, ss. 47 (5) (b), 89 (2), 124 (1), 174 (2) (3) & Pensions Act 2004, ss. 258 (7), 315 (2), 318 (1). - Issued: 12.04.2014. Made: 06.03.2014. Laid: 12.03.2014. Coming into force: 06.04.2014. Effect: S.I. 1996/1715; 1997/784; 2005/649, 678 amended. Territorial extent & classification: E/W/S. General. - 8p.: 30 cm. - 978-0-11-111143-7 £4.00

The Occupational Pensions (Revaluation) Order 2014 No. 2014/3078. - Enabling power: Pension Schemes Act 1993, sch. 3, para. 2 (1). - Issued: 25.11.2014. Made: 18.11.2014. Laid: 25.11.2014. Coming into force: 01.01.2015. Effect: None. Territorial extent & classification: E/W/S. General. - 2p.: 30 cm. - 978-0-11-112361-4 £4.25

The Payment of Pension Levies for Past Periods Regulations 2014 No. 2014/2939. - Enabling power: Pensions Act 2014, ss. 45 (1) (2) (b), 54 (5) (6). - Issued: 17.11.2014. Made: 10.11.2014. Laid: 17.11.2014. Coming into force: 08.12.2014. Effect: None. Territorial extent & classification: E/W/S. General. - EC note: These regulations implement Decision 55/2007/EC. - 4p.: 30 cm. - 978-0-11-112319-5 £4.25

The Pension Protection Fund and Occupational Pension Schemes (Levy Ceiling and Compensation Cap) Order 2014 No. 2014/10. - Enabling power: Pensions Act 2004, ss. 178 (1) (6), 315 (2) (5), sch. 7, paras 26 (7), 27 (2) (3). - Issued: 14.01.2014. Made: 08.01.2014. Laid: 14.01.2014. Coming into force: In accord. with art. 1 (2). Effect: S.I. 2013/105 revoked (01.04.2014). Territorial extent & classification: E/W/S. General. - Partially revoked by SI 2015/66 (ISBN 9780111128022). - 4p.: 30 cm. - 978-0-11-110812-3 £4.00

The Pension Protection Fund (Entry Rules) (Amendment) Regulations 2014 No. 2014/1664. - Enabling power: Pensions Act 2004, ss. 121 (5) (9) (b), 315 (2) (5), 318 (1). - Issued: 02.07.2014. Made: 25.06.2014. Laid: 30.06.2014. Coming into force: 21.07.2014. Effect: S.I. 2005/590 amended. Territorial extent & classification: E/W/S. General. - 4p.: 30 cm. - 978-0-11-111723-1 £4.25

The Pensions Act 2004 (Code of Practice) (Funding Defined Benefits) Appointed Day Order 2014 No. 2014/1926. - Enabling power: Pensions Act 2004, s. 91 (9). Bringing Code of practice no. 3 (funding defined benefits, 2nd issue) into effect on 29.07.2014. - Issued: 25.07.2014. Made: 21.07.2014. Effect: None. Territorial extent & classification: E/W/S. General. - 2p.: 30 cm. - 978-0-11-111899-3 £4.25

The Pensions Act 2004 (Commencement No. 15) Order 2014 No. 2014/1636 (C.66). - Enabling power: Pension Act 2004, ss. 315 (2), 322 (1). Bringing into operation various provisions of the 2004 Act on 25.06.2014. - Issued: 30.06.2014. Made: 24.06.2014. Effect: None. Territorial extent & classification: E/W/S. General. - 16p.: 30 cm. - 978-0-11-111705-7 £6.00

The Pensions Act 2008 (Commencement No.15) Order 2014 No. 2014/463 (C.22). - Enabling power: Pensions Act 2008, ss. 149 (1). Bringing into operation various provisions of the 2008 Act on 13.03.2014 in accord. with art. 2. - Issued: 10.03.2014. Made: 03.03.2014. Effect: None. Territorial extent & classification: E/W/S. General. - 4p.: 30 cm. - 978-0-11-111073-7 £4.00

The Pensions Act 2011 (Commencement No. 5) Order 2014 No. 2014/1683 (C.71). - Enabling power: Pensions Act 2011, s. 38 (4). Bringing into operation various provisions of the 2011 Act on 24.07.2014 in accord. with art. 2. - Issued: 04.07.2014. Made: 30.06.2014. Effect: None. Territorial extent & classification: E/W/S. General. - 2p.: 30 cm. - 978-0-11-111734-7 £4.25

The Pensions Act 2011 (Consequential and Supplementary Provisions) Regulations 2014 No. 2014/1954. - Enabling power: Pensions Act 2011, ss. 31 (1), 33 (1) (a) (b) (c). - Issued: 29.07.2014. Made: 23.07.2014. Coming into force: 24.07.2014 in accord. with reg. 1 (2). Effect: 1993 c.48; 2004 c.35 amended. Territorial extent & classification: E/W/S. General. - Supersedes draft S.I. (ISBN 9780111116647) issued 20.06.2014. - 4p.: 30 cm. - 978-0-11-111917-4 £4.25

The Pensions Act 2011 (Transitional, Consequential and Supplementary Provisions) Regulations 2014 No. 2014/1711. - Enabling power: Pensions Schemes Act 1993, ss. 74 (5), 97 (1) (2) (b) (3) (c), 101AF (1) (3) (b) (4) (b), 101I, 101L (1) (2) (b), 113 (1), 153 (1) (2) (c), 181 (1), 182 (2) (3), 183 (1) & Pensions Act 1995, ss. 10 (3), 37 (4) (a) to (c) (e) (8), 47 (5) (a), 73 (6) (7) (8) (a), 75 (5) (10), 124 (1), 174 (2) (3) & Welfare Reform and Pensions Act 1999, ss. 23 (1) (b), 26 (1), 30 (1), 83 (4) (6) & Pensions Act 2004, ss. 117, 126 (1) (b) (5), 135 (4), 138 (10) (a), 146 (1), 161 (3) (b), 179 (1) (a) (3), 189 (11) (b), 190 (1), 207, 232, 315 (2) (4) (5), 318 (1), sch. 7, paras 12 (3A) (b), 17 (3A) (b), 20 (7), 33 (1) & Equality Act 2010, s. 212 (1) (s), sch. 7, para. 5 (2) & Pensions Act 2011, ss. 30 (1) (2), 31 (1), 33 (1) (a) (b) (d). - Issued: 08.07.2014. Made: 01.07.2014. Laid: 03.07.2014. Coming into force: In accord. with reg. 1 (1). Effect: 1993 c.48; 2004 c.35; S.I. 1991/167, 168; 1996/1655, 1715, 1847; 2005/590, 669, 670, 3337; 2006/33, 802; 2010/2132; 2013/2734 amended & S.I. 1995/3183 modified. Territorial extent & classification: E/W/S/NI. General. - Supersedes draft SI (ISBN 9780111114568) issued 09/06/14. This Statutory Instrument supersedes in part the draft of the Pensions Act 2011 (Transitional, Consequential and Supplementary Provisions) regulations 2014 which was laid before Parliament on 6th May 2014 and published on 9th May (ISBN 978-0-11-111456-8). It is being issued free of charge to all known recipients of that draft statutory instrument. - 58p.: 30 cm. - 978-0-11-111749-1 £10.00

The Pensions Act 2014 (Commencement No. 2) Order 2014 No. 2014/2377 (C.102). - Enabling power: Pensions Act 2014, s. 56 (1) (4) (7). Bringing into operation various provisions of the 2014 Act on 11.09.2014, 12.09.2014, 01.10.2014. - Issued: 11.09.2014. Made: 04.09.2014. Effect: None. Territorial extent & classification: E/W/S. General. - 4p.: 30 cm. - 978-0-11-112036-1 £4.25

The Pensions Act 2014 (Commencement No. 3) Order 2014 No. 2014/2727 (C.119). - Enabling power: Pensions Act 2014, s. 56 (1). Bringing into operation various provisions of the 2014 Act on 13.10.2014, in accord. with art. 2. - Issued: 17.10.2014. Made: 11.10.2014. Effect: None. Territorial extent & classification: E/W/S. General. - 2p.: 30 cm. - 978-0-11-112171-9 £4.25

The Pensions Increase (Commissioners of Irish Lights) Regulations 2014 No. 2014/563. - Enabling power: Pensions (Increase) Act 1971, s. 5 (3). - Issued: 17.03.2014. Made: 10.03.2014. Laid: 11.03.2014. Coming into force: 01.04.2014. Effect: 1971 c.56 modified. Territorial extent & classification: E/W/S/NI. General. - 4p.: 30 cm. - 978-0-11-111162-8 £4.00

The Pensions Increase (Review) Order 2014 No. 2014/668. - Enabling power: Social Security Pensions Act 1975, s. 59 (1) (2) (5) (5ZA). - Issued: 21.03.2014. Made: 13.03.2014. Laid: 17.03.2014. Coming into force: 07.04.2014. Effect: None. Territorial extent & classification: E/W/S/NI. General. - 8p.: 30 cm. - 978-0-11-111232-8 £5.75

The Personal Injuries (Civilians) Scheme (Amendment) Order 2014 No. 2014/444. - Enabling power: Personal Injuries (Emergency Provisions) Act 1939, ss. 1, 2. - Issued: 05.03.2014. Made: 26.02.2014. Laid: 03.03.2014. Coming into force: 07.04.2014. Effect: S.I. 1983/686 amended. Territorial extent & classification: E/W/S/NI. General. - 8p.: 30 cm. - 978-0-11-111052-2 £5.75

The Public Service Pensions (Record Keeping and Miscellaneous Amendments) Regulations 2014 No. 2014/3138. - Enabling power: Pensions Act 1995, ss. 49 (9) (b), 124 (1), 174 (2) & Public Service Pensions Act 2013, s. 16 (1). - Issued: 03.12.2014. Made: 26.11.2014. Laid: 03.12.2014. Coming into force: 01.04.2015. Effect: S.I. 1996/1715 amended. Territorial extent & classification: E/W/S/NI. General. - 8p.: 30 cm. - 978-0-11-112412-3 £4.25

The Superannuation (Admission to Schedule 1 to the Superannuation Act 1972) Order 2014 No. 2014/555. - Enabling power: Superannuation Act 1972, s. 1 (5). - Issued: 14.03.2014. Made: 10.03.2014. Laid: 11.03.2014. Coming into force: 01.04.2014. Effect: 1972 c.11 amended. Territorial extent & classification: UK. General. - 2p.: 30 cm. - 978-0-11-111152-9 £4.00

Pensions, England

The Firefighters' Compensation Scheme (England) (Amendment) Order 2014 No. 2014/447. - Enabling power: Fire and Rescue Services Act 2004, ss. 34, 60. - Issued: 07.03.2014. Made: 28.02.2014. Laid: 06.03.2014. Coming into force: 01.04.2014. Effect: S.I. 2006/1811 amended. Territorial extent & classification: E. General. - 8p.: 30 cm. - 978-0-11-111074-4 £5.75

The Firefighters' Pension Scheme (Amendment) (England) Order 2014 No. 2014/446. - Enabling power: Fire Services Act 1947, s. 26 (1) to (5)- Issued: 07.03.2014. Made: 28.02.2014. Laid: 06.03.2014. Coming into force: 01.04.2014. Effect: S.I. 1992/129 amended in relation to England. Territorial extent & classification: E. General. - 4p.: 30 cm. - 978-0-11-111071-3 £4.00

The Firefighters' Pension Scheme (Amendment) (No. 2) (England) Order 2013 (correction slip) No. 2013/1392 Cor.. - 1 sheet.: 30 cm. Free

The Firefighters' Pension Scheme (England) (Amendment) (No. 2) Order 2013 (correction slip) No. 2013/1393 Cor.. - 1 sheet.: 30 cm. Free

The Firefighters' Pension Scheme (England) (Amendment) Order 2014 No. 2014/445. - Enabling power: Fire and Rescue Services Act 2004, ss. 34, 60. - Issued: 07.03.2014. Made: 28.02.2014. Laid: 06.03.2014. Coming into force: 01.04.2014. Effect: S.I. 2006/3432 amended. Territorial extent & classification: E. General. - 36p.: 30 cm. - 978-0-11-111072-0 £9.75

Pensions, England and Wales

The Police Pensions (Amendment) (No. 2) Regulations 2014 No. 2014/381. - Enabling power: Police Pensions Act 1976, s. 1. - Issued: 27.20.2014. Made: 13.02.2014. Laid: 25.02.2014. Coming into force: 01.04.2014. Effect: S.I. 1987/257; 2006/3415 amended. Territorial extent & classification: E/W. General. - 4p.: 30 cm. - 978-0-11-111011-9 £4.00

The Police Pensions (Amendment) Regulations 2014 No. 2014/79. - Enabling power: Police Pensions Act 1976, ss. 1 to 7. - Issued: 24.01.2014. Made: 15.01.2014. Laid: 23.01.2014. Coming into force: 13.03.2014. Effect: S.I. 1987/257; 2006/932 amended. Territorial extent & classification: E/W. General. - 8p.: 30 cm. - 978-0-11-110852-9 £4.00

Pensions, Wales

The Firefighters' Compensation Scheme (Wales) (Amendment) Order 2014 No. 2014/3256 (W.331). - Enabling power: Fire and Rescue Services Act 2004, ss. 34, 60, 62. - Issued: 30.12.2014. Made: 08.12.2014. Laid before the National Assembly for Wales: 10.12.2014. Coming into force: 31.12.2014. Effect: S.I. 2007/1073 (W.111) amended. Territorial extent & classification: W. General. - In English and Welsh. Welsh title: Gorchymyn Cynllun Digolledu'r Diffoddwyr Tân (Cymru) (Diwygio) 2014. - 16p.; 30 cm. - 978-0-348-11034-0 £6.00

The Firefighters' Pension Scheme (Wales) (Amendment) Order 2014 No. 2014/3254 (W.330). - Enabling power: Fire and Rescue Services Act 2004, ss. 34, 60, 62. - Issued: 26.01.2015. Made: 08.12.2014. Laid before the National Assembly for Wales: 10.12.2014. Coming into force: 31.12.2014. Effect: S.I. 2007/1072 (W.110) amended. Territorial extent & classification: W. General. - In English and Welsh. Welsh title: Gorchymyn Cynllun Pensiwn y Diffoddwyr Tân (Cymru) (Diwygio) 2014. - 68p.; 30 cm. - 978-0-348-11039-5 £11.00

The Firefighters' Pension (Wales) Scheme (Amendment) Order 2014 No. 2014/3242 (W.329). - Enabling power: Fire Services Act 1947, s. 26(1) to (5) & Superannuation Act 1972, s. 12. - Issued: 26.01.2015. Made: 08.12.2015. Laid: 10.12.2015. Coming into force: 31.12.2015. Effect: S.I. 1992/129 amended. Territorial extent & classification: W. General. - In English and Welsh. Welsh language title: Gorchymyn Cynllun Pensiwn y Dynion Tân (Cymru) (Diwygio) 2014. - 40p.: 30 cm. - 978-0-348-11038-8 £10.00

The Firefighters' Pension (Wales) Scheme (Contributions) (Amendment) Order 2014 No. 2014/523 (W.64). - Enabling power: Fire and Rescue Services Act 2004, ss. 34, 60, 62. - Issued: 25.03.2014. Made: 04.03.2014. Laid before the National Assembly for Wales: 07.03.2014. Coming into force: 01.04.2014. Effect: S.I. 2007/1072 (W.110) amended. Territorial extent & classification: W. General. - In English and Welsh. Welsh title: Gorchymyn Cynllun Pensiwn y Dynion Tân (Cymru) (Cyfraniadau) (Diwygio) 2014. - 4p.: 30 cm. - 978-0-348-10919-1 £4.00

The Firefighters' Pension (Wales) Scheme (Contributions) (Amendment) Order 2014 No. 2014/522 (W.63). - Enabling power: Fire Services Act 1947, s. 26 (1). - Issued: 26.03.2015. Made: 04.03.2014. Laid before the National Assembly for Wales: 07.03.2014. Coming into force: 01.04.2014. Effect: S.I. 1992/129 amended in relation to Wales. Territorial extent & classification: W. General. - In English and Welsh. Welsh title: Gorchymyn Cynllun Pensiwn y Dynion Tân (Cymru) (Cyfraniadau) (Diwygio) 2014. - 4p.: 30 cm. - 978-0-348-10924-5 £4.00

Petroleum

The Petroleum Licensing (Exploration and Production) (Landward Areas) Regulations 2014 No. 2014/1686. - Enabling power: Petroleum Act 1998, s. 4. - Issued: 07.07.2014. Made: 20.06.2014. Laid: 02.07.2014. Coming into force: 17.07.2014. Effect: None. Territorial extent & classification: E/W/S. General. - 36p.: 30 cm. - 978-0-11-111737-8 £10.00

Petroleum revenue tax

The Double Taxation Relief and International Tax Enforcement (Belgium) Order 2014 No. 2014/1875. - Enabling power: Taxation (International and Other Provisions) Act 2010, s. 2 & Finance Act 2006, s. 173 (1) to (3). - Issued: 23.07.2014. Made: 16.07.2014. Effect: None. Territorial extent & classification: E/W/S/NI. General. - Supersedes draft SI (ISBN 9780111116272) issued 13/06/14. - 8p.: 30 cm. - 978-0-11-111837-5 £4.25

The Double Taxation Relief and International Tax Enforcement (Canada) Order 2014 No. 2014/3274. - Enabling power: Taxation (International and Other Provisions) Act 2010, s. 2 & Finance Act 2006, s. 173 (1) to (3). - Issued: 17.12.2014. Made: 10.12.2014. Coming into force: 10.12.2014. Effect: 1980/709 amended. Territorial extent & classification: E/W/S/NI. - Supersedes draft S.I. (ISBN 9780111121801) issued 20/10/14. - 20p.: 30 cm. - 978-0-11-112537-3 £6.00

Pipe-lines

The Public Gas Transporter Pipe-line Works (Environmental Impact Assessment) (Amendment) (England) Regulations 2014 No. 2014/557. - Enabling power: European Communities Act 1972, s. 2 (2). - Issued: 14.03.2014. Made: 06.03.2014. Laid: 10.03.2014. Coming into force: 06.04.2014. Effect: S.I. 1999/1672 amended. Territorial extent & classification: E/W/S. General. - 4p.: 30 cm. - 978-0-11-111155-0 £4.00

The Submarine Pipelines (Designated Owners) (Revocation) Order 2014 No. 2014/422. - Enabling power: Petroleum Act 1998, s. 27 (1). - Issued: 04.03.2014. Made: 26.02.2014. Coming into force: 06.04.2014. Effect: S.I. 2010/3048 revoked. Territorial extent & classification: E/W/S/NI. General. - 2p.: 30 cm. - 978-0-11-111038-6 £4.00

The Submarine Pipe-lines (Electricity Generating Stations) (Revocation) Regulations 2014 No. 2014/430. - Enabling power: Petroleum Act 1998, s. 24 (3). - Issued: 05.03.2014. Made: 26.02.2014. Coming into force: 28.02.2014. Effect: S.I. 1981/750 revoked. Territorial extent & classification: E/W/S/NI. General. - 4p.: 30 cm. - 978-0-11-111041-6 £4.00

Plant health, England

The Plant Health (England) (Amendment) (No. 2) Order 2014 No. 2014/2385. - Enabling power: Plant Health Act 1967, ss. 2, 3 (1) & European Communities Act 1972, sch. 2 para. 1A. - Issued: 12.09.2014. Made: 03.09.2014. Laid: 08.09.2014. Coming into force: 01.10.2014. Effect: S.I. 2005/2530 amended. Territorial extent & classification: E. General. - 20p.; 30 cm. - 978-0-11-112044-6 £6.00

The Plant Health (England) (Amendment) Order 2014 No. 2014/979. - Enabling power: Plant Health Act 1967, ss. 2 (1), 3 (1). - Issued: 16.04.2014. Made: 07.04.2014. Laid: 14.04.2014. Coming into force: In accord. with art. 1 (2). Effect: S.I. 2005/2530 amended. Territorial extent & classification: E. General. - 4p.: 30 cm. - 978-0-11-111409-4 £4.25

The Plant Health (Export Certification) (England) (Amendment) Order 2014 No. 2014/609. - Enabling power: Plant Health Act 1967, ss. 3 (1), 4A. - Issued: 19.03.2014. Made: 11.03.2014. Laid: 14.03.2014. Coming into force: 06.04.2014. Effect: S.I. 2004/1404 amended. Territorial extent & classification: E. General. - 4p.: 30 cm. - 978-0-11-111211-3 £4.00

The Plant Health (Fees) (England) (Amendment) Regulations 2014 No. 2014/3243. - Enabling power: Finance Act 1973, s. 56 (1). - Issued: 15.12.2014. Made: 08.12.2014. Laid: 09.12.2014. Coming into force: 01.01.2015. Effect: S.I. 2014/601 amended. Territorial extent & classification: E. General. - 8p.: 30 cm. - 978-0-11-112502-1 £4.25

The Plant Health (Fees) (England) Regulations 2014 No. 2014/601. - Enabling power: Finance Act 1973, s. 56 (1) (2). - Issued: 19.03.2014. Made: 11.03.2014. Laid: 14.03.2014. Coming into force: 06.04.2014. Effect: S.I. 2013/494, 3050 revoked. Territorial extent & classification: E. General. - 12p.: 30 cm. - 978-0-11-111201-4 £5.75

The Plant Health (Fees) (Forestry) (Amendment) (England and Scotland) Regulations 2014 No. 2014/589. - Enabling power: European Communities Act 1972, s. 2 (2). - Issued: 18.03.2014. Made: 10.03.2014. Laid: 14.03.2014. Coming into force: 07.04.2014. Effect: S.I. 2006/2697 amended. Territorial extent & classification: E/S. General. - Revoked by S.I. 2015/350 (ISBN 9780111130384) in re to E/S. - 4p.: 30 cm. - 978-0-11-111193-2 £4.00

The Plant Health (Forestry) (Amendment) (England and Scotland) Order 2014 No. 2014/2420. - Enabling power: Plant Health Act 1967 ss. 2, 3 (1), European Communities Act 1972, sch. 2 para. 1A. - Issued: 16.09.2014. Made: 09.09.2014. Laid: 11.09.2014. Coming into force: 03.10.2014. Effect: S.I. 2005/2517 amended. Territorial extent & classification: E/S. General. - EC note: This Order amends S.I. 2005/2517 in relation to England and Scotland to implement Directive 2014/78/EU amending Annexes I, II, III, IV, and V to Council Directive 2000/29/EC on protective measures against the introduction into the Community of organisms harmful to plants or plant products and against their spread within the Community; and Directive 2014/83/EU amending Annexes I, II, III, IV, and V to Council Directive 2000/29/EC on protective measures against the introduction into the Community of organisms harmful to plants or plant products and against their spread within the Community. - 20p.: 30 cm. - 978-0-11-112065-1 £6.00

The Plant Health (Phytophthora kernovii Management Zone) (England) (Revocation) Order 2014 No. 2014/2875. - Enabling power: Plant Health Act 1967, ss. 3 (1) (2) (4), 4 (1). - Issued: 04.11.2014. Made: 17.10.2014. Laid: 30.10.2014. Coming into force: 01.12.2014. Effect: S.I. 2004/3367 revoked. Territorial extent & classification: E. General. - 2p.: 30 cm. - 978-0-11-112264-8 £4.25

The Seeds and Vegetable Plant Material (Nomenclature Changes) Regulations 2014 No. 2014/487. - Enabling power: Plant Varieties and Seeds Act 1964, ss. 16 (1) (1A) & European Communities Act 1972, s. 2 (2). - Issued: 11.03.2014. Made: 04.03.2014. Laid: 06.03.2014. Coming into force: 31.03.2014. Effect: S.I. 1995/2652; 2001/3510; 2011/463 amended. Territorial extent and classification: E/W/S/NI. General. - EC note: These regulations implement Commission Implementing Directive 2013/45/EU amending Council Directives 2002/55/EC and 2008/72/EC and Commission Directive 2009/145/EC. - 4p.: 30 cm. - 978-0-11-111091-1 £4.00

Plant health, Scotland

The Plant Health (Fees) (Forestry) (Amendment) (England and Scotland) Regulations 2014 No. 2014/589. - Enabling power: European Communities Act 1972, s. 2 (2). - Issued: 18.03.2014. Made: 10.03.2014. Laid: 14.03.2014. Coming into force: 07.04.2014. Effect: S.I. 2006/2697 amended. Territorial extent & classification: E/S. General. - Revoked by S.I. 2015/350 (ISBN 9780111130384) in re to E/S. - 4p.: 30 cm. - 978-0-11-111193-2 £4.00

The Plant Health (Forestry) (Amendment) (England and Scotland) Order 2014 No. 2014/2420. - Enabling power: Plant Health Act 1967 ss. 2, 3 (1), European Communities Act 1972, sch. 2 para. 1A. - Issued: 16.09.2014. Made: 09.09.2014. Laid: 11.09.2014. Coming into force: 03.10.2014. Effect: S.I. 2005/2517 amended. Territorial extent & classification: E/S. General. - EC note: This Order amends S.I. 2005/2517 in relation to England and Scotland to implement Directive 2014/78/EU amending Annexes I, II, III, IV, and V to Council Directive 2000/29/EC on protective measures against the introduction into the Community of organisms harmful to plants or plant products and against their spread within the Community; and Directive 2014/83/EU amending Annexes I, II, III, IV, and V to Council Directive 2000/29/EC on protective measures against the introduction into the Community of organisms harmful to plants or plant products and against their spread within the Community. - 20p.: 30 cm. - 978-0-11-112065-1 £6.00

Plant health, Wales

The Plant Health (Export Certification) (Wales) (Amendment) Order 2014 No. 2014/1759 (W.174). - Enabling power: Plant Health Act 1967, ss. 3 (1), 4A. - Issued: 11.07.2014. Made: 02.07.2014. Laid before the National Assembly for Wales: 04.07.2014. Coming into force: 31.07.2014. Effect: W.S.I. 2006/1701 (W.163) amended. Territorial extent & classification: W. General. - In English & Welsh. Welsh title: Gorchymyn lechyd Planhigion (Tystysgrifau Allforio) (Cymru) (Diwygio) 2014. - 4p.: 30 cm. - 978-0-348-10961-0 £4.25

The Plant Health (Fees) (Wales) Regulations 2014 No. 2014/1792 (W.185). - Enabling power: Finance Act 1973, ss. 56 (1) (2). - Issued: 18.07.2014. Made: 06.07.2014. Laid before the National Assembly for Wales: 08.07.2014. Coming into force: 02.08.2014. Effect: S.I. 2013/1700 (W.164) revoked. Territorial extent & classification: W. General. - In English & Welsh. Welsh title: Rheoliadau lechyd Planhigion (Ffioedd) (Cymru) 2014. - 24p.: 30 cm. - 978-0-348-10968-9 £6.00

The Plant Health (Miscellaneous Amendments) (Wales) Order 2014 No. 2014/1463 (W.144). - Enabling power: European Communities Act 1972, s. 2 (2). - Issued: 13.06.2014. Made: 05.06.2014. Laid before the National Assembly for Wales: 09.06.2014. Coming into force: 04.07.2014. Effect: S.I. 2004/2245 (W.209) amended. Territorial extent & classification: W. General. - In English & Welsh. Welsh title: Rheoliadau lechyd Planhigion (Diwygiadau Amrywiol) (Cymru) 2014. - 8p.: 30 cm. - 978-0-348-10952-8 £6.00

The Plant Health (Wales) (Amendment) (No. 2) Order 2014 No. 2014/1186 (W.115). - Enabling power: Plant Health Act 1967, ss. 2, 3 (1). - Issued: 15.05.2014. Made: 06.05.2014. Laid before the National Assembly for Wales: 08.05.2014. Coming into force: 31.05.2014. Effect: S.I. 2006/1643 (W.158) amended. Territorial extent & classification: W. General. - In English & Welsh. Welsh title: Gorchymyn lechyd Planhigion (Cymru) (Diwygio) (Rhif 2) 2014. - 8p.: 30 cm. - 978-0-348-10942-9 £4.25

The Plant Health (Wales) (Amendment) (No. 3) Order 2014 No. 2014/2368 (W.231). - Enabling power: Plant Health Act 1967, ss. 2, 3 (1) & European Communities Act 1972, sch. 2 para. 1A. - Issued: 22.09.2014. Made: 05.09.2014. Laid before the National Assembly for Wales: 05.09.2014. Coming into force: 01.10.2014. Effect: S.I. 2006/1643 (W.158) amended. Territorial extent & classification: W. General. - In English & Welsh. Welsh title: Gorchymyn lechyd Planhigion (Cymru) (Diwygio) (Rhif 3) 2014. - 36p.: 30 cm. - 978-0-348-10990-0 £10.00

The Plant Health (Wales) (Amendment) Order 2014 No. 2014/521 (W.62). - Enabling power: Plant Health Act 1967, ss. 2, 3 (1) & European Communities Act 1972, sch. 2, para. 1A. - Issued: 17.03.2014. Made: 05.03.2014. Laid before the National Assembly for Wales: 07.03.2014. Coming into force: 28.03.2014. Effect: S.I. 2006/1643 (W.158) amended. Territorial extent & classification: W. General. - In English & Welsh. Welsh title: Gorchymyn lechyd Planhigion (Cymru) (Diwygio) 2014. - 24p.: 30 cm. - 978-0-348-10915-3 £5.75

Police

The Anti-social Behaviour, Crime and Policing Act 2014 (Commencement No.1) Order 2014 No. 2014/630 (C.25). - Enabling power: Anti-social Behaviour, Crime and Policing Act 2014, s. 185 (1). Bringing into operation various provisions of the 2014 Act on 14.03.2014, 20.03.2014. - Issued: 19.03.2014. Made: 13.03.2014. Effect: None. Territorial extent & classification: E/W/S/NI. General. - 2p.: 30 cm. - 978-0-11-111220-5 £4.00

The Anti-social Behaviour, Crime and Policing Act 2014 (Commencement No. 4 and Transitional Provisions) Order 2014 No. 2014/1916 (C.87). - Enabling power: Anti-social Behaviour, Crime and Policing Act 2014, s. 185 (1) (7). Bringing into operation various provisions of the 2014 Act on 21.07.2014, 31.07.2014, and 01.04.2015. - Issued: 25.07.2014. Made: 18.07.2014. Effect: None. Territorial extent & classification: E/W/S/NI. General. - 8p.: 30 cm. - 978-0-11-111888-7 £4.25

Police, England and Wales

The Anti-social Behaviour, Crime and Policing Act 2014 (Commencement No. 2, Transitional and Transitory Provisions) Order 2014 No. 2014/949 (C.43). - Enabling power: Anti-social Behaviour, Crime and Policing Act 2014, s. 185 (1) (7). Bringing into operation various provisions of the 2014 Act on 13.05.2014, 01.06.2014, 16.06.2014, 14.07.2014, in accord. with arts. 2 to 6. - Issued: 14.04.2014. Made: 08.04.2014. Effect: None. Territorial extent & classification: E/W/S/NI. General. - 8p.: 30 cm. - 978-0-11-111401-8 £6.00

The Anti-social Behaviour, Crime and Policing Act 2014 (Commencement No. 5) Order 2014 No. 2014/2125 (C.96). - Enabling power: Anti-social Behaviour, Crime and Policing Act 2014, s. 185 (1). Bringing into operation various provisions of the 2014 Act on 01.09.2014. - Issued: 14.08.2014. Made: 07.08.2014. Effect: None. Territorial extent & classification: E/W/S/NI. General. - 8p.: 30 cm. - 978-0-11-111977-8 £4.25

The Anti-social Behaviour, Crime and Policing Act 2014 (Commencement No. 7, Saving and Transitional Provisions) (Amendment) Order 2014 No. 2014/2754 (C.121). - Enabling power: Anti-social Behaviour, Crime and Policing Act 2014, s. 185 (1) (7). - Issued: 20.10.2014. Made: 14.10.2014. Coming into force: 20.10.2014. Effect: S.I. 2014/2590 (C.113) amended. Territorial extent & classification: E/W. General. - This Statutory Instrument corrects errors in SI. 2014/2590 (C.113) which was made on 24th September 2014 and published on 29th September 2014 (ISBN 9780111121078). It is being issued free of charge to all known recipients of that Statutory Instrument. - 4p.: 30 cm. - 978-0-11-112185-6 £4.25

The Anti-social Behaviour, Crime and Policing Act 2014 (Commencement No. 7, Saving and Transitional Provisions) Order 2014 No. 2014/2590 (C.113). - Enabling power: Anti-social Behaviour, Crime and Policing Act 2014, s. 185 (1) (7). Bringing into operation various provisions of the 2014 Act on 20.10.2014, in accord. with art. 2. - Issued: 01.10.2014. Made: 24.09.2014. Effect: None. Territorial extent & classification: E/W. General. - 8p.: 30 cm. - 978-0-11-112107-8 £6.00

The Appointment of Chief Officers of Police (Overseas Police Forces) Regulations 2014 No. 2014/2376. - Enabling power: Police Reform and Social Responsibility Act 2011, ss. 42 (3B) (3C), sch. 8 paras. 2 (1B) (1C). - Issued: 11.09.2014. Made: 01.09.2014. Laid: 08.09.2014. Coming into force: 01.10.2014. Effect: None. Territorial extent & classification: E/W. General. - 8p.: 30 cm. - 978-0-11-112035-4 £6.00

The Crime and Security Act 2010 (Commencement No. 7) Order 2014 No. 2014/478 (C.23). - Enabling power: Crime and Security Act 2010, s. 59 (1). Bringing various provisions of the 2010 Act into operation on 08.03.2014, in accord. with art. 2. - Issued: 10.03.2014. Made: 04.03.2014. Effect: None. Territorial extent & classification: E/W. General. - 2p.: 30 cm. - 978-0-11-111078-2 £4.00

The Independent Police Complaints Commission (Investigation of Offences) Order 2014 No. 2014/2402. - Enabling power: Police Reform Act 2002, sch. 3 paras. 19 (6) (6A). - Issued: 15.09.2014. Made: 09.09.2014. Laid: 10.09.2014. Coming into force: 01.10.2014. Effect: None. Territorial extent & classification: E/W. - 4p.: 30 cm. - 978-0-11-112054-5 £4.25

The Police Act 1996 (Equipment) (Amendment) Regulations 2014 No. 2014/395. - Enabling power: Police Act 1996, s. 53 (1) (1A) (2A). - Issued: 03.03.2011. Made: 24.02.2014. Laid: 26.02.2014. Coming into force: 19.03.2014. Effect: S.I. 2011/300 amended. Territorial extent & classification: E/W. General. - 2p.: 30 cm. - 978-0-11-111022-5 £4.00

The Police Act 1997 (Commencement No. 12) (England and Wales) Order 2014 No. 2014/237 (C.8). - Enabling power: Police Act 1997, s. 135. Bringing into operation various provisions of the 1997 Act on 10.03.2014. - Issued: 13.02.2014. Made: 05.02.2014. Effect: None. Territorial extent & classification: E/W. General. - 4p.: 30 cm. - 978-0-11-110937-3 £3.00

The Police Act 1997 (Criminal Records) (Amendment No. 2) Regulations 2014 No. 2014/955. - Enabling power: Police Act 1997, ss. 113B (2) (b), 125. - Issued: 15.04.2014. Made: 08.04.2014. Laid: 11.04.2014. Coming into force: 06.05.2014. Effect: S.I. 2002/233 amended. Territorial extent & classification: E/W. General. - 2p.: 30 cm. - 978-0-11-111407-0 £4.25

The Police Act 1997 (Criminal Records) (Amendment No. 3) Regulations 2014 No. 2014/2122. - Enabling power: Police Act 1997, ss. 113B (2) (b), 125. - Issued: 13.08.2014. Made: 05.08.2014. Laid: 08.08.2014. Coming into force: 01.09.2014. Effect: S.I. 2002/233 amended. Territorial extent & classification: E/W. General. - 2p.: 30 cm. - 978-0-11-111971-6 £4.25

The Police Act 1997 (Criminal Records) (Amendment) Regulations 2014 No. 2014/239. - Enabling power: Police Act 1997, ss. 112 (1) (b) (2) (a) (3), 125. - Issued: 13.02.2014. Made: 05.02.2014. Laid: 13.02.2014. Coming into force: 10.03.2014. Effect: S.I. 2002/233 amended. Territorial extent & classification: E/W. General. - 4p.: 30 cm. - 978-0-11-110939-7 £4.00

The Police (Amendment) Regulations 2014 No. 2014/2372. - Enabling power: Police Act 1996, s. 50 (1) (2) (b) (c) (4). - Issued: 10.09.2014. Made: 01.09.2014. Laid: 08.09.2014. Coming into force: 01.10.2014. Effect: S.I. 2003/527 amended. Territorial extent & classification: E/W. General. - 4p.: 30 cm. - 978-0-11-112031-6 £4.25

The Police and Crime Commissioner Elections (Amendment) (No. 2) Order 2014 No. 2014/1963. - Enabling power: Police Reform and Social Responsibility Act 2011, ss. 58 (1), 154 (5). - Issued: 30.07.2014. Made: 23.07.2014. Coming into force: 24.07.2014, in accord. with art. 1. Effect: S.I. 2012/1917 amended. Territorial extent & classification: E/W. General. - Supersedes draft (ISBN 9780111117651) issued 11.07.2014. - 8p.: 30 cm. - 978-0-11-111924-2 £4.25

The Police and Crime Commissioner Elections (Amendment) Order 2014 No. 2014/921. - Enabling power: Police Reform and Social Responsibility Act 2011, ss. 58 (1) (5), 154 (5). - Issued: 10.04.2014. Made: 03.04.2014. Coming into force: In accord. with art. 1. Effect: S.I. 2012/1917 amended. Territorial extent & classification: E/W. General. - Supersedes draft SI (ISBN 9780111109960) issued 25/02/14. - 32p.: 30 cm. - 978-0-11-111384-4 £6.00

The Police and Criminal Evidence Act 1984 (Codes of Practice) (Revisions of Codes C and H) Order 2014 No. 2014/1237. - Enabling power: Police and Criminal Evidence Act 1984, s. 67 (5). - Issued: 20.05.2014. Made: 14.05.2014. Laid: 14.05.2014. Coming into force: 02.06.2014. Effect: None. Territorial extent & classification: E/W. General. - 2p.: 30 cm. - 978-0-11-111490-2 £4.25

The Police and Criminal Evidence Act 1984 (Remote Reviews of Detention) Regulations 2014 No. 2014/3279. - Enabling power: Police and Criminal Evidence Act 1984, s. 45A. - Issued: 17.12.2014. Made: 11.12.2014. Laid: 15.12.2014. Coming into force: 08.01.2015. Effect: None. Territorial extent & classification: E/W. General. - 2p.: 30 cm. - 978-0-11-112540-3 £4.25

The Police (Complaints and Misconduct) (Amendment) Regulations 2014 No. 2014/2406. - Enabling power: Police Reform Act 2002, s. 29 (1), sch. 3, para. 28A (4). - Issued: 15.09.2014. Made: 09.09.2014. Laid: 10.09.2014. Coming into force: 01.10.2014. Effect: S.I. 2012/1204 amended. Territorial extent & classification: E/W. General. - 4p.: 30 cm. - 978-0-11-112058-3 £4.25

The Police (Conduct) (Amendment) Regulations 2014 No. 2014/3347. - Enabling power: Police Act 1996, ss. 50, 51. - Issued: 24.12.2014. Made: 16.12.2014. Laid: 22.12.2014. Coming into force: 12.01.2015. Effect: S.I. 2012/2632 amended. Territorial extent & classification: E/W. General. - 4p.: 30 cm. - 978-0-11-112636-3 £4.25

The Police Pensions (Amendment) (No. 2) Regulations 2014 No. 2014/381. - Enabling power: Police Pensions Act 1976, s. 1. - Issued: 27.20.2014. Made: 13.02.2014. Laid: 25.02.2014. Coming into force: 01.04.2014. Effect: S.I. 1987/257; 2006/3415 amended. Territorial extent & classification: E/W. General. - 4p.: 30 cm. - 978-0-11-111011-9 £4.00

The Police Pensions (Amendment) Regulations 2014 No. 2014/79. - Enabling power: Police Pensions Act 1976, ss. 1 to 7. - Issued: 24.01.2014. Made: 15.01.2014. Laid: 23.01.2014. Coming into force: 13.03.2014. Effect: S.I. 1987/257; 2006/932 amended. Territorial extent & classification: E/W. General. - 8p.: 30 cm. - 978-0-11-110852-9 £4.00

The Police (Performance) (Amendment) Regulations 2014 No. 2014/2403. - Enabling power: Police Act 1996, ss. 50, 51, 84. - Issued: 15.09.2014. Made: 09.09.2014. Laid: 10.09.2014. Coming into force: 01.10.2014. Effect: S.I. 2012/2631 amended. Territorial extent & classification: E/W. General. - 4p.: 30 cm. - 978-0-11-112055-2 £4.25

The Police (Promotion) (Amendment) Regulations 2014 No. 2014/2373. - Enabling power: Police Act 1996, s. 50 (2) (b). - Issued: 10.09.2014. Made: 01.09.2014. Laid: 08.09.2014. Coming into force: 01.10.2014. Effect: S.I. 1996/1685 amended. Territorial extent & classification: E/W. General. - 2p.: 30 cm. - 978-0-11-112032-3 £4.25

Police, Northern Ireland

The Anti-social Behaviour, Crime and Policing Act 2014 (Commencement No. 5) Order 2014 No. 2014/2125 (C.96). - Enabling power: Anti-social Behaviour, Crime and Policing Act 2014, s. 185 (1). Bringing into operation various provisions of the 2014 Act on 01.09.2014. - Issued: 14.08.2014. Made: 07.08.2014. Effect: None. Territorial extent & classification: E/W/S/NI. General. - 8p.: 30 cm. - 978-0-11-111977-8 £4.25

The Protection of Freedoms Act 2012 (Commencement No. 10) Order 2014 No. 2014/3315 (C.153). - Enabling power: Protection of Freedoms Act 2012, s. 120 (1). Bringing into operation various provisions of the 2012 Act on 16.12.2014, in accord. with art. 2. - Issued: 22.12.2014. Made: 15.12.2014. Effect: None. Territorial extent & classification: E/W/S/NI. General. - 8p.: 30 cm. - 978-0-11-112597-7 £4.25

Political parties

The Political Donations and Regulated Transactions (Anonymous Electors) Regulations 2014 No. 2014/1806. - Enabling power: Political Parties, Elections and Referendums Act 2000, s. 65 (2A), sch. 6, paras 2 (3B) (3C), 3 (2) (3), sch 6A, para. 2 (3), 3 (2), sch. 7, para. 10 (4A), sch. 11, para. 10 (4), sch. 15, 10 (4). - Issued: 16.07.2014. Made: 09.07.2014. Laid: 14.07.2014. Coming into force: 15.09.2014. Effect: S.I. 2008/2869 revoked. Territorial extent & classification: E/W/S/NI. General. - 4p.: 30 cm. - 978-0-11-111797-2 £4.25

Political parties, Northern Ireland

The Electoral Administration Act 2006 (Commencement No. 2) (Northern Ireland) Order 2014 No. 2014/1809 (C.83). - Enabling power: Electoral Administration Act 2006, ss. 77 (2) (4). Bringing into operation various provisions of the 2006 Act, so far as they extend to Northern Ireland, on 15.09.2014, in accord. with art. 2. - Issued: 17.07.2014. Made: 09.07.2014. Effect: None. Territorial extent & classification: NI. General. - 4p.: 30 cm. - 978-0-11-111807-8 £4.25

Presumption of death

The Presumption of Death Act 2013 (Commencement and Transitional and Saving Provision) Order 2014 No. 2014/1810 (C.79). - Enabling power: Presumption of Death Act 2013, s. 22 (2) to (4). Bringing into operation various provisions of this Act on 01.10.2014, in accord. with art. 2. - Issued: 15.07.2014. Made: 08.07.2014. Effect: None. Territorial extent & classification: E/W/S/NI. General. - 2p.: 30 cm. - 978-0-11-111782-8 £4.25

Prevention and suppression of terrorism

The Anti-social Behaviour, Crime and Policing Act 2014 (Commencement No. 2, Transitional and Transitory Provisions) Order 2014 No. 2014/949 (C.43). - Enabling power: Anti-social Behaviour, Crime and Policing Act 2014, s. 185 (1) (7). Bringing into operation various provisions of the 2014 Act on 13.05.2014, 01.06.2014, 16.06.2014, 14.07.2014, in accord. with arts. 2 to 6. - Issued: 14.04.2014. Made: 08.04.2014. Effect: None. Territorial extent & classification: E/W/S/NI. General. - 8p.: 30 cm. - 978-0-11-111401-8 £6.00

The Proscribed Organisations (Name Changes) (No. 2) Order 2014 No. 2014/2210. - Enabling power: Terrorism Act 2000, s. 3 (6). - Issued: 26.08.2014. Made: 19.08.2014. Laid: 19.08.2014. Coming into force: 20.08.2014. Effect: None. Territorial extent & classification: E/W/S/NI. General. - 2p.: 30 cm. - 978-0-11-111993-8 £4.25

The Proscribed Organisations (Name Changes) Order 2014 No. 2014/1612. - Enabling power: Terrorism Act 2000, s. 3 (6). - Issued: 27.06.2014. Made: 07.06.2014. Laid: 26.06.2014. Coming into force: 27.06.2014. Effect: None. Territorial extent & classification: E/W/S/NI. General. - 2p.: 30 cm. - 978-0-11-111688-3 £4.25

The Protection of Freedoms Act 2012 (Guidance on the Making of Renewing of National Security Determinations) Order 2014 No. 2014/198. - Enabling power: Protection of Freedoms Act 2012, s. 22 (6). - Issued: 07.02.2014. Made: 03.02.2014. Coming into force: 04.02.2014. Effect: None. Territorial extent & classification: E/W/S/NI. General. - 2p.: 30 cm. - 978-0-11-110917-5 £4.00

The Terrorism Act 2000 (Code of Practice for Examining Officers and Review Officers) Order 2014 No. 2014/1838. - Enabling power: Terrorism Act 2000, s. 123 (1) (b), sch. 14, para. 7 (3) (4). - Issued: 18.07.2014. Made: 09.07.2014. Coming into force: 31.07.2014. Effect: Bringing the 'Code of Practice for Examining Officers and Review Officers under Schedule 7 to the Terrorism Act 2000' into operation on 31.07.2014. Territorial extent & classification: E/W/S/NI. General. - Supersedes draft S.I. (ISBN 9780111116463) issued 17.06.2014. - 4p.: 30 cm. - 978-0-11-111815-3 £4.25

The Terrorism Act 2000 (Proscribed Organisations) (Amendment) (No. 2) Order 2014 No. 2014/1624. - Enabling power: Terrorism Act 2000, s. 3 (3) (a). - Issued: 30.06.2014. Made: 19.06.2014. Coming into force: 20.06.2014. Effect: 2011 c.11 amended. Territorial extent & classification: E/W/S/NI. General - Supersedes draft S.I. (ISBN 9780111116616) issued 19.06.2014. - 2p.: 30 cm. - 978-0-11-111698-2 £4.25

The Terrorism Act 2000 (Proscribed Organisations) (Amendment) (No. 3) Order 2014 No. 2014/3189. - Enabling power: Terrorism Act 2000, s. 3 (3) (a). - Issued: 05.12.2014. Made: 27.11.2014. Coming into force: 28.11.2014. Effect: 2011 c.11 amended. Territorial extent & classification: E/W/S/NI. General. - Supersedes draft S.I. (ISBN 9780111123737) issued 26.11.2014. - 2p.: 30 cm. - 978-0-11-112439-0 £4.25

The Terrorism Act 2000 (Proscribed Organisations) (Amendment) Order 2014 No. 2014/927. - Enabling power: Terrorism Act 2000, s. 3 (3) (a). - Issued: 11.04.2014. Made: 03.04.2014. Coming into force: 04.04.2014. Effect: 2000 c.11 amended. Territorial extent & classification: E/W/S/NI. General. - Supersedes draft SI (ISBN 9780111112960) issued 02/04/14. - 2p.: 30 cm. - 978-0-11-111385-1 £4.25

Prisons, England and Wales

The Closure of Prisons (No. 2) Order 2014 No. 2014/2340. - Enabling power: Prison Act 1952, s. 37 (1). - Issued: 09.09.2014. Made: 28.08.2014. Laid: 03.09.2014. Coming into force: 28.09.2014. Effect: None. Territorial extent & classification: E/W. General. - 2p.: 30 cm. - 978-0-11-112014-9 £4.25

The Closure of Prisons Order 2014 No. 2014/3. - Enabling power: Prison Act 1952, s. 37 (1) (2). - Issued: 10.01.2014. Made: 06.01.2014. Laid: 09.01.2014. Coming into force: 31.01.2014. Effect: None. Territorial extent & classification: E/W. General. - 2p.: 30 cm. - 978-0-11-110804-8 £4.00

The Parole Board (Amendment) Rules 2014 No. 2014/240. - Enabling power: Criminal Justice Act 2003, s. 239 (5). - Issued: 13.02.2014. Made: 05.02.2014. Laid: 10.02.2014. Coming into force: 01.04.2014. Effect: S.I. 2011/2947 amended. Territorial extent & classification: E/W. General. - 2p.: 30 cm. - 978-0-11-110940-3 £4.00

The Prison and Young Offender Institution (Amendment) Rules 2014 No. 2014/2169. - Enabling power: Prison Act 1952, s. 47. - Issued: 19.08.2014. Made: 12.08.2014. Laid: 13.08.2014. Coming into force: 13.08.2014, at 5.00 pm. Effect: S.I. 1997/728; 2000/3371 amended. Territorial extent & classification: E/W. General. - 8p.: 30 cm. - 978-0-11-111990-7 £6.00

Probation, England and Wales

The Offender Management Act 2007 (Approved Premises) Regulations 2014 No. 2014/1198. - Enabling power: Offender Management Act 2007, ss. 13 (2), 36 (2) (a). - Issued: 14.05.2014. Made: 06.05.2014. Laid: 09.05.2008. Coming into force: 01.06.2014. Effect: S.I. 2008/1263 revoked. Territorial extent & classification: E/W. General. - 8p.: 30 cm. - 978-0-11-111472-8 £4.25

The Offender Management Act 2007 (Dissolution of Probation Trusts) Order 2014 No. 2014/2704. - Enabling power: Offender Management Act 2007, ss. 5 (1) (c), 36 (2). - Issued: 15.10.2014. Made: 08.10.2014. Laid: 10.10.2014. Coming into force: 31.10.2014. Effect: None. Territorial extent & classification: E/W. General. - 4p.: 30 cm. - 978-0-11-112142-9 £4.25

Proceeds of crime

The Crime and Courts Act 2013 (Commencement No. 11) Order 2014 No. 2014/3098 (C.134). - Enabling power: Crime and Courts Act 2013, s. 61 (2). Bringing into operation various provisions of the 2013 Act on 22.11.2014. - Issued: 27.11.2014. Made: 20.11.2014. Effect: None. Territorial extent & classification: E/W/S/NI. General. - 8p.: 30 cm. - 978-0-11-112374-4 £4.25

The Driving Standards Agency and the Vehicle and Operator Services Agency (Merger) (Consequential Amendments) Order 2014 No. 2014/467. - Enabling power: Regulation of Investigatory Powers Act 2000, ss. 30 (1) (3) (6), 46 (4), 78 (5) & Proceeds of Crime Act 2002, ss. 453 (1) (2), 459 (1) (2). - Issued: 07.03.2014. Made: 03.03.2014. Laid: 06.03.2014. Coming into force: 01.04.2014. Effect: S.I. 2007/934; 2009/975; 2010/521 amended. Territorial extent & classification: E/W/S/NI. General. - Incorrect price printed on document. - 8p.: 30 cm. - 978-0-11-111077-5 £4.00

The Policing and Crime Act 2009 (Commencement No. 9) Order 2014 No. 2014/3101 (C.135). - Enabling power: Policing and Crime Act 2009, s. 116 (1) (7). Bringing into operation various provisions of the 2009 Act on 22.11.2014. - Issued: 28.11.2014. Made: 20.11.2014. Effect: None. Territorial extent & classification: E/W/S/NI. General. - 8p.: 30 cm. - 978-0-11-112379-9 £4.25

Proceeds of crime, England and Wales

The Proceeds of Crime Act 2002 (External Investigations) Order 2014 No. 2014/1893. - Enabling power: Proceeds of Crime Act 2002, ss. 445, 459 (2). - Issued: 23.07.2014. Made: 16.07.2014. Laid: 23.07.2014. Coming into force: 13.08.2014. Effect: None. Territorial extent & classification: E/W/S. General. - 20p.: 30 cm. - 978-0-11-111855-9 £6.00

The Proceeds of Crime (Disclosure Orders: Confiscation Investigations) (Specified Person) Order 2014 No. 2014/3207. - Enabling power: Proceeds of Crime Act 2002, s. 357 (9). - Issued: 10.12.2014. Made: 03.12.2014. Laid: 05.12.2014. Coming into force: 01.01.2015. Effect: None. Territorial extent & classification: E/W/NI. General. - 2p.: 30 cm. - 978-0-11-112458-1 £4.25

Proceeds of crime, Northern Ireland

The Proceeds of Crime Act 2002 (External Investigations) Order 2014 No. 2014/1893. - Enabling power: Proceeds of Crime Act 2002, ss. 445, 459 (2). - Issued: 23.07.2014. Made: 16.07.2014. Laid: 23.07.2014. Coming into force: 13.08.2014. Effect: None. Territorial extent & classification: E/W/S. General. - 20p.: 30 cm. - 978-0-11-111855-9 £6.00

The Proceeds of Crime (Disclosure Orders: Confiscation Investigations) (Specified Person) Order 2014 No. 2014/3207. - Enabling power: Proceeds of Crime Act 2002, s. 357 (9). - Issued: 10.12.2014. Made: 03.12.2014. Laid: 05.12.2014. Coming into force: 01.01.2015. Effect: None. Territorial extent & classification: E/W/NI. General. - 2p.: 30 cm. - 978-0-11-112458-1 £4.25

Protection of vulnerable adults, England and Wales

The Protection of Freedoms Act 2012 (Commencement No. 3) (Amendment) Order 2014 No. 2014/831 (C.35). - Enabling power: Protection of Freedoms Act 2012, ss. 116 (1). Bringing into operation various provisions of the 2012 Act on 31.12.2014. - Issued: 01.04.2014. Made: 24.03.2014. Coming into force: 31.03.2014. Effect: S.I. 2012/2234 C.89 amended. Territorial extent & classification: E/W/NI. General. - 2p.: 30 cm. - 978-0-11-111286-1 £4.00

Protection of vulnerable adults, Northern Ireland

The Protection of Freedoms Act 2012 (Commencement No. 3) (Amendment) Order 2014 No. 2014/831 (C.35). - Enabling power: Protection of Freedoms Act 2012, ss. 116 (1). Bringing into operation various provisions of the 2012 Act on 31.12.2014. - Issued: 01.04.2014. Made: 24.03.2014. Coming into force: 31.03.2014. Effect: S.I. 2012/2234 C.89 amended. Territorial extent & classification: E/W/NI. General. - 2p.: 30 cm. - 978-0-11-111286-1 £4.00

Protection of wrecks, England

The Protection of Wrecks (Designation) (England) Order 2014 No. 2014/753. - Enabling power: Protection of Wrecks Act 1973, s. 1 (1) (2) (4). - Issued: 25.03.2014. Made: 18.03.2014. Laid: 20.03.2014. Coming into force: 21.03.2014. Effect: None. Territorial extent & classification: E. General. - 2p.: 30 cm. - 978-0-11-111248-9 £4.00

Provision of services

The Provision of Services (Amendment) Regulations 2014 No. 2014/1937. - Enabling power: European Communities Act 1972, s. 2 (2). - Issued: 28.07.2014. Made: 21.07.2014. Laid: 22.07.2014. Coming into force: 06.04.2016. Effect: S.I. 2009/2999 amended. Territorial extent & classification: E/W/S/NI. General. - EC note: These Regulations amend S.I. 2009/2999 which implemented Directive 2006/123/EC on services in the internal market. - 2p.: 30 cm. - 978-0-11-111908-2 £4.25

Public audit, Wales

The Public Audit (Wales) Act 2013 (Approved European Body of Accountants) Order 2014 No. 2014/890 (W.88). - Enabling power: Public Audit (Wales) Act 2013, ss. 19 (9), 30. - Issued: 15.04.2014. Made: 01.04.2014. Laid before the National Assembly for Wales: 02.04.2014. Coming into force: 23.04.2014. Effect: None. Territorial extent & classification: W. General. - In English and Welsh. Welsh title: Gorchymyn Deddf Archwilio Cyhoeddus (Cymru) 2013 (Corff Cyfrifwyr Ewropeaidd Cymeradwy) 2014. - 4p.: 30 cm. - 978-0-348-10933-7 £4.25

The Public Audit (Wales) Act 2013 (Consequential Amendments) Order 2014 No. 2014/77 (W.8). - Enabling power: Public Audit (Wales) Act 2013, ss. 30 (2), 33 (2). - Issued: 23.01.2014. Made: 14.01.2014. Coming into force: 01.04.2014. Effect: 1998 c.38; 2004 c.23 amended. Territorial extent & classification: W. General. - In English and Welsh. Welsh title: Gorchymyn Deddf Archwilio Cyhoeddus (Cymru) 2013 (Diwygiadau Canlyniadol) 2014. - 4p.: 30 cm. - 978-0-348-10854-5 £4.00

Public bodies

The Public Bodies (Abolition of Food from Britain) Order 2014 No. 2014/1924. - Enabling power: Public Bodies Act 2011, ss. 1 (1), 6 (1) (5), 24 (1), 35 (2). - Issued: 25.07.2014. Made: 17.07.2014. Coming into force: 18.07.2014 & 19.07.2014, in accord. with art. 1. Effect: 1967 c.13, 22; 1975 c.24, 25; 1986 c.49; 2000 c.36; 2002 asp 11; 2006 c.16; 2011 c.24 partially repealed & 1983 c.3 repealed & S.I. 1991/1997; 1993/1572; 1999/1319, 1747; 2001/1294; 2002/794; 2002/2812 (C.86), 2843; 2003/1326; 2008/948 partially revoked & S.I. 1983/366 (C.13); 1986/1596 (C.57) 1998/879 (C.19) revoked. Territorial extent & classification: E/W/S/NI. General. - Supersedes draft S.I. (ISBN 9780111114599) issued 09.05.2014. - 8p.: 30 cm. - 978-0-11-111897-9 £4.25

The Public Bodies (Abolition of the Committee on Agricultural Valuation) Order 2014 No. 2014/1068. - Enabling power: Public Bodies Act 2011, ss. 1 (1), 6 (1) (5), 35 (2). - Issued: 29.04.2014. Made: 22.04.2014. Coming into force: In accord. with art. 1. Effect: 1986 c.5; 2000 c.36; 2011 c.24 partially repealed. Territorial extent & classification: E/W. General. - Supersedes draft S.I. 2014 (ISBN 9780111109359) issued 14.02.2014. - 4p.: 30 cm. - 978-0-11-111426-1 £4.00

The Public Bodies (Abolition of the National Consumer Council and Transfer of the Office of Fair Trading's Functions in relation to Estate Agents etc) Order 2014 No. 2014/631. - Enabling power: Public Bodies Act 2011, ss. 1 (1) (2), 5 (1) (b), 6 (1) (2) (5), 35 (2). - Issued: 19.03.2014. Made: 13.03.2014. Coming into force: In accord. with art. 1 (2) to (6). Effect: 18 UK Acts, 6 asps & 12 SIs amended. Territorial extent & classification: E/W/S/NI. General. - Supersedes draft S.I. (ISBN 9780111106723) issued 10.12.2013; Partially revoked by SI 2015/699 (ISBN 9780111134436). - 48p.: 30 cm. - 978-0-11-111221-2 £9.75

The Public Bodies (Marine Management Organisation) (Fees) Order 2014 No. 2014/2555. - Enabling power: Public Bodies Act 2011, ss. 4 (1) (3) (b), 6 (1). - Issued: 26.09.2014. Made: 14.09.2014. Coming into force: in accord. with art. 1. Effect: None. Territorial extent & classification: E/W/S/NI. General. - Supersedes draft S.I. (ISBN 9780111114797) issued on 16.05.2014. - 8p.: 30 cm. - 978-0-11-112100-9 £6.00

The Public Bodies (Merger of the Director of Public Prosecutions and the Director of Revenue and Customs Prosecutions) Order 2014 No. 2014/834. - Enabling power: Public Bodies Act 2011, ss. 2 (1), 6 (1) (2), 23 (1) (2) (5) (6), 24 (1), 35 (2). - Issued: 02.04.2014. Made: 26.03.2014. Coming into force: 27.03.2014 in accord. with art. 1. Effect: 29 Acts amended & 19 SIs amended. Territorial extent & classification: E/W/S/NI. General. - Supersedes draft SI (ISBN 9780111107041) issued 02/04/14. - 20p.: 30 cm. - 978-0-11-111289-2 £5.75

Public health, England

The Care Quality Commission (Reviews and Performance Assessments) Regulations 2014 No. 2014/1788. - Enabling power: Health and Social Care Act 2008, ss. 46 (1) (2), 161 (4). - Issued: 14.07.2014. Made: 07.07.2014. Laid: 11.07.2014. Coming into force: 01.10.2014. Effect: None. Territorial extent & classification: E. General. - 4p.: 30 cm. - 978-0-11-111771-2 £4.25

The Control of Noise (Code of Practice on Noise from Audible Intruder Alarms) (Revocation) (England) Order 2014 No. 2014/2123. - Enabling power: Control of Pollution Act 1974, s. 71 (3). - Issued: 20.08.2014. Made: 29.07.2014. Laid: 07.08.2014. Coming into force: 01.10.2014. Effect: S.I. 1981/1829 revoked. Territorial extent & classification: E. General. - 2p.: 30 cm. - 978-0-11-111972-3 £4.25

The Health and Social Care Act 2008 (Regulated Activities) Regulations 2014 No. 2014/2936. - Enabling power: Health and Social Care Act 2008, ss. 8, 20 (1) to (5A), 35, 86 (2) (4), 87 (1) (2), 161 (3) (4). - Issued: 13.11.2014. Made: 06.11.2014. Coming into force: In accord. with reg. 1. Effect: None. Territorial extent & classification: E. General. - 32p.: 30 cm. - 978-0-11-112316-4 £10.00

The Healthy Start Vitamins (Charging) Regulations 2014 No. 2014/3099. - Enabling power: National Health Service Act 2006, ss. 187, 272 (7) (8). - Issued: 26.11.2014. Made: 18.11.2014. Laid: 26.11.2014. Coming into force: 05.01.2015. Effect: S.I. 1976/516 shall cease to apply to England. Territorial extent & classification: E. General. - 4p.: 30 cm. - 978-0-11-112375-1 £4.25

The HIV Testing Kits and Services (Revocation) (England) Regulations 2014 No. 2014/451. - Enabling power: Health and Medicines Act 1988, s. 23 (1). - Issued: 06.03.2014. Made: 26.02.2014. Laid: 06.03.2014. Coming into force: 06.04.2014. Effect: S.I. 1992/460 revoked in relation to England. Territorial extent & classification: E. General. - 2p.: 30 cm. - 978-0-11-111061-4 £4.00

Public health, England and Wales

The Care Act 2014 (Commencement No.1) Order 2014 No. 2014/1714 (C.73). - Enabling power: Care Act 2014, s. 127 (1) (5). Bringing into operation various provisions of the 2014 Act on 07.07.2014, 15.07.2014, 01.10.2014, in accord. with arts 2, 3, 4. - Issued: 08.07.2014. Made: 02.07.2014. Effect: None. Territorial extent & classification: E/W. General. - 4p.: 30 cm. - 978-0-11-111750-7 £4.25

The Care Act 2014 (Commencement No.2) Order 2014 No. 2014/2473 (C.111). - Enabling power: Care Act 2014, ss. 124 (1) (2), 127 (1) (5). Bringing into operation various provisions of the 2014 Act on 01.10.2014, 01.01.2015 in accord. with arts 2, 3, 4, 5, 6. - Issued: 22.09.2014. Made: 12.09.2014. Effect: None. Territorial extent & classification: E/W. General. - 8p.: 30 cm. - 978-0-11-112089-7 £6.00

Public health, Wales

The Animal By-Products (Enforcement) (Wales) Regulations 2014 No. 2014/517 (W.60). - Enabling power: European Communities Act 1972, s. 2 (2), sch. 2, para. 1A. - Issued: 20.03.2014. Made: 05.03.2014. Laid before the National Assembly for Wales: 07.03.2014. Coming into force: 28.03.2014. Effect: S.I. 2006/179 (W.30), 180 (W.31), 3309 (W.299), 3310 (W.300); 2007/842 (W.74), 3544; W.S.I. 2008/3154 (W.282); S.I. 2010/675; W.S.I. 2010/900 (W.93) amended & S.I. 1995/614 revoked in relation to Wales & S.I. 2002/1472 (W.146); 2003/1849 (W.199); 2003/2754 (W.265); W.S.I. 2011/2377 (W.250) revoked. Territorial extent & classification: W. General. - EC note: These Regulations continue to enforce, in Wales, Regulation 1069/2009 laying down health rules as regards animal by-products and derived products not intended for human consumption and repealing Regulation 1774/2002. They also continue to enforce, in Wales, Regulation 142/2011 implementing Regulation 1069/2009 and implementing Council Directive 97/78/EC as regards certain samples and items exempt from veterinary checks at the border. - In English and Welsh. Welsh title: Rheoliadau Sgil-gynhyrchion Anifeiliaid (Gorfodi) (Cymru) 2014. - 40p.: 30 cm. - 978-0-348-10916-0 £9.75

The HIV Testing Kits and Services Regulations 1992 (Revocation) (Wales) Regulations 2014 No. 2014/256 (W.34). - Enabling power: Health and Medicines Act 1988, s. 23 (1) to (3). - Issued: 18.02.2014. Made: 10.02.2014. Laid before the National Assembly for Wales: 11.02.2014. Coming into force: 06.04.2014. Effect: S.I. 1992/460 revoked in relation to Wales. Territorial extent & classification: W. General. - In English and Welsh. Welsh title: Rheoliadau Rheoliadau Citiau a Gwasanaethau Profi am HIV 1992 (Dirymu) (Cymru) 2014. - 4p.: 30 cm. - 978-0-348-10887-3 £4.00

Public passenger transport

The Public Service Vehicles (Operators' Licences) (Fees) (Amendment) Regulations 2014 No. 2014/2118. - Enabling power: Public Passenger Vehicles Act 1981, ss. 52 (1), 60. - Issued: 19.08.2014. Made: 06.08.2014. Laid: 19.08.2014. Coming into force: 01.10.2014. Effect: S.I. 1995/2909 amended. Territorial extent & classification: E/W/S. General. - 2p.: 30 cm. - 978-0-11-111982-2 £4.25

The Public Service Vehicles (Traffic Commissioners: Publication and Inquiries) (Amendment) Regulations 2014 No. 2014/3142. - Enabling power: Public Passenger Vehicles Act 1981, ss. 52 (1), 60 (1) (2). - Issued: 03.12.2014. Made: 26.11.2014. Laid: 02.12.2014. Coming into force: 30.12.2014. Effect: S.I. 1986/1629 amended. Territorial extent & classification: E/W/S. General. - 2p.: 30 cm. - 978-0-11-112420-8 £4.25

Public procurement

The Single Source Contract Regulations 2014 No. 2014/3337. - Enabling power: Defence Reform Act 2014, ss. 14 (2) (b) (c) (6) (8), 15, 16 (1), 17 (1) (2), 18 (2) (c) (3) (4), 21, 23 (1) (4) (5), 24 (1) to (3) (4) (a), 25 (1) (2) (4) (6), 27 (1) (3), 28 (3) (c) (d), (4) (c) (d) (5), 29, 30 (2) (a) (3) to (5), 31 (3) (a) (b) (5), 32 (5), 33 (1) (6), 35 (1), 38, 41, 42 (1) (2), 43 (2), sch. 5 para. 1 (1) (c). - Issued: 23.12.2014. Made: 17.12.2014. Coming into force: In accord. with reg. 1. Effect: None. Territorial extent & classification: E/W/S/NI. General. - Supersedes draft SI (ISBN 9780111122440) issued 31/10/14- 56p.: 30 cm. - 978-0-11-112626-4 £10.00

Public records

The Constitutional Reform and Governance Act 2010 (Commencement No. 9)Order 2014 No. 2014/3245 (C.146). - Enabling power: Constitutional Reform and Governance Act 2010, s. 52 (2). Bringing into operation various provisions of the 2010 Act on 01.01.2015, in accord. with art. 2. - Issued: 15.12.2014. Made: 08.12.2014. Effect: None. Territorial extent & classification: E/W/S/NI. General. - 4p.: 30 cm. - 978-0-11-112507-6 £4.25

The Public Records (Transfer to the Public Record Office) (Transitional and Saving Provisions) Order 2014 No. 2014/3249. - Enabling power: Constitutional Reform and Governance Act 2010, s. 45 (2) (3). - Issued: 15.12.2014. Made: 08.12.2014. Laid: 10.12.2014. Coming into force: 01.01.2015. Effect: None. Territorial extent & classification: E/W. General. - 4p.: 30 cm. - 978-0-11-112511-3 £4.25

Public service pensions

The Pensions Act 2014 (Commencement No. 1) Order 2014 No. 2014/1965 (C.92). - Enabling power: Pensions Act 2011, s. 56 (6). Bringing into operation various provisions of the 2014 Act on 23.07.2014 in accord. with art 2. - Issued: 31.07.2014. Made: 22.07.2014. Effect: None. Territorial extent & classification: E/W/S. General. - 2p.: 30 cm. - 978-0-11-111926-6 £4.25

The Public Service (Civil Servants and Others) Pensions Regulations 2014 No. 2014/1964. - Enabling power: Public Service Pensions Act 2013, ss. 1 (1) (2) (a), 2 (1), 3 (1) (2) (3) (a) (c), 4 (3) (6), 5 (2) (c) (5A), 8 (1) (a), 12 (6) (7), 18 (5) (6) (7), 25 (3), sch. 2, para. 1, sch. 3, sch 7, paras 1 (2) (ii), 5 (1). - Issued: 30.07.2014. Made: 23.07.2014. Laid: 24.07.2014. Coming into force: In accord with reg. 1 (2) (3). Effect: None. Territorial extent & classification: E/W/S/NI. General. - With correction slips dated August 2014 and December 2014. - 120p.: 30 cm. - 978-0-11-111925-9 £19.00

The Public Service Pensions Act 2013 (Commencement No. 3) Order 2014 No. 2014/433 (C.19). - Enabling power: Public Service Pensions Act 2013, s. 41 (2) (3). Bringing into operation various provisions of the 2013 Act on 28.02.2014. - Issued: 05.03.2014. Made: 27.02.2014. Effect: None. Territorial extent & classification: E/W/S/NI. General. - 4p.: 30 cm. - 978-0-11-111044-7 £4.00

The Public Service Pensions Act 2013 (Commencement No. 4) Order 2014 No. 2014/839 (C.36). - Enabling power: Public Service Pensions Act 2013, s. 41 (2) (3). Bringing into operation various provisions of the 2013 Act on 01.04.2014. - Issued: 02.04.2014. Made: 26.03.2014. Effect: None. Territorial extent & classification: E/W/S/NI. General. - 8p.: 30 cm. - 978-0-11-111294-6 £4.00

The Public Service Pensions Act 2013 (Commencement No. 5) Order 2014 No. 2014/1912 (C.86). - Enabling power: Public Service Pensions Act 2013, s. 41 (2) (3). Bringing into operation various provisions of the 2013 Act on 31.07.2014, 01.04.2015. - Issued: 24.07.2014. Made: 17.07.2014. Effect: None. Territorial extent & classification: E/W/S/NI. General. - 4p.: 30 cm. - 978-0-11-111881-8 £4.25

The Public Service Pensions (Employer Cost Cap) Regulations 2014 No. 2014/575. - Enabling power: Public Service Pensions Act 2013, s. 12 (5). - Issued: 17.03.2014. Made: 10.03.2014. Laid: 11.03.2014. Coming into force: 01.04.2014. Effect: None. Territorial extent & classification: E/W/S/NI. General. - 2p.: 30 cm. - 978-0-11-111174-1 £4.00

Public service pensions, England

The Firefighters' Pension Scheme (England) Regulations 2014 No. 2014/2848. - Enabling power: Public Service Pensions Act 2013, ss. 1 (1) (2) (f), 2 (1), 3 (1) (2) (3) (a) (c), 4 (1) (5) (6), 8(1) (a), 18 (5) (5A) (6) (7), sch. 2, 3, para. 6(a). - Issued: 29.10.2014. Made: 23.10.2014. Laid: 28.10.2014. Coming into force: 01.04.2015. Effect: None. Territorial extent & classification: E. General. - 100p.: 30 cm. - 978-0-11-112230-3 £16.50

Public service pensions, England and Wales

The Local Government Pension Scheme (Miscellaneous Amendments) Regulations 2014 No. 2014/44. - Enabling power: Superannuation Act 1972, ss. 7, 12. - Issued: 20.01.2014. Made: 14.01.2014. Laid: 17.01.2014. Coming into force: 10.02.2014. Effect: S.I. 2007/1166; 2008/239; 2013/2356 amended. Territorial extent & classification: E/W. General. - 8p.: 30 cm. - 978-0-11-110841-3 £5.75

The Local Government Pension Scheme (Offender Management) Regulations 2014 No. 2014/1146. - Enabling power: Public Service Pensions Act 2013, ss. 1,3, sch. 3. - Issued: 20.05.2014. Made: 01.05.2014. Laid: 06.05.2014. Coming into force: 01.06.2014. Effect: S.I. 2013/2356 amended. Territorial extent & classification: E/W. General. - 8p.: 30 cm. - 978-0-11-111458-2 £6.00

The Local Government Pension Scheme (Transitional Provisions, Savings and Amendment) Regulations 2014 No. 2014/525. - Enabling power: Superannuation Act 1972, ss. 7, 12, sch. 3. - Issued: 13.03.2014. Made: 05.03.2014. Laid: 10.03.2014. Coming into force: 01.04.2014. Effect: S.I. 1997/1612 revoked with savings; S.I. 1995/1019; 2007/1166; 2008/239, 1083, 2425, 2989, 3245; 2009/447, 1025, 3150; 2010/528, 2090; 2011/561; 2012/1989 revoked. Territorial extent & classification: E/W. General. - 24p.: 30 cm. - 978-0-11-111123-9 £5.75

The Teachers' Pension Scheme (Amendment) Regulations 2014 No. 2014/2652. - Enabling power: Public Service Pensions Act 2013, ss. 1 (1) (2) (d) (3) (4), 2, 3 (1) (2) (3) (a) (c) (4), 4 (1) (3), 5 (1), 7 (1), 8 (1) (a) (2) (a), 11 (1) (a) (2), 12 (1), (2), (3), (6), (7), 18 (1) (2) (4) (b) (5) to (9), 37 (c), sch. 1, para. 4, sch. 2, para. 4 (a), sch. 3, sch. 5, para. 18, sch. 7, paras. 1 (2) (ii), 2 (2) (ii), 5. - Issued: 06.10.2014. Made: 29.09.2014. Laid: 03.10.2014. Coming into force: 01.04.2015. Effect: None. Territorial extent & classification: E/W. General. - 12p.: 30 cm. - 978-0-11-112119-1 £6.00

The Teachers' Pension Scheme Regulations 2014 No. 2014/512. - Enabling power: Public Service Pensions Act 2013, ss. 1 (1) (2) (d) (3) (4), 2, 3 (1) (2) (3) (a) (c) (4), 4 (1) (3), 5 (1) (2) (4), 7 (1) (4), 8 (1) (a) (2) (a), 14, 18 (1) (2) (4) (b) (5) to (9), 37 (c), sch. 1, para. 4, sch. 2, para. 4 (a), sch. 3, sch. 5, para. 18, sch. 6, para. 6, sch. 7, paras. 1 (2) (ii), 2 (2) (ii), 5. - Issued: 12.03.2014. Made: 05.03.2014. Laid: 07.03.2014. Coming into force: In accord, with with reg. 1 (2). Effect: None. Territorial extent & classification: E/W. General. - 120p.: 30 cm. - 978-0-11-111116-1 £18.50

Rating and valuation, England

The Council Tax and Non-Domestic Rating (Demand Notices) (England) (Amendment) Regulations 2014 No. 2014/404. - Enabling power: Local Government Finance Act 1988, s. 143 (1), sch. 9, paras 1, 2 (2) (ga). - Issued: 03.03.2014. Made: 24.02.2014. Laid: 03.03.2014. Coming into force: 01.04.2014. Effect: S.I. 2003/2613 amended. Territorial extent & classification: E. General. - 12p.: 30 cm. - 978-0-11-111024-9 £5.75

The Local Government Finance Act 1988 (Non-Domestic Rating Multipliers) (England) Order 2014 No. 2014/2. - Enabling power: Local Government Finance Act 1988, sch. 7, para. 5 (3). - Issued: 14.02.2014. Made: 06.01.2014. Laid: 07.01.2014. Coming into force: In accord. with art. 1. Effect: None. Territorial extent & classification: E. General. - Approved by the House of Commons. Supersedes version laid before the House for approval (ISBN 9780111108024), published on 13.01.2014. - 2p.: 30 cm. - 978-0-11-154041-1 £4.00

The Local Government Finance Act 1988 (Non-Domestic Rating Multipliers) (England) Order 2014 No. 2014/2. - Enabling power: Local Government Finance Act 1988, s. sch. 7, para. 5 (3). - Issued: 13.01.2014. Made: 06.01.2014. Laid: 07.01.2014. Coming into force: In accord. with art. 1. Effect: None. Territorial extent & classification: E. General. - Superseded by approved version (ISBN 9780111540411) issued 14.02.2014. - 2p.: 30 cm. - 978-0-11-110802-4 £4.00

The Local Government Finance Act 2012 (Transitional Provisions) Order 2014 No. 2014/939. - Enabling power: Local Government Finance Act 2012, s. 20 (1). - Issued: 14.04.2014. Made: 08.04.2013. Coming into force: 08.04.2013. Effect: 1988 c.41 modified. Territorial extent & classification: E. General. - 2p.: 30 cm. - 978-0-11-111396-7 £4.25

The Non-Domestic Rating (Collection and Enforcement) (Amendment) (England) Regulations 2014 No. 2014/479. - Enabling power: Local Government Finance Act 1988, s. 143 (1), sch. 9, paras 1, 2 (2) (a) (b) (e). - Issued: 10.03.2014. Made: 03.03.2014. Laid: 10.03.2014. Coming into force: 01.04.2014. Effect: S.I. 1989/1058, 2260 amended. Territorial extent & classification: E. General. - 4p.: 30 cm. - 978-0-11-111079-9 £4.00

The Non-Domestic Rating (Designated Areas) Regulations 2014 No. 2014/98. - Enabling power: Local Government Finance Act 1988, sch. 7B, para. 39. - Issued: 24.01.2014. Made: 20.01.2014. Laid: 24.01.2014. Coming into force: 17.02.2014. Effect: None. Territorial extent & classification: E. General. - 8p.: 30 cm. - 978-0-11-110864-2 £5.75

The Non-Domestic Rating (Levy and Safety Net) (Amendment) Regulations 2014 No. 2014/822. - Enabling power: Local Government Finance Act 1988, s. 143 (1) (2), sch. 7B, paras. 22, 25, 37 (1) (2). - Issued: 01.04.2014. Made: 26.03.2014. Coming into force: 27.03.2014 in accord. with reg. 1. Effect: S.I. 2013/737 amended. Territorial extent & classification: E. General. - Supersedes draft SI (ISBN 9780111108819) issued 39/01/14. - 4p.: 30 cm. - 978-0-11-111280-9 £4.00

The Non-Domestic Rating (Rates Retention) (Amendment) Regulations 2014 No. 2014/96. - Enabling power: Local Government Finance Act 1988, s. 99 (3). - Issued: 24.01.2014. Made: 20.01.2014. Laid: 23.01.2014. Coming into force: 30.01.2014. Effect: S.I. 2013/452 amended. Territorial extent & classification: E. General. - 2p.: 30 cm. - 978-0-11-110863-5 £4.00

The Non-Domestic Rating (Small Business Rate Relief) (England) (Amendment) Order 2014 No. 2014/43. - Enabling power: Local Government Finance Act 1988, ss. 43 (4B) (a), 44 (9) (a), 143 (1). - Issued: 20.01.2014. Made: 14.01.2014. Laid: 20.01.2014. Coming into force: 14.02.2014. Effect: S.I. 2012/148 amended. Territorial extent & classification: E. General. - 4p.: 30 cm. - 978-0-11-110840-6 £4.00

The Rating Lists (Valuation Date) (England) Order 2014 No. 2014/2841. - Enabling power: Local Government Finance Act 1988, s. 143 (1), sch. 6, para. 2 (3) (b). - Issued: 28.10.2014. Made: 22.10.2014. Laid: 28.10.2014. Coming into force: 21.11.2014. Effect: S.I. 2008/216 revoked. Territorial extent & classification: E. General. - 2p.: 30 cm. - 978-0-11-112222-8 £4.25

Rating and valuation, Wales

The Non-Domestic Rating (Collection and Enforcement) (Local Lists) (Amendment) (Wales) Regulations 2014 No. 2014/379 (W.44). - Enabling power: Local Government Finance Act 1988, ss. 62, 143 (1) (2), sch. 9, paras 1, 2 (2) (gf) (h). - Issued: 06.03.2014. Made: 20.02.2014. Laid before the National Assembly for Wales: 24.02.2014. Coming into force: 17.03.2014. Effect: S.I. 1989/1058 amended in relation to Wales. Territorial extent & classification: W. General. - In English and Welsh: Welsh title: Rheoliadau Ardrethu Annomestig (Casglu a Gorfodi) (Rhestri Lleol) (Diwygio) (Cymru) 2014. - 4p.: 30 cm. - 978-0-348-10894-1 £4.00

The Non-Domestic Rating Contributions (Wales) (Amendment) Regulations 2014 No. 2014/3193 (W.323). - Enabling power: Local Government Finance Act 1988, s. 60, sch. 8, paras 4, 6. - Issued: 12.12.2014. Made: 28.11.2014. Laid before the National Assembly for Wales: 03.12.2014. Coming into force: 31.12.2014. Effect: S.I. 1992/3238 amended. Territorial extent & classification: W. General. - In English and Welsh: Welsh title: Rheoliadau Cyfraniadau Ardrethu Annomestig (Cymru) (Diwygio) 2014. - 8p.: 30 cm. - 978-0-348-11028-9 £6.00

The Non-Domestic Rating (Multiplier) (Wales) (No. 2) Order 2014 No. 2014/3492 (W.350). - Enabling power: Local Government Finance Act 1988, sch. 7, para. 5 (3). - Issued: 16.02.2015. Made: 23.12.2014. Laid before the National Assembly for Wales: 23.12.2014. Coming into force: In accord. with art. 1. Effect: None. Territorial extent & classification: W. General. - In English and Welsh: Welsh title: Gorchymyn Ardrethu Annomestig (Lluosydd) (Cymru) (Rhif 2) 2014. - 4p.: 30 cm. - 978-0-348-11045-6 £4.25

The Non-Domestic Rating (Multiplier) (Wales) Order 2014 No. 2014/124 (W.14). - Enabling power: Local Government Finance Act 1988, sch. 7, para. 5 (3). - Issued: 30.01.2014. Made: 22.01.2014. Coming into force: In accord. with art. 1. Effect: None. Territorial extent & classification: W. General. - In English and Welsh: Welsh title: Rheoliadau Cyfraniadau Ardrethu Annomestig (Cymru) (Diwygio) 2013. - 4p.: 30 cm. - 978-0-348-10860-6 £4.00

The Non-Domestic Rating (Small Business Relief) (Wales) (Amendment) Order 2014 No. 2014/372 (W.40). - Enabling power: Local Government Finance Act 1988, ss. 43 (4B) (b), 44 (9), 143 (1), 146 (6). - Issued: 06.03.2014. Made: 19.02.2014. Laid before the National Assembly for Wales: 21.02.2014. Coming into force: 14.03.2014. Effect: S.I. 2008/2770 (W.246) amended. Territorial extent & classification: W. General. - Revoked with savings by S.I. 2015/229 (W.11) (ISBN 9780348110487). - In English and Welsh: Welsh title: Gorchymyn Ardrethu Annomestig (Rhyddhad Ardrethi i Fusnesau Bach) (Cymru) (Diwygio) 2014. - 4p.: 30 cm. - 978-0-348-10893-4 £4.00

The Rating Lists (Postponement of Compilation) (Wales) Order 2014 No. 2014/1370 (W.139). - Enabling power: Local Government Finance Act 1988, s. 54A (1). - Issued: 09.06.2014. Made: 23.05.2014. Coming into force: In accord. with art. 1 (1). Effect: None. Territorial extent & classification: W. General. - In English and Welsh: Welsh title: Gorchymyn Rhestrau Ardrethu (Gohirio Gwneud Rhestrau) (Cymru) 2014. - 4p.: 30 cm. - 978-0-348-10949-8 £4.25

The Rating Lists (Valuation Date) (Wales) Order 2014 No. 2014/2917 (W.297). - Enabling power: Local Government Finance Act 1988, sch. 6, para. 2 (3) (b). - Issued: 14.11.2014. Made: 05.11.2014. Laid before the National Assembly for Wales: 07.11.2014. Coming into force: 01.12.2014. Effect: S.I. 2007/3153 (W.269) revoked. Territorial extent & classification: W. General. - In English and Welsh: Welsh title: Gorchymyn y Rhestrau Ardrethu (Dyddiad Prisio) (Cymru) 2014. - 4p.: 30 cm. - 978-0-348-11015-9 £4.25

Registration of births, deaths, marriages, etc.

The Legislative Reform (Overseas Registration of Births and Deaths) Order 2014 No. 2014/542. - Enabling power: Legislative and Regulatory Reform Act 2006, ss. 1, 2. - Issued: 12.03.2014. Made: 05.03.2014. Coming into force: 01.04.2014. Effect: 1981 c.61 amended. Territorial extent & classification: E/W/S/NI. General. - Supersedes draft S.I. (ISBN 9780111106600) issued 06.12.2013. - 2p.: 30 cm. - 978-0-11-111144-4 £4.00

The Registration of Overseas Births and Deaths Regulations 2014 No. 2014/511. - Enabling power: British Nationality Act 1981, s. 41 (1) (g) (h). - Issued: 12.03.2014. Made: 05.03.2014. Laid: 07.03.2014. Coming into force: 01.04.2014. Effect: S.I. 1982/1123; 1985/1574; 1997/1466 revoked. Territorial extent & classification: E/W/S/NI. General. - 8p.: 30 cm. - 978-0-11-111115-4 £5.75

Registration of births, deaths, marriages, etc., England and Wales

The Marriage of Same Sex Couples (Conversion of Civil Partnership) Regulations 2014 No. 2014/3181. - Enabling power: Marriage (Same Sex Couples) Act 2013, ss. 9 (1) (2) (4) (5), 18 (4) (a) (c). - Issued: 05.12.2014. Made: 29.11.2014. Coming into force: 10.12.2014. Effect: None. Territorial extent & classification: E/W. General. - Supersedes draft S.I. (ISBN 9780111121948) issued 22.10.2014. - 20p.: 30 cm. - 978-0-11-112432-1 £6.00

The Marriage of Same Sex Couples (Registration of Buildings and Appointment of Authorised Persons) (Amendment) Regulations 2014 No. 2014/1791. - Enabling power: Marriage Act 1949, s. 43D (1) (2). - Issued: 14.07.2014. Made: 07.07.2014. Laid: 10.07.2014. Coming into force: 01.09.2014. Effect: S.I. 2014/106 amended. Territorial extent & classification: E/W. General. - 2p.: 30 cm. - 978-0-11-111776-7 £4.25

The Marriage of Same Sex Couples (Registration of Buildings and Appointment of Authorised Persons) Regulations 2014 No. 2014/106. - Enabling power: Marriage Act 1949, s. 43D (1) (2). - Issued: 28.01.2014. Made: 21.01.2014. Laid: 23.01.2014. Coming into force: 13.03.2014. Effect: 1949 c.76 modified. Territorial extent & classification: E/W. General. - 8p.: 30 cm. - 978-0-11-110867-3 £5.75

The Marriage of Same Sex Couples (Registration of Shared Buildings) Regulations 2014 No. 2014/544. - Enabling power: Marriage Act 1949, ss. 44B (7), 44C (1) (2), 44D (2) to (5). - Issued: 12.03.2014. Made: 06.03.2014. Coming into force: 13.03.2014. Effect: None. Territorial extent & classification: E/W. General. - Supersedes draft S.I. (ISBN 9780111108734) issued 28.01.2014. - 8p.: 30 cm. - 978-0-11-111146-8 £5.75

The Marriage of Same Sex Couples (Use of Armed Forces' Chapels) Regulations 2014 No. 2014/815. - Enabling power: Marriage Act 1949, s. 70A (5) (6). - Issued: 31.03.2014. Made: 24.03.2014. Coming into force: 03.06.2014. Effect: None. Territorial extent & classification: E/W. General. - Supersedes draft SI (ISBN 9780111108710) issued 28/01/14. - 4p.: 30 cm. - 978-0-11-111278-6 £4.00

The Register of Presumed Deaths (Fees) Regulations 2014 No. 2014/2386. - Enabling power: Presumption of Death Act 2013. - Issued: 12.09.2014. Made: 05.09.2014. Laid: 09.09.2014. Coming into force: 01.10.2014. Effect: None. Territorial extent & classification: E/W. General. - 2p.: 30 cm. - 978-0-11-112045-3 £4.25

The Register of Presumed Deaths (Prescribed Information) Regulations 2014 No. 2014/2387. - Enabling power: Presumption of Death Act 2013 sch. 1 paras. 1 (1) (b), 1 (2) (a), 1 (3), 2 (1) (b), 2 (4). - Issued: 12.09.2014. Made: 05.09.2014. Coming into force: 01.10.2014. Effect: None. Territorial extent & classification: E/W. General. - 4p.: 30 cm. - 978-0-11-112046-0 £4.25

The Registration of Births, Deaths and Marriages (Fees) (Amendment) Order 2014 No. 2014/1790. - Enabling power: Public Expenditure and Receipts Act 1968, s. 5 (1) (2), sch. 3, paras 1, 2 & Marriage Act 1949, s. 31 (5F). - Issued: 14.07.2014. Made: 07.07.2014. Laid: 10.07.2014. Coming into force: 01.09.2012. Effect: S.I. 2010/441 amended. Territorial extent & classification: E/W. General. - 8p.: 30 cm. - 978-0-11-111778-1 £6.00

The Reporting of Suspicious Marriages and Civil Partnerships (Amendment) Regulations 2014 No. 2014/1660. - Enabling power: Immigration and Asylum Act 1999, ss. 24 (3), 24 (4) (a), 24A (3), (4) (a). - Issued: 02.07.2014. Made: 26.06.2014. Laid: - Coming into force: 21.07.2014. Effect: S.I. 2000/3164; 2005/3174 amended. Territorial extent & classification: E/W. General. - 2p.: 30 cm. - 978-0-11-111716-3 £4.25

Regulatory reform

The Co-ordination of Regulatory Enforcement (Enforcement Action) (Amendment) (No. 2) Order 2014 No. 2014/3070. - Enabling power: Regulatory Enforcement and Sanctions Act 2008, ss. 28 (6). - Issued: 24.11.2014. Made: 18.11.2014. Laid: 20.11.2014. Coming into force: 13.12.2014. Effect: S.I. 2009/261 amended. Territorial extent & classification: E/W/S/NI. General. - 4p.: 30 cm. - 978-0-11-112349-2 £4.25

The Co-ordination of Regulatory Enforcement (Enforcement Action) Order 2014 No. 2014/573. - Enabling power: Regulatory Enforcement and Sanctions Act 2008, ss. 28 (6), 29 (1). - Issued: 17.03.2014. Made: 07.03.2014. Laid: 11.03.2014. Coming into force: 06.04.2014. Effect: S.I. 2009/665 amended. Territorial extent & classification: E/W/S/NI. General. - 4p.: 30 cm. - 978-0-11-111169-7 £4.00

The Legislative and Regulatory Reform Code of Practice (Appointed Day) Order 2014 No. 2014/929 (C.41). - Enabling power: Legislative and Regulatory Reform Act 2006, s. 23 (6). Bringing into force the code of practice entitled the Regulators' Code on 13.04.2014. - Issued: 11.04.2014. Made: 25.03.2014. Effect: None. Territorial extent & classification: E/W/S/NI. General. - With correction slip dated January 2015. - 2p.: 30 cm. - 978-0-11-111387-5 £4.25

The Legislative and Regulatory Reform (Regulatory Functions) (Amendment) Order 2014 No. 2014/860. - Enabling power: Legislative and Regulatory Reform Act 2006, s. 24 (2). - Issued: 03.04.2014. Made: 25.03.2014. Coming into force: 06.04.2014. Effect: S.I. 2007/3544 amended. Territorial extent & classification: E/W/S/NI. General. - Supersedes Draft (ISBN 9780111108666) issued 27.01.2014. - 2p.: 30 cm. - 978-0-11-111316-5 £4.00

The Legislative Reform (Clinical Commissioning Groups) Order 2014 No. 2014/2436. - Enabling power: Legislative and Regulatory Reform Act 2006, s. 1. - Issued: 17.09.2014. Made: 10.09.2014. Laid: -Coming into force: 01.10.2014. Effect: 2006 c.41 amended. Territorial extent & classification: E/W/S/NI. General. - Supersedes draft S.I. (ISBN 9780111111789) issued 17.03.2014. - 4p.: 30 cm. - 978-0-11-112070-5 £4.25

The Legislative Reform (Overseas Registration of Births and Deaths) Order 2014 No. 2014/542. - Enabling power: Legislative and Regulatory Reform Act 2006, ss. 1, 2. - Issued: 12.03.2014. Made: 05.03.2014. Coming into force: 01.04.2014. Effect: 1981 c.61 amended. Territorial extent & classification: E/W/S/NI. General. - Supersedes draft S.I. (ISBN 9780111106600) issued 06.12.2013. - 2p.: 30 cm. - 978-0-11-111144-4 £4.00

The Legislative Reform (Payments by Parish Councils, Community Councils and Charter Trustees) Order 2014 No. 2014/580. - Enabling power: Legislative and Regulatory Reform Act 2006, s. 1. - Issued: 17.03.2014. Made: 11.03.2014. Coming into force: In accord. with art. 1(c). Effect: 1972 c.70; S.I. 1996/263 amended. Territorial extent & classification: E/W. General. - Supersedes draft SI (ISBN 9780111105825) issued 12/11/2013. - 4p.: 30 cm. - 978-0-11-111184-0 £4.00

Rehabilitation of offenders

The Legal Aid, Sentencing and Punishment of Offenders Act 2012 (Commencement No. 9, Saving Provision and Specification of Commencement Date) Order 2014 No. 2014/423 (C.18). - Enabling power: Legal Aid, Sentencing and Punishment of Offenders Act 2012, ss. 141 (12), 151 (1) (5) (b). Bringing into operation various provisions of the 2012 Act on 10.03.2014. - Issued: 04.03.2014. Made: 26.02.2014. Effect: None. Territorial extent & classification: E/W/S/NI. General. - 4p.: 30 cm. - 978-0-11-111039-3 £4.00

Rehabilitation of offenders, England and Wales

The Rehabilitation of Offenders Act 1974 (Exceptions) Order 1975 (Amendment) (England and Wales) Order 2014 No. 2014/1707. - Enabling power: Rehabilitation of Offenders Act 1974, ss. 4 (4), 7 (4), 10 (1), sch. 2, paras 4, 6 (4). - Issued: 07.07.2014. Made: 30.06.2014. Coming into force: In accord. with art. 1. Effect: S.I. 1975/1023 amended. Territorial extent & classification: E/W. General. - Supersedes draft SI (ISBN 9780111114575) issued on 09.05.2014. - 8p.: 30 cm. - 978-0-11-111744-6 £4.25

Representation of the people

The Donations to Candidates (Anonymous Registration) Regulations 2014 No. 2014/1805. - Enabling power: Representation of the People Act 1983, sch. 2A, para. 10 (2). - Issued: 17.07.2014. Made: 09.07.2014. Coming into force: 15.09.2014. Effect: S.I. 2001/341, 497 partially revoked. Territorial extent & classification: E/W/S/NI. General. - Supersedes draft SI (ISBN 9780111115671) issued 06.06.14. - 4p.: 30 cm. - 978-0-11-111801-6 £4.25

The Elections (Policy Development Grants Scheme) (Amendment) Order 2014 No. 2014/556. - Enabling power: Political Parties, Elections and Referendums Act 2000, s.12. - Issued: 13.03.2014. Made: 06.03.2014. Laid: 11.03.2014. Coming into force: 01.04.2014. Effect: S.I. 2006/602 amended. Territorial extent & classification: E/W/S/NI. General. - 4p.: 30 cm. - 978-0-11-111154-3 £4.00

The Electoral Registration and Administration Act 2013 (Commencement No.4 and Consequential Provision) Order 2014 No. 2014/336 (C.13). - Enabling power: Electoral Registration and Administration Act 2013, ss. 25 (1), 27 (1) (5) (6) (10). Bringing into operation various provisions of the 2013 Act on 22.05.2014, in accord. with art. 2. - Issued: 21.02.2014. Made: 13.02.2014. Coming into force: In accord. with art 1 (2). Effect: 1983 c.2 amended. Territorial extent & classification: E/W/S/NI. General. - Supersedes draft (ISBN 9780111105764) issued 11.11.2013. - 4p.: 30 cm. - 978-0-11-110988-5 £4.00

The Electoral Registration and Administration Act 2013 (Commencement No.5 and Transitory Provisions) Order 2014 No. 2014/414 (C.16). - Enabling power: Electoral Registration and Administration Act 2013, ss. 25 (1), 27 (1) (4) (10). Bringing into operation various provisions of the 2013 Act on 26.02.2014, 06.04.2014, 10.06.2014 (England), 19.09.2014 (Scotland). - Issued: 04.03.2014. Made: 25.02.2014. Effect: None. Territorial extent & classification: E/W/S/NI. General. - 4p.: 30 cm. - 978-0-11-111032-4 £4.00

The Electoral Registration and Administration Act 2013 (Transitional Provisions) (Amendment) Order 2014 No. 2014/449. - Enabling power: Electoral Registration and Administration Act 2013, s. 11 (3) (5), sch. 5, paras 4, 29. - Issued: 06.03.2014. Made: 27.02.2014. Coming into force: 28.02.2014, in accord. with art. 1. Effect: S.I. 2013/3197 amended. Territorial extent & classification: E/W/S. General. - This Statutory Instrument is being issued free of charge to all known recipients of SI 2013/3197 (ISBN 9780111107874), which it amends. - 4p.: 30 cm. - 978-0-11-111059-1 £4.00

The Electoral Registration Pilot Scheme Order 2014 No. 2014/3178. - Enabling power: Electoral Registration and Administration Act 2013, ss. 10, 11 (3). - Issued: 05.12.2014. Made: 25.11.2014. Coming into force: In accord. with art 1. Effect: None. Territorial extent & classification: E/W/S/NI. General. - Supersedes draft S.I. (ISBN 9780111118948) issued 25.07.2014. - 8p.: 30 cm. - 978-0-11-112431-4 £4.25

The European Parliamentary Election Petition (Amendment) Rules 2014 No. 2014/1129 (L.23). - Enabling power: S.I. 2004/293, reg. 120. - Issued: 07.05.2014. Made: 28.04.2014. Laid: 01.05.2014. Coming into force: 22.05.2014. Effect: S.I. 1979/521 amended in relation to England and Wales & Gibraltar. Territorial extent & classification: E/W/Gib. General. - 2p.: 30 cm. - 978-0-11-111449-0 £4.25

The European Parliamentary Elections (Amendment) Regulations 2014 No. 2014/923. - Enabling power: European Parliamentary Elections Act 2002, ss. 6 (5), 7 (1) & Political Parties, Elections and Referendums Act 2000, s. 7 (1) (2) (a). - Issued: 10.04.2014. Made: 03.04.2014. Coming into force: In accord. with reg. 1 (2). Effect: 2002 c.24; S.I. 2004/293 amended. Territorial extent & classification: E/W/S/Gibraltar. General. - This Statutory Instrument has been made in consequence of defects in S.I. 2013/2876 (ISBN 9780111105894) and is being issued free of charge to all known recipients of that Statutory Instrument. Supersedes draft (ISBN 9780111109939) issued 25.02.2014. - 4p.: 30 cm. - 978-0-11-111380-6 £4.25

The European Parliamentary Elections (Returning Officers' and Local Returning Officers' Charges) (Great Britain and Gibraltar) Order 2014 No. 2014/325. - Enabling power: European Parliamentary Elections Regulations 2004, reg. 15 (1). - Issued: 20.02.2014. Made: 13.02.2014. Coming into force: 14.02.2014 in accord. with art. 1 (1). Effect: S.I. 2009/1069, 1077, 1120 (S.7) revoked. Territorial extent & classification: E/W/S/Gib. General. - With correction slip dated October 2014. - 16p.: 30 cm. - 978-0-11-110982-3 £5.75

The European Parliamentary Elections (Welsh Forms) Order 2014 No. 2014/704. - Enabling power: Welsh Language Act 1993, s. 26 (2). - Issued: 24.03.2014. Made: 13.03.2014. Laid: 20.03.2014. Coming into force: 01.04.2014. Effect: S.I. 2009/781 revoked. Territorial extent & classification: W. General. - In English and Welsh. - 44p.: 30 cm. - 978-0-11-111243-4 £9.75

The Local Elections (Communities) (Welsh Forms) (Amendment) Order 2014 No. 2014/919. - Enabling power: Welsh Language Act 1993, ss. 26 (2) (as applied by s. 22 of the Representation of the People Act 1985). - Issued: 10.04.2014. Made: 03.04.2014. Laid: 07.04.2014. Coming into force: In accord. with art. 1 (2). Effect: S.I. 2007/1013 amended. Territorial extent & classification: W. General. - 36p.: 30 cm. - 978-0-11-111378-3 £10.00

The Local Elections (Principal Areas) (Welsh Forms) (Amendment) Order 2014 No. 2014/918. - Enabling power: Welsh Language Act 1993, ss. 26 (2) (as applied by. s. 22 of the Representation of the People Act 1985). - Issued: 10.04.2014. Made: 03.04.2014. Laid: 07.04.2014. Coming into force: In accord. with art. 1 (2). Effect: S.I. 2007/1015 amended. Territorial extent & classification: W. General. - 36p.: 30 cm. - 978-0-11-111377-6 £10.00

The Political Parties, Elections and Referendums (Civil Sanctions) (Amendment) (No.2) Order 2014 No. 2014/2448. - Enabling power: Political Parties, Elections and Referendums Act 2000, sch. 19C, paras 1, 5, 10, 15, 16. - Issued: 18.09.2014. Made: 10.09.2014. Coming into force: 19.09.2014. Effect: S.I. 2010/2860 amended. Territorial extent & classification: E/W/S/NI. General. - 4p.: 30 cm. - 978-0-11-112080-4 £4.25

The Political Parties, Elections and Referendums (Civil Sanctions) (Amendment) Order 2014 No. 2014/335. - Enabling power: Political Parties, Elections and Referendums Act 2000, sch. 19C, paras 1, 5, 16, 18. - Issued: 21.02.2014. Made: 13.02.2014. Coming into force: 14.02.2014 in accord. with art. 1. Effect: S.I. 2010/2860 amended. Territorial extent & classification: E/W/S/NI. General. - Supersedes draft S.I. (ISBN 9780111101568) issued 19.07.2013. - 2p.: 30 cm. - 978-0-11-110987-8 £4.00

The Representation of the People (Supply of Information) Regulations 2014 No. 2014/2764. - Enabling power: Representation of the People Act 1983, s. 53 (1) (3), sch. 2, paras. 10B (1) (2), 11A. - Issued: 21.10.2014. Made: 15.10.2014. Coming into force: 01.01.2015. Effect: None. Territorial extent & classification: E/W/S. General. - Supersedes draft (ISBN 9780111114308) issued 06.05.2014. - 4p.: 30 cm. - 978-0-11-112188-7 £4.25

The Representation of the People (Variation of Limits of Candidates' Election Expenses) Order 2014 No. 2014/1870. - Enabling power: Representation of the People Act 1983, s. 76A (1) (a). - Issued: 22.07.2014. Made: 14.07.2014. Coming into force: 04.08.2014. Effect: 1983 c.2 varied & S.I. 2005/269 revoked. Territorial extent & classification: E/W/S/NI. General. - 4p.: 30 cm. - 978-0-11-111834-4 £4.25

The Transparency of Lobbying, Non-Party Campaigning and Trade Union Administration Act 2014 (Commencement and Transitional Provision No. 1) Order 2014 No. 2014/1236 (C.49). - Enabling power: Transparency of Lobbying, Non-Party Campaigning and Trade Union Administration Act 2014, s. 45 (1) (2). Bringing into operation various provisions of the 2014 Act on 23.05.2014, 01.07.2014, in accord. with art 2. - Issued: 19.05.2014. Made: 11.05.2014. Effect: None. Territorial extent & classification: E/W/S/NI. General. - 2p.: 30 cm. - 978-0-11-111488-9 £4.25

Representation of the people, England and Wales

The Local Elections (Parishes and Communities) (England and Wales) (Amendment) Rules 2014 No. 2014/492. - Enabling power: Representation of the People Act 1983, s. 36 (1) (2). - Issued: 11.03.2014. Made: 28.02.2014. Laid: 07.3.2014. Coming into force: In accord with rule 1 (2). Effect: S.I. 2006/3305 amended. Territorial extent & classification: E/W. General. - 40p.: 30 cm. - 978-0-11-111096-6 £9.75

The Local Elections (Principal Areas) (England and Wales) (Amendment) Rules 2014 No. 2014/494. - Enabling power: Representation of the People Act 1983, s. 36 (1) (2). - Issued: 11.03.2014. Made: 28.02.2014. Laid: 07.03.2014. Coming into force: In accord. with rule 1 (2). Effect: S.I. 2006/3304 amended. Territorial extent & classification: E/W. General. - 40p.: 30 cm. - 978-0-11-111097-3 £9.75

The Representation of the People (Combination of Polls) (England and Wales) (Amendment) Regulations 2014 No. 2014/920. - Enabling power: Representation of the People Act 1985, s. 15 (5) & Local Government Act 2000, ss. 9HE (1) (a) (2) (d) (3) (a) (b), 9MG (2) (3) (4), 44 (1) (a) (2) (d) (3) (a) (b), 105 (2) (a). - Issued: 10.04.2014. Made: 03.04.2014. Coming into force: In accord. with reg. 1 (1). Effect: S.I. 2004/294 amended & S.I. 2006/3278 partially revoked. Territorial extent & classification: E/W. General. - Supersedes draft SI (ISBN 9780111110010) issued 10/04/14. - 8p.: 30 cm. - 978-0-11-111388-2 £6.00

The Representation of the People (England and Wales) (Amendment No. 2) Regulations 2014 No. 2014/3161. - Enabling power: Representation of the People Act 1983, ss. 16 (g), 202 (1), 53 (1) (3), sch. 2 paras 2A, 4 (1)- Issued: 03.12.2014. Made: 25.11.2014. Coming into force: in accord. with reg. 1. Effect: S.I. 2001/341 amended. Territorial extent & classification: E/W. General. - Supersedes draft S.I. (ISBN 9780111120910) issued 13.11.2014. - 4p.: 30 cm. - 978-0-11-112425-3 £4.25

The Representation of the People (England and Wales) (Amendment) Regulations 2014 No. 2014/1234. - Enabling power: Representation of the People Act 1983, ss. 9E (2), 53 (1) (3), 201 (3), sch. 2, paras. 1 (4), 1A. - Issued: 19.05.2014. Made: 13.05.2014. Coming into force: 14.05.2014 in accord. with reg. 1. Effect: S.I. 2001/341; 2013/3198 amended. Territorial extent & classification: E/W/S/NI. General. - Supersedes draft (ISBN 9780111112595) issued 27.03.2014. - 4p.: 30 cm. - 978-0-11-111487-2 £4.25

Representation of the people, Northern Ireland

The Anonymous Registration (Northern Ireland) (No. 2) Order 2014 No. 2014/1880. - Enabling power: Northern Ireland Act 1998, s. 84 (1) (3) & Northern Ireland (Miscellaneous Provisions) Act 2006, s. 1. - Issued: 23.07.2014. Made: 16.07.2014. Coming into force: 15.09.2014. Effect: 1962 c.14 (N.I.); 1983 c.2; S.I. 1985/454 amended. Territorial extent & classification: NI. General. - This Statutory Instrument corrects omissions in S.I. 2014/1116 (ISBN 978-0-11-111444-5) and is being issued free of charge to all known recipients of that Statutory Instrument. - 4p.: 30 cm. - 978-0-11-111842-9 £4.25

The Anonymous Registration (Northern Ireland) Order 2014 No. 2014/1116. - Enabling power: Northern Ireland Act 1998, s. 84 (1) (1A) (3) & Northern Ireland (Miscellaneous Provisions) Act 2006, s. 1. - Issued: 06.05.2014. Made: 28.04.2014. Coming into force: 15.09.2014. Effect: 1962 c.14 (N.I.); 1983 c.2; 1985 c.50; 1989 c.3; 2001 c.7; 2006 c.22; S.I. 1985/454; 1996/1141 (N.I. 6); 2001/2599; 2013/3156 amended & 2013 c.6 partially repealed. Territorial extent & classification: NI. General. - Supersedes draft SI (ISBN 9780111110041) issued 26/02/14. Corrected by SI 2014/1880 (ISBN 9780111118429) which is being issued free of charge to all known recipients of 2014/1116. - 24p.: 30 cm. - 978-0-11-111444-5 £6.00

The Electoral Registration (Disclosure of Electoral Registers) (Amendment) Regulations 2014 No. 2014/450. - Enabling power: Representation of the People Act 1983, s. 53 (1) (3), sch. 2, para. 1A. - Issued: 06.03.2014. Made: 27.02.2014. Coming into force: 28.02.2014, in accord. with reg. 1. Effect: S.I. 2013/760 amended. Territorial extent & classification: E/W/S. General. - 2p.: 30 cm. - 978-0-11-111060-7 £4.00

The European Parliamentary Elections (Anonymous Registration) (Northern Ireland) Regulations 2014 No. 2014/1803. - Enabling power: European Parliamentary Elections Act 2002, ss. 6 (5), 7 (1) (2) (a) (3) (4A) & European Parliament (Representation) Act 2003, ss. 17, 18 & European Communities Act 1972, s. 2 (2). - Issued: 18.07.2014. Made: 09.07.2014. Coming into force: 15.09.2014. Effect: S.I. 2001/1184; 2004/293, 1267 amended. Territorial extent & classification: UK. General. - Supersedes draft S.I. (ISBN 9780111115503) issued 05.06.2014. - 20p.: 30 cm. - 978-0-11-111813-9 £6.00

The European Parliamentary Elections (Returning Officer's Charges) (Northern Ireland) Order 2014 No. 2014/794. - Enabling power: S.I. 2004/1267, reg. 16 (1) (5). - Issued: 28.03.2014. Made: 20.03.2014. Coming into force: 21.03.2014 in accord. with reg. 1 (2). Effect: S.I. 2009/1143 revoked. Territorial extent & classification: NI. General. - 2p.: 30 cm. - 978-0-11-111265-6 £4.00

The Representation of the People (Northern Ireland) (Amendment) Regulations 2014 No. 2014/1808. - Enabling power: Representation of the People Act 1983, ss. 9B, 9B (1A), 9C, 10A (1) (a), 13A (1) (a), 53, 201 (3), sch. 1, rules 24, 28, 55 (1) (f), 57, sch. 2, paras. 2B, 3A, 3B, 5 (1B), 5A, 7, 8, 8A, 9C, 10, 10B, 12 & Representation of the People Act 1985, ss. 6 (1) (c) (5), 7 (3), 8 (6) (7), 9 (4) (7) (8). - Issued: 24.07.2014. Made: 09.07.2014. Coming into force: 15.09.2014. Effect: S.I. 2008/1741 amended. Territorial extent & classification: NI. General. - Supersedes draft SI (ISBN 9780111115695) issued 06/06/14. - 24p.: 30 cm. - 978-0-11-111874-0 £6.00

Representation of the people, Scotland

The Representation of the People (Scotland) (Amendment No. 2) Regulations 2014 No. 2014/3124. - Enabling power: Representation of the People Act 1983, ss. 16 (g), 53 (1) (3), sch.2, paras 1A, 2A, 4 (1). - Issued: 01.12.2014. Made: 25.11.2014. Coming into force: In accord. with reg. 1. Effect: S.I. 2001/497 amended. Territorial extent & classification: S. General. - Supersedes draft S.I. 2014 (ISBN 9780111118719) issued 23.07.2014. - 4p.: 30 cm. - 978-0-11-112400-0 £4.25

The Representation of the People (Scotland) (Amendment) Regulations 2014 No. 2014/1250. - Enabling power: Representation of the People Act 1983, ss. 9E (2) (3) (6), 10ZC (2) (3), 10ZD (2) (3), 10ZE (4) (6) (a), 53 (1) (3), 201 (1) (3), sch. ZA1, sch.2, paras 1 (2) (2A), 1A, 3ZA, 8C, 10B, 11 (1) (2), 13 (1ZB) (1A). - Issued: 20.05.2014. Made: 13.05.2014. Coming into force: In accord. with reg. 1. Effect: S.I. 2013/3206 amended. Territorial extent & classification: S. General. - This Statutory Instrument is being issued free of charge to all known recipients of S.I. 2013/3206 (ISBN 9780111107744) which it amends. - 4p.: 30 cm. - 978-0-11-111492-6 £4.25

Revenue and customs

The Customs (Inspections by Her Majesty's Inspectors of Constabulary and the Scottish Inspectors) (Amendment) Regulations 2014 No. 2014/907. - Enabling power: Borders Citizenship and Immigration Act 2009, ss. 29, 37 (2) (c). - Issued: 08.04.2014. Made: 01.04.2014. Laid: 04.04.2014. Coming into force: 01.05.2014. Effect: None. Territorial extent & classification: E/W/S/NI - but there is no provision for Northern Ireland as there are no detention centres there. General. - 4p.: 30 cm. - 978-0-11-111371-4 £4.25

Revenue and customs, England and Wales

The Finance Act 2008, Section 127 and Part 1 of Schedule 43 (Appointed Day) Order 2014 No. 2014/906 (C.40). - Enabling power: Finance Act 2008, s. 129 (4) (5). Bringing into operation various provisions of the 2008 Act on 05.04.2014 & 06.04.2014. - Issued: 09.04.2014. Made: 03.04.2014. Effect: None. Territorial extent & classification: E/W. General. - 2p.: 30 cm. - 978-0-11-111370-7 £4.25

The Police and Criminal Evidence Act 1984 (Application to Revenue and Customs) (Amendment) Order 2014 No. 2014/788. - Enabling power: Police and Criminal Evidence Act 1984, s. 114 (2) (3). - Issued: 31.03.2014. Made: 20.03.2014. Laid: 21.03.2014. Coming into force: 11.04.2014. Effect: S.I. 2007/3175 amended. Territorial extent & classification: E/W. General. - 4p.: 30 cm. - 978-0-11-111260-1 £4.00

Rights in performances

The Copyright and Duration of Rights in Performances (Amendment) Regulations 2014 No. 2014/434. - Enabling power: European Communities Act 1972, s. 2 (2) & Enterprise and Regulatory Reform Act 2013, s. 78. - Issued: 05.03.2014. Made: 26.02.2014. Laid: 28.02.2014. Coming into force: 06.04.2014. Effect: 1988 c.48 amended. Territorial extent & classification: E/W/S/NI. General. - This Statutory Instrument has been printed to correct an error in S.I. 2013/1782 (ISBN 9780111101865) and is being issued free of charge to all known recipients of that Statutory Instrument. - 2p.: 30 cm. - 978-0-11-111045-4 £4.00

The Copyright and Rights in Performances (Certain Permitted Uses of Orphan Works) Regulations 2014 No. 2014/2861. - Enabling power: European Communities Act 1972, s. 2 (2). - Issued: 03.11.2014. Made: 27.10.14. Coming into force: 29.10.2014. Effect: 1988 c.48 amended. Territorial extent & classification: E/W/S/NI. General. - Supersedes draft S.I. (ISBN 9780111117682) issued 11.07.2014. - 8p.: 30 cm. - 978-0-11-112247-1 £6.00

The Copyright and Rights in Performances (Disability) Regulations 2014 No. 2014/1384. - Enabling power: European Communities Act 1972, s. 2 (2). - Issued: 06.06.2014. Made: 19.05.2014. Coming into force: 01.06.2014 at 00.01, in accord. with reg. 1. Effect: 1988 c.48 amended/partially repealed & S.I. 2003/2498; 2006/18 partially revoked & 2002 c.33 repealed. Territorial extent & classification: E/W/S/NI. General. - Supersedes draft SI (ISBN 9780111112694) issued 28/03/14- 12p.: 30 cm. - 978-0-11-111565-7 £6.00

The Copyright and Rights in Performances (Personal Copies for Private Use) Regulations 2014 No. 2014/2361. - Enabling power: European Communities Act 1972, s. 2 (2). - Issued: 10.09.2014. Made: 26.08.14. Coming into force: 01.10.2014. Effect: 1988 c.48 amended. Territorial extent & classification: E/W/S/NI. - Supersedes draft SI (ISBN 9780111116036) issued 10.06.2014. - 8p.: 30 cm. - 978-0-11-112023-1 £6.00

The Copyright and Rights in Performances (Quotation and Parody) Regulations 2014 No. 2014/2356. - Enabling power: European Communities Act 1972, s. 2 (2). - Issued: 10.09.2014. Made: 26.08.2014. Coming into force: 01.10.2014. Effect: 1988 c.48 amended. Territorial extent & classification: E/W/S/NI. General. - Supersedes draft SI (ISBN 928011116029) issued 10.06.2014. - 4p.: 30 cm. - 978-0-11-112022-4 £4.25

The Copyright and Rights in Performances (Research, Education, Libraries and Archives) Regulations 2014 No. 2014/1372. - Enabling power: European Communities Act 1972, s. 2 (2). - Issued: 04.06.2014. Made: 19.05.2014. Coming into force: In accord. with reg. 1. Effect: 1988 c.48; 1990 c.42; 2010 c.24; S.I. 1989/1067 amended & 1988 c.48 partially repealed & S.I. 2003/2498 partially revoked. Territorial extent & classification: E/W/S/NI. General. - Supersedes draft SI (ISBN 9780111112755) issued 31/03/14. - 20p.: 30 cm. - 978-0-11-111544-2 £6.00

River, England: Salmon and freshwater fisheries

The Prohibition of Keeping or Release of Live Fish (Specified Species) (England) (Amendment) Order 2014 No. 2014/3342. - Enabling power: Import of Live Fish (England and Wales) Act 1980, s. 1 (1). - Issued: 29.12.2014. Made: 14.12.2014. Laid: 19.12.2014. Coming into force: 19.01.2015. Effect: S.I. 2014/143 amended. Territorial extent & classification: E. General. - 4p.: 30 cm. - 978-0-11-112631-8 £4.25

The Prohibition of Keeping or Release of Live Fish (Specified Species) (England) Order 2014 No. 2014/143. - Enabling power: Import of Live Fish (England and Wales) Act 1980, s. 1 (2). - Issued: 31.01.2014. Made: 23.01.2014. Laid: 27.01.2014. Coming into force: 17.02.2014. Effect: S.I. 2011/2292 partially revoked & S.I. 1998/2409; 2003/25 revoked. Territorial extent & classification: E. General. - 4p.: 30 cm. - 978-0-11-110889-5 £4.00

River, Wales

The Keeping and Introduction of Fish (Wales) Regulations 2014 No. 2014/3303 (W.336). - Enabling power: Marine and Coastal Access Act 2009, ss. 232(1) (5) (a) (d) (e) (h) (i) (j) (7), 316 (1) (2). - Issued: 30.12.2014. Made: 09.12.2014. Coming into force: 20.01.2015. Effect: 1975 c.51 partially repealed. Territorial extent & classification: W. General. - In English and Welsh. Welsh title: Rheoliadau Cadw a Chyflwyno Pysgod (Cymru) 2014. - 20p.: 30 cm. - 978-0-348-11035-7 £6.00

Road traffic

The Cycle Racing on Highways (Tour de France 2014) Regulations 2014 No. 2014/887. - Enabling power: Road Traffic Act 1988, s. 31 (2) (3). - Issued: 04.04.2014. Made: 31.03.2014. Laid: 04.04.2014. Coming into force: 01.05.2014. Effect: S.I. 1960/250 modified. Territorial extent & classification: E. General. - 2p.: 30 cm. - 978-0-11-111352-3 £4.25

The Driving Standards Agency and the Vehicle and Operator Services Agency (Merger) (Consequential Amendments) Order 2014 No. 2014/467. - Enabling power: Regulation of Investigatory Powers Act 2000, ss. 30 (1) (3) (6), 46 (4), 78 (5) & Proceeds of Crime Act 2002, ss. 453 (1) (2), 459 (1) (2). - Issued: 07.03.2014. Made: 03.03.2014. Laid: 06.03.2014. Coming into force: 01.04.2014. Effect: S.I. 2007/934; 2009/975; 2010/521 amended. Territorial extent & classification: E/W/S/NI. General. - Incorrect price printed on document. - 8p.: 30 cm. - 978-0-11-111077-5 £4.00

The Driving Standards Agency and the Vehicle and Operator Services Agency (Merger) (Consequential Amendments) Regulations 2014 No. 2014/480. - Enabling power: Road Traffic Act 1988, ss. 41 (1) (2) (4) (5), 45, 46, 49, 89 (3) (4) (5), 91, 105 (1) (2) (3), 129 (5), 135 (1) (a) (b) (c), 141 & Public Passenger Vehicles Act 1981, ss. 10 (1), 60 & Vehicle Excise and Registration Act 1994, ss. 57, 61B (1) & European Communities Act 1972, s. 2 (2). - Issued: 10.03.2014. Made: 03.03.2014. Laid: 06.03.2014. Coming into force: 01.04.2014. Effect: S.I. 1981/257, 1694; 1988/1478; 1989/1796; 1998/1833; 1999/2864; 2002/2742; 2005/1902 amended. Territorial extent & classification: E/W/S/NI. General. - 16p., col. figs: 30 cm. - 978-0-11-111083-6 £8.25

The Driving Theory Test Fees (Various Amendments) Regulations 2014 No. 2014/1816. - Enabling power: Road Traffic Act 1988, ss. 89 (3) (4) (5) (5ZA), 105 (1) (3) (4), 132, 141 & European Communities Act 1972, s. 2 (2) & Finance Act 1973, s. 56 (1) (2). - Issued: 23.01.2014. Made: 07.07.2014. Laid: 23.07.2014. Coming into force: 20.08.2014. Effect: S.I. 1999/2864; 2005/1902; 2007/605 amended. Territorial extent & classification: E/W/S/NI. General. - 8p.: 30 cm. - 978-0-11-111788-0 £4.25

The Goods Vehicles (Licensing of Operators) (Fees) (Amendment) Regulations 2014 No. 2014/2119. - Enabling power: Goods Vehicles (Licensing of Operators) Act 1995, ss. 45 (1), 57 (1) (7), 58 (1). - Issued: 19.08.2014. Made: 06.08.2014. Laid: 19.08.2014. Coming into force: 01.10.2014. Effect: S.I. 1995/3000 amended. Territorial extent & classification: E/W/S. General. - 2p.: 30 cm. - 978-0-11-111983-9 £4.25

The Goods Vehicles (Plating and Testing) (Amendment) Regulations 2014 No. 2014/2115. - Enabling power: Road Traffic Act 1988, ss. 49, 51 (1), 63A. - Issued: 19.08.2014. Made: 06.08.2014. Laid: 19.08.2014. Coming into force: 01.10.2014. Effect: S.I. 1988/1478 amended. Territorial extent & classification: E/W/S. General. - 8p.: 30 cm. - 978-0-11-111979-2 £4.25

The HGV Road User Levy Act 2013 (Commencement No.1) Order 2014 No. 2014/175 (C.4). - Enabling power: HGV Road User Levy Act 2013, s. 21 (1). Bringing into operation various provisions of the 2013 Act on 30.01.2014, in accord. with art. 2. - Issued: 05.02.2014. Made: 29.01.2014. Effect: None. Territorial extent & classification: E/W/S/NI. General. - 2p.: 30 cm. - 978-0-11-110905-2 £4.00

The HGV Road User Levy Act 2013 (Commencement No.2) Order 2014 No. 2014/797 (C.31). - Enabling power: HGV Road User Levy Act 2013, s. 21 (1). Bringing into operation various provisions of the 2013 Act on 01.04.2014, in accord. with art. 2. - Issued: 28.03.2014. Made: 24.03.2014. Effect: None. Territorial extent & classification: E/W/S/NI. General. - 2p.: 30 cm. - 978-0-11-111266-3 £4.00

The HGV Road User Levy (Exemption of Specified Roads) Order 2014 No. 2014/800. - Enabling power: HGV Road User Levy Act 2013, s. 3 (2). - Issued: 28.03.2014. Made: 24.03.2014. Coming into force: 01.04.2014. Effect: None. Territorial extent & classification: E/W/S/NI. General. - Supersedes draft S.I. (ISBN 9780111107072) issued 18.12.2013. - 2p.: 30 cm. - 978-0-11-111268-7 £4.00

The HGV Road User Levy (Exemption of Vehicles) Regulations 2014 No. 2014/326. - Enabling power: HGV Road User Levy Act 2013, s. 8 (3). - Issued: 20.02.2014. Made: 12.02.2014. Laid: 19.02.2014. Coming into force: 01.04.2014. Effect: None. Territorial extent & classification: E/W/S/NI. General. - 2p.: 30 cm. - 978-0-11-110983-0 £4.00

The International Carriage of Dangerous Goods by Road (Fees) (Amendment) Regulations 2014 No. 2014/2117. - Enabling power: Finance Act 1973, s. 56 (1) (2). - Issued: 19.08.2014. Made: 06.08.2014. Laid: 19.08.2014. Coming into force: 01.10.2014. Effect: S.I. 1988/370 amended. Territorial extent & classification: E/W/S. General. - 4p.: 30 cm. - 978-0-11-111981-5 £4.25

The Motor Cars (Driving Instruction) (Amendment) Regulations 2014 No. 2014/2216. - Enabling power: Road Traffic Act 1988, ss. 132 (1) (2) (a), 141. - Issued: 03.09.2014. Made: 18.08.2014. Laid: 03.09.2014. Coming into force: 01.10.2014. Effect: S.I. 2005/1902 amended. Territorial extent & classification: E/W/S. General. - 2p.: 30 cm. - 978-0-11-111994-5 £4.25

The Motor Vehicles (Driving Licences) (Amendment) (No.2) Regulations 2014 No. 2014/2580. - Enabling power: Road Traffic Act 1988, ss. 97 (1), 99 (7ZA), 105 (1) (4) & S.I. 2003/2994. - Issued: 30.09.2014. Made: 19.09.2014. Laid: 30.09.2014. Coming into force: 31.10.2014. Effect: S.I. 1999/2864 amended. Territorial extent & classification: E/W/S. General. - 4p.: 30 cm. - 978-0-11-112104-7 £4.25

The Motor Vehicles (Driving Licences) (Amendment) Regulations 2014 No. 2014/613. - Enabling power: Road Traffic Act 1988, ss. 89 (3) (a) (4) (a), 92 (2) (4) (b), 101 (2) (3), 105 (1) (2) (a) (3). - Issued: 19.03.2014. Made: 13.03.2014. Laid: 19.03.2014. Coming into force: 10.04.2014. Effect: S.I. 1999/2864 amended. Territorial extent & classification: E/W/S. General. - 8p.: 30 cm. - 978-0-11-111215-1 £4.00

The Motor Vehicles (Tests) (Amendment) Regulations 2014 No. 2014/2114. - Enabling power: Road Traffic Act 1988, ss. 45 (7), 46 (1) (f) (7). - Issued: 19.08.2014. Made: 06.08.2014. Laid: 19.08.2014. Coming into force: 01.10.2014. Effect: S.I. 1981/1694 amended. Territorial extent & classification: E/W/S. General. - 4p.: 30 cm. - 978-0-11-111978-5 £4.25

The Passenger and Goods Vehicles (Recording Equipment) (Tachograph Card Fees) (Amendment) Regulations 2014 No. 2014/2557. - Enabling power: Finance Act 1973, s. 56 (1) (2). - Issued: 30.09.2014. Made: 19.09.2014. Laid: 30.09.2014. Coming into force: 31.10.2014. Effect: S.I. 2005/1140 amended. Territorial extent & classification: E/W/S. General. - 2p.: 30 cm. - 978-0-11-112101-6 £4.25

The Road Safety (Financial Penalty Deposit) (Amendment) Order 2014 No. 2014/267. - Enabling power: Road Traffic Offenders Act 1988, s. 90A (2) (b). - Issued: 18.02.2014. Made: 10.02.2014. Laid: 18.02.2014. Coming into force: 01.04.2014. Effect: S.I. 2009/491 amended. Territorial extent & classification: E/W/S. General. - 2p.: 30 cm. - 978-0-11-110971-7 £4.00

The Road Safety (Financial Penalty Deposit) (Appropriate Amount) (Amendment) (No. 2) Order 2014 No. 2014/2766. - Enabling power: Road Traffic Offenders Act 1988, ss. 90B(2), 90E(3). - Issued: 21.10.2014. Made: 01.10.2014. Coming into force: In accord. with art. 1. Effect: S.I. 2009/492 amended. Territorial extent & classification: E/W/S. General. - This Statutory Instrument has been made in consequence of a defect in S.I. 2013/2025 (ISBN 9780111102978) and is being issued free of charge to all known recipients of that Statutory Instrument. - 4p.: 30 cm. - 978-0-11-112192-4 £4.25

The Road Safety (Financial Penalty Deposit) (Appropriate Amount) (Amendment) Order 2014 No. 2014/802. - Enabling power: Road Traffic Offenders Act 1988, ss. 90B (2), 90E (3). - Issued: 28.03.2014. Made: -. Coming into force: 01.04.2014. Effect: S.I. 2009/492 amended. Territorial extent & classification: E/W/S. General. - Supersedes draft S.I. (ISBN 9780111107058) issued 18.12.2013. - 2p.: 30 cm. - 978-0-11-111272-4 £4.00

The Road Traffic Act 1988 and Motor Vehicles (Driving Licences) (Amendment) Regulations 2014 No. 2014/3190. - Enabling power: Road Traffic Act 1988, ss. 89 (3) (4), 105 (1) (2) (a) (2) (ee) (3) & European Communities Act 1972, s. 2 (2). - Issued: 08.12.2014. Made: 27.11.2014. Laid: 08.12.2014. Coming into force: 29.12.2014. Effect: 1988 c.52; S.I. 1999/2864 amended. Territorial extent & classification: E/W/S. General. - 8p.: 30 cm. - 978-0-11-112440-6 £4.25

The Road Traffic Offenders (Additional Offences) Order 2014 No. 2014/260. - Enabling power: Road Traffic Offenders Act 1988, s. 20 (3). - Issued: 18.02.2014. Made: 10.02.2014. Laid: 18.02.2014. Coming into force: 01.04.2014. Effect: 1988 c.53 amended. Territorial extent & classification: E/W/S. General. - 2p.: 30 cm. - 978-0-11-110964-9 £4.00

The Road Vehicles (Construction and Use) (Amendment No. 2) Regulations 2014 No. 2014/1862. - Enabling power: Road Traffic Act 1988, s. 41 (1) (2) (5). - Issued: 22.07.214. Made: 14.07.2014. Laid: 21.07.2014. Coming into force: 20.08.2014. Effect: S.I. 1986/1078 amended & S.I. 2012/1404 revoked. Territorial extent & classification: E/W/S. General. - 2p.: 30 cm. - 978-0-11-111828-3 £4.25

The Road Vehicles (Construction and Use) (Amendment) Regulations 2014 No. 2014/264. - Enabling power: Road Traffic Act 1988, s. 41 (1) (2). - Issued: 18.02.2014. Made: 10.02.2014. Laid: 18.02.2014. Coming into force: 01.04.2014. Effect: S.I. 1986/1078 amended. Territorial extent & classification: E/W/S. General. - 2p.: 30 cm. - 978-0-11-110968-7 £4.00

The Road Vehicles (Registration and Licensing) (Amendment) (No. 2) Regulations 2014 No. 2014/2676. - Enabling power: Vehicle Excise and Registration Act 1994, ss. 22 (1) (2), 57. - Issued: 08.10.2014. Made: 02.10.2014. Laid: 08.10.2014. Coming into force: 31.10.2014; 09.12.2014 in a ccord. with reg. 1 (2) (3). Effect: S.I. 2002/2742 amended. Territorial extent & classification: E/W/S/NI. General. - 4p.: 30 cm. - 978-0-11-112125-2 £4.25

The Road Vehicles (Registration and Licensing) (Amendment) Regulations 2014 No. 2014/2116. - Enabling power: Vehicle Excise and Registration Act 1994, ss. 57 (1) to (3), 61B (1) (d). - Issued: 19.08.2014. Made: 06.08.2014. Laid: 19.08.2014. Coming into force: 01.10.2014. Effect: S.I. 2002/2742 amended. Territorial extent & classification: E/W/S/NI. General. - 4p.: 30 cm. - 978-0-11-111980-8 £4.25

The Vehicle Drivers (Certificates of Professional Competence) (Amendment) Regulations 2014 No. 2014/2264. - Enabling power: European Communities Act 1972, s. 2 (2). - Issued: 05.09.2014. Made: 26.08.2014. Laid: 05.09.2014. Coming into force: 26.09.2014. Effect: 2007/605 amended. Territorial extent & classification: E/W/S/NI. General. - 4p.: 30 cm. - 978-0-11-112002-6 £4.25

The Vehicle Excise and Registration (Consequential Amendments) Regulations 2014 No. 2014/2358. - Enabling power: Vehicle Excise and Registration Act 1994, ss. 7 (6), 10 (1), 11 (1) (1A), 14 (4), 22 (1) (d) (1D) (2), 23 (5) (b), 26 (1) (1A) (2), 27 (2) (3) (d) (h), 33 (1) (b) (1A) (c) (4), 57 (1) (2) (3), sch. 2A, paras, 1, 3, 5. - Issued: 09.09.2014. Made: 03.09.2014. Laid: 08.09.2014. Coming into force: 01.10.2014. Effect: S.I. 1993//987; 1995/2880; 1997/2439; 2002/2742 amended. Territorial extent & classification: E/W/S. General. - 8p.: 30 cm. - 978-0-11-112020-0 £4.25

Road traffic: Speed limits

The A1 and A14 Trunk Roads (Junction 21 Brampton Hut Interchange, Cambridgeshire) (Derestriction and Variation) Order 2014 No. 2014/1046. - Enabling power: Road Traffic Regulation Act 1984, ss. 82 (2) (a), 83 (1), sch. 9, para. 27. - Issued: 17.04.2014. Made: 04.04.2014. Coming into force: 18.04.2014. Effect: S.I. 2006/2881 varied. Territorial extent & classification: E. Local. - Available at http://www.legislation.gov.uk/uksi/2014/1046/contents/made Non-print

The A1 Trunk Road (Southoe to Buckden, Cambridgeshire) (60 Miles Per Hour Speed Limit) Order 2014 No. 2014/726. - Enabling power: Road Traffic Regulation Act 1984, ss. 84 (1) (a) (2). - Issued: 12.03.2014. Made: 07.03.2014. Coming into force: 21.03.2014. Effect: None. Territorial extent & classification: E. Local. - Available at http://www.legislation.gov.uk/uksi/2014/726/contents/made Non-print

The A5 Trunk Road (Potsgrove, Bedfordshire) (Derestriction) Order 2014 No. 2014/1011. - Enabling power: Road Traffic Regulation Act 1984, s. 82 (2) (a), 83 (1). - Issued: 16.04.2014. Made: 21.03.2014. Coming into force: 04.04.2014. Effect: None. Territorial extent & classification: E. Local. - Available at http://www.legislation.gov.uk/uksi/2014/1011/contents/made Non-print

The A11 Trunk Road (Barton Mills, Suffolk) (50 Miles Per Hour Speed Limit) Order 2014 No. 2014/2198. - Enabling power: Road Traffic Regulation Act 1984, s. 84 (1) (a) (2), sch. 9, para. 27. - Issued: 20.08.2014. Made: 08.08.2014. Coming into force: 22.08.2014. Effect: S.I. 2003/2162 revoked. Territorial extent & classification: E. Local. - Available at http://www.legislation.gov.uk/uksi/2014/2198/contents/made Non-print

The A13 Trunk Road (Wennington Interchange - Stifford Interchange) (50 Miles Per Hour Speed Limit) Order 2014 No. 2014/3553. - Enabling power: Road Traffic Regulation Act 1984, ss. 84 (1) (a) (2), 126, sch. 9, para. 27 (1). - Issued: 12.02.2015. Made: 16.12.2015. Coming into force: 06.01.2015. Effect: None. Territorial extent & classification: E. Local. - Available at http://www.legislation.gov.uk/uksi/2014/3553/contents/made Non-print

The A14 Trunk Road (Junction 15 Bythorn, Cambridgeshire) (Derestriction) Order 2014 No. 2014/1028. - Enabling power: Road Traffic Regulation Act 1984, ss. 82 (2) (a), 83 (1). - Issued: 17.04.2014. Made: 28.03.2014. Coming into force: 11.04.2014. Effect: None. Territorial extent & classification: E. Local. - Available at http://www.legislation.gov.uk/uksi/2014/1028/contents/made Non-print

The A23 Trunk Road (Handcross to Warninglid Section) (Derestriction) Order 2014 No. 2014/2305. - Enabling power: Road Traffic Regulation Act 1984, s. 82 (2), 83 (1)- Issued: 02.09.2014. Made: 20.08.2014. Coming into force: 05.09.2014. Effect: None. Territorial extent & classification: E. Local. - Available at http://www.legislation.gov.uk/uksi/2014/2305/contents/made Non-print

The A35 Trunk Road (Wilmington) (30 and 40 Miles Per Hour Speed Limits) Order 1998 (Variation) Order 2014 No. 2014/2148. - Enabling power: Road Traffic Regulation Act 1984, s. 84 (1) (a), 2, sch. 9, para. 27 (1). - Issued: 14.08.2014. Made: 21.07.2014. Coming into force: 01.08.2014. Effect: None. Territorial extent & classification: E. Local. - Available at http://www.legislation.gov.uk/uksi/2014/2148/contents/made Non-print

The A38 Trunk Road (Hilliard's Cross to Branston Interchange, Staffordshire) (30 and 60 Miles Per Hour Speed Limit and Derestriction) Order 2014 No. 2014/1034. - Enabling power: Road Traffic Regulation Act 1984, ss. 82 (2), 83 (1), 84 (1) (a) (2), sch. 9, para. 27 (1). - Issued: 17.04.2014. Made: 27.03.2014. Coming into force: 10.04.2014. Effect: None. Territorial extent & classification: E. Local. - Available at http://www.legislation.gov.uk/uksi/2014/1034/contents/made Non-print

The A46 Trunk Road (Coventry Eastern Bypass) (40 Miles Per Hour, 50 Miles Per Hour, 60 Miles Per Hour Speed Limit and Derestriction) Order 2014 No. 2014/136. - Enabling power: Road Traffic Regulation Act 1984, ss. 82 (2), 83 (1), 84 (1) (a) (2). - Issued: 24.01.2014. Made: 16.01.2014. Coming into force: 30.01.2014. Effect: S.I. 1990/2174; 2011/1325 revoked. Territorial extent & classification: E. Local. - Available at http://www.legislation.gov.uk/uksi/2014/136/contents/made Non-print

The A49 Trunk Road (Bromfield, Shropshire) (50 Miles Per Hour Speed Limit) Order 2014 No. 2014/3018. - Enabling power: Road Traffic Regulation Act 1984, s. 84 (1) (a) (2). - Issued: 13.11.2014. Made: 31.10.2014. Coming into force: 14.11.2014. Effect: None. Territorial extent & classification: E. Local. - Available at http://www.legislation.gov.uk/uksi/2014/3018/contents/made Non-print

The A120 Trunk Road (Hare Green to Horsley Cross, Essex) (50 Miles Per Hour Speed Limit) Order 2014 No. 2014/3439. - Enabling power: Road Traffic Regulation Act 1984, ss. 84 (1) (a) (2). - Issued: 03.12.2014. Made: 01.12.2014. Coming into force: 15.12.2014. Effect: None. Territorial extent & classification: E. Local. - Available at http://www.legislation.gov.uk/uksi/2014/3439/contents/made Non-print

The A282 Trunk Road (Dartford - Thurrock Crossing and Approach Roads) (Speed Limits) Order 2014 No. 2014/2519. - Enabling power: Road Traffic Regulation Act 1984, ss. 84 (1) (a) (2), 126, sch. 9 para. 27 (1). - Issued: 15.09.2014. Made: 08.09.2014. Coming into force: 26.10.2014. Effect: S.I. 2008/1503 revoked. Territorial extent & classification: E. Local. - Available at http://www.legislation.gov.uk/uksi/2014/2519/contents/made Non-print

The A428 Trunk Road (Cambourne, Cambridgeshire) (Derestriction) Order 2014 No. 2014/1013. - Enabling power: Road Traffic Regulation Act 1984, ss. 82 (2) (a), 83 (1). - Issued: 16.04.2014. Made: 21.03.2014. Coming into force: 04.04.2014. Effect: None. Territorial extent & classification: E. Local. - Available at http://www.legislation.gov.uk/uksi/2014/1013/contents/made Non-print

The A428 Trunk Road (Caxton Gibbet, Cambridgeshire) (Derestriction and Variation) Order 2014 No. 2014/1027. - Enabling power: Road Traffic Regulation Act 1984, ss. 82 (2) (a), 83 (1), sch. 9, para. 27. - Issued: 17.04.2014. Made: 28.03.2014. Coming into force: 11.04.2014. Effect: None. Territorial extent & classification: E. Local. - Available at http://www.legislation.gov.uk/uksi/2014/1027/contents/made Non-print

The A428 Trunk Road (Wyboston, Bedfordshire) (Derestriction) Order 2014 No. 2014/1047. - Enabling power: Road Traffic Regulation Act 1984, s. 82 (2) (a). - Issued: 22.04.2014. Made: 04.04.2014. Coming into force: 18.04.2014. Effect: None. Territorial extent & classification: E. Local. - Available at http://www.legislation.gov.uk/uksi/2014/1047/contents/made Non-print

The A500 Trunk Road (A527 Reginald Mitchell Way, Staffordshire) (Slip Roads) (40 Miles Per Hour Speed Limit) Order 2014 No. 2014/1033. - Enabling power: Road Traffic Regulation Act 1984, s. 84 (1) (a) (2), sch. 9, para. 27 (1). - Issued: 17.04.2014. Made: 27.03.2014. Coming into force: 10.04.2014. Effect: None. Territorial extent & classification: E. Local. - Available at http://www.legislation.gov.uk/uksi/2014/1033/contents/made Non-print

The A590 Trunk Road (Newlands) (50 Miles Per Hour Speed Limit) Order 2014 No. 2014/2033. - Enabling power: Road Traffic Regulation Act 1984, s. 84 (1) (a) (2). - Issued: 01.08.2014. Made: 16.06.2014. Coming into force: 27.06.2014. Effect: None. Territorial extent & classification: E. Local. - Available at http://www.legislation.gov.uk/uksi/2014/2033/contents/made Non-print

The A595 Trunk Road (Egremont) (40 Miles Per Hour Speed Limit) Order 2014 No. 2014/1041. - Enabling power: Road Traffic Regulation Act 1984, s. 84 (1) (a) (2). - Issued: 22.04.2014. Made: 03.04.2014. Coming into force: 14.04.2014. Effect: None. Territorial extent & classification: E. Local. - Available at http://www.legislation.gov.uk/uksi/2014/1041/contents/made Non-print

The A2070 Trunk Road (Bad Munstereifel Road) (50 Miles Per Hour Speed Limit) Order 2014 No. 2014/3402. - Enabling power: Road Traffic Regulation Act 1984, ss. 84 (1) (a) (2), sch. 9 para. 27, 122A. - Issued: 24.11.2014. Made: 17.11.2014. Coming into force: 01.12.2014. Effect: None. Territorial extent & classification: E. Local. - Available at http://www.legislation.gov.uk/uksi/2014/3402/contents/made Non-print

The A2070 Trunk Road (Park Farm Roundabout) (50 Miles Per Hour Speed Limit) Order 2014 No. 2014/1722. - Enabling power: Road Traffic Regulation Act 1984, s. 84 (1) (a) (2). - Issued: 02.07.2014. Made: 13.06.2014. Coming into force: 27.06.2014. Effect: None. Territorial extent & classification: E. Local. - Available at http://www.legislation.gov.uk/uksi/2014/1722/contents/made Non-print

Road traffic: Traffic regulation

The A1 and A52 Trunk Roads (Barrowby, Lincolnshire) (Slip Road) (Temporary Prohibition of Traffic) Order 2014 No. 2014/202. - Enabling power: Road Traffic Regulation Act 1984, s. 14 (1) (a). - Issued: 05.02.2014. Made: 20.01.2014. Coming into force: 27.01.2014. Effect: None. Territorial extent & classification: E. Local. - Available at http://www.legislation.gov.uk/uksi/2014/202/contents/made Non-print

The A1 and the A46 Trunk Roads (Winthorpe to Harlaxton) (Temporary Restriction and Prohibition of Traffic) Order 2014 No. 2014/2177. - Enabling power: Road Traffic Regulation Act 1984, s. 14 (1) (a). - Issued: 15.08.2014. Made: 28.07.2014. Coming into force: 04.08.2014. Effect: None. Territorial extent & classification: E. Local. - Available at http://www.legislation.gov.uk/uksi/2014/2177/contents/made Non-print

The A1(M) Motorway and The A1 Trunk Road (A1(M) Junction 2 and A1(M) Junction 1 - A1 Rowley Lane Junction) (Temporary Prohibition of Traffic) Order 2014 No. 2014/1553. - Enabling power: Road Traffic Regulation Act 1984, s. 14 (1) (a). - Issued: 16.06.2014. Made: 26.05.2014. Coming into force: 14.06.2014. Effect: None. Territorial extent & classification: E. Local. - Available at http://www.legislation.gov.uk/uksi/2014/1553/contents/made Non-print

The A1(M) Motorway and the A1 Trunk Road (Dishforth to Barton) (Temporary Restriction and Prohibition of Traffic and Pedestrians) Order 2014 No. 2014/993. - Enabling power: Road Traffic Regulation Act 1984, s. 14 (1) (a), 15 (2) & S.I. 1982/1163, reg. 16 (2). - Issued: 15.04.2014. Made: 20.03.2014. Coming into force: 02.04.2014. Effect: None. Territorial extent & classification: E. Local. - Available at http://www.legislation.gov.uk/uksi/2014/993/contents/made Non-print

The A1(M) Motorway and the A1 Trunk Road (Junction 56 to Junction 59) (Temporary Restriction and Prohibition of Traffic) Order 2014 No. 2014/1733. - Enabling power: Road Traffic Regulation Act 1984, s. 14 (1) (a) & S.I. 1982/1163, reg. 16 (2). - Issued: 02.07.2014. Made: 19.06.2014. Coming into force: 29.06.2014. Effect: None. Territorial extent & classification: E. Local. - Available at http://www.legislation.gov.uk/uksi/2014/1733/contents/made Non-print

The A1(M) Motorway and the A64 Trunk Road (Bramham Crossroads to Selby Fork) (Temporary Restriction and Prohibition of Traffic) Order 2014 No. 2014/1125. - Enabling power: Road Traffic Regulation Act 1984, s. 14 (1) (a). - Issued: 01.05.2014. Made: 17.04.2014. Coming into force: 27.04.2014. Effect: None. Territorial extent & classification: E. Local. - Available at http://www.legislation.gov.uk/uksi/2014/1125/contents/made Non-print

The A1(M) Motorway and the M62 Motorway (Holmfield Interchange) (Temporary Prohibition of Traffic) Order 2014 No. 2014/1324. - Enabling power: Road Traffic Regulation Act 1984, s. 14 (1) (a). - Issued: 27.05.2014. Made: 08.05.2014. Coming into force: 18.05.2014. Effect: None. Territorial extent & classification: E. Local. - Available at http://www.legislation.gov.uk/uksi/2014/1324/contents/made Non-print

The A1(M) Motorway (Between Junction 9 and Junction 10) (Temporary 50 Miles Per Hour Speed Restriction) Order 2014 No. 2014/3041. - Enabling power: Road Traffic Regulation Act 1984, s. 14 (1) (a). - Issued: 17.11.2014. Made: 10.11.2014. Coming into force: 17.11.2014. Effect: None. Territorial extent & classification: E. Local. - Available at http://www.legislation.gov.uk/uksi/2014/3041/contents/made Non-print

The A1(M) Motorway (Eighton Lodge to Blind Lane) and the A194 (M) Motorway (Peareth Hall Road to Birtley) (Temporary Restriction and Prohibition of Traffic) Order 2014 No. 2014/2683. - Enabling power: Road Traffic Regulation Act 1984, s. 14 (1) (a). - Issued: 07.10.2014. Made: 25.09.2014. Coming into force: 05.10.2014. Effect: None. Territorial extent & classification: E. Local. - Available at http://www.legislation.gov.uk/uksi/2014/2683/contents/made Non-print

The A1(M) Motorway (Great Yorkshire Show) (Temporary Restriction of Traffic) Order 2014 No. 2014/1783. - Enabling power: Road Traffic Regulation Act 1984, s. 16A (2) (a). - Issued: 09.07.2014. Made: 26.06.2014. Coming into force: 07.07.2014. Effect: None. Territorial extent & classification: E. Local. - Available at http://www.legislation.gov.uk/uksi/2014/1783/contents/made Non-print

The A1(M) Motorway (Hatfield Tunnel) (Temporary Prohibition of Traffic) Order 2014 No. 2014/1338. - Enabling power: Road Traffic Regulation Act 1984, s. 14 (1) (a). - Issued: 27.05.2014. Made: 12.05.2014. Coming into force: 01.06.2014. Effect: None. Territorial extent & classification: E. Local. - Available at http://www.legislation.gov.uk/uksi/2014/1338/contents/made Non-print

The A1(M) Motorway (Junction 4 to Junction 6) (Temporary Restriction and Prohibition of Traffic) Order 2014 No. 2014/2972. - Enabling power: Road Traffic Regulation Act 1984, s. 14 (1) (a) (7) & S.I. 1982/1163, reg. 16 (2). - Issued: 29.10.2014. Made: 27.10.2014. Coming into force: 03.11.2014. Effect: None. Territorial extent & classification: E. Local. - Revoked by SI 2015/1104 (Non-print) (ISBN 9786666731953). - Available at
http://www.legislation.gov.uk/uksi/2014/2972/contents/made
Non-print

The A1(M) Motorway (Junction 7 Stevenage, Hertfordshire) Slip Roads (Temporary Prohibition of Traffic) Order 2014 No. 2014/1746. - Enabling power: Road Traffic Regulation Act 1984, s. 14 (1) (b). - Issued: 03.07.2014. Made: 23.06.2014. Coming into force: 30.06.2014. Effect: None. Territorial extent & classification: E. Local. - Available at
http://www.legislation.gov.uk/uksi/2014/1746/contents/made
Non-print

The A1(M) Motorway (Junction 7 to Junction 6, Hertfordshire) Southbound (Temporary Prohibition of Traffic) Order 2014 No. 2014/2265. - Enabling power: Road Traffic Regulation Act 1984, s. 14 (1) (a). - Issued: 27.08.2014. Made: 18.08.2014. Coming into force: 26.08.2014. Effect: None. Territorial extent & classification: E. Local. - Available at
http://www.legislation.gov.uk/uksi/2014/2265/contents/made
Non-print

The A1(M) Motorway (Junction 7 to Junction 8, Hertfordshire) (Temporary Prohibition of Traffic) Order 2014 No. 2014/2332. - Enabling power: Road Traffic Regulation Act 1984, s. 14 (1) (a). - Issued: 04.09.2014. Made: 01.09.2014. Coming into force: 08.09.2014. Effect: None. Territorial extent & classification: E. Local. - Available at
http://www.legislation.gov.uk/uksi/2014/2332/contents/made
Non-print

The A1(M) Motorway (Junction 7 to Junction 9) (Temporary 50 Miles Per Hour Speed Restriction) Order 2014 No. 2014/190. - Enabling power: Road Traffic Regulation Act 1984, s. 14 (1) (a). - Issued: 04.02.2014. Made: 24.01.2014. Coming into force: 31.01.2014. Effect: None. Territorial extent & classification: E. Local. - Available at
http://www.legislation.gov.uk/uksi/2014/190/contents/made Non-print

The A1(M) Motorway (Junction 9 to Junction 8) Southbound (Temporary Restriction and Prohibition of Traffic) Order 2014 No. 2014/134. - Enabling power: Road Traffic Regulation Act 1984, s. 14 (1) (a). - Issued: 24.01.2014. Made: 20.01.2014. Coming into force: 27.01.2014. Effect: None. Territorial extent & classification: E. Local. - Available at
http://www.legislation.gov.uk/uksi/2014/134/contents/made Non-print

The A1(M) Motorway (Junction 10) (Temporary Prohibition of Traffic) Order 2014 No. 2014/2477. - Enabling power: Road Traffic Regulation Act 1984, s. 14 (1) (a)- Issued: 11.09.2014. Made: 08.09.2014. Coming into force: 15.09.2014. Effect: None. Territorial extent & classification: E. Local. - Available at
http://www.legislation.gov.uk/uksi/2014/2477/contents/made
Non-print

The A1(M) Motorway (Junction 14) and The A1 Trunk Road (Alconbury to Brampton) Cambridgeshire (Temporary Prohibition of Traffic) Order 2014 No. 2014/2751. - Enabling power: Road Traffic Regulation Act 1984, s. 14 (1) (a). - Issued: 13.10.2014. Made: 29.09.2014. Coming into force: 06.10.2014. Effect: None. Territorial extent & classification: E. Local. - Available at
http://www.legislation.gov.uk/uksi/2014/2751/contents/made
Non-print

The A1(M) Motorway (Junction 14) to the A14 Trunk Road (Junction 23 Spittals Interchange) Cambridgeshire (Temporary Prohibition of Traffic) Order 2014 No. 2014/3451. - Enabling power: Road Traffic Regulation Act 1984, s. 14 (1) (a). - Issued: 19.12.2014. Made: 15.12.2014. Coming into force: 29.12.2014. Effect: None. Territorial extent & classification: E. Local. - Available at
http://www.legislation.gov.uk/uksi/2014/3451/contents/made
Non-print

The A1(M) Motorway (Junction 15 Sawtry, Cambridgeshire) and the A1 Trunk Road (Junction 17 Fletton Parkway, City of Peterborough) Northbound Slip Roads (Temporary Prohibition of Traffic) Order 2014 No. 2014/3355. - Enabling power: Road Traffic Regulation Act 1984, s. 14 (1) (a). - Issued: 11.12.2014. Made: 06.10.2014. Coming into force: 13.10.2014. Effect: None. Territorial extent & classification: E. Local. - Available at
http://www.legislation.gov.uk/uksi/2014/3355/contents/made
Non-print

The A1(M) Motorway (Junction 15 Sawtry, Cambridgeshire) Southbound (Temporary Restriction and Prohibition of Traffic) Order 2014 No. 2014/2266. - Enabling power: Road Traffic Regulation Act 1984, s. 14 (1) (a). - Issued: 27.08.2014. Made: 18.08.2014. Coming into force: 26.08.2014. Effect: None. Territorial extent & classification: E. Local. - Available at
http://www.legislation.gov.uk/uksi/2014/2266/contents/made
Non-print

The A1(M) Motorway (Junction 15 to Junction 17) and the A14(M) Motorway (Alconbury, Cambridgeshire) (Temporary Prohibition of Traffic) Order 2014 No. 2014/1473. - Enabling power: Road Traffic Regulation Act 1984, s. 14 (1) (a). - Issued: 05.06.2014. Made: 19.05.2014. Coming into force: 26.05.2014. Effect: None. Territorial extent & classification: E. Local. - Available at
http://www.legislation.gov.uk/uksi/2014/1473/contents/made
Non-print

The A1(M) Motorway (Junction 17 Fletton Parkway, City of Peterborough) Northbound(Temporary Restriction and Prohibition of Traffic) Order 2014 No. 2014/225. - Enabling power: Road Traffic Regulation Act 1984, s. 14 (1) (a) & S.I. 1982/1163, reg. 16 (2). - Issued: 10.02.2014. Made: 03.02.2014. Coming into force: 10.02.2014. Effect: None. Territorial extent & classification: E. Local. - Available at
http://www.legislation.gov.uk/uksi/2014/225/contents/made Non-print

The A1(M) Motorway (Junction 17 Fletton Parkway, City of Peterborough) Northbound(Temporary Restriction and Prohibition of Traffic) Variation Order 2014 No. 2014/2272. - Enabling power: Road Traffic Regulation Act 1984, s. 14 (1) (a), sch. 9, para. 27 (1). - Issued: 27.08.2014. Made: 18.08.2014. Coming into force: 29.08.2014. Effect: None. Territorial extent & classification: E. Local. - Available at
http://www.legislation.gov.uk/uksi/2014/2272/contents/made
Non-print

The A1(M) Motorway (Junction 34 to Junction 35) (Temporary Prohibition of Traffic) (No.2) Order 2014 No. 2014/2817. - Enabling power: Road Traffic Regulation Act 1984, s. 14 (1) (a). - Issued: 20.10.2014. Made: 16.10.2014. Coming into force: 24.10.2014. Effect: None. Territorial extent & classification: E. Local. - Available at
http://www.legislation.gov.uk/uksi/2014/2817/contents/made
Non-print

The A1(M) Motorway (Junction 34 to Junction 35) (Temporary Prohibition of Traffic) Order 2014 No. 2014/2507. - Enabling power: Road Traffic Regulation Act 1984, s. 14 (1) (a)- Issued: 15.09.2014. Made: 11.09.2014. Coming into force: 21.09.2014. Effect: None. Territorial extent & classification: E. Local. - Available at
http://www.legislation.gov.uk/uksi/2014/2507/contents/made
Non-print

The A1(M) Motorway (Junction 34 to Junction 38) (Temporary Prohibition of Traffic) Order 2014 No. 2014/2808. - Enabling power: Road Traffic Regulation Act 1984, s. 14 (1) (a). - Issued: 14.10.2014. Made: 09.10.2014. Coming into force: 19.10.2014. Effect: None. Territorial extent & classification: E. Local. - Available at
http://www.legislation.gov.uk/uksi/2014/2808/contents/made
Non-print

The A1(M) Motorway (Junction 36, Warmsworth) (Temporary Prohibition of Traffic) Order 2014 No. 2014/69. - Enabling power: Road Traffic Regulation Act 1984, s. 14 (1) (a). - Issued: 20.01.2014. Made: 09.01.2014. Coming into force: 12.01.2014. Effect: None. Territorial extent & classification: E. Local. - Available at
http://www.legislation.gov.uk/uksi/2014/69/contents/made Non-print

The A1(M) Motorway (Junction 37) (Temporary Prohibition of Traffic) (No.2) Order 2014 No. 2014/2316. - Enabling power: Road Traffic Regulation Act 1984, s. 14 (1) (a). - Issued: 01.09.2014. Made: 28.08.2014. Coming into force: 07.09.2014. Effect: None. Territorial extent & classification: E. Local. - Available at
http://www.legislation.gov.uk/uksi/2014/2316/contents/made
Non-print

The A1(M) Motorway (Junction 37) (Temporary Prohibition of Traffic) Order 2014 No. 2014/2194. - Enabling power: Road Traffic Regulation Act 1984, s. 14 (1) (a). - Issued: 20.08.2014. Made: 07.08.2014. Coming into force: 17.08.2014. Effect: None. Territorial extent & classification: E. Local. - Available at
http://www.legislation.gov.uk/uksi/2014/2194/contents/made
Non-print

The A1(M) Motorway (Junction 37 to Junction 36) (Temporary Prohibition of Traffic) Order 2014 No. 2014/1123. - Enabling power: Road Traffic Regulation Act 1984, s. 14 (1) (a). - Issued: 01.05.2014. Made: 17.04.2014. Coming into force: 27.04.2014. Effect: None. Territorial extent & classification: E. Local. - Available at http://www.legislation.gov.uk/uksi/2014/1123/contents/made Non-print

The A1(M) Motorway (Junction 37 to Junction 38) (Temporary Prohibition of Traffic) (No.2) Order 2014 No. 2014/776. - Enabling power: Road Traffic Regulation Act 1984, s. 14 (1) (a). - Issued: 11.03.2014. Made: 06.03.2014. Coming into force: 09.03.2014. Effect: None. Territorial extent & classification: E. Local. - Available at http://www.legislation.gov.uk/uksi/2014/776/contents/made Non-print

The A1(M) Motorway (Junction 37 to Junction 38) (Temporary Prohibition of Traffic) Order 2014 No. 2014/152. - Enabling power: Road Traffic Regulation Act 1984, s. 14 (1) (a). - Issued: 30.01.2014. Made: 23.01.2014. Coming into force: 02.02.2014. Effect: None. Territorial extent & classification: E. Local. - Available at http://www.legislation.gov.uk/uksi/2014/152/contents/made Non-print

The A1(M) Motorway (Junction 43 to Junction 41) (Temporary Restriction and Prohibition of Traffic) Order 2014 No. 2014/1490. - Enabling power: Road Traffic Regulation Act 1984, s. 14 (1) (a) & S.I. 1982/1163, reg. 16 (2). - Issued: 09.06.2014. Made: 22.05.2014. Coming into force: 01.06.2014. Effect: None. Territorial extent & classification: E. Local. - Available at http://www.legislation.gov.uk/uksi/2014/1490/contents/made Non-print

The A1(M) Motorway (Junction 43 to Junction 42) (Temporary Prohibition of Traffic) Order 2014 No. 2014/3543. - Enabling power: Road Traffic Regulation Act 1984, s. 14 (1) (a). - Issued: 22.01.2015. Made: 29.12.2014. Coming into force: 13.01.2015. Effect: None. Territorial extent & classification: E. Local. - Available at http://www.legislation.gov.uk/uksi/2014/3543/contents/made Non-print

The A1(M) Motorway (Junction 44) (Temporary Prohibition of Traffic) (No.2) Order 2014 No. 2014/1482. - Enabling power: Road Traffic Regulation Act 1984, s. 14 (1) (a). - Issued: 30.05.2014. Made: 15.05.2014. Coming into force: 27.05.2014. Effect: None. Territorial extent & classification: E. Local. - Available at http://www.legislation.gov.uk/uksi/2014/1482/contents/made Non-print

The A1(M) Motorway (Junction 44) (Temporary Prohibition of Traffic) (No.3) Order 2014 No. 2014/3422. - Enabling power: Road Traffic Regulation Act 1984, s. 14 (1) (a)- Issued: 03.12.2014. Made: 27.11.2014. Coming into force: 09.12.2014. Effect: None. Territorial extent & classification: E. Local. - Available at http://www.legislation.gov.uk/uksi/2014/3422/contents/made Non-print

The A1(M) Motorway (Junction 44) (Temporary Prohibition of Traffic) Order 2014 No. 2014/1310. - Enabling power: Road Traffic Regulation Act 1984, s. 14 (1) (a). - Issued: 27.05.2014. Made: 17.04.2014. Coming into force: 27.04.2014. Effect: None. Territorial extent & classification: E. Local. - Available at http://www.legislation.gov.uk/uksi/2014/1310/contents/made Non-print

The A1(M) Motorway (Junction 44 to Junction 46) (Temporary Restriction and Prohibition of Traffic) Order 2014 No. 2014/2183. - Enabling power: Road Traffic Regulation Act 1984, s. 14 (1) (a). - Issued: 18.08.2014. Made: 10.07.2014. Coming into force: 20.07.2014. Effect: None. Territorial extent & classification: E. Local. - Available at http://www.legislation.gov.uk/uksi/2014/2183/contents/made Non-print

The A1(M) Motorway (Junction 45 to Junction 42) (Temporary Prohibition of Traffic) Order 2014 No. 2014/2165. - Enabling power: Road Traffic Regulation Act 1984, s. 14 (1) (a). - Issued: 12.08.2014. Made: 31.07.2014. Coming into force: 11.08.2014. Effect: None. Territorial extent & classification: E. Local. - Available at http://www.legislation.gov.uk/uksi/2014/2165/contents/made Non-print

The A1(M) Motorway (Junction 45 to Junction 46) (Temporary Prohibition of Traffic) Order 2014 No. 2014/1114. - Enabling power: Road Traffic Regulation Act 1984, s. 14 (1) (a). - Issued: 01.05.2014. Made: 10.04.2014. Coming into force: 21.04.2014. Effect: None. Territorial extent & classification: E. Local. - Available at http://www.legislation.gov.uk/uksi/2014/1114/contents/made Non-print

The A1(M) Motorway (Junction 46 to Junction 48) (Temporary Restriction and Prohibition of Traffic) Order 2014 No. 2014/1104. - Enabling power: Road Traffic Regulation Act 1984, s. 14 (1) (a) & S.I. 1982/1163, reg. 16 (2). - Issued: 30.04.2014. Made: 10.04.2014. Coming into force: 21.04.2014. Effect: None. Territorial extent & classification: E. Local. - Available at http://www.legislation.gov.uk/uksi/2014/1104/contents/made Non-print

The A1(M) Motorway (Junction 47) (Temporary Prohibition of Traffic) (No.2) Order 2014 No. 2014/3400. - Enabling power: Road Traffic Regulation Act 1984, s. 14 (1) (a)- Issued: 25.11.2014. Made: 20.11.2014. Coming into force: 30.11.2014. Effect: None. Territorial extent & classification: E. Local. - Available at http://www.legislation.gov.uk/uksi/2014/3400/contents/made Non-print

The A1(M) Motorway (Junction 47) (Temporary Prohibition of Traffic) Order 2014 No. 2014/986. - Enabling power: Road Traffic Regulation Act 1984, s. 14 (1) (a). - Issued: 04.04.2014. Made: 20.03.2014. Coming into force: 03.04.2014. Effect: None. Territorial extent & classification: E. Local. - Available at http://www.legislation.gov.uk/uksi/2014/986/contents/made Non-print

The A1(M) Motorway (Junction 48) (Temporary Prohibition of Traffic) Order 2014 No. 2014/2666. - Enabling power: Road Traffic Regulation Act 1984, s. 14 (1) (a). - Issued: 03.10.2014. Made: 25.09.2014. Coming into force: 05.10.2014. Effect: None. Territorial extent & classification: E. Local. - Available at http://www.legislation.gov.uk/uksi/2014/2666/contents/made Non-print

The A1(M) Motorway (Junction 57 to Junction 58) (Temporary Restriction and Prohibition of Traffic) Order 2014 No. 2014/2525. - Enabling power: Road Traffic Regulation Act 1984, s. 14 (1) (a). - Issued: 16.09.2014. Made: 11.09.2014. Coming into force: 24.09.2014. Effect: None. Territorial extent & classification: E. Local. - Available at http://www.legislation.gov.uk/uksi/2014/2525/contents/made Non-print

The A1(M) Motorway (Junction 57 to Junction 64) (Temporary Restriction and Prohibition of Traffic) Order 2014 No. 2014/3370. - Enabling power: Road Traffic Regulation Act 1984, s. 14 (1) (a). - Issued: 03.12.2014. Made: 13.11.2014. Coming into force: 24.11.2014. Effect: None. Territorial extent & classification: E. Local. - Available at http://www.legislation.gov.uk/uksi/2014/3370/contents/made Non-print

The A1(M) Motorway (Junction 58) (Temporary Restriction and Prohibition of Traffic) Order 2014 No. 2014/2802. - Enabling power: Road Traffic Regulation Act 1984, s. 14 (1) (a). - Issued: 14.10.2014. Made: 09.10.2014. Coming into force: 19.10.2014. Effect: None. Territorial extent & classification: E. Local. - Available at http://www.legislation.gov.uk/uksi/2014/2802/contents/made Non-print

The A1(M) Motorway (Junction 59) (Temporary Prohibition of Traffic) (No.4) Order 2014 No. 2014/2586. - Enabling power: Road Traffic Regulation Act 1984, s. 14 (1) (a)- Issued: 25.09.2014. Made: 18.09.2014. Coming into force: 28.09.2014. Effect: None. Territorial extent & classification: E. Local. - Available at http://www.legislation.gov.uk/uksi/2014/2586/contents/made Non-print

The A1(M) Motorway (Junction 59) (Temporary Restriction and Prohibition of Traffic) (No.2) Order 2014 No. 2014/1569. - Enabling power: Road Traffic Regulation Act 1984, s. 14 (1) (a). - Issued: 17.06.2014. Made: 29.05.2014. Coming into force: 08.06.2014. Effect: None. Territorial extent & classification: E. Local. - Available at http://www.legislation.gov.uk/uksi/2014/1569/contents/made Non-print

The A1(M) Motorway (Junction 59) (Temporary Restriction and Prohibition of Traffic) (No.3) Order 2014 No. 2014/1863. - Enabling power: Road Traffic Regulation Act 1984, s. 14 (1) (a). - Issued: 17.07.2014. Made: 26.06.2014. Coming into force: 15.07.2014. Effect: None. Territorial extent & classification: E. Local. - Available at http://www.legislation.gov.uk/uksi/2014/1863/contents/made Non-print

The A1(M) Motorway (Junction 59) (Temporary Restriction and Prohibition of Traffic) Order 2014 No. 2014/770. - Enabling power: Road Traffic Regulation Act 1984, s. 14 (1) (a). - Issued: 10.03.2014. Made: 27.02.2014. Coming into force: 09.03.2014. Effect: None. Territorial extent & classification: E. Local. - Available at http://www.legislation.gov.uk/uksi/2014/770/contents/made Non-print

The A1(M) Motorway (Junction 59 to Junction 57) (Temporary Prohibition of Traffic) Order 2014 No. 2014/3172. - Enabling power: Road Traffic Regulation Act 1984, s. 14 (1) (a). - Issued: 24.11.2014. Made: 13.11.2014. Coming into force: 23.11.2014. Effect: None. Territorial extent & classification: E. Local. - Available at http://www.legislation.gov.uk/uksi/2014/3172/contents/made Non-print

The A1(M) Motorway (Junction 59 to Junction 60) (Temporary Restriction and Prohibition of Traffic) Order 2014 No. 2014/1856. - Enabling power: Road Traffic Regulation Act 1984, s. 14 (1) (a) & S.I. 1982/1163, reg. 16 (2). - Issued: 16.07.2014. Made: 26.06.2014. Coming into force: 13.07.2014. Effect: None. Territorial extent & classification: E. Local. - Available at http://www.legislation.gov.uk/uksi/2014/1856/contents/made Non-print

The A1(M) Motorway (Junction 60) (Temporary 50 Miles Per Hour and 40 Miles Per Hour Speed Restriction) Order 2014 No. 2014/1306. - Enabling power: Road Traffic Regulation Act 1984, s. 14 (1) (a). - Issued: 23.05.2014. Made: 08.05.2014. Coming into force: 18.05.2014. Effect: None. Territorial extent & classification: E. Local. - Available at http://www.legislation.gov.uk/uksi/2014/1306/contents/made Non-print

The A1(M) Motorway (Junction 60 to Junction 59) (Temporary Prohibition of Traffic) Order 2014 No. 2014/3430. - Enabling power: Road Traffic Regulation Act 1984, s. 14 (1) (a). - Issued: 10.12.2014. Made: 04.12.2014. Coming into force: 11.12.2014. Effect: None. Territorial extent & classification: E. Local. - Available at http://www.legislation.gov.uk/uksi/2014/3430/contents/made Non-print

The A1(M) Motorway (Junction 60 to Junction 61) (Temporary Prohibition of Traffic) Order 2014 No. 2014/3407. - Enabling power: Road Traffic Regulation Act 1984, s. 14 (1) (a). - Issued: 25.11.2014. Made: 20.11.2014. Coming into force: 02.12.2014. Effect: None. Territorial extent & classification: E. Local. - Available at http://www.legislation.gov.uk/uksi/2014/3407/contents/made Non-print

The A1(M) Motorway (Junction 60 to Junction 61) (Temporary Restriction and Prohibition of Traffic) Order 2014 No. 2014/289. - Enabling power: Road Traffic Regulation Act 1984, s. 14 (1) (a). - Issued: 14.02.2014. Made: 07.02.2014. Coming into force: 16.02.2014. Effect: None. Territorial extent & classification: E. Local. - Available at http://www.legislation.gov.uk/uksi/2014/289/contents/made Non-print

The A1(M) Motorway (Junction 61) (Temporary Restriction and Prohibition of Traffic) Order 2014 No. 2014/2090. - Enabling power: Road Traffic Regulation Act 1984, s. 14 (1) (a). - Issued: 07.08.2014. Made: 17.07.2014. Coming into force: 03.08.2014. Effect: None. Territorial extent & classification: E. Local. - Available at http://www.legislation.gov.uk/uksi/2014/2090/contents/made Non-print

The A1(M) Motorway (Junction 61 to Junction 60) (Temporary Prohibition of Traffic) Order 2014 No. 2014/3043. - Enabling power: Road Traffic Regulation Act 1984, s. 14 (1) (a). - Issued: 13.11.2014. Made: 06.11.2014. Coming into force: 18.11.2014. Effect: None. Territorial extent & classification: E. Local. - Available at http://www.legislation.gov.uk/uksi/2014/3043/contents/made Non-print

The A1(M) Motorway (Junction 61 to Junction 62) (Temporary 50 Miles Per Hour Speed Restriction) Order 2014 No. 2014/1570. - Enabling power: Road Traffic Regulation Act 1984, s. 14 (1) (a). - Issued: 17.06.2014. Made: 29.05.2014. Coming into force: 08.06.2014. Effect: None. Territorial extent & classification: E. Local. - Available at http://www.legislation.gov.uk/uksi/2014/1570/contents/made Non-print

The A1(M) Motorway (Junction 61 to Junction 63) (Temporary 50 Miles Per Hour Speed Restriction) Order 2014 No. 2014/252. - Enabling power: Road Traffic Regulation Act 1984, s. 14 (1) (a). - Issued: 10.02.2014. Made: 30.01.2014. Coming into force: 13.02.2014. Effect: None. Territorial extent & classification: E. Local. - Available at http://www.legislation.gov.uk/uksi/2014/252/contents/made Non-print

The A1(M) Motorway (Junction 61 to Junction 63) (Temporary Restriction and Prohibition of Traffic) Order 2014 No. 2014/3175. - Enabling power: Road Traffic Regulation Act 1984, s. 14 (1) (a) & S.I. 1982/1163, reg. 16 (2). - Issued: 24.11.2014. Made: 13.11.2014. Coming into force: 24.11.2014. Effect: None. Territorial extent & classification: E. Local. - Available at http://www.legislation.gov.uk/uksi/2014/3175/contents/made Non-print

The A1(M) Motorway (Junction 61 to Junction 64) (Temporary Restriction and Prohibition of Traffic) Order 2014 No. 2014/2870. - Enabling power: Road Traffic Regulation Act 1984, s. 14 (1) (a) & S.I. 1982/1163, reg. 16 (2). - Issued: 20.10.2014. Made: 16.10.2014. Coming into force: 28.10.2014. Effect: None. Territorial extent & classification: E. Local. - Available at http://www.legislation.gov.uk/uksi/2014/2870/contents/made Non-print

The A1(M) Motorway (Junction 62) (Temporary Restriction and Prohibition of Traffic) Order 2014 No. 2014/2685. - Enabling power: Road Traffic Regulation Act 1984, s. 14 (1) (a). - Issued: 07.10.2014. Made: 25.09.2014. Coming into force: 05.10.2014. Effect: None. Territorial extent & classification: E. Local. - Available at http://www.legislation.gov.uk/uksi/2014/2685/contents/made Non-print

The A1(M) Motorway (Junction 62 to Junction 63) (Temporary Restriction and Prohibition of Traffic) Order 2014 No. 2014/3032. - Enabling power: Road Traffic Regulation Act 1984, s. 14 (1) (a) & S.I. 1982/1163, reg. 16 (2). - Issued: 13.11.2014. Made: 06.11.2014. Coming into force: 16.11.2014. Effect: None. Territorial extent & classification: E. Local. - Available at http://www.legislation.gov.uk/uksi/2014/3032/contents/made Non-print

The A1(M) Motorway (Junction 63 to Junction 62) (Temporary Prohibition of Traffic) Order 2014 No. 2014/3408. - Enabling power: Road Traffic Regulation Act 1984, s. 14 (1) (a). - Issued: 25.11.2014. Made: 20.11.2014. Coming into force: 03.12.2014. Effect: None. Territorial extent & classification: E. Local. - Available at http://www.legislation.gov.uk/uksi/2014/3408/contents/made Non-print

The A1(M) Motorway (Junction 63 to Junction 64) (Temporary Restriction and Prohibition of Traffic) Order 2014 No. 2014/1982. - Enabling power: Road Traffic Regulation Act 1984, s. 14 (1) (a). - Issued: 21.07.2014. Made: 10.07.2014. Coming into force: 20.07.2014. Effect: None. Territorial extent & classification: E. Local. - Available at http://www.legislation.gov.uk/uksi/2014/1982/contents/made Non-print

The A1(M) Motorway (Junction 63 to Junction 65) and the A194(M) Motorway (Havannah to Birtley) (Temporary Restriction and Prohibition of Traffic) (No.2) Order 2014 No. 2014/2684. - Enabling power: Road Traffic Regulation Act 1984, s. 14 (1) (a). - Issued: 07.10.2014. Made: 25.09.2014. Coming into force: 05.10.2014. Effect: None. Territorial extent & classification: E. Local. - Available at http://www.legislation.gov.uk/uksi/2014/2684/contents/made Non-print

The A1(M) Motorway (Junction 63 to Junction 65) and the A194(M) Motorway (Havannah to Birtley) (Temporary Restriction and Prohibition of Traffic) Order 2014 No. 2014/1970. - Enabling power: Road Traffic Regulation Act 1984, s. 14 (1) (a). - Issued: 18.07.2014. Made: 03.07.2014. Coming into force: 13.07.2014. Effect: None. Territorial extent & classification: E. Local. - Available at http://www.legislation.gov.uk/uksi/2014/1970/contents/made Non-print

The A1(M) Motorway (Junction 64) (Temporary Restriction and Prohibition of Traffic) Order 2014 No. 2014/2195. - Enabling power: Road Traffic Regulation Act 1984, s. 14 (1) (a). - Issued: 20.08.2014. Made: 07.08.2014. Coming into force: 17.08.2014. Effect: None. Territorial extent & classification: E. Local. - Available at http://www.legislation.gov.uk/uksi/2014/2195/contents/made Non-print

The A1(M) Motorway (Junctions 3 - 4) (Temporary Prohibition of Traffic) Order 2014 No. 2014/2100. - Enabling power: Road Traffic Regulation Act 1984, s. 14 (1) (a). - Issued: 07.08.2014. Made: 21.07.2014. Coming into force: 09.08.2014. Effect: None. Territorial extent & classification: E. Local. - Available at http://www.legislation.gov.uk/uksi/2014/2100/contents/made Non-print

The A1(M) Motorway (South Mimms Interchange, Slip Road) (Temporary Prohibition of Traffic) Order 2014 No. 2014/1280. - Enabling power: Road Traffic Regulation Act 1984, s. 14 (1) (a). - Issued: 19.05.2014. Made: 05.05.2014. Coming into force: 24.05.2014. Effect: None. Territorial extent & classification: E. Local. - Available at http://www.legislation.gov.uk/uksi/2014/1280/contents/made Non-print

ROAD TRAFFIC: TRAFFIC REGULATION

The A1(M) Motorway (Tour de France) (Temporary Restriction and Prohibition of Traffic) Order 2014 No. 2014/2001. - Enabling power: Road Traffic Regulation Act 1984, s. 16A (2) (a) & S.I. 1982/1163, reg. 16 (2). - Issued: 30.07.2014. Made: 26.06.2014. Coming into force: 04.07.2014. Effect: None. Territorial extent & classification: E. Local. - Available at http://www.legislation.gov.uk/uksi/2014/2001/contents/made Non-print

The A1(M) Motorway (Yorkshire Festival of Cycling) (Temporary Restriction of Traffic) Order 2014 No. 2014/1784. - Enabling power: Road Traffic Regulation Act 1984, s. 16A (2) (a) & S.I. 1982/1163, reg. 16 (2). - Issued: 09.07.2014. Made: 26.06.2014. Coming into force: 04.07.2014. Effect: None. Territorial extent & classification: E. Local. - Available at http://www.legislation.gov.uk/uksi/2014/1784/contents/made Non-print

The A1 Trunk Road (Alnwick to Guyzance) (Temporary Restriction and Prohibition of Traffic) (No.2) Order 2014 No. 2014/2192. - Enabling power: Road Traffic Regulation Act 1984, s. 14 (1) (a). - Issued: 20.08.2014. Made: 07.08.2014. Coming into force: 16.08.2014. Effect: None. Territorial extent & classification: E. Local. - Available at http://www.legislation.gov.uk/uksi/2014/2192/contents/made Non-print

The A1 Trunk Road (Alnwick to Guyzance) (Temporary Restriction and Prohibition of Traffic) Order 2014 No. 2014/1486. - Enabling power: Road Traffic Regulation Act 1984, s. 14 (1) (a). - Issued: 09.06.2014. Made: 22.05.2014. Coming into force: 31.05.2014. Effect: None. Territorial extent & classification: E. Local. - Available at http://www.legislation.gov.uk/uksi/2014/1486/contents/made Non-print

The A1 Trunk Road and A1(M) Motorway (Barnet By-Pass) (Temporary Prohibition of Traffic) Order 2014 No. 2014/1213. - Enabling power: Road Traffic Regulation Act 1984, s. 14 (1) (a). - Issued: 13.05.2014. Made: 17.03.2014. Coming into force: 05.04.2014. Effect: None. Territorial extent & classification: E. Local. - Available at http://www.legislation.gov.uk/uksi/2014/1213/contents/made Non-print

The A1 Trunk Road and the A1(M) Motorway (A5135 Junction - Junction 6) (Temporary Prohibition of Traffic) Order 2014 No. 2014/2668. - Enabling power: Road Traffic Regulation Act 1984, s. 14 (1) (a). - Issued: 30.09.2014. Made: 22.09.2014. Coming into force: 14.10.2014. Effect: None. Territorial extent & classification: E. Local. - Available at http://www.legislation.gov.uk/uksi/2014/2668/contents/made Non-print

The A1 Trunk Road and the A1(M) Motorway (Barnsdale Bar Interchange to Junction 41) (Temporary Restriction and Prohibition of Traffic) Order 2014 No. 2014/961. - Enabling power: Road Traffic Regulation Act 1984, s. 14 (1) (a). - Issued: 01.04.2014. Made: 13.03.2014. Coming into force: 20.03.2014. Effect: None. Territorial extent & classification: E. Local. - Available at http://www.legislation.gov.uk/uksi/2014/961/contents/made Non-print

The A1 Trunk Road and the A1(M) Motorway (Junctions 1, 3 and 4, Northbound Slip Roads) (Temporary Prohibition of Traffic) Order 2014 No. 2014/998. - Enabling power: Road Traffic Regulation Act 1984, s. 14 (1) (a). - Issued: 04.04.2014. Made: 24.03.2014. Coming into force: 16.04.2014. Effect: None. Territorial extent & classification: E. Local. - Available at http://www.legislation.gov.uk/uksi/2014/998/contents/made Non-print

The A1 Trunk Road and the A19 Trunk Road (Seaton Burn Interchange) (Temporary Restriction and Prohibition of Traffic) (No.2) Order 2014 No. 2014/1297. - Enabling power: Road Traffic Regulation Act 1984, s. 14 (1) (a). - Issued: 23.05.2014. Made: 01.05.2014. Coming into force: 11.05.2014. Effect: None. Territorial extent & classification: E. Local. - Available at http://www.legislation.gov.uk/uksi/2014/1297/contents/made Non-print

The A1 Trunk Road and the A19 Trunk Road (Seaton Burn Interchange) (Temporary Restriction and Prohibition of Traffic) Order 2014 No. 2014/233. - Enabling power: Road Traffic Regulation Act 1984, s. 14 (1) (a). - Issued: 10.02.2014. Made: 30.01.2014. Coming into force: 30.01.2014. Effect: None. Territorial extent & classification: E. Local. - Available at http://www.legislation.gov.uk/uksi/2014/233/contents/made Non-print

The A1 Trunk Road (Apleyhead - Blyth, Nottinghamshire) (Temporary Restriction and Prohibition of Traffic) Order 2014 No. 2014/1721. - Enabling power: Road Traffic Regulation Act 1984, s. 14 (1) (a). - Issued: 03.07.2014. Made: 16.06.2014. Coming into force: 23.06.2014. Effect: None. Territorial extent & classification: E. Local. - Available at http://www.legislation.gov.uk/uksi/2014/1721/contents/made Non-print

The A1 Trunk Road (Bannister Lane Junction to Hampole Balk Lane Junction) (Temporary Prohibition of Traffic) Order 2014 No. 2014/1321. - Enabling power: Road Traffic Regulation Act 1984, s. 14 (1) (a). - Issued: 27.05.2014. Made: 08.05.2014. Coming into force: 20.05.2014. Effect: None. Territorial extent & classification: E. Local. - Available at http://www.legislation.gov.uk/uksi/2014/1321/contents/made Non-print

The A1 Trunk Road (Barnsdale Bar Interchange) (Temporary Prohibition of Traffic) (No.2) Order 2014 No. 2014/3373. - Enabling power: Road Traffic Regulation Act 1984, s. 14 (1) (a). - Issued: 17.11.2014. Made: 13.11.2014. Coming into force: 25.11.2014. Effect: None. Territorial extent & classification: E. Local. - Available at http://www.legislation.gov.uk/uksi/2014/3373/contents/made Non-print

The A1 Trunk Road (Barnsdale Bar Interchange) (Temporary Prohibition of Traffic) Order 2014 No. 2014/2998. - Enabling power: Road Traffic Regulation Act 1984, s. 14 (1) (a). - Issued: 04.11.2014. Made: 30.10.2014. Coming into force: 09.11.2014. Effect: None. Territorial extent & classification: E. Local. - Available at http://www.legislation.gov.uk/uksi/2014/2998/contents/made Non-print

The A1 Trunk Road (Beeston, Sandy, Bedfordshire) (Temporary Restriction and Prohibition of Traffic) Order 2014 No. 2014/3494. - Enabling power: Road Traffic Regulation Act 1984, s. 14 (1) (a). - Issued: 16.01.2015. Made: 06.10.2014. Coming into force: 13.10.2014. Effect: None. Territorial extent & classification: E. Local. - Available at http://www.legislation.gov.uk/uksi/2014/3494/contents/made Non-print

The A1 Trunk Road (Beeston, Sandy, Bedfordshire) (Temporary Restriction of Traffic and Prohibition of Pedestrians) Order 2014 No. 2014/689. - Enabling power: Road Traffic Regulation Act 1984, s. 14 (1) (a). - Issued: 06.03.2014. Made: 24.02.2014. Coming into force: 03.03.2014. Effect: None. Territorial extent & classification: E. Local. - Available at http://www.legislation.gov.uk/uksi/2014/689/contents/made Non-print

The A1 Trunk Road (Blaydon Interchange to Gosforth Park Interchange) (Temporary Restriction and Prohibition of Traffic) Order 2014 No. 2014/681. - Enabling power: Road Traffic Regulation Act 1984, s. 14 (1) (a). - Issued: 04.03.2014. Made: 20.02.2014. Coming into force: 02.03.2014. Effect: None. Territorial extent & classification: E. Local. - Available at http://www.legislation.gov.uk/uksi/2014/681/contents/made Non-print

The A1 Trunk Road (Bloody Oaks Junction, Lincolnshire) (Temporary Restriction and Prohibition of Traffic) Order 2014 No. 2014/1540. - Enabling power: Road Traffic Regulation Act 1984, s. 14 (1) (a). - Issued: 13.06.2014. Made: 23.05.2014. Coming into force: 30.05.2014. Effect: None. Territorial extent & classification: E. Local. - Available at http://www.legislation.gov.uk/uksi/2014/1540/contents/made Non-print

The A1 Trunk Road (Blunham to Wyboston) and the A421 Trunk Road (Renhold/Great Barford Interchange to Black Cat Roundabout) (Bedfordshire) (Temporary Restriction and Prohibition of Traffic) Order 2014 No. 2014/1218. - Enabling power: Road Traffic Regulation Act 1984, s. 14 (1) (a). - Issued: 13.05.2014. Made: 28.04.2014. Coming into force: 05.05.2014. Effect: None. Territorial extent & classification: E. Local. - Available at http://www.legislation.gov.uk/uksi/2014/1218/contents/made Non-print

The A1 Trunk Road (Blyth, Nottinghamshire) (Temporary Prohibition of Traffic) Order 2014 No. 2014/364. - Enabling power: Road Traffic Regulation Act 1984, s. 14 (1) (a). - Issued: 20.02.2014. Made: 11.02.2014. Coming into force: 18.02.2014. Effect: None. Territorial extent & classification: E. Local. - Available at http://www.legislation.gov.uk/uksi/2014/364/contents/made Non-print

The A1 Trunk Road (Brampton Hut) Southbound and the A14 Trunk Road (Junction 20 Ellington) Eastbound (Cambridgeshire) (Temporary Prohibition of Traffic) Order 2014 No. 2014/2627. - Enabling power: Road Traffic Regulation Act 1984, s. 14 (1) (b). - Issued: 29.09.2014. Made: 22.09.2014. Coming into force: 29.09.2014. Effect: None. Territorial extent & classification: E. Local. - Available at http://www.legislation.gov.uk/uksi/2014/2627/contents/made Non-print

The A1 Trunk Road (Carpenter's Lodge to Stamford) (Temporary Restriction and Prohibition of Traffic) Order 2014 No. 2014/2298. - Enabling power: Road Traffic Regulation Act 1984, s. 14 (1) (b). - Issued: 28.08.2014. Made: 26.08.2014. Coming into force: 01.09.2014. Effect: None. Territorial extent & classification: E. Local. - Available at http://www.legislation.gov.uk/uksi/2014/2298/contents/made Non-print

The A1 Trunk Road (Catterick North Interchange) (Temporary Prohibition of Traffic) Order 2014 No. 2014/63. - Enabling power: Road Traffic Regulation Act 1984, s. 14 (1) (a). - Issued: 20.01.2014. Made: 07.01.2014. Coming into force: 12.01.2014. Effect: None. Territorial extent & classification: E. Local. - Available at http://www.legislation.gov.uk/uksi/2014/63/contents/made Non-print

The A1 Trunk Road (Coalhouse Interchange to Lobley Hill Interchange) (Temporary Prohibition of Traffic) Order 2014 No. 2014/345. - Enabling power: Road Traffic Regulation Act 1984, s. 14 (1) (a). - Issued: 19.02.2014. Made: 13.02.2014. Coming into force: 24.02.2014. Effect: None. Territorial extent & classification: E. Local. - Available at http://www.legislation.gov.uk/uksi/2014/345/contents/made Non-print

The A1 Trunk Road (Coddington, Nottinghamshire) (No.2) (Temporary Prohibition of Traffic) Order 2014 No. 2014/2226. - Enabling power: Road Traffic Regulation Act 1984, s. 14 (1) (a). - Issued: 27.08.2014. Made: 01.08.2014. Coming into force: 08.08.2014. Effect: None. Territorial extent & classification: E. Local. - Available at http://www.legislation.gov.uk/uksi/2014/2226/contents/made Non-print

The A1 Trunk Road (Coddington, Nottinghamshire) (No.3) (Temporary Prohibition of Traffic) Order 2014 No. 2014/3019. - Enabling power: Road Traffic Regulation Act 1984, s. 14 (1) (a). - Issued: 14.11.2014. Made: 07.11.2014. Coming into force: 14.11.2014. Effect: None. Territorial extent & classification: E. Local. - Available at http://www.legislation.gov.uk/uksi/2014/3019/contents/made Non-print

The A1 Trunk Road (Coddington, Nottinghamshire) (Temporary Prohibition of Traffic) Order 2014 No. 2014/1073. - Enabling power: Road Traffic Regulation Act 1984, s. 14 (1) (a). - Issued: 28.04.2014. Made: 08.04.2014. Coming into force: 15.04.2014. Effect: None. Territorial extent & classification: E. Local. - Available at http://www.legislation.gov.uk/uksi/2014/1073/contents/made Non-print

The A1 Trunk Road (Colsterworth, Lincolnshire) (Slip Roads) (Temporary Prohibition of Traffic) Order 2014 No. 2014/639. - Enabling power: Road Traffic Regulation Act 1984, s. 14 (1) (a). - Issued: 05.03.2014. Made: 17.02.2014. Coming into force: 24.02.2014. Effect: None. Territorial extent & classification: E. Local. - Available at http://www.legislation.gov.uk/uksi/2014/639/contents/made Non-print

The A1 Trunk Road (Colsterworth Services, Lincolnshire) (Slip Roads) (Temporary Prohibition of Traffic) Order 2014 No. 2014/629. - Enabling power: Road Traffic Regulation Act 1984, s. 14 (1) (a). - Issued: 05.03.2014. Made: 17.02.2014. Coming into force: 24.02.2014. Effect: None. Territorial extent & classification: E. Local. - Available at http://www.legislation.gov.uk/uksi/2014/629/contents/made Non-print

The A1Trunk Road (Denwick Interchange to Hemelspeth Junction) (Temporary Restriction and Prohibition of Traffic) Order 2014 No. 2014/2312. - Enabling power: Road Traffic Regulation Act 1984, s. 14 (1) (a). - Issued: 01.09.2014. Made: 28.08.2014. Coming into force: 07.09.2014. Effect: None. Territorial extent & classification: E. Local. - Available at http://www.legislation.gov.uk/uksi/2014/2312/contents/made Non-print

The A1 Trunk Road (Denwick to Wandylaw) (Temporary Restriction and Prohibition of Traffic) (No.2) Order 2014 No. 2014/3034. - Enabling power: Road Traffic Regulation Act 1984, s. 14 (1) (a). - Issued: 13.11.2014. Made: 06.11.2014. Coming into force: 16.11.2014. Effect: None. Territorial extent & classification: E. Local. - Available at http://www.legislation.gov.uk/uksi/2014/3034/contents/made Non-print

The A1 Trunk Road (Denwick to Wandylaw) (Temporary Restriction and Prohibition of Traffic) Order 2014 No. 2014/1175. - Enabling power: Road Traffic Regulation Act 1984, s. 14 (1) (a). - Issued: 06.05.2014. Made: 24.04.2014. Coming into force: 05.05.2014. Effect: None. Territorial extent & classification: E. Local. - Available at http://www.legislation.gov.uk/uksi/2014/1175/contents/made Non-print

The A1 Trunk Road (Derwenthaugh Interchange to Swalwell Interchange) (Temporary Prohibition of Traffic) Order 2014 No. 2014/1645. - Enabling power: Road Traffic Regulation Act 1984, s. 14 (1) (a). - Issued: 18.06.2014. Made: 05.06.2014. Coming into force: 15.06.2014. Effect: None. Territorial extent & classification: E. Local. - Available at http://www.legislation.gov.uk/uksi/2014/1645/contents/made Non-print

The A1 Trunk Road (Derwenthaugh to Eighton Lodge) (Temporary Restriction and Prohibition of Traffic) Order 2014 No. 2014/2221. - Enabling power: Road Traffic Regulation Act 1984, ss. 14 (1) (a), 15 (2). - Issued: 22.08.2014. Made: 04.07.2014. Coming into force: 12.07.2014. Effect: None. Territorial extent & classification: E. Local. - Available at http://www.legislation.gov.uk/uksi/2014/2221/contents/made Non-print

The A1 Trunk Road (Duddo Junction to Denwick Interchange) Temporary Restriction and Prohibition of Traffic) Order 2014 No. 2014/1647. - Enabling power: Road Traffic Regulation Act 1984, s. 14 (1) (a). - Issued: 26.06.2014. Made: 05.06.2014. Coming into force: 17.06.2014. Effect: None. Territorial extent & classification: E. Local. - Available at http://www.legislation.gov.uk/uksi/2014/1647/contents/made Non-print

The A1 Trunk Road (Dunston Interchange) (Temporary Prohibition of Traffic) Order 2014 No. 2014/744. - Enabling power: Road Traffic Regulation Act 1984, s. 14 (1) (a). - Issued: 10.03.2014. Made: 27.02.2014. Coming into force: 12.03.2014. Effect: None. Territorial extent & classification: E. Local. - Available at http://www.legislation.gov.uk/uksi/2014/744/contents/made Non-print

The A1 Trunk Road (East Ord Roundabout to Highfields Roundabout) (Temporary Restriction and Prohibition of Traffic) Order 2014 No. 2014/2779. - Enabling power: Road Traffic Regulation Act 1984, s. 14 (1) (a). - Issued: 13.10.2014. Made: 02.10.2014. Coming into force: 11.10.2014. Effect: None. Territorial extent & classification: E. Local. - Available at http://www.legislation.gov.uk/uksi/2014/2779/contents/made Non-print

The A1 Trunk Road (Eighton Lodge Interchange to Seaton Burn Interchange) (Temporary Restriction and Prohibition of Traffic) Order 2014 No. 2014/53. - Enabling power: Road Traffic Regulation Act 1984, s. 14 (1) (a). - Issued: 17.01.2014. Made: 09.01.2014. Coming into force: 19.01.2014. Effect: None. Territorial extent & classification: E. Local. - Available at http://www.legislation.gov.uk/uksi/2014/53/contents/made Non-print

The A1 Trunk Road (Eighton Lodge to Birtley Junction) (Temporary Restriction and Prohibition of Traffic) Order 2014 No. 2014/2426. - Enabling power: Road Traffic Regulation Act 1984, s. 14 (1) (a). - Issued: 10.09.2014. Made: 04.09.2014. Coming into force: 14.09.2014. Effect: None. Territorial extent & classification: E. Local. - Available at http://www.legislation.gov.uk/uksi/2014/2426/contents/made Non-print

The A1 Trunk Road (Elkesley, Nottinghamshire) (Temporary Restriction and Prohibition of Traffic) Order 2014 No. 2014/1242. - Enabling power: Road Traffic Regulation Act 1984, s. 14 (1) (a). - Issued: 16.05.2014. Made: 28.04.2014. Coming into force: 05.05.2014. Effect: None. Territorial extent & classification: E. Local. - Revoked by SI 2015/1199 (Non-print). - Available at http://www.legislation.gov.uk/uksi/2014/1242/contents/made Non-print

The A1 Trunk Road (Fairmoor to Clifton Lane) (Temporary Prohibition of Traffic) Order 2014 No. 2014/1315. - Enabling power: Road Traffic Regulation Act 1984, s. 14 (1) (a). - Issued: 27.05.2014. Made: 08.05.2014. Coming into force: 18.05.2014. Effect: None. Territorial extent & classification: E. Local. - Available at http://www.legislation.gov.uk/uksi/2014/1315/contents/made Non-print

ROAD TRAFFIC: TRAFFIC REGULATION

The A1 Trunk Road (Fair Moor to Clifton) (Temporary Restriction and Prohibition of Traffic) (No.2) Order 2014 No. 2014/1968. - Enabling power: Road Traffic Regulation Act 1984, s. 14 (1) (a) (7). - Issued: 21.07.2014. Made: 03.07.2014. Coming into force: 12.07.2014. Effect: None. Territorial extent & classification: E. Local. - Available at http://www.legislation.gov.uk/uksi/2014/1968/contents/made
Non-print

The A1 Trunk Road (Felton North to Clifton) (Temporary Restriction and Prohibition of Traffic) Order 2014 No. 2014/2499. - Enabling power: Road Traffic Regulation Act 1984, s. 14 (1) (a). - Issued: 10.09.2014. Made: 04.09.2014. Coming into force: 16.09.2014. Effect: None. Territorial extent & classification: E. Local. - Available at http://www.legislation.gov.uk/uksi/2014/2499/contents/made
Non-print

The A1 Trunk Road (Felton to Alnwick) (Temporary Restriction and Prohibition of Traffic) Order 2014 No. 2014/3153. - Enabling power: Road Traffic Regulation Act 1984, s. 14 (1) (a) (7). - Issued: 24.11.2014. Made: 13.11.2014. Coming into force: 22.11.204. Effect: None. Territorial extent & classification: E. Local. - Available at http://www.legislation.gov.uk/uksi/2014/3153/contents/made
Non-print

The A1 Trunk Road (Fenrother Lane to Felton Junction) (Temporary Restriction and Prohibition of Traffic) Order 2014 No. 2014/3151. - Enabling power: Road Traffic Regulation Act 1984, s. 14 (1) (a). - Issued: 24.11.2014. Made: 13.11.2014. Coming into force: 22.11.204. Effect: None. Territorial extent & classification: E. Local. - Available at http://www.legislation.gov.uk/uksi/2014/3151/contents/made
Non-print

The A1 Trunk Road (Fenwick Junction to Elwick Junction) (Temporary Restriction and Prohibition of Traffic) Order 2014 No. 2014/2967. - Enabling power: Road Traffic Regulation Act 1984, s. 14 (1) (a). - Issued: 27.10.2014. Made: 23.10.2014. Coming into force: 02.11.2014. Effect: None. Territorial extent & classification: E. Local. - Available at http://www.legislation.gov.uk/uksi/2014/2967/contents/made
Non-print

The A1 Trunk Road (Fenwick Junction to Scremerston Roundabout) (Temporary Restriction and Prohibition of Traffic) Order 2014 No. 2014/2581. - Enabling power: Road Traffic Regulation Act 1984, s. 14 (1) (a). - Issued: 25.09.2014. Made: 18.09.2014. Coming into force: 27.09.2014. Effect: None. Territorial extent & classification: E. Local. - Available at http://www.legislation.gov.uk/uksi/2014/2581/contents/made
Non-print

The A1 Trunk Road (Gateshead Quays Interchange) (Temporary Prohibition of Traffic) (No.2) Order 2014 No. 2014/1296. - Enabling power: Road Traffic Regulation Act 1984, s. 14 (1) (a). - Issued: 23.05.2014. Made: 01.05.2014. Coming into force: 11.05.2014. Effect: None. Territorial extent & classification: E. Local. - Available at http://www.legislation.gov.uk/uksi/2014/1296/contents/made
Non-print

The A1 Trunk Road (Gateshead Quays Interchange) (Temporary Prohibition of Traffic) Order 2014 No. 2014/975. - Enabling power: Road Traffic Regulation Act 1984, s. 14 (1) (a). - Issued: 31.03.2014. Made: 13.03.2014. Coming into force: 25.03.2014. Effect: None. Territorial extent & classification: E. Local. - Available at http://www.legislation.gov.uk/uksi/2014/975/contents/made Non-print

The A1 Trunk Road (Grantham, Lincolnshire) (Temporary Restriction and Prohibition of Traffic) Order 2014 No. 2014/2739. - Enabling power: Road Traffic Regulation Act 1984, s. 14 (1) (a). - Issued: 14.10.2014. Made: 22.09.2014. Coming into force: 29.09.2014. Effect: None. Territorial extent & classification: E. Local. - Available at http://www.legislation.gov.uk/uksi/2014/2739/contents/made
Non-print

The A1 Trunk Road (Kingsway Interchange) (Temporary Restriction and Prohibition of Traffic) Order 2014 No. 2014/1841. - Enabling power: Road Traffic Regulation Act 1984, s. 14 (1) (a). - Issued: 16.07.2014. Made: 26.06.2014. Coming into force: 04.07.2014. Effect: None. Territorial extent & classification: E. Local. - Available at http://www.legislation.gov.uk/uksi/2014/1841/contents/made
Non-print

The A1 Trunk Road (Leeming to Catterick) (Prohibition of Use of Gaps in the Central Reservation) Order 2014 No. 2014/2151. - Enabling power: Road Traffic Regulation Act 1984, ss. 1 (1), 2 (1). - Issued: 14.08.2014. Made: 01.08.2014. Coming into force: 08.08.2014. Effect: None. Territorial extent & classification: E. Local. - Available at http://www.legislation.gov.uk/uksi/2014/2151/contents/made
Non-print

The A1 Trunk Road (Lobley Hill Interchange to Derwenthaugh Interchange) (Temporary Prohibition of Traffic) Order 2014 No. 2014/1071. - Enabling power: Road Traffic Regulation Act 1984, s. 14 (1) (a). - Issued: 28.04.2014. Made: 10.04.2014. Coming into force: 21.04.2014. Effect: None. Territorial extent & classification: E. Local. - Available at http://www.legislation.gov.uk/uksi/2014/1071/contents/made
Non-print

The A1 Trunk Road (Markham Moor to Winthorpe, Nottinghamshire) (Temporary Restriction and Prohibition of Traffic) Order 2014 No. 2014/319. - Enabling power: Road Traffic Regulation Act 1984, s. 14 (1) (a). - Issued: 18.02.2014. Made: 03.02.2014. Coming into force: 10.02.2014. Effect: None. Territorial extent & classification: E. Local. - Available at http://www.legislation.gov.uk/uksi/2014/319/contents/made Non-print

The A1 Trunk Road (Marston, Lincolnshire) (Temporary Prohibition of Traffic) (No.2) Order 2014 No. 2014/2730. - Enabling power: Road Traffic Regulation Act 1984, s. 14 (1) (a). - Issued: 14.10.2014. Made: 22.09.2014. Coming into force: 29.09.2014. Effect: None. Territorial extent & classification: E. Local. - Available at http://www.legislation.gov.uk/uksi/2014/2730/contents/made
Non-print

The A1 Trunk Road (Marston, Lincolnshire) (Temporary Prohibition of Traffic) Order 2014 No. 2014/114. - Enabling power: Road Traffic Regulation Act 1984, s. 14 (1) (a). - Issued: 24.01.2014. Made: 10.01.2014. Coming into force: 17.01.2014. Effect: None. Territorial extent & classification: E. Local. - Available at http://www.legislation.gov.uk/uksi/2014/114/contents/made Non-print

The A1 Trunk Road (Metro Centre Interchange) (Temporary Prohibition of Traffic) (No.2) Order 2014 No. 2014/2160. - Enabling power: Road Traffic Regulation Act 1984, s. 14 (1) (a). - Issued: 12.08.2014. Made: 31.07.2014. Coming into force: 10.08.2014. Effect: None. Territorial extent & classification: E. Local. - Available at http://www.legislation.gov.uk/uksi/2014/2160/contents/made
Non-print

The A1 Trunk Road (Metro Centre Interchange) (Temporary Prohibition of Traffic) Order 2014 No. 2014/745. - Enabling power: Road Traffic Regulation Act 1984, s. 14 (1) (a). - Issued: 12.03.2014. Made: 06.03.2014. Coming into force: 19.03.2014. Effect: None. Territorial extent & classification: E. Local. - Available at http://www.legislation.gov.uk/uksi/2014/745/contents/made Non-print

The A1 Trunk Road (Metro Centre Interchange to Stannington Interchange) (Temporary Restriction and Prohibition of Traffic) Order 2014 No. 2014/759. - Enabling power: Road Traffic Regulation Act 1984, s. 14 (1) (a). - Issued: 10.03.2014. Made: 27.02.2014. Coming into force: 08.03.2014. Effect: None. Territorial extent & classification: E. Local. - Available at http://www.legislation.gov.uk/uksi/2014/759/contents/made Non-print

The A1 Trunk Road (Morpeth to Alnwick) (Temporary Restriction and Prohibition of Traffic) Order 2014 No. 2014/2324. - Enabling power: Road Traffic Regulation Act 1984, s. 14 (1) (a). - Issued: 01.09.2014. Made: 28.08.2014. Coming into force: 10.09.2014. Effect: None. Territorial extent & classification: E. Local. - Available at http://www.legislation.gov.uk/uksi/2014/2324/contents/made
Non-print

The A1 Trunk Road (New Road, Sandy, Bedfordshire) (Prohibition of "U" Turn) Order 2014 No. 2014/741. - Enabling power: Road Traffic Regulation Act 1984, ss. 1 (1) (2), 2 (1) (2), sch. 9, para. 27 (1). - Issued: 10.03.2014. Made: 03.03.2014. Coming into force: 17.03.2014. Effect: None. Territorial extent & classification: E. Local. - Available at http://www.legislation.gov.uk/uksi/2014/741/contents/made Non-print

The A1 Trunk Road (New Road, Sandy, Bedfordshire) (Temporary Prohibition of Traffic) Order 2014 No. 2014/1646. - Enabling power: Road Traffic Regulation Act 1984, s. 14 (1) (a). - Issued: 26.06.2014. Made: 09.06.2014. Coming into force: 16.06.2014. Effect: None. Territorial extent & classification: E. Local. - Available at http://www.legislation.gov.uk/uksi/2014/1646/contents/made
Non-print

ROAD TRAFFIC: TRAFFIC REGULATION

The A1 Trunk Road (Newton on the Moor North to Alnwick) (Temporary Restriction and Prohibition of Traffic) Order 2014 No. 2014/2088. - Enabling power: Road Traffic Regulation Act 1984, s. 14 (1) (a). - Issued: 06.08.2014. Made: 17.07.2014. Coming into force: 26.07.2014. Effect: None. Territorial extent & classification: E. Local. - Available at
http://www.legislation.gov.uk/uksi/2014/2088/contents/made
Non-print

The A1 Trunk Road (Newton on the Moor North to Charlton Mires) (Temporary Restriction and Prohibition of Traffic) Order 2014 No. 2014/978. - Enabling power: Road Traffic Regulation Act 1984, s. 14 (1) (a). - Issued: 04.04.2014. Made: 20.03.2014. Coming into force: 30.03.2014. Effect: None. Territorial extent & classification: E. Local. - Available at
http://www.legislation.gov.uk/uksi/2014/978/contents/made Non-print

The A1 Trunk Road (Newton-on-the-Moor North to Deanmoor Junction) (Temporary Restriction and Prohibition of Traffic) Order 2014 No. 2014/740. - Enabling power: Road Traffic Regulation Act 1984, s. 14 (1) (a). - Issued: 12.03.2014. Made: 06.03.2014. Coming into force: 16.03.2014. Effect: None. Territorial extent & classification: E. Local. - Available at
http://www.legislation.gov.uk/uksi/2014/740/contents/made Non-print

The A1 Trunk Road (northbound carriageway south of Seaton Burn Interchange) (Closure of Layby) Order 2014 No. 2014/2610. - Enabling power: Road Traffic Regulation Act 1984, ss. 1 (1), 2 (1) (2). - Issued: 30.09.2014. Made: 22.09.2014. Coming into force: 06.10.2014. Effect: None. Territorial extent & classification: E. Local. - Available at
http://www.legislation.gov.uk/uksi/2014/2610/contents/made
Non-print

The A1 Trunk Road (Redhouse Interchange to Darrington Interchange Laybys) (Temporary Prohibition of Traffic) Order 2014 No. 2014/3536. - Enabling power: Road Traffic Regulation Act 1984, s. 14 (1) (a). - Issued: 22.01.2015. Made: 29.12.2014. Coming into force: 11.01.2015. Effect: None. Territorial extent & classification: E. Local. - Available at
http://www.legislation.gov.uk/uksi/2014/3536/contents/made
Non-print

The A1 Trunk Road (Sandy, Bedfordshire) (Temporary Prohibition of Pedestrians) Order 2014 No. 2014/249. - Enabling power: Road Traffic Regulation Act 1984, s. 14 (1) (a). - Issued: 10.02.2014. Made: 03.02.2014. Coming into force: 10.02.2014. Effect: None. Territorial extent & classification: E. Local. - Available at
http://www.legislation.gov.uk/uksi/2014/249/contents/made Non-print

The A1 Trunk Road (Sandy Roundabout, Bedfordshire) (Temporary Prohibition of Traffic) Order 2014 No. 2014/1285. - Enabling power: Road Traffic Regulation Act 1984, s. 14 (1) (a). - Issued: 21.05.2014. Made: 06.05.2014. Coming into force: 13.05.2014. Effect: None. Territorial extent & classification: E. Local. - Available at
http://www.legislation.gov.uk/uksi/2014/1285/contents/made
Non-print

The A1 Trunk Road (Scotswood Interchange) (Temporary Prohibition of Traffic) Order 2014 No. 2014/2859. - Enabling power: Road Traffic Regulation Act 1984, s. 14 (1) (a). - Issued: 28.10.2014. Made: 25.09.2014. Coming into force: 05.10.2014. Effect: None. Territorial extent & classification: E. Local. - Available at
http://www.legislation.gov.uk/uksi/2014/2859/contents/made
Non-print

The A1 Trunk Road (Scotswood to Seaton Burn) (Temporary Restriction and Prohibition of Traffic) Order 2014 No. 2014/2500. - Enabling power: Road Traffic Regulation Act 1984, s. 14 (1) (a). - Issued: 10.09.2014. Made: 04.09.2014. Coming into force: 18.09.2014. Effect: None. Territorial extent & classification: E. Local. - Available at
http://www.legislation.gov.uk/uksi/2014/2500/contents/made
Non-print

The A1 Trunk Road (Scremerston Roundabout to East Ord Roundabout) (Temporary Restriction and Prohibition of Traffic) Order 2014 No. 2014/2323. - Enabling power: Road Traffic Regulation Act 1984, s. 14 (1) (a), 5 (b). - Issued: 01.09.2014. Made: 28.08.2014. Coming into force: 10.09.2014. Effect: None. Territorial extent & classification: E. Local. - Available at
http://www.legislation.gov.uk/uksi/2014/2323/contents/made
Non-print

The A1 Trunk Road (Seaton Burn Interchange to Fairmoor Junction) (Temporary Restriction and Prohibition of Traffic) Order 2014 No. 2014/679. - Enabling power: Road Traffic Regulation Act 1984, s. 14 (1) (a). - Issued: 04.03.2014. Made: 20.02.2014. Coming into force: 02.03.2014. Effect: None. Territorial extent & classification: E. Local. - Available at
http://www.legislation.gov.uk/uksi/2014/679/contents/made Non-print

The A1 Trunk Road (Seaton Burn to Clifton) (Temporary Restriction and Prohibition of Traffic) Order 2014 No. 2014/2835. - Enabling power: Road Traffic Regulation Act 1984, s. 14 (1) (a). - Issued: 23.10.2014. Made: 16.10.2014. Coming into force: 26.10.2014. Effect: None. Territorial extent & classification: E. Local. - Available at
http://www.legislation.gov.uk/uksi/2014/2835/contents/made
Non-print

The A1 Trunk Road (South Witham, Lincolnshire) (Temporary Restriction of Traffic) Order 2014 No. 2014/2145. - Enabling power: Road Traffic Regulation Act 1984, s. 14 (1) (a). - Issued: 14.08.2014. Made: 21.05.2014. Coming into force: 28.05.2014. Effect: None. Territorial extent & classification: E. Local. - Available at
http://www.legislation.gov.uk/uksi/2014/2145/contents/made
Non-print

The A1 Trunk Road (Stamford to Grantham, Lincolnshire) (Temporary Prohibition of Traffic) Order 2014 No. 2014/1401. - Enabling power: Road Traffic Regulation Act 1984, s. 14 (1) (a). - Issued: 04.06.2014. Made: 02.05.2014. Coming into force: 09.05.2014. Effect: None. Territorial extent & classification: E. Local. - Available at
http://www.legislation.gov.uk/uksi/2014/1401/contents/made
Non-print

The A1 Trunk Road (Stannington Interchange) (Temporary Restriction and Prohibition of Traffic) Order 2014 No. 2014/2876. - Enabling power: Road Traffic Regulation Act 1984, s. 14 (1) (a). - Issued: 31.10.2014. Made: 11.09.2014. Coming into force: 20.09.2014. Effect: None. Territorial extent & classification: E. Local. - Available at
http://www.legislation.gov.uk/uksi/2014/2876/contents/made
Non-print

The A1 Trunk Road (Stretton, Lincolnshire) (Temporary Restriction and Prohibition of Traffic) Order 2014 No. 2014/1529. - Enabling power: Road Traffic Regulation Act 1984, s. 14 (1) (a). - Issued: 11.06.2014. Made: 27.05.2014. Coming into force: 03.06.2014. Effect: None. Territorial extent & classification: E. Local. - Available at
http://www.legislation.gov.uk/uksi/2014/1529/contents/made
Non-print

The A1 Trunk Road (Stretton, Rutland) (Slip Roads) (Temporary Prohibition of Traffic) Order 2014 No. 2014/2227. - Enabling power: Road Traffic Regulation Act 1984, s. 14 (1) (a). - Issued: 27.08.2014. Made: 12.08.2014. Coming into force: 19.08.2014. Effect: None. Territorial extent & classification: E. Local. - Available at
http://www.legislation.gov.uk/uksi/2014/2227/contents/made
Non-print

The A1 Trunk Road (The Scottish Border to Duns Road Junction) (Temporary Restriction and Prohibition of Traffic) Order 2014 No. 2014/3544. - Enabling power: Road Traffic Regulation Act 1984, s. 14 (1) (a) (7). - Issued: 10.02.2015. Made: 29.12.2014. Coming into force: 10.01.2015. Effect: None. Territorial extent & classification: E. Local. - Available at
http://www.legislation.gov.uk/uksi/2014/3544/contents/made
Non-print

The A1 Trunk Road (The Scottish Border to Haggerston Junction) Temporary Restriction and Prohibition of Traffic) Order 2014 No. 2014/1496. - Enabling power: Road Traffic Regulation Act 1984, s. 14 (1) (a). - Issued: 09.06.2014. Made: 22.05.2014. Coming into force: 31.05.2014. Effect: None. Territorial extent & classification: E. Local. - Available at
http://www.legislation.gov.uk/uksi/2014/1496/contents/made
Non-print

The A1 Trunk Road (Tinwell, Rutland) (Slip Roads) (Temporary Prohibition of Traffic) Order 2014 No. 2014/2446. - Enabling power: Road Traffic Regulation Act 1984, s. 14 (1) (a). - Issued: 15.09.2014. Made: 26.08.2014. Coming into force: 02.09.2014. Effect: None. Territorial extent & classification: E. Local. - Available at
http://www.legislation.gov.uk/uksi/2014/2446/contents/made
Non-print

ROAD TRAFFIC: TRAFFIC REGULATION

The A1 Trunk Road (Tinwell - Wothorpe) (Temporary Prohibition of Traffic) Order 2014 No. 2014/2074. - Enabling power: Road Traffic Regulation Act 1984, s. 14 (1) (a). - Issued: 06.08.2014. Made: 11.07.2014. Coming into force: 18.07.2014. Effect: None. Territorial extent & classification: E. Local. - Available at http://www.legislation.gov.uk/uksi/2014/2074/contents/made Non-print

The A1 Trunk Road (Wansford - Harlaxton) (Temporary Restriction and Prohibition of Traffic) Order 2014 No. 2014/1720. - Enabling power: Road Traffic Regulation Act 1984, s. 14 (1) (a). - Issued: 03.07.2014. Made: 16.06.2014. Coming into force: 23.06.2014. Effect: None. Territorial extent & classification: E. Local. - Available at http://www.legislation.gov.uk/uksi/2014/1720/contents/made Non-print

The A1 Trunk Road (Warreners House Junction to Seaton Burn Interchange) (Temporary Restriction and Prohibition of Traffic) Order 2014 No. 2014/680. - Enabling power: Road Traffic Regulation Act 1984, s. 14 (1) (a). - Issued: 04.03.2014. Made: 20.02.2014. Coming into force: 02.03.2014. Effect: None. Territorial extent & classification: E. Local. - Available at http://www.legislation.gov.uk/uksi/2014/680/contents/made Non-print

The A1 Trunk Road (Warreners House) (Temporary Restriction and Prohibition of Traffic) (No.2) Order 2014 No. 2014/2969. - Enabling power: Road Traffic Regulation Act 1984, s. 14 (1) (a). - Issued: 27.10.2014. Made: 23.10.2014. Coming into force: 02.11.2014. Effect: None. Territorial extent & classification: E. Local. - Available at http://www.legislation.gov.uk/uksi/2014/2969/contents/made Non-print

The A1 Trunk Road (Warreners House) (Temporary Restriction and Prohibition of Traffic) Order 2014 No. 2014/2256. - Enabling power: Road Traffic Regulation Act 1984, s. 14 (1) (a). - Issued: 22.08.2014. Made: 14.08.2014. Coming into force: 25.08.2014. Effect: None. Territorial extent & classification: E. Local. - Available at http://www.legislation.gov.uk/uksi/2014/2256/contents/made Non-print

The A1 Trunk Road (Washington to Seaton Burn) (Temporary Restriction and Prohibition of Traffic) Order 2014 No. 2014/3475. - Enabling power: Road Traffic Regulation Act 1984, s. 14 (1) (a). - Issued: 30.12.2014. Made: 24.12.2014. Coming into force: 01.01.2015. Effect: None. Territorial extent & classification: E. Local. - Available at http://www.legislation.gov.uk/uksi/2014/3475/contents/made Non-print

The A1 Trunk Road (Wentbridge Junction) (Temporary Prohibition of Traffic) Order 2014 No. 2014/2997. - Enabling power: Road Traffic Regulation Act 1984, s. 14 (1) (a). - Issued: 04.11.2014. Made: 30.10.2014. Coming into force: 09.11.2014. Effect: None. Territorial extent & classification: E. Local. - Available at http://www.legislation.gov.uk/uksi/2014/2997/contents/made Non-print

The A1 Trunk Road (Went Edge Road Bridge Junction) (Temporary Prohibition of Traffic) Order 2014 No. 2014/3036. - Enabling power: Road Traffic Regulation Act 1984, s. 14 (1) (a). - Issued: 13.11.2014. Made: 06.11.2014. Coming into force: 16.11.2014. Effect: None. Territorial extent & classification: E. Local. - Available at http://www.legislation.gov.uk/uksi/2014/3036/contents/made Non-print

The A1 Trunk Road (Westerhope Interchange) (Temporary Prohibition of Traffic) Order 2014 No. 2014/743. - Enabling power: Road Traffic Regulation Act 1984, s. 14 (1) (a). - Issued: 10.03.2014. Made: 06.03.2014. Coming into force: 18.03.2014. Effect: None. Territorial extent & classification: E. Local. - Available at http://www.legislation.gov.uk/uksi/2014/743/contents/made Non-print

The A1 Trunk Road (Winthorpe, Nottinghamshire) (Slip Road) (Temporary Prohibition of Traffic) Order 2014 No. 2014/337. - Enabling power: Road Traffic Regulation Act 1984, s. 14 (1) (a). - Issued: 19.02.2014. Made: 24.01.2014. Coming into force: 31.01.2014. Effect: None. Territorial extent & classification: E. Local. - Available at http://www.legislation.gov.uk/uksi/2014/337/contents/made Non-print

The A1 Trunk Road (Wyboston, Bedfordshire to Buckden, Cambridgeshire) Northbound (Temporary Prohibition of Traffic) Order 2014 No. 2014/1474. - Enabling power: Road Traffic Regulation Act 1984, s. 14 (1) (a). - Issued: 02.06.2014. Made: 19.05.2014. Coming into force: 26.05.2014. Effect: None. Territorial extent & classification: E. Local. - Available at http://www.legislation.gov.uk/uksi/2014/1474/contents/made Non-print

The A2, A20 and the A282 Trunk Roads and the M20 and the M25 Motorways (Near Dartford) (Temporary Prohibition of Traffic) Order 2014 No. 2014/2800. - Enabling power: Road Traffic Regulation Act 1984, s. 14 (1) (a). - Issued: 13.10.2014. Made: 29.09.2014. Coming into force: 18.10.2014. Effect: None. Territorial extent & classification: E. Local. - Available at http://www.legislation.gov.uk/uksi/2014/2800/contents/made Non-print

The A2 Trunk Road and the M25 and M20 Motorways (Dartford Heath Interchange, M25 Junctions 2 and M20 Junction 1) (Temporary Restriction and Prohibition of Traffic) Order 2014 No. 2014/1757. - Enabling power: Road Traffic Regulation Act 1984, s. 14 (1) (a). - Issued: 04.07.2014. Made: 23.06.2014. Coming into force: 12.07.2014. Effect: None. Territorial extent & classification: E. Local. - Available at http://www.legislation.gov.uk/uksi/2014/1757/contents/made Non-print

The A2 Trunk Road (Bean Interchange - Darenth Interchange) (Temporary Restriction and Prohibition of Traffic) Order 2014 No. 2014/2959. - Enabling power: Road Traffic Regulation Act 1984, s. 14 (1) (a). - Issued: 16.10.2014. Made: 13.10.2014. Coming into force: 01.11.2014. Effect: None. Territorial extent & classification: E. Local. - Available at http://www.legislation.gov.uk/uksi/2014/2959/contents/made Non-print

The A2 Trunk Road (Bean Interchange) (Temporary Prohibition of Traffic) Order 2014 No. 2014/733. - Enabling power: Road Traffic Regulation Act 1984, s. 14 (1) (a). - Issued: 10.03.2014. Made: 03.03.2014. Coming into force: 22.03.2014. Effect: None. Territorial extent & classification: E. Local. - Available at http://www.legislation.gov.uk/uksi/2014/733/contents/made Non-print

The A2 Trunk Road (Brenley Corner Interchange - Stuppington Lane Bridge) (Temporary Restriction and Prohibition of Traffic) Order 2014 No. 2014/2541. - Enabling power: Road Traffic Regulation Act 1984, s. 14 (1) (a), sch. 9 para 27 (1). - Issued: 22.09.2014. Made: 08.09.2014. Coming into force: 01.10.2014. Effect: None. Territorial extent & classification: E. Local. - Available at http://www.legislation.gov.uk/uksi/2014/2541contents/made Non-print

The A2 Trunk Road (Brenley Corner Interchange - Thanington Interchange) (Temporary Restriction and Prohibition of Traffic) Order 2014 No. 2014/99. - Enabling power: Road Traffic Regulation Act 1984, s. 14 (1) (a). - Issued: 22.01.2014. Made: 20.01.2014. Coming into force: 08.02.2014. Effect: None. Territorial extent & classification: E. Local. - Available at http://www.legislation.gov.uk/uksi/2014/99/contents/made Non-print

The A2 Trunk Road (Cobham Interchange - Cycle Track) (Temporary Prohibition of Traffic) Order 2014 No. 2014/3556. - Enabling power: Road Traffic Regulation Act 1984, s. 14 (1) (a). - Issued: 18.02.2015. Made: 15.12.2014. Coming into force: 17.01.2015. Effect: None. Territorial extent & classification: E. Local. - Available at http://www.legislation.gov.uk/uksi/2014/3556/contents/made Non-print

The A2 Trunk Road (Darenth Interchange and Bean Junction) (Temporary Prohibition of Traffic) Order 2014 No. 2014/3459. - Enabling power: Road Traffic Regulation Act 1984, s. 14 (1) (a). - Issued: 18.12.2014. Made: 15.12.2014. Coming into force: 09.01.2015. Effect: None. Territorial extent & classification: E. Local. - Available at http://www.legislation.gov.uk/uksi/2014/3459/contents/made Non-print

The A2 Trunk Road (Darenth Interchange, Westbound Link Road) (Temporary Restriction and Prohibition of Traffic) Order 2014 No. 2014/102. - Enabling power: Road Traffic Regulation Act 1984, s. 14 (1) (a). - Issued: 22.01.2014. Made: 20.01.2014. Coming into force: 08.02.2014. Effect: None. Territorial extent & classification: E. Local. - Available at http://www.legislation.gov.uk/uksi/2014/102/contents/made Non-print

The A2 Trunk Road (Dartford Heath, Slip Roads) (Temporary Prohibition of Traffic) Order 2014 No. 2014/1592. - Enabling power: Road Traffic Regulation Act 1984, s. 14 (1) (a). - Issued: 18.06.2014. Made: 02.06.2014. Coming into force: 30.06.2014. Effect: None. Territorial extent & classification: E. Local. - Available at http://www.legislation.gov.uk/uksi/2014/1592/contents/made Non-print

The A2 Trunk Road (Dover Road) (Temporary Prohibition of Traffic) Order 2014 No. 2014/3546. - Enabling power: Road Traffic Regulation Act 1984, s. 14 (1) (a). - Issued: 22.01.2015. Made: 29.12.2014. Coming into force: 17.01.2015. Effect: None. Territorial extent & classification: E. Local. - Available at http://www.legislation.gov.uk/uksi/2014/3546/contents/made Non-print

The A2 Trunk Road (Ebbsfleet Link Road Roundabout) (Temporary Prohibition of Traffic) Order 2014 No. 2014/3432. - Enabling power: Road Traffic Regulation Act 1984, s. 14 (1) (a). - Issued: 28.11.2014. Made: 24.11.2014. Coming into force: 13.12.2014. Effect: None. Territorial extent & classification: E. Local. - Available at http://www.legislation.gov.uk/uksi/2014/3432/contents/made Non-print

The A2 Trunk Road (Guston Roundabout - Eastern Docks Roundabout) (Temporary Prohibition of Traffic) Order 2014 No. 2014/3463. - Enabling power: Road Traffic Regulation Act 1984, s. 14 (1) (a). - Issued: 18.12.2014. Made: 15.12.2014. Coming into force: 03.01.2015. Effect: None. Territorial extent & classification: E. Local. - Available at http://www.legislation.gov.uk/uksi/2014/3463/contents/made Non-print

The A2 Trunk Road (Jubilee Way, Coastbound Carriageway) (Temporary Prohibition of Traffic) Order 2014 No. 2014/2552. - Enabling power: Road Traffic Regulation Act 1984, s. 14 (1) (a). - Issued: 24.09.2014. Made: 08.09.2014. Coming into force: 01.10.2014. Effect: None. Territorial extent & classification: E. Local. - Available at http://www.legislation.gov.uk/uksi/2014/2552/contents/made Non-print

The A2 Trunk Road (Jubilee Way, Coastbound Carriageway) (Temporary Prohibition of Traffic) Order 2014 No. 2014/2662. - Enabling power: Road Traffic Regulation Act 1984, s. 14 (1) (a). - Issued: 02.10.2014. Made: 08.09.2014. Coming into force: 01.10.2014. Effect: None. Territorial extent & classification: E. Local. - Available at http://www.legislation.gov.uk/uksi/2014/2662/contents/made Non-print

The A2 Trunk Road (Pepperhill Junction) (Temporary Prohibition of Traffic) Order 2014 No. 2014/2108. - Enabling power: Road Traffic Regulation Act 1984, s. 14 (1) (a). - Issued: 07.08.2014. Made: 21.07.2014. Coming into force: 10.08.2014. Effect: None. Territorial extent & classification: E. Local. - Available at http://www.legislation.gov.uk/uksi/2014/2108/contents/made Non-print

The A2 Trunk Road (Tollgate Junction - Pepper Hill Interchange) (Temporary 50 Miles Per Hour Speed Restriction) Order 2014 No. 2014/33. - Enabling power: Road Traffic Regulation Act 1984, s. 14 (1) (a). - Issued: 15.01.2014. Made: 13.01.2014. Coming into force: 01.02.2014. Effect: None. Territorial extent & classification: E. Local. - Available at http://www.legislation.gov.uk/uksi/2014/33/contents/made Non-print

The A2 Trunk Road (Upper Harbledown - Whitfield, Slip Roads) (Temporary Prohibition of Traffic) Order 2014 No. 2014/3442. - Enabling power: Road Traffic Regulation Act 1984, s. 14 (1) (a). - Issued: 01.12.2014. Made: 24.11.2014. Coming into force: 17.12.2014. Effect: None. Territorial extent & classification: E. Local. - Available at http://www.legislation.gov.uk/uksi/2014/3442/contents/made Non-print

The A2 Trunk Road (Watling Street) (Temporary Prohibition of Traffic) Order 2014 No. 2014/2641. - Enabling power: Road Traffic Regulation Act 1984, ss. 14 (1) (a), 5 (b) (7). - Issued: 30.09.2014. Made: 22.09.2014. Coming into force: 11.10.2014. Effect: None. Territorial extent & classification: E. Local. - Available at http://www.legislation.gov.uk/uksi/2014/2641/contents/made Non-print

The A3 and the A30 Trunk Roads and the M25 Motorway (A3 Ockham - Wisley, A30 Crooked Billet Roundabout - A308 Runnymede Roundabout and M25 Junctions 7 - 13) (Temporary Prohibition of Traffic) Order 2014 No. 2014/3512. - Enabling power: Road Traffic Regulation Act 1984, s. 14 (1) (a). - Issued: 22.01.2014. Made: 20.10.2014. Coming into force: 08.11.2014. Effect: None. Territorial extent & classification: E. Local. - Available at http://www.legislation.gov.uk/uksi/2014/3512/contents/made Non-print

The A3(M) Motorway (Junction 3) (Temporary Prohibition of Traffic) Order 2014 No. 2014/3545. - Enabling power: Road Traffic Regulation Act 1984, s. 14 (1) (a). - Issued: 22.01.2015. Made: 29.12.2014. Coming into force: 17.01.2015. Effect: None. Territorial extent & classification: E. Local. - Available at http://www.legislation.gov.uk/uksi/2014/3545/contents/made Non-print

The A3(M) Motorway (Junctions 2 - 4) (Temporary Prohibition of Traffic) Order 2014 No. 2014/749. - Enabling power: Road Traffic Regulation Act 1984, s. 14 (1) (a). - Issued: 04.03.2014. Made: 24.02.2014. Coming into force: 15.03.2014. Effect: None. Territorial extent & classification: E. Local. - Available at http://www.legislation.gov.uk/uksi/2014/749/contents/made Non-print

The A3(M) Motorway (Junctions 3- 5) (Temporary Prohibition of Traffic) Order 2014 No. 2014/2350. - Enabling power: Road Traffic Regulation Act 1984, s. 14 (1) (a). - Issued: 29.08.2014. Made: 26.08.2014. Coming into force: 13.09.2014. Effect: None. Territorial extent & classification: E. Local. - Available at http://www.legislation.gov.uk/uksi/2014/2350/contents/made Non-print

The A3 Trunk Road and the A3(M) Motorway (A272 Berelands Interchange - A3(M) Junction 3) (Temporary Prohibition of Traffic) Order 2014 No. 2014/2203. - Enabling power: Road Traffic Regulation Act 1984, s. 14 (1) (a). - Issued: 15.08.2014. Made: 04.08.2014. Coming into force: 24.08.2014. Effect: None. Territorial extent & classification: E. Local. - Available at http://www.legislation.gov.uk/uksi/2014/2203/contents/made Non-print

The A3 Trunk Road (Burpham Interchange - Hog's Back Link Road) (Temporary Prohibition of Traffic) Order 2014 No. 2014/1934. - Enabling power: Road Traffic Regulation Act 1984, s. 14 (1) (a). - Issued: 22.07.2014. Made: 30.06.2014. Coming into force: 19.07.2014. Effect: None. Territorial extent & classification: E. Local. - Available at http://www.legislation.gov.uk/uksi/2014/1934/contents/made Non-print

The A3 Trunk Road (Chalton Slip Roads) (Temporary Prohibition of Traffic) Order 2014 No. 2014/1755. - Enabling power: Road Traffic Regulation Act 1984, s. 14 (1) (a). - Issued: 04.07.2014. Made: 23.06.2014. Coming into force: 12.07.2014. Effect: None. Territorial extent & classification: E. Local. - Available at http://www.legislation.gov.uk/uksi/2014/1755/contents/made Non-print

The A3 Trunk Road (Compton Interchange - Stoke Interchange) (Temporary Prohibition of Traffic) Order 2014 No. 2014/1325. - Enabling power: Road Traffic Regulation Act 1984, s. 14 (1) (a). - Issued: 27.05.2014. Made: 12.05.2014. Coming into force: 31.05.2014. Effect: None. Territorial extent & classification: E. Local. - Available at http://www.legislation.gov.uk/uksi/2014/1325/contents/made Non-print

The A3 Trunk Road (Dennis Interchange - Ockham Interchange) (Temporary Prohibition of Traffic) Order 2014 No. 2014/2036. - Enabling power: Road Traffic Regulation Act 1984, s. 14 (1) (a). - Issued: 01.08.2014. Made: 14.07.2014. Coming into force: 02.08.2014. Effect: None. Territorial extent & classification: E. Local. - Available at http://www.legislation.gov.uk/uksi/2014/2036/contents/made Non-print

The A3 Trunk Road (Esher Common) (Temporary Prohibition of Traffic) Order 2014 No. 2014/2056. - Enabling power: Road Traffic Regulation Act 1984, s. 16A (2) (a). - Issued: 04.08.2014. Made: 14.07.2014. Coming into force: 10.08.2014. Effect: None. Territorial extent & classification: E. Local. - Available at http://www.legislation.gov.uk/uksi/2014/2056/contents/made Non-print

The A3 Trunk Road (Esher - Ockham) (Temporary Prohibition of Traffic) Order 2014 No. 2014/3474. - Enabling power: Road Traffic Regulation Act 1984, s. 14 (1) (a). - Issued: 19.12.2014. Made: 15.12.2014. Coming into force: 15.01.2015. Effect: None. Territorial extent & classification: E. Local. - Available at http://www.legislation.gov.uk/uksi/2014/3474/contents/made Non-print

The A3 Trunk Road (Hammer Lane Junction - A3(M) Junction 1) (Temporary Restriction and Prohibition of Traffic) Order 2014 No. 2014/2041. - Enabling power: Road Traffic Regulation Act 1984, s. 14 (1) (a). - Issued: 04.08.2014. Made: 14.07.2014. Coming into force: 08.08.2014. Effect: None. Territorial extent & classification: E. Local. - Available at http://www.legislation.gov.uk/uksi/2014/2041/contents/made Non-print

ROAD TRAFFIC: TRAFFIC REGULATION

The A3 Trunk Road (Hazel Grove Interchange - Thursley Interchange) (Temporary Prohibition of Traffic) Order 2014 No. 2014/1591. - Enabling power: Road Traffic Regulation Act 1984, s. 14 (1) (a). - Issued: 18.06.2014. Made: 02.06.2014. Coming into force: 21.06.2014. Effect: None. Territorial extent & classification: E. Local. - Available at http://www.legislation.gov.uk/uksi/2014/1591/contents/made Non-print

The A3 Trunk Road (Hindhead Tunnel) (Temporary Restriction and Prohibition of Traffic) Order 2014 No. 2014/2424. - Enabling power: Road Traffic Regulation Act 1984, s. 14 (1) (a). - Issued: 08.09.2014. Made: 18.08.2014. Coming into force: 12.09.2014. Effect: None. Territorial extent & classification: E. Local. - Available at http://www.legislation.gov.uk/uksi/2014/2424/contents/made Non-print

The A3 Trunk Road (Hog's Back Interchange - Longmoor Interchange) (Temporary Prohibition of Traffic) Order 2014 No. 2014/2139. - Enabling power: Road Traffic Regulation Act 1984, s. 14 (1) (a). - Issued: 13.08.2014. Made: 14.07.2014. Coming into force: 02.08.2014. Effect: None. Territorial extent & classification: E. Local. - Available at http://www.legislation.gov.uk/uksi/2014/2139/contents/made Non-print

The A3 Trunk Road (Hook Rise Junction - Esher Common Junction) (Temporary Prohibition of Traffic) Order 2014 No. 2014/995. - Enabling power: Road Traffic Regulation Act 1984, s. 14 (1) (a). - Issued: 10.04.2014. Made: 24.03.2014. Coming into force: 12.04.2014. Effect: None. Territorial extent & classification: E. Local. - Available at http://www.legislation.gov.uk/uksi/2014/995/contents/made Non-print

The A3 Trunk Road (Liphook Interchange - Sheet Interchange) (Temporary Prohibition of Traffic) Order 2014 No. 2014/2106. - Enabling power: Road Traffic Regulation Act 1984, s. 14 (1) (a). - Issued: 07.08.2014. Made: 21.07.2014. Coming into force: 09.08.2014. Effect: None. Territorial extent & classification: E. Local. - Available at http://www.legislation.gov.uk/uksi/2014/2106/contents/made Non-print

The A3 Trunk Road (M25 Junction 10 - Hammer Lane Junction) (Temporary Restriction and Prohibition of Traffic) Order 2014 No. 2014/2188. - Enabling power: Road Traffic Regulation Act 1984, s. 14 (1) (a). - Issued: 18.08.2014. Made: 07.07.2014. Coming into force: 01.08.2014. Effect: None. Territorial extent & classification: E. Local. - Available at http://www.legislation.gov.uk/uksi/2014/2188/contents/made Non-print

The A3 Trunk Road (Ockham - Painshill) (Temporary Prohibition of Traffic) Order 2014 No. 2014/3465. - Enabling power: Road Traffic Regulation Act 1984, s. 14 (1) (a). - Issued: 18.12.2014. Made: 15.12.2014. Coming into force: 03.01.2015. Effect: None. Territorial extent & classification: E. Local. - Available at http://www.legislation.gov.uk/uksi/2014/3465/contents/made Non-print

The A3 Trunk Road (Painshill Interchange, Slip Roads) (Temporary Prohibition of Traffic) Order 2014 No. 2014/46. - Enabling power: Road Traffic Regulation Act 1984, s. 14 (1) (a). - Issued: 16.01.2014. Made: 13.01.2014. Coming into force: 01.02.2014. Effect: None. Territorial extent & classification: E. Local. - Available at http://www.legislation.gov.uk/uksi/2014/46/contents/made Non-print

The A3 Trunk Road (Queen Elizabeth Country Park, Slip Roads) (Temporary Prohibition of Traffic) Order 2014 No. 2014/2326. - Enabling power: Road Traffic Regulation Act 1984, s. 16A (2) (a). - Issued: 22.08.2014. Made: 18.08.2014. Coming into force: 13.09.2014. Effect: None. Territorial extent & classification: E. Local. - Available at http://www.legislation.gov.uk/uksi/2014/2326/contents/made Non-print

The A3 Trunk Road (Ripley By-Pass) (Temporary Prohibition of Traffic) (Amendment) Order 2014 No. 2014/2419. - Enabling power: Road Traffic Regulation Act 1984, s. 14 (1) (a). - Issued: 12.09.2014. Made: 05.09.2014. Coming into force: 08.09.2014. Effect: None. Territorial extent & classification: E. Local. - Available at http://www.legislation.gov.uk/uksi/2014/2419/contents/made Non-print

The A3 Trunk Road (Ripley By-Pass) (Temporary Prohibition of Traffic) Order 2014 No. 2014/2035. - Enabling power: Road Traffic Regulation Act 1984, s. 14 (1) (a). - Issued: 01.08.2014. Made: 14.07.2014. Coming into force: 02.08.2014. Effect: None. Territorial extent & classification: E. Local. - Available at http://www.legislation.gov.uk/uksi/2014/2035/contents/made Non-print

The A3 Trunk Road (Sheet Link) (Temporary Prohibition of Traffic) Order 2014 No. 2014/2034. - Enabling power: Road Traffic Regulation Act 1984, s. 14 (1) (a). - Issued: 01.08.2014. Made: 14.07.2014. Coming into force: 02.08.2014. Effect: None. Territorial extent & classification: E. Local. - Available at http://www.legislation.gov.uk/uksi/2014/2034/contents/made Non-print

The A3 Trunk Road (Weston Interchange - Sheet Interchange) (Temporary Prohibition of Traffic) Order 2014 No. 2014/2199. - Enabling power: Road Traffic Regulation Act 1984, s. 14 (1) (a). - Issued: 15.08.2014. Made: 04.08.2014. Coming into force: 23.08.2014. Effect: None. Territorial extent & classification: E. Local. - Available at http://www.legislation.gov.uk/uksi/2014/2199/contents/made Non-print

The A5 and A38 Trunk Roads and the M6 Toll Motorway (Weeford, Staffordshire) (Temporary Restriction of Traffic) Order 2014 No. 2014/2496. - Enabling power: Road Traffic Regulation Act 1984, s. 14 (1) (a). - Issued: 15.09.2014. Made: 08.09.2014. Coming into force: 15.09.2014. Effect: None. Territorial extent & classification: E. Local. - Available at http://www.legislation.gov.uk/uksi/2014/2496/contents/made Non-print

The A5 and A43 Trunk Roads (Towcester, Northamptonshire) (Temporary Restriction and Prohibition of Traffic) Order 2014 No. 2014/329. - Enabling power: Road Traffic Regulation Act 1984, s. 14 (1) (a). - Issued: 18.02.2014. Made: 27.01.2014. Coming into force: 03.02.2014. Effect: None. Territorial extent & classification: E. Local. - Available at http://www.legislation.gov.uk/uksi/2014/329/contents/made Non-print

The A5 and A483 Trunk Roads (Mile End, Shropshire) (Temporary Restriction and Prohibition of Traffic) Order 2014 No. 2014/1844. - Enabling power: Road Traffic Regulation Act 1984, s. 14 (1) (a). - Issued: 16.07.2014. Made: 17.06.2014. Coming into force: 24.06.2014. Effect: None. Territorial extent & classification: E. Local. - Available at http://www.legislation.gov.uk/uksi/2014/1844/contents/made Non-print

The A5 and A5148 Trunk Roads (Muckley Corner to Weeford, Staffordshire) (Temporary Restriction and Prohibition of Traffic) Order 2014 No. 2014/113. - Enabling power: Road Traffic Regulation Act 1984, s. 14 (1) (a). - Issued: 24.01.2014. Made: 06.01.2014. Coming into force: 13.01.2014. Effect: None. Territorial extent & classification: E. Local. - Available at http://www.legislation.gov.uk/uksi/2014/113/contents/made Non-print

The A5 Trunk Road (A505 Dunstable, Central Bedfordshire to A4146 Milton Keynes) (Temporary Restriction and Prohibition of Traffic) Order 2014 No. 2014/12. - Enabling power: Road Traffic Regulation Act 1984, s. 14 (1) (a). - Issued: 10.01.2014. Made: 02.01.2014. Coming into force: 09.01.2014. Effect: None. Territorial extent & classification: E. Local. - Available at http://www.legislation.gov.uk/uksi/2014/12/contents/made Non-print

The A5 Trunk Road (A508 Old Stratford Roundabout to A4146 Kelly's Kitchen Roundabout, Milton Keynes) (Temporary Restriction and Prohibition of Traffic) Order 2014 No. 2014/3000. - Enabling power: Road Traffic Regulation Act 1984, s. 14 (1) (a). - Issued: 11.11.2014. Made: 03.11.2014. Coming into force: 10.11.2014. Effect: None. Territorial extent & classification: E. Local. - Available at http://www.legislation.gov.uk/uksi/2014/3000/contents/made Non-print

The A5 Trunk Road (A4146 Kelly's Kitchen Roundabout to A422 Abbey Hill Roundabout, Milton Keynes) (Temporary Prohibition of Traffic) Order 2014 No. 2014/1379. - Enabling power: Road Traffic Regulation Act 1984, s. 14 (1) (a). - Issued: 03.06.2014. Made: 06.05.2014. Coming into force: 13.05.2014. Effect: None. Territorial extent & classification: E. Local. - Available at http://www.legislation.gov.uk/uksi/2014/1379/contents/made Non-print

ROAD TRAFFIC: TRAFFIC REGULATION

The A5 Trunk Road and M54 Motorway (Shrewsbury, Shropshire) (Temporary Restriction and Prohibition of Traffic) Order 2014 No. 2014/1245. - Enabling power: Road Traffic Regulation Act 1984, s. 14 (1) (a). - Issued: 16.05.2014. Made: 28.04.2014. Coming into force: 05.05.2014. Effect: None. Territorial extent & classification: E. Local. - Available at
http://www.legislation.gov.uk/uksi/2014/1245/contents/made
Non-print

The A5 Trunk Road and the M6 Toll Motorway (Churchbridge, Staffordshire) (Temporary Prohibition of Traffic) Order 2014 No. 2014/1724. - Enabling power: Road Traffic Regulation Act 1984, s. 14 (1) (a). - Issued: 03.07.2014. Made: 16.06.2014. Coming into force: 23.06.2014. Effect: None. Territorial extent & classification: E. Local. - Available at
http://www.legislation.gov.uk/uksi/2014/1724/contents/made
Non-print

The A5 Trunk Road (Atherstone, Warwickshire) (Temporary Prohibition of Traffic) Order 2014 No. 2014/180. - Enabling power: Road Traffic Regulation Act 1984, s. 14 (1) (a). - Issued: 03.02.2014. Made: 20.01.2014. Coming into force: 27.01.2014. Effect: None. Territorial extent & classification: E. Local. - Available at
http://www.legislation.gov.uk/uksi/2014/180/contents/made Non-print

The A5 Trunk Road (Brownhills, Staffordshire) (Temporary Restriction and Prohibition of Traffic) Order 2014 No. 2014/1412. - Enabling power: Road Traffic Regulation Act 1984, s. 14 (1) (a). - Issued: 04.06.2014. Made: 06.05.2014. Coming into force: 13.05.2014. Effect: None. Territorial extent & classification: E. Local. - Available at
http://www.legislation.gov.uk/uksi/2014/1412/contents/made
Non-print

The A5 Trunk Road (Caldecote - Mancetter) (Temporary Prohibition of Traffic) No. 2014/2738. - Enabling power: Road Traffic Regulation Act 1984, s. 14 (1) (a). - Issued: 14.10.2014. Made: 22.09.2014. Coming into force: 29.09.2014. Effect: None. Territorial extent & classification: E. Local. - Available at
http://www.legislation.gov.uk/uksi/2014/2738/contents/made
Non-print

The A5 Trunk Road (Caldecote - Mancetter) (Temporary Prohibition of Traffic) (No.2) Order 2014 No. 2014/3555. - Enabling power: Road Traffic Regulation Act 1984, s. 14 (1) (a). - Issued: 18.02.2015. Made: 29.12.2014. Coming into force: 05.01.2015. Effect: None. Territorial extent & classification: E. Local. - Available at
http://www.legislation.gov.uk/uksi/2014/3555/contents/made
Non-print

The A5 Trunk Road (Catthorpe, Warwickshire) (Temporary Restriction of Traffic) Order 2014 No. 2014/2620. - Enabling power: Road Traffic Regulation Act 1984, s. 14 (1) (a). - Issued: 30.09.2014. Made: 15.09.2014. Coming into force: 22.09.2014. Effect: None. Territorial extent & classification: E. Local. - Available at
http://www.legislation.gov.uk/uksi/2014/2620/contents/made
Non-print

The A5 Trunk Road (Chalk Hill, Dunstable, Bedfordshire) (Temporary 10 Miles Per Hour Speed Restriction) Order 2014 No. 2014/1927. - Enabling power: Road Traffic Regulation Act 1984, s. 14 (1) (a). - Issued: 23.07.2014. Made: 30.06.2014. Coming into force: 07.07.2014. Effect: None. Territorial extent & classification: E. Local. - Available at
http://www.legislation.gov.uk/uksi/2014/1927/contents/made
Non-print

The A5 Trunk Road (Churchbridge, Staffordshire) (Temporary Prohibition of Traffic) Order 2014 No. 2014/2760. - Enabling power: Road Traffic Regulation Act 1984, s. 14 (1) (a). - Issued: 14.10.2014. Made: 29.09.2014. Coming into force: 06.10.2014. Effect: None. Territorial extent & classification: E. Local. - Available at
http://www.legislation.gov.uk/uksi/2014/2760/contents/made
Non-print

The A5 Trunk Road (Dordon, Warwickshire) (Temporary Restriction and Prohibition of Traffic) Order 2014 No. 2014/2619. - Enabling power: Road Traffic Regulation Act 1984, s. 14 (1) (a). - Issued: 30.09.2014. Made: 15.09.2014. Coming into force: 22.09.2014. Effect: None. Territorial extent & classification: E. Local. - Available at
http://www.legislation.gov.uk/uksi/2014/2619/contents/made
Non-print

The A5 Trunk Road (Dunstable, Bedfordshire and Markyate, Hertfordshire) (Temporary Restriction and Prohibition of Traffic) Order 2014 No. 2014/1547. - Enabling power: Road Traffic Regulation Act 1984, s. 14 (1) (a). - Issued: 13.06.2014. Made: 27.05.2014. Coming into force: 03.06.2014. Effect: None. Territorial extent & classification: E. Local. - Available at
http://www.legislation.gov.uk/uksi/2014/1547/contents/made
Non-print

The A5 Trunk Road (Felton Butler - Churncote, Shropshire) (Temporary Prohibition of Traffic) Order 2014 No. 2014/3489. - Enabling power: Road Traffic Regulation Act 1984, s. 14 (1) (a). - Issued: 07.01.2015. Made: 23.12.2014. Coming into force: 30.12.2014. Effect: None. Territorial extent & classification: E. Local. - Available at
http://www.legislation.gov.uk/uksi/2014/3489/contents/made
Non-print

The A5 Trunk Road (Gledrid, Shropshire) (Temporary Prohibition of Traffic) Order 2014 No. 2014/1093. - Enabling power: Road Traffic Regulation Act 1984, s. 14 (1) (a). - Issued: 25.04.2014. Made: 02.04.2014. Coming into force: 09.04.2014. Effect: None. Territorial extent & classification: E. Local. - Available at
http://www.legislation.gov.uk/uksi/2014/1093/contents/made
Non-print

The A5 Trunk Road (Grendon, Warwickshire) (Temporary Prohibition of Traffic) Order 2014 No. 2014/1269. - Enabling power: Road Traffic Regulation Act 1984, s. 14 (1) (a). - Issued: 19.05.2014. Made: 28.04.2014. Coming into force: 05.05.2014. Effect: None. Territorial extent & classification: E. Local. - Available at
http://www.legislation.gov.uk/uksi/2014/1269/contents/made
Non-print

The A5 Trunk Road (Higham-On-The-Hill) (Temporary Prohibition of Traffic) Order 2014 No. 2014/3445. - Enabling power: Road Traffic Regulation Act 1984, s. 14 (1) (b). - Issued: 30.12.2014. Made: 19.12.2014. Coming into force: 27.12.2014. Effect: None. Territorial extent & classification: E. Local. - Available at
http://www.legislation.gov.uk/uksi/2014/3445/contents/made
Non-print

The A5 Trunk Road (Higham, Warwickshire) (Temporary Restriction and Prohibition of Traffic) Order 2014 No. 2014/321. - Enabling power: Road Traffic Regulation Act 1984, s. 14 (1) (a). - Issued: 18.02.2014. Made: 31.01.2014. Coming into force: 07.02.2014. Effect: None. Territorial extent & classification: E. Local. - Available at
http://www.legislation.gov.uk/uksi/2014/321/contents/made Non-print

The A5 Trunk Road (High Street, Dunstable, Bedfordshire) (Temporary Prohibition of Traffic) Order 2014 No. 2014/2258. - Enabling power: Road Traffic Regulation Act 1984, s. 14 (1) (a). - Issued: 27.08.2014. Made: 18.08.2014. Coming into force: 25.08.2014. Effect: None. Territorial extent & classification: E. Local. - Available at
http://www.legislation.gov.uk/uksi/2014/2258/contents/made
Non-print

The A5 Trunk Road (High Street North, Dunstable, Bedfordshire) (Temporary Prohibition of Traffic) Order 2014 No. 2014/1475. - Enabling power: Road Traffic Regulation Act 1984, s. 14 (1) (a). - Issued: 02.06.2014. Made: 19.05.2014. Coming into force: 26.05.2014. Effect: None. Territorial extent & classification: E. Local. - Available at
http://www.legislation.gov.uk/uksi/2014/1475/contents/made
Non-print

The A5 Trunk Road (Hinckley, Leicestershire) (Temporary Prohibition of Traffic) Order 2014 No. 2014/2271. - Enabling power: Road Traffic Regulation Act 1984, s. 14 (1) (a). - Issued: 29.08.2014. Made: 19.08.2014. Coming into force: 26.08.2014. Effect: None. Territorial extent & classification: E. Local. - Available at
http://www.legislation.gov.uk/uksi/2014/2271/contents/made
Non-print

The A5 Trunk Road (Hockley, Tamworth, Staffordshire) (Temporary Prohibition of Traffic) Order 2014 No. 2014/2031. - Enabling power: Road Traffic Regulation Act 1984, s. 14 (1) (a). - Issued: 01.08.2014. Made: 30.06.2014. Coming into force: 07.07.2014. Effect: None. Territorial extent & classification: E. Local. - Available at
http://www.legislation.gov.uk/uksi/2014/2031/contents/made
Non-print

The A5 Trunk Road (Lay-by east of Llanfairpwllgwyngyll, Isle of Anglesey) (Prohibition of Vehicles) Order 2014 No. 2014/2678 (W.266). - Enabling power: Road Traffic Regulation Act 1984, ss. 1 (1), 2 (1), 2 (2). - Issued: 07.10.2014. Made: 30.09.2014. Coming into force: 02.10.2014. Effect: None. Territorial extent & classification: W. Local. - Welsh title: Gorchymyn Cefnffordd yr A5 (Cilfan i'r dwyrain o Lanfair Pwllgwyngyll, Ynys Môn) (Gwahardd Cerbydau) 2014. - Available at
http://www.legislation.gov.uk/wsi/2014/2678/contents/made Non-print

The A5 Trunk Road (Lilbourne, Northamptonshire) (Temporary Restriction and Prohibition of Traffic) Order 2014 No. 2014/2621. - Enabling power: Road Traffic Regulation Act 1984, s. 14 (1) (a). - Issued: 30.09.2014. Made: 15.09.2014. Coming into force: 22.09.2014. Effect: None. Territorial extent & classification: E. Local. - Available at http://www.legislation.gov.uk/uksi/2014/2621/contents/made
Non-print

The A5 Trunk Road (Little Brickhill, Milton Keynes) Northbound (Temporary Prohibition of Traffic) Order 2014 No. 2014/2915. - Enabling power: Road Traffic Regulation Act 1984, s. 14 (1) (a). - Issued: 24.10.2014. Made: 20.10.2014. Coming into force: 27.10.2014. Effect: None. Territorial extent & classification: E. Local. - Available at http://www.legislation.gov.uk/uksi/2014/2915/contents/made
Non-print

The A5 Trunk Road (Longford, Staffordshire) (Temporary Prohibition of Traffic) Order 2014 No. 2014/1127. - Enabling power: Road Traffic Regulation Act 1984, s. 14 (1) (a). - Issued: 01.05.2014. Made: 11.04.2014. Coming into force: 18.04.2014. Effect: None. Territorial extent & classification: E. Local. - Available at http://www.legislation.gov.uk/uksi/2014/1127/contents/made
Non-print

The A5 Trunk Road (Longford to Churchbridge, Staffordshire) (Temporary Restriction and Prohibition of Traffic) Order 2014 No. 2014/2979. - Enabling power: Road Traffic Regulation Act 1984, s. 14 (1) (a). - Issued: 13.11.2014. Made: 27.10.2014. Coming into force: 03.11.2014. Effect: None. Territorial extent & classification: E. Local. - Available at http://www.legislation.gov.uk/uksi/2014/2979/contents/made
Non-print

The A5 Trunk Road (Lutterworth, Leicestershire) (Temporary Prohibition of Traffic) Order 2014 No. 2014/2451. - Enabling power: Road Traffic Regulation Act 1984, s. 14 (1) (a). - Issued: 15.09.2014. Made: 02.09.2014. Coming into force: 09.09.2014. Effect: None. Territorial extent & classification: E. Local. - Available at http://www.legislation.gov.uk/uksi/2014/2451/contents/made
Non-print

The A5 Trunk Road (M42 - Bonehill, Staffordshire) (Temporary Prohibition of Traffic) Order 2014 No. 2014/3515. - Enabling power: Road Traffic Regulation Act 1984, s. 14 (1) (a). - Issued: 23.01.2015. Made: 17.11.2014. Coming into force: 24.11.2014. Effect: None. Territorial extent & classification: E. Local. - Available at http://www.legislation.gov.uk/uksi/2014/3515/contents/made
Non-print

The A5 Trunk Road (Nescliffe, Shropshire) (Temporary Prohibition of Traffic) Order 2014 No. 2014/1268. - Enabling power: Road Traffic Regulation Act 1984, s. 14 (1) (a). - Issued: 19.05.2014. Made: 28.04.2014. Coming into force: 05.05.2014. Effect: None. Territorial extent & classification: E. Local. - Available at http://www.legislation.gov.uk/uksi/2014/1268/contents/made
Non-print

The A5 Trunk Road (Norton Canes, Staffordshire) (Temporary Prohibition of Traffic) Order 2014 No. 2014/1171. - Enabling power: Road Traffic Regulation Act 1984, s. 14 (1) (a). - Issued: 07.05.2014. Made: 22.04.2014. Coming into force: 29.04.2014. Effect: None. Territorial extent & classification: E. Local. - Available at http://www.legislation.gov.uk/uksi/2014/1171/contents/made
Non-print

The A5 Trunk Road (Nuneaton, Warwickshire and Hinckley, Leicestershire) (Temporary Restriction and Prohibition of Traffic) Order 2014 No. 2014/2435. - Enabling power: Road Traffic Regulation Act 1984, s. 14 (1) (a). - Issued: 15.09.2014. Made: 22.08.2014. Coming into force: 29.09.2014. Effect: None. Territorial extent & classification: E. Local. - Available at http://www.legislation.gov.uk/uksi/2014/2435/contents/made
Non-print

The A5 Trunk Road (Old Stratford - Bradwell Abbey, Northamptonshire) (Temporary Prohibition of Traffic) Order 2014 No. 2014/3369. - Enabling power: Road Traffic Regulation Act 1984, s. 14 (1) (a). - Issued: 28.11.2014. Made: 17.11.2014. Coming into force: 24.11.2014. Effect: None. Territorial extent & classification: E. Local. - Available at http://www.legislation.gov.uk/uksi/2014/3369/contents/made
Non-print

The A5 Trunk Road (Rye Hill, Northamptonshire) (Temporary Restriction of Traffic) (No.2) Order 2014 No. 2014/2957. - Enabling power: Road Traffic Regulation Act 1984, s. 14 (1) (a). - Issued: 13.11.2014. Made: 24.10.2014. Coming into force: 31.10.2014. Effect: None. Territorial extent & classification: E. Local. - Available at http://www.legislation.gov.uk/uksi/2014/2957/contents/made
Non-print

The A5 Trunk Road (Rye Hill, Northamptonshire) (Temporary Restriction of Traffic) Order 2014 No. 2014/2019. - Enabling power: Road Traffic Regulation Act 1984, s. 14 (1) (a). - Issued: 31.07.2014. Made: 30.06.2014. Coming into force: 07.07.2014. Effect: None. Territorial extent & classification: E. Local. - Available at http://www.legislation.gov.uk/uksi/2014/2019/contents/made
Non-print

The A5 Trunk Road (South East of Atherstone, Warwickshire) (Temporary Prohibition of Traffic) Order 2014 No. 2014/2945. - Enabling power: Road Traffic Regulation Act 1984, s. 14 (1) (a). - Issued: 27.10.2014. Made: 20.10.2014. Coming into force: 27.10.2014. Effect: None. Territorial extent & classification: E. Local. - Available at http://www.legislation.gov.uk/uksi/2014/2945/contents/made
Non-print

The A5 Trunk Road (South of Hinckley, Leicestershire) (Temporary Restriction and Prohibition of Traffic) Order 2014 No. 2014/2442. - Enabling power: Road Traffic Regulation Act 1984, s. 14 (1) (a). - Issued: 15.09.2014. Made: 22.08.2014. Coming into force: 29.08.2014. Effect: None. Territorial extent & classification: E. Local. - Available at http://www.legislation.gov.uk/uksi/2014/2442/contents/made
Non-print

The A5 Trunk Road (South of Tamworth, Staffordshire) (Temporary Prohibition of Traffic) Order 2014 No. 2014/3014. - Enabling power: Road Traffic Regulation Act 1984, s. 14 (1) (a). - Issued: 14.11.2014. Made: 04.11.2014. Coming into force: 11.11.2014. Effect: None. Territorial extent & classification: E. Local. - Available at http://www.legislation.gov.uk/uksi/2014/3014/contents/made
Non-print

The A5 Trunk Road (Tamworth, Staffordshire) (Slip Roads) (Temporary Prohibition of Traffic) Order 2014 No. 2014/185. - Enabling power: Road Traffic Regulation Act 1984, s. 14 (1) (a). - Issued: 04.02.2014. Made: 20.01.2014. Coming into force: 27.01.2014. Effect: None. Territorial extent & classification: E. Local. - Available at http://www.legislation.gov.uk/uksi/2014/185/contents/made Non-print

The A5 Trunk Road (Tamworth, Staffordshire) (Temporary Prohibition of Traffic) (No.2) Order 2014 No. 2014/3431. - Enabling power: Road Traffic Regulation Act 1984, s. 14 (1) (a). - Issued: 15.12.2014. Made: 05.12.2014. Coming into force: 12.12.2014. Effect: None. Territorial extent & classification: E. Local. - Available at http://www.legislation.gov.uk/uksi/2014/3431/contents/made
Non-print

The A5 Trunk Road (Tamworth, Staffordshire) (Temporary Prohibition of Traffic) Order 2014 No. 2014/642. - Enabling power: Road Traffic Regulation Act 1984, s. 14 (1) (a). - Issued: 06.03.2014. Made: 17.02.2014. Coming into force: 24.02.2014. Effect: None. Territorial extent & classification: E. Local. - Available at http://www.legislation.gov.uk/uksi/2014/642/contents/made Non-print

The A5 Trunk Road (Telford, Shropshire) (Slip Road) (Temporary Prohibition of Traffic) Order 2014 No. 2014/659. - Enabling power: Road Traffic Regulation Act 1984, s. 14 (1) (a). - Issued: 07.03.2014. Made: 21.02.2014. Coming into force: 28.02.2014. Effect: None. Territorial extent & classification: E. Local. - Available at http://www.legislation.gov.uk/uksi/2014/659/contents/made Non-print

The A5 Trunk Road (Towcester - Heathencote, Northamptonshire) (Temporary Prohibition of Traffic) Order 2014 No. 2014/2231. - Enabling power: Road Traffic Regulation Act 1984, s. 14 (1) (a). - Issued: 27.08.2014. Made: 04.08.2014. Coming into force: 11.08.2014. Effect: None. Territorial extent & classification: E. Local. - Available at http://www.legislation.gov.uk/uksi/2014/2231/contents/made
Non-print

The A5 Trunk Road (Towcester, Northamptonshire) (Temporary Prohibition of Traffic) Order 2014 No. 2014/2133. - Enabling power: Road Traffic Regulation Act 1984, s. 14 (1) (a). - Issued: 12.08.2014. Made: 21.07.2014. Coming into force: 28.07.2014. Effect: None. Territorial extent & classification: E. Local. - Available at http://www.legislation.gov.uk/uksi/2014/2133/contents/made
Non-print

ROAD TRAFFIC: TRAFFIC REGULATION

The A5 Trunk Road (Towcester to Stony Stratford) (Temporary Prohibition of Traffic) Order 2014 No. 2014/2617. - Enabling power: Road Traffic Regulation Act 1984, s. 14 (1) (a). - Issued: 30.09.2014. Made: 15.09.2014. Coming into force: 22.09.2014. Effect: None. Territorial extent & classification: E. Local. - Available at http://www.legislation.gov.uk/uksi/2014/2617/contents/made Non-print

The A5 Trunk Road (Upton Magna, Shropshire) (Temporary Prohibition of Traffic) Order 2014 No. 2014/807. - Enabling power: Road Traffic Regulation Act 1984, s. 14 (1) (a). - Issued: 26.03.2014. Made: 10.03.2014. Coming into force: 17.03.2014. Effect: None. Territorial extent & classification: E. Local. - Available at http://www.legislation.gov.uk/uksi/2014/807/contents/made Non-print

The A5 Trunk Road (Weedon Bec to Towcester, Northamptonshire) (Temporary Restriction and Prohibition of Traffic) Order 2014 No. 2014/3412. - Enabling power: Road Traffic Regulation Act 1984, s. 14 (1) (a). - Issued: 03.12.2014. Made: 28.11.2014. Coming into force: 05.12.2014. Effect: None. Territorial extent & classification: E. Local. - Available at http://www.legislation.gov.uk/uksi/2014/3412/contents/made Non-print

The A5 Trunk Road (Weedon, Northamptonshire) (Temporary Restriction and Prohibition of Traffic) Order 2014 No. 2014/627. - Enabling power: Road Traffic Regulation Act 1984, s. 14 (1) (a). - Issued: 05.03.2014. Made: 17.02.2014. Coming into force: 24.02.2014. Effect: None. Territorial extent & classification: E. Local. - Available at http://www.legislation.gov.uk/uksi/2014/627/contents/made Non-print

The A5 Trunk Road (Weirbrook to East of Nesscliffe, Shropshire) (24 Hours Clearway) Order 2014 No. 2014/2469. - Enabling power: Road Traffic Regulation Act 1984, ss. 1 (1), 2 (1) (2), 4 (1), sch. 9 para. 27 (1). - Issued: 18.09.2014. Made: 14.09.2014. Coming into force: 28.08.2014. Effect: S.I. 1969/1576 varied & S.I. 2001/3119, 2003/2687 revoked. Territorial extent & classification: E. Local. - Available at http://www.legislation.gov.uk/uksi/2014/2469/contents/made Non-print

The A5 Trunk Road (West Felton, Shropshire) (Temporary Prohibition of Traffic) Order 2014 No. 2014/1517. - Enabling power: Road Traffic Regulation Act 1984, s. 14 (1) (a). - Issued: 11.06.2014. Made: 19.05.2014. Coming into force: 26.05.2014. Effect: None. Territorial extent & classification: E. Local. - Available at http://www.legislation.gov.uk/uksi/2014/1517/contents/made Non-print

The A5 Trunk Road (West of Crick to Weedon Bec, Northamptonshire) (Temporary Prohibition of Traffic) Order 2014 No. 2014/2616. - Enabling power: Road Traffic Regulation Act 1984, s. 14 (1) (a). - Issued: 30.09.2014. Made: 15.09.2014. Coming into force: 22.09.2014. Effect: None. Territorial extent & classification: E. Local. - Available at http://www.legislation.gov.uk/uksi/2014/2616/contents/made Non-print

The A6 and A5111 Trunk Roads (Thulston to Alvaston, Derbyshire) (Temporary Prohibition of Traffic) Order 2014 No. 2014/3358. - Enabling power: Road Traffic Regulation Act 1984, s. 14 (1) (a). - Issued: 28.11.2014. Made: 17.11.2014. Coming into force: 24.11.2014. Effect: None. Territorial extent & classification: E. Local. - Available at http://www.legislation.gov.uk/uksi/2014/3358/contents/made Non-print

The A11 Trunk Road (A14 Junction 38 Waterhall Interchange to Newmarket Road Junction, Suffolk) Northbound (Temporary Prohibition of Traffic) Order 2014 No. 2014/3356. - Enabling power: Road Traffic Regulation Act 1984, s. 14 (1) (a). - Issued: 11.12.2014. Made: 06.10.2014. Coming into force: 13.10.2014. Effect: None. Territorial extent & classification: E. Local. - Available at http://www.legislation.gov.uk/uksi/2014/3356/contents/made Non-print

The A11 Trunk Road (Attleborough, Norfolk) Slip Roads (Temporary Prohibition of Traffic) Order 2014 No. 2014/1271. - Enabling power: Road Traffic Regulation Act 1984, s. 14 (1) (a). - Issued: 19.05.2014. Made: 06.05.2014. Coming into force: 13.05.2014. Effect: None. Territorial extent & classification: E. Local. - Available at http://www.legislation.gov.uk/uksi/2014/1271/contents/made Non-print

The A11 Trunk Road (Attleborough to Spooner Row, Norfolk) (Temporary Prohibition of Traffic) Order 2014 No. 2014/2914. - Enabling power: Road Traffic Regulation Act 1984, s. 14 (1) (a). - Issued: 24.10.2014. Made: 20.10.2014. Coming into force: 27.10.2014. Effect: None. Territorial extent & classification: E. Local. - Available at http://www.legislation.gov.uk/uksi/2014/2914/contents/made Non-print

The A11 Trunk Road (Fiveways to Thetford Improvement) (Temporary Restriction and Prohibition of Traffic) Order 2014 No. 2014/1018. - Enabling power: Road Traffic Regulation Act 1984, ss. 14 (1) (a), 122 (A). - Issued: 16.04.2014. Made: 31.03.2014. Coming into force: 07.04.2014. Effect: None. Territorial extent & classification: E. Local. - Available at http://www.legislation.gov.uk/uksi/2014/1018/contents/made Non-print

The A11 Trunk Road (Fulbourn, Cambridgeshire) Exit Slip Roads (Temporary Prohibition of Traffic) Order 2014 No. 2014/779. - Enabling power: Road Traffic Regulation Act 1984, s. 14 (1) (a). - Issued: 10.03.2014. Made: 03.03.2014. Coming into force: 10.03.2014. Effect: None. Territorial extent & classification: E. Local. - Available at http://www.legislation.gov.uk/uksi/2014/779/contents/made Non-print

The A11 Trunk Road (Tuttles Lane Interchange, Wymondham, Norfolk) Connecting Roads (Temporary Prohibition of Traffic) Order 2014 No. 2014/2786. - Enabling power: Road Traffic Regulation Act 1984, s. 14 (1) (a). - Issued: 13.10.2014. Made: 06.10.2014. Coming into force: 13.10.2014. Effect: None. Territorial extent & classification: E. Local. - Available at http://www.legislation.gov.uk/uksi/2014/2786/contents/made Non-print

The A11 Trunk Road (Wymondham Bypass, B1172 Spooner Row to B1135 Tuttles Lane, Norfolk) (Temporary Restriction and Prohibition of Traffic) Order 2014 No. 2014/3005. - Enabling power: Road Traffic Regulation Act 1984, s. 14 (1) (a). - Issued: 12.11.2014. Made: 03.11.2014. Coming into force: 10.11.2014. Effect: None. Territorial extent & classification: E. Local. - Available at http://www.legislation.gov.uk/uksi/2014/3005/contents/made Non-print

The A12 and A120 Trunk Roads (Junction 27 Spring Lane Interchange to Junction 29 Crown Interchange, Colchester, Essex) (Temporary Prohibition of Traffic) Order 2014 No. 2014/2628. - Enabling power: Road Traffic Regulation Act 1984, s. 14 (1) (a). - Issued: 29.09.2014. Made: 22.09.2014. Coming into force: 29.09.2014. Effect: None. Territorial extent & classification: E. Local. - Available at http://www.legislation.gov.uk/uksi/2014/2628/contents/made Non-print

The A12 Trunk Road (Bascule Bridge, Lowestoft, Suffolk) (Temporary Prohibition of Traffic and Pedestrians) Order 2014 No. 2014/756. - Enabling power: Road Traffic Regulation Act 1984, s. 14 (1) (a). - Issued: 17.03.2014. Made: 10.03.2014. Coming into force: 17.03.2014. Effect: None. Territorial extent & classification: E. Local. - Available at http://www.legislation.gov.uk/uksi/2014/756/contents/made Non-print

The A12 Trunk Road (Breydon Bridge, Great Yarmouth, Norfolk) (Temporary Prohibition of Traffic and Pedestrians) Order 2014 No. 2014/1571. - Enabling power: Road Traffic Regulation Act 1984, s. 14 (1) (a) (7). - Issued: 18.06.2014. Made: 02.06.2014. Coming into force: 09.06.2014. Effect: None. Territorial extent & classification: E. Local. - Available at http://www.legislation.gov.uk/uksi/2014/1571/contents/made Non-print

The A12 Trunk Road (Colchester Bypass, Essex) Northbound (Temporary Restriction and Prohibition of Traffic) Order 2014 No. 2014/222. - Enabling power: Road Traffic Regulation Act 1984, s. 14 (1) (a). - Issued: 07.02.2014. Made: 03.02.2014. Coming into force: 10.02.2014. Effect: None. Territorial extent & classification: E. Local. - Available at http://www.legislation.gov.uk/uksi/2014/222/contents/made Non-print

The A12 Trunk Road (Corton, Suffolk) (Temporary Restriction and Prohibition of Traffic) Order 2014 No. 2014/2758. - Enabling power: Road Traffic Regulation Act 1984, s. 14 (1) (a) (7). - Issued: 13.10.2014. Made: 29.09.2014. Coming into force: 06.10.2014. Effect: None. Territorial extent & classification: E. Local. - Available at http://www.legislation.gov.uk/uksi/2014/2758/contents/made Non-print

The A12 Trunk Road (Corton, Suffolk to Hopton, Norfolk) (Temporary Restriction and Prohibition of Traffic) Order 2014 No. 2014/3450. - Enabling power: Road Traffic Regulation Act 1984, s. 14 (1) (a). - Issued: 19.12.2014. Made: 15.12.2014. Coming into force: 29.12.2014. Effect: None. Territorial extent & classification: E. Local. - Available at
http://www.legislation.gov.uk/uksi/2014/3450/contents/made
Non-print

The A12 Trunk Road (Dedham, Essex to Four Sisters Interchange, Suffolk) Northbound (Temporary Restriction and Prohibition of Traffic) Order 2014 No. 2014/283. - Enabling power: Road Traffic Regulation Act 1984, s. 14 (1) (a). - Issued: 14.02.2014. Made: 10.02.2014. Coming into force: 17.02.2014. Effect: None. Territorial extent & classification: E. Local. - Available at
http://www.legislation.gov.uk/uksi/2014/283/contents/made Non-print

The A12 Trunk Road (Junction 11 Brook Street Interchange to Junction 15 Webbs Farm Interchange) Essex (Temporary Restriction and Prohibition of Traffic) Order 2014 No. 2014/3371. - Enabling power: Road Traffic Regulation Act 1984, s. 14 (1) (a). - Issued: 03.12.2014. Made: 17.11.2014. Coming into force: 24.11.2014. Effect: None. Territorial extent & classification: E. Local. - Available at
http://www.legislation.gov.uk/uksi/2014/3371/contents/made
Non-print

The A12 Trunk Road (Junction 12 Marylands Interchange, Mountnessing, Essex) Southbound Exit Slip Road (Temporary 50 Miles Per Hour Speed Restriction) Order 2014 No. 2014/2639. - Enabling power: Road Traffic Regulation Act 1984, s. 14 (2) (b). - Issued: 30.09.2014. Made: 24.09.2014. Coming into force: 01.10.2014. Effect: None. Territorial extent & classification: E. Local. - Available at
http://www.legislation.gov.uk/uksi/2014/2639/contents/made
Non-print

The A12 Trunk Road (Junction 18 Sandon, Chelmsford, Essex) Northbound Entry Slip Road (Temporary Prohibition of Traffic) Order 2014 No. 2014/3448. - Enabling power: Road Traffic Regulation Act 1984, s. 14 (1) (a). - Issued: 19.12.2014. Made: 15.12.2014. Coming into force: 29.12.2014. Effect: None. Territorial extent & classification: E. Local. - Available at
http://www.legislation.gov.uk/uksi/2014/3448/contents/made
Non-print

The A12 Trunk Road (Junction 18 Sandon Interchange to Junction 19 Boreham Interchange, Chelmsford, Essex) (Temporary Restriction and Prohibition of Traffic) Order 2014 No. 2014/1469. - Enabling power: Road Traffic Regulation Act 1984, s. 14 (1) (a). - Issued: 04.06.2014. Made: 19.05.2014. Coming into force: 26.05.2014. Effect: None. Territorial extent & classification: E. Local. - Available at
http://www.legislation.gov.uk/uksi/2014/1469/contents/made
Non-print

The A12 Trunk Road (Junction 19 Boreham Interchange to Junction 24 Kelvedon North Interchange, Essex) Northbound (Temporary Restriction and Prohibition of Traffic) Order 2014 No. 2014/778. - Enabling power: Road Traffic Regulation Act 1984, s. 14 (1) (a). - Issued: 10.03.2014. Made: 03.03.2014. Coming into force: 10.03.2014. Effect: None. Territorial extent & classification: E. Local. - Available at
http://www.legislation.gov.uk/uksi/2014/778/contents/made Non-print

The A12 Trunk Road (Junction 22 Coleman's Interchange Witham, Essex) Southbound Lay-by (Temporary Prohibition of Traffic) Order 2014 No. 2014/682. - Enabling power: Road Traffic Regulation Act 1984, s. 14 (1) (a). - Issued: 06.03.2014. Made: 24.02.2014. Coming into force: 03.03.2014. Effect: None. Territorial extent & classification: E. Local. - Available at
http://www.legislation.gov.uk/uksi/2014/682/contents/made Non-print

The A12 Trunk Road (Junction 22 Coleman's Interchange, Witham to Junction 24 Kelvedon, Essex) (Temporary Prohibition of Traffic) Order 2014 No. 2014/3447. - Enabling power: Road Traffic Regulation Act 1984, s. 14 (1) (a). - Issued: 19.12.2014. Made: 15.12.2014. Coming into force: 29.12.2014. Effect: None. Territorial extent & classification: E. Local. - Available at
http://www.legislation.gov.uk/uksi/2014/3447/contents/made
Non-print

The A12 Trunk Road (Junction 22 Witham North Interchange, Essex) Southbound (Temporary Prohibition of Traffic) Order 2014 No. 2014/97. - Enabling power: Road Traffic Regulation Act 1984, s. 14 (1) (a). - Issued: 22.01.2014. Made: 20.01.2014. Coming into force: 27.01.2014. Effect: None. Territorial extent & classification: E. Local. - Available at http://www.legislation.gov.uk/uksi/2014/97/contents/made Non-print

The A12 Trunk Road (Junction 27 Spring Lane Interchange to Junction 29 Crown Interchange) and the A120 Trunk Road (Colchester) Essex (Temporary Restriction and Prohibition of Traffic) Order 2014 No. 2014/3176. - Enabling power: Road Traffic Regulation Act 1984, s. 14 (1) (a). - Issued: 24.11.2014. Made: 17.11.2014. Coming into force: 24.11.204. Effect: None. Territorial extent & classification: E. Local. - Available at
http://www.legislation.gov.uk/uksi/2014/3176/contents/made
Non-print

The A12 Trunk Road (Junction 28 Severalls Interchange, Colchester, Essex) Southbound (Temporary Prohibition of Traffic) Order 2014 No. 2014/390. - Enabling power: Road Traffic Regulation Act 1984, s. 14 (1) (a). - Issued: 27.02.2014. Made: 17.02.2014. Coming into force: 24.02.2014. Effect: None. Territorial extent & classification: E. Local. - Available at
http://www.legislation.gov.uk/uksi/2014/390/contents/made Non-print

The A12 Trunk Road (Junction 30 Stratford St Mary to Junction 33 Copdock Mill Interchange, Ipswich, Suffolk) (Temporary Restriction and Prohibition of Traffic) Order 2014 No. 2014/3403. - Enabling power: Road Traffic Regulation Act 1984, s. 14 (1) (a). - Issued: 28.11.2014. Made: 24.11.2014. Coming into force: 01.12.2014. Effect: None. Territorial extent & classification: E. Local. - Available at
http://www.legislation.gov.uk/uksi/2014/3403/contents/made
Non-print

The A12 Trunk Road (Old London Road, Marks Tey, Colchester, Essex) (Temporary Prohibition of Traffic) Order 2014 No. 2014/291. - Enabling power: Road Traffic Regulation Act 1984, s. 14 (1) (a). - Issued: 14.02.2014. Made: 10.02.2014. Coming into force: 17.02.2014. Effect: None. Territorial extent & classification: E. Local. - Available at
http://www.legislation.gov.uk/uksi/2014/291/contents/made Non-print

The A12 Trunk Road (Stanway Bypass, Colchester, Essex) Lay-bys (Temporary Prohibition of Traffic) Order 2014 No. 2014/135. - Enabling power: Road Traffic Regulation Act 1984, s. 14 (1) (a). - Issued: 24.01.2014. Made: 20.01.2014. Coming into force: 27.01.2014. Effect: None. Territorial extent & classification: E. Local. - Available at
http://www.legislation.gov.uk/uksi/2014/135/contents/made Non-print

The A12 Trunk Road (St Peters Street to Station Square, Lowestoft, Suffolk) (Temporary Prohibition of Traffic) Order 2014 No. 2014/3129. - Enabling power: Road Traffic Regulation Act 1984, s. 14 (1) (a). - Issued: 27.11.2014. Made: 20.10.2014. Coming into force: 27.10.2014. Effect: None. Territorial extent & classification: E. Local. - Available at
http://www.legislation.gov.uk/uksi/2014/3129/contents/made
Non-print

The A13 and the A1089 Trunk Roads and the M25 Motorway (A13 Dumb-Bell Interchange - Baker Street Interchange, A1089 Marshfoot Interchange - Baker Street Interchange and M25 Junctions 29 and 30) (Temporary Prohibition of Traffic) Order 2014 No. 2014/2202. - Enabling power: Road Traffic Regulation Act 1984, s. 14 (1) (a). - Issued: 15.08.2014. Made: 04.08.2014. Coming into force: 24.08.2014. Effect: None. Territorial extent & classification: E. Local. - Available at
http://www.legislation.gov.uk/uksi/2014/2202/contents/made
Non-print

The A13 and the A1089 Trunk Roads (Wennington Interchange - Marshfoot Interchange) (Temporary Prohibition of Traffic) Order 2014 No. 2014/3017. - Enabling power: Road Traffic Regulation Act 1984, s. 14 (1) (a). - Issued: 23.10.2014. Made: 20.10.2014. Coming into force: 14.11.2014. Effect: None. Territorial extent & classification: E. Local. - Available at
http://www.legislation.gov.uk/uksi/2014/3017/contents/made
Non-print

The A13 Trunk Road (Lakeside Junction - North Stifford Interchange) (Temporary Prohibition of Traffic) Order 2014 No. 2014/736. - Enabling power: Road Traffic Regulation Act 1984, s. 14 (1) (a). - Issued: 17.03.2014. Made: 10.03.2014. Coming into force: 29.03.2014. Effect: None. Territorial extent & classification: E. Local. - Available at
http://www.legislation.gov.uk/uksi/2014/736/contents/made Non-print

The A13 Trunk Road (Wennington Interchange - Stifford Interchange) (Temporary Restriction and Prohibition of Traffic) Order 2014 No. 2014/2053. - Enabling power: Road Traffic Regulation Act 1984, s. 14 (1) (a). - Issued: 04.08.2014. Made: 14.07.2014. Coming into force: 02.08.2014. Effect: None. Territorial extent & classification: E. Local. - Available at
http://www.legislation.gov.uk/uksi/2014/2053/contents/made
Non-print

ROAD TRAFFIC: TRAFFIC REGULATION

The A13 Trunk Road (Wennington Interchange) (Temporary Prohibition of Traffic) Order 2014 No. 2014/2902. - Enabling power: Road Traffic Regulation Act 1984, s. 14 (1) (a). - Issued: 24.10.2014. Made: 29.09.2014. Coming into force: 19.10.2014. Effect: None. Territorial extent & classification: E. Local. - Available at http://www.legislation.gov.uk/uksi/2014/2902/contents/made Non-print

The A14 and A11 Trunk Roads (Waterhall Interchange, Suffolk to Thickthorn Interchange, Norfolk) (Temporary Restriction and Prohibition of Traffic) Order 2014 No. 2014/224. - Enabling power: Road Traffic Regulation Act 1984, s. 14 (1) (a). - Issued: 10.02.2014. Made: 03.02.2014. Coming into force: 10.02.2014. Effect: None. Territorial extent & classification: E. Local. - Available at http://www.legislation.gov.uk/uksi/2014/224/contents/made Non-print

The A14 Trunk Road (Barton Seagrave, Northamptonshire) (Slip Road) (Temporary Prohibition of Traffic) Order 2014 No. 2014/647. - Enabling power: Road Traffic Regulation Act 1984, s. 14 (1) (a). - Issued: 05.03.2014. Made: 17.02.2014. Coming into force: 24.02.2014. Effect: None. Territorial extent & classification: E. Local. - Available at http://www.legislation.gov.uk/uksi/2014/647/contents/made Non-print

The A14 Trunk Road (Junction 10, Kettering, Northamptonshire) (Temporary Restriction and Prohibition of Traffic) Order 2014 No. 2014/2076. - Enabling power: Road Traffic Regulation Act 1984, s. 14 (1) (a). - Issued: 06.08.2014. Made: 14.07.2014. Coming into force: 21.07.2014. Effect: None. Territorial extent & classification: E. Local. - Available at http://www.legislation.gov.uk/uksi/2014/2076/contents/made Non-print

The A14 Trunk Road (Junction 11, Kettering, Northamptonshire) (Temporary Restriction and Prohibition of Traffic) Order 2014 No. 2014/2275. - Enabling power: Road Traffic Regulation Act 1984, s. 14 (1) (a). - Issued: 01.09.2014. Made: 19.08.2014. Coming into force: 26.08.2014. Effect: None. Territorial extent & classification: E. Local. - Available at http://www.legislation.gov.uk/uksi/2014/2275/contents/made Non-print

The A14 Trunk Road (Junction 11, Northamptonshire) (Temporary Prohibition of Traffic) Order 2014 No. 2014/2164. - Enabling power: Road Traffic Regulation Act 1984, s. 14 (1) (a). - Issued: 12.08.2014. Made: 04.08.2014. Coming into force: 11.08.2014. Effect: None. Territorial extent & classification: E. Local. - Available at http://www.legislation.gov.uk/uksi/2014/2164/contents/made Non-print

The A14 Trunk Road (Junction 16 Catworth/Molesworth to Junction 24 Godmanchester, Cambridgeshire) (Temporary Restriction and Prohibition of Traffic) Order 2014 No. 2014/1974. - Enabling power: Road Traffic Regulation Act 1984, s. 14 (1) (a). - Issued: 21.07.2014. Made: 07.07.2014. Coming into force: 14.07.2014. Effect: None. Territorial extent & classification: E. Local. - Available at http://www.legislation.gov.uk/uksi/2014/1974/contents/made Non-print

The A14 Trunk Road (Junction 16 Catworth/Molesworth to Junction 24 Godmanchester, Cambridgeshire) (Temporary Restriction and Prohibition of Traffic) Variation Order 2014 No. 2014/2488. - Enabling power: Road Traffic Regulation Act 1984, s. 14 (1) (a), sch. 9 para. 27 (1). - Issued: 12.09.2014. Made: 08.09.2014. Coming into force: 15.09.2014. Effect: S.I. 2014/1974 varied. Territorial extent & classification: E. Local. - Available at http://www.legislation.gov.uk/uksi/2014/2488/contents/made Non-print

The A14 Trunk Road (Junction 23 Spittals Interchange to Junction 24 Godmanchester, Cambridgeshire) (Temporary Prohibition of Traffic) (No.2) Order 2014 No. 2014/2347. - Enabling power: Road Traffic Regulation Act 1984, s. 14 (1) (a). - Issued: 04.09.2014. Made: 01.09.2014. Coming into force: 08.09.2014. Effect: None. Territorial extent & classification: E. Local. - Available at http://www.legislation.gov.uk/uksi/2014/2347/contents/made Non-print

The A14 Trunk Road (Junction 23 Spittals Interchange to Junction 24 Godmanchester, Cambridgeshire) (Temporary Prohibition of Traffic) Order 2014 No. 2014/1485. - Enabling power: Road Traffic Regulation Act 1984, s. 14 (1) (a). - Issued: 05.06.2014. Made: 19.05.2014. Coming into force: 26.05.2014. Effect: None. Territorial extent & classification: E. Local. - Available at http://www.legislation.gov.uk/uksi/2014/1485/contents/made Non-print

The A14 Trunk Road (Junction 25 Hemingford Abbots, Cambridgeshire to Junction 38 Waterhall Interchange, Suffolk) the A428 Trunk Road (Girton Interchange) the M11 Motorway (Junction 11 to Junction 14) and the A11 Trunk Road (Nine Mile Hill to Six Mile Bottom) (Cambridgeshire) (Temporary Restriction and Prohibition of Traffic) Order 2014 No. 2014/2008. - Enabling power: Road Traffic Regulation Act 1984, s. 14 (1) (a), sch. 9, para. 27 (1). - Issued: 31.07.2014. Made: 14.07.2014. Coming into force: 21.07.2014. Effect: S.I. 2014/985, 1546 revoked. Territorial extent & classification: E. Local. - Available at http://www.legislation.gov.uk/uksi/2014/2008/contents/made Non-print

The A14 Trunk Road (Junction 26 St Ives to Junction 29 Bar Hill, Cambridgeshire) (Temporary Prohibition of Traffic) Order 2014 No. 2014/1546. - Enabling power: Road Traffic Regulation Act 1984, s. 14 (1) (a). - Issued: 13.06.2014. Made: 27.05.2014. Coming into force: 03.06.2014. Effect: None. Territorial extent & classification: E. Local. - Revoked by S.I. 2014/2008 (non-print). - Available at http://www.legislation.gov.uk/uksi/2014/1546/contents/made Non-print

The A14 Trunk Road (Junction 31 Girton to Junction 37 Exning) and the A428 Trunk Road/M11 Motorway (Girton Interchange) (Cambridgeshire) (Temporary Restriction and Prohibition of Traffic) Order 2014 No. 2014/985. - Enabling power: Road Traffic Regulation Act 1984, s. 14 (1) (a). - Issued: 07.04.2014. Made: 24.03.2014. Coming into force: 31.03.2014. Effect: None. Territorial extent & classification: E. Local. - Revoked by S.I. 2014/2008 (non-print). - Available at http://www.legislation.gov.uk/uksi/2014/985/contents/made Non-print

The A14 Trunk Road (Junction 36 Nine Mile Hill, Cambridgeshire) Westbound Entry Slip Road (Temporary Prohibition of Traffic) Order 2014 No. 2014/31. - Enabling power: Road Traffic Regulation Act 1984, s. 14 (1) (a). - Issued: 14.01.2014. Made: 06.01.2014. Coming into force: 13.01.2014. Effect: None. Territorial extent & classification: E. Local. - Available at http://www.legislation.gov.uk/uksi/2014/31/contents/made Non-print

The A14 Trunk Road (Junction 37 Exning to Junction 39 Kentford) Suffolk (Temporary Prohibition of Traffic) Order 2014 No. 2014/2810. - Enabling power: Road Traffic Regulation Act 1984, s. 14 (1) (a). - Issued: 16.10.2014. Made: 13.10.2014. Coming into force: 20.10.2014. Effect: None. Territorial extent & classification: E. Local. - Available at http://www.legislation.gov.uk/uksi/2014/2810/contents/made Non-print

The A14 Trunk Road (Junction 39 Kentford to Junction 37 Exning, Westbound) and the A11 Trunk Road (Waterhall Interchange, Southbound) Suffolk (Temporary Restriction and Prohibition of Traffic) Order 2014 No. 2014/281. - Enabling power: Road Traffic Regulation Act 1984, s. 14 (1) (a). - Issued: 14.02.2014. Made: 10.02.2014. Coming into force: 17.02.2014. Effect: None. Territorial extent & classification: E. Local. - Available at http://www.legislation.gov.uk/uksi/2014/281/contents/made Non-print

The A14 Trunk Road (Junction 42 Westley Interchange to Junction 43 St Saviours Interchange, Bury St Edmunds, Suffolk) (Temporary Restriction and Prohibition of Traffic) Order 2014 No. 2014/968. - Enabling power: Road Traffic Regulation Act 1984, s. 14 (1) (a). - Issued: 01.04.2014. Made: 17.03.2014. Coming into force: 24.03.2014. Effect: None. Territorial extent & classification: E. Local. - Available at http://www.legislation.gov.uk/uksi/2014/968/contents/made Non-print

The A14 Trunk Road (Junction 43 St Saviours Interchange to Junction 47 Woolpit Interchange, Suffolk) (Temporary Restriction and Prohibition of Traffic) Order 2014 No. 2014/56. - Enabling power: Road Traffic Regulation Act 1984, s. 14 (1) (a) (5) (b) (7). - Issued: 17.01.2014. Made: 13.01.2014. Coming into force: 20.01.2014. Effect: None. Territorial extent & classification: E. Local. - Available at http://www.legislation.gov.uk/uksi/2014/56/contents/made Non-print

The A14 Trunk Road (Junction 44 Moreton Hall Interchange to Junction 47 Woolpit Interchange, Suffolk) (Temporary Prohibition of Traffic) Order 2014 No. 2014/3177. - Enabling power: Road Traffic Regulation Act 1984, s. 14 (1) (a). - Issued: 24.11.2014. Made: 17.11.2014. Coming into force: 24.11.204. Effect: None. Territorial extent & classification: E. Local. - Available at http://www.legislation.gov.uk/uksi/2014/3177/contents/made Non-print

ROAD TRAFFIC: TRAFFIC REGULATION

The A14 Trunk Road (Junction 46 Thurston, Suffolk) (Temporary Restriction and Prohibition of Traffic) Order 2014 No. 2014/3040. - Enabling power: Road Traffic Regulation Act 1984, s. 14 (1) (a). - Issued: 17.11.2014. Made: 10.11.2014. Coming into force: 17.11.2014. Effect: None. Territorial extent & classification: E. Local. - Available at http://www.legislation.gov.uk/uksi/2014/3040/contents/made Non-print

The A14 Trunk Road (Junction 51 Beacon Hill, Needham Market, Suffolk) Westbound (Temporary Prohibition of Traffic) Order 2014 No. 2014/2531. - Enabling power: Road Traffic Regulation Act 1984, s. 14 (1) (a). - Issued: 23.09.2014. Made: 15.09.2014. Coming into force: 22.09.2014. Effect: None. Territorial extent & classification: E. Local. - Available at http://www.legislation.gov.uk/uksi/2014/2531/contents/made Non-print

The A14 Trunk Road (Junction 53 Whitehouse Interchange to Junction 58 Levington Interchange, Ipswich, Suffolk) (Temporary Prohibition of Traffic) Order 2014 No. 2014/145. - Enabling power: Road Traffic Regulation Act 1984, s. 14 (1) (a). - Issued: 29.01.2014. Made: 06.01.2014. Coming into force: 13.01.2014. Effect: None. Territorial extent & classification: E. Local. - Available at http://www.legislation.gov.uk/uksi/2014/145/contents/made Non-print

The A14 Trunk Road (Junction 56 Wherstead to Junction 57 Nacton, Ipswich, Suffolk) Eastbound (Temporary Prohibition of Traffic and Pedestrians) Order 2014 No. 2014/3008. - Enabling power: Road Traffic Regulation Act 1984, s. 14 (1) (a). - Issued: 12.11.2014. Made: 03.11.2014. Coming into force: 10.11.2014. Effect: None. Territorial extent & classification: E. Local. - Available at http://www.legislation.gov.uk/uksi/2014/3008/contents/made Non-print

The A14 Trunk Road (Kelmarsh - Rothwell, Northamptonshire) (Temporary Restriction and Prohibition of Traffic) Order 2014 No. 2014/2229. - Enabling power: Road Traffic Regulation Act 1984, s. 14 (1) (a). - Issued: 27.08.2014. Made: 01.08.2014. Coming into force: 08.08.2014. Effect: None. Territorial extent & classification: E. Local. - Available at http://www.legislation.gov.uk/uksi/2014/2229/contents/made Non-print

The A14 Trunk Road (Kettering, Northamptonshire) (Temporary Prohibition of Traffic) (Slip Road) Order 2014 No. 2014/648. - Enabling power: Road Traffic Regulation Act 1984, s. 14 (1) (a). - Issued: 05.03.2014. Made: 17.02.2014. Coming into force: 24.02.2014. Effect: None. Territorial extent & classification: E. Local. - Available at http://www.legislation.gov.uk/uksi/2014/648/contents/made Non-print

The A14 Trunk Road (Rothwell - Kettering, Northamptonshire) (Temporary Restriction and Prohibition of Traffic) Order 2014 No. 2014/2230. - Enabling power: Road Traffic Regulation Act 1984, s. 14 (1) (a). - Issued: 27.08.2014. Made: 04.08.2014. Coming into force: 11.08.2014. Effect: None. Territorial extent & classification: E. Local. - Available at http://www.legislation.gov.uk/uksi/2014/2230/contents/made Non-print

The A14 Trunk Road (Rothwell, Northamptonshire) (Temporary Prohibition of Traffic) Order 2014 No. 2014/1521. - Enabling power: Road Traffic Regulation Act 1984, s. 14 (1) (a). - Issued: 11.06.2014. Made: 21.05.2014. Coming into force: 28.05.2014. Effect: None. Territorial extent & classification: E. Local. - Available at http://www.legislation.gov.uk/uksi/2014/1521/contents/made Non-print

The A14 Trunk Road (Thrapston, Northamptonshire) (Temporary Prohibition of Traffic) Order 2014 No. 2014/625. - Enabling power: Road Traffic Regulation Act 1984, s. 14 (1) (a). - Issued: 05.03.2014. Made: 17.02.2014. Coming into force: 24.02.2014. Effect: None. Territorial extent & classification: E. Local. - Available at http://www.legislation.gov.uk/uksi/2014/625/contents/made Non-print

The A14 Trunk Road (Thrapston, Northamptonshire) (Temporary Restriction and Prohibition of Traffic) Order 2014 No. 2014/3411. - Enabling power: Road Traffic Regulation Act 1984, s. 14 (1) (a). - Issued: 03.12.2014. Made: 28.11.2014. Coming into force: 05.12.2014. Effect: None. Territorial extent & classification: E. Local. - Available at http://www.legislation.gov.uk/uksi/2014/3411/contents/made Non-print

The A19 Trunk Road and the A66 Trunk Road (Stockton Road Interchange) (Temporary Prohibition of Traffic) Order 2014 No. 2014/193. - Enabling power: Road Traffic Regulation Act 1984, s. 14 (1) (a). - Issued: 04.02.2014. Made: 23.01.2014. Coming into force: 02.02.2014. Effect: None. Territorial extent & classification: E. Local. - Available at http://www.legislation.gov.uk/uksi/2014/193/contents/made Non-print

The A19 Trunk Road and the A174 Trunk Road (Blue Bell Interchange to Parkway Interchange) (Temporary Restriction and Prohibition of Traffic) Order 2014 No. 2014/1307. - Enabling power: Road Traffic Regulation Act 1984, s. 14 (1) (a). - Issued: 23.05.2014. Made: 08.05.2014. Coming into force: 18.05.2014. Effect: None. Territorial extent & classification: E. Local. - Available at http://www.legislation.gov.uk/uksi/2014/1307/contents/made Non-print

The A19 Trunk Road (Chester Road Interchange to Herrington Interchange) (Temporary Prohibition of Traffic) Order 2014 No. 2014/755. - Enabling power: Road Traffic Regulation Act 1984, s. 14 (1) (a). - Issued: 12.03.2014. Made: 06.03.2014. Coming into force: 16.03.2014. Effect: None. Territorial extent & classification: E. Local. - Available at http://www.legislation.gov.uk/uksi/2014/755/contents/made Non-print

The A19 Trunk Road (Crathorne Interchange) (Temporary Prohibition of Traffic) Order 2014 No. 2014/247. - Enabling power: Road Traffic Regulation Act 1984, s. 14 (1) (a). - Issued: 10.02.2014. Made: 30.01.2014. Coming into force: 09.02.2014. Effect: None. Territorial extent & classification: E. Local. - Available at http://www.legislation.gov.uk/uksi/2014/247/contents/made Non-print

The A19 Trunk Road (Crathorne Interchange to Parkway Interchange) (Temporary Restriction and Prohibition of Traffic) (No.2) Order 2014 No. 2014/1113. - Enabling power: Road Traffic Regulation Act 1984, s. 14 (1) (a). - Issued: 01.05.2014. Made: 10.04.2014. Coming into force: 22.04.2014. Effect: None. Territorial extent & classification: E. Local. - Available at http://www.legislation.gov.uk/uksi/2014/1113/contents/made Non-print

The A19 Trunk Road (Crathorne Interchange to Parkway Interchange) (Temporary Restriction and Prohibition of Traffic) Order 2014 No. 2014/747. - Enabling power: Road Traffic Regulation Act 1984, s. 14 (1) (a). - Issued: 12.03.2014. Made: 06.03.2014. Coming into force: 20.03.2014. Effect: None. Territorial extent & classification: E. Local. - Available at http://www.legislation.gov.uk/uksi/2014/747/contents/made Non-print

The A19 Trunk Road (Downhill Lane Interchange) (Temporary Prohibition of Traffic) Order 2014 No. 2014/1319. - Enabling power: Road Traffic Regulation Act 1984, s. 14 (1) (a). - Issued: 27.05.2014. Made: 08.05.2014. Coming into force: 16.05.2014. Effect: None. Territorial extent & classification: E. Local. - Available at http://www.legislation.gov.uk/uksi/2014/1319/contents/made Non-print

The A19 Trunk Road (Dudley Lane Interchange) (Temporary Prohibition of Traffic) Order 2014 No. 2014/3538. - Enabling power: Road Traffic Regulation Act 1984, s. 14 (1) (a). - Issued: 22.01.2015. Made: 29.12.2014. Coming into force: 11.01.2015. Effect: None. Territorial extent & classification: E. Local. - Available at http://www.legislation.gov.uk/uksi/2014/3538/contents/made Non-print

The A19 Trunk Road (Elwick South Junction) (Temporary Prohibition of Traffic) Order 2014 No. 2014/705. - Enabling power: Road Traffic Regulation Act 1984, s. 14 (1) (a). - Issued: 20.03.2014. Made: 20.02.2014. Coming into force: 28.02.2014. Effect: None. Territorial extent & classification: E. Local. - Available at http://www.legislation.gov.uk/uksi/2014/705/contents/made Non-print

The A19 Trunk Road (Killingworth Interchange to Holystone Interchange) (Temporary Prohibition of Traffic) Order 2014 No. 2014/742. - Enabling power: Road Traffic Regulation Act 1984, s. 14 (1) (a). - Issued: 10.03.2014. Made: 06.03.2014. Coming into force: 17.03.2014. Effect: None. Territorial extent & classification: E. Local. - Available at http://www.legislation.gov.uk/uksi/2014/742/contents/made Non-print

The A19 Trunk Road (Killingworth Interchange to Silverlink Interchange) (Temporary Prohibition of Traffic) Order 2014 No. 2014/2682. - Enabling power: Road Traffic Regulation Act 1984, s. 14 (1) (a). - Issued: 07.10.2014. Made: 25.09.2014. Coming into force: 5.10.2014. Effect: None. Territorial extent & classification: E. Local. - Available at http://www.legislation.gov.uk/uksi/2014/2682/contents/made Non-print

The A19 Trunk Road (Laybys between Osmotherley and Nether Silton) (Temporary Prohibition of Traffic) Order 2014 No. 2014/2964. - Enabling power: Road Traffic Regulation Act 1984, s. 14 (1) (a). - Issued: 27.10.2014. Made: 23.10.2014. Coming into force: 02.11.2014. Effect: None. Territorial extent & classification: E. Local. - Available at http://www.legislation.gov.uk/uksi/2014/2964/contents/made
Non-print

The A19 Trunk Road (Moor Farm to Fisher Lane) (Temporary Restriction and Prohibition of Traffic) Order 2014 No. 2014/2787. - Enabling power: Road Traffic Regulation Act 1984, s. 14 (1) (a). - Issued: 13.10.2014. Made: 02.10.2014. Coming into force: 12.10.2014. Effect: None. Territorial extent & classification: E. Local. - Available at http://www.legislation.gov.uk/uksi/2014/2787/contents/made
Non-print

The A19 Trunk Road (Parkway Interchange to Tontine Interchange) (Temporary Prohibition of Traffic) Order 2014 No. 2014/1316. - Enabling power: Road Traffic Regulation Act 1984, s. 14 (1) (a). - Issued: 27.05.2014. Made: 08.05.2014. Coming into force: 16.05.2014. Effect: None. Territorial extent & classification: E. Local. - Available at http://www.legislation.gov.uk/uksi/2014/1316/contents/made
Non-print

The A19 Trunk Road (Seaton Lane Interchange) (Temporary Prohibition of Traffic) Order 2014 No. 2014/2224. - Enabling power: Road Traffic Regulation Act 1984, s. 14 (1) (a). - Issued: 22.08.2014. Made: 14.07.2014. Coming into force: 24.07.2014. Effect: None. Territorial extent & classification: E. Local. - Available at http://www.legislation.gov.uk/uksi/2014/2224/contents/made
Non-print

The A19 Trunk Road (Sheraton Interchange) (Temporary Prohibition of Traffic) Order 2014 No. 2014/1703. - Enabling power: Road Traffic Regulation Act 1984, s. 14 (1) (a). - Issued: 01.07.2014. Made: 12.06.2014. Coming into force: 22.06.2014. Effect: None. Territorial extent & classification: E. Local. - Available at http://www.legislation.gov.uk/uksi/2014/1703/contents/made
Non-print

The A19 Trunk Road (South Kilvington Interchange to Osmotherley Interchange) (Temporary Restriction and Prohibition of Traffic) Order 2014 No. 2014/2003. - Enabling power: Road Traffic Regulation Act 1984, s. 14 (1) (a). - Issued: 30.07.2014. Made: 26.06.2014. Coming into force: 12.07.2014. Effect: None. Territorial extent & classification: E. Local. - Available at http://www.legislation.gov.uk/uksi/2014/2003/contents/made
Non-print

The A19 Trunk Road (Stockton Interchange to Wolviston Interchange) (Temporary Restriction and Prohibition of Traffic) Order 2014 No. 2014/1284. - Enabling power: Road Traffic Regulation Act 1984, s. 14 (1) (a). - Issued: 21.05.2014. Made: 01.05.2014. Coming into force: 05.05.2014. Effect: None. Territorial extent & classification: E. Local. - Available at http://www.legislation.gov.uk/uksi/2014/1284/contents/made
Non-print

The A19 Trunk Road (Stockton Ring Road Interchange) (Temporary Restriction and Prohibition of Traffic) Order 2014 No. 2014/1736. - Enabling power: Road Traffic Regulation Act 1984, s. 14 (1) (a). - Issued: 02.07.2014. Made: 19.06.2014. Coming into force: 29.06.2014. Effect: None. Territorial extent & classification: E. Local. - Available at http://www.legislation.gov.uk/uksi/2014/1736/contents/made
Non-print

The A19 Trunk Road (Stockton Road Interchange to Portrack Interchange) (No.2) (Temporary Prohibition of Traffic) Order 2014 No. 2014/3535. - Enabling power: Road Traffic Regulation Act 1984, s. 14 (1) (a). - Issued: 22.01.2015. Made: 29.12.2014. Coming into force: 11.01.2015. Effect: None. Territorial extent & classification: E. Local. - Available at http://www.legislation.gov.uk/uksi/2014/3535/contents/made
Non-print

The A19 Trunk Road (Stockton Road Interchange to Portrack Interchange) (Temporary Prohibition of Traffic) Order 2014 No. 2014/49. - Enabling power: Road Traffic Regulation Act 1984, s. 14 (1) (a). - Issued: 16.01.2014. Made: 09.01.2014. Coming into force: 12.01.2014. Effect: None. Territorial extent & classification: E. Local. - Available at http://www.legislation.gov.uk/uksi/2014/49/contents/made
Non-print

The A19 Trunk Road (Wellfield Interchange to Easington Interchange) (Temporary Restriction and Prohibition of Traffic) Order 2014 No. 2014/1301. - Enabling power: Road Traffic Regulation Act 1984, s. 14 (1) (a). - Issued: 23.05.2014. Made: 01.05.2014. Coming into force: 10.05.2014. Effect: None. Territorial extent & classification: E. Local. - Available at http://www.legislation.gov.uk/uksi/2014/1301/contents/made
Non-print

The A19 Trunk Road (York Road Interchange to South Kilvington Interchange) (Temporary Restriction and Prohibition of Traffic) Order 2014 No. 2014/1700. - Enabling power: Road Traffic Regulation Act 1984, s. 14 (1) (a). - Issued: 01.07.2014. Made: 12.06.2014. Coming into force: 21.06.2014. Effect: None. Territorial extent & classification: E. Local. - Available at http://www.legislation.gov.uk/uksi/2014/1700/contents/made
Non-print

The A20 Trunk Road (A260 Interchange - B2011 Interchange) (Temporary Restriction and Prohibition of Traffic) Order 2014 No. 2014/2990. - Enabling power: Road Traffic Regulation Act 1984, s. 14 (1) (a). - Issued: 24.10.2014. Made: 20.10.2014. Coming into force: 08.11.2014. Effect: None. Territorial extent & classification: E. Local. - Available at http://www.legislation.gov.uk/uksi/2014/2990/contents/made
Non-print

The A20 Trunk Road (Alkham Valley Interchange and Courtwood Interchange, Slip Roads) (Temporary Prohibition of Traffic) Order 2014 No. 2014/3467. - Enabling power: Road Traffic Regulation Act 1984, s. 14 (1) (a). - Issued: 18.12.2014. Made: 15.12.2014. Coming into force: 21.01.2015. Effect: None. Territorial extent & classification: E. Local. - Available at http://www.legislation.gov.uk/uksi/2014/3467/contents/made
Non-print

The A20 Trunk Road (B2011 Underbridge - Limekiln Roundabout) (Temporary Prohibition of Traffic) Order 2014 No. 2014/3415. - Enabling power: Road Traffic Regulation Act 1984, s. 14 (1) (a). - Issued: 24.11.2014. Made: 17.11.2014. Coming into force: 06.12.2014. Effect: None. Territorial extent & classification: E. Local. - Available at http://www.legislation.gov.uk/uksi/2014/3415/contents/made
Non-print

The A20 Trunk Road (Hawkinge Roundabout) (Temporary Restriction and Prohibition of Traffic) Order 2014 No. 2014/1312. - Enabling power: Road Traffic Regulation Act 1984, s. 14 (1) (a). - Issued: 27.05.2014. Made: 14.04.2014. Coming into force: 03.05.2014. Effect: None. Territorial extent & classification: E. Local. - Available at http://www.legislation.gov.uk/uksi/2014/1312/contents/made
Non-print

The A20 Trunk Road (Limekiln Roundabout - Lord Warden Square) (Temporary Prohibition of Traffic) Order 2014 No. 2014/1575. - Enabling power: Road Traffic Regulation Act 1984, s. 14 (1) (a). - Issued: 18.06.2014. Made: 02.06.2014. Coming into force: 21.06.2014. Effect: None. Territorial extent & classification: E. Local. - Available at http://www.legislation.gov.uk/uksi/2014/1575/contents/made
Non-print

The A20 Trunk Road (Petham Court Bridge, Lay-By) (Temporary Prohibition of Traffic) Order 2014 No. 2014/1747. - Enabling power: Road Traffic Regulation Act 1984, s. 14 (1) (a). - Issued: 02.07.2014. Made: 16.06.2014. Coming into force: 09.07.2014. Effect: None. Territorial extent & classification: E. Local. - Available at http://www.legislation.gov.uk/uksi/2014/1747/contents/made
Non-print

The A20 Trunk Road (Roundhill Tunnel - Eastern Docks Roundabout) (Temporary Restriction and Prohibition of Traffic) Order 2014 No. 2014/2214. - Enabling power: Road Traffic Regulation Act 1984, s. 14 (1) (a). - Issued: 21.08.2014. Made: 11.08.2014. Coming into force: 30.08.2014. Effect: None. Territorial extent & classification: E. Local. - Available at http://www.legislation.gov.uk/uksi/2014/2214/contents/made
Non-print

The A20 Trunk Road (Swanley Interchange - Crittall's Corner) (Temporary Prohibition of Traffic) Order 2014 No. 2014/731. - Enabling power: Road Traffic Regulation Act 1984, s. 14 (1) (a). - Issued: 10.03.2014. Made: 03.03.2014. Coming into force: 22.03.2014. Effect: None. Territorial extent & classification: E. Local. - Available at http://www.legislation.gov.uk/uksi/2014/731/contents/made Non-print

ROAD TRAFFIC: TRAFFIC REGULATION

The A21 Trunk Road and the M25 Motorway (A21 Philpots Lane - M25 Junction 5) (Temporary Restriction and Prohibition of Traffic) Order 2014 No. 2014/3464. - Enabling power: Road Traffic Regulation Act 1984, s. 14 (1) (a). - Issued: 18.12.2014. Made: 15.12.2014. Coming into force: 03.01.2015. Effect: None. Territorial extent & classification: E. Local. - Available at http://www.legislation.gov.uk/uksi/2014/3464/contents/made Non-print

The A21 Trunk Road (B2089 - Whatlington Road) (Temporary Restriction and Prohibition of Traffic) Order 2014 No. 2014/392. - Enabling power: Road Traffic Regulation Act 1984, s. 14 (1) (a). - Issued: 27.02.2014. Made: 17.02.2014. Coming into force: 08.03.2014. Effect: None. Territorial extent & classification: E. Local. - Available at http://www.legislation.gov.uk/uksi/2014/392/contents/made Non-print

The A21 Trunk Road (Bessels Green Interchange) (Temporary Prohibition of Traffic) Order 2014 No. 2014/2795. - Enabling power: Road Traffic Regulation Act 1984, s. 14 (1) (a). - Issued: 13.10.2014. Made: 29.09.2014. Coming into force: 18.10.2014. Effect: None. Territorial extent & classification: E. Local. - Available at http://www.legislation.gov.uk/uksi/2014/2795/contents/made Non-print

The A21 Trunk Road (Flimwell Crossroads - A2100 Junction Road) (Temporary Prohibition of Traffic) Order 2014 No. 2014/1753. - Enabling power: Road Traffic Regulation Act 1984, s. 14 (1) (a). - Issued: 03.07.2014. Made: 23.06.2014. Coming into force: 12.07.2014. Effect: None. Territorial extent & classification: E. Local. - Available at http://www.legislation.gov.uk/uksi/2014/1753/contents/made Non-print

The A21 Trunk Road (Forstal Farm Roundabout - B2087 Junction) (Temporary Prohibition of Traffic) Order 2014 No. 2014/2211. - Enabling power: Road Traffic Regulation Act 1984, s. 14 (1) (a). - Issued: 21.08.2014. Made: 26.05.2014. Coming into force: 14.06.2014. Effect: None. Territorial extent & classification: E. Local. - Available at http://www.legislation.gov.uk/uksi/2014/2211/contents/made Non-print

The A21 Trunk Road (John's Cross Road) (Temporary Restriction and Prohibition of Traffic) Order 2014 No. 2014/103. - Enabling power: Road Traffic Regulation Act 1984, s. 14 (1) (a). - Issued: 22.01.2014. Made: 20.01.2014. Coming into force: 08.02.2014. Effect: None. Territorial extent & classification: E. Local. - Available at http://www.legislation.gov.uk/uksi/2014/103/contents/made Non-print

The A21 Trunk Road (London Road, Flimwell) (Temporary Restriction and Prohibition of Traffic) Order 2014 No. 2014/3024. - Enabling power: Road Traffic Regulation Act 1984, s. 14 (1) (a). - Issued: 29.10.2014. Made: 27.10.2014. Coming into force: 15.11.2014. Effect: None. Territorial extent & classification: E. Local. - Available at http://www.legislation.gov.uk/uksi/2014/3024/contents/made Non-print

The A21 Trunk Road (Merriments Lane - Northbridge Street Roundabout) (Temporary Restriction and Prohibition of Traffic) Order 2014 No. 2014/228. - Enabling power: Road Traffic Regulation Act 1984, s. 14 (1) (a). - Issued: 07.02.2014. Made: 03.02.2014. Coming into force: 22.02.2014. Effect: None. Territorial extent & classification: E. Local. - Available at http://www.legislation.gov.uk/uksi/2014/228/contents/made Non-print

The A21 Trunk Road (Morley's Interchange - Pembury Road Interchange, Slip Roads) (Temporary Prohibition of Traffic) Order 2014 No. 2014/3462. - Enabling power: Road Traffic Regulation Act 1984, s. 14 (1) (a). - Issued: 18.12.2014. Made: 15.12.2014. Coming into force: 04.02.2015. Effect: None. Territorial extent & classification: E. Local. - Available at http://www.legislation.gov.uk/uksi/2014/3462/contents/made Non-print

The A21 Trunk Road (Morley's Interchange) (Temporary Prohibition of Traffic) Order 2014 No. 2014/95. - Enabling power: Road Traffic Regulation Act 1984, s. 14 (1) (a). - Issued: 22.01.2014. Made: 20.01.2014. Coming into force: 08.02.2014. Effect: None. Territorial extent & classification: E. Local. - Available at http://www.legislation.gov.uk/uksi/2014/95/contents/made Non-print

The A21 Trunk Road (Northbridge Street Roundabout) (Temporary Prohibition of Traffic) Order 2014 No. 2014/2993. - Enabling power: Road Traffic Regulation Act 1984, s. 16A (2) (a). - Issued: 16.10.2014. Made: 13.10.2014. Coming into force: 09.11.2014. Effect: None. Territorial extent & classification: E. Local. - Available at http://www.legislation.gov.uk/uksi/2014/2993/contents/made Non-print

The A21 Trunk Road (Pembury Interchange, Slip Roads) (Temporary Prohibition of Traffic) Order 2014 No. 2014/1573. - Enabling power: Road Traffic Regulation Act 1984, s. 14 (1) (a). - Issued: 17.06.2014. Made: 26.05.2014. Coming into force: 14.06.2014. Effect: None. Territorial extent & classification: E. Local. - Available at http://www.legislation.gov.uk/uksi/2014/1573/contents/made Non-print

The A21 Trunk Road (Pembury Road, 40mph Speed) (Temporary Restriction of Traffic) Order 2014 No. 2014/2353. - Enabling power: Road Traffic Regulation Act 1984, s. 14 (1) (a), sch. 9 para. 27(1). - Issued: 04.09.2014. Made: 01.09.2014. Coming into force: 20.09.2014. Effect: None. Territorial extent & classification: E. Local. - Available at http://www.legislation.gov.uk/uksi/2014/2353/contents/made Non-print

The A21 Trunk Road (Scotney Castle Roundabout - Flimwell Crossroads) (Temporary Prohibition of Traffic) Order 2014 No. 2014/1396. - Enabling power: Road Traffic Regulation Act 1984, s. 14 (1) (a). - Issued: 02.06.2014. Made: 19.05.2014. Coming into force: 07.06.2014. Effect: None. Territorial extent & classification: E. Local. - Available at http://www.legislation.gov.uk/uksi/2014/1396/contents/made Non-print

The A21 Trunk Road (Vauxhall Interchange - Morley Road Interchange) (Temporary Prohibition of Traffic) Order 2014 No. 2014/2533. - Enabling power: Road Traffic Regulation Act 1984, s. 14 (1) (a). - Issued: 12.09.2014. Made: 08.09.2014. Coming into force: 01.10.2014. Effect: None. Territorial extent & classification: E. Local. - Available at http://www.legislation.gov.uk/uksi/2014/2533/contents/made Non-print

The A21 Trunk Road (Whatlington - Sedlescombe) (Temporary Restriction and Prohibition of Traffic) Order 2014 No. 2014/2645. - Enabling power: Road Traffic Regulation Act 1984, s. 14 (1) (a). - Issued: 30.09.2014. Made: 22.09.2014. Coming into force: 11.10.2014. Effect: None. Territorial extent & classification: E. Local. - Available at http://www.legislation.gov.uk/uksi/2014/2645/contents/made Non-print

The A23 Trunk Road (A2300 Jobs Lane, Hickstead) (Temporary Restriction of Traffic) Order 2014 No. 2014/2545. - Enabling power: Road Traffic Regulation Act 1984, s. 14 (1) (a). - Issued: 23.09.2014. Made: 08.09.2014. Coming into force: 27.09.2014. Effect: None. Territorial extent & classification: E. Local. - Available at http://www.legislation.gov.uk/uksi/2014/2545/contents/made Non-print

The A23 Trunk Road and the A27 Trunk Road (Patcham Interchange, Link Roads) (Temporary Prohibition of Traffic) Order 2014 No. 2014/3477. - Enabling power: Road Traffic Regulation Act 1984, s. 14 (1) (a). - Issued: 19.12.2014. Made: 15.12.2014. Coming into force: 21.01.2015. Effect: None. Territorial extent & classification: E. Local. - Available at http://www.legislation.gov.uk/uksi/2014/3477/contents/made Non-print

The A23 Trunk Road and the M23 Motorway (Junctions 9 - 11, Slip Roads) (Temporary Prohibition of Traffic) Order 2014 No. 2014/3480. - Enabling power: Road Traffic Regulation Act 1984, s. 14 (1) (a). - Issued: 19.12.2014. Made: 15.12.2014. Coming into force: 28.01.2015. Effect: None. Territorial extent & classification: E. Local. - Available at http://www.legislation.gov.uk/uksi/2014/3480/contents/made Non-print

The A23 Trunk Road (B2100 - M23 Junction 11) (Temporary Restriction and Prohibition of Traffic) Order 2014 No. 2014/138. - Enabling power: Road Traffic Regulation Act 1984, s. 14 (1) (a). - Issued: 24.01.2014. Made: 20.01.2014. Coming into force: 08.02.2014. Effect: None. Territorial extent & classification: E. Local. - Available at http://www.legislation.gov.uk/uksi/2014/138/contents/made Non-print

The A23 Trunk Road (Bolney Interchange - Hickstead Interchange) (Temporary Restriction and Prohibition of Traffic) Order 2014 No. 2014/174. - Enabling power: Road Traffic Regulation Act 1984, s. 14 (1) (a). - Issued: 03.02.2014. Made: 27.01.2014. Coming into force: 15.02.2014. Effect: None. Territorial extent & classification: E. Local. - Available at http://www.legislation.gov.uk/uksi/2014/174/contents/made Non-print

The A23 Trunk Road (Brighton Road) (Temporary Prohibition of Traffic) Order 2014 No. 2014/1750. - Enabling power: Road Traffic Regulation Act 1984, s. 14 (1) (a). - Issued: 02.07.2014. Made: 16.06.2014. Coming into force: 05.07.2014. Effect: None. Territorial extent & classification: E. Local. - Available at http://www.legislation.gov.uk/uksi/2014/1750/contents/made
Non-print

The A23 Trunk Road (Handcross to Warninglid Section) (Restriction on Use of Outside Lane) Order 2014 No. 2014/2304. - Enabling power: Road Traffic Regulation Act 1984, s. 1 (1), 2 (1) (2), 4 (1), 122A sch. 9 para. 27 (1). - Issued: 02.09.2014. Made: 20.08.2014. Coming into force: 05.09.2014. Effect: None. Territorial extent & classification: E. Local. - Available at http://www.legislation.gov.uk/uksi/2014/2304/contents/made
Non-print

The A23 Trunk Road (Handcross to Warninglid Section Slip Roads) (24 Hours Clearway) Order 2014 No. 2014/2306. - Enabling power: Road Traffic Regulation Act 1984, s. 1 (1), 2 (1) (2), 4 (1), 122A, sch. 9, para. 27 (1)- Issued: 02.09.2014. Made: 20.08.2014. Coming into force: 05.09.2014. Effect: None. Territorial extent & classification: E. Local. - Available at http://www.legislation.gov.uk/uksi/2014/2306/contents/made
Non-print

The A23 Trunk Road (Pyecombe Junction - M23 Junction 11) (Temporary Prohibition of Traffic) Order 2014 No. 2014/3022. - Enabling power: Road Traffic Regulation Act 1984, s. 14 (1) (a). - Issued: 29.10.2014. Made: 27.10.2014. Coming into force: 15.11.2014. Effect: None. Territorial extent & classification: E. Local. - Available at http://www.legislation.gov.uk/uksi/2014/3022/contents/made
Non-print

The A23 Trunk Road (Stalkers Copse - Patcham Interchange) (Temporary Restriction and Prohibition of Traffic) Order 2014 No. 2014/1109. - Enabling power: Road Traffic Regulation Act 1984, s. 14 (1) (a). - Issued: 30.04.2014. Made: 14.04.2014. Coming into force: 03.05.2014. Effect: None. Territorial extent & classification: E. Local. - Available at http://www.legislation.gov.uk/uksi/2014/1109/contents/made
Non-print

The A23 Trunk Road (Warninglid Interchange - Hickstead Interchange, Slip Roads) (Temporary Prohibition of Traffic) Order 2014 No. 2014/3509. - Enabling power: Road Traffic Regulation Act 1984, s. 14 (1) (a). - Issued: 19.01.2015. Made: 17.11.2014. Coming into force: 21.01.2015. Effect: None. Territorial extent & classification: E. Local. - Available at http://www.legislation.gov.uk/uksi/2014/3509/contents/made
Non-print

The A23 Trunk Road (Warninglid Junction - Pease Pottage Interchange) (Temporary Prohibition of Cyclists and Pedestrians) Order 2014 No. 2014/2107. - Enabling power: Road Traffic Regulation Act 1984, s. 14 (1) (b). - Issued: 07.08.2014. Made: 21.07.2014. Coming into force: 09.08.2014. Effect: None. Territorial extent & classification: E. Local. - Available at http://www.legislation.gov.uk/uksi/2014/2107/contents/made
Non-print

The A27 and the A259 Trunk Roads (Jubilee Roundabout - Pevensey Roundabout) (Temporary Restriction and Prohibition of Traffic) Order 2014 No. 2014/302. - Enabling power: Road Traffic Regulation Act 1984, s. 14 (1) (a). - Issued: 13.02.2014. Made: 10.02.2014. Coming into force: 01.03.2014. Effect: None. Territorial extent & classification: E. Local. - Available at http://www.legislation.gov.uk/uksi/2014/302/contents/made Non-print

The A27 (Temple Bar Interchange - Fontwell Western Roundabout) (Temporary Prohibition of Traffic) Order 2014 No. 2014/307. - Enabling power: Road Traffic Regulation Act 1984, s. 14 (1) (a). - Issued: 13.02.2014. Made: 10.02.2014. Coming into force: 01.03.2014. Effect: None. Territorial extent & classification: E. Local. - Available at http://www.legislation.gov.uk/uksi/2014/307/contents/made Non-print

The A27 Trunk Road (A285) (Temple Bar Interchange) (Temporary Prohibition of Traffic) Order 2014 No. 2014/65. - Enabling power: Road Traffic Regulation Act 1984, s. 14 (1) (a). - Issued: 20.01.2014. Made: 07.01.2014. Coming into force: 18.01.2014. Effect: None. Territorial extent & classification: E. Local. - Available at http://www.legislation.gov.uk/uksi/2014/65/contents/made Non-print

The A27 Trunk Road (Adur Interchange - A293 Junction) (Temporary Prohibition of Traffic) Order 2014 No. 2014/1786. - Enabling power: Road Traffic Regulation Act 1984, s. 14 (1) (a). - Issued: 09.07.2014. Made: 23.06.2014. Coming into force: 12.07.2014. Effect: None. Territorial extent & classification: E. Local. - Available at http://www.legislation.gov.uk/uksi/2014/1786/contents/made
Non-print

The A27 Trunk Road (Adur Interchange) (Temporary Prohibition of Traffic) Order 2014 No. 2014/2528. - Enabling power: Road Traffic Regulation Act 1984, s. 14 (1) (a). - Issued: 18.09.2014. Made: 15.09.2014. Coming into force: 04.10.2014. Effect: None. Territorial extent & classification: E. Local. - Available at http://www.legislation.gov.uk/uksi/2014/2528/contents/made
Non-print

The A27 Trunk Road (Arundel Road, Crockerhill) (Temporary Prohibition of Traffic) Order 2014 No. 2014/1785. - Enabling power: Road Traffic Regulation Act 1984, s. 14 (1) (a). - Issued: 09.07.2014. Made: 23.06.2014. Coming into force: 12.07.2014. Effect: None. Territorial extent & classification: E. Local. - Available at http://www.legislation.gov.uk/uksi/2014/1785/contents/made
Non-print

The A27 Trunk Road (Beddingham Roundabout - Polegate) (Temporary Prohibition of Traffic) Order 2014 No. 2014/1548. - Enabling power: Road Traffic Regulation Act 1984, s. 14 (1) (a). - Issued: 13.06.2014. Made: 26.05.2014. Coming into force: 14.06.2014. Effect: None. Territorial extent & classification: E. Local. - Available at http://www.legislation.gov.uk/uksi/2014/1548/contents/made
Non-print

The A27 Trunk Road (Coldean Interchange - Patcham Interchange) (Temporary Prohibition of Traffic) Order 2014 (Temporary Restriction and Prohibition of Traffic) Order 2014 No. 2014/2310. - Enabling power: Road Traffic Regulation Act 1984, s. 14 (1) (a). - Issued: 22.08.2014. Made: 18.08.2014. Coming into force: 06.09.2014. Effect: None. Territorial extent & classification: E. Local. - Available at http://www.legislation.gov.uk/uksi/2014/2310/contents/made
Non-print

The A27 Trunk Road (Cop Hall Roundabout, Dedicated Link Road) (Temporary Prohibition of Traffic) Order 2014 No. 2014/3561. - Enabling power: Road Traffic Regulation Act 1984, s. 14 (1) (a). - Issued: 19.01.2015. Made: 17.11.2014. Coming into force: 28.01.2015. Effect: None. Territorial extent & classification: E. Local. - Available at http://www.legislation.gov.uk/uksi/2014/3561/contents/made
Non-print

The A27 Trunk Road (Cophall Roundabout - Pevensey Roundabout) (Temporary Prohibition of Traffic) Order 2014 No. 2014/2307. - Enabling power: Road Traffic Regulation Act 1984, s. 14 (1) (a). - Issued: 22.08.2014. Made: 18.08.2014. Coming into force: 06.09.2014. Effect: None. Territorial extent & classification: E. Local. - Available at http://www.legislation.gov.uk/uksi/2014/2307/contents/made
Non-print

The A27 Trunk Road (Copse Lane Junction - Fontwell Roundabout) (Temporary Restriction and Prohibition of Traffic) Order 2014 No. 2014/3476. - Enabling power: Road Traffic Regulation Act 1984, s. 14 (1) (a). - Issued: 22.12.2014. Made: 15.12.2014. Coming into force: 10.01.2015. Effect: None. Territorial extent & classification: E. Local. - Available at http://www.legislation.gov.uk/uksi/2014/3476/contents/made
Non-print

The A27 Trunk Road (Crossbush Interchange - A280 Overbridge) (Temporary Restriction and Prohibition of Traffic) Order 2014 No. 2014/3473. - Enabling power: Road Traffic Regulation Act 1984, s. 14 (1) (a), sch. 9 para. 27 (1). - Issued: 19.12.2014. Made: 15.12.2014. Coming into force: 04.01.2015. Effect: None. Territorial extent & classification: E. Local. - Available at http://www.legislation.gov.uk/uksi/2014/3473/contents/made
Non-print

The A27 Trunk Road (Eastbourne Road Junction - Golden Jubilee Way Roundabout) (Temporary Prohibition of Traffic) Order 2014 No. 2014/2104. - Enabling power: Road Traffic Regulation Act 1984, s. 14 (1) (a). - Issued: 07.08.2014. Made: 21.07.2014. Coming into force: 09.08.2014. Effect: None. Territorial extent & classification: E. Local. - Available at http://www.legislation.gov.uk/uksi/2014/2104/contents/made
Non-print

ROAD TRAFFIC: TRAFFIC REGULATION

The A27 Trunk Road (Falmer Interchange - Southerham Roundabout) (Temporary Prohibition of Traffic) Order 2014 No. 2014/2878. - Enabling power: Road Traffic Regulation Act 1984, s. 14 (1) (a) (5) (b) (7). - Issued: 24.10.2014. Made: 29.09.2014. Coming into force: 18.10.2014. Effect: None. Territorial extent & classification: E. Local. - Available at
http://www.legislation.gov.uk/uksi/2014/2878/contents/made
Non-print

The A27 Trunk Road (Fontwell Carriageway) (Temporary Restriction and Prohibition of Traffic) Order 2014 No. 2014/309. - Enabling power: Road Traffic Regulation Act 1984, s. 14 (1) (a). - Issued: 13.02.2014. Made: 10.02.2014. Coming into force: 02.03.2014. Effect: None. Territorial extent & classification: E. Local. - Available at
http://www.legislation.gov.uk/uksi/2014/309/contents/made Non-print

The A27 Trunk Road (Fontwell East Roundabout - Crossbush Interchange) (Temporary Prohibition of Traffic) Order 2014 No. 2014/2527. - Enabling power: Road Traffic Regulation Act 1984, s. 14 (1) (a). - Issued: 17.09.2014. Made: 15.09.2014. Coming into force: 04.10.2014. Effect: None. Territorial extent & classification: E. Local. - Available at
http://www.legislation.gov.uk/uksi/2014/2527/contents/made
Non-print

The A27 Trunk Road (Fontwell Roundabout, Westbound Lay-by) (Temporary Prohibition of Traffic) Order 2014 No. 2014/168. - Enabling power: Road Traffic Regulation Act 1984, s. 14 (1) (a). - Issued: 30.01.2014. Made: 27.01.2014. Coming into force: 15.02.2014. Effect: None. Territorial extent & classification: E. Local. - Available at
http://www.legislation.gov.uk/uksi/2014/168/contents/made Non-print

The A27 Trunk Road (Holmbush Interchange to Hangleton) (Temporary Prohibition of Traffic) Order 2014 No. 2014/723. - Enabling power: Road Traffic Regulation Act 1984, s. 14 (1) (a). - Issued: 17.03.2014. Made: 10.03.2014. Coming into force: 01.04.2014. Effect: None. Territorial extent & classification: E. Local. - Available at
http://www.legislation.gov.uk/uksi/2014/723/contents/made Non-print

The A27 Trunk Road (Jarvis Road - Ford Roundabout) (Temporary Prohibition of Traffic) Order 2014 No. 2014/171. - Enabling power: Road Traffic Regulation Act 1984, s. 14 (1) (a). - Issued: 30.01.2014. Made: 27.01.2014. Coming into force: 15.02.2014. Effect: None. Territorial extent & classification: E. Local. - Available at
http://www.legislation.gov.uk/uksi/2014/171/contents/made Non-print

The A27 Trunk Road (Langstone Interchange, Slip Roads) (Temporary Prohibition of Traffic) Order 2014 No. 2014/3020. - Enabling power: Road Traffic Regulation Act 1984, s. 14 (1) (a). - Issued: 24.10.2014. Made: 20.10.2014. Coming into force: 15.11.2014. Effect: None. Territorial extent & classification: E. Local. - Available at
http://www.legislation.gov.uk/uksi/2014/3020/contents/made
Non-print

The A27 Trunk Road (Old Shoreham Road and Shoreham Bypass) (Temporary Restriction and Prohibition of Traffic) Order 2014 No. 2014/2168. - Enabling power: Road Traffic Regulation Act 1984, s. 14 (1) (b). - Issued: 14.08.2014. Made: 04.08.2014. Coming into force: 23.08.2014. Effect: None. Territorial extent & classification: E. Local. - Available at
http://www.legislation.gov.uk/uksi/2014/2168/contents/made
Non-print

The A27 Trunk Road (Patcham Interchange - Hangleton Interchange) (Temporary Prohibition of Traffic) Order 2014 No. 2014/2532. - Enabling power: Road Traffic Regulation Act 1984, s. 14 (1) (a). - Issued: 12.09.2014. Made: 08.09.2014. Coming into force: 27.09.2014. Effect: None. Territorial extent & classification: E. Local. - Available at
http://www.legislation.gov.uk/uksi/2014/2532/contents/made
Non-print

The A27 Trunk Road (Patcham Interchange - Hollingbury Interchange, Slip Roads) (Temporary Prohibition of Traffic) Order 2014 No. 2014/748. - Enabling power: Road Traffic Regulation Act 1984, s. 14 (1) (a). - Issued: 04.03.2014. Made: 24.02.2014. Coming into force: 15.03.2014. Effect: None. Territorial extent & classification: E. Local. - Available at
http://www.legislation.gov.uk/uksi/2014/748/contents/made Non-print

The A27 Trunk Road (Patcham Interchange, Northern Roundabout) (Temporary Prohibition of Traffic) Order 2014 No. 2014/1754. - Enabling power: Road Traffic Regulation Act 1984, s. 14 (1) (a). - Issued: 03.07.2014. Made: 23.06.2014. Coming into force: 12.07.2014. Effect: None. Territorial extent & classification: E. Local. - Available at
http://www.legislation.gov.uk/uksi/2014/1754/contents/made
Non-print

The A27 Trunk Road (Portfield Roundabout - Bognor Road Roundabout) (Temporary Restriction and Prohibition of Traffic) Order 2014 No. 2014/300. - Enabling power: Road Traffic Regulation Act 1984, s. 14 (1) (a). - Issued: 13.02.2014. Made: 10.02.2014. Coming into force: 01.03.2014. Effect: None. Territorial extent & classification: E. Local. - Available at
http://www.legislation.gov.uk/uksi/2014/300/contents/made Non-print

The A27 Trunk Road (Portfield Roundabout - Whyke Roundabout) (Temporary Restriction of Traffic) Order 2014 No. 2014/2037. - Enabling power: Road Traffic Regulation Act 1984, s. 14 (1) (a), sch. 9, para. 27 (1). - Issued: 01.08.2014. Made: 14.07.2014. Coming into force: 03.08.2014. Effect: S.I. 2014/300 revoked. Territorial extent & classification: E. Local. - Available at
http://www.legislation.gov.uk/uksi/2014/2037/contents/made
Non-print

The A27 Trunk Road (Portsbridge Roundabout - Eastern Road Interchange) (Temporary Prohibition of Traffic) Order 2014 No. 2014/2218. - Enabling power: Road Traffic Regulation Act 1984, s. 14 (1) (a). - Issued: 21.08.2014. Made: 11.08.2014. Coming into force: 30.08.2014. Effect: None. Territorial extent & classification: E. Local. - Available at
http://www.legislation.gov.uk/uksi/2014/2218/contents/made
Non-print

The A27 Trunk Road (Southerham Roundabout - Hollingbury Interchange) (Temporary Prohibition of Traffic) Order 2014 No. 2014/3534. - Enabling power: Road Traffic Regulation Act 1984, s. 14 (1) (a) (5) (b) (7). - Issued: 23.01.2015. Made: 15.12.2014. Coming into force: 10.01.2015. Effect: None. Territorial extent & classification: E. Local. - Available at
http://www.legislation.gov.uk/uksi/2014/3534/contents/made
Non-print

The A27 Trunk Road (Stockbridge Roundabout - Bognor Road Roundabout) (Temporary Restriction and Prohibition of Traffic) Order 2014 No. 2014/3504. - Enabling power: Road Traffic Regulation Act 1984, s. 14 (1) (a). - Issued: 20.01.2015. Made: 15.12.2014. Coming into force: 03.01.2015. Effect: None. Territorial extent & classification: E. Local. - Available at
http://www.legislation.gov.uk/uksi/2014/3504/contents/made
Non-print

The A27 Trunk Road (Upper Brighton Road/Old Shoreham Road) (Temporary Restriction and Prohibition of Traffic) Order 2014 No. 2014/226. - Enabling power: Road Traffic Regulation Act 1984, s. 14 (1) (a). - Issued: 07.02.2014. Made: 03.02.2014. Coming into force: 22.02.2014. Effect: None. Territorial extent & classification: E. Local. - Available at
http://www.legislation.gov.uk/uksi/2014/226/contents/made Non-print

The A27 Trunk Road (Upper Brighton Road) (Temporary Prohibition of Traffic) Order 2014 No. 2014/3021. - Enabling power: Road Traffic Regulation Act 1984, s. 14 (1) (a). - Issued: 29.10.2014. Made: 27.10.2014. Coming into force: 15.11.2014. Effect: None. Territorial extent & classification: E. Local. - Available at
http://www.legislation.gov.uk/uksi/2014/3021/contents/made
Non-print

The A27 Trunk Road (Warblington Interchange - Falmer Interchange, Slip Roads) (Temporary Prohibition of Traffic) Order 2014 No. 2014/3479. - Enabling power: Road Traffic Regulation Act 1984, s. 14 (1) (a). - Issued: 19.12.2014. Made: 15.12.2014. Coming into force: 28.01.2015. Effect: None. Territorial extent & classification: E. Local. - Available at
http://www.legislation.gov.uk/uksi/2014/3479/contents/made
Non-print

The A27 Trunk Road (Warblington Interchange-Stockbridge Roundabout) (Temporary Restriction and Prohibition of Traffic) Order 2014 No. 2014/2352. - Enabling power: Road Traffic Regulation Act 1984, s. 14 (1) (a). - Issued: 04.09.2014. Made: 01.09.2014. Coming into force: 20.09.2014. Effect: None. Territorial extent & classification: E. Local. - Available at
http://www.legislation.gov.uk/uksi/2014/2352/contents/made
Non-print

The A30 Trunk Road, A316 Trunk Road and A3113 Trunk Road (Staines By-Pass, Country Way and Airport Way) (Temporary Prohibition of Traffic) Order 2014 No. 2014/1989. - Enabling power: Road Traffic Regulation Act 1984, s. 14 (1) (a). - Issued: 21.07.2014. Made: 07.07.2014. Coming into force: 26.07.2014. Effect: None. Territorial extent & classification: E. Local. - Available at
http://www.legislation.gov.uk/uksi/2014/1989/contents/made
Non-print

The A30 Trunk Road (Avers Junction, Redruth) (Temporary Prohibition of Traffic) Order 2014 No. 2014/2605. - Enabling power: Road Traffic Regulation Act 1984, s. 14 (1) (a). - Issued: 30.09.2014. Made: 23.09.2014. Coming into force: 27.09.2014. Effect: None. Territorial extent & classification: E. Local. - Available at http://www.legislation.gov.uk/uksi/2014/2605/contents/made Non-print

The A30 Trunk Road (Camborne to Chiverton Roundabout, Cornwall) (Temporary Restriction and Prohibition of Traffic) Order 2014 No. 2014/758. - Enabling power: Road Traffic Regulation Act 1984, s. 14 (1) (a). - Issued: 11.03.2014. Made: 04.03.2014. Coming into force: 07.03.2014. Effect: None. Territorial extent & classification: E. Local. - Available at http://www.legislation.gov.uk/uksi/2014/758/contents/made Non-print

The A30 Trunk Road (Camborne to Hayle) (Temporary Restriction and Prohibition of Traffic) Order 2014 No. 2014/419. - Enabling power: Road Traffic Regulation Act 1984, s. 14 (1) (a). - Issued: 27.02.2014. Made: 18.02.2014. Coming into force: 21.02.2014. Effect: None. Territorial extent & classification: E. Local. - Available at http://www.legislation.gov.uk/uksi/2014/419/contents/made Non-print

The A30 Trunk Road (Carland Cross Roundabout, Cornwall) (Temporary Restriction and Prohibition of Traffic) Order 2014 No. 2014/425. - Enabling power: Road Traffic Regulation Act 1984, s. 14 (1) (a). - Issued: 27.02.2014. Made: 18.02.2014. Coming into force: 22.02.2014. Effect: None. Territorial extent & classification: E. Local. - Available at http://www.legislation.gov.uk/uksi/2014/425/contents/made Non-print

The A30 Trunk Road (Carland Cross to Chiverton Cross, Cornwall) (Temporary Prohibition of Traffic) Order 2014 No. 2014/2909. - Enabling power: Road Traffic Regulation Act 1984, s. 14 (1) (a). - Issued: 24.10.2014. Made: 21.10.2014. Coming into force: 25.10.2014. Effect: None. Territorial extent & classification: E. Local. - Available at http://www.legislation.gov.uk/uksi/2014/2909/contents/made Non-print

The A30 Trunk Road (Carminow Cross Eastbound Exit Slip Road, Bodmin) (Temporary Prohibition of Traffic) Order 2014 No. 2014/408. - Enabling power: Road Traffic Regulation Act 1984, s. 14 (1) (a). - Issued: 27.02.2014. Made: 18.02.2014. Coming into force: 21.02.2014. Effect: None. Territorial extent & classification: E. Local. - Available at http://www.legislation.gov.uk/uksi/2014/408/contents/made Non-print

The A30 Trunk Road (Chiverton Roundabout to Zelah, Cornwall) (Temporary Restriction and Prohibition of Traffic) Order 2014 No. 2014/342. - Enabling power: Road Traffic Regulation Act 1984, s. 14 (1) (a). - Issued: 19.02.2014. Made: 11.02.2014. Coming into force: 14.02.2014. Effect: None. Territorial extent & classification: E. Local. - Available at http://www.legislation.gov.uk/uksi/2014/342/contents/made Non-print

The A30 Trunk Road (Daisymount to Honiton) (Temporary Prohibition of Traffic) Order 2014 No. 2014/2297. - Enabling power: Road Traffic Regulation Act 1984, s. 14 (1) (a). - Issued: 28.08.2014. Made: 26.08.2014. Coming into force: 01.09.2014. Effect: None. Territorial extent & classification: E. Local. - Available at http://www.legislation.gov.uk/uksi/2014/2297/contents/made Non-print

The A30 Trunk Road (Fingle Glen Junction, Devon) (Temporary Prohibition of Traffic) Order 2014 No. 2014/3433. - Enabling power: Road Traffic Regulation Act 1984, s. 14 (1) (a). - Issued: 17.12.2014. Made: 10.12.2014. Coming into force: 13.12.2014. Effect: None. Territorial extent & classification: E. Local. - Available at http://www.legislation.gov.uk/uksi/2014/3433/contents/made Non-print

The A30 Trunk Road (Fingle Glen to Alphington, Devon) (Temporary Prohibition of Traffic) Order 2014 No. 2014/969. - Enabling power: Road Traffic Regulation Act 1984, s. 14 (1) (a). - Issued: 01.04.2014. Made: 18.03.2014. Coming into force: 24.03.2014. Effect: None. Territorial extent & classification: E. Local. - Available at http://www.legislation.gov.uk/uksi/2014/969/contents/made Non-print

The A30 Trunk Road (Honiton to Exeter) (Temporary Prohibition of Traffic) Order 2014 No. 2014/2273. - Enabling power: Road Traffic Regulation Act 1984, s. 14 (1) (a). - Issued: 28.08.2014. Made: 26.08.2014. Coming into force: 29.08.2014. Effect: None. Territorial extent & classification: E. Local. - Available at http://www.legislation.gov.uk/uksi/2014/2273/contents/made Non-print

The A30 Trunk Road (Innis Downs to Callywith, Near Bodmin) (Temporary Restriction and Prohibition of Traffic) Order 2014 No. 2014/2743. - Enabling power: Road Traffic Regulation Act 1984, s. 14 (1) (a). - Issued: 14.10.2014. Made: 30.09.2014. Coming into force: 02.10.2014. Effect: None. Territorial extent & classification: E. Local. - Available at http://www.legislation.gov.uk/uksi/2014/2743/contents/made Non-print

The A30 Trunk Road (Launceston to Liftondown) (Temporary Restriction and Prohibition of Traffic) Order 2014 No. 2014/429. - Enabling power: Road Traffic Regulation Act 1984, s. 14 (1) (a). - Issued: 27.02.2014. Made: 19.02.2014. Coming into force: 26.02.2014. Effect: None. Territorial extent & classification: E. Local. - Available at http://www.legislation.gov.uk/uksi/2014/429/contents/made Non-print

The A30 Trunk Road (Launceston to Okehampton) (Temporary Restriction and Prohibition of Traffic) Order 2014 No. 2014/2432. - Enabling power: Road Traffic Regulation Act 1984, s. 14 (1) (a). - Issued: 12.09.2014. Made: 09.09.2014. Coming into force: 13.09.2014. Effect: None. Territorial extent & classification: E. Local. - Available at http://www.legislation.gov.uk/uksi/2014/2432/contents/made Non-print

The A30 Trunk Road (Liftondown to M5 Junction 31) (Temporary Restriction and Prohibition of Traffic) Order 2014 No. 2014/1228. - Enabling power: Road Traffic Regulation Act 1984, s. 14 (1) (a). - Issued: 14.05.2014. Made: 30.04.2014. Coming into force: 03.05.2014. Effect: None. Territorial extent & classification: E. Local. - Available at http://www.legislation.gov.uk/uksi/2014/1228/contents/made Non-print

The A30 Trunk Road (Loggans Moor Roundabout, Hayle) (Temporary Restriction and Prohibition of Traffic) Order 2014 No. 2014/1342. - Enabling power: Road Traffic Regulation Act 1984, s. 14 (1) (a). - Issued: 29.05.2014. Made: 13.05.2014. Coming into force: 17.05.2014. Effect: None. Territorial extent & classification: E. Local. - Available at http://www.legislation.gov.uk/uksi/2014/1342/contents/made Non-print

The A30 Trunk Road (Loggans Moor Roundabout, Hayle, to Tolvaddon Junction, Camborne) (Temporary Restriction and Prohibition of Traffic) Order 2014 No. 2014/343. - Enabling power: Road Traffic Regulation Act 1984, s. 14 (1) (a). - Issued: 19.02.2014. Made: 11.02.2014. Coming into force: 15.02.2014. Effect: None. Territorial extent & classification: E. Local. - Available at http://www.legislation.gov.uk/uksi/2014/343/contents/made Non-print

The A30 Trunk Road (M25 Junction 13, Link Road) (Temporary Prohibition of Traffic) Order 2014 No. 2014/724. - Enabling power: Road Traffic Regulation Act 1984, s. 14 (1) (a). - Issued: 17.03.2014. Made: 10.03.2014. Coming into force: 02.04.2014. Effect: None. Territorial extent & classification: E. Local. - Available at http://www.legislation.gov.uk/uksi/2014/724/contents/made Non-print

The A30 Trunk Road (Mitchell to Summercourt, Cornwall) (Temporary Restriction of Traffic) Order 2014 No. 2014/244. - Enabling power: Road Traffic Regulation Act 1984, s. 14 (1) (a). - Issued: 11.02.2014. Made: 04.02.2014. Coming into force: 07.02.2014. Effect: None. Territorial extent & classification: E. Local. - Available at http://www.legislation.gov.uk/uksi/2014/244/contents/made Non-print

The A30 Trunk Road (Monkton, Devon) (Temporary Restriction and Prohibition of Traffic) Order 2014 No. 2014/1952. - Enabling power: Road Traffic Regulation Act 1984, s. 14 (1) (a). - Issued: 18.07.2014. Made: 01.07.2014. Coming into force: 07.07.2014. Effect: None. Territorial extent & classification: E. Local. - Available at http://www.legislation.gov.uk/uksi/2014/1952/contents/made Non-print

The A30 Trunk Road (Monkton, Near Honiton, Devon) (Temporary Prohibition of Traffic) (Number 2) Order 2014 No. 2014/762. - Enabling power: Road Traffic Regulation Act 1984, s. 14 (1) (a). - Issued: 11.03.2014. Made: 04.03.2014. Coming into force: 08.03.2014. Effect: None. Territorial extent & classification: E. Local. - Available at http://www.legislation.gov.uk/uksi/2014/762/contents/made Non-print

The A30 Trunk Road (Monkton, Near Honiton, Devon) (Temporary Prohibition of Traffic) Order 2014 No. 2014/15. - Enabling power: Road Traffic Regulation Act 1984, s. 14 (1) (a). - Issued: 10.01.2014. Made: 06.01.2014. Coming into force: 09.01.2014. Effect: None. Territorial extent & classification: E. Local. - Available at http://www.legislation.gov.uk/uksi/2014/15/contents/made Non-print

ROAD TRAFFIC: TRAFFIC REGULATION

The A30 Trunk Road (Penzance to Launceston, Cornwall) (Temporary Restriction of Traffic) Order 2014 No. 2014/1346. - Enabling power: Road Traffic Regulation Act 1984, s. 14 (1) (a). - Issued: 29.05.2014. Made: 14.05.2014. Coming into force: 17.05.2014. Effect: None. Territorial extent & classification: E. Local. - Available at http://www.legislation.gov.uk/uksi/2014/1346/contents/made Non-print

The A30 Trunk Road (Penzance to Launceston) (Temporary Prohibition of Traffic) Order 2014 No. 2014/1589. - Enabling power: Road Traffic Regulation Act 1984, s. 14 (1) (a). - Issued: 18.06.2014. Made: 04.06.2014. Coming into force: 07.06.2014. Effect: None. Territorial extent & classification: E. Local. - Available at http://www.legislation.gov.uk/uksi/2014/1589/contents/made Non-print

The A30 Trunk Road (Rawridge Hill, Near Honiton) (Temporary Restriction and Prohibition of Traffic) Order 2014 No. 2014/189. - Enabling power: Road Traffic Regulation Act 1984, s. 14 (1) (a). - Issued: 04.02.2014. Made: 28.01.2014. Coming into force: 31.01.2014. Effect: None. Territorial extent & classification: E. Local. - Available at http://www.legislation.gov.uk/uksi/2014/189/contents/made Non-print

The A30 Trunk Road (Redruth to Chiverton Roundabout, Cornwall) (Temporary Restriction and Prohibition of Traffic) Order 2014 No. 2014/799. - Enabling power: Road Traffic Regulation Act 1984, s. 14 (1) (a). - Issued: 26.03.2014. Made: 11.03.2014. Coming into force: 14.03.2014. Effect: None. Territorial extent & classification: E. Local. - Available at http://www.legislation.gov.uk/uksi/2014/799/contents/made Non-print

The A30 Trunk Road (Scorrier Junction, Redruth) (Temporary Prohibition of Traffic) Order 2014 No. 2014/3417. - Enabling power: Road Traffic Regulation Act 1984, s. 14 (1) (a). - Issued: 01.12.2014. Made: 26.11.2014. Coming into force: 06.12.2014. Effect: None. Territorial extent & classification: E. Local. - Available at http://www.legislation.gov.uk/uksi/2014/3417/contents/made Non-print

The A30 Trunk Road (Sowton to Daisymount) (Temporary Prohibition of Traffic) Order 2014 No. 2014/3025. - Enabling power: Road Traffic Regulation Act 1984, s. 14 (1) (a). - Issued: 14.11.2014. Made: 10.11.2014. Coming into force: 15.11.2014. Effect: None. Territorial extent & classification: E. Local. - Available at http://www.legislation.gov.uk/uksi/2014/3025/contents/made Non-print

The A30 Trunk Road (Treswithian Junction, Camborne) (Temporary Prohibition of Traffic) Order 2014 No. 2014/2961. - Enabling power: Road Traffic Regulation Act 1984, s. 14 (1) (a). - Issued: 30.10.2014. Made: 28.10.2014. Coming into force: 01.11.2014. Effect: None. Territorial extent & classification: E. Local. - Available at http://www.legislation.gov.uk/uksi/2014/2961/contents/made Non-print

The A30 Trunk Road (Trewint to Treguddick, Cornwall) (Temporary Restriction of Traffic) Order 2014 No. 2014/3048. - Enabling power: Road Traffic Regulation Act 1984, s. 14 (1) (a). - Issued: 17.11.2014. Made: 12.11.2014. Coming into force: 22.11.2014. Effect: None. Territorial extent & classification: E. Local. - Available at http://www.legislation.gov.uk/uksi/2014/3048/contents/made Non-print

The A30 Trunk Road (Two Bridges to Fivelanes, Near Launceston) (Temporary Restriction and Prohibition of Traffic) Order 2014 No. 2014/672. - Enabling power: Road Traffic Regulation Act 1984, s. 14 (1) (a). - Issued: 07.03.2014. Made: 25.02.2014. Coming into force: 01.03.2014. Effect: None. Territorial extent & classification: E. Local. - Available at http://www.legislation.gov.uk/uksi/2014/672/contents/made Non-print

The A30 Trunk Road (Victoria Junction, Near Roche) (Temporary Prohibition of Traffic) Order 2014 No. 2014/1019. - Enabling power: Road Traffic Regulation Act 1984, s. 14 (1) (a). - Issued: 17.04.2014. Made: 01.04.2014. Coming into force: 05.04.2014. Effect: None. Territorial extent & classification: E. Local. - Available at http://www.legislation.gov.uk/uksi/2014/1019/contents/made Non-print

The A30 Trunk Road (Whiddon Down to Launceston) (Temporary Prohibition of Traffic) Order 2014 No. 2014/2278. - Enabling power: Road Traffic Regulation Act 1984, s. 14 (1) (a). - Issued: 28.08.2014. Made: 26.08.2014. Coming into force: 30.08.2014. Effect: None. Territorial extent & classification: E. Local. - Available at http://www.legislation.gov.uk/uksi/2014/2278/contents/made Non-print

The A31 Trunk Road and M27 Motorway (M27 Junction 2 - Ashley Heath Roundabout) (Temporary Prohibition of Traffic) Order 2014 No. 2014/2111. - Enabling power: Road Traffic Regulation Act 1984, s. 14 (1) (a). - Issued: 07.08.2014. Made: 28.07.2014. Coming into force: 16.08.2014. Effect: None. Territorial extent & classification: E. Local. - Available at http://www.legislation.gov.uk/uksi/2014/2111/contents/made Non-print

The A31 Trunk Road (Bere Regis Roundabout - Roundhouse Roundabout) (Temporary Prohibition of Traffic) Order 2014 No. 2014/1756. - Enabling power: Road Traffic Regulation Act 1984, s. 14 (1) (a). - Issued: 04.07.2014. Made: 23.06.2014. Coming into force: 12.07.2014. Effect: None. Territorial extent & classification: E. Local. - Available at http://www.legislation.gov.uk/uksi/2014/1756/contents/made Non-print

The A31 Trunk Road (Cadnam - Verwood Interchange) (Temporary Restriction and Prohibition of Traffic) Order 2014 No. 2014/311. - Enabling power: Road Traffic Regulation Act 1984, s. 14 (1) (a). - Issued: 13.02.2013. Made: 10.02.2014. Coming into force: 05.03.2014. Effect: None. Territorial extent & classification: E. Local. - Available at http://www.legislation.gov.uk/uksi/2014/311/contents/made Non-print

The A31 Trunk Road (Canford Bottom Roundabout) (Temporary Prohibition of Traffic) Order 2014 No. 2014/1118. - Enabling power: Road Traffic Regulation Act 1984, s. 14 (1) (a). - Issued: 01.05.2014. Made: 14.04.2014. Coming into force: 03.05.2014. Effect: None. Territorial extent & classification: E. Local. - Available at http://www.legislation.gov.uk/uksi/2014/1118/contents/made Non-print

The A31 Trunk Road (Merley Roundabout - Roundhouse Roundabout) (Temporary Prohibition of Traffic) Order 2014 No. 2014/2201. - Enabling power: Road Traffic Regulation Act 1984, s. 14 (1) (a). - Issued: 15.08.2014. Made: 04.08.2014. Coming into force: 23.08.2014. Effect: None. Territorial extent & classification: E. Local. - Available at http://www.legislation.gov.uk/uksi/2014/2201/contents/made Non-print

The A31 Trunk Road (Ringwood Road, Slip Road) (Temporary Prohibition of Traffic) Order 2014 No. 2014/2205. - Enabling power: Road Traffic Regulation Act 1984, s. 14 (1) (a). - Issued: 15.08.2014. Made: 08.08.2014. Coming into force: 27.08.2014. Effect: None. Territorial extent & classification: E. Local. - Available at http://www.legislation.gov.uk/uksi/2014/2205/contents/made Non-print

The A31 Trunk Road (Stag Gate - Almer Cross Roads) (Temporary 40 Miles Per Hour Speed Restriction) Order 2014 No. 2014/1656. - Enabling power: Road Traffic Regulation Act 1984, s. 16A (2) (a). - Issued: 30.06.2014. Made: 16.06.2014. Coming into force: 05.07.2014. Effect: None. Territorial extent & classification: Local. - Available at http://www.legislation.gov.uk/uksi/2014/1656/contents/made Non-print

The A31 Trunk Road (Verwood Interchange - Bere Regis Roundabout) (Temporary Restriction and Prohibition of Traffic) Order 2014 No. 2014/393. - Enabling power: Road Traffic Regulation Act 1984, s. 14 (1) (a). - Issued: 26.02.2014. Made: 17.02.2014. Coming into force: 12.03.2014. Effect: None. Territorial extent & classification: E. Local. - Available at http://www.legislation.gov.uk/uksi/2014/393/contents/made Non-print

The A34 Trunk Road (A343 Interchange-Tufton Interchange) (Temporary Prohibition of Traffic) Order 2014 No. 2014/2349. - Enabling power: Road Traffic Regulation Act 1984, s. 14 (1) (a). - Issued: 28.08.2014. Made: 26.08.2014. Coming into force: 13.09.2014. Effect: None. Territorial extent & classification: E. Local. - Available at http://www.legislation.gov.uk/uksi/2014/2349/contents/made Non-print

The A34 Trunk Road (Chieveley Interchange) (Temporary Prohibition of Traffic) Order 2014 No. 2014/2300. - Enabling power: Road Traffic Regulation Act 1984, s. 14 (1) (a). - Issued: 02.09.2014. Made: 11.08.2014. Coming into force: 02.09.2014. Effect: None. Territorial extent & classification: E. Local. - Available at http://www.legislation.gov.uk/uksi/2014/2300/contents/made Non-print

The A34 Trunk Road (Chilton Interchange - Milton Interchange) (Temporary Restriction and Prohibition of Traffic) Order 2014 No. 2014/2681. - Enabling power: Road Traffic Regulation Act 1984, s. 14 (1) (a). - Issued: 07.10.2014. Made: 07.07.2014. Coming into force: 26.07.2014. Effect: None. Territorial extent & classification: E. Local. - Available at http://www.legislation.gov.uk/uksi/2014/2681/contents/made
Non-print

The A34 Trunk Road (East Ilsley Interchange - Abingdon North Interchange) (Temporary Restriction and Prohibition of Traffic) Order 2014 No. 2014/3434. - Enabling power: Road Traffic Regulation Act 1984, s. 14 (1) (a). - Issued: 24.11.2014. Made: 17.11.2014. Coming into force: 14.12.2014. Effect: None. Territorial extent & classification: E. Local. - Available at http://www.legislation.gov.uk/uksi/2014/3434/contents/made
Non-print

The A34 Trunk Road (Great Barr, Sandwell) (Temporary Prohibition of Traffic) Order 2014 No. 2014/1586. - Enabling power: Road Traffic Regulation Act 1984, s. 14 (1) (a). - Issued: 18.06.2014. Made: 30.05.2014. Coming into force: 06.06.2014. Effect: None. Territorial extent & classification: E. Local. - Available at http://www.legislation.gov.uk/uksi/2014/1586/contents/made
Non-print

The A34 Trunk Road (Headbourne Worthy Lay-by) (Temporary Prohibition of Traffic) Order 2014 No. 2014/2503. - Enabling power: Road Traffic Regulation Act 1984, s. 14 (1) (a). - Issued: 05.09.2014. Made: 01.09.2014. Coming into force: 20.09.2014. Effect: None. Territorial extent & classification: E. Local. - Available at http://www.legislation.gov.uk/uksi/2014/2503/contents/made
Non-print

The A34 Trunk Road (Hinksey Hill Interchange - Peartree Interchange) (Temporary Prohibition of Traffic) Order 2014 No. 2014/2530. - Enabling power: Road Traffic Regulation Act 1984, s. 14 (1) (a). - Issued: 18.09.2014. Made: 15.09.2014. Coming into force: 04.10.2014. Effect: None. Territorial extent & classification: E. Local. - Available at http://www.legislation.gov.uk/uksi/2014/2530/contents/made
Non-print

The A34 Trunk Road (M3 Junction 9 - Andover Road Interchange) (Temporary Prohibition of Traffic) Order 2014 No. 2014/1738. - Enabling power: Road Traffic Regulation Act 1984, s. 14 (1) (a). - Issued: 04.07.2014. Made: 23.06.2014. Coming into force: 20.07.2014. Effect: None. Territorial extent & classification: E. Local. - Available at http://www.legislation.gov.uk/uksi/2014/1738/contents/made
Non-print

The A34 Trunk Road (M3 Junction 9 - M40 Junction 9, Lay-Bys) (Temporary Prohibition of Traffic) Order 2014 No. 2014/3449. - Enabling power: Road Traffic Regulation Act 1984, s. 14 (1) (a). - Issued: 28.11.2014. Made: 24.11.2014. Coming into force: 20.12.2014. Effect: None. Territorial extent & classification: E. Local. - Available at http://www.legislation.gov.uk/uksi/2014/3449/contents/made
Non-print

The A34 Trunk Road (M3 Junction 9 - Tot Hill Interchange) (Temporary Speed Restrictions) Order 2014 No. 2014/3386. - Enabling power: Road Traffic Regulation Act 1984, s. 14 (1) (a). - Issued: 06.11.2014. Made: 03.11.2014. Coming into force: 29.11.2014. Effect: None. Territorial extent & classification: E. Local. - Available at http://www.legislation.gov.uk/uksi/2014/3386/contents/made
Non-print

The A34 Trunk Road (M40 Junction 9 - West Ilsley) (Temporary Restriction and Prohibition of Traffic) Order 2014 No. 2014/999. - Enabling power: Road Traffic Regulation Act 1984, s. 14 (1) (a). - Issued: 03.04.2014. Made: 24.03.2014. Coming into force: 16.04.2014. Effect: None. Territorial extent & classification: E. Local. - Available at http://www.legislation.gov.uk/uksi/2014/999/contents/made Non-print

The A34 Trunk Road (Peartree Interchange) (Temporary Prohibition of Traffic) Order 2014 No. 2014/730. - Enabling power: Road Traffic Regulation Act 1984, s. 14 (1) (a). - Issued: 10.03.2014. Made: 03.03.2014. Coming into force: 22.03.2014. Effect: None. Territorial extent & classification: E. Local. - Available at http://www.legislation.gov.uk/uksi/2014/730/contents/made Non-print

The A34 Trunk Road (Speen - East Ilsley, Slip Roads) (Temporary Prohibition of Traffic) Order 2014 No. 2014/1765. - Enabling power: Road Traffic Regulation Act 1984, s. 14 (1) (a). - Issued: 04.07.2014. Made: 23.06.2014. Coming into force: 14.07.2014. Effect: None. Territorial extent & classification: E. Local. - Available at http://www.legislation.gov.uk/uksi/2014/1765/contents/made
Non-print

The A34 Trunk Road (Tot Hill Interchange - West Ilsley Interchange) (Temporary Restriction of Traffic) Order 2014 No. 2014/1339. - Enabling power: Road Traffic Regulation Act 1984, s. 14 (1) (a). - Issued: 27.05.2014. Made: 12.05.2014. Coming into force: 02.06.2014. Effect: None. Territorial extent & classification: E. Local. - Available at http://www.legislation.gov.uk/uksi/2014/1339/contents/made
Non-print

The A34 Trunk Road (Wendlebury) (Closure of Lay-by) Order 2014 No. 2014/1397. - Enabling power: Road Traffic Regulation Act 1984, ss. 1 (1), 2 (1) (2). - Issued: 02.06.2014. Made: 19.05.2014. Coming into force: 02.06.2014. Effect: None. Territorial extent & classification: E. Local. - Available at http://www.legislation.gov.uk/uksi/2014/1397/contents/made
Non-print

The A35 Trunk Road (Axminster to Bridport) (Temporary Restriction and Prohibition of Traffic) Order 2014 No. 2014/2345. - Enabling power: Road Traffic Regulation Act 1984, s. 14 (1) (a). - Issued: 04.09.2014. Made: 02.09.2014. Coming into force: 05.09.2014. Effect: None. Territorial extent & classification: E. Local. - Available at http://www.legislation.gov.uk/uksi/2014/2345/contents/made
Non-print

The A35 Trunk Road (Bridport Bypass, Dorset) (Temporary Restriction and Prohibition of Traffic) Order 2014 No. 2014/2630. - Enabling power: Road Traffic Regulation Act 1984, s. 14 (1) (b). - Issued: 30.09.2014. Made: 24.09.2014. Coming into force: 29.09.2014. Effect: None. Territorial extent & classification: E. Local. - Available at http://www.legislation.gov.uk/uksi/2014/2630/contents/made
Non-print

The A35 Trunk Road (Bridport) (Temporary Prohibition of Traffic) Order 2014 No. 2014/2413. - Enabling power: Road Traffic Regulation Act 1984, s. 14 (1) (a). - Issued: 09.09.2014. Made: 03.09.2014. Coming into force: 06.09.2014. Effect: None. Territorial extent & classification: E. Local. - Available at http://www.legislation.gov.uk/uksi/2014/2413/contents/made
Non-print

The A35 Trunk Road (Bridport to Dorchester) (Temporary Restriction and Prohibition of Traffic) Order 2014 No. 2014/2538. - Enabling power: Road Traffic Regulation Act 1984, s. 14 (1) (a). - Issued: 23.09.2014. Made: 03.09.2014. Coming into force: 06.09.2014. Effect: None. Territorial extent & classification: E. Local. - Available at http://www.legislation.gov.uk/uksi/2014/2538/contents/made
Non-print

The A35 Trunk Road (Dorchester Bypass) (Temporary Restriction and Prohibition of Traffic) (Number 2) Order 2014 No. 2014/2521. - Enabling power: Road Traffic Regulation Act 1984, s. 14 (1) (a). - Issued: 19.09.2014. Made: 16.09.2014. Coming into force: 22.09.2014. Effect: None. Territorial extent & classification: E. Local. - Available at http://www.legislation.gov.uk/uksi/2014/2521/contents/made
Non-print

The A35 Trunk Road (Dorchester Bypass) (Temporary Restriction and Prohibition of Traffic) Order 2014 No. 2014/1166. - Enabling power: Road Traffic Regulation Act 1984, s. 14 (1) (a). - Issued: 06.05.2014. Made: 23.04.2014. Coming into force: 29.04.2014. Effect: None. Territorial extent & classification: E. Local. - Available at http://www.legislation.gov.uk/uksi/2014/1166/contents/made
Non-print

The A35 Trunk Road (Honiton) (Temporary Prohibition of Traffic) Order 2014 No. 2014/2213. - Enabling power: Road Traffic Regulation Act 1984, s. 14 (1) (a). - Issued: 21.08.2014. Made: 12.08.2014. Coming into force: 15.08.2014. Effect: None. Territorial extent & classification: E. Local. - Available at http://www.legislation.gov.uk/uksi/2014/2213/contents/made
Non-print

The A35 Trunk Road (Honiton to Axminster) (Temporary Prohibition of Traffic) Order 2014 No. 2014/2296. - Enabling power: Road Traffic Regulation Act 1984, s. 14 (1) (a). - Issued: 28.08.2014. Made: 26.08.2014. Coming into force: 01.09.2014. Effect: None. Territorial extent & classification: E. Local. - Available at http://www.legislation.gov.uk/uksi/2014/2296/contents/made
Non-print

The A35 Trunk Road (Litton Cheney, Dorset) (Temporary Restriction and Prohibition of Traffic) Order 2014 No. 2014/2453. - Enabling power: Road Traffic Regulation Act 1984, s. 14 (1) (a). - Issued: 15.09.2014. Made: 10.09.2014. Coming into force: 13.09.2014. Effect: None. Territorial extent & classification: E. Local. - Available at http://www.legislation.gov.uk/uksi/2014/2453/contents/made
Non-print

ROAD TRAFFIC: TRAFFIC REGULATION

The A35 Trunk Road (Puddletown, Dorset) (Temporary Prohibition of Traffic) Order 2014 No. 2014/2502. - Enabling power: Road Traffic Regulation Act 1984, s. 14 (1) (a). - Issued: 19.09.2014. Made: 16.09.2014. Coming into force: 19.09.2014. Effect: None. Territorial extent & classification: E. Local. - Available at http://www.legislation.gov.uk/uksi/2014/2502/contents/made Non-print

The A36 Trunk Road (Brickworth Road to Ower) (Temporary Restriction and Prohibition of Traffic) Order 2014 No. 2014/1302. - Enabling power: Road Traffic Regulation Act 1984, s. 14 (1) (a). - Issued: 23.05.2014. Made: 07.05.2014. Coming into force: 10.05.2014. Effect: None. Territorial extent & classification: E. Local. - Available at http://www.legislation.gov.uk/uksi/2014/1302/contents/made Non-print

The A36 Trunk Road (Churchill Way North, Salisbury) (Temporary Prohibition of Traffic) Order 2014 No. 2014/192. - Enabling power: Road Traffic Regulation Act 1984, s. 14 (1) (a). - Issued: 04.02.2014. Made: 29.01.2014. Coming into force: 01.02.2014. Effect: None. Territorial extent & classification: E. Local. - Available at http://www.legislation.gov.uk/uksi/2014/192/contents/made Non-print

The A36 Trunk Road (Crawley Hill, Hampshire) (Temporary Prohibition of Traffic) (Number 2) Order 2014 No. 2014/2570. - Enabling power: Road Traffic Regulation Act 1984, s. 14 (1) (a). - Issued: 25.09.2014. Made: 18.09.2014. Coming into force: 24.09.2014. Effect: None. Territorial extent & classification: E. Local. - Available at http://www.legislation.gov.uk/uksi/2014/2570/contents/made Non-print

The A36 Trunk Road (Crawley Hill, Hampshire) (Temporary Prohibition of Traffic) Order 2014 No. 2014/132. - Enabling power: Road Traffic Regulation Act 1984, s. 14 (1) (a). - Issued: 24.01.2014. Made: 22.01.2014. Coming into force: 25.01.2014. Effect: None. Territorial extent & classification: E. Local. - Available at http://www.legislation.gov.uk/uksi/2014/132/contents/made Non-print

The A36 Trunk Road (Deptford Junction to Wilton, Salisbury) (Temporary Prohibition of Traffic) Order 2014 No. 2014/344. - Enabling power: Road Traffic Regulation Act 1984, s. 14 (1) (a). - Issued: 19.02.2014. Made: 11.02.2014. Coming into force: 17.02.2014. Effect: None. Territorial extent & classification: E. Local. - Available at http://www.legislation.gov.uk/uksi/2014/344/contents/made Non-print

The A36 Trunk Road (Heytesbury to Deptford, Wiltshire) (Temporary Prohibition of Traffic) Order 2014 No. 2014/2093. - Enabling power: Road Traffic Regulation Act 1984, s. 14 (1) (a). - Issued: 07.08.2014. Made: 22.07.2014. Coming into force: 26.07.2014. Effect: None. Territorial extent & classification: E. Local. - Available at http://www.legislation.gov.uk/uksi/2014/2093/contents/made Non-print

The A36 Trunk Road (Monkton Combe to Hinton Charterhouse) (Temporary Prohibition of Traffic) Order 2014 No. 2014/2745. - Enabling power: Road Traffic Regulation Act 1984, s. 14 (1) (a). - Issued: 13.10.2014. Made: 01.10.2014. Coming into force: 04.10.2014. Effect: None. Territorial extent & classification: E. Local. - Available at http://www.legislation.gov.uk/uksi/2014/2745/contents/made Non-print

The A36 Trunk Road (Monkton Combe to Limpley Stoke) (Temporary Prohibition of Traffic) Order 2014 No. 2014/2423. - Enabling power: Road Traffic Regulation Act 1984, s. 16A (2) (a). - Issued: 11.09.2014. Made: 08.09.2014. Coming into force: 10.09.2014. Effect: None. Territorial extent & classification: E. Local. - Available at http://www.legislation.gov.uk/uksi/2014/2423/contents/made Non-print

The A36 Trunk Road (Standerwick, Near Frome) (Temporary Prohibition of Traffic) Order 2014 No. 2014/2783. - Enabling power: Road Traffic Regulation Act 1984, s. 14 (1) (a). - Issued: 14.10.2014. Made: 08.10.2014. Coming into force: 11.10.2014. Effect: None. Territorial extent & classification: E. Local. - Available at http://www.legislation.gov.uk/uksi/2014/2783/contents/made Non-print

The A36 Trunk Road (Wilton Road, Salisbury) (Temporary Restriction of Traffic) Order 2014 No. 2014/2253. - Enabling power: Road Traffic Regulation Act 1984, s. 14 (1) (a). - Issued: 27.08.2014. Made: 19.08.2014. Coming into force: 23.08.2014. Effect: None. Territorial extent & classification: E. Local. - Available at http://www.legislation.gov.uk/uksi/2014/2253/contents/made Non-print

The A38 and A30 Trunk Roads (Kennford Bypass, Devon) and M5 Motorway (Junction 31) (Temporary Restriction and Prohibition of Traffic) Order 2014 No. 2014/2276. - Enabling power: Road Traffic Regulation Act 1984, s. 14 (1) (a). - Issued: 27.08.2014. Made: 22.08.2014. Coming into force: 30.08.2014. Effect: None. Territorial extent & classification: E. Local. - Available at http://www.legislation.gov.uk/uksi/2014/2276/contents/made Non-print

The A38 and A516 Trunk Roads (Mickleover - Findern, Derbyshire) (Temporary Prohibition of Traffic) Order 2014 No. 2014/2740. - Enabling power: Road Traffic Regulation Act 1984, s. 14 (1) (a). - Issued: 14.10.2014. Made: 22.09.2014. Coming into force: 29.09.2014. Effect: None. Territorial extent & classification: E. Local. - Available at http://www.legislation.gov.uk/uksi/2014/2740/contents/made Non-print

The A38 Trunk Road (Allestree, Derbyshire) (Slip Roads) (Temporary Prohibition of Traffic) Order 2014 No. 2014/640. - Enabling power: Road Traffic Regulation Act 1984, s. 14 (1) (a). - Issued: 06.03.2014. Made: 17.02.2014. Coming into force: 24.02.2014. Effect: None. Territorial extent & classification: E. Local. - Available at http://www.legislation.gov.uk/uksi/2014/640/contents/made Non-print

The A38 Trunk Road (Alrewas, Staffordshire) (Temporary Prohibition of Traffic) (No.2) Order 2014 No. 2014/3440. - Enabling power: Road Traffic Regulation Act 1984, s. 14 (1) (a). - Issued: 15.12.2014. Made: 08.12.2014. Coming into force: 15.12.2014. Effect: None. Territorial extent & classification: E. Local. - Available at http://www.legislation.gov.uk/uksi/2014/3440/contents/made Non-print

The A38 Trunk Road (Alrewas, Staffordshire) (Temporary Prohibition of Traffic) Order 2014 No. 2014/1176. - Enabling power: Road Traffic Regulation Act 1984, s. 14 (1) (a). - Issued: 07.05.2014. Made: 22.04.2014. Coming into force: 29.04.2014. Effect: None. Territorial extent & classification: E. Local. - Available at http://www.legislation.gov.uk/uksi/2014/1176/contents/made Non-print

The A38 Trunk Road (Ashburton) (Temporary Restriction of Traffic) Order 2014 No. 2014/767. - Enabling power: Road Traffic Regulation Act 1984, s. 14 (1) (a). - Issued: 17.03.2014. Made: 10.03.2014. Coming into force: 13.03.2014. Effect: None. Territorial extent & classification: E. Local. - Available at http://www.legislation.gov.uk/uksi/2014/767/contents/made Non-print

The A38 Trunk Road (Barton Turn to Branston, Staffordshire) (Closure of Gaps in the Central Reservation and Verge) Order 2014 No. 2014/1029. - Enabling power: Road Traffic Regulation Act 1984, ss. 1 (1), 2 (1) (2). - Issued: 17.04.2014. Made: 27.03.2014. Coming into force: 10.04.2014. Effect: None. Territorial extent & classification: E. Local. - Available at http://www.legislation.gov.uk/uksi/2014/1029/contents/made Non-print

The A38 Trunk Road (Barton-Under-Needwood to Branston, Staffordshire) (Temporary Restriction and Prohibition of Traffic) Order 2014 No. 2014/2625. - Enabling power: Road Traffic Regulation Act 1984, s. 14 (1) (a). - Issued: 30.09.2014. Made: 17.09.2014. Coming into force: 24.09.2014. Effect: None. Territorial extent & classification: E. Local. - Available at http://www.legislation.gov.uk/uksi/2014/2625/contents/made Non-print

The A38 Trunk Road (Barton-Under-Needwood to Branston) (Temporary Restriction and Prohibition of Traffic) Order 2014 No. 2014/3490. - Enabling power: Road Traffic Regulation Act 1984, s. 14 (1) (a). - Issued: 07.01.2015. Made: 24.12.2014. Coming into force: 31.12.2014. Effect: None. Territorial extent & classification: E. Local. - Available at http://www.legislation.gov.uk/uksi/2014/3490/contents/made Non-print

The A38 Trunk Road (Branston, Staffordshire) (Temporary Prohibition of Traffic) Order 2014 No. 2014/3383. - Enabling power: Road Traffic Regulation Act 1984, s. 14 (1) (a). - Issued: 28.11.2014. Made: 21.11.2014. Coming into force: 28.11.2014. Effect: None. Territorial extent & classification: E. Local. - Available at http://www.legislation.gov.uk/uksi/2014/3383/contents/made Non-print

The A38 Trunk Road (Burton-On-Trent, Staffordshire) (Slip Roads) (Temporary Prohibition of Traffic) Order 2014 No. 2014/121. - Enabling power: Road Traffic Regulation Act 1984, s. 14 (1) (a). - Issued: 24.01.2014. Made: 17.01.2014. Coming into force: 24.01.2014. Effect: None. Territorial extent & classification: E. Local. - Available at http://www.legislation.gov.uk/uksi/2014/121/contents/made Non-print

The A38 Trunk Road (Carkeel Roundabout to Saltash Tunnel) (Temporary Prohibition of Traffic) Order 2014 No. 2014/1782. - Enabling power: Road Traffic Regulation Act 1984, s. 14 (1) (a). - Issued: 09.07.2014. Made: 26.06.2014. Coming into force: 02.07.2014. Effect: None. Territorial extent & classification: E. Local. - Available at http://www.legislation.gov.uk/uksi/2014/1782/contents/made Non-print

The A38 Trunk Road (Carkeel Roundabout to Saltash Tunnel) (Temporary Restriction and Prohibition of Traffic) Order (No 2) 2014 No. 2014/3483. - Enabling power: Road Traffic Regulation Act 1984, s. 14 (1) (a). - Issued: 29.12.2014. Made: 23.12.2014. Coming into force: 03.01.2015. Effect: None. Territorial extent & classification: E. Local. - Available at http://www.legislation.gov.uk/uksi/2014/3483/contents/made Non-print

The A38 Trunk Road (Chudleigh Station Eastbound Exit Slip Road) (Temporary Prohibition of Traffic) Order 2014 No. 2014/191. - Enabling power: Road Traffic Regulation Act 1984, s. 14 (1) (a). - Issued: 04.02.2014. Made: 29.01.2014. Coming into force: 01.02.2014. Effect: None. Territorial extent & classification: E. Local. - Available at http://www.legislation.gov.uk/uksi/2014/191/contents/made Non-print

The A38 Trunk Road (Clay Mills, Staffordshire) (Temporary Restriction and Prohibition of Traffic) (Slip Road) Order 2014 No. 2014/650. - Enabling power: Road Traffic Regulation Act 1984, s. 14 (1) (a). - Issued: 07.03.2014. Made: 17.02.2014. Coming into force: 24.02.2014. Effect: None. Territorial extent & classification: E. Local. - Available at http://www.legislation.gov.uk/uksi/2014/650/contents/made Non-print

The A38 Trunk Road (Coxbench, Derbyshire) (Temporary Prohibition of Traffic) Order 2014 No. 2014/3144. - Enabling power: Road Traffic Regulation Act 1984, s. 14 (1) (a). - Issued: 24.11.2014. Made: 10.11.2014. Coming into force: 17.11.204. Effect: None. Territorial extent & classification: E. Local. - Available at http://www.legislation.gov.uk/uksi/2014/3144/contents/made Non-print

The A38 Trunk Road (Devon Expressway at Haldon Junction and Chudleigh Knighton) and A30 Trunk Road (Sourton Cross) (Temporary Prohibition of Traffic) Order 2014 No. 2014/2344. - Enabling power: Road Traffic Regulation Act 1984, s. 14 (1) (b). - Issued: 04.09.2014. Made: 01.09.2014. Coming into force: 10.09.2014. Effect: None. Territorial extent & classification: E. Local. - Available at http://www.legislation.gov.uk/uksi/2014/2344/contents/made Non-print

The A38 Trunk Road (Dobwalls Bypass, Cornwall) (Temporary Restriction and Prohibition of Traffic) Order 2014 No. 2014/2626. - Enabling power: Road Traffic Regulation Act 1984, s. 14 (1) (a). - Issued: 01.10.2014. Made: 24.09.2014. Coming into force: 27.09.2014. Effect: None. Territorial extent & classification: E. Local. - Available at http://www.legislation.gov.uk/uksi/2014/2626/contents/made Non-print

The A38 Trunk Road (Dobwalls to Saltash, Cornwall) (Temporary Restriction and Prohibition of Traffic) Order 2014 No. 2014/1690. - Enabling power: Road Traffic Regulation Act 1984, s. 14 (1) (a). - Issued: 01.07.2014. Made: 11.06.2014. Coming into force: 14.06.2014. Effect: None. Territorial extent & classification: E. Local. - Available at http://www.legislation.gov.uk/uksi/2014/1690/contents/made Non-print

The A38 Trunk Road (Drumbridges Roundabout, near Chudleigh Knighton, Devon) (Temporary Restriction and Prohibition of Traffic) Order 2014 No. 2014/2159. - Enabling power: Road Traffic Regulation Act 1984, s. 14 (1) (a). - Issued: 14.08.2014. Made: 04.08.2014. Coming into force: 08.08.2014. Effect: None. Territorial extent & classification: E. Local. - Available at http://www.legislation.gov.uk/uksi/2014/2159/contents/made Non-print

The A38 Trunk Road (Efflinch, Staffordshire) (Temporary Prohibition of Traffic) Order 2014 No. 2014/354. - Enabling power: Road Traffic Regulation Act 1984, s. 14 (1) (a). - Issued: 20.02.2014. Made: 07.02.2014. Coming into force: 14.02.2014. Effect: None. Territorial extent & classification: E. Local. - Available at http://www.legislation.gov.uk/uksi/2014/354/contents/made Non-print

The A38 Trunk Road (Egginton, Derbyshire) (Temporary Prohibition of Traffic) Order 2014 No. 2014/3015. - Enabling power: Road Traffic Regulation Act 1984, s. 14 (1) (a). - Issued: 14.11.2014. Made: 04.11.2014. Coming into force: 11.11.2014. Effect: None. Territorial extent & classification: E. Local. - Available at http://www.legislation.gov.uk/uksi/2014/3015/contents/made Non-print

The A38 Trunk Road (Egginton to Branston, Staffordshire) (Temporary Prohibition of Traffic) Order 2014 No. 2014/277. - Enabling power: Road Traffic Regulation Act 1984, s. 14 (1) (a). - Issued: 14.02.2014. Made: 03.02.2014. Coming into force: 10.02.2014. Effect: None. Territorial extent & classification: E. Local. - Available at http://www.legislation.gov.uk/uksi/2014/277/contents/made Non-print

The A38 Trunk Road (Fradley to Stretton) (Temporary Restriction and Prohibition of Traffic) Order 2014 No. 2014/2978. - Enabling power: Road Traffic Regulation Act 1984, s. 14 (1) (a). - Issued: 13.11.2014. Made: 27.10.2014. Coming into force: 03.11.2014. Effect: None. Territorial extent & classification: E. Local. - Available at http://www.legislation.gov.uk/uksi/2014/2978/contents/made Non-print

The A38 Trunk Road (Glynn Valley, Near Bodmin) (Temporary Restriction and Prohibition of Traffic) Order 2014 No. 2014/2782. - Enabling power: Road Traffic Regulation Act 1984, s. 14 (1) (a). - Issued: 14.10.2014. Made: 08.10.2014. Coming into force: 11.10.2014. Effect: None. Territorial extent & classification: E. Local. - Available at http://www.legislation.gov.uk/uksi/2014/2782/contents/made Non-print

The A38 Trunk Road (Haldon Hill and Harcombe Cross, Devon) (Temporary Restriction and Prohibition of Traffic) Order 2014 No. 2014/1159. - Enabling power: Road Traffic Regulation Act 1984, s. 14 (1) (a). - Issued: 06.05.2014. Made: 23.04.2014. Coming into force: 26.04.2014. Effect: None. Territorial extent & classification: E. Local. - Available at http://www.legislation.gov.uk/uksi/2014/1159/contents/made Non-print

The A38 Trunk Road (Hilliard's Cross, Staffordshire) (Temporary Restriction and Prohibition of Traffic) Order 2014 No. 2014/2622. - Enabling power: Road Traffic Regulation Act 1984, s. 14 (1) (a). - Issued: 30.09.2014. Made: 15.09.2014. Coming into force: 22.09.2014. Effect: None. Territorial extent & classification: E. Local. - Available at http://www.legislation.gov.uk/uksi/2014/2622/contents/made Non-print

The A38 Trunk Road (Holbrook - Allestree, Derbyshire) (Temporary Restriction and Prohibition of Traffic) Order 2014 No. 2014/2131. - Enabling power: Road Traffic Regulation Act 1984, s. 14 (1) (a). - Issued: 12.08.2014. Made: 21.07.2014. Coming into force: 28.07.2014. Effect: None. Territorial extent & classification: E. Local. - Available at http://www.legislation.gov.uk/uksi/2014/2131/contents/made Non-print

The A38 Trunk Road (Holbrook, Derbyshire) (Slip Roads) (Temporary Prohibition of Traffic) Order 2014 No. 2014/641. - Enabling power: Road Traffic Regulation Act 1984, s. 14 (1) (a). - Issued: 06.03.2014. Made: 17.02.2014. Coming into force: 24.02.2014. Effect: None. Territorial extent & classification: E. Local. - Available at http://www.legislation.gov.uk/uksi/2014/641/contents/made Non-print

The A38 Trunk Road (Ivybridge to Ashburton) (Temporary Prohibition of Traffic) Order 2014 No. 2014/2991. - Enabling power: Road Traffic Regulation Act 1984, s. 14 (1) (a). - Issued: 12.11.2014. Made: 05.11.2014. Coming into force: 08.11.2014. Effect: None. Territorial extent & classification: E. Local. - Available at http://www.legislation.gov.uk/uksi/2014/2991/contents/made Non-print

The A38 Trunk Road (Ivybridge to Wrangaton) (Temporary Prohibition of Traffic) Order 2014 No. 2014/1969. - Enabling power: Road Traffic Regulation Act 1984, s. 14 (1) (a). - Issued: 21.07.2014. Made: 09.07.2014. Coming into force: 12.07.2014. Effect: None. Territorial extent & classification: E. Local. - Available at http://www.legislation.gov.uk/uksi/2014/1969/contents/made Non-print

The A38 Trunk Road (Kingsway, Mickleover, Derbyshire) (Temporary Prohibition of Traffic) Order 2014 No. 2014/1022. - Enabling power: Road Traffic Regulation Act 1984, s. 14 (1) (a). - Issued: 17.04.2014. Made: 17.03.2014. Coming into force: 24.03.2014. Effect: None. Territorial extent & classification: E. Local. - Available at http://www.legislation.gov.uk/uksi/2014/1022/contents/made Non-print

The A38 Trunk Road (Liskeard to Saltash) (Temporary Prohibition of Traffic) Order 2014 No. 2014/1702. - Enabling power: Road Traffic Regulation Act 1984, s. 14 (1) (a). - Issued: 02.07.2014. Made: 18.06.2014. Coming into force: 21.06.2014. Effect: None. Territorial extent & classification: E. Local. - Available at http://www.legislation.gov.uk/uksi/2014/1702/contents/made Non-print

ROAD TRAFFIC: TRAFFIC REGULATION

The A38 Trunk Road (Manadon Interchange, Plymouth) (Temporary Restriction and Prohibition of Traffic) Order 2014 No. 2014/2274. - Enabling power: Road Traffic Regulation Act 1984, s. 14 (1) (a). - Issued: 27.08.2014. Made: 21.08.2014. Coming into force: 30.08.2014. Effect: None. Territorial extent & classification: E. Local. - Available at http://www.legislation.gov.uk/uksi/2014/2274/contents/made Non-print

The A38 Trunk Road (Markeaton, Derby) (Temporary Prohibition of Traffic) Order 2014 No. 2014/2084. - Enabling power: Road Traffic Regulation Act 1984, s. 14 (1) (a). - Issued: 06.08.2014. Made: 14.07.2014. Coming into force: 21.07.2014. Effect: None. Territorial extent & classification: E. Local. - Available at http://www.legislation.gov.uk/uksi/2014/2084/contents/made Non-print

The A38 Trunk Road (Marley Head to Dartbridge, Devon) (Temporary Restriction and Prohibition of Traffic) Order 2014 No. 2014/2282. - Enabling power: Road Traffic Regulation Act 1984, s. 14 (1) (a). - Issued: 29.08.2014. Made: 27.08.2014. Coming into force: 30.08.2014. Effect: None. Territorial extent & classification: E. Local. - Available at http://www.legislation.gov.uk/uksi/2014/2282/contents/made Non-print

The A38 Trunk Road (Near Saltash) (Temporary Restriction and Prohibition of Traffic) Order 2014 No. 2014/674. - Enabling power: Road Traffic Regulation Act 1984, s. 14 (1) (a). - Issued: 07.03.2014. Made: 26.02.2014. Coming into force: 01.03.2014. Effect: None. Territorial extent & classification: E. Local. - Available at http://www.legislation.gov.uk/uksi/2014/674/contents/made Non-print

The A38 Trunk Road (Plymouth, Devon) (Temporary Restriction and Prohibition of Traffic) Order 2014 No. 2014/2138. - Enabling power: Road Traffic Regulation Act 1984, s. 14 (1) (a). - Issued: 12.08.2014. Made: 30.07.2014. Coming into force: 02.08.2014. Effect: None. Territorial extent & classification: E. Local. - Available at http://www.legislation.gov.uk/uksi/2014/2138/contents/made Non-print

The A38 Trunk Road (Plymouth) (Temporary Restriction of Traffic) Order 2014 No. 2014/673. - Enabling power: Road Traffic Regulation Act 1984, s. 14 (1) (a). - Issued: 07.03.2014. Made: 25.02.2014. Coming into force: 01.03.2014. Effect: None. Territorial extent & classification: E. Local. - Available at http://www.legislation.gov.uk/uksi/2014/673/contents/made Non-print

The A38 Trunk Road (Plympton to Plymouth) (Temporary Prohibition of Traffic) Order 2014 No. 2014/1040. - Enabling power: Road Traffic Regulation Act 1984, s. 14 (1) (a). - Issued: 22.04.2014. Made: 09.04.2014. Coming into force: 13.04.2014. Effect: None. Territorial extent & classification: E. Local. - Available at http://www.legislation.gov.uk/uksi/2014/1040/contents/made Non-print

The A38 Trunk Road (Ripley - Alfreton, Derbyshire) (Temporary Restriction and Prohibition of Traffic) Order 2014 No. 2014/2073. - Enabling power: Road Traffic Regulation Act 1984, s. 14 (1) (a). - Issued: 06.08.2014. Made: 07.07.2014. Coming into force: 21.07.2014. Effect: None. Territorial extent & classification: E. Local. - Available at http://www.legislation.gov.uk/uksi/2014/2073/contents/made Non-print

The A38 Trunk Road (Ripley, Derbyshire) (Temporary Prohibition of Traffic) Order 2014 No. 2014/1719. - Enabling power: Road Traffic Regulation Act 1984, s. 14 (1) (a). - Issued: 03.07.2014. Made: 16.06.2014. Coming into force: 23.06.2014. Effect: None. Territorial extent & classification: E. Local. - Available at http://www.legislation.gov.uk/uksi/2014/1719/contents/made Non-print

The A38 Trunk Road (Saltash to Exeter, Devon) (Temporary Restriction and Prohibition of Traffic) Order 2014 No. 2014/1735. - Enabling power: Road Traffic Regulation Act 1984, s. 14 (1) (a). - Issued: 04.07.2014. Made: 25.06.2014. Coming into force: 28.06.2014. Effect: None. Territorial extent & classification: E. Local. - Available at http://www.legislation.gov.uk/uksi/2014/1735/contents/made Non-print

The A38 Trunk Road (Saltash to Exeter) (Temporary Prohibition of Traffic) Order 2014 No. 2014/1566. - Enabling power: Road Traffic Regulation Act 1984, s. 14 (1) (a). - Issued: 17.06.2014. Made: 28.05.2014. Coming into force: 31.05.2014. Effect: None. Territorial extent & classification: E. Local. - Available at http://www.legislation.gov.uk/uksi/2014/1566/contents/made Non-print

The A38 Trunk Road (South of Burton-Upon-Trent, Staffordshire) (Temporary Prohibition of Traffic) Order 2014 No. 2014/1090. - Enabling power: Road Traffic Regulation Act 1984, s. 14 (1) (a). - Issued: 25.04.2014. Made: 31.03.2014. Coming into force: 07.04.2014. Effect: None. Territorial extent & classification: E. Local. - Available at http://www.legislation.gov.uk/uksi/2014/1090/contents/made Non-print

The A38 Trunk Road (Southwest of Burton-on-Trent, Staffordshire) (Temporary Restriction and Prohibition of Traffic) Order 2014 No. 2014/664. - Enabling power: Road Traffic Regulation Act 1984, s. 14 (1) (a). - Issued: 10.03.2014. Made: 21.02.2014. Coming into force: 28.02.2014. Effect: None. Territorial extent & classification: E. Local. - Available at http://www.legislation.gov.uk/uksi/2014/664/contents/made Non-print

The A38 Trunk Road (Streethay, Staffordshire) (Temporary Prohibition of Traffic) Order 2014 No. 2014/3011. - Enabling power: Road Traffic Regulation Act 1984, s. 14 (1) (a). - Issued: 17.11.2014. Made: 03.11.2014. Coming into force: 10.11.2014. Effect: None. Territorial extent & classification: E. Local. - Available at http://www.legislation.gov.uk/uksi/2014/3011/contents/made Non-print

The A38 Trunk Road (Streethay, Staffordshire) (Temporary Restriction and Prohibition of Traffic) Order 2014 No. 2014/1091. - Enabling power: Road Traffic Regulation Act 1984, s. 14 (1) (a). - Issued: 25.04.2014. Made: 31.03.2014. Coming into force: 07.04.2014. Effect: None. Territorial extent & classification: E. Local. - Available at http://www.legislation.gov.uk/uksi/2014/1091/contents/made Non-print

The A38 Trunk Road (Swinfen - Weeford, Staffordshire) (Temporary Prohibition of Traffic) Order 2014 No. 2014/2143. - Enabling power: Road Traffic Regulation Act 1984, s. 14 (1) (a). - Issued: 12.08.2014. Made: 28.07.2014. Coming into force: 04.08.2014. Effect: None. Territorial extent & classification: E. Local. - Available at http://www.legislation.gov.uk/uksi/2014/2143/contents/made Non-print

The A38 Trunk Road (Willington, Derbyshire) (Temporary Prohibition of Traffic) Order 2014 No. 2014/457. - Enabling power: Road Traffic Regulation Act 1984, s. 14 (1) (a). - Issued: 04.03.2014. Made: 07.02.2014. Coming into force: 14.02.2014. Effect: None. Territorial extent & classification: E. Local. - Available at http://www.legislation.gov.uk/uksi/2014/457/contents/made Non-print

The A38 Trunk Road (Willington, Derbyshire) (Temporary Restriction and Prohibition of Traffic) Order 2014 No. 2014/2794. - Enabling power: Road Traffic Regulation Act 1984, s. 14 (1) (a). - Issued: 14.10.2014. Made: 06.10.2014. Coming into force: 13.10.2014. Effect: None. Territorial extent & classification: E. Local. - Available at http://www.legislation.gov.uk/uksi/2014/2794/contents/made Non-print

The A40 Trunk Road and M50 Motorway (Ross-On-Wye, Herefordshire) (Temporary Prohibition of Traffic) Order 2014 No. 2014/963. - Enabling power: Road Traffic Regulation Act 1984, s. 14 (1) (a). - Issued: 07.04.2014. Made: 14.03.2014. Coming into force: 21.03.2014. Effect: None. Territorial extent & classification: E. Local. - Available at http://www.legislation.gov.uk/uksi/2014/963/contents/made Non-print

The A40 Trunk Road (Churcham, Gloucestershire) (Temporary Restriction of Traffic) Order 2014 No. 2014/60. - Enabling power: Road Traffic Regulation Act 1984, s. 14 (1) (a). - Issued: 20.01.2014. Made: 07.01.2014. Coming into force: 11.01.2014. Effect: None. Territorial extent & classification: E. Local. - Available at http://www.legislation.gov.uk/uksi/2014/60/contents/made Non-print

The A40 Trunk Road (Denham Court Drive, Denham) (Temporary Prohibition of Traffic) Order 2014 No. 2014/735. - Enabling power: Road Traffic Regulation Act 1984, s. 14 (1) (a). - Issued: 11.03.2014. Made: 05.03.2014. Coming into force: 24.03.2014. Effect: None. Territorial extent & classification: E. Local. - Available at http://www.legislation.gov.uk/uksi/2014/735/contents/made Non-print

The A40 Trunk Road (Denham Roundabout) (Temporary Prohibition of Traffic) Order 2014 No. 2014/1992. - Enabling power: Road Traffic Regulation Act 1984, s. 14 (1) (a). - Issued: 21.07.2014. Made: 07.07.2014. Coming into force: 01.08.2014. Effect: None. Territorial extent & classification: E. Local. - Available at http://www.legislation.gov.uk/uksi/2014/1992/contents/made Non-print

ROAD TRAFFIC: TRAFFIC REGULATION

The A40 Trunk Road (Doward near Whitchurch, Herefordshire) (Temporary Prohibition of Traffic) (Slip Road) Order 2014 No. 2014/323. - Enabling power: Road Traffic Regulation Act 1984, s. 14 (1) (a). - Issued: 18.02.2014. Made: 27.01.2014. Coming into force: 03.02.2014. Effect: None. Territorial extent & classification: E. Local. - Available at http://www.legislation.gov.uk/uksi/2014/323/contents/made Non-print

The A40 Trunk Road (Eastbound Exit Slip Road to M5 Junction 11) (Temporary Prohibition of Traffic) Order 2014 No. 2014/1737. - Enabling power: Road Traffic Regulation Act 1984, s. 14 (1) (a). - Issued: 04.07.2014. Made: 25.06.2014. Coming into force: 28.06.2014. Effect: None. Territorial extent & classification: E. Local. - Available at http://www.legislation.gov.uk/uksi/2014/1737/contents/made Non-print

The A40 Trunk Road (Elmbridge Court Roundabout to Over Roundabout, Gloucester) (Temporary Prohibition of Traffic) Order 2014 No. 2014/3388. - Enabling power: Road Traffic Regulation Act 1984, s. 14 (1) (a). - Issued: 01.12.2014. Made: 26.11.2014. Coming into force: 29.11.2014. Effect: None. Territorial extent & classification: E. Local. - Available at http://www.legislation.gov.uk/uksi/2014/3388/contents/made Non-print

The A40 Trunk Road (Glewstone, Herefordshire) (Temporary Restriction and Prohibition of Traffic) Order 2014 No. 2014/696. - Enabling power: Road Traffic Regulation Act 1984, s. 14 (1) (a). - Issued: 07.03.2014. Made: 24.02.2014. Coming into force: 03.03.2014. Effect: None. Territorial extent & classification: E. Local. - Available at http://www.legislation.gov.uk/uksi/2014/696/contents/made Non-print

The A40 Trunk Road (Highnam Right Turn Bans, Gloucestershire) (Temporary Prohibition of Traffic) Order 2014 No. 2014/1739. - Enabling power: Road Traffic Regulation Act 1984, s. 14 (1) (a). - Issued: 04.07.2014. Made: 25.06.2014. Coming into force: 28.06.2014. Effect: None. Territorial extent & classification: E. Local. - Available at http://www.legislation.gov.uk/uksi/2014/1739/contents/made Non-print

The A40 Trunk Road (Huntley to Highnam, Gloucestershire) (Temporary Prohibition of Traffic) Order 2014 No. 2014/2799. - Enabling power: Road Traffic Regulation Act 1984, s. 14 (1) (a). - Issued: 21.10.2014. Made: 01.10.2014. Coming into force: 04.10.2014. Effect: None. Territorial extent & classification: E. Local. - Available at http://www.legislation.gov.uk/uksi/2014/2799/contents/made Non-print

The A40 Trunk Road (Huntley to Lea) (Temporary Prohibition of Traffic) Order 2014 No. 2014/1732. - Enabling power: Road Traffic Regulation Act 1984, s. 14 (1) (a). - Issued: 04.07.2014. Made: 24.06.2014. Coming into force: 28.06.2014. Effect: None. Territorial extent & classification: E. Local. - Available at http://www.legislation.gov.uk/uksi/2014/1732/contents/made Non-print

The A40 Trunk Road (Longford Roundabout to Over Roundabout, Gloucester) (Temporary Prohibition of Traffic) Order 2014 No. 2014/3485. - Enabling power: Road Traffic Regulation Act 1984, s. 14 (1) (a). - Issued: 02.01.2015. Made: 29.12.2014. Coming into force: 03.01.2015. Effect: None. Territorial extent & classification: E. Local. - Available at http://www.legislation.gov.uk/uksi/2014/3485/contents/made Non-print

The A40 Trunk Road (M5 Junction 11) (Temporary Prohibition of Traffic) Order 2014 No. 2014/51. - Enabling power: Road Traffic Regulation Act 1984, s. 14 (1) (a). - Issued: 17.01.2014. Made: 14.01.2014. Coming into force: 18.01.2014. Effect: None. Territorial extent & classification: E. Local. - Available at http://www.legislation.gov.uk/uksi/2014/51/contents/made Non-print

The A40 Trunk Road (Whitchurch, Herefordshire) (Temporary Restriction and Prohibition of Traffic) Order 2014 No. 2014/1247. - Enabling power: Road Traffic Regulation Act 1984, s. 14 (1) (a). - Issued: 16.05.2014. Made: 30.04.2014. Coming into force: 07.05.2014. Effect: None. Territorial extent & classification: E. Local. - Available at http://www.legislation.gov.uk/uksi/2014/1247/contents/made Non-print

The A40 Trunk Road (Wilton to Whitchurch, Herefordshire) (Temporary Prohibition of Traffic) Order 2014 No. 2014/2744. - Enabling power: Road Traffic Regulation Act 1984, s. 14 (1) (a). - Issued: 14.10.2014. Made: 26.09.2014. Coming into force: 03.10.2014. Effect: None. Territorial extent & classification: E. Local. - Available at http://www.legislation.gov.uk/uksi/2014/2744/contents/made Non-print

The A42 Trunk Road (Ashby-De-La-Zouch, Leicestershire) (Temporary Restriction and Prohibition of Traffic) Order 2014 No. 2014/179. - Enabling power: Road Traffic Regulation Act 1984, s. 14 (1) (a). - Issued: 03.02.2014. Made: 20.01.2014. Coming into force: 27.01.2014. Effect: None. Territorial extent & classification: E. Local. - Available at http://www.legislation.gov.uk/uksi/2014/179/contents/made Non-print

The A42 Trunk Road (Ashby-de-la-Zouch to Diseworth, Leicestershire) (Temporary Prohibition of Traffic) Order 2014 No. 2014/2186. - Enabling power: Road Traffic Regulation Act 1984, s. 14 (1) (a). - Issued: 19.08.2014. Made: 21.07.2014. Coming into force: 25.07.2014. Effect: None. Territorial extent & classification: E. Local. - Available at http://www.legislation.gov.uk/uksi/2014/2186/contents/made Non-print

The A43 and A5 Trunk Roads (Silverstone - Rothersthorpe, Northamptonshire) (Temporary Restriction and Prohibition of Traffic) Order 2014 No. 2014/2674. - Enabling power: Road Traffic Regulation Act 1984, s. 14 (1) (a). - Issued: 06.10.2014. Made: 05.09.2014. Coming into force: 12.09.2014. Effect: None. Territorial extent & classification: E. Local. - Available at http://www.legislation.gov.uk/uksi/2014/2674/contents/made Non-print

The A43 and A5 Trunk Roads (Towcester - Rothersthorpe, Northamptonshire) (Temporary Restriction and Prohibition of Traffic) Order 2014 No. 2014/2075. - Enabling power: Road Traffic Regulation Act 1984, s. 14 (1) (a). - Issued: 06.08.2014. Made: 14.07.2014. Coming into force: 21.07.2014. Effect: None. Territorial extent & classification: E. Local. - Available at http://www.legislation.gov.uk/uksi/2014/2075/contents/made Non-print

The A43 Trunk Road (Abthorpe Roundabout - Silverstone, Northamptonshire) (Temporary Restriction and Prohibition of Traffic) Order 2014 No. 2014/2729. - Enabling power: Road Traffic Regulation Act 1984, s. 14 (1) (a). - Issued: 13.10.2014. Made: 22.09.2014. Coming into force: 29.09.2014. Effect: None. Territorial extent & classification: E. Local. - Available at http://www.legislation.gov.uk/uksi/2014/2729/contents/made Non-print

The A43 Trunk Road and M40 Motorway (M40 Junction 10, Oxfordshire) (Temporary Restriction and Prohibition of Traffic) Order 2014 No. 2014/2478. - Enabling power: Road Traffic Regulation Act 1984, s. 14 (1) (a). - Issued: 18.09.2014. Made: 19.08.2014. Coming into force: 26.082014. Effect: None. Territorial extent & classification: E. Local. - Available at http://www.legislation.gov.uk/uksi/2014/2478/contents/made. - Revoked by SI 2015/1009 (Non-print) Non-print

The A43 Trunk Road (Brackley, Northamptonshire) (Temporary Prohibition of Traffic) (No.2) Order 2014 No. 2014/2944. - Enabling power: Road Traffic Regulation Act 1984, s. 14 (1) (b). - Issued: 27.10.2014. Made: 20.10.2014. Coming into force: 27.10.2014. Effect: None. Territorial extent & classification: E. Local. - Available at http://www.legislation.gov.uk/uksi/2014/2944/contents/made Non-print

The A43 Trunk Road (Brackley, Northamptonshire) (Temporary Prohibition of Traffic) Order 2014 No. 2014/964. - Enabling power: Road Traffic Regulation Act 1984, s. 14 (1) (a). - Issued: 07.04.2014. Made: 14.03.2014. Coming into force: 21.03.2014. Effect: None. Territorial extent & classification: E. Local. - Available at http://www.legislation.gov.uk/uksi/2014/964/contents/made Non-print

The A43 Trunk Road (Brackley to Towcester, Northamptonshire) (Silverstone British Grand Prix) (Temporary Restriction and Prohibition of Traffic) Order 2014 No. 2014/1717. - Enabling power: Road Traffic Regulation Act 1984, s. 14 (1) (b). - Issued: 03.07.2014. Made: 16.06.2014. Coming into force: 23.06.2014. Effect: None. Territorial extent & classification: E. Local. - Available at http://www.legislation.gov.uk/uksi/2014/1717/contents/made Non-print

The A43 Trunk Road (Brackley to Towcester, Northamptonshire) (Temporary Restriction and Prohibition of Traffic) Order 2014 No. 2014/353. - Enabling power: Road Traffic Regulation Act 1984, s. 14 (1) (a). - Issued: 20.02.2014. Made: 03.02.2014. Coming into force: 10.02.2014. Effect: None. Territorial extent & classification: E. Local. - Available at http://www.legislation.gov.uk/uksi/2014/353/contents/made Non-print

ROAD TRAFFIC: TRAFFIC REGULATION

The A43 Trunk Road (Silverstone, Northamptonshire) (Temporary Restriction of Traffic) Order 2014 No. 2014/2262. - Enabling power: Road Traffic Regulation Act 1984, s. 14 (1) (b). - Issued: 29.08.2014. Made: 15.08.2014. Coming into force: 22.08.2014. Effect: None. Territorial extent & classification: E. Local. - Available at http://www.legislation.gov.uk/uksi/2014/2262/contents/made Non-print

The A43 Trunk Road (Syresham, Northamptonshire) (Slip Road) (No.2) (Temporary Prohibition of Traffic) Order 2014 No. 2014/1619. - Enabling power: Road Traffic Regulation Act 1984, s. 14 (1) (a). - Issued: 25.06.2014. Made: 02.06.2014. Coming into force: 09.06.2014. Effect: None. Territorial extent & classification: E. Local. - Available at http://www.legislation.gov.uk/uksi/2014/1619/contents/made Non-print

The A43 Trunk Road (Syresham, Northamptonshire) (Slip Road) (Temporary Prohibition of Traffic) Order 2014 No. 2014/1161. - Enabling power: Road Traffic Regulation Act 1984, s. 14 (1) (a). - Issued: 07.05.2014. Made: 21.04.2014. Coming into force: 28.04.2014. Effect: None. Territorial extent & classification: E. Local. - Available at http://www.legislation.gov.uk/uksi/2014/1161/contents/made Non-print

The A43 Trunk Road (Towcester, Northamptonshire) (Temporary Restriction and Prohibition of Traffic) Order 2014 No. 2014/1243. - Enabling power: Road Traffic Regulation Act 1984, s. 14 (1) (a). - Issued: 16.05.2014. Made: 28.04.2014. Coming into force: 05.05.2014. Effect: None. Territorial extent & classification: E. Local. - Available at http://www.legislation.gov.uk/uksi/2014/1243/contents/made Non-print

The A45 and A14 Trunk Roads (Higham Ferrers - Thrapston, Northamptonshire) (Temporary Restriction and Prohibition of Traffic) Order 2014 No. 2014/2078. - Enabling power: Road Traffic Regulation Act 1984, s. 14 (1) (a). - Issued: 06.08.2014. Made: 14.07.2014. Coming into force: 21.07.2014. Effect: None. Territorial extent & classification: E. Local. - Available at http://www.legislation.gov.uk/uksi/2014/2078/contents/made Non-print

The A45 and A423 Trunk Roads (Ryton, Warwickshire) (Temporary Prohibition of Traffic) Order 2014 No. 2014/1425. - Enabling power: Road Traffic Regulation Act 1984, s. 14 (1) (a). - Issued: 04.06.2014. Made: 06.05.2014. Coming into force: 13.05.2014. Effect: None. Territorial extent & classification: E. Local. - Available at http://www.legislation.gov.uk/uksi/2014/1425/contents/made Non-print

The A45 and A452 Trunk Roads (Stonebridge) (Temporary Prohibition of Traffic) Order 2014 No. 2014/652. - Enabling power: Road Traffic Regulation Act 1984, s. 14 (1) (a). - Issued: 06.03.2014. Made: 19.02.2014. Coming into force: 26.02.2014. Effect: None. Territorial extent & classification: E. Local. - Available at http://www.legislation.gov.uk/uksi/2014/652/contents/made Non-print

The A45 Trunk Road (A45 Wellingborough, Northamptonshire) (Temporary Restriction and Prohibition of Traffic) Order 2014 No. 2014/173. - Enabling power: Road Traffic Regulation Act 1984, s. 14 (1) (a). - Issued: 03.02.2014. Made: 21.01.2014. Coming into force: 28.01.2014. Effect: None. Territorial extent & classification: E. Local. - Available at http://www.legislation.gov.uk/uksi/2014/173/contents/made Non-print

The A45 Trunk Road and the M42 Motorway (Middle Bickenhill, Warwickshire) (Temporary Prohibition of Traffic) Order 2014 No. 2014/1725. - Enabling power: Road Traffic Regulation Act 1984, s. 14 (1) (a). - Issued: 03.07.2014. Made: 16.06.2014. Coming into force: 23.06.2014. Effect: None. Territorial extent & classification: E. Local. - Available at http://www.legislation.gov.uk/uksi/2014/1725/contents/made Non-print

The A45 Trunk Road and the M45 Motorway (Dunchurch, Warwickshire) (Temporary Prohibition of Traffic) Order 2014 No. 2014/2063. - Enabling power: Road Traffic Regulation Act 1984, s. 14 (1) (a). - Issued: 05.08.2014. Made: 07.07.2014. Coming into force: 14.07.2014. Effect: None. Territorial extent & classification: E. Local. - Available at http://www.legislation.gov.uk/uksi/2014/2063/contents/made Non-print

The A45 Trunk Road (Brackmills to Billing, Northamptonshire) (Temporary Restriction of Traffic) Order 2014 No. 2014/356. - Enabling power: Road Traffic Regulation Act 1984, s. 14 (1) (a). - Issued: 20.02.2014. Made: 07.02.2014. Coming into force: 14.02.2014. Effect: None. Territorial extent & classification: E. Local. - Available at http://www.legislation.gov.uk/uksi/2014/356/contents/made Non-print

The A45 Trunk Road (Doddington, Northamptonshire) (Temporary Prohibition of Traffic) (Slip Road) Order 2014 No. 2014/361. - Enabling power: Road Traffic Regulation Act 1984, s. 14 (1) (a). - Issued: 20.02.2014. Made: 10.02.2014. Coming into force: 17.02.2014. Effect: None. Territorial extent & classification: E. Local. - Available at http://www.legislation.gov.uk/uksi/2014/361/contents/made Non-print

The A45 Trunk Road (Earls Barton - Great Billing, Northamptonshire) (Temporary Prohibition of Traffic) Order 2014 No. 2014/2443. - Enabling power: Road Traffic Regulation Act 1984, s. 14 (1) (a). - Issued: 15.09.2014. Made: 26.08.2014. Coming into force: 02.09.2014. Effect: None. Territorial extent & classification: E. Local. - Available at http://www.legislation.gov.uk/uksi/2014/2443/contents/made Non-print

The A45 Trunk Road (Earls Barton, Northamptonshire) (Slip Roads) (Temporary Prohibition of Traffic) Order 2014 No. 2014/3147. - Enabling power: Road Traffic Regulation Act 1984, s. 14 (1) (a). - Issued: 24.11.2014. Made: 12.11.2014. Coming into force: 19.11.204. Effect: None. Territorial extent & classification: E. Local. - Available at http://www.legislation.gov.uk/uksi/2014/3147/contents/made Non-print

The A45 Trunk Road (Earls Barton, Northamptonshire) (Temporary Prohibition of Traffic) Order 2014 No. 2014/2267. - Enabling power: Road Traffic Regulation Act 1984, s. 14 (1) (a). - Issued: 29.08.2014. Made: 18.08.2014. Coming into force: 25.08.2014. Effect: None. Territorial extent & classification: E. Local. - Available at http://www.legislation.gov.uk/uksi/2014/2267/contents/made Non-print

The A45 Trunk Road (Great Billing, Northamptonshire) (Temporary Prohibition of Traffic) Order 2014 No. 2014/2140. - Enabling power: Road Traffic Regulation Act 1984, s. 14 (1) (a). - Issued: 12.08.2014. Made: 28.07.2014. Coming into force: 04.08.2014. Effect: None. Territorial extent & classification: E. Local. - Available at http://www.legislation.gov.uk/uksi/2014/2140/contents/made Non-print

The A45 Trunk Road (Great Billing, Northampton) (Temporary Restriction and Prohibition of Traffic) Order 2014 No. 2014/2869. - Enabling power: Road Traffic Regulation Act 1984, s. 14 (1) (a). - Issued: 27.10.2014. Made: 06.10.2014. Coming into force: 13.10.2014. Effect: None. Territorial extent & classification: E. Local. - Available at http://www.legislation.gov.uk/uksi/2014/2869/contents/made Non-print

The A45 Trunk Road (Great Billing to Wilby) (Temporary Restriction and Prohibition of Traffic) Order 2014 No. 2014/2976. - Enabling power: Road Traffic Regulation Act 1984, s. 14 (1) (a). - Issued: 13.11.2014. Made: 27.10.2014. Coming into force: 03.11.2014. Effect: None. Territorial extent & classification: E. Local. - Available at http://www.legislation.gov.uk/uksi/2014/2976/contents/made Non-print

The A45 Trunk Road (Hardingstone, Northamptonshire) (Temporary Prohibition of Traffic) Order 2014 No. 2014/167. - Enabling power: Road Traffic Regulation Act 1984, s. 14 (1) (a). - Issued: 31.01.2014. Made: 20.01.2014. Coming into force: 27.01.2014. Effect: None. Territorial extent & classification: E. Local. - Available at http://www.legislation.gov.uk/uksi/2014/167/contents/made Non-print

The A45 Trunk Road (Higham Ferrers, Northamptonshire) (Temporary Prohibition of Traffic) Order 2014 No. 2014/2943. - Enabling power: Road Traffic Regulation Act 1984, s. 14 (1) (a). - Issued: 27.10.2014. Made: 20.10.2014. Coming into force: 27.10.2014. Effect: None. Territorial extent & classification: E. Local. - Available at http://www.legislation.gov.uk/uksi/2014/2943/contents/made Non-print

The A45 Trunk Road (Irchester, Northamptonshire) (Temporary Restriction of Traffic) Order 2014 No. 2014/2023. - Enabling power: Road Traffic Regulation Act 1984, s. 14 (1) (a). - Issued: 31.07.2014. Made: 17.06.2014. Coming into force: 24.06.2014. Effect: None. Territorial extent & classification: E. Local. - Available at http://www.legislation.gov.uk/uksi/2014/2023/contents/made Non-print

The A45 Trunk Road (Irthlingborough, Northamptonshire) (Temporary Prohibition of Traffic) (No.2) Order 2014 No. 2014/2489. - Enabling power: Road Traffic Regulation Act 1984, s. 14 (1) (a). - Issued: 15.09.2014. Made: 08.09.2014. Coming into force: 15.09.2014. Effect: None. Territorial extent & classification: E. Local. - Available at http://www.legislation.gov.uk/uksi/2014/2489/contents/made Non-print

The A45 Trunk Road (Junction 14, Wellingborough, Northamptonshire) (Slip Road) (Temporary Prohibition of Traffic) Order 2014 No. 2014/148. - Enabling power: Road Traffic Regulation Act 1984, s. 14 (1) (a). - Issued: 30.01.2014. Made: 10.01.2014. Coming into force: 12.01.2014. Effect: None. Territorial extent & classification: E. Local. - Available at http://www.legislation.gov.uk/uksi/2014/148/contents/made Non-print

The A45 Trunk Road (M42 Junction 6) (Temporary Prohibition of Traffic) Order 2014 No. 2014/1590. - Enabling power: Road Traffic Regulation Act 1984, s. 14 (1) (a). - Issued: 19.06.2014. Made: 02.06.2014. Coming into force: 09.06.2014. Effect: None. Territorial extent & classification: E. Local. - Available at http://www.legislation.gov.uk/uksi/2014/1590/contents/made Non-print

The A45 Trunk Road (Nene Bridge, Northampton) (Temporary Restriction and Prohibition of Traffic) (Slip Road) Order 2014 No. 2014/1135. - Enabling power: Road Traffic Regulation Act 1984, s. 14 (1) (a). - Issued: 02.05.2014. Made: 14.04.2014. Coming into force: 21.04.2014. Effect: None. Territorial extent & classification: E. Local. - Available at http://www.legislation.gov.uk/uksi/2014/1135/contents/made Non-print

The A45 Trunk Road (Northampton) (Temporary Restriction and Prohibition of Traffic) Order 2014 No. 2014/1525. - Enabling power: Road Traffic Regulation Act 1984, s. 14 (1) (a). - Issued: 11.06.2014. Made: 21.05.2014. Coming into force: 28.05.2014. Effect: None. Territorial extent & classification: E. Local. - Available at http://www.legislation.gov.uk/uksi/2014/1525/contents/made Non-print

The A45 Trunk Road (North of Rushden, Northamptonshire) (Temporary Restriction and Prohibition of Traffic) Order 2014 No. 2014/1632. - Enabling power: Road Traffic Regulation Act 1984, s. 14 (1) (a). - Issued: 25.06.2014. Made: 02.06.2014. Coming into force: 09.06.2014. Effect: None. Territorial extent & classification: E. Local. - Available at http://www.legislation.gov.uk/uksi/2014/1632/contents/made Non-print

The A45 Trunk Road (Rushden, Northamptonshire) (Slip Road) (Temporary Prohibition of Traffic) Order 2014 No. 2014/727. - Enabling power: Road Traffic Regulation Act 1984, s. 14 (1) (a). - Issued: 07.03.2014. Made: 26.02.2014. Coming into force: 05.03.2014. Effect: None. Territorial extent & classification: E. Local. - Available at http://www.legislation.gov.uk/uksi/2014/727/contents/made Non-print

The A45 Trunk Road (Ryton-On-Dunsmore, Warwickshire) (Temporary Prohibition of Traffic) Order 2014 No. 2014/221. - Enabling power: Road Traffic Regulation Act 1984, s. 14 (1) (a). - Issued: 07.02.2014. Made: 20.01.2014. Coming into force: 27.01.2014. Effect: None. Territorial extent & classification: E. Local. - Available at http://www.legislation.gov.uk/uksi/2014/221/contents/made Non-print

The A45 Trunk Road (South of Irthlingborough, Northamptonshire) (Temporary Restriction and Prohibition of Traffic) Order 2014 No. 2014/2062. - Enabling power: Road Traffic Regulation Act 1984, s. 14 (1) (a). - Issued: 05.08.2014. Made: 07.07.2014. Coming into force: 14.07.2014. Effect: None. Territorial extent & classification: E. Local. - Available at http://www.legislation.gov.uk/uksi/2014/2062/contents/made Non-print

The A45 Trunk Road (South of Wellingborough, Northamptonshire) (Temporary Prohibition of Traffic) Order 2014 No. 2014/645. - Enabling power: Road Traffic Regulation Act 1984, s. 14 (1) (a). - Issued: 06.03.2014. Made: 17.02.2014. Coming into force: 24.02.2014. Effect: None. Territorial extent & classification: E. Local. - Available at http://www.legislation.gov.uk/uksi/2014/645/contents/made Non-print

The A45 Trunk Road (Stanwick to Thrapston, Northamptonshire) (Temporary Prohibition of Traffic) Order 2014 No. 2014/2061. - Enabling power: Road Traffic Regulation Act 1984, s. 14 (1) (a). - Issued: 05.08.2014. Made: 07.07.2014. Coming into force: 14.07.2014. Effect: None. Territorial extent & classification: E. Local. - Available at http://www.legislation.gov.uk/uksi/2014/2061/contents/made Non-print

The A45 Trunk Road (Stonebridge Highway, Coventry) (Temporary Prohibition of Traffic) Order 2014 No. 2014/338. - Enabling power: Road Traffic Regulation Act 1984, ss. 14 (1) (a), 15 (2). - Issued: 19.02.2014. Made: 24.01.2014. Coming into force: 31.01.2014. Effect: None. Territorial extent & classification: E. Local. - Available at http://www.legislation.gov.uk/uksi/2014/338/contents/made Non-print

The A45 Trunk Road (Stretton-On-Dunsmore, Warwickshire) (Temporary Prohibition of Traffic) Order 2014 No. 2014/1266. - Enabling power: Road Traffic Regulation Act 1984, s. 14 (1) (a). - Issued: 19.05.2014. Made: 25.04.2014. Coming into force: 02.05.2014. Effect: None. Territorial extent & classification: E. Local. - Available at http://www.legislation.gov.uk/uksi/2014/1266/contents/made Non-print

The A45 Trunk Road (Tollbar End to Thurlaston, Warwickshire) (Temporary Prohibition of Traffic) Order 2014 No. 2014/3457. - Enabling power: Road Traffic Regulation Act 1984, s. 14 (1) (a). - Issued: 02.01.2015. Made: 22.12.2014. Coming into force: 29.12.2014. Effect: None. Territorial extent & classification: E. Local. - Available at http://www.legislation.gov.uk/uksi/2014/3457/contents/made Non-print

The A45 Trunk Road (Wellingborough, Northamptonshire) (Temporary Restriction and Prohibition of Traffic) Order 2014 No. 2014/2241. - Enabling power: Road Traffic Regulation Act 1984, s. 14 (1) (a). - Issued: 27.08.2014. Made: 04.08.2014. Coming into force: 11.08.2014. Effect: None. Territorial extent & classification: E. Local. - Available at http://www.legislation.gov.uk/uksi/2014/2241/contents/made Non-print

The A45 Trunk Road (Wootton, Northamptonshire) (Temporary Prohibition of Traffic) Order 2014 No. 2014/2242. - Enabling power: Road Traffic Regulation Act 1984, s. 14 (1) (a). - Issued: 27.08.2014. Made: 04.08.2014. Coming into force: 11.08.2014. Effect: None. Territorial extent & classification: E. Local. - Available at http://www.legislation.gov.uk/uksi/2014/2242/contents/made Non-print

The A45 Trunk Road (Wootton to Weston Favell, Northampton) (Temporary Prohibition of Traffic) Order 2014 No. 2014/2851. - Enabling power: Road Traffic Regulation Act 1984, s. 14 (1) (a). - Issued: 24.10.2014. Made: 03.10.2014. Coming into force: 10.10.2014. Effect: None. Territorial extent & classification: E. Local. - Available at http://www.legislation.gov.uk/uksi/2014/2851/contents/made Non-print

The A46 and A1 Trunk Roads (Newark-On-Trent, Nottinghamshire) (Temporary Prohibition of Traffic) Order 2014 No. 2014/3496. - Enabling power: Road Traffic Regulation Act 1984, s. 14 (1) (a). - Issued: 20.01.2015. Made: 17.11.2015. Coming into force: 24.11.2015. Effect: None. Territorial extent & classification: E. Local. - Available at http://www.legislation.gov.uk/uksi/2015/3496/contents/made Non-print

The A46 Trunk Road (Alcester, Warwickshire) (Temporary Prohibition of Traffic) Order 2014 No. 2014/1585. - Enabling power: Road Traffic Regulation Act 1984, s. 14 (1) (a). - Issued: 19.06.2014. Made: 14.05.2014. Coming into force: 21.05.2014. Effect: None. Territorial extent & classification: E. Local. - Available at http://www.legislation.gov.uk/uksi/2014/1585/contents/made Non-print

The A46 Trunk Road (Ashchurch, Gloucestershire) (Temporary Prohibition of Traffic) Order 2014 No. 2014/1430. - Enabling power: Road Traffic Regulation Act 1984, s. 14 (1) (a). - Issued: 03.06.2014. Made: 13.05.2014. Coming into force: 20.05.2014. Effect: None. Territorial extent & classification: E. Local. - Available at http://www.legislation.gov.uk/uksi/2014/1430/contents/made Non-print

The A46 Trunk Road (Bishopton, Warwickshire) (Temporary Prohibition of Traffic) Order 2014 No. 2014/1543. - Enabling power: Road Traffic Regulation Act 1984, s. 14 (1) (a). - Issued: 13.06.2014. Made: 27.05.2014. Coming into force: 03.06.2014. Effect: None. Territorial extent & classification: E. Local. - Available at http://www.legislation.gov.uk/uksi/2014/1543/contents/made Non-print

The A46 Trunk Road (Cold Ashton Roundabout to London Road Junction, Bath) (Temporary Prohibition of Traffic) Order 2014 No. 2014/245. - Enabling power: Road Traffic Regulation Act 1984, s. 14 (1) (a). - Issued: 10.02.2014. Made: 04.02.2014. Coming into force: 08.02.2014. Effect: None. Territorial extent & classification: E. Local. - Available at http://www.legislation.gov.uk/uksi/2014/245/contents/made Non-print

The A46 Trunk Road (Cossington, Leicestershire) (Temporary Restriction and Prohibition of Traffic) (Slip Road) Order 2014 No. 2014/320. - Enabling power: Road Traffic Regulation Act 1984, s. 14 (1) (a). - Issued: 18.02.2014. Made: 31.01.2014. Coming into force: 07.02.2014. Effect: None. Territorial extent & classification: E. Local. - Available at http://www.legislation.gov.uk/uksi/2014/320/contents/made Non-print

ROAD TRAFFIC: TRAFFIC REGULATION

The A46 Trunk Road (Cossington to Widmerpool) (Temporary Restriction and Prohibition of Traffic) Order 2014 No. 2014/628. - Enabling power: Road Traffic Regulation Act 1984, s. 14 (1) (a). - Issued: 05.03.2014. Made: 17.02.2014. Coming into force: 24.02.2014. Effect: None. Territorial extent & classification: E. Local. - Available at http://www.legislation.gov.uk/uksi/2014/628/contents/made Non-print

The A46 Trunk Road (Farndon, Nottinghamshire) (Temporary Restriction of Traffic) Order 2014 No. 2014/1025. - Enabling power: Road Traffic Regulation Act 1984, s. 14 (1) (a). - Issued: 17.04.2014. Made: 03.03.2014. Coming into force: 10.03.2014. Effect: None. Territorial extent & classification: E. Local. - Available at http://www.legislation.gov.uk/uksi/2014/1025/contents/made Non-print

The A46 Trunk Road (Glenfield, Leicestershire) (Temporary Prohibition of Traffic) Order 2014 No. 2014/464. - Enabling power: Road Traffic Regulation Act 1984, s. 14 (1) (a). - Issued: 04.03.2014. Made: 17.02.2014. Coming into force: 24.02.2014. Effect: None. Territorial extent & classification: E. Local. - Available at http://www.legislation.gov.uk/uksi/2014/464/contents/made Non-print

The A46 Trunk Road (Grafton, Worcestershire) (Temporary Prohibition of Traffic) Order 2014 No. 2014/1409. - Enabling power: Road Traffic Regulation Act 1984, s. 14 (1) (a). - Issued: 04.06.2014. Made: 06.05.2014. Coming into force: 13.05.2014. Effect: None. Territorial extent & classification: E. Local. - Available at http://www.legislation.gov.uk/uksi/2014/1409/contents/made Non-print

The A46 Trunk Road (Groby, Leicestershire) (Temporary Prohibition of Traffic) Order 2014 No. 2014/2132. - Enabling power: Road Traffic Regulation Act 1984, s. 14 (1) (a). - Issued: 12.08.2014. Made: 21.07.2014. Coming into force: 28.07.2014. Effect: None. Territorial extent & classification: E. Local. - Available at http://www.legislation.gov.uk/uksi/2014/2132/contents/made Non-print

The A46 Trunk Road (Harvington, Worcestershire) (Temporary Prohibition of Traffic) Order 2014 No. 2014/1404. - Enabling power: Road Traffic Regulation Act 1984, s. 14 (1) (a). - Issued: 04.06.2014. Made: 06.05.2014. Coming into force: 12.05.2014. Effect: None. Territorial extent & classification: E. Local. - Available at http://www.legislation.gov.uk/uksi/2014/1404/contents/made Non-print

The A46 Trunk Road (Leek Wootton, Warwickshire) (Slip Roads) (Temporary Prohibition of Traffic) Order 2014 No. 2014/1542. - Enabling power: Road Traffic Regulation Act 1984, s. 14 (1) (b). - Issued: 13.06.2014. Made: 27.05.2014. Coming into force: 03.06.2014. Effect: None. Territorial extent & classification: E. Local. - Available at http://www.legislation.gov.uk/uksi/2014/1542/contents/made Non-print

The A46 Trunk Road (M4 Junction 18 to Cold Ashton Roundabout) (Temporary Prohibition of Traffic) Order 2014 No. 2014/804. - Enabling power: Road Traffic Regulation Act 1984, s. 14 (1) (a). - Issued: 26.03.2014. Made: 11.03.2014. Coming into force: 15.03.2014. Effect: None. Territorial extent & classification: E. Local. - Available at http://www.legislation.gov.uk/uksi/2014/804/contents/made Non-print

The A46 Trunk Road (near Baginton, Warwickshire) (Temporary Prohibition of Traffic) Order 2014 No. 2014/2618. - Enabling power: Road Traffic Regulation Act 1984, s. 14 (1) (a). - Issued: 30.09.2014. Made: 12.09.2014. Coming into force: 19.09.2014. Effect: None. Territorial extent & classification: E. Local. - Available at http://www.legislation.gov.uk/uksi/2014/2618/contents/made Non-print

The A46 Trunk Road (Northeast of Kenilworth, Warwickshire) (Temporary Prohibition of Traffic) Order 2014 No. 2014/2592. - Enabling power: Road Traffic Regulation Act 1984, s. 14 (1) (a). - Issued: 26.09.2014. Made: 06.05.2014. Coming into force: 13.05.2014. Effect: None. Territorial extent & classification: E. Local. - Available at http://www.legislation.gov.uk/uksi/2014/2592/contents/made Non-print

The A46 Trunk Road (Ratcliffe-On-The-Wreake, Leicestershire) (Slip Road) (Temporary Prohibition of Traffic) Order 2014 No. 2014/624. - Enabling power: Road Traffic Regulation Act 1984, s. 14 (1) (a). - Issued: 05.03.2014. Made: 17.02.2014. Coming into force: 24.02.2014. Effect: None. Territorial extent & classification: E. Local. - Available at http://www.legislation.gov.uk/uksi/2014/624/contents/made Non-print

The A46 Trunk Road (Salford Priors to Oversley) (Temporary Prohibition of Traffic) Order 2014 No. 2014/2737. - Enabling power: Road Traffic Regulation Act 1984, s. 14 (1) (a). - Issued: 14.10.2014. Made: 22.09.2014. Coming into force: 29.10.2014. Effect: None. Territorial extent & classification: E. Local. - Available at http://www.legislation.gov.uk/uksi/2014/2737/contents/made Non-print

The A46 Trunk Road (Salford Priors, Worcestershire) (Temporary Prohibition of Traffic) Order 2014 No. 2014/1246. - Enabling power: Road Traffic Regulation Act 1984, s. 14 (1) (a). - Issued: 16.05.2014. Made: 28.04.2014. Coming into force: 05.05.2014. Effect: None. Territorial extent & classification: E. Local. - Available at http://www.legislation.gov.uk/uksi/2014/1246/contents/made Non-print

The A46 Trunk Road (Sedgeberrow, Worcestershire) (Temporary Restriction and Prohibition of Traffic) Order 2014 No. 2014/1009. - Enabling power: Road Traffic Regulation Act 1984, s. 14 (1) (a). - Issued: 16.04.2014. Made: 21.03.2014. Coming into force: 28.03.2014. Effect: None. Territorial extent & classification: E. Local. - Available at http://www.legislation.gov.uk/uksi/2014/1009/contents/made Non-print

The A46 Trunk Road (Six Hills, Leicestershire) (Slip Roads) (Temporary Prohibition of Traffic) Order 2014 No. 2014/626. - Enabling power: Road Traffic Regulation Act 1984, s. 14 (1) (a). - Issued: 05.03.2014. Made: 17.02.2014. Coming into force: 24.02.2014. Effect: None. Territorial extent & classification: E. Local. - Available at http://www.legislation.gov.uk/uksi/2014/626/contents/made Non-print

The A46 Trunk Road (Skellingthorpe, Lincolnshire) (Temporary Restriction and Prohibition of Traffic) Order 2014 No. 2014/1538. - Enabling power: Road Traffic Regulation Act 1984, s. 14 (1) (a). - Issued: 13.06.2014. Made: 23.05.2014. Coming into force: 30.05.2014. Effect: None. Territorial extent & classification: E. Local. - Available at http://www.legislation.gov.uk/uksi/2014/1538/contents/made Non-print

The A46 Trunk Road (Snitterfield, Warwickshire) (Temporary Restriction and Prohibition of Traffic) Order 2014 No. 2014/1248. - Enabling power: Road Traffic Regulation Act 1984, s. 14 (1) (a). - Issued: 16.05.2014. Made: 28.04.2014. Coming into force: 05.05.2014. Effect: None. Territorial extent & classification: E. Local. - Available at http://www.legislation.gov.uk/uksi/2014/1248/contents/made Non-print

The A46 Trunk Road (Stoneleigh, Warwickshire) (Temporary Prohibition of Traffic) Order 2014 No. 2014/808. - Enabling power: Road Traffic Regulation Act 1984, s. 14 (1) (a). - Issued: 26.03.2014. Made: 10.03.2014. Coming into force: 17.03.2014. Effect: None. Territorial extent & classification: E. Local. - Available at http://www.legislation.gov.uk/uksi/2014/808/contents/made Non-print

The A46 Trunk Road (Teddington - Evesham) (Temporary Prohibition of Traffic) Order 2014 No. 2014/3149. - Enabling power: Road Traffic Regulation Act 1984, s. 14 (1) (a). - Issued: 24.11.2014. Made: 14.11.2014. Coming into force: 21.11.204. Effect: None. Territorial extent & classification: E. Local. - Available at http://www.legislation.gov.uk/uksi/2014/3149/contents/made Non-print

The A46 Trunk Road (Wanlip, Leicestershire) (Temporary Prohibition of Traffic) (No.2) Order 2014 No. 2014/3143. - Enabling power: Road Traffic Regulation Act 1984, s. 14 (1) (a). - Issued: 24.11.2014. Made: 10.11.2014. Coming into force: 17.11.204. Effect: None. Territorial extent & classification: E. Local. - Available at http://www.legislation.gov.uk/uksi/2014/3143/contents/made Non-print

The A46 Trunk Road (Wanlip, Leicestershire) (Temporary Prohibition of Traffic) Order 2014 No. 2014/181. - Enabling power: Road Traffic Regulation Act 1984, s. 14 (1) (a). - Issued: 03.02.2014. Made: 20.01.2014. Coming into force: 27.01.2014. Effect: None. Territorial extent & classification: E. Local. - Available at http://www.legislation.gov.uk/uksi/2014/181/contents/made Non-print

The A46 Trunk Road (Warwick Bypass) (Slip Roads) (Temporary Prohibition of Traffic) Order 2014 No. 2014/2025. - Enabling power: Road Traffic Regulation Act 1984, s. 14 (1) (a). - Issued: 31.07.2014. Made: 20.06.2014. Coming into force: 27.06.2014. Effect: None. Territorial extent & classification: E. Local. - Available at http://www.legislation.gov.uk/uksi/2014/2025/contents/made Non-print

ROAD TRAFFIC: TRAFFIC REGULATION

The A46 Trunk Road (Warwick Bypass) (Slip Road) (Temporary Prohibition of Traffic) Order 2014 No. 2014/188. - Enabling power: Road Traffic Regulation Act 1984, s. 14 (1) (a). - Issued: 04.02.2014. Made: 21.01.2014. Coming into force: 28.01.2014. Effect: None. Territorial extent & classification: E. Local. - Available at http://www.legislation.gov.uk/uksi/2014/188/contents/made Non-print

The A46 Trunk Road (Warwick Bypass) (Temporary Prohibition of Traffic) Order 2014 No. 2014/1527. - Enabling power: Road Traffic Regulation Act 1984, s. 14 (1) (a). - Issued: 11.06.2014. Made: 27.05.2014. Coming into force: 03.06.2014. Effect: None. Territorial extent & classification: E. Local. - Available at http://www.legislation.gov.uk/uksi/2014/1527/contents/made Non-print

The A46 Trunk Road (Warwick Bypass, Warwickshire) (Temporary Restriction and Prohibition of Traffic) Order 2014 No. 2014/1023. - Enabling power: Road Traffic Regulation Act 1984, s. 14 (1) (a). - Issued: 17.04.2014. Made: 21.03.2014. Coming into force: 28.03.2014. Effect: None. Territorial extent & classification: E. Local. - Available at http://www.legislation.gov.uk/uksi/2014/1023/contents/made Non-print

The A46 Trunk Road (West of Leicester, Leicestershire) (Temporary Prohibition of Traffic) Order 2014 No. 2014/1483. - Enabling power: Road Traffic Regulation Act 1984, s. 14 (1) (a). - Issued: 10.06.2014. Made: 19.05.2014. Coming into force: 26.05.2014. Effect: None. Territorial extent & classification: E. Local. - Available at http://www.legislation.gov.uk/uksi/2014/1483/contents/made Non-print

The A46 Trunk Road (Widmerpool, Nottinghamshire) (Temporary Prohibition of Traffic) (No.2) Order 2014 No. 2014/3379. - Enabling power: Road Traffic Regulation Act 1984, s. 14 (1) (a). - Issued: 28.11.2014. Made: 17.11.2014. Coming into force: 26.11.2014. Effect: None. Territorial extent & classification: E. Local. - Available at http://www.legislation.gov.uk/uksi/2014/3379/contents/made Non-print

The A46 Trunk Road (Widmerpool, Nottinghamshire) (Temporary Prohibition of Traffic) Order 2014 No. 2014/2245. - Enabling power: Road Traffic Regulation Act 1984, s. 14 (1) (a). - Issued: 27.08.2014. Made: 04.08.2014. Coming into force: 11.08.2014. Effect: None. Territorial extent & classification: E. Local. - Available at http://www.legislation.gov.uk/uksi/2014/2245/contents/made Non-print

The A46 Trunk Road (Widmerpool, Nottinghamshire) (Temporary Prohibition of Traffic) (Slip Road) Order 2014 No. 2014/644. - Enabling power: Road Traffic Regulation Act 1984, s. 14 (1) (a). - Issued: 06.03.2014. Made: 17.02.2014. Coming into force: 24.02.2014. Effect: None. Territorial extent & classification: E. Local. - Available at http://www.legislation.gov.uk/uksi/2014/644/contents/made Non-print

The A46 Trunk Road (Widmerpool - Six Hills) (Temporary Prohibition of Traffic) (No.2) Order 2014 No. 2014/3009. - Enabling power: Road Traffic Regulation Act 1984, s. 14 (1) (a). - Issued: 14.11.2014. Made: 03.11.2014. Coming into force: 10.11.2014. Effect: None. Territorial extent & classification: E. Local. - Available at http://www.legislation.gov.uk/uksi/2014/3009/contents/made Non-print

The A46 Trunk Road (Widmerpool - Six Hills) (Temporary Prohibition of Traffic) Order 2014 No. 2014/2490. - Enabling power: Road Traffic Regulation Act 1984, s. 14 (1) (a). - Issued: 15.09.2014. Made: 08.09.2014. Coming into force: 15.09.2014. Effect: None. Territorial extent & classification: E. Local. - Available at http://www.legislation.gov.uk/uksi/2014/2490/contents/made Non-print

The A46 Trunk Road (Winthorpe, Nottinghamshire) (Temporary Restriction and Prohibition of Traffic) Order 2014 No. 2014/1539. - Enabling power: Road Traffic Regulation Act 1984, s. 14 (1) (a). - Issued: 13.06.2014. Made: 23.05.2014. Coming into force: 30.05.2014. Effect: None. Territorial extent & classification: E. Local. - Available at http://www.legislation.gov.uk/uksi/2014/1539/contents/made Non-print

The A47 and A10 Trunk Roads (Hardwick Roundabout to New Road, Kings Lynn, Norfolk) (Temporary Prohibition of Traffic) Order 2014 No. 2014/2482. - Enabling power: Road Traffic Regulation Act 1984, s. 14 (1) (a). - Issued: 11.09.2014. Made: 08.09.2014. Coming into force: 15.09.2014. Effect: None. Territorial extent & classification: E. Local. - Available at http://www.legislation.gov.uk/uksi/2014/2482/contents/made Non-print

The A47 Trunk Road (A140 Ipswich Road Interchange to A146 Trowse Interchange, Norwich, Norfolk) (Temporary Prohibition of Traffic) Order 2014 No. 2014/2661. - Enabling power: Road Traffic Regulation Act 1984, s. 14 (1) (a). - Issued: 03.10.2014. Made: 22.09.2014. Coming into force: 29.09.2014. Effect: None. Territorial extent & classification: E. Local. - Available at http://www.legislation.gov.uk/uksi/2014/2661/contents/made Non-print

The A47 Trunk Road and the A1 Trunk Road (Wansford to Sutton, City of Peterborough) (Temporary Prohibition of Traffic) Order 2014 No. 2014/3532. - Enabling power: Road Traffic Regulation Act 1984, s. 14 (1) (a). - Issued: 23.01.2015. Made: 29.12.2014. Coming into force: 05.01.2015. Effect: None. Territorial extent & classification: E. Local. - Available at http://www.legislation.gov.uk/uksi/2014/3532/contents/made Non-print

The A47 Trunk Road (Brundall to Acle, Norfolk) (Temporary Prohibition of Traffic) Order 2014 No. 2014/2910. - Enabling power: Road Traffic Regulation Act 1984, s. 14 (1) (a). - Issued: 24.10.2014. Made: 20.10.2014. Coming into force: 27.10.2014. Effect: None. Territorial extent & classification: E. Local. - Available at http://www.legislation.gov.uk/uksi/2014/2910/contents/made Non-print

The A47 Trunk Road (Dogsthorpe Roundabout, City of Peterborough to Guyhirn Roundabout, Cambridgeshire) (Temporary Prohibition of Traffic) Order 2014 No. 2014/3004. - Enabling power: Road Traffic Regulation Act 1984, s. 14 (1) (a). - Issued: 12.11.2014. Made: 03.11.2014. Coming into force: 10.11.2014. Effect: None. Territorial extent & classification: E. Local. - Available at http://www.legislation.gov.uk/uksi/2014/3004/contents/made Non-print

The A47 Trunk Road (Kings Lynn to Swaffham, Norfolk) (Temporary Prohibition of Traffic) Order 2014 No. 2014/690. - Enabling power: Road Traffic Regulation Act 1984, s. 14 (1) (a). - Issued: 07.03.2014. Made: 24.02.2014. Coming into force: 03.03.2014. Effect: None. Territorial extent & classification: E. Local. - Available at http://www.legislation.gov.uk/uksi/2014/690/contents/made Non-print

The A47 Trunk Road (Newmarket Road Interchange to Ipswich Road Interchange, Norwich Southern Bypass, Norfolk) (Temporary Prohibition of Traffic) Order 2014 No. 2014/3357. - Enabling power: Road Traffic Regulation Act 1984, s. 14 (1) (a). - Issued: 17.12.2014. Made: 20.10.2014. Coming into force: 27.10.2014. Effect: None. Territorial extent & classification: E. Local. - Available at http://www.legislation.gov.uk/uksi/2014/3357/contents/made Non-print

The A47 Trunk Road (Norwich Southern Bypass, Norfolk) Lay-bys (Temporary Prohibition of Traffic) Order 2014 No. 2014/2484. - Enabling power: Road Traffic Regulation Act 1984, s. 14 (1) (a). - Issued: 11.09.2014. Made: 08.09.2014. Coming into force: 15.09.2014. Effect: None. Territorial extent & classification: E. Local. - Available at http://www.legislation.gov.uk/uksi/2014/2484/contents/made Non-print

The A47 Trunk Road (Peterborough to Wisbech) (Temporary Restriction and Prohibition of Traffic) Order 2014 No. 2014/248. - Enabling power: Road Traffic Regulation Act 1984, s. 14 (1) (a). - Issued: 10.02.2014. Made: 03.02.2014. Coming into force: 10.02.2014. Effect: None. Territorial extent & classification: E. Local. - Available at http://www.legislation.gov.uk/uksi/2014/248/contents/made Non-print

The A47 Trunk Road (Pullover Roundabout to Hardwick Interchange, Kings Lynn Bypass, Norfolk) (Temporary Restriction and Prohibition of Traffic) Order 2014 No. 2014/1476. - Enabling power: Road Traffic Regulation Act 1984, s. 14 (1) (a). - Issued: 05.06.2014. Made: 19.05.2014. Coming into force: 26.05.2014. Effect: None. Territorial extent & classification: E. Local. - Available at http://www.legislation.gov.uk/uksi/2014/1476/contents/made Non-print

The A47 Trunk Road (Soke Parkway, Junction 17 Bretton Way to Junction 18 Lincoln Road, Peterborough) (Temporary Prohibition of Traffic) No. 2014/3180. - Enabling power: Road Traffic Regulation Act 1984, s. 14 (1) (a). - Issued: 24.11.2014. Made: 17.11.2014. Coming into force: 24.11.204. Effect: None. Territorial extent & classification: E. Local. - Available at http://www.legislation.gov.uk/uksi/2014/3180/contents/made Non-print

ROAD TRAFFIC: TRAFFIC REGULATION

The A47 Trunk Road (Swaffham Interchange to Toftwood Interchange, Norfolk) (Temporary Prohibition of Traffic) Order 2014 No. 2014/2597. - Enabling power: Road Traffic Regulation Act 1984, s. 14 (1) (a). - Issued: 26.09.2014. Made: 22.09.2014. Coming into force: 29.09.2014. Effect: None. Territorial extent & classification: E. Local. - Available at http://www.legislation.gov.uk/uksi/2014/2597/contents/made Non-print

The A47 Trunk Road (Swaffham to Great Yarmouth, Norfolk) (Temporary Restriction and Prohibition of Traffic) Order 2014 No. 2014/232. - Enabling power: Road Traffic Regulation Act 1984, s. 14 (1) (a). - Issued: 10.02.2014. Made: 03.02.2014. Coming into force: 10.02.2014. Effect: None. Territorial extent & classification: E. Local. - Available at http://www.legislation.gov.uk/uksi/2014/232/contents/made Non-print

The A47 Trunk Road (Thickthorn Interchange) and A11 Trunk Road (Wymondham to Cringleford, Norfolk) (Temporary Restriction and Prohibition of Traffic) Order 2014 No. 2014/30. - Enabling power: Road Traffic Regulation Act 1984, ss. 14 (1) (a). - Issued: 14.01.2014. Made: 06.01.2014. Coming into force: 13.01.2014. Effect: None. Territorial extent & classification: E. Local. - Available at http://www.legislation.gov.uk/uksi/2014/30/contents/made Non-print

The A47 Trunk Road (Tilney All Saints to Hardwick Interchange, Kings Lynn, Norfolk) (Temporary Prohibition of Traffic) Order 2014 No. 2014/2913. - Enabling power: Road Traffic Regulation Act 1984, s. 14 (1) (a). - Issued: 24.10.2014. Made: 20.10.2014. Coming into force: 27.10.2014. Effect: None. Territorial extent & classification: E. Local. - Available at http://www.legislation.gov.uk/uksi/2014/2913/contents/made Non-print

The A47 Trunk Road (Trowse Interchange to Brundall, Norfolk) (Temporary Restriction and Prohibition of Traffic and Pedestrians) (No.2) Order 2014 No. 2014/2699. - Enabling power: Road Traffic Regulation Act 1984, s. 14 (1) (a), sch. 9 para. 27 (1). - Issued: 10.10.2014. Made: 29.09.2014. Coming into force: 06.10.2014. Effect: None. Territorial extent & classification: E. Local. - Available at http://www.legislation.gov.uk/uksi/2014/2699/contents/made Non-print

The A47 Trunk Road (Trowse Interchange to Brundall, Norfolk) (Temporary Restriction and Prohibition of Traffic and Pedestrians) Order 2014 No. 2014/398. - Enabling power: Road Traffic Regulation Act 1984, ss. 14 (1) (a), 15 (2). - Issued: 27.02.2014. Made: 17.02.2014. Coming into force: 24.02.2014. Effect: None. Territorial extent & classification: E. Local. - Available at http://www.legislation.gov.uk/uksi/2014/398/contents/made Non-print

The A47 Trunk Road (Wendling to Dereham, Norfolk) (Temporary Restriction and Prohibition of Traffic) Order 2014 No. 2014/701. - Enabling power: Road Traffic Regulation Act 1984, s. 14 (1) (a). - Issued: 20.03.2014. Made: 24.02.2014. Coming into force: 03.03.2014. Effect: None. Territorial extent & classification: E. Local. - Available at http://www.legislation.gov.uk/uksi/2014/701/contents/made Non-print

The A49 Trunk Road (Ashford Bowdler, Shropshire) (Temporary Prohibition of Traffic) Order 2014 No. 2014/108. - Enabling power: Road Traffic Regulation Act 1984, s. 14 (1) (a). - Issued: 24.01.2014. Made: 03.01.2014. Coming into force: 10.01.2014. Effect: None. Territorial extent & classification: E. Local. - Available at http://www.legislation.gov.uk/uksi/2014/108/contents/made Non-print

The A49 Trunk Road (Dinmore, Herefordshire) (Temporary Prohibition of Traffic in Layby) Order 2014 No. 2014/620. - Enabling power: Road Traffic Regulation Act 1984, s. 14 (1) (a). - Issued: 06.03.2014. Made: 20.01.2014. Coming into force: 27.01.2014. Effect: None. Territorial extent & classification: E. Local. - Available at http://www.legislation.gov.uk/uksi/2014/620/contents/made Non-print

The A49 Trunk Road (Dorrington, Shropshire) (Temporary Prohibition of Traffic) Order 2014 No. 2014/1089. - Enabling power: Road Traffic Regulation Act 1984, s. 14 (1) (a). - Issued: 25.04.2014. Made: 31.03.2014. Coming into force: 07.04.2014. Effect: None. Territorial extent & classification: E. Local. - Available at http://www.legislation.gov.uk/uksi/2014/1089/contents/made Non-print

The A49 Trunk Road (Hereford, Herefordshire) (Temporary Prohibition of Traffic) Order 2014 No. 2014/1254. - Enabling power: Road Traffic Regulation Act 1984, s. 14 (1) (a). - Issued: 16.05.2014. Made: 28.04.2014. Coming into force: 05.05.2014. Effect: None. Territorial extent & classification: E. Local. - Available at http://www.legislation.gov.uk/uksi/2014/1254/contents/made Non-print

The A49 Trunk Road (Holmer, Herefordshire) (Temporary Prohibition of Traffic) Order 2014 No. 2014/1524. - Enabling power: Road Traffic Regulation Act 1984, s. 14 (1) (a). - Issued: 11.06.2014. Made: 19.05.2014. Coming into force: 26.05.2014. Effect: None. Territorial extent & classification: E. Local. - Available at http://www.legislation.gov.uk/uksi/2014/1524/contents/made Non-print

The A49 Trunk Road (Holmer Road, Hereford) (Prohibition of Waiting) Order 2014 No. 2014/2907. - Enabling power: Road Traffic Regulation Act 1984, ss. 1 (1), 2 (1) (2), 4 (1) (2). - Issued: 27.10.2014. Made: 09.10.2014. Coming into force: 23.10.2014. Effect: None. Territorial extent & classification: E. Local. - Available at http://www.legislation.gov.uk/uksi/2014/2907/contents/made Non-print

The A49 Trunk Road (Kimbolton, Herefordshire) (Temporary Prohibition of Traffic) Order 2014 No. 2014/1523. - Enabling power: Road Traffic Regulation Act 1984, s. 14 (1) (a). - Issued: 11.06.2014. Made: 19.05.2014. Coming into force: 26.05.2014. Effect: None. Territorial extent & classification: E. Local. - Available at http://www.legislation.gov.uk/uksi/2014/1523/contents/made Non-print

The A49 Trunk Road (Leominster, Herefordshire) (Temporary Prohibition of Traffic) (No.2) Order 2014 No. 2014/2732. - Enabling power: Road Traffic Regulation Act 1984, s. 14 (1) (a). - Issued: 14.10.2014. Made: 22.09.2014. Coming into force: 29.09.2014. Effect: None. Territorial extent & classification: E. Local. - Available at http://www.legislation.gov.uk/uksi/2014/2732/contents/made Non-print

The A49 Trunk Road (Leominster, Herefordshire) (Temporary Prohibition of Traffic) Order 2014 No. 2014/312. - Enabling power: Road Traffic Regulation Act 1984, s. 14 (1) (a). - Issued: 17.02.2014. Made: 03.02.2014. Coming into force: 10.02.2014. Effect: None. Territorial extent & classification: E. Local. - Available at http://www.legislation.gov.uk/uksi/2014/312/contents/made Non-print

The A49 Trunk Road (Ludlow - Craven Arms, Shropshire) (Temporary Restriction and Prohibition of Traffic) Order 2014 No. 2014/3148. - Enabling power: Road Traffic Regulation Act 1984, s. 14 (1) (a). - Issued: 24.11.2014. Made: 14.11.2014. Coming into force: 21.11.204. Effect: None. Territorial extent & classification: E. Local. - Available at http://www.legislation.gov.uk/uksi/2014/3148/contents/made Non-print

The A49 Trunk Road (Ludlow, Shropshire) (Temporary Prohibition of Traffic) Order 2014 No. 2014/1244. - Enabling power: Road Traffic Regulation Act 1984, s. 14 (1) (a). - Issued: 16.05.2014. Made: 28.04.2014. Coming into force: 05.05.2014. Effect: None. Territorial extent & classification: E. Local. - Available at http://www.legislation.gov.uk/uksi/2014/1244/contents/made Non-print

The A49 Trunk Road (Ludlow to Woofferton, Shropshire) (Temporary Prohibition of Traffic) Order 2014 No. 2014/2778. - Enabling power: Road Traffic Regulation Act 1984, s. 14 (1) (a). - Issued: 14.10.2014. Made: 03.10.2014. Coming into force: 10.10.2014. Effect: None. Territorial extent & classification: E. Local. - Available at http://www.legislation.gov.uk/uksi/2014/2778/contents/made Non-print

The A49 Trunk Road (Onibury, Shropshire) (Temporary Prohibition of Traffic) Order 2014 No. 2014/1437. - Enabling power: Road Traffic Regulation Act 1984, s. 14 (1) (a). - Issued: 30.05.2014. Made: 14.05.2014. Coming into force: 21.05.2014. Effect: None. Territorial extent & classification: E. Local. - Available at http://www.legislation.gov.uk/uksi/2014/1437/contents/made Non-print

The A49 Trunk Road (Onibury, Shropshire) (Temporary Prohibition of Traffic) Variation Order 2014 No. 2014/1588. - Enabling power: Road Traffic Regulation Act 1984, s. 14 (1) (a). - Issued: 19.06.2014. Made: 02.06.2014. Coming into force: 09.06.2014. Effect: S.I. 2014/1437 varied. Territorial extent & classification: E. Local. - Available at http://www.legislation.gov.uk/uksi/2014/1588/contents/made Non-print

The A49 Trunk Road (Peterstow, Herefordshire) (Temporary Prohibition of Traffic) Order 2014 No. 2014/1631. - Enabling power: Road Traffic Regulation Act 1984, s. 14 (1) (a). - Issued: 25.06.2014. Made: 02.06.2014. Coming into force: 09.06.2014. Effect: None. Territorial extent & classification: E. Local. - Available at http://www.legislation.gov.uk/uksi/2014/1631/contents/made Non-print

ROAD TRAFFIC: TRAFFIC REGULATION

The A49 Trunk Road (Redhill, Herefordshire) (Temporary Prohibition of Traffic) Order 2014 No. 2014/1173. - Enabling power: Road Traffic Regulation Act 1984, s. 14 (1) (a). - Issued: 07.05.2014. Made: 22.04.2014. Coming into force: 29.04.2014. Effect: None. Territorial extent & classification: E. Local. - Available at http://www.legislation.gov.uk/uksi/2014/1173/contents/made Non-print

The A49 Trunk Road (South of Little Stretton, Shropshire) (Temporary Prohibition of Traffic) Order 2014 No. 2014/2790. - Enabling power: Road Traffic Regulation Act 1984, s. 14 (1) (a). - Issued: 14.10.2014. Made: 06.10.2014. Coming into force: 13.10.2014. Effect: None. Territorial extent & classification: E. Local. - Available at http://www.legislation.gov.uk/uksi/2014/2790/contents/made Non-print

The A49 Trunk Road (Stapleton, Shropshire) (Temporary Prohibition of Traffic) Order 2014 No. 2014/1405. - Enabling power: Road Traffic Regulation Act 1984, s. 14 (1) (a). - Issued: 04.06.2014. Made: 06.05.2014. Coming into force: 13.05.2014. Effect: None. Territorial extent & classification: E. Local. - Available at http://www.legislation.gov.uk/uksi/2014/1405/contents/made Non-print

The A49 Trunk Road (Wistantow, Shropshire) (Temporary Restriction and Prohibition of Traffic) Order 2014 No. 2014/314. - Enabling power: Road Traffic Regulation Act 1984, s. 14 (1) (a). - Issued: 17.02.2014. Made: 03.02.2014. Coming into force: 10.02.2014. Effect: None. Territorial extent & classification: E. Local. - Available at http://www.legislation.gov.uk/uksi/2014/314/contents/made Non-print

The A50 and A500 Trunk Roads (Stoke-On-Trent, Staffordshire) (Temporary Prohibition of Traffic) Order 2014 No. 2014/698. - Enabling power: Road Traffic Regulation Act 1984, s. 14 (1) (a). - Issued: 07.03.2014. Made: 24.02.2014. Coming into force: 03.03.2014. Effect: None. Territorial extent & classification: E. Local. - Available at http://www.legislation.gov.uk/uksi/2014/698/contents/made Non-print

The A50 Trunk Road and M1 Motorway (M1 Junction 24a, Leicestershire) (Temporary Prohibition of Traffic) Order 2014 No. 2014/1267. - Enabling power: Road Traffic Regulation Act 1984, s. 14 (1) (a). - Issued: 19.05.2014. Made: 28.04.2014. Coming into force: 05.05.2014. Effect: None. Territorial extent & classification: E. Local. - Available at http://www.legislation.gov.uk/uksi/2014/1267/contents/made Non-print

The A50 Trunk Road (Aston-On-Trent, Derbyshire) (Temporary Prohibition of Traffic) Order 2014 No. 2014/1400. - Enabling power: Road Traffic Regulation Act 1984, s. 14 (1) (a). - Issued: 04.06.2014. Made: 02.05.2014. Coming into force: 09.05.2014. Effect: None. Territorial extent & classification: E. Local. - Available at http://www.legislation.gov.uk/uksi/2014/1400/contents/made Non-print

The A50 Trunk Road (Blythe Bridge Bypass, Staffordshire) (Temporary Prohibition of Traffic) Order 2014 No. 2014/3533. - Enabling power: Road Traffic Regulation Act 1984, s. 14 (1) (a). - Issued: 23.01.2015. Made: 31.12.2014. Coming into force: 07.01.2015. Effect: None. Territorial extent & classification: E. Local. - Available at http://www.legislation.gov.uk/uksi/2014/3533/contents/made Non-print

The A50 Trunk Road (Blythe Bridge, Staffordshire) (Slip Roads) (Temporary Prohibition of Traffic) Order 2014 No. 2014/737. - Enabling power: Road Traffic Regulation Act 1984, s. 14 (1) (a). - Issued: 10.03.2014. Made: 28.02.2014. Coming into force: 07.03.2014. Effect: None. Territorial extent & classification: E. Local. - Available at http://www.legislation.gov.uk/uksi/2014/737/contents/made Non-print

The A50 Trunk Road (Blythe Bridge, Staffordshire) (Temporary Restriction of Traffic) Order 2014 No. 2014/3530. - Enabling power: Road Traffic Regulation Act 1984, s. 14 (1) (a). - Issued: 22.01.2015. Made: 29.12.2015. Coming into force: 05.01.2015. Effect: None. Territorial extent & classification: E. Local. - Available at http://www.legislation.gov.uk/uksi/2014/3550/contents/made Non-print

The A50 Trunk Road (Burnaston, Derbyshire) (Temporary Prohibition of Traffic) Order 2014 No. 2014/1520. - Enabling power: Road Traffic Regulation Act 1984, s. 14 (1) (a). - Issued: 11.06.2014. Made: 19.05.2014. Coming into force: 26.05.2014. Effect: None. Territorial extent & classification: E. Local. - Available at http://www.legislation.gov.uk/uksi/2014/1520/contents/made Non-print

The A50 Trunk Road (Caverswall, Staffordshire) (Temporary Prohibition of Traffic) Order 2014 No. 2014/1256. - Enabling power: Road Traffic Regulation Act 1984, s. 14 (1) (a). - Issued: 16.05.2014. Made: 28.04.2014. Coming into force: 05.05.2014. Effect: None. Territorial extent & classification: E. Local. - Available at http://www.legislation.gov.uk/uksi/2014/1256/contents/made Non-print

The A50 Trunk Road (Doveridge, Derbyshire) (Temporary Prohibition of Traffic) Order 2014 No. 2014/1516. - Enabling power: Road Traffic Regulation Act 1984, s. 14 (1) (a). - Issued: 11.06.2014. Made: 19.05.2014. Coming into force: 26.05.2014. Effect: None. Territorial extent & classification: E. Local. - Available at http://www.legislation.gov.uk/uksi/2014/1516/contents/made Non-print

The A50 Trunk Road (East of Meir, Stoke-On-Trent) (Temporary Prohibition of Traffic) Order 2014 No. 2014/1545. - Enabling power: Road Traffic Regulation Act 1984, s. 14 (1) (a). - Issued: 13.06.2014. Made: 27.05.2014. Coming into force: 03.06.2014. Effect: None. Territorial extent & classification: E. Local. - Available at http://www.legislation.gov.uk/uksi/2014/1545/contents/made Non-print

The A50 Trunk Road (Findern, Derbyshire) (Slip Roads) (Temporary Prohibition of Traffic) Order 2014 No. 2014/1536. - Enabling power: Road Traffic Regulation Act 1984, s. 14 (1) (a). - Issued: 12.06.2014. Made: 19.05.2014. Coming into force: 26.05.2014. Effect: None. Territorial extent & classification: E. Local. - Available at http://www.legislation.gov.uk/uksi/2014/1536/contents/made Non-print

The A50 Trunk Road (Foston, Derbyshire) (Temporary Restriction and Prohibition of Traffic) Order 2014 No. 2014/1480. - Enabling power: Road Traffic Regulation Act 1984, s. 14 (1) (a). - Issued: 10.06.2014. Made: 19.05.2014. Coming into force: 26.05.2014. Effect: None. Territorial extent & classification: E. Local. - Available at http://www.legislation.gov.uk/uksi/2014/1480/contents/made Non-print

The A50 Trunk Road (Lockington, Leicestershire) (Temporary Prohibition of Traffic) Order 2014 No. 2014/637. - Enabling power: Road Traffic Regulation Act 1984, s. 14 (1) (a). - Issued: 05.03.2014. Made: 17.02.2014. Coming into force: 24.02.2014. Effect: None. Territorial extent & classification: E. Local. - Available at http://www.legislation.gov.uk/uksi/2014/637/contents/made Non-print

The A50 Trunk Road (Longton, Staffordshire) (Temporary Prohibition of Traffic) Order 2014 No. 2014/1402. - Enabling power: Road Traffic Regulation Act 1984, s. 14 (1) (a). - Issued: 04.06.2014. Made: 06.05.2014. Coming into force: 12.05.2014. Effect: None. Territorial extent & classification: E. Local. - Available at http://www.legislation.gov.uk/uksi/2014/1402/contents/made Non-print

The A50 Trunk Road (Longton, Stoke-On-Trent) (Temporary Prohibition of Traffic) (No.2) Order 2014 No. 2014/3182. - Enabling power: Road Traffic Regulation Act 1984, s. 14 (1) (a). - Issued: 28.11.2014. Made: 17.11.2014. Coming into force: 24.11.204. Effect: None. Territorial extent & classification: E. Local. - Available at http://www.legislation.gov.uk/uksi/2014/3182/contents/made Non-print

The A50 Trunk Road (Longton, Stoke-On-Trent) (Temporary Prohibition of Traffic) Order 2014 No. 2014/1617. - Enabling power: Road Traffic Regulation Act 1984, s. 14 (1) (a). - Issued: 25.06.2014. Made: 02.06.2014. Coming into force: 09.06.2014. Effect: None. Territorial extent & classification: E. Local. - Available at http://www.legislation.gov.uk/uksi/2014/1617/contents/made Non-print

The A50 Trunk Road (Meir, Staffordshire) (Temporary Prohibition of Traffic) Order 2014 No. 2014/663. - Enabling power: Road Traffic Regulation Act 1984, s. 14 (1) (a). - Issued: 07.03.2014. Made: 21.02.2014. Coming into force: 28.02.2014. Effect: None. Territorial extent & classification: E. Local. - Available at http://www.legislation.gov.uk/uksi/2014/663/contents/made Non-print

The A50 Trunk Road (Meir, Stoke-On-Trent) (Temporary Prohibition of Traffic) (No.2) Order 2014 No. 2014/2905. - Enabling power: Road Traffic Regulation Act 1984, s. 14 (1) (a). - Issued: 27.10.2014. Made: 13.10.2014. Coming into force: 20.10.2014. Effect: None. Territorial extent & classification: E. Local. - Available at http://www.legislation.gov.uk/uksi/2014/2905/contents/made Non-print

The A50 Trunk Road (Meir, Stoke-On-Trent) (Temporary Prohibition of Traffic) Order 2014 No. 2014/2028. - Enabling power: Road Traffic Regulation Act 1984, s. 14 (1) (a). - Issued: 31.07.2014. Made: 27.06.2014. Coming into force: 04.07.2014. Effect: None. Territorial extent & classification: E. Local. - Available at http://www.legislation.gov.uk/uksi/2014/2028/contents/made Non-print

The A50 Trunk Road (Meir to Tean, Staffordshire) (Temporary Prohibition of Traffic) Order 2014 No. 2014/1479. - Enabling power: Road Traffic Regulation Act 1984, s. 14 (1) (a). - Issued: 10.06.2014. Made: 19.05.2014. Coming into force: 26.05.2014. Effect: None. Territorial extent & classification: E. Local. - Available at http://www.legislation.gov.uk/uksi/2014/1479/contents/made Non-print

The A50 Trunk Road (Normacot, Staffordshire) (Temporary Prohibition of Traffic) Order 2014 No. 2014/782. - Enabling power: Road Traffic Regulation Act 1984, s. 14 (1) (a). - Issued: 10.03.2014. Made: 03.03.2014. Coming into force: 10.03.2014. Effect: None. Territorial extent & classification: E. Local. - Available at http://www.legislation.gov.uk/uksi/2014/782/contents/made Non-print

The A50 Trunk Road (North of Uttoxeter, Staffordshire) (Temporary Prohibition of Traffic) Order 2014 No. 2014/1477. - Enabling power: Road Traffic Regulation Act 1984, s. 14 (1) (a). - Issued: 05.06.2014. Made: 20.05.2014. Coming into force: 27.05.2014. Effect: None. Territorial extent & classification: E. Local. - Available at http://www.legislation.gov.uk/uksi/2014/1477/contents/made Non-print

The A50 Trunk Road (North West of Sudbury, Derbyshire) (Temporary Prohibition of Traffic) Order 2014 No. 2014/2623. - Enabling power: Road Traffic Regulation Act 1984, s. 14 (1) (a). - Issued: 30.09.2014. Made: 15.09.2014. Coming into force: 22.09.2014. Effect: None. Territorial extent & classification: E. Local. - Available at http://www.legislation.gov.uk/uksi/2014/2623/contents/made Non-print

The A50 Trunk Road (Sawley, Derbyshire) (Temporary Prohibition of Traffic) Order 2014 No. 2014/1481. - Enabling power: Road Traffic Regulation Act 1984, s. 14 (1) (a). - Issued: 10.06.2014. Made: 19.05.2014. Coming into force: 26.05.2014. Effect: None. Territorial extent & classification: E. Local. - Available at http://www.legislation.gov.uk/uksi/2014/1481/contents/made Non-print

The A50 Trunk Road (Shardlow, Derbyshire) (Slip Roads) (Temporary Prohibition of Traffic) Order 2014 No. 2014/332. - Enabling power: Road Traffic Regulation Act 1984, s. 14 (1) (a). - Issued: 18.02.2014. Made: 24.01.2014. Coming into force: 31.01.2014. Effect: None. Territorial extent & classification: E. Local. - Available at http://www.legislation.gov.uk/uksi/2014/332/contents/made Non-print

The A50 Trunk Road (Sideway, Stoke on Trent) (Temporary Prohibition of Traffic) Order 2014 No. 2014/2986. - Enabling power: Road Traffic Regulation Act 1984, s. 14 (1) (a). - Issued: 13.11.2014. Made: 28.10.2014. Coming into force: 04.11.2014. Effect: None. Territorial extent & classification: E. Local. - Available at http://www.legislation.gov.uk/uksi/2014/2986/contents/made Non-print

The A50 Trunk Road (South of Derby, Derbyshire) (Temporary Prohibition of Traffic) Order 2014 No. 2014/2029. - Enabling power: Road Traffic Regulation Act 1984, s. 14 (1) (a). - Issued: 01.08.2014. Made: 27.06.2014. Coming into force: 04.07.2014. Effect: None. Territorial extent & classification: E. Local. - Available at http://www.legislation.gov.uk/uksi/2014/2029/contents/made Non-print

The A50 Trunk Road (Southwest of Derby, Derbyshire) (Temporary Prohibition of Traffic) Order 2014 No. 2014/796. - Enabling power: Road Traffic Regulation Act 1984, s. 14 (1) (a). - Issued: 26.03.2014. Made: 07.03.2014. Coming into force: 14.03.2014. Effect: None. Territorial extent & classification: E. Local. - Available at http://www.legislation.gov.uk/uksi/2014/796/contents/made Non-print

The A50 Trunk Road (Sudbury, Derbyshire) (Temporary Prohibition of Traffic) Order 2014 No. 2014/3443. - Enabling power: Road Traffic Regulation Act 1984, s. 14 (1) (a). - Issued: 17.12.2014. Made: 12.12.2014. Coming into force: 19.12.2014. Effect: None. Territorial extent & classification: E. Local. - Available at http://www.legislation.gov.uk/uksi/2014/3443/contents/made Non-print

The A50 Trunk Road (Tean, Staffordshire) (Temporary Prohibition of Traffic) Order 2014 No. 2014/2129. - Enabling power: Road Traffic Regulation Act 1984, s. 14 (1) (a). - Issued: 12.08.2014. Made: 18.07.2014. Coming into force: 25.07.2014. Effect: None. Territorial extent & classification: E. Local. - Available at http://www.legislation.gov.uk/uksi/2014/2129/contents/made Non-print

The A50 Trunk Road (Thulston, Derbyshire) (Temporary Restriction and Prohibition of Traffic) Order 2014 No. 2014/662. - Enabling power: Road Traffic Regulation Act 1984, s. 14 (1) (a). - Issued: 07.03.2014. Made: 21.02.2014. Coming into force: 28.02.2014. Effect: None. Territorial extent & classification: E. Local. - Available at http://www.legislation.gov.uk/uksi/2014/662/contents/made Non-print

The A50 Trunk Road (Uttoxeter, Staffordshire) (Temporary Prohibition of Traffic) Order 2014 No. 2014/1086. - Enabling power: Road Traffic Regulation Act 1984, s. 14 (1) (a). - Issued: 25.04.2014. Made: 28.03.2014. Coming into force: 04.04.2014. Effect: None. Territorial extent & classification: E. Local. - Available at http://www.legislation.gov.uk/uksi/2014/1086/contents/made Non-print

The A50 Trunk Road (Uttoxeter to Sudbury) (Temporary Prohibition of Traffic) Order 2014 No. 2014/2082. - Enabling power: Road Traffic Regulation Act 1984, s. 14 (1) (a). - Issued: 07.08.2014. Made: 11.07.2014. Coming into force: 18.07.2014. Effect: None. Territorial extent & classification: E. Local. - Available at http://www.legislation.gov.uk/uksi/2014/2082/contents/made Non-print

The A52 and A5111 Trunk Roads (Spondon to Sandiacre, Derbyshire) (Temporary Prohibition of Traffic) Order 2014 No. 2014/3359. - Enabling power: Road Traffic Regulation Act 1984, s. 14 (1) (a). - Issued: 28.11.2014. Made: 17.11.2014. Coming into force: 24.11.2014. Effect: None. Territorial extent & classification: E. Local. - Available at http://www.legislation.gov.uk/uksi/2014/3359/contents/made Non-print

The A52 Trunk Road and M1 Motorway (Borrowash, Derbyshire) (Temporary Restriction and Prohibition of Traffic) Order 2014 No. 2014/1074. - Enabling power: Road Traffic Regulation Act 1984, s. 14 (1) (a). - Issued: 28.04.2014. Made: 08.04.2014. Coming into force: 15.04.2014. Effect: None. Territorial extent & classification: E. Local. - Available at http://www.legislation.gov.uk/uksi/2014/1074/contents/made Non-print

The A52 Trunk Road and M1 Motorway (Near Borrowash, Derbyshire) (Temporary Restriction and Prohibition of Traffic) (Slip Road) Order 2014 No. 2014/686. - Enabling power: Road Traffic Regulation Act 1984, s. 14 (1) (a). - Issued: 20.03.2014. Made: 17.02.2014. Coming into force: 24.02.2014. Effect: None. Territorial extent & classification: E. Local. - Available at http://www.legislation.gov.uk/uksi/2014/686/contents/made Non-print

The A52 Trunk Road (Bingham - Barrowby) (Temporary Prohibition of Traffic) (No.2) Order 2014 No. 2014/3501. - Enabling power: Road Traffic Regulation Act 1984, s. 14 (1) (a). - Issued: 21.01.2014. Made: 17.11.2014. Coming into force: 24.11.2014. Effect: None. Territorial extent & classification: E. Local. - Available at http://www.legislation.gov.uk/uksi/2014/3501/contents/made Non-print

The A52 Trunk Road (Bingham - Barrowby) (Temporary Prohibition of Traffic) Order 2014 No. 2014/2149. - Enabling power: Road Traffic Regulation Act 1984, s. 14 (1) (a). - Issued: 12.08.2014. Made: 29.07.2014. Coming into force: 05.08.2014. Effect: None. Territorial extent & classification: E. Local. - Available at http://www.legislation.gov.uk/uksi/2014/2149/contents/made Non-print

The A52 Trunk Road (Bingham, Nottinghamshire) (Temporary Restriction and Prohibition of Traffic) Order 2014 No. 2014/2728. - Enabling power: Road Traffic Regulation Act 1984, s. 14 (1) (a). - Issued: 13.10.2014. Made: 22.09.2014. Coming into force: 29.09.2014. Effect: None. Territorial extent & classification: E. Local. - Available at http://www.legislation.gov.uk/uksi/2014/2728/contents/made Non-print

The A52 Trunk Road (Bramcote, Nottinghamshire) (Temporary Prohibition of Traffic) Order 2014 No. 2014/3528. - Enabling power: Road Traffic Regulation Act 1984, s. 14 (1) (a). - Issued: 22.01.2015. Made: 29.12.2014. Coming into force: 05.01.2015. Effect: None. Territorial extent & classification: E. Local. - Available at http://www.legislation.gov.uk/uksi/2014/3528/contents/made Non-print

ROAD TRAFFIC: TRAFFIC REGULATION

The A52 Trunk Road (Edwalton - Gamston, Nottinghamshire) (Temporary Prohibition of Traffic) Order 2014 No. 2014/2906. - Enabling power: Road Traffic Regulation Act 1984, s. 14 (1) (a). - Issued: 27.10.2014. Made: 13.10.2014. Coming into force: 20.10.2014. Effect: None. Territorial extent & classification: E. Local. - Available at http://www.legislation.gov.uk/uksi/2014/2906/contents/made Non-print

The A52 Trunk Road (Edwalton, Nottinghamshire) (Temporary Prohibition of Traffic) Order 2014 No. 2014/1075. - Enabling power: Road Traffic Regulation Act 1984, s. 14 (1) (a). - Issued: 28.04.2014. Made: 08.04.2014. Coming into force: 15.04.2014. Effect: None. Territorial extent & classification: E. Local. - Available at http://www.legislation.gov.uk/uksi/2014/1075/contents/made Non-print

The A52 Trunk Road (Lenton Lane, Nottingham) (Temporary Prohibition of Traffic) Order 2014 No. 2014/3198. - Enabling power: Road Traffic Regulation Act 1984, s. 14 (1) (a). - Issued: 04.12.2014. Made: 10.11.2014. Coming into force: 17.11.2014. Effect: None. Territorial extent & classification: E. Local. - Available at http://www.legislation.gov.uk/uksi/2014/3198/contents/made Non-print

The A52 Trunk Road (Nottingham) (Temporary Prohibition of Traffic) Order 2014 No. 2014/2973. - Enabling power: Road Traffic Regulation Act 1984, s. 14 (1) (a). - Issued: 13.11.2014. Made: 27.10.2014. Coming into force: 03.11.2014. Effect: None. Territorial extent & classification: E. Local. - Available at http://www.legislation.gov.uk/uksi/2014/2973/contents/made Non-print

The A52 Trunk Road (Ockbrook, Derbyshire) (Temporary Prohibition of Traffic) Order 2014 No. 2014/2624. - Enabling power: Road Traffic Regulation Act 1984, s. 14 (1) (a). - Issued: 30.09.2014. Made: 15.09.2014. Coming into force: 22.09.2014. Effect: None. Territorial extent & classification: E. Local. - Available at http://www.legislation.gov.uk/uksi/2014/2624/contents/made Non-print

The A52 Trunk Road (Radcliffe-On-Trent, Nottinghamshire) (Temporary Prohibition of Traffic) Order 2014 No. 2014/2789. - Enabling power: Road Traffic Regulation Act 1984, s. 14 (1) (a). - Issued: 14.10.2014. Made: 06.10.2014. Coming into force: 13.10.2014. Effect: None. Territorial extent & classification: E. Local. - Available at http://www.legislation.gov.uk/uksi/2014/2789/contents/made Non-print

The A52 Trunk Road (Radcliffe-On-Trent to Harlequin, Nottinghamshire) (Temporary Prohibition of Traffic) Order 2014 No. 2014/2940. - Enabling power: Road Traffic Regulation Act 1984, s. 14 (1) (a). - Issued: 27.10.2014. Made: 20.10.2014. Coming into force: 27.10.2014. Effect: None. Territorial extent & classification: E. Local. - Available at http://www.legislation.gov.uk/uksi/2014/2940/contents/made Non-print

The A52 Trunk Road (Southwest of Nottingham) (Temporary Prohibition of Traffic) Order 2014 No. 2014/3529. - Enabling power: Road Traffic Regulation Act 1984, s. 14 (1) (a). - Issued: 22.01.2015. Made: 29.12.2014. Coming into force: 05.01.2015. Effect: None. Territorial extent & classification: E. Local. - Available at http://www.legislation.gov.uk/uksi/2014/3529/contents/made Non-print

The A52 Trunk Road (Spondon, Derbyshire) (Temporary Prohibition of Traffic) Order 2014 No. 2014/1522. - Enabling power: Road Traffic Regulation Act 1984, s. 14 (1) (a). - Issued: 11.06.2014. Made: 19.05.2014. Coming into force: 26.05.2014. Effect: None. Territorial extent & classification: E. Local. - Available at http://www.legislation.gov.uk/uksi/2014/1522/contents/made Non-print

The A52 Trunk Road (Spondon to Long Eaton, Derbyshire) (Temporary Prohibition of Traffic) Order 2014 No. 2014/1699. - Enabling power: Road Traffic Regulation Act 1984, s. 14 (1) (a). - Issued: 03.07.2014. Made: 09.06.2014. Coming into force: 16.06.2014. Effect: None. Territorial extent & classification: E. Local. - Available at http://www.legislation.gov.uk/uksi/2014/1699/contents/made Non-print

The A52 Trunk Road (Stapleford to Bramcote, Nottinghamshire) (Temporary Restriction and Prohibition of Traffic) Order 2014 No. 2014/3012. - Enabling power: Road Traffic Regulation Act 1984, s. 14 (1) (a). - Issued: 14.11.2014. Made: 03.11.2014. Coming into force: 10.11.2014. Effect: None. Territorial extent & classification: E. Local. - Available at http://www.legislation.gov.uk/uksi/2014/3012/contents/made Non-print

The A52 Trunk Road (West Bridgford, Nottinghamshire) (Layby) (Temporary Prohibition of Traffic) Order 2014 No. 2014/2250. - Enabling power: Road Traffic Regulation Act 1984, s. 14 (1) (a). - Issued: 27.08.2014. Made: 12.08.2014. Coming into force: 19.08.2014. Effect: None. Territorial extent & classification: E. Local. - Available at http://www.legislation.gov.uk/uksi/2014/2250/contents/made Non-print

The A52 Trunk Road (Wheatcroft, Nottinghamshire) (Temporary Prohibition of Traffic) Order 2014 No. 2014/120. - Enabling power: Road Traffic Regulation Act 1984, s. 14 (1) (a). - Issued: 24.01.2014. Made: 17.01.2014. Coming into force: 24.01.2014. Effect: None. Territorial extent & classification: E. Local. - Available at http://www.legislation.gov.uk/uksi/2014/120/contents/made Non-print

The A52 Trunk Road (Wilford, Nottinghamshire) (Slip Road) (Temporary Prohibition of Traffic) Order 2014 No. 2014/643. - Enabling power: Road Traffic Regulation Act 1984, s. 14 (1) (a). - Issued: 06.03.2014. Made: 17.02.2014. Coming into force: 24.02.2014. Effect: None. Territorial extent & classification: E. Local. - Available at http://www.legislation.gov.uk/uksi/2014/643/contents/made Non-print

The A52 Trunk Road (Wilford, Nottingham) (Temporary Prohibition of Traffic) Order 2014 No. 2014/2136. - Enabling power: Road Traffic Regulation Act 1984, s. 14 (1) (a). - Issued: 12.08.2014. Made: 22.07.2014. Coming into force: 29.07.2014. Effect: None. Territorial extent & classification: E. Local. - Available at http://www.legislation.gov.uk/uksi/2014/2136/contents/made Non-print

The A55 Trunk Road (Junction 38 Eastbound and Westbound Carriageways and Slip Roads) and the A483 Trunk Road (Temporary Prohibition and Restriction of Traffic) Order 2014 No. 2014/2346. - Enabling power: Road Traffic Regulation Act 1984, s. 14 (1) (a), 122A. - Issued: 04.09.2014. Made: 28.08.2014. Coming into force: 31.08.2014. Effect: None. Territorial extent & classification: E. Local. - Available at http://www.legislation.gov.uk/uksi/2014/2346/contents/made Non-print

The A55 Trunk Road (Junction 38 Roundabout and Footway/Cycleway) (Temporary Prohibition of Traffic) Order 2014 No. 2014/2185. - Enabling power: Road Traffic Regulation Act 1984, s. 14 (1) (a). - Issued: 19.08.2014. Made: 17.07.2014. Coming into force: 24.07.2014. Effect: None. Territorial extent & classification: E. Local. - Available at http://www.legislation.gov.uk/uksi/2014/2185/contents/made Non-print

The A55 Trunk Road (Junction 40, Southbound Entry Slip Road) (Temporary Prohibition of Traffic) Order 2014 No. 2014/3002. - Enabling power: Road Traffic Regulation Act 1984, s. 14 (1) (a). - Issued: 17.11.2014. Made: 05.11.2014. Coming into force: 09.11.2014. Effect: None. Territorial extent & classification: E. Local. - Available at http://www.legislation.gov.uk/uksi/2014/3002/contents/made Non-print

The A55 Trunk Road (Junctions 40-36a Westbound and Eastbound Carriageways) (Temporary Restriction of Traffic) Order 2014 No. 2014/3174. - Enabling power: Road Traffic Regulation Act 1984, s. 14 (1) (a). - Issued: 17.11.2014. Made: 05.11.2014. Coming into force: 24.11.2014. Effect: None. Territorial extent & classification: E. Local. - Available at http://www.legislation.gov.uk/uksi/2014/3174/contents/made Non-print

The A55 Trunk Road (Lay-bys near Junction 9 (Treborth) & Junction 11 (Llandygai), Gwynedd) (Prohibition of Waiting) Order 2014 No. 2014/2694 (W.269). - Enabling power: Road Traffic Regulation Act 1984, ss. 1(1), 2(1) (2), 4 (2). - Issued: 13.10.2014. Made: 07.10.2014. Coming into force: 09.10.2014. Effect: None. Territorial extent & classification: W. Local. - Welsh title: Gorchymyn Cefnffordd yr A55 (Cilfannau ger Cyffordd 9 (Treborth) a Chyffordd 11 (Llandygai), Gwynedd) (Gwahardd Aros) 2014. - Available at http://www.legislation.gov.uk/uksi/2014/2694/contents/made Non-print

ROAD TRAFFIC: TRAFFIC REGULATION

The A55 Trunk Road (Pen-y-clip Tunnel, Conwy County Borough) (Temporary Traffic Prohibitions & Restriction) (No.2) Order 2014 No. 2014/3377 (W.340). - Enabling power: Road Traffic Regulation Act 1984, ss. 14 (1) (4)(7), 124, sch. 9 para. 27. - Issued: 30.12.2014. Made: 02.12.2014. Coming into force: 09.12.2014. Effect: None. Territorial extent & classification: W. Local. - Welsh title: Gorchymyn Cefnffordd yr A55 (Twnnel Pen-y-clip, Bwrdeistref Sirol Conwy) (Gwaharddiadau a Chyfyngiad Traffig Dros Dro) (Rhif 2) 2014. - Available at http://www.legislation.gov.uk/uksi/2014/3377/contents/made Non-print

The A55 Trunk Road (Westbound On-Slip Roads at Junction 23a, Dundonald Avenue and Junction 24, Faenol, Abergele, Conwy) (Temporary Prohibition of Vehicles, Cyclists and Pedestrians) Order 2014 No. 2014/3414 (W.346). - Enabling power: Road Traffic Regulation Act 1984, s. 14 (1) (4). - Issued: 02.01.2015. Made: 29.12.2014. Coming into force: 06.01.2015. Effect: None. Territorial extent & classification: W. Local. - Available at http://www.legislation.gov.uk/uksi/2014/3414/contents/made. - In English and Welsh. Welsh title: Gorchymyn Cefnffordd yr A55 (Ffyrdd Ymuno tua'r Gorllewin wrth Gyffordd 23a, Dundonald Avenue a Chyffordd 24, y Faenol, Abergele, Conwy) (Gwahardd Cerbydau, Beicwyr a Cherddwyr Dros Dro) 2014 Non-print

The A56 Trunk Road and the M66 Motorway (Northbound and Southbound) and the M65 (Junction 8) (Temporary Prohibition of Traffic) Order 2014 No. 2014/2086. - Enabling power: Road Traffic Regulation Act 1984, s. 14 (1) (a). - Issued: 07.08.2014. Made: 17.07.2014. Coming into force: 22.07.2014. Effect: None. Territorial extent & classification: E. Local. - Available at http://www.legislation.gov.uk/uksi/2014/2086/contents/made Non-print

The A56 Trunk Road (Northbound and Southbound) and the M65 Motorway (Junction 8 Eastbound and Westbound Slip Roads and Circulatory Carriageway) (Temporary Prohibition of Traffic) Order 2014 No. 2014/396. - Enabling power: Road Traffic Regulation Act 1984, s. 14 (1) (a). - Issued: 27.02.2014. Made: 13.02.2014. Coming into force: 16.02.2014. Effect: None. Territorial extent & classification: E. Local. - Available at http://www.legislation.gov.uk/uksi/2014/396/contents/made Non-print

The A57 Trunk Road and the A628 Trunk Road (Tour de France) (Temporary Prohibition of Traffic) Order 2014 No. 2014/1846. - Enabling power: Road Traffic Regulation Act 1984, ss. 16A (2) (a). - Issued: 16.07.2014. Made: 26.06.2014. Coming into force: 05.07.2014. Effect: None. Territorial extent & classification: E. Local. - Available at http://www.legislation.gov.uk/uksi/2014/1846/contents/made Non-print

The A63 Trunk Road and the A1033 Trunk Road (Daltry Street Flyover to Salt End Roundabout) (24-Hours Clearway) Order 2004 (Amendment) Order 2014 No. 2014/137. - Enabling power: Road Traffic Regulation Act 1984, ss. 1 (1), 2 (1) (2), sch. 9, para. 27 (1). - Issued: 24.01.2014. Made: 17.01.2014. Coming into force: 31.01.2014. Effect: S.I. 2004/1467 amended. Territorial extent & classification: E. Local. - Available at http://www.legislation.gov.uk/uksi/2014/137/contents/made Non-print

The A63 Trunk Road and the M62 Motorway (South Cave Interchange to North Cave Interchange) (Temporary Prohibition of Traffic) Order 2014 No. 2014/84. - Enabling power: Road Traffic Regulation Act 1984, s. 14 (1) (a). - Issued: 21.01.2014. Made: 16.01.2014. Coming into force: 29.01.2014. Effect: None. Territorial extent & classification: E. Local. - Available at http://www.legislation.gov.uk/uksi/2014/84/contents/made Non-print

The A63 Trunk Road (Austhorpe) (Temporary Prohibition of Traffic) Order 2014 No. 2014/1728. - Enabling power: Road Traffic Regulation Act 1984, s. 14 (1) (a). - Issued: 01.07.2014. Made: 12.06.2014. Coming into force: 24.06.2014. Effect: None. Territorial extent & classification: E. Local. - Available at http://www.legislation.gov.uk/uksi/2014/1728/contents/made Non-print

The A63 Trunk Road (Brighton Street Interchange to Mytongate Gyratory) (Temporary Prohibition of Traffic) Order 2014 No. 2014/2573. - Enabling power: Road Traffic Regulation Act 1984, s. 14 (1) (a). - Issued: 25.09.2014. Made: 18.09.2014. Coming into force: 28.09.2014. Effect: None. Territorial extent & classification: E. Local. - Available at http://www.legislation.gov.uk/uksi/2014/2573/contents/made Non-print

The A63 Trunk Road (Daltry Street Interchange) (Temporary Prohibition of Traffic) Order 2014 No. 2014/991. - Enabling power: Road Traffic Regulation Act 1984, s. 14 (1) (a). - Issued: 10.04.2014. Made: 27.03.2014. Coming into force: 06.04.2014. Effect: None. Territorial extent & classification: E. Local. - Available at http://www.legislation.gov.uk/uksi/2014/991/contents/made Non-print

The A63 Trunk Road (Garrison Roundabout to Southcoates Roundabout) (Temporary Prohibition of Traffic) Order 2014 No. 2014/754. - Enabling power: Road Traffic Regulation Act 1984, s. 14 (1) (a). - Issued: 11.03.2014. Made: 06.03.2014. Coming into force: 16.03.2014. Effect: None. Territorial extent & classification: E. Local. - Available at http://www.legislation.gov.uk/uksi/2014/754/contents/made Non-print

The A63 Trunk Road (Hull Jane Tomlinson 10k Run) (Temporary Prohibition of Traffic) Order 2014 No. 2014/1567. - Enabling power: Road Traffic Regulation Act 1984, s. 16A (2) (a). - Issued: 17.06.2014. Made: 29.05.2014. Coming into force: 07.06.2014. Effect: None. Territorial extent & classification: E. Local. - Available at http://www.legislation.gov.uk/uksi/2014/1567/contents/made Non-print

The A63 Trunk Road (Market Place to Garrison Road Roundabout) (Temporary Prohibition of Traffic and Pedestrians) Order 2014 No. 2014/1215. - Enabling power: Road Traffic Regulation Act 1984, s. 14 (1) (a). - Issued: 13.05.2014. Made: 17.04.2014. Coming into force: 26.04.2014. Effect: None. Territorial extent & classification: E. Local. - Available at http://www.legislation.gov.uk/uksi/2014/1215/contents/made Non-print

The A63 Trunk Road (Mount Pleasant Interchange) (Temporary Prohibition of Traffic) Order 2014 No. 2014/2572. - Enabling power: Road Traffic Regulation Act 1984, s. 14 (1) (a). - Issued: 25.09.2014. Made: 18.09.2014. Coming into force: 28.09.2014. Effect: None. Territorial extent & classification: E. Local. - Available at http://www.legislation.gov.uk/uksi/2014/2572/contents/made Non-print

The A63 Trunk Road (Mytongate to Western Interchange) (Temporary Prohibition of Traffic) Order 2014 No. 2014/1731. - Enabling power: Road Traffic Regulation Act 1984, s. 14 (1) (a). - Issued: 02.07.2014. Made: 19.06.2014. Coming into force: 29.06.2014. Effect: None. Territorial extent & classification: E. Local. - Available at http://www.legislation.gov.uk/uksi/2014/1731/contents/made Non-print

The A63 Trunk Road (North Cave Interchange to South Cave Interchange) (Temporary Restriction and Prohibition of Traffic) Order 2014 No. 2014/1634. - Enabling power: Road Traffic Regulation Act 1984, s. 14 (1) (a). - Issued: 25.06.2014. Made: 05.06.2014. Coming into force: 15.06.2014. Effect: None. Territorial extent & classification: E. Local. - Available at http://www.legislation.gov.uk/uksi/2014/1634/contents/made Non-print

The A63 Trunk Road (North Cave to South Cave) (Temporary Prohibition of Traffic) (No.2) Order 2014 No. 2014/2288. - Enabling power: Road Traffic Regulation Act 1984, s. 14 (1) (a). - Issued: 27.08.2014. Made: 21.08.2014. Coming into force: 31.08.2014. Effect: None. Territorial extent & classification: E. Local. - Available at http://www.legislation.gov.uk/uksi/2014/2288/contents/made Non-print

The A63 Trunk Road (Priory Way Interchange to Brighton Street Interchange) (Temporary Prohibition of Traffic) Order 2014 No. 2014/2508. - Enabling power: Road Traffic Regulation Act 1984, s. 14 (1) (a). - Issued: 15.09.2014. Made: 11.09.2014. Coming into force: 21.09.2014. Effect: None. Territorial extent & classification: E. Local. - Available at http://www.legislation.gov.uk/uksi/2014/2508/contents/made Non-print

The A63 Trunk Road (South Cave Interchange to Brighton Street Interchange) (Temporary Prohibition of Traffic) Order 2014 No. 2014/2197. - Enabling power: Road Traffic Regulation Act 1984, s. 14 (1) (a). - Issued: 20.08.2014. Made: 07.08.2014. Coming into force: 20.08.2014. Effect: None. Territorial extent & classification: E. Local. - Available at http://www.legislation.gov.uk/uksi/2014/2197/contents/made Non-print

ROAD TRAFFIC: TRAFFIC REGULATION

The A63 Trunk Road (South Cave to Western) (Temporary Prohibition of Traffic) Order 2014 No. 2014/1983. - Enabling power: Road Traffic Regulation Act 1984, s. 14 (1) (a). - Issued: 21.07.2014. Made: 10.07.2014. Coming into force: 20.07.2014. Effect: None. Territorial extent & classification: E. Local. - Available at http://www.legislation.gov.uk/uksi/2014/1983/contents/made Non-print

The A64 Trunk Road (Barton Hill to Crossgates) (Temporary Restriction and Prohibition of Traffic) Order 2014 No. 2014/3045. - Enabling power: Road Traffic Regulation Act 1984, s. 14 (1) (a). - Issued: 13.11.2014. Made: 06.11.2014. Coming into force: 19.11.2014. Effect: None. Territorial extent & classification: E. Local. - Available at http://www.legislation.gov.uk/uksi/2014/3045/contents/made Non-print

The A64 Trunk Road (Brambling Fields Interchange) (Temporary Prohibition of Traffic) Order 2014 No. 2014/350. - Enabling power: Road Traffic Regulation Act 1984, s. 14 (1) (a). - Issued: 19.02.2014. Made: 13.02.2014. Coming into force: 20.02.2014. Effect: None. Territorial extent & classification: E. Local. - Available at http://www.legislation.gov.uk/uksi/2014/350/contents/made Non-print

The A64 Trunk Road (Bramham to Askham Bryan) (Temporary Prohibition of Traffic) Order 2014 No. 2014/2287. - Enabling power: Road Traffic Regulation Act 1984, s. 14 (1) (a). - Issued: 27.08.2014. Made: 21.08.2014. Coming into force: 31.08.2014. Effect: None. Territorial extent & classification: E. Local. - Available at http://www.legislation.gov.uk/uksi/2014/2287/contents/made Non-print

The A64 Trunk Road (Chestnut Avenue to Pickering Interchange) (Temporary Restriction and Prohibition of Traffic) Order 2014 No. 2014/1320. - Enabling power: Road Traffic Regulation Act 1984, s. 14 (1) (a). - Issued: 27.05.2014. Made: 08.05.2014. Coming into force: 18.05.2014. Effect: None. Territorial extent & classification: E. Local. - Available at http://www.legislation.gov.uk/uksi/2014/1320/contents/made Non-print

The A64 Trunk Road (Claxton) (Temporary Restriction and Prohibition of Traffic) Order 2014 No. 2014/1081. - Enabling power: Road Traffic Regulation Act 1984, s. 14 (1) (a). - Issued: 28.04.2014. Made: 10.04.2014. Coming into force: 27.04.2014. Effect: None. Territorial extent & classification: E. Local. - Available at http://www.legislation.gov.uk/uksi/2014/1081/contents/made Non-print

The A64 Trunk Road (Claxton to Malton) (Temporary Restriction and Prohibition of Traffic) Order 2014 No. 2014/2663. - Enabling power: Road Traffic Regulation Act 1984, s. 14 (1) (a). - Issued: 03.10.2014. Made: 25.09.2014. Coming into force: 02.10.2014. Effect: None. Territorial extent & classification: E. Local. - Available at http://www.legislation.gov.uk/uksi/2014/2663/contents/made Non-print

The A64 Trunk Road (Fulford Interchange) (Temporary Prohibition of Traffic) Order 2014 No. 2014/3399. - Enabling power: Road Traffic Regulation Act 1984, s. 14 (1) (a). - Issued: 25.11.2014. Made: 20.11.2014. Coming into force: 30.11.2014. Effect: None. Territorial extent & classification: E. Local. - Available at http://www.legislation.gov.uk/uksi/2014/3399/contents/made Non-print

The A64 Trunk Road (Ganton) (Temporary 40 Miles Per Hour and 10 Miles Per Hour Speed Restriction) Order 2014 No. 2014/1336. - Enabling power: Road Traffic Regulation Act 1984, s. 14 (1) (a). - Issued: 27.05.2014. Made: 24.04.2014. Coming into force: 04.05.2014. Effect: None. Territorial extent & classification: E. Local. - Available at http://www.legislation.gov.uk/uksi/2014/1336/contents/made Non-print

The A64 Trunk Road (Grimston Bar Interchange) (Temporary Prohibition of Traffic) Order 2014 No. 2014/3527. - Enabling power: Road Traffic Regulation Act 1984, s. 14 (1) (a). - Issued: 23.01.2015. Made: 18.12.2014. Coming into force: 04.01.2015. Effect: None. Territorial extent & classification: E. Local. - Available at http://www.legislation.gov.uk/uksi/2014/3527/contents/made Non-print

The A64 Trunk Road (Grimston Interchange to Hopgrove Roundabout) (Temporary Prohibition of Traffic) Order 2014 No. 2014/2317. - Enabling power: Road Traffic Regulation Act 1984, s. 14 (1) (a). - Issued: 01.09.2014. Made: 28.08.2014. Coming into force: 07.09.2014. Effect: None. Territorial extent & classification: E. Local. - Available at http://www.legislation.gov.uk/uksi/2014/2317/contents/made Non-print

The A64 Trunk Road (Headley Bar Interchange) (Temporary Prohibition of Traffic) (No.2) Order 2014 No. 2014/1716. - Enabling power: Road Traffic Regulation Act 1984, s. 14 (1) (a). - Issued: 02.07.2014. Made: 12.06.2014. Coming into force: 22.06.2014. Effect: None. Territorial extent & classification: E. Local. - Available at http://www.legislation.gov.uk/uksi/2014/1716/contents/made Non-print

The A64 Trunk Road (Headley Bar Interchange) (Temporary Prohibition of Traffic) Order 2014 No. 2014/935. - Enabling power: Road Traffic Regulation Act 1984, s. 14 (1) (a). - Issued: 02.04.2014. Made: 27.02.2014. Coming into force: 09.03.2014. Effect: None. Territorial extent & classification: E. Local. - Available at http://www.legislation.gov.uk/uksi/2014/935/contents/made Non-print

The A64 Trunk Road (Pickering Interchange to Rillington Fields) (Temporary Restriction and Prohibition of Traffic) Order 2014 No. 2014/2571. - Enabling power: Road Traffic Regulation Act 1984, s. 14 (1) (a). - Issued: 25.09.2014. Made: 18.09.2014. Coming into force: 28.09.2014. Effect: None. Territorial extent & classification: E. Local. - Available at http://www.legislation.gov.uk/uksi/2014/2571/contents/made Non-print

The A64 Trunk Road (Rillington Fields) (Temporary Restriction and Prohibition of Traffic) Order 2014 No. 2014/1122. - Enabling power: Road Traffic Regulation Act 1984, s. 14 (1) (a). - Issued: 01.05.2014. Made: 17.04.2014. Coming into force: 04.05.2014. Effect: None. Territorial extent & classification: E. Local. - Available at http://www.legislation.gov.uk/uksi/2014/1122/contents/made Non-print

The A64 Trunk Road (Steelmoor Lane to Barton Hill) (Temporary Restriction and Prohibition of Traffic) Order 2014 No. 2014/2314. - Enabling power: Road Traffic Regulation Act 1984, s. 14 (1) (a). - Issued: 01.09.2014. Made: 28.08.2014. Coming into force: 07.09.2014. Effect: None. Territorial extent & classification: E. Local. - Available at http://www.legislation.gov.uk/uksi/2014/2314/contents/made Non-print

The A66(M) Motorway and the A66 Trunk Road (Blackwell Spur to Blands Corner Roundabout) (Temporary Prohibition of Traffic) Order 2014 No. 2014/2166. - Enabling power: Road Traffic Regulation Act 1984, s. 14 (1) (a). - Issued: 12.08.2014. Made: 31.07.2014. Coming into force: 13.08.2014. Effect: None. Territorial extent & classification: E. Local. - Available at http://www.legislation.gov.uk/uksi/2014/2166/contents/made Non-print

The A66(M) Motorway (Blackwell Spur to Blackwell Roundabout) (Temporary Prohibition of Traffic) Order 2014 No. 2014/2582. - Enabling power: Road Traffic Regulation Act 1984, s. 14 (1) (a). - Issued: 25.09.2014. Made: 18.09.2014. Coming into force: 28.09.2014. Effect: None. Territorial extent & classification: E. Local. - Available at http://www.legislation.gov.uk/uksi/2014/2582/contents/made Non-print

The A66 Trunk Road and the A595 Trunk Road (Chapel Brow Roundabout) (Temporary Prohibition and Restriction of Traffic) Order 2014 No. 2014/2820. - Enabling power: Road Traffic Regulation Act 1984, s. 14 (1) (a). - Issued: 16.10.2014. Made: 09.10.2014. Coming into force: 26.10.2014. Effect: None. Territorial extent & classification: E. Local. - Available at http://www.legislation.gov.uk/uksi/2014/2820/contents/made Non-print

The A66 Trunk Road (Appleby Bypass Westbound Resurfacing) (Temporary Prohibition and Restriction of Traffic) Order 2014 No. 2014/2479. - Enabling power: Road Traffic Regulation Act 1984, s. 14 (1) (a). - Issued: 18.09.2014. Made: 11.09.2014. Coming into force: 14.09.2014. Effect: None. Territorial extent & classification: E. Local. - Available at http://www.legislation.gov.uk/uksi/2014/2479/contents/made Non-print

The A66 Trunk Road (Barras Junction to Bluegrass Resurfacing) (Temporary Prohibition and Restriction of Traffic) Order 2014 No. 2014/1979. - Enabling power: Road Traffic Regulation Act 1984, s. 14 (1) (a). - Issued: 21.07.2014. Made: 03.07.2014. Coming into force: 20.07.2014. Effect: None. Territorial extent & classification: E. Local. - Available at http://www.legislation.gov.uk/uksi/2014/1979/contents/made Non-print

The A66 Trunk Road (Barras Junction to County Boundary) (Temporary Prohibition and Restriction of Traffic) Order 2014 No. 2014/1216. - Enabling power: Road Traffic Regulation Act 1984, s. 14 (1) (a). - Issued: 14.05.2014. Made: 06.03.2014. Coming into force: 09.03.2014. Effect: None. Territorial extent & classification: E. Local. - Available at http://www.legislation.gov.uk/uksi/2014/1216/contents/made Non-print

The A66 Trunk Road (Bassenthwaite Lake Layby) (Temporary Prohibition of Traffic) Order 2014 No. 2014/3435. - Enabling power: Road Traffic Regulation Act 1984, s. 14 (1) (a). - Issued: 03.12.2014. Made: 27.11.2014. Coming into force: 14.12.2014. Effect: None. Territorial extent & classification: E. Local. - Available at http://www.legislation.gov.uk/uksi/2014/3435/contents/made Non-print

The A66 Trunk Road (Bassenthwaite Lake) (Temporary Prohibition and Restriction of Traffic) (No.2) Order 2014 No. 2014/2551. - Enabling power: Road Traffic Regulation Act 1984, ss. 14 (1) (a). - Issued: 24.09.2014. Made: 28.09.2014. Coming into force: 31.08.2014. Effect: None. Territorial extent & classification: E. Local. - Available at http://www.legislation.gov.uk/uksi/2014/2551/contents/made Non-print

The A66 Trunk Road (Bassenthwaite Lake) (Temporary Prohibition and Restriction of Traffic) Order 2014 No. 2014/937. - Enabling power: Road Traffic Regulation Act 1984, s. 14 (1) (a). - Issued: 01.04.2014. Made: 13.03.2014. Coming into force: 16.03.2014. Effect: None. Territorial extent & classification: E. Local. - Available at http://www.legislation.gov.uk/uksi/2014/937/contents/made Non-print

The A66 Trunk Road (Beck Wythop to Woodend Brow) (Temporary Prohibition and Restriction of Traffic) Order 2014 No. 2014/1949. - Enabling power: Road Traffic Regulation Act 1984, s. 14 (1) (a). - Issued: 21.07.2014. Made: 03.07.2014. Coming into force: 06.07.2014. Effect: None. Territorial extent & classification: E. Local. - Available at http://www.legislation.gov.uk/uksi/2014/1949/contents/made Non-print

The A66 Trunk Road (Boathouse Lane Interchange to Thornaby Road Interchange) (Temporary Prohibition of Traffic) Order 2014 No. 2014/1972. - Enabling power: Road Traffic Regulation Act 1984, s. 14 (1) (a). - Issued: 21.07.2014. Made: 03.07.2014. Coming into force: 13.07.2014. Effect: None. Territorial extent & classification: E. Local. - Available at http://www.legislation.gov.uk/uksi/2014/1972/contents/made Non-print

The A66 Trunk Road (Bowes Interchange) (Temporary Restriction and Prohibition of Traffic) Order 2014 No. 2014/2428. - Enabling power: Road Traffic Regulation Act 1984, s. 14 (1) (a) (7). - Issued: 10.09.2014. Made: 04.09.2014. Coming into force: 14.09.2014. Effect: None. Territorial extent & classification: E. Local. - Available at http://www.legislation.gov.uk/uksi/2014/2428/contents/made Non-print

The A66 Trunk Road (Braithwaite to Portinscale) (Temporary Prohibition and Restriction of Traffic) Order 2014 No. 2014/294. - Enabling power: Road Traffic Regulation Act 1984, s. 14 (1) (a). - Issued: 11.02.2014. Made: 07.02.2014. Coming into force: 23.02.2014. Effect: None. Territorial extent & classification: E. Local. - Available at http://www.legislation.gov.uk/uksi/2014/294/contents/made Non-print

The A66 Trunk Road (Briery Interchange, Keswick) (Temporary Prohibition and Restriction of Traffic) Order 2014 No. 2014/1150. - Enabling power: Road Traffic Regulation Act 1984, s. 14 (1) (a). - Issued: 06.05.2014. Made: 13.02.2014. Coming into force: 16.02.2014. Effect: None. Territorial extent & classification: E. Local. - Available at http://www.legislation.gov.uk/uksi/2014/1150/contents/made Non-print

The A66 Trunk Road (Briery Interchange to Greta Bridge Resurfacing) (Temporary Prohibition and Restriction of Traffic) Order 2014 No. 2014/3123. - Enabling power: Road Traffic Regulation Act 1984, s. 14 (1) (a). - Issued: 21.11.2014. Made: 06.11.2014. Coming into force: 09.11.2014. Effect: None. Territorial extent & classification: E. Local. - Available at http://www.legislation.gov.uk/uksi/2014/3123/contents/made Non-print

The A66 Trunk Road (Brough Bypass Resurfacing) (Temporary Restriction and Prohibition of Traffic) Order 2014 No. 2014/2633. - Enabling power: Road Traffic Regulation Act 1984, s. 14 (1) (a). - Issued: 01.10.2014. Made: 24.08.2014. Coming into force: 10.08.2014. Effect: None. Territorial extent & classification: E. Local. - Available at http://www.legislation.gov.uk/uksi/2014/2633/contents/made Non-print

The A66 Trunk Road (Brough Bypass Westbound) (Temporary Prohibition and Restriction of Traffic) Order 2014 No. 2014/295. - Enabling power: Road Traffic Regulation Act 1984, s. 14 (1) (a). - Issued: 11.02.2014. Made: 06.02.2014. Coming into force: 23.02.2014. Effect: None. Territorial extent & classification: E. Local. - Available at http://www.legislation.gov.uk/uksi/2014/295/contents/made Non-print

The A66 Trunk Road (Broughton Cross) (Temporary Prohibition and Restriction of Traffic) Order 2014 No. 2014/858. - Enabling power: Road Traffic Regulation Act 1984, s. 14 (1) (a). - Issued: 31.03.2014. Made: 12.03.2014. Coming into force: 16.03.2014. Effect: None. Territorial extent & classification: E. Local. - Available at http://www.legislation.gov.uk/uksi/2014/858/contents/made Non-print

The A66 Trunk Road (Brough to Stainmore) (Temporary Prohibition and Restriction of Traffic) Order 2014 No. 2014/2293. - Enabling power: Road Traffic Regulation Act 1984, s. 14 (1) (a). - Issued: 01.09.2014. Made: 21.08.2014. Coming into force: 26.08.2014. Effect: None. Territorial extent & classification: E. Local. - Available at http://www.legislation.gov.uk/uksi/2014/2293/contents/made Non-print

The A66 Trunk Road (Cross Lanes to Dyson Lane) (Temporary Restriction and Prohibition of Traffic) Order 2014 No. 2014/3132. - Enabling power: Road Traffic Regulation Act 1984, s. 14 (1) (a). - Issued: 24.11.2014. Made: 06.11.2014. Coming into force: 16.11.2014. Effect: None. Territorial extent & classification: E. Local. - Available at http://www.legislation.gov.uk/uksi/2014/3132/contents/made Non-print

The A66 Trunk Road (Crosthwaite Roundabout to Briery Interchange) (Temporary Prohibition and Restriction of Traffic) Order 2014 No. 2014/2476. - Enabling power: Road Traffic Regulation Act 1984, s. 14 (1) (a). - Issued: 18.09.2014. Made: 11.09.2014. Coming into force: 14.09.2014. Effect: None. Territorial extent & classification: E. Local. - Available at http://www.legislation.gov.uk/uksi/2014/2476/contents/made Non-print

The A66 Trunk Road (Eaglescliffe Interchange to Yarm Road Interchange) (Temporary 50 Miles Per Hour Speed Restriction) Order 2014 No. 2014/70. - Enabling power: Road Traffic Regulation Act 1984, s. 14 (1) (a). - Issued: 20.01.2014. Made: 09.01.2014. Coming into force: 19.01.2014. Effect: None. Territorial extent & classification: E. Local. - Available at http://www.legislation.gov.uk/uksi/2014/70/contents/made Non-print

The A66 Trunk Road (Elton Interchange to Eaglescliffe Interchange) (Temporary Prohibition of Traffic) Order 2014 No. 2014/2196. - Enabling power: Road Traffic Regulation Act 1984, s. 14 (1) (a). - Issued: 20.08.2014. Made: 07.08.2014. Coming into force: 17.08.2014. Effect: None. Territorial extent & classification: E. Local. - Available at http://www.legislation.gov.uk/uksi/2014/2196/contents/made Non-print

The A66 Trunk Road (Fitz Roundabout to Lamplugh Roundabout) (Temporary Restriction of Traffic) Order 2014 No. 2014/3003. - Enabling power: Road Traffic Regulation Act 1984, s. 14 (1) (a). - Issued: 17.11.2014. Made: 06.11.2014. Coming into force: 09.11.2014. Effect: None. Territorial extent & classification: E. Local. - Available at http://www.legislation.gov.uk/uksi/2014/3003/contents/made Non-print

The A66 Trunk Road (Greta Bridge Eastbound and Westbound Carriageways) (Temporary Prohibition and Restriction of Traffic) Order 2014 No. 2014/3497. - Enabling power: Road Traffic Regulation Act 1984, s. 14 (1) (a). - Issued: 19.01.2015. Made: 20.11.2014. Coming into force: 06.12.2014. Effect: None. Territorial extent & classification: E. Local. - Available at http://www.legislation.gov.uk/uksi/2014/3497/contents/made Non-print

The A66 Trunk Road (Greta Viaduct, Keswick) (Temporary Prohibition and Restriction of Traffic) Order 2014 No. 2014/665. - Enabling power: Road Traffic Regulation Act 1984, s. 14 (1) (a). - Issued: 27.02.2014. Made: 21.02.2014. Coming into force: 01.03.2014. Effect: None. Territorial extent & classification: E. Local. - Available at http://www.legislation.gov.uk/uksi/2014/665/contents/made Non-print

The A66 Trunk Road (Hutton and Greystoke Right Turn Lanes Eastbound and Westbound Carriageways) (Temporary Prohibition and Restriction of Traffic) Order 2014 No. 2014/2804. - Enabling power: Road Traffic Regulation Act 1984, s. 14 (1) (a). - Issued: 14.10.2014. Made: 03.10.2014. Coming into force: 19.10.2014. Effect: None. Territorial extent & classification: E. Local. - Available at http://www.legislation.gov.uk/uksi/2014/2804/contents/made Non-print

ROAD TRAFFIC: TRAFFIC REGULATION

The A66 Trunk Road (Keswick Bypass to Kentigern Bridge) (Temporary Prohibition and Restriction of Traffic) Order 2014 No. 2014/967. - Enabling power: Road Traffic Regulation Act 1984, s. 14 (1) (a). - Issued: 01.04.2014. Made: 18.03.2014. Coming into force: 23.03.2014. Effect: None. Territorial extent & classification: E. Local. - Available at http://www.legislation.gov.uk/uksi/2014/967/contents/made Non-print

The A66 Trunk Road (Kirkby Thore to Long Marton) (Temporary Prohibition and Restriction of Traffic) Order 2014 No. 2014/2547. - Enabling power: Road Traffic Regulation Act 1984, s. 14 (1) (a). - Issued: 23.09.2014. Made: 28.08.2014. Coming into force: 14.09.2014. Effect: None. Territorial extent & classification: E. Local. - Available at http://www.legislation.gov.uk/uksi/2014/2547/contents/made Non-print

The A66 Trunk Road (Lamplugh Roundabout to Westray Farm) (Temporary Prohibition and Restriction of Traffic) (No 2) Order 2014 No. 2014/1745. - Enabling power: Road Traffic Regulation Act 1984, s. 14 (1) (a). - Issued: 02.07.2014. Made: 12.06.2014. Coming into force: 30.06.2014. Effect: None. Territorial extent & classification: E. Local. - Available at http://www.legislation.gov.uk/uksi/2014/1745/contents/made Non-print

The A66 Trunk Road (Lamplugh Roundabout to Westray Farm) (Temporary Prohibition and Restriction of Traffic) (No.3) Order 2014 No. 2014/3375. - Enabling power: Road Traffic Regulation Act 1984, s. 14 (1) (a). - Issued: 17.11.2014. Made: 06.11.2014. Coming into force: 26.11.2014. Effect: None. Territorial extent & classification: E. Local. - Available at http://www.legislation.gov.uk/uksi/2014/3375/contents/made Non-print

The A66 Trunk Road (Lamplugh Roundabout to Westray Farm) (Temporary Prohibition and Restriction of Traffic) Order 2014 No. 2014/156. - Enabling power: Road Traffic Regulation Act 1984, s. 14 (1) (a). - Issued: 30.01.2014. Made: 23.01.2014. Coming into force: 09.02.2014. Effect: None. Territorial extent & classification: E. Local. - Available at http://www.legislation.gov.uk/uksi/2014/156/contents/made Non-print

The A66 Trunk Road (Little Burdon Interchange to Sadberge Interchange) (Temporary 50 Miles Per Hour Speed Restriction) Order 2014 No. 2014/2156. - Enabling power: Road Traffic Regulation Act 1984, s. 14 (1) (a). - Issued: 12.08.2014. Made: 31.07.2014. Coming into force: 10.08.2014. Effect: None. Territorial extent & classification: E. Local. - Available at http://www.legislation.gov.uk/uksi/2014/2156/contents/made Non-print

The A66 Trunk Road (Little Burdon Roundabout to Long Newton Interchange) (Temporary Restriction and Prohibition of Traffic) Order 2014 No. 2014/67. - Enabling power: Road Traffic Regulation Act 1984, s. 14 (1) (a). - Issued: 20.01.2014. Made: 09.01.2014. Coming into force: 19.01.2014. Effect: None. Territorial extent & classification: E. Local. - Available at http://www.legislation.gov.uk/uksi/2014/67/contents/made Non-print

The A66 Trunk Road (Little Burdon Roundabout to Morton Palms Roundabout) (Temporary Prohibition of Traffic) Order 2014 No. 2014/2429. - Enabling power: Road Traffic Regulation Act 1984, s. 14 (1) (a). - Issued: 10.09.2014. Made: 04.09.2014. Coming into force: 14.09.2014. Effect: None. Territorial extent & classification: E. Local. - Available at http://www.legislation.gov.uk/uksi/2014/2429/contents/made Non-print

The A66 Trunk Road (Long Newton Interchange) (Temporary Prohibition of Traffic) Order 2014 No. 2014/2968. - Enabling power: Road Traffic Regulation Act 1984, s. 14 (1) (a). - Issued: 27.10.2014. Made: 23.10.2014. Coming into force: 02.11.2014. Effect: None. Territorial extent & classification: E. Local. - Available at http://www.legislation.gov.uk/uksi/2014/2968/contents/made Non-print

The A66 Trunk Road (Long Newton Interchange to Boathouse Lane Interchange) (Temporary Restriction and Prohibition of Traffic) Order 2014 No. 2014/2585. - Enabling power: Road Traffic Regulation Act 1984, s. 14 (1) (a) (7). - Issued: 25.09.2014. Made: 18.09.2014. Coming into force: 28.09.2014. Effect: None. Territorial extent & classification: E. Local. - Available at http://www.legislation.gov.uk/uksi/2014/2585/contents/made Non-print

The A66 Trunk Road (Mount Pleasant to Stainmore)(Temporary Prohibition and Restriction of Traffic) Order 2014 No. 2014/2286. - Enabling power: Road Traffic Regulation Act 1984, s. 14 (1) (a). - Issued: 21.08.2014. Made: 14.08.2014. Coming into force: 31.08.2014. Effect: None. Territorial extent & classification: E. Local. - Available at http://www.legislation.gov.uk/uksi/2014/2286/contents/made Non-print

The A66 Trunk Road (Mungrisdale Eastbound Resurfacing) (Temporary Prohibition and Restriction of Traffic) Order 2014 No. 2014/2600. - Enabling power: Road Traffic Regulation Act 1984, s. 14 (1) (a)- Issued: 29.09.2014. Made: 18.09.2014. Coming into force: 05.10.2014. Effect: None. Territorial extent & classification: E. Local. - Available at http://www.legislation.gov.uk/uksi/2014/2600/contents/made Non-print

The A66 Trunk Road (Neasham Road Roundabout to Morton Palms Roundabout) (Temporary Restriction and Prohibition of Traffic) (No.2) Order 2014 No. 2014/2193. - Enabling power: Road Traffic Regulation Act 1984, s. 14 (1) (a) (7). - Issued: 20.08.2014. Made: 07.08.2014. Coming into force: 17.08.2014. Effect: None. Territorial extent & classification: E. Local. - Available at http://www.legislation.gov.uk/uksi/2014/2193/contents/made Non-print

The A66 Trunk Road (Neasham Road Roundabout to Morton Palms Roundabout) (Temporary Restriction and Prohibition of Traffic) Order 2014 No. 2014/1672. - Enabling power: Road Traffic Regulation Act 1984, s. 14 (1) (a). - Issued: 01.07.2014. Made: 05.06.2014. Coming into force: 18.06.2014. Effect: None. Territorial extent & classification: E. Local. - Available at http://www.legislation.gov.uk/uksi/2014/1672/contents/made Non-print

The A66 Trunk Road (Newsham Grange to Gatherley Moor) (Temporary Restriction and Prohibition of Traffic) Order 2014 No. 2014/960. - Enabling power: Road Traffic Regulation Act 1984, s. 14 (1) (a). - Issued: 31.03.2014. Made: 13.03.2014. Coming into force: 20.03.2014. Effect: None. Territorial extent & classification: E. Local. - Available at http://www.legislation.gov.uk/uksi/2014/960/contents/made Non-print

The A66 Trunk Road (Rokeby Junction to Dick Scot Lane Junction) (Temporary Restriction and Prohibition of Traffic) Order 2014 No. 2014/2512. - Enabling power: Road Traffic Regulation Act 1984, ss. 14 (1) (a), 7. - Issued: 16.09.2014. Made: 11.09.2014. Coming into force: 21.09.2014. Effect: None. Territorial extent & classification: E. Local. - Available at http://www.legislation.gov.uk/uksi/2014/2512/contents/made Non-print

The A66 Trunk Road (Sandford to Warcop) (Temporary Prohibition and Restriction of Traffic) Order 2014 No. 2014/3510. - Enabling power: Road Traffic Regulation Act 1984, s. 14 (1) (a). - Issued: 22.01.2015. Made: 10.10.2014. Coming into force: 26.10.2014. Effect: None. Territorial extent & classification: E. Local. - Available at http://www.legislation.gov.uk/uksi/2014/3510/contents/made Non-print

The A66 Trunk Road (Scotch Corner Roundabout) (Temporary Restriction and Prohibition of Traffic) (No.2) Order 2014 No. 2014/773. - Enabling power: Road Traffic Regulation Act 1984, s. 14 (1) (a). - Issued: 10.03.2014. Made: 27.02.2014. Coming into force: 09.03.2014. Effect: None. Territorial extent & classification: E. Local. - Available at http://www.legislation.gov.uk/uksi/2014/773/contents/made Non-print

The A66 Trunk Road (Scotch Corner Roundabout) (Temporary Restriction and Prohibition of Traffic) Order 2014 No. 2014/29. - Enabling power: Road Traffic Regulation Act 1984, s. 14 (1) (a). - Issued: 10.01.2014. Made: 03.01.2014. Coming into force: 12.01.2014. Effect: None. Territorial extent & classification: E. Local. - Available at http://www.legislation.gov.uk/uksi/2014/29/contents/made Non-print

The A66 Trunk Road (Smallways to Rokeby) (Temporary Restriction and Prohibition of Traffic) Order 2014 No. 2014/734. - Enabling power: Road Traffic Regulation Act 1984, s. 14 (1) (a). - Issued: 10.03.2014. Made: 20.02.2014. Coming into force: 06.03.2014. Effect: None. Territorial extent & classification: E. Local. - Available at http://www.legislation.gov.uk/uksi/2014/734/contents/made Non-print

ROAD TRAFFIC: TRAFFIC REGULATION

The A66 Trunk Road (Stainburn Roundabout to Chapel Brow Roundabout) (Temporary Prohibition of Traffic) Order 2014 No. 2014/2455. - Enabling power: Road Traffic Regulation Act 1984, s. 14 (1) (a). - Issued: 17.09.2014. Made: 28.08.2014. Coming into force: 31.08.2014. Effect: None. Territorial extent & classification: E. Local. - Available at http://www.legislation.gov.uk/uksi/2014/2455/contents/made Non-print

The A66 Trunk Road (Temple Sowerby to Crackenthorpe) (Temporary Restriction of Traffic) Order 2014 No. 2014/1214. - Enabling power: Road Traffic Regulation Act 1984, s. 14 (1) (a). - Issued: 14.05.2014. Made: 06.03.2014. Coming into force: 09.03.2014. Effect: None. Territorial extent & classification: E. Local. - Available at http://www.legislation.gov.uk/uksi/2014/1214/contents/made Non-print

The A66 Trunk Road (The County Boundary to Palliard Resurfacing) (Temporary Prohibition and Restriction of Traffic) Order 2014 No. 2014/1950. - Enabling power: Road Traffic Regulation Act 1984, s. 14 (1) (a). - Issued: 21.07.2014. Made: 03.07.2014. Coming into force: 06.07.2014. Effect: None. Territorial extent & classification: E. Local. - Available at http://www.legislation.gov.uk/uksi/2014/1950/contents/made Non-print

The A66 Trunk Road (The M6 Junction 40 Roundabout to Kemplay Roundabout Eastbound Carriageway) (Temporary Prohibition and Restriction of Traffic) Order 2014 No. 2014/2700. - Enabling power: Road Traffic Regulation Act 1984, s. 14 (1) (a). - Issued: 09.10.2014. Made: 18.09.2014. Coming into force: 09.10.2014. Effect: None. Territorial extent & classification: E. Local. - Available at http://www.legislation.gov.uk/uksi/2014/2700/contents/made Non-print

The A66 Trunk Road (Warreners Lane Junction to Dick Scot Lane Junction) (Temporary Restriction and Prohibition of Traffic) Order 2014 No. 2014/3554. - Enabling power: Road Traffic Regulation Act 1984, s. 14 (1) (a). - Issued: 17.02.2015. Made: 06.11.2014. Coming into force: 16.11.2014. Effect: None. Territorial extent & classification: E. Local. - Available at http://www.legislation.gov.uk/uksi/2014/3554/contents/made Non-print

The A66 Trunk Road (West of Threlkeld to Scales Resurfacing) (Temporary Prohibition and Restriction of Traffic) Order 2014 No. 2014/1343. - Enabling power: Road Traffic Regulation Act 1984, s. 14 (1) (a). - Issued: 29.05.2014. Made: 02.05.2014. Coming into force: 05.05.2014. Effect: None. Territorial extent & classification: E. Local. - Available at http://www.legislation.gov.uk/uksi/2014/1343/contents/made Non-print

The A69 Trunk Road (Constantius Bridge to Coastley Junction) (Temporary Restriction and Prohibition of Traffic) Order 2014 No. 2014/1299. - Enabling power: Road Traffic Regulation Act 1984, s. 14 (1) (a). - Issued: 23.05.2014. Made: 01.05.2014. Coming into force: 05.05.2014. Effect: None. Territorial extent & classification: E. Local. - Available at http://www.legislation.gov.uk/uksi/2014/1299/contents/made Non-print

The A69 Trunk Road (Denton Burn Interchange to Rose Hill Interchange) (Temporary Restriction and Prohibition of Traffic) Order 2014 No. 2014/984. - Enabling power: Road Traffic Regulation Act 1984, s. 14 (1) (a). - Issued: 04.04.2014. Made: 20.03.2014. Coming into force: 31.03.2014. Effect: None. Territorial extent & classification: E. Local. - Available at http://www.legislation.gov.uk/uksi/2014/984/contents/made Non-print

The A69 Trunk Road (Northumberland County Show) (Temporary Restriction and Prohibition of Traffic) Order 2014 No. 2014/1348. - Enabling power: Road Traffic Regulation Act 1984, s. 16A (2) (a). - Issued: 29.05.2014. Made: 15.05.2014. Coming into force: 25.05.2014. Effect: None. Territorial extent & classification: E. Local. - Available at http://www.legislation.gov.uk/uksi/2014/1348/contents/made Non-print

The A69 Trunk Road (Throckley Interchange to Lemington Interchange) (Temporary Prohibition of Traffic) Order 2014 No. 2014/2150. - Enabling power: Road Traffic Regulation Act 1984, s. 14 (1) (a). - Issued: 14.08.2014. Made: 31.07.2014. Coming into force: 08.08.2014. Effect: None. Territorial extent & classification: E. Local. - Available at http://www.legislation.gov.uk/uksi/2014/2150/contents/made Non-print

The A69 Trunk Road (Warwick Bridge and Gelt Bridge) (Temporary Prohibition of Traffic) Order 2014 No. 2014/1697. - Enabling power: Road Traffic Regulation Act 1984, s. 14 (1) (a). - Issued: 01.07.2014. Made: 12.06.2014. Coming into force: 20.06.2014. Effect: None. Territorial extent & classification: E. Local. - Available at http://www.legislation.gov.uk/uksi/2014/1697/contents/made Non-print

The A69 Trunk Road (West Denton Interchange to Denton Burn Interchange) (Temporary Prohibition of Traffic) Order 2014 No. 2014/1300. - Enabling power: Road Traffic Regulation Act 1984, s. 14 (1) (a). - Issued: 23.05.2014. Made: 01.05.2014. Coming into force: 09.05.2014. Effect: None. Territorial extent & classification: E. Local. - Available at http://www.legislation.gov.uk/uksi/2014/1300/contents/made Non-print

The A120 Trunk Road (Crown Interchange to Little Bentley, Colchester, Essex) (Temporary Restriction and Prohibition of Traffic) Order 2014 No. 2014/3455. - Enabling power: Road Traffic Regulation Act 1984, s. 14 (1) (a). - Issued: 19.12.2014. Made: 15.12.2014. Coming into force: 29.12.2014. Effect: None. Territorial extent & classification: E. Local. - Available at http://www.legislation.gov.uk/uksi/2014/3455/contents/made Non-print

The A120 Trunk Road (Hare Green Interchange to Horsley Cross Roundabout, Essex) (Temporary Restriction and Prohibition of Traffic) (No. 2) Order 2014 No. 2014/1582. - Enabling power: Road Traffic Regulation Act 1984, s. 14 (1) (a). - Issued: 18.06.2014. Made: 02.06.2014. Coming into force: 09.06.2014. Effect: None. Territorial extent & classification: E. Local. - Available at http://www.legislation.gov.uk/uksi/2014/1582/contents/made Non-print

The A120 Trunk Road (Hare Green Interchange to Horsley Cross Roundabout, Essex) (Temporary Restriction and Prohibition of Traffic) Order 2014 No. 2014/391. - Enabling power: Road Traffic Regulation Act 1984, s. 14 (1) (a). - Issued: 27.02.2014. Made: 17.02.2014. Coming into force: 24.02.2014. Effect: None. Territorial extent & classification: E. Local. - Available at http://www.legislation.gov.uk/uksi/2014/391/contents/made Non-print

The A120 Trunk Road (Horsley Cross Roundabout to Ramsey Roundabout, Essex) (Temporary Prohibition of Traffic) Order 2014 No. 2014/2788. - Enabling power: Road Traffic Regulation Act 1984, s. 14 (1) (a), 5 (b) (7). - Issued: 14.10.2014. Made: 06.10.2014. Coming into force: 13.10.2014. Effect: None. Territorial extent & classification: E. Local. - Available at http://www.legislation.gov.uk/uksi/2014/2788/contents/made Non-print

The A120 Trunk Road (Stansted, Essex) (Temporary Restriction and Prohibition of Traffic) Order 2014 No. 2014/763. - Enabling power: Road Traffic Regulation Act 1984, s. 14 (1) (a). - Issued: 11.03.2014. Made: 03.03.2014. Coming into force: 10.03.2014. Effect: None. Territorial extent & classification: E. Local. - Available at http://www.legislation.gov.uk/uksi/2014/763/contents/made Non-print

The A160 Trunk Road (Eastfield Road to Habrough Road Roundabout) (Temporary Prohibition of Traffic) Order 2014 No. 2014/2543. - Enabling power: Road Traffic Regulation Act 1984, s. 14 (1) (a). - Issued: 23.09.2014. Made: 28.08.2014. Coming into force: 07.09.2014. Effect: None. Territorial extent & classification: E. Local. - Available at http://www.legislation.gov.uk/uksi/2014/2543/contents/made Non-print

The A168 Trunk Road (Asenby Interchange to York Road Interchange) (Temporary Restriction and Prohibition of Traffic) Order 2014 No. 2014/1489. - Enabling power: Road Traffic Regulation Act 1984, s. 14 (1) (a) (7). - Issued: 09.06.2014. Made: 22.05.2014. Coming into force: 28.05.2014. Effect: None. Territorial extent & classification: E. Local. - Available at http://www.legislation.gov.uk/uksi/2014/1489/contents/made Non-print

The A168 Trunk Road (Topcliffe Interchange to York Road Interchange) (Temporary Restriction and Prohibition of Traffic) Order 2014 No. 2014/2510. - Enabling power: Road Traffic Regulation Act 1984, s. 14 (1) (a). - Issued: 16.09.2014. Made: 11.09.2014. Coming into force: 21.09.2014. Effect: None. Territorial extent & classification: E. Local. - Available at http://www.legislation.gov.uk/uksi/2014/2510/contents/made Non-print

The A174 Trunk Road (Blue Bell Interchange and Stainton Interchange) (Temporary Prohibition of Traffic) Order 2014 No. 2014/74. - Enabling power: Road Traffic Regulation Act 1984, s. 14 (1) (a). - Issued: 20.01.2014. Made: 09.01.2014. Coming into force: 18.01.2014. Effect: None. Territorial extent & classification: E. Local. - Available at http://www.legislation.gov.uk/uksi/2014/74/contents/made Non-print

The A174 Trunk Road (eastbound carriageway east of Parkway Interchange) (Closure of Layby) Order 2014 No. 2014/2612. - Enabling power: Road Traffic Regulation Act 1984, ss. 1 (1), 2 (1) (2). - Issued: 30.09.2014. Made: 22.09.2014. Coming into force: 06.10.2014. Effect: None. Territorial extent & classification: E. Local. - Available at http://www.legislation.gov.uk/uksi/2014/2612/contents/made Non-print

The A174 Trunk Road (Stokesley Road Interchange to Blue Bell Interchange) (Temporary Restriction and Prohibition of Traffic) Order 2014 No. 2014/2002. - Enabling power: Road Traffic Regulation Act 1984, s. 14 (1) (a). - Issued: 30.07.2014. Made: 26.06.2014. Coming into force: 05.07.2014. Effect: None. Territorial extent & classification: E. Local. - Available at http://www.legislation.gov.uk/uksi/2014/2002/contents/made Non-print

The A180 Trunk Road and the M180 Motorway (Barnetby to Brocklesby) (Temporary Prohibition of Traffic) (No.2) Order 2014 No. 2014/2299. - Enabling power: Road Traffic Regulation Act 1984, s. 14 (1) (a). - Issued: 02.09.2014. Made: 24.07.2014. Coming into force: 07.08.2014. Effect: None. Territorial extent & classification: E. Local. - Available at http://www.legislation.gov.uk/uksi/2014/2299/contents/made Non-print

The A180 Trunk Road and the M180 Motorway (Barnetby to Brocklesby) (Temporary Prohibition of Traffic) Order 2014 No. 2014/2175. - Enabling power: Road Traffic Regulation Act 1984, s. 14 (1) (a). - Issued: 15.08.2014. Made: 24.07.2014. Coming into force: 03.08.2014. Effect: None. Territorial extent & classification: E. Local. - Available at http://www.legislation.gov.uk/uksi/2014/2175/contents/made Non-print

The A180 Trunk Road (Barnetby to Great Coates) (Temporary Prohibition of Traffic) Order 2014 No. 2014/732. - Enabling power: Road Traffic Regulation Act 1984, s. 14 (1) (a). - Issued: 28.02.2014. Made: 20.02.2014. Coming into force: 06.03.2014. Effect: None. Territorial extent & classification: E. Local. - Available at http://www.legislation.gov.uk/uksi/2014/732/contents/made Non-print

The A180 Trunk Road (Brocklesby Interchange) (Temporary Prohibition of Traffic) Order 2014 No. 2014/1303. - Enabling power: Road Traffic Regulation Act 1984, s. 14 (1) (a). - Issued: 23.05.2014. Made: 01.05.2014. Coming into force: 11.05.2014. Effect: None. Territorial extent & classification: E. Local. - Available at http://www.legislation.gov.uk/uksi/2014/1303/contents/made Non-print

The A180 Trunk Road (Brocklesby Interchange to Stallingborough Interchange) (Temporary Prohibition of Traffic) Order 2014 No. 2014/2051. - Enabling power: Road Traffic Regulation Act 1984, s. 14 (1) (a). - Issued: 05.08.2014. Made: 17.07.2014. Coming into force: 31.07.2014. Effect: None. Territorial extent & classification: E. Local. - Available at http://www.legislation.gov.uk/uksi/2014/2051/contents/made Non-print

The A180 Trunk Road (Pyewipe Roundabout to Stallingborough Interchange) (Temporary Prohibition of Traffic) Order 2014 No. 2014/2154. - Enabling power: Road Traffic Regulation Act 1984, s. 14 (1) (a). - Issued: 12.08.2014. Made: 31.07.2014. Coming into force: 10.08.2014. Effect: None. Territorial extent & classification: E. Local. - Available at http://www.legislation.gov.uk/uksi/2014/2154/contents/made Non-print

The A184 Trunk Road and the A194(M) Motorway (Follingsby to Whitemare Pool) (Temporary Restriction and Prohibition of Traffic) Order 2014 No. 2014/2797. - Enabling power: Road Traffic Regulation Act 1984, s. 14 (1) (a). - Issued: 13.10.2014. Made: 02.10.2014. Coming into force: 14.10.2014. Effect: None. Territorial extent & classification: E. Local. - Available at http://www.legislation.gov.uk/uksi/2014/2797/contents/made Non-print

The A194(M) Motorway (Havannah Interchange) (Temporary Restriction and Prohibition of Traffic) (No.2) Order 2014 No. 2014/3136. - Enabling power: Road Traffic Regulation Act 1984, s. 14 (1) (a). - Issued: 28.11.2014. Made: 23.10.2014. Coming into force: 02.11.2014. Effect: None. Territorial extent & classification: E. Local. - Available at http://www.legislation.gov.uk/uksi/2014/3136/contents/made Non-print

The A194(M) Motorway (Havannah Interchange) (Temporary Restriction and Prohibition of Traffic) Order 2014 No. 2014/775. - Enabling power: Road Traffic Regulation Act 1984, s. 14 (1) (a). - Issued: 10.03.2014. Made: 27.02.2014. Coming into force: 09.03.2014. Effect: None. Territorial extent & classification: E. Local. - Available at http://www.legislation.gov.uk/uksi/2014/775/contents/made Non-print

The A194(M) Motorway (Havannah to Whitemare Pool) (Temporary Restriction and Prohibition of Traffic) Order 2014 No. 2014/2834. - Enabling power: Road Traffic Regulation Act 1984, s. 14 (1) (a) & S.I. 1982/1163, reg. 16 (2). - Issued: 20.10.2014. Made: 16.10.2014. Coming into force: 26.10.2014. Effect: None. Territorial extent & classification: E. Local. - Available at http://www.legislation.gov.uk/uksi/2014/2834/contents/made Non-print

The A249 Trunk Road and M2 Motorway (Stockbury Roundabout and M2 Junction 5) (Temporary Restriction and Prohibition of Traffic) Order 2014 No. 2014/989. - Enabling power: Road Traffic Regulation Act 1984, s. 14 (1) (a). - Issued: 01.04.2014. Made: 17.03.2014. Coming into force: 05.04.2014. Effect: None. Territorial extent & classification: E. Local. - Available at http://www.legislation.gov.uk/uksi/2014/989/contents/made Non-print

The A249 Trunk Road (Key Street - Cowstead Roundabout) (Temporary Prohibition of Traffic) Order 2014 No. 2014/3507. - Enabling power: Road Traffic Regulation Act 1984, s. 14 (1) (a). - Issued: 19.01.2015. Made: 17.11.2014. Coming into force: 21.01.2015. Effect: None. Territorial extent & classification: E. Local. - Available at http://www.legislation.gov.uk/uksi/2014/3507/contents/made Non-print

The A249 Trunk Road (Key Street Junction - Grovehurst Junction) (Temporary Prohibition of Traffic) Order 2014 No. 2014/2900. - Enabling power: Road Traffic Regulation Act 1984, s. 14 (1) (a). - Issued: 04.11.2014. Made: 21.07.2014. Coming into force: 09.08.2014. Effect: None. Territorial extent & classification: E. Local. - Available at http://www.legislation.gov.uk/uksi/2014/2900/contents/made Non-print

The A249 Trunk Road (Kingsferry Junction - Cowstead Corner Roundabout) (Temporary Prohibition of Traffic) Order 2014 No. 2014/1219. - Enabling power: Road Traffic Regulation Act 1984, s. 14 (1) (a). - Issued: 14.05.2014. Made: 28.04.2014. Coming into force: 17.05.2014. Effect: None. Territorial extent & classification: E. Local. - Available at http://www.legislation.gov.uk/uksi/2014/1219/contents/made Non-print

The A249 Trunk Road (Queenborough Junction - Whiteway Roundabout) (Temporary Prohibition of Traffic) Order 2014 No. 2014/2146. - Enabling power: Road Traffic Regulation Act 1984, s. 14 (1) (a). - Issued: 14.08.2014. Made: 16.08.2014. Coming into force: 05.07.2014. Effect: None. Territorial extent & classification: E. Local. - Available at http://www.legislation.gov.uk/uksi/2014/2146/contents/made Non-print

The A259 Trunk Road (Camber Road Junction - A2070 Brenzett Roundabout) (Temporary Prohibition of Traffic) Order 2014 No. 2014/2640. - Enabling power: Road Traffic Regulation Act 1984, s. 14 (1) (a). - Issued: 29.09.2014. Made: 22.09.2014. Coming into force: 11.10.2014. Effect: None. Territorial extent & classification: E. Local. - Available at http://www.legislation.gov.uk/uksi/2014/2640/contents/made Non-print

The A259 Trunk Road (King Offa Way/De La Warr Road) (Temporary Prohibition of Traffic) Order 2014 No. 2014/101. - Enabling power: Road Traffic Regulation Act 1984, s. 14 (1) (a). - Issued: 22.01.2014. Made: 20.01.2014. Coming into force: 08.02.2014. Effect: None. Territorial extent & classification: E. Local. - Available at http://www.legislation.gov.uk/uksi/2014/101/contents/made Non-print

ROAD TRAFFIC: TRAFFIC REGULATION

The A259 Trunk Road (Lamb Inn-Hooe Junction) (Temporary Restriction of Traffic) Order 2014 No. 2014/2351. - Enabling power: Road Traffic Regulation Act 1984, s. 14 (1) (a). - Issued: 05.09.2014. Made: 25.08.2014. Coming into force: 13.09.2014. Effect: None. Territorial extent & classification: E. Local. - Available at http://www.legislation.gov.uk/uksi/2014/2351/contents/made Non-print

The A259 Trunk Road (Level Crossings) (Temporary Prohibition of Traffic) Order 2014 No. 2014/2930. - Enabling power: Road Traffic Regulation Act 1984, s. 14 (1) (a). - Issued: 24.10.2014. Made: 06.10.2014. Coming into force: 31.10.2014. Effect: None. Territorial extent & classification: E. Local. - Available at http://www.legislation.gov.uk/uksi/2014/2930/contents/made Non-print

The A259 Trunk Road (Little Common Road, Bexhill) (Temporary Prohibition of Traffic) Order 2014 No. 2014/2994. - Enabling power: Road Traffic Regulation Act 1984, s. 16A (2) (a). - Issued: 16.10.2014. Made: 13.10.2014. Coming into force: 09.11.2014. Effect: None. Territorial extent & classification: E. Local. - Available at http://www.legislation.gov.uk/uksi/2014/2994/contents/made Non-print

The A259 Trunk Road (Little Common Road) (Temporary Prohibition of Traffic and Pedestrians) Order 2014 No. 2014/3046. - Enabling power: Road Traffic Regulation Act 1984, s. 14 (1) (a). - Issued: 06.11.2014. Made: 03.11.2014. Coming into force: 22.11.2014. Effect: None. Territorial extent & classification: E. Local. - Available at http://www.legislation.gov.uk/uksi/2014/3046/contents/made Non-print

The A259 Trunk Road (Martineau Lane - North Lane) (Temporary Restriction and Prohibition of Traffic) Order 2014 No. 2014/172. - Enabling power: Road Traffic Regulation Act 1984, s. 14 (1) (a). - Issued: 31.01.2014. Made: 27.01.2014. Coming into force: 15.02.2014. Effect: None. Territorial extent & classification: E. Local. - Available at http://www.legislation.gov.uk/uksi/2014/172/contents/made Non-print

The A259 Trunk Road (Various Roads, Rye) (Temporary Restriction and Prohibition of Traffic) Order 2014 No. 2014/2989. - Enabling power: Road Traffic Regulation Act 1984, s. 16A (2) (a). - Issued: 16.10.2014. Made: 13.10.2014. Coming into force: 08.11.2014. Effect: None. Territorial extent & classification: E. Local. - Available at http://www.legislation.gov.uk/uksi/2014/2989/contents/made Non-print

The A282 Trunk Road (Dartford - Thurrock Crossing) (Weight Restriction and One Way Traffic) Order 2014 No. 2014/2518. - Enabling power: Road Traffic Regulation Act 1984, ss. 1 (1), 2 (1) (2), sch. 9 para. 27 (1). - Issued: 15.09.2014. Made: 08.09.2014. Coming into force: 26.10.2014. Effect: S.I. 1995/2417. S.I. 1996/301, S.I. 1994/515 revoked. Territorial extent & classification: E. Local. - Available at http://www.legislation.gov.uk/uksi/2014/2518/contents/made Non-print

The A282 Trunk Road (Junctions 1A - 2) (Temporary Prohibition of Traffic) Order 2014 No. 2014/2294. - Enabling power: Road Traffic Regulation Act 1984, s. 14 (1) (a). - Issued: 21.08.2014. Made: 11.08.2014. Coming into force: 01.09.2014. Effect: None. Territorial extent & classification: E. Local. - Available at http://www.legislation.gov.uk/uksi/2014/2294/contents/made Non-print

The A282 Trunk Road (M25 Junction 31-A282 Junction 1a) (Temporary Prohibition of Traffic) Order 2014 No. 2014/2333. - Enabling power: Road Traffic Regulation Act 1984, s. 14 (1) (a). - Issued: 04.09.2014. Made: 01.09.2014. Coming into force: 23.09.2014. Effect: None. Territorial extent & classification: E. Local. - Available at http://www.legislation.gov.uk/uksi/2014/2333/contents/made Non-print

The A303 Trunk Road and A36 Trunk Road (Deptford Junction Slip Roads) (Temporary Prohibition of Traffic) (Number 2) Order 2014 No. 2014/3502. - Enabling power: Road Traffic Regulation Act 1984, s. 14 (1) (a). - Issued: 19.01.2014. Made: 16.12.2014. Coming into force: 18.12.2014. Effect: None. Territorial extent & classification: E. Local. - Available at http://www.legislation.gov.uk/uksi/2014/3502/contents/made Non-print

The A303 Trunk Road and A36 Trunk Road (Deptford Junction Slip Roads) (Temporary Prohibition of Traffic) Order 2014 No. 2014/1471. - Enabling power: Road Traffic Regulation Act 1984, s. 14 (1) (a). - Issued: 09.06.2014. Made: 20.05.2014. Coming into force: 24.05.2014. Effect: None. Territorial extent & classification: E. Local. - Available at http://www.legislation.gov.uk/uksi/2014/1471/contents/made Non-print

The A303 Trunk Road (Bullington Cross Interchange - Picket Twenty Interchange) (Temporary Prohibition of Traffic) Order 2014 No. 2014/2101. - Enabling power: Road Traffic Regulation Act 1984, s. 14 (1) (a). - Issued: 07.08.2014. Made: 21.07.2014. Coming into force: 09.08.2014. Effect: None. Territorial extent & classification: E. Local. - Available at http://www.legislation.gov.uk/uksi/2014/2101/contents/made Non-print

The A303 Trunk Road (Cartgate Roundabout, near Martock, Somerset) (40 and 50 Miles Per Hour Speed Limit) Order 2014 No. 2014/2171. - Enabling power: Road Traffic Regulation Act 1984, s. 14 (1) (a). - Issued: 15.08.2014. Made: 06.08.2014. Coming into force: 18.08.2014. Effect: None. Territorial extent & classification: E. Local. - Available at http://www.legislation.gov.uk/uksi/2014/2171/contents/made Non-print

The A303 Trunk Road (Cartgate Roundabout, near Martock, Somerset) (Temporary Restriction of Traffic) (Number 2) Order 2014 No. 2014/3471. - Enabling power: Road Traffic Regulation Act 1984, s. 14 (1) (a). - Issued: 19.12.2014. Made: 17.12.2014. Coming into force: 02.01.2015. Effect: None. Territorial extent & classification: E. Local. - Available at http://www.legislation.gov.uk/uksi/2014/3471/contents/made Non-print

The A303 Trunk Road (Eagle Cross, Near Buckland St Mary) (Temporary Prohibition of Traffic) Order 2014 No. 2014/52. - Enabling power: Road Traffic Regulation Act 1984, s. 14 (1) (b). - Issued: 17.01.2014. Made: 14.01.2014. Coming into force: 18.01.2014. Effect: None. Territorial extent & classification: E. Local. - Available at http://www.legislation.gov.uk/uksi/2014/52/contents/made Non-print

The A303 Trunk Road (Horton Layby, Somerset) (Temporary Prohibition of Traffic) Order 2014 No. 2014/3444. - Enabling power: Road Traffic Regulation Act 1984, s. 14 (1) (b). - Issued: 19.12.2014. Made: 17.12.2014. Coming into force: 22.12.2014. Effect: None. Territorial extent & classification: E. Local. - Available at http://www.legislation.gov.uk/uksi/2014/3444/contents/made Non-print

The A303 Trunk Road (Hundred Acre Interchange - Parkhouse Cross Interchange) (Temporary Prohibition of Traffic) Order 2014 No. 2014/2204. - Enabling power: Road Traffic Regulation Act 1984, s. 14 (1) (a). - Issued: 15.08.2014. Made: 04.08.2014. Coming into force: 24.08.2014. Effect: None. Territorial extent & classification: E. Local. - Available at http://www.legislation.gov.uk/uksi/2014/2204/contents/made Non-print

The A303 Trunk Road (Ilchester Interchange) (Temporary Prohibition of Traffic) Order 2014 No. 2014/2277. - Enabling power: Road Traffic Regulation Act 1984, s. 14 (1) (a). - Issued: 28.08.2014. Made: 26.08.2014. Coming into force: 30.08.2014. Effect: None. Territorial extent & classification: E. Local. - Available at http://www.legislation.gov.uk/uksi/2014/2277/contents/made Non-print

The A303 Trunk Road (Ilminster Laybys) (Temporary Prohibition of Traffic) Order 2014 No. 2014/3380. - Enabling power: Road Traffic Regulation Act 1984, s. 14 (1) (a). - Issued: 28.11.2014. Made: 21.11.2014. Coming into force: 28.11.2014. Effect: None. Territorial extent & classification: E. Local. - Available at http://www.legislation.gov.uk/uksi/2014/3380/contents/made Non-print

The A303 Trunk Road (Ilminster to Prophet's Lane) (Temporary Prohibition of Traffic) Order 2014 No. 2014/3418. - Enabling power: Road Traffic Regulation Act 1984, s. 14 (1) (a). - Issued: 05.12.2014. Made: 02.12.2014. Coming into force: 06.12.2014. Effect: None. Territorial extent & classification: E. Local. - Available at http://www.legislation.gov.uk/uksi/2014/3418/contents/made Non-print

ROAD TRAFFIC: TRAFFIC REGULATION

The A303 Trunk Road (Ilminster to South Petherton) (Temporary Prohibition of Traffic) Order 2014 No. 2014/1470. - Enabling power: Road Traffic Regulation Act 1984, s. 14 (1) (a). - Issued: 09.06.2014. Made: 20.05.2014. Coming into force: 24.05.2014. Effect: None. Territorial extent & classification: E. Local. - Available at http://www.legislation.gov.uk/uksi/2014/1470/contents/made Non-print

The A303 Trunk Road (M3 Junction 8 - Bullington Cross Interchange) (Temporary Prohibition of Traffic) Order 2014 No. 2014/1598. - Enabling power: Road Traffic Regulation Act 1984, s. 14 (1) (a). - Issued: 19.06.2014. Made: 19.05.2014. Coming into force: 07.06.2014. Effect: None. Territorial extent & classification: E. Local. - Available at http://www.legislation.gov.uk/uksi/2014/1598/contents/made Non-print

The A303 Trunk Road (M3 Junction 8 - Parkhouse Interchange) (Temporary Restriction and Prohibition of Traffic) Order 2014 No. 2014/1554. - Enabling power: Road Traffic Regulation Act 1984, s. 14 (1) (a). - Issued: 13.06.2014. Made: 26.05.2014. Coming into force: 20.06.2014. Effect: None. Territorial extent & classification: E. Local. - Available at http://www.legislation.gov.uk/uksi/2014/1554/contents/made Non-print

The A303 Trunk Road (Picket Twenty Interchange - Salisbury Road Interchange) (Temporary Prohibition of Traffic) Order 2014 No. 2014/227. - Enabling power: Road Traffic Regulation Act 1984, s. 14 (1) (a). - Issued: 07.02.2014. Made: 03.02.2014. Coming into force: 22.02.2014. Effect: None. Territorial extent & classification: E. Local. - Available at http://www.legislation.gov.uk/uksi/2014/227/contents/made Non-print

The A303 Trunk Road (Sparkford to Mere) (Temporary Prohibition of Traffic) Order 2014 No. 2014/2280. - Enabling power: Road Traffic Regulation Act 1984, s. 14 (1) (a). - Issued: 28.08.2014. Made: 26.08.2014. Coming into force: 30.08.2014. Effect: None. Territorial extent & classification: E. Local. - Available at http://www.legislation.gov.uk/uksi/2014/2280/contents/made Non-print

The A303 Trunk Road (Stonehenge Summer Solstice, Wiltshire) (Temporary Restriction and Prohibition of Traffic) Order 2014 No. 2014/1695. - Enabling power: Road Traffic Regulation Act 1984, s. 14 (1) (b). - Issued: 01.07.2014. Made: 10.06.2014. Coming into force: 17.06.2014. Effect: None. Territorial extent & classification: E. Local. - Available at http://www.legislation.gov.uk/uksi/2014/1695/contents/made Non-print

The A303 Trunk Road (Stonehenge Winter Solstice, Wiltshire) (Temporary Restriction and Prohibition of Traffic) Order 2014 No. 2014/3446. - Enabling power: Road Traffic Regulation Act 1984, s. 14 (1) (b). - Issued: 17.12.2014. Made: 10.12.2014. Coming into force: 18.12.2014. Effect: None. Territorial extent & classification: E. Local. - Available at http://www.legislation.gov.uk/uksi/2014/3446/contents/made Non-print

The A303 Trunk Road (Upottery to Ilminster) (Temporary Prohibition of Traffic) Order 2014 No. 2014/59. - Enabling power: Road Traffic Regulation Act 1984, s. 14 (1) (a). - Issued: 20.01.2014. Made: 07.01.2014. Coming into force: 15.01.2014. Effect: None. Territorial extent & classification: E. Local. - Available at http://www.legislation.gov.uk/uksi/2014/59/contents/made Non-print

The A303 Trunk Road (Wincanton Junction Slip Roads) (Temporary Prohibition of Traffic) Order 2014 No. 2014/1468. - Enabling power: Road Traffic Regulation Act 1984, s. 14 (1) (a). - Issued: 05.06.2014. Made: 20.05.2014. Coming into force: 24.05.2014. Effect: None. Territorial extent & classification: E. Local. - Available at http://www.legislation.gov.uk/uksi/2014/1468/contents/made Non-print

The A404(M) Motorway (M4 Junction 8/9) (Temporary Prohibition of Traffic) Order 2014 No. 2014/2200. - Enabling power: Road Traffic Regulation Act 1984, s. 14 (1) (a). - Issued: 15.08.2014. Made: 04.08.2014. Coming into force: 23.08.2014. Effect: None. Territorial extent & classification: E. Local. - Available at http://www.legislation.gov.uk/uksi/2014/2200/contents/made Non-print

The A404 Trunk Road and the A404(M) Motorway (A404(M) Junction 9B - M40 Junction 4) (Temporary Restriction and Prohibition of Traffic) Order 2014 No. 2014/2517. - Enabling power: Road Traffic Regulation Act 1984, s. 14 (1) (a). - Issued: 18.09.2014. Made: 15.09.2014. Coming into force: 08.10.2014. Effect: None. Territorial extent & classification: E. Local. - Available at http://www.legislation.gov.uk/uksi/2014/2517/contents/made Non-print

The A404 Trunk Road and the A404(M) Motorway (M4 Junction 8/9 - M40 Junction 4, Handy Cross Interchange) (Temporary Restriction and Prohibition of Traffic) Order 2014 No. 2014/2675. - Enabling power: Road Traffic Regulation Act 1984, s. 14 (1) (a), sch. 9 para. 27 (1). - Issued: 06.10.2014. Made: 25.08.2014. Coming into force: 13.09.2014. Effect: None. Territorial extent & classification: E. Local. - Available at http://www.legislation.gov.uk/uksi/2014/2675/contents/made Non-print

The A405 Trunk Road (M1 Junction 6) (Temporary Prohibition of Traffic) Order 2014 No. 2014/1119. - Enabling power: Road Traffic Regulation Act 1984, s. 14 (1) (a). - Issued: 01.05.2014. Made: 14.04.2014. Coming into force: 04.05.2014. Effect: None. Territorial extent & classification: E. Local. - Available at http://www.legislation.gov.uk/uksi/2014/1119/contents/made Non-print

The A406 Trunk Road (M11 Junction 4) (Temporary Prohibition of Traffic) Order 2014 No. 2014/2970. - Enabling power: Road Traffic Regulation Act 1984, s. 14 (1) (a). - Issued: 16.10.2014. Made: 13.10.2014. Coming into force: 03.11.2014. Effect: None. Territorial extent & classification: E. Local. - Available at http://www.legislation.gov.uk/uksi/2014/2970/contents/made Non-print

The A417 and A419 Trunk Roads (Gloucester to Swindon) (Temporary Prohibition of Traffic) Order 2014 No. 2014/1227. - Enabling power: Road Traffic Regulation Act 1984, s. 14 (1) (a). - Issued: 14.05.2014. Made: 29.04.2014. Coming into force: 03.05.2014. Effect: None. Territorial extent & classification: E. Local. - Available at http://www.legislation.gov.uk/uksi/2014/1227/contents/made Non-print

The A417 Trunk Road (A46 Shurdington Road Junction to B4070 Junction, Gloucestershire) (Temporary Prohibition of Traffic) Order 2014 No. 2014/2416. - Enabling power: Road Traffic Regulation Act 1984, s. 16A (2) (a). - Issued: 10.09.2014. Made: 05.09.2014. Coming into force: 08.09.2014. Effect: None. Territorial extent & classification: E. Local. - Available at http://www.legislation.gov.uk/uksi/2014/2416/contents/made Non-print

The A417 Trunk Road (M5 Junction 11A) (Temporary Prohibition of Traffic) Order 2014 No. 2014/250. - Enabling power: Road Traffic Regulation Act 1984, s. 14 (1) (a). - Issued: 10.02.2014. Made: 0402.2014. Coming into force: 10.02.2014. Effect: None. Territorial extent & classification: E. Local. - Available at http://www.legislation.gov.uk/uksi/2014/250/contents/made Non-print

The A419 Trunk Road (Castle Eaton, Kingshill and Lower Widhill Farm Junctions, Near Cricklade, Wiltshire) (Temporary Prohibition of Traffic) Order 2014 No. 2014/1953. - Enabling power: Road Traffic Regulation Act 1984, s. 14 (1) (b). - Issued: 18.07.2014. Made: 02.07.2014. Coming into force: 09.07.2014. Effect: None. Territorial extent & classification: E. Local. - Available at http://www.legislation.gov.uk/uksi/2014/1953/contents/made Non-print

The A421 Trunk Road (Bedford Southern Bypass, Bedfordshire) (Temporary Restriction and Prohibition of Traffic) (No.2) Order 2014 No. 2014/2792. - Enabling power: Road Traffic Regulation Act 1984, s. 14 (1) (a), sch. 9 para. 27 (1). - Issued: 14.10.2014. Made: 06.10.2014. Coming into force: 13.10.2014. Effect: None. Territorial extent & classification: E. Local. - Available at http://www.legislation.gov.uk/uksi/2014/2792/contents/made Non-print

The A421 Trunk Road (Bedford Southern Bypass, Bedfordshire) (Temporary Restriction and Prohibition of Traffic) (No.3) Order 2014 No. 2014/2999. - Enabling power: Road Traffic Regulation Act 1984, s. 14 (1) (a), sch. 9, para. 27 (1). - Issued: 11.11.2014. Made: 03.11.2014. Coming into force: 10.11.2014. Effect: None. Territorial extent & classification: E. Local. - Available at http://www.legislation.gov.uk/uksi/2014/2999/contents/made Non-print

ROAD TRAFFIC: TRAFFIC REGULATION

The A421 Trunk Road (Bedford Southern Bypass, Bedfordshire) (Temporary Restriction and Prohibition of Traffic) Order 2014 No. 2014/2608. - Enabling power: Road Traffic Regulation Act 1984, s. 14 (1) (a). - Issued: 29.09.2014. Made: 22.09.2014. Coming into force: 29.09.2014. Effect: None. Territorial extent & classification: E. Local. - Available at
http://www.legislation.gov.uk/uksi/2014/2608/contents/made
Non-print

The A428 Trunk Road (Eltisley to Caxton Gibbet, Cambridgeshire) Eastbound (Temporary Prohibition of Traffic) Order 2014 No. 2014/32. - Enabling power: Road Traffic Regulation Act 1984, s. 14 (1) (a). - Issued: 14.01.2013. Made: 06.01.2014. Coming into force: 13.01.2014. Effect: None. Territorial extent & classification: E. Local. - Available at http://www.legislation.gov.uk/uksi/2014/32/contents/made
Non-print

The A446 and A452 Trunk Roads (East of Birmingham, Warwickshire) (Temporary Prohibition of Traffic) Order 2014 No. 2014/1432. - Enabling power: Road Traffic Regulation Act 1984, s. 14 (1) (a). - Issued: 30.05.2014. Made: 13.05.2014. Coming into force: 20.05.2014. Effect: None. Territorial extent & classification: E. Local. - Available at
http://www.legislation.gov.uk/uksi/2014/1432/contents/made
Non-print

The A446 Trunk Road (South of Coleshill, Warwickshire) (Temporary Restriction and Prohibition of Traffic) Order 2014 No. 2014/330. - Enabling power: Road Traffic Regulation Act 1984, s. 14 (1) (a). - Issued: 18.02.2014. Made: 31.01.2014. Coming into force: 07.02.2014. Effect: None. Territorial extent & classification: E. Local. - Available at
http://www.legislation.gov.uk/uksi/2014/330/contents/made Non-print

The A449 (Coven Heath - Four Ashes, Staffordshire) (Temporary Restriction and Prohibition of Traffic) Order 2014 No. 2014/2767. - Enabling power: Road Traffic Regulation Act 1984, s. 14 (1) (a). - Issued: 17.10.2014. Made: 22.09.2014. Coming into force: 29.09.2014. Effect: None. Territorial extent & classification: E. Local. - Available at
http://www.legislation.gov.uk/uksi/2014/2767/contents/made
Non-print

The A449 Trunk Road and M50 Motorway (M50 Junctions 2 - 4) (Temporary Prohibition of Traffic) Order 2014 No. 2014/3381. - Enabling power: Road Traffic Regulation Act 1984, s. 14 (1) (a). - Issued: 28.11.2014. Made: 21.11.2014. Coming into force: 28.11.2014. Effect: None. Territorial extent & classification: E. Local. - Available at
http://www.legislation.gov.uk/uksi/2014/3381/contents/made
Non-print

The A449 Trunk Road (Coven Heath, Staffordshire) (Temporary Prohibition of Traffic) Order 2014 No. 2014/1541. - Enabling power: Road Traffic Regulation Act 1984, s. 14 (1) (a). - Issued: 13.06.2014. Made: 26.05.2014. Coming into force: 02.06.2014. Effect: None. Territorial extent & classification: E. Local. - Available at
http://www.legislation.gov.uk/uksi/2014/1541/contents/made
Non-print

The A449 Trunk Road (Coven, Staffordshire) (Temporary Prohibition of Traffic) Order 2014 No. 2014/340. - Enabling power: Road Traffic Regulation Act 1984, s. 14 (1) (a). - Issued: 19.02.2014. Made: 27.02.2014. Coming into force: 03.02.2014. Effect: None. Territorial extent & classification: E. Local. - Available at
http://www.legislation.gov.uk/uksi/2014/340/contents/made Non-print

The A452 and the A446 Trunk Roads (Packington, Warwickshire) (Temporary Restriction of Traffic) Order 2014 No. 2014/1435. - Enabling power: Road Traffic Regulation Act 1984, s. 14 (1) (a). - Issued: 02.06.2014. Made: 13.05.2014. Coming into force: 20.05.2014. Effect: None. Territorial extent & classification: E. Local. - Available at
http://www.legislation.gov.uk/uksi/2014/1435/contents/made
Non-print

The A453 Trunk Road (Ratcliffe on Soar, Nottinghamshire) (Temporary Restriction of Traffic) Order 2014 No. 2014/2021. - Enabling power: Road Traffic Regulation Act 1984, s. 14 (1) (a). - Issued: 31.07.2014. Made: 13.06.2014. Coming into force: 20.06.2014. Effect: None. Territorial extent & classification: E. Local. - Available at
http://www.legislation.gov.uk/uksi/2014/2021/contents/made
Non-print

The A458 Trunk Road (West of Shrewsbury, Shropshire) (Temporary Prohibition of Traffic) Order 2014 No. 2014/1154. - Enabling power: Road Traffic Regulation Act 1984, s. 14 (1) (a). - Issued: 02.05.2014. Made: 16.04.2014. Coming into force: 23.04.2014. Effect: None. Territorial extent & classification: E. Local. - Available at
http://www.legislation.gov.uk/uksi/2014/1154/contents/made
Non-print

The A470 Trunk Road (Llanrwst, Conwy) (Temporary Prohibition of Vehicles, Cyclists and Pedestrians) Order 2014 No. 2014/2756 (W.278). - Enabling power: Road Traffic Regulation Act 1984, s. 14 (1) (4). - Issued: 20.10.2014. Made: 10.10.2014. Coming into force: 19.10.2014. Effect: None. Territorial extent & classification: W. Local. - Welsh title: Gorchymyn Cefnffordd yr A470 (Llanrwst, Conwy) (Gwahardd Cerbydau, Beicwyr a Cherddwyr Dros Dro) 2014. - Available at
http://www.legislation.gov.uk/wsi/2014/2756/contents/made Non-print

The A483 Trunk Road (Llanymynech to Mile End, Oswestry, Shropshire) (Temporary Prohibition of Traffic) Order 2014 No. 2014/1408. - Enabling power: Road Traffic Regulation Act 1984, s. 14 (1) (a). - Issued: 04.06.2014. Made: 06.05.2014. Coming into force: 13.05.2014. Effect: None. Territorial extent & classification: E. Local. - Available at
http://www.legislation.gov.uk/uksi/2014/1408/contents/made
Non-print

The A483 Trunk Road (near Morda, Shropshire) (Temporary Prohibition of Traffic) Order 2014 No. 2014/1178. - Enabling power: Road Traffic Regulation Act 1984, s. 14 (1) (a). - Issued: 07.05.2014. Made: 23.04.2014. Coming into force: 30.04.2014. Effect: None. Territorial extent & classification: E. Local. - Available at
http://www.legislation.gov.uk/uksi/2014/1178/contents/made
Non-print

The A483 Trunk Road (Wrexham Road, Eccleston, Chester) (50 Miles Per Hour Speed Limit) Order 2014 No. 2014/2819. - Enabling power: Road Traffic Regulation Act 1984, s. 14 (1) (a). - Issued: 21.10.2014. Made: 10.10.2014. Coming into force: 24.10.2014. Effect: None. Territorial extent & classification: E. Local. - Available at
http://www.legislation.gov.uk/uksi/2014/2819/contents/made
Non-print

The A483 Trunk Road (Wrexham Road, Eccleston, Chester) (Prohibition of Movements and Revocation) Order 2014 No. 2014/2946. - Enabling power: Road Traffic Regulation Act 1984, ss. 1 (1), 2 (1) (2), sch. 9 para. 27 (1). - Issued: 13.11.2014. Made: 13.10.2014. Coming into force: 27.10.2014. Effect: None. Territorial extent & classification: E. Local. - Available at
http://www.legislation.gov.uk/uksi/2014/2946/contents/made
Non-print

The A487 Trunk Road (Great Darkgate Street, Aberystwyth, Ceredigion) (Temporary Prohibition of Vehicles) Order 2014 No. 2014/2755 (W.277). - Enabling power: Road Traffic Regulation Act 1984, s. 14 (1) (4)- Issued: 20.10.2014. Made: 10.10.2014. Coming into force: 20.10.2014. Effect: None. Territorial extent & classification: W. Local. - Welsh title: Gorchymyn Cefnffordd yr A487 (Y Stryd Fawr, Aberystwyth, Ceredigion) (Gwahardd Cerbydau Dros Dro) 2014. - Available at
http://www.legislation.gov.uk/wsi/2014/2755/contents/made Non-print

The A494 Trunk Road (Chester Half Marathon) (Temporary Prohibition of Traffic) Order 2014 No. 2014/1380. - Enabling power: Road Traffic Regulation Act 1984, s. 16A (2) (a). - Issued: 02.06.2014. Made: 15.05.2014. Coming into force: 17.05.2014. Effect: None. Territorial extent & classification: E. Local. - Available at
http://www.legislation.gov.uk/uksi/2014/1380/contents/made
Non-print

The A500 Trunk Road (A53 Etruria Road, Stoke-on-Trent) (Temporary Prohibition of Traffic) Order 2014 No. 2014/186. - Enabling power: Road Traffic Regulation Act 1984, s. 14 (1) (a). - Issued: 04.02.2014. Made: 20.01.2014. Coming into force: 27.01.2014. Effect: None. Territorial extent & classification: E. Local. - Available at http://www.legislation.gov.uk/uksi/2014/186/contents/made Non-print

The A500 Trunk Road and M6 Motorway (Barthomley, Cheshire) (Temporary Restriction and Prohibition of Traffic) (Slip Road) (No.2) Order 2014 No. 2014/3130. - Enabling power: Road Traffic Regulation Act 1984, s. 14 (1) (a). - Issued: 27.11.2014. Made: 24.10.2014. Coming into force: 31.10.2014. Effect: None. Territorial extent & classification: E. Local. - Available at
http://www.legislation.gov.uk/uksi/2014/3130/contents/made
Non-print

The A500 Trunk Road and M6 Motorway (Barthomley, Cheshire) (Temporary Restriction and Prohibition of Traffic) (Slip Road) Order 2014 No. 2014/1410. - Enabling power: Road Traffic Regulation Act 1984, s. 14 (1) (a). - Issued: 04.06.2014. Made: 06.05.2014. Coming into force: 13.05.2014. Effect: None. Territorial extent & classification: E. Local. - Available at
http://www.legislation.gov.uk/uksi/2014/1410/contents/made
Non-print

ROAD TRAFFIC: TRAFFIC REGULATION

The A500 Trunk Road (Etruria, Stoke-on-Trent) (Temporary Prohibition of Traffic) Order 2014 No. 2014/2774. - Enabling power: Road Traffic Regulation Act 1984, s. 14 (1) (a). - Issued: 14.10.2014. Made: 03.10.2014. Coming into force: 10.10.2014. Effect: None. Territorial extent & classification: E. Local. - Available at http://www.legislation.gov.uk/uksi/2014/2774/contents/made Non-print

The A500 Trunk Road (Etruria, Stoke-on-Trent) (Temporary Restriction and Prohibition of Traffic) Order 2014 No. 2014/2742. - Enabling power: Road Traffic Regulation Act 1984, s. 14 (1) (a). - Issued: 14.10.2014. Made: 24.09.2014. Coming into force: 01.10.2014. Effect: None. Territorial extent & classification: E. Local. - Available at http://www.legislation.gov.uk/uksi/2014/2742/contents/made Non-print

The A500 Trunk Road (Hanchurch, Staffordshire) (Temporary Prohibition of Traffic) Order 2014 No. 2014/1433. - Enabling power: Road Traffic Regulation Act 1984, s. 14 (1) (a). - Issued: 30.05.2014. Made: 13.05.2014. Coming into force: 20.05.2014. Effect: None. Territorial extent & classification: E. Local. - Available at http://www.legislation.gov.uk/uksi/2014/1433/contents/made Non-print

The A500 Trunk Road (Porthill, Staffordshire) (Temporary Prohibition of Traffic) Order 2014 No. 2014/617. - Enabling power: Road Traffic Regulation Act 1984, s. 14 (1) (a). - Issued: 11.03.2014. Made: 17.01.2014. Coming into force: 24.01.2014. Effect: None. Territorial extent & classification: E. Local. - Available at http://www.legislation.gov.uk/uksi/2014/617/contents/made Non-print

The A500 Trunk Road (Porthill, Stoke on Trent) (Slip Road) (Temporary Prohibition of Traffic) Order 2014 No. 2014/118. - Enabling power: Road Traffic Regulation Act 1984, s. 14 (1) (a). - Issued: 24.01.2014. Made: 13.01.2014. Coming into force: 20.01.2014. Effect: None. Territorial extent & classification: E. Local. - Available at http://www.legislation.gov.uk/uksi/2014/118/contents/made Non-print

The A500 Trunk Road (South of Stoke-On-Trent, Staffordshire) (Slip Road) (Temporary Prohibition of Traffic) Order 2014 No. 2014/1618. - Enabling power: Road Traffic Regulation Act 1984, s. 14 (1) (a). - Issued: 25.06.2014. Made: 02.06.2014. Coming into force: 09.06.2014. Effect: None. Territorial extent & classification: E. Local. - Available at http://www.legislation.gov.uk/uksi/2014/1618/contents/made Non-print

The A500 Trunk Road (Stoke-On-Trent, Staffordshire) (Temporary Prohibition of Traffic) (No.2) Order 2014 No. 2014/3426. - Enabling power: Road Traffic Regulation Act 1984, s. 14 (1) (a). - Issued: 05.12.2014. Made: 01.12.2014. Coming into force: 08.12.2014. Effect: None. Territorial extent & classification: E. Local. - Available at http://www.legislation.gov.uk/uksi/2014/3426/contents/made Non-print

The A500 Trunk Road (Stoke-On-Trent, Staffordshire) (Temporary Prohibition of Traffic) Order 2014 No. 2014/1411. - Enabling power: Road Traffic Regulation Act 1984, s. 14 (1) (a). - Issued: 04.06.2014. Made: 06.05.2014. Coming into force: 13.05.2014. Effect: None. Territorial extent & classification: E. Local. - Available at http://www.legislation.gov.uk/uksi/2014/1411/contents/made Non-print

The A500 Trunk Road (Talke Roundabout, Staffordshire) (Temporary Restriction and Prohibition of Traffic) Order 2014 No. 2014/3063. - Enabling power: Road Traffic Regulation Act 1984, s. 14 (1) (a). - Issued: 19.11.2014. Made: 24.10.2014. Coming into force: 31.10.2014. Effect: None. Territorial extent & classification: E. Local. - Available at http://www.legislation.gov.uk/uksi/2014/3063/contents/made Non-print

The A500 Trunk Road (Talke, Staffordshire) (Temporary Prohibition of Traffic) Order 2014 No. 2014/1526. - Enabling power: Road Traffic Regulation Act 1984, s. 14 (1) (a). - Issued: 11.06.2014. Made: 27.05.2014. Coming into force: 03.06.2014. Effect: None. Territorial extent & classification: E. Local. - Available at http://www.legislation.gov.uk/uksi/2014/1526/contents/made Non-print

The A556 Trunk Road (Between the A5034 and the A556/A56/M56 Bowdon Roundabout) and the M56 Motorway (Temporary Prohibition and Restriction of Traffic) Order 2014 No. 2014/3064. - Enabling power: Road Traffic Regulation Act 1984, ss. 14 (1) (a), 15 (2). - Issued: 19.11.2014. Made: 04.11.2014. Coming into force: 09.11.2014. Effect: None. Territorial extent & classification: E. Local. - Available at http://www.legislation.gov.uk/uksi/2014/3064/contents/made Non-print

The A556 Trunk Road (M6 Junction 19 Roundabout to the A56/A50 Bowdon Roundabout) and the M56 Motorway (Temporary Prohibition of Traffic) Order 2014 No. 2014/2050. - Enabling power: Road Traffic Regulation Act 1984, s. 14 (1) (a). - Issued: 04.08.2014. Made: 15.07.2014. Coming into force: 31.07.2014. Effect: None. Territorial extent & classification: E. Local. - Available at http://www.legislation.gov.uk/uksi/2014/2050/contents/made Non-print

The A585 Trunk Road (Amounderness Way) (Prohibition of U Turns) Order 2014 No. 2014/3472. - Enabling power: Road Traffic Regulation Act 1984, ss. 1 (1), 2 (1) (2). - Issued: 29.12.2014. Made: 18.12.2014. Coming into force: 01.01.2015. Effect: None. Territorial extent & classification: E. Local. - Available at http://www.legislation.gov.uk/uksi/2014/3472/contents/made Non-print

The A585 Trunk Road (Anchorsholme to Morrisons)(Temporary Prohibition of Traffic) Order 2014 No. 2014/1217. - Enabling power: Road Traffic Regulation Act 1984, s. 14 (1) (a). - Issued: 14.05.2014. Made: 06.03.2014. Coming into force: 09.03.2014. Effect: None. Territorial extent & classification: E. Local. - Available at http://www.legislation.gov.uk/uksi/2014/1217/contents/made Non-print

The A585 Trunk Road (Bourne Way Junction to Eros Roundabout) (Temporary Prohibition of Traffic) Order 2014 No. 2014/1222. - Enabling power: Road Traffic Regulation Act 1984, s. 14 (1) (a). - Issued: 14.05.2014. Made: 13.03.2014. Coming into force: 17.03.2014. Effect: None. Territorial extent & classification: E. Local. - Available at http://www.legislation.gov.uk/uksi/2014/1222/contents/made Non-print

The A585 Trunk Road (Eros and Morrisons Roundabouts)(Temporary Prohibition of Traffic) Order 2014 No. 2014/1221. - Enabling power: Road Traffic Regulation Act 1984, s. 14 (1) (a). - Issued: 14.05.2014. Made: 06.03.2014. Coming into force: 14.03.2014. Effect: None. Territorial extent & classification: E. Local. - Available at http://www.legislation.gov.uk/uksi/2014/1221/contents/made Non-print

The A585 Trunk Road (Greenhalgh Lane to Mile Road) (Temporary Prohibition and Restriction of Traffic) Order 2014 No. 2014/3044. - Enabling power: Road Traffic Regulation Act 1984, s. 14 (1) (a). - Issued: 12.11.2014. Made: 30.10.2014. Coming into force: 19.11.2014. Effect: None. Territorial extent & classification: E. Local. - Available at http://www.legislation.gov.uk/uksi/2014/3044/contents/made Non-print

The A585 Trunk Road (The M55 Junction 3 Roundabout to Fleetwood Road Northbound and Southbound Carriageways) (Temporary Prohibition and Restriction of Traffic) Order 2014 No. 2014/3031. - Enabling power: Road Traffic Regulation Act 1984, s. 14 (1) (a). - Issued: 12.11.2014. Made: 30.10.2014. Coming into force: 16.11.2014. Effect: None. Territorial extent & classification: E. Local. - Available at http://www.legislation.gov.uk/uksi/2014/3031/contents/made Non-print

The A585 Trunk Road (Windy Harbour Improvement Scheme) (Temporary Restriction of Traffic) Order 2014 No. 2014/3478. - Enabling power: Road Traffic Regulation Act 1984, s. 14 (1) (a). - Issued: 24.12.2014. Made: 18.12.2014. Coming into force: 03.01.2015. Effect: None. Territorial extent & classification: E. Local. - Available at http://www.legislation.gov.uk/uksi/2014/3478/contents/made Non-print

The A590 Trunk Road (Askam and Dalton Roundabouts) (Temporary Restriction of Traffic) Order 2014 No. 2014/1951. - Enabling power: Road Traffic Regulation Act 1984, s. 14 (1) (a). - Issued: 21.07.2014. Made: 03.07.2014. Coming into force: 06.07.2014. Effect: None. Territorial extent & classification: E. Local. - Available at http://www.legislation.gov.uk/uksi/2014/1951/contents/made Non-print

ROAD TRAFFIC: TRAFFIC REGULATION

The A590 Trunk Road (Askham Roundabout to Dalton Roundabout and Laybys) (Temporary Prohibition and Restriction of Traffic) Order 2014 No. 2014/3049. - Enabling power: Road Traffic Regulation Act 1984, s. 14 (1) (a). - Issued: 17.11.2014. Made: 05.11.2014. Coming into force: 23.11.2014. Effect: None. Territorial extent & classification: E. Local. - Available at http://www.legislation.gov.uk/uksi/2014/3049/contents/made Non-print

The A590 Trunk Road (Booths Roundabout to Swan Street, Ulverston) (Temporary Prohibition and Restriction of Traffic) Order 2014 No. 2014/75. - Enabling power: Road Traffic Regulation Act 1984, s. 14 (1) (a). - Issued: 20.01.2014. Made: 08.01.2014. Coming into force: 26.01.2014. Effect: None. Territorial extent & classification: E. Local. - Available at http://www.legislation.gov.uk/uksi/2014/75/contents/made Non-print

The A590 Trunk Road (Brettargh Holt Roundabout) (Temporary Restriction of Traffic) Order 2014 No. 2014/1048. - Enabling power: Road Traffic Regulation Act 1984, s. 14 (1) (a). - Issued: 22.04.2014. Made: 02.04.2014. Coming into force: 22.04.2014. Effect: None. Territorial extent & classification: E. Local. - Available at http://www.legislation.gov.uk/uksi/2014/1048/contents/made Non-print

The A590 Trunk Road (Brettargh Holt Roundabout to Junction 36 with the M6 Motorway) (Temporary Prohibition and Restriction of Traffic) Order 2014 No. 2014/3121. - Enabling power: Road Traffic Regulation Act 1984, s. 14 (1) (a). - Issued: 21.11.2014. Made: 29.10.2014. Coming into force: 02.11.2014. Effect: None. Territorial extent & classification: E. Local. - Available at http://www.legislation.gov.uk/uksi/2014/3121/contents/made Non-print

The A590 Trunk Road (Brettargh Holt to the A6 Junction Resurfacing) (Temporary Prohibition and Restriction of Traffic) Order 2014 No. 2014/2752. - Enabling power: Road Traffic Regulation Act 1984, s. 14 (1) (a). - Issued: 16.10.2014. Made: 02.10.2014. Coming into force: 05.10.2014. Effect: None. Territorial extent & classification: E. Local. - Available at http://www.legislation.gov.uk/uksi/2014/2752/contents/made Non-print

The A590 Trunk Road (Greenodd Picnic Site) (Temporary Prohibition of Traffic) Order 2014 No. 2014/2962. - Enabling power: Road Traffic Regulation Act 1984, s. 14 (1) (a). - Issued: 16.10.2014. Made: 14.10.2014. Coming into force: 02.11.2014. Effect: None. Territorial extent & classification: E. Local. - Available at http://www.legislation.gov.uk/uksi/2014/2962/contents/made Non-print

The A590 Trunk Road (Greenodd Resurfacing Scheme) (Temporary Prohibition of Traffic) Order 2014 No. 2014/3409. - Enabling power: Road Traffic Regulation Act 1984, s. 14 (1) (a). - Issued: 25.11.2014. Made: 12.11.2014. Coming into force: 04.12.2014. Effect: None. Territorial extent & classification: E. Local. - Available at http://www.legislation.gov.uk/uksi/2014/3409/contents/made Non-print

The A590 Trunk Road (Hoad Lane to Arrad Foot) (Temporary Prohibition and Restriction of Traffic) Order 2014 No. 2014/3131. - Enabling power: Road Traffic Regulation Act 1984, s. 14 (1) (a). - Issued: 21.11.2014. Made: 30.10.2014. Coming into force: 16.11.2014. Effect: None. Territorial extent & classification: E. Local. - Available at http://www.legislation.gov.uk/uksi/2014/3131/contents/made Non-print

The A590 Trunk Road (Levens to Lindale) (Temporary Restriction of Traffic) Order 2014 No. 2014/223. - Enabling power: Road Traffic Regulation Act 1984, s. 14 (1) (a). - Issued: 07.02.2014. Made: 29.01.2014. Coming into force: 16.02.2014. Effect: None. Territorial extent & classification: E. Local. - Available at http://www.legislation.gov.uk/uksi/2014/223/contents/made Non-print

The A590 Trunk Road (Lindale Hill Westbound Resurfacing) (Temporary Prohibition and Restriction of Traffic) Order 2014 No. 2014/2414. - Enabling power: Road Traffic Regulation Act 1984, s. 14 (1) (a). - Issued: 10.09.2014. Made: 03.09.2014. Coming into force: 07.09.2014. Effect: None. Territorial extent & classification: E. Local. - Available at http://www.legislation.gov.uk/uksi/2014/2414/contents/made Non-print

The A590 Trunk Road (M6 Junction 36 to Park Road) (Temporary Prohibition and Restriction of Traffic) Order 2014 No. 2014/3523. - Enabling power: Road Traffic Regulation Act 1984, s. 14 (1) (a). - Issued: 23.01.2015. Made: 31.12.2014. Coming into force: 04.01.2015. Effect: None. Territorial extent & classification: E. Local. - Available at http://www.legislation.gov.uk/uksi/2014/3523/contents/made Non-print

The A590 Trunk Road (Newby Bridge to Backbarrow) (Temporary Prohibition and Restriction of Traffic) Order 2014 No. 2014/3514. - Enabling power: Road Traffic Regulation Act 1984, s. 14 (1) (a). - Issued: 23.01.2014. Made: 19.11.2014. Coming into force: 23.11.2014. Effect: None. Territorial extent & classification: E. Local. - Available at http://www.legislation.gov.uk/uksi/2014/3514/contents/made Non-print

The A590 Trunk Road (Ulverston Road Bus Stop Laybys) (Temporary Prohibition of Traffic) Order 2014 No. 2014/2781. - Enabling power: Road Traffic Regulation Act 1984, s. 14 (1) (a). - Issued: 13.10.2014. Made: 24.09.2014. Coming into force: 11.10.2014. Effect: None. Territorial extent & classification: E. Local. - Available at http://www.legislation.gov.uk/uksi/2014/2781/contents/made Non-print

The A590 Trunk Road (Witherslack to Gilpin Drainage) (Temporary Restriction and Prohibition of Traffic) Order 2014 No. 2014/3505. - Enabling power: Road Traffic Regulation Act 1984, s. 14 (1) (a). - Issued: 20.01.2015. Made: 17.12.2014. Coming into force: 04.01.2015. Effect: None. Territorial extent & classification: E. Local. - Available at http://www.legislation.gov.uk/uksi/2014/3505/contents/made Non-print

The A595 Trunk Road (Blackbeck to Nursery Road) (Temporary Prohibition and Restriction of Traffic) Order 2014 No. 2014/3516. - Enabling power: Road Traffic Regulation Act 1984, s. 14 (1) (a). - Issued: 23.01.2014. Made: 19.11.2014. Coming into force: 07.12.2014. Effect: None. Territorial extent & classification: E. Local. - Available at http://www.legislation.gov.uk/uksi/2014/3516/contents/made Non-print

The A595 Trunk Road (Crossbarrow) (Temporary Prohibition and Restriction of Traffic) Order 2014 No. 2014/2153. - Enabling power: Road Traffic Regulation Act 1984, s. 14 (1) (a). - Issued: 12.08.2014. Made: 25.07.2014. Coming into force: 10.08.2014. Effect: None. Territorial extent & classification: E. Local. - Available at http://www.legislation.gov.uk/uksi/2014/2153/contents/made Non-print

The A595 Trunk Road (Dobies Roundabout to Lillyhall Roundabout) (Temporary Restriction and Prohibition of Traffic) Order 2014 No. 2014/3562. - Enabling power: Road Traffic Regulation Act 1984, s. 14 (1) (a). - Issued: 07.04.2015. Made: 31.12.2015. Coming into force: 18.01.2015. Effect: None. Territorial extent & classification: E. Local. - Available at http://www.legislation.gov.uk/uksi/2014/3562/contents/made Non-print

The A595 Trunk Road (Egremont to Bigrigg Resurfacing) (Temporary Prohibition and Restriction of Traffic) Order 2014 No. 2014/2480. - Enabling power: Road Traffic Regulation Act 1984, s. 14 (1) (a). - Issued: 18.09.2014. Made: 11.09.2014. Coming into force: 14.09.2014. Effect: None. Territorial extent & classification: E. Local. - Available at http://www.legislation.gov.uk/uksi/2014/2480/contents/made Non-print

The A595 Trunk Road (Howgate Roundabout to Hensingham Roundabout) (Temporary Restriction and Prohibition of Traffic) Order 2014 No. 2014/2048. - Enabling power: Road Traffic Regulation Act 1984, s. 14 (1) (a). - Issued: 04.08.2014. Made: 11.07.2014. Coming into force: 26.07.2014. Effect: None. Territorial extent & classification: E. Local. - Available at http://www.legislation.gov.uk/uksi/2014/2048/contents/made Non-print

The A595 Trunk Road (Loop Road, Whitehaven) (Temporary Restriction and Prohibition of Traffic) Order 2014 No. 2014/3030. - Enabling power: Road Traffic Regulation Act 1984, s. 14 (1) (a). - Issued: 12.11.2014. Made: 29.10.2014. Coming into force: 16.11.2014. Effect: None. Territorial extent & classification: E. Local. - Available at http://www.legislation.gov.uk/uksi/2014/3030/contents/made Non-print

ROAD TRAFFIC: TRAFFIC REGULATION

The A595 Trunk Road (Needless Bridge to Mirehouse) (Temporary Prohibition and Restriction of Traffic) Order 2014 No. 2014/2292. - Enabling power: Road Traffic Regulation Act 1984, s. 14 (1) (a). - Issued: 02.09.2014. Made: 21.08.2014. Coming into force: 25.08.2014. Effect: None. Territorial extent & classification: E. Local. - Available at http://www.legislation.gov.uk/uksi/2014/2292/contents/made
Non-print

The A595 Trunk Road (Parton to Pelican Garage) (Temporary Prohibition and Restriction of Traffic) Order 2014 No. 2014/3154. - Enabling power: Road Traffic Regulation Act 1984, s. 14 (1) (a). - Issued: 17.11.2014. Made: 06.11.2014. Coming into force: 23.11.2014. Effect: None. Territorial extent & classification: E. Local. - Available at http://www.legislation.gov.uk/uksi/2014/3154/contents/made
Non-print

The A616 Trunk Road (Deepcar Interchange) (Temporary Prohibition of Traffic) Order 2014 No. 2014/2995. - Enabling power: Road Traffic Regulation Act 1984, s. 14 (1) (a). - Issued: 04.11.2014. Made: 30.10.2014. Coming into force: 09.11.2014. Effect: None. Territorial extent & classification: Local. - Available at http://www.legislation.gov.uk/uksi/2014/2995/contents/made
Non-print

The A616 Trunk Road (Flouch Roundabout to Deepcar Junction) (Temporary Restriction and Prohibition of Traffic) Order 2014 No. 2014/1298. - Enabling power: Road Traffic Regulation Act 1984, s. 14 (1) (a). - Issued: 23.05.2014. Made: 01.05.2014. Coming into force: 05.05.2014. Effect: None. Territorial extent & classification: E. Local. - Available at http://www.legislation.gov.uk/uksi/2014/1298/contents/made
Non-print

The A616 Trunk Road (Stocksbridge) (Temporary Restriction and Prohibition of Traffic) Order 2014 No. 2014/1322. - Enabling power: Road Traffic Regulation Act 1984, s. 14 (1) (a). - Issued: 27.05.2014. Made: 08.05.2014. Coming into force: 18.05.2014. Effect: None. Territorial extent & classification: E. Local. - Available at http://www.legislation.gov.uk/uksi/2014/1322/contents/made
Non-print

The A616 Trunk Road (Westwood Roundabout to Deepcar Junction) (Temporary Restriction and Prohibition of Traffic) Order 2014 No. 2014/2785. - Enabling power: Road Traffic Regulation Act 1984, s. 14 (1) (a). - Issued: 13.10.2014. Made: 02.10.2014. Coming into force: 12.10.2014. Effect: None. Territorial extent & classification: E. Local. - Available at http://www.legislation.gov.uk/uksi/2014/2785/contents/made
Non-print

The A627(M) Motorway (Junction 1 Southbound Carriageway and Slattocks Link Roads) (Temporary Prohibition of Traffic) Order 2014 No. 2014/1584. - Enabling power: Road Traffic Regulation Act 1984, s. 14 (1) (a). - Issued: 18.06.2014. Made: 30.05.2014. Coming into force: 01.06.2014. Effect: None. Territorial extent & classification: E. Local. - Available at http://www.legislation.gov.uk/uksi/2014/1584/contents/made
Non-print

The A627(M) Motorway (Junction 1 to the A664 (Edinburgh Way) Northbound and Southbound Carriageways and Slip Roads) (Temporary Prohibition of Traffic) Order 2014 No. 2014/2560. - Enabling power: Road Traffic Regulation Act 1984, s. 14 (1) (a). - Issued: 24.09.2014. Made: 29.08.2014. Coming into force: 31.08.2014. Effect: None. Territorial extent & classification: E. Local. - Available at http://www.legislation.gov.uk/uksi/2014/2560/contents/made
Non-print

The A627(M) Motorway (Northbound Carriageway between the M62 Junction 20 Roundabout and the A664 Edinburgh Way) (Temporary Prohibition of Traffic) Order 2014 No. 2014/1741. - Enabling power: Road Traffic Regulation Act 1984, s. 14 (1) (a). - Issued: 04.07.2014. Made: 20.06.2014. Coming into force: 06.07.2014. Effect: None. Territorial extent & classification: E. Local. - Available at http://www.legislation.gov.uk/uksi/2014/1741/contents/made
Non-print

The A628 Trunk Road and the A616 Trunk Road (Tour de France) (Temporary Prohibition of Traffic) Order 2014 No. 2014/1851. - Enabling power: Road Traffic Regulation Act 1984, s. 16A (2) (a). - Issued: 16.07.2014. Made: 26.06.2014. Coming into force: 05.07.2014. Effect: None. Territorial extent & classification: E. Local. - Available at http://www.legislation.gov.uk/uksi/2014/1851/contents/made
Non-print

The A628 Trunk Road and the A616 Trunk Road (Tour de France) (Temporary Restriction of Waiting) Order 2014 No. 2014/1743. - Enabling power: Road Traffic Regulation Act 1984, s. 16A (2) (a) (9). - Issued: 02.07.2014. Made: 19.06.2014. Coming into force: 29.06.2014. Effect: None. Territorial extent & classification: E. Local. - Available at http://www.legislation.gov.uk/uksi/2014/1743/contents/made
Non-print

The A628 Trunk Road (Chapel Brow Junction to West Drive Junction) (Temporary Restriction and Prohibition of Traffic) Order 2014 No. 2014/1079. - Enabling power: Road Traffic Regulation Act 1984, s. 14 (1) (a). - Issued: 28.04.2014. Made: 10.04.2014. Coming into force: 21.04.2014. Effect: None. Territorial extent & classification: E. Local. - Available at http://www.legislation.gov.uk/uksi/2014/1079/contents/made
Non-print

The A628 Trunk Road (Flouch Roundabout to Gunn Inn Junction) (Temporary Restriction and Prohibition of Traffic) (No.2) Order 2014 No. 2014/2471. - Enabling power: Road Traffic Regulation Act 1984, s. 14 (1) (a). - Issued: 10.09.2014. Made: 04.09.2014. Coming into force: 14.09.2014. Effect: None. Territorial extent & classification: E. Local. - Available at http://www.legislation.gov.uk/uksi/2014/2471/contents/made
Non-print

The A628 Trunk Road (Flouch Roundabout to Gunn Inn Junction) (Temporary Restriction and Prohibition of Traffic) Order 2014 No. 2014/157. - Enabling power: Road Traffic Regulation Act 1984, s. 14 (1) (a). - Issued: 30.01.2014. Made: 23.01.2014. Coming into force: 02.02.2014. Effect: None. Territorial extent & classification: E. Local. - Available at http://www.legislation.gov.uk/uksi/2014/157/contents/made Non-print

The A628 Trunk Road (Manchester Road) (Temporary Restriction and Prohibition of Traffic) Order 2014 No. 2014/1072. - Enabling power: Road Traffic Regulation Act 1984, s. 14 (1) (a). - Issued: 28.04.2014. Made: 10.04.2014. Coming into force: 21.04.2014. Effect: None. Territorial extent & classification: E. Local. - Available at http://www.legislation.gov.uk/uksi/2014/1072/contents/made
Non-print

The A638 Trunk Road (Redhouse Interchange) (Temporary Prohibition of Traffic) (No.2) Order 2014 No. 2014/2058. - Enabling power: Road Traffic Regulation Act 1984, s. 14 (1) (a). - Issued: 04.08.2014. Made: 17.07.2014. Coming into force: 31.07.2014. Effect: None. Territorial extent & classification: E. Local. - Available at http://www.legislation.gov.uk/uksi/2014/2058/contents/made
Non-print

The A638 Trunk Road (Redhouse Interchange) (Temporary Prohibition of Traffic) Order 2014 No. 2014/750. - Enabling power: Road Traffic Regulation Act 1984, s. 14 (1) (a). - Issued: 11.03.2014. Made: 06.03.2014. Coming into force: 16.03.2014. Effect: None. Territorial extent & classification: E. Local. - Available at http://www.legislation.gov.uk/uksi/2014/750/contents/made Non-print

The A638 Trunk Road, the A1 Trunk Road and the A1(M) Motorway (Redhouse Interchange) (Temporary Prohibition of Traffic) Order 2014 No. 2014/2191. - Enabling power: Road Traffic Regulation Act 1984, s. 14 (1) (a). - Issued: 20.08.2014. Made: 07.08.2014. Coming into force: 16.08.2014. Effect: None. Territorial extent & classification: E. Local. - Available at http://www.legislation.gov.uk/uksi/2014/2191/contents/made
Non-print

The A1033 Trunk Road (Craven Street South to Salt End Roundabout) (Temporary Prohibition of Traffic) Order 2014 No. 2014/677. - Enabling power: Road Traffic Regulation Act 1984, s. 14 (1) (a). - Issued: 04.03.2014. Made: 20.02.2014. Coming into force: 02.03.2014. Effect: None. Territorial extent & classification: E. Local. - Available at http://www.legislation.gov.uk/uksi/2014/677/contents/made Non-print

The A1033 Trunk Road (Marfleet Roundabout to South Coates Roundabout) (Temporary Prohibition of Traffic) Order 2014 No. 2014/1980. - Enabling power: Road Traffic Regulation Act 1984, s. 14 (1) (a). - Issued: 21.07.2014. Made: 10.07.2014. Coming into force: 20.07.2014. Effect: None. Territorial extent & classification: E. Local. - Available at http://www.legislation.gov.uk/uksi/2014/1980/contents/made
Non-print

ROAD TRAFFIC: TRAFFIC REGULATION

The A1033 Trunk Road (Salt End Roundabout to Somerden Roundabout) (Temporary Prohibition of Traffic) Order 2014 No. 2014/2049. - Enabling power: Road Traffic Regulation Act 1984, s. 14 (1) (a). - Issued: 05.08.2014. Made: 17.07.2014. Coming into force: 27.07.2014. Effect: None. Territorial extent & classification: E. Local. - Available at http://www.legislation.gov.uk/uksi/2014/2049/contents/made Non-print

The A1089 Trunk Road (Marshfoot Interchange - Tilbury Port Access Road) (No 2) (Temporary Restriction and Prohibition of Traffic) Order 2014 No. 2014/2173. - Enabling power: Road Traffic Regulation Act 1984, s. 14 (1) (a), sch. 9, para. 27 (1). - Issued: 14.08.2014. Made: 04.08.2014. Coming into force: 23.08.2014. Effect: None. Territorial extent & classification: E. Local. - Available at http://www.legislation.gov.uk/uksi/2014/2173/contents/made Non-print

The A2070 Trunk Road (A2042 Junction, Slip Roads) (Temporary Prohibition of Traffic) Order 2014 No. 2014/3441. - Enabling power: Road Traffic Regulation Act 1984, s. 14 (1) (a). - Issued: 28.11.2014. Made: 24.11.2014. Coming into force: 17.12.2014. Effect: None. Territorial extent & classification: E. Local. - Available at http://www.legislation.gov.uk/uksi/2014/3441/contents/made Non-print

The A2070 Trunk Road (Bad Munstereifel Road, 50mph Speed) (Temporary Restriction of Traffic) Order 2014 No. 2014/2102. - Enabling power: Road Traffic Regulation Act 1984, s. 14 (1) (a), sch. 9, para. 27 (1). - Issued: 07.08.2014. Made: 21.07.2014. Coming into force: 09.08.2014. Effect: None. Territorial extent & classification: E. Local. - Available at http://www.legislation.gov.uk/uksi/2014/2102/contents/made Non-print

The A2070 Trunk Road (Bad Munstereifel Road) (Prohibition of 'U' Turns and Bus Lane) Order 2014 No. 2014/3401. - Enabling power: Road Traffic Regulation Act 1984, ss. 1 (1), 2 (1), 4 (1), 122A. - Issued: 24.11.2014. Made: 17.11.2014. Coming into force: 01.12.2014. Effect: None. Territorial extent & classification: E. Local. - Available at http://www.legislation.gov.uk/uksi/2014/3401/contents/made Non-print

The A2070 Trunk Road (Near Ashford) (Temporary Restriction and Prohibition of Traffic) Order 2014 No. 2014/1392. - Enabling power: Road Traffic Regulation Act 1984, s. 14 (1) (a). - Issued: 02.06.2014. Made: 19.05.2014. Coming into force: 07.06.2014. Effect: None. Territorial extent & classification: E. Local. - Available at http://www.legislation.gov.uk/uksi/2014/1392/contents/made Non-print

The A4123 Link Road (M5 Junction 2, Oldbury) (Temporary Prohibition of Traffic) Order 2014 No. 2014/2741. - Enabling power: Road Traffic Regulation Act 1984, s. 14 (1) (a). - Issued: 14.10.2014. Made: 23.09.2014. Coming into force: 30.09.2014. Effect: None. Territorial extent & classification: E. Local. - Available at http://www.legislation.gov.uk/uksi/2014/2741/contents/made Non-print

The A4510 Trunk Road (M54 Junction 2) (Link Roads) (24 Hours Clearway) Order 2014 No. 2014/3384. - Enabling power: Road Traffic Regulation Act 1984, ss. 1 (1), 2 (1) (2), 4 (1), 122A, sch. 9, para. 27. - Issued: 05.12.2014. Made: 14.11.2014. Coming into force: 28.11.2014. Effect: None. Territorial extent & classification: E. Local. - Available at http://www.legislation.gov.uk/uksi/2014/3384/contents/made Non-print

The A4510 Trunk Road (M54 Junction 2) (Link Roads) (40 Miles Per Hour Speed Limit) Order 2014 No. 2014/3385. - Enabling power: Road Traffic Regulation Act 1984, s. 14 (1) (a). - Issued: 05.12.2014. Made: 14.11.2014. Coming into force: 28.11.2014. Effect: None. Territorial extent & classification: E. Local. - Available at http://www.legislation.gov.uk/uksi/2014/3385/contents/made Non-print

The A5036 Trunk Road (Crosby Road to Switch Island) (Temporary Prohibition of Traffic) Order 2014 No. 2014/3539. - Enabling power: Road Traffic Regulation Act 1984, s. 14 (1) (a). - Issued: 10.02.2015. Made: 30.12.2014. Coming into force: 04.01.2015. Effect: None. Territorial extent & classification: E. Local. - Available at http://www.legislation.gov.uk/uksi/2014/3539/contents/made Non-print

The A5036 Trunk Road (Princess Way/Church Road Roundabout and Westbound and Eastbound Carriageways) (Temporary Prohibition and Restriction of Traffic) Order 2014 No. 2014/2343. - Enabling power: Road Traffic Regulation Act 1984, s. 14 (1) (a). - Issued: 04.09.2014. Made: 28.08.2014. Coming into force: 31.08.2014. Effect: None. Territorial extent & classification: E. Local. - Available at http://www.legislation.gov.uk/uksi/2014/2343/contents/made Non-print

The A5036 Trunk Road (Westbound Carriageway between the A5038 Netherton Way and Orrell Road, Litherland (Temporary Prohibition of Traffic) Order 2014 No. 2014/2567. - Enabling power: Road Traffic Regulation Act 1984, s. 14 (1) (a). - Issued: 24.09.2014. Made: 10.09.2014. Coming into force: 17.09.2014. Effect: None. Territorial extent & classification: E. Local. - Available at http://www.legislation.gov.uk/uksi/2014/2567/contents/made Non-print

The A5103 Trunk Road (Princess Road) and the M60 Motorway (Junction 5 Entry Slip Roads) (Temporary Prohibition of Traffic) Order 2014 No. 2014/2505. - Enabling power: Road Traffic Regulation Act 1984, s. 14 (1) (a). - Issued: 10.09.2014. Made: 03.09.2014. Coming into force: 21.09.2014. Effect: None. Territorial extent & classification: E. Local. - Available at http://www.legislation.gov.uk/uksi/2014/2505/contents/made Non-print

The A5111 and A52 Trunk Roads (Derby) (Temporary Prohibition of Traffic) Order 2014 No. 2014/341. - Enabling power: Road Traffic Regulation Act 1984, s. 14 (1) (a). - Issued: 19.02.2014. Made: 28.01.2014. Coming into force: 04.02.2014. Effect: None. Territorial extent & classification: E. Local. - Available at http://www.legislation.gov.uk/uksi/2014/341/contents/made Non-print

The A5111 Trunk Road (Spondon - Alvaston, Derby) (Temporary Prohibition of Traffic) Order 2014 No. 2014/2268. - Enabling power: Road Traffic Regulation Act 1984, s. 14 (1) (a). - Issued: 29.08.2014. Made: 18.08.2014. Coming into force: 26.08.2014. Effect: None. Territorial extent & classification: E. Local. - Available at http://www.legislation.gov.uk/uksi/2014/2268/contents/made Non-print

The M1 and M6 Motorways and the A14 Trunk Road (Catthorpe) (Temporary Restriction and Prohibition of Traffic) Order 2014 No. 2014/1164. - Enabling power: Road Traffic Regulation Act 1984, ss. 14 (1) (a), 15 (2), 122A, sch. 9, para. 27 (1) & S.I. 1982/1163, reg. 16 (2). - Issued: 07.05.2014. Made: 19.04.2014. Coming into force: 26.04.2014. Effect: None. Territorial extent & classification: E. Local. - Available at http://www.legislation.gov.uk/uksi/2014/1164/contents/made Non-print

The M1 and M45 Motorways (M1 Junction 17 to M45 Junction 1) (Temporary Restriction and Prohibition of Traffic) Order 2014 No. 2014/2977. - Enabling power: Road Traffic Regulation Act 1984, s. 14 (1) (a). - Issued: 13.11.2014. Made: 27.10.2014. Coming into force: 03.11.2014. Effect: None. Territorial extent & classification: E. Local. - Available at http://www.legislation.gov.uk/uksi/2014/2977/contents/made Non-print

The M1 and M45 Motorways (M1 Junctions 15a to 18) (Temporary Restriction and Prohibition of Traffic) Order 2014 No. 2014/1689. - Enabling power: Road Traffic Regulation Act 1984, ss. 14 (1) (a), 15 (2) & S.I. 1982/1163, reg. 16 (2). - Issued: 03.07.2014. Made: 06.06.2014. Coming into force: 13.06.2014. Effect: None. Territorial extent & classification: E. Local. - Available at http://www.legislation.gov.uk/uksi/2014/1689/contents/made Non-print

The M1 and M45 Motorways (M1 Junctions 18 to 16, Northamptonshire) (Temporary Restriction and Prohibition of Traffic) Order 2014 No. 2014/115. - Enabling power: Road Traffic Regulation Act 1984, s. 14 (1) (a) & S.I. 1982/1163, reg. 16 (2). - Issued: 24.01.2014. Made: 10.01.2014. Coming into force: 17.01.2014. Effect: None. Territorial extent & classification: E. Local. - Available at http://www.legislation.gov.uk/uksi/2014/115/contents/made Non-print

The M1 Motorway and A42 Trunk Road (M1 Junction 23a, Leicestershire) (Temporary Prohibition of Traffic) Order 2014 No. 2014/2759. - Enabling power: Road Traffic Regulation Act 1984, s. 14 (1) (a). - Issued: 13.10.2014. Made: 29.09.2014. Coming into force: 06.10.2014. Effect: None. Territorial extent & classification: E. Local. - Available at http://www.legislation.gov.uk/uksi/2014/2759/contents/made Non-print

ROAD TRAFFIC: TRAFFIC REGULATION

The M1 Motorway and A43 Trunk Road, Rothersthorpe (Northampton Motorway Service Area) (Temporary Restriction and Prohibition of Traffic) Order 2014 No. 2014/2956. - Enabling power: Road Traffic Regulation Act 1984, s. 14 (1) (a). - Issued: 13.11.2014. Made: 24.10.2014. Coming into force: 31.10.2014. Effect: None. Territorial extent & classification: E. Local. - Available at http://www.legislation.gov.uk/uksi/2014/2956/contents/made Non-print

The M1 Motorway and A46 Trunk Road (M1 Junction 21a, Kirby Muxloe) (Temporary Prohibition of Traffic) Order 2014 No. 2014/2047. - Enabling power: Road Traffic Regulation Act 1984, s. 14 (1) (a). - Issued: 04.08.2014. Made: 09.07.2014. Coming into force: 16.07.2014. Effect: None. Territorial extent & classification: E. Local. - Available at http://www.legislation.gov.uk/uksi/2014/2047/contents/made Non-print

The M1 Motorway and A46 Trunk Road (M1 Junctions 21 to 22, Leicestershire) (Temporary Restriction and Prohibition of Traffic) Order 2014 No. 2014/2974. - Enabling power: Road Traffic Regulation Act 1984, s. 14 (1) (a). - Issued: 13.11.2014. Made: 27.10.2014. Coming into force: 03.11.2014. Effect: None. Territorial extent & classification: E. Local. - Available at http://www.legislation.gov.uk/uksi/2014/2974/contents/made Non-print

The M1 Motorway and A52 Trunk Road (Sandiacre, Derbyshire) (Temporary Prohibition of Traffic) Order 2014 No. 2014/2190. - Enabling power: Road Traffic Regulation Act 1984, s. 14 (1) (a). - Issued: 18.08.2014. Made: 28.07.2014. Coming into force: 04.08.2014. Effect: None. Territorial extent & classification: E. Local. - Available at http://www.legislation.gov.uk/uksi/2014/2190/contents/made Non-print

The M1 Motorway and the A50 and A453 Trunk Roads (M1 Junction 24, Kegworth) (Temporary Restriction and Prohibition of Traffic) Order 2014 No. 2014/1537. - Enabling power: Road Traffic Regulation Act 1984, s. 14 (1) (a). - Issued: 13.06.2014. Made: 23.05.2014. Coming into force: 30.05.2014. Effect: None. Territorial extent & classification: E. Local. - Available at http://www.legislation.gov.uk/uksi/2014/1537/contents/made Non-print

The M1 Motorway and the A50 and A453 Trunk Roads (M1 Junction 24, Kegworth) (Temporary Restriction and Prohibition of Traffic) Variation Order 2014 No. 2014/2187. - Enabling power: Road Traffic Regulation Act 1984, s. 14 (1) (a). - Issued: 19.08.2014. Made: 20.07.2014. Coming into force: 27.07.2014. Effect: S.I. 2014/1537 varied. Territorial extent & classification: E. Local. - Available at http://www.legislation.gov.uk/uksi/2014/2187/contents/made Non-print

The M1 Motorway and the A63 Trunk Road (East Leeds Link) (Temporary Restriction and Prohibition of Traffic) Order 2014 No. 2014/983. - Enabling power: Road Traffic Regulation Act 1984, s. 14 (1) (a). - Issued: 04.04.2014. Made: 20.03.2014. Coming into force: 30.03.2014. Effect: None. Territorial extent & classification: E. Local. - Available at http://www.legislation.gov.uk/uksi/2014/983/contents/made Non-print

The M1 Motorway and the A421 Trunk Road (Junction 13, Central Bedfordshire) (Temporary Prohibition of Traffic) Order 2014 No. 2014/2259. - Enabling power: Road Traffic Regulation Act 1984, s. 14 (1) (a). - Issued: 27.08.2014. Made: 18.08.2014. Coming into force: 26.08.2014. Effect: None. Territorial extent & classification: E. Local. - Available at http://www.legislation.gov.uk/uksi/2014/2259/contents/made Non-print

The M1 Motorway and the M18 Motorway (Thurcroft Interchange) (Temporary Prohibition of Traffic) Order 2014 No. 2014/752. - Enabling power: Road Traffic Regulation Act 1984, s. 14 (1) (a). - Issued: 11.03.2014. Made: 06.03.2014. Coming into force: 16.03.2014. Effect: None. Territorial extent & classification: E. Local. - Available at http://www.legislation.gov.uk/uksi/2014/752/contents/made Non-print

The M1 Motorway and the M18 Motorway (Thurcroft to Bramley) (Temporary Restriction and Prohibition of Traffic) Order 2014 No. 2014/1644. - Enabling power: Road Traffic Regulation Act 1984, s. 14 (1) (a) & S.I. 1982/1163, reg. 16 (2). - Issued: 25.06.2014. Made: 05.06.2014. Coming into force: 15.06.2014. Effect: None. Territorial extent & classification: E. Local. - Available at http://www.legislation.gov.uk/uksi/2014/1644/contents/made Non-print

The M1 Motorway (Between Junctions 11 and 13) (Temporary 50 Miles Per Hour Speed Restriction) Order 2014 No. 2014/3042. - Enabling power: Road Traffic Regulation Act 1984, s. 14 (1) (a) (7) & S.I. 1982/1163, reg. 16 (2). - Issued: 17.11.2014. Made: 10.11.2014. Coming into force: 17.11.2014. Effect: None. Territorial extent & classification: E. Local. - Available at http://www.legislation.gov.uk/uksi/2014/3042/contents/made Non-print

The M1 Motorway (Enderby, Leicestershire) (Temporary Restriction and Prohibition of Traffic) Order 2014 No. 2014/2980. - Enabling power: Road Traffic Regulation Act 1984, s. 14 (1) (a). - Issued: 13.11.2014. Made: 27.10.2014. Coming into force: 03.11.2014. Effect: None. Territorial extent & classification: E. Local. - Available at http://www.legislation.gov.uk/uksi/2014/2980/contents/made Non-print

The M1 Motorway (Junction 2, Slip Roads) (Temporary Prohibition of Traffic) Order 2014 No. 2014/400. - Enabling power: Road Traffic Regulation Act 1984, s. 14 (1) (a). - Issued: 27.02.2014. Made: 17.02.2014. Coming into force: 08.03.2014. Effect: None. Territorial extent & classification: E. Local. - Available at http://www.legislation.gov.uk/uksi/2014/400/contents/made Non-print

The M1 Motorway (Junction 6, Slip Roads) (Temporary Prohibition of Traffic) Order 2014 No. 2014/203. - Enabling power: Road Traffic Regulation Act 1984, s. 14 (1) (a). - Issued: 05.02.2014. Made: 20.01.2014. Coming into force: 08.02.2014. Effect: None. Territorial extent & classification: E. Local. - Available at http://www.legislation.gov.uk/uksi/2014/203/contents/made Non-print

The M1 Motorway (Junction 6, Southbound Entry Slip Road) (Temporary Prohibition of Traffic) Order 2014 No. 2014/738. - Enabling power: Road Traffic Regulation Act 1984, s. 14 (1) (a). - Issued: 17.03.2014. Made: 10.03.2014. Coming into force: 29.03.2014. Effect: None. Territorial extent & classification: E. Local. - Available at http://www.legislation.gov.uk/uksi/2014/738/contents/made Non-print

The M1 Motorway (Junction 10 to 10A Spur) (Temporary Restriction and Prohibition of Traffic) Order 2014 No. 2014/948. - Enabling power: Road Traffic Regulation Act 1984, s. 14 (1) (a) & S.I. 1982/1163, reg. 16 (2). - Issued: 10.04.2014. Made: 24.02.2014. Coming into force: 03.03.2014. Effect: None. Territorial extent & classification: E. Local. - Available at http://www.legislation.gov.uk/uksi/2014/948/contents/made Non-print

The M1 Motorway (Junction 15a, Northamptonshire) (Temporary Prohibition of Traffic) Order 2014 No. 2014/359. - Enabling power: Road Traffic Regulation Act 1984, s. 14 (1) (a). - Issued: 20.02.2014. Made: 10.02.2014. Coming into force: 17.02.2014. Effect: None. Territorial extent & classification: E. Local. - Available at http://www.legislation.gov.uk/uksi/2014/359/contents/made Non-print

The M1 Motorway (Junction 15a, Northamptonshire) (Temporary Prohibition of Traffic) Order 2014 No. 2014/1678. - Enabling power: Road Traffic Regulation Act 1984, s. 14 (1) (a). - Issued: 01.07.2014. Made: 10.02.2014. Coming into force: 17.02.2014. Effect: None. Territorial extent & classification: E. Local. - Available at http://www.legislation.gov.uk/uksi/2014/1678/contents/made Non-print

The M1 Motorway (Junction 15a, Rothersthorpe) (Temporary Prohibition of Traffic) Order 2014 No. 2014/2142. - Enabling power: Road Traffic Regulation Act 1984, s. 14 (1) (a). - Issued: 12.08.2014. Made: 28.07.2014. Coming into force: 04.08.2014. Effect: None. Territorial extent & classification: E. Local. - Available at http://www.legislation.gov.uk/uksi/2014/2142/contents/made Non-print

The M1 Motorway (Junction 15, Collingtree, Northamptonshire) (Temporary Restriction and Prohibition of Traffic) Order 2014 No. 2014/1478. - Enabling power: Road Traffic Regulation Act 1984, s. 14 (1) (a). - Issued: 09.06.2014. Made: 19.05.2014. Coming into force: 26.05.2014. Effect: None. Territorial extent & classification: E. Local. - Available at http://www.legislation.gov.uk/uksi/2014/1478/contents/made Non-print

The M1 Motorway (Junction 15, Collingtree) (Temporary Restriction and Prohibition of Traffic) Order 2014 No. 2014/1094. - Enabling power: Road Traffic Regulation Act 1984, s. 14 (1) (a). - Issued: 25.04.2014. Made: 01.04.2014. Coming into force: 08.04.2014. Effect: None. Territorial extent & classification: E. Local. - Available at http://www.legislation.gov.uk/uksi/2014/1094/contents/made Non-print

ROAD TRAFFIC: TRAFFIC REGULATION

The M1 Motorway (Junction 15, Northamptonshire) (Slip Road) (Temporary Prohibition of Traffic) Order 2014 No. 2014/638. - Enabling power: Road Traffic Regulation Act 1984, s. 14 (1) (a). - Issued: 05.03.2014. Made: 17.02.2014. Coming into force: 24.02.2014. Effect: None. Territorial extent & classification: E. Local. - Available at http://www.legislation.gov.uk/uksi/2014/638/contents/made Non-print

The M1 Motorway (Junction 15, South of Northampton, Northamptonshire) (Temporary Prohibition of Traffic) Order 2014 No. 2014/2017. - Enabling power: Road Traffic Regulation Act 1984, s. 14 (1) (a). - Issued: 31.07.2014. Made: 02.07.2014. Coming into force: 09.07.2014. Effect: None. Territorial extent & classification: E. Local. - Available at http://www.legislation.gov.uk/uksi/2014/2017/contents/made Non-print

The M1 Motorway (Junction 15 to Junction 14, Northamptonshire) (Temporary Restriction and Prohibition of Traffic) Order 2014 No. 2014/616. - Enabling power: Road Traffic Regulation Act 1984, s. 14 (1) (a). - Issued: 11.03.2014. Made: 10.01.2014. Coming into force: 17.01.2014. Effect: None. Territorial extent & classification: E. Local. - Available at http://www.legislation.gov.uk/uksi/2014/616/contents/made Non-print

The M1 Motorway (Junction 15 to Junction 14, Northamptonshire) (Temporary Restriction and Prohibition of Traffic) Order 2014 No. 2014/116. - Enabling power: Road Traffic Regulation Act 1984, s. 14 (1) (a). - Issued: 24.01.2014. Made: 10.01.2014. Coming into force: 17.01.2014. Effect: None. Territorial extent & classification: E. Local. - Available at http://www.legislation.gov.uk/uksi/2014/116/contents/made Non-print

The M1 Motorway (Junction 16 Northamptonshire) (Slip Road) (Temporary Prohibition of Traffic) Order 2014 No. 2014/2220. - Enabling power: Road Traffic Regulation Act 1984, s. 14 (1) (a). - Issued: 21.08.2014. Made: 30.07.2014. Coming into force: 06.08.2014. Effect: None. Territorial extent & classification: E. Local. - Available at http://www.legislation.gov.uk/uksi/2014/2220/contents/made Non-print

The M1 Motorway (Junction 20) (Slip Road) (Temporary Prohibition of Traffic) Order 2014 No. 2014/362. - Enabling power: Road Traffic Regulation Act 1984, s. 14 (1) (a). - Issued: 20.02.2014. Made: 10.02.2014. Coming into force: 17.02.2014. Effect: None. Territorial extent & classification: E. Local. - Available at http://www.legislation.gov.uk/uksi/2014/362/contents/made Non-print

The M1 Motorway (Junction 21a, Leicestershire) (Link Road) (Temporary Prohibition of Traffic) Order 2014 No. 2014/3531. - Enabling power: Road Traffic Regulation Act 1984, s. 14 (1) (a). - Issued: 22.01.2015. Made: 29.12.2015. Coming into force: 05.01.2015. Effect: None. Territorial extent & classification: E. Local. - Available at http://www.legislation.gov.uk/uksi/2014/3531/contents/made Non-print

The M1 Motorway (Junction 21a, Leicestershire) (Slip Road) (Temporary Prohibition of Traffic) Order 2014 No. 2014/903. - Enabling power: Road Traffic Regulation Act 1984, s. 14 (1) (a). - Issued: 01.04.2014. Made: 17.02.2014. Coming into force: 24.02.2014. Effect: None. Territorial extent & classification: E. Local. - Available at http://www.legislation.gov.uk/uksi/2014/903/contents/made Non-print

The M1 Motorway (Junction 21a, Leicestershire) (Temporary Prohibition of Traffic) Order 2014 No. 2014/2982. - Enabling power: Road Traffic Regulation Act 1984, s. 14 (1) (a). - Issued: 13.11.2014. Made: 27.10.2014. Coming into force: 03.11.2014. Effect: None. Territorial extent & classification: E. Local. - Available at http://www.legislation.gov.uk/uksi/2014/2982/contents/made Non-print

The M1 Motorway (Junction 23a, West Meadow Viaduct) (Temporary Restriction and Prohibition of Traffic) Order 2014 No. 2014/1442. - Enabling power: Road Traffic Regulation Act 1984, s. 14 (1) (a). - Issued: 02.06.2014. Made: 16.05.2014. Coming into force: 23.05.2014. Effect: None. Territorial extent & classification: E. Local. - Available at http://www.legislation.gov.uk/uksi/2014/1442/contents/made Non-print

The M1 Motorway (Junction 28, Derbyshire) (Temporary Prohibition of Traffic) Order 2014 No. 2014/972. - Enabling power: Road Traffic Regulation Act 1984, s. 14 (1) (a). - Issued: 10.04.2014. Made: 17.03.2014. Coming into force: 24.03.2014. Effect: None. Territorial extent & classification: E. Local. - Available at http://www.legislation.gov.uk/uksi/2014/972/contents/made Non-print

The M1 Motorway (Junction 33) (Temporary Prohibition of Traffic) Order 2014 No. 2014/3428. - Enabling power: Road Traffic Regulation Act 1984, s. 14 (1) (a). - Issued: 03.12.2014. Made: 27.11.2014. Coming into force: 10.12.2014. Effect: None. Territorial extent & classification: E. Local. - Available at http://www.legislation.gov.uk/uksi/2014/3428/contents/made Non-print

The M1 Motorway (Junction 34) (Temporary Prohibition of Traffic) Order 2014 No. 2014/285. - Enabling power: Road Traffic Regulation Act 1984, s. 14 (1) (a). - Issued: 14.02.2014. Made: 06.02.2014. Coming into force: 15.02.2014. Effect: None. Territorial extent & classification: E. Local. - Available at http://www.legislation.gov.uk/uksi/2014/285/contents/made Non-print

The M1 Motorway (Junction 34) (Temporary Restriction and Prohibition of Traffic) Order 2014 No. 2014/657. - Enabling power: Road Traffic Regulation Act 1984, s. 14 (1) (a) & S.I. 1982/1163, reg. 16 (2). - Issued: 04.03.2014. Made: 20.02.2014. Coming into force: 28.02.2014. Effect: None. Territorial extent & classification: E. Local. - Available at http://www.legislation.gov.uk/uksi/2014/657/contents/made Non-print

The M1 Motorway (Junction 35A) (Temporary Prohibition of Traffic) Order 2014 No. 2014/2509. - Enabling power: Road Traffic Regulation Act 1984, s. 14 (1) (a)- Issued: 15.09.2014. Made: 11.09.2014. Coming into force: 21.09.2014. Effect: None. Territorial extent & classification: E. Local. - Available at http://www.legislation.gov.uk/uksi/2014/2509/contents/made Non-print

The M1 Motorway (Junction 35 to Junction 34) (Temporary Restriction and Prohibition of Traffic) Order 2014 No. 2014/2313. - Enabling power: Road Traffic Regulation Act 1984, s. 14 (1) (a) & S.I. 1982/1163, reg. 16 (2). - Issued: 01.09.2014. Made: 28.08.2014. Coming into force: 07.09.2014. Effect: None. Territorial extent & classification: E. Local. - Available at http://www.legislation.gov.uk/uksi/2014/2313/contents/made Non-print

The M1 Motorway (Junction 36) (Temporary Prohibition of Traffic) Order 2014 No. 2014/1128. - Enabling power: Road Traffic Regulation Act 1984, s. 14 (1) (a). - Issued: 01.05.2014. Made: 17.04.2014. Coming into force: 27.04.2014. Effect: None. Territorial extent & classification: E. Local. - Available at http://www.legislation.gov.uk/uksi/2014/1128/contents/made Non-print

The M1 Motorway (Junction 36 to Junction 34) (Temporary Restriction and Prohibition of Traffic) Order 2014 No. 2014/751. - Enabling power: Road Traffic Regulation Act 1984, s. 14 (1) (a) & S.I. 1982/1163, reg. 16 (2). - Issued: 11.03.2014. Made: 06.03.2014. Coming into force: 16.03.2014. Effect: None. Territorial extent & classification: E. Local. - Available at http://www.legislation.gov.uk/uksi/2014/751/contents/made Non-print

The M1 Motorway (Junction 36 to Junction 35a) (Temporary Restriction and Prohibition of Traffic) Order 2014 No. 2014/1853. - Enabling power: Road Traffic Regulation Act 1984, ss. 14 (1) (a) & S.I. 1982/1163, reg. 16 (2). - Issued: 16.07.2014. Made: 26.06.2014. Coming into force: 06.07.2014. Effect: None. Territorial extent & classification: E. Local. - Available at http://www.legislation.gov.uk/uksi/2014/1853/contents/made Non-print

The M1 Motorway (Junction 36 to Junction 38) (Temporary Restriction and Prohibition of Traffic) Order 2014 No. 2014/2583. - Enabling power: Road Traffic Regulation Act 1984, s. 14 (1) (a) & S.I. 1982/1163 reg. 16 (2). - Issued: 25.09.2014. Made: 18.09.2014. Coming into force: 30.09.2014. Effect: None. Territorial extent & classification: E. Local. - Available at http://www.legislation.gov.uk/uksi/2014/2583/contents/made Non-print

The M1 Motorway (Junction 37) (Temporary Prohibition of Traffic) Order 2014 No. 2014/3537. - Enabling power: Road Traffic Regulation Act 1984, ss. 14 (1) (a). - Issued: 22.01.2015. Made: 29.12.2014. Coming into force: 11.01.2015. Effect: None. Territorial extent & classification: E. Local. - Available at http://www.legislation.gov.uk/uksi/2014/3537/contents/made Non-print

The M1 Motorway (Junction 37 to Junction 36) (Temporary Restriction and Prohibition of Traffic) (No.2) Order 2014 No. 2014/2965. - Enabling power: Road Traffic Regulation Act 1984, s. 14 (1) (a) & S.I. 1982/1163, reg. 16 (2). - Issued: 27.10.2014. Made: 23.10.2014. Coming into force: 02.11.2014. Effect: None. Territorial extent & classification: E. Local. - Available at http://www.legislation.gov.uk/uksi/2014/2965/contents/made Non-print

The M1 Motorway (Junction 37 to Junction 36) (Temporary Restriction and Prohibition of Traffic) Order 2014 No. 2014/2157. - Enabling power: Road Traffic Regulation Act 1984, ss. 14 (1) (a) & S.I. 1982/1163, reg. 16 (2). - Issued: 12.08.2014. Made: 31.07.2014. Coming into force: 10.08.2014. Effect: None. Territorial extent & classification: E. Local. - Available at http://www.legislation.gov.uk/uksi/2014/2157/contents/made Non-print

The M1 Motorway (Junction 37 to Junction 38) (Temporary Restriction and Prohibition of Traffic) Order 2014 No. 2014/1956. - Enabling power: Road Traffic Regulation Act 1984, s. 14 (1) (a). - Issued: 21.07.2014. Made: 03.07.2014. Coming into force: 10.07.2014. Effect: None. Territorial extent & classification: E. Local. - Available at http://www.legislation.gov.uk/uksi/2014/1956/contents/made Non-print

The M1 Motorway (Junction 38) (Temporary Restriction and Prohibition of Traffic) Order 2014 No. 2014/2470. - Enabling power: Road Traffic Regulation Act 1984, s. 14 (1) (a) & S.I. 1982/1163, reg. 16 (2). - Issued: 10.09.2014. Made: 04.09.2014. Coming into force: 14.09.2014. Effect: None. Territorial extent & classification: E. Local. - Available at http://www.legislation.gov.uk/uksi/2014/2470/contents/made Non-print

The M1 Motorway (Junction 38 to Junction 39) (Temporary Restriction and Prohibition of Traffic) (No.2) Order 2014 No. 2014/3065. - Enabling power: Road Traffic Regulation Act 1984, s. 14 (1) (a) & S.I. 1982/1163, reg. 16 (2). - Issued: 19.11.2014. Made: 30.10.2014. Coming into force: 09.11.2014. Effect: None. Territorial extent & classification: E. Local. - Available at http://www.legislation.gov.uk/uksi/2014/3065/contents/made Non-print

The M1 Motorway (Junction 38 to Junction 39) (Temporary Restriction and Prohibition of Traffic) Order 2014 No. 2014/2099. - Enabling power: Road Traffic Regulation Act 1984, s. 14 (1) (a). - Issued: 07.08.2014. Made: 24.07.2014. Coming into force: 07.08.2014. Effect: None. Territorial extent & classification: E. Local. - Available at http://www.legislation.gov.uk/uksi/2014/2099/contents/made Non-print

The M1 Motorway (Junction 42) (Temporary Prohibition of Traffic) (No.2) Order 2014 No. 2014/3468. - Enabling power: Road Traffic Regulation Act 1984, s. 14 (1) (a). - Issued: 22.12.2014. Made: 18.12.2014. Coming into force: 04.01.2015. Effect: None. Territorial extent & classification: E. Local. - Available at http://www.legislation.gov.uk/uksi/2014/3468/contents/made Non-print

The M1 Motorway (Junction 42) (Temporary Prohibition of Traffic) Order 2014 No. 2014/2167. - Enabling power: Road Traffic Regulation Act 1984, ss. 14 (1) (a). - Issued: 12.08.2014. Made: 31.07.2014. Coming into force: 13.08.2014. Effect: None. Territorial extent & classification: E. Local. - Available at http://www.legislation.gov.uk/uksi/2014/2167/contents/made Non-print

The M1 Motorway (Junction 42 to Junction 44) (Temporary Restriction and Prohibition of Traffic) (No.2) Order 2014 No. 2014/2098. - Enabling power: Road Traffic Regulation Act 1984, s. 14 (1) (a). - Issued: 07.08.2014. Made: 24.07.2014. Coming into force: 03.08.2014. Effect: None. Territorial extent & classification: E. Local. - Available at http://www.legislation.gov.uk/uksi/2014/2098/contents/made Non-print

The M1 Motorway (Junction 42 to Junction 44) (Temporary Restriction and Prohibition of Traffic) (No.3) Order 2014 No. 2014/2427. - Enabling power: Road Traffic Regulation Act 1984, s. 14 (1) (a). - Issued: 10.09.2014. Made: 04.09.2014. Coming into force: 14.09.2014. Effect: None. Territorial extent & classification: E. Local. - Available at http://www.legislation.gov.uk/uksi/2014/2427/contents/made Non-print

The M1 Motorway (Junction 42 to Junction 44) (Temporary Restriction and Prohibition of Traffic) Order 2014 No. 2014/352. - Enabling power: Road Traffic Regulation Act 1984, s. 14 (1) (a). - Issued: 19.02.2014. Made: 13.02.2014. Coming into force: 27.02.2014. Effect: None. Territorial extent & classification: E. Local. - Available at http://www.legislation.gov.uk/uksi/2014/352/contents/made Non-print

The M1 Motorway (Junction 42 to Junction 47) (Temporary Prohibition of Traffic) Order 2014 No. 2014/1349. - Enabling power: Road Traffic Regulation Act 1984, s. 14 (1) (a). - Issued: 29.05.2014. Made: 15.05.2014. Coming into force: 27.05.2014. Effect: None. Territorial extent & classification: E. Local. - Available at http://www.legislation.gov.uk/uksi/2014/1349/contents/made Non-print

The M1 Motorway (Junction 43 to Junction 44) (Temporary Prohibition of Traffic) Order 2014 No. 2014/3542. - Enabling power: Road Traffic Regulation Act 1984, s. 14 (1) (a). - Issued: 22.01.2015. Made: 29.12.2014. Coming into force: 13.01.2015. Effect: None. Territorial extent & classification: E. Local. - Available at http://www.legislation.gov.uk/uksi/2014/3542/contents/made Non-print

The M1 Motorway (Junction 44) (Temporary Prohibition of Traffic) Order 2014 No. 2014/1742. - Enabling power: Road Traffic Regulation Act 1984, s. 14 (1) (a). - Issued: 02.07.2014. Made: 19.06.2014. Coming into force: 29.06.2014. Effect: None. Territorial extent & classification: E. Local. - Available at http://www.legislation.gov.uk/uksi/2014/1742/contents/made Non-print

The M1 Motorway (Junction 45) (Temporary Prohibition of Traffic) (No.2) Order 2014 No. 2014/1572. - Enabling power: Road Traffic Regulation Act 1984, ss. 14 (1) (a). - Issued: 17.06.2014. Made: 29.05.2014. Coming into force: 11.06.2014. Effect: None. Territorial extent & classification: E. Local. - Available at http://www.legislation.gov.uk/uksi/2014/1572/contents/made Non-print

The M1 Motorway (Junction 45) (Temporary Prohibition of Traffic) Order 2014 No. 2014/1126. - Enabling power: Road Traffic Regulation Act 1984, s. 14 (1) (a). - Issued: 01.05.2014. Made: 17.04.2014. Coming into force: 30.04.2014. Effect: None. Territorial extent & classification: E. Local. - Available at http://www.legislation.gov.uk/uksi/2014/1126/contents/made Non-print

The M1 Motorway (Junction 45 to Junction 44) (Temporary Restriction and Prohibition of Traffic) Order 2014 No. 2014/980. - Enabling power: Road Traffic Regulation Act 1984, s. 14 (1) (a). - Issued: 04.04.2014. Made: 20.03.2014. Coming into force: 30.03.2014. Effect: None. Territorial extent & classification: E. Local. - Available at http://www.legislation.gov.uk/uksi/2014/980/contents/made Non-print

The M1 Motorway (Junction 45 to Junction 46) (Temporary Restriction and Prohibition of Traffic) Order 2014 No. 2014/199. - Enabling power: Road Traffic Regulation Act 1984, s. 14 (1) (a) & S.I. 1982/1163, reg. 16 (2). - Issued: 05.02.2014. Made: 09.01.2014. Coming into force: 13.01.2014. Effect: None. Territorial extent & classification: E. Local. - Available at http://www.legislation.gov.uk/uksi/2014/199/contents/made Non-print

The M1 Motorway (Junction 46) (Temporary Restriction and Prohibition of Traffic) (No.2) Order 2014 No. 2014/1080. - Enabling power: Road Traffic Regulation Act 1984, s. 14 (1) (a). - Issued: 28.04.2014. Made: 10.04.2014. Coming into force: 23.04.2014. Effect: None. Territorial extent & classification: E. Local. - Available at http://www.legislation.gov.uk/uksi/2014/1080/contents/made Non-print

The M1 Motorway (Junction 46) (Temporary Restriction and Prohibition of Traffic) Order 2014 No. 2014/64. - Enabling power: Road Traffic Regulation Act 1984, s. 14 (1) (a) & S.I. 1982/1163, reg. 16 (2). - Issued: 20.01.2014. Made: 06.01.2014. Coming into force: 14.01.2014. Effect: None. Territorial extent & classification: E. Local. - Available at http://www.legislation.gov.uk/uksi/2014/64/contents/made Non-print

The M1 Motorway (Junction 46 to Junction 45) (Temporary Prohibition of Traffic) Order 2014 No. 2014/2290. - Enabling power: Road Traffic Regulation Act 1984, s. 14 (1) (a). - Issued: 27.08.2014. Made: 21.08.2014. Coming into force: 31.08.2014. Effect: None. Territorial extent & classification: E. Local. - Available at http://www.legislation.gov.uk/uksi/2014/2290/contents/made Non-print

The M1 Motorway (Junction 47, Parlington) (Temporary Restriction and Prohibition of Traffic) Order 2014 No. 2014/346. - Enabling power: Road Traffic Regulation Act 1984, s. 14 (1) (a) & S.I. 1982/1163, reg. 16 (2). - Issued: 19.02.2014. Made: 13.02.2014. Coming into force: 20.02.2014. Effect: None. Territorial extent & classification: E. Local. - Available at http://www.legislation.gov.uk/uksi/2014/346/contents/made Non-print

The M1 Motorway (Junction 47) (Temporary Prohibition of Traffic) Order 2014 No. 2014/2161. - Enabling power: Road Traffic Regulation Act 1984, ss. 14 (1) (a). - Issued: 12.08.2014. Made: 31.07.2014. Coming into force: 10.08.2014. Effect: None. Territorial extent & classification: E. Local. - Available at http://www.legislation.gov.uk/uksi/2014/2161/contents/made Non-print

The M1 Motorway (Junction 47) (Temporary Restriction and Prohibition of Traffic) (No.2) Order 2014 No. 2014/3035. - Enabling power: Road Traffic Regulation Act 1984, s. 14 (1) (a). - Issued: 13.11.2014. Made: 06.11.2014. Coming into force: 16.11.2014. Effect: None. Territorial extent & classification: E. Local. - Available at http://www.legislation.gov.uk/uksi/2014/3035/contents/made Non-print

The M1 Motorway (Junction 47 to Junction 48) (Temporary Prohibition of Traffic) (No.2) Order 2014 No. 2014/2664. - Enabling power: Road Traffic Regulation Act 1984, s. 14 (1) (a). - Issued: 03.10.2014. Made: 25.10.2014. Coming into force: 05.10.2014. Effect: None. Territorial extent & classification: E. Local. - Available at http://www.legislation.gov.uk/uksi/2014/2664/contents/made Non-print

The M1 Motorway (Junction 47 to Junction 48) (Temporary Restriction and Prohibition of Traffic) Order 2014 No. 2014/153. - Enabling power: Road Traffic Regulation Act 1984, s. 14 (1) (a) & S.I. 1982/1163, reg. 16 (2). - Issued: 30.01.2014. Made: 23.01.2014. Coming into force: 02.02.2014. Effect: None. Territorial extent & classification: E. Local. - Available at http://www.legislation.gov.uk/uksi/2014/153/contents/made Non-print

The M1 Motorway (Junction 48 to Junction 47) and the A1(M) Motorway (Junction 43 to Junction 42) (Temporary Restriction and Prohibition of Traffic) Order 2014 No. 2014/292. - Enabling power: Road Traffic Regulation Act 1984, s. 14 (1) (a) & S.I. 1982/1163, reg. 16 (2). - Issued: 14.02.2014. Made: 06.02.2014. Coming into force: 18.02.2014. Effect: None. Territorial extent & classification: E. Local. - Available at http://www.legislation.gov.uk/uksi/2014/292/contents/made Non-print

The M1 Motorway (Junctions 1 - 4, Slip Roads) (Temporary Prohibition of Traffic) Order 2014 No. 2014/722. - Enabling power: Road Traffic Regulation Act 1984, s. 14 (1) (a). - Issued: 17.03.2014. Made: 10.03.2014. Coming into force: 01.04.2014. Effect: None. Territorial extent & classification: E. Local. - Available at http://www.legislation.gov.uk/uksi/2014/722/contents/made Non-print

The M1 Motorway (Junctions 1 - 6A) (Temporary Prohibition of Traffic) Order 2014 No. 2014/1552. - Enabling power: Road Traffic Regulation Act 1984, s. 14 (1) (a). - Issued: 16.06.2014. Made: 26.05.2014. Coming into force: 14.06.2014. Effect: None. Territorial extent & classification: E. Local. - Available at http://www.legislation.gov.uk/uksi/2014/1552/contents/made Non-print

The M1 Motorway (Junctions 5 - 6a, Link/Slip Roads) (Temporary Prohibition of Traffic) Order 2014 No. 2014/1990. - Enabling power: Road Traffic Regulation Act 1984, s. 14 (1) (a). - Issued: 21.07.2014. Made: 07.07.2014. Coming into force: 01.08.2014. Effect: None. Territorial extent & classification: E. Local. - Available at http://www.legislation.gov.uk/uksi/2014/1990/contents/made Non-print

The M1 Motorway (Junctions 6 - 6A) (Temporary Prohibition of Traffic) Order 2014 No. 2014/988. - Enabling power: Road Traffic Regulation Act 1984, s. 14 (1) (a). - Issued: 31.03.2014. Made: 17.03.2014. Coming into force: 05.04.2014. Effect: None. Territorial extent & classification: E. Local. - Available at http://www.legislation.gov.uk/uksi/2014/988/contents/made Non-print

The M1 Motorway (Junctions 6a, Link Road) (Temporary Prohibition of Traffic) Order 2014 No. 2014/306. - Enabling power: Road Traffic Regulation Act 1984, s. 14 (1) (a). - Issued: 13.02.2014. Made: 10.02.2014. Coming into force: 01.03.2014. Effect: None. Territorial extent & classification: E. Local. - Available at http://www.legislation.gov.uk/uksi/2014/306/contents/made Non-print

The M1 Motorway (Junctions 11 to 13) (Temporary Prohibition of Traffic) Order 2014 No. 2014/3524. - Enabling power: Road Traffic Regulation Act 1984, s. 14 (1) (a). - Issued: 22.01.2015. Made: 29.12.2015. Coming into force: 05.01.2015. Effect: None. Territorial extent & classification: E. Local. - Available at http://www.legislation.gov.uk/uksi/2014/3524/contents/made Non-print

The M1 Motorway (Junctions 14 - 15, Northamptonshire) (Temporary Prohibition of Traffic) Order 2014 No. 2014/2606. - Enabling power: Road Traffic Regulation Act 1984, s. 14 (1) (a). - Issued: 30.09.2014. Made: 15.09.2014. Coming into force: 22.09.2014. Effect: None. Territorial extent & classification: E. Local. - Available at http://www.legislation.gov.uk/uksi/2014/2606/contents/made Non-print

The M1 Motorway (Junctions 15-16, Northamptonshire) (Temporary Restriction and Prohibition of Traffic) Order 2014 No. 2014/2985. - Enabling power: Road Traffic Regulation Act 1984, ss. 14 (1) (a), 15 (2) & S.I. 1982/1163, reg. 16 (2). - Issued: 13.11.2014. Made: 27.10.2014. Coming into force: 03.11.2014. Effect: None. Territorial extent & classification: E. Local. - Available at http://www.legislation.gov.uk/uksi/2014/2985/contents/made Non-print

The M1 Motorway (Junctions 15-16, Northamptonshire) (Temporary Restriction and Prohibition of Traffic) Order 2014 No. 2014/2984. - Enabling power: Road Traffic Regulation Act 1984, ss. 14 (1) (a), 15 (2) & S.I. 1982/1163, reg. 16 (2). - Issued: 13.11.2014. Made: 27.10.2014. Coming into force: 03.11.2014. Effect: None. Territorial extent & classification: E. Local. - Available at http://www.legislation.gov.uk/uksi/2014/2984/contents/made Non-print

The M1 Motorway (Junctions 22 to 21a, Leicestershire) (Temporary Prohibition of Traffic) Order 2014 No. 2014/2981. - Enabling power: Road Traffic Regulation Act 1984, s. 14 (1) (a). - Issued: 13.11.2014. Made: 27.10.2014. Coming into force: 03.11.2014. Effect: None. Territorial extent & classification: E. Local. - Available at http://www.legislation.gov.uk/uksi/2014/2981/contents/made Non-print

The M1 Motorway (Junctions 22 to 23, Leicestershire) (Temporary Restriction and Prohibition of Traffic) Order 2014 No. 2014/1723. - Enabling power: Road Traffic Regulation Act 1984, s. 14 (1) (a). - Issued: 03.07.2014. Made: 16.06.2014. Coming into force: 23.06.2014. Effect: None. Territorial extent & classification: E. Local. - Available at http://www.legislation.gov.uk/uksi/2014/1723/contents/made Non-print

The M1 Motorway (Junctions 24a and 25) (Slip Roads) (Temporary Prohibition of Traffic) Order 2014 No. 2014/3360. - Enabling power: Road Traffic Regulation Act 1984, s. 14 (1) (a). - Issued: 28.11.2014. Made: 17.11.2014. Coming into force: 24.11.2014. Effect: None. Territorial extent & classification: E. Local. - Available at http://www.legislation.gov.uk/uksi/2014/3360/contents/made Non-print

The M1 Motorway (Junctions 24 to 23a, Kegworth, Leicestershire) (Temporary Restriction and Prohibition of Traffic) Order 2014 No. 2014/2134. - Enabling power: Road Traffic Regulation Act 1984, s. 14 (1) (a). - Issued: 12.08.2014. Made: 21.07.2014. Coming into force: 28.07.2014. Effect: None. Territorial extent & classification: E. Local. - Available at http://www.legislation.gov.uk/uksi/2014/2134/contents/made Non-print

The M1 Motorway (Junctions 24 to 25, Leicestershire) (Temporary Restriction and Prohibition of Traffic) Order 2014 No. 2014/1726. - Enabling power: Road Traffic Regulation Act 1984, s. 14 (1) (a) (7) & S.I. 1982/1163, reg. 16 (2). - Issued: 03.07.2014. Made: 16.06.2014. Coming into force: 23.06.2014. Effect: None. Territorial extent & classification: E. Local. - Available at http://www.legislation.gov.uk/uksi/2014/1726/contents/made Non-print

The M1 Motorway (M1 Junctions 21 to 20) (Temporary Restriction of Traffic) Order 2014 No. 2014/2248. - Enabling power: Road Traffic Regulation Act 1984, ss. 14 (1) (a). - Issued: 27.08.2014. Made: 12.08.2014. Coming into force: 19.08.2014. Effect: None. Territorial extent & classification: E. Local. - Available at http://www.legislation.gov.uk/uksi/2014/2248/contents/made Non-print

The M1 Motorway (North of Junction 14) (Temporary 50 Miles Per Hour Speed Restriction) Order 2014 No. 2014/3006. - Enabling power: Road Traffic Regulation Act 1984, s. 14 (1) (a) (7) & S.I. 1982/1163, reg. 16 (2). - Issued: 12.11.2014. Made: 03.11.2014. Coming into force: 10.11.2014. Effect: None. Territorial extent & classification: E. Local. - Available at http://www.legislation.gov.uk/uksi/2014/3006/contents/made Non-print

The M1 Motorway (North of Junction 22, Markfield, Leicestershire) (Temporary Restriction of Traffic) Order 2014 No. 2014/2135. - Enabling power: Road Traffic Regulation Act 1984, s. 14 (1) (a). - Issued: 12.08.2014. Made: 21.07.2014. Coming into force: 28.07.2014. Effect: None. Territorial extent & classification: E. Local. - Available at http://www.legislation.gov.uk/uksi/2014/2135/contents/made Non-print

The M1 Motorway (Trowell, Nottinghamshire) (Temporary Prohibition of Traffic) Order 2014 No. 2014/2452. - Enabling power: Road Traffic Regulation Act 1984, s. 14 (1) (a). - Issued: 15.09.2014. Made: 02.09.2014. Coming into force: 09.09.2014. Effect: None. Territorial extent & classification: E. Local. - Available at http://www.legislation.gov.uk/uksi/2014/2452/contents/made Non-print

The M2 Motorway and the A2 Trunk Road (Junctions 1 - 4, Slip Roads) (Temporary Prohibition of Traffic) Order 2014 No. 2014/1000. - Enabling power: Road Traffic Regulation Act 1984, s. 14 (1) (a). - Issued: 07.04.2014. Made: 24.03.2014. Coming into force: 16.04.2014. Effect: None. Territorial extent & classification: E. Local. - Available at http://www.legislation.gov.uk/uksi/2014/1000/contents/made Non-print

The M2 Motorway (Junction 2) (Temporary Prohibition of Traffic) Order 2014 No. 2014/1653. - Enabling power: Road Traffic Regulation Act 1984, ss. 14 (1) (a). - Issued: 26.08.2014. Made: 09.06.2014. Coming into force: 28.06.2014. Effect: None. Territorial extent & classification: E. Local. - Available at http://www.legislation.gov.uk/uksi/2014/1653/contents/made Non-print

The M2 Motorway (Junctions 4 - 6) (Temporary Restriction and Prohibition of Traffic) Order 2014 No. 2014/3547. - Enabling power: Road Traffic Regulation Act 1984, ss. 14 (1) (a). - Issued: 22.01.2015. Made: 29.12.2014. Coming into force: 17.01.2015. Effect: None. Territorial extent & classification: E. Local. - Available at http://www.legislation.gov.uk/uksi/2014/3547/contents/made Non-print

The M2 Motorway (Junctions 5 - 6) (Temporary Restriction of Traffic) Order 2014 No. 2014/3503. - Enabling power: Road Traffic Regulation Act 1984, s. 14 (1) (b). - Issued: 22.01.2015. Made: 17.11.2014. Coming into force: 06.12.2014. Effect: None. Territorial extent & classification: E. Local. - Available at http://www.legislation.gov.uk/uksi/2014/3503/contents/made Non-print

The M2 Motorway (Junctions 5 - 7, Slip Roads) (Temporary Prohibition of Traffic) Order 2014 No. 2014/996. - Enabling power: Road Traffic Regulation Act 1984, s. 14 (1) (a). - Issued: 04.04.2014. Made: 24.03.2014. Coming into force: 16.04.2014. Effect: None. Territorial extent & classification: E. Local. - Available at http://www.legislation.gov.uk/uksi/2014/996/contents/made Non-print

The M2 Motorway (Junctions 6 - 7) (Temporary Restriction and Prohibition of Traffic) Order 2014 No. 2014/37. - Enabling power: Road Traffic Regulation Act 1984, s. 14 (1) (a). - Issued: 15.01.2014. Made: 13.01.2014. Coming into force: 01.02.2014. Effect: None. Territorial extent & classification: E. Local. - Available at http://www.legislation.gov.uk/uksi/2014/37/contents/made Non-print

The M3 Motorway and the A316 Trunk Road (Junction 1, Slip Roads) (Temporary Prohibition of Traffic) Order 2014 No. 2014/3461. - Enabling power: Road Traffic Regulation Act 1984, s. 14 (1) (a). - Issued: 18.12.2014. Made: 15.12.2014. Coming into force: 15.01.2015. Effect: None. Territorial extent & classification: E. Local. - Available at http://www.legislation.gov.uk/uksi/2014/3461/contents/made Non-print

The M3 Motorway and the M27 Motorway (Chilworth Interchange - M3 Junction 14, Northbound) (Temporary Prohibition of Traffic) Order 2014 No. 2014/1053. - Enabling power: Road Traffic Regulation Act 1984, s. 14 (1) (a). - Issued: 22.04.2014. Made: 07.04.2014. Coming into force: 01.05.2014. Effect: None. Territorial extent & classification: E. Local. - Available at http://www.legislation.gov.uk/uksi/2014/1053/contents/made Non-print

The M3 Motorway (Junction 2, Westbound Carriageway) (Temporary Prohibition of Traffic) Order 2014 No. 2014/2971. - Enabling power: Road Traffic Regulation Act 1984, s. 14 (1) (a). - Issued: 13.10.2014. Made: 06.10.2014. Coming into force: 01.11.2014. Effect: None. Territorial extent & classification: E. Local. - Available at http://www.legislation.gov.uk/uksi/2014/2971/contents/made Non-print

The M3 Motorway (Junction 4 - Kitsmead Lane, Carriageways) (Temporary Restriction of Traffic) Order 2014 No. 2014/151. - Enabling power: Road Traffic Regulation Act 1984, s. 14 (1) (a). - Issued: 30.01.2014. Made: 21.01.2014. Coming into force: 15.02.2014. Effect: None. Territorial extent & classification: E. Local. - Available at http://www.legislation.gov.uk/uksi/2014/151/contents/made Non-print

The M3 Motorway (Junction 4, Slip Roads) (Temporary Prohibition of Traffic) Order 2014 No. 2014/1050. - Enabling power: Road Traffic Regulation Act 1984, s. 14 (1) (a). - Issued: 22.04.2014. Made: 07.04.2014. Coming into force: 26.04.2014. Effect: None. Territorial extent & classification: E. Local. - Available at http://www.legislation.gov.uk/uksi/2014/1050/contents/made Non-print

The M3 Motorway (Junction 6, Spur Road) (Temporary Prohibition of Traffic) (No.2) Order 2014 No. 2014/2504. - Enabling power: Road Traffic Regulation Act 1984, s. 14 (1) (a). - Issued: 09.09.2014. Made: 01.09.2014. Coming into force: 20.09.2014. Effect: None. Territorial extent & classification: E. Local. - Available at http://www.legislation.gov.uk/uksi/2014/2504/contents/made Non-print

The M3 Motorway (Junction 6, Spur Road) (Temporary Prohibition of Traffic) (No.3) Order 2014 No. 2014/3499. - Enabling power: Road Traffic Regulation Act 1984, s. 14 (1) (a). - Issued: 19.01.2014. Made: 24.11.2014. Coming into force: 13.12.2014. Effect: None. Territorial extent & classification: E. Local. - Available at http://www.legislation.gov.uk/uksi/2014/3499/contents/made Non-print

The M3 Motorway (Junction 6, Spur Road) (Temporary Restriction of Traffic) Order 2014 No. 2014/1655. - Enabling power: Road Traffic Regulation Act 1984, s. 14 (1) (a). - Issued: 26.06.2014. Made: 09.06.2014. Coming into force: 28.06.2014. Effect: None. Territorial extent & classification: E. Local. - Available at http://www.legislation.gov.uk/uksi/2014/1655/contents/made Non-print

The M3 Motorway (Junctions 3 - 13, Slip Roads) (Temporary Prohibition of Traffic) Order 2014 No. 2014/305. - Enabling power: Road Traffic Regulation Act 1984, s. 14 (1) (a). - Issued: 13.02.2014. Made: 10.02.2014. Coming into force: 01.03.2014. Effect: None. Territorial extent & classification: E. Local. - Available at http://www.legislation.gov.uk/uksi/2014/305/contents/made Non-print

The M3 Motorway (Junctions 4 - 5) (Temporary Prohibition of Traffic) Order 2014 No. 2014/2215. - Enabling power: Road Traffic Regulation Act 1984, s. 14 (1) (a). - Issued: 21.08.2014. Made: 11.08.2014. Coming into force: 30.08.2014. Effect: None. Territorial extent & classification: E. Local. - Available at http://www.legislation.gov.uk/uksi/2014/2215/contents/made Non-print

The M3 Motorway (Junctions 9 - 8) (Temporary Prohibition of Traffic) Order 2014 No. 2014/1124. - Enabling power: Road Traffic Regulation Act 1984, s. 14 (1) (a). - Issued: 01.05.2014. Made: 14.04.2014. Coming into force: 07.05.2014. Effect: None. Territorial extent & classification: E. Local. - Available at http://www.legislation.gov.uk/uksi/2014/1124/contents/made Non-print

The M3 Motorway (Junctions 13 and 14, Slip/Link Roads) (Temporary Prohibition of Traffic) Order 2014 No. 2014/1323. - Enabling power: Road Traffic Regulation Act 1984, s. 14 (1) (a). - Issued: 27.05.2014. Made: 12.05.2014. Coming into force: 05.06.2014. Effect: None. Territorial extent & classification: E. Local. - Available at http://www.legislation.gov.uk/uksi/2014/1323/contents/made Non-print

ROAD TRAFFIC: TRAFFIC REGULATION

The M3 Motorway (Junctions 14 - 4, Carriageways) (Temporary Restriction of Traffic) Order 2014 No. 2014/3394. - Enabling power: Road Traffic Regulation Act 1984, s. 14 (1) (a). - Issued: 06.11.2014. Made: 03.11.2014. Coming into force: 30.11.2014. Effect: None. Territorial extent & classification: E. Local. - Available at http://www.legislation.gov.uk/uksi/2014/3394/contents/made Non-print

The M4 and M25 Motorways (M4 Junctions 4 and 5 and M25 Junctions 14, 17 and 18) (Temporary Restriction and Prohibition of Traffic) Order 2014 No. 2014/2219. - Enabling power: Road Traffic Regulation Act 1984, s. 14 (1) (a). - Issued: 21.08.2014. Made: 11.08.2014. Coming into force: 30.08.2014. Effect: None. Territorial extent & classification: E. Local. - Available at http://www.legislation.gov.uk/uksi/2014/2219/contents/made Non-print

The M4 Motorway and the A34 Trunk Road (M4 Junction 13) (Temporary Prohibition of Traffic) Order 2014 No. 2014/2529. - Enabling power: Road Traffic Regulation Act 1984, s. 14 (1) (a). - Issued: 18.09.2014. Made: 15.09.2014. Coming into force: 04.10.2014. Effect: None. Territorial extent & classification: E. Local. - Available at http://www.legislation.gov.uk/uksi/2014/2529/contents/made Non-print

The M4 Motorway and the A34 Trunk Road (M4 Junctions 12 - 14) (Temporary Restriction and Prohibition of Traffic) Order 2014 No. 2014/3454. - Enabling power: Road Traffic Regulation Act 1984, s. 14 (1) (a) (7). - Issued: 17.12.2014. Made: 15.12.2014. Coming into force: 03.01.2015. Effect: None. Territorial extent & classification: E. Local. - Available at http://www.legislation.gov.uk/uksi/2014/3454/contents/made Non-print

The M4 Motorway (Junction 2, Elevated Section) (Temporary Prohibition of Traffic) Order 2014 No. 2014/1758. - Enabling power: Road Traffic Regulation Act 1984, s. 14 (1) (a). - Issued: 04.07.2014. Made: 23.06.2014. Coming into force: 12.07.2014. Effect: None. Territorial extent & classification: E. Local. - Available at http://www.legislation.gov.uk/uksi/2014/1758/contents/made Non-print

The M4 Motorway (Junction 5-West of Junction 14), Carriageways (Temporary Restriction of Traffic) Order 2014 No. 2014/2334. - Enabling power: Road Traffic Regulation Act 1984, s. 14 (1) (a). - Issued: 04.09.2014. Made: 01.09.2014. Coming into force: 22.09.2014. Effect: None. Territorial extent & classification: E. Local. - Available at http://www.legislation.gov.uk/uksi/2014/2334/contents/made Non-print

The M4 Motorway (Junction 10, Link Roads) (Temporary Prohibition of Traffic) Order 2014 No. 2014/3456. - Enabling power: Road Traffic Regulation Act 1984, s. 14 (1) (a). - Issued: 15.12.2014. Made: 08.12.2014. Coming into force: 01.02.2015. Effect: None. Territorial extent & classification: E. Local. - Available at http://www.legislation.gov.uk/uksi/2014/3456/contents/made Non-print

The M4 Motorway (Junction 14 - 15) (Temporary Prohibition of Traffic) Order 2014 No. 2014/1049. - Enabling power: Road Traffic Regulation Act 1984, s. 14 (1) (a). - Issued: 22.04.2014. Made: 07.04.2014. Coming into force: 26.04.2014. Effect: None. Territorial extent & classification: E. Local. - Available at http://www.legislation.gov.uk/uksi/2014/1049/contents/made Non-print

The M4 Motorway (Junction 15 - West of Junction 14) (Temporary Restriction and Prohibition of Traffic) Order 2014 No. 2014/2537. - Enabling power: Road Traffic Regulation Act 1984, s. 14 (1) (a). - Issued: 12.09.2014. Made: 08.09.2014. Coming into force: 03.10.2014. Effect: None. Territorial extent & classification: E. Local. - Available at http://www.legislation.gov.uk/uksi/2014/2537/contents/made Non-print

The M4 Motorway (Junction 16 Westbound Entry Slip Road) (Temporary Prohibition of Traffic) Order 2014 No. 2014/3387. - Enabling power: Road Traffic Regulation Act 1984, s. 14 (1) (a). - Issued: 25.11.2014. Made: 20.11.2014. Coming into force: 29.11.2014. Effect: None. Territorial extent & classification: E. Local. - Available at http://www.legislation.gov.uk/uksi/2014/3387/contents/made Non-print

The M4 Motorway (Junction 16 Westbound Exit Slip Road) (Temporary Prohibition of Traffic) Order 2014 No. 2014/1778. - Enabling power: Road Traffic Regulation Act 1984, s. 14 (1) (a). - Issued: 09.07.2014. Made: 25.06.2014. Coming into force: 28.06.2014. Effect: None. Territorial extent & classification: E. Local. - Available at http://www.legislation.gov.uk/uksi/2014/1778/contents/made Non-print

The M4 Motorway (Junction 17 Exit Slip Roads) (Temporary Prohibition of Traffic) Order 2014 No. 2014/1734. - Enabling power: Road Traffic Regulation Act 1984, s. 14 (1) (a). - Issued: 04.07.2014. Made: 24.06.2014. Coming into force: 28.06.2014. Effect: None. Territorial extent & classification: E. Local. - Available at http://www.legislation.gov.uk/uksi/2014/1734/contents/made Non-print

The M4 Motorway (Junction 18 Slip Roads) (Temporary Prohibition of Traffic) (Number 2) Order 2014 No. 2014/760. - Enabling power: Road Traffic Regulation Act 1984, s. 14 (1) (a). - Issued: 11.03.2014. Made: 04.03.2014. Coming into force: 08.03.2014. Effect: None. Territorial extent & classification: E. Local. - Available at http://www.legislation.gov.uk/uksi/2014/760/contents/made Non-print

The M4 Motorway (Junction 18 Slip Roads) (Temporary Prohibition of Traffic) Order 2014 No. 2014/426. - Enabling power: Road Traffic Regulation Act 1984, s. 14 (1) (a). - Issued: 27.02.2014. Made: 18.02.2014. Coming into force: 22.02.2014. Effect: None. Territorial extent & classification: E. Local. - Available at http://www.legislation.gov.uk/uksi/2014/426/contents/made Non-print

The M4 Motorway (Junction 18) (Temporary Restriction and Prohibition of Traffic) Order 2014 No. 2014/246. - Enabling power: Road Traffic Regulation Act 1984, s. 14 (1) (a) & S.I. 1982/1163, reg. 16 (2). - Issued: 11.02.2014. Made: 04.02.2014. Coming into force: 08.02.2014. Effect: None. Territorial extent & classification: E. Local. - Available at http://www.legislation.gov.uk/uksi/2014/246/contents/made Non-print

The M4 Motorway (Junction 19 Eastbound Slip Roads) (Temporary Prohibition of Traffic) Order 2014 No. 2014/1776. - Enabling power: Road Traffic Regulation Act 1984, s. 14 (1) (a). - Issued: 09.07.2014. Made: 25.06.2014. Coming into force: 28.06.2014. Effect: None. Territorial extent & classification: E. Local. - Available at http://www.legislation.gov.uk/uksi/2014/1776/contents/made Non-print

The M4 Motorway (Junction 19 Westbound Entry Slip Road) (Temporary Prohibition of Traffic) Order 2014 No. 2014/1673. - Enabling power: Road Traffic Regulation Act 1984, s. 14 (1) (a). - Issued: 01.07.2014. Made: 10.06.2014. Coming into force: 14.06.2014. Effect: None. Territorial extent & classification: E. Local. - Available at http://www.legislation.gov.uk/uksi/2014/1673/contents/made Non-print

The M4 Motorway (Junction 22 Slip Roads) (Temporary Prohibition of Traffic) Order 2014 No. 2014/1691. - Enabling power: Road Traffic Regulation Act 1984, s. 14 (1) (a). - Issued: 01.07.2014. Made: 10.06.2014. Coming into force: 14.06.2014. Effect: None. Territorial extent & classification: E. Local. - Available at http://www.legislation.gov.uk/uksi/2014/1691/contents/made Non-print

The M4 Motorway (Junction 22) (Temporary Prohibition of Traffic) Order 2014 No. 2014/976. - Enabling power: Road Traffic Regulation Act 1984, s. 14 (1) (a). - Issued: 10.04.2014. Made: 26.03.2014. Coming into force: 29.03.2014. Effect: None. Territorial extent & classification: E. Local. - Available at http://www.legislation.gov.uk/uksi/2014/976/contents/made Non-print

The M4 Motorway (Junctions 1 - 3) (Temporary Prohibition of Traffic) Order 2014 No. 2014/720. - Enabling power: Road Traffic Regulation Act 1984, s. 14 (1) (a). - Issued: 10.03.2014. Made: 03.03.2014. Coming into force: 01.04.2014. Effect: None. Territorial extent & classification: E. Local. - Available at http://www.legislation.gov.uk/uksi/2014/720/contents/made Non-print

The M4 Motorway (Junctions 3 - 5, Link and Slip Roads) (Temporary Prohibition of Traffic) Order 2014 No. 2014/1993. - Enabling power: Road Traffic Regulation Act 1984, s. 14 (1) (a). - Issued: 21.07.2014. Made: 07.07.2014. Coming into force: 02.08.2014. Effect: None. Territorial extent & classification: E. Local. - Available at http://www.legislation.gov.uk/uksi/2014/1993/contents/made Non-print

ROAD TRAFFIC: TRAFFIC REGULATION

The M4 Motorway (Junctions 5 and 6) (Temporary Prohibition and Restriction of Traffic) Order 2014 No. 2014/2327. - Enabling power: Road Traffic Regulation Act 1984, s. 14 (1) (a). - Issued: 28.08.2014. Made: 26.08.2014. Coming into force: 13.09.2014. Effect: None. Territorial extent & classification: E. Local. - Available at http://www.legislation.gov.uk/uksi/2014/2327/contents/made
Non-print

The M4 Motorway (Junctions 8/9 - 10) (Temporary Prohibition of Traffic) Order 2014 No. 2014/1752. - Enabling power: Road Traffic Regulation Act 1984, s. 14 (1) (a). - Issued: 03.07.2014. Made: 23.06.2014. Coming into force: 12.07.2014. Effect: None. Territorial extent & classification: E. Local. - Revoked by S.I. 2014/2412 (Non-print). - Available at http://www.legislation.gov.uk/uksi/2014/1752/contents/made
Non-print

The M4 Motorway (Junctions 8/9 - 10) (Temporary Restriction and Prohibition of Traffic) (No.2) Order 2014 No. 2014/2412. - Enabling power: Road Traffic Regulation Act 1984, s. 14 (1) (a), sch. 9 para. 27 (1). - Issued: 08.09.2014. Made: 18.09.2014. Coming into force: 06.09.2014. Effect: S.I. 2014/1752 revoked. Territorial extent & classification: E. Local. - Available at http://www.legislation.gov.uk/uksi/2014/2412/contents/made
Non-print

The M4 Motorway (Junctions 10 - 11) (No 2) (Temporary Restriction and Prohibition of Traffic) Order 2014 No. 2014/1654. - Enabling power: Road Traffic Regulation Act 1984, s. 14 (1) (a), sch. 9, para. 27 (1). - Issued: 26.06.2014. Made: 09.06.2014. Coming into force: 28.06.2014. Effect: None. Territorial extent & classification: E. Local. - Available at http://www.legislation.gov.uk/uksi/2014/1654/contents/made
Non-print

The M4 Motorway (Junctions 10 - 11) (Temporary Restriction and Prohibition of Traffic) Order 2014 No. 2014/169. - Enabling power: Road Traffic Regulation Act 1984, s. 14 (1) (a). - Issued: 30.01.2014. Made: 27.01.2014. Coming into force: 15.02.2014. Effect: None. Territorial extent & classification: E. Local. - Available at http://www.legislation.gov.uk/uksi/2014/169/contents/made Non-print

The M4 Motorway (Junctions 10) (Temporary Restriction and Prohibition of Traffic) Order 2014 No. 2014/1658. - Enabling power: Road Traffic Regulation Act 1984, s. 14 (1) (a). - Issued: 30.06.2014. Made: 09.06.2014. Coming into force: 29.06.2014. Effect: None. Territorial extent & classification: E. Local. - Available at http://www.legislation.gov.uk/uksi/2014/1658/contents/made
Non-print

The M4 Motorway (Junctions 12 - 10) (Temporary Prohibition of Traffic) Order 2014 No. 2014/1177. - Enabling power: Road Traffic Regulation Act 1984, s. 14 (1) (a). - Issued: 02.05.2014. Made: 21.04.2014. Coming into force: 10.05.2014. Effect: None. Territorial extent & classification: E. Local. - Available at http://www.legislation.gov.uk/uksi/2014/1177/contents/made
Non-print

The M4 Motorway (Junctions 13 - 14) (Temporary Restriction and Prohibition of Traffic) Order 2014 No. 2014/2105. - Enabling power: Road Traffic Regulation Act 1984, s. 14 (1) (a). - Issued: 07.08.2014. Made: 21.07.2014. Coming into force: 09.08.2014. Effect: None. Territorial extent & classification: E. Local. - Available at http://www.legislation.gov.uk/uksi/2014/2105/contents/made
Non-print

The M4 Motorway (Junctions 15-16) (Temporary Restriction of Traffic) Order 2014 No. 2014/1701. - Enabling power: Road Traffic Regulation Act 1984, s. 14 (1) (a). - Issued: 02.07.2014. Made: 17.06.2014. Coming into force: 21.06.2014. Effect: None. Territorial extent & classification: E. Local. - Available at http://www.legislation.gov.uk/uksi/2014/1701/contents/made
Non-print

The M4 Motorway (Junctions 15-18) (Temporary Restriction and Prohibition of Traffic) Order 2014 No. 2014/3519. - Enabling power: Road Traffic Regulation Act 1984, s. 14 (1) (a) & Motorways Traffic (England and Wales) Regulations 1982, reg. 16 (2). - Issued: 22.01.2015. Made: 30.12.2014. Coming into force: 03.01.2015. Effect: None. Territorial extent & classification: E. Local. - Available at http://www.legislation.gov.uk/uksi/2014/3519/contents/made
Non-print

The M4 Motorway (Junctions 16-17) (Temporary Restriction of Traffic) (Number 2) Order 2014 No. 2014/3419. - Enabling power: Road Traffic Regulation Act 1984, s. 14 (1) (a) & S.I. 1982/1163 reg. 16 (2). - Issued: 05.12.2014. Made: 02.12.2014. Coming into force: 06.12.2014. Effect: None. Territorial extent & classification: E. Local. - Available at http://www.legislation.gov.uk/uksi/2014/3419/contents/made
Non-print

The M4 Motorway (Junctions 16-17) (Temporary Restriction of Traffic) Order 2014 No. 2014/1163. - Enabling power: Road Traffic Regulation Act 1984, s. 14 (1) (a) & S.I. 1982/1163, reg. 16 (2). - Issued: 02.05.2014. Made: 22.04.2014. Coming into force: 29.04.2014. Effect: None. Territorial extent & classification: E. Local. - Available at http://www.legislation.gov.uk/uksi/2014/1163/contents/made
Non-print

The M4 Motorway (Junctions 17-18) (Temporary Restriction and Prohibition of Traffic) (No. 2) Order 2014 No. 2014/3518. - Enabling power: Road Traffic Regulation Act 1984, s. 14 (1) (a) & S.I. 1982/1163, reg. 16 (2). - Issued: 22.01.2015. Made: 29.12.2014. Coming into force: 02.01.2015. Effect: None. Territorial extent & classification: E. Local. - Available at http://www.legislation.gov.uk/uksi/2014/3518/contents/made
Non-print

The M4 Motorway (Junctions 17-18) (Temporary Restriction and Prohibition of Traffic) (Number 2) Order 2014 No. 2014/3557. - Enabling power: Road Traffic Regulation Act 1984, s. 14 (1) (a) & S.I. 1982/1163, reg. 16 (2). - Issued: 24.02.2014. Made: 29.12.2014. Coming into force: 02.01.2015. Effect: None. Territorial extent & classification: E. Local. - Available at http://www.legislation.gov.uk/uksi/2014/3557/contents/made
Non-print

The M4 Motorway (Junctions 17-18) (Temporary Restriction and Prohibition of Traffic) Order 2014 No. 2014/803. - Enabling power: Road Traffic Regulation Act 1984, s. 14 (1) (a). - Issued: 26.03.2014. Made: 11.03.2014. Coming into force: 14.03.2014. Effect: None. Territorial extent & classification: E. Local. - Available at http://www.legislation.gov.uk/uksi/2014/803/contents/made Non-print

The M4 Motorway (Junctions 19-18) (Temporary Restriction and Prohibition of Traffic) Order 2014 No. 2014/2992. - Enabling power: Road Traffic Regulation Act 1984, s. 14 (1) (a) & S.I. 1982/1163, reg. 16 (2). - Issued: 12.11.2014. Made: 05.11.2014. Coming into force: 08.11.2014. Effect: None. Territorial extent & classification: E. Local. - Available at http://www.legislation.gov.uk/uksi/2014/2992/contents/made
Non-print

The M4 Motorway (Second Severn Crossing) (Temporary Prohibition of Traffic) Order 2014 No. 2014/2798. - Enabling power: Road Traffic Regulation Act 1984, s. 14 (1) (a). - Issued: 16.10.2014. Made: 14.10.2014. Coming into force: 18.10.2014. Effect: None. Territorial extent & classification: E. Local. - Available at http://www.legislation.gov.uk/uksi/2014/2798/contents/made
Non-print

The M5 and M6 Motorways (Ray Hall Interchange, Sandwell) (Link Road) (Temporary Prohibition of Traffic) Order 2014 No. 2014/717. - Enabling power: Road Traffic Regulation Act 1984, s. 14 (1) (a). - Issued: 10.03.2014. Made: 24.02.2014. Coming into force: 03.03.2014. Effect: None. Territorial extent & classification: E. Local. - Available at http://www.legislation.gov.uk/uksi/2014/717/contents/made Non-print

The M5 and M42 Motorways (Bromsgrove, Worcestershire) (Link Road) (Temporary Prohibition of Traffic) Order 2014 No. 2014/801. - Enabling power: Road Traffic Regulation Act 1984, s. 14 (1) (a). - Issued: 26.03.2014. Made: 10.03.2014. Coming into force: 17.03.2014. Effect: None. Territorial extent & classification: E. Local. - Available at http://www.legislation.gov.uk/uksi/2014/801/contents/made Non-print

The M5 and M42 Motorways (M5 Junctions 3 to 5, Worcestershire) (Temporary Restriction and Prohibition of Traffic) Order 2014 No. 2014/1138. - Enabling power: Road Traffic Regulation Act 1984, s. 14 (1) (a). - Issued: 02.05.2014. Made: 14.04.2014. Coming into force: 21.04.2014. Effect: None. Territorial extent & classification: E. Local. - Available at http://www.legislation.gov.uk/uksi/2014/1138/contents/made
Non-print

The M5 Motorway and A46 Trunk Road (Ashchurch, Gloucestershire) (Temporary Prohibition of Traffic) Order 2014 No. 2014/806. - Enabling power: Road Traffic Regulation Act 1984, s. 14 (1) (a). - Issued: 26.03.2014. Made: 10.03.2014. Coming into force: 17.03.2014. Effect: None. Territorial extent & classification: E. Local. - Available at http://www.legislation.gov.uk/uksi/2014/806/contents/made Non-print

The M5 Motorway and A46 Trunk Road (M5 Junction 9, Gloucestershire) (Temporary Prohibition of Traffic) Order 2014 No. 2014/3405. - Enabling power: Road Traffic Regulation Act 1984, s. 14 (1) (a). - Issued: 28.11.2014. Made: 24.11.2014. Coming into force: 01.12.2014. Effect: None. Territorial extent & classification: E. Local. - Available at http://www.legislation.gov.uk/uksi/2014/3405/contents/made Non-print

The M5 Motorway (Gloucester Gateway Services) (Temporary Restriction and Prohibition of Traffic) Order 2014 No. 2014/977. - Enabling power: Road Traffic Regulation Act 1984, s. 14 (1) (a). - Issued: 10.04.2014. Made: 26.03.2014. Coming into force: 29.03.2014. Effect: None. Territorial extent & classification: E. Local. - Available at http://www.legislation.gov.uk/uksi/2014/977/contents/made Non-print

The M5 Motorway (Great Barr) (Link Road) (Temporary Prohibition of Traffic) Order 2014 No. 2014/279. - Enabling power: Road Traffic Regulation Act 1984, s. 14 (1) (a). - Issued: 14.02.2014. Made: 03.02.2014. Coming into force: 10.02.2014. Effect: None. Territorial extent & classification: E. Local. - Available at http://www.legislation.gov.uk/uksi/2014/279/contents/made Non-print

The M5 Motorway (Junction 1, Sandwell) (Slip Road) (Temporary Prohibition of Traffic) Order 2014 No. 2014/1157. - Enabling power: Road Traffic Regulation Act 1984, s. 14 (1) (a). - Issued: 07.05.2014. Made: 18.04.2014. Coming into force: 25.04.2014. Effect: None. Territorial extent & classification: E. Local. - Available at http://www.legislation.gov.uk/uksi/2014/1157/contents/made Non-print

The M5 Motorway (Junction 1, Sandwell) (Temporary Prohibition of Traffic) Order 2014 No. 2014/2611. - Enabling power: Road Traffic Regulation Act 1984, s. 14 (1) (a). - Issued: 30.09.2014. Made: 15.09.2014. Coming into force: 22.09.2014. Effect: None. Territorial extent & classification: E. Local. - Available at http://www.legislation.gov.uk/uksi/2014/2611/contents/made Non-print

The M5 Motorway (Junction 1, West Bromwich) (Slip Road) (Temporary Prohibition of Traffic) Order 2014 No. 2014/1439. - Enabling power: Road Traffic Regulation Act 1984, s. 14 (1) (a). - Issued: 30.05.2014. Made: 14.05.2014. Coming into force: 21.05.2014. Effect: None. Territorial extent & classification: E. Local. - Available at http://www.legislation.gov.uk/uksi/2014/1439/contents/made Non-print

The M5 Motorway (Junction 2) (Slip Road) (Temporary Prohibition of Traffic) Order 2014 No. 2014/729. - Enabling power: Road Traffic Regulation Act 1984, s. 14 (1) (a). - Issued: 10.03.2014. Made: 26.02.2014. Coming into force: 05.03.2014. Effect: None. Territorial extent & classification: E. Local. - Available at http://www.legislation.gov.uk/uksi/2014/729/contents/made Non-print

The M5 Motorway (Junction 3, Quinton) (Temporary Prohibition of Traffic) (No.2) Order 2014 No. 2014/2762. - Enabling power: Road Traffic Regulation Act 1984, s. 14 (1) (a). - Issued: 14.10.2014. Made: 29.09.2014. Coming into force: 06.10.2014. Effect: None. Territorial extent & classification: E. Local. - Available at http://www.legislation.gov.uk/uksi/2014/2762/contents/made Non-print

The M5 Motorway (Junction 3, Quinton) (Temporary Prohibition of Traffic) Order 2014 No. 2014/117. - Enabling power: Road Traffic Regulation Act 1984, s. 14 (1) (a). - Issued: 24.01.2014. Made: 10.01.2014. Coming into force: 17.01.2014. Effect: None. Territorial extent & classification: E. Local. - Available at http://www.legislation.gov.uk/uksi/2014/117/contents/made Non-print

The M5 Motorway (Junction 4, Bromsgrove) (Slip Road) (Temporary Prohibition of Traffic) Order 2014 No. 2014/1260. - Enabling power: Road Traffic Regulation Act 1984, s. 14 (1) (a). - Issued: 19.05.2014. Made: 25.04.2014. Coming into force: 02.05.2014. Effect: None. Territorial extent & classification: E. Local. - Available at http://www.legislation.gov.uk/uksi/2014/1260/contents/made Non-print

The M5 Motorway (Junction 5, Worcestershire) (Temporary Prohibition of Traffic) Order 2014 No. 2014/1429. - Enabling power: Road Traffic Regulation Act 1984, s. 14 (1) (a). - Issued: 30.05.2014. Made: 13.05.2014. Coming into force: 20.05.2014. Effect: None. Territorial extent & classification: E. Local. - Available at http://www.legislation.gov.uk/uksi/2014/1429/contents/made Non-print

The M5 Motorway (Junction 5, Wychbold, Worcestershire) (Temporary Prohibition of Traffic) Order 2014 No. 2014/1544. - Enabling power: Road Traffic Regulation Act 1984, s. 14 (1) (a). - Issued: 13.06.2014. Made: 27.05.2014. Coming into force: 03.06.2014. Effect: None. Territorial extent & classification: E. Local. - Available at http://www.legislation.gov.uk/uksi/2014/1544/contents/made Non-print

The M5 Motorway (Junction 6, Worcester) (Slip Road) (Temporary Prohibition of Traffic) Order 2014 No. 2014/2614. - Enabling power: Road Traffic Regulation Act 1984, s. 14 (1) (a). - Issued: 30.09.2014. Made: 17.09.2014. Coming into force: 24.09.2014. Effect: None. Territorial extent & classification: E. Local. - Available at http://www.legislation.gov.uk/uksi/2014/2614/contents/made Non-print

The M5 Motorway (Junction 7, Worcestershire) (Temporary Prohibition of Traffic) Order 2014 No. 2014/1434. - Enabling power: Road Traffic Regulation Act 1984, s. 14 (1) (a). - Issued: 30.05.2014. Made: 13.05.2014. Coming into force: 20.05.2014. Effect: None. Territorial extent & classification: E. Local. - Available at http://www.legislation.gov.uk/uksi/2014/1434/contents/made Non-print

The M5 Motorway (Junction 10 Slip Roads) (Temporary Prohibition of Traffic) Order 2014 No. 2014/1668. - Enabling power: Road Traffic Regulation Act 1984, s. 14 (1) (a). - Issued: 30.06.2014. Made: 10.06.2014. Coming into force: 16.06.2014. Effect: None. Territorial extent & classification: E. Local. - Available at http://www.legislation.gov.uk/uksi/2014/1668/contents/made Non-print

The M5 Motorway (Junction 10) (Temporary Restriction and Prohibition of Traffic) (Number 2) Order 2014 No. 2014/1305. - Enabling power: Road Traffic Regulation Act 1984, s. 14 (1) (a) & S.I. 1982/1163, reg. 16 (2). - Issued: 23.05.2014. Made: 08.05.2014. Coming into force: 14.05.2014. Effect: None. Territorial extent & classification: E. Local. - Available at http://www.legislation.gov.uk/uksi/2014/1305/contents/made Non-print

The M5 Motorway (Junction 10) (Temporary Restriction and Prohibition of Traffic) Order 2014 No. 2014/653. - Enabling power: Road Traffic Regulation Act 1984, s. 14 (1) (a) & S.I. 1982/1163, reg. 16 (2). - Issued: 27.02.2014. Made: 19.02.2014. Coming into force: 27.02.2014. Effect: None. Territorial extent & classification: E. Local. - Available at http://www.legislation.gov.uk/uksi/2014/653/contents/made Non-print

The M5 Motorway (Junction 11A Southbound Entry and Exit Slip Roads) (Temporary Prohibition of Traffic) Order 2014 No. 2014/2222. - Enabling power: Road Traffic Regulation Act 1984, ss. 14 (1) (a). - Issued: 22.08.2014. Made: 06.08.2014. Coming into force: 15.08.2014. Effect: None. Territorial extent & classification: E. Local. - Available at http://www.legislation.gov.uk/uksi/2014/2222/contents/made Non-print

The M5 Motorway (Junction 11A Southbound Exit Slip Road) (Temporary Prohibition of Traffic) Order 2014 No. 2014/1948. - Enabling power: Road Traffic Regulation Act 1984, s. 14 (1) (a). - Issued: 18.07.2014. Made: 01.07.2014. Coming into force: 05.07.2014. Effect: None. Territorial extent & classification: E. Local. - Available at http://www.legislation.gov.uk/uksi/2014/1948/contents/made Non-print

The M5 Motorway (Junction 11 Slip Roads) (Temporary Prohibition of Traffic) Order 2014 No. 2014/761. - Enabling power: Road Traffic Regulation Act 1984, s. 14 (1) (a). - Issued: 11.03.2014. Made: 04.03.2014. Coming into force: 08.03.2014. Effect: None. Territorial extent & classification: E. Local. - Available at http://www.legislation.gov.uk/uksi/2014/761/contents/made Non-print

The M5 Motorway (Junction 11 Southbound Exit Slip Road) (Temporary Prohibition of Traffic) Order 2014 No. 2014/1781. - Enabling power: Road Traffic Regulation Act 1984, s. 14 (1) (a). - Issued: 09.07.2014. Made: 25.06.2014. Coming into force: 28.07.2014. Effect: None. Territorial extent & classification: E. Local. - Available at http://www.legislation.gov.uk/uksi/2014/1781/contents/made Non-print

The M5 Motorway (Junction 14) (Temporary Prohibition of Traffic) Order 2014 No. 2014/1671. - Enabling power: Road Traffic Regulation Act 1984, s. 14 (1) (a). - Issued: 01.07.2014. Made: 10.06.2014. Coming into force: 16.06.2014. Effect: None. Territorial extent & classification: E. Local. - Available at http://www.legislation.gov.uk/uksi/2014/1671/contents/made Non-print

The M5 Motorway (Junction 16 Slip Road) (Temporary Prohibition of Traffic) Order 2014 No. 2014/3495. - Enabling power: Road Traffic Regulation Act 1984, s. 14 (1) (a). - Issued: 20.01.2015. Made: 27.11.2014. Coming into force: 05.12.2014. Effect: None. Territorial extent & classification: E. Local. - Available at http://www.legislation.gov.uk/uksi/2014/3495/contents/made Non-print

The M5 Motorway (Junction 18 'V' Loop Slip Road) (Temporary Prohibition of Traffic) Order 2014 No. 2014/1780. - Enabling power: Road Traffic Regulation Act 1984, s. 14 (1) (a). - Issued: 09.07.2014. Made: 25.06.2014. Coming into force: 28.07.2014. Effect: None. Territorial extent & classification: E. Local. - Available at http://www.legislation.gov.uk/uksi/2014/1780/contents/made Non-print

The M5 Motorway (Junction 19 Slip Roads) (Temporary Prohibition of Traffic) Order 2014 No. 2014/3390. - Enabling power: Road Traffic Regulation Act 1984, s. 14 (1) (a). - Issued: 01.12.2014. Made: 26.11.2014. Coming into force: 29.11.2014. Effect: None. Territorial extent & classification: E. Local. - Available at http://www.legislation.gov.uk/uksi/2014/3390/contents/made Non-print

The M5 Motorway (Junction 20 Southbound Exit Slip Road) (Temporary Prohibition of Traffic) Order 2014 No. 2014/3392. - Enabling power: Road Traffic Regulation Act 1984, s. 14 (1) (a). - Issued: 01.12.2014. Made: 26.11.2014. Coming into force: 29.11.2014. Effect: None. Territorial extent & classification: E. Local. - Available at http://www.legislation.gov.uk/uksi/2014/3392/contents/made Non-print

The M5 Motorway (Junction 21 Slip Roads) (No 2) (Temporary Prohibition of Traffic) Order 2014 No. 2014/1729. - Enabling power: Road Traffic Regulation Act 1984, s. 14 (1) (a). - Issued: 02.07.2014. Made: 18.06.2014. Coming into force: 28.06.2014. Effect: None. Territorial extent & classification: E. Local. - Available at http://www.legislation.gov.uk/uksi/2014/1729/contents/made Non-print

The M5 Motorway (Junction 21 Slip Roads) (Temporary Prohibition of Traffic) Order 2014 No. 2014/965. - Enabling power: Road Traffic Regulation Act 1984, s. 14 (1) (a). - Issued: 01.04.2014. Made: 18.03.2014. Coming into force: 22.03.2014. Effect: None. Territorial extent & classification: E. Local. - Available at http://www.legislation.gov.uk/uksi/2014/965/contents/made Non-print

The M5 Motorway (Junction 23 Slip Roads) (Temporary Prohibition of Traffic) Order 2014 No. 2014/780. - Enabling power: Road Traffic Regulation Act 1984, s. 14 (1) (a). - Issued: 10.03.2014. Made: 03.03.2014. Coming into force: 10.03.2014. Effect: None. Territorial extent & classification: E. Local. - Available at http://www.legislation.gov.uk/uksi/2014/780/contents/made Non-print

The M5 Motorway (Junction 26 Southbound Entry Slip Road) (Temporary Prohibition of Traffic) Order 2014 No. 2014/2279. - Enabling power: Road Traffic Regulation Act 1984, s. 14 (1) (a). - Issued: 28.08.2014. Made: 26.08.2014. Coming into force: 30.08.2014. Effect: None. Territorial extent & classification: E. Local. - Available at http://www.legislation.gov.uk/uksi/2014/2279/contents/made Non-print

The M5 Motorway (Junction 27 Slip Roads) (Temporary Prohibition of Traffic) Order 2014 No. 2014/3559. - Enabling power: Road Traffic Regulation Act 1984, s. 14 (1) (a). - Issued: 24.02.2015. Made: 16.12.2015. Coming into force: 02.01.2015. Effect: None. Territorial extent & classification: E. Local. - Available at http://www.legislation.gov.uk/uksi/2014/3559/contents/made Non-print

The M5 Motorway (Junction 28 Slip Roads) (Temporary Prohibition of Traffic) Order 2014 No. 2014/3152. - Enabling power: Road Traffic Regulation Act 1984, s. 14 (1) (a). - Issued: 24.11.2014. Made: 17.11.2014. Coming into force: 22.11.2014. Effect: None. Territorial extent & classification: E. Local. - Available at http://www.legislation.gov.uk/uksi/2014/3152/contents/made Non-print

The M5 Motorway (Junction 29 Slip Roads) (Temporary Restriction and Prohibition of Traffic) Order 2014 No. 2014/1467. - Enabling power: Road Traffic Regulation Act 1984, s. 14 (1) (a) & S.I. 1982/1163, reg. 16 (2). - Issued: 05.06.2014. Made: 20.05.2014. Coming into force: 24.05.2014. Effect: None. Territorial extent & classification: E. Local. - Available at http://www.legislation.gov.uk/uksi/2014/1467/contents/made Non-print

The M5 Motorway (Junctions 1 to 2, Sandwell) (Temporary Restriction and Prohibition of Traffic) Order 2014 No. 2014/339. - Enabling power: Road Traffic Regulation Act 1984, s. 14 (1) (a) & S.I. 1982/1163, reg. 16 (2). - Issued: 19.02.2014. Made: 27.01.2014. Coming into force: 03.02.2014. Effect: None. Territorial extent & classification: E. Local. - Available at http://www.legislation.gov.uk/uksi/2014/339/contents/made Non-print

The M5 Motorway (Junctions 2 to 3, Oldbury) (Temporary 50 Miles Per Hour Speed Restriction) Order 2014 No. 2014/363. - Enabling power: Road Traffic Regulation Act 1984, s. 14 (1) (a). - Issued: 20.02.2014. Made: 10.02.2014. Coming into force: 17.02.2014. Effect: None. Territorial extent & classification: E. Local. - Available at http://www.legislation.gov.uk/uksi/2014/363/contents/made Non-print

The M5 Motorway (Junctions 2 to 3, Oldbury to Quinton) (Temporary Prohibition of Traffic) Order 2014 No. 2014/1077. - Enabling power: Road Traffic Regulation Act 1984, s. 14 (1) (a). - Issued: 28.04.2014. Made: 08.04.2014. Coming into force: 15.04.2014. Effect: None. Territorial extent & classification: E. Local. - Available at http://www.legislation.gov.uk/uksi/2014/1077/contents/made Non-print

The M5 Motorway (Junctions 6 - 9) (Temporary Prohibition of Traffic) Order 2014 No. 2014/3517. - Enabling power: Road Traffic Regulation Act 1984, s. 14 (1) (a). - Issued: 23.01.2015. Made: 22.12.2014. Coming into force: 29.12.2014. Effect: None. Territorial extent & classification: E. Local. - Available at http://www.legislation.gov.uk/uksi/2014/3517/contents/made Non-print

The M5 Motorway (Junctions 6 to 5, Worcestershire) (Temporary Prohibition of Traffic) Order 2014 No. 2014/1083. - Enabling power: Road Traffic Regulation Act 1984, s. 14 (1) (a). - Issued: 25.04.2014. Made: 28.03.2014. Coming into force: 04.04.2014. Effect: None. Territorial extent & classification: E. Local. - Available at http://www.legislation.gov.uk/uksi/2014/1083/contents/made Non-print

The M5 Motorway (Junctions 6 to 7, Worcestershire) (Temporary Prohibition of Traffic) Order 2014 No. 2014/3365. - Enabling power: Road Traffic Regulation Act 1984, s. 14 (1) (a). - Issued: 28.11.2014. Made: 17.11.2014. Coming into force: 24.11.2014. Effect: None. Territorial extent & classification: E. Local. - Available at http://www.legislation.gov.uk/uksi/2014/3365/contents/made Non-print

The M5 Motorway (Junctions 7 to 8, Worcestershire) (Temporary Prohibition of Traffic) Order 2014 No. 2014/1255. - Enabling power: Road Traffic Regulation Act 1984, s. 14 (1) (a). - Issued: 16.05.2014. Made: 28.04.2014. Coming into force: 05.05.2014. Effect: None. Territorial extent & classification: E. Local. - Available at http://www.legislation.gov.uk/uksi/2014/1255/contents/made Non-print

The M5 Motorway (Junctions 8 to 6, Worcestershire) (Slip Roads) (Temporary Prohibition of Traffic) Order 2014 No. 2014/660. - Enabling power: Road Traffic Regulation Act 1984, s. 14 (1) (a). - Issued: 07.03.2014. Made: 21.02.2014. Coming into force: 28.02.2014. Effect: None. Territorial extent & classification: E. Local. - Available at http://www.legislation.gov.uk/uksi/2014/660/contents/made Non-print

The M5 Motorway (Junctions 8 to 7, South of Worcester) (Temporary Prohibition of Traffic) Order 2014 No. 2014/1156. - Enabling power: Road Traffic Regulation Act 1984, s. 14 (1) (a). - Issued: 07.05.2014. Made: 18.04.2014. Coming into force: 25.04.2014. Effect: None. Territorial extent & classification: E. Local. - Available at http://www.legislation.gov.uk/uksi/2014/1156/contents/made Non-print

The M5 Motorway (Junctions 8 to 7, Worcestershire) (Temporary Prohibition of Traffic) Order 2014 No. 2014/3488. - Enabling power: Road Traffic Regulation Act 1984, s. 14 (1) (a). - Issued: 07.01.2015. Made: 22.12.2014. Coming into force: 29.12.2014. Effect: None. Territorial extent & classification: E. Local. - Available at http://www.legislation.gov.uk/uksi/2014/3488/contents/made Non-print

ROAD TRAFFIC: TRAFFIC REGULATION

The M5 Motorway (Junctions 9 to 8) (Temporary Restriction and Prohibition of Traffic) Order 2014 No. 2014/2615. - Enabling power: Road Traffic Regulation Act 1984, s. 14 (1) (a) & S.I. 1982/1163, reg. 16 (2). - Issued: 30.09.2014. Made: 19.09.2014. Coming into force: 26.09.2014. Effect: None. Territorial extent & classification: E. Local. - Available at http://www.legislation.gov.uk/uksi/2014/2615/contents/made Non-print

The M5 Motorway (Junctions 10-11) (Temporary Restriction and Prohibition of Traffic) Order 2014 No. 2014/61. - Enabling power: Road Traffic Regulation Act 1984, s. 14 (1) (a) & S.I. 1982/1163, reg. 16 (2). - Issued: 20.01.2014. Made: 07.01.2014. Coming into force: 11.01.2014. Effect: None. Territorial extent & classification: E. Local. - Available at http://www.legislation.gov.uk/uksi/2014/61/contents/made Non-print

The M5 Motorway (Junctions 11-10) (Temporary Restriction and Prohibition of Traffic) Order 2014 No. 2014/428. - Enabling power: Road Traffic Regulation Act 1984, s. 14 (1) (a). - Issued: 27.02.2014. Made: 20.02.2014. Coming into force: 25.02.2014. Effect: None. Territorial extent & classification: E. Local. - Available at http://www.legislation.gov.uk/uksi/2014/428/contents/made Non-print

The M5 Motorway (Junctions 11A & 12 Slip Roads) and A417 Trunk Road (Temporary Prohibition of Traffic) Order 2014 No. 2014/1670. - Enabling power: Road Traffic Regulation Act 1984, s. 14 (1) (a). - Issued: 30.06.2014. Made: 10.06.2014. Coming into force: 16.06.2014. Effect: None. Territorial extent & classification: E. Local. - Available at http://www.legislation.gov.uk/uksi/2014/1670/contents/made Non-print

The M5 Motorway (Junctions 11A-12) (Temporary Prohibition of Traffic) Order 2014 No. 2014/1165. - Enabling power: Road Traffic Regulation Act 1984, s. 14 (1) (b). - Issued: 06.05.2014. Made: 24.04.2014. Coming into force: 29.04.2014. Effect: None. Territorial extent & classification: E. Local. - Available at http://www.legislation.gov.uk/uksi/2014/1165/contents/made Non-print

The M5 Motorway (Junctions 11A-12) (Temporary Restriction and Prohibition of Traffic) (Number 2) Order 2013 Variation Order 2014 No. 2014/420. - Enabling power: Road Traffic Regulation Act 1984, s. 14 (1) (a), sch. 9, para. 27 & S.I. 1982/1163, reg. 16 (2). - Issued: 27.02.2014. Made: 18.02.2014. Coming into force: 21.02.2014. Effect: S.I. 2013/3287 varied. Territorial extent & classification: E. Local. - Available at http://www.legislation.gov.uk/uksi/2014/420/contents/made Non-print

The M5 Motorway (Junctions 13-15) (Temporary Restriction and Prohibition of Traffic) Order 2014 No. 2014/3560. - Enabling power: Road Traffic Regulation Act 1984, s. 14 (1) (a) & S.I. 1982/1163, reg. 16 (2). - Issued: 26.02.2015. Made: 17.12.2014. Coming into force: 31.12.2014. Effect: None. Territorial extent & classification: E. Local. - Available at http://www.legislation.gov.uk/uksi/2014/3560/contents/made Non-print

The M5 Motorway (Junctions 18 & 18A Slip Roads) (Temporary Prohibition of Traffic) Order 2014 No. 2014/1669. - Enabling power: Road Traffic Regulation Act 1984, s. 14 (1) (a). - Issued: 30.06.2014. Made: 10.06.2014. Coming into force: 16.06.2014. Effect: None. Territorial extent & classification: E. Local. - Available at http://www.legislation.gov.uk/uksi/2014/1669/contents/made Non-print

The M5 Motorway (Junctions 19 and 20 Slip Roads) (Temporary Prohibition of Traffic) Order 2014 No. 2014/1443. - Enabling power: Road Traffic Regulation Act 1984, s. 14 (1) (a). - Issued: 05.06.2014. Made: 20.05.2014. Coming into force: 24.05.2014. Effect: None. Territorial extent & classification: E. Local. - Available at http://www.legislation.gov.uk/uksi/2014/1443/contents/made Non-print

The M5 Motorway (Junctions 20-21) (Temporary Prohibition of Traffic) Order 2014 No. 2014/2431. - Enabling power: Road Traffic Regulation Act 1984, s. 14 (1) (a). - Issued: 12.09.2014. Made: 09.09.2014. Coming into force: 12.09.2014. Effect: None. Territorial extent & classification: E. Local. - Available at http://www.legislation.gov.uk/uksi/2014/2431/contents/made Non-print

The M5 Motorway (Junctions 21 and 22 Slip Roads) (Temporary Prohibition of Traffic) Order 2014 No. 2014/1466. - Enabling power: Road Traffic Regulation Act 1984, s. 14 (1) (a). - Issued: 05.06.2014. Made: 20.05.2014. Coming into force: 24.05.2014. Effect: None. Territorial extent & classification: E. Local. - Available at http://www.legislation.gov.uk/uksi/2014/1466/contents/made Non-print

The M5 Motorway (Junctions 23-24) (Temporary Restriction and Prohibition of Traffic) Order 2014 No. 2014/2331. - Enabling power: Road Traffic Regulation Act 1984, s. 14 (1) (a) & S.I. 1982/1163, reg. 16 (2). - Issued: 04.09.2014. Made: 01.09.2014. Coming into force: 06.09.2014. Effect: None. Territorial extent & classification: E. Local. - Available at http://www.legislation.gov.uk/uksi/2014/2331/contents/made Non-print

The M5 Motorway (Junctions 24, 25 and 27 Slip Roads) (Temporary Prohibition of Traffic) Order 2014 No. 2014/2180. - Enabling power: Road Traffic Regulation Act 1984, s. 14 (1) (a). - Issued: 19.08.2014. Made: 01.07.2014. Coming into force: 05.07.2014. Effect: None. Territorial extent & classification: E. Local. - Available at http://www.legislation.gov.uk/uksi/2014/2180/contents/made Non-print

The M5 Motorway (Junctions 24-27) (Temporary Restriction and Prohibition of Traffic) Order 2014 No. 2014/3520. - Enabling power: Road Traffic Regulation Act 1984, s. 14 (1) (a) & Motorways Traffic (England and Wales) Regulations 1982, s. 16 (2). - Issued: 22.01.2015. Made: 30.12.2015. Coming into force: 03.01.2015. Effect: None. Territorial extent & classification: E. Local. - Available at http://www.legislation.gov.uk/uksi/2014/3520/contents/made Non-print

The M5 Motorway (Junctions 26-29) (Temporary Restriction and Prohibition of Traffic) Order 2014 No. 2014/3521. - Enabling power: Road Traffic Regulation Act 1984, s. 14 (1) (a) & Motorways Traffic (England and Wales) Regulations 1982, s. 16 (2). - Issued: 22.01.2015. Made: 30.12.2015. Coming into force: 03.01.2015. Effect: None. Territorial extent & classification: E. Local. - Available at http://www.legislation.gov.uk/uksi/2014/3521/contents/made Non-print

The M5 Motorway (Junctions 27-26) (Temporary Restriction and Prohibition of Traffic) Order 2014 No. 2014/671. - Enabling power: Road Traffic Regulation Act 1984, s. 14 (1) (a) & S.I. 1982/1163, reg. 16 (2). - Issued: 07.03.2014. Made: 25.02.2014. Coming into force: 01.03.2014. Effect: None. Territorial extent & classification: E. Local. - Available at http://www.legislation.gov.uk/uksi/2014/671/contents/made Non-print

The M5 Motorway (Junctions 27-28) (Temporary Restriction and Prohibition of Traffic) Order 2014 No. 2014/1642. - Enabling power: Road Traffic Regulation Act 1984, s. 14 (1) (a) & S.I. 1982/1163, reg. 16 (2). - Issued: 26.06.2014. Made: 09.06.2014. Coming into force: 12.06.2014. Effect: None. Territorial extent & classification: E. Local. - Available at http://www.legislation.gov.uk/uksi/2014/1642/contents/made Non-print

The M5 Motorway (Junctions 29 - 30) (Temporary Restriction and Prohibition of Traffic) Order 2014 No. 2014/3429. - Enabling power: Road Traffic Regulation Act 1984, s. 14 (1) (a). - Issued: 05.12.2014. Made: 02.12.2014. Coming into force: 10.12.2014. Effect: None. Territorial extent & classification: E. Local. - Available at http://www.legislation.gov.uk/uksi/2014/3429/contents/made Non-print

The M5 Motorway (Junctions 30-31) (Temporary Restriction of Traffic) Order 2014 No. 2014/1225. - Enabling power: Road Traffic Regulation Act 1984, ss. 14 (1) (a) & S.I. 1982/1163, reg. 16 (2). - Issued: 14.05.2014. Made: 29.04.2014. Coming into force: 03.05.2014. Effect: None. Territorial extent & classification: E. Local. - Available at http://www.legislation.gov.uk/uksi/2014/1225/contents/made Non-print

The M6 and M5 Motorways (M6 Junction 8, Sandwell) (Temporary Prohibition of Traffic) (No. 2) Order 2014 No. 2014/2733. - Enabling power: Road Traffic Regulation Act 1984, s. 14 (1) (a) & S.I. 1982/1163. - Issued: 14.10.2014. Made: 22.09.2014. Coming into force: 29.09.2014. Effect: None. Territorial extent & classification: E. Local. - Available at http://www.legislation.gov.uk/uksi/2014/2733/contents/made Non-print

ROAD TRAFFIC: TRAFFIC REGULATION

The M6 and M5 Motorways (M6 Junction 8, Sandwell) (Temporary Prohibition of Traffic) Order 2014 No. 2014/1259. - Enabling power: Road Traffic Regulation Act 1984, s. 14 (1) (a). - Issued: 19.05.2014. Made: 28.04.2014. Coming into force: 05.05.2014. Effect: None. Territorial extent & classification: E. Local. - Available at http://www.legislation.gov.uk/uksi/2014/1259/contents/made Non-print

The M6 and M5 Motorways (M6 Junction 8, Walsall) (Temporary Prohibition of Traffic) Order 2014 No. 2014/970. - Enabling power: Road Traffic Regulation Act 1984, s. 14 (1) (a). - Issued: 07.04.2014. Made: 17.03.2014. Coming into force: 24.03.2014. Effect: None. Territorial extent & classification: E. Local. - Available at http://www.legislation.gov.uk/uksi/2014/970/contents/made Non-print

The M6 and M42 Motorways (M6 Junction 4, Warwickshire) (Temporary Prohibition of Traffic) Order 2014 No. 2014/3404. - Enabling power: Road Traffic Regulation Act 1984, s. 14 (1) (a). - Issued: 28.11.2014. Made: 24.11.2014. Coming into force: 01.12.2014. Effect: None. Territorial extent & classification: E. Local. - Available at http://www.legislation.gov.uk/uksi/2014/3404/contents/made Non-print

The M6 and M42 Motorways (M6 Junctions 2 -4) (Temporary Restriction and Prohibition of Traffic) Order 2014 No. 2014/2734. - Enabling power: Road Traffic Regulation Act 1984, s. 14 (1) (a). - Issued: 14.10.2014. Made: 22.09.2014. Coming into force: 29.09.2014. Effect: None. Territorial extent & classification: E. Local. - Available at http://www.legislation.gov.uk/uksi/2014/2734/contents/made Non-print

The M6 and M42 Motorways (M6 Junctions 4a to 3a, Warwickshire) (Temporary Prohibition of Traffic) Order 2014 No. 2014/2016. - Enabling power: Road Traffic Regulation Act 1984, s. 14 (1) (a). - Issued: 31.07.2014. Made: 13.06.2014. Coming into force: 20.06.2014. Effect: None. Territorial extent & classification: E. Local. - Available at http://www.legislation.gov.uk/uksi/2014/2016/contents/made Non-print

The M6 and M54 Motorways (Junctions 10 to 11, Walsall) (Temporary Restriction and Prohibition of Traffic) Order 2014 No. 2014/328. - Enabling power: Road Traffic Regulation Act 1984, s. 14 (1) (a) (7) & S.I. 1982/1163, reg. 16 (2). - Issued: 18.02.2014. Made: 31.01.2014. Coming into force: 07.02.2014. Effect: None. Territorial extent & classification: E. Local. - Available at http://www.legislation.gov.uk/uksi/2014/328/contents/made Non-print

The M6 Motorway (Corley Services) (Slip Road) (Temporary Prohibition of Traffic) Order 2014 No. 2014/201. - Enabling power: Road Traffic Regulation Act 1984, s. 14 (1) (a). - Issued: 05.02.2014. Made: 15.01.2014. Coming into force: 22.01.2014. Effect: None. Territorial extent & classification: E. Local. - Available at http://www.legislation.gov.uk/uksi/2014/201/contents/made Non-print

The M6 Motorway (Hanchurch - Barthomley, Staffordshire) (Temporary Restriction and Prohibition of Traffic) Order 2014 No. 2014/1039. - Enabling power: Road Traffic Regulation Act 1984, s. 14 (1) (a). - Issued: 22.04.2014. Made: 24.03.2014. Coming into force: 31.03.2014. Effect: None. Territorial extent & classification: E. Local. - Available at http://www.legislation.gov.uk/uksi/2014/1039/contents/made Non-print

The M6 Motorway (Junction 1, Warwickshire) (Temporary Prohibition of Traffic) Order 2014 No. 2014/1519. - Enabling power: Road Traffic Regulation Act 1984, s. 14 (1) (a). - Issued: 11.06.2014. Made: 16.05.2014. Coming into force: 23.05.2014. Effect: None. Territorial extent & classification: E. Local. - Available at http://www.legislation.gov.uk/uksi/2014/1519/contents/made Non-print

The M6 Motorway (Junction 1, Warwickshire) (Temporary Restriction of Traffic) Order 2014 No. 2014/3367. - Enabling power: Road Traffic Regulation Act 1984, s. 14 (1) (a). - Issued: 28.11.2014. Made: 17.11.2014. Coming into force: 24.11.2014. Effect: None. Territorial extent & classification: E. Local. - Available at http://www.legislation.gov.uk/uksi/2014/3367/contents/made Non-print

The M6 Motorway (Junction 2 to 4) (Temporary Prohibition of Traffic) Order 2014 No. 2014/355. - Enabling power: Road Traffic Regulation Act 1984, s. 14 (1) (a). - Issued: 20.02.2014. Made: 07.02.2014. Coming into force: 14.02.2014. Effect: None. Territorial extent & classification: E. Local. - Available at http://www.legislation.gov.uk/uksi/2014/355/contents/made Non-print

The M6 Motorway (Junction 2, Warwickshire) (Temporary Restriction of Traffic) Order 2014 No. 2014/1169. - Enabling power: Road Traffic Regulation Act 1984, ss. 14 (1) (a). - Issued: 07.05.2014. Made: 22.04.2014. Coming into force: 29.04.2014. Effect: None. Territorial extent & classification: E. Local. - Available at http://www.legislation.gov.uk/uksi/2014/1169/contents/made Non-print

The M6 Motorway (Junction 3, Bedworth) (Slip Roads) (Temporary Prohibition of Traffic) Order 2014 No. 2014/1436. - Enabling power: Road Traffic Regulation Act 1984, s. 14 (1) (a). - Issued: 30.05.2014. Made: 14.05.2014. Coming into force: 21.05.2014. Effect: None. Territorial extent & classification: E. Local. - Available at http://www.legislation.gov.uk/uksi/2014/1436/contents/made Non-print

The M6 Motorway (Junction 3, Warwickshire) (Slip Road) (Temporary Prohibition of Traffic) Order 2014 No. 2014/1167. - Enabling power: Road Traffic Regulation Act 1984, s. 14 (1) (b). - Issued: 07.05.2014. Made: 22.04.2014. Coming into force: 29.04.2014. Effect: None. Territorial extent & classification: E. Local. - Available at http://www.legislation.gov.uk/uksi/2014/1167/contents/made Non-print

The M6 Motorway (Junction 4a, Birmingham) (Link Road) (Temporary Prohibition of Traffic) Order 2014 No. 2014/327. - Enabling power: Road Traffic Regulation Act 1984, s. 14 (1) (a). - Issued: 18.02.2014. Made: 27.01.2014. Coming into force: 03.02.2014. Effect: None. Territorial extent & classification: E. Local. - Available at http://www.legislation.gov.uk/uksi/2014/327/contents/made Non-print

The M6 Motorway (Junction 4, Coleshill) (Slip Road) (Temporary Prohibition of Traffic) Order 2014 No. 2014/2182. - Enabling power: Road Traffic Regulation Act 1984, s. 14 (1) (a). - Issued: 19.08.2014. Made: 09.07.2014. Coming into force: 16.07.2014. Effect: None. Territorial extent & classification: E. Local. - Available at http://www.legislation.gov.uk/uksi/2014/2182/contents/made Non-print

The M6 Motorway (Junction 4, Warwickshire) (Link Road) (Temporary Prohibition of Traffic) Order 2014 No. 2014/119. - Enabling power: Road Traffic Regulation Act 1984, s. 14 (1) (a). - Issued: 24.01.2014. Made: 13.01.2014. Coming into force: 20.01.2014. Effect: None. Territorial extent & classification: E. Local. - Available at http://www.legislation.gov.uk/uksi/2014/119/contents/made Non-print

The M6 Motorway (Junction 5, Birmingham) (Temporary Prohibition of Traffic) Order 2014 No. 2014/3469. - Enabling power: Road Traffic Regulation Act 1984, s. 14 (1) (a). - Issued: 02.01.2015. Made: 22.12.2014. Coming into force: 29.12.2014. Effect: None. Territorial extent & classification: E. Local. - Available at http://www.legislation.gov.uk/uksi/2014/3469/contents/made Non-print

The M6 Motorway (Junction 6, Birmingham) (Link Road) (Temporary Prohibition of Traffic) Order 2014 No. 2014/324. - Enabling power: Road Traffic Regulation Act 1984, s. 14 (1) (a). - Issued: 18.02.2014. Made: 27.01.2014. Coming into force: 03.02.2014. Effect: None. Territorial extent & classification: E. Local. - Available at http://www.legislation.gov.uk/uksi/2014/324/contents/made Non-print

The M6 Motorway (Junction 6, Birmingham) (Temporary Prohibition of Traffic) Order 2014 No. 2014/1587. - Enabling power: Road Traffic Regulation Act 1984, s. 14 (1) (a). - Issued: 18.06.2014. Made: 30.05.2014. Coming into force: 06.06.2014. Effect: None. Territorial extent & classification: E. Local. - Available at http://www.legislation.gov.uk/uksi/2014/1587/contents/made Non-print

The M6 Motorway (Junction 6, Gravelly Hill) (Link Roads) (Temporary Prohibition of Traffic) Order 2014 No. 2014/2731. - Enabling power: Road Traffic Regulation Act 1984, s. 14 (1) (a). - Issued: 14.10.2014. Made: 22.09.2014. Coming into force: 29.09.2014. Effect: None. Territorial extent & classification: E. Local. - Available at http://www.legislation.gov.uk/uksi/2014/2731/contents/made Non-print

The M6 Motorway (Junction 6, Gravelly Hill) (Link Roads) (Temporary Restriction and Prohibition of Traffic) Order 2014 No. 2014/3406. - Enabling power: Road Traffic Regulation Act 1984, s. 14 (1) (a). - Issued: 01.12.2014. Made: 24.11.2014. Coming into force: 01.12.2014. Effect: None. Territorial extent & classification: E. Local. - Available at http://www.legislation.gov.uk/uksi/2014/3406/contents/made Non-print

ROAD TRAFFIC: TRAFFIC REGULATION

The M6 Motorway (Junction 6, Gravelly Hill) (Slip Road) (Temporary Prohibition of Traffic) Order 2014 No. 2014/1441. - Enabling power: Road Traffic Regulation Act 1984, s. 14 (1) (a). - Issued: 02.06.2014. Made: 16.05.2014. Coming into force: 23.05.2014. Effect: None. Territorial extent & classification: E. Local. - Available at http://www.legislation.gov.uk/uksi/2014/1441/contents/made Non-print

The M6 Motorway (Junction 6, Gravelly Hill) (Temporary Prohibition of Traffic) Order 2014 No. 2014/795. - Enabling power: Road Traffic Regulation Act 1984, s. 14 (1) (a). - Issued: 26.03.2014. Made: 07.03.2014. Coming into force: 14.03.2014. Effect: None. Territorial extent & classification: E. Local. - Available at http://www.legislation.gov.uk/uksi/2014/795/contents/made Non-print

The M6 Motorway (Junction 7, Great Barr) (Slip Road) (Temporary Prohibition of Traffic) Order 2014 No. 2014/646. - Enabling power: Road Traffic Regulation Act 1984, s. 14 (1) (a). - Issued: 06.03.2014. Made: 17.02.2014. Coming into force: 24.02.2014. Effect: None. Territorial extent & classification: E. Local. - Available at http://www.legislation.gov.uk/uksi/2014/646/contents/made Non-print

The M6 Motorway (Junction 9, Bescot, Walsall) (Temporary Prohibition of Traffic) Order 2014 No. 2014/3558. - Enabling power: Road Traffic Regulation Act 1984, s. 14 (1) (a). - Issued: 20.02.2015. Made: 29.12.2014. Coming into force: 05.01.2015. Effect: None. Territorial extent & classification: E. Local. - Available at http://www.legislation.gov.uk/uksi/2014/3558/contents/made Non-print

The M6 Motorway (Junction 9, Walsall) (Slip Road) (Temporary Prohibition of Traffic) Order 2014 No. 2014/3145. - Enabling power: Road Traffic Regulation Act 1984, s. 14 (1) (a). - Issued: 24.11.2014. Made: 10.11.2014. Coming into force: 17.11.2014. Effect: None. Territorial extent & classification: E. Local. - Available at http://www.legislation.gov.uk/uksi/2014/3145/contents/made Non-print

The M6 Motorway (Junction 9, Walsall) (Temporary Prohibition of Traffic) Order 2014 No. 2014/2607. - Enabling power: Road Traffic Regulation Act 1984, s. 14 (1) (a). - Issued: 30.09.2014. Made: 17.09.2014. Coming into force: 24.09.2014. Effect: None. Territorial extent & classification: E. Local. - Available at http://www.legislation.gov.uk/uksi/2014/2607/contents/made Non-print

The M6 Motorway (Junction 10 to Junction 9) (Temporary Restriction and Prohibition of Traffic) (No.2) Order 2014 No. 2014/2449. - Enabling power: Road Traffic Regulation Act 1984, s. 14 (1) (a) & S.I. 1982/1163, reg. 16 (2). - Issued: 15.09.2014. Made: 26.08.2014. Coming into force: 02.09.2014. Effect: None. Territorial extent & classification: E. Local. - Available at http://www.legislation.gov.uk/uksi/2014/2449/contents/made Non-print

The M6 Motorway (Junction 10 to Junction 9) (Temporary Restriction and Prohibition of Traffic) Order 2014 No. 2014/721. - Enabling power: Road Traffic Regulation Act 1984, s. 14 (1) (a) & S.I. 1982/1163, s. 16 (2). - Issued: 07.03.2014. Made: 25.02.2014. Coming into force: 04.03.2014. Effect: None. Territorial extent & classification: E. Local. - Available at http://www.legislation.gov.uk/uksi/2014/721/contents/made Non-print

The M6 Motorway (Junction 10 to Junction 9, Walsall) (Temporary Restriction and Prohibition of Traffic) Order 2014 No. 2014/1155. - Enabling power: Road Traffic Regulation Act 1984, s. 14 (1) (a) (7). - Issued: 02.05.2014. Made: 17.04.2014. Coming into force: 24.04.2014. Effect: None. Territorial extent & classification: E. Local. - Available at http://www.legislation.gov.uk/uksi/2014/1155/contents/made Non-print

The M6 Motorway (Junction 10, Walsall) (Northbound Entry Slip Road) (Temporary Prohibition of Traffic) Order 2014 No. 2014/1399. - Enabling power: Road Traffic Regulation Act 1984, s. 14 (1) (a). - Issued: 04.06.2014. Made: 06.05.2014. Coming into force: 13.05.2014. Effect: None. Territorial extent & classification: E. Local. - Available at http://www.legislation.gov.uk/uksi/2014/1399/contents/made Non-print

The M6 Motorway (Junction 13 to 14, Staffordshire) (Temporary Restriction Prohibition of Traffic) Order 2014 No. 2014/1021. - Enabling power: Road Traffic Regulation Act 1984, s. 14 (1) (a) & S.I. 1982/1163, reg. 16 (2). - Issued: 17.04.2014. Made: 18.03.2014. Coming into force: 25.03.2014. Effect: None. Territorial extent & classification: E. Local. - Available at http://www.legislation.gov.uk/uksi/2014/1021/contents/made Non-print

The M6 Motorway (Junction 14, Staffordshire) (Temporary Prohibition of Traffic) Order 2014 No. 2014/2953. - Enabling power: Road Traffic Regulation Act 1984, s. 14 (1) (a). - Issued: 27.10.2014. Made: 22.10.2014. Coming into force: 29.10.2014. Effect: None. Territorial extent & classification: E. Local. - Available at http://www.legislation.gov.uk/uksi/2014/2953/contents/made Non-print

The M6 Motorway (Junction 15, Staffordshire) (Slip Roads) (Temporary Prohibition of Traffic) Order 2014 No. 2014/697. - Enabling power: Road Traffic Regulation Act 1984, s. 14 (1) (a). - Issued: 07.03.2014. Made: 24.02.2014. Coming into force: 03.03.2014. Effect: None. Territorial extent & classification: E. Local. - Available at http://www.legislation.gov.uk/uksi/2014/697/contents/made Non-print

The M6 Motorway (Junction 16, Staffordshire) (Slip Road) (Temporary Prohibition of Traffic) Order 2014 No. 2014/1088. - Enabling power: Road Traffic Regulation Act 1984, s. 14 (1) (a). - Issued: 25.04.2014. Made: 31.03.2014. Coming into force: 07.04.2014. Effect: None. Territorial extent & classification: E. Local. - Available at http://www.legislation.gov.uk/uksi/2014/1088/contents/made Non-print

The M6 Motorway (Junction 20 Northbound Entry Slip Road) (Temporary Prohibition of Traffic) Order 2014 No. 2014/3549. - Enabling power: Road Traffic Regulation Act 1984, ss. 14 (1) (a). - Issued: 23.01.2015. Made: 31.12.2014. Coming into force: 18.01.2015. Effect: None. Territorial extent & classification: E. Local. - Available at http://www.legislation.gov.uk/uksi/2014/3549/contents/made Non-print

The M6 Motorway (Junction 23 Haydock Island) and the A580 Trunk Road (Temporary Prohibition and Restriction of Traffic) Order 2014 No. 2014/3173. - Enabling power: Road Traffic Regulation Act 1984, s. 14 (1) (a). - Issued: 28.11.2014. Made: 04.11.2014. Coming into force: 23.11.2014. Effect: None. Territorial extent & classification: E. Local. - Available at http://www.legislation.gov.uk/uksi/2014/3173/contents/made Non-print

The M6 Motorway (Junction 26) (Orrell Interchange) and the M58 Motorway (Eastbound and Westbound) (Temporary Prohibition and Restriction of Traffic) Order 2014 No. 2014/87. - Enabling power: Road Traffic Regulation Act 1984, s. 14 (1) (a). - Issued: 21.01.2014. Made: 16.01.2014. Coming into force: 01.02.2014. Effect: None. Territorial extent & classification: E. Local. - Available at http://www.legislation.gov.uk/uksi/2014/87/contents/made Non-print

The M6 Motorway (Junction 27-26 Southbound Carriageway and Junction 27 Southbound Entry Slip Road) (Temporary Prohibition of Traffic) Order 2014 No. 2014/1153. - Enabling power: Road Traffic Regulation Act 1984, s. 14 (1) (a). - Issued: 06.05.2014. Made: 12.02.2014. Coming into force: 28.02.2014. Effect: None. Territorial extent & classification: E. Local. - Available at http://www.legislation.gov.uk/uksi/2014/1153/contents/made Non-print

The M6 Motorway (Junction 36) and the A590 Trunk Road (Farleton Interchange) (Temporary Prohibition and Restriction of Traffic) Order 2014 No. 2014/3526. - Enabling power: Road Traffic Regulation Act 1984, ss. 14 (1) (a). - Issued: 27.01.2015. Made: 30.10.2014. Coming into force: 16.11.2014. Effect: None. Territorial extent & classification: E. Local. - Available at http://www.legislation.gov.uk/uksi/2014/3526/contents/made Non-print

The M6 Motorway (Junction 36 Northbound Entry and Exit Slip Roads) (Temporary Prohibition and Restriction of Traffic) Order 2014 No. 2014/85. - Enabling power: Road Traffic Regulation Act 1984, s. 14 (1) (a). - Issued: 21.01.2014. Made: 15.01.2014. Coming into force: 30.01.2014. Effect: None. Territorial extent & classification: E. Local. - Available at http://www.legislation.gov.uk/uksi/2014/85/contents/made Non-print

The M6 Motorway (Junction 37 Northbound Carriageway) (Highgill North Bridge) (Temporary Prohibition and Restriction of Traffic) Order 2014 No. 2014/764. - Enabling power: Road Traffic Regulation Act 1984, s. 14 (1) (a) (7). - Issued: 27.02.2014. Made: 20.02.2014. Coming into force: 09.03.2014. Effect: None. Territorial extent & classification: E. Local. - Available at http://www.legislation.gov.uk/uksi/2014/764/contents/made Non-print

ROAD TRAFFIC: TRAFFIC REGULATION

The M6 Motorway (Junction 43 Northbound and Southbound Carriageways) (Temporary Prohibition and Restriction of Traffic) Order 2014 No. 2014/2506. - Enabling power: Road Traffic Regulation Act 1984, s. 14 (1) (a). - Issued: 10.09.2014. Made: 04.09.2014. Coming into force: 21.09.2014. Effect: None. Territorial extent & classification: E. Local. - Available at
http://www.legislation.gov.uk/uksi/2014/2506/contents/made
Non-print

The M6 Motorway (Junction 44 Southbound Carriageway) (Temporary Restriction of Traffic) Order 2014 No. 2014/1026. - Enabling power: Road Traffic Regulation Act 1984, s. 14 (1) (a). - Issued: 17.04.2014. Made: 28.03.2014. Coming into force: 30.03.2014. Effect: None. Territorial extent & classification: E. Local. - Available at
http://www.legislation.gov.uk/uksi/2014/1026/contents/made
Non-print

The M6 Motorway (Junctions 1 to 2, Rugby) (Temporary Restriction and Prohibition of Traffic) Order 2014 No. 2014/971. - Enabling power: Road Traffic Regulation Act 1984, s. 14 (1) (a) & S.I. 1982/1163, reg. 16 (2). - Issued: 10.04.2014. Made: 17.03.2014. Coming into force: 24.03.2014. Effect: None. Territorial extent & classification: E. Local. - Available at
http://www.legislation.gov.uk/uksi/2014/971/contents/made Non-print

The M6 Motorway (Junctions 1 to 2, Warwickshire) (Temporary Prohibition of Traffic) Order 2014 No. 2014/313. - Enabling power: Road Traffic Regulation Act 1984, s. 14 (1) (a). - Issued: 17.02.2014. Made: 03.02.2014. Coming into force: 10.02.2014. Effect: None. Territorial extent & classification: E. Local. - Available at
http://www.legislation.gov.uk/uksi/2014/313/contents/made Non-print

The M6 Motorway (Junctions 7 to 10) (Temporary Restriction and Prohibition of Traffic) Order 2014 No. 2014/1630. - Enabling power: Road Traffic Regulation Act 1984, s. 14 (1) (a) (7) & S.I. 1982/1163, reg. 16 (2). - Issued: 25.06.2014. Made: 02.06.2014. Coming into force: 09.06.2014. Effect: None. Territorial extent & classification: E. Local. - Available at
http://www.legislation.gov.uk/uksi/2014/1630/contents/made
Non-print

The M6 Motorway (Junctions 10 to 8, Walsall) (Temporary Prohibition of Traffic) Order 2014 No. 2014/3146. - Enabling power: Road Traffic Regulation Act 1984, s. 14 (1) (a). - Issued: 24.11.2014. Made: 10.11.2014. Coming into force: 17.11.2014. Effect: None. Territorial extent & classification: E. Local. - Available at
http://www.legislation.gov.uk/uksi/2014/3146/contents/made
Non-print

The M6 Motorway (Junctions 13 - 12), the M54 Motorway (Junctions 2 - 4 and 4 - 3), the A5 Trunk Road and the A449 Trunk Road (Temporary Prohibition of Traffic) Order 2014 No. 2014/2244. - Enabling power: Road Traffic Regulation Act 1984, s. 14 (1) (b) & S.I. 1982/1163, reg. 16 (2). - Issued: 27.08.2014. Made: 04.08.2014. Coming into force: 11.08.2014. Effect: None. Territorial extent & classification: E. Local. - Available at
http://www.legislation.gov.uk/uksi/2014/2244/contents/made
Non-print

The M6 Motorway (Junctions 14 to 15, Staffordshire) (Temporary Restriction and Prohibition of Traffic) Order 2014 No. 2014/621. - Enabling power: Road Traffic Regulation Act 1984, s. 14 (1) (a) & S.I. 1982/1163, reg. 16 (2). - Issued: 07.03.2014. Made: 07.02.2014. Coming into force: 14.02.2014. Effect: None. Territorial extent & classification: E. Local. - Available at
http://www.legislation.gov.uk/uksi/2014/621/contents/made Non-print

The M6 Motorway (Junctions 14 to 15, Stafford to Stoke-On-Trent) (Temporary Prohibition of Traffic) Order 2014 No. 2014/1038. - Enabling power: Road Traffic Regulation Act 1984, s. 14 (1) (a). - Issued: 22.04.2014. Made: 24.03.2014. Coming into force: 31.03.2014. Effect: None. Territorial extent & classification: E. Local. - Available at
http://www.legislation.gov.uk/uksi/2014/1038/contents/made
Non-print

The M6 Motorway (Junctions 16-18 Northbound and Southbound Carriageways and Slip Roads) and Sandbach Service Area (Temporary Prohibition and Restriction of Traffic) (No.2) Order 2014 No. 2014/2546. - Enabling power: Road Traffic Regulation Act 1984, s. 14 (1) (a) (7). - Issued: 23.09.2014. Made: 09.09.2014. Coming into force: 11.09.2014. Effect: None. Territorial extent & classification: E. Local. - Available at
http://www.legislation.gov.uk/uksi/2014/2546/contents/made
Non-print

The M6 Motorway (Junctions 16-18 Northbound and Southbound Carriageways and Slip Roads) and Sandbach Service Area (Temporary Prohibition and Restriction of Traffic) Order No. 2014/2217. - Enabling power: Road Traffic Regulation Act 1984, s. 14 (1) (a) (7). - Issued: 21.08.2014. Made: 12.08.2014. Coming into force: 27.08.2014. Effect: None. Territorial extent & classification: E. Local. - Available at
http://www.legislation.gov.uk/uksi/2014/2217/contents/made
Non-print

The M6 Motorway (Junctions 16-18 Northbound and Southbound Carriageways and Slip Roads) (Temporary Prohibition and Restriction of Traffic) Order 2014 No. 2014/2784. - Enabling power: Road Traffic Regulation Act 1984, s. 14 (1) (a) (7). - Issued: 13.10.2014. Made: 24.10.2014. Coming into force: 12.10.2014. Effect: None. Territorial extent & classification: E. Local. - Available at
http://www.legislation.gov.uk/uksi/2014/2784/contents/made
Non-print

The M6 Motorway (Junctions 18-19 Northbound and Southbound Carriageways) (Temporary Prohibition and Restriction of Traffic) Order 2014 No. 2014/2302. - Enabling power: Road Traffic Regulation Act 1984, s. 14 (1) (a). - Issued: 26.08.2014. Made: 26.08.2014. Coming into force: 04.09.2014. Effect: None. Territorial extent & classification: E. Local. - Available at
http://www.legislation.gov.uk/uksi/2014/2302/contents/made
Non-print

The M6 Motorway (Junctions 18-21A Northbound and Southbound Carriageways and Slip Roads) and Knutsford Service Area (Temporary Prohibition and Restriction of Traffic) Order 2014 No. 2014/1984. - Enabling power: Road Traffic Regulation Act 1984, s. 14 (1) (a) (7). - Issued: 18.07.2014. Made: 02.07.2014. Coming into force: 21.07.2014. Effect: None. Territorial extent & classification: E. Local. - Available at
http://www.legislation.gov.uk/uksi/2014/1984/contents/made
Non-print

The M6 Motorway (Junctions 20-21a Northbound and Southbound Carriageways, Link and Slip Roads) and the M62 and M56 Link Roads (Temporary Prohibition and Restriction of Traffic) Order 2014 No. 2014/397. - Enabling power: Road Traffic Regulation Act 1984, s. 14 (1) (a) (7). - Issued: 27.02.2014. Made: 12.02.2014. Coming into force: 19.02.2014. Effect: None. Territorial extent & classification: E. Local. - Available at
http://www.legislation.gov.uk/uksi/2014/397/contents/made Non-print

The M6 Motorway (Junctions 21A-23 Northbound and Southbound Carriageways and Slip Roads) and the M62 Link Roads (Temporary Prohibition and Restriction of Traffic) Order 2014 No. 2014/2826. - Enabling power: Road Traffic Regulation Act 1984, s. 14 (1) (a). - Issued: 16.10.2014. Made: 08.10.2014. Coming into force: 26.10.2014. Effect: None. Territorial extent & classification: E. Local. - Available at
http://www.legislation.gov.uk/uksi/2014/2826/contents/made
Non-print

The M6 Motorway (Junctions 23-26 Northbound and Southbound Entry and Exit Slip Roads) (Temporary Prohibition of Traffic) Order 2014 No. 2014/3122. - Enabling power: Road Traffic Regulation Act 1984, s. 14 (1) (a). - Issued: 21.11.2014. Made: 15.10.2014. Coming into force: 02.11.2014. Effect: None. Territorial extent & classification: E. Local. - Available at
http://www.legislation.gov.uk/uksi/2014/3122/contents/made
Non-print

The M6 Motorway (Junctions 25-28 Northbound and Southbound Carriageways and Slip Roads) (Temporary Prohibition and Restriction of Traffic) Order 2014 No. 2014/3028. - Enabling power: Road Traffic Regulation Act 1984, s. 14 (1) (a) & S.I. 1982/1163, reg. 16 (2). - Issued: 12.11.2014. Made: 28.10.2014. Coming into force: 16.11.2014. Effect: None. Territorial extent & classification: E. Local. - Available at
http://www.legislation.gov.uk/uksi/2014/3028/contents/made
Non-print

The M6 Motorway (Junctions 27-29 Northbound and Southbound Carriageways and Slip Roads) (Temporary Prohibition and Restriction of Traffic) Order 2014 No. 2014/3410. - Enabling power: Road Traffic Regulation Act 1984, s. 14 (1) (a) & S.I. 1982/1163, reg. 16 (2). - Issued: 25.11.2014. Made: 19.11.2014. Coming into force: 04.12.2014. Effect: None. Territorial extent & classification: E. Local. - Available at
http://www.legislation.gov.uk/uksi/2014/3410/contents/made
Non-print

The M6 Motorway (Junctions 29-30 Northbound and Southbound Carriageways and Slip Roads) (Temporary Prohibition of Traffic) Order 2014 No. 2014/2209. - Enabling power: Road Traffic Regulation Act 1984, s. 14 (1) (a). - Issued: 20.08.2014. Made: 07.07.2014. Coming into force: 28.08.2014. Effect: None. Territorial extent & classification: E. Local. - Available at http://www.legislation.gov.uk/uksi/2014/2209/contents/made Non-print

The M6 Motorway (Junctions 32-33 Northbound Carriageway) and M55 Eastbound Link Road to the M6 Northbound (Temporary Prohibition and Restriction of Traffic) Order 2014 No. 2014/1224. - Enabling power: Road Traffic Regulation Act 1984, ss. 14 (1) (a). - Issued: 14.05.2014. Made: 06.03.2014. Coming into force: 20.03.2014. Effect: None. Territorial extent & classification: E. Local. - Available at http://www.legislation.gov.uk/uksi/2014/1224/contents/made Non-print

The M6 Motorway (Junctions 33-32 Southbound Carriageway) (Temporary Restriction of Traffic) Order 2014 No. 2014/2654. - Enabling power: Road Traffic Regulation Act 1984, s. 14 (1) (a) (7). - Issued: 03.10.2014. Made: 04.09.2014. Coming into force: 07.09.2014. Effect: None. Territorial extent & classification: E. Local. - Available at http://www.legislation.gov.uk/uksi/2014/2654/contents/made Non-print

The M6 Motorway (Junctions 33-34 Northbound and Southbound Carriageways) (Temporary Restriction of Traffic) Order 2014 No. 2014/2318. - Enabling power: Road Traffic Regulation Act 1984, s. 14 (1) (a). - Issued: 01.09.2014. Made: 21.08.2014. Coming into force: 07.09.2014. Effect: None. Territorial extent & classification: E. Local. - Available at http://www.legislation.gov.uk/uksi/2014/2318/contents/made Non-print

The M6 Motorway (Junctions 33-34 Northbound Carriageway) (Temporary Prohibition and Restriction of Traffic) Order 2014 No. 2014/3481. - Enabling power: Road Traffic Regulation Act 1984, s. 14 (1) (a) & S.I. 1982/1163, reg. 16 (2). - Issued: 24.12.2014. Made: 18.12.2014. Coming into force: 04.01.2015. Effect: None. Territorial extent & classification: E. Local. - Available at http://www.legislation.gov.uk/uksi/2014/3481/contents/made Non-print

The M6 Motorway (Junctions 33-34 Northbound Carriageway) (Temporary Restriction of Traffic) Order 2014 No. 2014/2569. - Enabling power: Road Traffic Regulation Act 1984, s. 14 (1) (a). - Issued: 24.09.2014. Made: 12.09.2014. Coming into force: 27.09.2014. Effect: None. Territorial extent & classification: E. Local. - Available at http://www.legislation.gov.uk/uksi/2014/2569/contents/made Non-print

The M6 Motorway (Junctions 33-35 Northbound and Southbound Carriageways and Junction 34 Slip Roads) (Temporary Prohibition and Restriction of Traffic) Order 2014 No. 2014/1680. - Enabling power: Road Traffic Regulation Act 1984, s. 14 (1) (a), 15 (2). - Issued: 01.07.2014. Made: 05.06.2014. Coming into force: 09.06.2014. Effect: None. Territorial extent & classification: E. Local. - Available at http://www.legislation.gov.uk/uksi/2014/1680/contents/made Non-print

The M6 Motorway (Junctions 34-36 Northbound and Southbound Carriageways) (Temporary Restriction of Traffic) Order 2014 No. 2014/3525. - Enabling power: Road Traffic Regulation Act 1984, s. 14 (1) (a). - Issued: 27.01.2014. Made: 10.10.2014. Coming into force: 26.10.2014. Effect: None. Territorial extent & classification: E. Local. - Available at http://www.legislation.gov.uk/uksi/2014/3525/contents/made Non-print

The M6 Motorway (Junctions 35-36 Northbound Exit Slip Road to Burton-in-Kendal Services) (Temporary Prohibition of Traffic) Order 2014 No. 2014/1347. - Enabling power: Road Traffic Regulation Act 1984, s. 14 (1) (a). - Issued: 29.05.2014. Made: 30.04.2014. Coming into force: 18.05.2014. Effect: None. Territorial extent & classification: E. Local. - Available at http://www.legislation.gov.uk/uksi/2014/1347/contents/made Non-print

The M6 Motorway (Junctions 36-37 Northbound and Southbound Carriageways) (Temporary Restriction of Traffic) Order 2014 No. 2014/3425. - Enabling power: Road Traffic Regulation Act 1984, s. 14 (1) (a). - Issued: 28.11.2014. Made: 19.11.2014. Coming into force: 07.12.2014. Effect: None. Territorial extent & classification: E. Local. - Available at http://www.legislation.gov.uk/uksi/2014/3425/contents/made Non-print

The M6 Motorway (Junctions 37-39 Northbound and Southbound Carriageways and Slip Roads) (Temporary Restriction of Traffic) Order 2014 No. 2014/2092. - Enabling power: Road Traffic Regulation Act 1984, s. 14 (1) (a). - Issued: 07.08.2014. Made: 16.07.2014. Coming into force: 03.08.2014. Effect: None. Territorial extent & classification: E. Local. - Available at http://www.legislation.gov.uk/uksi/2014/2092/contents/made Non-print

The M6 Motorway (Junctions 37-39 Northbound and Southbound Carriageways) (Temporary Restriction of Traffic) (No.2) Order 2014 No. 2014/2425. - Enabling power: Road Traffic Regulation Act 1984, s. 14 (1) (a). - Issued: 10.09.2014. Made: 04.09.2014. Coming into force: 12.09.2014. Effect: None. Territorial extent & classification: E. Local. - Available at http://www.legislation.gov.uk/uksi/2014/2425/contents/made Non-print

The M6 Motorway (Junctions 37-39 Northbound and Southbound Carriageways) (Temporary Restriction of Traffic) Order 2014 No. 2014/1692. - Enabling power: Road Traffic Regulation Act 1984, s. 14 (1) (a). - Issued: 02.07.2014. Made: 12.06.2014. Coming into force: 14.06.2014. Effect: None. Territorial extent & classification: E. Local. - Available at http://www.legislation.gov.uk/uksi/2014/1692/contents/made Non-print

The M6 Motorway (Junctions 38-37 Southbound Carriageway and Junction 38 Southbound Entry Slip Road) (Temporary Restriction of Traffic) Order 2014 No. 2014/2815. - Enabling power: Road Traffic Regulation Act 1984, s. 14 (1) (a). - Issued: 22.10.2014. Made: 26.09.2014. Coming into force: 11.10.2014. Effect: None. Territorial extent & classification: E. Local. - Available at http://www.legislation.gov.uk/uksi/2014/2815/contents/made Non-print

The M6 Motorway (Junctions 39-38 Southbound Carriageway) (Temporary Restriction of Traffic) Order 2014 No. 2014/3423. - Enabling power: Road Traffic Regulation Act 1984, s. 14 (1) (a). - Issued: 28.11.2014. Made: 19.11.2014. Coming into force: 07.12.2014. Effect: None. Territorial extent & classification: E. Local. - Available at http://www.legislation.gov.uk/uksi/2014/3423/contents/made Non-print

The M6 Motorway (Junctions 39-40 Northbound and Southbound Carriageways) (Temporary Restriction of Traffic) (No.2) Order 2014 No. 2014/2390. - Enabling power: Road Traffic Regulation Act 1984, s. 14 (1) (a). - Issued: 08.09.2014. Made: 14.08.2014. Coming into force: 30.09.2014. Effect: None. Territorial extent & classification: E. Local. - Available at http://www.legislation.gov.uk/uksi/2014/2390/contents/made Non-print

The M6 Motorway (Junctions 39-40 Northbound and Southbound Carriageways) (Temporary Restriction of Traffic) Order 2014 No. 2014/71. - Enabling power: Road Traffic Regulation Act 1984, s. 14 (1) (a). - Issued: 20.01.2014. Made: 08.01.2014. Coming into force: 26.01.2014. Effect: None. Territorial extent & classification: E. Local. - Available at http://www.legislation.gov.uk/uksi/2014/71/contents/made Non-print

The M6 Motorway (Junctions 39-40 Northbound Carriageway) (Temporary Restriction of Traffic) (No.2) Order 2014 No. 2014/2408. - Enabling power: Road Traffic Regulation Act 1984, s. 14 (1) (a). - Issued: 05.09.2014. Made: 21.09.2014. Coming into force: 06.09.2014. Effect: None. Territorial extent & classification: E. Local. - Available at http://www.legislation.gov.uk/uksi/2014/2408/contents/made Non-print

The M6 Motorway (Junctions 39-40 Northbound Carriageway) (Temporary Restriction of Traffic) Order 2014 No. 2014/293. - Enabling power: Road Traffic Regulation Act 1984, s. 14 (1) (a). - Issued: 11.02.2014. Made: 07.02.2014. Coming into force: 22.02.2014. Effect: None. Territorial extent & classification: E. Local. - Available at http://www.legislation.gov.uk/uksi/2014/293/contents/made Non-print

The M6 Motorway (Junctions 39-41 Northbound and Southbound Carriageways) (Temporary Restriction of Traffic) Order 2014 No. 2014/957. - Enabling power: Road Traffic Regulation Act 1984, s. 14 (1) (a). - Issued: 01.04.2014. Made: 13.03.2014. Coming into force: 16.03.2014. Effect: None. Territorial extent & classification: E. Local. - Available at http://www.legislation.gov.uk/uksi/2014/957/contents/made Non-print

The M6 Motorway (Junctions 40-39 Southbound Carriageway) (Temporary Restriction of Traffic) Order 2014 No. 2014/2564. - Enabling power: Road Traffic Regulation Act 1984, s. 14 (1) (a). - Issued: 24.09.2014. Made: 28.08.2014. Coming into force: 31.08.2014. Effect: None. Territorial extent & classification: E. Local. - Available at http://www.legislation.gov.uk/uksi/2014/2564/contents/made Non-print

The M6 Motorway (Junctions 40-42 Northbound Carriageway and Junction 41 Northbound Entry Slip Road) (Temporary Restriction of Traffic) Order 2014 No. 2014/2563. - Enabling power: Road Traffic Regulation Act 1984, s. 14 (1) (a). - Issued: 24.09.2014. Made: 28.08.2014. Coming into force: 31.08.2014. Effect: None. Territorial extent & classification: E. Local. - Available at http://www.legislation.gov.uk/uksi/2014/2563/contents/made Non-print

The M6 Motorway (Junctions 40-42 Northbound Carriageway and Slip Roads) and Southwaite Services Slip Roads (Temporary Prohibition and Restriction of Traffic) Order 2014 No. 2014/1223. - Enabling power: Road Traffic Regulation Act 1984, ss. 14 (1) (a). - Issued: 14.05.2014. Made: 07.03.2014. Coming into force: 09.03.2014. Effect: None. Territorial extent & classification: E. Local. - Available at http://www.legislation.gov.uk/uksi/2014/1223/contents/made Non-print

The M6 Motorway (Junctions 40-42 Northbound Carriageway and Slip Roads) (Temporary Prohibition and Restriction of Traffic) Order 2014 No. 2014/947. - Enabling power: Road Traffic Regulation Act 1984, s. 14 (1) (a). - Issued: 01.04.2014. Made: 14.03.2014. Coming into force: 16.03.2014. Effect: None. Territorial extent & classification: E. Local. - Available at http://www.legislation.gov.uk/uksi/2014/947/contents/made Non-print

The M6 Motorway (Junctions 42-41 Southbound Carriageway) (Temporary Restriction of Traffic) (No.2) Order 2014 No. 2014/2723. - Enabling power: Road Traffic Regulation Act 1984, s. 14 (1) (a). - Issued: 13.10.2014. Made: 25.09.2014. Coming into force: 28.09.2014. Effect: None. Territorial extent & classification: E. Local. - Available at http://www.legislation.gov.uk/uksi/2014/2723/contents/made Non-print

The M6 Motorway (Junctions 42-41 Southbound Carriageway) (Temporary Restriction of Traffic) Order 2014 No. 2014/2638. - Enabling power: Road Traffic Regulation Act 1984, s. 14 (1) (a). - Issued: 01.10.2014. Made: 24.07.2014. Coming into force: 10.08.2014. Effect: None. Territorial extent & classification: E. Local. - Available at http://www.legislation.gov.uk/uksi/2014/2638/contents/made Non-print

The M6 Motorway (Junctions 43-44 Northbound Carriageway and Junction 43 Northbound Entry Slip Road) (Temporary Restriction of Traffic) Order 2014 No. 2014/297. - Enabling power: Road Traffic Regulation Act 1984, s. 14 (1) (a). - Issued: 11.02.2014. Made: 06.02.2014. Coming into force: 22.02.2014. Effect: None. Territorial extent & classification: E. Local. - Available at http://www.legislation.gov.uk/uksi/2014/297/contents/made Non-print

The M6 Motorway (Junctions 43-45 Northbound and Southbound Carriageways and Slip Roads) (Temporary Restriction of Traffic) Order 2014 No. 2014/2877. - Enabling power: Road Traffic Regulation Act 1984, s. 14 (1) (a) (7). - Issued: 24.10.2014. Made: 02.10.2014. Coming into force: 18.10.2014. Effect: None. Territorial extent & classification: E. Local. - Available at http://www.legislation.gov.uk/uksi/2014/2877/contents/made Non-print

The M6 Motorway (Junctions 44-45 Northbound and Southbound Carriageways) (Temporary Restriction of Traffic) Order 2014 No. 2014/2487. - Enabling power: Road Traffic Regulation Act 1984, s. 14 (1) (a). - Issued: 19.09.2014. Made: 11.09.2014. Coming into force: 14.09.2014. Effect: None. Territorial extent & classification: E. Local. - Available at http://www.legislation.gov.uk/uksi/2014/2487/contents/made Non-print

The M6 Motorway (Junctions 44-45 Northbound Carriageway) (Temporary Restriction of Traffic) Order 2014 No. 2014/3421. - Enabling power: Road Traffic Regulation Act 1984, s. 14 (1) (a). - Issued: 28.11.2014. Made: 20.11.2014. Coming into force: 07.12.2014. Effect: None. Territorial extent & classification: E. Local. - Available at http://www.legislation.gov.uk/uksi/2014/3421/contents/made Non-print

The M6 Motorway (Junctions 44-45 Southbound Carriageway) (Temporary Restriction of Traffic) Order 2014 No. 2014/1160. - Enabling power: Road Traffic Regulation Act 1984, s. 14 (1) (a). - Issued: 06.05.2014. Made: 24.04.2014. Coming into force: 26.04.2014. Effect: None. Territorial extent & classification: E. Local. - Available at http://www.legislation.gov.uk/uksi/2014/1160/contents/made Non-print

The M6 Motorway (M6 Junction 4, Warwickshire) (Temporary Prohibition of Traffic) (Slip Road) Order 2014 No. 2014/973. - Enabling power: Road Traffic Regulation Act 1984, s. 14 (1) (a). - Issued: 10.04.2014. Made: 17.03.2014. Coming into force: 24.03.2014. Effect: None. Territorial extent & classification: E. Local. - Available at http://www.legislation.gov.uk/uksi/2014/973/contents/made Non-print

The M6 Motorway, M42 Motorway and the M6 Toll Motorway (Water Orton) (Temporary Restriction and Prohibition of Traffic) Order 2014 No. 2014/2022. - Enabling power: Road Traffic Regulation Act 1984, s. 14 (1) (a). - Issued: 01.08.2014. Made: 13.06.2014. Coming into force: 20.06.2014. Effect: None. Territorial extent & classification: E. Local. - Available at http://www.legislation.gov.uk/uksi/2014/2022/contents/made Non-print

The M6 Motorway (South of Junction 10a) (Temporary Restriction and Prohibition of Traffic) Order 2014 No. 2014/2447. - Enabling power: Road Traffic Regulation Act 1984, s. 14 (1) (a) & S.I. 1982/1163, reg. 16 (2). - Issued: 15.09.2014. Made: 26.08.2014. Coming into force: 02.09.2014. Effect: None. Territorial extent & classification: E. Local. - Available at http://www.legislation.gov.uk/uksi/2014/2447/contents/made Non-print

The M6 Motorway (South of Junction 16, Staffordshire) (Temporary Prohibition and Restriction of Traffic) Order 2014 No. 2014/2024. - Enabling power: Road Traffic Regulation Act 1984, s. 14 (1) (a). - Issued: 01.08.2014. Made: 13.06.2014. Coming into force: 20.06.2014. Effect: None. Territorial extent & classification: E. Local. - Available at http://www.legislation.gov.uk/uksi/2014/2024/contents/made Non-print

The M6 Toll Motorway (Junctions T1 to T3) (Temporary Restriction and Prohibition of Traffic) Order 2014 No. 2014/1688. - Enabling power: Road Traffic Regulation Act 1984, s. 14 (1) (a) & S.I. 1982/1163, reg. 16 (2). - Issued: 02.07.2014. Made: 02.06.2014. Coming into force: 09.06.2014. Effect: None. Territorial extent & classification: E. Local. - Available at http://www.legislation.gov.uk/uksi/2014/1688/contents/made Non-print

The M6 Toll Motorway (Junction T3 to M42) (Temporary Prohibition of Traffic) Order 2014 No. 2014/1265. - Enabling power: Road Traffic Regulation Act 1984, s. 14 (1) (a). - Issued: 19.05.2014. Made: 22.04.2014. Coming into force: 29.04.2014. Effect: None. Territorial extent & classification: E. Local. - Available at http://www.legislation.gov.uk/uksi/2014/1265/contents/made Non-print

The M6 Toll Motorway (Slip Roads) (Temporary Prohibition of Traffic) Order 2014 No. 2014/1428. - Enabling power: Road Traffic Regulation Act 1984, s. 14 (1) (a). - Issued: 30.05.2014. Made: 13.05.2014. Coming into force: 20.05.2014. Effect: None. Territorial extent & classification: E. Local. - Available at http://www.legislation.gov.uk/uksi/2014/1428/contents/made Non-print

The M11 Motorway and The A406 Trunk Road (M11 Junction 4) (Temporary Restriction and Prohibition of Traffic) Order 2014 No. 2014/2094. - Enabling power: Road Traffic Regulation Act 1984, s. 14 (1) (a). - Issued: 07.08.2014. Made: 21.07.2014. Coming into force: 13.08.2014. Effect: None. Territorial extent & classification: E. Local. - Available at http://www.legislation.gov.uk/uksi/2014/2094/contents/made Non-print

The M11 Motorway (between Junction 6 and Junction 7) (Temporary 50 Miles Per Hour Speed Restriction) Order 2014 No. 2014/2433. - Enabling power: Road Traffic Regulation Act 1984, s. 14 (1) (a) (7), Motorway Traffic (England and Wales) Regulations 1982, 16 (2). - Issued: 04.09.2014. Made: 01.09.2014. Coming into force: 08.09.2014. Effect: None. Territorial extent & classification: E. Local. - Available at http://www.legislation.gov.uk/uksi/2014/2433/contents/made Non-print

ROAD TRAFFIC: TRAFFIC REGULATION

The M11 Motorway (between Junction 10 and Junction 11) (Temporary 50 Miles Per Hour Speed Restriction) Order 2014 No. 2014/3039. - Enabling power: Road Traffic Regulation Act 1984, s. 14 (1) (a). - Issued: 17.11.2014. Made: 10.11.2014. Coming into force: 17.11.2014. Effect: None. Territorial extent & classification: E. Local. - Available at http://www.legislation.gov.uk/uksi/2014/3039/contents/made Non-print

The M11 Motorway (Junction 7, Essex) Slip Roads (Temporary Prohibition of Traffic) Order 2014 No. 2014/2860. - Enabling power: Road Traffic Regulation Act 1984, s. 14 (1) (a). - Issued: 24.10.2014. Made: 06.10.2014. Coming into force: 13.10.2014. Effect: None. Territorial extent & classification: E. Local. - Available at http://www.legislation.gov.uk/uksi/2014/2860/contents/made Non-print

The M11 Motorway (Junction 11 to Junction 12, Cambridgeshire) (Temporary Restriction and Prohibition of Traffic) Order 2014 No. 2014/57. - Enabling power: Road Traffic Regulation Act 1984, s. 14 (1) (a) & S.I. 1982/1163, reg. 16 (2). - Issued: 17.01.2014. Made: 13.01.2014. Coming into force: 20.01.2014. Effect: None. Territorial extent & classification: E. Local. - Available at http://www.legislation.gov.uk/uksi/2014/57/contents/made Non-print

The M11 Motorway (Junctions 4 - 6) (Temporary Prohibition of Traffic) Order 2014 No. 2014/2109. - Enabling power: Road Traffic Regulation Act 1984, s. 14 (1) (a). - Issued: 07.08.2014. Made: 21.07.2014. Coming into force: 14.08.2014. Effect: None. Territorial extent & classification: E. Local. - Available at http://www.legislation.gov.uk/uksi/2014/2109/contents/made Non-print

The M11 Motorway (Junctions 7 to 11) and the A11 Trunk Road (Stumps Cross, Pampisford and Waterhall Interchange) Connecting Roads (Temporary Prohibition of Traffic) Order 2014 No. 2014/1748. - Enabling power: Road Traffic Regulation Act 1984, ss. 14 (1) (a). - Issued: 03.07.2014. Made: 23.06.2014. Coming into force: 30.06.2014. Effect: None. Territorial extent & classification: E. Local. - Available at http://www.legislation.gov.uk/uksi/2014/1748/contents/made Non-print

The M11 Motorway (Junctions 8 to 9) Northbound (Temporary Prohibition of Traffic) Order 2014 No. 2014/2811. - Enabling power: Road Traffic Regulation Act 1984, s. 14 (1) (a). - Issued: 16.10.2014. Made: 13.10.2014. Coming into force: 20.10.2014. Effect: None. Territorial extent & classification: E. Local. - Available at http://www.legislation.gov.uk/uksi/2014/2811/contents/made Non-print

The M11 Motorway (Junctions 10 to 8) Southbound (Temporary Prohibition of Traffic) Order 2014 No. 2014/54. - Enabling power: Road Traffic Regulation Act 1984, s. 14 (1) (a). - Issued: 17.01.2014. Made: 13.01.2014. Coming into force: 20.01.2014. Effect: None. Territorial extent & classification: E. Local. - Available at http://www.legislation.gov.uk/uksi/2014/54/contents/made Non-print

The M11 Motorway (Junctions 11 to 14) Northbound (Temporary Prohibition of Traffic) Order 2014 No. 2014/1286. - Enabling power: Road Traffic Regulation Act 1984, ss. 14 (1) (a). - Issued: 21.05.2014. Made: 06.05.2014. Coming into force: 13.05.2014. Effect: None. Territorial extent & classification: E. Local. - Available at http://www.legislation.gov.uk/uksi/2014/1286/contents/made Non-print

The M18 (Junction 5 to Junction 4) (Temporary Prohibition of Traffic) Order 2014 No. 2014/2809. - Enabling power: Road Traffic Regulation Act 1984, s. 14 (1) (a). - Issued: 14.10.2014. Made: 09.10.2014. Coming into force: 19.10.2014. Effect: None. Territorial extent & classification: E. Local. - Available at http://www.legislation.gov.uk/uksi/2014/2809/contents/made Non-print

The M18 Motorway and the A1(M) Motorway (Wadworth) (Temporary Prohibition of Traffic) Order 2014 No. 2014/994. - Enabling power: Road Traffic Regulation Act 1984, s. 14 (1) (a). - Issued: 10.04.2014. Made: 27.03.2014. Coming into force: 06.04.2014. Effect: None. Territorial extent & classification: E. Local. - Available at http://www.legislation.gov.uk/uksi/2014/994/contents/made Non-print

The M18 Motorway and the M62 Motorway (Langham Interchange) (Temporary Restriction and Prohibition of Traffic) Order 2014 No. 2014/2005. - Enabling power: Road Traffic Regulation Act 1984, s. 14 (1) (a) & S.I. 1982/1163 reg. 16 (2). - Issued: 30.07.2014. Made: 10.07.2014. Coming into force: 21.07.2014. Effect: None. Territorial extent & classification: E. Local. - Available at http://www.legislation.gov.uk/uksi/2014/2005/contents/made Non-print

The M18 Motorway (Junction 1 to Junction 2) (Temporary Restriction and Prohibition of Traffic) Order 2014 No. 2014/1633. - Enabling power: Road Traffic Regulation Act 1984, s. 14 (1) (a) & S.I. 1982/1163, reg. 16 (2). - Issued: 25.06.2014. Made: 05.06.2014. Coming into force: 15.06.2014. Effect: None. Territorial extent & classification: E. Local. - Available at http://www.legislation.gov.uk/uksi/2014/1633/contents/made Non-print

The M18 Motorway (Junction 2 to Junction 3) (Temporary Restriction and Prohibition of Traffic) Order 2014 No. 2014/1696. - Enabling power: Road Traffic Regulation Act 1984, s. 14 (1) (a). - Issued: 02.07.2014. Made: 12.06.2014. Coming into force: 19.06.2014. Effect: None. Territorial extent & classification: E. Local. - Available at http://www.legislation.gov.uk/uksi/2014/1696/contents/made Non-print

The M18 Motorway (Junction 2, Wadworth) (Temporary Prohibition of Traffic) (No.2) Order 2014 No. 2014/133. - Enabling power: Road Traffic Regulation Act 1984, s. 14 (1) (a). - Issued: 24.01.2014. Made: 16.01.2014. Coming into force: 26.01.2014. Effect: None. Territorial extent & classification: E. Local. - Available at http://www.legislation.gov.uk/uksi/2014/133/contents/made Non-print

The M18 Motorway (Junction 2, Wadworth) (Temporary Prohibition of Traffic) (No.3) Order 2014 No. 2014/2966. - Enabling power: Road Traffic Regulation Act 1984, s. 14 (1) (a). - Issued: 27.10.2014. Made: 23.10.2014. Coming into force: 02.11.2014. Effect: None. Territorial extent & classification: E. Local. - Available at http://www.legislation.gov.uk/uksi/2014/2966/contents/made Non-print

The M18 Motorway (Junction 2, Wadworth) (Temporary Restriction and Prohibition of Traffic) Order 2014 No. 2014/284. - Enabling power: Road Traffic Regulation Act 1984, s. 14 (1) (a) & S.I. 1982/1163, reg. 16 (2). - Issued: 14.02.2014. Made: 06.02.2014. Coming into force: 16.02.2014. Effect: None. Territorial extent & classification: E. Local. - Available at http://www.legislation.gov.uk/uksi/2014/284/contents/made Non-print

The M18 Motorway (Junction 3, St. Catherines) (Temporary Prohibition of Traffic) Order 2014 No. 2014/73. - Enabling power: Road Traffic Regulation Act 1984, s. 14 (1) (a). - Issued: 20.01.2014. Made: 09.01.2014. Coming into force: 10.01.2014. Effect: None. Territorial extent & classification: E. Local. - Available at http://www.legislation.gov.uk/uksi/2014/73/contents/made Non-print

The M18 Motorway (Junction 3) (Temporary Prohibition of Traffic) (No.2) Order 2014 No. 2014/3398. - Enabling power: Road Traffic Regulation Act 1984, s. 14 (1) (a). - Issued: 25.11.2014. Made: 20.11.2014. Coming into force: 30.11.2014. Effect: None. Territorial extent & classification: E. Local. - Available at http://www.legislation.gov.uk/uksi/2014/3398/contents/made Non-print

The M18 Motorway (Junction 4) (Temporary Prohibition of Traffic) Order 2014 No. 2014/2584. - Enabling power: Road Traffic Regulation Act 1984, s. 14 (1) (a). - Issued: 25.09.2014. Made: 18.09.2014. Coming into force: 30.09.2014. Effect: None. Territorial extent & classification: E. Local. - Available at http://www.legislation.gov.uk/uksi/2014/2584/contents/made Non-print

The M18 Motorway (Junction 4 to Junction 3) (Temporary Restriction and Prohibition of Traffic) (No.2) Order 201 No. 2014/3069. - Enabling power: Road Traffic Regulation Act 1984, s. 14 (1) (a) & S.I. 1982/1163, reg. 16 (2). - Issued: 20.11.2014. Made: 30.10.2014. Coming into force: 09.11.2014. Effect: None. Territorial extent & classification: E. Local. - Available at http://www.legislation.gov.uk/uksi/2014/3069/contents/made Non-print

The M18 Motorway (Junction 4 to Junction 3) (Temporary Restriction and Prohibition of Traffic) Order 2014 No. 2014/1987. - Enabling power: Road Traffic Regulation Act 1984, s. 14 (1) (a) & S.I. 1982/1163, reg. 16 (2). - Issued: 29.07.2014. Made: 10.07.2014. Coming into force: 20.07.2014. Effect: None. Territorial extent & classification: E. Local. - Available at
http://www.legislation.gov.uk/uksi/2014/1987/contents/made
Non-print

The M18 Motorway (Junction 4 to Junction 5) (Temporary Prohibition of Traffic) Order 2014 No. 2014/2315. - Enabling power: Road Traffic Regulation Act 1984, s. 14 (1) (a). - Issued: 01.09.2014. Made: 28.08.2014. Coming into force: 07.09.2014. Effect: None. Territorial extent & classification: E. Local. - Available at
http://www.legislation.gov.uk/uksi/2014/2315/contents/made
Non-print

The M18 Motorway (Junction 5) and the M180 Motorway (Junction 1) (Temporary Prohibition of Traffic) Order 2014 No. 2014/1568. - Enabling power: Road Traffic Regulation Act 1984, s. 14 (1) (a). - Issued: 17.06.2014. Made: 29.05.2014. Coming into force: 08.06.2014. Effect: None. Territorial extent & classification: E. Local. - Available at
http://www.legislation.gov.uk/uksi/2014/1568/contents/made
Non-print

The M18 Motorway (Junction 5) (Temporary Restriction and Prohibition of Traffic) Order 2014 No. 2014/3438. - Enabling power: Road Traffic Regulation Act 1984, s. 14 (1) (a) & S.I. 1982/1163, reg. 16 (2). - Issued: 10.12.2014. Made: 04.12.2014. Coming into force: 14.12.2014. Effect: None. Territorial extent & classification: E. Local. - Available at
http://www.legislation.gov.uk/uksi/2014/3438/contents/made
Non-print

The M18 Motorway (Junction 6 to Junction 7) (Temporary Restriction and Prohibition of Traffic) Order 2014 No. 2014/2155. - Enabling power: Road Traffic Regulation Act 1984, s. 14 (1) (a). - Issued: 12.08.2014. Made: 31.07.2014. Coming into force: 10.08.2014. Effect: None. Territorial extent & classification: E. Local. - Available at
http://www.legislation.gov.uk/uksi/2014/2155/contents/made
Non-print

The M18 Motorway (Langham Interchange) (Temporary Prohibition of Traffic) Order 2014 No. 2014/347. - Enabling power: Road Traffic Regulation Act 1984, s. 14 (1) (a). - Issued: 19.02.2014. Made: 13.02.2014. Coming into force: 23.02.2014. Effect: None. Territorial extent & classification: E. Local. - Available at
http://www.legislation.gov.uk/uksi/2014/347/contents/made Non-print

The M18 Motorway (Thurcroft) (Temporary Restriction and Prohibition of Traffic) Order 2014 No. 2014/678. - Enabling power: Road Traffic Regulation Act 1984, s. 14 (1) (a) & S.I. 1982/1163, reg. 16 (2). - Issued: 04.03.2014. Made: 20.02.2014. Coming into force: 02.03.2014. Effect: None. Territorial extent & classification: E. Local. - Available at
http://www.legislation.gov.uk/uksi/2014/678/contents/made Non-print

The M18 Motorway (Thurcroft to Wadworth) (Temporary Restriction and Prohibition of Traffic) Order 2014 No. 2014/2066. - Enabling power: Road Traffic Regulation Act 1984, ss. 14 (1) (a) & S.I. 1982/1163, reg. 16 (2). - Issued: 05.08.2014. Made: 17.07.2014. Coming into force: 31.07.2014. Effect: None. Territorial extent & classification: E. Local. - Available at
http://www.legislation.gov.uk/uksi/2014/2066/contents/made
Non-print

The M20 Motorway and the A20 Trunk Road (Junctions 9 - 13, Slip Roads) (Temporary Prohibition of Traffic) Order 2014 No. 2014/997. - Enabling power: Road Traffic Regulation Act 1984, s. 14 (1) (a). - Issued: 04.04.2014. Made: 24.03.2014. Coming into force: 16.04.2014. Effect: None. Territorial extent & classification: E. Local. - Available at http://www.legislation.gov.uk/uksi/2014/997/contents/made Non-print

The M20 Motorway and the A20 Trunk Road (Junctions 12 and 13, Slip Roads) (Temporary Prohibition of Traffic) Order 2014 No. 2014/100. - Enabling power: Road Traffic Regulation Act 1984, s. 14 (1) (a). - Issued: 22.01.2014. Made: 20.01.2014. Coming into force: 08.02.2014. Effect: None. Territorial extent & classification: E. Local. - Available at
http://www.legislation.gov.uk/uksi/2014/100/contents/made Non-print

The M20 Motorway and the A20 Trunk Road (Roundhill Tunnels) (Temporary Restriction and Prohibition of Traffic) Order 2014 No. 2014/3498. - Enabling power: Road Traffic Regulation Act 1984, ss. 14 (1) (a). - Issued: 20.01.2015. Made: 10.11.2014. Coming into force: 07.12.2014. Effect: None. Territorial extent & classification: E. Local. - Available at
http://www.legislation.gov.uk/uksi/2014/3498/contents/made
Non-print

The M20 Motorway and the A20 Trunk Road (Southeast of Junction 10 - Capel-le-Ferne) (Temporary Restriction and Prohibition of Traffic) Order 2014 No. 2014/304. - Enabling power: Road Traffic Regulation Act 1984, s. 14 (1) (a) (b). - Issued: 13.02.2014. Made: 10.02.2014. Coming into force: 01.03.2014. Effect: None. Territorial extent & classification: E. Local. - Available at
http://www.legislation.gov.uk/uksi/2014/304/contents/made Non-print

The M20 Motorway (Junction 1, Londonbound Link Road) (Temporary Prohibition of Traffic) Order 2014 No. 2014/303. - Enabling power: Road Traffic Regulation Act 1984, s. 14 (1) (a). - Issued: 13.02.2014. Made: 10.02.2013. Coming into force: 01.03.2014. Effect: None. Territorial extent & classification: E. Local. - Available at
http://www.legislation.gov.uk/uksi/2014/303/contents/made Non-print

The M20 Motorway (Junction 2, Slip Roads) (Temporary Prohibition of Traffic) Order 2014 No. 2014/1994. - Enabling power: Road Traffic Regulation Act 1984, ss. 14 (1) (a). - Issued: 21.07.2014. Made: 07.07.2014. Coming into force: 02.08.2014. Effect: None. Territorial extent & classification: E. Local. - Available at
http://www.legislation.gov.uk/uksi/2014/1994/contents/made
Non-print

The M20 Motorway (Junction 8) (Temporary Restriction and Prohibition of Traffic) Order 2014 No. 2014/170. - Enabling power: Road Traffic Regulation Act 1984, s. 14 (1) (a). - Issued: 30.01.2014. Made: 27.01.2014. Coming into force: 15.02.2014. Effect: None. Territorial extent & classification: E. Local. - Available at
http://www.legislation.gov.uk/uksi/2014/170/contents/made Non-print

The M20 Motorway (Junction 10 - Church Lane underbridge) (Temporary Restriction and Prohibition of Traffic) Order 2014 No. 2014/2644. - Enabling power: Road Traffic Regulation Act 1984, s. 14 (1) (a). - Issued: 30.09.2014. Made: 22.09.2014. Coming into force: 16.10.2014. Effect: None. Territorial extent & classification: E. Local. - Available at
http://www.legislation.gov.uk/uksi/2014/2644/contents/made
Non-print

The M20 Motorway (Junction 10, Slip Road) (Temporary Prohibition of Traffic) Order 2014 No. 2014/2539. - Enabling power: Road Traffic Regulation Act 1984, s. 14 (1) (a). - Issued: 12.09.2014. Made: 08.09.2014. Coming into force: 29.09.2014. Effect: None. Territorial extent & classification: E. Local. - Available at
http://www.legislation.gov.uk/uksi/2014/2539/contents/made
Non-print

The M20 Motorway (Junctions 4 - 6) (Temporary Restriction and Prohibition of Traffic) Order 2014 No. 2014/394. - Enabling power: Road Traffic Regulation Act 1984, s. 14 (1) (a). - Issued: 27.02.2014. Made: 17.02.2014. Coming into force: 12.03.2014. Effect: None. Territorial extent & classification: E. Local. - Available at
http://www.legislation.gov.uk/uksi/2014/394/contents/made Non-print

The M20 Motorway (Junctions 4 - 7) (Temporary Restriction and Prohibition of Traffic) (No.2) Order 2014 No. 2014/2549. - Enabling power: Road Traffic Regulation Act 1984, s. 14 (1) (a), sch. 9, para. 27 (1). - Issued: 24.09.2014. Made: 08.09.2014. Coming into force: 27.09.2014. Effect: None. Territorial extent & classification: E. Local. - Available at
http://www.legislation.gov.uk/uksi/2014/2549/contents/made
Non-print

The M20 Motorway (Junctions 4 - 7) (Temporary Restriction and Prohibition of Traffic) Order 2014 No. 2014/104. - Enabling power: Road Traffic Regulation Act 1984, s. 14 (1) (a). - Issued: 22.01.2014. Made: 20.01.2014. Coming into force: 08.02.2014. Effect: None. Territorial extent & classification: E. Local. - Available at
http://www.legislation.gov.uk/uksi/2014/104/contents/made Non-print

The M20 Motorway (Junctions 4 - 7) (Temporary Restriction and Prohibition of Traffic) Order 2014 No. 2014/1168. - Enabling power: Road Traffic Regulation Act 1984, s. 14 (1) (a). - Issued: 07.05.2014. Made: 21.04.2014. Coming into force: 10.05.2014. Effect: None. Territorial extent & classification: E. Local. - Available at
http://www.legislation.gov.uk/uksi/2014/1168/contents/made
Non-print

The M20 Motorway (Junctions 4 - 8) (Temporary Prohibition of Traffic) Order 2014 No. 2014/725. - Enabling power: Road Traffic Regulation Act 1984, s. 14 (1) (a). - Issued: 17.03.2014. Made: 10.03.2014. Coming into force: 02.04.2014. Effect: None. Territorial extent & classification: E. Local. - Available at http://www.legislation.gov.uk/uksi/2014/725/contents/made Non-print

The M20 Motorway (Junctions 5 - 7) (Temporary Restriction and Prohibition of Traffic) (No 2) Order 2014 No. 2014/3023. - Enabling power: Road Traffic Regulation Act 1984, s. 14 (1) (a). - Issued: 29.10.2014. Made: 27.10.2014. Coming into force: 15.11.2014. Effect: None. Territorial extent & classification: E. Local. - Available at http://www.legislation.gov.uk/uksi/2014/3023/contents/made Non-print

The M20 Motorway (Junctions 5 - 7) (Temporary Restriction and Prohibition of Traffic) Order 2014 No. 2014/405. - Enabling power: Road Traffic Regulation Act 1984, s. 14 (1) (a), sch. 9, para. 27 (1). - Issued: 27.02.2014. Made: 10.02.2014. Coming into force: 02.03.2014. Effect: S.I. 2013/1999 revoked. Territorial extent & classification: E. Local. - Available at http://www.legislation.gov.uk/uksi/2014/405/contents/made Non-print

The M20 Motorway (Junctions 8 - 9) (Temporary Restriction and Prohibition of Traffic) Order 2014 No. 2014/2163. - Enabling power: Road Traffic Regulation Act 1984, ss. 14 (1) (a). - Issued: 15.08.2014. Made: 30.06.2014. Coming into force: 19.07.2014. Effect: None. Territorial extent & classification: E. Local. - Available at http://www.legislation.gov.uk/uksi/2014/2163/contents/made Non-print

The M23 Motorway and the A23 Trunk Road (Junctions 11 - 10A, Northbound) (Temporary Restriction and Prohibition of Traffic) Order 2014 No. 2014/38. - Enabling power: Road Traffic Regulation Act 1984, s. 14 (1) (a). - Issued: 15.01.2014. Made: 13.01.2014. Coming into force: 01.02.2014. Effect: None. Territorial extent & classification: E. Local. - Available at http://www.legislation.gov.uk/uksi/2014/38/contents/made Non-print

The M23 Motorway and the A23 Trunk Road (Merstham Interchange - Brighton Road, Hooley) (Temporary Prohibition of Traffic) Order 2014 No. 2014/1117. - Enabling power: Road Traffic Regulation Act 1984, s. 14 (1) (a). - Issued: 30.04.2014. Made: 14.04.2014. Coming into force: 03.05.2014. Effect: None. Territorial extent & classification: E. Local. - Available at http://www.legislation.gov.uk/uksi/2014/1117/contents/made Non-print

The M23 Motorway (Junctions 8 - 9) (Temporary Restriction and Prohibition of Traffic) Order 2014 No. 2014/1174. - Enabling power: Road Traffic Regulation Act 1984, s. 14 (1) (a). - Issued: 06.05.2014. Made: 21.04.2014. Coming into force: 14.05.2014. Effect: None. Territorial extent & classification: E. Local. - Available at http://www.legislation.gov.uk/uksi/2014/1174/contents/made Non-print

The M23 Motorway (Junctions 9 - 11) (Temporary Restriction and Prohibition of Traffic) Order 2014 No. 2014/3047. - Enabling power: Road Traffic Regulation Act 1984, s. 14 (1) (a). - Issued: 06.11.2014. Made: 03.11.2014. Coming into force: 22.11.2014. Effect: None. Territorial extent & classification: E. Local. - Available at http://www.legislation.gov.uk/uksi/2014/3047/contents/made Non-print

The M25 and M3 Motorways (M25 Junctions 12 - 14 and M3 Junction 2) (Temporary Restriction and Prohibition of Traffic) Order 2014 No. 2014/1170. - Enabling power: Road Traffic Regulation Act 1984, ss. 14 (1) (a). - Issued: 06.05.2014. Made: 21.04.2014. Coming into force: 10.05.2014. Effect: None. Territorial extent & classification: E. Local. - Available at http://www.legislation.gov.uk/uksi/2014/1170/contents/made Non-print

The M25 and M20 Motorways and the A20 Trunk Road (Swanley Interchange) (Temporary Prohibition of Traffic) Order 2014 No. 2014/1282. - Enabling power: Road Traffic Regulation Act 1984, ss. 14 (1) (a). - Issued: 21.05.2014. Made: 06.05.2014. Coming into force: 01.06.2014. Effect: None. Territorial extent & classification: E. Local. - Available at http://www.legislation.gov.uk/uksi/2014/1282/contents/made Non-print

The M25 and M26 Motorway (Junctions 5 and 2) (Temporary Restriction and Prohibition of Traffic) Order 2014 No. 2014/718. - Enabling power: Road Traffic Regulation Act 1984, s. 14 (1) (a). - Issued: 17.03.2014. Made: 10.03.2014. Coming into force: 29.03.2014. Effect: None. Territorial extent & classification: E. Local. - Available at http://www.legislation.gov.uk/uksi/2014/718/contents/made Non-print

The M25 and the M1 Motorways and the A10 Trunk Road (M25 Junctions 15 - 25 and M1 Junction 4) (Temporary Prohibition of Traffic) Order 2014 No. 2014/2803. - Enabling power: Road Traffic Regulation Act 1984, s. 14 (1) (a). - Issued: 13.10.2014. Made: 29.09.2014. Coming into force: 18.10.2014. Effect: None. Territorial extent & classification: E. Local. - Available at http://www.legislation.gov.uk/uksi/2014/2803/contents/made Non-print

The M25 and the M1 Motorways (M25 Junction 21 and M1 Junction 6A) (Temporary Prohibition of Traffic) Order 2014 No. 2014/2516. - Enabling power: Road Traffic Regulation Act 1984, s. 14 (1) (a). - Issued: 18.09.2014. Made: 15.09.2014. Coming into force: 05.10.2014. Effect: None. Territorial extent & classification: E. Local. - Available at http://www.legislation.gov.uk/uksi/2014/2516/contents/made Non-print

The M25 and the M26 Motorways (Junctions 4 and 5) (Temporary Prohibition of Traffic) Order 2014 No. 2014/1015. - Enabling power: Road Traffic Regulation Act 1984, s. 14 (1) (a). - Issued: 16.04.2014. Made: 31.03.2014. Coming into force: 23.04.2014. Effect: None. Territorial extent & classification: E. Local. - Available at http://www.legislation.gov.uk/uksi/2014/1015/contents/made Non-print

The M25 (Junctions 10 - 8) (Temporary Restriction and Prohibition of Traffic) Order 2014 No. 2014/1749. - Enabling power: Road Traffic Regulation Act 1984, ss. 14 (1) (a). - Issued: 02.07.2014. Made: 16.06.2014. Coming into force: 05.07.2014. Effect: None. Territorial extent & classification: E. Local. - Available at http://www.legislation.gov.uk/uksi/2014/1749/contents/made Non-print

The M25 Motorway and the A2 and A282 Trunk Roads (Junctions 1B - 5) (Temporary Prohibition of Traffic) Order 2014 No. 2014/728. - Enabling power: Road Traffic Regulation Act 1984, s. 14 (1) (a). - Issued: 04.03.2014. Made: 24.02.2014. Coming into force: 22.03.2014. Effect: None. Territorial extent & classification: E. Local. - Available at http://www.legislation.gov.uk/uksi/2014/728/contents/made Non-print

The M25 Motorway and the A2 and the A282 Trunk Roads (Junction 2) (Temporary Prohibition of Traffic) Order 2014 No. 2014/1014. - Enabling power: Road Traffic Regulation Act 1984, s. 14 (1) (a). - Issued: 16.04.2014. Made: 31.03.2014. Coming into force: 21.04.2014. Effect: None. Territorial extent & classification: E. Local. - Available at http://www.legislation.gov.uk/uksi/2014/1014/contents/made Non-print

The M25 Motorway and the A2 Trunk Road (M25 Junction 2) (Temporary Prohibition of Traffic) Order 2014 No. 2014/296. - Enabling power: Road Traffic Regulation Act 1984, s. 14 (1) (a). - Issued: 07.02.2014. Made: 03.02.2014. Coming into force: 25.02.2014. Effect: None. Territorial extent & classification: E. Local. - Available at http://www.legislation.gov.uk/uksi/2014/296/contents/made Non-print

The M25 Motorway and the A30 Trunk Road (Junction 13 Slip Road and A30 Link Road) (Temporary Prohibition of Traffic) Order 2014 No. 2014/2311. - Enabling power: Road Traffic Regulation Act 1984, s. 14 (1) (a). - Issued: 27.08.2014. Made: 18.08.2014. Coming into force: 06.09.2014. Effect: None. Territorial extent & classification: E. Local. - Available at http://www.legislation.gov.uk/uksi/2014/2311/contents/made Non-print

The M25 Motorway and the A40 Trunk Road (M25 Junctions 19, 22 and 23 and Denham Roundabout) (Temporary Prohibition of Traffic) Order 2014 No. 2014/1001. - Enabling power: Road Traffic Regulation Act 1984, s. 14 (1) (a). - Issued: 10.04.2014. Made: 24.03.2014. Coming into force: 16.04.2014. Effect: None. Territorial extent & classification: E. Local. - Available at http://www.legislation.gov.uk/uksi/2014/1001/contents/made Non-print

The M25 Motorway and the A282 Trunk Road (Dartford - Thurrock Crossing) (Temporary Restriction and Prohibition of Traffic) Order 2014 No. 2014/3458. - Enabling power: Road Traffic Regulation Act 1984, s. 14 (1) (a). - Issued: 17.12.2014. Made: 08.12.2014. Coming into force: 04.01.2015. Effect: None. Territorial extent & classification: E. Local. - Available at http://www.legislation.gov.uk/uksi/2014/3458/contents/made Non-print

The M25 Motorway and the A282 Trunk Road (Junctions 2 - 31) (Temporary Prohibition of Traffic) Order 2014 No. 2014/1115. - Enabling power: Road Traffic Regulation Act 1984, s. 14 (1) (a). - Issued: 30.04.2014. Made: 14.04.2014. Coming into force: 03.05.2014. Effect: None. Territorial extent & classification: E. Local. - Available at http://www.legislation.gov.uk/uksi/2014/1115/contents/made Non-print

The M25 Motorway and the A282 Trunk Road (Junctions 26 - 31) (Temporary Prohibition of Traffic) Order 2014 No. 2014/2960. - Enabling power: Road Traffic Regulation Act 1984, s. 14 (1) (a). - Issued: 16.10.2014. Made: 13.10.2014. Coming into force: 01.11.2014. Effect: None. Territorial extent & classification: E. Local. - Available at http://www.legislation.gov.uk/uksi/2014/2960/contents/made Non-print

The M25 Motorway and the A282 Trunk Road (Junctions 30 - 2) (Temporary Restriction and Prohibition of Traffic) Order 2014 No. 2014/50. - Enabling power: Road Traffic Regulation Act 1984, s. 14 (1) (a). - Issued: 16.01.2014. Made: 13.01.2014. Coming into force: 01.02.2014. Effect: None. Territorial extent & classification: E. Local. - Available at http://www.legislation.gov.uk/uksi/2014/50/contents/made Non-print

The M25 Motorway and the A282 Trunk Road (M25 Junctions 4 - 5/A282 Junction 1A) (Temporary Restriction and Prohibition of Traffic) Order 2014 No. 2014/298. - Enabling power: Road Traffic Regulation Act 1984, s. 14 (1) (a). - Issued: 13.02.2014. Made: 10.02.2014. Coming into force: 01.03.2014. Effect: None. Territorial extent & classification: E. Local. - Available at http://www.legislation.gov.uk/uksi/2014/298/contents/made Non-print

The M25 Motorway and The M11 Motorway (M25 Junction 26 and M11 Junction 5) (Temporary Prohibition of Traffic) Order 2014 No. 2014/1967. - Enabling power: Road Traffic Regulation Act 1984, s. 16A. - Issued: 28.07.2014. Made: 09.06.2014. Coming into force: 06.07.2014. Effect: None. Territorial extent & classification: E. Local. - Available at http://www.legislation.gov.uk/uksi/2014/1967/contents/made Non-print

The M25 Motorway (Bell Common Tunnel) (Temporary Restriction and Prohibition of Traffic) Order 2014 No. 2014/3508. - Enabling power: Road Traffic Regulation Act 1984, s. 14 (1) (a). - Issued: 22.01.2014. Made: 08.12.2014. Coming into force: 04.01.2015. Effect: None. Territorial extent & classification: E. Local. - Available at http://www.legislation.gov.uk/uksi/2014/3508/contents/made Non-print

The M25 Motorway (Holmesdale Tunnel) (Temporary Restriction and Prohibition of Traffic) Order 2014 No. 2014/2189. - Enabling power: Road Traffic Regulation Act 1984, s. 14 (1) (a). - Issued: 20.08.2014. Made: 07.07.2014. Coming into force: 01.08.2014. Effect: None. Territorial extent & classification: E. Local. - Available at http://www.legislation.gov.uk/uksi/2014/2189/contents/made Non-print

The M25 Motorway (Junction 12) (M3 Junction 2 Slip Road) (Temporary Prohibition of Traffic) Order 2014 No. 2014/1864. - Enabling power: Road Traffic Regulation Act 1984, ss. 14 (1) (a). - Issued: 16.07.2014. Made: 30.06.2014. Coming into force: 19.07.2014. Effect: None. Territorial extent & classification: E. Local. - Available at http://www.legislation.gov.uk/uksi/2014/1864/contents/made Non-print

The M25 Motorway (Junction 14 and Terminal 5 Spur Roads) (Temporary Prohibition of Traffic) Order 2014 No. 2014/1774. - Enabling power: Road Traffic Regulation Act 1984, s. 14 (1) (a). - Issued: 09.07.2014. Made: 23.06.2014. Coming into force: 17.07.2014. Effect: None. Territorial extent & classification: E. Local. - Available at http://www.legislation.gov.uk/uksi/2014/1774/contents/made Non-print

The M25 Motorway (Junction 15) (Temporary Prohibition of Traffic) Order 2014 No. 2014/2534. - Enabling power: Road Traffic Regulation Act 1984, s. 14 (1) (a). - Issued: 12.09.2014. Made: 08.09.2014. Coming into force: 28.09.2014. Effect: None. Territorial extent & classification: E. Local. - Available at http://www.legislation.gov.uk/uksi/2014/2534/contents/made Non-print

The M25 Motorway (Junction 21) (Temporary Prohibition of Traffic) Order 2014 No. 2014/301. - Enabling power: Road Traffic Regulation Act 1984, s. 14 (1) (a). - Issued: 13.02.2014. Made: 10.02.2014. Coming into force: 01.03.2014. Effect: None. Territorial extent & classification: E. Local. - Available at http://www.legislation.gov.uk/uksi/2014/301/contents/made Non-print

The M25 Motorway (Junctions 6 - 10, Slip Roads) (Temporary Prohibition of Traffic) Order 2014 No. 2014/3460. - Enabling power: Road Traffic Regulation Act 1984, s. 14 (1) (a). - Issued: 18.12.2014. Made: 15.12.2014. Coming into force: 15.01.2015. Effect: None. Territorial extent & classification: E. Local. - Available at http://www.legislation.gov.uk/uksi/2014/3460/contents/made Non-print

The M25 Motorway (Junctions 17 - 25) (Temporary Prohibition of Traffic) Order 2014 No. 2014/1991. - Enabling power: Road Traffic Regulation Act 1984, s. 14 (1) (a). - Issued: 21.07.2014. Made: 07.07.2014. Coming into force: 01.08.2014. Effect: None. Territorial extent & classification: E. Local. - Available at http://www.legislation.gov.uk/uksi/2014/1991/contents/made Non-print

The M25 Motorway (Junctions 30 - 2) (Temporary Prohibition of Traffic) Order 2014 No. 2014/2207. - Enabling power: Road Traffic Regulation Act 1984, s. 14 (1) (a). - Issued: 21.08.2014. Made: 04.08.2014. Coming into force: 24.08.2014. Effect: None. Territorial extent & classification: E. Local. - Available at http://www.legislation.gov.uk/uksi/2014/2207/contents/made Non-print

The M25 Motorway, the M3 Motorway, the M4 Motorway and the M40 Motorway (M25 Junctions 10 - 16, M3 Junction 2, M4 Junction 4B and M40 Junction 1A) (Temporary Prohibition of Traffic) Order 2014 No. 2014/299. - Enabling power: Road Traffic Regulation Act 1984, s. 14 (1) (a). - Issued: 13.02.2014. Made: 10.02.2014. Coming into force: 01.03.2014. Effect: None. Territorial extent & classification: E. Local. - Available at http://www.legislation.gov.uk/uksi/2014/299/contents/made Non-print

The M25 Motorway , the M23 Motorway and the M3 Motorway (M25 Junctions 7-13, Slip/Link Roads) (Temporary Restriction and Prohibition of Traffic) Order 2014 No. 2014/2335. - Enabling power: Road Traffic Regulation Act 1984, s. 14 (1) (a). - Issued: 04.09.2014. Made: 01.09.2014. Coming into force: 22.09.2014. Effect: None. Territorial extent & classification: E. Local. - Available at http://www.legislation.gov.uk/uksi/2014/2335/contents/made Non-print

The M26 and M25 Motorways (M25 Junction 5 - M20 Junction 3) (Temporary Prohibition of Traffic) Order 2014 No. 2014/2643. - Enabling power: Road Traffic Regulation Act 1984, s. 14 (1) (a)- Issued: 30.09.2014. Made: 22.09.2014. Coming into force: 11.10.2014. Effect: None. Territorial extent & classification: E. Local. - Available at http://www.legislation.gov.uk/uksi/2014/2643/contents/made Non-print

The M26 Motorway (Junction 2A, Slip Roads) (Temporary Prohibition of Traffic) Order 2014 No. 2014/1674. - Enabling power: Road Traffic Regulation Act 1984, s. 14 (1) (a). - Issued: 30.06.2014. Made: 09.06.2014. Coming into force: 04.07.2014. Effect: None. Territorial extent & classification: E. Local. - Available at http://www.legislation.gov.uk/uksi/2014/1674/contents/made Non-print

The M27 Motorway and the M271 Motorway (M27 Junction 3 and M271 Junction 1 - A3057 Junction) (Temporary Restriction and Prohibition of Traffic) Order 2014 No. 2014/1279. - Enabling power: Road Traffic Regulation Act 1984, s. 14 (1) (a). - Issued: 19.05.2014. Made: 05.05.2014. Coming into force: 24.05.2014. Effect: None. Territorial extent & classification: E. Local. - Available at http://www.legislation.gov.uk/uksi/2014/1279/contents/made Non-print

The M27 Motorway (Junction 1, Westbound Exit Slip Road) (Temporary Prohibition of Traffic) Order 2014 No. 2014/1051. - Enabling power: Road Traffic Regulation Act 1984, s. 14 (1) (a). - Issued: 22.04.2014. Made: 07.04.2014. Coming into force: 01.05.2014. Effect: None. Territorial extent & classification: E. Local. - Available at http://www.legislation.gov.uk/uksi/2014/1051/contents/made Non-print

The M27 Motorway (Junction 5) (Temporary Restriction and Prohibition of Traffic) Order 2014 No. 2014/719. - Enabling power: Road Traffic Regulation Act 1984, s. 14 (1) (a). - Issued: 17.03.2014. Made: 10.03.2014. Coming into force: 29.03.2014. Effect: None. Territorial extent & classification: E. Local. - Available at http://www.legislation.gov.uk/uksi/2014/719/contents/made Non-print

The M27 Motorway (Junction 9) (Temporary Restriction and Prohibition of Traffic) Order 2014 No. 2014/3522. - Enabling power: Road Traffic Regulation Act 1984, s. 14 (1) (a). - Issued: 23.01.2015. Made: 15.12.2014. Coming into force: 03.01.2015. Effect: None. Territorial extent & classification: E. Local. - Available at http://www.legislation.gov.uk/uksi/2014/3522/contents/made Non-print

The M27 Motorway (Junction 12, Link Roads) (Temporary Prohibition of Traffic) Order 2014 No. 2014/2354. - Enabling power: Road Traffic Regulation Act 1984, s. 14 (1) (a). - Issued: 04.09.2014. Made: 01.09.2014. Coming into force: 20.09.2014. Effect: None. Territorial extent & classification: E. Local. - Available at http://www.legislation.gov.uk/uksi/2014/2354/contents/made Non-print

The M27 Motorway (Junction 12, Portsbridge Viaduct) (Temporary Prohibition of Traffic) Order 2014 No. 2014/2642. - Enabling power: Road Traffic Regulation Act 1984, s. 14 (1) (a). - Issued: 30.09.2014. Made: 22.09.2014. Coming into force: 11.10.2014. Effect: None. Territorial extent & classification: E. Local. - Available at http://www.legislation.gov.uk/uksi/2014/2642/contents/made Non-print

The M27 Motorway (Junctions 1 - 12, Carriageways) (Temporary Restriction of Traffic) Order 2014 No. 2014/1988. - Enabling power: Road Traffic Regulation Act 1984, s. 14 (1) (a). - Issued: 21.07.2014. Made: 07.07.2014. Coming into force: 26.07.2014. Effect: None. Territorial extent & classification: E. Local. - Available at http://www.legislation.gov.uk/uksi/2014/1988/contents/made Non-print

The M27 Motorway (Junctions 11 - 9) (Temporary Prohibition of Traffic) Order 2014 No. 2014/2515. - Enabling power: Road Traffic Regulation Act 1984, s. 14 (1) (a). - Issued: 18.09.2014. Made: 15.09.2014. Coming into force: 04.10.2014. Effect: None. Territorial extent & classification: E. Local. - Available at http://www.legislation.gov.uk/uksi/2014/2515/contents/made Non-print

The M27 Motorway (Junctions 11 and 12, Slip/Link Roads) (Temporary Prohibition of Traffic) Order 2014 No. 2014/1220. - Enabling power: Road Traffic Regulation Act 1984, s. 14 (1) (a). - Issued: 14.05.2014. Made: 28.04.2014. Coming into force: 21.05.2014. Effect: None. Territorial extent & classification: E. Local. - Available at http://www.legislation.gov.uk/uksi/2014/1220/contents/made Non-print

The M27 Motorway (Ower Interchange - Nursling Interchange) (Temporary Restriction and Prohibition of Traffic) Order 2014 No. 2014/2032. - Enabling power: Road Traffic Regulation Act 1984, s. 14 (1) (a). - Issued: 01.08.2014. Made: 14.07.2014. Coming into force: 02.08.2014. Effect: None. Territorial extent & classification: E. Local. - Available at http://www.legislation.gov.uk/uksi/2014/2032/contents/made Non-print

The M32 Motorway (Junction 1 Northbound Exit Slip Road) (Temporary Prohibition of Traffic) Order 2014 No. 2014/2818. - Enabling power: Road Traffic Regulation Act 1984, s. 14 (1) (a). - Issued: 22.10.2014. Made: 10.09.2014. Coming into force: 18.10.2014. Effect: None. Territorial extent & classification: E. Local. - Available at http://www.legislation.gov.uk/uksi/2014/2818/contents/made Non-print

The M32 Motorway (Junction 1) (Temporary Prohibition of Traffic) Order 2014 No. 2014/1565. - Enabling power: Road Traffic Regulation Act 1984, s. 14 (1) (a). - Issued: 17.06.2014. Made: 28.05.2014. Coming into force: 31.05.2014. Effect: None. Territorial extent & classification: E. Local. - Available at http://www.legislation.gov.uk/uksi/2014/1565/contents/made Non-print

The M32 Motorway (Junction 1) (Temporary Prohibition of Traffic) Order 2014 No. 2014/2152. - Enabling power: Road Traffic Regulation Act 1984, s. 14 (1) (a). - Issued: 12.08.2014. Made: 28.07.2014. Coming into force: 09.08.2014. Effect: None. Territorial extent & classification: E. Local. - Available at http://www.legislation.gov.uk/uksi/2014/2152/contents/made Non-print

The M32 Motorway (Junctions 1-3) (Temporary Prohibition of Traffic) Order 2014 No. 2014/805. - Enabling power: Road Traffic Regulation Act 1984, s. 14 (1) (a). - Issued: 26.03.2014. Made: 12.03.2014. Coming into force: 15.03.2014. Effect: None. Territorial extent & classification: E. Local. - Available at http://www.legislation.gov.uk/uksi/2014/805/contents/made Non-print

The M32 Motorway (Junctions 1-3) (Temporary Restriction of Traffic) Order 2014 No. 2014/2421. - Enabling power: Road Traffic Regulation Act 1984, s. 14 (1) (b). - Issued: 10.09.2014. Made: 05.09.2014. Coming into force: 09.09.2014. Effect: None. Territorial extent & classification: E. Local. - Available at http://www.legislation.gov.uk/uksi/2014/2421/contents/made Non-print

The M40 and M42 Motorways (Junction 3a) (Link Road) (Temporary Prohibition of Traffic) Order 2014 No. 2014/636. - Enabling power: Road Traffic Regulation Act 1984, s. 14 (1) (a). - Issued: 05.03.2014. Made: 17.02.2014. Coming into force: 24.02.2014. Effect: None. Territorial extent & classification: E. Local. - Available at http://www.legislation.gov.uk/uksi/2014/636/contents/made Non-print

The M40 and M42 Motorways (Sherbourne to Hockley Heath, Warwickshire) (Temporary Restriction and Prohibition of Traffic) Order 2014 No. 2014/661. - Enabling power: Road Traffic Regulation Act 1984, s. 14 (1) (a) & S.I. 1982/1163, reg. 16 (2). - Issued: 07.03.2014. Made: 21.02.2014. Coming into force: 28.02.2014. Effect: None. Territorial extent & classification: E. Local. - Available at http://www.legislation.gov.uk/uksi/2014/661/contents/made Non-print

The M40 Motorway and the A34 Trunk Road (Junction 9 - Weston-on-the-Green) (Temporary Restriction and Prohibition of Traffic) Order 2014 No. 2014/365. - Enabling power: Road Traffic Regulation Act 1984, s. 14 (1) (a). - Issued: 20.02.2014. Made: 17.02.2014. Coming into force: 08.03.2014. Effect: None. Territorial extent & classification: E. Local. - Available at http://www.legislation.gov.uk/uksi/2014/365/contents/made Non-print

The M40 Motorway (Junctions 1 to 4) (Temporary Prohibition of Traffic) Order 2014 No. 2014/1393. - Enabling power: Road Traffic Regulation Act 1984, s. 14 (1) (a). - Issued: 04.06.2014. Made: 19.05.2014. Coming into force: 01.06.2014. Effect: None. Territorial extent & classification: E. Local. - Available at http://www.legislation.gov.uk/uksi/2014/1393/contents/made Non-print

The M40 Motorway (Junctions 1 to 6) (Temporary Prohibition of Traffic) Order 2014 No. 2014/688. - Enabling power: Road Traffic Regulation Act 1984, s. 14 (1) (a). - Issued: 06.03.2014. Made: 24.02.2014. Coming into force: 03.03.2014. Effect: None. Territorial extent & classification: E. Local. - Available at http://www.legislation.gov.uk/uksi/2014/688/contents/made Non-print

The M40 Motorway (Junctions 5 to 6) (Temporary Restriction and Prohibition of Traffic) (No. 2) Order 2014 No. 2014/2360. - Enabling power: Road Traffic Regulation Act 1984, s. 14 (1) (a) (7), S.I. 1982/1163, s. 16 (2). - Issued: 08.09.2014. Made: 22.08.2014. Coming into force: 01.09.2014. Effect: None. Territorial extent & classification: E/W. Local. - Available at http://www.legislation.gov.uk/uksi/2014/2360/contents/made Non-print

The M40 Motorway (Junctions 5 to 6) (Temporary Restriction and Prohibition of Traffic) Order 2014 No. 2014/1010. - Enabling power: Road Traffic Regulation Act 1984, s. 14 (1) (a) & S.I. 1982/1163, reg. 16 (2). - Issued: 16.04.2014. Made: 31.03.2014. Coming into force: 07.04.2014. Effect: None. Territorial extent & classification: E. Local. - Available at http://www.legislation.gov.uk/uksi/2014/1010/contents/made Non-print

The M40 Motorway (Junctions 6 to 9) (Temporary Prohibition of Traffic) Order 2014 No. 2014/2514. - Enabling power: Road Traffic Regulation Act 1984, s. 14 (1) (a) (7) & S.I. 1982/1163, reg. 16 (2). - Issued: 17.09.2014. Made: 15.09.2014. Coming into force: 22.09.2014. Effect: None. Territorial extent & classification: E. Local. - Available at http://www.legislation.gov.uk/uksi/2014/2514/contents/made Non-print

The M40 Motorway (Junctions 7 to 9) (Temporary Prohibition of Traffic) (No 2) Order 2014 No. 2014/1394. - Enabling power: Road Traffic Regulation Act 1984, s. 14 (1) (a). - Issued: 04.06.2014. Made: 19.05.2014. Coming into force: 01.06.2014. Effect: None. Territorial extent & classification: E. Local. - Available at http://www.legislation.gov.uk/uksi/2014/1394/contents/made Non-print

The M40 Motorway (Junctions 7 to 9) (Temporary Prohibition of Traffic) Order 2014 No. 2014/687. - Enabling power: Road Traffic Regulation Act 1984, s. 14 (1) (a). - Issued: 06.03.2014. Made: 24.02.2014. Coming into force: 03.03.2014. Effect: None. Territorial extent & classification: E. Local. - Available at http://www.legislation.gov.uk/uksi/2014/687/contents/made Non-print

The M40 Motorway (Junctions 10 to 15) Slip Roads (Temporary Prohibition of Traffic) (No. 2) Order 2014 No. 2014/1395. - Enabling power: Road Traffic Regulation Act 1984, s. 14 (1) (a). - Issued: 05.06.2014. Made: 19.05.2014. Coming into force: 01.06.2014. Effect: None. Territorial extent & classification: E. Local. - Available at http://www.legislation.gov.uk/uksi/2014/1395/contents/made Non-print

The M40 Motorway (Junctions 10 to 15) Slip Roads (Temporary Prohibition of Traffic) Order 2014 No. 2014/399. - Enabling power: Road Traffic Regulation Act 1984, s. 14 (1) (a). - Issued: 27.02.2014. Made: 17.02.2014. Coming into force: 24.02.2014. Effect: None. Territorial extent & classification: E. Local. - Available at http://www.legislation.gov.uk/uksi/2014/399/contents/made Non-print

The M40 Motorway (Junctions 11 to 15) Slip Roads (Temporary Prohibition of Traffic) Order 2014 No. 2014/2602. - Enabling power: Road Traffic Regulation Act 1984, s. 14 (1) (a). - Issued: 29.09.2014. Made: 22.09.2014. Coming into force: 29.09.2014. Effect: None. Territorial extent & classification: E. Local. - Available at http://www.legislation.gov.uk/uksi/2014/2602/contents/made Non-print

The M42 and M5 Motorways (M5 Junction 4a) (Link Road) (Temporary Prohibition of Traffic) Order 2014 No. 2014/280. - Enabling power: Road Traffic Regulation Act 1984, s. 14 (1) (a). - Issued: 14.02.2014. Made: 04.02.2014. Coming into force: 11.02.2014. Effect: None. Territorial extent & classification: E. Local. - Available at http://www.legislation.gov.uk/uksi/2014/280/contents/made Non-print

The M42 and M5 Motorways (M42 Junction 1 - 2, Worcestershire) (Temporary Prohibition of Traffic) Order 2014 No. 2014/3368. - Enabling power: Road Traffic Regulation Act 1984, s. 14 (1) (a). - Issued: 28.11.2014. Made: 17.11.2014. Coming into force: 24.11.2014. Effect: None. Territorial extent & classification: E. Local. - Available at http://www.legislation.gov.uk/uksi/2014/3368/contents/made Non-print

The M42 and M6 Motorways (M42 Junction 7a) (Temporary Prohibition of Traffic) Order 2014 No. 2014/1694. - Enabling power: Road Traffic Regulation Act 1984, s. 14 (1) (a). - Issued: 03.07.2014. Made: 09.06.2014. Coming into force: 16.06.2014. Effect: None. Territorial extent & classification: E. Local. - Available at http://www.legislation.gov.uk/uksi/2014/1694/contents/made Non-print

The M42 and M6 Motorways (M42 Junction 7) (Link Road) (Temporary Prohibition of Traffic) Order 2014 No. 2014/282. - Enabling power: Road Traffic Regulation Act 1984, s. 14 (1) (a). - Issued: 14.02.2014. Made: 04.02.2014. Coming into force: 13.02.2014. Effect: None. Territorial extent & classification: E. Local. - Available at http://www.legislation.gov.uk/uksi/2014/282/contents/made Non-print

The M42 and M6 Motorways (M42 to M6 Link Road) (Temporary Restriction and Prohibition of Traffic) Order 2014 No. 2014/3010. - Enabling power: Road Traffic Regulation Act 1984, s. 14 (1) (a) & S.I. 1982/1163, reg. 16 (2). - Issued: 14.11.2014. Made: 03.11.2014. Coming into force: 10.11.2014. Effect: None. Territorial extent & classification: E. Local. - Available at http://www.legislation.gov.uk/uksi/2014/3010/contents/made Non-print

The M42 and M40 Motorways (M42 Junctions 1 to 8) (Temporary Restriction and Prohibition of Traffic) (Slip Road) Order 2014 No. 2014/739. - Enabling power: Road Traffic Regulation Act 1984, s. 14 (1) (a) & S.I. 1982/1163, reg. 16 (2). - Issued: 10.03.2014. Made: 28.02.2014. Coming into force: 07.03.2014. Effect: None. Territorial extent & classification: E. Local. - Available at http://www.legislation.gov.uk/uksi/2014/739/contents/made Non-print

The M42, M6 and M6 Toll Motorways (M42 Junctions 7 to 9, Coleshill) (Temporary Prohibition of Traffic) Order 2014 No. 2014/3453. - Enabling power: Road Traffic Regulation Act 1984, s. 14 (1) (a). - Issued: 02.01.2015. Made: 22.12.2014. Coming into force: 29.12.2014. Effect: None. Territorial extent & classification: E. Local. - Available at http://www.legislation.gov.uk/uksi/2014/3453/contents/made Non-print

The M42 Motorway and A5 Trunk Road (Glascote to Grendon, Warwickshire) (Temporary Prohibition of Traffic) Order 2014 No. 2014/1082. - Enabling power: Road Traffic Regulation Act 1984, s. 14 (1) (a). - Issued: 25.04.2014. Made: 27.03.2014. Coming into force: 03.04.2014. Effect: None. Territorial extent & classification: E. Local. - Available at http://www.legislation.gov.uk/uksi/2014/1082/contents/made Non-print

The M42 Motorway and A45 Trunk Road (M42 Junction 6, Solihull) (Temporary Restriction and Prohibition of Traffic) Order 2014 No. 2014/1095. - Enabling power: Road Traffic Regulation Act 1984, s. 14 (1) (a). - Issued: 25.04.2014. Made: 04.04.2014. Coming into force: 11.04.2014. Effect: None. Territorial extent & classification: E. Local. - Revoked by S.I. 2014/3382 (non-print). - Available at http://www.legislation.gov.uk/uksi/2014/1095/contents/made Non-print

The M42 Motorway and A45 Trunk Road (M42 Junction 6, Solihull) (Temporary Restriction and Prohibition of Traffic) (No.2) Order 2014 No. 2014/3382. - Enabling power: Road Traffic Regulation Act 1984, s. 14 (1) (a). - Issued: 28.11.2014. Made: 21.11.2014. Coming into force: 28.11.2014. Effect: S.I. 2014/1095 revoked. Territorial extent & classification: E. Local. - Available at http://www.legislation.gov.uk/uksi/2014/3382/contents/made Non-print

The M42 Motorway (Coleshill, Warwickshire) (Temporary Prohibition of Traffic) Order 2014 No. 2014/2174. - Enabling power: Road Traffic Regulation Act 1984, s. 14 (1) (a). - Issued: 15.08.2014. Made: 28.07.2014. Coming into force: 04.08.2014. Effect: None. Territorial extent & classification: E. Local. - Available at http://www.legislation.gov.uk/uksi/2014/2174/contents/made Non-print

The M42 Motorway (Junction 2, Hopwood) (Slip Road) (Temporary Prohibition of Traffic) (No.2) Order 2014 No. 2014/2770. - Enabling power: Road Traffic Regulation Act 1984, s. 14 (1) (a). - Issued: 14.10.2014. Made: 03.10.2014. Coming into force: 10.10.2014. Effect: None. Territorial extent & classification: E. Local. - Available at http://www.legislation.gov.uk/uksi/2014/2770/contents/made Non-print

The M42 Motorway (Junction 2, Hopwood) (Slip Road) (Temporary Prohibition of Traffic) Order 2014 No. 2014/781. - Enabling power: Road Traffic Regulation Act 1984, s. 14 (1) (a). - Issued: 10.03.2014. Made: 03.03.2014. Coming into force: 10.03.2014. Effect: None. Territorial extent & classification: E. Local. - Available at http://www.legislation.gov.uk/uksi/2014/781/contents/made Non-print

The M42 Motorway (Junction 3a) (Link Road) (Temporary Prohibition of Traffic) (No.2) Order 2014 No. 2014/3179. - Enabling power: Road Traffic Regulation Act 1984, s. 14 (1) (a). - Issued: 28.11.2014. Made: 17.11.2014. Coming into force: 24.11.2014. Effect: None. Territorial extent & classification: E. Local. - Available at http://www.legislation.gov.uk/uksi/2014/3179/contents/made Non-print

The M42 Motorway (Junction 3a, Warwickshire) (Link Road) (Temporary Prohibition of Traffic) Order 2014 No. 2014/316. - Enabling power: Road Traffic Regulation Act 1984, s. 14 (1) (a). - Issued: 17.02.2014. Made: 03.02.2014. Coming into force: 10.02.2014. Effect: None. Territorial extent & classification: E. Local. - Available at http://www.legislation.gov.uk/uksi/2014/316/contents/made Non-print

The M42 Motorway (Junction 4, Solihull) (Slip Road) (Temporary Prohibition of Traffic) Order 2014 No. 2014/1092. - Enabling power: Road Traffic Regulation Act 1984, s. 14 (1) (a). - Issued: 25.04.2014. Made: 04.04.2014. Coming into force: 11.04.2014. Effect: None. Territorial extent & classification: E. Local. - Available at http://www.legislation.gov.uk/uksi/2014/1092/contents/made Non-print

The M42 Motorway (Junction 5, Solihull) (Temporary Prohibition of Traffic) Order 2014 No. 2014/691. - Enabling power: Road Traffic Regulation Act 1984, s. 14 (1) (a). - Issued: 20.03.2014. Made: 17.02.2014. Coming into force: 24.02.2014. Effect: None. Territorial extent & classification: E. Local. - Available at http://www.legislation.gov.uk/uksi/2014/691/contents/made Non-print

The M42 Motorway (Junction 6, Solihull) (Slip Road) (Temporary Prohibition of Traffic) Order 2014 No. 2014/1518. - Enabling power: Road Traffic Regulation Act 1984, s. 14 (1) (a). - Issued: 11.06.2014. Made: 19.05.2014. Coming into force: 26.05.2014. Effect: None. Territorial extent & classification: E. Local. - Available at http://www.legislation.gov.uk/uksi/2014/1518/contents/made Non-print

The M42 Motorway (Junction 6, Solihull) (Temporary Prohibition of Traffic) Order 2014 No. 2014/765. - Enabling power: Road Traffic Regulation Act 1984, s. 14 (1) (a). - Issued: 11.03.2014. Made: 04.03.2014. Coming into force: 11.03.2014. Effect: None. Territorial extent & classification: E. Local. - Available at http://www.legislation.gov.uk/uksi/2014/765/contents/made Non-print

ROAD TRAFFIC: TRAFFIC REGULATION

The M42 Motorway (Junction 8, Warwickshire) (Link Road) (Temporary Prohibition of Traffic) Order 2014 No. 2014/1407. - Enabling power: Road Traffic Regulation Act 1984, s. 14 (1) (a). - Issued: 04.06.2014. Made: 06.05.2014. Coming into force: 13.05.2014. Effect: None. Territorial extent & classification: E. Local. - Available at http://www.legislation.gov.uk/uksi/2014/1407/contents/made Non-print

The M42 Motorway (Junction 9, Warwickshire) (Temporary Prohibition of Traffic) Order 2014 No. 2014/1085. - Enabling power: Road Traffic Regulation Act 1984, s. 14 (1) (a). - Issued: 25.04.2014. Made: 28.03.2014. Coming into force: 04.04.2014. Effect: None. Territorial extent & classification: E. Local. - Available at http://www.legislation.gov.uk/uksi/2014/1085/contents/made Non-print

The M42 Motorway (Junction 11, Leicestershire) (Slip Roads) (Temporary Prohibition of Traffic) Order 2014 No. 2014/1698. - Enabling power: Road Traffic Regulation Act 1984, s. 14 (1) (a). - Issued: 03.07.2014. Made: 09.06.2014. Coming into force: 16.06.2014. Effect: None. Territorial extent & classification: E. Local. - Available at http://www.legislation.gov.uk/uksi/2014/1698/contents/made Non-print

The M42 Motorway (Junction 11, Leicestershire) (Temporary Prohibition of Traffic) Order 2014 No. 2014/3208. - Enabling power: Road Traffic Regulation Act 1984, s. 14 (1) (a). - Issued: 28.11.2014. Made: 17.11.2014. Coming into force: 24.11.2014. Effect: None. Territorial extent & classification: E. Local. - Available at http://www.legislation.gov.uk/uksi/2014/3208/contents/made Non-print

The M42 Motorway (Junctions 2 to 3) (Temporary Prohibition of Traffic) Order 2014 No. 2014/3366. - Enabling power: Road Traffic Regulation Act 1984, s. 14 (1) (a). - Issued: 28.11.2014. Made: 17.11.2014. Coming into force: 24.11.2014. Effect: None. Territorial extent & classification: E. Local. - Available at http://www.legislation.gov.uk/uksi/2014/3366/contents/made Non-print

The M42 Motorway (Junctions 5 - 6, Catherine-De-Barnes) (Temporary Restriction and Prohibition of Traffic) Order 2014 No. 2014/1845. - Enabling power: Road Traffic Regulation Act 1984, s. 14 (1) (a). - Issued: 16.07.2014. Made: 23.06.2014. Coming into force: 30.06.2014. Effect: None. Territorial extent & classification: E. Local. - Available at http://www.legislation.gov.uk/uksi/2014/1845/contents/made Non-print

The M42 Motorway (Junctions 5 to 6, Solihull) (Temporary Restriction and Prohibition of Traffic) Order 2014 No. 2014/757. - Enabling power: Road Traffic Regulation Act 1984, s. 14 (1) (a) & S.I. 1982/1163, reg. 16 (2). - Issued: 21.03.2014. Made: 26.02.2014. Coming into force: 05.03.2014. Effect: None. Territorial extent & classification: E. Local. - Available at http://www.legislation.gov.uk/uksi/2014/757/contents/made Non-print

The M42 Motorway (Junctions 7 to 6, Solihull) (Temporary Restriction and Prohibition of Traffic) Order 2014 No. 2014/200. - Enabling power: Road Traffic Regulation Act 1984, s. 14 (1) (a) & S.I. 1982/1163, reg. 16 (2). - Issued: 05.02.2014. Made: 06.01.2014. Coming into force: 13.01.2014. Effect: None. Territorial extent & classification: E. Local. - Available at http://www.legislation.gov.uk/uksi/2014/200/contents/made Non-print

The M42 Motorway (Junctions 7 to 8, Warwickshire) (Temporary Restriction and Prohibition of Traffic) Order 2014 No. 2014/1096. - Enabling power: Road Traffic Regulation Act 1984, s. 14 (1) (a) & S.I. 1982/1163, reg. 16 (2). - Issued: 25.04.2014. Made: 04.04.2014. Coming into force: 11.04.2014. Effect: None. Territorial extent & classification: E. Local. - Available at http://www.legislation.gov.uk/uksi/2014/1096/contents/made Non-print

The M42 Motorway (Junctions 9 to 6) (Temporary Prohibition of Traffic) Order 2014 No. 2014/1032. - Enabling power: Road Traffic Regulation Act 1984, s. 14 (1) (a). - Issued: 22.04.2014. Made: 20.01.2014. Coming into force: 27.01.2014. Effect: None. Territorial extent & classification: E. Local. - Available at http://www.legislation.gov.uk/uksi/2014/1032/contents/made Non-print

The M42 Motorway (Junctions 9 to 10, Warwickshire) (Temporary Prohibition of Traffic) Order 2014 No. 2014/1440. - Enabling power: Road Traffic Regulation Act 1984, s. 14 (1) (a). - Issued: 02.06.2014. Made: 14.05.2014. Coming into force: 21.05.2014. Effect: None. Territorial extent & classification: E. Local. - Available at http://www.legislation.gov.uk/uksi/2014/1440/contents/made Non-print

The M42 Motorway (Junctions 9 to 11, West Midlands) (Temporary Restriction and Prohibition of Traffic) Order 2014 No. 2014/1162. - Enabling power: Road Traffic Regulation Act 1984, s. 14 (1) (a) & S.I. 1982/1163, reg. 16 (2). - Issued: 07.05.2014. Made: 21.04.2014. Coming into force: 28.04.2014. Effect: None. Territorial extent & classification: E. Local. - Available at http://www.legislation.gov.uk/uksi/2014/1162/contents/made Non-print

The M42 Motorway (M42 Junction 4 to Junction 3a, West Midlands) (Temporary Restriction and Prohibition of Traffic) Order 2014 No. 2014/1084. - Enabling power: Road Traffic Regulation Act 1984, s. 14 (1) (a) & S.I. 1982/1163, reg. 16 (2). - Issued: 25.04.2014. Made: 28.03.2014. Coming into force: 04.04.2014. Effect: None. Territorial extent & classification: E. Local. - Available at http://www.legislation.gov.uk/uksi/2014/1084/contents/made Non-print

The M45 Motorway (Dunchurch - M1) (Temporary Prohibition of Traffic) Order 2014 No. 2014/2176. - Enabling power: Road Traffic Regulation Act 1984, s. 14 (1) (a). - Issued: 15.08.2014. Made: 28.07.2014. Coming into force: 04.08.2014. Effect: None. Territorial extent & classification: E. Local. - Available at http://www.legislation.gov.uk/uksi/2014/2176/contents/made Non-print

The M45 Motorway (Thurlaston to M1 Junction 17) (Temporary Restriction and Prohibition of Traffic) Order 2014 No. 2014/2184. - Enabling power: Road Traffic Regulation Act 1984, s. 14 (1) (a). - Issued: 19.08.2014. Made: 14.07.2014. Coming into force: 21.07.2014. Effect: None. Territorial extent & classification: E. Local. - Available at http://www.legislation.gov.uk/uksi/2014/2184/contents/made Non-print

The M48 Motorway (Junction 1 Eastbound Exit Slip Road) (Temporary Prohibition of Traffic) Order 2014 No. 2014/1775. - Enabling power: Road Traffic Regulation Act 1984, s. 14 (1) (a). - Issued: 09.07.2014. Made: 25.06.2014. Coming into force: 28.06.2014. Effect: None. Territorial extent & classification: E. Local. - Available at http://www.legislation.gov.uk/uksi/2014/1775/contents/made Non-print

The M48 Motorway (Junction 1 Slip Roads) (Temporary Prohibition of Traffic) Order 2014 No. 2014/1682. - Enabling power: Road Traffic Regulation Act 1984, s. 14 (1) (a). - Issued: 01.07.2014. Made: 10.06.2014. Coming into force: 14.06.2014. Effect: None. Territorial extent & classification: E. Local. - Available at http://www.legislation.gov.uk/uksi/2014/1682/contents/made Non-print

The M48 Motorway (Severn Bridge) (Temporary Prohibition of Traffic) Order 2014 No. 2014/2251. - Enabling power: Road Traffic Regulation Act 1984, ss. 16 (2) (a). - Issued: 27.08.2014. Made: 21.08.2014. Coming into force: 22.08.2014. Effect: None. Territorial extent & classification: E. Local. - Available at http://www.legislation.gov.uk/uksi/2014/2251/contents/made Non-print

The M48 Motorway (Severn Bridge) (Temporary Restriction of Traffic) Order 2014 No. 2014/1488. - Enabling power: Road Traffic Regulation Act 1984, s. 14 (1) (a). - Issued: 05.06.2014. Made: 20.05.2014. Coming into force: 28.05.2014. Effect: None. Territorial extent & classification: E. Local. - Available at http://www.legislation.gov.uk/uksi/2014/1488/contents/made Non-print

The M49 Motorway and M4 Motorway (Junction 22) (Temporary Prohibition of Traffic) Order 2014 No. 2014/2283. - Enabling power: Road Traffic Regulation Act 1984, s. 14 (1) (a). - Issued: 29.08.2014. Made: 27.08.2014. Coming into force: 30.08.2014. Effect: None. Territorial extent & classification: E. Local. - Available at http://www.legislation.gov.uk/uksi/2014/2283/contents/made Non-print

The M49 Motorway (M4 Junction 22 to M5 Junction 18) (Temporary Prohibition of Traffic) Order 2014 No. 2014/427. - Enabling power: Road Traffic Regulation Act 1984, s. 14 (1) (a). - Issued: 27.02.2014. Made: 19.02.2014. Coming into force: 24.02.2014. Effect: None. Territorial extent & classification: E. Local. - Available at http://www.legislation.gov.uk/uksi/2014/427/contents/made Non-print

ROAD TRAFFIC: TRAFFIC REGULATION

The M49 Motorway (M5 Junction 18A to M4 Junction 22) (Temporary Prohibition of Traffic) Order 2014 No. 2014/1730. - Enabling power: Road Traffic Regulation Act 1984, s. 14 (1) (a). - Issued: 04.07.2014. Made: 25.06.2014. Coming into force: 28.06.2014. Effect: None. Territorial extent & classification: E. Local. - Available at http://www.legislation.gov.uk/uksi/2014/1730/contents/made Non-print

The M50 Motorway (Junction 1, Tewkesbury) (Temporary Prohibition of Traffic) Order 2014 No. 2014/315. - Enabling power: Road Traffic Regulation Act 1984, s. 14 (1) (a). - Issued: 17.02.2014. Made: 03.02.2014. Coming into force: 10.02.2014. Effect: None. Territorial extent & classification: E. Local. - Available at http://www.legislation.gov.uk/uksi/2014/315/contents/made Non-print

The M50 Motorway (Junction 1, Twyning, Gloucestershire) (Slip Road) (Temporary Prohibition of Traffic) Order 2014 No. 2014/2079. - Enabling power: Road Traffic Regulation Act 1984, s. 14 (1) (a). - Issued: 06.08.2014. Made: 14.07.2014. Coming into force: 21.07.2014. Effect: None. Territorial extent & classification: E. Local. - Available at http://www.legislation.gov.uk/uksi/2014/2079/contents/made Non-print

The M50 Motorway (Junction 2, Bury Court) (Temporary Restriction of Traffic) Order 2014 No. 2014/2181. - Enabling power: Road Traffic Regulation Act 1984, s. 14 (1) (a). - Issued: 19.08.2014. Made: 07.07.2014. Coming into force: 14.07.2014. Effect: None. Territorial extent & classification: E. Local. - Available at http://www.legislation.gov.uk/uksi/2014/2181/contents/made Non-print

The M50 Motorway (Junction 2, Gloucestershire) (Temporary Restriction of Traffic) Order 2014 No. 2014/2629. - Enabling power: Road Traffic Regulation Act 1984, s. 14 (1) (a). - Issued: 30.09.2014. Made: 22.09.2014. Coming into force: 29.09.2014. Effect: None. Territorial extent & classification: E. Local. - Available at http://www.legislation.gov.uk/uksi/2014/2629/contents/made Non-print

The M50 Motorway (Junction 2 to 3) (Temporary Prohibition of Traffic) Order 2014 No. 2014/125. - Enabling power: Road Traffic Regulation Act 1984, s. 14 (1) (a). - Issued: 24.01.2014. Made: 17.01.2014. Coming into force: 24.01.2014. Effect: None. Territorial extent & classification: E. Local. - Available at http://www.legislation.gov.uk/uksi/2014/125/contents/made Non-print

The M50 Motorway (Junctions 1 - 2) (Temporary Restriction and Prohibition of Traffic) Order 2014 No. 2014/2246. - Enabling power: Road Traffic Regulation Act 1984, ss. 14 (1) (a). - Issued: 27.08.2014. Made: 11.08.2014. Coming into force: 15.08.2014. Effect: None. Territorial extent & classification: E. Local. - Available at http://www.legislation.gov.uk/uksi/2014/2246/contents/made Non-print

The M50 Motorway (Junctions 2 to 4) (Temporary Restriction and Prohibition of Traffic) Order 2014 No. 2014/2497. - Enabling power: Road Traffic Regulation Act 1984, s. 14 (1) (a)- Issued: 15.09.2014. Made: 08.09.2014. Coming into force: 15.09.2014. Effect: None. Territorial extent & classification: E. Local. - Available at http://www.legislation.gov.uk/uksi/2014/2497/contents/made Non-print

The M50 Motorway (Junctions 3 - 4, Herefordshire) (Temporary Prohibition of Traffic) Order 2014 No. 2014/2137. - Enabling power: Road Traffic Regulation Act 1984, s. 14 (1) (a). - Issued: 12.08.2014. Made: 23.07.2014. Coming into force: 30.07.2014. Effect: None. Territorial extent & classification: E. Local. - Available at http://www.legislation.gov.uk/uksi/2014/2137/contents/made Non-print

The M50 Motorway (Ledbury, Herefordshire) (Temporary Prohibition of Traffic) Order 2014 No. 2014/708. - Enabling power: Road Traffic Regulation Act 1984, s. 14 (1) (a). - Issued: 10.03.2014. Made: 24.02.2014. Coming into force: 03.03.2014. Effect: None. Territorial extent & classification: E. Local. - Available at http://www.legislation.gov.uk/uksi/2014/708/contents/made Non-print

The M50 Motorway (M5 Junction 8 - M50 Junction 1) (Temporary Prohibition of Traffic) Order 2014 No. 2014/2772. - Enabling power: Road Traffic Regulation Act 1984, s. 14 (1) (a). - Issued: 14.10.2014. Made: 03.10.2014. Coming into force: 10.10.2014. Effect: None. Territorial extent & classification: E. Local. - Available at http://www.legislation.gov.uk/uksi/2014/2772/contents/made Non-print

The M50 Motorway (M5 Junction 8 - M50 Junction 1) (Temporary Restriction and Prohibition of Traffic) (No.2) Order 2014 No. 2014/3452. - Enabling power: Road Traffic Regulation Act 1984, s. 14 (1) (a). - Issued: 30.12.2014. Made: 22.12.2014. Coming into force: 29.12.2014. Effect: None. Territorial extent & classification: E. Local. - Available at http://www.legislation.gov.uk/uksi/2014/3452/contents/made Non-print

The M50 Motorway (M5 Junction 8 - M50 Junction 4) (Temporary Prohibition of Traffic) Order 2014 No. 2014/3413. - Enabling power: Road Traffic Regulation Act 1984, s. 14 (1) (a)- Issued: 05.12.2014. Made: 28.11.2014. Coming into force: 05.12.2014. Effect: None. Territorial extent & classification: E. Local. - Available at http://www.legislation.gov.uk/uksi/2014/3413/contents/made Non-print

The M53 Motorway (Junction 2 Southbound Exit Slip Road) (Moreton Spur) (Temporary Restriction of Traffic) Order 2014 No. 2014/2801. - Enabling power: Road Traffic Regulation Act 1984, s. 14 (1) (b). - Issued: 21.10.2014. Made: 24.09.2014. Coming into force: 01.10.2014. Effect: None. Territorial extent & classification: E. Local. - Available at http://www.legislation.gov.uk/uksi/2014/2801/contents/made Non-print

The M53 Motorway (Junction 5-9 Southbound Carriageway and Slip Roads and the A41 Trunk Road Northbound and Southbound Carriageways from the junction with M53 Junction 5 to the A550) (Temporary Prohibition of Traffic) Order 2014 No. 2014/1151. - Enabling power: Road Traffic Regulation Act 1984, s. 14 (1) (a). - Issued: 06.05.2014. Made: 11.02.2014. Coming into force: 16.02.2014. Effect: None. Territorial extent & classification: E. Local. - Available at http://www.legislation.gov.uk/uksi/2014/1151/contents/made Non-print

The M53 Motorway (Junction 5, Southbound Carriageway and Southbound and Northbound Slip Roads) (Temporary Prohibition of Traffic) Order 2014 No. 2014/2085. - Enabling power: Road Traffic Regulation Act 1984, s. 14 (1) (a). - Issued: 07.08.2014. Made: 16.07.2014. Coming into force: 20.07.2014. Effect: None. Territorial extent & classification: E. Local. - Available at http://www.legislation.gov.uk/uksi/2014/2085/contents/made Non-print

The M53 Motorway (Junction 7 Southbound Carriageway) (Temporary Prohibition of Traffic) Order 2014 No. 2014/2566. - Enabling power: Road Traffic Regulation Act 1984, s. 14 (1) (a). - Issued: 24.09.2014. Made: 28.08.2014. Coming into force: 04.09.2014. Effect: None. Territorial extent & classification: E. Local. - Available at http://www.legislation.gov.uk/uksi/2014/2566/contents/made Non-print

The M53 Motorway (Junction 9, Southbound Exit Slip Road) (Temporary Prohibition of Traffic) Order 2014 No. 2014/1494. - Enabling power: Road Traffic Regulation Act 1984, s. 14 (1) (a). - Issued: 05.06.2014. Made: 20.05.2014. Coming into force: 08.06.2014. Effect: None. Territorial extent & classification: E. Local. - Available at http://www.legislation.gov.uk/uksi/2014/1494/contents/made Non-print

The M53 Motorway (Junctions 4-1 Northbound and Southbound Carriageways and Slip Roads) (Temporary Prohibition and Restriction of Traffic) Order 2014 No. 2014/1978. - Enabling power: Road Traffic Regulation Act 1984, s. 14 (1) (a). - Issued: 18.07.2014. Made: 02.07.2014. Coming into force: 20.07.2014. Effect: None. Territorial extent & classification: E. Local. - Available at http://www.legislation.gov.uk/uksi/2014/1978/contents/made Non-print

The M53 Motorway (Junctions 6-7 Northbound and Southbound Exit Slip Roads) (Temporary Prohibition of Traffic) Order 2014 No. 2014/1054. - Enabling power: Road Traffic Regulation Act 1984, s. 14 (1) (a). - Issued: 22.04.2014. Made: 25.03.2014. Coming into force: 30.03.2014. Effect: None. Territorial extent & classification: E. Local. - Available at http://www.legislation.gov.uk/uksi/2014/1054/contents/made Non-print

The M53 Motorway (Junctions 8-4 Northbound and Southbound Carriageways and Slip Roads) (Temporary Prohibition of Traffic) Order 2014 No. 2014/2498. - Enabling power: Road Traffic Regulation Act 1984, s. 14 (1) (a). - Issued: 18.09.2014. Made: 10.09.2014. Coming into force: 15.09.2014. Effect: None. Territorial extent & classification: E. Local. - Available at http://www.legislation.gov.uk/uksi/2014/2498/contents/made Non-print

ROAD TRAFFIC: TRAFFIC REGULATION

The M53 Motorway (Junctions 11-12 Northbound and Southbound Carriageways, Slip and Link Roads) and the M56 Motorway (Junction 15 Westbound Link to M53) (Temporary Prohibition of Traffic) Order 2014 No. 2014/1152. - Enabling power: Road Traffic Regulation Act 1984, s. 14 (1) (a). - Issued: 06.05.2014. Made: 12.02.2014. Coming into force: 18.02.2014. Effect: None. Territorial extent & classification: E. Local. - Available at http://www.legislation.gov.uk/uksi/2014/1152/contents/made Non-print

The M54 Motorway and A5 Trunk Road (M54 Junction 7, Telford) (Temporary Restriction and Prohibition of Traffic) Order 2014 No. 2014/2724. - Enabling power: Road Traffic Regulation Act 1984, s. 14 (1) (a). - Issued: 13.10.2014. Made: 22.09.2014. Coming into force: 29.09.2014. Effect: None. Territorial extent & classification: E. Local. - Available at http://www.legislation.gov.uk/uksi/2014/2724/contents/made Non-print

The M54 Motorway (Essington, Staffordshire) (Temporary 50 Miles Per Hour Speed Restriction) Order 2014 No. 2014/276. - Enabling power: Road Traffic Regulation Act 1984, s. 14 (1) (a). - Issued: 14.02.2014. Made: 20.01.2014. Coming into force: 27.01.2014. Effect: None. Territorial extent & classification: E. Local. - Available at http://www.legislation.gov.uk/uksi/2014/276/contents/made Non-print

The M54 Motorway (Junction 1, Staffordshire) (Temporary Prohibition of Traffic) Order 2014 No. 2014/3150. - Enabling power: Road Traffic Regulation Act 1984, s. 14 (1) (a). - Issued: 24.11.2014. Made: 14.11.2014. Coming into force: 22.11.2014. Effect: None. Territorial extent & classification: E. Local. - Available at http://www.legislation.gov.uk/uksi/2014/3150/contents/made Non-print

The M54 Motorway (Junction 2) and A449 Trunk Road (Link Roads) (Temporary Restriction of Traffic) Order 2014 No. 2014/2243. - Enabling power: Road Traffic Regulation Act 1984, ss. 14 (1) (b), 122A. - Issued: 27.08.2014. Made: 04.08.2014. Coming into force: 11.08.2014. Effect: None. Territorial extent & classification: E. Local. - Available at http://www.legislation.gov.uk/uksi/2014/2243/contents/made Non-print

The M54 Motorway (Junction 2 to Junction 6) (Temporary Restriction and Prohibition of Traffic) Order 2014 No. 2014/2791. - Enabling power: Road Traffic Regulation Act 1984, s. 14 (1) (a) & S.I. 1982/1163, reg. 16 (2). - Issued: 14.10.2014. Made: 06.10.2014. Coming into force: 13.10.2014. Effect: None. Territorial extent & classification: E. Local. - Available at http://www.legislation.gov.uk/uksi/2014/2791/contents/made Non-print

The M54 Motorway (Junction 4, Telford, Shropshire) (Slip Road) (Temporary Prohibition of Traffic) Order 2014 No. 2014/2763. - Enabling power: Road Traffic Regulation Act 1984, s. 14 (1) (a). - Issued: 14.10.2014. Made: 29.09.2014. Coming into force: 06.10.2014. Effect: None. Territorial extent & classification: E. Local. - Available at http://www.legislation.gov.uk/uksi/2014/2763/contents/made Non-print

The M54 Motorway (Junction 6) (Temporary Restriction and Prohibition of Traffic) Order 2014 No. 2014/187. - Enabling power: Road Traffic Regulation Act 1984, s. 14 (1) (a) & S.I. 1982/1163, reg. 16 (2). - Issued: 04.02.2014. Made: 20.01.2014. Coming into force: 27.01.2014. Effect: None. Territorial extent & classification: E. Local. - Available at http://www.legislation.gov.uk/uksi/2014/187/contents/made Non-print

The M54 Motorway (Junctions 1 to 2, Staffordshire) (Temporary Prohibition of Traffic) Order 2014 No. 2014/1427. - Enabling power: Road Traffic Regulation Act 1984, s. 14 (1) (a). - Issued: 30.05.2014. Made: 13.05.2014. Coming into force: 20.05.2014. Effect: None. Territorial extent & classification: E. Local. - Available at http://www.legislation.gov.uk/uksi/2014/1427/contents/made Non-print

The M54 Motorway (Junctions 3 to 2, Staffordshire) (Temporary Restriction of Traffic) Order 2014 No. 2014/2736. - Enabling power: Road Traffic Regulation Act 1984, s. 14 (1) (a). - Issued: 14.10.2014. Made: 22.09.2014. Coming into force: 29.10.2014. Effect: None. Territorial extent & classification: E. Local. - Available at http://www.legislation.gov.uk/uksi/2014/2736/contents/made Non-print

The M54 Motorway (Junctions 3 to 4, Shropshire) (Temporary Restriction and Prohibition of Traffic) Order 2014 No. 2014/1158. - Enabling power: Road Traffic Regulation Act 1984, s. 14 (1) (a). - Issued: 07.05.2014. Made: 18.04.2014. Coming into force: 25.04.2014. Effect: None. Territorial extent & classification: E. Local. - Available at http://www.legislation.gov.uk/uksi/2014/1158/contents/made Non-print

The M55 Motorway (Junction 1 Eastbound and Westbound Exit and Entry Slip Roads) (Temporary Prohibition of Traffic) Order 2014 No. 2014/987. - Enabling power: Road Traffic Regulation Act 1984, s. 14 (1) (a). - Issued: 10.04.2014. Made: 27.03.2014. Coming into force: 03.04.2014. Effect: None. Territorial extent & classification: E. Local. - Available at http://www.legislation.gov.uk/uksi/2014/987/contents/made Non-print

The M55 Motorway (Junctions 4-1 Eastbound Carriageway and Junction 3 Eastbound Entry Slip Road) (Temporary Prohibition and Restriction of Traffic) Order 2014 No. 2014/3540. - Enabling power: Road Traffic Regulation Act 1984, s. 14 (1) (a). - Issued: 22.01.2015. Made: 24.12.2014. Coming into force: 11.01.2015. Effect: None. Territorial extent & classification: E. Local. - Available at http://www.legislation.gov.uk/uksi/2014/3540/contents/made Non-print

The M56 Motorway (Junction 6, Eastbound Entry Slip Road) (Temporary Prohibition of Traffic) Order 2014 No. 2014/3551. - Enabling power: Road Traffic Regulation Act 1984, s. 14 (1) (a). - Issued: 23.01.2015. Made: 31.12.2014. Coming into force: 20.01.2015. Effect: None. Territorial extent & classification: E. Local. - Available at http://www.legislation.gov.uk/uksi/2014/3551/contents/made Non-print

The M56 Motorway (Junction 9 Eastbound Link Road to the M6 Northbound and Southbound) (Temporary Prohibition of Traffic) Order 2014 No. 2014/2208. - Enabling power: Road Traffic Regulation Act 1984, s. 14 (1) (a). - Issued: 20.08.2014. Made: 06.07.2014. Coming into force: 28.08.2014. Effect: None. Territorial extent & classification: E. Local. - Available at http://www.legislation.gov.uk/uksi/2014/2208/contents/made Non-print

The M56 Motorway (Junction 10 Westbound and Eastbound Exit and Entry Slip Roads) (Temporary Prohibition of Traffic) No. 2014/2548. - Enabling power: Road Traffic Regulation Act 1984, s. 14 (1) (a). - Issued: 23.09.2014. Made: 10.09.2014. Coming into force: 14.09.2014. Effect: None. Territorial extent & classification: E. Local. - Available at http://www.legislation.gov.uk/uksi/2014/2548/contents/made Non-print

The M56 Motorway (Junction 12, Eastbound Exit Slip Road) (Temporary Prohibition of Traffic) Order 2014 No. 2014/2046. - Enabling power: Road Traffic Regulation Act 1984, s. 14 (1) (a). - Issued: 04.08.2014. Made: 09.07.2014. Coming into force: 12.07.2014. Effect: None. Territorial extent & classification: S. Local. - Available at: http://www.legislation.gov.uk/uksi/2014/2046/contents/made Non-print

The M56 Motorway (Junctions 1-3 Westbound and Eastbound Carriageways and Slip Roads) (Temporary Prohibition and Restriction of Traffic) Order 2014 No. 2014/401. - Enabling power: Road Traffic Regulation Act 1984, s. 14 (1) (a) (7). - Issued: 27.02.2014. Made: 18.02.2014. Coming into force: 21.02.2014. Effect: None. Territorial extent & classification: E. Local. - Available at http://www.legislation.gov.uk/uksi/2014/401/contents/made Non-print

The M56 Motorway (Junctions 1-6 Westbound and Eastbound Carriageways and Slip Roads) (Temporary Prohibition and Restriction of Traffic) Order 2014 No. 2014/3511. - Enabling power: Road Traffic Regulation Act 1984, s. 14 (1) (a) & Motorway Traffic (England and Wales) Regulations 1982, reg. 16 (2). - Issued: 23.01.2014. Made: 08.10.2014. Coming into force: 26.10.2014. Effect: None. Territorial extent & classification: E. Local. - Available at http://www.legislation.gov.uk/uksi/2014/3511/contents/made Non-print

The M56 Motorway (Junctions 3-3a) and the A5103 Trunk Road (Northbound and Southbound) (Temporary Prohibition and Restriction of Traffic) Order 2014 No. 2014/2596. - Enabling power: Road Traffic Regulation Act 1984, s. 14 (1) (a). - Issued: 26.09.2014. Made: 16.09.2014. Coming into force: 06.10.2014. Effect: None. Territorial extent & classification: E. Local. - Available at http://www.legislation.gov.uk/uksi/2014/2596/contents/made Non-print

The M56 Motorway (Junctions 4-8 Eastbound and Westbound Carriageways and Slip Roads) (Temporary Prohibition and Restriction of Traffic) Order 2014 No. 2014/1947. - Enabling power: Road Traffic Regulation Act 1984, s. 14 (1) (a) (7). - Issued: 18.07.2014. Made: 01.07.2014. Coming into force: 03.07.2014. Effect: None. Territorial extent & classification: E. Local. - Available at http://www.legislation.gov.uk/uksi/2014/1947/contents/made
Non-print

The M56 Motorway (Junctions 6 Westbound Entry Slip Road) (Temporary Prohibition of Traffic) Order 2014 No. 2014/1344. - Enabling power: Road Traffic Regulation Act 1984, s. 14 (1) (a). - Issued: 29.05.2014. Made: 29.04.2014. Coming into force: 04.05.2014. Effect: None. Territorial extent & classification: E. Local. - Available at http://www.legislation.gov.uk/uksi/2014/1344/contents/made
Non-print

The M56 Motorway (Junctions 7- 8 Westbound Carriageway) (Temporary Prohibition of Traffic) Order 2014 No. 2014/2415. - Enabling power: Road Traffic Regulation Act 1984, s. 14 (1) (a). - Issued: 10.09.2014. Made: 03.09.2014. Coming into force: 07.09.2014. Effect: None. Territorial extent & classification: E. Local. - Available at http://www.legislation.gov.uk/uksi/2014/2415/contents/made
Non-print

The M56 Motorway (Junctions 9-6 Eastbound Carriageway and Slip Roads) (Temporary Prohibition and Restriction of Traffic) Order 2014 No. 2014/2814. - Enabling power: Road Traffic Regulation Act 1984, s. 14 (1) (a) (7). - Issued: 22.10.2014. Made: 07.10.2014. Coming into force: 12.10.2014. Effect: None. Territorial extent & classification: E. Local. - Available at http://www.legislation.gov.uk/uksi/2014/2814/contents/made
Non-print

The M56 Motorway (Junctions 10-12 Westbound and Eastbound Carriageways and Slip Roads) (Temporary Prohibition and Restriction of Traffic) Order 2014 No. 2014/2285. - Enabling power: Road Traffic Regulation Act 1984, s. 14 (1) (a) (7). - Issued: 21.08.2014. Made: 13.08.2014. Coming into force: 31.08.2014. Effect: None. Territorial extent & classification: E. Local. - Available at http://www.legislation.gov.uk/uksi/2014/2285/contents/made
Non-print

The M56 Motorway (Junctions 11-16 Westbound and Eastbound Carriageways, Link and Slip Roads), the M53 (Link Roads) and the A494 Trunk Road (Temporary Prohibition and Restriction of Traffic) Order 2014 No. 2014/1744. - Enabling power: Road Traffic Regulation Act 1984, s. 14 (1) (a) & S.I. 1982/1163, reg. 16 (2). - Issued: 04.07.2014. Made: 19.06.2014. Coming into force: 06.07.2014. Effect: None. Territorial extent & classification: E. Local. - Available at http://www.legislation.gov.uk/uksi/2014/1744/contents/made
Non-print

The M56 Motorway (Junctions 14-16 Westbound and Eastbound) and the M53 Link Roads (Temporary Prohibition and Restriction of Traffic) Order 2014 No. 2014/2536. - Enabling power: Road Traffic Regulation Act 1984, s. 14 (1) (a) (7). - Issued: 18.09.2014. Made: 11.09.2014. Coming into force: 02.10.2014. Effect: None. Territorial extent & classification: E. Local. - Available at http://www.legislation.gov.uk/uksi/2014/2536/contents/made
Non-print

The M57 Motorway (Junction 1 Southbound Carriageway to the A5300 Knowsley Expressway) (Temporary Prohibition of Traffic) Order 2014 No. 2014/2812. - Enabling power: Road Traffic Regulation Act 1984, s. 14 (1) (a). - Issued: 16.10.2014. Made: 08.10.2014. Coming into force: 23.10.2014. Effect: None. Territorial extent & classification: E. Local. - Available at http://www.legislation.gov.uk/uksi/2014/2812/contents/made
Non-print

The M57 Motorway (Junction 2 Southbound Carriageway and Junction 2 Entry Slip Road) (Temporary Prohibition of Traffic) Order 2014 No. 2014/1426. - Enabling power: Road Traffic Regulation Act 1984, s. 14 (1) (a). - Issued: 02.06.2014. Made: 15.05.2014. Coming into force: 18.05.2014. Effect: None. Territorial extent & classification: E. Local. - Available at http://www.legislation.gov.uk/uksi/2014/1426/contents/made
Non-print

The M57 Motorway (Junction 4 Northbound and Southbound Exit and Entry Slip Roads) (Temporary Prohibition of Traffic) Order 2014 No. 2014/3541. - Enabling power: Road Traffic Regulation Act 1984, s. 14 (1) (a). - Issued: 23.01.2015. Made: 24.12.2014. Coming into force: 11.01.2015. Effect: None. Territorial extent & classification: E. Local. - Available at http://www.legislation.gov.uk/uksi/2014/3541/contents/made
Non-print

The M57 Motorway (Junctions 2-6 Northbound and Southbound Entry and Exit Slip Roads) and Link Roads (Temporary Prohibition of Traffic) Order 2014 No. 2014/2963. - Enabling power: Road Traffic Regulation Act 1984, s. 14 (1) (a). - Issued: 21.10.2014. Made: 15.10.2014. Coming into force: 02.11.2014. Effect: None. Territorial extent & classification: E. Local. - Available at http://www.legislation.gov.uk/uksi/2014/2963/contents/made
Non-print

The M57 Motorway (Junctions 3-7 Northbound and Southbound Carriageways and Slip Roads) (Temporary Prohibition and Restriction of Traffic) Order 2014 No. 2014/2091. - Enabling power: Road Traffic Regulation Act 1984, s. 14 (1) (a) (7). - Issued: 07.08.2014. Made: 17.07.2014. Coming into force: 03.08.2014. Effect: None. Territorial extent & classification: E. Local. - Available at http://www.legislation.gov.uk/uksi/2014/2091/contents/made
Non-print

The M57 Motorway (Junctions 7-6 Southbound Carriageway) (Temporary Prohibition and Restriction of Traffic) Order 2014 No. 2014/2695. - Enabling power: Road Traffic Regulation Act 1984, s. 14 (1) (a) (7). - Issued: 09.10.2014. Made: 03.07.2014. Coming into force: 22.07.2014. Effect: None. Territorial extent & classification: E. Local. - Available at http://www.legislation.gov.uk/uksi/2014/2695/contents/made
Non-print

The M58 Motorway (Junction 3 - The M6 Motorway Junction 26 (Orrell Interchange) Eastbound and Westbound Carriageways and Slip Roads) (Temporary Prohibition of Traffic) (No.2) Order 2014 No. 2014/3397. - Enabling power: Road Traffic Regulation Act 1984, s. 14 (1) (a). - Issued: 25.11.2014. Made: 11.11.2014. Coming into force: 30.11.2014. Effect: None. Territorial extent & classification: E. Local. - Available at http://www.legislation.gov.uk/uksi/2014/3397/contents/made
Non-print

The M58 Motorway (Junction 3 - The M6 Motorway Junction 26 (Orrell Interchange) Eastbound and Westbound Carriageways and Slip Roads) (Temporary Prohibition of Traffic) Order 2014 No. 2014/1564. - Enabling power: Road Traffic Regulation Act 1984, s. 14 (1) (a). - Issued: 17.06.2014. Made: 22.05.2014. Coming into force: 26.05.2014. Effect: None. Territorial extent & classification: E. Local. - Available at http://www.legislation.gov.uk/uksi/2014/1564/contents/made
Non-print

The M58 Motorway (Junctions 0-1 Eastbound and Westbound Carriageways) (Temporary Prohibition of Traffic) Order 2014 No. 2014/2561. - Enabling power: Road Traffic Regulation Act 1984, s. 14 (1) (a). - Issued: 24.09.2014. Made: 27.08.2014. Coming into force: 31.08.2014. Effect: None. Territorial extent & classification: E. Local. - Available at http://www.legislation.gov.uk/uksi/2014/2561/contents/made
Non-print

The M58 Motorway (Junctions 3 - 6 Eastbound and Westbound Carriageways and Slip Roads) (Temporary Prohibition and Restriction of Traffic) Order 2014 No. 2014/2952. - Enabling power: Road Traffic Regulation Act 1984, s. 14 (1) (a) (7). - Issued: 20.10.2014. Made: 09.10.2014. Coming into force: 29.10.2014. Effect: None. Territorial extent & classification: E. Local. - Available at http://www.legislation.gov.uk/uksi/2014/2952/contents/made
Non-print

The M60, M62, M61 and M602 Motorways (Manchester Smart Motorway Scheme) (Temporary Prohibition and Restriction of Traffic) Order 2014 No. 2014/2052. - Enabling power: Road Traffic Regulation Act 1984, ss. 14 (1) (a), 15 (2) & S.I. 1982/1163, reg. 16 (2). - Issued: 05.08.2014. Made: 19.06.2014. Coming into force: 22.06.2014. Effect: None. Territorial extent & classification: E. Local. - Revoked by SI (2015/136) (Non-print). - Available at http://www.legislation.gov.uk/uksi/2014/2052/contents/made
Non-print

The M60 Motorway (Junction 3, Clockwise Entry Slip Road from the A34 Northbound) (Temporary Prohibition of Traffic) Order 2014 No. 2014/2055. - Enabling power: Road Traffic Regulation Act 1984, ss. 14 (1) (a). - Issued: 04.08.2014. Made: 15.07.2014. Coming into force: 03.08.2014. Effect: None. Territorial extent & classification: E. Local. - Available at http://www.legislation.gov.uk/uksi/2014/2055/contents/made
Non-print

The M60 Motorway (Junction 7-6 Anticlockwise Collector-Distributor Road and Exit Slip Road) (Temporary Prohibition of Traffic) Order 2014 No. 2014/1037. - Enabling power: Road Traffic Regulation Act 1984, s. 14 (1) (a). - Issued: 22.04.2014. Made: 03.04.2014. Coming into force: 06.04.2014. Effect: None. Territorial extent & classification: E. Local. - Available at http://www.legislation.gov.uk/uksi/2014/1037/contents/made Non-print

The M60 Motorway (Junction 7 Clockwise Exit and Anticlockwise Entry Slip Roads) (Greater Manchester Marathon) (Temporary Prohibition of Traffic) Order 2014 No. 2014/1036. - Enabling power: Road Traffic Regulation Act 1984, s. 16A (2) (a). - Issued: 22.04.2014. Made: 03.04.2014. Coming into force: 05.04.2014. Effect: None. Territorial extent & classification: E. Local. - Available at http://www.legislation.gov.uk/uksi/2014/1036/contents/made Non-print

The M60 Motorway (Junction 11 Anticlockwise and Clockwise Exit and Entry Slip Roads) (Temporary Prohibition of Traffic) Order 2014 No. 2014/2636. - Enabling power: Road Traffic Regulation Act 1984, ss. 14 (1) (a), 15 (2). - Issued: 01.10.2014. Made: 23.07.2014. Coming into force: 31.07.2014. Effect: None. Territorial extent & classification: E. Local. - Available at http://www.legislation.gov.uk/uksi/2014/2636/contents/made Non-print

The M60 Motorway (Junction 13 Clockwise Entry Slip Road) and M62 (Junction 12 Eastbound Link Road to the M60 Clockwise) (Temporary Prohibition of Traffic) Order 2014 No. 2014/2565. - Enabling power: Road Traffic Regulation Act 1984, s. 14 (1) (a). - Issued: 24.09.2014. Made: 28.08.2014. Coming into force: 14.09.2014. Effect: None. Territorial extent & classification: E. Local. - Available at http://www.legislation.gov.uk/uksi/2014/2565/contents/made Non-print

The M60 Motorway (Junction 18, Clockwise Exit Slip Road and Dedicated Entry Slip Road to the M66 Northbound) and the Junction 18 Roundabout (Simister Island) (Temporary Prohibition of Traffic) Order 2014 No. 2014/1955. - Enabling power: Road Traffic Regulation Act 1984, s. 14 (1) (a). - Issued: 18.07.2014. Made: 02.07.2014. Coming into force: 09.07.2014. Effect: None. Territorial extent & classification: E. Local. - Available at http://www.legislation.gov.uk/uksi/2014/1955/contents/made Non-print

The M60 Motorway (Junction 24 Anticlockwise and Clockwise Slip Roads), the M67 (Junctions 2-1A Westbound) and the A57 Trunk Road (Temporary Prohibition and Restriction of Traffic) Order 2014 No. 2014/1172. - Enabling power: Road Traffic Regulation Act 1984, ss. 14 (1) (a), 122A. - Issued: 06.05.2014. Made: 23.04.2014. Coming into force: 14.05.2014. Effect: None. Territorial extent & classification: E. Local. - Available at http://www.legislation.gov.uk/uksi/2014/1172/contents/made Non-print

The M60 Motorway (Junction 24 to 1, Clockwise and Anticlockwise Carriageways and Slip Roads) (Temporary Prohibition and Restriction of Traffic) Order 2014 No. 2014/1147. - Enabling power: Road Traffic Regulation Act 1984, s. 14 (1) (a) (7). - Issued: 06.05.2014. Made: 11.02.2014. Coming into force: 16.02.2014. Effect: None. Territorial extent & classification: E. Local. - Available at http://www.legislation.gov.uk/uksi/2014/1147/contents/made Non-print

The M60 Motorway (Junction 25 Anticlockwise and Clockwise Exit and Entry Slip Roads) (Temporary Prohibition of Traffic) Order 2014 No. 2014/2595. - Enabling power: Road Traffic Regulation Act 1984, s. 14 (1) (a). - Issued: 26.09.2014. Made: 16.09.2014. Coming into force: 05.10.2014. Effect: None. Territorial extent & classification: E. Local. - Available at http://www.legislation.gov.uk/uksi/2014/2595/contents/made Non-print

The M60 Motorway (Junction 25, Clockwise Exit Slip Road) (Temporary Prohibition of Traffic) Order 2014 No. 2014/938. - Enabling power: Road Traffic Regulation Act 1984, s. 14 (1) (a). - Issued: 01.04.2014. Made: 11.03.2014. Coming into force: 16.03.2014. Effect: None. Territorial extent & classification: E. Local. - Available at http://www.legislation.gov.uk/uksi/2014/938/contents/made Non-print

The M60 Motorway (Junction 26 Clockwise Exit and Entry Slip Roads) (Temporary Prohibition of Traffic) Order 2014 No. 2014/3071. - Enabling power: Road Traffic Regulation Act 1984, s. 14 (1) (a). - Issued: 19.11.2014. Made: 28.10.2014. Coming into force: 16.11.2014. Effect: None. Territorial extent & classification: E. Local. - Available at http://www.legislation.gov.uk/uksi/2014/3071/contents/made Non-print

The M60 Motorway (Junctions 4-5 Clockwise and Anticlockwise Carriageways and Slip Road) (Temporary Prohibition and Restriction of Traffic) Order 2014 No. 2014/2593. - Enabling power: Road Traffic Regulation Act 1984, s. 14 (1) (a) (7). - Issued: 29.09.2014. Made: 16.09.2014. Coming into force: 21.09.2014. Effect: None. Territorial extent & classification: E. Local. - Available at http://www.legislation.gov.uk/uksi/2014/2593/contents/made Non-print

The M60 Motorway (Junctions 5-12, Clockwise and Anticlockwise Carriageways, Slip and Link Roads) (Temporary Prohibition and Restriction of Traffic) Order 2014 No. 2014/62. - Enabling power: Road Traffic Regulation Act 1984, s. 14 (1) (a) (7). - Issued: 20.01.2014. Made: 07.01.2014. Coming into force: 12.01.2014. Effect: None. Territorial extent & classification: E. Local. - Available at http://www.legislation.gov.uk/uksi/2014/62/contents/made Non-print

The M60 Motorway (Junctions 14-17 Clockwise and Anticlockwise) and the M61 Link Road (Temporary Prohibition and Restriction of Traffic) Order 2014 No. 2014/2599. - Enabling power: Road Traffic Regulation Act 1984, s. 14 (1) (a) (7). - Issued: 29.09.2014. Made: 18.09.2014. Coming into force: 05.10.2014. Effect: None. Territorial extent & classification: E. Local. - Available at http://www.legislation.gov.uk/uksi/2014/2599/contents/made Non-print

The M60 Motorway (Junctions 14-17 Clockwise and Anticlockwise Carriageways, Slip and Link Roads) (Temporary Prohibition and Restriction of Traffic) Order 2014 No. 2014/1681. - Enabling power: Road Traffic Regulation Act 1984, s. 14 (1) (a) (7). - Issued: 01.07.2014. Made: 05.06.2014. Coming into force: 10.06.2014. Effect: None. Territorial extent & classification: E. Local. - Available at http://www.legislation.gov.uk/uksi/2014/1681/contents/made Non-print

The M60 Motorway (Junctions 23-24 Clockwise Carriageway and Slip Roads) (Temporary Prohibition and Restriction of Traffic) Order 2014 No. 2014/2951. - Enabling power: Road Traffic Regulation Act 1984, s. 14 (1) (a) (7). - Issued: 16.10.2014. Made: 08.10.2014. Coming into force: 28.10.2014. Effect: None. Territorial extent & classification: E. Local. - Available at http://www.legislation.gov.uk/uksi/2014/2951/contents/made Non-print

The M60 Motorway (Junctions 25-4 Clockwise and Anticlockwise Slip Roads) (Temporary Prohibition of Traffic) Order 2014 No. 2014/2284. - Enabling power: Road Traffic Regulation Act 1984, s. 14 (1) (a). - Issued: 21.08.2014. Made: 12.08.2014. Coming into force: 31.08.2014. Effect: None. Territorial extent & classification: E. Local. - Available at http://www.legislation.gov.uk/uksi/2014/2284/contents/made Non-print

The M61 Motorway (Junction 2 Northbound and Junction 3 Southbound Links to the A666) (Temporary Prohibition of Traffic) Order 2014 No. 2014/946. - Enabling power: Road Traffic Regulation Act 1984, s. 14 (1) (a). - Issued: 01.04.2014. Made: 13.03.2014. Coming into force: 16.03.2014. Effect: None. Territorial extent & classification: E. Local. - Available at http://www.legislation.gov.uk/uksi/2014/946/contents/made Non-print

The M61 Motorway (Junction 4 Northbound and Southbound Exit Slip Roads) (Temporary Prohibition of Traffic) Order 2014 No. 2014/3491. - Enabling power: Road Traffic Regulation Act 1984, s. 14 (1) (a). - Issued: 07.01.2015. Made: 18.12.2014. Coming into force: 05.01.2015. Effect: None. Territorial extent & classification: E. Local. - Available at http://www.legislation.gov.uk/uksi/2014/3491/contents/made Non-print

The M61 Motorway (Junction 5 Northbound and Southbound Exit and Entry Slip Roads) (Temporary Prohibition of Traffic) Order 2014 No. 2014/959. - Enabling power: Road Traffic Regulation Act 1984, s. 14 (1) (a). - Issued: 04.04.2014. Made: 13.03.2014. Coming into force: 17.03.2014. Effect: None. Territorial extent & classification: E. Local. - Available at http://www.legislation.gov.uk/uksi/2014/959/contents/made Non-print

ROAD TRAFFIC: TRAFFIC REGULATION

The M61 Motorway (Junction 5, Northbound Entry Slip Road) (Temporary Prohibition of Traffic) Order 2014 No. 2014/3372. - Enabling power: Road Traffic Regulation Act 1984, s. 14 (1) (a). - Issued: 12.11.2014. Made: 05.11.2014. Coming into force: 25.11.2014. Effect: None. Territorial extent & classification: E. Local. - Available at http://www.legislation.gov.uk/uksi/2014/3372/contents/made Non-print

The M61 Motorway (Junction 6 Southbound Dedicated Exit Slip Road) (Temporary Prohibition of Traffic) Order 2014 No. 2014/2526. - Enabling power: Road Traffic Regulation Act 1984, s. 14 (1) (b). - Issued: 09.09.2014. Made: 04.09.2014. Coming into force: 25.09.2014. Effect: None. Territorial extent & classification: E. Local. - Available at http://www.legislation.gov.uk/uksi/2014/2526/contents/made Non-print

The M61 Motorway (Junctions 1-3 Northbound and Southbound Carriageways, Link and Slip Roads) and M60 Link Roads (Temporary Prohibition and Restriction of Traffic) Order 2014 No. 2014/1679. - Enabling power: Road Traffic Regulation Act 1984, s. 14 (1) (a). - Issued: 01.07.2014. Made: 05.06.2014. Coming into force: 08.06.2014. Effect: None. Territorial extent & classification: E. Local. - Available at http://www.legislation.gov.uk/uksi/2014/1679/contents/made Non-print

The M61 Motorway (Junctions 2-4 Northbound Carriageway and M61/A666 Link Roads) (Temporary Prohibition of Traffic) Order 2014 No. 2014/3072. - Enabling power: Road Traffic Regulation Act 1984, s. 14 (1) (a). - Issued: 20.11.2014. Made: 30.10.2014. Coming into force: 16.11.2014. Effect: None. Territorial extent & classification: E. Local. - Available at http://www.legislation.gov.uk/uksi/2014/3072/contents/made Non-print

The M61 Motorway (Junctions 9-6 Southbound Carriageway and Slip Roads) (Temporary Prohibition and Restriction of Traffic) Order 2014 No. 2014/2601. - Enabling power: Road Traffic Regulation Act 1984, s. 14 (1) (a) (7). - Issued: 29.09.2014. Made: 18.09.2014. Coming into force: 09.10.2014. Effect: None. Territorial extent & classification: E. Local. - Available at http://www.legislation.gov.uk/uksi/2014/2601/contents/made Non-print

The M61 Motorway (Kearsley Spur) (Southbound and Northbound Link Roads) and the M60 Junction 14 Link Roads (Temporary Prohibition of Traffic) Order 2014 No. 2014/1946. - Enabling power: Road Traffic Regulation Act 1984, s. 14 (1) (a). - Issued: 18.07.2014. Made: 26.06.2014. Coming into force: 02.07.2014. Effect: None. Territorial extent & classification: E. Local. - Available at http://www.legislation.gov.uk/uksi/2014/1946/contents/made Non-print

The M61 Motorway (Links from Junction 2 Southbound and A666 Southbound to the A580 Eastbound)(Temporary Prohibition of Traffic) Order 2014 No. 2014/962. - Enabling power: Road Traffic Regulation Act 1984, s. 14 (1) (a). - Issued: 04.04.2014. Made: 13.03.2014. Coming into force: 21.03.2014. Effect: None. Territorial extent & classification: E. Local. - Available at http://www.legislation.gov.uk/uksi/2014/962/contents/made Non-print

The M61 Motorway (Northbound and Southbound Link Roads) and the M60 (Junction 15 Anticlockwise Link Road) (Temporary Prohibition of Traffic) Order 2014 No. 2014/2698. - Enabling power: Road Traffic Regulation Act 1984, s. 14 (1) (a). - Issued: 09.10.2014. Made: 18.09.2014. Coming into force: 23.09.2014. Effect: None. Territorial extent & classification: E. Local. - Available at http://www.legislation.gov.uk/uksi/2014/2698/contents/made Non-print

The M61 Motorway (Northbound and Southbound Link Roads from and to the A580 Westbound and Eastbound) (Temporary Prohibition of Traffic) Order 2014 No. 2014/958. - Enabling power: Road Traffic Regulation Act 1984, s. 14 (1) (a). - Issued: 04.04.2014. Made: 12.03.2014. Coming into force: 16.03.2014. Effect: None. Territorial extent & classification: E. Local. - Available at http://www.legislation.gov.uk/uksi/2014/958/contents/made Non-print

The M62 Motorway and M18 Motorway (Langham Interchange) (Temporary Prohibition of Traffic) Order 2014 No. 2014/2805. - Enabling power: Road Traffic Regulation Act 1984, s. 14 (1) (a) & S.I. 1982/1163, reg. 16 (2). - Issued: 14.10.2014. Made: 09.10.2014. Coming into force: 19.10.2014. Effect: None. Territorial extent & classification: E. Local. - Available at http://www.legislation.gov.uk/uksi/2014/2805/contents/made Non-print

The M62 Motorway and the A1(M) Motorway (Castleford to Holmfield) (Temporary Prohibition of Traffic) Order 2014 No. 2014/1718. - Enabling power: Road Traffic Regulation Act 1984, s. 14 (1) (a). - Issued: 02.07.2014. Made: 12.06.2014. Coming into force: 22.06.2014. Effect: None. Territorial extent & classification: E. Local. - Available at http://www.legislation.gov.uk/uksi/2014/1718/contents/made Non-print

The M62 Motorway and the A1(M) Motorway (Holmfield Interchange) (Temporary Prohibition of Traffic) Order 2014 No. 2014/3424. - Enabling power: Road Traffic Regulation Act 1984, s. 14 (1) (a). - Issued: 05.11.2014. Made: 27.11.2014. Coming into force: 07.12.2014. Effect: None. Territorial extent & classification: E. Local. - Available at http://www.legislation.gov.uk/uksi/2014/3424/contents/made Non-print

The M62 Motorway Junction 6 (Tarbock Island) and the M57 (Junction 1 Slip Roads) (Temporary Prohibition of Traffic) Order 2014 No. 2014/2831. - Enabling power: Road Traffic Regulation Act 1984, s. 14 (1) (a). - Issued: 16.10.2014. Made: 08.10.2014. Coming into force: 26.10.2014. Effect: None. Territorial extent & classification: E. Local. - Available at http://www.legislation.gov.uk/uksi/2014/2831/contents/made Non-print

The M62 Motorway (Junction 7 Eastbound and Westbound Exit and Entry Slip Roads) (Temporary Prohibition of Traffic) Order 2014 No. 2014/1581. - Enabling power: Road Traffic Regulation Act 1984, s. 14 (1) (a). - Issued: 18.06.2014. Made: 28.05.2014. Coming into force: 03.06.2014. Effect: None. Territorial extent & classification: E. Local. - Available at http://www.legislation.gov.uk/uksi/2014/1581/contents/made Non-print

The M62 Motorway (Junction 11 Eastbound Entry Slip Road) (Temporary Prohibition of Traffic) Order 2014 No. 2014/3506. - Enabling power: Road Traffic Regulation Act 1984, s. 14 (1) (a). - Issued: 20.01.2015. Made: 17.12.2014. Coming into force: 04.01.2015. Effect: None. Territorial extent & classification: E. Local. - Available at http://www.legislation.gov.uk/uksi/2014/3506/contents/made Non-print

The M62 Motorway (Junction 21 Eastbound Exit Slip Road and Designated Exit Slip Road to the A6193 Sir Isaac Newton Way) (Temporary Prohibition of Traffic) Order 2014 No. 2014/1345. - Enabling power: Road Traffic Regulation Act 1984, s. 14 (1) (a). - Issued: 29.05.2014. Made: 02.05.2014. Coming into force: 05.05.2014. Effect: None. Territorial extent & classification: E. Local. - Available at http://www.legislation.gov.uk/uksi/2014/1345/contents/made Non-print

The M62 Motorway (Junction 22) (No. 2) (Temporary Prohibition of Traffic) Order 2014 No. 2014/2688. - Enabling power: Road Traffic Regulation Act 1984, s. 14 (1) (a). - Issued: 07.10.2014. Made: 25.09.2014. Coming into force: 05.10.2014. Effect: None. Territorial extent & classification: E. Local. - Available at http://www.legislation.gov.uk/uksi/2014/2688/contents/made Non-print

The M62 Motorway (Junction 22) (Temporary Prohibition of Traffic) Order 2014 No. 2014/150. - Enabling power: Road Traffic Regulation Act 1984, s. 14 (1) (a). - Issued: 30.01.2014. Made: 23.01.2014. Coming into force: 02.02.2014. Effect: None. Territorial extent & classification: E. Local. - Available at http://www.legislation.gov.uk/uksi/2014/150/contents/made Non-print

The M62 Motorway (Junction 22) (Temporary Restriction and Prohibition of Traffic) Order 2014 No. 2014/1311. - Enabling power: Road Traffic Regulation Act 1984, s. 14 (1) (a) & S.I. 1982/1163, reg. 16 (2). - Issued: 27.05.2014. Made: 17.04.2014. Coming into force: 27.04.2014. Effect: None. Territorial extent & classification: E. Local. - Available at http://www.legislation.gov.uk/uksi/2014/1311/contents/made Non-print

The M62 Motorway (Junction 22 to Junction 23) (Temporary Restriction and Prohibition of Traffic) Order 2014 No. 2014/351. - Enabling power: Road Traffic Regulation Act 1984, s. 14 (1) (a) & S.I. 1982/1163, reg. 16 (2). - Issued: 19.02.2014. Made: 13.02.2014. Coming into force: 22.02.2014. Effect: None. Territorial extent & classification: E. Local. - Available at http://www.legislation.gov.uk/uksi/2014/351/contents/made Non-print

The M62 Motorway (Junction 23 to Junction 24) (Temporary Restriction and Prohibition of Traffic) Order 2014 No. 2014/2348. - Enabling power: Road Traffic Regulation Act 1984, s. 14 (1) (a). - Issued: 04.09.2014. Made: 28.08.2014. Coming into force: 10.09.2014. Effect: None. Territorial extent & classification: E. Local. - Available at http://www.legislation.gov.uk/uksi/2014/2348/contents/made Non-print

The M62 Motorway (Junction 24) (Temporary Prohibition of Traffic) Order 2014 No. 2014/1179. - Enabling power: Road Traffic Regulation Act 1984, s. 14 (1) (a). - Issued: 06.05.2014. Made: 24.04.2014. Coming into force: 05.05.2014. Effect: None. Territorial extent & classification: E. Local. - Available at http://www.legislation.gov.uk/uksi/2014/1179/contents/made Non-print

The M62 Motorway (Junction 24) (Temporary Restriction and Prohibition of Traffic) (No.2) Order 2014 No. 2014/3170. - Enabling power: Road Traffic Regulation Act 1984, s. 14 (1) (a) & S.I. 1982/1163, s. 16 (2). - Issued: 24.11.2014. Made: 13.11.2014. Coming into force: 23.11.2014. Effect: None. Territorial extent & classification: E. Local. - Available at http://www.legislation.gov.uk/uksi/2014/3170/contents/made Non-print

The M62 Motorway (Junction 24 to Junction 25) (Temporary Restriction and Prohibition of Traffic) Order 2014 No. 2014/317. - Enabling power: Road Traffic Regulation Act 1984, s. 14 (1) (a) & S.I. 1982/1163, reg. 16 (2). - Issued: 17.02.2014. Made: 06.02.2014. Coming into force: 20.02.2014. Effect: None. Territorial extent & classification: E. Local. - Available at http://www.legislation.gov.uk/uksi/2014/317/contents/made Non-print

The M62 Motorway (Junction 25 and Junction 28) (Temporary Prohibition of Traffic) Order 2014 No. 2014/3436. - Enabling power: Road Traffic Regulation Act 1984, s. 14 (1) (a). - Issued: 10.12.2014. Made: 04.12.2014. Coming into force: 14.12.2014. Effect: None. Territorial extent & classification: E. Local. - Available at http://www.legislation.gov.uk/uksi/2014/3436/contents/made Non-print

The M62 Motorway (Junction 25 to Junction 26) (Temporary Prohibition of Traffic) Order 2014 No. 2014/2903. - Enabling power: Road Traffic Regulation Act 1984, s. 14 (1) (a). - Issued: 31.10.2014. Made: 09.10.2014. Coming into force: 19.10.2014. Effect: None. Territorial extent & classification: E. Local. - Available at http://www.legislation.gov.uk/uksi/2014/2903/contents/made Non-print

The M62 Motorway (Junction 25 to Junction 27) (Temporary Restriction and Prohibition of Traffic) Order 2014 No. 2014/1472. - Enabling power: Road Traffic Regulation Act 1984, s. 14 (1) (a) & S.I. 1982/1163, reg. 16 (2). - Issued: 30.05.2014. Made: 15.05.2014. Coming into force: 26.05.2014. Effect: None. Territorial extent & classification: E. Local. - Available at http://www.legislation.gov.uk/uksi/2014/1472/contents/made Non-print

The M62 Motorway (Junction 26) (Temporary Prohibition of Traffic) Order 2014 No. 2014/3171. - Enabling power: Road Traffic Regulation Act 1984, s. 14 (1) (a). - Issued: 24.11.2014. Made: 13.11.2014. Coming into force: 23.11.2014. Effect: None. Territorial extent & classification: E. Local. - Available at http://www.legislation.gov.uk/uksi/2014/3171/contents/made Non-print

The M62 Motorway (Junction 27) (Temporary Prohibition of Traffic) Order 2014 No. 2014/2686. - Enabling power: Road Traffic Regulation Act 1984, s. 14 (1) (a). - Issued: 07.10.2014. Made: 25.09.2014. Coming into force: 05.10.2014. Effect: None. Territorial extent & classification: E. Local. - Available at http://www.legislation.gov.uk/uksi/2014/2686/contents/made Non-print

The M62 Motorway (Junction 28 to Junction 29) (Temporary Prohibition of Traffic) Order 2014 No. 2014/1351. - Enabling power: Road Traffic Regulation Act 1984, s. 14 (1) (a). - Issued: 29.05.2014. Made: 15.05.2014. Coming into force: 27.05.2014. Effect: None. Territorial extent & classification: E. Local. - Available at http://www.legislation.gov.uk/uksi/2014/1351/contents/made Non-print

The M62 Motorway (Junction 28 to Junction 29) (Temporary Restriction and Prohibition of Traffic) (No.2) Order 2014 No. 2014/2170. - Enabling power: Road Traffic Regulation Act 1984, s. 14 (1) (a). - Issued: 15.08.2014. Made: 05.08.2014. Coming into force: 13.08.2014. Effect: None. Territorial extent & classification: E. Local. - Available at http://www.legislation.gov.uk/uksi/2014/2170/contents/made Non-print

The M62 Motorway (Junction 29) (Temporary Prohibition of Traffic) (No.2) Order 2014 No. 2014/3500. - Enabling power: Road Traffic Regulation Act 1984, ss. 14 (1) (a). - Issued: 19.01.2015. Made: 04.12.2014. Coming into force: 17.12.2014. Effect: None. Territorial extent & classification: E. Local. - Available at http://www.legislation.gov.uk/uksi/2014/3500/contents/made Non-print

The M62 Motorway (Junction 29) (Temporary Prohibition of Traffic) Order 2014 No. 2014/86. - Enabling power: Road Traffic Regulation Act 1984, s. 14 (1) (a). - Issued: 21.01.2014. Made: 16.01.2014. Coming into force: 30.01.2014. Effect: None. Territorial extent & classification: E. Local. - Available at http://www.legislation.gov.uk/uksi/2014/86/contents/made Non-print

The M62 Motorway (Junction 29 to Junction 28) (Temporary Restriction and Prohibition of Traffic) Order 2014 No. 2014/2988. - Enabling power: Road Traffic Regulation Act 1984, s. 14 (1) (a). - Issued: 27.10.2014. Made: 23.10.2014. Coming into force: 06.11.2014. Effect: None. Territorial extent & classification: E. Local. - Available at http://www.legislation.gov.uk/uksi/2014/2988/contents/made Non-print

The M62 Motorway (Junction 30) (Temporary Prohibition of Traffic) Order 2014 No. 2014/2501. - Enabling power: Road Traffic Regulation Act 1984, s. 14 (1) (a). - Issued: 10.09.2014. Made: 04.09.2014. Coming into force: 19.09.2014. Effect: None. Territorial extent & classification: E. Local. - Available at http://www.legislation.gov.uk/uksi/2014/2501/contents/made Non-print

The M62 Motorway (Junction 30 to Junction 32) (Temporary Restriction and Prohibition of Traffic) Order 2014 No. 2014/3016. - Enabling power: Road Traffic Regulation Act 1984, s. 14 (1) (a) (7) & S.I. 1982/1163, reg. 16 (2). - Issued: 04.11.2014. Made: 30.10.2014. Coming into force: 11.11.2014. Effect: None. Territorial extent & classification: E. Local. - Available at http://www.legislation.gov.uk/uksi/2014/3016/contents/made Non-print

The M62 Motorway (Junction 32 to Junction 33) (Temporary Prohibition of Traffic) Order 2014 No. 2014/2690. - Enabling power: Road Traffic Regulation Act 1984, s. 14 (1) (a). - Issued: 09.10.2014. Made: 25.09.2014. Coming into force: 05.10.2014. Effect: None. Territorial extent & classification: E. Local. - Available at http://www.legislation.gov.uk/uksi/2014/2690/contents/made Non-print

The M62 Motorway (Junction 33) (Temporary Prohibition of Traffic) Order 2014 No. 2014/966. - Enabling power: Road Traffic Regulation Act 1984, s. 14 (1) (a). - Issued: 31.03.2014. Made: 13.03.2014. Coming into force: 23.03.2014. Effect: None. Territorial extent & classification: E. Local. - Available at http://www.legislation.gov.uk/uksi/2014/966/contents/made Non-print

The M62 Motorway (Junction 34 to Junction 33) (Temporary Restriction and Prohibition of Traffic) Order 2014 No. 2014/2064. - Enabling power: Road Traffic Regulation Act 1984, ss. 14 (1) (a) & S.I. 1982/1163, reg. 16 (2). - Issued: 05.08.2014. Made: 17.07.2014. Coming into force: 27.07.2014. Effect: None. Territorial extent & classification: E. Local. - Available at http://www.legislation.gov.uk/uksi/2014/2064/contents/made Non-print

The M62 Motorway (Junction 34 to Junction 35) (Temporary Restriction and Prohibition of Traffic) Order 2014 No. 2014/2004. - Enabling power: Road Traffic Regulation Act 1984, s. 14 (1) (a) & S.I. 1982/1163, reg. 16 (2). - Issued: 30.07.2014. Made: 10.07.2014. Coming into force: 18.07.2014. Effect: None. Territorial extent & classification: E. Local. - Available at http://www.legislation.gov.uk/uksi/2014/2004/contents/made Non-print

The M62 Motorway (Junction 34 to Junction 36) (Temporary Prohibition of Traffic) Order 2014 No. 2014/2322. - Enabling power: Road Traffic Regulation Act 1984, s. 14 (1) (a). - Issued: 01.09.2014. Made: 28.08.2014. Coming into force: 09.09.2014. Effect: None. Territorial extent & classification: E. Local. - Available at http://www.legislation.gov.uk/uksi/2014/2322/contents/made Non-print

The M62 Motorway (Junction 34, Whitley) (Temporary Prohibition of Traffic) Order 2014 No. 2014/2472. - Enabling power: Road Traffic Regulation Act 1984, s. 14 (1) (a). - Issued: 15.09.2014. Made: 04.09.2014. Coming into force: 14.09.2014. Effect: None. Territorial extent & classification: E. Local. - Available at http://www.legislation.gov.uk/uksi/2014/2472/contents/made Non-print

The M62 Motorway (Junction 37) (No.4) (Temporary Prohibition of Traffic) Order 2014 No. 2014/3484. - Enabling power: Road Traffic Regulation Act 1984, s. 14 (1) (a). - Issued: 02.01.2015. Made: 29.12.2014. Coming into force: 11.01.2015. Effect: None. Territorial extent & classification: E. Local. - Available at http://www.legislation.gov.uk/uksi/2014/3484/contents/made Non-print

The M62 Motorway (Junction 37) (Temporary Prohibition of Traffic) (No.2) Order 2014 No. 2014/1035. - Enabling power: Road Traffic Regulation Act 1984, s. 14 (1) (a). - Issued: 17.04.2014. Made: 03.04.2014. Coming into force: 13.04.2014. Effect: None. Territorial extent & classification: E. Local. - Available at http://www.legislation.gov.uk/uksi/2014/1035/contents/made Non-print

The M62 Motorway (Junction 37) (Temporary Prohibition of Traffic) (No.3) Order 2014 No. 2014/1854. - Enabling power: Road Traffic Regulation Act 1984, s. 14 (1) (a). - Issued: 16.07.2014. Made: 26.06.2014. Coming into force: 06.07.2014. Effect: None. Territorial extent & classification: E. Local. - Available at http://www.legislation.gov.uk/uksi/2014/1854/contents/made Non-print

The M62 Motorway (Junction 37) (Temporary Prohibition of Traffic) Order 2014 No. 2014/769. - Enabling power: Road Traffic Regulation Act 1984, s. 14 (1) (a). - Issued: 07.03.2014. Made: 27.02.2014. Coming into force: 09.03.2014. Effect: None. Territorial extent & classification: E. Local. - Available at http://www.legislation.gov.uk/uksi/2014/769/contents/made Non-print

The M62 Motorway (Junction 37 to Junction 36) (Temporary Prohibition of Traffic) Order 2014 No. 2014/2301. - Enabling power: Road Traffic Regulation Act 1984, s. 14 (1) (a). - Issued: 27.08.2014. Made: 21.08.2014. Coming into force: 04.09.2014. Effect: None. Territorial extent & classification: E. Local. - Available at http://www.legislation.gov.uk/uksi/2014/2301/contents/made Non-print

The M62 Motorway (Junction 38 to Junction 37) (Temporary Prohibition of Traffic) Order 2014 No. 2014/2255. - Enabling power: Road Traffic Regulation Act 1984, ss. 14 (1) (a). - Issued: 22.08.2014. Made: 14.08.2014. Coming into force: 25.08.2014. Effect: None. Territorial extent & classification: E. Local. - Available at http://www.legislation.gov.uk/uksi/2014/2255/contents/made Non-print

The M62 Motorway (Junction 6-8 Eastbound and Westbound Carriageways) (Temporary Prohibition and Restriction of Traffic) Order 2014 No. 2014/3563. - Enabling power: Road Traffic Regulation Act 1984, s. 14 (1) (a) (7). - Issued: 23.06.2015. Made: 25.06.2014. Coming into force: 14.07.2014. Effect: None. Territorial extent & classification: E. Local. - Replaces withdrawn SI 2014/1861. - Available at http://www.legislation.gov.uk/uksi/2014/3563/contents/made Non-print

The M62 Motorway (Junctions 7- 6 Westbound Carriageway and Junction 7 Westbound Entry Slip Road) (Temporary Prohibition of Traffic) Order 2014 No. 2014/2550. - Enabling power: Road Traffic Regulation Act 1984, s. 14 (1) (a). - Issued: 23.09.2014. Made: 10.09.2014. Coming into force: 28.09.2014. Effect: None. Territorial extent & classification: E. Local. - Available at http://www.legislation.gov.uk/uksi/2014/2550/contents/made Non-print

The M62 Motorway (Junctions 8-9 Eastbound Carriageway and Eastbound and Westbound Slip Roads (Temporary Prohibition of Traffic) Order 2014 No. 2014/2325. - Enabling power: Road Traffic Regulation Act 1984, s. 14 (1) (a). - Issued: 02.09.2014. Made: 27.08.2014. Coming into force: 12.09.2014. Effect: None. Territorial extent & classification: E. Local. - Available at http://www.legislation.gov.uk/uksi/2014/2325/contents/made Non-print

The M62 Motorway (Junctions 11 - 12 Eastbound and Westbound Carriageways and Slip Roads) (Temporary Prohibition and Restriction of Traffic) Order 2013 Amendment Order 2014 No. 2014/127. - Enabling power: Road Traffic Regulation Act 1984, s. 14 (1) (a). - Issued: 24.01.2014. Made: 20.01.2014. Coming into force: 24.01.2014. Effect: S.I. 2013/2608 amended. Territorial extent & classification: E. Local. - Available at http://www.legislation.gov.uk/uksi/2014/127/contents/made Non-print

The M62 Motorway (Junctions 20-21 Eastbound and Westbound Carriageways and Slip Roads) (Temporary Prohibition and Restriction of Traffic) Order 2014 No. 2014/1145. - Enabling power: Road Traffic Regulation Act 1984, s. 14 (1) (a) (7). - Issued: 06.05.2014. Made: 11.02.2014. Coming into force: 13.02.2014. Effect: None. Territorial extent & classification: E. Local. - Available at http://www.legislation.gov.uk/uksi/2014/1145/contents/made Non-print

The M62 Motorway (Langham Interchange) (Temporary Prohibition of Traffic) Order 2014 No. 2014/154. - Enabling power: Road Traffic Regulation Act 1984, s. 14 (1) (a). - Issued: 30.01.2014. Made: 23.01.2014. Coming into force: 02.02.2014. Effect: None. Territorial extent & classification: E. Local. - Available at http://www.legislation.gov.uk/uksi/2014/154/contents/made Non-print

The M62 Motorway (Langham Interchange) (Temporary Restriction and Prohibition of Traffic) (No.2) Order 2014 No. 2014/655. - Enabling power: Road Traffic Regulation Act 1984, s. 14 (1) (a). - Issued: 04.03.2014. Made: 20.02.2014. Coming into force: 28.02.2014. Effect: None. Territorial extent & classification: E. Local. - Available at http://www.legislation.gov.uk/uksi/2014/655/contents/made Non-print

The M62 Motorway (Langham Interchange) (Temporary Restriction and Prohibition of Traffic) Order 2014 No. 2014/155. - Enabling power: Road Traffic Regulation Act 1984, s. 14 (1) (a). - Issued: 30.01.2014. Made: 23.01.2014. Coming into force: 02.02.2014. Effect: None. Territorial extent & classification: E. Local. - Available at http://www.legislation.gov.uk/uksi/2014/155/contents/made Non-print

The M62 Motorway (Tour de France) (Temporary Prohibition of Traffic) Order 2014 No. 2014/1852. - Enabling power: Road Traffic Regulation Act 1984, s. 16A (2) (a). - Issued: 16.07.2014. Made: 26.07.2014. Coming into force: 05.07.2014. Effect: None. Territorial extent & classification: E. Local. - Available at http://www.legislation.gov.uk/uksi/2014/1852/contents/made Non-print

The M65 Motorway (Junction 4 Westbound Entry Slip Road) (Temporary Prohibition of Traffic) Order 2014 No. 2014/3029. - Enabling power: Road Traffic Regulation Act 1984, s. 14 (1) (a). - Issued: 12.11.2014. Made: 29.10.2014. Coming into force: 16.11.2014. Effect: None. Territorial extent & classification: E. Local. - Available at http://www.legislation.gov.uk/uksi/2014/3029/contents/made Non-print

The M65 Motorway (Junction 5 Eastbound and Westbound Entry and Exit Slip Roads) (Temporary Prohibition of Traffic) Order 2014 No. 2014/3482. - Enabling power: Road Traffic Regulation Act 1984, s. 14 (1) (a). - Issued: 24.12.2014. Made: 18.12.2014. Coming into force: 08.01.2015. Effect: None. Territorial extent & classification: E. Local. - Available at http://www.legislation.gov.uk/uksi/2014/3482/contents/made Non-print

The M65 Motorway (Junction 8 Eastbound and Westbound Exit and Entry Slip Roads) (Temporary Prohibition of Traffic) Order 2014 No. 2014/3548. - Enabling power: Road Traffic Regulation Act 1984, ss. 14 (1) (a). - Issued: 23.01.2015. Made: 31.12.2014. Coming into force: 18.01.2015. Effect: None. Territorial extent & classification: E. Local. - Available at http://www.legislation.gov.uk/uksi/2014/3548/contents/made Non-print

ROAD TRAFFIC: TRAFFIC REGULATION

The M65 Motorway (Junctions 3-7 Eastbound and Westbound Carriageways and Slip Roads) (Temporary Prohibition of Traffic) Order 2014 No. 2014/2535. - Enabling power: Road Traffic Regulation Act 1984, s. 14 (1) (a). - Issued: 18.09.2014. Made: 11.09.2014. Coming into force: 01.10.2014. Effect: None. Territorial extent & classification: E. Local. - Available at http://www.legislation.gov.uk/uksi/2014/2535/contents/made Non-print

The M65 Motorway (Junctions 9-10 Eastbound and Westbound Carriageways and Slip Roads) (Temporary Prohibition of Traffic) Order 2014 No. 2014/1148. - Enabling power: Road Traffic Regulation Act 1984, s. 14 (1) (a). - Issued: 06.05.2014. Made: 13.02.2014. Coming into force: 16.02.2014. Effect: None. Territorial extent & classification: E. Local. - Available at http://www.legislation.gov.uk/uksi/2014/1148/contents/made Non-print

The M66 Motorway (Junction 2 - A56 Northbound Carriageway and Junction 2 Northbound Entry Slip Road) (Temporary Prohibition of Traffic) Order 2014 No. 2014/1693. - Enabling power: Road Traffic Regulation Act 1984, s. 14 (1) (a). - Issued: 02.07.2014. Made: 11.06.2014. Coming into force: 15.06.2014. Effect: None. Territorial extent & classification: E. Local. - Available at http://www.legislation.gov.uk/uksi/2014/1693/contents/made Non-print

The M66 Motorway (Junction 4, Northbound Carriageway) (Simister Island) (Temporary Prohibition of Traffic) Order 2014 No. 2014/1487. - Enabling power: Road Traffic Regulation Act 1984, s. 14 (1) (a). - Issued: 09.06.2014. Made: 21.05.2014. Coming into force: 26.05.2014. Effect: None. Territorial extent & classification: E. Local. - Available at http://www.legislation.gov.uk/uksi/2014/1487/contents/made Non-print

The M66 Motorway (Junction 18 Southbound Dedicated Link Road to the M62 Eastbound) (Temporary Prohibition of Traffic) Order 2014 No. 2014/2223. - Enabling power: Road Traffic Regulation Act 1984, ss. 14 (1) (a). - Issued: 22.08.2014. Made: 14.08.2014. Coming into force: 20.08.2014. Effect: None. Territorial extent & classification: E. Local. - Available at http://www.legislation.gov.uk/uksi/2014/2223/contents/made Non-print

The M66 Motorway (Junctions 1-2 Northbound and Southbound Carriageways and Slip Roads) (Temporary Prohibition of Traffic) Order 2014 No. 2014/1149. - Enabling power: Road Traffic Regulation Act 1984, s. 14 (1) (a). - Issued: 06.05.2014. Made: 12.02.2014. Coming into force: 16.02.2014. Effect: None. Territorial extent & classification: E. Local. - Available at http://www.legislation.gov.uk/uksi/2014/1149/contents/made Non-print

The M67 Motorway (Junction 3 Eastbound Entry and Westbound Exit Slip Roads) (Temporary Prohibition of Traffic) Order 2014 No. 2014/3396. - Enabling power: Road Traffic Regulation Act 1984, s. 14 (1) (a). - Issued: 25.11.2014. Made: 11.11.2014. Coming into force: 30.11.2014. Effect: None. Territorial extent & classification: E. Local. - Available at http://www.legislation.gov.uk/uksi/2014/3396/contents/made Non-print

The M67 Motorway (Junctions 0-4 Eastbound and Westbound Carriageways and Slip Roads) (Temporary Prohibition of Traffic) Order 2014 No. 2014/2598. - Enabling power: Road Traffic Regulation Act 1984, s. 14 (1) (a). - Issued: 26.09.2014. Made: 16.09.2014. Coming into force: 02.10.2014. Effect: None. Territorial extent & classification: E. Local. - Available at http://www.legislation.gov.uk/uksi/2014/2598/contents/made Non-print

The M67 Motorway (Junctions 2-1A Westbound and Eastbound), the M60 (Junction 24) and the A57 Trunk Road (Temporary Prohibition of Traffic) Order 2014 No. 2014/2655. - Enabling power: Road Traffic Regulation Act 1984, ss. 14 (1) (a), 122. - Issued: 03.10.2014. Made: 17.09.2014. Coming into force: 21.09.2014. Effect: None. Territorial extent & classification: E. Local. - Available at http://www.legislation.gov.uk/uksi/2014/2655/contents/made Non-print

The M69 and M6 Motorways (M6 Junction 2, Warwickshire) (Link Road) (Temporary Prohibition of Traffic) Order 2014 No. 2014/278. - Enabling power: Road Traffic Regulation Act 1984, s. 14 (1) (a). - Issued: 14.02.2014. Made: 03.02.2014. Coming into force: 10.02.2014. Effect: None. Territorial extent & classification: E. Local. - Available at http://www.legislation.gov.uk/uksi/2014/278/contents/made Non-print

The M69 and M6 Motorways (South of Hinckley) (Temporary Prohibition of Traffic) Order 2014 No. 2014/1020. - Enabling power: Road Traffic Regulation Act 1984, s. 14 (1) (a). - Issued: 17.04.2014. Made: 21.03.2014. Coming into force: 28.03.2014. Effect: None. Territorial extent & classification: E. Local. - Available at http://www.legislation.gov.uk/uksi/2014/1020/contents/made Non-print

The M69 Motorway (Hinckley, Leicestershire) (Temporary Restriction and Prohibition of Traffic) Order 2014 No. 2014/716. - Enabling power: Road Traffic Regulation Act 1984, s. 14 (1) (a) & S.I. 1982/1163, reg. 16 (2). - Issued: 10.03.2014. Made: 24.02.2014. Coming into force: 03.03.2014. Effect: None. Territorial extent & classification: E. Local. - Available at http://www.legislation.gov.uk/uksi/2014/716/contents/made Non-print

The M69 Motorway (Junction 1) (Temporary Prohibition of Traffic) Order 2014 No. 2014/1727. - Enabling power: Road Traffic Regulation Act 1984, s. 14 (1) (a). - Issued: 03.07.2014. Made: 20.06.2014. Coming into force: 27.06.2014. Effect: None. Territorial extent & classification: E. Local. - Available at http://www.legislation.gov.uk/uksi/2014/1727/contents/made Non-print

The M69 Motorway (Junction 1, West Midlands) (Temporary Prohibition of Traffic) Order 2014 No. 2014/1406. - Enabling power: Road Traffic Regulation Act 1984, s. 14 (1) (a). - Issued: 04.06.2014. Made: 06.05.2014. Coming into force: 13.05.2014. Effect: None. Territorial extent & classification: E. Local. - Available at http://www.legislation.gov.uk/uksi/2014/1406/contents/made Non-print

The M69 Motorway (M6 Junction 2) (Link Road) (Temporary Prohibition of Traffic) Order 2014 No. 2014/706. - Enabling power: Road Traffic Regulation Act 1984, s. 14 (1) (a). - Issued: 10.03.2014. Made: 24.02.2014. Coming into force: 03.03.2014. Effect: None. Territorial extent & classification: E. Local. - Available at http://www.legislation.gov.uk/uksi/2014/706/contents/made Non-print

The M69 Motorway (West of M1 Junction 21, Leicestershire) (Temporary Restriction of Traffic) Order 2014 No. 2014/2261. - Enabling power: Road Traffic Regulation Act 1984, s. 14 (1) (a). - Issued: 29.08.2014. Made: 18.08.2014. Coming into force: 25.08.2014. Effect: None. Territorial extent & classification: E. Local. - Available at http://www.legislation.gov.uk/uksi/2014/2261/contents/made Non-print

The M180 Motorway and the M18 Motorway (North Ings to Broughton) (Temporary Restriction and Prohibition of Traffic) Order 2014 No. 2014/2089. - Enabling power: Road Traffic Regulation Act 1984, s. 14 (1) (a). - Issued: 06.08.2014. Made: 17.07.2014. Coming into force: 31.07.2014. Effect: None. Territorial extent & classification: E. Local. - Available at http://www.legislation.gov.uk/uksi/2014/2089/contents/made Non-print

The M180 Motorway (Junction 3 to Junction 4) (Temporary Restriction and Prohibition of Traffic) Order 2014 No. 2014/3013. - Enabling power: Road Traffic Regulation Act 1984, s. 14 (1) (a) (7) & S.I. 1982/1163, reg. 16 (2). - Issued: 04.11.2014. Made: 30.10.2014. Coming into force: 11.11.2014. Effect: None. Territorial extent & classification: E. Local. - Available at http://www.legislation.gov.uk/uksi/2014/3013/contents/made Non-print

The M180 Motorway (Junction 4) (Temporary Prohibition of Traffic) Order 2014 No. 2014/2289. - Enabling power: Road Traffic Regulation Act 1984, s. 14 (1) (a). - Issued: 27.08.2014. Made: 21.08.2014. Coming into force: 31.08.2014. Effect: None. Territorial extent & classification: E. Local. - Available at http://www.legislation.gov.uk/uksi/2014/2289/contents/made Non-print

The M181 Motorway (Midmoor to Frodingham) (Temporary Restriction and Prohibition of Traffic) Order 2014 No. 2014/2955. - Enabling power: Road Traffic Regulation Act 1984, s. 14 (1) (a). - Issued: 27.10.2014. Made: 23.10.2014. Coming into force: 31.10.2014. Effect: None. Territorial extent & classification: E. Local. - Available at http://www.legislation.gov.uk/uksi/2014/2955/contents/made Non-print

The M271 Motorway (Junction 1 - Redbridge Roundabout) (Temporary Prohibition of Traffic) Order 2014 No. 2014/2110. - Enabling power: Road Traffic Regulation Act 1984, s. 14 (1) (a). - Issued: 07.08.2014. Made: 28.07.2014. Coming into force: 16.08.2014. Effect: None. Territorial extent & classification: E. Local. - Available at http://www.legislation.gov.uk/uksi/2014/2110/contents/made Non-print

The M602 Motorway (Junctions 2 - 3 Eastbound and Westbound Carriageways and Slip Roads) (Temporary Prohibition of Traffic) Order 2014 No. 2014/1381. - Enabling power: Road Traffic Regulation Act 1984, s. 14 (1) (a). - Issued: 02.06.2014. Made: 15.05.2014. Coming into force: 18.05.2014. Effect: None. Territorial extent & classification: E. Local. - Available at http://www.legislation.gov.uk/uksi/2014/1381/contents/made Non-print

The M606 Motorway (Junction 1) (Temporary Prohibition of Traffic) Order 2014 No. 2014/68. - Enabling power: Road Traffic Regulation Act 1984, s. 14 (1) (a). - Issued: 20.01.2014. Made: 09.01.2014. Coming into force: 18.01.2014. Effect: None. Territorial extent & classification: E. Local. - Available at http://www.legislation.gov.uk/uksi/2014/68/contents/made Non-print

The M606 Motorway (Junction 1 to Junction 3) (Temporary Prohibition of Traffic) Order 2014 No. 2014/2806. - Enabling power: Road Traffic Regulation Act 1984, s. 14 (1) (a). - Issued: 14.10.2014. Made: 09.10.2014. Coming into force: 19.10.2014. Effect: None. Territorial extent & classification: E. Local. - Available at http://www.legislation.gov.uk/uksi/2014/2806/contents/made Non-print

The M621 Motorway (Gildersome Interchange to Junction 1) (Temporary Prohibition of Traffic) Order 2014 No. 2014/766. - Enabling power: Road Traffic Regulation Act 1984, s. 14 (1) (a). - Issued: 11.03.2014. Made: 06.03.2014. Coming into force: 13.03.2014. Effect: None. Territorial extent & classification: E. Local. - Available at http://www.legislation.gov.uk/uksi/2014/766/contents/made Non-print

The M621 Motorway (Gildersome to Stourton) (Temporary Prohibition of Traffic) (No.2) Order 2014 No. 2014/2769. - Enabling power: Road Traffic Regulation Act 1984, s. 14 (1) (a). - Issued: 13.10.2014. Made: 02.10.2014. Coming into force: 10.10.2014. Effect: None. Territorial extent & classification: E. Local. - Available at http://www.legislation.gov.uk/uksi/2014/2769/contents/made Non-print

The M621 Motorway (Gildersome to Stourton) (Temporary Restriction and Prohibition of Traffic) Order 2014 No. 2014/83. - Enabling power: Road Traffic Regulation Act 1984, s. 14 (1) (a) & S.I. 1982/1163, reg. 16 (2). - issued: 21.01.2014. Made: 16.01.2014. Coming into force: 21.01.2014. Effect: None. Territorial extent & classification: E. Local. - Available at http://www.legislation.gov.uk/uksi/2014/83/contents/made Non-print

The M621 Motorway (Junction 1 and Junction 6) (Temporary Prohibition of Traffic) Order 2014 No. 2014/2987. - Enabling power: Road Traffic Regulation Act 1984, s. 14 (1) (a). - Issued: 04.11.2014. Made: 30.10.2014. Coming into force: 07.11.2014. Effect: None. Territorial extent & classification: E. Local. - Available at http://www.legislation.gov.uk/uksi/2014/2987/contents/made Non-print

The M621 Motorway (Junction 1) (Temporary Prohibition of Traffic) (No.2) Order 2014 No. 2014/1985. - Enabling power: Road Traffic Regulation Act 1984, s. 14 (1) (a). - Issued: 21.07.2014. Made: 10.07.2014. Coming into force: 21.07.2014. Effect: None. Territorial extent & classification: E. Local. - Available at http://www.legislation.gov.uk/uksi/2014/1985/contents/made Non-print

The M621 Motorway (Junction 1) (Temporary Prohibition of Traffic) Order 2014 No. 2014/676. - Enabling power: Road Traffic Regulation Act 1984, s. 14 (1) (a). - Issued: 28.02.2014. Made: 20.02.2014. Coming into force: 02.03.2014. Effect: None. Territorial extent & classification: E. Local. - Available at http://www.legislation.gov.uk/uksi/2014/676/contents/made Non-print

The M621 Motorway (Junction 2) (Temporary Prohibition of Traffic) (No. 2) Order 2014 No. 2014/3550. - Enabling power: Road Traffic Regulation Act 1984, s. 14 (1) (a). - Issued: 11.02.2015. Made: 29.12.2014. Coming into force: 12.01.2015. Effect: None. Territorial extent & classification: E. Local. - Available at http://www.legislation.gov.uk/uksi/2014/3550/contents/made Non-print

The M621 Motorway (Junction 2) (Temporary Prohibition of Traffic) Order 2014 No. 2014/777. - Enabling power: Road Traffic Regulation Act 1984, s. 14 (1) (a). - Issued: 07.03.2014. Made: 27.02.2014. Coming into force: 10.03.2014. Effect: None. Territorial extent & classification: E. Local. - Available at http://www.legislation.gov.uk/uksi/2014/777/contents/made Non-print

The M621 Motorway (Junction 4) (Temporary Prohibition of Traffic) Order 2014 No. 2014/990. - Enabling power: Road Traffic Regulation Act 1984, s. 14 (1) (a). - Issued: 10.04.2014. Made: 27.03.2014. Coming into force: 05.04.2014. Effect: None. Territorial extent & classification: E. Local. - Available at http://www.legislation.gov.uk/uksi/2014/990/contents/made Non-print

The M621 Motorway (Junction 7, Stourton) (Temporary Prohibition of Traffic) Order 2014 No. 2014/1350. - Enabling power: Road Traffic Regulation Act 1984, s. 14 (1) (a). - Issued: 29.05.2014. Made: 15.05.2014. Coming into force: 27.05.2014. Effect: None. Territorial extent & classification: E. Local. - Available at http://www.legislation.gov.uk/uksi/2014/1350/contents/made Non-print

The A2 Trunk Road (Ebbsfleet Interchange) (Temporary Prohibition of Traffic) Order 2014 No. 2014/3470. - Enabling power: Road Traffic Regulation Act 1984, s. 14 (1) (a). - Issued: 18.12.2014. Made: 15.12.2014. Coming into force: 03.02.2015. Effect: None. Territorial extent & classification: E. Local. - Available at http://www.legislation.gov.uk/uksi/2014/3470/contents/made Non-print

The A5 Trunk Road (Markyate, Hertfordshire) Northbound Lay-by (Temporary Prohibition of Traffic) Order 2014 No. 2014/2911. - Enabling power: Road Traffic Regulation Act 1984, s. 14 (1) (a). - Issued: 24.10.2014. Made: 20.10.2014. Coming into force: 27.10.2014. Effect: None. Territorial extent & classification: E. Local. - Available at http://www.legislation.gov.uk/uksi/2014/2911/contents/made Non-print

The M1 Motorway (Junction 42 to Junction 47) (Temporary Prohibition of Traffic) (No.2) Order 2014 No. 2014/3437. - Enabling power: Road Traffic Regulation Act 1984, s. 14 (1) (a). - Issued: 10.12.2014. Made: 04.12.2014. Coming into force: 14.12.2014. Effect: None. Territorial extent & classification: E. Local. - Available at http://www.legislation.gov.uk/uksi/2014/3437/contents/made Non-print

The M6 Motorway (Junctions 31-33 Northbound and Southbound) and the M55 (Junction 1 Eastbound) Carriageways, Slip and Link Roads (Temporary Prohibition and Restriction of Traffic) Order 2014 No. 2014/3353. - Enabling power: Road Traffic Regulation Act 1984, s. 14 (1) (a) (7). - Issued: 09.12.2014. Made: 13.05.2014. Coming into force: 16.05.2014. Effect: None. Territorial extent & classification: E. Local. - Available at http://www.legislation.gov.uk/uksi/2014/3353/contents/made Non-print

The M40 Motorway (Junctions 1 to 4) (Temporary Prohibition of Traffic) (No.2) Order 2014 No. 2014/2513. - Enabling power: Road Traffic Regulation Act 1984, s. 14 (1) (a). - Issued: 17.09.2014. Made: 15.09.2014. Coming into force: 22.09.2014. Effect: None. Territorial extent & classification: E. Local. - Available at http://www.legislation.gov.uk/uksi/2014/2513/contents/made Non-print

Road traffic, England

The A6055 Trunk Road (A1(M) Junction 51, Leeming Interchange) (Trunking) Order 2014 No. 2014/1708. - Enabling power: Highways Act 1980, ss. 10, 41. - Issued: 08.07.2014. Made: 09.06.2014. Coming into force: 30.06.2014. Effect: None. Territorial extent & classification: E. Local. - 4p., 1 plan: 30 cm. - 978-0-11-111746-0 £4.25

The Civil Enforcement of Parking Contraventions Designation Order 2014 No. 2014/3205. - Enabling power: Traffic Management Act 2004, s. 89 (3), sch. 8, para. 8 (1), sch. 10, para. 3 (1). - Issued: 08.12.2014. Made: 02.12.2014. Laid: 08.12.2014. Coming into force: 29.12.2014, for arts 1, 2, 3; 19.01.2015, for art. 4. Effect: S.I. 2004/2424 revoked. Territorial extent & classification: E. General. - 8p.: 30 cm. - 978-0-11-112454-3 £4.25

The M275 and M27 Motorway (Speed Limit and Bus Lane) Regulations 2014 No. 2014/790. - Enabling power: Road Traffic Regulation Act 1984, s. 17 (2) (3). - Issued: 27.03.2014. Made: 19.03.2014. Laid: 24.03.2014. Coming into force: 14.04.2014. Effect: S.I. 2005/1999 revoked. Territorial extent & classification: E. Local. - Revoked by SI 2015/405 (ISBN 9780111130926). - 8p.: 30 cm. - 978-0-11-111261-8 £4.00

The Motor Vehicles (Variation of Speed Limits) (England and Wales) Regulations 2014 No. 2014/3552. - Enabling power: Road Traffic Regulation Act 1984, s. 86 (2). - Issued: 16.02.2015. Made: 30.11.2014. Laid: 03.12.2014. Coming into force: 06.04.2015. Effect: 1984 c.27 amended. Territorial extent & classification: E/W. General. - Supersedes S.I. draft (ISBN 9780111124444) issued 08/12/14. - 2p.: 30 cm. - 978-0-11-112920-3 £4.25

The Motor Vehicles (Variation of Speed Limits) (England and Wales) Regulations 2014 No. 2014/Un-numbered. - Enabling power: Road Traffic Regulation Act 1984, s. 86 (2). - Issued: 08.12.2014. Made: 30.11.2014. Laid: 03.12.2014. Coming into force: in accord. with reg. 1. Effect: 1984 c.27 amended. Territorial extent & classification: E/W. General. - Superseded by S.I. 2014/3552 (ISBN 9780111129203) issued 16/02/15. - 2p.: 30 cm. - 978-0-11-112444-4 £4.25

The Road User Charging Schemes (Penalty Charges, Adjudication and Enforcement) (England) (Amendment) Regulations 2014 No. 2014/81. - Enabling power: Transport Act 2000, ss. 163 (2), 173 (1) to (3), 197 (1). - Issued: 23.01.2014. Made: 15.01.2014. Laid: 21.01.2014. Coming into force: 14.02.2014. Effect: S.I. 2013/1783 amended. Territorial extent & classification: E. General. - This Statutory Instrument has been printed to correct errors in S.I. 2013/1783 (ISBN 9780111101872) and is being issued free of charge to all known recipients of that Statutory Instrument. - 4p.: 30 cm. - 978-0-11-110855-0 £4.00

Road traffic, England and Wales

The Drug Driving (Specified Limits) (England and Wales) Regulations 2014 No. 2014/2868. - Enabling power: Road Traffic Act 1988, s. 5A. - Issued: 03.11.2014. Made: 24.10.2014. Coming into force: 02.03.2015. Effect: None. Territorial extent & classification: E/W. General. - Supersedes draft S.I. (ISBN 9780111117422) issued 07.07.2014. - 2p.: 30 cm. - 978-0-11-112258-7 £4.25

Road traffic, Wales

The Civil Enforcement of Bus Lane and Moving Traffic Contraventions (City and Count of Cardiff) (Wales) Order 2014 No. 2014/2725 (W.276). - Enabling power: Traffic Management Act 2004, sch. 8, paras 9 (1), 10 (1). - Issued: 22.10.2014. Made: 08.10.2014. Laid before the National Assembly for Wales: 14.10.2014. Coming into force: 10.11.2014. Effect: None. Territorial extent & classification: W. General. - In English and Welsh. Welsh title: Gorchymyn Dynodi Gorfodi Sifil ar Dramgwyddau Lonydd Bysiau a Traffig sy'n Symud (Dinas a Sir Caerdydd) 2014. - 4p.: 30 cm. - 978-0-348-11005-0 £4.25

The Civil Enforcement of Parking Contraventions (City and County of Cardiff) Designation (Amendment) Order 2014 No. 2014/2722 (W.275). - Enabling power: Traffic Management Act 2004, sch. 10 para. 3 (1). - Issued: 22.10.2014. Made: 08.10.2014. Laid before the National Assembly for Wales: 14.11.2014. Coming into force: 07.10.2014. Effect: S.I. 2010/1461 (W.133) amended. Territorial extent & classification: W. General. - In English and Welsh. Welsh title: Gorchymyn Dynodi Gorfodi Sifil ar Dramgwyddau Parcio (Dinas a Sir Caerdydd) (Diwygio) 2014. - 4p.: 30 cm. - 978-0-348-11004-3 £4.25

The Disabled Persons (Badges for Motor Vehicles) (Wales) (Amendment) Regulations 2014 No. 2014/3082 (W.306). - Enabling power: Chronically Sick and Disabled Persons Act 1970, s. 21. - Issued: 28.11.2014. Made: 18.11.2014. Laid before the National Assembly for Wales: 20.11.2014. Coming into force: 17.12.2014. Effect: S.I. 2000/1786 (W.123) amended. Territorial extent & classification: W. General. - In English and Welsh. Welsh title: Rheoliadau Personau Anabl (Bathodynnau ar gyfer Cerbydau Modur) (Cymru) (Diwygio) 2014. - 8p.: 30 cm. - 978-0-348-11017-3 £4.25

The Removal and Disposal of Vehicles (Amendment) (Wales) Regulations 2014 No. 2014/1388 (W.141). - Enabling power: Road Traffic Regulation Act 1984, s. 99 (1) (2). - Issued: 12.06.2014. Made: 30.05.2014. Laid before the National Assembly for Wales: 03.06.2014. Coming into force: 27.06.2014. Effect: S.I. 1986/183 amended. Territorial extent & classification: W. General. - In English and Welsh. Welsh title: Rheoliadau Symud Ymaith a Gwaredu Cerbydau (Diwygio) (Cymru) 2014. - 4p.: 30 cm. - 978-0-348-10951-1 £4.25

Road traffic, Wales: Speed limits

The A470 and A40 Trunk Roads (Tarell Roundabout, Brecon, Powys) (40 mph Speed Limit) Order 2014 No. 2014/1503 (W.153). - Enabling power: Road Traffic Regulation Act 1984, s. 84 (1) (2)- Issued: 12.06.2014. Made: 04.06.2014. Coming into force: 06.06.2014. Effect: None. Territorial extent & classification: W. Local. - Available at http://www.legislation.gov.uk/wsi/2014/1503/contents/made. - In English and Welsh. Welsh title: Gorchymyn Cefnffyrdd yr A470 a'r A40 (Cylchfan Tarell, Aberhonddu, Powys) (Terfyn Cyflymder 40 mya) 2014 Non-print

The A470 Trunk Road (Ganllwyd, Gwynedd) (Restricted Road & 40 mph Speed Limit) Order 2014 No. 2014/1650 (W.168). - Enabling power: Road Traffic Regulation Act 1984, ss. 82 (1) (2), 83 (1), 84 (1) (2), 124, sch. 9, para. 27. - Issued: 30.06.2014. Made: 25.06.2014. Coming into force: 27.06.2014. Effect: None. Territorial extent & classification: W. Local. - Available at http://www.legislation.gov.uk/wsi/2014/1650/contents/made. - In English and Welsh. Welsh title: Gorchymyn Cefnffordd yr A470 (Y Ganllwyd, Gwynedd) (Ffordd Gyfyngedig a Therfyn Cyflymder o 40 mya) 2014 Non-print

The A470 Trunk Road (Llandinam, Powys) (30 MPH and 40 MPH Speed Limits) Order 2014 No. 2014/348 (W.37). - Enabling power: Road Traffic Regulation Act 1984, ss. 84 (1) (2), 124, sch. 9, para. 27. - Issued: 24.02.2014. Made: 11.02.2014. Coming into force: 19.02.2014. Effect: S.I. 1984/690 revoked. Territorial extent & classification: W. Local. - Available at http://www.legislation.gov.uk/wsi/2014/348/contents/made. - In English and Welsh. Welsh title: Gorchymyn Cefnffordd yr A470 (Llandinam, Powys) (Terfynau Cyflymder 30 MYA a 40 MYA) 2014 Non-print

The A470 Trunk Road (Newbridge-on-Wye, Powys) (30 mph Speed Limit) Order 2014 No. 2014/3116 (W.315). - Enabling power: Road Traffic Regulation Act 1984, ss. 84 (1) (2), 124, sch. 9, para. 27- Issued: 27.11.2014. Made: 19.11.2014. Coming into force: 20.11.2014. Effect: S.I. 1991/2847 revoked. Territorial extent & classification: W. Local. - Available at http://www.legislation.gov.uk/wsi/2014/3116/contents/made. - In English and Welsh. Welsh title: Gorchymyn Cefnffordd yr A470 (Pontnewydd ar Wy, Powys) (Terfyn Cyflymder o 30 mya) 2014 Non-print

The A483 Trunk Road (Llandybie, Carmarthenshire) (40 MPH Speed Limit) Order 2014 No. 2014/2893 (W.294). - Enabling power: Road Traffic Regulation Act 1984, ss. 84 (1) (2), 124, sch. 9, para. 27. - Issued: 05.11.2014. Made: 28.10.2014. Coming into force: 30.10.2014. Effect: S.I. 1978/1555; 2000/2664 (W.173); 2004/940 revoked. Territorial extent & classification: W. Local. - Available at http://www.legislation.gov.uk/wsi/2014/2893/contents/made. - In English and Welsh. Welsh title: Gorchymyn Cefnffordd yr A483 (Llandybïe, Sir Gaerfyrddin) (Terfyn Cyflymder o 40 MYA) 2014 Non-print

The A483 Trunk Road (Pontardulais Road, Ty-Croes, Ammanford, Carmarthenshire) (De-restriction and 40 MPH Speed Limit) Order 2014 No. 2014/1455 (W.142). - Enabling power: Road Traffic Regulation Act 1984, ss. 82 (2), 83 (1), 84 (1) (2), 124, sch. 9, para. 27. - Issued: 09.06.2014. Made: 27.05.2014. Coming into force: 29.05.2014. Effect: S.I. 2002/2664 (W.256) revoked. Territorial extent & classification: W. Local. - Available at http://www.legislation.gov.uk/wsi/2014/1455/contents/made. - In English and Welsh. Welsh title: Gorchymyn Cefnffordd yr A483 (Heol Pontarddulais, Ty-croes, Rhydaman, Sir Gaerfyrddin) (Dileu Cyfyngiad a Therfyn Cyflymder 40 MYA) 2014 Non-print

The A487 Trunk Road (Blaenporth, Ceredigion) (De-Restriction and 40 mph Speed Limit) Order 2014 No. 2014/2855 (W.291). - Enabling power: Road Traffic Regulation Act 1984, ss. 82 (2), 83 (1), 84 (1) (2). - Issued: 29.10.2014. Made: 23.10.2014. Coming into force: 30.10.2014. Effect: None. Territorial extent & classification: W. Local. - Available at http://www.legislation.gov.uk/wsi/2014/2855/contents/made. - In English and Welsh. Welsh title: Gorchymyn Cefnffordd yr A487 (Blaen-porth, Ceredigion) (Codi Cyfyngiad a Chyflwyno Terfyn Cyflymder o 40 mya) 2014 Non-print

Road traffic, Wales: Traffic regulation

The A5 & A494 Trunk Roads (Druid Junction, Druid, Denbighshire) (Temporary Traffic Prohibitions & Restrictions) Order 2014 No. 2014/72 (W.7). - Enabling power: Road Traffic Regulation Act 1984, s. 14 (1) (4). - Issued: 20.01.2014. Made: 13.01.2014. Coming into force: 20.01.2014. Effect: None. Territorial extent & classification: W. Local. - Available at http://www.legislation.gov.uk/wsi/2014/72/contents/made. - In English and Welsh. Welsh title: Gorchymyn Cefnffyrdd yr A5 a'r A494 (Cyffordd y Ddwyryd, Y Ddwyryd, Sir Ddinbych) (Gwaharddiadau a Chyfyngiadau Traffig Dros Dro) 2014 Non-print

The A5 and A494 Trunk Roads (Tyn-y-cefn, Denbighshire) (Temporary Traffic Restrictions & Prohibitions) Order 2014 No. 2014/2813 (W.285). - Enabling power: Road Traffic Regulation Act 1984, s. 14 (1) (a). - Issued: 22.10.2014. Made: 17.10.2014. Coming into force: 29.10.2014. Effect: None. Territorial extent & classification: W. Local. - http://www.legislation.gov.uk/wsi/2014/2813/contents/made Non-print

The A5 Trunk Road (Chirk Bypass, Wrexham County Borough) (Temporary Prohibition of Vehicles & Cyclists) Order 2014 No. 2014/811 (W.82). - Enabling power: Road Traffic Regulation Act 1984, s. 14 (1) (4). - Issued: 27.03.2014. Made: 24.03.2014. Coming into force: 31.03.2014. Effect: None. Territorial extent & classification: W. Local. - Available at http://www.legislation.gov.uk/wsi/2014/811/contents/made. - In English and Welsh. Welsh title: Gorchymyn Cefnffordd yr A5 (Ffordd Osgoi'r Waun, Bwrdeistref Sirol Wrecsam) (Gwahardd Cerbydau a Beicwyr Dros Dro) 2014 Non-print

The A5 Trunk Road (Druid Junction, Druid, Denbighshire) (Temporary Prohibition of High Vehicles) Order 2014 No. 2014/1289 (W.133). - Enabling power: Road Traffic Regulation Act 1984, ss. 14 (1) (4). - Issued: 22.05.2014. Made: 19.05.2014. Coming into force: 25.05.2014. Effect: None. Territorial extent & classification: W. Local. - Available at http://www.legislation.gov.uk/wsi/2014/1289/contents/made. - In English and Welsh. Welsh title: Gorchymyn Cefnffordd yr A5 (Cyffordd y Ddwyryd, y Ddwyryd, Sir Ddinbych) (Gwahardd Cerbydau Uchel Dros Dro) 2014 Non-print

The A5 Trunk Road (Froncysyllte, Wrexham to Glyndyfrdwy, Denbighshire) (Temporary Traffic Restrictions & Prohibitions) Order 2014 No. 2014/2575 (W.251). - Enabling power: Road Traffic Regulation Act 1984, s. 14 (1) (4). - Issued: 25.09.2014. Made: 26.08.2014. Coming into force: 01.09.2014. Effect: None. Territorial extent & classification: W. Local. - Available at http://www.legislation.gov.uk/wsi/2014/2575/contents/made. - In English and Welsh. Welsh title: Gorchymyn Cefnffordd yr A5 (Froncysyllte, Wrecsam i Lyndyfrdwy, Sir Ddinbych) (Cyfyngiadau a Gwaharddiadau Traffig Dros Dro) 2014 Non-print

The A5 Trunk Road (Halton Roundabout to Whitehurst Roundabout, Chirk, Wrexham County Borough) (Temporary Prohibition of Vehicles) Order 2014 No. 2014/161 (W.22). - Enabling power: Road Traffic Regulation Act 1984, s. 14 (1) (4). - Issued: 31.01.2014. Made: 27.01.2014. Coming into force: 03.02.2014. Effect: None. Territorial extent & classification: W. Local. - Available at http://www.legislation.gov.uk/wsi/2014/161/contents/made. - In English and Welsh. Welsh title: Gorchymyn Cefnffordd yr A5 (Cylchfan Halton i Gylchfan Whitehurst, Y Waun, Bwrdeistref Sirol Wrecsam) (Gwahardd Cerbydau Dros Dro) 2014 Non-print

The A5 Trunk Road (Holyhead Road, Betws-y-Coed, Conwy) (Prohibition of Waiting) Order 2014 No. 2014/2938 (W.299). - Enabling power: Road Traffic Regulation Act 1984, ss. 1 (1), 2 (1) (2), 4 (2). - Issued: 12.11.2014. Made: 31.10.2014. Coming into force: 06.11.2014. Effect: None. Territorial extent & classification: W. Local. - Available at http://www.legislation.gov.uk/wsi/2014/2938/contents/made. - In English and Welsh. Welsh title: Gorchymyn Cefnffordd yr A5 (Ffordd Caergybi, Betws-y-Coed, Conwy) (Gwahardd Aros) 2014 Non-print

The A5 Trunk Road (Llidiart y Parc to Corwen, Denbighshire) (Temporary Traffic Restrictions & Prohibitions) Order 2014 No. 2014/2542 (W.245). - Enabling power: Road Traffic Regulation Act 1984, s. 14 (1) (4). - Issued: 23.09.2014. Made: 19.09.2014. Coming into force: 29.09.2014. Effect: None. Territorial extent & classification: W. Local. - Available at http://www.legislation.gov.uk/wsi/2014/2542/contents/made. - In English and Welsh. Welsh title: Gorchymyn Cefnffordd yr A5 (Llidiart-y-parc i Gorwen, Sir Ddinbych) (Cyfyngiadau a Gwaharddiadau Traffig Dros Dro) 2014 Non-print

The A5 Trunk Road (Llidiart y Parc to Glyndyfrdwy, Denbighshire) (Temporary Traffic Restrictions and No Overtaking) Order 2014 No. 2014/146 (W.18). - Enabling power: Road Traffic Regulation Act 1984, s. 14 (1) (4). - Issued: 03.03.2014. Made: 24.01.2014. Coming into force: 03.02.2014. Effect: None. Territorial extent & classification: W. Local. - Available at http://www.legislation.gov.uk/wsi/2014/146/contents/made. - In English and Welsh. Welsh title: Gorchymyn Cefnffordd yr A5 (Llidiart-y-parc i Lyndyfrdwy, Sir Ddinbych) (Cyfyngiadau Traffig Dros Dro a Dim Goddiweddyd) 2014 Non-print

The A5 Trunk Road (Near Maerdy, Conwy) (Temporary Traffic Restrictions and No Overtaking) Order 2014 No. 2014/1493 (W.147). - Enabling power: Road Traffic Regulation Act 1984, s. 14 (1) (4). - Issued: 11.06.2014. Made: 23.05.2014. Coming into force: 02.06.2014. Effect: None. Territorial extent & classification: W. Local. - Available at http://www.legislation.gov.uk/wsi/2014/1493/contents/made. - In English and Welsh. Welsh title: Gorchymyn Cefnffordd yr A5 (Ger Maerdy, Conwy) (Cyfyngiadau Traffig Dros Dro a Dim Goddiweddyd) 2014 Non-print

The A5 Trunk Road (Pentrefoelas, Conwy) (Temporary Traffic Restrictions and No Overtaking) Order 2014 No. 2014/3164 (W.319). - Enabling power: Road Traffic Regulation Act 1984, ss. 14 (1) (4). - Issued: 03.12.2014. Made: 24.11.2014. Coming into force: 01.12.2014. Effect: None. Territorial extent & classification: W. Local. - Available at http://www.legislation.gov.uk/wsi/2014/3164/contents/made. - In English and Welsh. Welsh title: Gorchymyn Cefnffordd yr A5 (Pentrefoelas, Conwy) (Cyfyngiadau Traffig Dros Dro a Dim Goddiweddyd) 2014 Non-print

The A5 Trunk Road (South of Cerrigydrudion, Conwy) (Temporary Traffic Restrictions and No Overtaking) Order 2014 No. 2014/3165 (W.320). - Enabling power: Road Traffic Regulation Act 1984, ss. 14 (1) (4). - Issued: 03.12.2014. Made: 24.11.2014. Coming into force: 01.12.2014. Effect: None. Territorial extent & classification: W. Local. - Available at http://www.legislation.gov.uk/wsi/2014/3165/contents/made. - In English and Welsh. Welsh title: Gorchymyn Cefnffordd yr A5 (Man i'r De o Gerrigydrudion, Conwy) (Cyfyngiadau Traffig Dros Dro a Dim Goddiweddyd) 2014 Non-print

The A5 Trunk Road (West of Llangollen, Denbighshire) (Temporary Traffic Restrictions & No Overtaking) Order 2014 No. 2014/477 (W.57). - Enabling power: Road Traffic Regulation Act 1984, s. 14 (1) (4). - Issued: 07.03.2014. Made: 03.03.2014. Coming into force: 10.03.2014. Effect: None. Territorial extent & classification: W. Local. - Available at http://www.legislation.gov.uk/wsi/2014/477/contents/made. - In English and Welsh. Welsh title: Gorchymyn Cefnffordd yr A5 (Man i'r Gorllewin o Langollen, Sir Ddinbych) (Cyfyngiadau Traffig Dros Dro a Dim Goddiweddyd) 2014 Non-print

The A40 and A449 Trunk Roads (East of Glangrwyney, Powys to Raglan, Monmouthshire and Raglan to South of Ganarew, Monmouthshire) (Temporary Traffic Restrictions and Prohibitions) Order 2014 No. 2014/2466 (W.235). - Enabling power: Road Traffic Regulation Act 1984, s. 14 (1) (4) (7). - Issued: 19.09.2014. Made: 05.09.2014. Coming into force: 14.09.2014. Effect: None. Territorial extent & classification: W. Local. - Available at http://www.legislation.gov.uk/wsi/2014/2466/contents/made. - In English and Welsh. Welsh title: Gorchymyn Cefnffyrdd yr A40 a'r A449 (Man i'r Dwyrain o Langrwyne, Powys i Raglan, Sir Fynwy a Rhaglan i Fan i'r De o Ganarew, Sir Fynwy) (Cyfyngiadau a Gwaharddiadau Traffig Dros Dro) 2014 Non-print

The A40 Trunk Road (East of Llandovery, Carmarthenshire) (Temporary Traffic Restrictions and Prohibitions) Order 2014 No. 2014/2540 (W.244). - Enabling power: Road Traffic Regulation Act 1984, s. 14 (1) (4). - Issued: 23.09.2014. Made: 19.09.2014. Coming into force: 26.09.2014. Effect: None. Territorial extent & classification: W. Local. - Available at http://www.legislation.gov.uk/wsi/2014/2540/contents/made. - In English and Welsh. Welsh title: Gorchymyn Cefnffordd yr A40 (Man i'r Dwyrain o Lanymddyfri, Sir Gaerfyrddin) (Cyfyngiadau a Gwaharddiadau Traffig Dros Dro) 2014 Non-print

The A40 Trunk Road (Gibraltar Tunnels, Monmouth, Monmouthshire) (Temporary Prohibition of Vehicles & 40 mph Speed Limit) Order 2014 No. 2014/1500 (W.150). - Enabling power: Road Traffic Regulation Act 1984, ss. 14 (1) (4) (7). - Issued: 12.06.2014. Made: 02.06.2014. Coming into force: 08.06.2014. Effect: None. Territorial extent & classification: W. Local. - Available at http://www.legislation.gov.uk/wsi/2014/1500/contents/made. - In English and Welsh. Welsh title: Gorchymyn Cefnffordd yr A40 (Twneli Gibraltar, Trefynwy, Sir Fynwy) (Gwahardd Cerbydau a Therfyn Cyflymder 40 mya Dros Dro) 2014 Non-print

The A40 Trunk Road (Glangwili Roundabout to Broad Oak, Carmarthenshire) (Temporary Traffic Restrictions and Prohibition) Order 2014 No. 2014/128 (W.16). - Enabling power: Road Traffic Regulation Act 1984, s. 14 (1) (4). - Issued: 31.01.2014. Made: 23.01.2014. Coming into force: 29.01.2014. Effect: None. Territorial extent & classification: W. Local. - Available at http://www.legislation.gov.uk/wsi/2014/128/contents/made. - In English and Welsh. Welsh title: Gorchymyn Cefnffordd yr A40 (Cylchfan Glangwili i Dderwen-fawr, Sir Gaerfyrddin) (Cyfyngiadau a Gwaharddiad Traffig Dros Dro) 2014 Non-print

The A40 Trunk Road (Junction of Cross Street and Monk Street, Abergavenny, Monmouthshire) (Temporary Prohibition of Vehicles and Cyclists) Order 2014 No. 2014/1031 (W.94). - Enabling power: Road Traffic Regulation Act 1984, ss. 14 (1) (4). - Issued: 22.04.2014. Made: 01.04.2014. Coming into force: 10.04.2014. Effect: None. Territorial extent & classification: W. Local. - Available at http://www.legislation.gov.uk/wsi/2014/1031/contents/made. - In English and Welsh. Welsh title: Gorchymyn Cefnffordd yr A40 (Cyffordd Cross Street a Monk Street, y Fenni, Sir Fynwy) (Gwahardd Cerbydau a Beicwyr Dros Dro) 2014 Non-print

The A40 Trunk Road (Llandovery Level Crossing, Llandovery, Carmarthenshire) (Temporary Prohibition of Vehicles) Order 2014 No. 2014/1203 (W.119). - Enabling power: Road Traffic Regulation Act 1984, ss. 14 (1) (4). - Issued: 20.05.2014. Made: 02.05.2014. Coming into force: 10.05.2014. Effect: None. Territorial extent & classification: W. Local. - Available at http://www.legislation.gov.uk/wsi/2014/1203/contents/made. - In English and Welsh. Welsh title: Gorchymyn Cefnffordd yr A40 (Croesfan Reilffordd Llanymddyfri, Llanymddyfri, Sir Gaerfyrddin) (Gwahardd Cerbydau Dros Dro) 2014 Non-print

The A40 Trunk Road (Llanwrda to Llandovery, Carmarthenshire) (Temporary Traffic Restrictions and Prohibitions) Order 2014 No. 2014/2659 (W.264). - Enabling power: Road Traffic Regulation Act 1984, s. 14 (1) (4). - Issued: 06.10.2014. Made: 29.09.2014. Coming into force: 06.10.2014. Effect: None. Territorial extent & classification: W. Local. - Available at http://www.legislation.gov.uk/wsi/2014/2659/contents/made. - In English and Welsh. Welsh title: Gorchymyn Cefnffordd yr A40 (Llanwrda i Lanymddyfri, Sir Gaerfyrddin) (Cyfyngiadau a Gwaharddiadau Traffig Dros Dro) 2014 Non-print

The A40 Trunk Road (Monmouth, Monmouthshire) (Temporary Prohibition of Vehicles) Order 2014 No. 2014/1600 (W.162). - Enabling power: Road Traffic Regulation Act 1984, s. 14 (1) (4). - Issued: 20.06.2014. Made: 17.06.2014. Coming into force: 22.06.2014. Effect: None. Territorial extent & classification: W. Local. - Available at http://www.legislation.gov.uk/wsi/2014/1600/contents/made. - In English and Welsh. Welsh title: Gorchymyn Cefnffordd yr A40 (Trefynwy, Sir Fynwy) (Gwahardd Cerbydau Dros Dro) 2014 Non-print

The A40 Trunk Road (Pensarn Roundabout to Traveller's Rest, Carmarthenshire) (Temporary Traffic Prohibitions and Restrictions) Order 2014 No. 2014/3416 (W.347). - Enabling power: Road Traffic Regulation Act 1984, ss. 14 (1) (4) (7). - Issued: 02.01.2015. Made: 29.12.2014. Coming into force: 05.01.2015. Effect: None. Territorial extent & classification: W. Local. - Available at http://www.legislation.gov.uk/wsi/2014/3416/contents/made. - In English and Welsh. Welsh title: Gorchymyn Cefnffordd yr A40 (Cylchfan Pensarn i Traveller's Rest, Sir Gaerfyrddin) (Gwaharddiadau a Chyfyngiadau Traffig Dros Dro) 2014 Non-print

The A40 Trunk Road (Powys/Monmouthshire County Boundary, Glangrwyney to Tarell Roundabout, Brecon, Powys) (Temporary Speed Restrictions and No Overtaking) Order 2014 No. 2014/1341 (W.138). - Enabling power: Road Traffic Regulation Act 1984, s. 14 (1) (4). - Issued: 02.06.2014. Made: 23.05.2014. Coming into force: 02.06.2014. Effect: None. Territorial extent & classification: W. Local. - Available at http://www.legislation.gov.uk/wsi/2014/1341/contents/made. - In English and Welsh. Welsh title: Gorchymyn Cefnffordd yr A40 (Ffin Sirol Powys/Sir Fynwy, Llangrwyne i Gylchfan Tarell, Aberhonddu, Powys) (Cyfyngiadau Cyflymder a Gwahardd Goddiweddyd Dros Dro) 2014 Non-print

The A40 Trunk Road (Raglan Interchange, Monmouthshire) (Temporary Prohibition of Vehicles and Right and Left Hand Turns) Order 2014 No. 2014/2837 (W.288). - Enabling power: Road Traffic Regulation Act 1984, s. 14 (1) (4). - Issued: 24.10.2014. Made: 21.10.2014. Coming into force: 27.10.2014. Effect: None. Territorial extent & classification: W. Local. - Available at http://www.legislation.gov.uk/wsi/2014/2837/contents/made. - In English and Welsh. Welsh title: Gorchymyn Cefnffordd yr A40 (Cyfnewidfa Rhaglan, Sir Fynwy) (Gwahardd Cerbydau a Throi i'r Dde ac i'r Chwith Dros Dro) 2014 Non-print

The A40 Trunk Road (Raglan Roundabout to Hardwick Roundabout, Abergavenny, Monmouthshire) (Temporary Prohibition of Vehicles) Order 2014 No. 2014/2648 (W.259). - Enabling power: Road Traffic Regulation Act 1984, s. 14 (1) (4). - Issued: 03.10.2014. Made: 29.09.2014. Coming into force: 06.10.2014. Effect: None. Territorial extent & classification: W. Local. - Available at http://www.legislation.gov.uk/wsi/2014/2648/contents/made. - In English and Welsh. Welsh title: Gorchymyn Cefnffordd yr A40 (Cylchfan Rhaglan i Gylchfan Hardwick, Y Fenni, Sir Fynwy) (Gwahardd Cerbydau Dros Dro) 2014 Non-print

The A40 Trunk Road (Scethrog to Llanhamlach, Powys) (Temporary Traffic Restrictions & Prohibitions) Order 2014 No. 2014/1491 (W.146). - Enabling power: Road Traffic Regulation Act 1984, s. 14 (1) (4). - Issued: 11.06.2014. Made: 23.05.2014. Coming into force: 01.06.2014. Effect: None. Territorial extent & classification: W. Local. - Available at http://www.legislation.gov.uk/wsi/2014/1491/contents/made. - In English and Welsh. Welsh title: Gorchymyn Cefnffordd yr A40 (Scethrog i Lanhamlach, Powys) (Cyfyngiadau a Gwaharddiadau Traffig Dros Dro) 2014 Non-print

The A40 Trunk Road (St Clears Roundabout to Llanboidy Road Roundabout, Carmarthenshire) (Temporary Speed Restrictions & No Overtaking) Order 2014 No. 2014/2556 (W.248). - Enabling power: Road Traffic Regulation Act 1984, s. 14 (1) (4). - Issued: 24.09.2014. Made: 22.09.2014. Coming into force: 29.09.2014. Effect: None. Territorial extent & classification: W. Local. - Available at http://www.legislation.gov.uk/wsi/2014/2556/contents/made. - In English and Welsh. Welsh title: Gorchymyn Cefnffordd yr A40 (Cylchfan Sanclêr i Gylchfan Heol Llanboidy, Sir Gaerfyrddin) (Cyfyngiadau Cyflymder Dros Dro a Dim Goddiweddyd) 2014 Non-print

The A40 Trunk Road (Tarrell Roundabout, Brecon to County Border at Pont Wen, Halfway, Powys) (Temporary Traffic Restrictions and No Overtaking) Order 2014 No. 2014/1373 (W.140). - Enabling power: Road Traffic Regulation Act 1984, ss. 14 (1) (4). - Issued: 16.06.2014. Made: 23.05.2014. Coming into force: 02.06.2014. Effect: None. Territorial extent & classification: W. Local. - Available at http://www.legislation.gov.uk/wsi/2014/1373/contents/made. - In English and Welsh. Welsh title: Gorchymyn Cefnffordd yr A40 (Cylchfan Tarrell, Aberhonddu i'r Ffin Sirol ym Mhont Wen, Halfway, Powys) (Cyfyngiadau Traffig Dros Dro a Dim Goddiweddyd) 2014 Non-print

The A44 Trunk Road (Between Llangurig and Eisteddfa Gurig, Powys) (Temporary Traffic Prohibitions and Restrictions) Order 2014 No. 2014/3113 (W.312). - Enabling power: Road Traffic Regulation Act 1984, s. 14 (1) (4). - Issued: 26.11.2014. Made: 14.11.2014. Coming into force: 24.11.2014. Effect: None. Territorial extent & classification: W. Local. - Available at http://www.legislation.gov.uk/wsi/2014/3113/contents/made. - In English and Welsh. Welsh title: Gorchymyn Cefnffordd yr A44 (Rhwng Llangurig ac Eisteddfa Gurig, Powys) (Gwaharddiadau a Chyfyngiadau Traffig Dros Dro) 2014 Non-print

The A44 Trunk Road (Llangurig to Eisteddfa Gurig, Powys) (Temporary Traffic Restrictions and No Overtaking) Order 2014 No. 2014/3201 (W.324). - Enabling power: Road Traffic Regulation Act 1984, s. 14 (1) (4). - Issued: 05.12.2014. Made: 01.12.2014. Coming into force: 08.12.2014. Effect: None. Territorial extent & classification: W. Local. - Available at http://www.legislation.gov.uk/wsi/2014/3201/contents/made. - In English and Welsh. Welsh title: Gorchymyn Cefnffordd yr A44 (Llangurig i Eisteddfa Gurig, Powys) (Cyfyngiadau Traffig a Dim Goddiweddyd Dros Dro) 2014 Non-print

The A44 Trunk Road (Lovesgrove, East of Aberystwyth, Ceredigion) (Temporary 40 MPH Speed Limit) Order 2014 No. 2014/1504 (W.154). - Enabling power: Road Traffic Regulation Act 1984, s. 14 (1) (4). - Issued: 12.06.2014. Made: 06.06.2014. Coming into force: 13.06.2014. Effect: None. Territorial extent & classification: W. Local. - Available at http://www.legislation.gov.uk/wsi/2014/1504/contents/made. - In English and Welsh. Welsh title: Gorchymyn Cefnffordd yr A44 (Gelli Angharad, i'r Dwyrain o Aberystwyth, Ceredigion) (Terfyn Cyflymder o 40 MYA Dros Dro) 2014 Non-print

The A48 and A40 Trunk Road (Pont Abraham, Carmarthenshire to Penblewin, Pembrokeshire) (Temporary Prohibition of Vehicles) Order 2014 No. 2014/2232 (W.215). - Enabling power: Road Traffic Regulation Act 1984, ss. 14 (1) (4). - Issued: 28.08.2014. Made: 21.08.2014. Coming into force: 01.09.2014. Effect: None. Territorial extent & classification: W. Local. - Available at http://www.legislation.gov.uk/wsi/2014/2232/contents/made. - In English and Welsh. Welsh title: Gorchymyn Cefnffordd yr A48 a'r A40 (Pont Abraham, Sir Gaerfyrddin i Benblewin, Sir Benfro) (Gwahardd Cerbydau Dros Dro) 2014 Non-print

The A55, A494 and A550 Trunk Roads (Northop Interchange to the Wales/England Border, Flintshire) (Temporary Traffic Prohibitions and Restrictions) Order 2014 No. 2014/2018 (W.203). - Enabling power: Road Traffic Regulation Act 1984, ss. 14 (1) (4). - Issued: 31.07.2014. Made: 28.07.2014. Coming into force: 04.08.2014. Effect: None. Territorial extent & classification: W. Local. - Available at http://www.legislation.gov.uk/wsi/2014/2018/contents/made. - In English and Welsh. Welsh title: Gorchymyn Cefnffyrdd yr A55, yr A494 a'r A550 (Cyfnewidfa Northop i Ffin Cymru/Lloegr, Sir y Fflint) (Gwahardiadau a Chyfyngiadau Traffig Dros Dro) 2014 Non-print

The A55 and A494 Trunk Roads (St Davids Park Interchange to Pinfold Lane Junction, Flintshire) (Temporary Traffic Prohibitions and 40 MPH Speed Limit) Order 2014 No. 2014/2579 (W.255). - Enabling power: Road Traffic Regulation Act 1984, s. 14 (1) (4). - Issued: 25.09.2014. Made: 23.09.2014. Coming into force: 30.09.2014. Effect: None. Territorial extent & classification: W. Local. - Available at http://www.legislation.gov.uk/wsi/2014/2579/contents/made. - In English and Welsh. Welsh title: Gorchymyn Cefnffyrdd yr A55 a'r A494 (Cyfnewidfa Parc Dewi Sant i Gyffordd Pinfold Lane, Sir y Fflint) (Gwahardiadau Traffig Dros Dro a Therfyn Cyflymder 40 MYA) 2014 Non-print

The A55 Trunk Road (Broughton, Flintshire) (Temporary Prohibition of Vehicles, Cyclists & Pedestrians) Order 2014 No. 2014/1779 (W.184). - Enabling power: Road Traffic Regulation Act 1984, ss. 14 (1) (4). - Issued: 22.08.2014. Made: 07.07.2014. Coming into force: 13.07.2014. Effect: None. Territorial extent & classification: W. Local. - Available at http://www.legislation.gov.uk/wsi/2014/1779/contents/made. - In English and Welsh. Welsh title: Gorchymyn Cefnffordd yr A55 (Brychdyn, Sir y Fflint) (Gwahardd Cerbydau, Beicwyr a Cherddwyr Dros Dro) 2014 Non-print

The A55 Trunk Road (Conwy Tunnel, Conwy) (Temporary Traffic Prohibitions and Restrictions) Order 2014 No. 2014/2892 (W.293). - Enabling power: Road Traffic Regulation Act 1984, ss. 14 (1) (4) (7), 124, sch. 9, para. 27. - Issued: 05.11.2014. Made: 27.10.2014. Coming into force: 02.11.2014. Effect: S.I. 1985/824; 1990/1586 part suspended & S.I. 2013/3238 (W.318) revoked. Territorial extent & classification: W. Local. - Available at http://www.legislation.gov.uk/wsi/2014/2892/contents/made. - In English and Welsh. Welsh title: Gorchymyn Cefnffordd yr A55 (Twnnel Conwy, Conwy) (Gwahardiadau a Chyfyngiadau Traffig Dros Dro) 2014 Non-print

The A55 Trunk Road (Eastbound Carriageway between Junction 30 (Travellers' Inn Junction) and Junction 33 (Northop, Flintshire) (Temporary Traffic Prohibitions & Restriction) Order 2014 No. 2014/712 (W.79). - Enabling power: Road Traffic Regulation Act 1984, s. 14 (1) (4). - Issued: 24.03.2014. Made: 17.03.2014. Coming into force: 23.03.2014. Effect: None. Territorial extent & classification: W. Local. - Available at http://www.legislation.gov.uk/wsi/2014/712/contents/made. - In English and Welsh. Welsh title: Gorchymyn Cefnffordd yr A55 (Y Gerbytffordd tua'r Dwyrain rhwng Cyffordd 30 (Cyffordd Travellers' Inn) a Chyffordd 33 (Llaneurgain), Sir y Fflint) (Gwaharddiadau a Chyfyngiad Traffig Dros Dro) 2014 Non-print

The A55 Trunk Road (Junction 7, Cefn Du Interchange, Isle of Anglesey to Junction 10, Caernarfon Road Interchange, Gwynedd) (Temporary Traffic Prohibitions and Restrictions) Order 2014 No. 2014/1549 (W.158). - Enabling power: Road Traffic Regulation Act 1984, ss. 14 (1) (4). - Issued: 16.06.2014. Made: 12.06.2014. Coming into force: 21.06.2014. Effect: None. Territorial extent & classification: W. Local. - Available at http://www.legislation.gov.uk/wsi/2014/1549/contents/made. - In English and Welsh. Welsh title: Gorchymyn Cefnffordd yr A55 (Cyffordd 7, Cyfnewidfa Cefn Du, Ynys Môn i Gyffordd 10, Cyfnewidfa Ffordd Caernarfon, Gwynedd) (Gwaharddiadau a Chyfyngiadau Traffig Dros Dro) 2014 Non-print

The A55 Trunk Road (Junction 8 (Pant Lodge Interchange), Anglesey to Junction 9 (Treborth Interchange), Gwynedd) (Prohibition of Pedestrians) Order 2014 No. 2014/2927 (W.298). - Enabling power: Road Traffic Regulation Act 1984, ss. 1 (1), 2 (3), 124, sch. 9, para. 27. - Issued: 12.11.2014. Made: 04.11.2014. Coming into force: 06.11.2014. Effect: S.I. 1983/1771, 1932 revoked. Territorial extent & classification: W. Local. - Available at http://www.legislation.gov.uk/wsi/2014/2927/contents/made. - In English and Welsh. Welsh title: Gorchymyn Cefnffordd yr A55 (Cyffordd 8 (Cyfnewidfa Pant Lodge), Ynys Môn i Gyffordd 9 (Cyfnewidfa Treborth), Gwynedd) (Gwahardd Cerddwyr) 2014 Non-print

The A55 Trunk Road (Junction 9 (Treborth Interchange) to Britannia Bridge, Gwynedd) (Temporary Prohibition of Vehicles, Cyclists and Pedestrians) Order 2014 No. 2014/1136 (W.113). - Enabling power: Road Traffic Regulation Act 1984, s. 14 (1) (4). - Issued: 06.05.2014. Made: 29.04.2014. Coming into force: 06.05.2014. Effect: None. Territorial extent & classification: W. Local. - Available at http://www.legislation.gov.uk/wsi/2014/1136/contents/made. - In English and Welsh. Welsh title: Gorchymyn Cefnffordd yr A55 (Cyffordd 9 (Cyfnewidfa Treborth) i Bont Britannia, Gwynedd) (Gwahardd Cerbydau, Beicwyr a Cherddwyr Dros Dro) 2014 Non-print

The A55 Trunk Road (Junction 11 (Llys y Gwynt Interchange), Bangor, Gwynedd to Junction 33a (Northop) Flintshire) and The A494/A550 Trunk Road (Drome Corner to the Wales / England Border, Flintshire) (Temporary Prohibition of Vehicles, Cyclists and Pedestrians) Order 2014 No. 2014/1078 (W.107). - Enabling power: Road Traffic Regulation Act 1984, s. 14 (1) (4). - Issued: 02.05.2014. Made: 23.04.2014. Coming into force: 06.05.2014. Effect: None. Territorial extent & classification: W. Local. - Available at http://www.legislation.gov.uk/wsi/2014/1078/contents/made. - In English and Welsh. Welsh title: Gorchymyn Cefnffordd yr A55 (Cyffordd 11 (Cyfnewidfa Llys y Gwynt), Bangor, Gwynedd i Gyffordd 33a (Llaneurgain) Sir y Fflint) a Chefnffordd yr A494/A550 (Drome Corner i Ffin Cymru / Lloegr, Sir y Fflint) (Gwahardd Cerbydau, Beicwyr a Cherddwyr Dros Dro) 2014 Non-print

The A55 Trunk Road (Junction 11 (Llys y Gwynt Interchange), Bangor, Gwynedd to the Wales/England Border) and the A494/A550 Trunk Road (Ewloe Interchange, Flintshire) (Temporary 40 mph Speed Limit & Prohibition of Vehicles) Order 2014 No. 2014/915 (W.91). - Enabling power: Road Traffic Regulation Act 1984, s. 14 (1) (4). - Issued: 08.04.2014. Made: 25.03.2014. Coming into force: 01.04.2014. Effect: None. Territorial extent & classification: W. Local. - Available at http://www.legislation.gov.uk/wsi/2014/915/contents/made. - In English and Welsh. Welsh title: Gorchymyn Cefnffordd yr A55 (Cyffordd 11 (Cyfnewidfa Llys y Gwynt), Bangor, Gwynedd i Ffin Cymru/Lloegr) a Chefnffordd yr A494/A550 (Cyfnewidfa Ewloe, Sir y Fflint) (Terfyn Cyflymder 40 mya a Gwahardd Cerbydau Dros Dro) 2014 Non-print

ROAD TRAFFIC, WALES: TRAFFIC REGULATION

The A55 Trunk Road (Junction 19 (Glan Conwy) to Junction 17 (Conwy Morfa), Conwy County Borough) (Temporary Prohibition of Vehicles & 40 mph Speed Limit) Order 2014 No. 2014/2467 (W.236). - Enabling power: Road Traffic Regulation Act 1984, s. 14 (1) (4) (7). - Issued: 19.09.2014. Made: 08.09.2014. Coming into force: 15.09.2014. Effect: None. Territorial extent & classification: W. Local. - Available at http://www.legislation.gov.uk/wsi/2014/2467/contents/made. - In English and Welsh. Welsh title: Gorchymyn Cefnffordd yr A55 (Cyffordd 19 (Llansanffraid Glan Conwy) i Gyffordd 17 (Morfa Conwy), Bwrdeistref Sirol Conwy) (Gwahardd Cerbydau a Therfyn Cyflymder o 40 mya Dros Dro) 2014 Non-print

The A55 Trunk Road (Junction 20, Brompton Avenue, Colwyn Bay, Conwy) (Temporary Prohibition of Vehicles, Cyclists and Pedestrians) Order 2014 No. 2014/709 (W.76). - Enabling power: Road Traffic Regulation Act 1984, s. 14 (1) (4). - Issued: 07.04.2014. Made: 10.03.2014. Coming into force: 17.03.2014. Effect: None. Territorial extent & classification: W. Local. - Available at http://www.legislation.gov.uk/wsi/2014/709/contents/made. - In English and Welsh. Welsh title: Gorchymyn Cefnffordd yr A55 (Cyffordd 20, Brompton Avenue, Bae Colwyn, Conwy) (Gwahardd Cerbydau, Beicwyr a Cherddwyr Dros Dro) 2014 Non-print

The A55 Trunk Road (Junction 20, Conway Road, Colwyn Bay, Conwy) (Temporary Prohibition of Vehicles, Cyclists and Pedestrians) Order 2014 No. 2014/1055 (W.95). - Enabling power: Road Traffic Regulation Act 1984, s. 14 (1) (4). - Issued: 23.04.2014. Made: 01.04.2014. Coming into force: 08.04.2014. Effect: None. Territorial extent & classification: W. Local. - Available at http://www.legislation.gov.uk/wsi/2014/1055/contents/made. - In English and Welsh. Welsh title: Gorchymyn Cefnffordd yr A55 (Cyffordd 20, Ffordd Conwy, Bae Colwyn, Conwy) (Gwahardd Cerbydau, Beicwyr a Cherddwyr Dros Dro) 2014 Non-print

The A55 Trunk Road (Junction 27, Denbighshire to Junction 31, Flintshire) (Temporary Traffic Prohibitions and Restriction) Order 2014 No. 2014/541 (W.65). - Enabling power: Road Traffic Regulation Act 1984, s. 14 (1) (4). - Issued: 12.03.2014. Made: 07.03.2014. Coming into force: 16.03.2014. Effect: None. Territorial extent & classification: W. Local. - Available at http://www.legislation.gov.uk/wsi/2014/541/contents/made. - In English and Welsh. Welsh title: Gorchymyn Cefnffordd yr A55 (Cyffordd 27, Sir Ddinbych i Gyffordd 31, Sir y Fflint) (Gwaharddiadau a Chyfyngiad Traffig Dros Dro) 2014 Non-print

The A55 Trunk Road (Junction 27, St Asaph, Denbighshire, Eastbound On Slip Road) (Temporary Prohibition of Vehicles, Cyclists and Pedestrians) Order 2014 No. 2014/34 (W.2). - Enabling power: Road Traffic Regulation Act 1984, s. 14 (1) (4). - Issued: 15.01.2014. Made: 06.01.2014. Coming into force: 12.01.2014. Effect: None. Territorial extent & classification: W. Local. - Available at http://www.legislation.gov.uk/wsi/2014/34/contents/made. - In English and Welsh. Welsh title: Gorchymyn Cefnffordd yr A55 (Cyffordd 27, Llanelwy, Sir Ddinbych, Ffordd Ymuno tua'r Dwyrain) (Gwahardd Cerbydau, Beicwyr a Cherddwyr Dros Dro) 2014 Non-print

The A55 Trunk Road (Junction 27 (Talardy Interchange), Denbighshire to Junction 24 (Faenol Interchange), Conwy) (Temporary Prohibition of Vehicles, Cyclists & Pedestrians) Order 2014 No. 2014/2578 (W.254). - Enabling power: Road Traffic Regulation Act 1984, s. 14 (1) (4). - Issued: 25.09.2014. Made: 26.08.2014. Coming into force: 01.09.2014. Effect: None. Territorial extent & classification: W. Local. - Available at http://www.legislation.gov.uk/wsi/2014/2578/contents/made. - In English and Welsh. Welsh title: Gorchymyn Cefnffordd yr A55 (Cyffordd 27 (Cyfnewidfa Talardy), Sir Ddinbych i Gyffordd 24 (Cyfnewidfa'r Faenol), Conwy) (Gwahardd Cerbydau, Beicwyr a Cherddwyr Dros Dro) 2014 Non-print

The A55 Trunk Road (Junction 33b, Alltami and Junction 34, Ewloe, Flintshire) (Temporary Prohibition of Vehicles, Cyclists and Pedestrians) Order 2014 No. 2014/2836 (W.287). - Enabling power: Road Traffic Regulation Act 1984, s. 14 (1) (4). - Issued: 24.10.2014. Made: 21.10.2014. Coming into force: 27.10.2014. Effect: None. Territorial extent & classification: W. Local. - Available at http://www.legislation.gov.uk/wsi/2014/2836/contents/made. - In English and Welsh. Welsh title: Gorchymyn Cefnffordd yr A55 (Cyffordd 33b, Alltami a Chyffordd 34, Ewlo, Sir y Fflint) (Gwahardd Cerbydau, Beicwyr a Cherddwyr Dros Dro) 2014 Non-print

The A55 Trunk Road (Junction 34, Ewloe Interchange, Flintshire) (Temporary Prohibition of Vehicles, Cyclists and Pedestrians) Order 2014 No. 2014/1498 (W.148). - Enabling power: Road Traffic Regulation Act 1984, s. 14 (1) (4). - Issued: 11.06.2014. Made: 28.05.2014. Coming into force: 03.06.2014. Effect: None. Territorial extent & classification: W. Local. - Available at http://www.legislation.gov.uk/wsi/2014/1498/contents/made. - In English and Welsh. Welsh title: Gorchymyn Cefnffordd yr A55 (Cyffordd 34, Cyfnewidfa Ewloe, Sir y Fflint) (Gwahardd Cerbydau, Beicwyr a Cherddwyr Dros Dro) 2014 Non-print

The A55 Trunk Road (Junction 35 (Dobshill) to the Wales/England Border, Flintshire) (Temporary Traffic Prohibitions & Restriction) Order 2014 No. 2014/126 (W.15). - Enabling power: Road Traffic Regulation Act 1984, s. 14 (1) (4). - Issued: 31.01.2014. Made: 22.01.2014. Coming into force: 26.01.2014. Effect: None. Territorial extent & classification: W. Local. - Available at http://www.legislation.gov.uk/wsi/2014/126/contents/made. - In English and Welsh. Welsh title: Gorchymyn Cefnffordd yr A55 (Cyffordd 35 (Dobshill) i Ffin Cymru/Lloegr, Sir y Fflint) (Gwaharddiadau a Chyfyngiad Traffig Dros Dro) 2014 Non-print

The A55 Trunk Road (Junction 35 to the Wales/England Border, Flintshire) (Temporary Traffic Prohibition & 40 MPH Speed Limit) Order 2014 No. 2014/3166 (W.321). - Enabling power: Road Traffic Regulation Act 1984, ss. 14 (1) (4). - Issued: 03.12.2014. Made: 24.11.2014. Coming into force: 01.12.2014. Effect: None. Territorial extent & classification: W. Local. - Available at http://www.legislation.gov.uk/wsi/2014/3166/contents/made. - In English and Welsh. Welsh title: Gorchymyn Cefnffordd yr A55 (Cyffordd 35 i Ffin Cymru/Lloegr, Sir y Fflint) (Gwahardd Traffig Dros Dro a Therfyn Cyflymder o 40 mya) 2014 Non-print

The A55 Trunk Road (Junction 36A, Broughton, Flintshire) (Temporary Prohibition of Vehicles, Cyclists and Pedestrians) Order 2014 No. 2014/2544 (W.246). - Enabling power: Road Traffic Regulation Act 1984, s. 14 (1) (4). - Issued: 24.09.2014. Made: 18.09.2014. Coming into force: 29.09.2014. Effect: None. Territorial extent & classification: W. Local. - Available at http://www.legislation.gov.uk/wsi/2014/2544/contents/made. - In English and Welsh. Welsh title: Gorchymyn Cefnffordd yr A55 (Cyffordd 36A, Brychdyn, Sir y Fflint) (Gwahardd Cerbydau, Beicwyr a Cherddwyr Dros Dro) 2014 Non-print

The A55 Trunk Road (Kingsland Roundabout to Junction 7, Cefn Du Interchange, Isle of Anglesey) (Temporary Traffic Prohibitions and Restrictions) Order 2014 No. 2014/2649 (W.260). - Enabling power: Road Traffic Regulation Act 1984, s. 14 (1) (4) (7). - Issued: 03.10.2014. Made: 26.09.2014. Coming into force: 03.10.2014. Effect: None. Territorial extent & classification: W. Local. - Available at http://www.legislation.gov.uk/wsi/2014/2649/contents/made. - In English and Welsh. Welsh title: Gorchymyn Cefnffordd yr A55 (Cylchfan Kingsland i Gyffordd 7, Cyfnewidfa Cefn Du, Ynys Môn) (Cyfyngiadau a Gwaharddiadau Traffig Dros Dro) 2014 Non-print

The A55 Trunk Road (Pen-y-clip Tunnel, Conwy County Borough) (Temporary Traffic Prohibitions & Restriction) Order 2014 No. 2014/827 (W.85). - Enabling power: Road Traffic Regulation Act 1984, s. 14 (1) (4) (7). - Issued: 31.03.2014. Made: 26.03.2014. Coming into force: 02.04.2014. Effect: None. Territorial extent & classification: W. Local. - Available at http://www.legislation.gov.uk/wsi/2014/827/contents/made. - In English and Welsh. Welsh title: Gorchymyn Cefnffordd yr A55 (Twnnel Pen-y-clip, Bwrdeistref Sirol Conwy) (Gwaharddiadau a Chyfyngiad Traffig Dros Dro) 2014 Non-print

The A55 Trunk Road (Slip Roads at Junction 13, Abergwyngregyn and Junction 14, Madryn Interchange, Gwynedd) (Temporary Prohibition of Vehicles, Cyclists and Pedestrians) Order 2014 No. 2014/2895 (W.296). - Enabling power: Road Traffic Regulation Act 1984, s. 14 (1) (4). - Issued: 05.11.2014. Made: 03.11.2014. Coming into force: 09.11.2014. Effect: None. Territorial extent & classification: W. Local. - Available at http://www.legislation.gov.uk/wsi/2014/2895/contents/made. - In English and Welsh. Welsh title: Gorchymyn Cefnffordd yr A55 (Ffyrdd Ymuno ac Ymadael wrth Gyffordd 13, Abergwyngregyn a Chyffordd 14, Cyfnewidfa Madryn, Gwynedd) (Gwahardd Cerbydau, Beicwyr a Cherddwyr Dros Dro) 2014 Non-print

The A55 Trunk Road (Slip Roads at Junction 27 (St Asaph), Denbighshire) (Temporary Prohibition of Vehicles, Cyclists & Pedestrians) Order 2014 No. 2014/1499 (W.149). - Enabling power: Road Traffic Regulation Act 1984, s. 14 (1) (4). - Issued: 12.06.2014. Made: 28.05.2014. Coming into force: 04.06.2014. Effect: None. Territorial extent & classification: W. Local. - Available at http://www.legislation.gov.uk/wsi/2014/1499/contents/made. - In English and Welsh. Welsh title: Gorchymyn Cefnffordd yr A55 (Slipffyrdd wrth Gyffordd 27 (Llanelwy), Sir Ddinbych) (Gwahardd Cerbydau, Beicwyr a Cherddwyr Dros Dro) 2014 Non-print

The A449 Trunk Road (Abernant Interchange, Newport) (Temporary 50 mph Speed Limit) Order 2014 No. 2014/1340 (W.137). - Enabling power: Road Traffic Regulation Act 1984, s. 14 (1) (4). - Issued: 30.05.2014. Made: 23.05.2014. Coming into force: 01.06.2014. Effect: None. Territorial extent & classification: W. Local. - Available at http://www.legislation.gov.uk/wsi/2014/1340/contents/made. - In English and Welsh. Welsh title: Gorchymyn Cefnffordd yr A449 (Cyfnewidfa Aber-nant, Casnewydd) (Terfyn Cyflymder 50 mya Dros Dro) 2014 Non-print

The A449 Trunk Road (Coldra Interchange, Newport to Usk Interchange, Monmouthshire) (Temporary Traffic Prohibitions & Restriction) Order 2014 No. 2014/789 (W.80). - Enabling power: Road Traffic Regulation Act 1984, s. 14 (1) (4). - Issued: 26.03.2014. Made: 18.03.2014. Coming into force: 25.03.2014. Effect: None. Territorial extent & classification: W. Local. - Available at http://www.legislation.gov.uk/wsi/2014/789/contents/made. - In English and Welsh. Welsh title: Gorchymyn Cefnffordd yr A449 (Cyfnewidfa Coldra, Casnewydd i Gyfnewidfa Brynbuga, Sir Fynwy) (Gwaharddiadau a Chyfyngiad Traffig Dros Dro) 2014 Non-print

The A449 Trunk Road (Northbound Carriageway between Coldra Interchange, Newport and Usk Interchange, Monmouthshire) (Temporary Prohibition of Vehicles) Order 2014 No. 2014/2474 (W.238). - Enabling power: Road Traffic Regulation Act 1984, s. 14 (1) (4). - Issued: 19.09.2014. Made: 12.09.2014. Coming into force: 19.09.2014. Effect: None. Territorial extent & classification: W. Local. - Available at http://www.legislation.gov.uk/wsi/2014/2474/contents/made. - In English and Welsh. Welsh title: Gorchymyn Cefnffordd yr A449 (Y Gerbytffordd tua'r Gogledd rhwng Cyfnewidfa Coldra, Casnewydd a Chyfnewidfa Brynbuga, Sir Fynwy) (Gwahardd Cerbydau Dros Dro) 2014 Non-print

The A458 Trunk Road (Buttington Roundabout, Powys to the Powys/Shropshire Border) (Temporary Speed Restrictions & No Overtaking) Order 2014 No. 2014/3378 (W.341). - Enabling power: Road Traffic Regulation Act 1984, s. 14 (1) (4). - Issued: 30.12.2014. Made: 02.12.2014. Coming into force: 08.12.2014. Effect: None. Territorial extent & classification: W. Local. - Available at http://www.legislation.gov.uk/wsi/2014/3378/contents/made. - In English and Welsh. Welsh title: Gorchymyn Cefnffordd yr A458 (Cylchfan Tal-y-bont, Powys hyd at Ffin Powys/Swydd Amwythig) (Cyfyngiadau Cyflymder a Dim Goddiweddyd Dros Dro) 2014 Non-print

The A458 Trunk Road (East of Mallwyd, Gwynedd) (Temporary Speed Restrictions & No Overtaking) Order 2014 No. 2014/1676 (W.169). - Enabling power: Road Traffic Regulation Act 1984, s. 14 (1) (4). - Issued: 02.07.2014. Made: 27.06.2014. Coming into force: 03.07.2014. Effect: None. Territorial extent & classification: W. Local. - Available at http://www.legislation.gov.uk/wsi/2014/1676/contents/made. - In English and Welsh. Welsh title: Gorchymyn Cefnffordd yr A458 (Man i'r Dwyrain o Fallwyd, Gwynedd) (Cyfyngiadau Cyflymder Dros Dro a Dim Goddiweddyd) 2014 Non-print

The A458 Trunk Road (Salop Road, Welshpool, Powys) (Temporary Prohibition of Vehicles) Order 2014 No. 2014/2492 (W.240). - Enabling power: Road Traffic Regulation Act 1984, s. 14 (1) (4). - Issued: 22.09.2014. Made: 15.09.2014. Coming into force: 22.09.2014. Effect: None. Territorial extent & classification: W. Local. - Available at http://www.legislation.gov.uk/wsi/2014/2492/contents/made. - In English and Welsh. Welsh title: Gorchymyn Cefnffordd yr A458 (Salop Road, Y Trallwng, Powys) (Gwahardd Cerbydau Dros Dro) 2014 Non-print

The A458 Trunk Road (Welshpool, Powys to the Powys/Gwynedd Border) (Temporary Speed Restrictions & No Overtaking) Order 2014 No. 2014/3393 (W.344). - Enabling power: Road Traffic Regulation Act 1984, s. 14 (1) (4). - Issued: 30.12.2014. Made: 02.12.2014. Coming into force: 08.12.2014. Effect: None. Territorial extent & classification: W. Local. - Available at http://www.legislation.gov.uk/wsi/2014/3393/contents/made. - In English and Welsh. Welsh title: Gorchymyn Cefnffordd yr A458 (Y Trallwng, Powys hyd at Ffin Powys/Gwynedd) (Cyfyngiadau Cyflymder a Dim Goddiweddyd Dros Dro) 2014 Non-print

The A465 Trunk Road (Aberdulais Interchange to Neath Abbey Interchange, Neath Port Talbot) (Temporary Prohibition of Vehicles, Pedestrians and Cyclists) Order 2014 No. 2014/710 (W.77). - Enabling power: Road Traffic Regulation Act 1984, s. 14 (1) (4). - Issued: 24.03.2014. Made: 10.03.2014. Coming into force: 18.03.2014. Effect: None. Territorial extent & classification: W. Local. - Available at http://www.legislation.gov.uk/wsi/2014/710/contents/made. - In English and Welsh. Welsh title: Gorchymyn Cefnffordd yr A465 (Cyfnewidfa Aberdulais i Gyfnewidfa Mynachlog Nedd, Castell-nedd Port Talbot) (Gwahardd Cerbydau, Cerddwyr a Beicwyr Dros Dro) 2014 Non-print

The A465 Trunk Road (Hirwaun, Rhondda Cynon Taf) (Prohibition of Right Hand Turns) Order 2014 No. 2014/1064 (W.103). - Enabling power: Road Traffic Regulation Act 1984, ss. 1 (1), 2 (1) (2). - Issued: 24.04.2014. Made: 11.04.2014. Coming into force: 16.04.2014. Effect: None. Territorial extent & classification: W. Local. - Available at http://www.legislation.gov.uk/wsi/2014/1064/contents/made. - In English and Welsh. Welsh title: Gorchymyn Cefnffordd yr A465 (Hirwaun, Rhondda Cynon Taf) (Gwahardd Troi i'r Dde) 2014 Non-print

The A465 Trunk Road (Hirwaun Roundabout to Rhigos Roundabout, Rhondda Cynon Taf) (Temporary Prohibition of Vehicles) Order 2014 No. 2014/2853 (W.290). - Enabling power: Road Traffic Regulation Act 1984, s. 14 (1) (4) (7). - Issued: 29.10.2014. Made: 24.10.2014. Coming into force: 03.11.2014. Effect: None. Territorial extent & classification: W. Local. - Available at http://www.legislation.gov.uk/wsi/2014/2853/contents/made. - In English and Welsh. Welsh title: Gorchymyn Cefnffordd yr A465 (Cylchfan Hirwaun i Gylchfan Rhigos, Rhondda Cynon Taf) (Gwahardd Cerbydau Dros Dro) 2014 Non-print

The A465 Trunk Road (Llanfoist, Monmouthshire to Brynmawr, Blaenau Gwent) (Temporary Speed Restrictions & No Overtaking) Order 2014 No. 2014/3420 (W.348). - Enabling power: Road Traffic Regulation Act 1984, ss. 14 (1) (4) (7). - Issued: 02.01.2015. Made: 29.12.2014. Coming into force: 05.01.2015. Effect: None. Territorial extent & classification: W. Local. - Available at http://www.legislation.gov.uk/wsi/2014/3420/contents/made. - In English and Welsh. Welsh title: Gorchymyn Cefnffordd yr A465 (Llan-ffwyst, Sir Fynwy i Fryn-mawr, Blaenau Gwent) (Cyfyngiadau Cyflymder Dros Dro a Dim Goddiweddyd) 2014 Non-print

The A465 Trunk Road (Neath Abbey Interchange to Llandarcy Interchange, Neath Port Talbot) (Temporary Prohibition of Vehicles) Order 2014 No. 2014/2212 (W.213). - Enabling power: Road Traffic Regulation Act 1984, ss. 14 (1) (4). - Issued: 21.05.2014. Made: 19.08.2014. Coming into force: 26.08.2014. Effect: None. Territorial extent & classification: W. Local. - Available at http://www.legislation.gov.uk/wsi/2014/2212/contents/made. - In English and Welsh. Welsh title: Gorchymyn Cefnffordd yr A465 (Cyfnewidfa Mynachlog Nedd i Gyfnewidfa Llandarcy, Castell-nedd Port Talbot) (Gwahardd Cerbydau Dros Dro) 2014 Non-print

The A465 Trunk Road (Neath Interchange, Neath Port Talbot) (Temporary Prohibition of Vehicles) Order 2014 No. 2014/441 (W.50). - Enabling power: Road Traffic Regulation Act 1984, s. 14 (1) (4). - Issued: 07.03.2014. Made: 25.02.2014. Coming into force: 08.03.2014. Effect: None. Territorial extent & classification: W. Local. - Available at http://www.legislation.gov.uk/wsi/2014/441/contents/made. - In English and Welsh. Welsh title: Gorchymyn Cefnffordd yr A465 (Cyfnewidfa Castell-nedd, Castell-nedd Port Talbot) (Gwahardd Cerbydau Dros Dro) 2014 Non-print

The A465 Trunk Road (Pandy to Llangua, Monmouthshire) (Temporary Speed Restrictions & No Overtaking) Order 2014 No. 2014/3203 (W.326). - Enabling power: Road Traffic Regulation Act 1984, s. 14 (1) (4). - Issued: 05.12.2014. Made: 28.11.2014. Coming into force: 04.12.2014. Effect: None. Territorial extent & classification: W. Local. - Available at http://www.legislation.gov.uk/wsi/2014/3203/contents/made. - In English and Welsh. Welsh title: Gorchymyn Cefnffordd yr A465 (Pandy i Langiwa, Sir Fynwy) (Cyfyngiadau Cyflymder a Dim Goddiweddyd Dros Dro) 2014 Non-print

The A465 Trunk Road (Rhigos Roundabout, Rhondda Cynon Taf to Glynneath Interchange, Neath Port Talbot) (Temporary Prohibition of Vehicles) Order 2014 No. 2014/1944 (W.196). - Enabling power: Road Traffic Regulation Act 1984, ss. 14 (1) (4). - Issued: 31.07.2014. Made: 22.07.2014. Coming into force: 30.07.2014. Effect: None. Territorial extent & classification: W. Local. - Available at http://www.legislation.gov.uk/wsi/2014/1944/contents/made. - In English and Welsh. Welsh title: Gorchymyn Cefnffordd yr A465 (Cylchfan y Rhigos, Rhondda Cynon Taf i Gyfnewidfa Glyn-nedd, Castell-nedd Port Talbot) (Gwahardd Cerbydau Dros Dro) 2014 Non-print

The A465 Trunk Road (Rhymney Interchange, Caerphilly County Borough) (Temporary Prohibition of Vehicles) Order 2014 No. 2014/1251 (W.131). - Enabling power: Road Traffic Regulation Act 1984, ss. 14 (1) (4). - Issued: 19.05.2014. Made: 14.05.2014. Coming into force: 19.05.2014. Effect: None. Territorial extent & classification: W. Local. - Available at http://www.legislation.gov.uk/wsi/2014/1251/contents/made. - In English and Welsh. Welsh title: Gorchymyn Cefnffordd yr A465 (Cyfnewidfa Rhymni, Bwrdeistref Sirol Caerffili) (Gwahardd Cerbydau Dros Dro) 2014 Non-print

The A465 Trunk Road (Slip Roads at Llanfoist Interchange, Monmouthshire) (Temporary Prohibition of Vehicles) Order 2014 No. 2014/2463 (W.232). - Enabling power: Road Traffic Regulation Act 1984, s. 14 (1) (4). - Issued: 19.09.2014. Made: 28.08.2014. Coming into force: 07.09.2014. Effect: None. Territorial extent & classification: W. Local. - Available at http://www.legislation.gov.uk/wsi/2014/2463/contents/made. - In English and Welsh. Welsh title: Gorchymyn Cefnffordd yr A465 (Ffyrdd Ymuno ac Ymadael wrth Gyfnewidfa Llan-ffwyst, Sir Fynwy) (Gwahardd Cerbydau Dros Dro) 2014 Non-print

The A465 Trunk Road (Tredegar Roundabout, Blaenau Gwent to Rhymney Interchange, Caerphilly) (Temporary Prohibition of Vehicles, Cyclists and Pedestrians) Order 2014 No. 2014/3395 (W.345). - Enabling power: Road Traffic Regulation Act 1984, s. 14 (1) (4). - Issued: 30.12.2014. Made: 12.12.2014. Coming into force: 19.12.2014. Effect: None. Territorial extent & classification: W. Local. - Available at http://www.legislation.gov.uk/wsi/2014/3395/contents/made. - In English and Welsh. Welsh title: Gorchymyn Cefnffordd yr A465 (Cylchfan Tredegar, Blaenau Gwent i Gyfnewidfa Rhymni, Caerffili) (Gwahardd Cerbydau, Beicwyr a Cherddwyr Dros Dro) 2014 Non-print

The A465 Trunk Road (Tredegar Roundabout, Blaenau Gwent to Rhymney Roundabout, Caerphilly) (Temporary Prohibition of Vehicles and Cyclists) Order 2014 No. 2014/1060 (W.100). - Enabling power: Road Traffic Regulation Act 1984, s. 14 (1) (4). - Issued: 24.04.2014. Made: 07.04.2014. Coming into force: 16.04.2014. Effect: None. Territorial extent & classification: W. Local. - Available at http://www.legislation.gov.uk/wsi/2014/1060/contents/made. - In English and Welsh. Welsh title: Gorchymyn Cefnffordd yr A465 (Cylchfan Tredegar, Blaenau Gwent i Gylchfan Rhymni, Caerffili) (Gwahardd Cerbydau a Beicwyr Dros Dro) 2014 Non-print

The A470 Trunk Road (Abercanaid Roundabout to Cefn Coed Roundabout, Merthyr Tydfil) (Temporary Prohibition of Vehicles) Order 2014 No. 2014/1211 (W.127). - Enabling power: Road Traffic Regulation Act 1984, ss. 14 (1) (4). - Issued: 19.05.2014. Made: 07.05.2014. Coming into force: 13.05.2014. Effect: None. Territorial extent & classification: W. Local. - Available at http://www.legislation.gov.uk/wsi/2014/1211/contents/made. - In English and Welsh. Welsh title: Gorchymyn Cefnffordd yr A470 (Cylchfan Abercannaid i Gylchfan Cefncoedycymer, Merthyr Tudful) (Gwahardd Cerbydau Dros Dro) 2014 Non-print

The A470 Trunk Road (Abercynon Roundabout, Rhondda Cynon Taf to Abercanaid Roundabout, Merthyr Tydfil) (Temporary Prohibition of Vehicles, Cyclists and Pedestrians) Order 2014 No. 2014/1202 (W.118). - Enabling power: Road Traffic Regulation Act 1984, ss. 14 (1) (4). - Issued: 20.05.2014. Made: 02.05.2014. Coming into force: 09.05.2014. Effect: None. Territorial extent & classification: W. Local. - Available at http://www.legislation.gov.uk/wsi/2014/1202/contents/made. - In English and Welsh. Welsh title: Gorchymyn Cefnffordd yr A470 (Cylchfan Abercynon, Rhondda Cynon Taf i Gylchfan Abercannaid, Merthyr Tudful) (Gwahardd Cerbydau, Beicwyr a Cherddwyr Dros Dro) 2014 Non-print

The A470 Trunk Road (Builth Wells to Llangurig, Powys) (Temporary Traffic Restrictions and No Overtaking) Order 2014 No. 2014/2239 (W.221). - Enabling power: Road Traffic Regulation Act 1984, ss. 14 (1) (4). - Issued: 01.09.2014. Made: 22.08.2014. Coming into force: 01.09.2014. Effect: None. Territorial extent & classification: W. Local. - Available at http://www.legislation.gov.uk/wsi/2014/2239/contents/made. - In English and Welsh. Welsh title: Gorchymyn Cefnffordd yr A470 (Llanfair-ym-Muallt i Langurig, Powys) (Cyfyngiadau Traffig Dros Dro a Dim Goddiweddyd) 2014 Non-print

The A470 Trunk Road (Caersws to Cemmaes Road, Powys) (Temporary Speed Restrictions & No Overtaking) Order 2014 No. 2014/2568 (W.249). - Enabling power: Road Traffic Regulation Act 1984, ss. 14 (1) (4). - Issued: 25.09.2014. Made: 26.08.2014. Coming into force: 01.09.2014. Effect: None. Territorial extent & classification: W. Local. - Available at http://www.legislation.gov.uk/wsi/2014/2568/contents/made. - In English and Welsh. Welsh title: Gorchymyn Cefnffordd yr A470 (Caers?s i Lantwymyn, Powys) (Cyfyngiadau Cyflymder Dros Dro a Dim Goddiweddyd) 2014 Non-print

The A470 Trunk Road (Cemmaes Road Roundabout to County Border, South of Mallwyd, Powys) (Temporary Traffic Restrictions and No Overtaking) Order 2014 No. 2014/1550 (W.159). - Enabling power: Road Traffic Regulation Act 1984, ss. 14 (1) (4). - Issued: 16.06.2014. Made: 12.06.2014. Coming into force: 16.06.2014. Effect: None. Territorial extent & classification: W. Local. - Available at http://www.legislation.gov.uk/wsi/2014/1550/contents/made. - In English and Welsh. Welsh title: Gorchymyn Cefnffordd yr A470 (Cylchfan Glantwymyn i'r Ffin Sirol, Man i'r De o Fallwyd, Powys) (Cyfyngiadau Traffig Dros Dro a Dim Goddiweddyd) 2014 Non-print

The A470 Trunk Road (Coryton Interchange, Cardiff) (Temporary Prohibition of Left and Right Hand Turns and 40 MPH Speed Limit) Order 2014 No. 2014/2000 (W.201). - Enabling power: Road Traffic Regulation Act 1984, ss. 14 (1) (4). - Issued: 31.07.2014. Made: 24.07.2014. Coming into force: 31.07.2014. Effect: None. Territorial extent & classification: W. Local. - Available at http://www.legislation.gov.uk/wsi/2014/2000/contents/made. - In English and Welsh. Welsh title: Gorchymyn Cefnffordd yr A470 (Cyfnewidfa Coryton, Caerdydd) (Gwahardd Dros Dro Droi i'r Chwith a Throi i'r Dde a Therfyn Cyflymder 40 MYA Dros Dro) 2014 Non-print

The A470 Trunk Road (Derlwyn Junction, Carno, Powys) (Temporary Prohibition of Vehicles) Order 2014 No. 2014/349 (W.38). - Enabling power: Road Traffic Regulation Act 1984, ss. 14 (1) (4). - Issued: 20.02.2014. Made: 17.02.2014. Coming into force: 24.02.2014. Effect: None. Territorial extent & classification: W. Local. - Available at http://www.legislation.gov.uk/wsi/2014/349/contents/made. - In English and Welsh. Welsh title: Gorchymyn Cefnffordd yr A470 (Cyffordd Derlwyn, Carno, Powys) (Gwahardd Cerbydau Dros Dro) 2014 Non-print

The A470 Trunk Road (Glan Conwy, Conwy) (Temporary Traffic Prohibitions and Restrictions) Order 2014 No. 2014/164 (W.23). - Enabling power: Road Traffic Regulation Act 1984, ss. 14 (1) (4). - Issued: 31.01.2014. Made: 28.01.2014. Coming into force: 03.02.2014. Effect: None. Territorial extent & classification: Local. - Available at http://www.legislation.gov.uk/wsi/2014/164/contents/made. - In English and Welsh. Welsh title: Gorchymyn Cefnffordd yr A470 (Llansanffraid Glan Conwy, Conwy) (Gwaharddiadau a Chyfyngiadau Traffig Dros Dro) 2014 Non-print

The A470 Trunk Road (Llanffestiniog to Ty Nant Junction, Gwynedd) (Temporary Traffic Prohibitions and Restrictions) Order 2014 No. 2014/235 (W.31). - Enabling power: Road Traffic Regulation Act 1984, s. 14 (1) (4). - Issued: 12.02.2014. Made: 06.02.2014. Coming into force: 17.02.2014. Effect: None. Territorial extent & classification: W. Local. - Available at http://www.legislation.gov.uk/wsi/2014/235/contents/made. - In English and Welsh. Welsh title: Gorchymyn Cefnffordd yr A470 (Llanffestiniog i Gyffordd Ty Nant, Gwynedd) (Gwaharddiadau a Chyfyngiadau Traffig Dros Dro) 2014 Non-print

The A470 Trunk Road (Llangurig to Caersws, Powys) (Temporary Speed Restrictions & No Overtaking) Order 2014 No. 2014/2574 (W.250). - Enabling power: Road Traffic Regulation Act 1984, s. 14 (1) (4). - Issued: 25.09.2014. Made: 26.08.2014. Coming into force: 01.09.2014. Effect: None. Territorial extent & classification: W. Local. - Available at http://www.legislation.gov.uk/wsi/2014/2574/contents/made. - In English and Welsh. Welsh title: Gorchymyn Cefnffordd yr A470 (Llangurig i Gaers?s, Powys) (Cyfyngiadau Cyflymder Dros Dro a Dim Goddiweddyd) 2014 Non-print

The A470 Trunk Road (Llanrwst Road, Llansanffraid Glan Conwy, Conwy) (Prohibition of Waiting) Order 2014 No. 2014/1059 (W.99). - Enabling power: Road Traffic Regulation Act 1984, ss. 1 (1), 2 (1) (2), 4 (2), 124, sch. 9, para. 27. - Issued: 23.04.2014. Made: 31.03.2014. Coming into force: 07.04.2014. Effect: S.I. 1994/3019 revoked. Territorial extent & classification: W. Local. - Available at http://www.legislation.gov.uk/wsi/2014/1059/contents/made. - In English and Welsh. Welsh title: Gorchymyn Cefnffordd yr A470 (Ffordd Llanrwst, Llansanffraid Glan Conwy, Conwy) (Gwahardd Aros) 2014 Non-print

The A470 Trunk Road (Llansanffraid Glan Conwy to Bodnant, Conwy County Borough) (Temporary Traffic Restrictions and Prohibitions) Order 2014 No. 2014/159 (W.20). - Enabling power: Road Traffic Regulation Act 1984, s. 14 (1) (4). - Issued: 31.01.2014. Made: 24.01.2014. Coming into force: 30.01.2014. Effect: None. Territorial extent & classification: W. Local. - Available at http://www.legislation.gov.uk/wsi/2014/159/contents/made. - In English and Welsh. Welsh title: Gorchymyn Cefnffordd yr A470 (Llansanffraid Glan Conwy i Fodnant, Bwrdeistref Sirol Conwy) (Cyfyngiadau a Gwaharddiadau Traffig Dros Dro) 2014 Non-print

The A470 Trunk Road (Llyswen Powys) (Temporary Traffic Prohibitions and Restrictions) Order 2014 No. 2014/1288 (W.132). - Enabling power: Road Traffic Regulation Act 1984, ss. 14 (1) (4). - Issued: 22.05.2014. Made: 19.05.2014. Coming into force: 27.05.2014. Effect: None. Territorial extent & classification: W. Local. - Available at http://www.legislation.gov.uk/wsi/2014/1288/contents/made. - In English and Welsh. Welsh title: Gorchymyn Cefnffordd yr A470 (Llys-wen, Powys) (Gwaharddiadau a Chyfyngiadau Traffig Dros Dro) 2014 Non-print

The A470 Trunk Road (Newbridge-on-Wye, Powys) (Temporary 30 MPH Speed Limit) Order 2014 No. 2014/241 (W.33). - Enabling power: Road Traffic Regulation Act 1984, ss. 14 (1) (4) (7). - Issued: 12.02.2014. Made: 07.02.2014. Coming into force: 17.02.2014. Effect: None. Territorial extent & classification: W. Local. - Available at http://www.legislation.gov.uk/wsi/2014/241/contents/made. - In English and Welsh. Welsh title: Gorchymyn Cefnffordd yr A470 (Pontnewydd ar Wy, Powys) (Terfyn Cyflymder 30 MYA Dros Dro) 2014 Non-print

The A470 Trunk Road (Powys/Merthyr Tydfil County Boundary to Builth Wells, Powys) (Temporary Speed Restrictions & No Overtaking) Order 2014 No. 2014/2576 (W.252). - Enabling power: Road Traffic Regulation Act 1984, s. 14 (1) (4). - Issued: 25.09.2014. Made: 26.08.2014. Coming into force: 01.09.2014. Effect: None. Territorial extent & classification: W. Local. - Available at http://www.legislation.gov.uk/wsi/2014/2576/contents/made. - In English and Welsh. Welsh title: Gorchymyn Cefnffordd yr A470 (Ffin Sirol Powys/Merthyr Tudful i Lanfair-ym-Muallt, Powys) (Cyfyngiadau Cyflymder Dros Dro a Dim Goddiweddyd) 2014 Non-print

The A470 Trunk Road (Rhyd y Creuau to Hafod, Conwy) (Temporary Traffic Restrictions and No Overtaking) Order 2014 No. 2014/1205 (W.121). - Enabling power: Road Traffic Regulation Act 1984, ss. 14 (1) (4). - Issued: 19.05.2014. Made: 02.05.2014. Coming into force: 12.05.2014. Effect: None. Territorial extent & classification: W. Local. - Available at http://www.legislation.gov.uk/wsi/2014/1205/contents/made. - In English and Welsh. Welsh title: Gorchymyn Cefnffordd yr A470 (Rhyd-y-creuau i Hafod, Conwy) (Cyfyngiadau Traffig Dros Dro a Gwahardd Goddiweddyd) 2014 Non-print

The A470 Trunk Road (Trawsfynydd, Gwynedd) (Temporary Traffic Restrictions & No Overtaking) Order 2014 No. 2014/234 (W.30). - Enabling power: Road Traffic Regulation Act 1984, s. 14 (1) (4). - Issued: 12.02.2014. Made: 06.02.2014. Coming into force: 13.02.2013. Effect: None. Territorial extent & classification: W. Local. - Available at http://www.legislation.gov.uk/wsi/2014/234/contents/made. - In English and Welsh. Welsh title: Gorchymyn Cefnffordd yr A470 (Trawsfynydd, Gwynedd) (Cyfyngiadau Traffig Dros Dro a Dim Goddiweddyd) 2014 Non-print

The A477 Trunk Road (Llanddowror to Red Roses, Carmarthenshire) (Temporary Speed Restrictions & No Overtaking) Order 2014 No. 2014/1058 (W.98). - Enabling power: Road Traffic Regulation Act 1984, s. 14 (1) (4). - Issued: 23.04.2014. Made: 03.04.2014. Coming into force: 07.04.2014. Effect: None. Territorial extent & classification: W. Local. - Available at http://www.legislation.gov.uk/wsi/2014/1058/contents/made. - In English and Welsh. Welsh title: Gorchymyn Cefnffordd yr A477 (Llanddowror i Ros-goch, Sir Gaerfyrddin) (Cyfyngiadau Cyflymder Dros Dro a Dim Goddiweddyd) 2014 Non-print

The A477 Trunk Road (St Clears Roundabout, Carmarthenshire to Kilgetty Roundabout, Pembrokeshire) (Temporary Prohibition of Wide Vehicles) Order 2014 No. 2014/207 (W.28). - Enabling power: Road Traffic Regulation Act 1984, s. 14 (1) (4). - Issued: 06.02.2014. Made: 30.01.2014. Coming into force: 31.01.2014. Effect: None. Territorial extent & classification: W. Local. - Available at http://www.legislation.gov.uk/wsi/2014/207/contents/made. - In English and Welsh. Welsh title: Gorchymyn Cefnffordd yr A477 (Cylchfan Sanclêr, Sir Gaerfyrddin i Gylchfan Cilgeti, Sir Benfro) (Gwahardd Cerbydau Llydan Dros Dro) 2014 Non-print

The A479 Trunk Road (Glanusk Park to Llyswen, Powys) (Temporary Traffic Restrictions and No Overtaking) Order 2014 No. 2014/2240 (W.222). - Enabling power: Road Traffic Regulation Act 1984, ss. 14 (1) (4). - Issued: 01.09.2014. Made: 22.08.2014. Coming into force: 01.09.2014. Effect: None. Territorial extent & classification: W. Local. - Available at http://www.legislation.gov.uk/wsi/2014/2240/contents/made. - In English and Welsh. Welsh title: Gorchymyn Cefnffordd yr A479 (Parc Glan-wysg i Lys-wen, Powys) (Cyfyngiadau Traffig Dros Dro a Dim Goddiweddyd) 2014 Non-print

The A483 Trunk Road (Broad Street & High Street, Builth Wells, Powys) (Temporary Prohibition of Vehicles) Order 2014 No. 2014/2464 (W.233). - Enabling power: Road Traffic Regulation Act 1984, s. 14 (1) (4) (7). - Issued: 19.09.2014. Made: 01.09.2014. Coming into force: 08.09.2014. Effect: None. Territorial extent & classification: W. Local. - Available at http://www.legislation.gov.uk/wsi/2014/2464/contents/made. - In English and Welsh. Welsh title: Gorchymyn Cefnffordd yr A483 (Stryd Lydan a Stryd Fawr, Llanfair-ym-Muallt, Powys) (Gwahardd Cerbydau Dros Dro) 2014 Non-print

The A483 Trunk Road (Cilyrychen Level Crossing, Llandeilo Road, Near Llandybie, Carmarthenshire) (Temporary Prohibition of Vehicles) Order 2014 No. 2014/1056 (W.96). - Enabling power: Road Traffic Regulation Act 1984, s. 14 (1) (4). - Issued: 23.04.2014. Made: 03.04.2014. Coming into force: 09.04.2014. Effect: None. Territorial extent & classification: W. Local. - Available at http://www.legislation.gov.uk/wsi/2014/1056/contents/made. - In English and Welsh. Welsh title: Gorchymyn Cefnffordd yr A483 (Croesfan Reilffordd Cilyrychen, Heol Llandeilo, Ger Llandybie, Sir Gaerfyrddin) (Gwahardd Cerbydau Dros Dro) 2014 Non-print

The A483 Trunk Road (Derwydd, Llandybie, Dyfed) (De-Restriction) Order 1995 Revocation Order 2014 No. 2014/1065 (W.104). - Enabling power: Road Traffic Regulation Act 1984, s. 124, sch. 9, para. 27. - Issued: 24.04.2014. Made: 04.04.2014. Coming into force: 11.04.2014. Effect: None. Territorial extent & classification: W. Local. - Available at http://www.legislation.gov.uk/wsi/2014/1065/contents/made. - In English and Welsh. Welsh title: Gorchymyn Dirymu Gorchymyn Cefnffordd yr A483 (Derwydd, Llandybïe, Dyfed) (Codi Cyfyngiad) 1995 2014 Non-print

The A483 Trunk Road (Dolfor Road, Newtown, Powys) (Temporary Prohibition of Vehicles, Cyclists & Pedestrians) Order 2014 No. 2014/3115 (W.314). - Enabling power: Road Traffic Regulation Act 1984, s. 14 (1) (4). - Issued: 26.11.2014. Made: 17.11.2014. Coming into force: 24.11.2014. Effect: None. Territorial extent & classification: W. Local. - Available at http://www.legislation.gov.uk/wsi/2014/3115/contents/made. - In English and Welsh. Welsh title: Gorchymyn Cefnffordd yr A483 (Ffordd Dolfor, Y Drenewydd, Powys) (Gwahardd Cerbydau, Beicwyr a Cherddwyr Dros Dro) 2014 Non-print

ROAD TRAFFIC, WALES: TRAFFIC REGULATION

The A483 Trunk Road (Ffairfach to Derwydd, Carmarthenshire) (Temporary Traffic Restrictions and Prohibitions) Order 2014 No. 2014/2656 (W.262). - Enabling power: Road Traffic Regulation Act 1984, s. 14 (1) (4). - Issued: 06.10.2014. Made: 29.09.2014. Coming into force: 06.10.2014. Effect: None. Territorial extent & classification: W. Local. - Available at http://www.legislation.gov.uk/wsi/2014/2656/contents/made. - In English and Welsh. Welsh title: Gorchymyn Cefnffordd yr A483 (Ffair-fach i Dderwydd, Sir Gaerfyrddin) (Cyfyngiadau a Gwaharddiadau Traffig Dros Dro) 2014 Non-print

The A483 Trunk Road (Junction 1 to Wales/England Border, Wrexham County Borough) (Temporary Traffic Restriction and Prohibitions) Order 2014 No. 2014/810 (W.81). - Enabling power: Road Traffic Regulation Act 1984, s. 14 (1) (4). - Issued: 27.03.2014. Made: 25.03.2014. Coming into force: 01.04.2014. Effect: None. Territorial extent & classification: W. Local. - Available at http://www.legislation.gov.uk/wsi/2014/810/contents/made. - In English and Welsh. Welsh title: Gorchymyn Cefnffordd yr A483 (Cyffordd 1 i Ffin Cymru/Lloegr, Bwrdeistref Sirol Wrecsam) (Cyfyngiad a Gwaharddiadau Traffig Dros Dro) 2014 Non-print

The A483 Trunk Road (Junction 3 to Junction 4, Wrexham County Borough) (Temporary Traffic Prohibitions & Restriction) Order 2014 No. 2014/388 (W.47). - Enabling power: Road Traffic Regulation Act 1984, s. 14 (1) (4). - Issued: 07.03.2014. Made: 24.02.2014. Coming into force: 02.03.2014. Effect: None. Territorial extent & classification: W. Local. - Available at http://www.legislation.gov.uk/wsi/2014/388/contents/made. - In English and Welsh. Welsh title: Gorchymyn Cefnffordd yr A483 (Cyffordd 3 i Gyffordd 4, Bwrdeistref Sirol Wrecsam) (Gwaharddiadau a Chyfyngiad Traffig Dros Dro) 2014 Non-print

The A483 Trunk Road (Junction 5 (Mold Road Interchange) to Junction 6 (Gresford Interchange), Wrexham County Borough) (Temporary Prohibition of Vehicles) Order 2014 No. 2014/403 (W.48). - Enabling power: Road Traffic Regulation Act 1984, s. 14 (1) (4). - Issued: 07.03.2014. Made: 25.02.2014. Coming into force: 03.03.2014. Effect: None. Territorial extent & classification: W. Local. - Available at http://www.legislation.gov.uk/wsi/2014/403/contents/made. - In English and Welsh. Welsh title: Gorchymyn Cefnffordd yr A483 (Cyffordd 5 (Cyfnewidfa Ffordd yr Wyddgrug) i Gyffordd 6 (Cyfnewidfa Gresffordd), Bwrdeistref Sirol Wrecsam) (Gwahardd Cerbydau Dros Dro) 2014 Non-print

The A483 Trunk Road (Junction 7, Rossett Interchange to the Wales/England Border, Wrexham County Borough) (Temporary Prohibition of Vehicles and 40 MPH Speed Limit) Order 2014 No. 2014/2233 (W.216). - Enabling power: Road Traffic Regulation Act 1984, s. 14 (1) (4). - Issued: 28.08.2014. Made: 21.08.2014. Coming into force: 01.09.2014. Effect: None. Territorial extent & classification: W. Local. - Available at http://www.legislation.gov.uk/wsi/2014/2233/contents/made. - In English and Welsh. Welsh title: Gorchymyn Cefnffordd yr A483 (Cyffordd 7, Cyfnewidfa'r Orsedd i Ffin Cymru/Lloegr, Bwrdeistref Sirol Wrecsam) (Gwahardd Cerbydau a Therfyn Cyflymder o 40 mya Dros Dro) 2014 Non-print

The A483 Trunk Road (Junction 7, Rossett Interchange to the Wales/England Border, Wrexham County Borough) (Temporary Prohibition of Vehicles) Order 2014 No. 2014/711 (W.78). - Enabling power: Road Traffic Regulation Act 1984, s. 14 (1) (4). - Issued: 02.06.2014. Made: 17.03.2014. Coming into force: 24.03.2014. Effect: None. Territorial extent & classification: W. Local. - Available at http://www.legislation.gov.uk/wsi/2014/711/contents/made. - In English and Welsh. Welsh title: Gorchymyn Cefnffordd yr A483 (Cyffordd 7, Cyfnewidfa'r Orsedd i Ffin Cymru/Lloegr, Bwrdeistref Sirol Wrecsam) (Gwahardd Cerbydau Dros Dro) 2014 Non-print

The A483 Trunk Road (Llandovery to Sugar Loaf, Carmarthenshire) (Temporary Traffic Restrictions and Prohibitions) Order 2014 No. 2014/2891 (W.292). - Enabling power: Road Traffic Regulation Act 1984, s. 14 (1) (4). - Issued: 05.11.2014. Made: 27.10.2014. Coming into force: 03.11.2014. Effect: None. Territorial extent & classification: W. Local. - Available at http://www.legislation.gov.uk/wsi/2014/2891/contents/made. - In English and Welsh. Welsh title: Gorchymyn Cefnffordd yr A483 (Llanymddyfri i Ddinas-y-bwlch, Sir Gaerfyrddin) (Cyfyngiadau a Gwaharddiadau Traffig Dros Dro) 2014 Non-print

The A483 Trunk Road (Newbridge Bypass, Wrexham County Borough) (Temporary Prohibition of Vehicles) Order 2014 No. 2014/914 (W.90). - Enabling power: Road Traffic Regulation Act 1984, s. 14 (1) (4). - Issued: 08.04.2014. Made: 25.03.2014. Coming into force: 01.04.2014. Effect: None. Territorial extent & classification: W. Local. - Available at http://www.legislation.gov.uk/wsi/2014/914/contents/made. - In English and Welsh. Welsh title: Gorchymyn Cefnffordd yr A483 (Ffordd Osgoi Newbridge, Bwrdeistref Sirol Wrecsam) (Gwahardd Cerbydau Dros Dro) 2014 Non-print

The A483 Trunk Road (Newtown to Llanymynech, Powys) (Temporary Speed Restrictions & No Overtaking) Order 2014 No. 2014/3391 (W.343). - Enabling power: Road Traffic Regulation Act 1984, s. 14 (1) (4). - Issued: 30.12.2014. Made: 02.12.2014. Coming into force: 08.12.2014. Effect: None. Territorial extent & classification: W. Local. - Available at http://www.legislation.gov.uk/wsi/2014/3391/contents/made. - In English and Welsh. Welsh title: Gorchymyn Cefnffordd yr A483 (Y Drenewydd i Lanymynech, Powys) (Cyfyngiadau Cyflymder a Dim Goddiweddyd Dros Dro) 2014 Non-print

The A483 Trunk Road (Powys/Carmarthenshire Border to Newtown, Powys) (Temporary Speed Restrictions & No Overtaking) Order 2014 No. 2014/3374 (W.338). - Enabling power: Road Traffic Regulation Act 1984, s. 14 (1) (4). - Issued: 30.12.2014. Made: 02.12.2014. Coming into force: 08.12.2014. Effect: None. Territorial extent & classification: W. Local. - Available at http://www.legislation.gov.uk/wsi/2014/3374/contents/made. - In English and Welsh. Welsh title: Gorchymyn Cefnffordd yr A483 (Ffin Powys/Sir Gaerfyrddin i'r Drenewydd, Powys) (Cyfyngiadau Cyflymder a Dim Goddiweddyd Dros Dro) 2014 Non-print

The A483 Trunk Road (Rhosmaen Street, Llandeilo, Carmarthenshire) (Temporary Prohibition of Vehicles) Order 2014 No. 2014/1204 (W.120). - Enabling power: Road Traffic Regulation Act 1984, ss. 14 (1) (4). - Issued: 19.05.2014. Made: 02.05.2014. Coming into force: 11.05.2014. Effect: None. Territorial extent & classification: W. Local. - Available at http://www.legislation.gov.uk/wsi/2014/1204/contents/made. - In English and Welsh. Welsh title: Gorchymyn Cefnffordd yr A483 (Stryd Rhosmaen, Llandeilo, Sir Gaerfyrddin) (Gwahardd Cerbydau Dros Dro) 2014 Non-print

The A483 Trunk Road (Various Roads in Builth Wells, Powys) (Temporary Traffic Prohibitions) Order 2014 No. 2014/2757 (W.279). - Enabling power: Road Traffic Regulation Act 1984, s. 14 (1) (4) (7). - Issued: 20.10.2014. Made: 13.10.2014. Coming into force: 20.10.2014. Effect: None. Territorial extent & classification: W. Local. - Welsh title: Gorchymyn Cefnffordd yr A483 (Amrywiol Ffyrdd yn Llanfair-ym-Muallt, Powys) (Gwaharddiadau Traffig Dros Dro) 2014. - Available at http://www.legislation.gov.uk/wsi/2014/2757/contents/made Non-print

The A487 Trunk Road (Aberarth, Ceredigion) (Temporary Prohibition of Vehicles) Order 2014 No. 2014/2249 (W.224). - Enabling power: Road Traffic Regulation Act 1984, s. 14 (1) (4). - Issued: 19.09.2014. Made: 22.08.2014. Coming into force: 01.09.2014. Effect: None. Territorial extent & classification: W. Local. - Available at http://www.legislation.gov.uk/wsi/2014/2249/contents/made. - In English and Welsh. Welsh title: Gorchymyn Cefnffordd yr A487 (Aber-arth, Ceredigion) (Gwahardd Cerbydau Dros Dro) 2014 Non-print

The A487 Trunk Road (Bangor Road, Caernarfon, Gwynedd) (Temporary Traffic Prohibitions and Restrictions) Order 2014 No. 2014/3513 (W.351). - Enabling power: Road Traffic Regulation Act 1984, s. 14 (1) (4). - Issued: 27.01.2015. Made: 30.12.2014. Coming into force: 06.01.2015. Effect: None. Territorial extent & classification: W. Local. - Available at http://www.legislation.gov.uk/wsi/2014/3513/contents/made. - In English and Welsh. Welsh title: Gorchymyn Cefnffordd yr A487 (Ffordd Bangor, Caernarfon, Gwynedd) (Gwaharddiadau a Chyfyngiadau Traffig Dros Dro) 2014 Non-print

The A487 Trunk Road (Blaenannerch, Ceredigion) (Temporary Traffic Restrictions & No Overtaking) Order 2014 No. 2014/454 (W.52). - Enabling power: Road Traffic Regulation Act 1984, s. 14 (1) (4) (7). - Issued: 07.03.2014. Made: 28.02.2014. Coming into force: 06.03.2014. Effect: None. Territorial extent & classification: W. Local. - Available at http://www.legislation.gov.uk/wsi/2014/454/contents/made. - In English and Welsh. Welsh title: Gorchymyn Cefnffordd yr A487 (Blaenannerch, Ceredigion) (Cyfyngiadau Traffig Dros Dro a Dim Goddiweddyd) 2014 Non-print

The A487 Trunk Road (Bontnewydd, Gwynedd) (Temporary 10 mph Speed Limit & No Overtaking) Order 2014 No. 2014/1087 (W.108). - Enabling power: Road Traffic Regulation Act 1984, s. 14 (1) (4). - Issued: 02.05.2014. Made: 23.04.2014. Coming into force: 28.04.2014. Effect: None. Territorial extent & classification: W. Local. - Available at http://www.legislation.gov.uk/wsi/2014/1087/contents/made. - In English and Welsh. Welsh title: Gorchymyn Cefnffordd yr A487 (Y Bontnewydd, Gwynedd) (Terfyn Cyflymder 10 mya Dros Dro a Dim Goddiweddyd) 2014 Non-print

The A487 Trunk Road (Bridge Street, Aberystwyth, Ceredigion) (Temporary Prohibition of Vehicles) (No.2) Order 2014 No. 2014/2465 (W.234). - Enabling power: Road Traffic Regulation Act 1984, s. 14 (1) (4). - Issued: 19.09.2014. Made: 01.09.2014. Coming into force: 08.09.2014. Effect: None. Territorial extent & classification: W. Local. - Available at http://www.legislation.gov.uk/wsi/2014/2465/contents/made. - In English and Welsh. Welsh title: Gorchymyn Cefnffordd yr A487 (Stryd y Bont, Aberystwyth, Ceredigion) (Gwahardd Cerbydau Dros Dro) (Rhif 2) 2014 Non-print

The A487 Trunk Road (Bridge Street, Aberystwyth, Ceredigion) (Temporary Prohibition of Vehicles) Order 2014 No. 2014/1574 (W.160). - Enabling power: Road Traffic Regulation Act 1984, s. 14 (1) (4). - Issued: 19.06.2014. Made: 16.06.2014. Coming into force: 23.06.2014. Effect: None. Territorial extent & classification: W. Local. - Available at http://www.legislation.gov.uk/wsi/2014/1574/contents/made. - In English and Welsh. Welsh title: Gorchymyn Cefnffordd yr A487 (Stryd y Bont, Aberystwyth, Ceredigion) (Gwahardd Cerbydau Dros Dro) 2014 Non-print

The A487 Trunk Road (Corris Uchaf to Rhiw Gwgan, Gwynedd) (Temporary Traffic Restrictions & No Overtaking) Order 2014 No. 2014/1502 (W.152). - Enabling power: Road Traffic Regulation Act 1984, s. 14 (1) (4). - Issued: 16.06.2014. Made: 02.06.2014. Coming into force: 09.06.2014. Effect: None. Territorial extent & classification: W. Local. - Available at http://www.legislation.gov.uk/wsi/2014/1502/contents/made. - In English and Welsh. Welsh title: Gorchymyn Cefnffordd yr A487 (Corris Uchaf i Riw Gwgan, Gwynedd) (Cyfyngiadau Traffig Dros Dro a Dim Goddiweddyd) 2014 Non-print

The A487 Trunk Road (Llanllyfni Bypass, Gwynedd) (Temporary Speed Restrictions & No Overtaking) Order 2014 No. 2014/1677 (W.170). - Enabling power: Road Traffic Regulation Act 1984, s. 14 (1) (4). - Issued: 02.07.2014. Made: 27.06.2014. Coming into force: 03.07.2014. Effect: None. Territorial extent & classification: W. Local. - Available at http://www.legislation.gov.uk/wsi/2014/1677/contents/made. - In English and Welsh. Welsh title: Gorchymyn Cefnffordd yr A487 (Ffordd Osgoi Llanllyfni, Gwynedd) (Cyfyngiadau Cyflymder Dros Dro a Dim Goddiweddyd) 2014 Non-print

The A487 Trunk Road (Llanrhystud to Llanfarian, Ceredigion) (Temporary Speed Restrictions & No Overtaking) Order 2014 No. 2014/1501 (W.151). - Enabling power: Road Traffic Regulation Act 1984, s. 14 (1) (4) (7). - Issued: 12.06.2014. Made: 02.06.2014. Coming into force: 09.06.2014. Effect: S.I. S.I. 2003/480 (W.66) suspended with savings. Territorial extent & classification: W. Local. - Available at http://www.legislation.gov.uk/wsi/2014/1501/contents/made. - In English and Welsh. Welsh title: Gorchymyn Cefnffordd yr A487 (Llanrhystud i Lanfarian, Ceredigion) (Cyfyngiadau Cyflymder Dros Dro a Dim Goddiweddyd) 2014 Non-print

The A487 Trunk Road (Mill Street, Aberystwyth, Ceredigion) (Temporary Prohibition of Vehicles) Order 2014 No. 2014/3427 (W.349). - Enabling power: Road Traffic Regulation Act 1984, s. 14 (1) (4). - Issued: 02.01.2015. Made: 29.12.2014. Coming into force: 05.01.2015. Effect: None. Territorial extent & classification: W. Local. - Available at http://www.legislation.gov.uk/wsi/2014/3427/contents/made. - In English and Welsh. Welsh title: Gorchymyn Cefnffordd yr A487 (Dan Dre, Aberystwyth, Ceredigion) (Gwahardd Cerbydau Dros Dro) 2014 Non-print

The A487 Trunk Road (Newport, Pembrokeshire) (Temporary Prohibition of Vehicles) (No. 2) Order 2014 No. 2014/2647 (W.258). - Enabling power: Road Traffic Regulation Act 1984, s. 14 (1) (4). - Issued: 03.10.2014. Made: 26.09.2014. Coming into force: 05.10.2014. Effect: None. Territorial extent & classification: W. Local. - Available at http://www.legislation.gov.uk/wsi/2014/2647/contents/made. - In English and Welsh. Welsh title: Gorchymyn Cefnffordd yr A487 (Trefdraeth, Sir Benfro) (Gwahardd Cerbydau Dros Dro) (Rhif 2) 2014 Non-print

The A487 Trunk Road (Newport, Pembrokeshire) (Temporary Prohibition of Vehicles) Order 2014 No. 2014/1061 (W.101). - Enabling power: Road Traffic Regulation Act 1984, s. 14 (1) (4). - Issued: 24.04.2014. Made: 07.04.2014. Coming into force: 13.04.2014. Effect: None. Territorial extent & classification: W. Local. - Available at http://www.legislation.gov.uk/wsi/2014/1061/contents/made. - In English and Welsh. Welsh title: Gorchymyn Cefnffordd yr A487 (Trefdraeth, Sir Benfro) (Gwahardd Cerbydau Dros Dro) 2014 Non-print

The A487 Trunk Road (Powys-Ceredigion Border to Dyfi Bridge, North of Machynlleth, Powys) (Temporary Traffic Restrictions and No Overtaking) Order 2014 No. 2014/3376 (W.339). - Enabling power: Road Traffic Regulation Act 1984, s. 14 (1) (4). - Issued: 30.12.2014. Made:01.12.2014. Coming into force: 08.12.2014. Effect: None. Territorial extent & classification: W. Local. - Available at http://www.legislation.gov.uk/wsi/2014/3376/contents/made. - In English and Welsh. Welsh title: Gorchymyn Cefnffordd yr A487 (Ffin Powys/Ceredigion i Bont ar Ddyfi, i'r Gogledd o Fachynlleth, Powys) (Cyfyngiadau Traffig a Dim Goddiweddyd Dros Dro) 2014 Non-print

The A487 Trunk Road (Ty'n y Maes to Rhiw Staerdywyll, Corris, Gwynedd) (Temporary 30 MPH Speed Limit and No Overtaking) Order 2014 No. 2014/2468 (W.237). - Enabling power: Road Traffic Regulation Act 1984, s. 14 (1) (4). - Issued: 19.09.2014. Made: 09.09.2014. Coming into force: 15.09.2014. Effect: None. Territorial extent & classification: W. Local. - Available at http://www.legislation.gov.uk/wsi/2014/2468/contents/made. - In English and Welsh. Welsh title: Gorchymyn Cefnffordd yr A487 (Ty'n-y-maes i Riw Staerdywyll, Corris, Gwynedd) (Terfyn Cyflymder o 30 MYA Dros Dro a Dim Goddiweddyd) 2014 Non-print

The A487 Trunk Road (Y Felinheli Bypass, Gwynedd) (Temporary Traffic Restrictions & Prohibition) Order 2014 No. 2014/236 (W.32). - Enabling power: Road Traffic Regulation Act 1984, s. 14 (1) (4). - Issued: 12.02.2014. Made: 06.02.2014. Coming into force: 12.02.2014. Effect: None. Territorial extent & classification: W. Local. - Available at http://www.legislation.gov.uk/wsi/2014/236/contents/made. - In English and Welsh. Welsh title: Gorchymyn Cefnffordd yr A487 (Ffordd Osgoi'r Felinheli, Gwynedd) (Cyfyngiadau a Gwaharddiad Traffig Dros Dro) 2014 Non-print

The A489 Trunk Road (Cemmaes Road to Machynlleth, Powys) (Temporary Traffic Restrictions and No Overtaking) Order 2014 No. 2014/3202 (W.325). - Enabling power: Road Traffic Regulation Act 1984, s. 14 (1) (4). - Issued: 05.12.2014. Made: 01.12.2014. Coming into force: 08.12.2014. Effect: None. Territorial extent & classification: W. Local. - Available at http://www.legislation.gov.uk/wsi/2014/3202/contents/made. - In English and Welsh. Welsh title: Gorchymyn Cefnffordd yr A489 (Glantwymyn i Fachynlleth, Powys) (Cyfyngiadau Traffig a Dim Goddiweddyd Dros Dro) 2014 Non-print

The A489 Trunk Road (Llanidloes Road, Newtown, Powys) (Temporary Prohibition of Vehicles) Order 2014 No. 2014/2941 (W.300). - Enabling power: Road Traffic Regulation Act 1984, s. 14 (1) (4). - Issued: 12.11.2014. Made: 10.11.2014. Coming into force: 17.11.2014. Effect: None. Territorial extent & classification: W. Local. - Available at http://www.legislation.gov.uk/wsi/2014/2941/contents/made. - In English and Welsh. Welsh title: Gorchymyn Cefnffordd yr A489 (Ffordd Llanidloes, Y Drenewydd, Powys) (Gwahardd Cerbydau Dros Dro) 2014 Non-print

The A489 Trunk Road (Newtown to Caersws, Powys) (Temporary Speed Restrictions & No Overtaking) Order 2014 No. 2014/3389 (W.342). - Enabling power: Road Traffic Regulation Act 1984, s. 14 (1) (4). - Issued: 30.12.2014. Made: 02.12.2014. Coming into force: 08.12.2014. Effect: None. Territorial extent & classification: W. Local. - Available at http://www.legislation.gov.uk/wsi/2014/3389/contents/made. - In English and Welsh. Welsh title: Gorchymyn Cefnffordd yr A489 (Y Drenewydd i Gaersws, Powys) (Cyfyngiadau Cyflymder a Dim Goddiweddyd Dros Dro) 2014 Non-print

The A494 and A55 Trunk Roads (St Davids Park Interchange to Junction 33a (Brookside Junction), Flintshire) (Temporary Traffic Prohibitions and Restriction) Order 2014 No. 2014/2491 (W.239). - Enabling power: Road Traffic Regulation Act 1984, s. 14 (1) (4). - Issued: 22.09.2014. Made: 15.09.2014. Coming into force: 21.09.2014. Effect: None. Territorial extent & classification: W. Local. - Available at http://www.legislation.gov.uk/wsi/2014/2491/contents/made. - In English and Welsh. Welsh title: Gorchymyn Cefnffyrdd yr A494 a'r A55 (Cyfnewidfa Parc Dewi Sant i Gyffordd 33a (CyfforddBrookside), Sir y Fflint) (Gwaharddiadau a Chyfyngiad Traffig Dros Dro) 2014 Non-print

ROAD TRAFFIC, WALES: TRAFFIC REGULATION

The A494 and A550 Trunk Roads (Queensferry Interchange to Deeside Park Interchange, Flintshire) (Temporary Traffic Prohibitions and 40 MPH Speed Limit) (Amendment) Order 2014 No. 2014/1201 (W.117). - Enabling power: Road Traffic Regulation Act 1984, ss. 14 (1) (4) (7). - Issued: 20.05.2014. Made: 08.05.2014. Coming into force: 10.05.2014. Effect: W.S.I. 2014/1200 (W.116) amended. Territorial extent & classification: W. Local. - Available at http://www.legislation.gov.uk/wsi/2014/1201/contents/made. - In English and Welsh. Welsh title: Gorchymyn Cefnffyrdd yr A494 a'r A550 (Cyfnewidfa Queensferry i Gyfnewidfa Parc Glannau Dyfrdwy, Sir y Fflint) (Gwaharddiadau Traffig Dros Dro a Therfyn Cyflymder 40 MYA) (Diwygio) 2014 Non-print

The A494 and A550 Trunk Roads (Queensferry Interchange to Deeside Park Interchange, Flintshire) (Temporary Traffic Prohibitions and 40 MPH Speed Limit) Order 2014 No. 2014/1200 (W.116). - Enabling power: Road Traffic Regulation Act 1984, ss. 14 (1) (4) (7). - Issued: 20.05.2014. Made: 01.05.2014. Coming into force: 10.05.2014. Effect: None. Territorial extent & classification: W. Local. - Available at http://www.legislation.gov.uk/wsi/2014/1200/contents/made. - In English and Welsh. Welsh title: Gorchymyn Cefnffyrdd yr A494 a'r A550 (Cyfnewidfa Queensferry i Gyfnewidfa Parc Glannau Dyfrdwy, Sir y Fflint) (Gwaharddiadau Traffig Dros Dro a Therfyn Cyflymder 40 MYA) 2014 Non-print

The A494 Trunk Road (Bala, Gwynedd) (Temporary 30 mph Speed Limit & No Overtaking) Order 2014 No. 2014/1062 (W.102). - Enabling power: Road Traffic Regulation Act 1984, ss. 14 (1) (4). - Issued: 24.04.2014. Made: 14.04.2014. Coming into force: 22.04.2014. Effect: None. Territorial extent & classification: W. Local. - Available at http://www.legislation.gov.uk/wsi/2014/1062/contents/made. - In English and Welsh. Welsh title: Gorchymyn Cefnffordd yr A494 (Y Bala, Gwynedd) (Terfyn Cyflymder 30 mya Dros Dro a Dim Goddiweddyd) 2014 Non-print

The A494 Trunk Road (Bala to Bethel, Gwynedd) (Temporary Traffic Restrictions and No Overtaking) Order 2014 No. 2014/2493 (W.241). - Enabling power: Road Traffic Regulation Act 1984, ss. 14 (1) (4). - Issued: 22.09.2014. Made: 16.09.2014. Coming into force: 22.10.2014. Effect: None. Territorial extent & classification: W. Local. - Available at http://www.legislation.gov.uk/wsi/2014/2493/contents/made. - In English and Welsh. Welsh title: Gorchymyn Cefnffordd yr A494 (Y Bala i Fethel, Gwynedd) (Cyfyngiadau Traffig Dros Dro a Dim Goddiweddyd) 2014 Non-print

The A494 Trunk Road (Bala Triathlon, Gwynedd) (Temporary Prohibition of Vehicles) Order 2014 No. 2014/2281 (W.225). - Enabling power: Road Traffic Regulation Act 1984, s. 16A. - Issued: 01.09.2014. Made: 27.08.2014. Coming into force: 07.09.2014. Effect: None. Territorial extent & classification: W. Local. - Available at http://www.legislation.gov.uk/wsi/2014/2281/contents/made. - In English and Welsh. Welsh title: Gorchymyn Cefnffordd yr A494 (Triathlon y Bala, Gwynedd) (Gwahardd Cerbydau Dros Dro) 2014 Non-print

The A494 Trunk Road (Bethel to Braich Ddu, Glan-yr-Afon, Gwynedd) (Temporary Traffic Prohibition and Restrictions) Order 2014 No. 2014/177 (W.25). - Enabling power: Road Traffic Regulation Act 1984, s. 14 (1) (4). - Issued: 05.02.2014. Made: 30.01.2014. Coming into force: 06.02.2014. Effect: None. Territorial extent & classification: W. Local. - Available at http://www.legislation.gov.uk/wsi/2014/177/contents/made. - In English and Welsh. Welsh title: Gorchymyn Cefnffordd yr A494 (Bethel i Fraich Ddu, Glan-yr-afon, Gwynedd) (Gwaharddiad a Chyfyngiadau Traffig Dros Dro) 2014 Non-print

The A494 Trunk Road (Clawdd Poncen, Corwen, Denbighshire) (Temporary Speed Restrictions & No Overtaking) Order 2014 No. 2014/2838 (W.289). - Enabling power: Road Traffic Regulation Act 1984, ss. 14 (1) (4). - Issued: 24.10.2014. Made: 21.10.2014. Coming into force: 27.10.2014. Effect: None. Territorial extent & classification: W. Local. - Available at http://www.legislation.gov.uk/wsi/2014/2838/contents/made. - In English and Welsh. Welsh title: Gorchymyn Cefnffordd yr A494 (Clawdd Poncen, Corwen, Sir Ddinbych) (Cyfyngiadau Cyflymder Dros Dro a Dim Goddiweddyd) 2014 Non-print

The A494 Trunk Road (Dee Bridge, Queensferry, Flintshire) (Temporary 50 mph Speed Limit) Order 2014 No. 2014/3167 (W.322). - Enabling power: Road Traffic Regulation Act 1984, ss. 14 (1) (4). - Issued: 03.12.2014. Made: 25.11.2014. Coming into force: 01.12.2014. Effect: None. Territorial extent & classification: W. Local. - Available at http://www.legislation.gov.uk/wsi/2014/3167/contents/made. - In English and Welsh. Welsh title: Gorchymyn Cefnffordd yr A494 (Pont Afon Dyfrdwy, Queensferry, Sir y Fflint) (Terfyn Cyflymder 50 mya Dros Dro) 2014 Non-print

The A494 Trunk Road (Deeside Park Interchange, Flintshire) (Temporary Prohibition of Vehicles, Cyclists and Pedestrians) Order 2014 No. 2014/1137 (W.114). - Enabling power: Road Traffic Regulation Act 1984, ss. 14 (1) (4). - Issued: 06.05.2014. Made: 29.04.2014. Coming into force: 07.05.2014. Effect: None. Territorial extent & classification: W. Local. - Available at http://www.legislation.gov.uk/wsi/2014/1137/contents/made. - In English and Welsh. Welsh title: Gorchymyn Cefnffordd yr A494 (Cyfnewidfa Parc Glannau Dyfrdwy, Sir y Fflint) (Gwahardd Cerbydau, Beicwyr a Cherddwyr Dros Dro) 2014 Non-print

The A494 Trunk Road (Eastbound Entry Slip Road at Deeside Park Interchange, Flintshire) (Temporary Prohibition of Vehicles, Cyclists & Pedestrians) Order 2014 No. 2014/1210 (W.126). - Enabling power: Road Traffic Regulation Act 1984, ss. 14 (1) (4). - Issued: 19.05.2014. Made: 06.05.2014. Coming into force: 12.05.2014. Effect: None. Territorial extent & classification: W. Local. - Available at http://www.legislation.gov.uk/wsi/2014/1210/contents/made. - In English and Welsh. Welsh title: Gorchymyn Cefnffordd yr A494 (Y Ffordd Ymuno tua'r Dwyrain wrth Gyfnewidfa Parc Glannau Dyfrdwy, Sir y Fflint) (Gwahardd Cerbydau, Beicwyr a Cherddwyr Dros Dro) 2014 Non-print

The A494 Trunk Road (Gwyddelwern, Denbighshire) (Temporary Traffic Restriction & Prohibitions) Order 2014 No. 2014/197 (W.27). - Enabling power: Road Traffic Regulation Act 1984, s. 14 (1) (4). - Issued: 05.02.2014. Made: 03.02.2014. Coming into force: 10.02.2014. Effect: None. Territorial extent & classification: W. Local. - Available at http://www.legislation.gov.uk/wsi/2014/197/contents/made. - In English and Welsh. Welsh title: Gorchymyn Cefnffordd yr A494 (Gwyddelwern, Sir Ddinbych) (Cyfyngiad a Gwaharddiadau Traffig Dros Dro) 2014 Non-print

The A494 Trunk Road (Mold Bypass, Flintshire) (Temporary Prohibition of Vehicles & Cyclists) (No.2) Order 2014 No. 2014/1649 (W.167). - Enabling power: Road Traffic Regulation Act 1984, ss. 14 (1) (4). - Issued: 30.06.2014. Made: 25.06.2014. Coming into force: 30.06.2014. Effect: None. Territorial extent & classification: W. Local. - Available at http://www.legislation.gov.uk/wsi/2014/1649/contents/made. - In English and Welsh. Welsh title: Gorchymyn Cefnffordd yr A494 (Ffordd Osgoi'r Wyddgrug, Sir y Fflint) (Gwahardd Cerbydau a Beicwyr Dros Dro) (Rhif 2) 2014 Non-print

The A494 Trunk Road (Mold Bypass, Flintshire) (Temporary Prohibition of Vehicles & Cyclists) Order 2014 No. 2014/1206 (W.122). - Enabling power: Road Traffic Regulation Act 1984, ss. 14 (1) (4). - Issued: 19.05.2014. Made: 06.05.2014. Coming into force: 12.05.2014. Effect: None. Territorial extent & classification: W. Local. - Available at http://www.legislation.gov.uk/wsi/2014/1206/contents/made. - In English and Welsh. Welsh title: Gorchymyn Cefnffordd yr A494 (Ffordd Osgoi'r Wyddgrug, Sir y Fflint) (Gwahardd Cerbydau a Beicwyr Dros Dro) 2014 Non-print

The A494 Trunk Road (Pandy'r Capel, Denbighshire) (Temporary Traffic Prohibitions & Restrictions) Order 2014 No. 2014/160 (W.21). - Enabling power: Road Traffic Regulation Act 1984, s. 14 (1) (4). - Issued: 31.01.2014. Made: 27.01.2014. Coming into force: 03.02.2014. Effect: None. Territorial extent & classification: W. Local. - Available at http://www.legislation.gov.uk/wsi/2014/160/contents/made. - In English and Welsh. Welsh title: Gorchymyn Cefnffordd yr A494 (Pandy'r Capel, Sir Ddinbych) (Gwaharddiadau a Chyfyngiadau Traffig Dros Dro) 2014 Non-print

ROAD TRAFFIC, WALES: TRAFFIC REGULATION

The A494 Trunk Road (Plough Lane Junction, Aston, Deeside, Flintshire) (Temporary Prohibition of Vehicles, Cyclists and Pedestrians) Order 2014 No. 2014/1207 (W.123). - Enabling power: Road Traffic Regulation Act 1984, ss. 14 (1) (4). - Issued: 19.05.2014. Made: 05.05.2014. Coming into force: 15.05.2014. Effect: None. Territorial extent & classification: W. Local. - Available at http://www.legislation.gov.uk/wsi/2014/1207/contents/made. - In English and Welsh. Welsh title: Gorchymyn Cefnffordd yr A494 (Cyffordd Plough Lane, Aston, Glannau Dyfrdwy, Sir y Fflint) (Gwahardd Cerbydau, Beicwyr a Cherddwyr Dros Dro) 2014 Non-print

The A494 Trunk Road (Pont Rhyd-sarn to Pont Fronwydd, Gwynedd) (Temporary Traffic Restrictions and No Overtaking) Order 2014 No. 2014/1767 (W.180). - Enabling power: Road Traffic Regulation Act 1984, s. 14 (1) (4). - Issued: 10.07.2014. Made: 04.07.2014. Coming into force: 07.07.2014. Effect: None. Territorial extent & classification: W. Local. - Available at http://www.legislation.gov.uk/wsi/2014/1767/contents/made. - In English and Welsh. Welsh title: Gorchymyn Cefnffordd yr A494 (Pont Rhyd-sarn i Bont Fronwydd, Gwynedd) (Cyfyngiadau Traffig Dros Dro a Dim Goddiweddyd) 2014 Non-print

The A494 Trunk Road (Pwll-glâs, Denbighshire) (Temporary Traffic Prohibitions and Restrictions) Order 2014 No. 2014/3114 (W.313). - Enabling power: Road Traffic Regulation Act 1984, s. 14 (1) (4). - Issued: 26.11.2014. Made: 18.11.2014. Coming into force: 24.11.2014. Effect: None. Territorial extent & classification: W. Local. - Available at http://www.legislation.gov.uk/wsi/2014/3114/contents/made. - In English and Welsh. Welsh title: Gorchymyn Cefnffordd yr A494 (Pwll-glas, Sir Ddinbych) (Gwahardddiadau a Chyfyngiadau Traffig Dros Dro) 2014 Non-print

The A4042 Trunk Road (Crown Roundabout to Mamhilad Roundabout, Torfaen) (Temporary Traffic Prohibitions & Restrictions) Order 2014 No. 2014/1209 (W.125). - Enabling power: Road Traffic Regulation Act 1984, ss. 14 (1) (4). - Issued: 19.05.2014. Made: 06.05.2014. Coming into force: 12.05.2014. Effect: None. Territorial extent & classification: W. Local. - Available at http://www.legislation.gov.uk/wsi/2014/1209/contents/made. - In English and Welsh. Welsh title: Gorchymyn Cefnffordd yr A4042 (Cylchfan Crown i Gylchfan Mamheilad, Torfaen) (Gwaharddiadau a Chyfyngiadau Traffig Dros Dro) 2014 Non-print

The A4042 Trunk Road (Malpas Relief Road, Newport) (Temporary Traffic Restrictions) Order 2014 No. 2014/1326 (W.136). - Enabling power: Road Traffic Regulation Act 1984, s. 14 (1) (4). - Issued: 02.06.2014. Made: 13.05.2014. Coming into force: 14.05.2014. Effect: None. Territorial extent & classification: W. Local. - Available at http://www.legislation.gov.uk/wsi/2014/1326/contents/made. - In English and Welsh. Welsh title: Gorchymyn Cefnffordd yr A4042 (Ffordd Liniaru Malpas, Casnewydd) (Cyfyngiadau Traffig Dros Dro) 2014 Non-print

The A4042 Trunk Road (Mamhilad Roundabout to Court Farm Roundabout, Torfaen) (Temporary Traffic Restrictions & Prohibition) Order 2014 No. 2014/111 (W.11). - Enabling power: Road Traffic Regulation Act 1984, s. 14 (1) (4). - Issued: 28.01.2014. Made: 22.01.2014. Coming into force: 27.01.2014. Effect: None. Territorial extent & classification: W. Local. - Available at http://www.legislation.gov.uk/wsi/2014/111/contents/made. - In English and Welsh. Welsh title: Gorchymyn Cefnffordd yr A4042 (Cylchfan Mamheilad i Gylchfan Court Farm, Torfaen) (Cyfyngiadau a Gwarddiad Traffig Dros Dro) 2014 Non-print

The A4042 Trunk Road (Southbound Lay-by between Edlogan Way Roundabout and Turnpike Roundabout, Near Croesyceiliog, Torfaen) (Temporary Prohibition of Vehicles) Order 2014 No. 2014/2030 (W.204). - Enabling power: Road Traffic Regulation Act 1984, ss. 14 (1) (4). - Issued: 04.08.2014. Made: 25.07.2014. Coming into force: 04.08.2014. Effect: None. Territorial extent & classification: W. Local. - Available at http://www.legislation.gov.uk/wsi/2014/2030/contents/made. - In English and Welsh. Welsh title: Gorchymyn Cefnffordd yr A4042 (Cilfan y Gerbytffordd tua'r De rhwng Cylchfan Edlogan Way a Chylchfan y Tyrpeg, Ger Croesyceiliog, Torfaen) (Gwahardd Cerbydau Dros Dro) 2014 Non-print

The A4076 Trunk Road (Johnston to Steynton, Pembrokeshire) (Temporary Traffic Restrictions & No Overtaking) Order 2014 No. 2014/2065 (W.205). - Enabling power: Road Traffic Regulation Act 1984, ss. 14 (1) (4). - Issued: 22.08.2014. Made: 01.08.2014. Coming into force: 11.08.2014. Effect: None. Territorial extent & classification: W. Local. - Available at http://www.legislation.gov.uk/wsi/2014/2065/contents/made. - In English and Welsh. Welsh title: Gorchymyn Cefnffordd yr A4076 (Johnston i Steynton, Sir Benfro) (Cyfyngiadau Traffig Dros Dro a Dim Goddiweddyd) 2014 Non-print

The A4076 Trunk Road (South of Johnston, Pembrokeshire) (Temporary Traffic Prohibitions & Restriction) Order 2014 No. 2014/2247 (W.223). - Enabling power: Road Traffic Regulation Act 1984, s. 14 (1) (4). - Issued: 01.09.2014. Made: 22.08.2014. Coming into force: 01.09.2014. Effect: None. Territorial extent & classification: W. Local. - Available at http://www.legislation.gov.uk/wsi/2014/2247/contents/made. - In English and Welsh. Welsh title: Gorchymyn Cefnffordd yr A4076 (Man i'r De o Johnston, Sir Benfro) (Gwahardddiadau a Chyfyngiad Traffig Dros Dro) 2014 Non-print

The A4810 Steelworks Access Road (Queen's Way), (Llanwern, Newport) (Prohibition of U-Turns) Order 2014 No. 2014/2658 (W.263). - Enabling power: Road Traffic Regulation Act 1984, ss. 1 (1), 2 (1) (2). - Issued: 06.10.2014. Made: 25.09.2014. Coming into force: 30.09.2014. Effect: None. Territorial extent & classification: W. Local. - Available at http://www.legislation.gov.uk/wsi/2014/2658/contents/made. - In English and Welsh. Welsh title: Gorchymyn Ffordd Fynediad Gwaith Dur yr A4810 (Queen's Way), (Llan-wern, Casnewydd) (Gwahardd Troadau Pedol) 2014 Non-print

The M4 Motorway & A48 Trunk Road (Earlswood Junction to Briton Ferry Roundabout, Neath Port Talbot) (Temporary 50 mph Speed Limit) Order 2014 No. 2014/1914 (W.195). - Enabling power: Road Traffic Regulation Act 1984, s. 14 (1) (4). - Issued: 23.07.2014. Made: 21.07.2014. Coming into force: 29.07.2014. Effect: None. Territorial extent & classification: W. Local. - Available at http://www.legislation.gov.uk/wsi/2014/1914/contents/made. - In English and Welsh. Welsh title: Gorchymyn Traffordd yr M4 a Chefnffordd yr A48 (Cyffordd Earlswood i Gylchfan Llansawel, Castell-nedd Port Talbot) (Terfyn Cyflymder 50 mya Dros Dro) 2014 Non-print

The M4 Motorway (Eastbound Carriageway between Junction 28 (Tredegar Park) & Junction 24 (Coldra), Newport) (Temporary Prohibition of Vehicles) Order 2014 No. 2014/2983 (W.301). - Enabling power: Road Traffic Regulation Act 1984, s. 14 (1) (4). - Issued: 14.11.2014. Made: 07.11.2014. Coming into force: 13.11.2014. Effect: None. Territorial extent & classification: W. Local. - Available at http://www.legislation.gov.uk/wsi/2014/2983/contents/made. - In English and Welsh. Welsh title: Gorchymyn Traffordd yr M4 (Y Gerbytffordd tua'r Dwyrain rhwng Cyffordd 28 (Parc Tredegar) a Chyffordd 24 (Coldra), Casnewydd) (Gwahardd Cerbydau Dros Dro) 2014 Non-print

The M4 Motorway (Eastbound Entry Slip Road at Junction 24 (Coldra), Newport) (Temporary Prohibition of Vehicles) Order 2014 No. 2014/2577 (W.253). - Enabling power: Road Traffic Regulation Act 1984, s. 14 (1) (4) (7). - Issued: 25.09.2014. Made: 22.09.2014. Coming into force: 29.09.2014. Effect: None. Territorial extent & classification: W. Local. - Available at http://www.legislation.gov.uk/wsi/2014/2577/contents/made. - In English and Welsh. Welsh title: Gorchymyn Traffordd yr M4 (Ffordd Ymuno Tua'r Dwyrain wrth Gyffordd 24 (Y Coldra), Casnewydd) (Gwahardd Cerbydau Dros Dro) 2014 Non-print

The M4 Motorway (Junction 23a, Magor, Monmouthshire and Junction 25, Caerleon, Newport), the M48 Motorway (Junction 2, Chepstow, Monmouthshire), the A449 Trunk Road (Coldra, Newport) and the A40 Trunk Road (Raglan, Monmouthshire) (Temporary Traffic Prohibition and Restrictions) Order 2014 No. 2014/1515 (W.156). - Enabling power: Road Traffic Regulation Act 1984, s. 14 (1) (4) (7)- Issued: 12.06.2014. Made: 04.06.2014. Coming into force: 08.06.2014. Effect: None. Territorial extent & classification: W. Local. - Available at http://www.legislation.gov.uk/wsi/2014/1515/contents/made. - In English and Welsh. Welsh title: Gorchymyn Traffordd yr M4 (Cyffordd 23a, Magwyr, Sir Fynwy a Chyffordd 25, Caerllion, Casnewydd), Traffordd yr M48 (Cyffordd 2, Cas-gwent, Sir Fynwy), Cefnffordd yr A449 (Coldra, Casnewydd) a Chefnffordd yr A40 (Rhaglan, Sir Fynwy) (Gwahardddiad a Chyfyngiadau Traffig Dros Dro) 2014 Non-print

ROAD TRAFFIC, WALES: TRAFFIC REGULATION

The M4 Motorway (Junction 23A, Magor, Monmouthshire) (Temporary Prohibition of Vehicles) Order 2014 No. 2014/2144 (W.210). - Enabling power: Road Traffic Regulation Act 1984, s. 14 (1) (4). - Issued: 14.08.2014. Made: 11.08.2014. Coming into force: 15.08.2014. Effect: None. Territorial extent & classification: W. Local. - Available at http://www.legislation.gov.uk/wsi/2014/2144/contents/made. - In English and Welsh. Welsh title: Gorchymyn Trafford yr M4 (Cyffordd 23A, Magwyr, Sir Fynwy) (Gwahardd Cerbydau Dros Dro) 2014 Non-print

The M4 Motorway (Junction 25a (Grove Park) to Junction 26 (Malpas), Newport) (Temporary Prohibition of Vehicles) Order 2014 No. 2014/2308 (W.228). - Enabling power: Road Traffic Regulation Act 1984, ss. 14 (1) (4), 124, sch. 9, para. 27. - Issued: 05.09.2014. Made: 29.08.2014. Coming into force: 05.09.2014. Effect: WSI. 2013/3271 (W.321) revoked. Territorial extent & classification: W. Local. - Available at http://www.legislation.gov.uk/wsi/2014/2308/contents/made. - In English and Welsh. Welsh title: Gorchymyn Trafford yr M4 (Cyffordd 25a (Grove Park) i Gyffordd 26 (Malpas), Casnewydd) (Gwahardd Cerbydau Dros Dro) 2014 Non-print

The M4 Motorway (Junction 30, Cardiff Gate Business Park, Cardiff) (Temporary Traffic Restrictions) Order 2014 No. 2014/1317 (W.135). - Enabling power: Road Traffic Regulation Act 1984, s. 14 (1) (4). - Issued: 02.06.2014. Made: 13.05.2014. Coming into force: 14.05.2014. Effect: None. Territorial extent & classification: W. Local. - Available at http://www.legislation.gov.uk/wsi/2014/1317/contents/made. - In English and Welsh. Welsh title: Gorchymyn Trafford yr M4 (Cyffordd 30, Parc Busnes Porth Caerdydd) (Cyfyngiadau Traffig Dros Dro) 2014 Non-print

The M4 Motorway (Junction 32, Coryton) and the A470 Trunk Road (Coryton Interchange, Cardiff) (Temporary Traffic Prohibitions and Restriction) Order 2014 No. 2014/2494 (W.242). - Enabling power: Road Traffic Regulation Act 1984, s. 14 (1) (4). - Issued: 22.09.2014. Made: 16.09.2014. Coming into force: 22.09.2014. Effect: None. Territorial extent & classification: W. Local. - Available at http://www.legislation.gov.uk/wsi/2014/2494/contents/made. - In English and Welsh. Welsh title: Gorchymyn Trafford yr M4 (Cyffordd 32, Coryton) a Chefnffordd yr A470 (Cyfnewidfa Coryton, Caerdydd) (Gwaharddiadau a Chyfyngiad Traffig Dros Dro) 2014 Non-print

The M4 Motorway (Junction 33 (Capel Llanilltern Interchange)) & The A4232 Trunk Road (Capel Llanilltern to Culverhouse Cross, Cardiff) (Temporary Traffic Prohibitions & Restrictions) Order 2014 No. 2014/176 (W.24). - Enabling power: Road Traffic Regulation Act 1984, s. 14 (1) (4) (7). - Issued: 05.02.2014. Made: 30.01.2014. Coming into force: 03.02.2014. Effect: None. Territorial extent & classification: W. Local. - Available at http://www.legislation.gov.uk/wsi/2014/176/contents/made. - In English and Welsh. Welsh title: Gorchymyn Trafford yr M4 (Cyffordd 33 (Cyfnewidfa Capel Llanilltern)) a Chefnffordd yr A4232 (Capel Llanilltern i Groes Cwrlwys, Caerdydd) (Gwaharddiadau a Chyfyngiadau Traffig Dros Dro) 2014 Non-print

The M4 Motorway (Junction 34, Miskin, Rhondda Cynon Taf and the Vale of Glamorgan) (Temporary Prohibition of Vehicles) Order 2014 No. 2014/1859 (W.193). - Enabling power: Road Traffic Regulation Act 1984, s. 14 (1) (4). - Issued: 22.08.2014. Made: 15.07.2014. Coming into force: 19.07.2014. Effect: None. Territorial extent & classification: W. Local. - Available at http://www.legislation.gov.uk/wsi/2014/1859/contents/made. - In English and Welsh. Welsh title: Gorchymyn Trafford yr M4 (Cyffordd 34, Meisgyn, Rhondda Cynon Taf a Bro Morgannwg) (Gwahardd Cerbydau Dros Dro) 2014 Non-print

The M4 Motorway (Junction 35 (Pencoed) to Junction 37 (Pyle), Bridgend County Borough) (Temporary Traffic Prohibitions and Restriction) Order 2014 No. 2014/1595 (W.161). - Enabling power: Road Traffic Regulation Act 1984, s. 14 (1) (4) (7). - Issued: 19.06.2014. Made: 17.06.2014. Coming into force: 18.06.2014. Effect: None. Territorial extent & classification: W. Local. - Available at http://www.legislation.gov.uk/wsi/2014/1595/contents/made. - In English and Welsh. Welsh title: Gorchymyn Trafford yr M4 (Cyffordd 35 (Pencoed) i Gyffordd 37 (y Pîl), Bwrdeistref Sirol Pen-y-bont ar Ogwr) (Gwaharddiadau a Chyfyngiad Traffig Dros Dro) 2014 Non-print

The M4 Motorway (Junction 38, Margam Interchange to Junction 39, Groes, Neath Port Talbot) (Temporary Prohibition of Vehicles) Order 2014 No. 2014/1057 (W.97). - Enabling power: Road Traffic Regulation Act 1984, s. 14 (1) (4). - Issued: 23.04.2014. Made: 03.04.2014. Coming into force: 10.04.2014. Effect: None. Territorial extent & classification: W. Local. - Available at http://www.legislation.gov.uk/wsi/2014/1057/contents/made. - In English and Welsh. Welsh title: Gorchymyn Trafford yr M4 (Cyffordd 38, Cyfnewidfa Margam i Gyffordd 39, Y Groes, Castell-nedd Port Talbot) (Gwahardd Cerbydau Dros Dro) 2014 Non-print

The M4 Motorway (Junction 38 (Margam) to Junction 41 (Pentyla), Neath Port Talbot) (Temporary Prohibition of Vehicles) Order 2014 No. 2014/1208 (W.124). - Enabling power: Road Traffic Regulation Act 1984, ss. 14 (1) (4). - Issued: 19.05.2014. Made: 06.05.2014. Coming into force: 12.05.2014. Effect: None. Territorial extent & classification: W. Local. - Available at http://www.legislation.gov.uk/wsi/2014/1208/contents/made. - In English and Welsh. Welsh title: Gorchymyn Trafford yr M4 (Cyffordd 38 (Margam) i Gyffordd 41 (Pentyla), Castell-nedd Port Talbot) (Gwahardd Cerbydau Dros Dro) 2014 Non-print

The M4 Motorway (Junction 41, Pentyla to Junction 42, Earlswood, Neath Port Talbot) (Temporary Prohibition of Vehicles) Order 2014 No. 2014/2495 (W.243). - Enabling power: Road Traffic Regulation Act 1984, s. 14 (1) (4). - Issued: 22.09.2014. Made: 16.09.2014. Coming into force: 23.09.2014. Effect: None. Territorial extent & classification: W. Local. - Available at http://www.legislation.gov.uk/wsi/2014/2495/contents/made. - In English and Welsh. Welsh title: Gorchymyn Trafford yr M4 (Cyffordd 41, Pentyla i Gyffordd 42, Earlswood, Castell-nedd Port Talbot) (Gwahardd Cerbydau Dros Dro) 2014 Non-print

The M4 Motorway (Junction 42, Earlswood Interchange to Junction 43, Llandarcy Interchange) and the A48 Trunk Road (Earlswood Interchange to Sunnycroft Roundabout), Neath Port Talbot (Temporary Prohibition of Vehicles) Order 2014 No. 2014/1839 (W.191). - Enabling power: Road Traffic Regulation Act 1984, s. 14 (1) (4). - Issued: 17.07.2014. Made: 14.07.2014. Coming into force: 21.07.2014. Effect: None. Territorial extent & classification: W. Local. - Available at http://www.legislation.gov.uk/wsi/2014/1839/contents/made. - In English and Welsh. Welsh title: Gorchymyn Trafford yr M4 (Cyffordd 42, Cyfnewidfa Earlswood i Gyffordd 43, Cyfnewidfa Llandarcy) a Chefnffordd yr A48 (Cyfnewidfa Earlswood i Gylchfan Sunnycroft), Castell-nedd Port Talbot (Gwahardd Cerbydau Dros Dro) 2014 Non-print

The M4 Motorway (Slip Roads between Junction 23a (Magor), Monmouthshire and Junction 28 (Tredegar Park), Newport) (Temporary Prohibition of Vehicles) Order 2014 No. 2014/873 (W.87). - Enabling power: Road Traffic Regulation Act 1984, s. 14 (1) (4). - Issued: 03.04.2014. Made: 31.03.2014. Coming into force: 04.04.2014. Effect: None. Territorial extent & classification: W. Local. - Available at http://www.legislation.gov.uk/wsi/2014/873/contents/made. - In English and Welsh. Welsh title: Gorchymyn Trafford yr M4 (Slipffyrdd rhwng Cyffordd 23a (Magwyr), Sir Fynwy a Chyffordd 28 (Parc Tredegar), Casnewydd) (Gwahardd Cerbydau Dros Dro) 2014 Non-print

The M4 Motorway (Slip Roads between Junction 38 (Margam) and Junction 43 (Llandarcy), Neath Port Talbot) (Temporary Prohibition of Vehicles) Order 2014 No. 2014/1535 (W.157). - Enabling power: Road Traffic Regulation Act 1984, s. 14 (1) (4). - Issued: 16.06.2014. Made: 11.06.2014. Coming into force: 16.06.2014. Effect: None. Territorial extent & classification: W. Local. - Available at http://www.legislation.gov.uk/wsi/2014/1535/contents/made. - In English and Welsh. Welsh title: Gorchymyn Trafford yr M4 (Slipffyrdd rhwng Cyffordd 38 (Margam) a Chyffordd 43 (Llandarsi), Castell-nedd Port Talbot) (Gwahardd Cerbydau Dros Dro) 2014 Non-print

The M4 Motorway (Westbound Entry Slip Road, Junction 41 (Pentyla), Neath Port Talbot) Experimental Traffic Order 2014 No. 2014/1995 (W.197). - Enabling power: Road Traffic Regulation Act 1984, s. 9 (1) (a). - Issued: 31.07.2014. Made: 21.07.2014. Coming into force: 04.08.2014. Effect: None. Territorial extent & classification: W. Local. - Available at http://www.legislation.gov.uk/wsi/2014/1995/contents/made. - In English and Welsh. Welsh title: Gorchymyn Traffig Arbrofol Trafford yr M4 (Ffordd Ymuno Tua'r Gorllewin, Cyffordd 41 (Pentyla), Castell-nedd Port Talbot) 2014 Non-print

The M4 Motorway (Westbound Slip Roads at Junction 35 (Pencoed), Bridgend County Borough) (Temporary Prohibition of Vehicles) Order 2014 No. 2014/387 (W.46). - Enabling power: Road Traffic Regulation Act 1984, s. 14 (1) (4). - Issued: 10.02.2014. Made: 24.02.2014. Coming into force: 03.03.2014. Effect: None. Territorial extent & classification: W. Local. - Available at http://www.legislation.gov.uk/wsi/2014/387/contents/made. - In English and Welsh. Welsh title: Gorchymyn Traffordd yr M4 (Slipffyrdd Tua'r Gorllewin wrth Gyffordd 35 (Pencoed), Bwrdeistref Sirol Pen-y-bont ar Ogwr) (Gwahardd Cerbydau Dros Dro) 2014 Non-print

The M4 Motorway (West of Junction 23A, Magor to East of Junction 29, Castleton, Newport) (Temporary 50 MPH Speed Limit) Order 2014 No. 2014/158 (W.19). - Enabling power: Road Traffic Regulation Act 1984, s. 14 (1) (4) (7). - Issued: 31.01.2014. Made: 28.01.2014. Coming into force: 31.01.2014. Effect: None. Territorial extent & classification: W. Local. - Available at http://www.legislation.gov.uk/wsi/2014/158/contents/made. - In English and Welsh. Welsh title: Gorchymyn Traffordd yr M4 (Man i'r Gorllewin o Gyffordd 23A, Magwyr i Fan i'r Dwyrain o Gyffordd 29, Cas-bach, Casnewydd) (Terfyn Cyflymder 50mya Dros Dro) 2014 Non-print

Salmon and freshwater Wales

The Keeping and Introduction of Fish (Wales) Regulations 2014 No. 2014/3303 (W.336). - Enabling power: Marine and Coastal Access Act 2009, ss. 232(1) (5) (a) (d) (e) (h) (i) (j) (7), 316 (1) (2). - Issued: 30.12.2014. Made: 09.12.2014. Coming into force: 20.01.2015. Effect: 1975 c.51 partially repealed. Territorial extent & classification: W. General. - In English and Welsh. Welsh title: Rheoliadau Cadw a Chyflwyno Pysgod (Cymru) 2014. - 20p.: 30 cm. - 978-0-348-11035-7 £6.00

Savings banks

The National Savings Bank (Investment Deposits) (Limits) (Amendment) Order 2014 No. 2014/484. - Enabling power: National Savings Bank Act 1971, ss. 4. - Issued: 11.03.2014. Made: 04.03.2014. Laid: 06.03.2014. Coming into force: 06.04.2014. Effect: S.I. 1977/1210 amended & S.I. 2009/2460; 2012/795 revoked. Territorial extent & classification: E/W/S/NI. General. - Revoked by SI 2015/623 (ISBN 9780111133316). - 2p.: 30 cm. - 978-0-11-111086-7 £4.00

Sea fisheries

The Sea Fishing (Points for Masters of Fishing Boats) Regulations 2014 No. 2014/3345. - Enabling power: Sea Fish (Conservation) Act 1967, s. 2 (2), sch. 2, para. 1A. - Issued: 29.12.2014. Made: 18.12.2014. Laid: 19.12.2014. Laid before the National Assembly of Wales: 19.12.2014. Coming into force: 12.01.2015. Effect: None. Territorial extent & classification: E. General. - 10p.: 30 cm. - 978-0-11-112634-9 £6.00

Sea fisheries, England: Sea fish industry

The Fishing Boats (Satellite-Tracking Devices and Electronic Reporting) (England) (Amendment) Scheme 2014 No. 2014/3363. - Enabling power: Fisheries Act 1981, s. 15 (1) (2). - Issued: 16.02.2015. Made: 18.12.2014. Laid: 06.01.2015. Coming into force: 19.12.2014 in accord with art. 1. Effect: S.I. 2012/1375 amended. Territorial extent & classification: E. General. - Approved by both Houses of Parliament. This version replaces the pre-approved version (same ISBN) issued 06.01.2015. EC note: This Scheme makes provision for state funding of the costs incurred by persons in charge of English fishing boats in complying with two EU obligations. - 2p.: 30 cm. - 978-0-11-112649-3 £4.25

Seeds

The Seeds and Vegetable Plant Material (Nomenclature Changes) Regulations 2014 No. 2014/487. - Enabling power: Plant Varieties and Seeds Act 1964, ss. 16 (1) (1A) & European Communities Act 1972, s. 2 (2). - Issued: 11.03.2014. Made: 04.03.2014. Laid: 06.03.2014. Coming into force: 31.03.2014. Effect: S.I. 1995/2652; 2001/3510; 2011/463 amended. Territorial extent and classification: E/W/S/NI. General. - EC note: These regulations implement Commission Implementing Directive 2013/45/EU amending Council Directives 2002/55/EC and 2008/72/EC and Commission Directive 2009/145/EC. - 4p.: 30 cm. - 978-0-11-111091-1 £4.00

Seeds, England

The Forest Reproductive Material (Great Britain) (Amendment) (England and Scotland) Regulations 2014 No. 2014/1833. - Enabling power: European Communities Act 1972, s. 2 (2). - Issued: 17.07.2014. Made: 09.07.2014. Laid: 15.07.2014. Coming into force: 01.09.2014. Effect: S.I. 2002/3026 amended. Territorial extent & classification: E/W/S. General. - EC note: Implements in relation to England and Scotland Council Decision 2008/971/EC in the equivalence of forest reproductive material produced in third countries. Implement in full derogation permitted by Commission Decision 2008/989/EC. - 12p.: 30 cm. - 978-0-11-111811-5 £6.00

Seeds, Scotland

The Forest Reproductive Material (Great Britain) (Amendment) (England and Scotland) Regulations 2014 No. 2014/1833. - Enabling power: European Communities Act 1972, s. 2 (2). - Issued: 17.07.2014. Made: 09.07.2014. Laid: 15.07.2014. Coming into force: 01.09.2014. Effect: S.I. 2002/3026 amended. Territorial extent & classification: E/W/S. General. - EC note: Implements in relation to England and Scotland Council Decision 2008/971/EC in the equivalence of forest reproductive material produced in third countries. Implement in full derogation permitted by Commission Decision 2008/989/EC. - 12p.: 30 cm. - 978-0-11-111811-5 £6.00

Seeds, Wales

The Seeds and Vegetable Plant Material (Nomenclature Changes) (Wales) Regulations 2014 No. 2014/519 (W.61). - Enabling power: Plant Varieties and Seeds Act 1964, ss. 16 (1) (1A) (2) (3) (4) (5) (5A), 36 & European Communities Act 1972, s. 2 (2), sch. 2, para. 1A. - Issued: 19.03.2014. Made: 05.03.2014. Laid before the National Assembly for Wales: 07.03.2014. Coming into force: 31.03.2014. Effect: S.I. 1995/2652; 2012/245 (W.39) amended. Territorial extent & classification: W. General. - EC note: These Regulations implement Directive 2013/45/EU which amends Directive 2002/55/EC, Directive 2008/72/EC, and Directive 2009/145/EC as regards the botanical name of tomato to reflect revisions to the international Code of Botanical Nomenclature. Directive 92/33/EEC has been repealed by Directive 2008/72/EC. - In English and Welsh. Welsh title: Rheoliadau Hadau Llysiau (Cymru) (Diwygio) 2011. - 4p.: 30 cm. - 978-0-348-10917-7 £4.00

Senior courts of England and Wales

The Access to Justice Act 1999 (Destination of Appeals) (Family Proceedings) Order 2014 No. 2014/602 (L.7). - Enabling power: Access to Justice Act 1999, s. 56 (1) (3). - Issued: 19.03.2014. Made: 12.03.2014. Coming into force: In accord. with rule 1. Effect: S.I. 2011/1044 amended. Territorial extent & classification: E/W. General. - 4p.: 30 cm. - 978-0-11-111202-1 £4.00

The Civil Courts Order 2014 No. 2014/819. - Enabling power: Senior Courts Act 1981, s. 99 (1). - Issued: 03.04.2014. Made: 27.03.2014. Laid: 31.03.2014. Coming into force: 22.04.2014. Effect: None. Territorial extent & classification: E/W. General. - 8p.: 30 cm. - 978-0-11-111313-4 £4.00

The Civil Procedure (Amendment No. 2) Rules 2014 No. 2014/482 (L.2). - Enabling power: Civil Procedure Act 1997, s. 2. - Issued: 10.03.2014. Made: 04.03.2014. Laid: 06.03.2014. Coming into force: 06.04.2014. Effect: S.I. 1998/3132 amended. Territorial extent & classification: E/W. General. - 8p.: 30 cm. - 978-0-11-111084-3 £4.00

SENIOR COURTS OF ENGLAND AND WALES

The Civil Procedure (Amendment No. 3) Rules 2014 No. 2014/610 (L.10). - Enabling power: Civil Procedure Act 1997, s. 2. - Issued: 19.03.2014. Made: 12.03.2014. Laid: 14.03.2014. Coming into force: 06.04.2014. Effect: S.I. 1998/3132 amended. Territorial extent & classification: E/W. General. - With correction slip dated October 2014. - 4p.: 30 cm. - 978-0-11-111212-0 £4.00

The Civil Procedure (Amendment No. 4) Rules 2014 No. 2014/867 (L.16). - Enabling power: Civil Procedure Act 1997, s. 2. - Issued: 04.04.2014. Made: 28.03.2014. Laid: 01.04.2014. Coming into force: 22.04.2014. Effect: S.I. 1998/3132 amended. Territorial extent & classification: E/W. General. - 8p.: 30 cm. - 978-0-11-111322-6 £5.75

The Civil Procedure (Amendment No. 5) Rules 2014 No. 2014/1233 (L.24). - Enabling power: Civil Procedure Act 1997, s. 2. - Issued: 19.05.2014. Made: 13.05.2014. Laid: 15.05.2014. Coming into force: 05.06.2014. Effect: S.I. 1998/3132; 2014/407, 867 amended. Territorial extent & classification: E/W. General. - 4p.: 30 cm. - 978-0-11-111485-8 £4.25

The Civil Procedure (Amendment No. 6) Rules 2014 No. 2014/2044 (L.28). - Enabling power: Civil Procedure Act 1997, s. 2 & Presumption of Death Act 1997, s. 9 (1) (2). - Issued: 07.08.2014. Made: 29.07.2014. Laid: 01.08.2014. Coming into force: 01.10.2014. Effect: S.I. 1998/3132 amended. Territorial extent & classification: E/W. General. - 12p.: 30 cm. - 978-0-11-111945-7 £6.00

The Civil Procedure (Amendment No. 7) Rules 2014 No. 2014/2948 (L.32). - Enabling power: Civil Procedure Act 1997, s. 2. - Issued: 17.11.2014. Made: 10.11.2014. Laid: 12.11.2014. Coming into force: 10.01.2015. Effect: S.I. 1998/3132 amended. Territorial extent & classification: E/W. General. - 8p.: 30 cm. - 978-0-11-112322-5 £6.00

The Civil Procedure (Amendment No. 8) Rules 2014 No. 2014/3299 (L.36). - Enabling power: Civil Procedure Act 1997, s. 2. - Issued: 23.12.2014. Made: 16.12.2014. Laid: 18.12.2014. Coming into force: In accord. with rule 2. Effect: S.I. 1998/3132 amended. Territorial extent & classification: E/W. General. - 32p.: 30 cm. - 978-0-11-112608-0 £6.00

The Civil Procedure (Amendment) Rules 2014 No. 2014/407 (L.1). - Enabling power: Civil Procedure Act 1997, s. 2. - Issued: 03.03.2014. Made: 24.02.2014. Laid: 27.02.2014. Coming into force: In accord. with rule 2. Effect: S.I. 1998/3132 amended. Territorial extent & classification: E/W. General. - 60p.: 30 cm. - 978-0-11-111026-3 £9.75

The Civil Proceedings Fees (Amendment No. 2) Order 2014 No. 2014/1834 (L.27). - Enabling power: Courts Act 2003, s. 92 & Insolvency Act 1986, ss. 414, 415. - Issued: 17.07.2014. Made: 10.07.2014. Laid: 14.07.2014. Coming into force: 04.08.2014. Effect: S.I. 2008/1053 (L.5) amended. Territorial extent & classification: E/W. General. - This Statutory Instrument has been made in consequence of a defect in S.I. 2013/2302 (ISBN 9780111103944) and is being issued free of charge to all known purchasers of that Statutory Instrument and of S.I. 2014/513 (ISBN 9780111111178) which was also affected by the defect. A defect in this SI (1834) has been corrected by SI 2014/2059 (L.29) (ISBN 9780111118122) which is being issued free of charge to all known recipients of 1834. - 4p.: 30 cm. - 978-0-11-111812-2 £4.25

The Civil Proceedings Fees (Amendment) Order 2014 No. 2014/874 (L.17). - Enabling power: Courts Act 2003, s. 92 & Insolvency Act 1986, ss. 414, 415. - Issued: 04.04.2014. Made: 27.03.2014. Laid: 01.04.2014. Coming into force: 22.04.2014. Effect: S.I. 2008/1053 (L.5) amended. Territorial extent & classification: E/W. General. - 12p.: 30 cm. - 978-0-11-111326-4 £6.00

The Courts and Tribunals Fees (Miscellaneous Amendments) Order 2014 No. 2014/590 (L.6). - Enabling power: Courts Act 2003, s. 92 & Insolvency Act 1986, ss. 414, 415 & Tribunals, Courts and Enforcement Act 2007, s. 42, 49 (3) & Constitutional Reform Act 2005, s. 52 & Mental Capacity Act 2005. s. 54 & Gender Recognition Act 2004, s. 7 (2). - Issued: 19.03.2014. Made: 11.03.2014. Laid: 13.03.2104. Coming into force: 06.04.2014. Effect: S.I. 2004/3120; 2006/758; 2007/1745; 2008/1052, 1053, 1054; 2009/213, 1114; 2010/42; 2011/2344; 2013/1179, 1893 amended. Territorial extent & classification: E/W. General. - 16p.: 30 cm. - 978-0-11-111194-9 £5.75

The Crime and Courts Act 2013 (Commencement No. 10 and Transitional Provision) Order 2014 No. 2014/954 (C.44). - Enabling power: Crime and Courts Act 2013, s. 61 (3). Bringing into operation various provisions of the 2013 Act on 22.04.2014. - Issued: 15.04.2014. Made: 09.04.2014. Effect: None. Territorial extent & classification: E/W. General. - 4p.: 30 cm. - 978-0-11-111406-3 £4.25

The Crime and Courts Act 2013 (Consequential, Transitional and Saving Provisions) Order 2014 No. 2014/820. - Enabling power: Crime and Courts Act 2013, ss. 59, 60. - Issued: 03.04.2014. Made: 27.03.2014. Coming into force: 22.04.2014. Effect: S.I. 1983/713 revoked with saving. Territorial extent & classification: E/W/S/NI. General. - 4p.: 30 cm. - 978-0-11-111314-1 £4.00

The Crime and Courts Act 2013 (Family Court: Consequential Provision) (No.2) Order 2014 No. 2014/879. - Enabling power: Crime and Courts Act 2013, ss. 58 (12) (c), 59. - Issued: 07.04.2014. Made: 31.03.2014. Laid: 01.04.2014. Coming into force: 22.04.2014. Effect: 35 SIs/SSIs amended & 3 SIs partially revoked & 12 SIs revoked. Territorial extent & classification: E/W. General. - 8p.: 30 cm. - With correction slip dated December 2014. - 978-0-11-111335-6 £6.00

The Crime and Courts Act 2013 (Family Court: Consequential Provision) Order 2014 No. 2014/605 (L.9). - Enabling power: Crime and Courts Act 2013, ss. 58 (12) (c), 59. - Issued: 19.03.2014. Made: 12.03.2014. Coming into force: In accord. with art. 1. Effect: 1970 c.31; 1971 c.32; 1972 c.18; 1974 c.47; 1978 c.22; 1979 c.53; 1982 c.53; 1985 c.61; 1990 c.41; 1992 c.12; 1995 c.18; 2007 c.15, c.29; 2012 c.10 amended. Territorial extent & classification: E/W. General. - Supersedes draft SI (ISBN 9780111108871) issued 30/01/14- 8p.: 30 cm. - 978-0-11-111208-3 £4.00

The Criminal Procedure Rules 2014 No. 2014/1610 (L.26). - Enabling power: Bail Act 1976, s. 5B (9) & Criminal Law Act 1977, s. 48 & Senior Courts Act 1981, ss. 19, 52, 66, 67, 73 (2), 74 (2) (3) (4), 87 (4) & Criminal Evidence Act 1984, s. 81 & Road Traffic Offenders Act 1988 s. 12 (1) & Criminal Procedure and Investigations Act 1996, ss. 19, 20 (3) & Powers of Criminal Courts (Sentencing) Act 2000, s. 155 (7) & Terrorism Act 2000, sch. 5, para. 10, sch. 6, para. 4, sch. 6A para. 5 & Proceeds of Crime Act 2002, ss. 91, 351 (2), 362 (2), 369 92), 375 (1) & Courts Act 2003, s. 69 & Criminal Justice Act 2003, ss. 30 (1), 132 (4), 132 (4), 174 (4) & Extradition Act 2003, ss. 36A, 36B (3), 118A (4), 118B (3)- Issued: 25.06.2014. Made: 11.06.2014. Laid: 25.06.2014. Coming into force: 06.10.2014. Effect: S.I. 2013/1554 revoked. Territorial extent and classification: E/W. General. - 392p.: 30 cm. - 978-0-11-111684-5 £39.25

The Family Court (Composition and Distribution of Business) (Amendment) Rules 2014 No. 2014/3297 (L.35). - Enabling power: Matrimonial and Family Proceedings Act 1984, ss. 31D (1) (3). - Issued: 24.12.2014. Made: 15.12.2014. Laid: 18.12.2014. Coming into force: 11.01.2015. Effect: None. Territorial extent & classification: E/W. General. - 4p.: 30 cm. - 978-0-11-112624-0 £4.25

The Family Court (Composition and Distribution of Business) Rules 2014 No. 2014/840 (L.13). - Enabling power: Matrimonial and Family Proceedings Act 1984, ss. 31D (1) (2) (3) (5) (a). - Issued: 04.04.2014. Made: 31.03.2014. Laid: 01.04.2014. Coming into force: 22.04.2014. Effect: None. Territorial extent & classification: E/W. General. - 16p.: 30 cm. - 978-0-11-111329-5 £6.00

The Family Procedure (Amendment No. 2) Rules 2014 No. 2014/667 (L.11). - Enabling power: Courts Act 2003, ss. 75, 76 & Access to Justice Act 1999, s. 54 (1). - Issued: 20.03.2014. Made: 13.03.2014. Laid: 18.03.2014. Coming into force: 22.04.2014. Effect: S.I. 2010/2955 amended. Territorial extent & classification: E/W. General. - 28p.: 30 cm. - With correction slip dated December 2014. - 978-0-11-111231-1 £5.75

The Family Procedure (Amendment No. 3) Rules 2014 No. 2014/843 (L.15). - Enabling power: Courts Act 2003, ss. 75, 76 & Children and Families Act 2014, s. 10. - Issued: 09.04.2014. Made: 31.03.2014. Laid: 01.04.2014. Coming into force: 22.04.2014. Effect: S.I. 2010/2955 amended. Territorial extent & classification: E/W/S/NI. General. - With correction slip dated October 2014. - 20p.: 30 cm. - 978-0-11-111325-7 £6.00

The Family Procedure (Amendment No. 4) Rules 2014 No. 2014/3296 (L.34). - Enabling power: Courts Act 2003, ss. 75, 76. - Issued: 23.12.2014. Made: 15.12.2014. Laid: 18.12.2014. Coming into force: In accord. with rule 1. Effect: S.I. 2010/2955 amended. Territorial extent & classification: E/W/S/NI. General. - 12p.: 30 cm. - 978-0-11-112611-0 £6.00

The Family Procedure (Amendment) Rules 2014 No. 2014/524 (L.5). - Enabling power: Courts Act 2003, ss. 75, 76. - Issued: 13.03.2014. Made: 06.03.2014. Laid: 10.03.2014. Coming into force: 13.03.2014. Effect: S.I. 2010/2955 amended. Territorial extent & classification: E/W. General. - 4p.: 30 cm. - 978-0-11-111122-2 £4.00

The Family Proceedings Fees (Amendment) Order 2014 No. 2014/877 (L.20). - Enabling power: Courts Act 2003, ss. 92, 108 (6). - Issued: 07.04.2014. Made: 27.03.2014. Laid: 01.04.2014. Coming into force: 22.04.2014. Effect: S.I. 2008/1054 (L.6) amended. Territorial extent & classification: E/W. General. - 12p.: 30 cm. - 978-0-11-111331-8 £6.00

The High Court and County Courts Jurisdiction (Amendment) Order 2014 No. 2014/821 (L.12). - Enabling power: Courts and Legal Services Act 1990, ss. 1, 120. - Issued: 10.04.2014. Made: 04.04.2014. Laid: 07.04.2014. Coming into force: 22.04.2014. Effect: S.I. 1991/724 amended. Territorial extent & classification: E/W. General. - 4p.: 30 cm. - 978-0-11-111383-7 £4.25

The High Court (Distribution of Business) Order 2014 No. 2014/3257 (L.33). - Enabling power: Senior Courts Act 1981, s. 61 (3). - Issued: 16.12.2014. Made: 08.12.2014. Laid: 11.12.2014. Coming into force: 06.04.2015. Effect: 1981 c.54 amended. Territorial extent & classification: E/W. General. - 4p.: 30 cm. - 978-0-11-112520-5 £4.25

The Non-Contentious Probate Fees (Amendment) Order 2014 No. 2014/876 (L.19). - Enabling power: Courts Act 2003, s. 92. - Issued: 04.04.2014. Made: 27.03.2014. Laid: 01.04.2014. Coming into force: 22.04.2014. Effect: S.I. 2004/3120 amended. Territorial extent & classification: E/W. General. - 2p.: 30 cm. - 978-0-11-111328-8 £4.25

Social care

The Care and Support (Cross-border Placements and Business Failure: Temporary Duty) (Dispute Resolution) Regulations 2014 No. 2014/2843. - Enabling power: Care Act 2014, ss. 39 (8), 125 (7) (8), sch. 1 paras 5 (9) to (11). - Issued: 28.10.2014. Made: 20.10.2014. Laid: 28.10.2014. Coming into force: in accord with reg. 1 (2). Effect: None. Territorial extent & classification: E/W/NI/S. General. - 12p.: 30 cm. - 978-0-11-112225-9 £6.00

The Care and Support (Cross-border Placements) (Business Failure Duties of Scottish Local Authorities) Regulations 2014 No. 2014/2839. - Enabling power: Care Act 2014, ss. 39 (8), 125 (7) (8), sch. 1, paras 1 (6) (7), 2(9) (10), 4 (5) (6). - Issued: 28.10.2014. Made: 20.10.2014. Laid: 28.10.2014. Coming into force: in accord with reg. 1 (2). Effect: None. Territorial extent & classification: E/W/S/NI. General. - 8p.: 30 cm. - 978-0-11-112220-4 £4.25

The Social Care (Self-directed Support) (Scotland) Act 2013 (Consequential Modifications and Savings) Order 2014 No. 2014/513. - Enabling power: Scotland Act 1998, ss. 104, 112 (1), 113 (2) (4) (5). - Issued: 11.03.2014. Made: 04.03.2014. Laid: 06.03.2014. Coming into force: 01.04.2014. Effect: S.I. 1987/1967, 1973; 1991/2887; 1992/1815; 1996/207, 2890; 2002/1792, 2006; 2004/3120; 2006/213, 214, 758; 2007/1745; 2008/794, 1052, 1053, 1054; 2009/1114, 2131; 2010/42; 2011/2344; 2012/2885; 2013/1179, 1893, 3029 (W.301), 3035 (W.303) amended. Territorial extent & classification: UK. General. - This SI was affected by a defect in SI 2013/2302 which has been corrected by SI 2014/1834 (L.27) (ISBN 9780111118122) which is being issued free of charge to all known recipients of SI 2013/2302 and SI 2014/513. - 12p.: 30 cm. - 978-0-11-111117-8 £5.75

Social care, England

The Adoption Information and Intermediary Services (Pre-Commencement Adoptions) (Amendment) Regulations 2014 No. 2014/2696. - Enabling power: Adoption and Children Act 2002, ss. 9 (1), 98 (1) (1A) (2) (3), 140 (7) (8). - Issued: 13.10.2014. Made: 02.10.2014. Laid: 09.10.2014. Coming into force: 31.10.2014. Effect: S.I. 2005/890 amended. Territorial extent & classification: E. General. - 8p.: 30 cm. - 978-0-11-112134-4 £4.25

The Adoption Support Services (Amendment) Regulations 2014 No. 2014/1563. - Enabling power: Adoption and Children Act 2002, s. 4B, 140 (7) (8). - Issued: 19.06.2014. Made: 09.06.2014. Laid: 18.06.2014. Coming into force: 25.07.2014. Effect: S.I. 2005/691 amended. Territorial extent & classification: E. General. - 4p.: 30 cm. - 978-0-11-111662-3 £4.25

The Care and Support and After-care (Choice of Accommodation) Regulations 2014 No. 2014/2670. - Enabling power: Mental Health Act 1983, ss. 117A (1) (2) (4) & Care Act 2014, ss. 30 (1) (2), 125 (7) (8). - Issued: 31.10.2014. Made: 22.10.2014. Laid: 30.10.2014. Coming into force: in accord with reg. 1 (2). Effect: None. Territorial extent & classification: E. General. - 8p.: 30 cm. - 978-0-11-112243-3 £6.00

The Care and Support (Assessment) Regulations 2014 No. 2014/2827. - Enabling power: Care Act 2014, ss. 12 (1) (2), 65 (1), 125 (7) (8). - Issued: 27.10.2014. Made: 06.10.2014. Laid: 27.10.2014. Coming into force: in accord with reg. 1 (1). Effect: None. Territorial extent & classification: E. General. - 8p.: 30 cm. - 978-0-11-112214-3 £4.25

The Care and Support (Charging and Assessment of Resources) Regulations 2014 No. 2014/2672. - Enabling power: Care Act 2014, ss. 14 (5) to (8), 17 (7) to (13), 125 (7) (8). - Issued: 30.10.2014. Made: 22.10.2014. Laid: 30.10.2014. Coming into force: in accord with reg. 1. Effect: None. Territorial extent & classification: E. General. - 24p.: 30 cm. - 978-0-11-112236-5 £6.00

The Care and Support (Continuity of Care) Regulations 2014 No. 2014/2825. - Enabling power: Care Act 2014, s. 38 (8). - Issued: 27.10.2014. Made: 06.10.2014. Laid: 27.10.2014. Coming into force: in accord with reg. 1 (1). Effect: None. Territorial extent & classification: E. General. - 4p.: 30 cm. - 978-0-11-112208-2 £4.25

The Care and Support (Deferred Payment) Regulations 2014 No. 2014/2671. - Enabling power: Care Act 2014, ss. 34 (1) (2) (4) to (8), 35, 125 (7) (8). - Issued: 04.11.2014. Made: 22.10.2014. Laid: 31.10.2014. Coming into force: in accord with reg. 1 (1). Effect: None. Territorial extent & classification: E. General. - 12p.: 30 cm. - 978-0-11-112261-7 £6.00

The Care and Support (Direct Payments) Regulations 2014 No. 2014/2871. - Enabling power: Care Act 2014, ss. 33 (1) (2), 75 (7), 125 (7) (8). - Issued: 03.11.2014. Made: 20.10.2014. Laid: 31.10.2014. Coming into force: In accord with reg. 1. Effect: None. Territorial extent & classification: E. General. - 12p.: 30 cm. - 978-0-11-112259-4 £6.00

The Care and Support (Discharge of Hospital Patients) Regulations 2014 No. 2014/2823. - Enabling power: Care Act 2014, s. 125 (7), sch. 3 paras 2 (5) (b), 4 (6), 6, 8. - Issued: 24.10.2014. Made: 06.10.2014. Laid: 24.10.2014. Coming into force: in accord with reg. 1 (1). Effect: None. Territorial extent & classification: E. General. - 8p.: 30 cm. - 978-0-11-112206-8 £6.00

The Care and Support (Disputes Between Local Authorities) Regulations 2014 No. 2014/2829. - Enabling power: Care Act 2014, ss. 40 (4), 125 (7) (8). - Issued: 27.10.2014. Made: 06.10.2014. Laid: 27.10.2014. Coming into force: in accord with reg. 1 (1). Effect: None. Territorial extent & classification: E. General. - 8p.: 30 cm. - 978-0-11-112216-7 £6.00

The Care and Support (Independent Advocacy Support) (No. 2) Regulations 2014 No. 2014/2889. - Enabling power: Care Act 2014, ss. 67 (7), 125 (7) (8). - Issued: 05.11.2014. Made: 29.10.2014. Laid: 05.11.2014. Coming into force: in accord with reg. 1 (1). Effect: None. Territorial extent & classification: E. General. - This Statutory Instrument has been made in consequence of a defect in S.I. 2014/2824 (ISBN 9780111122075) and is being issued free of charge to all known recipients of that Statutory Instrument. - 8p.: 30 cm. - 978-0-11-112274-7 £6.00

The Care and Support (Independent Advocacy Support) Regulations 2014 No. 2014/2824. - Enabling power: Care Act 2014, ss. 67 (7), 125 (7) (8). - Issued: 27.10.2014. Made: 06.10.2014. Laid: 27.10.2014. Coming into force: in accord with reg. 1 (1). Effect: None. Territorial extent & classification: E. General. - 8p.: 30 cm. - 978-0-11-112207-5 £6.00

The Care and Support (Market Oversight Information) Regulations 2014 No. 2014/2822. - Enabling power: Care Act 2014, ss. 55 (5), 125 (7) (8). - Issued: 24.10.2014. Made: 06.10.2014. Laid: 24.10.2014. Coming into force: in accord with reg. 1 (1). Effect: None. Territorial extent & classification: E. General. - 4p.: 30 cm. - 978-0-11-112205-1 £4.25

The Care and Support (Ordinary Residence) (Specified Accommodation) Regulations 2014 No. 2014/2828. - Enabling power: Care Act 2014, ss. 39 (1), 125 (7). - Issued: 27.10.2014. Made: 06.10.2014. Laid: 27.10.2014. Coming into force: in accord with reg. 1 (1). Effect: None. Territorial extent & classification: E. General. - 4p.: 30 cm. - 978-0-11-112215-0 £4.25

The Care and Support (Personal Budget: Exclusion of Costs) Regulations 2014 No. 2014/2840. - Enabling power: Care Act 2014, ss. 26 (4), 125 (7). - Issued: 28.10.2014. Made: 20.10.2014. Laid: 28.10.2014. Coming into force: in accord with reg. 1 (1). Effect: None. Territorial extent & classification: E. General. - 2p.: 30 cm. - 978-0-11-112221-1 £4.25

SOCIAL CARE, ENGLAND AND WALES

The Care and Support (Preventing Needs for Care and Support) Regulations 2014 No. 2014/2673. - Enabling power: Care Act 2014, ss. 2 (3) (4), 125 (7). - Issued: 30.10.2014. Made: 22.10.2014. Laid: 30.10.2014. Coming into force: in accord with reg. 1. Effect: None. Territorial extent & classification: E. General. - 4p.: 30 cm. - 978-0-11-112237-2 £4.25

The Care and Support (Provision of Health Services) Regulations 2014 No. 2014/2821. - Enabling power: Care Act 2014, ss. 22 (4) (a), 22 (6), 125 (7) (8). - Issued: 24.10.2014. Made: 06.10.2014. Laid: 24.10.2014. Coming into force: in accord with reg. 1 (1). Effect: None. Territorial extent & classification: E. General. - 8p.: 30 cm. - 978-0-11-112204-4 £4.25

The Care and Support (Sight-impaired and Severely Sight-impaired Adults) Regulations 2014 No. 2014/2854. - Enabling power: Care Act 2014, s. 77 (2). - Issued: 30.10.2014. Made: 22.10.2014. Laid: 30.10.2014. Coming into force: in accord with reg. 1 (1). Effect: None. Territorial extent & classification: E. General. - 2p.: 30 cm. - 978-0-11-112239-6 £4.25

The Care Quality Commission (Reviews and Performance Assessments) Regulations 2014 No. 2014/1788. - Enabling power: Health and Social Care Act 2008, ss. 46 (1) (2), 161 (4). - Issued: 14.07.2014. Made: 07.07.2014. Laid: 11.07.2014. Coming into force: 01.10.2014. Effect: None. Territorial extent & classification: E. General. - 4p.: 30 cm. - 978-0-11-111771-2 £4.25

The Children and Young Persons Act 2008 (Relevant Care Functions) (England) Regulations 2014 No. 2014/2407. - Enabling power: Children and Young Persons Act 2008, ss. 1 (6) (7), 40 (12). - Issued: 15.09.2014. Made: 09.09.2014. Coming into force: 10.09.2014. Effect: None. Territorial extent & classification: E. General. - Supersedes draft S.I. (ISBN 9780111116920) issued 27.06.2014. - 2p.: 30 cm. - 978-0-11-112059-0 £4.25

The Health and Social Care Act 2008 (Regulated Activities) Regulations 2014 No. 2014/2936. - Enabling power: Health and Social Care Act 2008, ss. 8, 20 (1) to (5A), 35, 86 (2) (4), 87 (1) (2), 161 (3) (4). - Issued: 13.11.2014. Made: 06.11.2014. Coming into force: In accord. with reg. 1. Effect: None. Territorial extent & classification: E. General. - 32p.: 30 cm. - 978-0-11-112316-4 £10.00

The Health Research Authority (Transfer of Staff, Property and Liabilities) and Care Act 2014 (Consequential Amendments) Order 2014 No. 2014/3090. - Enabling power: Care Act 2014, ss. 109 (4), 118, 125 (8). - Issued: 12.12.2014. Made: 18.11.2014. Coming into force: 01.01.2015. Effect: S.I. 1990/2024; 1995/2800; 1996/251; 1999/873, 874; 2011/2260 amended & S.I. 2012/1108, 1109 revoked. Territorial extent & classification: E. General. - This S.I. has been printed in substitution of the S.I. of the same number and ISBN issued 25.11.2014 and is being issued free of charge to all known recipients of that S.I. Partially revoked by SI 2015/559 (ISBN 9780111132296). - 8p.: 30 cm. - 978-0-11-112369-0 £4.25

Social care, England and Wales

The Care Act 2014 (Commencement No.1) Order 2014 No. 2014/1714 (C.73). - Enabling power: Care Act 2014, s. 127 (1) (5). Bringing into operation various provisions of the 2014 Act on 07.07.2014, 15.07.2014, 01.10.2014, in accord. with arts 2, 3, 4. - Issued: 08.07.2014. Made: 02.07.2014. Effect: None. Territorial extent & classification: E/W. General. - 4p.: 30 cm. - 978-0-11-111750-7 £4.25

The Care Act 2014 (Commencement No.2) Order 2014 No. 2014/2473 (C.111). - Enabling power: Care Act 2014, ss. 124 (1) (2), 127 (1) (5). Bringing into operation various provisions of the 2014 Act on 01.10.2014, 01.01.2015 in accord. with arts 2, 3, 4, 5, 6. - Issued: 22.09.2014. Made: 12.09.2014. Effect: None. Territorial extent & classification: E/W. General. - 8p.: 30 cm. - 978-0-11-112089-7 £6.00

Social care, Wales

The Children and Families (Wales) Measure 2010 (Commencement No. 8) Order 2014 No. 2014/373 (W.41). - Enabling power: Children and Families (Wales) Measure 2010, ss. 74 (2), 75 (3). Bringing into operation various provisions of the 2010 Measure on 28.02.2014. - Issued: 03.03.2014. Made: 18.02.2014. Effect: None. Territorial extent & classification: W. General. - In English and Welsh. Welsh title: Gorchymyn Mesur Plant a Theuluoedd (Cymru) 2010 (Cychwyn Rhif 8) 2014. - 8p.: 30 cm. - 978-0-348-10892-7 £5.75

The Children and Families (Wales) Measure 2010 (Commencement No. 9) Order 2014 No. 2014/1606 (W.164) (C.64). - Enabling power: Children and Families (Wales) Measure 2010, s. 75 (3). Bringing into operation various provisions of the 2010 Measure on 30.06.2014, 01.07.2014, in accord. with art. 2. - Issued: 26.06.2014. Made: 11.06.2014. Effect: None. Territorial extent & classification: W. General. - In English and Welsh. Welsh title: Gorchymyn Mesur Plant a Theuluoedd (Cymru) 2010 (Cychwyn Rhif 9) 2014. - 8p.: 30 cm. - 978-0-348-10955-9 £6.00

The Health and Social Care (Community Health and Standards) Act 2003 Commencement (Wales) (No. 6) Order 2014 No. 2014/1793 (W.186)(C.78). - Enabling power: Health and Social Care (Community Health and Standards) Act 2003, s. 199 (1). Bringing into force various provisions of the 2003 Act on 01.08.2014. - Issued: 18.07.2014. Made: 07.07.2014. Effect: None. Territorial extent & classification: W. General. - In English and Welsh. Welsh title: Gorchymyn Cychwyn Deddf Iechyd a Gofal Cymdeithasol (Iechyd Cymunedol a Safonau) 2003 (Cymru) (Rhif 6) 2014. - 12p.: 30 cm. - 978-0-348-10964-1 £6.00

The National Assistance (Sums for Personal Requirements) (Assessment of Resources) and Social Care Charges (Wales) (Miscellaneous Amendments) Regulations 2014 No. 2014/666 (W.73). - Enabling power: National Assistance Act 1948, ss. 22 (4) (5) & Social Care Charges (Wales) Measure 2010, ss. 2 (2), 7 (2), 12 (2), 17 (2). - Issued: 26.03.2014. Made: 14.03.2013. Laid before the National Assembly for Wales: 17.03.2013. Coming into force: 07.04.2013. Effect: S.I. 1992/2977; 2011/962 (W.136), 963 (W.137) amended & S.I. 2013/631 (W.68) partially revoked. Territorial extent & classification: W. General. - Partially revoked by WSI 2015/720 (ISBN 9780348110579). - In English & Welsh. Welsh title: Rheoliadau Cymorth Gwladol (Symiau at Anghenion Personol) (Asesu Adnoddau) a Ffioedd Gofal Cymdeithasol (Cymru) (Diwygiadau Amrywiol) 2014. - 8p.: 30 cm. - 978-0-348-10926-9 £5.75

The Representations Procedure (Wales) Regulations 2014 No. 2014/1795 (W.188). - Enabling power: Children Act 1989, ss. 24D (1A), 24D (2), 26(3A) (3B) (3C) (4A) (5) (5A) (6), 26A (3), 104 (4),104A. sch. 7, para. 6. - Issued: 25.07.2014. Made: 07.07.2014. Laid before the National Assembly for Wales: 09.07.2014. Coming into force: 01.08.2014. Effect: W.S.I. 2007/1357 (W.128) amended & W.S.I. 2005/3365 (W.262) revoked with saving. Territorial extent & classification: W. General. - In English and Welsh. Welsh title: Rheoliadau Gweithdrefn Sylwadau (Cymru) 2014. - 20p.: 30 cm. - 978-0-348-10973-3 £6.00

The Social Services and Well-being (Wales) Act 2014 (Commencement No. 1) Order 2014 No. 2014/2718 (W.274) (C.118). - Enabling power: Social Services and Well-being (Wales) Act 2014, s. 199 (2). Bringing into operation various provisions of the 2014 Act on 01.11.2014, in accord. with art. 2. - Issued: 17.10.2014. Made: 08.10.2014. Effect: None. Territorial extent & classification: W. General. - In English and Welsh. Welsh title: Gorchymyn Deddf Gwasanaethau Cymdeithasol a Llesiant (Cymru) 2014 (Cychwyn Rhif 1) 2014. - 4p.: 30 cm. - 978-0-348-11002-9 £4.25

The Social Services Complaints Procedure (Wales) Regulations 2014 No. 2014/1794 (W.187). - Enabling power: Health and Social Care (Community Health and Standards) Act 2003, ss. 114 (3) (4) (5) (b) (c), 115 (1) (2) (4) (5) (6), 195 (1) (b). - Issued: 23.07.2014. Made: 07.07.2014. Laid before the National Assembly for Wales: 09.07.2014. Coming into force: 01.08.2014. Effect: S.I. 2007/1357 (W.128); 2011/964 (W.138) amended & S.I. 2005/3366 (W.263) revoked with saving. Territorial extent & classification: W. General. - In English and Welsh. Welsh title: Rheoliadau Gweithdrefn Gwynion y Gwasanaethau Cymdeithasol (Cymru) 2014. - 20p.: 30 cm. - 978-0-348-10970-2 £6.00

Social security

The Child Benefit and Tax Credits Up-rating Order 2014 No. 2014/384. - Enabling power: Welfare Benefits Up-rating Act 2013, ss. 1 (1) (2) (3) (5) (7), 2 (1) (2) (3) (4) & Social Security Administration (Northern Ireland) Act 1992, s. 132 (1). - Issued: 28.02.2014. Made: 24.02.2014. Coming into force: 07.04.2014 for art. 2; 06.04.2014 for arts 3,4. Effect: S.I. 2002/2005, 2007; 2006/965 amended. Territorial extent & classification: E/W/S/NI. General. - 4p.: 30 cm. - 978-0-11-111015-7 £4.00

SOCIAL SECURITY

The Child Benefit (General) and Child Tax Credit (Amendment) Regulations 2014 No. 2014/1231. - Enabling power: Social Security Contributions and Benefits Act 1992, ss. 142 (2) (b), 175 (1) (3), sch. 9, para. 3 & Social Security Contributions and Benefits (Northern Ireland) Act 1992, ss. 138 (1) (b), 171 (1) (3), sch. 9, para. 3 & Tax Credits Act 2002, ss. 8 (4) (b), 65 (1) (7), 67. - Issued: 19.05.2014. Made: 12.05.2014. Laid: 14.05.2014. Coming into force: 04.06.2014. Effect: S.I. 2002/2007; 2006/223 amended. Territorial extent & classification: E/W/S/NI. General. - 4p.: 30 cm. - 978-0-11-111482-7 £4.25

The Child Benefit (General) and Tax Credits (Miscellaneous) Regulations 2014 No. 2014/2924. - Enabling power: Social Security Contributions and Benefits Act 1992, ss. 142 (2) (b), 175 (1) (1A) (3) & Social Security Contributions and Benefits (Northern Ireland) Act 1992, ss. 138 (1) (c), 171 (1) (3) & Tax Credits Act 2002, ss. 7 (8), 8 (4) (b), 9 (6), 11 (1), 12 (3), 65 (1) (7) (9), 67. - Issued: 12.11.2014. Made: 06.11.2014. Laid: 07.11.2014. Coming into force: 28.11.2014. Effect: S.I. 2002/2005, 2006, 2007; 2006/223 amended. Territorial extent & classification: E/W/S/NI. General. - 4p.: 30 cm. - 978-0-11-112304-1 £4.25

The Child Benefit (General) and the Tax Credits (Residence) (Amendment) Regulations 2014 No. 2014/1511. - Enabling power: Social Security Contributions and Benefits Act 1992, ss. 146 (3), 175 (1) (1A) (a) (3) (4) & Social Security Contributions and Benefits (Northern Ireland) Act 1992, ss. 142 (3), 171 (3) (4) (10) & Tax Credits Act 2002, ss. 3 (7), 65 (1) (7) (9). - Issued: 16.06.2014. Made: 09.06.2014. Laid: 10.06.2014. Coming into force: 01.07.2014. Effect: S.I. 2003/654; 2006/223 amended. Territorial extent & classification: E/W/S/NI. General. - 8p.: 30 cm. - 978-0-11-111635-7 £6.00

The Finance Act 2009, Sections 101 and 102 (Interest on Late Payments and Repayments), Appointed Days and Consequential Provisions Order 2014 No. 2014/992 (C.45). - Enabling power: Finance Act 2009, s. 104 (3) (4) (5) (6) (7). Bringing into operation various provisions of the 2009 Act on 06.05.2014, in accord. with art. 3. - Issued: 17.04.2014. Made: 10.04.2014. Laid: 14.04.2014. Coming into force: 06.05.2014. Effect: 1970 c.9; 1992 c.5, 8; 2005 c.5; S.I. 2001/1004; 2003/2682; 2005/2045 amended. Territorial extent & classification: E/W/S/NI. General. - 8p.: 30 cm. - 978-0-11-111412-4 £4.25

The Finance Act 2009, Sections 101 and 102 (Interest on Late Payments and Repayments) (Consequential Amendments) Order 2014 No. 2014/1283. - Enabling power: Finance Act 2009, s. 104 (5) (6) (7). - Issued: 23.05.2014. Made: 16.05.2014. Laid: 19.05.2014. Coming into force: 20.05.2014. Effect: 1992 c.4, c.5, c.7, c.8; 2005 c.5; 2009 c.4 amended. Territorial extent & classification: E/W/S/NI. General. - 4p.: 30 cm. - 978-0-11-111509-1 £4.25

The Guardian's Allowance Up-rating Order 2014 No. 2014/828. - Enabling power: Social Security Administration Act 1992, ss. 150 (9) (10) (a) (i), 189 (4). - Issued: 01.04.2014. Made: 26.03.2014. Coming into force: 07.04.2014. Effect: 1992 c.4 amended. Territorial extent & classification: E/W/S. General. - Supersedes draft SI (ISBN 9780111109472) issued 17/02/14. - 2p.: 30 cm. - 978-0-11-111283-0 £4.00

The Guardian's Allowance Up-rating Regulations 2014 No. 2014/881. - Enabling power: Social Security Contributions and Benefits Act 1992, ss. 113 (1), 175 (1) (3) (4) & Social Security Administration Act 1992, ss. 155 (3), 189 (1) (4) (5), 190, 191 & Social Security Contributions and Benefits (Northern Ireland) Act 1992, ss. 113 (1), 171 (1) (3) (4) & Social security Administration (Northern Ireland) Act 1992, ss. 135 (3), 165 (1) (4) (5), 167 (1). - Issued: 07.04.2013. Made: 01.04.2014. Laid: 02.04.2014. Coming into force: 07.04.2014. Effect: None. Territorial extent & classification: E/W/S. General. - 4p.: 30 cm. - 978-0-11-111342-4 £4.25

The Housing Benefit and Universal Credit (Supported Accommodation) (Amendment) Regulations 2014 No. 2014/771. - Enabling power: Welfare Reform Act 2012, ss. 11 (3) (a), 42 (1) (2), 96 (1) (4) (a) (10), 97 (1). - Issued: 25.03.2014. Made: 19.03.2014. Laid: 20.03.2014. Coming into force: In accord. with reg. 1. Effect: S.I. 2006/213; 2013/376 amended. Territorial extent & classification: E/W/S. General. - 8p.: 30 cm. - 978-0-11-111251-9 £4.00

The Housing Benefit (Habitual Residence) Amendment Regulations 2014 No. 2014/539. - Enabling power: Social Security Contributions and Benefits Act 1992, ss. 123 (1) (d), 137 (1) (2) (i), 175 (1) (3) (4). - Issued: 13.03.2014. Made: 05.03.2014. Laid: 11.03.2014. Coming into force: 01.04.2014. Effect: S.I. 2006/213 amended. Territorial extent & classification: E/W/S. General. - 2p.: 30 cm. - 978-0-11-111141-3 £4.00

The Housing Benefit (Miscellaneous Amendments) Regulations 2014 No. 2014/213. - Enabling power: Social Security Contributions and Benefits Act 1992; ss. 123 (1) (d), 130A (2) (3) (4), 135 (1) (6), 136 (3) (4), 137 (1), 175 (1) (3) & Social Security Administration Act 1992, ss. 5 (1) (a), 189 (1) (4) (6) & Social Security Act 1998, s. 79 (4) & Child Support, Pensions and Social Security Act 2000, sch. 7, paras 4 (4) (6), 20 (1), 23 (1). - Issued: 10.02.2014. Made: 30.01.2014. Laid: 06.02.2014. Coming into force: In accord. with reg. 1. Effect: S.I. 2001/1002; 2006/213, 214 amended. Territorial extent & classification: E/W/S. General. - 8p.: 30 cm. - 978-0-11-110927-4 £4.00

The Housing Benefit (Transitional Provisions) (Amendment) Regulations 2014 No. 2014/212. - Enabling power: Social Security Contributions and Benefits Act 1992, ss. 123 (1) (d), 130A (2) to (5), 137 (1), 175 (1) (3) (4). - Issued: 10.02.2014. Made: 04.02.2014. Laid: 05.02.2014. Coming into force: 03.03.2014. Effect: S.I. 2006/213, 217 amended. Territorial extent & classification: E/W/S. General. - 4p.: 30 cm. - 978-0-11-110925-0 £4.00

The Income-related Benefits (Subsidy to Authorities) and Discretionary Housing Payments (Grants) Amendment Order 2014 No. 2014/1667. - Enabling power: Social Security Administration Act 1992, ss. 140B (1) (3), 140C (1) (4), 140F (2), 189 (1) (4) (5) (7) & Child Support, Pensions and Social Security Act 2000, s. 70 (3) (a) (4) (6). - Issued: 03.07.2014. Made: 26.06.2014. Laid: 03.07.2014. Coming into force: 25.07.2014. Effect: S.I. 1998/562; 2001/2340 amended. Territorial extent & classification: E/W/S. General. - 16p.: 30 cm. - 978-0-11-111728-6 £6.00

The Income Support (Work-Related Activity) and Miscellaneous Amendments Regulations 2014 No. 2014/1097. - Enabling power: Social Security Administration Act 1992, ss. 2A (1) (3) (6) (8), 2D (1) (4) (a) (b) (d) (f) (h) (5) to (9)(c), 2E (3) (a) (b) (4) (5) (a) (d), 2G (2) (a) (4), 2H, 189 (1) (4) to (6), 191 & Social Security Act 1998, ss. 9 (1), 10 (3) (6), 84 & Welfare Reform Act 2007, ss. 11E (1) (a), 13 (2) (a), 24 (1), 25 (2) (3) & Welfare Reform Act 2012, ss. 20 (1) (a), 21 (1) (b) (5), 40, 42 (2) (3). - Issued: 02.05.2014. Made: 27.04.2014. Coming into force: 28.04.2014 in accord. with reg. 1 (1). Effect: S.I. 1999/991; 2000/1926; 2002/1703; 2011/1349; 2013/376, 379 amended. Territorial extent & classification: E/W/S. General. - Supersedes draft S.I. (ISBN 9780111108499) issued 22.01.2014. - 12p.: 30 cm. - 978-0-11-111431-5 £6.00

The Jobseeker's Allowance (18-21 Work Skills Pilot Scheme) Regulations 2014 No. 2014/3117. - Enabling power: Social Security Contributions and Benefits Act 1992, ss. 123 (1) (d), 136 (5) (a) (b), 137 (1), 175 (1) (3) (4) (6) & Jobseekers Act 1995, ss. 12 (4) (a) (b), 17A (1) (2) (5) (a) (b), 20E (3) (a), 29, 35 (1), 36 (2), (4) (4A) & Housing Grants, Construction and Regeneration Act 1996, ss. 30, 146 (1) (2). - Issued: 28.11.2014. Made: -. Coming into force: 25.11.2014 in accord. with reg. 1 (1). Effect: S.I. 1996/207, 2890; 2006/213 amended. Territorial extent & classification: E. General. - Supersedes draft S.I. (ISBN 9780111121368) issued 13.10.2014. - 12p.: 30 cm. - 978-0-11-112395-9 £6.00

The Jobseeker's Allowance (Habitual Residence) Amendment Regulations 2014 No. 2014/2735. - Enabling power: Jobseekers Act 1995, ss. 4 (5) (12), 35 (1), 36 (2). - Issued: 17.10.2014. Made: 13.10.2014. Laid: 17.10.2014. Coming into force: 09.11.2014. Effect: S.I. 1996/207 amended. Territorial extent & classification: E/W/S. General. - 4p.: 30 cm. - 978-0-11-112173-3 £4.25

The Jobseeker's Allowance (Homeless Claimants) Amendment Regulations 2014 No. 2014/1623. - Enabling power: Jobseekers Act 1995, ss. 6 (4), 35 (1), 36 (2) (4). - Issued: 30.06.2014. Made: 23.06.2014. Laid: 30.06.2014. Coming into force: 21.07.2014. Effect: S.I. 1996/207 amended. Territorial extent & classification: E/W/S. General. - 2p.: 30 cm. - 978-0-11-111697-5 £4.25

The Jobseeker's Allowance (Supervised Jobsearch Pilot Scheme) Regulations 2014 No. 2014/1913. - Enabling power: Social Security Contributions and Benefits Act 1992, ss. 123 (1) (d), 136 (5) (a) (b), 137 (1), 175 (1) (3) (4) (6) & Jobseekers Act 1995, ss. 12 (4) (a) (b), 17A (1) (2) (4) (5) (a), 20E (3) (a), 29, 35 (1), 36 (2) (4) (4A) & Housing Grants, Construction and Regeneration Act 1996, ss. 30, 146 (1) (2). - Issued: 24.07.2014. Made: 17.07.2014. Coming into force: 18.07.2014, in accord with reg. 1 (1). Effect: S.I. 1996/207, 2890; 2006/213 amended. Territorial extent & classification: E. General. - Supersedes draft (ISBN 9780111115367) issued 04.06.2014. - 8p.: 30 cm. - 978-0-11-111884-9 £6.00

The Maternity Allowance (Curtailment) Regulations 2014 No. 2014/3053. - Enabling power: Social Security Contributions and Benefits Act 1992, ss. 35 (3A) (3B) (3C) (3D), 175 (1) (3) (4) (5). - Issued: 25.11.2014. Made: 19.11.2014. Laid: 20.11.2014. Coming into force: 01.25.2014. Effect: None. Territorial extent & classification: E/W/S. General. - 4p.: 30 cm. - 978-0-11-112359-1 £4.25

SOCIAL SECURITY

The Mesothelioma Lump Sum Payments (Conditions and Amounts) (Amendment) Regulations 2014 No. 2014/868. - Enabling power: Child Maintenance and Other Payments Act 2008, ss. 46 (3), 53 (1) (2) (b). - Issued: 04.04.2014. Made: 31.03.2014. Coming into force: 01.04.2014, in accord. with reg. 1 (1). Effect: S.I. 2008/1963 amended. Territorial extent & classification: E/W/S. General. - Supersedes draft SI (ISBN 9780111109564) issued 07.02.2014. - 4p.: 30 cm. - 978-0-11-111334-9 £4.25

The Pensions Act 2014 (Consequential Amendments) (Units of Additional Pension) Order 2014 No. 2014/3213. - Enabling power: Pensions Act 2014, s. 53 (1) (2). - Issued: 11.12.2014. Made: 04.12.2014. Coming to force: 12.10.2015. Effect: 1992 c.4; 1993 c.48; S.I. 2001/1085 amended. Territorial extent & classification: E/W/S. General- 4p.: 30 cm. - 978-0-11-112463-5 £4.25

The Pneumoconiosis etc. (Workers' Compensation) (Payment of Claims) (Amendment) Regulations 2014 No. 2014/869. - Enabling power: Pneumoconiosis etc. (Workers' Compensation) Act 1979, ss. 1 (1) (2) (4), 7 (1) (2). - Issued: 04.04.2014. Made: 31.03.2014. Coming into force: In accord. with reg. 1 (1). Effect: S.I. 1988/668 amended. Territorial extent & classification: E/W/S. General. - Supersedes draft (ISBN 9780111109601) issued 18.02.2014. - 8p.: 30 cm. - 978-0-11-111336-3 £6.00

The Social Fund Cold Weather Payments (General) Amendment Regulations 2014 No. 2014/2687. - Enabling power: Social Security Contributions and Benefits Act 1992, ss. 138 (2) (4), 175 (1) (3) (4) (5). - Issued: 10.10.2014. Made: 29.09.2014. Laid: 07.10.2014. Coming into force: 01.11.2014. Effect: S.I. 1988/1724 amended. Territorial extent & classification: E/W/S. General. - 8p.: 30 cm. - 978-0-11-112130-6 £6.00

The Social Fund Winter Fuel Payment (Amendment) Regulations 2014 No. 2014/3270. - Enabling power: Social Security Contributions and Benefits Act 1992, ss. 138 (2) (4), 175 (1) (3). - Issued: 16.12.2014. Made: 10.12.2014. Laid: 15.12.2014. Coming into force: 21.09.2015. Effect: S.I. 2000/729 amended. Territorial extent & classification: E/W/S. General. - 4p.: 30 cm. - 978-0-11-112533-5 £4.25

The Social Security Benefits Up-rating Order 2014 No. 2014/516. - Enabling power: Social Security Administration Act 1992, ss. 150, 150A, 151, 189 (1) (4) (5). - Issued: 19.03.2014. Made: 11.03.2014. Coming into force: In accord. with art. 1. Effect: 1965 c.51; 1992 c.4; S.I. 1978/393; 1987/1967; 1991/2890; 1994/2946; 1995/310; 1996/207; 2002/1792; 2005/454; 2006/213, 214; 2008/794; 2010/2818; 2013/376, 377, 379 amended & S.I. 2013/574 revoked (14.04.2014). Territorial extent & classification: E/W/S. General. - Supersedes draft (ISBN 9780111108789) issued 29.01.2014; Revoked by SI 2015/457 (ISBN 9780111132043). - 48p.: 30 cm. - 978-0-11-111206-9 £9.75

The Social Security Benefits Up-rating Regulations 2014 No. 2014/618. - Enabling power: Social Security Contributions and Benefits Act 1992, ss. 90, 113 (1), 122 (1), 175 (1) (3) & Social Security Administration Act 1992, ss. 5 (1) (p), 155 (3), 189 (1) (4), 191. - Issued: 19.03.2014. Made: 13.03.2014. Laid: 17.03.2014. Coming into force: 07.04.2014. Effect: S.I. 1977/343; 1987/1968 amended & S.I. 2013/599 revoked. Territorial extent & classification: E/W/S. General. - Revoked by SI 2015/496 (ISBN 9780111131947). - 4p.: 30 cm. - 978-0-11-111218-2 £4.00

The Social Security (Categorisation of Earners) (Amendment) Regulations 2014 No. 2014/635. - Enabling power: Social Security Contributions and Benefits Act 1992, s. 2 (2) (b) (2A), 7 (2) (3), 175 (4) & Social Security Contributions and Benefits (Northern Ireland) Act 1992, ss. 2 (2) (b) (2A), 7 (2) (3), 171 (4). - Issued: 20.03.2014. Made: 13.03.2014. Laid: 14.03.2014. Coming into force: 06.04.2014. Effect: S.I. 1978/1689; S.R. 1978/401 amended & S.I. 2004/770 partially revoked & S.I. 1998/1728; 1999/3; 2003/733, 736; S.R 1998/250; 1999/2 revoked. Territorial extent & classification: E/W/S/NI. General. - 12p.: 30 cm. - 978-0-11-111224-3 £5.75

The Social Security Class 3A Contributions (Amendment) Regulations 2014 No. 2014/2746. - Enabling power: Social Security Contributions and Benefits Act 1992, ss. 14B (1) (2) (4), 14C (2) (3) & Social Security Contributions and Benefits (Northern Ireland) Act 1992, ss. 14B (1) (2) (4), 14C (2) (3). - Issued: 20.10.2014. Made: 13.10.2014. Laid: 14.10.2014. Coming into force: in accord. with reg. 1 (2) (3). Effect: 1992 c.4, c.7; S.I. 2001/1004 amended. Territorial extent & classification: E/W/S/NI. General. - 4p.: 30 cm. - 978-0-11-112178-8 £4.25

The Social Security Class 3A Contributions (Units of Additional Pension) Regulations 2014 No. 2014/3240. - Enabling power: Social Security Contributions and Benefits Act 1992, ss. 14A (3) (6), 45 (2A), sch. 1, para. 8 (1) (q) & Social Security Contributions and Benefits (Northern Ireland) Act 1992, ss. 14A (3) (6), sch. 1, para. 8 (1) (q). - Issued: 15.12.2014. Made: 08.12.2014. Coming into force: in accord. with reg. 1(2) (3). Effect: None. Territorial extent & classification: E/W/S/NI. General. - Supersedes draft S.I. (ISBN 9780111121689) issued 17/10/14. - 4p.: 30 cm. - 978-0-11-112499-4 £4.25

The Social Security (Contributions) (Amendment No. 2) Regulations 2014 No. 2014/572. - Enabling power: Social Security Contributions and Benefits Act 1992, s. 120 (1) (4), 175 (4). - Issued: 20.03.2014. Made: 14.03.2014. Laid: 14.03.2014. Coming into force: 06.04.2014. Effect: S.I. 2001/1004 amended. Territorial extent & classification: E/W/S/NI. General. - With correction slips dated March 2014 and April 2014. - 8p.: 30 cm. - 978-0-11-111226-7 £5.75

The Social Security (Contributions) (Amendment No. 3) Regulations 2014 No. 2014/1016. - Enabling power: Social Security Contributions and Benefits Act 1992, sch. 1, para. 6 (1) (2) & Social Security Contributions and Benefits (Northern Ireland) Act 1992, sch. 1, para. 6 (1) (2). - Issued: 22.04.2014. Made: 14.04.2014. Laid: 15.04.2014. Coming into force: 06.05.2014. Effect: S.I. 2001/1004 amended. Territorial extent & classification: E/W/S/NI. General. - 4p.: 30 cm. - 978-0-11-111414-8 £4.25

The Social Security (Contributions) (Amendment No. 4) Regulations 2014 No. 2014/2397. - Enabling power: Social Security Contributions and Benefits Act 1992, s. 175 (4), sch. 1 para. 6 (1) (2) & Social Security Contributions and Benefits (Northern Ireland) Act 1992, s. 171 (4), sch. 1 para. 6 (1) (2). - Issued: 17.09.2014. Made: 11.09.2014, 11.16 am. Laid: 12.09.2014. Coming into force: 06.10.2014. Effect: S.I. 2001/1004 amended. Territorial extent & classification: E/W/S/NI. General. - 4p.: 30 cm. - 978-0-11-112073-6 £4.25

The Social Security (Contributions) (Amendment No. 5) Regulations 2014 No. 2014/3196. - Enabling power: Social Security Contributions and Benefits Act 1992, ss 18A (1) (3), 175 (3) (4) & Social Security Contributions and Benefits (Northern Ireland) Act 1992, ss. 18A (1) (3), 171 (3) (4). - Issued: 08.12.2014. Made: 02.12.2014. Coming into force: 03.12.2014. Effect: S.I. 2001/1004 amended. Territorial extent & classification: E/W/S/NI. General. - 4p.: 30 cm. - 978-0-11-112448-2 £4.25

The Social Security (Contributions) (Amendment No. 6) Regulations 2014 No. 2014/3228. - Enabling power: Social Security Contributions and Benefits Act 1992, ss 3 (2) (3). - Issued: 15.12.2014. Made: 09.12.2014. Laid: 10.12.2014. Coming into force: 01.01.2015. Effect: S.I. 2001/1004 amended. Territorial extent & classification: E/W/S/NI. General. - 4p.: 30 cm. - 978-0-11-112514-4 £4.25

The Social Security (Contributions) (Amendment) Regulations 2014 No. 2014/608. - Enabling power: Social Security Contributions and Benefits Act 1992, ss. 3 (2) (3), 175, sch. 1, para. 6 (1) (2) & Social Security Contributions and Benefits (Northern Ireland) Act 1992, ss. 3 (2) (3), 171, sch. 1, para. 6 (1) (2). - Issued: 19.03.2014. Made: 13.03.2014. Laid: 13.03.2014. Coming into force: 06.04.2014. Effect: S.I. 2001/1004 amended. Territorial extent & classification: E/W/S/NI. General. - 8p.: 30 cm. - 978-0-11-111210-6 £5.75

The Social Security Contributions (Limited Liability Partnership) Regulations 2014 No. 2014/3159. - Enabling power: Social Security Contributions and Benefits Act 1992, ss. 4AA, 175 (3) (4) & Social Security Contributions and Benefits (Northern Ireland) Act 1992, ss. 4AA, 171 (3) (4). - Issued: 15.12.2014. Made: 04.12.2014. Coming into force: 05.12.2104. Effect: S.I. 2000/727, 728; 2001/1004 amended. Territorial extent & classification: E/W/S/NI. General. - Supersedes draft SI (ISBN 9780111121658) issued 17/10/14. - 8p.: 30 cm. - 978-0-11-112505-2 £6.00

The Social Security (Contributions) (Limits and Thresholds) (Amendment) Regulations 2014 No. 2014/569. - Enabling power: Social Security Contributions and Benefits Act 1992, ss. 5 (1) (4) to (6), 175 (3) & Social Security Contributions and Benefits (Northern Ireland) Act 1992, ss. 5 (1) (4) to (6), 171 (3) (10). - Issued: 17.03.2014. Made: 10.03.2014. Coming into force: 06.04.2014. Effect: S.I. 2001/1004 amended. Territorial extent & classification: E/W/S/NI. General. - Supersedes draft SI (ISBN 9780111108796) issued 30/01/14. - 2p.: 30 cm. - 978-0-11-111165-9 £4.00

SOCIAL SECURITY

The Social Security (Contributions) (Re-rating and National Insurance Funds Payments) Order 2014 No. 2014/475. - Enabling power: Social Security Administration Act 1992, ss. 141 (4) (5), 142 (2) (3) & Social Security Administration (Northern Ireland) Act 1992, s. 129 & Social Security Act 1993, ss. 2 (2) (3) & S.I. 1993/592 (N.I. 2), art. 4. - Issued: 14.03.2014. Made: -. Coming into force: 06.04.2014. Effect: 1992 c.4, 7 amended. Territorial extent & classification: E/W/S/NI. General. - Supersedes draft S.I. (ISBN 9780111108826) issued 30.01.2014. - 4p.: 30 cm. - 978-0-11-111164-2 £4.00

The Social Security (Contributions) (Re-Rating) Consequential Amendment Regulations 2014 No. 2014/634. - Enabling power: Social Security Contributions and Benefits Act 1992, ss. 117 (1), 175 (3) & Social Security Contributions and Benefits (Northern Ireland) Act 1992, ss. 117 (1), 171 (3) (10). - Issued: 19.03.2014. Made: 13.03.2014. Laid: 14.03.2014. Coming into force: 06.04.2014. Effect: S.I. 2001/1004 amended. Territorial extent & classification: E/W/S/NI. General. - 2p.: 30 cm. - 978-0-11-111223-6 £4.00

The Social Security (Fees Payable by Qualifying Lenders) (Amendment) Regulations 2014 No. 2014/485. - Enabling power: Social Security Administration Act 1992, ss. 15A (2) (b), 189 (1) (4). - Issued: 10.03.2014. Made: 03.03.2014. Laid: 10.03.2014. Coming into force: 01.04.2014. Effect: S.I. 1987/1968; 2013/380 amended. Territorial extent & classification: E/W/S. General. - 4p.: 30 cm. - 978-0-11-111087-4 £4.00

The Social Security (Habitual Residence) (Amendment) Regulations 2014 No. 2014/902. - Enabling power: Social Security Contributions and Benefits Act 1992, ss. 123 (1) (a) (2), 135 (1) (2), 137 (1), 175 (1) (3) (4) & Jobseekers Act 1995, ss. 4 (5) (12), 35 (1), 36 (2) & & Immigration and Asylum Act 1999, s. 115 (3) (4) (7) & State Pensions Credit Act 2002, ss. 1 (5) (a), 17 (1), 19 91) & Welfare Reform Act 2007, ss. 4 (3), 24, 25 (2) (3) & Welfare Reform Act 2012, ss. 30, 40, 42 (1) (2) (3), sch. 1, para. 7. - Issued: 08.04.2014. Made: 02.04.2014. Laid: 08.04.2014. Coming into force: 31.05.2014. Effect: S.I. 1987/1967; 1996/207; 2002/1792; 2006/213, 214; 2008/794; 2013/376 amended. Territorial extent & classification: E/W/S. General. - 4p.: 30 cm. - 978-0-11-111367-7 £4.25

The Social Security (Invalid Care Allowance) (Amendment) Regulations 2014 No. 2014/904. - Enabling power: Social Security Contributions and Benefits Act 1992, ss. 70 (8), 175 (1) (3). - Issued: 09.04.2014. Made: 03.04.2014. Laid: 03.04.2014. Coming into force: 20.05.2014. Effect: S.I. 1976/409 amended. Territorial extent & classification: E/W/S. General. - 2p.: 30 cm. - 978-0-11-111368-4 £4.25

The Social Security (Jobseeker's Allowance and Employment and Support Allowance) (Waiting Days) Amendment Regulations 2014 No. 2014/2309. - Jobseekers Act 1995, ss. 21, 35 (1) (36) (2) (4) (a), sch. 1 paras. 4, 10 (1), Welfare Reform Act 2007, ss. 22, 24 (1) 25 (2) (3) (5) (a), sch. 2 para. 2. - Issued: 08.09.2014. Made: 03.09.2014. Laid: 04.09.2014. Coming into force: 27.10.2014. Effect: S.I. 1996/207 amended. Territorial extent & classification: E/W/S. General- 4p.: 30 cm. - 978-0-11-112013-2 £4.25

The Social Security (Maternity Allowance) (Miscellaneous Amendments) Regulations 2014 No. 2014/884. - Enabling power: Child Support Act 1991, s. 42 (1), sch. 1, para. 4 (1) (b) & Social Security Contributions and Benefits Act 1992, ss. 35 (3), 35B (11), 175 (1) (3) (4) (5) & Jobseekers Act 1995, ss. 1 (2C), 6 (4), sch. 1, para. 3 & Welfare Reform Act 2007, sch. 2, para. 1 (a) & Welfare Reform Act 2012, ss. 12, 96, 97, sch. 1, paras. 2, 4 (1) (b). - Issued: 07.04.2014. Made: 01.04.2014. Laid: 02.04.2014. Coming into force: 18.05.2014. Effect: S.I. 1987/416; 1992/1815; 1996/207; 2001/155; 2008/794; 2012/2677; 2013/376, 378, 379 amended. Territorial extent & classification: E/W/S. General. - 4p.: 30 cm. - 978-0-11-111349-3 £4.25

The Social Security (Maternity Allowance) (Participating Wife or Civil Partner of Self-employed Earner) Regulations 2014 No. 2014/606. - Enabling power: European Communities Act 1972, s. 2 (2). - Issued: 20.03.2014. Made: 13.03.2014. Coming into force: 01.04.2014. Effect: 1992 c.4; 2003 c.1; 2012 c.5 amended. Territorial extent & classification: E/W/S. - Supersedes draft (ISBN 9780111108475) issued 22.01.2014. - 4p.: 30 cm. - 978-0-11-111234-2 £4.00

The Social Security (Miscellaneous Amendments) Regulations 2014 No. 2014/591. - Enabling power: Social Security Contributions and Benefits Act 1992, ss. 44C (3) (e), 123 (1) (a) (d), 136 (3) (4) (5), 136A, 137 (1), 175 (1) (3) (4) & Social Security Administration Act 1992, ss. 5 (1) (a), 115A (2) (b), 189 (1) (4) (6), 191 & Jobseeker's Act 1995, ss. 12 (4), 35 (1), 36 (1) (2) (4) (a) & State Pension Credit Act 2002, ss. 15 (3) (6), 17 (1), 19 (1) & Welfare Reform Act 2007, ss. 17 (1), 24 (1), 25 (2) (3) (5) (a). - Issued: 18.03.2014. Made: 11.03.2014. Laid: 18.03.2014. Coming into force: 28.04.2014. Effect: S.I. 1987/1967, 1968; 1996/207; 1997/2813; 2001/1323; 2002/1792; 2006/213, 214; 2008/794 amended. Territorial extent & classification: E/W/S. General. - 8p.: 30 cm. - 978-0-11-111195-6 £5.75

The Social Security Pensions (Flat Rate Accrual Amount) Order 2014 No. 2014/369. - Enabling power: Social Security Administration Act 1992, ss. 148AA (3) to (6), 189 (1) (4) (5). - Issued: 25.02.2014. Made: 19.02.2014. Laid: 25.02.2014. Coming into force: 06.04.2014. Effect: None. Territorial extent & classification: E/W/S. General. - 2p.: 30 cm. - 978-0-11-111000-3 £4.00

The Social Security Pensions (Low Earnings Threshold) Order 2014 No. 2014/368. - Enabling power: Social Security Administration Act 1992, s. 148A (3) to (5), 189 (1) (4) (5). - Issued: 25.02.2014. Made: 19.02.2014. Laid: 25.02.2014. Coming into force: 06.04.2014. Effect: None. Territorial extent & classification: E/W/S. General. - 2p.: 30 cm. - 978-0-11-110997-7 £4.00

The Social Security (Recovery of Benefits) (Lump Sum Payments) (Amendment) Regulations 2014 No. 2014/1456. - Enabling power: Social Security Administration Act 1992, s. 189 (4) (5) (6) & Social Security (Recovery of Benefits) Act 1997, ss. 1A (1) (3), 14 (2) (3) (4), 19, 21 (3), 23 (1) (2) (6A) (7), 29, 30 (4), sch. 1, para. 4. - Issued: 10.06.2014. Made: 04.06.2014. Laid: 10.06.2014. Coming into force: 01.07.2014. Effect: S.I. 2008/1596 amended. Territorial extent & classification: E/W/S. General. - 8p.: 30 cm. - 978-0-11-111604-3 £6.00

The Social Security Revaluation of Earnings Factors Order 2014 No. 2014/367. - Enabling power: Social Security Administration Act 1992, ss. 148 (3) (4), 189 (1) (4) (5). - Issued: 25.02.2014. Made: 19.02.2014. Laid: 25.02.2014. Coming into force: 06.04.2014. Effect: None. Territorial extent & classification: E/W/S. General. - 4p.: 30 cm. - 978-0-11-110998-4 £4.00

The Statutory Maternity Pay and Statutory Adoption Pay (Curtailment) Regulations 2014 No. 2014/3054. - Enabling power: Social Security Contributions and Benefits Act 1992, ss. 165 (3A) (3B) (3C) (3D), 171ZN (2A) (2B) (2C) (2D), 175 (1) (3) (4). - Issued: 25.11.2014. Made: 19.11.2014. Laid: 20.11.2014. Coming into force: 01.12.2014. Effect: None. Territorial extent & classification: E/W/S. General. - 8p.: 30 cm. - 978-0-11-112360-7 £6.00

The Statutory Shared Parental Pay (Administration) Regulations 2014 No. 2014/2929. - Enabling power: Employment Act 2002, ss. 7, 8, 10, 51 (1) & Social Security Contributions (Transfer of Functions, etc.) Act 1999, ss. 8 (1) (f) (ga), 25 (3) (6). - Issued: 12.11.2014. Made: 05.11.2014. Laid: 07.11.2014. Coming into force: 01.12.2014. Effect: None. Territorial extent & classification: E/W/S. General. - 8p.: 30 cm. - 978-0-11-112309-6 £6.00

The Statutory Sick Pay (Maintenance of Records) (Revocation) Regulations 2014 No. 2014/55. - Enabling power: Social Security Administration Act 1992, s. 130 (4). - Issued: 21.01.2014. Made: 07.01.2014. Laid: 15.01.2014. Coming into force: 06.04.2014. Effect: S.I. 1982/894 partially revoked. Territorial extent & classification: E/W/S. General. - 2p.: 30 cm. - 978-0-11-110845-1 £4.00

The Statutory Sick Pay Percentage Threshold (Revocations, Transitional and Saving Provisions) (Great Britain and Northern Ireland) Order 2014 No. 2014/897. - Enabling power: Social Security Contributions and Benefits Act 1992, s. 176 (1) (c) & Social Security Contributions and Benefits (Northern Ireland) Act 1992, s. 172 (11A). - Issued: 08.04.2014. Made: 01.04.2014. Coming into force: 06.04.2014. Effect: S.I. 1995/512; S.R. 1995/69 revoked. Territorial extent & classification: E/W/S/NI. General. - Supersedes draft S.I. (ISBN 9780111108468) issued 21.01.2014. - 4p.: 30 cm. - 978-0-11-111362-2 £4.25

The Tax Credits, Child Benefit and Guardian's Allowance Appeals (Appointed Day) (Northern Ireland) Order 2014 No. 2014/2881 (C.127). - Enabling power: S.I. 2014/886, art. 1 (2). Bringing into operation various provisions of the 2014 Order, so far as they extend to Northern Ireland, on 03.11.2014, in accord. with art. 2. - Issued: 05.11.2014. Made: 29.10.2014. Effect: None. Territorial extent & classification: NI. General. - 2p.: 30 cm. - 978-0-11-112267-9 £4.25

SOCIAL SECURITY, ENGLAND AND WALES

The Tax Credits, Child Benefit and Guardian's Allowance Reviews and Appeals Order 2014 No. 2014/886. - Enabling power: Finance Act 2008, s. 124 (1) (2) (6) (7). - Issued: 08.04.2014. Made: 01.04.2014. Coming into force: 06.04.2014. Effect: 1998 c.14; 2002 c.21 & S.I. 1998/1506 (N.I.10); 2003/916 amended & S.I. 2002/3119 amended in relation to Northern Ireland and revoked in relation to Great Britain. Territorial extent & classification: E/W/S/NI. General. - Supersedes draft SI (ISBN 9780111109571) issued 18/04/14. - 8p.: 30 cm. - 978-0-11-111351-6 £4.25

The Universal Credit and Miscellaneous Amendments (No. 2) Regulations 2014 No. 2014/2888. - Enabling power: Social Security Contributions and Benefits Act 1992, ss. 135 (1) (5) (6), 136 (3) (4), 136A (3), 137 (1), 175 (1) (3) (4) & Social Security Administration Act 1992, ss. 5 (1) (i) (p) (r) (1A) & Jobseekers Act 1995, ss. 4 (5), 35 (1), 36 (1) (2) (4) (a) & State Pension Credit Act 2002, ss. 2 (3) (b), 15 (3) (6) (b), 17 (1) & Welfare Reform Act 2007, ss. 4 (2) (a), 24 (1), 25 (2) (3) (5), sch. 2, para. 2 & Welfare Reform Act 2012, ss. 8 (3), 10 (2) (3), 11 (4), 19 (2) (d), 22 (2), 32, 40, 42, sch. 1, para. 4 (1) (3) (4). - Issued: 05.11.2014. Made: 29.10.2014. Laid: 04.11.2014. Coming into force: 26.11.2014. Effect: 1992 c.5; 2013 c.16; S.I. 1987/1967, 1968; 1996/207; 2002/1792; 2006/213, 214; 2007/572; 2008/794; 2013/376, 380, 383 amended. Territorial extent & classification: E/W/S. General. - With correction slip dated January 2015. - 16p.: 30 cm. - 978-0-11-112273-0 £6.00

The Universal Credit and Miscellaneous Amendments Regulations 2014 No. 2014/597. - Enabling power: Social Security Administration Act 1992, ss. 5 (1) (p), 189 (1) (5) (6) & Social Security Act 1998, ss. 10 (3), 79 (1) (4) (6) (7), 84 & Jobseekers Act 1995, ss. 6H (5) (6), 6J (5) (b), 6K (4) (b) (5), 12 (1) (2), 35 (1), 36 (2) (4) (a) & Welfare Reform Act 2007, ss. 11H (5) (6), 11J (3) (b) (4), 17 (1) (2), 24 (1), 25 (2) (3) & Welfare Reform Act 2012, ss. 9 (2), 10 (3), 11 (4), 12 (3), 18 (5), 22 (2), 24 (5) (6), 26 (6) (b), 27 (5) (b), 28, 37 (6), 40, 42 (1) (2) (3) (a). - Issued: 18.03.2014. Made: 11.03.2014. Laid: 18.03.2014. Coming into force: 28.04.2014. Effect: S.I. 2013/376, 378, 379, 380, 381 amended. Territorial extent & classification: E/W/S. General. - 8p.: 30 cm. - 978-0-11-111197-0 £5.75

The Universal Credit (Digital Service) Amendment Regulations 2014 No. 2014/2887. - Enabling power: Social Security Administration Act 1992, s. 1 (1) & Welfare Reform Act 2012, ss. 4 (3), 7 (3), 8 (3), 9 (2), 10 (3), 11 (4), 12 (1) (3), 19 (2) (d), 32 (1) (4), 42 (2) (3), sch. 1, para. 3 (2). - Issued: 05.11.2014. Made: 29.10.2014. Laid: 04.11.2104. Coming into force: 26.11.2014. Effect: None. Territorial extent & classification: E/W/S. General. - 8p.: 30 cm. - 978-0-11-112271-6 £6.00

The Universal Credit (Transitional Provisions) (Amendment) Regulations 2014 No. 2014/1626. - Enabling power: Welfare Reform Act 2012, s.42 (2) (3), sch. 6, paras 1 (1) (2) (b), 5 (1) (a), 6 (a). - Issued: 30.06.2014. Made: 23.06.2014. Laid: 30.06.2014. Coming into force: In accord. with reg 1. Effect: 2002 c.21; S.I. 2002/2006, 2008, 2014, 2173; 2003/654 modified & S.I. 2014/1230 amended. Territorial extent & classification: E/W/S. General. - 12p.: 30 cm. - 978-0-11-111700-2 £6.00

The Universal Credit (Transitional Provisions) Regulations 2014 No. 2014/1230. - Enabling power: Welfare Reform Act 2012, s.42 (2) (3), sch. 6, paras 1 (1) (2) (b), 3 (1) (a) to (c), 4 (1) (a), 5 (1) (2) (c) (d) (3) (a), 6. - Issued: 19.05.2014. Made: 12.05.2014. Laid: 14.05.2014. Coming into force: 16.06.2014. Effect: 2002 c.21 modified & S.I.2013/386 revoked with savings. Territorial extent & classification: E/W/S. General. - 36p.: 30 cm. - 978-0-11-111481-0 £10.00

The Welfare Benefits Up-Rating Order 2014 No. 2014/147. - Enabling power: Welfare Benefits Uprating Act 2013, s. 1. - Issued: 31.01.2014. Made: 24.01.2014. Coming into force: In accord. with art. 1. Effect: 1992 c.4; 1986/1960; 1987/1967; 1996/207; 2002/2818; 2006/213; 2008/794; 2013/376, 378, 379 amended. Territorial extent & classification: E/W/S. General. - Revoked by SI 2015/30 (ISBN 9780111127360). - 16p.: 30 cm. - 978-0-11-110892-5 £5.75

The Welfare Reform Act 2012 (Commencement No. 9, 11, 13 14, 16, 17 and 19 and Transitional and Transitory Provisions (Amendment)) Order 2014 No. 2014/3067 (C.129). - Enabling power: Welfare Reform Act 2012, s. 150 (3) (4) (a) (b) (i) (c). - Issued: 24.11.2014. Made: 17.11.2014. Coming into force: 24.11.2014. Effect: S.I. 2013/983 (C.41), 1511 (C.60), 2657 (C.107), 2846 (C.114); 2014/209 (C.7), 1583 (C.61), 2321 (C.99) amendment. Territorial extent & classification: E/W/S. General. - 16p.: 30 cm. - 978-0-11-112346-1 £6.00

The Welfare Reform Act 2012 (Commencement No. 9, 11, 13, 14, 16 and 17 and Transitional and Transitory Provisions (Amendment) (No. 2)) Order 2014 No. 2014/1923 (C.88). - Enabling power: Welfare Reform Act 2012, s. 150 (3) (4) (a) (b) (i) (c). - Issued: 25.07.2014. Made: 21.07.2014. Coming into force: 21.07.2014. Effect: S.I. 2013/983 (C.41), 1511 (C.60), 2657 (C.107), 2846 (C.114); 2014/209 (C.7), 1583 (C.61) amended. Territorial extent & classification: E/W/S. General. - 24p.: 30 cm. - 978-0-11-111895-5 £6.00

The Welfare Reform Act 2012 (Commencement No. 9, 11, 13, 14, 16 and 17 and Transitional and Transitory Provisions) (Amendment) Order 2014 No. 2014/1661 (C.69). - Enabling power: Welfare Reform Act 2012, s. 150 (3) (4) (a) (b) (i) (c). Bringing into operation various provisions of the 2012 Act on 30.06.2014. - Issued: 02.07.2014. Made: 26.06.2014. Effect: S.I. 2013/983 (C.41); 1511 (C.60), 2657 (C.107), 2846 (C.114); 2014/209 (C.7), 1583 (C.61) amended. Territorial extent & classification: E/W/S. General. - 24p.: 30 cm. - 978-0-11-111717-0 £6.00

The Welfare Reform Act 2012 (Commencement No. 9, 11, 13, 14 and 16 and Transitional and Transitory Provisions) (Amendment) Order 2014 No. 2014/1452 (C.56). - Enabling power: Welfare Reform Act 2012, s. 150 (3) (4) (b) (a) (b) (i). - Issued: 10.06.2014. Made: 04.06.2014. Coming into force: 04.06.2014. Effect: S.I. 2013/983 (C.41), 1511 (C.60), 2657 (C.107), 2846 (C.114); 2014/209 (C.7) amended. Territorial extent & classification: E/W/S. General. - 40p.: 30 cm. - 978-0-11-111598-5 £10.00

The Welfare Reform Act 2012 (Commencement No. 16 and Transitional and Transitory Provisions) Order 2014 No. 2014/209 (C.7). - Enabling power: Welfare Reform Act 2012, s. 150 (3) (4) (a) (b) (i) (c). Bringing into operation certain provisions of the 2012 Act on 04.02.2014 in accord. with art. 6. - Issued: 10.02.2014. Made: 03.02.2014. Effect: None. Territorial extent & classification: E/W/S. General. - 12p.: 30 cm. - 978-0-11-110923-6 £5.75

The Welfare Reform Act 2012 (Commencement No. 17 and Transitional and Transitory Provisions) Order 2014 No. 2014/1583 (C.61). - Enabling power: Welfare Reform Act 2012, s. 150 (3) (4) (a) (b) (i) (c). Bringing into operation certain provisions of the 2012 Act on the first day of the period in respect of which a claim is made. - Issued: 23.06.2014. Made: 16.06.2014. Effect: None. Territorial extent & classification: E/W/S. General. - 20p.: 30 cm. - 978-0-11-111666-1 £6.00

The Welfare Reform Act 2012 (Commencement No. 19 and Transitional and Transitory Provisions and Commencement No. 9 and Transitional and Transitory Provisions) Order 2014 No. 2014/2321 (C.99). - Enabling power: Welfare Reform Act 2012, s. 150 (3) (4) (a) (b) (i) (c). Bringing into operation various provisions of the 2012 Act on 15.09.2014. - Issued: 05.09.2014. Made: 01.09.2014. Effect: S.I. 2013/983 (C.41) amended. Territorial extent & classification: E/W/S. General. - 24p.: 30 cm. - 978-0-11-112007-1 £6.00

The Welfare Reform Act 2012 (Commencement No. 20 and Transitional and Transitory Provisions and Commencement No. 9 and Transitional and Transitory Provisions (Amendment)) Order 2014 No. 2014/3094 (C.133). - Enabling power: Welfare Reform Act 2012, s. 150 (3) (4) (a) (b) (i) (c). Bringing various provisions of the 2012 Act into operation in according with art. 3 (3). - Issued: 27.11.2014. Made: 21.11.2014. Effect: S.I. 2013/983 (C.41) amended. Territorial extent & classification: E/W/S. General. - 16p.: 30 cm. - 978-0-11-112372-0 £6.00

Social security, England and Wales

The Social Security (Graduated Retirement Benefit) (Married Same Sex Couples) Regulations 2014 No. 2014/76. - Enabling power: Social Security Contributions and Benefits Act 1992, ss. 62 (1) (ad) (ae), 175 (1) (3) (4). - Issued: 23.01.2014. Made: 14.01.2014. Laid: 23.01.2014. Coming into force: 13.03.2014. Effect: 1965 c.51; S.I. 1978/393 amended. Territorial extent & classification: E/W. General. - 4p.: 30 cm. - 978-0-11-110850-5 £4.00

Social security, Northern Ireland

The Guardian's Allowance Up-rating (Northern Ireland) Order 2014 No. 2014/838. - Enabling power: Social Security Administration (Northern Ireland) Act 1992, ss. 132 (1), 165 (4). - Issued: 02.04.2014. Made: 26.03.2014. Coming into force: 07.04.2014. Effect: 1992 c.7 amended. Territorial extent & classification: NI. General. - Supersedes draft (ISBN 9780111109502) issued 17.02.2014. - 4p.: 30 cm. - 978-0-11-111293-9 £4.00

SUPREME COURTS OF ENGLAND AND WALES

Sports grounds and sporting events, England and Wales

The Football Spectators (2014 World Cup Control Period) (Amendment) Order 2014 No. 2014/220. - Enabling power: Football Spectators Act 1989, ss. 14 (6). - Issued: 11.02.01.2014. Made: 04.02.2014. Laid: 06.02.2014. Coming into force: 24.02.2014. Effect: S.I. 2014/144 amended. Territorial extent & classification: E/W. General. - This Statutory Instrument has been made to correct an error in SI 2014/144 (ISBN 9780111108901) and is being issued free of charge to all known recipients of that Statutory Instrument. - 2p.: 30 cm. - 978-0-11-110929-8 £4.00

The Football Spectators (2014 World Cup Control Period) Order 2014 No. 2014/144. - Enabling power: Football Spectators Act 1989, ss. 14 (6), 22A (2). - Issued: 31.01.2014. Made: 24.01.2014. Laid: 29.01.2014. Coming into force: 22.02.2014. Effect: None. Territorial extent & classification: E/W. General. - This Statutory Instrument has been corrected by SI 2014/220 (ISBN 9780111109298) which is being issued free of charge to all known recipients of this SI 2014/144. - 2p.: 30 cm. - 978-0-11-110890-1 £4.00

The Safety of Sports Grounds (Designation) Order 2014 No. 2014/2523. - Enabling power: Safety of Sports Grounds Act 1975, s. 1 (1). - Issued: 25.09.2014. Made: 18.09.2014. Laid: 19.09.2014. Coming into force: 10.10.2014. Effect: None. Territorial extent & classification: E/W. General. - 2p.: 30 cm. - 978-0-11-112097-2 £4.25

Stamp duty

The Stamp Duty and Stamp Duty Reserve Tax (BX Swiss AG) (Recognised Foreign Exchange and Recognised Foreign Options Exchange) Regulations 2014 No. 2014/2942. - Enabling power: Finance Act 1986, s. 80B (3) (b) (4) (b). - Issued: 17.11.2014. Made: 10.11.2014. Laid: 11.11.2014. Coming into force: 02.12.2014. Effect: None. Territorial extent & classification: E/W/S/NI. General. - 2p.: 30 cm. - 978-0-11-112320-1 £4.25

The Stamp Duty and Stamp Duty Reserve Tax (European Central Counterparty N.V.) Regulations 2014 No. 2014/9. - Enabling power: Finance Act 1991, ss. 116, 117. - Issued: 14.01.2014. Made: 08.01.2014. Laid: 09.01.2014. Coming into force: 30.01.2014. Effect: S.I. 2011/668 revoked. Territorial extent & classification: UK. General. - 8p.: 30 cm. - 978-0-11-110811-6 £4.00

The Stamp Duty and Stamp Duty Reserve Tax (Exchange Traded Funds) (Exemption) Regulations 2014 No. 2014/911. - Enabling power: Finance Act 2013, ss. 217 (1) to (3) (7). - Issued: 10.04.2014. Made: 03.04.2014. Laid: 07.04.2014. Coming into force: 28.04.2014. Effect: None. Territorial extent & classification: UK. General. - 4p.: 30 cm. - 978-0-11-111374-5 £4.25

The Taxes (Definition of Charity) (Relevant Territories) (Amendment) Regulations 2014 No. 2014/1807. - Enabling power: Finance Act 2010, sch. 6, para. 2 (3) (b). - Issued: 15.07.2014. Made: 09.07.2014. Laid: 10.07.2014. Coming into force: 31.07.2014. Effect: S.I. 2010/1904 amended. Territorial extent & classification: E/W/S/NI. General. - 4p.: 30 cm. - 978-0-11-111781-1 £4.25

Stamp duty land tax

The Taxes (Definition of Charity) (Relevant Territories) (Amendment) Regulations 2014 No. 2014/1807. - Enabling power: Finance Act 2010, sch. 6, para. 2 (3) (b). - Issued: 15.07.2014. Made: 09.07.2014. Laid: 10.07.2014. Coming into force: 31.07.2014. Effect: S.I. 2010/1904 amended. Territorial extent & classification: E/W/S/NI. General. - 4p.: 30 cm. - 978-0-11-111781-1 £4.25

Stamp duty reserve tax

The Finance Act 2009, Schedules 55 and 56 and Sections 101 and 102 (Stamp Duty Reserve Tax) (Appointed Days, Consequential and Transitional Provision) (Amendment) Order 2014 No. 2014/3346. - Enabling power: Finance Act 2009, ss. 104 (3) to (6), 106 (2) to (6), 107 (2) to (6). - Issued: 29.12.2014. Made: 18.12.2014. Laid: 19.12.2014. Coming into force: 31.12.2014. Effect: S.I. 2014/3269 (c.151) amended. Territorial extent & classification: E/W/S/NI. General. - This Statutory Instrument has been made to correct errors in S.I. 2014/3269 (ISBN 9780111125328) and is being issued free of charge to all known recipients of that Statutory Instrument. - 2p.: 30 cm. - 978-0-11-112635-6 £4.25

The Finance Act 2009, Schedules 55 and 56 and Sections 101 and 102 (Stamp Duty Reserve Tax) (Appointed Days, Consequential and Transitional Provision) Order 2014 No. 2014/3269 (C.151). - Enabling power: Finance Act 2009, ss. 104 (3) to (6), 107 (2) to (6). Bringing into operation various provisions of the 2009 Act on 01.01.2015 in accordance with art. 2. - Issued: 17.12.2014. Made: 11.12.2014. Laid: 11.12.2014. Coming into force: 01.01.2015. Effect: S.I. 2011/702 partially revoked. Territorial extent & classification: E/W/S/NI. General. - 4p.: 30 cm. - 978-0-11-112532-8 £4.25

The Stamp Duty and Stamp Duty Reserve Tax (BX Swiss AG) (Recognised Foreign Exchange and Recognised Foreign Options Exchange) Regulations 2014 No. 2014/2942. - Enabling power: Finance Act 1986, s. 80B (3) (b) (4) (b). - Issued: 17.11.2014. Made: 10.11.2014. Laid: 11.11.2014. Coming into force: 02.12.2014. Effect: None. Territorial extent & classification: E/W/S/NI. General. - 2p.: 30 cm. - 978-0-11-112320-1 £4.25

The Stamp Duty and Stamp Duty Reserve Tax (European Central Counterparty N.V.) Regulations 2014 No. 2014/9. - Enabling power: Finance Act 1991, ss. 116, 117. - Issued: 14.01.2014. Made: 08.01.2014. Laid: 09.01.2014. Coming into force: 30.01.2014. Effect: S.I. 2011/668 revoked. Territorial extent & classification: UK. General. - 8p.: 30 cm. - 978-0-11-110811-6 £4.00

The Stamp Duty and Stamp Duty Reserve Tax (Exchange Traded Funds) (Exemption) Regulations 2014 No. 2014/911. - Enabling power: Finance Act 2013, ss. 217 (1) to (3) (7). - Issued: 10.04.2014. Made: 03.04.2014. Laid: 07.04.2014. Coming into force: 28.04.2014. Effect: None. Territorial extent & classification: UK. General. - 4p.: 30 cm. - 978-0-11-111374-5 £4.25

The Stamp Duty Reserve Tax (Finance Act 1999, Schedule 19) (Consequential Amendments) Regulations 2014 No. 2014/1932. - Enabling power: Finance Act 1986, s. 98 & Finance Act 1995, s. 152, & Finance (No. 2) Act 2005, s. 17 (3) & Finance Act 2014, s, 114 (5). - Issued: 28.07.2014. Made: 21.07.2014. Laid: 22.07.2014. Coming into force: 14.08.2014. Effect: S.I. 1986/1711; 1997/1156; 2006/964 amended. Territorial extent & classification: E/W/S/NI. General. - 4p.: 30 cm. - 978-0-11-111904-4 £4.25

The Taxes (Definition of Charity) (Relevant Territories) (Amendment) Regulations 2014 No. 2014/1807. - Enabling power: Finance Act 2010, sch. 6, para. 2 (3) (b). - Issued: 15.07.2014. Made: 09.07.2014. Laid: 10.07.2014. Coming into force: 31.07.2014. Effect: S.I. 2010/1904 amended. Territorial extent & classification: E/W/S/NI. General. - 4p.: 30 cm. - 978-0-11-111781-1 £4.25

Statistics of trade

The Statistics of Trade (Customs and Excise) (Amendment) Regulations 2014 No. 2014/3135. - Enabling power: European Communities Act 1972, s. 2 (2). - Issued: 02.12.2014. Made: 26.11.2014. Laid: 27.11.2014. Coming into force: 01.01.2015. Effect: S.I. 1992/2790 amended. Territorial extent & classification: E/W/S/NI. General. - 2p.: 30 cm. - 978-0-11-112407-9 £4.25

Supreme Court of the United Kingdom

The Courts and Tribunals Fees (Miscellaneous Amendments) Order 2014 No. 2014/590 (L.6). - Enabling power: Courts Act 2003, s. 92 & Insolvency Act 1986, ss. 414, 415 & Tribunals, Courts and Enforcement Act 2007, s. 42, 49 (3) & Constitutional Reform Act 2005, s. 52 & Mental Capacity Act 2005. s. 54 & Gender Recognition Act 2004, s. 7 (2). - Issued: 19.03.2014. Made: 11.03.2014. Laid: 13.03.2104. Coming into force: 06.04.2014. Effect: S.I. 2004/3120; 2006/758; 2007/1745; 2008/1052, 1053, 1054; 2009/213, 1114; 2010/42; 2011/2344; 2013/1179, 1893 amended. Territorial extent & classification: E/W. General. - 16p.: 30 cm. - 978-0-11-111194-9 £5.75

Supreme Courts of England and Wales

The European Parliamentary Election Petition (Amendment) Rules 2014 No. 2014/1129 (L.23). - Enabling power: S.I. 2004/293, reg. 120. - Issued: 07.05.2014. Made: 28.04.2014. Laid: 01.05.2014. Coming into force: 22.05.2014. Effect: S.I. 1979/521 amended in relation to England and Wales & Gibraltar. Territorial extent & classification: E/W/Gib. General. - 2p.: 30 cm. - 978-0-11-111449-0 £4.25

Tax credits

The Child Benefit and Tax Credits Up-rating Order 2014 No. 2014/384. - Enabling power: Welfare Benefits Up-rating Act 2013, ss. 1 (1) (2) (3) (5) (7), 2 (1) (2) (3) (4) & Social Security Administration (Northern Ireland) Act 1992, s. 132 (1). - Issued: 28.02.2014. Made: 24.02.2014. Coming into force: 07.04.2014 for art. 2; 06.04.2014 for arts 3,4. Effect: S.I. 2002/2005, 2007; 2006/965 amended. Territorial extent & classification: E/W/S/NI. General. - 4p.: 30 cm. - 978-0-11-111015-7 £4.00

The Child Benefit (General) and Child Tax Credit (Amendment) Regulations 2014 No. 2014/1231. - Enabling power: Social Security Contributions and Benefits Act 1992, ss. 142 (2) (b), 175 (1) (3), sch. 9, para. 3 & Social Security Contributions and Benefits (Northern Ireland) Act 1992, ss. 138 (1) (b), 171 (1) (3), sch. 9, para. 3 & Tax Credits Act 2002, ss. 8 (4) (b), 65 (1) (7), 67. - Issued: 19.05.2014. Made: 12.05.2014. Laid: 14.05.2014. Coming into force: 04.06.2014. Effect: S.I. 2002/2007; 2006/223 amended. Territorial extent & classification: E/W/S/NI. General. - 4p.: 30 cm. - 978-0-11-111482-7 £4.25

The Child Benefit (General) and Tax Credits (Miscellaneous) Regulations 2014 No. 2014/2924. - Enabling power: Social Security Contributions and Benefits Act 1992, ss. 142 (2) (b), 175 (1) (1A) (3) & Social Security Contributions and Benefits (Northern Ireland) Act 1992, ss. 138 (1) (c), 171 (1) (3) & Tax Credits Act 2002, ss. 7 (8), 8 (4) (b), 9 (6), 11 (1), 12 (3), 65 (1) (7) (9), 67. - Issued: 12.11.2014. Made: 06.11.2014. Laid: 07.11.2014. Coming into force: 28.11.2014. Effect: S.I. 2002/2005, 2006, 2007; 2006/223 amended. Territorial extent & classification: E/W/S/NI. General. - 4p.: 30 cm. - 978-0-11-112304-1 £4.25

The Child Benefit (General) and the Tax Credits (Residence) (Amendment) Regulations 2014 No. 2014/1511. - Enabling power: Social Security Contributions and Benefits Act 1992, ss. 146 (3), 175 (1) (1A) (a) (3) (4) & Social Security Contributions and Benefits (Northern Ireland) Act 1992, ss. 142 (3), 171 (3) (4) (10) & Tax Credits Act 2002, ss. 3 (7), 65 (1) (7) (9). - Issued: 16.06.2014. Made: 09.06.2014. Laid: 10.06.2014. Coming into force: 01.07.2014. Effect: S.I. 2003/654; 2006/223 amended. Territorial extent & classification: E/W/S/NI. General. - 8p.: 30 cm. - 978-0-11-111635-7 £6.00

The Tax Credits Act 2002 (Commencement and Transitional Provisions) (Partial Revocation) Order 2014 No. 2014/1848. - Enabling power: Tax Credits Act 2002, ss. 61, 62 (2). - Issued: 23.07.2014. Made: 14.07.2014. Effect: S.I. 2003/962 (C.51); 2008/3151; 2010/644 partially revoked & S.I. 2011/2910 revoked. Territorial extent & classification: E/W/S/NI. General. - 2p.: 30 cm. - 978-0-11-111821-4 £4.25

The Tax Credits, Child Benefit and Guardian's Allowance Appeals (Appointed Day) (Northern Ireland) Order 2014 No. 2014/2881 (C.127). - Enabling power: S.I. 2014/886, art. 1 (2). Bringing into operation various provisions of the 2014 Order, so far as they extend to Northern Ireland, on 03.11.2014, in accord. with art. 2. - Issued: 05.11.2014. Made: 29.10.2014. Effect: None. Territorial extent & classification: NI. General. - 2p.: 30 cm. - 978-0-11-112267-9 £4.25

The Tax Credits, Child Benefit and Guardian's Allowance Reviews and Appeals Order 2014 No. 2014/886. - Enabling power: Finance Act 2008, s. 124 (1) (2) (6) (7). - Issued: 08.04.2014. Made: 01.04.2014. Coming into force: 06.04.2014. Effect: 1998 c.14; 2002 c.21 & S.I. 1998/1506 (N.I.10); 2003/916 amended & S.I. 2002/3119 amended in relation to Northern Ireland and revoked in relation to Great Britain. Territorial extent & classification: E/W/S/NI. General. - Supersedes draft SI (ISBN 9780111109571) issued 18/04/14. - 8p.: 30 cm. - 978-0-11-111351-6 £4.25

The Tax Credits (Exercise of Functions) Order 2014 No. 2014/3280. - Enabling power: Welfare Reform Act 2012, ss. 126 (1) (2) (3) (a) (b) (i) (9). - Issued: 17.12.2014. Made: 10.12.2014. Laid: 17.12.2014. Coming into force: 01.04.2015. Effect: S.I. 2013/384 amended. Territorial extent & classification: E/W/S/NI. General. - 4p.: 30 cm. - 978-0-11-112541-0 £4.25

The Tax Credits (Late Appeals) Order 2014 No. 2014/885. - Enabling power: Finance Act 2008, s. 124 (1) (2) (6) (7). - Issued: 08.04.2014. Made: 01.04.2014. Coming into force: In accord. with art. 1. Effect: 2002 c.21 amended. Territorial extent & classification: E/W/S. General. - Supersedes draft SI (ISBN 9780111109595) issued 18/02/14. - 4p.: 30 cm. - 978-0-11-111350-9 £4.25

The Tax Credits (Miscellaneous Amendments) Regulations 2014 No. 2014/658. - Enabling power: Tax Credits Act 2002, ss. 7 (8) (9), 11, 42, 65 (1) (7) (9), 67. - Issued: 20.03.2014. Made: 14.03.2014. Laid: 14.03.2014. Coming into force: 06.04.2014. Effect: S.I. 2002/2006; 2003/653 amended & S.I. 2002/2005 partially revoked. Territorial extent & classification: E/W/S/NI. General. - 4p.: 30 cm. - 978-0-11-111230-4 £4.00

The Tax Credits (Settlement of Appeals) Regulations 2014 No. 2014/1933. - Enabling power: Tax Credits Act 2002, ss. 63 (8), 65 (2) (6). - Issued: 28.07.2014. Made: 21.07.2014. Laid: 22.07.2014. Coming into force: 12.08.2014. Effect: 1970 c.9 modified. Territorial extent & classification: E/W/S. General. - 4p.: 30 cm. - 978-0-11-111906-8 £4.25

The Tax Credits Up-rating Regulations 2014 No. 2014/845. - Enabling power: Tax Credits Act 2002, ss. 7 (1) (a) (3), 9, 11, 13, 65 (1), 67. - Issued: 02.04.2014. Made: 26.03.2014. Coming into force: 06.04.2014. Effect: S.I. 2002/2005, 2007, 2008 amended. Territorial extent & classification: E/W/S/NI. General. - Supersedes draft S.I. (ISBN 9780111109465) issued 17.02.2014. - 4p.: 30 cm. - 978-0-11-111298-4 £4.00

Taxes

The International Tax Compliance (Crown Dependencies and Gibraltar) Regulations 2014 No. 2014/520. - Enabling power: Finance Act 2013, ss. 222 (1) (c) (2) (3). - Issued: 12.03.2014. Made: 06.03.2014. Laid: 07.03.2014. Coming into force: 31.03.2014. Effect: None. Territorial extent & classification: E/W/S/NI. General. - 16p.: 30 cm. - 978-0-11-111121-5 £5.75

The International Tax Compliance (United States of America) Regulations 2014 No. 2014/1506. - Enabling power: Finance Act 2013, ss. 222 (1) (2) (3). - Issued: 13.06.2014. Made: 09.06.2014. Laid: 09.06.2014. Coming into force: 30.06.2014. Effect: S.I. 2013/1962 revoked. Territorial extent & classification: E/W/S/NI. General. - 16p.: 30 cm. - 978-0-11-111626-5 £6.00

The International Tax Enforcement (Gibraltar) Order 2014 No. 2014/1356. - Enabling power: Finance Act 2006, s. 173 (1) to (3). - Issued: 03.06.2014. Made: 27.05.2014. Coming into force: 03.06.2014. Effect: None. Territorial extent & classification: E/W/S/NI. General. - Supersedes draft SI (ISBN 9780111110553) issued 06.03.14. - 8p.: 30 cm. - 978-0-11-111528-2 £4.25

The International Tax Enforcement (Uruguay) Order 2014 No. 2014/1358. - Enabling power: Finance Act 2006, s. 173 (1) to (3). - Issued: 03.06.2014. Made: 27.05.2014. Coming into force: 03.06.2014. Effect: None. Territorial extent & classification: E/W/S/NI. General. - Supersedes draft SI (ISBN 9780111110577) issued 06.03.14. - 8p.: 30 cm. - 978-0-11-111530-5 £6.00

The Revenue Scotland and Tax Powers Act 2014 (Consequential Provisions and Modifications) Order 2014 No. 2014/3294. - Enabling power: Scotland Act 1998, ss. 104, 112 (1), 113 (2) (4) (5),114 (1). - Issued: 18.12.2014. Made: 11.12.2014. Coming into force: in accord. with art. 1 (2). Effect: None. Territorial extent & classification: E/W/S/NI. General. - Supersedes draft S.I. (ISBN 9780111121276) issued 15/10/14. - 8p.: 30 cm. - 978-0-11-112563-2 £4.25

Taxes: Tonnage tax

The Tonnage Tax (Training Requirement) (Amendment) Regulations 2014 No. 2014/2394. - Enabling power: Finance Act 2000, sch. 22, paras 29, 31, 36. - Issued: 15.09.2014. Made: 08.09.2014. Laid: 10.09.2014. Coming into force: 01.10.2014. Effect: S.I. 2000/2129 amended. Territorial extent & classification: E/W/S/NI. General. - 2p.: 30 cm. - 978-0-11-112049-1 £4.25

Terms and conditions of employment

The Children and Families Act 2014 (Commencement No. 3, Transitional Provisions and Savings) Order 2014 No. 2014/1640 (C.67). - Enabling power: Children and Families Act 2014, s. 137 (1), 139 (6). Bringing into operation various provisions of the 2014 Act on 30.06.2014; 01.10.2014; 01.12.2014; 05.04.2015. - Issued: 02.07.2014. Made: 26.06.2014. Effect: None. Territorial extent & classification: E/W/S. General. - 12p.: 30 cm. - 978-0-11-111719-4 £6.00

TERMS AND CONDITIONS OF EMPLOYMENT

The Code of Practice (Handling in a Reasonable Manner Requests to Work Flexibly) Order 2014 No. 2014/1665. - Enabling power: Trade Union and Labour Relations (Consolidation) Act 1992, s. 200 (5). - Issued: 02.07.2014. Made: 26.06.2014. Effect: None. Territorial extent & classification: E/W/S. General. - 4p.: 30 cm. - 978-0-11-111725-5 £4.25

The Collective Redundancies and Transfer of Undertakings (Protection of Employment) (Amendment) Regulations 2014 No. 2014/16. - Enabling power: European Communities Act 1972, s. 2 (2) & Employment Relations Act 1999, s. 38. - Issued: 15.01.2014. Made: 08.01.2014. Laid: 10.1.2014. Coming into force: 31.01.2014. Effect: 1992 c.52; S.I. 2006/246 amended. Territorial extent & classification: E/W/S. General. - 12p.: 30 cm. - 978-0-11-110814-7 £5.75

The Deduction from Wages (Limitation) Regulations 2014 No. 2014/3322. - Enabling power: European Communities Act 1972, s. 2 (2). - Issued: 23.12.2014. Made: 17.12.2014. Laid: 18.12.2014. Coming into force: 08.01.2015. Effect: 1996 c.18; S.I. 1998/1833 amended. Territorial extent & classification: E/W/S. General. - 4p.: 30 cm. - 978-0-11-112614-1 £4.25

The Employment Rights Act 1996 (Application of Sections 75A, 75B, 75G, 75H, 80A and 80B to Parental Order Cases) Regulations 2014 No. 2014/3095. - Enabling power: Employment Rights Act 1996, ss. 75A (8), 75B (9), 75H (18), 80B (9), 236 (5)- Issued: 10.12.2014. Made: 24.11.2014. Coming into force: 25.11.2014. Effect: 1996 c.18 modified. Territorial extent & classification: E/W/S. General. - Supersedes draft S.I. (ISBN 9780111121641) issued 16/10/14. - 8p.: 30 cm. - 978-0-11-112471-0 £4.25

The Employment Rights Act 1996 (Application of Sections 75G and 75H to Adoptions from Overseas) Regulations 2014 No. 2014/3091. - Enabling power: Employment Rights Act 1996, s. 75H (17). - Issued: 10.12.2014. Made: 24.11.2014. Coming into force: 25.11.2014. Effect: None. Territorial extent & classification: E/W/S. General. - Supersedes draft S.I. (ISBN 9780111121528) issued 15/10/14. - 4p.: 30 cm. - 978-0-11-112465-9 £4.25

The Employment Rights (Increase of Limits) Order 2014 No. 2014/382. - Enabling power: Employment Relations Act 1999, s. 34. - Issued: 28.02.2014. Made: 18.02.2014. Laid: 25.02.2014. Coming into force: 06.04.2014. Effect: S.I. 2012/3007 revoked. Territorial extent & classification: E/W/S. General. - Revoked by SI 2015/226 (ISBN 9780111129661). - With correction slip dated October 2014. - 8p.: 30 cm. - 978-0-11-111012-6 £4.00

The Employment Tribunals Act 1996 (Application of Conciliation Provisions) Order 2014 No. 2014/431. - Enabling power: Employment Tribunals Act 1996, ss. 18 (8) (9), 41 (4). - Issued: 05.03.2014. Made: 25.02.2014. Laid: 28.02.2014. Coming into force: 06.04.2014. Effect: 5 Acts & 14 SIs amended. Territorial extent & classification: E/W/S. General. - 12p.: 30 cm. - 978-0-11-111042-3 £5.75

The Enterprise and Regulatory Reform Act 2013 (Commencement No. 5, Transitional Provisions and Savings) Order 2014 No. 2014/253 (C.10). - Enabling power: Enterprise and Regulatory Reform Act 2013, ss. 100, 103 (3). Bringing into operation various provisions of the 2013 Act on 06.03.2014 & 06.04.2014. - Issued: 18.02.2014. Made: 11.02.2014. Effect: None. Territorial extent & classification: E/W/S/NI. General. - Commencement series no. '(C.10)' not printed on document. - With correction slip dated December 2014. - 8p.: 30 cm. - 978-0-11-110975-5 £4.00

The Enterprise and Regulatory Reform Act 2013 (Consequential Amendments) (Employment) (No. 2) Order 2014 No. 2014/853. - Enabling power: Enterprise and Regulatory Reform Act 2013, s. 99 (1) (2). - Issued: 03.04.2014. Made: 27.03.2014. Laid: 28.03.2014. Coming into force: 20.04.2014. Effect: S.I. 2006/246 amended. Territorial extent & classification: E/W/S. General. - 2p.: 30 cm. - 978-0-11-111304-2 £4.00

The Enterprise and Regulatory Reform Act 2013 (Consequential Amendments) (Employment) Order 2014 No. 2014/386. - Enabling power: Enterprise and Regulatory Reform Act 2013, s. 99 (1) (2). - Issued: 28.02.2014. Made: 18.02.2014. Laid: 25.02.2014. Coming into force: 06.04.2014. Effect: 21 S.I.s amended. Territorial extent & classification: E/W/S/NI. General. - 12p.: 30 cm. - 978-0-11-111017-1 £5.75

The Flexible Working Regulations 2014 No. 2014/1398. - Enabling power: Employment Rights Act 1996, ss. 80F (1) (b) (5) (8) (a), 80G (2) (3), 80(H) (3) (b), 80I (3), 236 (5). - Issued: 09.06.2014. Made: 02.06.2014. Laid: 04.06.2014. Coming into force: 30.06.2014. Effect: None. Territorial extent & classification: E/W/S. General. - 4p.: 30 cm. - 978-0-11-111570-1 £4.25

The Maternity and Adoption Leave (Curtailment of Statutory Rights to Leave) Regulations 2014 No. 2014/3052. - Enabling power: Employment Rights Act 1996, ss. 71 (2) (3) (ba) (bb) (3A), 73 (2) (3) (a) (aa) (3A), 75 (1) (a) (2), 75A (1A) (2) (2A) (2B), 75B (2) (3) (a) (aa) (3A), 75D (1) (a) (2). - Issued: 01.12.2014. Made: 18.11.2014. Coming into force: 01.12.2014. Effect: None. Territorial extent & classification: E/W/S. - Supersedes draft S.I. (ISBN 9780111118863) issued 25.07.2014. - 8p.: 30 cm. - 978-0-11-112399-7 £6.00

The Maternity and Parental Leave etc. (Amendment) Regulations 2014 No. 2014/3221. - Enabling power: Employment Rights Act 1996, ss. 71 (4) (c), 76 (1) (2), 77 (1) (c). - Issued: 11.12.2014. Made: 28.11.2014. Coming into force: 01.12.2014 for the purpose of regs 1, 2 & 5; 05.04.2015 for all other purposes. Effect: S.I. 1999/3312 amended. Territorial extent & classification: E/W/S. General. - Supersedes draft S.I. (ISBN 9780111121559) issued 15.10.2014. - 2p.: 30 cm. - 978-0-11-112478-9 £4.25

The National Minimum Wage (Amendment) (No. 2) Regulations 2014 No. 2014/2485. - Enabling power: National Minimum Wage Act 1998, ss. 1 (3), 2, 3, 51. - Issued: 23.09.2014. Made: 14.09.2014. Coming into force: 01.10.2014. Effect: S.I. 1999/584 amended. Territorial extent & classification: E/W/S/NI. General. - Supersedes draft S.I. (ISBN 9780111117323) issued on 04.07.2014; Revoked by SI 2015/621 (ISBN 9780111132845). - 2p.: 30 cm. - 978-0-11-112094-1 £4.25

The National Minimum Wage (Amendment) (No. 3) Regulations 2014 No. 2014/2832. - Enabling power: National Minimum Wage Act 1998, ss. 3, 51. - Issued: 27.10.2014. Made: 16.10.2014. Coming into force: 17.10.2014. Effect: S.I. 1999/584 amended. Territorial extent & classification: E/W/S/NI. General but applies to E only. - Supersedes draft S.I. (ISBN 9780111117453) issued 08.07.2014; Revoked by SI 2015/621 (ISBN 9780111132845). - 2p.: 30 cm. - 978-0-11-112217-4 £4.25

The National Minimum Wage (Amendment) Regulations 2014 No. 2014/546. - Enabling power: National Minimum Wage Act 1998, s. 3, 51 (1). - Issued: 12.03.2014. Made: 06.03.2014. Coming into force: 07.03.2014. Effect: S.I. 1999/584 amended. Territorial extent & classification: E/W/S/NI. General. - Supersedes draft (ISBN 9780111107553) issued 23.12.2013; Revoked by SI 2015/621(ISBN 9780111132845). - 4p.: 30 cm. - 978-0-11-111148-2 £4.00

The National Minimum Wage (Variation of Financial Penalty) Regulations 2014 No. 2014/547. - Enabling power: National Minimum Wage Act 1998, s. 51 (5). - Issued: 12.03.2014. Made: 06.03.2014. Coming into force: 07.03.2014. Effect: 1998 c.39 amended. Territorial extent & classification: E/W/S/NI. General. - Supersedes draft (ISBN 9780111108321) issued 17.01.2014. - 4p.: 30 cm. - 978-0-11-111149-9 £4.00

The Paternity, Adoption and Shared Parental Leave (Parental Order Cases) Regulations 2014 No. 2014/3096. - Enabling power: Employment Rights Act 1996, ss. 47C (2), 75A (1) (2) (2A) (2B) (3) (6) (7), 75B (1) (2) (3) (3A) (4) (7) (8), 75C (1) (2), 75D, 75G (1) to (6), 75H (1) (4) (7) to (14) (16), 75I (1) (4) (5), 75J, 75K (1) (6) (7), 80A (5) (aa), 80B (1) (2) (4a) (5), 80C (1) (6), 80D (1), 80E, 99. - Issued: 10.12.2014. Made: 28.11.2014. Coming into force: 01.12.2014. Effect: None. Territorial extent & classification: E/W. General. - Supersedes draft S.I. (ISBN 9780111121665) issued 17/10/14. - 12p.: 30 cm. - 978-0-11-112473-4 £6.00

The Paternity and Adoption Leave (Amendment) (No. 2) Regulations 2014 No. 2014/3206. - Enabling power: Employment Rights Act 1996, ss. 75A (1), (1A), 75D (2), 80B (1) (5) (aa) (6A) (6B). - Issued: 11.12.2014. Made: 28.11.2014. Coming into force: 05.04.2015. Effect: S.I. 2002/2788 amended. Territorial extent & classification: E/W/S. General. - 4p.: 30 cm. - 978-0-11-112479-6 £4.25

The Paternity and Adoption Leave (Amendment) Regulations 2014 No. 2014/2112. - Enabling power: Employment Rights Act 1996, ss. 47C (2) (aa) (ab), 75A (1) (3) (c), 75D (2), 80A (4A), 80B (4A) (5) (ba), 80C (1) (c), 80D (1), 99 (1) (2) (3) (aa) (ab). - Issued: 12.08.2014. Made: 05.08.2014. Coming into force: 01.10.2014, 01.12.2014 & 05.04.2015. Effect: S.I. 2002/2788 amended. Territorial extent & classification: E/W/S. - Supersedes draft (ISBN 9780111116913) issued 27.06.2014. - 4p.: 30 cm. - 978-0-11-111968-6 £4.25

The Public Interest Disclosure (Prescribed Persons) (Amendment) Order 2014 No. 2014/596. - Enabling power: Employment Rights Act 1996, s. 43F. - Issued: 19.03.2014. Made: 12.03.2014. Laid: 13.03.2014. Coming into force: 06.04.2014. Effect: S.I. 1999/1549 amended. Territorial extent & classification: E/W/S. General. - 2p.: 30 cm. - 978-0-11-111196-3 £4.00

The Public Interest Disclosure (Prescribed Persons) Order 2014 No. 2014/2418. - Enabling power: Employment Rights Act 1996, ss. 43F, 236 (5). - Issued: 16.09.2014. Made: 08.09.2014. Laid: 10.09.2014. Coming into force: 01.10.2014. Effect: S.I. 1999/1549 partially revoked. Territorial extent & classification: E/W/S. General. - 16p.: 30 cm. - 978-0-11-112064-4 £6.00

The Shared Parental Leave and Paternity and Adoption Leave (Adoptions from Overseas) Regulations 2014 No. 2014/3092. - Enabling power: Employment Rights Act 1996, ss. 47C (2), 75A (1) (2A) (2B), 75B (3) (a) (aa) (3A), 75D (1) (a) (2), 75G (1) to (6), 75H (1) (4), (7) to (14), (16) (17), 75I (1) (4) (5), 75J, 75K (1) (6), 80B (2) (4A), 99. - Issued: 10.12.2014. Made: 26.11.2014. Coming into force: 05.04.2015. Effect: S.I. 2014/3050, 3052 modified. Territorial extent & classification: E/W/S. General. - Supersedes draft SI (ISBN 9780111121542) issued 15/10/14 - 8p.: 30 cm. - 978-0-11-112467-3 £6.00

The Shared Parental Leave and Statutory Shared Parental Pay (Consequential Amendments to Subordinate Legislation) Order 2014 No. 2014/3255. - Enabling power: Children and Families Act 2014, ss. 135 (3), 136 (1) (2). - Issued: 16.12.2014. Made: 09.11.2014. Laid: 10.11.2014. Coming into force: In accord. with art. 1 (2) (3). Effect: S.I. 1975/556; 1982/894; 1986/1960; 1987/1967; 1992/1815; 1996/207; 2000/688; 2001/155; 2002/1792, 2005, 2006, 2821; 2003/499; 2005/438; 2006/213, 214; 2008/794; 2010/832, 990; 2012/762, 1796, 2885; 2013/376, 378, 379, 2356; 2014/512, 2336, 2848 amended & S.S.I. 2008/228; 2012/303, 319 amended. Territorial extent & classification: E/W/S/NI. General. - With correction slip dated December 2014. - 24p.: 30 cm. - 978-0-11-112519-9 £6.00

The Shared Parental Leave Regulations 2014 No. 2014/3050. - Enabling power: Employment Rights Act 1996, ss. 47C (2), 75E, 75F (1) (4) (7) to (14), 16, 75G (1) to (6), 75H (1) (4) (7) to (14) (16), 75I (1) (4) (5), 75J, 75K (1) (6), 99. - Issued: 25.11.2014. Made: 18.11.2014. Coming into force: 01.12.2014. Effect: None. Territorial extent & classification: E/W/S. General. - Supersedes draft S.I. (ISBN 9780111118856) issued 24.07.2014. - 40p.: 30 cm. - 978-0-11-112377-5 £10.00

The Social Security Contributions and Benefits Act 1992 (Application of Parts 12ZA, 12ZB and 12ZC to Parental Order Cases) Regulations 2014 No. 2014/2866. - Enabling power: Social Security Contributions and Benefits Act 1992, s. 171ZK (2), 171ZT (2), 171ZZ5 (2). - Issued: 03.11.2014. Made: 20.10.2014. Laid: 28.10.2014. Coming into force: In accord. with reg. 1. Effect: None. Territorial extent & classification: E/W/S. General. - With correction slip dated January 2015. - 12p.: 30 cm. - 978-0-11-112253-2 £6.00

The Social Security Contributions and Benefits Act 1992 (Application of Parts 12ZA and 12ZB to Adoptions from Overseas) (Amendment) Regulations 2014 No. 2014/2857. - Enabling power: Social Security Contributions and Benefits Act 1992, s. 171ZZ5(1). - Issued: 31.10.2014. Made: 20.10.2014. Laid: 28.10.2014. Coming into force: 19.11.2014. Effect: S.I. 2003/499 amended. Territorial extent & classification: E/W/S. General. - 4p.: 30 cm. - 978-0-11-112245-7 £4.25

The Statutory Paternity Pay and Statutory Adoption Pay (General) (Amendment) Regulations 2014 No. 2014/2862. - Enabling power: Social Security Contributions and Benefits Act 1992, ss. 171ZC (1A), 171ZC (3). - Issued: 03.11.2014. Made: 20.10.2014. Laid: 28.10.2014. Coming into force: 01.12.2014. Effect: S.I. 2002/2822 amended. Territorial extent & classification: E/W/S. General. - 4p.: 30 cm. - 978-0-11-112248-8 £4.25

The Statutory Paternity Pay and Statutory Adoption Pay (Parental Orders and Prospective Adopters) Regulations 2014 No. 2014/2934. - Enabling power: Social Security Contributions and Benefits Act 1992, ss. 171ZB (2) (a), 171ZC (1A) (3) (a) (c) (d) (f) (g), 171ZD (2) (3), 171ZE (2) (3) (7) (8), 171ZG (3), 171ZJ (1) (3) (4) (7) (8), 171ZL (8) (b) to (d) (f) (g), 171ZM (2) (3), 171ZN (2) (5) (6), 171ZP (6), 171ZS (1) (3) (4) (7) (8), 175 (4) & Social Security Administration Act 2002, s. 5 (1) (g) (i) (p) & Employment Act 2002, ss. 8 (1) (2) (c), 51 (1). - Issued: 13.11.2014. Made: 05.11.2014. Laid: 07.11.2014. Coming into force: 01.12.2014. Effect: S.I. 2002/2820, 2822 amended. Territorial extent & classification: E/W/S. General. - 12p.: 30 cm. - 978-0-11-112314-0 £6.00

The Statutory Shared Parental Pay (Administration) Regulations 2014 No. 2014/2929. - Enabling power: Employment Act 2002, ss. 7, 8, 10, 51 (1) & Social Security Contributions (Transfer of Functions, etc.) Act 1999, ss. 8 (1) (f) (ga), 25 (3) (6). - Issued: 12.11.2014. Made: 05.11.2014. Laid: 07.11.2014. Coming into force: 01.12.2014. Effect: None. Territorial extent & classification: E/W/S. General. - 8p.: 30 cm. - 978-0-11-112309-6 £6.00

The Statutory Shared Parental Pay (Adoption from Overseas) Regulations 2014 No. 2014/3093. - Enabling power: Social Security Contributions and Benefits Act 1992, ss. 171ZV (1) to (5), (12) to (15), 171ZW (1), 171ZX (2) (3), 171ZY (1), (3) to (5), 171ZZ1 (3), 171ZZ4 (3) (4) (7) (8), 175 (3) & Social Security Administration Act 1992, s. 5 (1) (g) (i) (l) (p). - Issued: 12.12.2014. Made: 26.11.2014. Coming into force: 05.04.2015. Effect: S.I. 2014/3051 modified. Territorial extent & classification: E/W/S. General. - Supersedes draft S.I. (ISBN 9780111121573) issued 15/10/14. - 8p.: 30 cm. - 978-0-11-112501-4 £4.25

The Statutory Shared Parental Pay (General) Regulations 2014 No. 2014/3051. - Enabling power: Social Security Contributions and Benefits Acct 1992, ss. 171ZU (1) (2) (3) (4) (5) (12) (13) (14) (15), 171ZV (1) (2) (3) (4) (5) (12) (13) (14) (15) (17), 171ZW (1) (a) to (f), 171ZX (2) (3), 171ZY (1) (3) (4) (5), 171ZZ1 (3), 171ZZ4 (3) (4) (7) (8), 175 (3) & Social Security Administration Act 1992, s. 5 (1) (g) (i) (l) (p). - Issued: 28.11.2014. Made: 18.11.2014. Coming into force: 01.12.2014. Effect: None. Territorial extent & classification: E/W/S. General. - Supersedes draft S.I. (ISBN 9780111118832) issued 24.07.2014. - 44p.: 30 cm. - 978-0-11-112389-8 £10.00

The Statutory Shared Parental Pay (Parental Order Cases) Regulations 2014 No. 2014/3097. - Enabling power: Social Security Contributions and Benefits Act 1992, ss. 171ZV (1) (2) (3) (4) (5) (12) (13) (14) (15), 171ZW (1) (a) to (f), 171ZX (2) (3), 171ZY (1) (3) (4) (5), 171ZZ1 (3), 171ZZ4 (3) (4) (7) (8), 175 (3) & Social Security Administration Act 1992, s. 5 (1) (g) (i) (l) (p). - Issued: 10.12.2014. Made: 26.11.2014. Coming into force: 01.12.2014. Effect: None. Territorial extent & classification: E/W/S. General. - Supersedes draft S.I. (ISBN 9780111121627) issued 16/10/14. - 8p.: 30 cm. - 978-0-11-112474-1 £6.00

The Statutory Shared Parental Pay (Persons Abroad and Mariners) Regulations 2014 No. 2014/3134. - Enabling power: Social Security Contributions and Benefits Acct 1992, ss. 171ZZ3 (1), 171ZZ4 (3 (b). - Issued: 02.12.2014. Made: 24.11.2014. Laid: 27.11.2014. Coming into force: 01.12.2014. Effect: S.I. 2002/2821 amended. Territorial extent & classification: E/W/S. General. - 12p.: 30 cm. - 978-0-11-112406-2 £6.00

The Transfer of Undertakings (Protection of Employment) (Transfer of Staff to the Department for Work and Pensions) Regulations 2014 No. 2014/1139. - Enabling power: Employment Relations Act 1999, s. 38. - Issued: 08.05.2014. Made: 01.05.2014 Laid: 06.05.2014. Coming into force: 27.06.2014. Effect: None. Territorial extent & classification: E/W/S. General. - 4p.: 30 cm. - 978-0-11-111455-1 £4.25

The Welfare Benefits Up-Rating Order 2014 No. 2014/147. - Enabling power: Welfare Benefits Uprating Act 2013, s. 1. - Issued: 31.01.2014. Made: 24.01.2014. Coming into force: In accord. with art. 1. Effect: 1992 c.4; 1986/1960; 1987/1967; 1996/207; 2002/2818; 2006/213; 2008/794; 2013/376, 378, 379 amended. Territorial extent & classification: E/W/S. General. - Revoked by SI 2015/30 (ISBN 9780111127360). - 16p.: 30 cm. - 978-0-11-110892-5 £5.75

Terms and conditions of employment, England

The Enterprise and Regulatory Reform Act 2013 (Commencement No. 4 and Saving Provision) (Amendment) Order 2014 No. 2014/824 (C.33). - Enabling power: Enterprise and Regulatory Reform Act 2013, s. 103 (3) (4). Bringing into operation various provisions of the 2013 Act on 31.03.2014, 30.09.2014, in accord. with art. 2. - Issued: 01.04.2014. Made: 26.03.2014. Effect: S.I. 2013/2979 (C.122) amended. Territorial extent & classification: E. General. - 4p.: 30 cm. - 978-0-11-111282-3 £4.00

The Enterprise and Regulatory Reform Act 2013 (Commencement No. 7 and Amendment) Order 2014 No. 2014/2481. - Enabling power: Enterprise and Regulatory Reform Act 2013, ss. 100, 103 (3) (4). Bringing into operation various provisions of the 2013 Act on 15.09.2014, 31.12.2014, in accord. with art. 2 & 3A. - Issued: 23.09.2014. Made: 14.09.2014. Effect: S.I. 2013/1455 (C.55), 2979 (C.122) amended. Territorial extent & classification: E. General. - 4p.: 30 cm. - 978-0-11-112092-7 £4.25

Territorial sea

The Territorial Sea Act 1987 (Guernsey) Order 2014 No. 2014/1105. - Enabling power: Territorial Sea Act 1987, s. 4 (4). - Issued: 06.05.2014. Made: 28.04.2014. Coming into force: 19.05.2014. Effect: None. Territorial extent & classification: Guernsey. General. - 2p.: 30 cm. - 978-0-11-111437-7 £4.25

The Territorial Sea (Baselines) Order 2014 No. 2014/1353. - Enabling power: Territorial Sea Act 1987, s. 1 (1) (b). - Issued: 03.06.2014. Made: 27.05.2014. Coming into force: 30.06.2014. Effect: None. Territorial extent & classification: Guernsey. General. - 4p.: 30 cm. - 978-0-11-111525-1 £4.25

Town and country planning

The Enterprise and Regulatory Reform Act 2013 (Commencement No. 6, Transitional Provisions and Savings) Order 2014 No. 2014/416 (C.17). - Enabling power: Enterprise and Regulatory Reform Act 2013, ss. 100, 103 (3). Bringing into operation various provisions of the 2013 Act on 01.04.2014 & 06.04.2014, in ac cord. with arts 2, 3. - Issued: 10.03.2014. Made: 03.03.2014. Effect: None. Territorial extent & classification: E/W/S/NI. General. - 16p.: 30 cm. - 978-0-11-111081-2 £5.75

Town and country planning, England

The Crossrail (Insertion of Review Clauses) Order 2014 No. 2014/1367. - Enabling power: Crossrail Act 2008, s. 39 (1), sch. 7, para. 1 (1). - Issued: 03.06.2014. Made: 26.05.2014. Coming into force: 30.06.2014. Effect: S.I. 2008/2034, 2036 amended. Territorial extent & classification: E. General. - 4p.: 30 cm. - 978-0-11-111541-1 £4.25

The Crossrail (Insertion of Review Clauses) Regulations 2014 No. 2014/1382. - Enabling power: Crossrail Act 2008, s. 12, sch. 7, paras 30 (1) (5), 34, 35 (1). - Issued: 06.06.2014. Made: 29.05.2014. Laid: 06.06.2014. Coming into force: 30.06.2014. Effect: S.I. 2008/2175, 2908 amended. Territorial extent & classification: E. General. - 4p.: 30 cm. - 978-0-11-111554-1 £4.25

The Enterprise and Regulatory Reform Act 2013 (Listed Buildings Certificate of Lawfulness) (Hearings and Inquiries Procedures) (Consequential Amendments) (England) Order 2014 No. 2014/553. - Enabling power: Enterprise and Regulatory reform Act 2013, s. 99. - Issued: 17.03.2014. Made: 10.03.2014. Laid: 13.03.2014. Coming into force: 06.04.2014. Effect: S.I. 2002/2684, 2685, 2686 amended. Territorial extent & classification: E/W. General. - 4p.: 30 cm. - 978-0-11-111171-0 £4.00

The Growth and Infrastructure Act 2013 (Commencement No. 6) Order 2014 No. 2014/1531 (C.60). - Enabling power: Growth and Infrastructure Act 2013, s. 35. Bringing into operation various provisions of the 2013 Act on 01.10.2014, in accord. with art 2. - Issued: 16.06.2014. Made: 09.06.2014. Effect: None. Territorial extent & classification: E. General. - 2p.: 30 cm. - 978-0-11-111643-2 £4.25

The Heavy Fuel Oil (Amendment) Regulations 2014 No. 2014/162. - Enabling power: European Communities Act 1972, s. 2 (2) & Health and Safety at Work etc. Act 1974, s. 15 (1) (2), sch. 3, para. 1 (1((b) & Planning (Hazardous Substances) Act 1990, ss. 5, 40. - Issued: 03.02.2014. Made: 28.01.2014. Laid: 30.01.2014. Coming into force: 20.02.2014. Effect: S.I. 1992/656; 1999/743 amended. Territorial extent & classification: E/W/S. General. - 4p.: 30 cm. - 978-0-11-110895-6 £4.00

The Neighbourhood Planning (Referendums) (Amendment) Regulations 2014 No. 2014/333. - Enabling power: Town and Country Planning Act 1990, s. 333 (2A), sch. 4B, para. 16 & Planning and Compulsory Purchase Act 2004, s. 38A (3). - Issued: 21.02.2014. Made: 13.02.2014. Coming into force: In accord. with reg. 1. Effect: S.I. 2012/2031 amended. Territorial extent & classification: E. General. - Supersedes draft SI (ISBN 9780111107584) issued 23.12.2013. - 44p.: 30 cm. - 978-0-11-110985-4 £9.75

The Planning (Listed Buildings and Conservation Areas) (Heritage Partnership Agreements) Regulations 2014 No. 2014/550. - Enabling power: Planning (Listed Buildings and Conservation Areas) Act 1990, ss. 26B (2), 93. - Issued: 17.03.2014. Made: 10.03.2014. Laid: 13.03.2014. Coming into force: 06.04.2014. Effect: 1990 c.9 modified. Territorial extent & classification: E. General. - 8p.: 30 cm. - 978-0-11-111177-2 £5.75

The Planning (Listed Buildings) (Certificates of Lawfulness of Proposed Works) Regulations 2014 No. 2014/552. - Enabling power: Planning (Listed Buildings and Conservation Areas) Act 1990, ss. 26I, 26K, 93, sch. 3. - Issued: 17.03.2014. Made: 10.03.2014. Laid: 13.03.2014. Coming into force: 06.04.2014. Effect: S.I. 1997/420 amended. Territorial extent & classification: E. General. - 8p.: 30 cm. - 978-0-11-111170-3 £5.75

The Planning (Local Listed Building Consent Orders) (Procedure) Regulations 2014 No. 2014/551. - Enabling power: Planning (Listed Buildings and Conservation Areas) Act 1990, ss. 28A, 93, sch. 2A. - Issued: 14.03.2014. Made: 10.03.2014. Laid: 13.03.2014. Coming into force: 06.04.2014. Effect: None. Territorial extent & classification: E. General. - 8p.: 30 cm. - 978-0-11-111168-0 £5.75

The Town and Country Planning (Compensation) (England) (Amendment) Regulations 2014 No. 2014/565. - Enabling power: Town and Country Planning Act 1990, s. 108 (2A) (3C) (5) (6). - Issued: 17.03.2014. Made: 10.03.2014. Laid: 13.03.2014. Coming into force: 06.04.2014. Effect: S.I. 2013/1102 amended. Territorial extent & classification: E. General. - Revoked by SI 2015/598 (ISBN 9780111134375). - 2p.: 30 cm. - 978-0-11-111175-8 £4.00

The Town and Country Planning (Development Management Procedure and Section 62A Applications) (England) (Amendment) Order 2014 No. 2014/1532. - Enabling power: Town and Country Planning Act 1990, ss. 59, 61 (1), 74 (1), 76C (3). - Issued: 16.06.2014. Made: 09.06.2014. Laid: 13.06.2014. Coming into force: 01.10.2014. Effect: S.I. 1990/1519; 2010/2184; 2013/2140 amended. Territorial extent & classification: E. General. - Partially revoked by SI 2015/595 (ISBN 9780111134399). - 16p.: 30 cm. - 978-0-11-111644-9 £6.00

The Town and Country Planning (Fees for Applications, Deemed Applications, Requests and Site Visits) (England) (Amendment) (No. 2) Regulations 2014 No. 2014/2026. - Enabling power: Town and Country Planning Act 1990, ss. 303 (1) (5), 333 (2A). - Issued: 05.08.2014. Made: 30.07.2014. Coming into force: 31.07.2014, in accord. with reg. 1. Effect: S.I. 2012/2920 amended. Territorial extent & classification: E. General. - Supersedes draft S.I. (ISBN 9780111116500) issued 17.06.2014. - 2p.: 30 cm. - 978-0-11-111937-2 £4.25

The Town and Country Planning (Fees for Applications, Deemed Applications, Requests and Site Visits) (England) (Amendment) Regulations 2014 No. 2014/357. - Enabling power: Town and Country Planning Act 1990, ss. 303 (1) (2) (3) (5), 333 (2A). - Issued: 24.02.2014. Made: 18.02.2014. Coming into force: 19.02.2014 in accord. with reg. 1. Effect: S.I. 2012/2920 amended. Territorial extent & classification: E. General. - Supersedes draft S.I. (ISBN 9780111107485) issued 20.12.2013. - 2p.: 30 cm. - 978-0-11-110989-2 £4.00

The Town and Country Planning (General Permitted Development) (Amendment and Consequential Provisions) (England) Order 2014 No. 2014/564. - Enabling power: Town and Country Planning Act 1990, ss. 59, 60, 61, 333 (7). - Issued: 17.03.2014. Made: 10.03.2014. Laid: 13.03.2014. Coming into force: 06.04.2014. Effect: S.I. 1995/418 amended. Territorial extent & classification: E. General. - Partially revoked by SI 2015/595 (9780111134399) in re to E; Revoked by SI 2015/596 (ISBN 9780111134467). - 16p.: 30 cm. - 978-0-11-111183-3 £5.75

The Town and Country Planning (Revocations) Order 2014 No. 2014/683. - Enabling power: Local Government Act 1972, s. 254 & Local Government, Planning and Land Act 1980, ss. 134 (3A) (5), 148 (2), 149, 170 (3) (b) & Town and Country Planning Act 1990, ss. 59, 60, 333 (7) & Coal Industry Act 1994, s. 67 (2). - Issued: 21.03.2014. Made: 17.03.2014. Laid: 20.03.2014. Coming into force: 14.04.2014. Effect: S.I. 1994/2567 partially revoked & S.I. 1974/460; 1982/817; 1988/900; 1997/2946; 1998/84; 2004/2355 revoked. Territorial extent & classification: E. General. - 4p.: 30 cm. - 978-0-11-111236-6 £4.00

The Town and Country Planning (Revocations) Regulations 2014 No. 2014/692. - Enabling power: Housing and Planning Act 1990, s. 42 & Town and Country Planning Act 1990, s. 303A (5) & Planning and Compulsory Purchase Act 2004, sch. 8, paras 17 (1) (2), 18 & Planning Act 2008, ss. 7, 232. - Issued: 21.03.2014. Made: 17.03.2014. Laid: 20.03.2014. Coming into force: 14.04.2014. Effect: S.I. 1988/1788; 1990/2027; 1994/642; 1996/24; 1998/2864; 1999/327 revoked in relation to England & S.I. 2000/3089; 2002/452; 2003/464; 2004/2205; 2009/1302 revoked. Territorial extent & classification: E. General. - 4p.: 30 cm. - 978-0-11-111238-0 £4.00

Town and country planning, England and Wales

The Channel Tunnel Rail Link (Planning Appeals and Assessment of Environmental Effects) (Revocation) Regulations 2014 No. 2014/1333. - Enabling power: European Communities Act 1972, s. 2 (2) & Channel Tunnel Rail Link Act 1996, s. 9 (5), sch. 6, paras 32 (1) (7), 36, 37 (1). - Issued: 06.06.2014. Made: 20.05.2014. Laid: 06.06.2014. Coming into force: 30.06.2014. Effect: S.I. 1997/821; 1999/107 revoked. Territorial extent & classification: E/W/S/NI. General. - 2p.: 30 cm. - 978-0-11-111522-0 £4.25

The Channel Tunnel Rail Link (Revocations) Order 2014 No. 2014/1332. - Enabling power: Channel Tunnel Rail Link Act 1996, ss. 9 (5), 34 (1) (4), sch. 6, para. 1 (1). - Issued: 30.05.2014. Made: 20.05.2014. Coming into force: 30.06.2014. Effect: S.I. 1997/8; 2003/2306, 2834; 2007/2920 revoked. Territorial extent & classification: E/W/S/NI. General. - 2p.: 30 cm. - 978-0-11-111521-3 £4.25

Town and country planning, Wales

The Planning Act 2008 (Commencement No. 2) (Wales) Order 2014 No. 2014/1769 (W.181)(C.76). - Enabling power: Planning Act 2008, s. 241 (3). Bringing into operation various provisions of the 2008 Act on 08.08.2014, in accord. with art. 2. - Issued: 15.06.2014. Made: 02.07.2014. Effect: None. Territorial extent & classification: W. General. - In English and Welsh. Welsh title: Gorchymyn Deddf Cynllunio 2008 (Cychwyn Rhif 2) (Cymru) 2014. - 8p.: 30 cm. - 978-0-348-10963-4 £6.00

The Planning Act 2008 (Commencement No. 3) (Wales) Order 2014 No. 2014/2780 (W.284)(C.123). - Enabling power: Planning Act 2008, s. 241 (3). Bringing into operation various provisions of the 2008 Act on 28.11.2014, in accord. with art. 2. - Issued: 24.10.2014. Made: 14.10.2014. Effect: None. Territorial extent & classification: W. General. - In English and Welsh. Welsh title: Gorchymyn Deddf Cynllunio 2008 (Cychwyn Rhif 3) (Cymru) 2014. - 8p.: 30 cm. - 978-0-348-11010-4 £6.00

The Planning (Hazardous Substances) (Amendment) (Wales) Regulations 2014 No. 2014/375 (W.43). - Enabling power: Planning (Hazardous Substances) Act 1990, ss. 5, 40. - Issued: 07.03.2014. Made: 20.02.2014. Laid before the National Assembly for Wales: 21.02.2014. Coming into force: 14.03.2014. Effect: S.I. 1992/656 amended in relation to Wales. Territorial extent & classification: W. General. - EC note: These Regulations contribute towards the implementation, in relation to Wales, of Article 30 of Directive 2012/18/EU of the European Parliament and of the Council on the control of major-accident hazards involving dangerous substances. - In English and Welsh. Welsh title: Rheoliadau Cynllunio (Sylweddau Peryglus) (Diwygio) (Cymru) 2014. - 4p.: 30 cm. - 978-0-348-10895-8 £4.00

The Planning (Hazardous Substances) (Determination of Procedure) (Prescribed Period) (Wales) Regulations 2014 No. 2014/2777 (W.283). - Enabling power: Planning (Hazardous Substances) Act 1990, s. 21B. - Issued: 27.10.2014. Made: 14.10.2014. Laid before the National Assembly for Wales: 17.10.2014. Coming into force: 12.11.2014. Effect: None. Territorial extent & classification: W. General. - In English and Welsh. Welsh title: Rheoliadau Cynllunio (Sylweddau Peryglus) (Pennu'r Weithdrefn) (Cyfnod Rhagnodedig) (Cymru) 2014. - 4p.: 30 cm. - 978-0-348-11011-1 £4.25

The Planning (Listed Buildings and Conservation Areas) (Determination of Procedure) (Prescribed Period) (Wales) Regulations 2014 No. 2014/2776 (W.282). - Enabling power: Planning (Listed Buildings and Conservation Areas) Act 1990, ss. 88E, 93. - Issued: 22.10.2014. Made: 14.10.2014. Laid before the National Assembly for Wales: 17.10.2014. Coming into force: 12.11.2014. Effect: None. Territorial extent & classification: W. General. - In English and Welsh. Welsh title: Rheoliadau Cynllunio (Adeiladau Rhestredig ac Ardaloedd Cadwraeth) (Pennu'r Weithdrefn) (Cyfnod Rhagnodedig) (Cymru) 2014. - 4p.: 30 cm. - 978-0-348-11008-1 £4.25

The Town and Country Planning (Compensation) (Wales) (No. 2) Regulations 2014 No. 2014/2693 (W.268). - Enabling power: Town and Country Planning Act 1990, s. 108. - Issued: 17.10.2014. Made: 29.09.2014. Laid before the National Assembly for Wales: 09.10.2014. Coming into force: 07.11.2014. Effect: W.S.I. 2014/593 (W.70) revoked. Territorial extent & classification: W. General. - In English and Welsh. Welsh language title: Rheoliadau Cynllunio Gwlad a Thref (Digolledu) (Cymru) (Rhif 2) 2014. - 8p.: 30 cm. - 978-0-348-10997-9 £6.00

The Town and Country Planning (Compensation) (Wales) Regulations 2014 No. 2014/593 (W.70). - Enabling power: Town and Country Planning Act 1990, s. 108. - Issued: 27.03.2014. Made: 11.03.2014. Laid before the National Assembly for Wales: 13.03.2014. Coming into force: 28.04.2014. Effect: W.S.I. 2012/2319 (W.253) revoked. Territorial extent & classification: W. General. - Revoked by WSI 2014/593 (ISBN 9780348109979). - In English and Welsh. Welsh language title: Rheoliadau Cynllunio Gwlad a Thref (Digolledu) (Cymru) 2014. - 8p.: 30 cm. - 978-0-348-10922-1 £4.00

The Town and Country Planning (Determination of Procedure) (Prescribed Period) (Wales) Regulations 2014 No. 2014/2775 (W.281). - Enabling power: Town and Country Planning Act 1990, ss. 319B, 333. - Issued: 22.10.2014. Made: 14.10.2014. Laid before the National Assembly for Wales: 17.10.2014. Coming into force: 12.11.2014. Effect: None. Territorial extent & classification: W. General. - In English and Welsh. Welsh language title: Rheoliadau Cynllunio Gwlad a Thref (Cyfnod Rhagnodedig) (Cymru) 2014. - 4p.: 30 cm. - 978-0-348-11006-7 £4.25

The Town and Country Planning (Determination of Procedure) (Wales) Order 2014 No. 2014/2773 (W.280). - Enabling power: Town and Country Planning Act 2008, ss. 203 (1) (6) (8). - Issued: 22.10.2014. Made: 14.10.2014. Coming into force: In accord. with art. 1 (2). Effect: 1990 c.8, c.10 amended. Territorial extent & classification: W. General. - In English and Welsh. Welsh language title: Gorchymyn Cynllunio Gwlad a Thref (Pennu'r Weithdrefn) (Cymru) 2014. - 16p.: 30 cm. - 978-0-348-11009-8 £6.00

The Town and Country Planning (Development Management Procedure) (Wales) (Amendment) Order 2014 No. 2014/1772 (W.183). - Enabling power: Town and Country Planning Act 1990, ss. 69, 96A, 333. - Issued: 25.07.2014. Made: 03.07.2014. Laid before the National Assembly for Wales: 07.07.2014. Coming into force: 01.09.2014. Effect: W.S.I. 2012/801 (W.110) amended. Territorial extent & classification: W. General. - In English and Welsh. Welsh language title: Gorchymyn Cynllunio Gwlad a Thref (Gweithdrefn Rheoli Datblygu) (Cymru) (Diwygio) 2014. - 4p.: 30 cm. - 978-0-348-10971-9 £4.25

The Town and Country Planning (Fees for Non-Material Changes) (Wales) Order 2014 No. 2014/1761 (W.176). - Enabling power: Town and Country Planning Act 1990, s. 303. - Issued: 28.07.2014. Made: 02.07.2014. Coming into force: 01.09.2014. Effect: None. Territorial extent & classification: W. General. - In English and Welsh. Welsh language title: Rheoliadau Cynllunio Gwlad a Thref (Ffioedd am Newidiadau Ansylweddol) (Cymru) 2014. - 8p.: 30 cm. - 978-0-348-10975-7 £4.25

The Town and Country Planning (General Permitted Development) (Amendment) (Wales) (No. 2) Order 2014 No. 2014/2692 (W.267). - Enabling power: Town and Country Planning Act 1990, ss. 59, 60, 61, 333. - Issued: 17.10.2014. Made: 29.09.2014. Laid before the National Assembly for Wales: 09.10.2014. Coming into force: 07.11.2014. Effect: S.I. 1995/418 amended in relation to Wales. Territorial extent & classification: W. General. - In English and Welsh. Welsh language title: Gorchymyn Cynllunio Gwlad a Thref (Datblygu Cyffredinol a Ganiateir) (Diwygio) (Cymru) 2014. - 16p.: 30 cm. - 978-0-348-11000-5 £6.00

The Town and Country Planning (General Permitted Development) (Amendment) (Wales) Order 2014 No. 2014/592 (W.69). - Enabling power: Town and Country Planning Act 1990, ss. 59, 60, 61, 333 (7). - Issued: 27.03.2014. Made: 11.03.2014. Laid before the National Assembly for Wales: 13.03.2014. Coming into force: 28.04.2014. Effect: S.I. 1995/418 amended in relation to Wales. Territorial extent & classification: W. General. - In English and Welsh. Welsh language title: Gorchymyn Cynllunio Gwlad a Thref (Datblygu Cyffredinol a Ganiateir) (Diwygio) (Cymru) 2014. - 20p.: 30 cm. - 978-0-348-10923-8 £5.75

The Town and Country Planning (Non-Material Changes and Correction of Errors) (Wales) Order 2014 No. 2014/1770 (W.182). - Enabling power: Planning Act 2008, s. 203. - Issued: 18.07.2014. Made: 02.07.2014. Coming into force: 01.09.2014. Effect: 1990 c.8; 2004, c.5 amended. Territorial extent & classification: W. General. - In English and Welsh. Welsh language title: Gorchymyn Cynllunio Gwlad a Thref (Newidiadau Ansylweddol a Chywiro Gwallau) (Cymru) 2014. - 4p.: 30 cm. - 978-0-348-10965-8 £4.25

Transport

The Rail Passengers' Rights and Obligations (Exemptions) Regulations 2014 No. 2014/2793. - With correction slip dated October 2014. - Enabling power: European Communities Act 1972, s. 2 (2). - Issued: 23.10.2014. Made: 17.10.2014. Laid: 22.10.2014. Coming into force: 04.12.2014. Effect: None. Territorial extent & classification: E/W/S. General. - With correction slip dated October 2014. - 4p.: 30 cm. - 978-0-11-112197-9 £4.25

The Rail Vehicle Accessibility (Non-Interoperable Rail System) (Blackpool Tramway) Exemption Order 2014 No. 2014/2660. - Enabling power: Equality Act 2010, ss. 183 (1) (2) (4) (a) (5), 207 (1) (4). - Issued: 10.10.2014. Made: 29.09.2014. Laid: 10.10.2014. Coming into force: 01.11.2014. Effect: None. Territorial extent & classification: E/W/S. General. - 4p.: 30 cm. - 978-0-11-112122-1 £4.25

The Railways and Rail Vehicles (Revocations and Consequential Amendments) Order 2014 No. 2014/3244. - Enabling power: Equality Act 2010, s. 184 (1) (2) (3) & S.I. 2008/2975, reg. 2 (1) (3) (c). - Issued: 15.12.2014. Made: 08.12.2014. Laid: 12.12.2014. Coming into force: 05.01.2015. Effect: S.I. 2001/3592 amended & S.I. 1994/2229; 1997/1531; 1999/2932; 2001/218, 1768; 2005/395 revoked. Territorial extent & classification: E/W/S. General. - 4p.: 30 cm. - 978-0-11-112506-9 £4.25

Transport: Railways

The Channel Tunnel Rail Link (Revocations) Order 2014 No. 2014/1332. - Enabling power: Channel Tunnel Rail Link Act 1996, ss. 9 (5), 34 (1) (4), sch. 6, para. 1 (1). - Issued: 30.05.2014. Made: 20.05.2014. Coming into force: 30.06.2014. Effect: S.I. 1997/8; 2003/2306, 2834; 2007/2920 revoked. Territorial extent & classification: E/W/S/NI. General. - 2p.: 30 cm. - 978-0-11-111521-3 £4.25

The Railways (Interoperability) (Amendment) Regulations 2014 No. 2014/3217. - Enabling power: Transport Act 2000, s. 247. - Issued: 11.12.2014. Made: 19.11.2014. Laid: 08.12.2014. Coming into force: 01.01.2015. Effect: S.I. 2011/3066 amended. Territorial extent & classification: E/W/S/NI. General. - 2p.: 30 cm. - 978-0-11-112469-7 £4.25

Transport and works, England

The Crossrail (Paddington Station Bakerloo Line Connection) Order 2014 No. 2014/310. - Enabling power: Transport and Works Act 1992, ss. 1, 5, sch. 1, paras. 1 to 5, 7, 8, 10, 11, 15, 16 & Crossrail Act 2008, s. 48. - Issued: 24.02.2014. Made: 18.02.2014. Coming into force: 11.03.2014. Effect: 1965 c.56; 1973 c.26; 2008 c.18 modified. Territorial extent & classification: E. General. - 24p.: 30 cm. - 978-0-11-110991-5 £5.75

The Felixstowe Branch Line (Land Acquisition) Order 2014 No. 2014/1821. - Enabling power: Transport and Works Act 1992, ss. 1, 5, sch. 1, paras 3 to 5, 7, 8, 11, 16. - Issued: 15.07.2014. Made: 08.07.2014. Coming into force: 29.07.2014. Effect: None. Territorial extent & classification: E. General. - 16p.: 30 cm. - 978-0-11-111792-7 £6.00

The London Underground (Northern Line Extension) Order 2014 No. 2014/3102. - Enabling power: Transport and Works Act 1992, ss. 1, 3, 5, sch. 1, paras 1 to 5, 7, 8, 10, 11, 15 to 17. - Issued: 02.12.2014. Made: 24.11.2014. Coming into force: 15.12.2014. Effect: None. Territorial extent & classification: E. General. - 76p.: 30 cm. - 978-0-11-112428-4 £14.25

The Network Rail (Huyton) Order 2014 No. 2014/2027. - Enabling power: Transport and Works Act 1992, 1, 5, sch. 1, paras 1 to 4, 7, 8, 10, 11, 16. - Issued: 06.08.2014. Made: 29.07.2014. Coming into force: 19.08.2014. Effect: 1965 c.56; 1973 c.26 modified. Territorial extent & classification: E. General. - 32p.: 30 cm. - 978-0-11-111938-9 £10.00

The Swanage Railway Order 2014 No. 2014/1604. - Enabling power: Transport and Works Act 1992, ss. 1, 5, sch. 1, paras 1, 8, 15, 17. - Issued: 24.06.2014. Made: 05.06.2014. Coming into force: 26.06.2014. Effect: None. Territorial extent & classification: E. General. - 8p.: 30 cm. - 978-0-11-111673-9 £4.25

Transport, England

The Barnsley, Doncaster, Rotherham and Sheffield Combined Authority Order 2014 No. 2014/863. - Enabling power: Local Transport Act 2008, ss. 84, 91, 93 & Local Democracy, Economic Development and Construction Act 2009, ss. 103 to 105, 114 to 116. - Issued: 04.04.2014. Made: 31.03.2014. Coming into force: In accord with art. 1. Effect: None. Territorial extent & classification: E. General. - Supersedes draft SI (ISBN 9780111111314) issued 12.03.2014. - 12p.: 30 cm. - 978-0-11-111340-0 £6.00

The Combined Authorities (Consequential Amendments) Order 2014 No. 2014/866. - Enabling power: Local Democracy, Economic Development and Construction Act 2009, ss. 114 to 116. - Issued: 04.04.2014. Made: 31.03.2014. Coming into force: 01.04.2014, in accord. with art. 1. Effect: 1968 c.73 amended. Territorial extent & classification: E. General. - Supersedes draft SI (ISBN 9780111111352) issued 12/03/14. - 4p.: 30 cm. - 978-0-11-111348-6 £4.25

The Crossrail (Insertion of Review Clauses) Order 2014 No. 2014/1367. - Enabling power: Crossrail Act 2008, s. 39 (1), sch. 7, para. 1 (1). - Issued: 03.06.2014. Made: 26.05.2014. Coming into force: 30.06.2014. Effect: S.I. 2008/2034, 2036 amended. Territorial extent & classification: E. General. - 4p.: 30 cm. - 978-0-11-111541-1 £4.25

The Crossrail (Paddington Station Bakerloo Line Connection) Order 2014 No. 2014/310. - Enabling power: Transport and Works Act 1992, ss. 1, 5, sch. 1, paras. 1 to 5, 7, 8, 10, 11, 15, 16 & Crossrail Act 2008, s. 48. - Issued: 24.02.2014. Made: 18.02.2014. Coming into force: 11.03.2014. Effect: 1965 c.56; 1973 c.26; 2008 c.18 modified. Territorial extent & classification: E. General. - 24p.: 30 cm. - 978-0-11-110991-5 £5.75

The Durham, Gateshead, Newcastle Upon Tyne, North Tyneside, Northumberland, South Tyneside and Sunderland Combined Authority Order 2014 No. 2014/1012. - Enabling power: Local Transport Act 2008, ss. 84, 91, 93 & Local Democracy, Economic Development and Construction Act 2009, ss. 103 to 105, 114 to 116. - Issued: 22.04.2014. Made: 14.04.2014. Coming into force: In accord. with art. 1. Effect: 1989 ch.42; S.I. 2013/2356 amended. Territorial extent & classification: E. General. - Supersedes draft SI (ISBN 9780111111819) issued 17.03.2014. - 12p.: 30 cm. - 978-0-11-111413-1 £6.00

The Felixstowe Branch Line (Land Acquisition) Order 2014 No. 2014/1821. - Enabling power: Transport and Works Act 1992, ss. 1, 5, sch. 1, paras 3 to 5, 7, 8, 11, 16. - Issued: 15.07.2014. Made: 08.07.2014. Coming into force: 29.07.2014. Effect: None. Territorial extent & classification: E. General. - 16p.: 30 cm. - 978-0-11-111792-7 £6.00

The Halton, Knowsley, Liverpool, St Helens, Sefton and Wirral Combined Authority Order 2014 No. 2014/865. - Enabling power: Local Transport Act 2008, ss. 84, 91, 93 & Local Democracy, Economic Development and Construction Act 2009, ss. 103 to 105, 114 to 116. - Issued: 04.04.2014. Made: 31.03.2014. Coming into force: In accord. with art. 1. Effect: None. Territorial extent & classification: E. - Supersedes draft SI (ISBN 9780111111345) issued 12/03/14. - 12p.: 30 cm. - 978-0-11-111347-9 £6.00

The London Underground (Northern Line Extension) Order 2014 No. 2014/3102. - Enabling power: Transport and Works Act 1992, ss. 1, 3, 5, sch. 1, paras 1 to 5, 7, 8, 10, 11, 15 to 17. - Issued: 02.12.2014. Made: 24.11.2014. Coming into force: 15.12.2014. Effect: None. Territorial extent & classification: E. General. - 76p.: 30 cm. - 978-0-11-112428-4 £14.25

The Network Rail (Huyton) Order 2014 No. 2014/2027. - Enabling power: Transport and Works Act 1992, 1, 5, sch. 1, paras 1 to 4, 7, 8, 10, 11, 16. - Issued: 06.08.2014. Made: 29.07.2014. Coming into force: 19.08.2014. Effect: 1965 c.56; 1973 c.26 modified. Territorial extent & classification: E. General. - 32p.: 30 cm. - 978-0-11-111938-9 £10.00

The Passenger Transport Executives (Exclusion of Bus Operating Powers) (Revocations) (England) Order 2014 No. 2014/1364. - Enabling power: Transport Act 1985, s. 60 (5). - Issued: 06.06.2014. Made: 25.05.2014. Laid: 06.06.2014. Coming into force: 30.06.2014. Effect: S.I. 1986/1648, 1649, 1650, 1651, 1652, 1653 revoked. Territorial extent & classification: E. General. - 4p.: 30 cm. - 978-0-11-111538-1 £4.25

The Swanage Railway Order 2014 No. 2014/1604. - Enabling power: Transport and Works Act 1992, ss. 1, 5, sch. 1, paras 1, 8, 15, 17. - Issued: 24.06.2014. Made: 05.06.2014. Coming into force: 26.06.2014. Effect: None. Territorial extent & classification: E. General. - 8p.: 30 cm. - 978-0-11-111673-9 £4.25

The West Yorkshire Combined Authority Order 2014 No. 2014/864. - Enabling power: Transport Act 1985, s. 85 & Local Transport Act 2008, ss. 84, 91, 93 & Local Democracy, Economic Development and Construction Act 2009, ss. 103 to 105, 114 to 116. - Issued: 07.04.2014. Made: 31.03.2014. Coming into force: In accord. with art. 1. Effect: None. Territorial extent & classification: E. General. - Supersedes draft SI (ISBN 9780111111420) issued 14/03/14. - 12p.: 30 cm. - 978-0-11-111346-2 £6.00

Transport, England and Wales

The West Midlands Integrated Transport Authority (Decrease in Number of Members) Order 2014 No. 2014/1180. - Enabling power: Local Government Act 1985, s. 29 (2). - Issued: 12.05.2014. Made: 06.05.2014. Laid: 12.05.2014. Coming into force: 04.06.2014. Effect: 1985 c.51 amended. Territorial extent & classification: E/W. General. - 2p.: 30 cm. - 978-0-11-111460-5 £4.25

Transport, Wales

The Public Transport Users' Committee for Wales (Abolition) Order 2014 No. 2014/595 (W.71). - Enabling power: Transport (Wales) Act 2006, ss. 8, 9. - Issued: 20.03.2014. Made: 12.03.2014. Laid before the National Assembly for Wales: 13.03.2014. Coming into force: 15.04.2014. Effect: W.S.I. 2009/2816 revoked. Territorial extent & classification: W. General. - In English and Welsh. Welsh title: Gorchymyn Pwyllgor Defnyddwyr Trafnidiaeth Gyhoeddus Cymru (Diddymu) 2014. - 4p.: 30 cm. - 978-0-348-10918-4 £4.00

The Regional Transport Planning (Wales) Order 2014 No. 2014/2178 (W.212). - Enabling power: Transport Act 2000, s. 113A. - Issued: 09.10.2014. Made: 07.08.2014. Laid before the National Assembly for Wales: 14.08.2014. Coming into force: 04.09.2014. Effect: S.I. 2006/2993 (W.280) revoked. Territorial extent & classification: W. General. - In English and Welsh. Welsh title: Gorchymyn Cynllunio Trafnidiaeth Rhanbarthol (Cymru) 2014. - 4p.: 30 cm. - 978-0-348-10993-1 £4.25

Tribunals and inquiries

The Courts and Tribunals Fees (Miscellaneous Amendments) Order 2014 No. 2014/590 (L.6). - Enabling power: Courts Act 2003, s. 92 & Insolvency Act 1986, ss. 414, 415 & Tribunals, Courts and Enforcement Act 2007, s. 42, 49 (3) & Constitutional Reform Act 2005, s. 52 & Mental Capacity Act 2005. s. 54 & Gender Recognition Act 2004, s. 7 (2). - Issued: 19.03.2014. Made: 11.03.2014. Laid: 13.03.2104. Coming into force: 06.04.2014. Effect: S.I. 2004/3120; 2006/758; 2007/1745; 2008/1052, 1053, 1054; 2009/213, 1114; 2010/42; 2011/2344; 2013/1179, 1893 amended. Territorial extent & classification: E/W. General. - 16p.: 30 cm. - 978-0-11-111194-9 £5.75

The First-tier Tribunal and Upper Tribunal (Chambers) (Amendment) Order 2014 No. 2014/1901. - Enabling power: Tribunals, Courts and Enforcement Act 2007, s. 7 (9). - Issued: 24.07.2014. Made: 14.07.2014. Laid: 18.07.2014. Coming into force: 08.08.2014. Effect: S.I. 2010/2655 amended. Territorial extent & classification: E/W/S/NI. General. - 2p.: 30 cm. - 978-0-11-111866-5 £4.25

The Tribunal Procedure (Amendment No. 2) Rules 2014 No. 2014/1505 (L.25). - Enabling power: Tribunals, Courts and Enforcement Act 2007, ss. 22, sch. 5. - Issued: 13.06.2014. Made: 09.06.2014. Laid: 09.06.2014. Coming into force: 30.06.2014. Effect: S.I. 2008/2698 amended. Territorial extent & classification: E/W/S/NI. General. - 2p.: 30 cm. - 978-0-11-111622-7 £4.25

The Tribunal Procedure (Amendment No. 3) Rules 2014 No. 2014/2128 (L.30). - Enabling power: Tribunals, Courts and Enforcement Act 2007, ss. 22, sch. 5. - Issued: 15.08.2014. Made: 07.08.2014. Laid: 11.08.2014. Coming into force: In accord. with rule 1. Effect: S.I. 2008/2685, 2698, 2699; 2009/1976; 2013/477, 1169 amended & S.I. 2012/1363 partially revoked. Territorial extent & classification: E/W/S/NI. General. - 12p.: 30 cm. - 978-0-11-111985-3 £6.00

The Tribunal Procedure (Amendment) Rules 2014 No. 2014/514 (L.4). - Enabling power: S.I. 2013/1389, reg. 44 (2) & S.R. 2013/208, reg. 44 (2) & Tribunals, Courts and Enforcement Act 2007, ss. 22, 29 (3), sch. 5. - Issued: 11.03.2014. Made: 04.03.2014. Laid: 10.03.2014. Coming into force: 06.04.2014. Effect: S.I. 2008/2685, 2698, 2699; 2010/2600; amended. Territorial extent & classification: E/W/S/NI. General. - With correction slip dated December 2014. - 8p.: 30 cm. - 978-0-11-111118-5 £5.75

The Tribunal Procedure (First-tier Tribunal) (Immigration and Asylum Chamber) Rules 2014 No. 2014/2604 (L.31). - Enabling power: Tribunals, Courts and Enforcement Act 2007, ss. 9, 22, 29 (3) (4), sch. 5 & Immigration Act 1971, sch. 2 para. 25 & Nationality, Immigration and Asylum Act 2002, s. 106 (3) & British Nationality Act 1981, s. 40A (3) & S.I. 2006/1003, sch. 1. - Issued: 01.10.2014. Made: 24.09.2014. Laid: 29.09.2014. Coming into force: 20.10.2014. Effect: S.I. 2010/44; 2653 partially revoked & 2005/230; 560; 2006/2788; 2789; 2007/835; 3170; 2008/1088; 1089; 2011/2840 revoked. Territorial extent & classification: E/W/S/NI. General. - 32p.: 30 cm. - 978-0-11-112110-8 £6.00

Tribunals and inquiries: Commercial rent arrears recovery

The Tribunals, Courts and Enforcement Act 2007 (Commencement No. 11) Order 2014 No. 2014/768 (C.27). - Enabling power: Tribunals, Courts and Enforcement Act 2007, s. 148 (5) (6). Bringing into operation various provisions of the 2007 Act on 06.04.2014 in accord. with art. 2. - Issued: 25.03.2014. Made: 19.03.2014. Effect: None. Territorial extent & classification: E/W/S/NI. General. - 4p.: 30 cm. - 978-0-11-111249-6 £4.00

Tribunals and inquiries: Taking control of goods

The Tribunals, Courts and Enforcement Act 2007 (Commencement No. 11) Order 2014 No. 2014/768 (C.27). - Enabling power: Tribunals, Courts and Enforcement Act 2007, s. 148 (5) (6). Bringing into operation various provisions of the 2007 Act on 06.04.2014 in accord. with art. 2. - Issued: 25.03.2014. Made: 19.03.2014. Effect: None. Territorial extent & classification: E/W/S/NI. General. - 4p.: 30 cm. - 978-0-11-111249-6 £4.00

Tribunals and inquiries, England

The First-tier Tribunal (Property Chamber) Fees (Amendment) Order 2014 No. 2014/182. - Enabling power: Tribunals, Courts and Enforcement Act 2007, s. 42. - Issued: 06.02.2014. Made: 30.01.2014. Laid: 03.02.2014. Coming into force: 25.02.2014. Effect: S.I. 2013/1179 amended. Territorial extent & classification: E. General. - 4p.: 30 cm. - 978-0-11-110906-9 £4.00

Tribunals and inquiries, England and Wales

The Judicial Appointments (Amendment) Order 2014 No. 2014/2898. - Enabling power: Tribunals, Courts and Enforcement Act 2007, s. 51 (1). - Issued: 07.11.2014. Made: 03.11.2014. Coming into force: In accord. with art. 1. Effect: S.I. 2008/2995 amended. Territorial extent & classification: E/W. General. - Supersedes draft SI (ISBN 9780111117590) issued 10/07/14 - 2p.: 30 cm. - 978-0-11-112288-4 £4.25

The Transfer of Tribunal Functions (Mobile Homes Act 2013 and Miscellaneous Amendments) Order 2014 No. 2014/1900. - Enabling power: Tribunals, Courts and Enforcement Act 2007, ss. 30 (1) (e) (4), 31 (9), 42 (1). - Issued: 24.07.2014. Made: 17.07.2014. Coming into force: 18.07.2014, in accord. with art. 1. Effect: 1960 c.62; 2004, c.34; 2013, c.14; S.I. 1997/194; 2013/1179 amended. Territorial extent & classification: E/W. General. - Supersedes draft (ISBN 9780111114896) issued 20.05.2014. - 8p.: 30 cm. - 978-0-11-111865-8 £6.00

The Tribunal Security Order 2014 No. 2014/786. - Enabling power: Coroners and Justice Act 2009, ss. 148 (1) (2), 176 (3). - Issued: 26.03.2014. Made: 19.03.2014. Coming into force: 20.3.02014 in accord. with art. 1. Effect: 2003 c.39; S.I. 2005/588; 2010/790 modified. Territorial extent & classification: E/W. General. - Supersedes draft SI (ISBN 9780111108383) issued 20/01/14. - 4p.: 30 cm. - 978-0-11-111256-4 £4.00

The Upper Tribunal (Immigration and Asylum Chamber) (Judicial Review) (England and Wales) Fees (Amendment) Order 2014 No. 2014/878 (L.21). - Enabling power: Tribunals, Courts and Enforcement Act 2007, s. 42. - Issued: 07.04.2014. Made: 27.03.2014. Laid: 01.04.2014. Coming into force: 22.04.2014. Effect: S.I. 2011/2344 amended. Territorial extent & classification: E/W. General. - 2p.: 30 cm. - 978-0-11-111333-2 £4.25

United Nations

The United Nations Sanctions (Revocations) Order 2014 No. 2014/2711. - Enabling power: United Nations Act 1946, s. 1 & Saint Helena Act 1833, s. 112 & British Settlements Acts 1887 & 1945. - Issued: 15.10.2014. Made: 08.10.2014. Laid: 15.10.2014. Laid before the Scottish Parliament: 15.10.2014. Coming into force: 06.11.2014. Effect: S.I. 1992/1302, 1304; 1993/1188, 1787; 1994/1323, 1637, 2673; 1996/1629; 1997/272, 273; 1998/1065, 1501, 1502; 1999/280; 2000/1106, 1556, 1820; 2002/111; 2008/3128 revoked. Territorial extent & classification: E/W/S/NI. General. - 4p.: 30 cm. - 978-0-11-112148-1 £4.25

Urban development, England

The Urban Development Corporations in England (Area and Constitution) Order 2014 No. 2014/1181. - Enabling power: Local Government, Planning and Land Act 1980, ss. 134, 135, sch. 26, para. 1. - Issued: 16.05.2014. Made: 04.02.2014. Laid: 10.02.2014. Coming into force: 31.03.2014. Effect: S.I. 2004/3370 partially revoked (31.03.2014) & S.I. 2003/2896; 2004/1642 revoked (31.03.2014) & S.I. 2004/3370; 2011/2752 revoked (31.07.2014). Territorial extent & classification: E. General. - Approved by resolution of each House of Parliament. Supersedes unnumbered SI issued 13.02.2014 (ISBN 9780111109410). - 4p.: 30 cm. - 978-0-11-111461-2 £4.25

The West Northamptonshire Development Corporation (Dissolution) Order 2014 No. 2014/857. - Enabling power: Local Government, Planning and Land Act 1980, s. 166. - Issued: 03.04.2014. Made: 28.03.2014. Coming into force: 31.03.2014. Effect: None. Territorial extent & classification: E. General. - 2p.: 30 cm. - 978-0-11-111312-7 £4.00

The West Northamptonshire Development Corporation (Transfer of Property, Rights and Liabilities) Order 2014 No. 2014/217. - Enabling power: Local Government, Planning and Land Act 1980, ss. 165A (1) (4), 165B (1) (4). - Issued: 11.02.2014. Made: 04.02.2014. Laid: 10.02.2014. Coming into force: 27.03.2014. Effect: None. Territorial extent & classification: E. General. - 8p.: 30 cm. - 978-0-11-110930-4 £5.75

Value added tax

The International Tax Enforcement (Anguilla) Order 2014 No. 2014/1357. - Enabling power: Finance Act 2006, s. 173 (1) to (3). - Issued: 03.06.2014. Made: 27.05.2014. Coming into force: 03.06.2014. Effect: None. Territorial extent & classification: E/W/S/NI. General. - Supersedes draft SI (ISBN 9780111110539) issued 06.03.14. - 8p.: 30 cm. - 978-0-11-111529-9 £6.00

The International Tax Enforcement (British Virgin Islands) Order 2014 No. 2014/1359. - Enabling power: Finance Act 2006, s. 173 (1) to (3). - Issued: 03.06.2014. Made: 27.05.2014. Coming into force: 03.06.2014. Effect: None. Territorial extent & classification: E/W/S/NI. General. - Supersedes draft SI (ISBN 9780111110546) issued 06.03.14. - 8p.: 30 cm. - 978-0-11-111531-2 £6.00

The International Tax Enforcement (Turks and Caicos Islands) Order 2014 No. 2014/1360. - Enabling power: Finance Act 2006, s. 173 (1) to (3). - Issued: 03.06.2014. Made: 27.05.2014. Coming into force: 03.06.2014. Effect: None. Territorial extent & classification: E/W/S/NI. General. - Supersedes draft SI (ISBN 9780111110560) issued 06.03.14. - 8p.: 30 cm. - 978-0-11-111532-9 £6.00

The Revenue and Customs (Amendment of Appeal Provisions for Out of Time Reviews) Order 2014 No. 2014/1264. - Enabling power: Finance Act 2008, s. 124 (1) (2) (6) (7) (b). - Issued: 21.05.2014. Made: 14.05.2014. Coming into force: In accord. with art. 1 (2). Effect: 1994 c.9, c.23; 1996 c.8; 2000 c.17; 2001 c.9; 2003 c.14; S.I. 2003/3102; 2007/1509, 2157, 3298 amended. Territorial extent & classification: E/W/S/NI. General. - Supersedes draft SI (ISBN 9780111112991) issued 03/04/14. - 8p.: 30 cm. - 978-0-11-111499-5 £6.00

The Taxes (Definition of Charity) (Relevant Territories) (Amendment) Regulations 2014 No. 2014/1807. - Enabling power: Finance Act 2010, sch. 6, para. 2 (3) (b). - Issued: 15.07.2014. Made: 09.07.2014. Laid: 10.07.2014. Coming into force: 31.07.2014. Effect: S.I. 2010/1904 amended. Territorial extent & classification: E/W/S/NI. General. - 4p.: 30 cm. - 978-0-11-111781-1 £4.25

The Value Added Tax (Amendment) (No. 2) Regulations 2014 No. 2014/1497. - Enabling power: Value Added Tax Act 1994, s. 25 (1), sch. 11, para. 2 (1) (3A) (3B) (11) & Finance Act 1999, ss. 132, 133 & Finance Act 2002, ss. 135, 136. - Issued: 12.06.2014. Made: 06.06.2014. Laid: 09.06.2014. Coming into force: 01.07.2014. Effect: S.I. 1995/2518 amended. Territorial extent & classification: E/W/S/NI. General. - 4p.: 30 cm. - 978-0-11-111618-0 £4.25

The Value Added Tax (Amendment) (No. 3) Regulations 2014 No. 2014/2430. - Enabling power: Value Added Tax Act 1994, ss. 36 (5) (a) (c) (f) (7) (b), 39 (1) (3), 80 (6), 80A (1) (3) to (7), sch. 3B paras 4 (5) (a) (b), 7 (3), 12 (4), 16C (4) (a) (b), 16J (1), 16K (5) (a) (b), 16L, sch. 3BA paras 5 (5) (a) (b), 6 (2), 10 (3) (b), 17 (4), 19, 23 (4) (a) (b), 30 (1), 31 (5) (a) (b), 32. - Issued: 17.09.2014. Made: 10.09.2014. Laid: 10.09.2014. Coming into force: 01.10.2014 , 01.01.2015 in accord. with reg. 1. Effect: S.I. 1995/2518 amended. Territorial extent & classification: E/W/S/NI. General. - 8p.: 30 cm. - 978-0-11-112067-5 £6.00

The Value Added Tax (Amendment) Regulations 2014 No. 2014/548. - Enabling power: Value Added Tax Act 1994, sch. 11, para. 2 (4) to (5B) (10) (b) (11) & Finance Act 1999, ss. 132, 133. - Issued: 14.03.2014. Made: 10.03.2014. Laid: 10.03.2014. Coming into force: 01.04.2014. Effect: S.I. 1995/2518 amended. Territorial extent & classification: E/W/S/NI. General. - 4p.: 30 cm. - 978-0-11-111150-5 £4.00

The Value Added Tax (Drugs and Medicines) Order 2014 No. 2014/1111. - Enabling power: Value Added Tax Act 1994, ss. 30 (4), 96 (9). - Issued: 06.05.2014. Made: 28.04.2014. Laid: 29.04.2014. Coming into force: 21.05.2014. Effect: 1994 c.23 amended. Territorial extent & classification: E/W/S/NI. General. - 2p.: 30 cm. - 978-0-11-111442-1 £4.25

The Value Added Tax (Imported Goods) Relief (Amendment) Order 2014 No. 2014/2364. - Enabling power: Value Added Tax Act 1994, s. 37. - Issued: 10.09.2014. Made: 04.09.2014. Laid before Parliament: 05.09.2014. Coming into force: 26.09.2014. Effect: S.I. 1984/746 amended. Territorial extent & classification: E/W/S/NI. General. - 4p.: 30 cm. - 978-0-11-112026-2 £4.25

The Value Added Tax (Increase of Registration Limits) Order 2014 No. 2014/703. - Enabling power: Value Added Tax Act 1994, sch. 1, para. 15, sch. 3, para. 9. - Issued: 24.03.2014. Made: 18.03.2014. Laid: 19.03.2014. Coming into force: 01.04.2014. Effect: 1994 c.23 amended. Territorial extent & classification: E/W/S/NI. General. - 2p.: 30 cm. - 978-0-11-111242-7 £4.00

The Value Added Tax (Place of Supply of Services) (Exceptions Relating to Supplies Not Made to Relevant Business Person) Order 2014 No. 2014/2726. - Enabling power: Value Added Tax Act 1994, s. 7A (6) (b). - Issued: 17.11.2014. Made: 13.10.2014. Laid: 14.10.2014. Coming into force: 01.01.2015. Effect: 1994 c.23 amended. Territorial extent & classification: E/W/S/NI. General. - Approved by the House of Commons. Supersedes earlier SI of the same no. and title (ISBN 9780111121702) issued 17.10.2014. - 4p.: 30 cm. - 978-0-11-154043-5 £4.25

The Value Added Tax (Place of Supply of Services) (Exceptions Relating to Supplies Not Made to Relevant Business Person) Order 2014 No. 2014/2726. - Enabling power: Value Added Tax Act 1994, s. 7A (6) (b). - Issued: 17.10.2014. Made: 13.10.2014. Laid: 14.10.2014. Coming into force: 01.01.2015. Effect: 1994 c.23 amended. Territorial extent & classification: E/W/S/NI. General. - For approval by resolution of that House within twenty-eight days beginning with the day on which the Order was made, subject to extension for periods of dissolution, prorogation or adjournment for more than four days. Superseded by approved version (ISBN 9780111540435) issued 17.11.2014. - 4p.: 30 cm. - 978-0-11-112170-2 £4.25

The Value Added Tax (Refund of Tax) Order 2014 No. 2014/1112. - Enabling power: Value Added Tax Act 1994, s. 33 (3) (k). - Issued: 06.05.2014. Made: 28.04.2014. Laid: 29.04.2014. Coming into force: 20.05.2014. Effect: None. Territorial extent & classification: E/W/S/NI. General. - 4p.: 30 cm. - 978-0-11-111443-8 £4.25

The Value Added Tax (Refund of Tax to Museums and Galleries) (Amendment) Order 2014 No. 2014/2858. - Enabling power: Value Added Tax Act 1994, s. 33A (9). - Issued: 03.11.2014. Made: 27.10.2014. Laid: 28.10.2014. Coming into force: 01.12.2014. Effect: S.I. 2001/2879 amended. Territorial extent & classification: E/W/S/NI. General. - 8p.: 30 cm. - 978-0-11-112246-4 £6.00

The Value Added Tax (Section 55A) (Specified Goods and Excepted Supplies) Order 2014 No. 2014/1458. - Enabling power: Value Added Tax Act 1994, s. 55A (9) (10) (11) (14). - Issued: 13.06.2014. Made: 09.06.2014. Laid: 09.06.2014. Coming into force: 01.07.2014. Effect: None. Territorial extent & classification: E/W/S/NI. General. - 8p.: 30 cm. - 978-0-11-111625-8 £4.25

The Value Added Tax (Sport) Order 2014 No. 2014/3185. - Enabling power: Value Added Tax Act 1994, ss. 31 (2), 96 (9). - Issued: 05.12.2014. Made: 01.12.2014. Laid: 02.12.2014. Coming into force: 01.01.2015. Effect: 1994 c.23 amended. Territorial extent & classification: E/W/S/NI. General. - 2p.: 30 cm. - 978-0-11-112436-9 £4.25

Veterinary surgeons

The Veterinary Surgeons and Veterinary Practitioners (Registration) Regulations Order of Council 2014 No. 2014/3493. - Enabling power: Veterinary Surgeons Act 1966, s. 11. - Issued: 22.01.2015. Made: 17.12.2015. Coming into force: 14.01.2015. Effect: S.I. 2010/2854 revoked. Territorial extent & classification: E/W/S/NI. General. - 8p.: 30 cm. - 978-0-11-112738-4 £6.00

Video recordings

The Video Recordings Act 1984 (Exempted Video Works) Regulations 2014 No. 2014/2097. - Enabling power: Video Recordings Act 1984, ss. 2 (4), 3 (13), 22A (2). - Issued: 12.08.2014. Made: 04.08.2014. Coming into force: 01.10.2014. Effect: 1984 c.39 amended. Territorial extent & classification: E/W/S/NI. General. - Supersedes draft (ISBN 9780111117309) issued 03.07.2014. - 4p.: 30 cm. - 978-0-11-111966-2 £4.25

Water, England and Wales

The Water Act 2014 (Commencement No. 1) Order 2014 No. 2014/1823 (C.82). - Enabling power: Water Act 2014, s. 94 (3) (6), sch. 12. Bringing into operation various provisions of the 2014 Act on 14.07.2014, 01.10.2014, in accord. with arts 2, 3. - Issued: 17.07.2014. Made: 08.07.2014. Effect: None. Territorial extent & classification: E. General. - 2p.: 30 cm. - 978-0-11-111795-8 £4.25

Water industry, England and Wales

The Flood and Water Management Act 2010 (Commencement No.9) Order 2014 No. 2014/3155 (W.317) (C.137). - Enabling power: Flood and Water Management Act 2010, s. 49 (3) (e). Bringing into operation various provisions of the 2010 Act on 01.01.2015. - Issued: 09.12.2014. Made: 02.12.2014. Effect: None. Territorial extent & classification: W. General. - In English and Welsh. Welsh title: Gorchymyn Deddf Rheoli Llifogydd a Dwr 2010 (Cychwyn Rhif 9) 2014. - 8p.: 30 cm. - 978-0-348-11025-8 £6.00

The South West Water Authority (Dissolution) Order 2014 No. 2014/2679. - Enabling power: Water Act 1989, s. 4 (3). - Issued: 09.10.2014. Made: 30.09.2014. Coming into force: 01.11.2014. Effect: None. Territorial extent & classification: E/W. General. - 2p.: 30 cm. - 978-0-11-112126-9 £4.25

The Water Act 2014 (Commencement No. 2 and Transitional Provisions) Order 2014 No. 2014/3320 (C.155). - Enabling power: Water Act 2014, ss. 91 (1), 94 (3) (6). Bringing into operation various provisions of the 2014 Act on 01.01.2015, in accord. with arts 2, 4. - Issued: 22.12.2014. Made: 15.12.2014. Effect: None. Territorial extent & classification: E/W. General. - 4p.: 30 cm. - 978-0-11-112605-9 £4.25

The Water Industry (Undertakers Wholly or Mainly in Wales) (Information about Non-owner Occupiers) Regulations 2014 No. 2014/3156 (W.318). - Enabling power: Water Industry Act 1991, s. 144C (4) (8) (b), 213 (2) (f). - Issued: 09.12.2014. Made: 02.12.2014. Laid before the National Assembly for Wales 03.12.2014. Coming into force: 01.01.2015. Effect: Territorial extent & classification: E/W. General. - In English and Welsh. Welsh title: Rheoliadau'r Diwydiant Dwr (Ymgymerwyr sy'n Gyfan Gwbl neu'n Bennaf yng Nghymru) (Gwybodaeth am Feddianwyr nad ydynt yn Berchenogion) 2014. - 4p.: 30 cm. - 978-0-348-11026-5 £4.25

Water resources, England

The Bathing Water (Amendment) (England) Regulations 2014 No. 2014/2363. - Enabling power: European Communities Act 1972, s. 2 (2). - Issued: 10.09.2014. Made: 02.09.2014. Laid before Parliament: 05.09.2014. Coming into force: 01.10.2014. Effect: S.I. 2013/1675 amended. Territorial extent & classification: E. General. - With correction slip dated December 2014. - 2p.: 30 cm. - 978-0-11-112025-5 £4.25

Water resources, England and Wales

The Water Act 2014 (Commencement No. 1) Order 2014 No. 2014/1823 (C.82). - Enabling power: Water Act 2014, s. 94 (3) (6), sch. 12. Bringing into operation various provisions of the 2014 Act on 14.07.2014, 01.10.2014, in accord. with arts 2, 3. - Issued: 17.07.2014. Made: 08.07.2014. Effect: None. Territorial extent & classification: E. General. - 2p.: 30 cm. - 978-0-11-111795-8 £4.25

Water resources, Wales

The Bathing Water (Amendment) (Wales) Regulations 2014 No. 2014/1067 (W.106). - Enabling power: European Communities Act 1972, s. 2 (2). - Issued: 09.05.2014. Made: 21.04.2014. Laid before the National Assembly for Wales: 24.04.2014. Coming into force: 15.05.2014. Effect: S.I. 2013/1675 amended in relation to Wales. Territorial extent & classification: W. General. - In English and Welsh. Welsh title: Rheoliadau Dyfroedd Ymdrochi (Diwygio) (Cymru) 2014. - 4p.: 30 cm. - 978-0-348-10941-2 £4.25

Weights and measures

The Weights and Measures (Food) (Amendment) Regulations 2014 No. 2014/2975. - Enabling power: European Communities Act 1972, s. 2 (2). - Issued: 18.11.2014. Made: 09.11.2014. Laid: 14.11.2014. Coming into force: 13.12.2014. Effect: 1985 c.72; S.I. 1984/1315; 1987/1538; 1988/2039, 2040; 2006/659 amended. Territorial extent & classification: E/W/S. General. - 16p.: 30 cm. - 978-0-11-112328-7 £6.00

Wildlife, England

The Wildlife and Countryside Act 1981 (Prohibition on Sale etc. of Invasive Non-native Plants) (England) Order 2014 No. 2014/538. - Enabling power: Wildlife and Countryside Act 1981, s. 14ZA (3) (b), 26. - Issued: 13.03.2014. Made: 03.03.2014. Laid before Parliament & National Assembly for Wales: 10.03.2014. Coming into force: 06.04.2014. Effect: None. Territorial extent & classification: E. General. - 4p.: 30 cm. - 978-0-11-111140-6 £4.00

Young offender institutions, England and Wales

The Prison and Young Offender Institution (Amendment) Rules 2014 No. 2014/2169. - Enabling power: Prison Act 1952, s. 47. - Issued: 19.08.2014. Made: 12.08.2014. Laid: 13.08.2014. Coming into force: 13.08.2014, at 5.00 pm. Effect: S.I. 1997/728; 2000/3371 amended. Territorial extent & classification: E/W. General. - 8p.: 30 cm. - 978-0-11-111990-7 £6.00

Statutory Instruments 2014

Arranged by Number

1	Enforcement, England and Wales
2	Rating and valuation, England
3	Prisons, England and Wales
4	Architects
5	Mobile homes, England
6	Cancelled
7	Legal aid and advice, England and Wales
8	Merchant shipping
9	Stamp duty
	Stamp duty reserve tax
10	Pensions
11 (W.1)(C.1)	Mobile homes, Wales
12	Road traffic
13	Civil aviation
14	Civil aviation
15	Road traffic
16	Terms and conditions of employment
17	Harbours, docks, piers and ferries
18	Local government, England
19	Local government, England
20	Local government, England
21	Local government, England
22	Local government, England
23	Local government, England
24	Local government, England
25	Local government, England
26	Local government, England
27	Local government, England
28	Civil aviation
29	Road traffic
30	Road traffic
31	Road traffic
32	Road traffic
33	Road traffic
34 (W.2)	Road traffic, Wales
35	Council tax, England
36	Civil aviation
37	Road traffic
38	Road traffic
39 (C.2)	National Health Service, England
40	Cancelled
41 (W.3)	Landlord and tenant, Wales
42 (W.4)	Education, Wales
43	Rating and valuation, England
44	Public service pensions, England and Wales
45	Betting, gaming and lotteries
46	Road traffic
47	Excise
48	Building societies
49	Road traffic
50	Road traffic
51	Road traffic
52	Road traffic
53	Road traffic
54	Road traffic
55	Social security
56	Road traffic
57	Road traffic
58 (W.5)	Building and buildings, Wales
59	Road traffic
60	Road traffic
61	Road traffic
62	Road traffic
63	Road traffic
64	Road traffic
65	Road traffic
66 (W.6)	Council tax, Wales
67	Road traffic
68	Road traffic
69	Road traffic
70	Road traffic
71	Road traffic
72 (W.7)	Road traffic, Wales
73	Road traffic
74	Road traffic
75	Road traffic
76	Social security, England and Wales
77 (W.8)	Public audit, Wales
78	National Health Service, England and Wales
79	Police, England and Wales
	Pensions, England and Wales
80	Education, England
81	Road traffic, England
82	Merchant shipping
83	Road traffic
84	Road traffic
85	Road traffic
86	Road traffic
87	Road traffic
88	Civil aviation
89	Civil aviation
90	Civil aviation
91	Mental health, England
	National Health Service, England
92	European Communities, Wales
93 (C.3)	Marriage
94	Electricity
95	Road traffic
96	Rating and valuation, England
97	Road traffic
98	Rating and valuation, England
99	Road traffic
100	Road traffic
101	Road traffic
102	Road traffic
103	Road traffic
104	Road traffic
105	Criminal law
106	Registration of births, deaths, marriages, etc., England and Wales
107	Marriage
	Civil partnership
108	Road traffic
109 (W.9)	National Health Service, Wales
110 (W.10)	Building and buildings, Wales
111 (W.11)	Road traffic, Wales
112	Agriculture, England
113	Road traffic
114	Road traffic
115	Road traffic
116	Road traffic

117	Road traffic	177 (W.25)	Road traffic, Wales
118	Road traffic	178 (W.26) (C.5)	Education, Wales
119	Road traffic	179	Road traffic
120	Road traffic	180	Road traffic
121	Road traffic	181	Road traffic
122 (W.12)	Council tax, Wales	182	Tribunals and inquiries, England
123 (W.13)	Food, Wales	183 (C.6)	Co-operative societies
124 (W.14)	Rating and valuation, Wales		Community benefit societies
125	Road traffic		Credit unions
126 (W.15)	Road traffic, Wales	184	Industrial and provident societies
127	Road traffic		Credit unions
128 (W.16)	Road traffic, Wales	185	Road traffic
129 (W.17)	Council tax, Wales	186	Road traffic
130	Criminal law, England and Wales	187	Road traffic
131	Legal aid and advice, England and Wales	188	Road traffic
132	Road traffic	189	Road traffic
133	Road traffic	190	Road traffic
134	Road traffic	191	Road traffic
135	Road traffic	192	Road traffic
136	Road traffic	193	Road traffic
137	Road traffic	194	Cancelled
138	Road traffic	195	Food
139	Civil aviation	196	National Health Service, England
140	Civil aviation	197 (W.27)	Road traffic, Wales
141	Civil aviation	198	Prevention and suppression of terrorism
142	Civil aviation	199	Road traffic
143	River, England	200	Road traffic
144	Sports grounds and sporting events, England and Wales	201	Road traffic
		202	Road traffic
145	Road traffic	203	Road traffic
146 (W.18)	Road traffic, Wales	204	National Health Service, England and Wales
147	Social security	205	Immigration
	Terms and conditions of employment	206	Financial services and markets
148	Road traffic	207 (W.28)	Road traffic, Wales
149	Cancelled	208	Financial services and markets
150	Road traffic	209 (C.7)	Social security
151	Road traffic	210	Industrial and provident societies
152	Road traffic	211	Income tax
153	Road traffic	212	Social security
154	Road traffic	213	Social security
155	Road traffic	214	Civil aviation
156	Road traffic	215	Civil aviation
157	Road traffic	216	Civil aviation
158 (W.19)	Road traffic, Wales	217	Urban development, England
159 (W.20)	Road traffic, Wales	218	Cancelled
160 (W.21)	Road traffic, Wales	219 (W.29)	Commons, Wales
161 (W.22)	Road traffic, Wales	220	Sports grounds and sporting events, England and Wales
162	Health and safety		
	Town and country planning, England	221	Road traffic
163	Criminal law, England and Wales	222	Road traffic
164 (W.23)	Road traffic, Wales	223	Road traffic
165	Local government, England	224	Road traffic
166	Education, England	225	Road traffic
167	Road traffic	226	Road traffic
168	Road traffic	227	Road traffic
169	Road traffic	228	Road traffic
170	Road traffic	229	Industrial and provident societies
171	Road traffic		Credit unions
172	Road traffic	230	National Health Service, England
173	Road traffic	231	Council tax, England
174	Road traffic	232	Road traffic
175 (C.4)	Road traffic	233	Road traffic
176 (W.24)	Road traffic, Wales	234 (W.30)	Road traffic, Wales

235 (W.31)	Road traffic, Wales	296	Road traffic
236 (W.32)	Road traffic, Wales	297	Road traffic
237 (C.8)	Police, England and Wales	298	Road traffic
238	Children and young persons, England and Wales	299	Road traffic
		300	Road traffic
239	Police, England and Wales	301	Road traffic
240	Prisons, England and Wales	302	Road traffic
241 (W.33)	Road traffic, Wales	303	Road traffic
242	Charities, England and Wales	304	Road traffic
243	Local government, England	305	Road traffic
244	Road traffic	306	Road traffic
245	Road traffic	307	Road traffic
246	Road traffic	308	Merchant shipping
247	Road traffic	309	Road traffic
248	Road traffic	310	Transport and works, England
249	Road traffic		Transport, England
250	Road traffic	311	Road traffic
251 (C.9)	Energy	312	Road traffic
252	Road traffic	313	Road traffic
253 (C.10)	Terms and conditions of employment	314	Road traffic
254	Employment tribunals	315	Road traffic
255	Environmental protection, England and Wales	316	Road traffic
256 (W.34)	Public health, Wales	317	Road traffic
257	Commons, England	318	Civil aviation
258 (C.11)	Criminal law	319	Road traffic
259	Criminal law	320	Road traffic
260	Road traffic	321	Road traffic
261	Education, England	322	Justices of the Peace, England and Wales
	Children and young persons, England	323	Road traffic
262 (C.12)	Civil aviation	324	Road traffic
263	Cancelled	325	Representation of the people
264	Road traffic	326	Road traffic
265	Merchant shipping	327	Road traffic
266	European Union	328	Road traffic
267	Road traffic	329	Road traffic
268	Ministers of the Crown	330	Road traffic
269	Overseas territories	331	Animals, England
270	Northern Ireland	332	Road traffic
271	Employment tribunals	333	Town and country planning, England
272	Civil aviation	334	Financial services and markets
273	Civil aviation	335	Representation of the people
274	Civil aviation	336 (C.13)	Representation of the people
275	Civil aviation	337	Road traffic
276	Road traffic	338	Road traffic
277	Road traffic	339	Road traffic
278	Road traffic	340	Road traffic
279	Road traffic	341	Road traffic
280	Road traffic	342	Road traffic
281	Road traffic	343	Road traffic
282	Road traffic	344	Road traffic
283	Road traffic	345	Road traffic
284	Road traffic	346	Road traffic
285	Road traffic	347	Road traffic
286 (W.35)	Landlord and tenant, Wales	348 (W.37)	Road traffic, Wales
287 (W.36)	Landlord and tenant, Wales	349 (W.38)	Road traffic, Wales
288	Pensions	350	Road traffic
289	Road traffic	351	Road traffic
290	Education, England	352	Road traffic
291	Road traffic	353	Road traffic
292	Road traffic	354	Road traffic
293	Road traffic	355	Road traffic
294	Road traffic	356	Road traffic
295	Road traffic		

357	Town and country planning, England
358	National Health Service, England
359	Road traffic
360	National Health Service, England
361	Road traffic
362	Road traffic
363	Road traffic
364	Road traffic
365	Road traffic
366	Financial services and markets
367	Social security
368	Social security
369	Social security
370	Local government, England and Wales
371 (W.39)	Agriculture, Wales
372 (W.40)	Rating and valuation, Wales
373 (W.41)	Social care, Wales
	National Health Service, Wales
	Children and young persons, Wales
374 (W.42)	Landlord and tenant, Wales
375 (W.43)	Town and country planning, Wales
376	Financial services and markets
377 (C.14)	Financial services and markets
378	Financial services and markets
379 (W.44)	Rating and valuation, Wales
380 (W.45) (C.15)	Local government, Wales
381	Police, England and Wales
	Pensions, England and Wales
382	Terms and conditions of employment
383	Criminal law
384	Social security
	Tax credits
385	Community infrastructure levy, England and Wales
386	Terms and conditions of employment
387 (W.46)	Road traffic, Wales
388 (W.47)	Road traffic, Wales
389	Council tax, England
	London Government
390	Road traffic
391	Road traffic
392	Road traffic
393	Road traffic
394	Road traffic
395	Police, England and Wales
396	Road traffic
397	Road traffic
398	Road traffic
399	Road traffic
400	Road traffic
401	Road traffic
402	Income tax
403 (W.48)	Road traffic, Wales
404	Rating and valuation, England
405	Road traffic
406	Equal opportunities and human rights
407 (L.1)	Senior courts of England and Wales
	County courts, England and Wales
408	Road traffic
409	Immigration
410	Cancelled
411	Criminal law, England and Wales
412	Pensions
413	National Health Service, England
414 (C.16)	Representation of the people
415	Legal aid and advice, England and Wales
416 (C.17)	Competition
	Equality
	Town and country planning
417	National Health Service, England
418	National Health Service, England
419	Road traffic
420	Road traffic
421	Enforcement, England and Wales
422	Pipe-lines
423 (C.18)	Rehabilitation of offenders
424	Education, England and Wales
425	Road traffic
426	Road traffic
427	Road traffic
428	Road traffic
429	Road traffic
430	Pipe-lines
431	Terms and conditions of employment
432	Government trading funds
433 (C.19)	Public service pensions
434	Copyright
	Rights in performances
435	Housing, England
436	Consumer credit
437	Civil aviation
438	Civil aviation
439	Civil aviation
440 (W.49)	Food, Wales
441 (W.50)	Road traffic, Wales
442	Mobile homes, England
443	National Health Service, England
444	Pensions
445	Fire and rescue services, England
	Pensions, England
446	Fire and rescue services, England
	Pensions, England
447	Fire and rescue services, England
	Pensions, England
448	Council tax, England
449	Representation of the people
450	Representation of the people, Northern Ireland
451	Public health, England
452	National Health Service, England
453 (W.51) (C.20)	Local government, Wales
454 (W.52)	Road traffic, Wales
455	Local government, England
456	Local government, England
457	Road traffic
458	Competition
459 (C.21)	Payment scheme
460 (W.53)	National Health Service, Wales
461 (W.54)	National Health Service, Wales
462 (W.55)	National Health Service, Wales
463 (C.22)	Pensions
464	Road traffic
465	National Health Service, England
466	Highways, England
467	Road traffic
	Investigatory powers
	Proceeds of crime

No.	Subject
468	Employment tribunals
469	Energy
470	Excise
471	Excise
472	Income tax
473	Cancelled
474	Income tax
475	Social security
476 (W.56)	Local government, Wales
477 (W.57)	Road traffic, Wales
478 (C.23)	Police, England and Wales
479	Rating and valuation, England
480	Road traffic
481 (W.58)	Local government, Wales
482 (L.2)	Senior courts of England and Wales
	County courts, England and Wales
483	Pensions
484	Savings banks
485	Social security
486	Health and safety
487	Agriculture
	Plant health, England
	Seeds
488	Inheritance tax
489	Income tax
490	Medicines
491	Clean air, England
492	Representation of the people, England and Wales
493 (W.59)	Landlord and tenant, Wales
494	Representation of the people, England and Wales
495	Climate change
496	Income tax
497	Overseas territories
498	Education, England
	Children and young persons, England
499	Merchant shipping
500	Ministers of the Crown
501 (S.1)	Constitutional law
	Devolution, Scotland
502	Climate change
503 (L.3)	County court, England and Wales
504	Clean air, England
505	Pensions
506	Financial services and markets
507	Criminal law
508	Civil aviation
509	Diplomatic Service
510	Electoral Commission
511	Registration of births, deaths, marriages, etc.
512	Public service pensions, England and Wales
	Education, England and Wales
513	Constitutional law
	Devolution, Scotland
	Social care
514 (L.4)	Tribunals and inquiries
515	Pensions
516	Social security
517 (W.60)	Animals, Wales
	Public health, Wales
518	Corporation tax
519 (W.61)	Seeds, Wales
520	Taxes
521 (W.62)	Plant health, Wales
522 (W.63)	Fire and rescue services, Wales
	Pensions, Wales
523 (W.64)	Fire and rescue services, Wales
	Pensions, Wales
524 (L.5)	Family proceedings, England and Wales
	Senior courts of England and Wales
	County courts, England and Wales
	Magistrates' courts, England and Wales
525	Public service pensions, England and Wales
526	Atomic energy and radioactive substances
527	Merchant shipping
528	Gas
529	Gas
530	Immigration
531	Government resources and accounts
532	Health care and associated professions
533	Competition
534	Competition
535	Criminal law
536	Competition
537	Competition
538	Wildlife, England
539	Social security
540	Pensions
541 (W.65)	Road traffic, Wales
542	Registration of births, deaths, marriages, etc.
	Regulatory reform
543	Judgments, England and Wales
	Family law, England and Wales
544	Registration of births, deaths, marriages, etc., England and Wales
545	National Health Service, England
546	Terms and conditions of employment
547	Terms and conditions of employment
548	Value added tax
549	Competition
550	Town and country planning, England
551	Town and country planning, England
552	Town and country planning, England
553	Town and country planning, England
554 (W.66)	Local government, Wales
555	Pensions
556	Representation of the people
557	Gas
	Pipe-lines
558	Competition
559	Competition
560	Marriage
	Civil partnership
	Human fertilisation and embryology
561	Government trading funds
562	Criminal law, England and Wales
563	Pensions
564	Town and country planning, England
565	Town and country planning, England
566 (W.67)	National Health Service, Wales
567 (W.68)	Children and young persons, Wales
568	Fees and charges
569	Social security
570	National Health Service, England and Wales
571	Countryside, England
572	Social security
573	Regulatory reform

574	Co-operative societies	617	Road traffic
	Community benefit societies	618	Social security
	Credit unions	619	Cancelled
575	Public service pensions	620	Road traffic
576 (C.24)	Family law	621	Road traffic
577	Merchant shipping	622	Cancelled
578	Patents	623	Pensions
579	Building and buildings, England and Wales	624	Road traffic
580	Regulatory reform	625	Road traffic
	Local government, England and Wales	626	Road traffic
581	Immigration	627	Road traffic
	Nationality	628	Road traffic
582	National assistance services, England	629	Road traffic
583	Insolvency, England and Wales	630 (C.25)	Police
584	Income tax	631	Public bodies
585	Capital gains tax	632 (W.72)	Animals, Wales
	Corporation tax	633 (C.26)	Criminal law, England and Wales
	Income tax	634	Social security
586	Legal aid and advice, England and Wales	635	Social security
587	Criminal law	636	Road traffic
588	National Health Service, England	637	Road traffic
589	Plant health, England	638	Road traffic
	Plant health, Scotland	639	Road traffic
590 (L.6)	Betting, gaming and lotteries	640	Road traffic
	County courts, England and Wales	641	Road traffic
	Family proceedings, England and Wales	642	Road traffic
	Gender recognition	643	Road traffic
	Magistrates' courts, England and Wales	644	Road traffic
	Mental capacity, England and Wales	645	Road traffic
	Senior courts of England and Wales	646	Road traffic
	Supreme Court of the United Kingdom	647	Road traffic
	Tribunals and inquiries	648	Road traffic
591	Social security	649	Child trust funds
592 (W.69)	Town and country planning, Wales	650	Road traffic
593 (W.70)	Town and country planning, Wales	651	Education
594	Cancelled	652	Road traffic
595 (W.71)	Transport, Wales	653	Road traffic
596	Terms and conditions of employment	654	Income tax
597	Social security		Capital gains tax
598	Healthcare and associated professions	655	Road traffic
599	Medicines	656	Environmental protection, England and Wales
600	Enforcement, England and Wales	657	Road traffic
601	Plant health, England	658	Tax credits
602 (L.7)	Family proceedings, England and Wales	659	Road traffic
	Senior courts of England and Wales	660	Road traffic
	County courts, England and Wales	661	Road traffic
603 (L.8)	Family court, England and Wales	662	Road traffic
604	Merchant shipping	663	Road traffic
605 (L.9)	Family proceedings	664	Road traffic
	Senior courts of England and Wales	665	Road traffic
	Family court, England and Wales	666 (W.73)	Social care, Wales
606	Social security	667 (L.11)	Family proceedings, England and Wales
607	Legal aid and advice, England and Wales		Senior courts of England and Wales
608	Social security		Family court, England and Wales
609	Plant health, England	668	Pensions
610 (L.10)	Senior courts of England and Wales	669	Criminal law, England and Wales
	County courts, England and Wales	670	Children and young persons, England
611	Employment tribunals	671	Road traffic
612	Family law	672	Road traffic
613	Road traffic	673	Road traffic
614	Family law	674	Road traffic
615	Environmental protection	675	Cancelled
	Licensing (marine)	676	Road traffic
	Marine pollution		
616	Road traffic		

677	Road traffic
678	Road traffic
679	Road traffic
680	Road traffic
681	Road traffic
682	Road traffic
683	Town and country planning, England
684 (W.74)	Clean air, Wales
685	Income tax
	Corporation tax
686	Road traffic
687	Road traffic
688	Road traffic
689	Road traffic
690	Road traffic
691	Road traffic
692	Town and country planning, England
693	Criminal law
694 (W.75)	Clean air, Wales
695	Electricity
	Gas
696	Road traffic
697	Road traffic
698	Road traffic
699	Education, England
700	Civil aviation
701	Road traffic
702	Customs
703	Value added tax
704	Representation of the people
705	Road traffic
706	Road traffic
707	Landfill tax
708	Road traffic
709 (W.76)	Road traffic, Wales
710 (W.77)	Road traffic, Wales
711 (W.78)	Road traffic, Wales
712 (W.79)	Road traffic, Wales
713	Excise
714	Animals, England
715	Pensions
716	Road traffic
717	Road traffic
718	Road traffic
719	Road traffic
720	Road traffic
721	Road traffic
722	Road traffic
723	Road traffic
724	Road traffic
725	Road traffic
726	Road traffic
727	Road traffic
728	Road traffic
729	Road traffic
730	Road traffic
731	Road traffic
732	Road traffic
733	Road traffic
734	Road traffic
735	Road traffic
736	Road traffic
737	Road traffic
738	Road traffic
739	Road traffic
740	Road traffic
741	Road traffic
742	Road traffic
743	Road traffic
744	Road traffic
745	Road traffic
746	Civil aviation
747	Road traffic
748	Road traffic
749	Road traffic
750	Road traffic
751	Road traffic
752	Road traffic
753	Protection of wrecks, England
754	Road traffic
755	Road traffic
756	Road traffic
757	Road traffic
758	Road traffic
759	Road traffic
760	Road traffic
761	Road traffic
762	Road traffic
763	Road traffic
764	Road traffic
765	Road traffic
766	Road traffic
767	Road traffic
768 (C.27)	Tribunals and inquiries
769	Road traffic
770	Road traffic
771	Social security
772 (C.28)	Consumer protection, England and Wales
	Legal services, England and Wales
773	Road traffic
774	Electronic communications
775	Road traffic
776	Road traffic
777	Road traffic
778	Road traffic
779	Road traffic
780	Road traffic
781	Road traffic
782	Road traffic
783	Civil aviation
784	National Health Service, England
785 (C.29)	Legal services, England and Wales
786	Tribunals and inquiries, England and Wales
787	Employment tribunals
788	Revenue and customs, England and Wales
789 (W.80)	Road traffic, Wales
790	Road traffic, England
791	Employment and training
792	National Health Service, England
793 (C.30)	Family proceedings
794	Representation of the people, Northern Ireland
795	Road traffic
796	Road traffic
797 (C.31)	Road traffic

798	Education, England	845	Tax credits
799	Road traffic	846	Countryside, England
800	Road traffic	847	Employment tribunals
801	Road traffic	848	Civil aviation
802	Road traffic	849	Civil aviation
803	Road traffic	850	Civil aviation
804	Road traffic	851	Countryside, England
805	Road traffic	852	Family proceedings, England and Wales
806	Road traffic	853	Terms and conditions of employment
807	Road traffic	854	Annual tax on enveloped dwellings
808	Road traffic	855	Defence
809	Civil aviation	856	Contracting out, Wales
810 (W.81)	Road traffic, Wales	857	Urban development, England
811 (W.82)	Road traffic, Wales	858	Road traffic
812	Legal aid and advice, England and Wales	859	Income tax
813	Ecclesiastical law, England	860	Regulatory reform
814	Legal aid and advice, England and Wales	861	Environmental protection Customs
815	Registration of births, deaths, marriages, etc., England and Wales	862	Defence
816	Mobile homes, England	863	Local government, England Transport, England
817	Insolvency, England and Wales	864	Local government, England Transport, England
818	County court, England and Wales		
819	Senior courts of England and Wales	865	Local government, England Transport, England
820	Senior courts of England and Wales County court, England and Wales	866	Local government, England Transport, England
821 (L.12)	Senior courts of England and Wales County courts, England and Wales	867 (L.16)	Senior courts of England and Wales County court, England and Wales
822	Rating and valuation, England	868	Social security
823 (C.32)	Financial services and markets Competition	869	Social security
		870	Consumer protection
824 (C.33)	Agricultural employment, England Landlord and tenant, England Terms and conditions of employment, England	871	Cancelled
		872 (W.86)	National Health Service, Wales
		873 (W.87)	Road traffic, Wales
825 (W.83)	Council tax, Wales	874 (L.17)	Senior courts of England and Wales County court, England and Wales
826 (W.84)	Housing, Wales		
827 (W.85)	Road traffic, Wales	875 (L.18)	Magistrates' courts, England and Wales
828	Social security	876 (L.19)	Senior courts of England and Wales
829	Contracting out, England	877 (L.20)	Family proceedings, England and Wales Senior courts of England and Wales
830 (C.34)	Enforcement, England and Wales		
831 (C.35)	Children and young persons, England and Wales Children and young persons, Northern Ireland Protection of vulnerable adults, England and Wales Protection of vulnerable adults, Northern Ireland	878 (L.21)	Tribunals and inquiries, England and Wales
		879	Family proceedings Senior courts of England and Wales Family court, England and Wales
		880	Building and buildings, England and Wales
832	Family proceedings, England and Wales Family court, England and Wales	881	Social security
		882	Financial services and markets
833	Family proceedings, England and Wales Family court, England and Wales	883	Financial services and markets
		884	Social security
834	Public bodies	885	Tax credits
835	Financial services and markets	886	Tax credits Social security
836	Aggregates levy		
837	Pensions	887	Road traffic
838	Social security, Northern Ireland	888 (C.37)	Coal industry
839 (C.36)	Public service pensions	889 (C.38)	Children and young persons Family proceedings
840 (L.13)	Family proceedings, England and Wales Senior courts of England and Wales Family court, England and Wales		
		890 (W.88)	Public audit, Wales
		891	Competition
841 (L.14)	Family court, England and Wales	892	Competition
842	Family court, England and Wales	893	Electricity, England and Wales
843 (L.15)	Family proceedings, England and Wales Senior courts of England and Wales Family court, England and Wales	894	Financial services and markets
		895	Ecclesiastical law, England
		896	Ecclesiastical law, England
844	Climate change levy		

897	Social security	950	Environmental protection
898	Copyright		Licensing (marine)
899	Housing, England		Marine pollution
900 (C.39)	Local government, England	951 (W.92)	Animals, Wales
901	Legal aid and advice, England and Wales	952	Energy
902	Social security	953	Electronic communications
903	Road traffic	954 (C.44)	County court, England and Wales
904	Social security		Family proceedings
905	Financial services and markets		Magistrates' courts, England and Wales
906 (C.40)	Revenue and customs, England and Wales		Senior courts of England and Wales
907	Revenue and customs	955	Police, England and Wales
908	Cancelled	956	Family court, England and Wales
909	Infrastructure planning, England	957	Road traffic
910 (W.89)	Landlord and tenant, Wales	958	Road traffic
911	Stamp duty	959	Road traffic
	Stamp duty reserve tax	960	Road traffic
912	Children and young persons, England	961	Road traffic
913	Children and young persons, England	962	Road traffic
914 (W.90)	Road traffic, Wales	963	Road traffic
915 (W.91)	Road traffic, Wales	964	Road traffic
916	Payment scheme	965	Road traffic
917	Payment scheme	966	Road traffic
918	Representation of the people	967	Road traffic
919	Representation of the people	968	Road traffic
920	Representation of the people, England and Wales	969	Road traffic
		970	Road traffic
921	Police, England and Wales	971	Road traffic
922	Immigration	972	Road traffic
	Nationality	973	Road traffic
923	Representation of the people	974	Cancelled
924	Local government, England	975	Road traffic
925	Local government, England	976	Road traffic
926	Highways, England	977	Road traffic
927	Prevention and suppression of terrorism	978	Road traffic
928	Energy	979	Plant health, England
929 (C.41)	Regulatory reform	980	Road traffic
930	Cancelled	981	Criminal law, England and Wales
931	National Health Service, England	982 (L.22)	County court, England and Wales
932	National Health Service, England	983	Road traffic
933	National Health Service, England	984	Road traffic
934	Defence	985	Road traffic
935	Road traffic	986	Road traffic
936	Health care and associated professions	987	Road traffic
937	Road traffic	988	Road traffic
938	Road traffic	989	Road traffic
939	Rating and valuation, England	990	Road traffic
940 (C.42)	Local government, England	991	Road traffic
941	Highways, England	992 (C.45)	Income tax
942	Education, England		Social security
943	Civil aviation	993	Road traffic
944	Civil aviation	994	Road traffic
945	Civil aviation	995	Road traffic
946	Road traffic	996	Road traffic
947	Road traffic	997	Road traffic
948	Road traffic	998	Road traffic
949 (C.43)	Arms and ammunition	999	Road traffic
	Criminal law, England and Wales	1000	Road traffic
	Defence	1001	Road traffic
	Dogs	1002	Civil aviation
	Dogs, England and Wales	1003	Civil aviation
	Family law, England and Wales	1004 (W.93)	Constitutional law
	Housing, England and Wales	1005	Civil aviation
	Police, England and Wales	1006	Civil aviation
	Prevention and suppression of terrorism		

1007	Civil aviation	1068	Public bodies
1008	Civil aviation		Landlord and tenant, England and Wales
1009	Road traffic	1069	Customs
1010	Road traffic	1070	Civil aviation
1011	Road traffic	1071	Road traffic
1012	Local government, England	1072	Road traffic
	Transport, England	1073	Road traffic
1013	Road traffic	1074	Road traffic
1014	Road traffic	1075	Road traffic
1015	Road traffic	1076	Harbours, docks, piers and ferries
1016	Social security	1077	Road traffic
1017	Income tax	1078 (W.107)	Road traffic, Wales
1018	Road traffic	1079	Road traffic
1019	Road traffic	1080	Road traffic
1020	Road traffic	1081	Road traffic
1021	Road traffic	1082	Road traffic
1022	Road traffic	1083	Road traffic
1023	Road traffic	1084	Road traffic
1024	Education, England	1085	Road traffic
1025	Road traffic	1086	Road traffic
1026	Road traffic	1087 (W.108)	Road traffic, Wales
1027	Road traffic	1088	Road traffic
1028	Road traffic	1089	Road traffic
1029	Road traffic	1090	Road traffic
1030	Land drainage, England	1091	Road traffic
1031 (W.94)	Road traffic, Wales	1092	Road traffic
1032	Road traffic	1093	Road traffic
1033	Road traffic	1094	Road traffic
1034	Road traffic	1095	Road traffic
1035	Road traffic	1096	Road traffic
1036	Road traffic	1097	Social security
1037	Road traffic	1098	Overseas territories
1038	Road traffic	1099 (W.109)	National Health Service, Wales
1039	Road traffic	1100	Overseas territories
1040	Road traffic	1101	Health care and associated professions
1041	Road traffic	1102 (W.110)	Food, Wales
1042	Family proceedings	1103	Education, England
1043	Highways, England		Children and young persons, England
1044	Highways, England	1104	Road traffic
1045	Highways, England	1105	Territorial sea
1046	Road traffic	1106	Dangerous drugs
1047	Road traffic	1107	Civil partnership
1048	Road traffic	1108	Marriage
1049	Road traffic	1109	Road traffic
1050	Road traffic	1110	Marriage
1051	Road traffic	1111	Value added tax
1052	Infrastructure planning	1112	Value added tax
1053	Road traffic	1113	Road traffic
1054	Road traffic	1114	Road traffic
1055 (W.95)	Road traffic, Wales	1115	Road traffic
1056 (W.96)	Road traffic, Wales	1116	Representation of the people, Northern Ireland
1057 (W.97)	Road traffic, Wales	1117	Road traffic
1058 (W.98)	Road traffic, Wales	1118	Road traffic
1059 (W.99)	Road traffic, Wales	1119	Road traffic
1060 (W.100)	Road traffic, Wales	1120	Capital gains tax
1061 (W.101)	Road traffic, Wales		Corporation tax
1062 (W.102)	Road traffic, Wales	1121	Cancelled
1063	Education, England and Wales	1122	Road traffic
1064 (W.103)	Road traffic, Wales	1123	Road traffic
1065 (W.104)	Road traffic, Wales	1124	Road traffic
1066 (W.105) (C.46)	Education, Wales	1125	Road traffic
1067 (W.106)	Water resources, Wales	1126	Road traffic

1127	Road traffic	1186 (W.115)	Plant health, Wales
1128	Road traffic	1187	Local government, England
1129 (L.23)	Representation of the people	1188	Local government, England
	Supreme Courts of England and Wales	1189	Local government, England
1130	Consumer protection	1190	Local government, England
1131	Electricity	1191	Civil aviation
	Gas	1192	Civil aviation
1132 (W.111)	Education, Wales	1193	Civil aviation
1133 (W.112)	Education, Wales	1194	Civil aviation
1134 (C.47)	Children and young persons	1195	Financial services and markets
	Family proceedings	1196	Civil aviation
1135	Road traffic	1197	Local government, England
1136 (W.113)	Road traffic, Wales	1198	Probation, England and Wales
1137 (W.114)	Road traffic, Wales	1199	Cancelled
1138	Road traffic	1200 (W.116)	Road traffic, Wales
1139	Terms and conditions of employment	1201 (W.117)	Road traffic, Wales
1140	Civil aviation	1202 (W.118)	Road traffic, Wales
1141	Civil aviation	1203 (W.119)	Road traffic, Wales
1142	Civil aviation	1204 (W.120)	Road traffic, Wales
1143	Civil aviation	1205 (W.121)	Road traffic, Wales
1144	Civil aviation	1206 (W.122)	Road traffic, Wales
1145	Road traffic	1207 (W.123)	Road traffic, Wales
1146	Public service pensions, England and Wales	1208 (W.124)	Road traffic, Wales
1147	Road traffic	1209 (W.125)	Road traffic, Wales
1148	Road traffic	1210 (W.126)	Road traffic, Wales
1149	Road traffic	1211 (W.127)	Road traffic, Wales
1150	Road traffic	1212 (W.128)	Education, Wales
1151	Road traffic	1213	Road traffic
1152	Road traffic	1214	Road traffic
1153	Road traffic	1215	Road traffic
1154	Road traffic	1216	Road traffic
1155	Road traffic	1217	Road traffic
1156	Road traffic	1218	Road traffic
1157	Road traffic	1219	Road traffic
1158	Road traffic	1220	Road traffic
1159	Road traffic	1221	Road traffic
1160	Road traffic	1222	Road traffic
1161	Road traffic	1223	Road traffic
1162	Road traffic	1224	Road traffic
1163	Road traffic	1225	Road traffic
1164	Road traffic	1226 (C.48)	Criminal law, England and Wales
1165	Road traffic	1227	Road traffic
1166	Road traffic	1228	Road traffic
1167	Road traffic	1229	Criminal law, England and Wales
1168	Road traffic	1230	Social security
1169	Road traffic	1231	Social security
1170	Road traffic		Tax credits
1171	Road traffic	1232	Cancelled
1172	Road traffic	1233 (L.24)	Senior courts of England and Wales
1173	Road traffic		County court, England and Wales
1174	Road traffic	1234	Representation of the people, England and Wales
1175	Road traffic		
1176	Road traffic	1235	Civil aviation
1177	Road traffic	1236 (C.49)	Consultant lobbying
1178	Road traffic		Representation of the people
1179	Road traffic	1237	Police, England and Wales
1180	Transport, England and Wales	1238	Cancelled
1181	Urban development, England	1239	Arms and ammunition
1182	National debt	1240	Animals, England
1183	Immigration	1241 (W.129) (C.50)	Housing, Wales
1184	Broadcasting	1242	Road traffic
1185	Legal services, England and Wales	1243	Road traffic
		1244	Road traffic

1245	Road traffic	1299	Road traffic
1246	Road traffic	1300	Road traffic
1247	Road traffic	1301	Road traffic
1248	Road traffic	1302	Road traffic
1249 (W.130)	Education, Wales	1303	Road traffic
1250	Representation of the people, Scotland	1304	Civil aviation
1251 (W.131)	Road traffic, Wales	1305	Road traffic
1252	Licences and licensing, England and Wales	1306	Road traffic
1253	Offshore installations	1307	Road traffic
1254	Road traffic	1308	Local government, England
1255	Road traffic	1309	Environmental protection
1256	Road traffic	1310	Road traffic
1257	Education, England	1311	Road traffic
1258	Animals, England	1312	Road traffic
1259	Road traffic	1313	Financial services and markets
1260	Road traffic	1314 (W.134)	Education, Wales
1261	Financial services and markets	1315	Road traffic
1262	Immigration	1316	Road traffic
1263 (C.51)	Family law	1317 (W.135)	Road traffic, Wales
1264	Aggregates levy	1318	Climate change levy
	Climate change levy	1319	Road traffic
	Customs and excise	1320	Road traffic
	Financial services	1321	Road traffic
	Insurance premium tax	1322	Road traffic
	Landfill tax	1323	Road traffic
	Value added tax	1324	Road traffic
1265	Road traffic	1325	Road traffic
1266	Road traffic	1326 (W.136)	Road traffic, Wales
1267	Road traffic	1327	National debt
1268	Road traffic	1328	Highways, England
1269	Road traffic	1329	Highways, England
1270	Health care and associated professions	1330	Highways, England
1271	Road traffic	1331	Highways, England
1272	Health care and associated professions	1332	Town and country planning, England and Wales
1273	Health care and associated professions		Transport
1274	Dangerous drugs	1333	Town and country planning, England and Wales
1275	Dangerous drugs	1334	Local government, England
1276	Health care and associated professions	1335	Local government, England
1277	Harbours, docks, piers and ferries	1336	Road traffic
1278	Civil aviation	1337	Highways, England
1279	Road traffic	1338	Road traffic
1280	Road traffic	1339	Road traffic
1281	Civil aviation	1340 (W.137)	Road traffic, Wales
1282	Road traffic	1341 (W.138)	Road traffic, Wales
1283	Income tax	1342	Road traffic
	Social security	1343	Road traffic
1284	Road traffic	1344	Road traffic
1285	Road traffic	1345	Road traffic
1286	Road traffic	1346	Road traffic
1287 (C.52)	Criminal law, England and Wales	1347	Road traffic
	Defence	1348	Road traffic
1288 (W.132)	Road traffic, Wales	1349	Road traffic
1289 (W.133)	Road traffic, Wales	1350	Road traffic
1290	Energy conservation	1351	Road traffic
1291 (C.53)	Criminal law, England and Wales	1352	Dangerous drugs
1292	Financial services and markets	1353	Territorial sea
1293	Electricity	1354	Education, England
	Gas		Children and young persons, England
1294	Licences and licensing, England	1355	Merchant shipping
1295	Electronic communications	1356	Taxes
1296	Road traffic	1357	Capital gains tax
1297	Road traffic		
1298	Road traffic		

	Corporation tax	1406	Road traffic
	Income tax	1407	Road traffic
	Inheritance tax	1408	Road traffic
	Value added tax	1409	Road traffic
1358	Taxes	1410	Road traffic
1359	Capital gains tax	1411	Road traffic
	Corporation tax	1412	Road traffic
	Income tax	1413	Energy
	Inheritance tax	1414	Cancelled
	Value added tax	1415	Cancelled
1360	Capital gains tax	1416	Cancelled
	Corporation tax	1417	Cancelled
	Income tax	1418	Cancelled
	Inheritance tax	1419	Cancelled
	Value added tax	1420	Cancelled
1361	Merchant shipping	1421	Cancelled
1362	European Union	1422	Cancelled
1363	Cancelled	1423	Family law
1364	Transport, England	1424	Cancelled
1365	Criminal law, England and Wales	1425	Road traffic
1366	International development	1426	Road traffic
1367	Town and country planning, England	1427	Road traffic
	Transport, England	1428	Road traffic
1368	Overseas territories	1429	Road traffic
1369	Ecclesiastical law, England	1430	Road traffic
1370 (W.139)	Rating and valuation, Wales	1431	Highways, England
1371	Licences and licensing, Wales	1432	Road traffic
1372	Copyright	1433	Road traffic
	Rights in performances	1434	Road traffic
1373 (W.140)	Road traffic, Wales	1435	Road traffic
1374	Cancelled	1436	Road traffic
1375	Local government, England	1437	Road traffic
1376	Dangerous drugs, England and Wales	1438	Merchant shipping
	Dangerous drugs, Scotland	1439	Road traffic
1377	Dangerous drugs	1440	Road traffic
1378	Housing, England	1441	Road traffic
1379	Road traffic	1442	Road traffic
1380	Road traffic	1443	Road traffic
1381	Road traffic	1444 (C.54)	Defence
1382	Town and country planning, England	1445	Cancelled
1383	Criminal law, England and Wales	1446	Financial services and markets
1384	Copyright	1447 (C.55)	Financial services and markets
	Rights in performances	1448	Financial services and markets
1385	Copyright	1449	Income tax
1386	Family law	1450	Income tax
1387	National Health Service, England		Capital gains tax
1388 (W.141)	Road traffic, Wales	1451	Immigration
1389	Legal aid and advice, England and Wales	1452 (C.56)	Social security
1390	National Health Service, England	1453	Child trust funds
1391	Energy	1454 (C.57)	National Health Service, England
1392	Road traffic	1455 (W.142)	Road traffic, Wales
1393	Road traffic	1456	Social security
1394	Road traffic	1457	Libraries
1395	Road traffic	1458	Value added tax
1396	Road traffic	1459	Human tissue
1397	Road traffic	1460 (C.58)	Energy
1398	Terms and conditions of employment	1461 (C.59)	Energy
1399	Road traffic	1462 (W.143)	Education, Wales
1400	Road traffic	1463 (W.144)	Plant health, Wales
1401	Road traffic	1464 (W.145)	Education, Wales
1402	Road traffic	1465	British nationality
1403	Energy	1466	Road traffic
1404	Road traffic		
1405	Road traffic		

1467	Road traffic	1528	Civil aviation
1468	Road traffic	1529	Road traffic
1469	Road traffic	1530	Education, England
1470	Road traffic	1531 (C.60)	Town and country planning, England
1471	Road traffic	1532	Town and country planning, England
1472	Road traffic	1533	Cancelled
1473	Road traffic	1534	National Health Service, England
1474	Road traffic	1535 (W.157)	Road traffic, Wales
1475	Road traffic	1536	Road traffic
1476	Road traffic	1537	Road traffic
1477	Road traffic	1538	Road traffic
1478	Road traffic	1539	Road traffic
1479	Road traffic	1540	Road traffic
1480	Road traffic	1541	Road traffic
1481	Road traffic	1542	Road traffic
1482	Road traffic	1543	Road traffic
1483	Road traffic	1544	Road traffic
1484	Electronic communications	1545	Road traffic
1485	Road traffic	1546	Road traffic
1486	Road traffic	1547	Road traffic
1487	Road traffic	1548	Road traffic
1488	Road traffic	1549 (W.158)	Road traffic, Wales
1489	Road traffic	1550 (W.159)	Road traffic, Wales
1490	Road traffic	1551	Cancelled
1491 (W.146)	Road traffic, Wales	1552	Road traffic
1492	Children and young persons, England	1553	Road traffic
1493 (W.147)	Road traffic, Wales	1554	Road traffic
1494	Road traffic	1555	Civil aviation
1495	Civil aviation	1556	Children and young persons, England
1496	Road traffic	1557	Companies
1497	Value added tax	1558	Civil aviation
1498 (W.148)	Road traffic, Wales	1559	Constitutional law Devolution, Scotland
1499 (W.149)	Road traffic, Wales	1560	Education, England Children and young persons, England
1500 (W.150)	Road traffic, Wales		
1501 (W.151)	Road traffic, Wales	1561	Cinema and films
1502 (W.152)	Road traffic, Wales	1562	Legal aid and advice, England and Wales
1503 (W.153)	Road traffic, Wales	1563	Children and young persons, England Social care, England
1504 (W.154)	Road traffic, Wales		
1505 (L.25)	Tribunals and inquiries	1564	Road traffic
1506	Taxes	1565	Road traffic
1507	Education, England	1566	Road traffic
1508	Industrial development	1567	Road traffic
1509	Fuel and electricity control	1568	Road traffic
1510	Betting, gaming and lotteries	1569	Road traffic
1511	Social security Tax credits	1570	Road traffic
		1571	Road traffic
1512	Merchant shipping	1572	Road traffic
1513	Immigration	1573	Road traffic
1514 (W.155)	Local government, Wales	1574 (W.160)	Road traffic, Wales
1515 (W.156)	Road traffic, Wales	1575	Road traffic
1516	Road traffic	1576	Cancelled
1517	Road traffic	1577	Civil aviation
1518	Road traffic	1578	Civil aviation
1519	Road traffic	1579	Civil aviation
1520	Road traffic	1580	Civil aviation
1521	Road traffic	1581	Road traffic
1522	Road traffic	1582	Road traffic
1523	Road traffic	1583 (C.61)	Social security
1524	Road traffic	1584	Road traffic
1525	Road traffic	1585	Road traffic
1526	Road traffic	1586	Road traffic
1527	Road traffic	1587	Road traffic

Number	Subject
1588	Road traffic
1589	Road traffic
1590	Road traffic
1591	Road traffic
1592	Road traffic
1593	Cancelled
1594	Cancelled
1595 (W.161)	Road traffic, Wales
1596 (C.62)	Local government, England and Wales
1597	National Health Service, England
1598	Road traffic
1599	Infrastructure planning
1600 (W.162)	Road traffic, Wales
1601	Electricity
1602	Companies
1603	Education, England
1604	Transport and works, England
	Transport, England
1605 (W.163) (C.63)	Education, Wales
1606 (W.164) (C.64)	Social care, Wales
	Children and young persons, Wales
1607	National Health Service, England and Wales
1608	Disclosure of information, England and Wales
1609 (W.165)	Education, Wales
1610 (L.26)	Senior courts of England and Wales
	Magistrates' courts, England and Wales
1611	National Health Service, England
1612	Prevention and suppression of terrorism
1613	Merchant shipping
1614	Merchant shipping
1615	Merchant shipping
1616	Merchant shipping
1617	Road traffic
1618	Road traffic
1619	Road traffic
1620	Cancelled
1621	Family law
1622 (W.166)	National Health Service, Wales
1623	Social security
1624	Prevention and suppression of terrorism
1625	National Health Service, England
1626	Social security
1627	Local government, England and Wales
1628	Local government, England and Wales
1629	Local government, England and Wales
1630	Road traffic
1631	Road traffic
1632	Road traffic
1633	Road traffic
1634	Road traffic
1635 (C.65)	Family law
1636 (C.66)	Pensions
1637	Health and safety
1638	Health and safety
1639	Health and safety
1640 (C.67)	Terms and conditions of employment
1641	Betting, gaming and lotteries, England and Wales
	Betting, gaming and lotteries, Scotland
1642	Road traffic
1643	Energy
1644	Road traffic
1645	Road traffic
1646	Road traffic
1647	Road traffic
1648	Electricity
	Gas
1649 (W.167)	Road traffic, Wales
1650 (W.168)	Road traffic, Wales
1651	Criminal law, England and Wales
1652	Education, England
1653	Road traffic
1654	Road traffic
1655	Road traffic
1656	Road traffic
1657	Civil aviation
1658	Road traffic
1659 (C.68)	Libraries
1660	Registration of births, deaths, marriages, etc., England and Wales
1661 (C.69)	Social security
1662 (C.70)	Marriage
1663	Health and safety
1664	Pensions
1665	Terms and conditions of employment
1666	Highways, England
1667	Social security
1668	Road traffic
1669	Road traffic
1670	Road traffic
1671	Road traffic
1672	Road traffic
1673	Road traffic
1674	Road traffic
1675	Betting, gaming and lotteries
1676 (W.169)	Road traffic, Wales
1677 (W.170)	Road traffic, Wales
1678	Road traffic
1679	Road traffic
1680	Road traffic
1681	Road traffic
1682	Road traffic
1683 (C.71)	Pensions
1684	Fees and charges
1685	Education, England
1686	Petroleum
1687	Income tax
	Corporation tax
1688	Road traffic
1689	Road traffic
1690	Road traffic
1691	Road traffic
1692	Road traffic
1693	Road traffic
1694	Road traffic
1695	Road traffic
1696	Road traffic
1697	Road traffic
1698	Road traffic
1699	Road traffic
1700	Road traffic
1701	Road traffic
1702	Road traffic
1703	Road traffic
1704	National Crime Agency
1705	Children and young persons, England

1706 (W.171)(C.72)	Education, Wales
1707	Rehabilitation of offenders, England and Wales
1708	Road traffic, England
1709	Electricity
1710	Local government, England and Wales
1711	Pensions
1712 (W.172)	Education, Wales
1713 (W.173)	Local government, Wales
1714 (C.73)	National Health Service, England and Wales
	Public health, England and Wales
	Social care, England and Wales
1715 (C.74)	Intellectual property
1716	Road traffic
1717	Road traffic
1718	Road traffic
1719	Road traffic
1720	Road traffic
1721	Road traffic
1722	Road traffic
1723	Road traffic
1724	Road traffic
1725	Road traffic
1726	Road traffic
1727	Road traffic
1728	Road traffic
1729	Road traffic
1730	Road traffic
1731	Road traffic
1732	Road traffic
1733	Road traffic
1734	Road traffic
1735	Road traffic
1736	Road traffic
1737	Road traffic
1738	Road traffic
1739	Road traffic
1740	Financial services and markets
1741	Road traffic
1742	Road traffic
1743	Road traffic
1744	Road traffic
1745	Road traffic
1746	Road traffic
1747	Road traffic
1748	Road traffic
1749	Road traffic
1750	Road traffic
1751 (C.75)	Defence
1752	Road traffic
1753	Road traffic
1754	Road traffic
1755	Road traffic
1756	Road traffic
1757	Road traffic
1758	Road traffic
1759 (W.174)	Plant health, Wales
1760 (W.175)	Mobile homes, Wales
1761 (W.176)	Town and country planning, Wales
1762 (W.177)	Mobile homes, Wales
1763 (W.178)	Mobile homes, Wales
1764 (W.179)	Mobile homes, Wales
1765	Road traffic
1766	Education, England
1767 (W.180)	Road traffic, Wales
1768	Cancelled
1769 (W.181)(C.76)	Town and country planning, Wales
1770 (W.182)	Town and country planning, Wales
1771	Environmental protection
1772 (W.183)	Town and country planning, Wales
1773	Family proceedings
	Civil proceedings
	Family court, England and Wales
	County court, England and Wales
1774	Road traffic
1775	Road traffic
1776	Road traffic
1777 (C.77)	Criminal law, England and Wales
1778	Road traffic
1779 (W.184)	Road traffic, Wales
1780	Road traffic
1781	Road traffic
1782	Road traffic
1783	Road traffic
1784	Road traffic
1785	Road traffic
1786	Road traffic
1787	Criminal law, England and Wales
1788	National Health Service, England
	Public health, England
	Social care, England
1789	Civil partnership, England and Wales
1790	Registration of births, deaths, marriages, etc., England and Wales
1791	Registration of births, deaths, marriages, etc., England and Wales
1792 (W.185)	Plant health, Wales
1793 (W.186)(C.78)	Social care, Wales
1794 (W.187)	Social care, Wales
	Children and young persons, Wales
1795 (W.188)	Social care, Wales
	Children and young persons, Wales
1796	Infrastructure planning, England
1797	Housing, England
1798	Immigration
1799	Highways, England
1800	Cancelled
1801	Cancelled
1802	Civil aviation
1803	Representation of the people, Northern Ireland
1804	Northern Ireland
1805	Representation of the people
1806	Political parties
1807	Charities
	Income tax
	Capital gains tax
	Corporation tax
	Value added tax
	Inheritance tax
	Stamp duty
	Stamp duty land tax
	Stamp duty reserve tax
	Annual tax on enveloped dwellings
1808	Representation of the people, Northern Ireland
1809 (C.83)	Political parties, Northern Ireland
1810 (C.79)	Presumption of death

1811	Merchant shipping
1812	Cancelled
1813	Cancelled
1814	Channel Tunnel
1815	Co-operative societies
	Community benefit societies
	Credit unions
1816	Road traffic
1817	Civil aviation
1818	Legal Services Commission, England and Wales
1819 (C.80)	Financial services and markets
1820 (C.81)	Immigration
1821	Transport and works, England
	Transport, England
1822	Co-operative societies
	Community benefit societies
	Credit unions
1823 (C.82)	Water, England and Wales
	Water resources, England and Wales
1824	Legal aid and advice, England and Wales
1825	Electronic communications
1826	Criminal law
1827	Criminal law
1828	Financial services and markets
1829	Housing, England
1830	Financial services and markets
1831	Financial services and markets
1832	Financial services and markets
1833	Seeds, England
	Seeds, Scotland
1834 (L.27)	Senior courts of England and Wales
	County court, England and Wales
1835 (W.189)	Agriculture, Wales
1836 (W.190)	Education, Wales
1837	Highways, England
1838	Prevention and suppression of terrorism
1839 (W.191)	Road traffic, Wales
1840	Civil aviation
1841	Road traffic
1842	Income tax
1843	Income tax
1844	Road traffic
1845	Road traffic
1846	Road traffic
1847 (C.84)	Financial services and markets
1848	Tax credits
1849	Immigration
1850	Financial services and markets
1851	Road traffic
1852	Road traffic
1853	Road traffic
1854	Road traffic
1855	Food, England
1856	Road traffic
1857	Highways, England
1858 (W.192)	Food, Wales
1859 (W.193)	Road traffic, Wales
1860 (C.85)	Local government, England
1861	Cancelled
1862	Road traffic
1863	Road traffic
1864	Road traffic
1865	Housing, England
1866	Education, England
1867	Education, England
1868	Income tax
	Corporation tax
1869	Income tax
	Corporation tax
1870	Representation of the people
1871	Highways, England
1872	Legal services, England and Wales
1873	Infrastructure planning
1874	Capital gains tax
	Corporation tax
	Income tax
1875	Capital gains tax
	Corporation tax
	Income tax
	Petroleum revenue tax
1876	Capital gains tax
	Corporation tax
	Income tax
1877	Education, England
	Children and young persons, England
1878	Medicines
1879	Capital gains tax
	Corporation tax
	Income tax
1880	Representation of the people, Northern Ireland
1881	Capital gains tax
	Corporation tax
	Income tax
1882	Defence
1883	European Union
1884	European Union
1885	European Union
1886	European Union
1887	Health care and associated professions
1888	Civil aviation
1889	European Union
1890	European Union
1891	International immunities and privileges
1892	Constitutional law
	Devolution, Scotland
	Employment
1893	Proceeds of crime, England and Wales
	Proceeds of crime, Northern Ireland
1894	Animals
1895 (W.194)	Education, Wales
1896	Customs
1897	Legal services, England and Wales
1898	Legal services, England and Wales
1899	Justices of the Peace, England and Wales
1900	Tribunals and inquiries, England and Wales
1901	Tribunals and inquiries
1902	Agriculture
1903	National Health Service, England
1904	National Health Service, England
1905	National Health Service, England
1906	Local government, England
1907	Local government, England
1908	Local government, England
1909	Local government, England
1910	Local government, England

1911	Local government, England	1968	Road traffic
1912 (C.86)	Public service pensions	1969	Road traffic
1913	Social security	1970	Road traffic
1914 (W.195)	Road traffic, Wales	1971	Cancelled
1915	Housing, England	1972	Road traffic
1916 (C.87)	Extradition	1973	Civil aviation
	Police	1974	Road traffic
1917	Children and young persons, England	1975	Environmental protection, England and Wales
1918	Highways, England	1976	Immigration
1919	Judicial appointments and discipline	1977	Education, England
1920	Children and young persons, England	1978	Road traffic
1921	Children and young persons, England	1979	Road traffic
1922	Children and young persons, England	1980	Road traffic
1923 (C.88)	Social security	1981	Health care and associated professions
1924	Agriculture	1982	Road traffic
	Public bodies	1983	Road traffic
1925	Legal services, England and Wales	1984	Road traffic
1926	Pensions	1985	Road traffic
1927	Road traffic	1986	Coal industry
1928	Income tax	1987	Road traffic
1929	Income tax	1988	Road traffic
1930	Excise	1989	Road traffic
1931	Income tax	1990	Road traffic
	Corporation tax	1991	Road traffic
	Capital gains tax	1992	Road traffic
1932	Stamp duty reserve tax	1993	Road traffic
1933	Tax credits	1994	Road traffic
1934	Road traffic	1995 (W.197)	Road traffic, Wales
1935	Cancelled	1996 (W.198)	Education, Wales
1936	Cancelled	1997	Patents
1937	Provision of services	1998 (W.199)	Education, Wales
1938	Civil aviation	1999 (W.200)	Education, Wales
1939	Civil aviation	2000 (W.201)	Road traffic, Wales
1940	Countryside, England	2001	Road traffic
1941	Education, England	2002	Road traffic
1942	Health and safety	2003	Road traffic
1943 (C.89)	Immigration	2004	Road traffic
1944 (W.196)	Road traffic, Wales	2005	Road traffic
1945	Libraries	2006	Education, England
1946	Road traffic	2007	Merchant shipping
1947	Road traffic	2008	Road traffic
1948	Road traffic	2009	Local government, England and Wales
1949	Road traffic		Companies
1950	Road traffic		Auditors
1951	Road traffic	2010	Electricity
1952	Road traffic	2011	Electricity
1953	Road traffic	2012	Electricity
1954	Pensions	2013	Electricity
1955	Road traffic	2014	Electricity
1956	Road traffic	2015 (W.202)	National Health Service, Wales
1957	Children and young persons, England	2016	Road traffic
1958	Corporation tax	2017	Road traffic
1959	Education, England	2018 (W.203)	Road traffic, Wales
1960	Banks and banking	2019	Road traffic
1961 (C.90)	Children and young persons, England and Wales	2020	Energy conservation
		2021	Road traffic
1962 (C.91)	Corporation tax	2022	Road traffic
1963	Police, England and Wales	2023	Road traffic
1964	Public service pensions	2024	Road traffic
1965 (C.92)	Public service pensions	2025	Road traffic
1966	Acquisition of land, England	2026	Town and country planning, England
	Compensation	2027	Transport and works, England
1967	Road traffic		Transport, England

2028	Road traffic	2089	Road traffic
2029	Road traffic	2090	Road traffic
2030 (W.204)	Road traffic, Wales	2091	Road traffic
2031	Road traffic	2092	Road traffic
2032	Road traffic	2093	Road traffic
2033	Road traffic	2094	Road traffic
2034	Road traffic	2095	Local government, England
2035	Road traffic	2096	Education, England
2036	Road traffic	2097	Video recordings
2037	Road traffic	2098	Road traffic
2038	Immigration	2099	Road traffic
2039 (C.93)	Family provision	2100	Road traffic
2040	Judicial appointments and discipline	2101	Road traffic
2041	Road traffic	2102	Road traffic
2042	Electronic communications	2103	Education, England
2043	Electricity	2104	Road traffic
2044 (L.28)	Senior courts of England and Wales County court, England and Wales	2105	Road traffic
		2106	Road traffic
2045	Education, England and Wales	2107	Road traffic
2046	Road traffic	2108	Road traffic
2047	Road traffic	2109	Road traffic
2048	Road traffic	2110	Road traffic
2049	Road traffic	2111	Road traffic
2050	Road traffic	2112	Terms and conditions of employment
2051	Road traffic	2113	Ecclesiastical law, England
2052	Road traffic	2114	Road traffic
2053	Road traffic	2115	Road traffic
2054	Criminal law	2116	Road traffic
2055	Road traffic	2117	Road traffic
2056	Road traffic	2118	Public passenger transport
2057	Cancelled	2119	Road traffic
2058	Road traffic	2120	Criminal law, England and Wales
2059 (L.29)	County court, England and Wales	2121 (W.207) (C.95)	Local government, Wales
2060	Local government, England	2122	Police, England and Wales
2061	Road traffic	2123	Public health, England
2062	Road traffic	2124 (W.208)	Animals, Wales
2063	Road traffic	2125 (C.96)	Criminal law, England and Wales Police, England and Wales Police, Northern Ireland
2064	Road traffic		
2065 (W.205)	Road traffic, Wales		
2066	Road traffic	2126 (W.209)	Education, Wales
2067	Education, England	2127	Highways, England
2068	Education, England	2128 (L.30)	Tribunals and inquiries
2069 (C.94)	Intellectual property	2129	Road traffic
2070	Cancelled	2130	Highways, England
2071 (W.206)	Education, Wales	2131	Road traffic
2072	Ecclesiastical law, England	2132	Road traffic
2073	Road traffic	2133	Road traffic
2074	Road traffic	2134	Road traffic
2075	Road traffic	2135	Road traffic
2076	Road traffic	2136	Road traffic
2077	Ecclesiastical law, England	2137	Road traffic
2078	Road traffic	2138	Road traffic
2079	Road traffic	2139	Road traffic
2080	Banks and banking	2140	Road traffic
2081	Dangerous drugs	2141	Highways, England
2082	Road traffic	2142	Road traffic
2083	Ecclesiastical law, England	2143	Road traffic
2084	Road traffic	2144 (W.210)	Road traffic, Wales
2085	Road traffic	2145	Road traffic
2086	Road traffic	2146	Road traffic
2087	Cancelled	2147	Children and young persons, England
2088	Road traffic	2148	Road traffic

2149	Road traffic
2150	Road traffic
2151	Road traffic
2152	Road traffic
2153	Road traffic
2154	Road traffic
2155	Road traffic
2156	Road traffic
2157	Road traffic
2158	Education, England
2159	Road traffic
2160	Road traffic
2161	Road traffic
2162 (W.211) (C.97)	Education, Wales
2163	Road traffic
2164	Road traffic
2165	Road traffic
2166	Road traffic
2167	Road traffic
2168	Road traffic
2169	Prisons, England and Wales
	Young offender institutions, England and Wales
2170	Road traffic
2171	Road traffic
2172	Local government, England
2173	Road traffic
2174	Road traffic
2175	Road traffic
2176	Road traffic
2177	Road traffic
2178 (W.212)	Transport, Wales
2179	Education, England
2180	Road traffic
2181	Road traffic
2182	Road traffic
2183	Road traffic
2184	Road traffic
2185	Road traffic
2186	Road traffic
2187	Road traffic
2188	Road traffic
2189	Road traffic
2190	Road traffic
2191	Road traffic
2192	Road traffic
2193	Road traffic
2194	Road traffic
2195	Road traffic
2196	Road traffic
2197	Road traffic
2198	Road traffic
2199	Road traffic
2200	Road traffic
2201	Road traffic
2202	Road traffic
2203	Road traffic
2204	Road traffic
2205	Road traffic
2206	Civil aviation
2207	Road traffic
2208	Road traffic
2209	Road traffic
2210	Prevention and suppression of terrorism
2211	Road traffic
2212 (W.213)	Road traffic, Wales
2213	Road traffic
2214	Road traffic
2215	Road traffic
2216	Road traffic
2217	Road traffic
2218	Road traffic
2219	Road traffic
2220	Road traffic
2221	Road traffic
2222	Road traffic
2223	Road traffic
2224	Road traffic
2225 (W.214)	Education, Wales
2226	Road traffic
2227	Road traffic
2228 (C.98)	Corporation tax
2229	Road traffic
2230	Road traffic
2231	Road traffic
2232 (W.215)	Road traffic, Wales
2233 (W.216)	Road traffic, Wales
2234	Government resources and accounts
2235 (W.217)	Education, Wales
2236 (W.218)	Education, Wales
2237 (W.219)	Education, Wales
2238 (W.220)	Education, Wales
2239 (W.221)	Road traffic, Wales
2240 (W.222)	Road traffic, Wales
2241	Road traffic
2242	Road traffic
2243	Road traffic
2244	Road traffic
2245	Road traffic
2246	Road traffic
2247 (W.223)	Road traffic, Wales
2248	Road traffic
2249 (W.224)	Road traffic, Wales
2250	Road traffic
2251	Road traffic
2252	Ecclesiastical law, England
2253	Road traffic
2254	Education, England
2255	Road traffic
2256	Road traffic
2257	Excise
2258	Road traffic
2259	Road traffic
2260	Offshore installations
2261	Road traffic
2262	Road traffic
2263	Criminal law, England and Wales
2264	Road traffic
2265	Road traffic
2266	Road traffic
2267	Road traffic
2268	Road traffic
2269	Infrastructure planning, England
2270	Education, England
2271	Road traffic

2272	Road traffic	2334	Road traffic
2273	Road traffic	2335	Road traffic
2274	Road traffic	2336	Pensions
2275	Road traffic	2337	Animals, England
2276	Road traffic	2338	Animals, England
2277	Road traffic	2339	Customs
2278	Road traffic	2340	Prisons, England and Wales
2279	Road traffic	2341	Licences and licensing, England and Wales
2280	Road traffic	2342	Education, England
2281 (W.225)	Road traffic, Wales	2343	Road traffic
2282	Road traffic	2344	Road traffic
2283	Road traffic	2345	Road traffic
2284	Road traffic	2346	Road traffic
2285	Road traffic	2347	Road traffic
2286	Road traffic	2348	Road traffic
2287	Road traffic	2349	Road traffic
2288	Road traffic	2350	Road traffic
2289	Road traffic	2351	Road traffic
2290	Road traffic	2352	Road traffic
2291 (W.226)	National Health Service, Wales	2353	Road traffic
2292	Road traffic	2354	Road traffic
2293	Road traffic	2355	Cancelled
2294	Road traffic	2356	Copyright
2295	Education, England		Rights in performances
2296	Road traffic	2357	Customs
2297	Road traffic	2358	Road traffic
2298	Road traffic	2359	Housing, England
2299	Road traffic	2360	Road traffic
2300	Road traffic	2361	Copyright
2301	Road traffic		Rights in performances
2302	Road traffic	2362	Building and buildings, England and Wales
2303 (W.227)	Food, Wales	2363	Water resources, England
2304	Road traffic	2364	Value added tax
2305	Road traffic	2365 (W.229)	Education, Wales
2306	Road traffic	2366	Clean air, England
2307	Road traffic	2367 (W.230)	Agriculture, Wales
2308 (W.228)	Road traffic, Wales	2368 (W.231)	Plant health, Wales
2309	Social security	2369	Consumer credit
2310	Road traffic	2370 (C.101)	Defence
2311	Road traffic	2371	Financial services and markets
2312	Road traffic	2372	Police, England and Wales
2313	Road traffic	2373	Police, England and Wales
2314	Road traffic	2374	Education, England
2315	Road traffic	2375	Cancelled
2316	Road traffic	2376	Police, England and Wales
2317	Road traffic	2377 (C.102)	Pensions
2318	Road traffic	2378	Consumer protection
2319	Children and young persons, England		Electricity
2320	Education, England		Gas
2321 (C.99)	Social security	2379 (C.103)	Education, England
2322	Road traffic	2380 (C.104)	Education, England
2323	Road traffic	2381	Infrastructure planning
2324	Road traffic	2382	Companies
2325	Road traffic	2383	Animals, England
2326	Road traffic	2384	Infrastructure planning
2327	Road traffic	2385	Plant health, England
2328	Pensions	2386	Registration of births, deaths, marriages, etc., England and Wales
2329	Intellectual property	2387	Registration of births, deaths, marriages etc., England and Wales
2330 (C.100)	Intellectual property	2388	Electricity
2331	Road traffic	2389	Civil aviation
2332	Road traffic	2390	Road traffic
2333	Road traffic		

2391	Civil aviation	2450	Civil aviation
2392	Civil aviation	2451	Road traffic
2393	Civil aviation	2452	Road traffic
2394	Taxes	2453	Road traffic
2395 (C.105)	Income tax	2454 (C.108)	Extradition, England and Wales
2396	Income tax		Housing, England
2397	Social security	2455	Road traffic
2398	Immigration	2456	International development
	Nationality	2457	International development
2399	Cancelled	2458 (C.109)	Financial services and markets
2400	Designs		Competition
2401	Patents	2459	National Health Service, England
2402	Police, England and Wales	2460	Highways, England
2403	Police, England and Wales	2461 (C.110)	Income tax
2404	Clean air, England		Capital gains tax
2405	Designs	2462	Highways, England
2406	Police, England and Wales	2463 (W.232)	Road traffic, Wales
2407	Children and young persons, England	2464 (W.233)	Road traffic, Wales
	Social care, England	2465 (W.234)	Road traffic, Wales
2408	Road traffic	2466 (W.235)	Road traffic, Wales
2409	Corporation tax	2467 (W.236)	Road traffic, Wales
2410	Defence	2468 (W.237)	Road traffic, Wales
2411	Patents	2469	Road traffic
2412	Road traffic	2470	Road traffic
2413	Road traffic	2471	Road traffic
2414	Road traffic	2472	Road traffic
2415	Road traffic	2473 (C.111)	National Health Service, England and Wales
2416	Road traffic		Public health, England and Wales
2417	Licences and licensing, England and Wales		Social care, England and Wales
2418	Terms and conditions of employment	2474 (W.238)	Road traffic, Wales
2419	Road traffic	2475	Immigration
2420	Plant health, England	2476	Road traffic
	Plant health, Scotland	2477	Road traffic
2421	Road traffic	2478	Road traffic
2422	Legal aid and advice, England and Wales	2479	Road traffic
2423	Road traffic	2480	Road traffic
2424	Road traffic	2481	Agricultural employment, England
2425	Road traffic		Landlord and tenant, England
2426	Road traffic		Terms and conditions of employment, England
2427	Road traffic	2482	Road traffic
2428	Road traffic	2483	Companies
2429	Road traffic	2484	Road traffic
2430	Value added tax	2485	Terms and conditions of employment
2431	Road traffic	2486	Civil aviation
2432	Road traffic	2487	Road traffic
2433	Road traffic	2488	Road traffic
2434	Infrastructure planning, England and Wales	2489	Road traffic
2435	Road traffic	2490	Road traffic
2436	Regulatory reform	2491 (W.239)	Road traffic, Wales
	National Health Service, England	2492 (W.240)	Road traffic, Wales
2437	Highways	2493 (W.241)	Road traffic, Wales
2438	Income tax	2494 (W.242)	Road traffic, Wales
2439 (C.106)	Northern Ireland	2495 (W.243)	Road traffic, Wales
2440	Licences and licensing, England and Wales	2496	Road traffic
2441	Infrastructure planning	2497	Road traffic
2442	Road traffic	2498	Road traffic
2443	Road traffic	2499	Road traffic
2444 (C.107)	Betting, gaming and lotteries	2500	Road traffic
2445	Criminal law	2501	Road traffic
2446	Road traffic	2502	Road traffic
2447	Road traffic	2503	Road traffic
2448	Representation of the people	2504	Road traffic
2449	Road traffic		

2505	Road traffic	2566	Road traffic
2506	Road traffic	2567	Road traffic
2507	Road traffic	2568 (W.249)	Road traffic, Wales
2508	Road traffic	2569	Road traffic
2509	Road traffic	2570	Road traffic
2510	Road traffic	2571	Road traffic
2511	Electricity	2572	Road traffic
2512	Road traffic	2573	Road traffic
2513	Road traffic	2574 (W.250)	Road traffic, Wales
2514	Road traffic	2575 (W.251)	Road traffic, Wales
2515	Road traffic	2576 (W.252)	Road traffic, Wales
2516	Road traffic	2577 (W.253)	Road traffic, Wales
2517	Road traffic	2578 (W.254)	Road traffic, Wales
2518	Road traffic	2579 (W.255)	Road traffic, Wales
2519	Road traffic	2580	Road traffic
2520	Civil aviation	2581	Road traffic
2521	Road traffic	2582	Road traffic
2522	Arms and ammunition, England and Wales	2583	Road traffic
	Arms and ammunition, Scotland	2584	Road traffic
2523	Sports grounds and sporting events, England and Wales	2585	Road traffic
		2586	Road traffic
2524	National Health Service, England	2587	Electricity
2525	Road traffic	2588	Copyright
2526	Road traffic	2589 (W.256) (C.112)	Highways, Wales
2527	Road traffic	2590 (C.113)	Environmental protection, England and Wales
2528	Road traffic		Housing, England and Wales
2529	Road traffic		Police, England and Wales
2530	Road traffic	2591	Environmental protection, England and Wales
2531	Road traffic	2592	Road traffic
2532	Road traffic	2593	Road traffic
2533	Road traffic	2594	Infrastructure planning, England
2534	Road traffic	2595	Road traffic
2535	Road traffic	2596	Road traffic
2536	Road traffic	2597	Road traffic
2537	Road traffic	2598	Road traffic
2538	Road traffic	2599	Road traffic
2539	Road traffic	2600	Road traffic
2540 (W.244)	Road traffic, Wales	2601	Road traffic
2541	Road traffic	2602	Road traffic
2542 (W.245)	Road traffic, Wales	2603 (W.257)	Housing, Wales
2543	Road traffic	2604 (L.31)	Tribunals and inquiries
2544 (W.246)	Road traffic, Wales	2605	Road traffic
2545	Road traffic	2606	Road traffic
2546	Road traffic	2607	Road traffic
2547	Road traffic	2608	Road traffic
2548	Road traffic	2609 (C.114)	Children and young persons
2549	Road traffic	2610	Road traffic
2550	Road traffic	2611	Road traffic
2551	Road traffic	2612	Road traffic
2552	Road traffic	2613 (C.115)	Northern Ireland
2553 (W.247)	Housing, Wales	2614	Road traffic
2554	Housing, England	2615	Road traffic
2555	Public bodies	2616	Road traffic
2556 (W.248)	Road traffic, Wales	2617	Road traffic
2557	Road traffic	2618	Road traffic
2558	Cancelled	2619	Road traffic
2559	Equality	2620	Road traffic
2560	Road traffic	2621	Road traffic
2561	Road traffic	2622	Road traffic
2562	Local government, England	2623	Road traffic
2563	Road traffic	2624	Road traffic
2564	Road traffic	2625	Road traffic
2565	Road traffic		

Number	Subject
2626	Road traffic
2627	Road traffic
2628	Road traffic
2629	Road traffic
2630	Road traffic
2631	Education, England
2632	Financial services and markets
2633	Road traffic
2634 (C.116)	Immigration
2635	Cancelled
2636	Road traffic
2637	Infrastructure planning, England
2638	Road traffic
2639	Road traffic
2640	Road traffic
2641	Road traffic
2642	Road traffic
2643	Road traffic
2644	Road traffic
2645	Road traffic
2646 (C.117)	Betting, gaming and lotteries
2647 (W.258)	Road traffic, Wales
2648 (W.259)	Road traffic, Wales
2649 (W.260)	Road traffic, Wales
2650	Education, England
2651	Education, England and Wales
2652	Public service pensions, England and Wales
	Education, England and Wales
2653 (W.261)	Council tax, Wales
2654	Road traffic
2655	Road traffic
2656 (W.262)	Road traffic, Wales
2657	Highways, England
2658 (W.263)	Road traffic, Wales
2659 (W.264)	Road traffic, Wales
2660	Disabled persons
	Transport
2661	Road traffic
2662	Road traffic
2663	Road traffic
2664	Road traffic
2665	Betting, gaming and lotteries
2666	Road traffic
2667	National Health Service, England
2668	Road traffic
2669	Civil aviation
2670	Mental health, England
	Social care, England
2671	Social care, England
2672	Social care, England
2673	Social care, England
2674	Road traffic
2675	Road traffic
2676	Road traffic
2677 (W.265)	Education, Wales
2678 (W.266)	Road traffic
2679	Water industry, England and Wales
2680	Local government, England
2681	Road traffic
2682	Road traffic
2683	Road traffic
2684	Road traffic
2685	Road traffic
2686	Road traffic
2687	Social security
2688	Road traffic
2689	Income tax
2690	Road traffic
2691 (S.2)	Cancelled
2692 (W.267)	Town and country planning, Wales
2693 (W.268)	Town and country planning, Wales
2694 (W.269)	Road traffic
2695	Road traffic
2696	Social care, England
	Children and young persons, England
2697	Education, England
2698	Road traffic
2699	Road traffic
2700	Road traffic
2701	Legal aid and advice, England and Wales
2702	Immigration
2703	Overseas territories
2704	Probation, England and Wales
2705	European Union
2706	International Criminal Court
2707	Overseas territories
2708	Ministers of the Crown
2709 (W.270)	Education, Wales
2710	Overseas territories
2711	United Nations
2712	Landlord and tenant, England
2713	Civil aviation
2714 (W.271)	Agriculture, Wales
	Food, Wales
2715	Electronic communications
2716 (W.272)	Highways, Wales
2717 (W.273)	Local government, Wales
2718 (W.274) (C.118)	Social care, Wales
2719	Education, England
2720	Harbours, docks, piers and ferries
2721	National Health Service, England
2722 (W.275)	Road traffic, Wales
2723	Road traffic
2724	Road traffic
2725 (W.276)	Road traffic, Wales
2726	Value added tax
2727 (C.119)	Pensions
2728	Road traffic
2729	Road traffic
2730	Road traffic
2731	Road traffic
2732	Road traffic
2733	Road traffic
2734	Road traffic
2735	Social security
2736	Road traffic
2737	Road traffic
2738	Road traffic
2739	Road traffic
2740	Road traffic
2741	Road traffic
2742	Road traffic
2743	Road traffic
2744	Road traffic
2745	Road traffic

2746	Social security	2799	Road traffic
2747	Constitutional law	2800	Road traffic
	Devolution, Scotland	2801	Road traffic
	Children and young persons	2802	Road traffic
2748	Agriculture, England	2803	Road traffic
	Food, England	2804	Road traffic
2749 (C.120)	Children and young persons	2805	Road traffic
	Family proceedings	2806	Road traffic
2750	Cancelled	2807	Competition
2751	Road traffic		Consumer protection
2752	Road traffic		Disclosure of information
2753 (S.3)	Constitutional law	2808	Road traffic
	Devolution, Scotland	2809	Road traffic
	Agriculture	2810	Road traffic
2754 (C.121)	Environmental protection, England and Wales	2811	Road traffic
	Housing, England and Wales	2812	Road traffic
	Police, England and Wales	2813 (W.285)	Road traffic, Wales
2755 (W.277)	Road traffic	2814	Road traffic
2756 (W.278)	Road traffic	2815	Road traffic
2757 (W.279)	Road traffic, Wales	2816	Immigration
2758	Road traffic	2817	Road traffic
2759	Road traffic	2818	Road traffic
2760	Road traffic	2819	Road traffic
2761	Immigration	2820	Road traffic
2762	Road traffic	2821	Social care, England
2763	Road traffic	2822	Social care, England
2764	Representation of the people	2823	Social care, England
2765	Education, England		National Health Service, England
2766	Road traffic	2824	Social care, England
2767	Road traffic	2825	Social care, England
2768	Immigration	2826	Road traffic
2769	Road traffic	2827	Social care, England
2770	Road traffic	2828	Social care, England
2771 (C.122)	Immigration	2829	Social care, England
2772	Road traffic	2830 (W.286) (C.130)	Housing, Wales
2773 (W.280)	Town and country planning, Wales	2831	Road traffic
2774	Road traffic	2832	Terms and conditions of employment
2775 (W.281)	Town and country planning, Wales	2833	Civil aviation
2776 (W.282)	Town and country planning, Wales		Disabled persons
2777 (W.283)	Town and country planning, Wales	2834	Road traffic
2778	Road traffic	2835	Road traffic
2779	Road traffic	2836 (W.287)	Road traffic, Wales
2780 (W.284)(C.123)	Town and country planning, Wales	2837 (W.288)	Road traffic, Wales
2781	Road traffic	2838 (W.289)	Road traffic, Wales
2782	Road traffic	2839	Social care
2783	Road traffic	2840	Social care, England
2784	Road traffic	2841	Rating and valuation, England
2785	Road traffic	2842	Cancelled
2786	Road traffic	2843	Social care
2787	Road traffic	2844	National Health Service, England
2788	Road traffic	2845	Local government, England and Wales
2789	Road traffic	2846	Infrastructure planning
2790	Road traffic	2847	Immigration
2791	Road traffic	2848	Public service pensions, England
2792	Road traffic	2849	National Health Service, England
2793	Transport	2850	Cancelled
2794	Road traffic	2851	Road traffic
2795	Road traffic	2852	Environmental protection, England
2796 (C.124)	Building societies	2853 (W.290)	Road traffic, Wales
	Friendly societies	2854	Social care, England
	Industrial and provident societies	2855 (W.291)	Road traffic, Wales
2797	Road traffic	2856	Insurance premium tax
2798	Road traffic	2857	Terms and conditions of employment

Number	Subject
2858	Value added tax
2859	Road traffic
2860	Road traffic
2861	Copyright
	Rights in performances
2862	Terms and conditions of employment
2863	Copyright
2864	Legal aid and advice, England and Wales
2865	Electricity
2866	Terms and conditions of employment
2867	Justices of the Peace, England and Wales
2868	Road traffic, England and Wales
2869	Road traffic
2870	Road traffic
2871	Social care, England
2872	Climate change levy
2873	Immigration
2874	Immigration
2875	Plant health, England
2876	Road traffic
2877	Road traffic
2878	Road traffic
2879	Financial services and markets
2880 (C.126)	Corporation tax
2881 (C.127)	Tax credits
	Social security
2882	Consumer protection
	Environmental protection
	Health and safety
2883	Human tissue
2884	Human fertilisation and embryology
2885	Food, England
2886	Education, England
2887	Social security
2888	Social security
2889	Social care, England
2890	Environmental protection
2891 (W.292)	Road traffic, Wales
2892 (W.293)	Road traffic, Wales
2893 (W.294)	Road traffic, Wales
2894 (W.295)	Agriculture, Wales
2895 (W.296)	Road traffic, Wales
2896	Income tax
2897	Electricity
	Gas
2898	Tribunals and inquiries, England and Wales
	Judicial appointments and discipline, England and Wales
2899	Highways, England
2900	Road traffic
2901	Cancelled
2902	Road traffic
2903	Road traffic
2904	Payment scheme
2905	Road traffic
2906	Road traffic
2907	Road traffic
2908	Consumer protection
2909	Road traffic
2910	Road traffic
2911	Road traffic
2912	Excise
2913	Road traffic
2914	Road traffic
2915	Road traffic
2916	Electronic communications
	Broadcasting
2917 (W.297)	Rating and valuation, Wales
2918	Constitutional law
	Devolution, Scotland
2919	Overseas territories
2920	Civil aviation
2921	Education, England
	Children and young persons, England
2922	Education, Wales
2923	Education, England
2924	Social security
	Tax credits
2925	Civil aviation
2926	Civil aviation
2927 (W.298)	Road traffic, Wales
2928	Immigration
2929	Terms and conditions of employment
	Social security
2930	Road traffic
2931	Criminal law, England and Wales
2932	Customs
2933	Harbours, docks, piers and ferries
2934	Terms and conditions of employment
2935	Infrastructure planning
	Harbours, docks, piers and ferries
2936	National Health Service, England
	Social care, England
	Public health, England
2937	Legal services, England and Wales
2938 (W.299)	Road traffic, Wales
2939	Pensions
2940	Road traffic
2941 (W.300)	Road traffic, Wales
2942	Stamp duty
	Stamp duty reserve tax
2943	Road traffic
2944	Road traffic
2945	Road traffic
2946	Road traffic
2947	Judgments
2948 (L.32)	Senior courts of England and Wales
	County courts, England and Wales
2949	Highways, England and Wales
2950	Infrastructure planning
2951	Road traffic
2952	Road traffic
2953	Road traffic
2954	Cancelled
2955	Road traffic
2956	Road traffic
2957	Road traffic
2958	Pensions
2959	Road traffic
2960	Road traffic
2961	Road traffic
2962	Road traffic
2963	Road traffic
2964	Road traffic
2965	Road traffic
2966	Road traffic

2967	Road traffic	3029	Road traffic
2968	Road traffic	3030	Road traffic
2969	Road traffic	3031	Road traffic
2970	Road traffic	3032	Road traffic
2971	Road traffic	3033 (W.302)	Local government, Wales
2972	Road traffic	3034	Road traffic
2973	Road traffic	3035	Road traffic
2974	Road traffic	3036	Road traffic
2975	Weights and measures	3037 (W.303)	Education, Wales
2976	Road traffic	3038	Commons, England
2977	Road traffic	3039	Road traffic
2978	Road traffic	3040	Road traffic
2979	Road traffic	3041	Road traffic
2980	Road traffic	3042	Road traffic
2981	Road traffic	3043	Road traffic
2982	Road traffic	3044	Road traffic
2983 (W.301)	Road traffic, Wales	3045	Road traffic
2984	Road traffic	3046	Road traffic
2985	Road traffic	3047	Road traffic
2986	Road traffic	3048	Road traffic
2987	Road traffic	3049	Road traffic
2988	Road traffic	3050	Terms and conditions of employment
2989	Road traffic	3051	Terms and conditions of employment
2990	Road traffic	3052	Terms and conditions of employment
2991	Road traffic	3053	Social security
2992	Road traffic	3054	Social security
2993	Road traffic	3055	International development
2994	Road traffic	3056	International development
2995	Road traffic	3057	Local government, England
2996	Cancelled	3058	Local government, England
2997	Road traffic	3059	Local government, England
2998	Road traffic	3060	Local government, England
2999	Road traffic	3061	Marriage
3000	Road traffic		Civil partnership
3001	Food, England		Devolution, Scotland
3002	Road traffic	3062	Income tax
3003	Road traffic	3063	Road traffic
3004	Road traffic	3064	Road traffic
3005	Road traffic	3065	Road traffic
3006	Road traffic	3066	Income tax
3007	Highways, England	3067 (C.129)	Social security
3008	Road traffic	3068	Defence
3009	Road traffic	3069	Road traffic
3010	Road traffic	3070	Regulatory reform
3011	Road traffic	3071	Road traffic
3012	Road traffic	3072	Road traffic
3013	Road traffic	3073	Mobile homes, England
3014	Road traffic	3074	Financial services and markets
3015	Road traffic		Immigration
3016	Road traffic	3075	Climate change
3017	Road traffic	3076	Merchant shipping
3018	Road traffic	3077	Legal services, England and Wales
3019	Road traffic	3078	Pensions
3020	Road traffic	3079 (W.304)	Food, Wales
3021	Road traffic	3080 (W.305)	Food, Wales
3022	Road traffic	3081	Financial services and markets
3023	Road traffic	3082 (W.306)	Road traffic, Wales
3024	Road traffic	3083	Cancelled
3025	Road traffic	3084 (W.307) (C.125)	Cancelled
3026 (C.128)	Commons, England	3085	Financial services and markets
3027	Highways, England		Immigration
3028	Road traffic	3086	Financial services and markets
			Immigration

Number	Subject
3087 (W.308)	Food, Wales
3088 (W.309) (C.131)	Nature conservation, Wales
3089 (W.310) (C.132)	Food, Wales
3090	Health services, England
	Social care, England
3091	Terms and conditions of employment
3092	Terms and conditions of employment
3093	Terms and conditions of employment
3094 (C.133)	Social security
3095	Terms and conditions of employment
3096	Terms and conditions of employment
3097	Terms and conditions of employment
3098 (C.134)	Proceeds of crime
3099	National Health Service, England
	Public health, England
3100	Cancelled
3101 (C.135)	Proceeds of crime
3102	Transport and works, England
	Transport, England
3103	Investigatory powers
3104	Food
3105	Highways, England
3106	Highways, England
3107	Highways, England
3108	Highways, England
3109	Highways, England
3110	Highways, England
3111 (W.311)	Local government, Wales
3112	Highways, England
3113 (W.312)	Road traffic, Wales
3114 (W.313)	Road traffic, Wales
3115 (W.314)	Road traffic, Wales
3116 (W.315)	Road traffic, Wales
3117	Social security
3118	Cancelled
3119	Investigatory powers
3120	Energy
3121	Road traffic
3122	Road traffic
3123	Road traffic
3124	Representation of the people, Scotland
3125	Climate change
3126	Housing
3127 (W.316)(C.136)	Housing, Wales
3128	Countryside, England
3129	Road traffic
3130	Road traffic
3131	Road traffic
3132	Road traffic
3133	Capital gains tax
3134	Terms and conditions of employment
3135	Statistics of trade
3136	Road traffic
3137	Broadcasting
3138	Pensions
3139	Health care and associated professions
3140	Companies
	Limited liability partnerships
	Business names
3141	Criminal law
	Data protection
3142	Public passenger transport
3143	Road traffic
3144	Road traffic
3145	Road traffic
3146	Road traffic
3147	Road traffic
3148	Road traffic
3149	Road traffic
3150	Road traffic
3151	Road traffic
3152	Road traffic
3153	Road traffic
3154	Road traffic
3155 (W.317) (C.137)	Water industry, England and Wales
3156 (W.318)	Water industry, England and Wales
3157	Coroners, England
3158	Animals
3159	Social security
3160 (C.138)	Banks and banking
3161	Representation of the people, England and Wales
3162 (C.139)	Defence
3163	Cancelled
3164 (W.319)	Road traffic, Wales
3165 (W.320)	Road traffic, Wales
3166 (W.321)	Road traffic, Wales
3167 (W.322)	Road traffic, Wales
3168	Marriage
	Civil partnership
	Devolution, Scotland
3169 (C.140)	Marriage
3170	Road traffic
3171	Road traffic
3172	Road traffic
3173	Road traffic
3174	Road traffic
3175	Road traffic
3176	Road traffic
3177	Road traffic
3178	Representation of the people
3179	Road traffic
3180	Road traffic
3181	Registration of births, deaths, marriages, etc., England and Wales
3182	Road traffic
3183	Corporation tax
3184	Olympic games and paralympic games
3185	Value added tax
3186 (C.141)	National Health Service, England
3187	Corporation tax
3188	Corporation tax
3189	Prevention and suppression of terrorism
3190	Road traffic
3191	Criminal law
	Data protection
3192 (C.142)	Criminal law
3193 (W.323)	Rating and valuation, Wales
3194	Land drainage, England and Wales
3195	Cancelled
3196	Social security
3197	Children and young persons, England
3198	Road traffic
3199	Local government, England
3200 (C.143)	Local government, England
3201 (W.324)	Road traffic, Wales

3202 (W.325)	Road traffic, Wales		Pensions, Wales
3203 (W.326)	Road traffic, Wales	3255	Terms and conditions of employment
3204	Local government, England	3256 (W.331)	Fire and rescue services, Wales
3205	Road traffic, England		Pensions, Wales
3206	Terms and conditions of employment	3257 (L.33)	Senior courts of England and Wales
3207	Proceeds of crime, England and Wales	3258	Customs
	Proceeds of crime, Northern Ireland	3259	Agriculture, England
3208	Road traffic	3260	Agriculture
3209	Companies	3261 (W.332)	Education, Wales
	Partnership	3262	Climate change
3210	Cancelled	3263	Agriculture
3211	Cancelled	3264 (C.149)	Cancelled
3212	Offshore installations	3265	Marriage
3213	Social security	3266 (W.333)	Animals, Wales
3214	National debt	3267 (W.334)	Education, Wales
3215	National Health Service, England	3268 (C.150)	Criminal law, England and Wales
3216	Education, England	3269 (C.151)	Stamp duty reserve tax
3217	Transport	3270	Social security
3218	National Health Service, England	3271	Dangerous drugs
3219	Electricity	3272	Health care and associated professions
	Gas	3273	Income tax
3220	Energy, England	3274	Capital gains tax
3221	Terms and conditions of employment		Corporation tax
3222 (W.327)	Agriculture, Wales		Income tax
3223 (W.328)	Agriculture, Wales		Petroleum revenue tax
3224	Local government, England and Wales	3275	Capital gains tax
3225	Civil aviation		Corporation tax
3226 (C.144)	Income tax		Income tax
3227	Income tax	3276	Dangerous drugs
3228	Social security	3277	Dangerous drugs
3229	Constitutional law	3278 (W.335)	Housing, Wales
	Devolution, Scotland	3279	Police, England and Wales
	Civil partnership	3280	Tax credits
	Marriage	3281	Civil aviation
3230	Criminal law	3282	Data protection
3231	Electricity	3283	Education, England
	Gas	3284	Licences and licensing, England and Wales
3232	Children and young persons	3285	Education, England
3233	Civil aviation	3286	Education, England
3234	Legal services, England and Wales	3287	Local government, England
3235	Legal services, England and Wales	3288	Local government, England
3236	Legal services, England and Wales	3289	Local government, England
3237	Corporation tax	3290	Local government, England
3238	Legal services, England and Wales	3291	Local government, England
3239	Consumer protection, England and Wales	3292	Cancelled
3240	Social security	3293	Financial services and markets
3241 (C.145)	Cancelled	3294	Constitutional law
3242 (W.329)	Fire and rescue services, Wales		Devolution, Scotland
	Pensions, Wales		Taxes
3243	Plant health, England	3295	Highways, England
3244	Disabled persons	3296 (L.34)	Family proceedings, England and Wales
	Transport		Senior courts of England and Wales
3245 (C.146)	Public records		Family court, England and Wales
3246	Education, England	3297 (L.35)	Family proceedings, England and Wales
3247	Education, England		Senior courts of England and Wales
3248	Health and safety		Family court, England and Wales
3249	Public records	3298	Judgments, England and Wales
3250 (C.147)	Constitutional law		Judgments, Northern Ireland
	Devolution, Scotland	3299 (L.36)	Senior courts of England and Wales
3251 (C.148)	Health care and associated professions		County court, England and Wales
3252	Cancelled	3300	Criminal law, England and Wales
3253	Licences and licensing, England and Wales	3301	Infrastructure planning, England
3254 (W.330)	Fire and rescue services, Wales	3302	Civil aviation
		3303 (W.336)	River, Wales

Number	Subject
	Salmon and freshwater Wales
3304	Cancelled
3305	Legal aid and advice, England and Wales
3306	Marine pollution
3307 (C.152)	Legal services, England and Wales
3308	London government
3309	Children and young persons, England
3310	Highways, England
3311	Highways, England
3312	Council tax, England
3313	Highways, England
3314	Government resources and accounts
3315 (C.153)	Police, Northern Ireland
3316	Legal services, England and Wales
3317	Fire and rescue services, England
3318	Clean air, England
3319 (C.154)	Local government, England and Wales
3320 (C.155)	Water industry, England and Wales
	Insurance
3321	Education, England
3322	Terms and conditions of employment
3323 (C.156)	Banks and banking
3324 (C.157)	Excise
3325	Corporation tax
3326	Cancelled
3327	Corporation tax
3328	Infrastructure planning
3329	Banks and banking
	Financial services and markets
3330	Banks and banking
3331	Infrastructure planning
3332	Electricity
	Gas
3333	Electricity
	Gas
3334	Local government, England
3335	Local government, England
3336	Local government, England
3337	Public procurement
3338	Local government, England
3339	Local government, England
3340	Financial services and markets
3341	Local government, England
3342	River, England
3343	Highways, England
3344	Financial services and markets
	Building societies
3345	Sea fisheries
3346	Stamp duty reserve tax
3347	Police, England and Wales
3348	Financial services and markets
3349	Criminal law
3350	Banks and banking
3351	Employment agencies, etc.
3352	Education, England
3353	Road traffic
3354	Electricity
3355	Road traffic
3356	Road traffic
3357	Road traffic
3358	Road traffic
3359	Road traffic
3360	Road traffic
3361	Education, England
3362 (W.337)	Local government, Wales
3363	Sea fisheries, England
3364 (C.158)	Education, England
3365	Road traffic
3366	Road traffic
3367	Road traffic
3368	Road traffic
3369	Road traffic
3370	Road traffic
3371	Road traffic
3372	Road traffic
3373	Road traffic
3374 (W.338)	Road traffic, Wales
3375	Road traffic
3376 (W.339)	Road traffic, Wales
3377 (W.340)	Road traffic
3378 (W.341)	Road traffic, Wales
3379	Road traffic
3380	Road traffic
3381	Road traffic
3382	Road traffic
3383	Road traffic
3384	Road traffic
3385	Road traffic
3386	Road traffic
3387	Road traffic
3388	Road traffic
3389 (W.342)	Road traffic, Wales
3390	Road traffic
3391 (W.343)	Road traffic, Wales
3392	Road traffic
3393 (W.344)	Road traffic, Wales
3394	Road traffic
3395 (W.345)	Road traffic, Wales
3396	Road traffic
3397	Road traffic
3398	Road traffic
3399	Road traffic
3400	Road traffic
3401	Road traffic
3402	Road traffic
3403	Road traffic
3404	Road traffic
3405	Road traffic
3406	Road traffic
3407	Road traffic
3408	Road traffic
3409	Road traffic
3410	Road traffic
3411	Road traffic
3412	Road traffic
3413	Road traffic
3414 (W.346)	Road traffic
3415	Road traffic
3416 (W.347)	Road traffic, Wales
3417	Road traffic
3418	Road traffic
3419	Road traffic
3420 (W.348)	Road traffic, Wales
3421	Road traffic
3422	Road traffic

3423	Road traffic
3424	Road traffic
3425	Road traffic
3426	Road traffic
3427 (W.349)	Road traffic, Wales
3428	Road traffic
3429	Road traffic
3430	Road traffic
3431	Road traffic
3432	Road traffic
3433	Road traffic
3434	Road traffic
3435	Road traffic
3436	Road traffic
3437	Road traffic
3438	Road traffic
3439	Road traffic
3440	Road traffic
3441	Road traffic
3442	Road traffic
3443	Road traffic
3444	Road traffic
3445	Road traffic
3446	Road traffic
3447	Road traffic
3448	Road traffic
3449	Road traffic
3450	Road traffic
3451	Road traffic
3452	Road traffic
3453	Road traffic
3454	Road traffic
3455	Road traffic
3456	Road traffic
3457	Road traffic
3458	Road traffic
3459	Road traffic
3460	Road traffic
3461	Road traffic
3462	Road traffic
3463	Road traffic
3464	Road traffic
3465	Road traffic
3466	Cancelled
3467	Road traffic
3468	Road traffic
3469	Road traffic
3470	Road traffic
3471	Road traffic
3472	Road traffic
3473	Road traffic
3474	Road traffic
3475	Road traffic
3476	Road traffic
3477	Road traffic
3478	Road traffic
3479	Road traffic
3480	Road traffic
3481	Road traffic
3482	Road traffic
3483	Road traffic
3484	Road traffic
3485	Road traffic
3486	Banks and banking
	Building societies
3487	National Health Service, England
3488	Road traffic
3489	Road traffic
3490	Road traffic
3491	Road traffic
3492 (W.350)	Rating and valuation, Wales
3493	Veterinary surgeons
3494	Road traffic
3495	Road traffic
3496	Road traffic
3497	Road traffic
3498	Road traffic
3499	Road traffic
3500	Road traffic
3501	Road traffic
3502	Road traffic
3503	Road traffic
3504	Road traffic
3505	Road traffic
3506	Road traffic
3507	Road traffic
3508	Road traffic
3509	Road traffic
3510	Road traffic
3511	Road traffic
3512	Road traffic
3513 (W.351)	Road traffic, Wales
3514	Road traffic
3515	Road traffic
3516	Road traffic
3517	Road traffic
3518	Road traffic
3519	Road traffic
3520	Road traffic
3521	Road traffic
3522	Road traffic
3523	Road traffic
3524	Road traffic
3525	Road traffic
3526	Road traffic
3527	Road traffic
3528	Road traffic
3529	Road traffic
3530	Road traffic
3531	Road traffic
3532	Road traffic
3533	Road traffic
3534	Road traffic
3535	Road traffic
3536	Road traffic
3537	Road traffic
3538	Road traffic
3539	Road traffic
3540	Road traffic
3541	Road traffic
3542	Road traffic
3543	Road traffic
3544	Road traffic
3545	Road traffic

3546	Road traffic	
3547	Road traffic	
3548	Road traffic	
3549	Road traffic	
3550	Road traffic	
3551	Road traffic	
3552	Road traffic, England	
3553	Road traffic	
3554	Road traffic	
3555	Road traffic	
3556	Road traffic	
3557	Road traffic	
3558	Road traffic	
3559	Road traffic	
3560	Road traffic	
3561	Road traffic	
3562	Road traffic	
3563	Road traffic	

Subsidiary Numbers

Commencement orders (bring an act or part of an act into operation) 2014

11 (W.1)(C.1)
39 (C.2)
93 (C.3)
175 (C.4)
178 (W.26) (C.5)
183 (C.6)
209 (C.7)
237 (C.8)
251 (C.9)
253 (C.10)
258 (C.11)
262 (C.12)
336 (C.13)
377 (C.14)
380 (W.45) (C.15)
414 (C.16)
416 (C.17)
423 (C.18)
433 (C.19)
453 (W.51) (C.20)
459 (C.21)
463 (C.22)
478 (C.23)
576 (C.24)
630 (C.25)
633 (C.26)
768 (C.27)
772 (C.28)
785 (C.29)
793 (C.30)
797 (C.31)
823 (C.32)
824 (C.33)
830 (C.34)
831 (C.35)
839 (C.36)
888 (C.37)
889 (C.38)
900 (C.39)
906 (C.40)
929 (C.41)
940 (C.42)
949 (C.43)
954 (C.44)
992 (C.45)
1066 (W.105) (C.46)
1134 (C.47)
1226 (C.48)
1236 (C.49)
1241 (W.129) (C.50)
1263 (C.51)
1287 (C.52)
1291 (C.53)
1444 (C.54)
1447 (C.55)
1452 (C.56)
1454 (C.57)
1460 (C.58)
1461 (C.59)
1531 (C.60)
1583 (C.61)
1596 (C.62)
1605 (W.163) (C.63)
1606 (W.164) (C.64)
1635 (C.65)
1636 (C.66)
1640 (C.67)
1659 (C.68)
1661 (C.69)
1662 (C.70)
1683 (C.71)
1706 (W.171)(C.72)
1714 (C.73)
1715 (C.74)
1751 (C.75)
1769 (W.181)(C.76)
1777 (C.77)
1793 (W.186)(C.78)
1809 (C.83)
1810 (C.79)
1819 (C.80)
1820 (C.81)
1823 (C.82)
1847 (C.84)
1860 (C.85)
1912 (C.86)
1916 (C.87)
1923 (C.88)
1943 (C.89)
1961 (C.90)
1962 (C.91)
1965 (C.92)
2039 (C.93)
2069 (C.94)
2121 (W.207) (C.95)
2125 (C.96)
2162 (W.211) (C.97)
2228 (C.98)
2321 (C.99)
2330 (C.100)
2370 (C.101)

2377 (C.102)
2379 (C.103)
2380 (C.104)
2395 (C.105)
2439 (C.106)
2444 (C.107)
2454 (C.108)
2458 (C.109)
2461 (C.110)
2473 (C.111)
2589 (W.256) (C.112)
2590 (C.113)
2609 (C.114)
2613 (C.115)
2634 (C.116)
2646 (C.117)
2718 (W.274) (C.118)
2727 (C.119)
2749 (C.120)
2754 (C.121)
2771 (C.122)
2780 (W.284)(C.123)
2796 (C.124)
3084 (W.307)(C.125) Cancelled
2830 (W.286) (C.130)
2880 (C.126)
2881 (C.127)
3026 (C.128)
3067 (C.129)
3088 (W.309) (C.131)
3089 (W.310) (C.132)
3094 (C.133)
3098 (C.134)
3101 (C.135)
3127 (W.316)(C.136)
3155 (W.317) (C.137)
3160 (C.138)
3162 (C.139)
3169 (C.140)
3186 (C.141)
3192 (C.142)
3200 (C.143)
3226 (C.144)
3241 (C.145) Cancelled
3245 (C.146)
3250 (C.147)
3251 (C.148)
3264 (C.149) Cancelled
3268 (C.150)
3269 (C.151)
3307 (C.152)
3315 (C.153)
3319 (C.154)
3320 (C.155)
3323 (C.156)
3324 (C.157)
3364 (C.158)

Instruments relating to fees or procedure in courts in England and Wales 2014

407 (L.1)
482 (L.2)
503 (L.3)
514 (L.4)
524 (L.5)
590 (L.6)
602 (L.7)
603 (L.8)
605 (L.9)
610 (L.10)
667 (L.11)
821 (L.12)
840 (L.13)
841 (L.14)
843 (L.15)
867 (L.16)
874 (L.17)
875 (L.18)
876 (L.19)
877 (L.20)
878 (L.21)
982 (L.22)
1129 (L.23)
1233 (L.24)
1505 (L.25)
1610 (L.26)
1834 (L.27)
2044 (L.28)
2059 (L.29)
2128 (L.30)
2604 (L.31)
2948 (L.32)
3257 (L.33)
3296 (L.34)
3297 (L.35)
3299 (L.36)

Instruments that extend only to Scotland 2014

501 (S.1)
2691 (S.2) Cancelled
2753 (S.3)

Instruments that extend only to Wales 2014

11 (W.1) (C.1)
34 (W.2)
41 (W.3)
42 (W.4)
58 (W.5)
66 (W.6)
72 (W.7)
77 (W.8)
109 (W.9)
110 (W.10)
111 (W.11)
122 (W.12)
123 (W.13)
124 (W.14)
126 (W.15)
128 (W.16)
129 (W.17)
146 (W.18)
158 (W.19)
159 (W.20)
160 (W.21)
161 (W.22)
164 (W.23)

176 (W.24)	910 (W.89)
177 (W.25)	914 (W.90)
178 (W.26) (C.5)	915 (W.91)
197 (W.27)	951 (W.92)
207 (W.28)	1004 (W.93)
219 (W.29)	1031 (W.94)
234 (W.30)	1055 (W.95)
235 (W.31)	1056 (W.96)
236 (W.32)	1057 (W.97)
241 (W.33)	1058 (W.98)
256 (W.34)	1059 (W.99)
286 (W.35)	1060 (W.100)
287 (W.36)	1061 (W.101)
348 (W.37)	1062 (W.102)
349 (W.38)	1064 (W.103)
371 (W.39)	1065 (W.104)
372 (W.40)	1066 (W.105) (C.46)
373 (W.41)	1067 (W.106)
374 (W.42)	1078 (W.107)
375 (W.43)	1087 (W.108)
379 (W.44)	1099 (W.109)
380 (W.45) (C.15)	1102 (W.110)
387 (W.46)	1132 (W.111)
388 (W.47)	1133 (W.112)
403 (W.48)	1136 (W.113)
440 (W.49)	1137 (W.114)
441 (W.50)	1186 (W.115)
453 (W.51) (C.20)	1200 (W.116)
454 (W.52)	1201 (W.117)
460 (W.53)	1202 (W.118)
461 (W.54)	1203 (W.119)
462 (W.55)	1204 (W.120)
476 (W.56)	1205 (W.121)
477 (W.57)	1206 (W.122)
481 (W.58)	1207 (W.123)
493 (W.59)	1208 (W.124)
517 (W.60)	1209 (W.125)
519 (W.61)	1210 (W.126)
521 (W.62)	1211 (W.127)
522 (W.63)	1212 (W.128)
523 (W.64)	1241 (W.129) (C.50)
541 (W.65)	1249 (W.130)
554 (W.66)	1251 (W.131)
566 (W.67)	1288 (W.132)
567 (W.68)	1289 (W.133)
592 (W.69)	1314 (W.134)
593 (W.70)	1317 (W.135)
595 (W.71)	1326 (W.136)
632 (W.72)	1340 (W.137)
666 (W.73)	1341 (W.138)
684 (W.74)	1370 (W.139)
694 (W.75)	1373 (W.140)
709 (W.76)	1388 (W.141)
710 (W.77)	1455 (W.142)
711 (W.78)	1462 (W.143)
712 (W.79)	1463 (W.144)
789 (W.80)	1464 (W.145)
810 (W.81)	1491 (W.146)
811 (W.82)	1493 (W.147)
825 (W.83)	1498 (W.148)
826 (W.84)	1499 (W.149)
827 (W.85)	1500 (W.150)
872 (W.86)	1501 (W.151)
873 (W.87)	1502 (W.152)
890 (W.88)	1503 (W.153)

1504 (W.154)	2237 (W.219)
1514 (W.155)	2238 (W.220)
1515 (W.156)	2239 (W.221)
1535 (W.157)	2240 (W.222)
1549 (W.158)	2247 (W.223)
1550 (W.159)	2249 (W.224)
1574 (W.160)	2281 (W.225)
1595 (W.161)	2291 (W.226)
1600 (W.162)	2303 (W.227)
1605 (W.163) (C.63)	2308 (W.228)
1606 (W.164) (C.64)	2365 (W.229)
1609 (W.165)	2367 (W.230)
1622 (W.166)	2368 (W.231)
1649 (W.167)	2463 (W.232)
1650 (W.168)	2464 (W.233)
1676 (W.169)	2465 (W.234)
1677 (W.170)	2466 (W.235)
1706 (W.171) (C.72)	2467 (W.236)
1712 (W.172)	2468 (W.237)
1713 (W.173)	2474 (W.238)
1759 (W.174)	2491 (W.239)
1760 (W.175)	2492 (W.240)
1761 (W.176)	2493 (W.241)
1762 (W.177)	2494 (W.242)
1763 (W.178)	2495 (W.243)
1764 (W.179)	2540 (W.244)
1767 (W.180)	2542 (W.245)
1769 (W.181)(C.76)	2544 (W.246)
1770 (W.182)	2553 (W.247)
1772 (W.183)	2556 (W.248)
1779 (W.184)	2568 (W.249)
1792 (W.185)	2574 (W.250)
1793 (W.186) (C.78)	2575 (W.251)
1794 (W.187)	2576 (W.252)
1795 (W.188)	2577 (W.253)
1835 (W.189)	2578 (W.254)
1836 (W.190)	2579 (W.255)
1839 (W.191)	2589 (W.256) (C.112)
1858 (W.192)	2603 (W.257)
1859 (W.193)	2647 (W.258)
1895 (W.194)	2648 (W.259)
1914 (W.195)	2649 (W.260)
1944 (W.196)	2653 (W.261)
1995 (W.197)	2656 (W.262)
1996 (W.198)	2658 (W.263)
1998 (W.199)	2659 (W.264)
1999 (W.200)	2677 (W.265)
2000 (W.201)	2678 (W.266)
2015 (W.202)	2692 (W.267)
2018 (W.203)	2693 (W.268)
2030 (W.204)	2694 (W.269)
2065 (W.205)	2709 (W.270)
2071 (W.206)	2714 (W.271)
2121 (W.207) (C.95)	2716 (W.272)
2124 (W.208)	2717 (W.273)
2126 (W.209)	2718 (W.274) (C.118)
2144 (W.210)	2722 (W.275)
2162 (W.211) (C.97)	2725 (W.276)
2178 (W.212)	2755 (W.277)
2212 (W.213)	2756 (W.278)
2225 (W.214)	2757 (W.279)
2232 (W.215)	2773 (W.280)
2233 (W.216)	2775 (W.281)
2235 (W.217)	2776 (W.282)
2236 (W.218)	2777 (W.283)

2780 (W.284) (C.123)
2813 (W.285)
2830 (W.286) (C.130)
2836 (W.287)
2837 (W.288)
2838 (W.289)
2853 (W.290)
2855 (W.291)
2891 (W.292)
2892 (W.293)
2893 (W.294)
2894 (W.295)
2895 (W.296)
2917 (W.297)
2927 (W.298)
2938 (W.299)
2941 (W.300)
2983 (W.301)
3033 (W.302)
3037 (W.303)
3079 (W.304)
3080 (W.305)
3082 (W.306)
3084 (W.307) Cancelled
3087 (W.308)
3088 (W.309) (C.131)
3089 (W.310) (C.132)
3111 (W.311)
3113 (W.312)
3114 (W.313)
3115 (W.314)
3116 (W.315)
3127 (W.316) (C.136)
3155 (W.317) (C.137)

3156 (W.318)
3164 (W.319)
3165 (W.320)
3166 (W.321)
3167 (W.322)
3193 (W.323)
3201 (W.324)
3202 (W.325)
3203 (W.326)
3222 (W.327)
3223 (W.328)
3242 (W.329)
3254 (W.330)
3256 (W.331)
3261 (W.332)
3266 (W.333)
3267 (W.334)
3278 (W.335)
3303 (W.336)
3362 (W.337)
3374 (W.338)
3376 (W.339)
3377 (W.340)
3378 (W.341)
3389 (W.342)
3391 (W.343)
3393 (W.344)
3395 (W.345)
3414 (W.346)
3416 (W.347)
3420 (W.348)
3427 (W.349)
3492 (W.350)
3513 (W.351)

SCOTTISH LEGISLATION

Acts of the Scottish Parliament

Acts of the Scottish Parliament 2014

Bankruptcy and Debt Advice (Scotland) Act 2014: 2014 asp 11. - iii, 75p.: 30 cm. - Royal assent, 29 April 2014. An Act of the Scottish Parliament to amend the Bankruptcy (Scotland) Act 1985. Explanatory notes to assist in the understanding of this Act will be available separately. - 978-0-10-590221-8 £14.25

Budget (Scotland) Act 2014: 2014 asp 6. - [12]p.: 30 cm. - Royal assent, 12 March 2014. An Act of the Scottish Parliament to make provision, for financial year 2014/15, for the use of resources by the Scottish Administration and certain bodies whose expenditure is payable out of the Scottish Consolidated Fund, for the maximum amounts of borrowing by certain statutory bodies and for authorising the payment of sums out of the Fund; to make provision, for financial year 2015/16, for authorising the payment of sums out of the Fund on a temporary basis. - 978-0-10-590213-3 £5.75

Buildings (Recovery of Expenses) (Scotland) Act 2014: 2014 asp 13. - [12]p.: 30 cm. - Royal assent, 24 July 2014. An Act of the Scottish Parliament to amend the Building (Scotland) Act 2003 to provide for expenses incurred by local authorities in connection with notices served or work carried out under that Act to be recovered by way of charging order. Explanatory notes to assist in the understanding of this Act are available separately (ISBN 9780105902317). - 978-0-10-590227-0 £6.00

Burrell Collection (Lending and Borrowing) (Scotland) Act 2014: 2014 asp 4. - [8]p.: 30 cm. - Royal assent, 25 February 2014. An Act of the Scottish Parliament to provide Glasgow City Council with additional powers to lend, including lending overseas, any items forming part of the Burrell Collection and to receive items on loan from others in both cases with agreement of the charity trustees of the Sir William Burrell Trust in accordance with a published code. Explanatory notes to assist in the understanding of the Act are available separately (ISBN 9780105902331). - 978-0-10-590211-9 £4.00

Children and Young People (Scotland) Act 2014: 2014 asp 8. - v, 72p.: 30 cm. - Royal assent, 27 March 2014. An Act of the Scottish Parliament to make provision about the rights of children and young people; to make provision about investigations by the Commissioner for Children and Young People in Scotland; to make provision for and about the provision of services and support for or in relation to children and young people; to make provision for an adoption register; to make provision about children's hearings, detention in secure accommodation and consultation on certain proposals in relation to schools. Explanatory notes have been produced to assist in the understanding of this Act and are available separately (ISBN 9780105902171). - 978-0-10-590215-7 £13.75

City of Edinburgh Council (Leith Links and Surplus Fire Fund) Act 2014: 2014 asp 7. - [2], 4p.: 30 cm. - Royal assent, 27 March 2014. An Act of the Scottish Parliament to amend the City of Edinburgh District Council Order Confirmation Act 1991 to create an exception to the prohibition on the construction of monuments on Leith Links; to amend the purposes for which the Surplus Fire Fund may be used; to transfer the property, rights, interests and liabilities of the Surplus Fire Fund to a successor charitable trust and then dissolve the Surplus Fire Fund. Explanatory notes to the Act are available separately (ISBN 9780105902324). - 978-0-10-590214-0 £5.75

City of Edinburgh (Portobello Park) Act 2014: 2014 asp 15. - [8]p.: 30 cm. - Royal assent, 1 August 2014. An Act of the Scottish Parliament to change the status of Portobello Park, so as to permit the City of Edinburgh Council to appropriate it for the purposes of the Council's functions as an education authority. Explanatory notes to assist in the understanding of the Act are available separately (ISBN 9780105902386). - 978-0-10-590229-4 £6.00

Courts Reform (Scotland) Act 2014: 2014 asp 18. - viii, [106]p.: 30 cm. - Royal assent, 10 November 2014. An Act of the Scottish Parliament to make provision about the sheriff courts; to establish a Sheriff Appeal Court; to make provision about civil court procedure; to make provision about appeals in civil proceedings; to make provision about appeals in criminal proceedings; to make provision about judges of the Court of Session; to make provision about the Scottish Land Court; to make provision about justice of the peace courts; to rename the Scottish Court Service and give it functions in relation to tribunals; to provide for assistants to the Judicial Appointments Board for Scotland. - 978-0-10-590239-3 £19.00

Disabled Persons' Parking Badges (Scotland) Act 2014: 2014 asp 17. - [8]p.: 30 cm. - Royal assent, 24 September 2014. An Act of the Scottish Parliament to make provision about badges for display on motor vehicles used by disabled persons. Explanatory notes to assist in the understanding of the Act are available separately (ISBN 9780105902379). - 978-0-10-590236-2 £4.25

Historic Environment (Scotland) Act 2014: 2014 asp 19. - iii, 54p.: 30 cm. - Royal assent, 9th December 2014. An Act of the Scottish Parliament to establish Historic Environment Scotland; to make minor amendments to the law relating to the historic environment. Explanatory notes are available separately (ISBN 9780105902416). - 978-0-10-590240-9 £10.00

Housing (Scotland) Act 2014: 2014 asp 14. - iv, 84p.: 30 cm. - Royal assent, 1 August 2014. An Act of the Scottish Parliament to make provision about housing, including provision about the abolition of the right to buy, social housing, the law affecting private housing, the regulation of letting agents and the licensing of sites for mobile homes. Explanatory notes to assist in the understanding of the Act are available separately (ISBN 9780105902300). - 978-0-10-590228-7 £16.00

Landfill Tax (Scotland) Act 2014: 2014 asp 2. - iii, 23p.: 30 cm. - Royal assent, 21 January 2014. An Act of the Scottish Parliament to make provision about the taxation of disposals to landfill. Explanatory notes to assist in the understanding of the Act are available separately (ISBN 9780105902256). - 978-0-10-590208-9 £6.25

Marriage and Civil Partnership (Scotland) Act 2014: 2014 asp 5. - iii, 50p.: 30 cm. - Royal assent, 12 March 2014. An Act of the Scottish Parliament to make provision for the marriage of persons of the same sex; to make further provision as to the persons who may solemnise marriage and as to marriage procedure and the places at which civil marriages may be solemnised; to make provision for the registration of civil partnerships by celebrants of religious or belief bodies; to make provision about gender change by married persons and civil partners; to make a minor correction in relation to registration information. Explanatory notes have been produced to assist in the understanding of this Act and are available separately (ISBN 9780105902249). - 978-0-10-590212-6 £9.75

Procurement Reform (Scotland) Act 2014: 2014 asp 12. - [1], iii, 23p.: 30 cm. - Royal assent, 17 June 2014. An Act of the Scottish Parliament to make provision about the procedures relating to the award of certain public contracts; to require certain authorities to produce procurement strategies and annual reports. Explanatory notes to assist in the understanding of this Act are available separately (ISBN 9780105902263). - 978-0-10-590223-2 £6.00

Public Bodies (Joint Working) (Scotland) Act 2014: 2014 asp 9. - iii, 42p.: 30 cm. - Royal assent, 1 April 2014. An Act of the Scottish Parliament to make provision in relation to the carrying out of functions of local authorities and Health Boards; to make further provision about certain functions of public bodies; to make further provision in relation to certain functions under the National Health Service (Scotland) Act 1978. Explanatory notes have been produced to assist in the understanding of this Act and are available separately (ISBN 9780105902201). - 978-0-10-590218-8 £10.00

Regulatory Reform (Scotland) Act 2014:2014 asp 3. - iii, 82p.: 30 cm. - Royal assent, 19 February 2014. An Act of the Scottish Parliament to enable provision to be made for the purpose of promoting regulatory consistency; to make provision in relation to primary authorities; to enable provision to be made, and to make provision, as respects regulatory activities, and offences, relating to the environment; to make provision about regulatory functions relating to marine licensing, planning and street traders' licences. Explanatory notes to assist in the understanding of the Act will be available separately. - 978-0-10-590210-2 £15.50

Revenue Scotland and Tax Powers Act 2014 :2014 asp 16. - [154]p.: 30 cm. - Royal assent, 24 September 2014. An Act of the Scottish Parliament to establish Scottish tax tribunals; to put in place a general anti-avoidance rule; to make provision about the collection management of devolved taxes. Explanatory notes to assist in the understanding of the Act will be available separately. With correction slip dated October 2014. - 978-0-10-590235-5 £23.25

Tribunals (Scotland) Act 2014:2014 asp 10. - v, 62p.: 30 cm. - Royal assent, 15 April 2014. An Act of the Scottish Parliament to establish the First-tier Tribunal for Scotland and the Upper Tribunal for Scotland. Explanatory notes to assist in the understanding of this Act are available separately (ISBN 9780105902225). - 978-0-10-590219-5 £11.00

Victims and Witnesses (Scotland) Act 2014:2014 asp 1. - iii, 31p.: 30 cm. - Royal assent, 17 January 2014. An Act of the Scottish Parliament to make provision for certain rights and support for victims and witnesses, including provision for implementing Directive 2012/29/EU of the European Parliament and the Council; and to make provision for the establishment of a committee of the Mental Welfare Commission with functions relating to persons who were placed in institutional care as children. Explanatory Notes have been produced to assist in the understanding of this Act and are available separately (ISBN 978010592164). - 978-0-10-590207-2 £9.75

Acts of the Scottish Parliament - Explanatory notes 2013

Land and Buildings Transaction Tax (Scotland) Act 2013 (asp 11): explanatory notes. - 64p.: 30 cm. - Land and Buildings Transaction Tax (Scotland) Act 2013 (asp 11) (ISBN 9780105902027) which received Royal assent on 31 July 2013. - 978-0-10-590246-1 £11.00

National Trust for Scotland (Governance etc.) Act 2013 (asp 9): explanatory notes. - 8p.: 30 cm. - These Notes relate to the National Trust for Scotland (Governance etc.) Act 2013 (asp 9) (ISBN 9780105902003) which received Royal assent on 28 June 2013. - 978-0-10-590234-8 £6.00

Scottish Independence Referendum Act 2013 (asp 14):explanatory notes. - 53p.: 30 cm. - These notes relate to the Scottish Independence Act 2013 (asp 14) (ISBN 9780105902065) which received Royal assent on 17 December 2013. - 978-0-10-590209-6 £9.75

Acts of the Scottish Parliament - Explanatory notes 2014

Buildings (Recovery of Expenses) (Scotland) Act 2014 (asp 13): explanatory notes. - 8p.: 30 cm. - These Notes relate to the Buildings (Recovery of Expenses) (Scotland) Act 2014 (asp 13) (ISBN 9780105902270) which received Royal assent on 24 July 2014. - 978-0-10-590231-7 £6.00

Burrell Collection (Lending and Borrowing) (Scotland) Act 2014 (asp 4):explanatory notes. - 34p.: 30 cm. - These Notes relate to the Burrell Collection (Lending and Borrowing) (Scotland) Act 2014 (asp 4) (ISBN 9780105902119) which received Royal assent on 25 February 2014. - 978-0-10-590233-1 £10.00

Children and Young People (Scotland) Act 2014 (asp 8):explanatory notes. - 55p.: 30 cm. - These notes relate to the Children and Young People (Scotland) Act 2014 (asp 8) (ISBN 9780105902157) which received Royal assent on 27 March 2014. - 978-0-10-590217-1 £10.00

City of Edinburgh Council (Leith Links and Surplus Fire Fund) Act 2014 (asp 7):explanatory notes. - [8]p.: 30 cm. - These Notes relate to the City of Edinburgh Council (Leith Links and Surplus Fire Fund) Act 2014 (asp 7) (ISBN 9780105902140) which received Royal assent on 27 March 2014. - 978-0-10-590232-4 £4.25

City of Edinburgh Council (Portobello Park) Act 2014 (asp 15): explanatory notes. - 8p.: 30 cm. - These Notes relate to the City of Edinburgh Council (Portobello Park) Act 2014 (asp 15) (ISBN 9780105902294) which received Royal assent on 1 August 2014. - 978-0-10-590238-6 £4.25

Disabled Persons' Parking Badges (Scotland) Act 2014 (asp 17): explanatory notes. - 6p.: 30 cm. - These notes relate to the Disabled Persons' Parking Badges (Scotland) Act 2014 (asp 17) (ISBN 9780105902362) which received Royal Assent on 24 September 2014. - 978-0-10-590237-9 £4.25

Historic Environment (Scotland) Act 2014 (asp 19):explanatory notes. - [27]p.: 30 cm. - These notes relate to the Historic Environment (Scotland) Act 2014 (asp 19) (ISBN 9780105902409) which received Royal assent on 9 December 2014. - 978-0-10-590241-6 £6.00

Housing (Scotland) Act 2014 (asp 14):explanatory notes. - 46p.: 30 cm. - These Notes relate to the Housing (Scotland) Act 2014 (asp 14) (ISBN 9780105902287) which received Royal assent on 1 August 2014. - 978-0-10-590230-0 £10.00

Landfill Tax (Scotland) Act 2014 (asp 2):explanatory notes. - 14p.: 30 cm. - These notes relate to the Landfill Tax (Scotland) Act 2014 (asp 9) (ISBN 9780105902089) which received Royal assent on 21 January 2014. - 978-0-10-590225-6 £6.00

Marriage and Civil Partnership (Scotland) Act 2014 (asp 5): explanatory notes. - 47p.: 30 cm. - These notes relate to the Marriage and Civil Partnership (Scotland) Act 2014 (asp 5) (ISBN 9780105902126) which received Royal assent on 12 March 2014. - 978-0-10-590224-9 £10.00

Procurement Reform (Scotland) Act 2014 (asp 12):explanatory notes. - 15, [1]p.: 30 cm. - These notes relate to the Procurement Reform (Scotland) Act 2014 (asp 12) (ISBN 9780105902232) which received Royal assent on 17 June 2014. - 978-0-10-590226-3 £6.00

Public Bodies (Joint Working) (Scotland) Act 2014 (asp 9): explanatory notes. - 30p.: 30 cm. - These Notes relate to the Public Bodies (Joint Working) (Scotland) Act 2014 (asp 9) (ISBN 9780105902188) which received Royal assent on 1 April 2014. - 978-0-10-590220-1 £6.00

Tribunals (Scotland) Act 2014 (asp 10):explanatory notes. - 36p.: 30 cm. - These notes relate to the Tribunals (Scotland) Act 2014 (asp 10) (ISBN 9780105902195) which received Royal assent on 15 April 2014. - 978-0-10-590222-5 £10.00

Victims and Witnesses (Scotland) Act 2014 (asp 1):explanatory notes. - 26p.: 30 cm. - These notes relate to the Victims and Witnesses (Scotland) Act 2014 (asp 1) (ISBN 9780105902072) which received Royal assent on 17 January 2014. - 978-0-10-590216-4 £6.00

Scottish Statutory Instruments

By Subject Heading

Adults with incapacity

The Adults with Incapacity (Supervision of Welfare Guardians etc. by Local Authorities) (Scotland) Amendment (No. 2) Regulations 2014 No. 2014/157. - Enabling power: Adults with Incapacity (Scotland) Act 2000, ss. 10 (3) (a), 86 (2). - Issued: 10.06.2014. Made: 03.06.2014. Laid: 05.06.2014. Coming into force: 12.08.2014. Effect: S.S.I. 2002/95 amended. Territorial extent & classification: S. General. - 2p.: 30 cm. - 978-0-11-102374-7 £4.25

The Adults with Incapacity (Supervision of Welfare Guardians etc. by Local Authorities) (Scotland) Amendment Regulations 2014 No. 2014/123. - Enabling power: Adults with Incapacity (Scotland) Act 2000, ss. 10 (3) (a) (b), 86 (2). - Issued: 13.05.2014. Made: 06.05.2014. Laid before the Scottish Parliament: 08.05.2014. Coming into force: 09.06.2014. Effect: S.S.I. 2002/95 amended. Territorial extent & classification: S. General. - 8p.: 30 cm. - 978-0-11-102339-6 £4.25

Agriculture

The Common Agricultural Policy (Cross-Compliance) (Scotland) Regulations 2014 No. 2014/325. - Enabling power: European Communities Act 1972, s. 2 (2), sch. 2, para. 1A. - Issued: 26.11.2014. Made: 19.11.2014. Laid before the Scottish Parliament: 21.11.2014. Coming into force: 01.01.2015. Effect: S.S.I. 2009/376 amended & S.S.I. 2011/415; 2014/6 revoked with savings. Territorial extent & classification: S. General. - EC note: These Regulations make provision in Scotland for the administration and enforcement of Council Regulation (EC) no. 1306/2013; Commission Delegated Reg. (EU) no. 640/2014 & Commission implementing Reg. (EU) no. 809/2014 in relation to cross compliance under Common Agricultural Policy. - 12p.: 30 cm. - 978-0-11-102516-1 £6.00

The Common Agricultural Policy Schemes (Cross-Compliance) (Scotland) Amendment Regulations 2014 No. 2014/6. - Enabling power: European Communities Act 1972, s. 2 (2). - Issued: 16.01.2014. Made: 09.01.2014. Laid before the Scottish Parliament: 13.01.2014. Coming into force: 21.02.2014. Effect: S.S.I. 2011/415 amended. Territorial extent & classification: S. General. - EC note: These Regulations make provision in Scotland for the administration and enforcement of Council Regulation (EC) no. 73/2009 and Commission Regulation (EC) no. 1122/2009 in relation to cross-compliance under the Common Agricultural Policy. - 4p.: 30 cm. - 978-0-11-102236-8 £4.00

The Less Favoured Area Support Scheme (Scotland) Amendment Regulations 2014 No. 2014/7. - Enabling power: European Communities Act 1972, s. 2 (2). - Issued: 16.01.2014. Made: 09.01.2014. Laid before the Scottish Parliament: 13.01.2014. Coming into force: 01.03.2014. Effect: S.S.I. 2009/376; 2010/273 amended. Territorial extent & classification: S. General. - 4p.: 30 cm. - 978-0-11-102237-5 £4.00

Ancient monuments

The Historic Environment Scotland Act 2014 (Commencement No. 1) Order 2014 No. 2014/368 (C.34). - Enabling power: Historic Environment Act 2014, s. 31 (2). Bringing into operation various provisions of the 2014 Act on 19.01.2015 in accord. with art. 2. - Issued: 22.12.2014. Made: 16.12.2014. Laid before the Scottish Parliament: 18.12.2104. Coming into force: 19.01.2015. Effect: None. Territorial extent & classification: S. General. - 2p.: 30 cm. - 978-0-11-102563-5 £4.25

Animals

The Tuberculosis (Scotland) Amendment Order 2014 No. 2014/71. - Enabling power: Animal Health Act 1981, ss. 1, 8 (1), 15 (4), 25, 83 (2). - Issued: 11.03.2014. Made: 05.03.2014. Laid before the Scottish Parliament: 07.03.2014. Coming into force: 06.04.2014. Effect: S.S.I. 2007/147 amended. Territorial extent & classification: S. General. - With correction slip dated December 2014. - 4p.: 30 cm. - 978-0-11-102298-6 £4.00

Animals: Animal health

The Brucellosis (Scotland) Amendment (No. 2) Order 2014 No. 2014/72. - Enabling power: European Communities Act 1972, s. 2 (2). - Issued: 18.03.2014. Made: 12.03.2014. Laid before the Scottish Parliament: 14.03.2014. Coming into force: 31.03.2014, for arts. 1, 2; 01.04.2014, for art. 3. Effect: S.S.I. 2009/232 amended & S.S.I. 2014/63 partially revoked (31.03.2014). Territorial extent & classification: S. General. - This Statutory Instrument has been made in consequence of a defect in S.S.I. 2014/63 (ISBN 9780111022894) and is being issued free of charge to all known recipients of that instrument. - 4p.: 30 cm. - 978-0-11-102300-6 £4.00

The Brucellosis (Scotland) Amendment Order 2014 No. 2014/63. - Enabling power: European Communities Act 1972, s. 2 (2) & Animal Health Act 1981, s. 88 (2). - Issued: 06.03.2014. Made: 27.02.2014. Laid before the Scottish Parliament: 03.03.2014. Coming into force: 01.04.2014. Effect: S.I. 2009/232 amended & S.I. 1971/531 revoked in relation to Scotland. Territorial extent & classification: S. General. - A defect in this SSI has been corrected by a partial revocation via SSI 2014/72 (ISBN 9780111023006) which is being sent free of charge to all known recipients of 2014/63. - 4p.: 30 cm. - 978-0-11-102289-4 £4.00

The Specified Diseases (Notification and Slaughter) (Amendment) and Compensation (Scotland) Order 2014 No. 2014/151. - Enabling power: Animal Health Act 1981, ss. 32 (2) (3), 87 (2) (a). - Issued: 04.06.2014. Made: 28.05.2014. Laid before the Scottish Parliament: 30.05.2014. Coming into force: 28.06.2014. Effect: S.I. 1992/3159 amended. Territorial extent & classification: S. General. - 4p.: 30 cm. - 978-0-11-102369-3 £4.25

Aquaculture

The Aquaculture and Fisheries (Scotland) Act 2013 (Specification of Commercially Damaging Species) Order 2014 No. 2014/176. - Enabling power: Aquaculture and Fisheries (Scotland) Act 2013, s. 11 (1). - Issued: 23.06.2014. Made: 17.06.2014. Laid before the Scottish Parliament: 18.06.2014. Coming into force: 23.08.2014. Effect: None. Territorial extent & classification: S. General. - 2p.: 30 cm. - 978-0-11-102393-8 £4.25

Bankruptcy

The Bankruptcy and Debt Advice (Scotland) Act 2014 (Commencement No. 1 and Saving) Order 2014 No. 2014/172 (C.13). - Enabling power: Bankruptcy and Debt Advice (Scotland) Act 2014, ss. 57 (2) (3). Bringing into operation various provisions of the 2014 Act on 30.06.2014, in accord. with art. 2. - Issued: 20.06.2014. Made: 16.06.2014. Laid before the Scottish Parliament: 18.06.2014. Coming into force: 30.06.2014. Effect: None. Territorial extent & classification: S. General. - 8p.: 30 cm. - 978-0-11-102391-4 £6.00

The Bankruptcy and Debt Advice (Scotland) Act 2014 (Commencement No. 2, Savings and Transitionals) Order 2014 No. 2014/261 (C.23). - Enabling power: Bankruptcy and Debt Advice (Scotland) Act 2014, s. 57 (2) (3). Bringing into operation various provisions of the 2014 Act on 01.04.2015, in accord. with art. 2. - Issued: 06.10.2014. Made: 29.09.2014. Laid before the Scottish Parliament: 01.10.2014. Coming into force: 01.04.2015. Effect: None. Territorial extent & classification: S. General. - 8p.: 30 cm. - 978-0-11-102449-2 £6.00

The Bankruptcy and Debt Advice (Scotland) Act 2014 (Consequential Provisions) Order 2014 No. 2014/293. - Enabling power: Bankruptcy and Debt Advice (Scotland) Act 2014, s. 55. - Issued: 12.11.2014. Made: 05.11.2014. Coming into force: 01.04.2015. Effect: 1980 c.44; 2001 asp 13; 2005 asp 10 & S.I. 1998/1451, 1594; S.S.I. 2003/344; 2005/393; 2006/333; 2007/154; 2008/228, 235; 2011/117; 2014/164 amended. Territorial extent & classification: S. General. - Supersedes draft S.S.I. (ISBN 9780111024331) issued 29.08.2014. - 8p.: 30 cm. - 978-0-11-102486-7 £6.00

The Bankruptcy and Diligence etc. (Scotland) Act 2007 (Commencement No. 9 and Savings Amendment) Order 2014 No. 2014/173 (C.14). - Enabling power: Bankruptcy and Diligence etc. (Scotland) Act 2007, ss. 224 (2), 227 (3) (4). Bringing into operation various provisions of the 2007 Act on 01.04.2015 in accord. with art. 2. - Issued: 20.06.2014. Made: 16.06.2014. Laid before the Scottish Parliament: 18.06.2014. Coming into force: 04.10.2014. Effect: S.S.I. 2008/115 amended. Territorial extent & classification: S. General. - 8p.: 30 cm. - 978-0-11-102392-1 £4.25

The Bankruptcy (Applications and Decisions) (Scotland) Regulations 2014 No. 2014/226. - Enabling power: Bankruptcy (Scotland) Act 1985, ss. 71C, 72 (1A), 72A. - Issued: 28.08.2014. Made: 20.08.2014. Laid before the Scottish Parliament: 21.08.2014. Coming into force: 01.05.2015. Effect: None. Territorial extent & classification: S. General. - 28p.: 30 cm. - 978-0-11-102426-3 £6.00

The Bankruptcy (Money Advice and Deduction from Income etc.) (Scotland) Regulations 2014 No. 2014/296. - Enabling power: Bankruptcy (Scotland) Act 1985, ss. 5A, 5B (5) (b) (2), 5C (1) (d) (2) (b), 32E (7), 39A (4) (a), 71C, 72 (1A). - Issued: 12.11.2014. Made: 05.11.2014. Coming into force: 01.04.2015. Effect: 1985 c.66; S.I. 2010/397 amended & S.S.I. 2013/137 partially revoked & S.S.I. 2008/81 revoked. Territorial extent & classification: S. General. - Supersedes draft SI (ISBN 9780111024386) issued 11/09/14. - 12p.: 30 cm. - 978-0-11-102489-8 £6.00

BUILDING AND BUILDINGS

The Bankruptcy (Scotland) Regulations 2014 No. 2014/225. - Enabling power: Bankruptcy (Scotland) Act 1985, ss. 1A (1) (b) (5), 2 (8), 5 (2ZA) (a) (ii) (2D) (6A), 6 (7), 7 (1) (d), 11 (1), 19 (2), 22 (2) (a) (6), 23 (1) (a), 32 (9A), 40 (3B), 43A (2), 43B (1), 45 (3) (a), 49 (3), 51 (7) (a), 54 (2), 54A (2), 54C (2), 54D (2) (a), 54E (2) (5), 69, 71C, 72 (1A), 73 (1), sch. 3, para. 5 (1), 6. - Issued: 28.08.2014. Made: 20.08.2014. Laid before the Scottish Parliament: 21.08.2014. Coming into force: 01.04.2014. Effect: S.S.I. 2008/82; 2010/367 partially revoked & S.S.I. 2008/334 revoked. Territorial extent & classification: S. General. - 148p.: 30 cm. - 978-0-11-102425-6 £23.25

The Common Financial Tool etc. (Scotland) Regulations 2014 No. 2014/290. - Enabling power: Bankruptcy (Scotland) Act 1985, ss. 5D, 71C, 72 (1A), sch. 5, para. 5 & Debt Arrangement and Attachment Act (Scotland) Act 2002, s. 7 (2) (bd). - Issued: 12.11.2014. Made: 05.11.2014. Coming into force: 01.04.2015. Effect: S.S.I. 2013/318 amended. Territorial extent & classification: S. General. - Supersedes draft SI (ISBN 9780111024348) issued 29/08/14. - 24p.: 30 cm. - 978-0-11-102484-3 £6.00

Building and buildings

The Building (Scotland) Act 2003 (Charging Orders) Regulations 2014 No. 2014/369. - Enabling power: Building (Scotland) Act 2003, ss. 33 (1) (b) (ii), 36 (1). - Issued: 23.12.2014. Made: 16.12.2014. Laid before the Scottish Parliament: 18.12.2014. Coming into force: 07.02.2015. Effect: None. Territorial extent & classification: S. General. - 8p.: 30 cm. - 978-0-11-102564-2 £4.25

The Building (Scotland) Amendment Regulations 2014 No. 2014/219. - Enabling power: Building (Scotland) Act 2003, ss. 1, 54 (2). - Issued: 19.08.2014. Made: 12.08.2014. Laid before the Scottish Parliament: 14.08.2014. Coming into force: 01.10.2015. Effect: S.S.I. 2004/406 amended. Territorial extent & classification: S. General. - 4p.: 30 cm. - 978-0-11-102421-8 £4.25

Charities

The Charities Accounts (Scotland) Amendment (No. 2) Regulations 2014 No. 2014/335. - Enabling power: Charities and Trustee Investment (Scotland) Act 2005, s. 44 (4) (5). - Issued: 03.12.2014. Made: 26.11.2014. Laid before the Scottish Parliament: 27.11.2014. Coming into force: 01.01.2015. Effect: S.S.I. 2006/218 amended & S.S.I. 2014/295 revoked. Territorial extent & classification: S. General. - This Scottish Statutory Instrument has been made in consequence of defects in S.S.I. 2014/295 (ISBN 9780111024881) issued 12.11.2014 and is being issued free of charge to all known recipients of that Instrument. - 4p.: 30 cm. - 978-0-11-102527-7 £4.25

The Charities Accounts (Scotland) Amendment Regulations 2014 No. 2014/295. - Enabling power: Charities and Trustee Investment (Scotland) Act 2005, s. 44 (4) (5). - Issued: 12.11.2014. Made: 05.11.2014. Laid before the Scottish Parliament: 07.11.2014. Coming into force: 01.01.2015. Effect: S.S.I. 2006/218 amended. Territorial extent & classification: S. General. - Revoked by SSI 2014/335 (ISBN 9780111025277). - 4p.: 30 cm. - 978-0-11-102488-1 £4.25

The Land and Buildings Transaction Tax (Definition of Charity) (Relevant Territories) (Scotland) Regulations 2014 No. 2014/352. - Enabling power: Land and Buildings Transaction Tax (Scotland) Act 2013, sch. 13 para. 15 (3) (d). - Issued: 11.12.2014. Made: 04.12.2014. Laid before the Scottish Parliament: 08.12.2014. Coming into force: 01.04.2015. Effect: None. Territorial extent & classification: S. General. - 2p.: 30 cm. - 978-0-11-102546-8 £4.25

Children and young persons

The Adoption and Children (Scotland) Act 2007 (Compulsory Supervision Order Reports in Applications for Permanence Orders) Regulations 2014 No. 2014/113. - Enabling power: Adoption and Children (Scotland) Act 2007, s. 95 (2). - Issued: 30.04.2014. Made: 23.04.2014. Laid before the Scottish Parliament: 25.04.2014. Coming into force: 02.06.2014. Effect: SSI 2009/169 revoked. Territorial extent & classification: S. General. - 4p.: 30 cm. - 978-0-11-102330-3 £4.25

The Children and Young People (Scotland) Act 2014 (Ancillary Provision) (No. 2) Order 2014 No. 2014/315. - Enabling power: Children and Young People (Scotland) Act 2014, s. 101 (a). - Issued: 25.11.2014. Made: 18.11.2014. Laid before the Scottish Parliament: 20.11.2014. Coming into force: 05.01.2015. Effect: S.S.I. 2008/400 revoked. Territorial extent & classification: S. General. - 2p.: 30 cm. - 978-0-11-102506-2 £4.25

The Children and Young People (Scotland) Act 2014 (Commencement No. 1 and Transitory Provisions) Order 2014 No. 2014/131 (C.9). - Enabling power: Children and Young People (Scotland) Act 2014, s. 102 (3) (4). Bringing into operation various provisions of the 2014 Act on 28.06.2014, 01.08.2014, in accord. with art. 2. - Issued: 22.05.2014. Made: 15.05.2014. Laid before the Scottish Parliament: 19.05.2014. Coming into force: 28.06.2014. Effect: 1968 c.49 modified. Territorial extent & classification: S. General. - 8p.: 30 cm. - 978-0-11-102344-0 £4.25

The Children and Young People (Scotland) Act 2014 (Commencement No. 3) Order 2014 No. 2014/251 (C.22). - Enabling power: Children and Young People (Scotland) Act 2014, s. 102 (3). Bringing into operation various provisions of the 2014 Act on 06.10.2014, in accord. with art. 1. - Issued: 30.09.2014. Made: 23.09.2014. Laid before the Scottish Parliament: 25.09.2014. Coming into force: 06.10.2014. Effect: None. Territorial extent & classification: S. General. - 4p.: 30 cm. - 978-0-11-102444-7 £4.25

The Children and Young People (Scotland) Act 2014 (Commencement No. 4) Order 2014 No. 2014/314 (C.29). - Enabling power: Children and Young People (Scotland) Act 2014, s. 102 (3). Bringing into operation various provisions of the 2014 Act on 05.01.2015, in accord. with art. 2. - Issued: 25.11.2014. Made: 18.11.2014. Laid before the Scottish Parliament: 20.11.2014. Effect: None. Territorial extent & classification: S. General. - 8p.: 30 cm. - 978-0-11-102505-5 £4.25

The Children and Young People (Scotland) Act 2014 (Commencement No. 5 and Saving Provision) Order 2014 No. 2014/353 (C.31). - Enabling power: Children and Young People (Scotland) Act 2014, s. 102 (3) (4). Bringing into operation various provisions of the 2014 Act on 09.01.2015, 26.01.2015, in accord. with art. 2. - Issued: 15.12.2014. Made: 09.12.2014. Laid before the Scottish Parliament: 10.12.2014. Coming into force: 09.01.2015. Effect: None. Territorial extent & classification: S. General. - 8p.: 30 cm. - 978-0-11-102549-9 £4.25

The Children and Young People (Scotland) Act 2014 (Commencement No. 6) Order 2014 No. 2014/365 (C.33). - Enabling power: Children and Young People (Scotland) Act 2014, s. 102 (3). Bringing into operation various provisions of the 2014 Act on 09.01.2015, in accord. with art. 2. - Issued: 22.12.2014. Made: 16.12.2014. Laid before the Scottish Parliament: 17.12.2014. Coming into force: 09.01.2015. Effect: None. Territorial extent & classification: S. General. - 4p.: 30 cm. - 978-0-11-102560-4 £4.25

The Children (Performances and Activities) (Scotland) Regulations 2014 No. 2014/372. - Enabling power: Children and Young People Act 1933, s. 25 (2) (8) & Children and Young Persons Act 1963, ss. 37 (3) (4) (5) (6), 39 (3) (5). - Issued: 23.12.2014. Made: 17.12.2014. Laid before the Scottish Parliament: 19.12.2014. Coming into force: 20.02.2015. Effect: S.I. 1968/178; 1998/1678 revoked in relation to Scotland. Territorial extent & classification: S. General. - 24p.: 30 cm. - 978-0-11-102567-3 £6.00

The Children's Hearings (Scotland) Act 2011 (Modification of Subordinate Legislation) Order 2014 No. 2014/112. - Enabling power: Children's Hearing (Scotland) Act 2011, s. 204. - Issued: 30.04.2014. Made: 23.04.2014. Laid before the Scottish Parliament: 25.04.2014. Coming into force: 02.06.2014. Effect: S.I. 2009/154, 210 amended. Territorial extent & classification: S. General. - 4p.: 30 cm. - 978-0-11-102329-7 £4.25

The Children's Hearings (Scotland) Act 2011 (Supplementary Provision) Order 2014 No. 2014/137. - Enabling power: Children's Hearing (Scotland) Act 2011, s. 204. - Issued: 28.05.2014. Made: 20.05.2014. Laid before the Scottish Parliament: 22.05.2014. Coming into force: 20.06.2014. Effect: None. Territorial extent & classification: S. General. - 4p.: 30 cm. - 978-0-11-102354-9 £4.25

The Looked After Children (Scotland) Amendment Regulations 2014 No. 2014/310. - Enabling power: Social Work (Scotland) Act 1968, s. 5 (2), (3) (4) & Children (Scotland) Act 1995, ss. 17 (1), 103 (2) (3). - Issued: 19.11.2014. Made: 12.11.2014. Laid before the Scottish Parliament: 14.11.2014. Coming into force: 29.12.2014. Effect: S.S.I. 2009/210 amended. Territorial extent & classification: S. General. - 4p.: 30 cm. - 978-0-11-102502-4 £4.25

The Protection of Vulnerable Groups (Scotland) Act 2007 (Miscellaneous Provisions) Amendment Order 2014 No. 2014/33. - Enabling power: European Communities Act 1972, s. 2 (2). - Issued: 11.02.2014. Made: 04.02.2014. Laid before the Scottish Parliament: 06.02.2014. Coming into force: 16.03.2014. Effect: S.S.I. 2010/446 amended. Territorial extent & classification: S. General. - 4p.: 30 cm. - 978-0-11-102256-6 £4.00

Civil partnership

The Marriage and Civil Partnership (Prescribed Forms) (Scotland) Regulations 2014 No. 2014/306. - Enabling power: Marriage and Civil Partnership (Scotland) Act 2014, s. 88 (1) (5), 95ZA & Local Electoral Administration and Registration Services (Scotland) Act 2006, s. 55 (2) & Marriage (Scotland) Act 1977, ss. 3 (1), 6 (1), 7 (2) & Registration of Births, Deaths and Marriages (Scotland) Act 1965, ss. 32 (1), 54 (1) (b). - Issued: 18.11.2014. Made: 11.11.2014. Laid before the Scottish Parliament: 13.11.2014. Coming into force: 16.12.2014. Effect: S.I. 1997/2348, 2349; S.S.I. 2005/458; 2008/386 amended. Territorial extent & classification: S. General. - 16p.: 30 cm. - 978-0-11-102499-7 £6.00

The Marriage and Civil Partnership (Scotland) Act 2014 (Commencement No. 1) Order 2014 No. 2014/121 (C.8). - Enabling power: Marriage and Civil Partnership (Scotland) Act 2014, s. 36 (2). Bringing into operation various provisions of the Act on 21.05.2014, in accord. with art. 2. - Issued: 09.05.2014. Made: 01.05.2014. Laid before the Scottish Parliament: 06.05.2014. Coming into force: 21.05.2014. Effect: None. Territorial extent & classification: S. General. - 2p.: 30 cm. - 978-0-11-102337-2 £4.25

The Marriage and Civil Partnership (Scotland) Act 2014 (Commencement No. 2 and Saving Provisions) Amendment Order 2014 No. 2014/218 (C.19). - Enabling power: Marriage and Civil Partnership (Scotland) Act 2014, s. 36 (2) (3). Bringing into operation various provisions of the 2014 Act on 01.09.2014. - Issued: 14.08.2014. Made: 07.08.2014. Laid before the Scottish Parliament: 11.08.2014. Coming into force: 01.09.2014. Effect: S.S.I. 2014/212 amended. Territorial extent & classification: S. General. - This S.S.I. has been made in consequence of defects in S.S.I. 2014/212 (ISBN 9780111024164, issued 29.07.2014) and is being issued free of charge to all known recipients of that instrument. - 8p.: 30 cm. - 978-0-11-102420-1 £6.00

The Marriage and Civil Partnership (Scotland) Act 2014 (Commencement No. 2 and Saving Provisions) Order 2014 No. 2014/212 (C.18). - Enabling power: Marriage and Civil Partnership (Scotland) Act 2014, s. 36 (2). Bringing into operation various provisions of the 2014 Act on 01.09.2014, in accord. with art. 2. - Issued: 29.07.2014. Made: 22.07.2014. Laid before the Scottish Parliament: 24.07.2014. Coming into force: 01.09.2014. Effect: None. Territorial extent & classification: S. General. - Corrected by SSI 2014/218 (ISBN 9780111024201) which is being sent free of charge to all known recipients of 2012/212. - 8p.: 30 cm. - 978-0-11-102416-4 £4.25

The Marriage and Civil Partnership (Scotland) Act 2014 (Commencement No. 3, Saving, Transitional Provision and Revocation) Order 2014 No. 2014/287 (C.28). - Enabling power: Marriage and Civil Partnership (Scotland) Act 2014, ss. 35, 36 (2) (3). Bringing into operation various provisions of the 2014 Act on 16.12.2014, in accord. with art. 3. - Issued: 05.11.2014. Made: 29.10.2014. Laid before the Scottish Parliament: 31.10.2014. Coming into force: 16.12.2014. Effect: S.S.I. 2002/260; 2005/657; 2006/573 amended. Territorial extent & classification: S. General. - 8p.: 30 cm. - 978-0-11-102477-5 £6.00

The Marriage Between Civil Partners (Procedure for Change and Fees) (Scotland) Regulations 2014 No. 2014/361. - Enabling power: Marriage and Civil Partnership (Scotland) Act 2014, s. 10. - Issued: 19.12.2014. Made: 15.12.2014. Coming into force: 16.12.2014. Effect: 1977 c.15; 2004 c.7 modified. Territorial extent & classification: S. General. - Supersedes draft SI (ISBN 9780111024805) issued 06/11/14. - 8p.: 30 cm. - 978-0-11-102557-4 £6.00

Clean air

The Smoke Control Areas (Authorised Fuels) (Scotland) Regulations 2014 No. 2014/317. - Enabling power: Clean Air Act 1993, s. 20 (6). - Issued: 25.11.2014. Made: 19.11.2014. Laid before the Scottish Parliament: 20.11.2014. Coming into force: 19.12.2014. Effect: S.S.I. 2010/271 revoked. Territorial extent & classification: S. General. - 20p.: 30 cm. - 978-0-11-102508-6 £6.00

The Smoke Control Areas (Exempt Fireplaces) (Scotland) Order 2014 No. 2014/316. - Enabling power: Clean Air Act 1993, s. 21 (5). - Issued: 26.11.2014. Made: 19.11.2014. Laid before the Scottish Parliament: 20.11.2014. Coming into force: 19.12.2014. Effect: S.S.I. 2010/272 revoked. Territorial extent & classification: S. General. - 156p.: 30 cm. - 978-0-11-102507-9 £23.25

Council tax

The Council Tax (Discounts) (Scotland) Amendment Order 2014 No. 2014/37. - Enabling power: Local Government Finance Act 1992, s. 113 (1) (2), sch. 1, para. 4. - Issued: 18.02.2014. Made: 11.02.2014. Laid before the Scottish Parliament: 13.02.2014. Coming into force: 01.04.2014. Effect: S.S.I. 2003/176 amended. Territorial extent & classification: S. General. - 4p.: 30 cm. - 978-0-11-102261-0 £4.00

The Council Tax Reduction (Scotland) Amendment Regulations 2014 No. 2014/35. - Enabling power: Local Government Finance Act 1992, ss. 80, 113 (1), sch. 2, para. 1. - Issued: 13.02.2014. Made: 06.02.2014. Laid before the Scottish Parliament: 10.02.2014. Coming into force: 01.04.2014. Effect: S.S.I. 2012/303, 319 amended. Territorial extent & classification: S. General. - 8p.: 30 cm. - 978-0-11-102259-7 £4.00

Court of Session

Act of Sederunt (Messengers-at-Arms and Sheriff Officers Rules) (Amendment) 2014 No. 2014/29. - Enabling power: Debtors (Scotland) Act 1987, s. 75. - Issued: 10.02.2014. Made: 04.02.2014. Laid before the Scottish Parliament: 06.02.2014. Coming into force: 17.03.2014. Effect: S.I. 1991/1397 amended. Territorial extent & classification: S. General. - 4p.: 30 cm. - 978-0-11-102252-8 £4.00

Act of Sederunt (Rules of the Court of Session Amendment) (Fees of Solicitors) 2014 No. 2014/15. - Enabling power: Court of Session Act 1988, s. 5. - Issued: 24.01.2014. Made: 20.01.2014. Laid before the Scottish Parliament: 21.01.2014. Coming into force: 01.03.2014. Effect: S.I. 1994/1443 amended. Territorial extent & classification: S. General. - 24p.: 30 cm. - 978-0-11-102243-6 £5.75

Act of Sederunt (Rules of the Court of Session and Sheriff Court Company Insolvency Rules Amendment) (Miscellaneous) 2014 No. 2014/119. - Enabling power: Sheriff Courts (Scotland) Act 1971, s. 32 & Court of Session Act 1988, s. 5. - Issued: 08.05.2014. Made: 01.05.2014. Laid before the Scottish Parliament: 02.05.2014. Coming into force: 30.05.2014. Effect: S.I. 1986/2297; 1994/1443 amended. Territorial extent & classification: S. General. - 4p.: 30 cm. - 978-0-11-102336-5 £4.25

Act of Sederunt (Rules of the Court of Session and Sheriff Court Rules Amendment) (Miscellaneous) 2014 No. 2014/201. - Enabling power: Sheriff Courts (Scotland) Act 1971, s. 32 & Court of Session Act 1988, s. 5. - Issued: 10.07.2014. Made: 04.07.2014. Laid before the Scottish Parliament: 07.07.2014. Coming into force: 01.08.2014. Effect: 1907 c.51; S.I. 1994/1443; 1997/291 amended. Territorial extent & classification: S. General. - 8p.: 30 cm. - 978-0-11-102412-6 £6.00

Act of Sederunt (Rules of the Court of Session and Sheriff Court Rules Amendment No. 2) (Marriage and Civil Partnership (Scotland) Act 2014) 2014 No. 2014/302. - Enabling power: Sheriff Courts (Scotland) Act 1971, s. 32 & & Court of Session Act 1988, s. 5 & Adoption and Children (Scotland) Act 2007, s. 114. - Issued: 18.11.2014. Made: 12.11.2014. Laid before the Scottish Parliament: 14.11.2014. Coming into force: 16.12.2014. Effect: 1907 c.51; S.I. 1994/1443; 1999/929; S.S.I. 2009/284 amended. Territorial extent & classification: S. General. - 12p.: 30 cm. - 978-0-11-102495-9 £6.00

Act of Sederunt (Rules of the Court of Session and Sheriff Court Rules Amendment No.2) (Miscellaneous) 2014 No. 2014/291. - Enabling power: Sheriff Courts (Scotland) Act 1971, s. 32 & Debtors (Scotland) Act 1987, s. 15K (3) (a) & Court of Session Act 1988, s. 5. - Issued: 11.11.2014. Made: 05.11.2014. Laid before the Scottish Parliament: 07.11.2014. Coming into force: 08.12.2014. Effect: 1907 c.51; S.I. 1994/1443; S.S.I. 2002/132, 133 amended. Territorial extent & classification: S. General. - 16p.: 30 cm. - 978-0-11-102483-6 £6.00

CRIMINAL LAW

Act of Sederunt (Rules of the Court of Session and Sheriff Court Rules Amendment No. 3) (Mutual Recognition of Protection Measures) 2014 No. 2014/371. - Enabling power: Sheriff Courts (Scotland) Act 1971, s. 32 & Court of Session Act 1988, s. 5 & Protection from Abuse (Scotland) Act 2001, ss. 2 (1), 3 (1). - Issued: 23.12.2014. Made: 17.12.2014. Laid before the Scottish Parliament: 19.12.2014. Coming into force: 11.01.2015. Effect: 1907 c.51; S.I. 1994/1443; 1999/929 amended. Territorial extent & classification: S. General. - 36p.: 30 cm. - 978-0-11-102566-6 £10.00

Act of Sederunt (Rules of the Court of Session, Ordinary Cause Rules and Summary Cause Rules Amendment) (Miscellaneous) 2014 No. 2014/152. - Enabling power: Sheriff Courts (Scotland) Act 1971, s. 32 & Court of Session Act 1988, s. 5. - Issued: 04.06.2014. Made: 28.05.2014. Laid before the Scottish Parliament: 30.05.2014. Coming into force: 07.07.2014. Effect: 1907 c.51; S.I. 1994/1443; S.S.I. 2002/132 amended. Territorial extent & classification: S. General. - 16p.: 30 cm. - 978-0-11-102370-9 £6.00

Criminal law

The Anti-social Behaviour, Crime and Policing Act 2014 (Commencement) (Scotland) Order 2014 No. 2014/221 (C.20). - Enabling power: Anti-social Behaviour, Crime and Policing Act 2014, s. 185 (6). Bringing into operation various provisions of the 2014 Act on 30.09.2014. - Issued: 19.08.2014. Made: 12.08.2014. Laid before the Scottish Parliament: 14.08.2014. Effect: None. Territorial extent & classification: S. General. - 2p.: 30 cm. - 978-0-11-102423-2 £4.25

The Right to Information (Suspects and Accused Persons) (Scotland) Regulations 2014 No. 2014/159. - Enabling power: European Communities Act 1972, s. 2 (2). - Issued: 10.06.2014. Made: 04.06.2014. Laid before the Scottish Parliament: 05.06.2014. Coming into force: 06.06.2014. Effect: None. Territorial extent & classification: S. General. - 4p.: 30 cm. - 978-0-11-102376-1 £4.25

The Right to Interpretation and Translation in Criminal Proceedings (Scotland) Regulations 2014 No. 2014/95. - Enabling power: European Communities Act 1972, s. 2 (2). - Issued: 07.04.2014. Made: 01.04.2014. Laid before the Scottish Parliament: 03.04.2014. Coming into force: 19.05.2014. Effect: None. Territorial extent & classification: S. General. - 8p.: 30 cm. - 978-0-11-102316-7 £6.00

The Sexual Offences Act 2003 (Prescribed Police Stations) (Scotland) Regulations 2014 No. 2014/147. - Enabling power: Sexual Offences Act 2003, ss. 87 (1) (a), 138 (4). - Issued: 03.06.2014. Made: 28.05.2014. Laid before the Scottish Parliament: 30.05.2014. Coming into force: 28.06.2014. Effect: S.S.I. 2013/119 partially revoked & S.S.I. 2008/128; 2012/50 revoked. Territorial extent & classification: S. General. - 8p.: 30 cm. - 978-0-11-102365-5 £6.00

The Victims and Witnesses (Scotland) Act 2014 (Commencement No. 2 and Transitional Provision) Order 2014 No. 2014/210 (C.17). - Enabling power: Victims and Witnesses (Scotland) Act 2014, s. 34 (2) (3). Bringing into operation various provisions of the 2014 Act on 13.08.2014. - Issued: 28.07.2014. Made: 22.07.2014. Laid before the Scottish Parliament: 24.07.2014. Coming into force: 13.08.2014. Effect: None. Territorial extent & classification: S. General. - 4p.: 30 cm. - 978-0-11-102415-7 £4.25

The Victims and Witnesses (Scotland) Act 2014 (Commencement No. 3 and Transitional Provision) Order 2014 No. 2014/359 (C.32). - Enabling power: Victims and Witnesses (Scotland) Act 2014, s. 34 (2) (3). Bringing into operation various provisions of the 2014 Act on 30.01.2015. - Issued: 19.12.2014. Made: 15.12.2014. Laid before the Scottish Parliament: 16.12.2014. Coming into force: 30.01.2015. Effect: None. Territorial extent & classification: S. General. - 8p.: 30 cm. - 978-0-11-102555-0 £4.25

The Victims and Witnesses (Scotland) Act 2014 (Prescribed Relatives) Order 2014 No. 2014/360. - Enabling power: Victims and Witnesses (Scotland) Act 2014, ss. 2 (6), 6 (2) (b). - Issued: 19.12.2014. Made: 15.12.2014. Laid before the Scottish Parliament: 16.12.2014. Coming into force: 30.01.2015. Effect: None. Territorial extent & classification: S. General. - 4p.: 30 cm. - 978-0-11-102556-7 £4.25

Criminal procedure

The Mutual Recognition of Criminal Financial Penalties in the European Union (Scotland) (No. 1) Order 2014 No. 2014/322. - Enabling power: Criminal Proceedings etc. (Reform) (Scotland) Act 2007, s. 56 (1). - Issued: 25.11.2014. Made: 18.11.2014. Coming into force: 01.12.2014. Effect: 1995 c.46 amended. Territorial extent & classification: S. General. - Supersedes draft S.S.I. (ISBN 9780111024508) issued 08.10.2014. - 4p.: 30 cm. - 978-0-11-102512-3 £4.25

The Mutual Recognition of Criminal Financial Penalties in the European Union (Scotland) (No. 2) Order 2014 No. 2014/336. - Enabling power: European Communities Act 1972, s. 2 (2). - Issued: 08.12.2014. Made: 01.12.2014. Laid before the Scottish Parliament: 01.12.2014. Coming into force: 01.12.2014. Effect: 1995 c.46 amended. Territorial extent & classification: S. General. - 4p.: 30 cm. - 978-0-11-102535-2 £4.25

The Mutual Recognition of Supervision Measures in the European Union (Scotland) Regulations 2014 No. 2014/337. - Enabling power: European Communities Act 1972, s. 2 (2), sch. 2, para. 1A. - Issued: 08.12.2014. Made: 01.12.2014. Laid before the Scottish Parliament: 01.12.2014. Coming into force: 01.12.2014. Effect: None. Territorial extent & classification: S. General. - 20p.: 30 cm. - 978-0-11-102536-9 £6.00

Debt

The Bankruptcy and Debt Advice (Scotland) Act 2014 (Commencement No. 1 and Saving) Order 2014 No. 2014/172 (C.13). - Enabling power: Bankruptcy and Debt Advice (Scotland) Act 2014, ss. 57 (2) (3). Bringing into operation various provisions of the 2014 Act on 30.06.2014, in accord. with art. 2. - Issued: 20.06.2014. Made: 16.06.2014. Laid before the Scottish Parliament: 18.06.2014. Coming into force: 30.06.2014. Effect: None. Territorial extent & classification: S. General. - 8p.: 30 cm. - 978-0-11-102391-4 £6.00

The Bankruptcy and Debt Advice (Scotland) Act 2014 (Commencement No. 2, Savings and Transitionals) Order 2014 No. 2014/261 (C.23). - Enabling power: Bankruptcy and Debt Advice (Scotland) Act 2014, s. 57 (2) (3). Bringing into operation various provisions of the 2014 Act on 01.04.2015, in accord. with art. 2. - Issued: 06.10.2014. Made: 29.09.2014. Laid before the Scottish Parliament: 01.10.2014. Coming into force: 01.04.2015. Effect: None. Territorial extent & classification: S. General. - 8p.: 30 cm. - 978-0-11-102449-2 £6.00

The Bankruptcy (Applications and Decisions) (Scotland) Regulations 2014 No. 2014/226. - Enabling power: Bankruptcy (Scotland) Act 1985, ss. 71C, 72 (1A), 72A. - Issued: 28.08.2014. Made: 20.08.2014. Laid before the Scottish Parliament: 21.08.2014. Coming into force: 01.05.2015. Effect: None. Territorial extent & classification: S. General. - 28p.: 30 cm. - 978-0-11-102426-3 £6.00

The Bankruptcy (Money Advice and Deduction from Income etc.) (Scotland) Regulations 2014 No. 2014/296. - Enabling power: Bankruptcy (Scotland) Act 1985, ss. 5A, 5B (5) (b) (2), 5C (1) (d) (2) (b), 32E (7), 39A (4) (a), 71C, 72 (1A). - Issued: 12.11.2014. Made: 05.11.2014. Coming into force: 01.04.2015. Effect: 1985 c.66; S.I. 2010/397 amended & S.S.I. 2013/137 partially revoked & S.S.I. 2008/81 revoked. Territorial extent & classification: S. General. - Supersedes draft SI (ISBN 9780111024386) issued 11/09/14. - 12p.: 30 cm. - 978-0-11-102489-8 £6.00

The Common Financial Tool etc. (Scotland) Regulations 2014 No. 2014/290. - Enabling power: Bankruptcy (Scotland) Act 1985, ss. 5D, 71C, 72 (1A), sch. 5, para. 5 & Debt Arrangement and Attachment Act (Scotland) Act 2002, s. 7 (2) (bd). - Issued: 12.11.2014. Made: 05.11.2014. Coming into force: 01.04.2015. Effect: S.S.I. 2013/318 amended. Territorial extent & classification: S. General. - Supersedes draft SI (ISBN 9780111024348) issued 29/08/14. - 24p.: 30 cm. - 978-0-11-102484-3 £6.00

The Debt Arrangement Scheme (Scotland) Amendment Regulations 2014 No. 2014/294. - Enabling power: Debt Arrangement and Attachment (Scotland) Act 2002, ss. 2 (3) (d), 4 (5), 5 (4), 7, 62 (2). - Issued: 12.11.2014. Made: 05.11.2014. Coming into force: 11.12.2014, for the purpose of reg. 1 (2); 01.04.2015, for the purpose of reg. 1 (3). Effect: S.S.I. 2011/141 amended & partially revoked. Territorial extent & classification: S. General. - Supersedes draft (ISBN 9780111024416) issued 24.09.2014. - 56p.: 30 cm. - 978-0-11-102487-4 £10.00

Education

The Additional Support for Learning (Sources of Information) (Scotland) Amendment Order 2014 No. 2014/103. - Enabling power: Education (Additional Support for Learning) (Scotland) Act 2004, s. 26 (2) (i). - Issued: 23.04.2014. Made: 15.04.2014. Laid before the Scottish Parliament: 17.04.2014. Coming into force: 21.05.2014. Effect: S.S.I. 2010/145 amended. Territorial extent & classification: S. General. - 2p.: 30 cm. - 978-0-11-102323-5 £4.25

The Assigned Colleges (Scotland) Order 2014 No. 2014/80. - Enabling power: Further and Higher Education (Scotland) Act 2005, ss. 7C (1), 34 (2). - Issued: 27.03.2014. Made: 20.03.2014. Laid before the Scottish Parliament: 24.03.2014. Coming into force: 01.08.2014. Effect: None. Territorial extent & classification: S. General. - 4p.: 30 cm. - 978-0-11-102304-4 £4.00

The Assigned Colleges (University of the Highlands and Islands) Order 2014 No. 2014/146. - Enabling power: Further and Higher Education (Scotland) Act 2005, ss. 7C (1), 34 (2). - Issued: 04.06.2014. Made: 28.05.2014. Laid before the Scottish Parliament: 30.05.2014. Coming into force: 01.08.2014. Effect: None. Territorial extent & classification: S. General. - 4p.: 30 cm. - 978-0-11-102364-8 £4.25

The Children and Young People (Scotland) Act 2014 (Ancillary Provision) (No. 2) Order 2014 No. 2014/315. - Enabling power: Children and Young People (Scotland) Act 2014, s. 101 (a). - Issued: 25.11.2014. Made: 18.11.2014. Laid before the Scottish Parliament: 20.11.2014. Coming into force: 05.01.2015. Effect: S.S.I. 2008/400 revoked. Territorial extent & classification: S. General. - 2p.: 30 cm. - 978-0-11-102506-2 £4.25

The Children and Young People (Scotland) Act 2014 (Ancillary Provision) Order 2014 No. 2014/132. - Enabling power: Children and Young People (Scotland) Act 2014, s. 101. - Issued: 22.05.2014. Made: 15.05.2014. Laid before the Scottish Parliament: 19.05.2014. Coming into force: 28.06.2014. Effect: None. Territorial extent & classification: S. General. - 4p.: 30 cm. - 978-0-11-102345-7 £4.25

The Children and Young People (Scotland) Act 2014 (Commencement No. 1 and Transitory Provisions) Order 2014 No. 2014/131 (C.9). - Enabling power: Children and Young People (Scotland) Act 2014, s. 102 (3) (4). Bringing into operation various provisions of the 2014 Act on 28.06.2014, 01.08.2014, in accord. with art. 2. - Issued: 22.05.2014. Made: 15.05.2014. Laid before the Scottish Parliament: 19.05.2014. Coming into force: 28.06.2014. Effect: 1968 c.49 modified. Territorial extent & classification: S. General. - 8p.: 30 cm. - 978-0-11-102344-0 £4.25

The Children and Young People (Scotland) Act 2014 (Commencement No. 2, Transitional and Transitory Provisions) Order 2014 No. 2014/165 (C.12). - Enabling power: Children and Young People (Scotland) Act 2014, s. 102 (3) (4). Bringing into operation various provisions of the 2014 Act on 01.08.2014, in accord. with art. 2. - Issued: 12.06.2014. Made: 05.06.2014. Laid before the Scottish Parliament: 09.06.2014. Coming into force: 01.08.2014. Effect: None. Territorial extent & classification: S. General. - 8p.: 30 cm. - 978-0-11-102382-2 £6.00

The Children and Young People (Scotland) Act 2014 (Commencement No. 3) Order 2014 No. 2014/251 (C.22). - Enabling power: Children and Young People (Scotland) Act 2014, s. 102 (3). Bringing into operation various provisions of the 2014 Act on 06.10.2014, in accord. with art. 1. - Issued: 30.09.2014. Made: 23.09.2014. Laid before the Scottish Parliament: 25.09.2014. Coming into force: 06.10.2014. Effect: None. Territorial extent & classification: S. General. - 4p.: 30 cm. - 978-0-11-102444-7 £4.25

The Children and Young People (Scotland) Act 2014 (Commencement No. 4) Order 2014 No. 2014/314 (C.29). - Enabling power: Children and Young People (Scotland) Act 2014, s. 102 (3). Bringing into operation various provisions of the 2014 Act on 05.01.2015, in accord. with art. 2. - Issued: 25.11.2014. Made: 18.11.2014. Laid before the Scottish Parliament: 20.11.2014. Effect: None. Territorial extent & classification: S. General. - 8p.: 30 cm. - 978-0-11-102505-5 £4.25

The Children and Young People (Scotland) Act 2014 (Commencement No. 5 and Saving Provision) Order 2014 No. 2014/353 (C.31). - Enabling power: Children and Young People (Scotland) Act 2014, s. 102 (3) (4). Bringing into operation various provisions of the 2014 Act on 09.01.2015, 26.01.2015, in accord. with art. 2. - Issued: 15.12.2014. Made: 09.12.2014. Laid before the Scottish Parliament: 10.12.2014. Coming into force: 09.01.2015. Effect: None. Territorial extent & classification: S. General. - 8p.: 30 cm. - 978-0-11-102549-9 £4.25

The Children and Young People (Scotland) Act 2014 (Commencement No. 6) Order 2014 No. 2014/365 (C.33). - Enabling power: Children and Young People (Scotland) Act 2014, s. 102 (3). Bringing into operation various provisions of the 2014 Act on 09.01.2015, in accord. with art. 2. - Issued: 22.12.2014. Made: 16.12.2014. Laid before the Scottish Parliament: 17.12.2014. Coming into force: 09.01.2015. Effect: None. Territorial extent & classification: S. General. - 4p.: 30 cm. - 978-0-11-102560-4 £4.25

The Coatbridge College (Transfer and Closure) (Scotland) Order 2014 No. 2014/52. - Enabling power: Further and Higher Education (Scotland) Act 1992, ss. 3 (1) (c), 25 (1) (1A) (2) (5), 60 (3). - Issued: 05.03.2014. Made: 26.02.2014. Laid before the Scottish Parliament: 28.02.2014. Coming into force: 01.04.2014. Effect: S.S.I. 2014/21 amended. Territorial extent & classification: S. General. - 4p.: 30 cm. - 978-0-11-102278-8 £4.00

The Convener of the School Closure Review Panels (Scotland) Regulations 2014 No. 2014/262. - Enabling power: Schools (Consultation) (Scotland) Act 2010, sch. 2A, para. 1 (9). - Issued: 14.10.2014. Made: 07.10.2014. Laid before the Scottish Parliament: 09.10.2014. Coming into force: 24.11.2014. Effect: None. Territorial extent & classification: S. General. - Supersedes draft SI (ISBN 9780111024003) issued 02.07.2014. - 4p.: 30 cm. - 978-0-11-102455-3 £4.25

The Designation of Regional Colleges (Scotland) Order 2014 No. 2014/22. - Enabling power: Further and Higher Education (Scotland) Act 2005, ss. 7A (1), 34 (2). - Issued: 29.01.2014. Made: 22.01.2014. Laid before the Scottish Parliament: 24.01.2014. Coming into force: 03.03.2014. Effect: None. Territorial extent & classification: S. General. - 4p.: 30 cm. - 978-0-11-102246-7 £4.00

The Education (Disapplication of section 53B) (Scotland) Regulations 2014 No. 2014/318. - Enabling power: Education (Scotland) Act 1980, s. 53B (1A). - Issued: 25.11.2014. Made: 18.11.2014. Laid before the Scottish Parliament: 20.11.2014. Coming into force: 05.01.2015. Effect: None. Territorial extent & classification: S. General. - 4p.: 30 cm. - 978-0-11-102509-3 £4.25

The Lanarkshire Colleges Order 2014 No. 2014/250. - Enabling power: Further and Higher Education (Scotland) Act 1992, ss. 3 (5), 60 (3) & Further and Higher Education (Scotland) Act 2005, ss. 7A (1), 7B (2), 7C (1), 34 (2). - Issued: 30.09.2014. Made: 23.09.2014. Coming into force: 01.10.2014. Effect: 1992 c.37 modified. Territorial extent & classification: S. General. - Supersedes draft S.I. (ISBN 9780111023907) issued 18/06/14. - 8p.: 30 cm. - 978-0-11-102443-0 £4.25

The Members of a School Closure Review Panel (Scotland) Regulations 2014 No. 2014/263. - Enabling power: Schools (Consultation) (Scotland) Act 2010, sch. 2A, para. 2 (5). - Issued: 14.10.2014. Made: 07.10.2014. Laid before the Scottish Parliament: 09.10.2014. Coming into force: 24.11.2014. Effect: None. Territorial extent & classification: S. General. - 4p.: 30 cm. - 978-0-11-102456-0 £4.25

The Post-16 Education (Scotland) Act 2013 (Commencement No. 3 and Transitory and Savings Provisions) Order 2014 No. 2014/21 (C.1). - Enabling power: Post-16 Education (Scotland) Act 2013, s. 23 (2) (3). Bringing into operation various provisions of this Act on 03.03.2014, in accord. with art. 2. - Issued: 29.01.2014. Made: 22.01.2014. Laid before the Scottish Parliament: 24.01.2014. Effect: None. Territorial extent & classification: S. General. - 12p.: 30 cm. - 978-0-11-102245-0 £5.75

The Post-16 Education (Scotland) Act 2013 (Commencement No. 4 and Transitory Provisions) Order 2014 No. 2014/79 (C.6). - Enabling power: Post-16 Education (Scotland) Act 2013, s. 23 (2) (3). Bringing into operation various provisions of this Act on 01.05.2014; 01.08.2014 in accord. with art. 2. - Issued: 27.03.2014. Made: 20.03.2014. Laid before the Scottish Parliament: 24.03.2014. Coming into force: 01.05.2014. Effect: 2005 asp 6 modified. Territorial extent & classification: S. General. - 8p.: 30 cm. - 978-0-11-102303-7 £5.75

The Post-16 Education (Scotland) Act 2013 (Commencement No. 5) Order 2014 No. 2014/144 (C.10). - Enabling power: Post-16 Education (Scotland) Act 2013, s. 23 (2). Bringing into operation various provisions of this Act on 01.08.2014 in accord. with art. 2. - Issued: 04.06.2014. Made: 28.05.2014. Laid before the Scottish Parliament: 30.05.2014. Coming into force: 01.08.2014. Effect: None. Territorial extent & classification: S. General. - 4p.: 30 cm. - 978-0-11-102363-1 £4.25

The Provision of Early Learning and Childcare (Specified Children) (Scotland) Order 2014 No. 2014/196. - Enabling power: Children and Young People (Scotland) Act 2014, ss. 47 (2) (c) (ii) (4), 99 (1). - Issued: 04.07.2014. Made: 30.06.2014. Coming into force: 01.08.2014 & 31.10.2014, in accord. with art. 1 (1). Effect: S.S.I. 2002/90; 2007/396 revoked (01.08.2014). Territorial extent & classification: S. General. - Supersedes draft S.S.I. (ISBN 9780111023945) issued 26.06.2014. - 8p.: 30 cm. - 978-0-11-102410-2 £6.00

The Royal Conservatoire of Scotland Order of Council 2014 No. 2014/268. - Enabling power: Further and Higher Education (Scotland) Act 1992, s. 45, 60 (3). - Issued: 21.10.2014. Made: 14.10.2014. Laid before the Scottish Parliament: 16.10.2014. Coming into force: 01.12.2014. Effect: S.I. 1995/2261 revoked. Territorial extent & classification: S. General. - 16p.: 30 cm. - 978-0-11-102461-4 £6.00

The St Mary's Music School (Aided Places) (Scotland) Amendment Regulations 2014 No. 2014/143. - Enabling power: Education (Scotland) Act 1980, ss. 73 (f), 74 (1). - Issued: 03.06.2014. Made: 27.05.2014. Laid before the Scottish Parliament: 29.05.2014. Coming into force: 01.08.2014. Effect: S.S.I. 2001/223 amended. Territorial extent & classification: S. General. - 4p.: 30 cm. - 978-0-11-102361-7 £4.25

The Young People's Involvement in Education and Training (Provision of Information) (Scotland) Order 2014 No. 2014/116. - Enabling power: Post-16 Education (Scotland) Act 2013, s. 20 (1) (3) (8). - Issued: 08.05.2014. Made: 30.04.2014. Coming into force: 01.05.2014. Effect: None. Territorial extent & classification: S. General. - Supersedes draft SI (ISBN 9780111022962) issued 11/03/14. - 8p.: 30 cm. - 978-0-11-102333-4 £6.00

Electricity

The Renewables Obligation (Scotland) Amendment Order 2014 No. 2014/94. - Enabling power: Electricity Act 1989, ss. 32 (1) (2), 32A (1) (2), 32B (1), 32C (1) to (6), 32D (1) (2), 32J (3), 32K (1) (3). - Issued: 07.04.2014. Made: 31.03.2014. Coming into force: 01.04.2014. Effect: S.I. 2009/140 amended. Territorial extent & classification: S. General. - Supersedes draft SI (ISBN 9780111022696) issued 25.02.2014. - 28p.: 30 cm. - 978-0-11-102315-0 £6.00

Electronic communications

The Electronic Documents (Scotland) Regulations 2014 No. 2014/83. - Enabling power: Requirements of Writing (Scotland) Act 1995, ss. 9B (2) (c), 9C (2), 9E (1) (d). - Issued: 01.04.2014. Made: 25.03.2014. Laid before the Scottish Parliament: 27.03.2014. Coming into force: 11.05.2014. Effect: None. Territorial extent & classification: S. General. - 4p.: 30 cm. - 978-0-11-102306-8 £4.00

Energy conservation

The Home Energy Assistance Scheme (Scotland) Amendment Regulations 2014 No. 2014/40. - Enabling power: Social Security Act 1990, s. 15 (1) (2) (c) (9) (b). - Issued: 25.02.2014. Made: 18.02.2014. Laid before the Scottish Parliament: 20.02.2014. Coming into force: 01.04.2014. Effect: S.S.I. 2013/148 amended. Territorial extent & classification: S. General. - 4p.: 30 cm. - 978-0-11-102265-8 £4.00

Environmental protection

The Controlled Waste (Fixed Penalty Notices) (Scotland) Order 2014 No. 2014/320. - Enabling power: Environment Protection Act 1990, s. 33A (8). - Issued: 26.11.2014. Made: 19.11.2014. Laid before the Scottish Parliament: 21.11.2014. Coming into force: 01.04.2015. Effect: S.S.I. 2004/426 revoked. Territorial extent & classification: S. General. - 4p.: 30 cm. - 978-0-11-102510-9 £4.25

The Environmental Protection (Duty of Care) Amendment (Scotland) Regulations 2014 No. 2014/4. - Enabling power: Environmental Protection Act 1990, s. 34 (5) & European Communities Act 1972, sch. 2, para. 1A. - Issued: 15.01.2014. Made: 08.01.2014. Laid before the Scottish Parliament: 10.01.2014. Coming into force: 01.03.2014. Effect: S.I. 1991/2839 revoked. Territorial extent & classification: S. General. - 8p.: 30 cm. - 978-0-11-102234-4 £4.00

The Environmental Regulation (Liability where Activity Carried Out by Arrangement with Another) (Scotland) Order 2014 No. 2014/323. - Enabling power: Regulatory Reform (Scotland) Act 2014, s. 39 (6) (b). - Issued: 26.11.2014. Made: 19.11.2014. Laid before the Scottish Parliament: 21.11.2014. Coming into force: 31.12.2014. Effect: None. Territorial extent & classification: S. General. - 4p.: 30 cm. - 978-0-11-102514-7 £4.25

The Environmental Regulation (Relevant Offences) (Scotland) Order 2014 No. 2014/319. - Enabling power: Regulatory Reform (Scotland) Act 2014, s. 53, 58 (1) (a). - Issued: 26.11.2014. Made: 19.11.2014. Laid before the Scottish Parliament: 21.11.2014. Coming into force: 31.12.2014. Effect: None. Territorial extent & classification: S. General. - 20p.: 30 cm. - 978-0-11-102513-0 £6.00

The Environmental Regulation (Significant Environmental Harm) (Scotland) Order 2014 No. 2014/324. - Enabling power: Regulatory Reform (Scotland) Act 2014, s. 40 (6) (c). - Issued: 26.11.2014. Made: 19.11.2014. Laid before the Scottish Parliament: 21.11.2014. Coming into force: 31.12.2014. Effect: None. Territorial extent & classification: S. General. - 4p.: 30 cm. - 978-0-11-102515-4 £4.25

The Litter (Fixed Penalty Notices) (Scotland) Order 2014 No. 2014/321. - Enabling power: Environmental Protection Act 1990, s. 88 (5). - Issued: 26.11.2014. Made: 19.11.2014. Laid before the Scottish Parliament: 21.11.2014. Coming into force: 01.04.2015. Effect: S.S.I. 2004/427 revoked. Territorial extent & classification: S. General. - 4p.: 30 cm. - 978-0-11-102511-6 £4.25

The Pollution Prevention and Control (Scotland) Amendment Regulations 2014 No. 2014/267. - Enabling power: Pollution Prevention and Control Act 1999, s. 2, sch. 1. - Issued: 15.10.2014. Made: 08.10.2014. Coming into force: 30.10.2014. Effect: None. Territorial extent & classification: S. General. - Supersedes draft SI (ISBN 9780111023990) issued 02/07/14. EC note: These regulations transpose art. 14 (5) of Directive 2012/27/EU and article 7 of Directive 2010/75. - 12p.: 30 cm. - 978-0-11-102459-1 £6.00

The Regulatory Reform (Scotland) Act 2014 (Commencement No. 1 and Transitional Provision) Order 2014 No. 2014/160 (C.11). - Enabling power: Regulatory Reform (Scotland) Act 2014, s. 61 (2). Bringing into operation various provisions of the Act on 30.06.2014; 01.04.2015, in accord. with art. 2. - Issued: 10.06.2014. Made: 04.06.2014. Laid before the Scottish Parliament: 06.06.2014. Coming into force: 30.06.2014. Effect: None. Territorial extent & classification: S. General. - 8p.: 30 cm. - 978-0-11-102377-8 £6.00

The Single Use Carrier Bags Charge (Scotland) Regulations 2014 No. 2014/161. - Enabling power: Climate Change (Scotland) Act 2009, ss. 88, 89, 90, 96 (2). - Issued: 11.06.2014. Made: 03.06.2014. Coming into force: 20.10.2014. Effect: None. Territorial extent & classification: S. General. - Supersedes draft S.S.I. (ISBN 9780111023211) issued 09.04.2014. - 12p.: 30 cm. - 978-0-11-102378-5 £6.00

The South Arran Marine Conservation (Amendment) Order 2014 No. 2014/297. - Enabling power: Marine (Scotland) Act 2010, ss. 85 (1) (a) (2) (4) (b) (c), 86 (1) (3), 92 (1). - Issued: 12.11.2014. Made: 06.11.2014. Laid before the Scottish Parliament: 07.11.2014. Coming into force: 06.12.2014. Effect: None. Territorial extent & classification: S. General. - 4p.: 30 cm. - 978-0-11-102490-4 £4.25

The South Arran Marine Conservation Order 2014 No. 2014/260. - Enabling power: Marine (Scotland) Act 2010, ss. 85 (1) (a) (2) (4), 86 (1) (3), 88 (1) (2), 92 (1) (5). - Issued: 06.10.2014. Made: 30.09.2014. Laid before the Scottish Parliament: 30.09.2014. Coming into force: 01.10.2014. Effect: None. Territorial extent & classification: S. General. - 8p.: 30 cm. - 978-0-11-102448-5 £8.50

The Sulphur Content of Liquid Fuels (Scotland) Regulations 2014 No. 2014/258. - Enabling power: European Communities Act 1972, s. 2 (2). - Issued: 02.10.2010. Made: 25.09.2014. Laid before the Scottish Parliament: 29.09.2014. Coming into force: 13.11.2014. Effect: S.S.I. 2007/27 revoked. Territorial extent & classification: S. General. - 8p.: 30 cm. - 978-0-11-102446-1 £6.00

Ethical standards

The Ethical Standards in Public Life etc. (Scotland) Act 2000 (Register of Interests) Amendment Regulations 2014 No. 2014/50. - Enabling power: Ethical Standards in Public Life etc. (Scotland) Act 2000, s. 7 (2). - Issued: 04.03.2014. Made: 25.02.2014. Laid before the Scottish Parliament: 27.02.2014. Coming into force: 01.04.2014. Effect: S.S.I. 2003/135 amended. Territorial extent & classification: S. General. - 8p.: 30 cm. - 978-0-11-102275-7 £4.00

Fire services

The Firefighters' Compensation Scheme (Scotland) Amendment Order 2014 No. 2014/109. - Enabling power: Fire and Rescue Services Act 2004, ss. 34 (1) to (4), 60 (2). - Issued: 29.04.2014. Made: 22.04.2014. Laid: 24.04.2014. Coming into force: 23.05.2014. Effect: S.S.I. 2006/338 amended. Territorial extent & classification: S. General. - 12p.: 30 cm. - 978-0-11-102326-6 £6.00

The Firefighters' Pension Scheme (Scotland) Amendment (No. 2) Order 2014 No. 2014/110. - Enabling power: Fire and Rescue Services Act 2004, ss. 34 (1) to (4), 60 (2). - Issued: 29.04.2014. Made: 22.04.2014. Laid before the Scottish Parliament: 24.04.2014. Coming into force: 23.05.2014. Effect: S.S.I. 2007/199 amended. Territorial extent & classification: S. General. - Errors in this SSI have been corrected by SSI 2014/149 (ISBN 9780111023679) which is being issued free of charge to all known recipients of 2014/110. - 36p.: 30 cm. - 978-0-11-102327-3 £10.00

The Firefighters' Pension Scheme (Scotland) Amendment (No. 3) Order 2014 No. 2014/149. - Enabling power: Fire and Rescue Services Act 2004, ss. 34 (1) to (4), 60 (2). - Issued: 04.06.2014. Made: 29.05.2014. Laid before the Scottish Parliament: 30.05.2014. Coming into force: 28.06.2014. Effect: S.S.I. 2007/199; 2014/110 amended. Territorial extent & classification: S. General. - This Statutory Instrument has been made in consequence of errors in S.S.I. 2014/110 (9780111023273, issued 29.04.2014) and is being issued free of charge to all known recipients of that Statutory Instrument. - 4p.: 30 cm. - 978-0-11-102367-9 £4.25

The Firefighters' Pension Scheme (Scotland) Amendment Order 2014 No. 2014/60. - Enabling power: Fire and Rescue Services Act 2004, ss. 34, 60. - Issued: 06.03.2014. Made: 27.02.2014. Laid before the Scottish Parliament: 03.03.2014. Coming into force: 01.04.2014. Effect: S.S.I. 2007/199 amended. Territorial extent & classification: S. General. - 4p.: 30 cm. - 978-0-11-102288-7 £4.00

The Firemen's Pension Scheme (Amendment No. 2) (Scotland) Order 2014 No. 2014/108. - Enabling power: Fire and Rescue Services Act 2004, s. 26 (1) to (5). - Issued: 29.04.2014. Made: 22.04.2014. Laid before the Scottish Parliament: 24.04.2014. Coming into force: 23.05.2014. Effect: S.I. 1992/129 amended. Territorial extent & classification: S. General. - 4p.: 30 cm. - 978-0-11-102325-9 £4.25

The Firemen's Pension Scheme (Amendment) (Scotland) Order 2014 No. 2014/59. - Enabling power: Fire Services Act 1947, s. 26 (1) to (5). - Issued: 06.03.2014. Made: 27.02.2014. Laid before the Scottish Parliament: 03.03.2014. Coming into force: 01.04.2014. Effect: S.I. 1992/129 amended in relation to Scotland. Territorial extent & classification: S. General. - 4p.: 30 cm. - 978-0-11-102287-0 £4.00

Fisheries

The Conservation of Salmon (Annual Close Time and Catch and Release) (Scotland) (Amendment) Regulations 2014 No. 2014/357. - Enabling power: Salmon and Freshwater Fisheries (Consolidation) (Scotland) Act 2003, s. 38 (1) (5) (c) (6) (c), sch. 1, paras 7 (b), 14 (1). - Issued: 17.12.2014. Made: 10.12.2014. Laid before the Scottish Parliament: 12.12.2014. Coming into force: 09.01.2015. Effect: None. Territorial extent & classification: S. General. - This S.S.I. has been printed to correct an error in S.S.I. 2014/327 (ISBN 9780111025185) and is being issued free of charge to all known recipients of that instrument. - 4p.: 30 cm. - 978-0-11-102553-6 £4.25

The Conservation of Salmon (Annual Close Time and Catch and Release) (Scotland) Regulations 2014 No. 2014/327. - Enabling power: Salmon and Freshwater Fisheries (Consolidation) (Scotland) Act 2003, s. 38 (1) (5) (c) (6) (c), sch. 1, paras 7 (b), 14 (1). - Issued: 28.11.2014. Made: 20.11.2014. Laid before the Scottish Parliament: 24.11.2014. Coming into force: 09.01.2015. Effect: None. Territorial extent & classification: S. General. - 24p.: 30 cm. - 978-0-11-102518-5 £6.00

Fish farming

The Aquaculture and Fisheries (Scotland) Act 2013 (Specification of Commercially Damaging Species) Order 2014 No. 2014/176. - Enabling power: Aquaculture and Fisheries (Scotland) Act 2013, s. 11 (1). - Issued: 23.06.2014. Made: 17.06.2014. Laid before the Scottish Parliament: 18.06.2014. Coming into force: 23.08.2014. Effect: None. Territorial extent & classification: S. General. - 2p.: 30 cm. - 978-0-11-102393-8 £4.25

Flood risk management

The Reservoirs (Scotland) Act 2011 (Commencement No. 1) Order 2014 No. 2014/348 (C.30). - Enabling power: Reservoirs (Scotland) Act 2011, s. 116 (1). Bringing into operation various provisions of the 2011 Act on 01.01.2015. - Issued: 09.12.2014. Made: 02.12.2014. Laid before the Scottish Parliament: 04.12.2014. Coming into force: 01.01.2015. Effect: None. Territorial extent & classification: S. General. - 4p.: 30 cm. - 978-0-11-102540-6 £4.25

Food

The Food Hygiene and Official Feed and Food Controls (Scotland) Amendment Regulations 2014 No. 2014/213. - Enabling power: European Communities Act 1972, s. 2 (2), sch. 2, para 1A. - Issued: 05.08.2014. Made: 29.07.2014. Laid before the Scottish Parliament: 31.07.2014. Coming into force: 01.10.2014. Effect: S.S.I. 2006/3; 2009/446 amended. Territorial extent & classification: S. General. - EC note: These Regulations implement Commission Regulations (EU) 704/2014 (amending 211/2013) and (EU) 579/2014. - 4p.: 30 cm. - 978-0-11-102417-1 £4.25

The Food Hygiene (Scotland) Amendment Regulations 2014 No. 2014/118. - Enabling power: European Communities Act 1972, s. 2 (2), sch. 2, para. 1A. - Issued: 08.05.2014. Made: 30.04.2014. Laid: 02.05.2014. Coming into force: 01.06.2014. Effect: S.S.I. 2006/3 amended/partially revoked. Territorial extent & classification: S. General. - 4p.: 30 cm. - 978-0-11-102335-8 £4.25

The Food Information (Scotland) Regulations 2014 No. 2014/312. - Enabling power: Food Safety Act 1990, ss. 6 (4), 16 (1), 17, 18, 26, 45, 48 (1) , sch. 1 paras 1 , 4 (b) & European Communities Act 1972, s. 2 (2), sch. 2, para. 1A. - Issued: 04.03.2015. Made: 12.11.2014. Laid before the Scottish Parliament: 14.11.2014. Coming into force: 13.12.2014; 13.12.2018 in accord. with reg. 1 (2) to (4). Effect: 5 SIs amended & 13 SSIs amended & 9 SIs partially revoked & 11 SSIs partially revoked & 5 SIs revoked & 10 SSIs revoked. Territorial extent & classification: S. General. - This S.S.I. has been printed in substitution of the S.S.I. of the same number and ISBN issued 19.11.2014 and is being issued free of charge to all known recipients of that instrument. Originally listed on DL 226/2014. - EC note: These Regulations make provision to enforce, in Scotland, certain provisions of Regulation (EU) no. 1169/2011 on the provision of food information to consumers, amending Regulations (EC) no. 1924/2006 & (EC) no. 1925/2006 and repealing Commission Directive 87/250/EEC, Council Directive 90/496/EEC, Commission Directive 1999/10/EC, Directive 2000/13/EC, Commission Directives 2002/67/EC and 2008/5/EC and Commission Regulation (EC) no. 608/2004. They also implement in Scotland, certain provisions of art. 6, Directive 1992/2/EC. - 32p.: 30 cm. - 978-0-11-102503-1 £10.00

The Infant Formula and Follow-on Formula (Scotland) Amendment Regulations 2014 No. 2014/12. - Enabling power: Food Safety Act 1990, ss. 16 (1) (e), 17 (1), 48 (1). - Issued: 21.01.2014. Made: 14.01.2014. Laid before the Scottish Parliament: 16.01.2014. Coming into force: 28.02.2014. Effect: S.S.I. 2007/549 amended. Territorial extent & classification: S. General. - 4p.: 30 cm. - 978-0-11-102240-5 £4.00

The Products Containing Meat etc. (Scotland) Regulations 2014 No. 2014/289. - Enabling power: Food Safety Act 1990, ss. 6 (4), 16 (1) (a) (e) (f), 26 (1) (a) (3), 48 (1). - Issued: 11.11.2014. Made: 03.11.2014. Laid before the Scottish Parliament: 05.11.2014. Coming into force: 13.12.2014. Effect: S.S.I. 2004/6; 2008/97; 2009/436 revoked. Territorial extent & classification: S. General. - 12p.: 30 cm. - 978-0-11-102482-9 £6.00

Freedom of information

The Freedom of Information (Scotland) Act 2002 (Scottish Public Authorities) Amendment Order 2014 No. 2014/354. - Enabling power: Freedom of Information (Scotland) Act 2002, s. 4 (1). - Issued: 15.12.2014. Made: 08.12.2014. Laid before the Scottish Parliament: 10.12.2014. Coming into force: 01.04.2015. Effect: None Territorial extent & classification: S. General. - 4p.: 30 cm. - 978-0-11-102550-5 £4.25

Gender recognition

The Marriage and Civil Partnership (Scotland) Act 2014 (Commencement No. 2 and Saving Provisions) Amendment Order 2014 No. 2014/218 (C.19). - Enabling power: Marriage and Civil Partnership (Scotland) Act 2014, s. 36 (2) (3). Bringing into operation various provisions of the 2014 Act on 01.09.2014. - Issued: 14.08.2014. Made: 07.08.2014. Laid before the Scottish Parliament: 11.08.2014. Coming into force: 01.09.2014. Effect: S.S.I. 2014/212 amended. Territorial extent & classification: S. General. - This S.S.I. has been made in consequence of defects in S.S.I. 2014/212 (ISBN 9780111024164, issued 29.07.2014) and is being issued free of charge to all known recipients of that instrument. - 8p.: 30 cm. - 978-0-11-102420-1 £6.00

The Marriage and Civil Partnership (Scotland) Act 2014 (Commencement No. 2 and Saving Provisions) Order 2014 No. 2014/212 (C.18). - Enabling power: Marriage and Civil Partnership (Scotland) Act 2014, s. 36 (2). Bringing into operation various provisions of the 2014 Act on 01.09.2014, in accord. with art. 2. - Issued: 29.07.2014. Made: 22.07.2014. Laid before the Scottish Parliament: 24.07.2014. Coming into force: 01.09.2014. Effect: None. Territorial extent & classification: S. General. - Corrected by SSI 2014/218 (ISBN 9780111024201) which is being sent free of charge to all known recipients of 2012/212. - 8p.: 30 cm. - 978-0-11-102416-4 £4.25

Harbours, docks, piers and ferries

The Harbour Authority Designation (Scotland) Order 2014 No. 2014/166. - Enabling power: Harbours Act 1964, s. 40A (4) (c). - Issued: 13.06.2014. Made: 09.06.2014. Coming into force: 16.06.2014. Effect: None. Territorial extent & classification: S. Local. - 2p.: 30 cm. - 978-0-11-102385-3 £4.25

The Pennan Harbour Revision Order 2014 No. 2014/158. - Enabling power: Harbours Act 1964, s. 14 (1) (2A) (3). - Issued: 10.06.2014. Made: 04.06.2014. Coming into force: 05.06.2014. Effect: 3 Edw. 7. c.129 partial repeal. Territorial extent & classification: S. Local. - 16p.: 30 cm. - 978-0-11-102375-4 £6.00

The Port of Ardersier Harbour Revision Order 2014 No. 2014/224. - Enabling power: Harbours Act 1964, s. 14 (1). - Issued: 22.08.2014. Made: 18.08.2014. Coming into force: 19.08.2014. Effect: S.S.I. 2008/361 revoked. Territorial extent & classification: S. Local. - 20p.: 30 cm. - 978-0-11-102424-9 £6.00

High Court of Justiciary

Act of Adjournal (Amendment of the Criminal Procedure (Scotland) Act 1995 and Criminal Procedure Rules 1996) (Miscellaneous) 2014 No. 2014/242. - Enabling power: Criminal Procedure (Scotland) Act 1995, s. 305 & Extradition Act 2003, s. 210. - Issued: 15.09.2014. Made: 09.09.2014. Laid before the Scottish Parliament: 11.09.2014. Coming into force: 10.10.2014. Effect: 1995 c.46 amended. Territorial extent & classification: S. General. - 8p.: 30 cm. - 978-0-11-102439-3 £4.25

Act of Adjournal (Criminal Procedure Rules Amendment No. 2) (Miscellaneous) 2014 No. 2014/349. - Enabling power: Criminal Procedure (Scotland) Act 1995, s. 305. - Issued: 09.12.2014. Made: 03.12.2014. Laid before the Scottish Parliament: 03.12.2014. Coming into force: 04.12.2014. Effect: S.I. 1996/513 amended. Territorial extent & classification: S. General. - 8p.: 30 cm. - 978-0-11-102542-0 £6.00

Act of Adjournal (Criminal Procedure Rules Amendment) (Regulatory Reform (Scotland) Act 2014) 2014 No. 2014/162. - Enabling power: Criminal Procedure (Scotland) Act 1995, s. 305. - Issued: 11.06.2014. Made: 05.06.2014. Laid before the Scottish Parliament: 06.06.2014. Coming into force: 30.06.2014. Effect: S.I. 1996/513 amended. Territorial extent & classification: S. General. - 8p.: 30 cm. - 978-0-11-102379-2 £6.00

High hedges

The High Hedges (Scotland) Act 2013 (Commencement) Order 2014 No. 2014/54 (C.5). - Enabling power: High Hedges (Scotland) Act 2013, s. 38 (2). Bringing into operation various provisions of the 2013 Act on 01.04.2014. - Issued: 05.03.2014. Made: 26.02.2014. Laid before the Scottish Parliament: 28.02.2014. Coming into force: 01.04.2014. Effect: None. Territorial extent & classification: S. General. - 2p.: 30 cm. - 978-0-11-102280-1 £4.00

The High Hedges (Scotland)Act 2013 (Supplementary Provision) Order 2014 No. 2014/55. - Enabling power: High Hedges (Scotland) Act 2013, s. 36 (1). - Issued: 05.03.2014. Made: 26.02.2014. Laid before the Scottish Parliament: 28.02.2014. Coming into force: 01.04.2014. Effect: None. Territorial extent & classification: S. General. - 2p.: 30 cm. - 978-0-11-102281-8 £4.00

Housing

The Homeless Persons (Unsuitable Accommodation) (Scotland) Order 2014 No. 2014/243. - Enabling power: Housing (Scotland) Act 1987, s. 29 (3) (4). - Issued: 17.09.2014. Made: 08.09.2014. Laid before the Scottish Parliament: 12.09.2014. Coming into force: 21.11.2014. Effect: S.S.I. 2004/489 revoked. Territorial extent & classification: S. General. - 4p.: 30 cm. - 978-0-11-102440-9 £4.25

The Housing (Scotland) Act 2014 (Commencement No. 1, Transitional and Saving Provisions) Order 2014 No. 2014/264 (C.24). - Enabling power: Housing (Scotland) Act 2014, s. 104 (3) to (5). - Issued: 14.10.2014. Made: 07.10.2014. Laid before the Scottish Parliament: 09.10.2014. Coming into force: 13.11.2014. Effect: None. Territorial extent & classification: S. General. - 6p.: 30 cm. - 978-0-11-102457-7 £6.00

Insolvency

The Bankruptcy and Debt Advice (Scotland) Act 2014 (Commencement No. 1 and Saving) Order 2014 No. 2014/172 (C.13). - Enabling power: Bankruptcy and Debt Advice (Scotland) Act 2014, ss. 57 (2) (3). Bringing into operation various provisions of the 2014 Act on 30.06.2014, in accord. with art. 2. - Issued: 20.06.2014. Made: 16.06.2014. Laid before the Scottish Parliament: 18.06.2014. Coming into force: 30.06.2014. Effect: None. Territorial extent & classification: S. General. - 8p.: 30 cm. - 978-0-11-102391-4 £6.00

The Bankruptcy and Debt Advice (Scotland) Act 2014 (Commencement No. 2, Savings and Transitionals) Order 2014 No. 2014/261 (C.23). - Enabling power: Bankruptcy and Debt Advice (Scotland) Act 2014, s. 57 (2) (3). Bringing into operation various provisions of the 2014 Act on 01.04.2015, in accord. with art. 2. - Issued: 06.10.2014. Made: 29.09.2014. Laid before the Scottish Parliament: 01.10.2014. Coming into force: 01.04.2015. Effect: None. Territorial extent & classification: S. General. - 8p.: 30 cm. - 978-0-11-102449-2 £6.00

The Bankruptcy and Diligence etc. (Scotland) Act 2007 (Commencement No. 9 and Savings Amendment) Order 2014 No. 2014/173 (C.14). - Enabling power: Bankruptcy and Diligence etc. (Scotland) Act 2007, ss. 224 (2), 227 (3) (4). Bringing into operation various provisions of the 2007 Act on 01.04.2015 in accord. with art. 2. - Issued: 20.06.2014. Made: 16.06.2014. Laid before the Scottish Parliament: 18.06.2014. Coming into force: 04.10.2014. Effect: S.S.I. 2008/115 amended. Territorial extent & classification: S. General. - 8p.: 30 cm. - 978-0-11-102392-1 £4.25

The Bankruptcy (Applications and Decisions) (Scotland) Regulations 2014 No. 2014/226. - Enabling power: Bankruptcy (Scotland) Act 1985, ss. 71C, 72 (1A), 72A. - Issued: 28.08.2014. Made: 20.08.2014. Laid before the Scottish Parliament: 21.08.2014. Coming into force: 01.05.2015. Effect: None. Territorial extent & classification: S. General. - 28p.: 30 cm. - 978-0-11-102426-3 £6.00

The Bankruptcy (Money Advice and Deduction from Income etc.) (Scotland) Regulations 2014 No. 2014/296. - Enabling power: Bankruptcy (Scotland) Act 1985, ss. 5A, 5B (5) (b) (2), 5C (1) (d) (2) (b), 32E (7), 39A (4) (a), 71C, 72 (1A). - Issued: 12.11.2014. Made: 05.11.2014. Coming into force: 01.04.2015. Effect: 1985 c.66;S.I. 2010/397 amended & S.S.I. 2013/137 partially revoked & S.S.I. 2008/81 revoked. Territorial extent & classification: S. General. - Supersedes draft SI (ISBN 9780111024386) issued 11/09/14. - 12p.: 30 cm. - 978-0-11-102489-8 £6.00

The Bankruptcy (Scotland) Regulations 2014 No. 2014/225. - Enabling power: Bankruptcy (Scotland) Act 1985, ss. 1A (1) (b) (5), 2 (8), 5 (2ZA) (a) (ii) (2D) (6A), 6 (7), 7 (1) (d), 11 (1), 19 (2), 22 (2) (a) (6), 23 (1) (a), 32 (9A), 40 (3B), 43A (2), 43B (1), 45 (3) (a), 49 (3), 51 (7) (a), 54 (2), 54A (2), 54C (2), 54D (2) (a), 54E (2) (5), 69, 71C, 72 (1A), 73 (1), sch. 3, para. 5 (1), 6. - Issued: 28.08.2014. Made: 20.08.2014. Laid before the Scottish Parliament: 21.08.2014. Coming into force: 01.04.2014. Effect: S.S.I. 2008/82; 2010/367 partially revoked & S.S.I. 2008/334 revoked. Territorial extent & classification: S. General. - 148p.: 30 cm. - 978-0-11-102425-6 £23.25

The Common Financial Tool etc. (Scotland) Regulations 2014 No. 2014/290. - Enabling power: Bankruptcy (Scotland) Act 1985, ss. 5D, 71C, 72 (1A), sch. 5, para. 5 & Debt Arrangement and Attachment Act (Scotland) Act 2002, s. 7 (2) (bd). - Issued: 12.11.2014. Made: 05.11.2014. Coming into force: 01.04.2015. Effect: S.S.I. 2013/318 amended. Territorial extent & classification: S. General. - Supersedes draft SI (ISBN 9780111024348) issued 29/08/14. - 24p.: 30 cm. - 978-0-11-102484-3 £6.00

Insolvency: Bankruptcy

The Bankruptcy Fees (Scotland) Regulations 2014 No. 2014/227. - Enabling power: Bankruptcy (Scotland) Act 1985, ss. 69A, 72 (1A). - Issued: 29.08.2014. Made: 20.08.2014. Laid before the Scottish Parliament: 21.08.2014. Coming into force: 01.04.2014. Effect: S.S.I. 2012/118 revoked with savings. Territorial extent & classification: S. General. - 12p.: 30 cm. - 978-0-11-102429-4 £6.00

Insolvency: Companies

The Insolvency (Scotland) Amendment Rules 2014 No. 2014/114. - Enabling power: Insolvency Act 1986, s. 411. - Issued: 07.05.2014. Made: 29.04.2014. Laid before the Scottish Parliament: 01.05.2014. Coming into force: 30.05.2014. Effect: S.I. 1986/1915 amended. Territorial extent & classification: S. General. - 24p.: 30 cm. - 978-0-11-102331-0 £6.00

Investigatory powers

The Regulation of Investigatory Powers (Authorisation of Covert Human Intelligence Sources) (Scotland) Order 2014 No. 2014/339. - Enabling power: Regulation of Investigatory Powers (Scotland) Act 2000, ss. 7 (4) (b), 8 (1) (2), 19 (8), 28 (4). - Issued: 04.12.2014. Made: 27.11.2014. Laid before the Scottish Parliament: 02.12.2014. Coming into force: 02.02.2015. Effect: 2000 c.7 modified & S.S.I. 2010/350 amended. Territorial extent & classification: S. General. - 12p.: 30 cm. - 978-0-11-102529-1 £6.00

Judgments

The Civil Jurisdiction and Judgments (Protection Measures) (Scotland) Regulations 2014 No. 2014/333. - Enabling power: European Communities Act 1972, s. 2 (2). - Issued: 02.12.2014. Made: 25.11.2014. Laid before the Scottish Parliament: 27.11.2014. Coming into force: 11.01.2015. Effect: None. Territorial extent & classification: S. General. - 4p.: 30 cm. - 978-0-11-102521-5 £4.25

The Marriage (Same Sex Couples) (Jurisdiction and Recognition of Judgments) (Scotland) Regulations 2014 No. 2014/362. - Enabling power: Domicile and Matrimonial Proceedings Act 1973. sch. 1B, para. 2. - Issued: 19.12.2014. Made: 15.12.2014. Coming into force: 16.12.2014. Effect: None. Territorial extent & classification: S. General. - Supersedes draft SI (ISBN 9780111024768) issued 04/11/14 - 4p.: 30 cm. - 978-0-11-102558-1 £4.25

Judicial appointments and discipline

Act of Sederunt (Fitness for Judicial Office Tribunal Rules) (No. 2) 2014 No. 2014/102. - Enabling power: Sheriff Courts (Scotland) Act 1971, s. 12 C (5) & Judiciary and Courts (Scotland) Act 2008 s. 37 (5). - Issued: 15.04.2014. Made: 09.04.2014. Laid before the Scottish Parliament: 11.04.2014. Coming into force: 19.05.2014 for rule 16; 01.06.2014 for remainder, in accord. with rule 1 (2) (3). Effect: S.S.I. 2014/99 revoked (19.05.2014). Territorial extent & classification: S. General. - This S.S.I. has been made to correct defects in S.S.I. 2014/99 (ISBN 9780111023181) and is being issued free of charge to all known recipients of that instrument; Revoked by SSI 2015/120 (ISBN 9780111027110). - 8p.: 30 cm. - 978-0-11-102322-8 £6.00

Justice of the Peace Court

Act of Adjournal (Amendment of the Criminal Procedure (Scotland) Act 1995 and Criminal Procedure Rules 1996) (Miscellaneous) 2014 No. 2014/242. - Enabling power: Criminal Procedure (Scotland) Act 1995, s. 305 & Extradition Act 2003, s. 210. - Issued: 15.09.2014. Made: 09.09.2014. Laid before the Scottish Parliament: 11.09.2014. Coming into force: 10.10.2014. Effect: 1995 c.46 amended. Territorial extent & classification: S. General. - 8p.: 30 cm. - 978-0-11-102439-3 £4.25

Act of Adjournal (Criminal Procedure Rules Amendment No. 2) (Miscellaneous) 2014 No. 2014/349. - Enabling power: Criminal Procedure (Scotland) Act 1995, s. 305. - Issued: 09.12.2014. Made: 03.12.2014. Laid before the Scottish Parliament: 03.12.2014. Coming into force: 04.12.2014. Effect: S.I. 1996/513 amended. Territorial extent & classification: S. General. - 8p.: 30 cm. - 978-0-11-102542-0 £6.00

The Judicial Pensions and Retirement Act 1993 (Part-time Sheriff, Stipendiary Magistrate and Justice of the Peace) Order 2014 No. 2014/155. - Enabling power: European Communities Act 1972, s. 2 (2) & Judicial Pensions and Retirement Act 1993, ss. 26 (9), 29 (3). - Issued: 05.06.2014. Made: 29.05.2014. Coming into force: 30.05.2014. Effect: 1971 c.58; 1993 c.8; 2007 asp 6 amended. Territorial extent & classification: S. General. - Supersedes draft SI (ISBN 9780111023242) issued 24/04/14. - 4p.: 30 cm. - 978-0-11-102373-0 £4.25

Land and buildings transaction tax

The Land and Buildings Transaction Tax (Administration) (Scotland) Regulations 2014 No. 2014/375. - Enabling power: Land and Buildings Transaction Tax (Scotland) Act 2013, s. 42 (1), sch. 8 paras 11 (1), 20, 21 (5) (6). - Issued: 24.12.2014. Made: 17.12.2014. Laid before the Scottish Parliament: 19.12.2014. Coming into force: 01.04.2015. Effect: None. Territorial extent & classification: S. General. - 8p.: 30 cm. - 978-0-11-102571-0 £6.00

The Land and Buildings Transaction Tax (Ancillary Provision) (Scotland) Order 2014 No. 2014/376. - Enabling power: Land and Buildings Transaction Tax (Scotland) Act 2013, s. 67 (1). - Issued: 24.12.2014. Made: 17.12.2014. Laid before the Scottish Parliament: 19.12.2014. Coming into force: 01.04.2015. Effect: None. Territorial extent & classification: S. General. - 2p.: 30 cm. - 978-0-11-102572-7 £4.25

The Land and Buildings Transaction Tax (Definition of Charity) (Relevant Territories) (Scotland) Regulations 2014 No. 2014/352. - Enabling power: Land and Buildings Transaction Tax (Scotland) Act 2013, sch. 13 para. 15 (3) (d). - Issued: 11.12.2014. Made: 04.12.2014. Laid before the Scottish Parliament: 08.12.2014. Coming into force: 01.04.2015. Effect: None. Territorial extent & classification: S. General. - 2p.: 30 cm. - 978-0-11-102546-8 £4.25

The Land and Buildings Transaction Tax (Prescribed Proportions) (Scotland) Order 2014 No. 2014/350. - Enabling power: Land and Buildings Transaction Tax (Scotland) Act 2013, sch. 5 para. 12, sch. 11 para 6 (3). - Issued: 11.12.2014. Made: 04.12.2014. Laid before the Scottish Parliament: 08.12.2014. Coming into force: 01.04.2015. Effect: None. Territorial extent & classification: S. General. - 2p.: 30 cm. - 978-0-11-102544-4 £4.25

The Land and Buildings Transaction Tax (Qualifying Public or Educational Bodies) (Scotland) Amendment Order 2014 No. 2014/351. - Enabling power: Land and Buildings Transaction Tax (Scotland) Act 2013, sch. 2 para. 17 (3) (c). - Issued: 11.12.2014. Made: 04.12.2014. Laid before the Scottish Parliament: 08.12.2014. Coming into force: 01.04.2014. Effect: None. Territorial extent & classification: S. General. - 2p.: 30 cm. - 978-0-11-102545-1 £4.25

The Land and Buildings Transaction Tax (Scotland) Act 2013 (Commencement No. 1) Order 2014 No. 2014/279 (C.27). - Enabling power: Land and Buildings Transaction Tax (Scotland) Act 2013, s. 70 (2). - Issued: 30.10.2014. Made: 24.10.2014. Laid before the Scottish Parliament: 27.10.2014. Coming into force: 07.11.2014. Effect: None. Territorial extent & classification: S. General. - 4p.: 30 cm. - 978-0-11-102470-6 £4.25

The Land and Buildings Transaction Tax (Transitional Provisions) (Scotland) Order 2014 No. 2014/377. - Enabling power: Land and Buildings Transaction Tax (Scotland) Act 2013, s. 67 (1). - Issued: 24.12.2014. Made: 17.12.2014. Laid before the Scottish Parliament: 19.12.2014. Coming into force: 01.04.2015. Effect: None. Territorial extent & classification: S. General. - 8p.: 30 cm. - 978-0-11-102573-4 £6.00

Landfill tax

The Landfill Tax (Scotland) Act 2014 (Commencement No. 1) Order 2014 No. 2014/277 (C.25). - Enabling power: Landfill Tax (Scotland) Act 2014, s. 43 (2). - Issued: 30.10.2014. Made: 24.10.2014. Laid before the Scottish Parliament: 27.10.2014. Coming into force: 07.11.2014. Effect: None. Territorial extent & classification: S. General. - 4p.: 30 cm. - 978-0-11-102467-6 £4.25

The Scottish Landfill Tax (Prescribed Landfill Site Activities) Order 2014 No. 2014/367. - Enabling power: Landfill Tax (Scotland) Act 2014, s. 6. - Issued: 23.12.2014. Made: 16.12.2014. Laid before the Scottish Parliament: 18.12.2014. Coming into force: 01.04.2015. Effect: None. Territorial extent & classification: S. General. - For approval by resolution of the Scottish Parliament within 28 days beginning with the day on which the Order was made, not taking into account periods of dissolution or recess for more than 4 days. - 4p.: 30 cm. - 978-0-11-102562-8 £4.25

Landlord and tenant

The Agricultural Holdings (Scotland) Act 2003 Remedial Order 2014 No. 2014/98. - Enabling power: Convention Rights (Compliance) (Scotland) Act 2001, s. 12 (1) (3). - Issued: 08.04.2014. Made: 02.04.2014. Coming into force: 03.04.2014. Effect: 2003 asp 11 amended. Territorial extent & classification: S. General. - Supersedes draft SI (ISBN 9780111022993) issued 08/04/14. - 8p.: 30 cm. - 978-0-11-102317-4 £4.25

Land reform

The Long Leases (Appeal Period) (Scotland) Order 2014 No. 2014/8. - Enabling power: Long Leases (Scotland) Act 2012, s. 78 (5) (b). - Issued: 16.01.2014. Made: 09.01.2014. Laid before the Scottish Parliament: 13.01.2014. Coming into force: 06.03.2014. Effect: None. Territorial extent & classification: S. General. - 2p.: 30 cm. - 978-0-11-102238-2 £4.00

The Long Leases (Prescribed Form of Notices etc.) (Scotland) Regulation 2013 No. 2014/9. - Enabling power: Long Leases (Scotland) Act 2012, ss. 8 (2), 14 (3) (a), 17 (4) (a), 23 (3) (a), 24 (2) (a), 25 (2) (a), 26 (2) (a), 27 (3) (a), 28 (3) (a), 45 (2) (4) (b), 50 (4) (b) (c), 54 (3) (b) (c), 56 (3) (a) (c), 57 (2), 63 (b), 64 (2) (a), 67 (1) (b), 68 (2) (b), 71 (1) (c) (ii), 74 (3) (a) (b), 75 (2) (b), 82 (1) (b). - Issued: 17.01.2014. Made: 09.01.2014. Laid before the Scottish Parliament: 13.01.2014. Coming into force: 21.02.2014. Effect: None. Territorial extent & classification: S. General. - 60p.: 30 cm. - 978-0-11-102239-9 £9.75

Land registration

The Land and Buildings Transaction Tax (Ancillary Provision) (Scotland) Order 2014 No. 2014/376. - Enabling power: Land and Buildings Transaction Tax (Scotland) Act 2013, s. 67 (1). - Issued: 24.12.2014. Made: 17.12.2014. Laid before the Scottish Parliament: 19.12.2014. Coming into force: 01.04.2015. Effect: None. Territorial extent & classification: S. General. - 2p.: 30 cm. - 978-0-11-102572-7 £4.25

The Land Register of Scotland (Automated Registration) etc. Regulations 2014 No. 2014/347. - Enabling power: Land Registration etc. (Scotland) Act 2012, ss. 99 (3), 100, 115 (1) (c) & Requirements of Writing (Scotland) Act 1995, ss. 9 E (1) (b), 9G (3) (5) (a). - Issued: 09.12.2014. Made: 02.12.2014. Coming into force: 08.12.2014. Effect: S.S.I. 2014/83, 150 amended. Territorial extent & classification: S. General. - Supersedes draft S.I. (ISBN 9780111024607) issued 16/10/14- 16p.: 30 cm. - 978-0-11-102538-3 £6.00

The Land Register of Scotland (Rate of Interest on Compensation) Regulations 2014 No. 2014/194. - Enabling power: Land Registration etc. (Scotland) Act 2012, ss. 79 (4), 84 (7), 95 (4). - Issued: 03.07.2014. Made: 26.06.2014. Coming into force: 08.12.2014. Effect: None. Territorial extent & classification: S. General. - Supersedes draft S.S.I. (ISBN 9780111023518) issued 23.05.2014. - 4p.: 30 cm. - 978-0-11-102409-6 £4.25

The Land Register Rules etc. (Scotland) Regulations 2014 No. 2014/150. - Enabling power: Land Registration etc. (Scotland) Act 2012, ss. 43 (7), 56 (4), 62 (2), 115 (1), 116 (1). - Issued: 04.06.2014. Made: 28.05.2014. Laid: 30.05.2014. Coming into force: 08.12.2014. Effect: None. Territorial extent & classification: S. General. - 28p.: 30 cm. - 978-0-11-102368-6 £6.00

The Land Registration etc. (Scotland) Act 2012 (Amendment and Transitional) Order 2014 No. 2014/346. - Enabling power: Land Registration etc. (Scotland) Act 2012, ss. 110 (1) (2), 116 (1), 117. - Issued: 09.12.2014. Made: 02.12.2014. Coming into force: 08.12.2014. Effect: 1995 c.7; 2012 asp 5 modified & S.S.I. 2014/150, 188 amended. Territorial extent & classification: S. General. - Supersedes draft S.I. (ISBN 9780111024683) issued 30/10/14 - 4p.: 30 cm. - 978-0-11-102537-6 £4.25

The Land Registration etc. (Scotland) Act 2012 (Commencement No. 2 and Transitional Provisions) Order 2014 No. 2014/41 (C.4). - Enabling power: Land Registration etc. (Scotland) Act 2012, ss. 116 (1), 117 (1), 123 (3). Bringing into operation certain provisions of the 2012 Act on 22.03.2014, 11.05.2014 and the 'designated day' in accord. with art. 2. - Issued: 25.02.2014. Made: 19.02.2014. Laid before the Scottish Parliament: 21.02.2014. Coming into force: 22.03.2014. Effect: None. Territorial extent & classification: S. General. - 8p.: 30 cm. - 978-0-11-102268-9 £4.00

The Land Registration etc. (Scotland) Act 2012 (Designated Day) Order 2014 No. 2014/127. - Enabling power: Land Registration etc. (Scotland) Act 2012, ss. 122. - Issued: 20.05.2014. Made: 14.05.2014. Laid before the Scottish Parliament: 16.05.2014. Coming into force: 28.5.2014. Effect: None. Territorial extent & classification: S. General. - 2p.: 30 cm. - 978-0-11-102340-2 £4.25

The Land Registration etc. (Scotland) Act 2012 (Incidental, Consequential and Transitional) Order 2014 No. 2014/190. - Enabling power: Land Registration etc. (Scotland) Act 2012, ss. 64 (1), 116 (1), 117 (1) & Long Leases (Scotland) Act 2012, s. 81 (1). - Issued: 03.07.2014. Made: 26.06.2014. Coming into force: 08.12.2014. Effect: 1973 c.52; 1995 c.7; 2012 asp 5; SSI 2004/318; 2012/297 amended. Territorial extent & classification: S. General. - Supersedes draft SI (ISBN 9780111023525) issued 03.07.14. - 12p.: 30 cm. - 978-0-11-102405-8 £6.00

The Registers of Scotland (Information and Access) Order 2014 No. 2014/189. - Enabling power: Land Registration etc. (Scotland) Act 2012, s. 107 (1). - Issued: 03.07.2014. Made: 26.06.2014. Coming into force: 08.12.2014. Effect: None. Territorial extent & classification: S. General. - Supersedes draft SI (ISBN 9780111023501) issued 03.07.14. - 4p.: 30 cm. - 978-0-11-102404-1 £4.25

Lands Tribunal

The Lands Tribunal for Scotland Amendment (Fees) Rules 2014 No. 2014/24. - Enabling power: Lands Tribunal Act 1949, s. 3 (6) (12) (e). - Issued: 30.01.2014. Made: 23.01.2014. Laid before the Scottish Parliament: 27.01.2014. Coming into force: 06.03.2014. Effect: S.I. 1971/218 amended. Territorial extent & classification: S. General. - 4p.: 30 cm. - 978-0-11-102248-1 £4.00

Legal aid and advice

The Criminal Legal Aid (Fixed Payments and Assistance by Way of Representation) (Scotland) (Miscellaneous Amendments) Regulations 2014 No. 2014/366. - Enabling power: Legal Aid (Scotland) Act 1986, ss. 9, 33 (3A), (3C), (3D), (3F) to (3H), 36 (1) (2) (a) (c) (e). - Issued: 22.12.2014. Made: 16.12.2014. Coming into force: 17.12.2014. Effect: S.I. 1999/491 & S.S.I. 2003/179 amended. Territorial extent and classification: S. General. - Supersedes draft SI (ISBN 9780111024812) issued 07/11/14. - 4p.: 30 cm. - 978-0-11-102561-1 £4.25

The Legal Aid and Assistance By Way of Representation (Fees for Time at Court and Travelling) (Scotland) Regulations 2014 No. 2014/257. - Enabling power: Legal Aid (Scotland) Act 1986, s. 33 (2) (a) (b) (3). - Issued: 01.10.2014. Made: 24.09.2014. Laid before the Scottish Parliament: 26.09.2014. Coming into force: 10.11.2014. Effect: S.I. 1989/1490; 1491; 1992/1228; 1996/2447 amended. Territorial extent & classification: S. General. - 4p.: 30 cm. - 978-0-11-102445-4 £3.00

Legal profession

The Legal Profession and Legal Aid (Scotland) Act 2007 (Membership of the Scottish Legal Complaints Commission) Amendment Order 2014 No. 2014/272. - Enabling power: Legal Profession and Legal Aid (Scotland) Act 2007, s. 1 (2), sch. 1, para. 2 (7). - Issued: 27.10.2014. Made: 21.10.2014. Coming into force: 22.10.2014. Effect: 2007 asp. 5 amended. Territorial extent & classification: S. General. - Supersedes draft S.I. (ISBN 9780111024133) issued 16.07.2014. - 2p.: 30 cm. - 978-0-11-102462-1 £4.25

The Scottish Legal Complaints Commission (Modification of Duties and Powers) Regulations 2014 No. 2014/232. - Enabling power: Legal Profession and Legal Aid (Scotland) Act 2007, s. 41 (1) (2). - Issued: 29.08.2014. Made: 20.08.2014. Coming into force: 01.01.2015. Effect: 2007 asp.5 modified. Territorial extent & classification: S. General. - Supersedes draft SSI (ISBN 9780111023846) issued 13.06.2014. - 8p.: 30 cm. - 978-0-11-102431-7 £6.00

Local government

The Children and Young People (Scotland) Act 2014 (Ancillary Provision) (No. 2) Order 2014 No. 2014/315. - Enabling power: Children and Young People (Scotland) Act 2014, s. 101 (a). - Issued: 25.11.2014. Made: 18.11.2014. Laid before the Scottish Parliament: 20.11.2014. Coming into force: 05.01.2015. Effect: S.S.I. 2008/400 revoked. Territorial extent & classification: S. General. - 2p.: 30 cm. - 978-0-11-102506-2 £4.25

The Ethical Standards in Public Life etc. (Scotland) Act 2000 (Register of Interests) Amendment Regulations 2014 No. 2014/50. - Enabling power: Ethical Standards in Public Life etc. (Scotland) Act 2000, s. 7 (2). - Issued: 04.03.2014. Made: 25.02.2014. Laid before the Scottish Parliament: 27.02.2014. Coming into force: 01.04.2014. Effect: S.S.I. 2003/135 amended. Territorial extent & classification: S. General. - 8p.: 30 cm. - 978-0-11-102275-7 £4.00

The Local Authority Accounts (Scotland) Amendment Regulations 2014 No. 2014/200. - Enabling power: Local Government (Scotland) Act 1973, s. 105 (1). - Issued: 10.07.2014. Made: 03.07.2014. Laid before the Scottish Parliament: 07.07.2014. Coming into force: 10.10.2014. Effect: S.S.I. 2013/119 partially revoked & S.I. 1985/267; 1997/1980; S.S.I. 2011/64 revoked. Territorial extent & classification: S. General. - 12p.: 30 cm. - 978-0-11-102411-9 £6.00

The Local Government Finance (Scotland) Amendment Order 2014 No. 2014/74. - Enabling power: Local Government Finance Act 1992, sch. 12, para. 1. - Issued: 25.03.2014. Made: 18.03.2014. Coming into force: 19.03.2014 in accord. with art. 1. Effect: S.S.I. 2014/36 amended. Territorial extent & classification: S. General. - Supersedes draft S.S.I. (ISBN 9780111022764) issued 04.03.2014. - 8p.: 30 cm. - 978-0-11-102302-0 £4.00

The Local Government Finance (Scotland) Order 2014 No. 2014/36. - Enabling power: Local Government Finance Act 1992, sch. 12, paras 1, 9 (4). - Issued: 18.02.2014. Made: 11.02.2014. Coming into force: 12.02.2014. Effect: S.S.I. 2013/44 partially revoked. Territorial extent & classification: S. General. - Supersedes draft (ISBN 9780111022443) issued 28.01.2014; Partially revoked by SSI 2015/56 (ISBN 9780111026380). - 8p.: 30 cm. - 978-0-11-102260-3 £4.00

Marine management

The South Arran Marine Conservation (Amendment) Order 2014 No. 2014/297. - Enabling power: Marine (Scotland) Act 2010, ss. 85 (1) (a) (2) (4) (b) (c), 86 (1) (3), 92 (1). - Issued: 12.11.2014. Made: 06.11.2014. Laid before the Scottish Parliament: 07.11.2014. Coming into force: 06.12.2014. Effect: None. Territorial extent & classification: S. General. - 4p.: 30 cm. - 978-0-11-102490-4 £4.25

The South Arran Marine Conservation Order 2014 No. 2014/260. - Enabling power: Marine (Scotland) Act 2010, ss. 85 (1) (a) (2) (4), 86 (1) (3), 88 (1) (2), 92 (1) (5). - Issued: 06.10.2014. Made: 30.09.2014. Laid before the Scottish Parliament: 30.09.2014. Coming into force: 01.10.2014. Effect: None. Territorial extent & classification: S. General. - 8p.: 30 cm. - 978-0-11-102448-5 £8.50

Marriage

The Civil Partnership (Prescribed Bodies) (Scotland) Regulations 2014 No. 2014/303. - Enabling power: Civil Partnership Act 2004, s. 94A (1) (a) (i). - Issued: 18.11.2014. Made: 11.11.2014. Laid before the Scottish Parliament: 13.11.2014. Coming into force: 16.12.2014. Effect: None. Territorial extent & classification: S. General. - 4p.: 30 cm. - 978-0-11-102496-6 £4.25

The Marriage and Civil Partnership (Prescribed Forms) (Scotland) Regulations 2014 No. 2014/306. - Enabling power: Marriage and Civil Partnership (Scotland) Act 2014, s. 88 (1) (5), 95ZA & Local Electoral Administration and Registration Services (Scotland) Act 2006, s. 55 (2) & Marriage (Scotland) Act 1977, ss. 3 (1), 6 (1), 7 (2) & Registration of Births, Deaths and Marriages (Scotland) Act 1965, ss. 32 (1), 54 (1) (b). - Issued: 18.11.2014. Made: 11.11.2014. Laid before the Scottish Parliament: 13.11.2014. Coming into force: 16.12.2014. Effect: S.I. 1997/2348, 2349; S.S.I. 2005/458; 2008/386 amended. Territorial extent & classification: S. General. - 16p.: 30 cm. - 978-0-11-102499-7 £6.00

The Marriage and Civil Partnership (Scotland) Act 2014 (Commencement No. 1) Order 2014 No. 2014/121 (C.8). - Enabling power: Marriage and Civil Partnership (Scotland) Act 2014, s. 36 (2). Bringing into operation various provisions of the Act on 21.05.2014, in accord. with art. 2. - Issued: 09.05.2014. Made: 01.05.2014. Laid before the Scottish Parliament: 06.05.2014. Coming into force: 21.05.2014. Effect: None. Territorial extent & classification: S. General. - 2p.: 30 cm. - 978-0-11-102337-2 £4.25

The Marriage and Civil Partnership (Scotland) Act 2014 (Commencement No. 2 and Saving Provisions) Amendment Order 2014 No. 2014/218 (C.19). - Enabling power: Marriage and Civil Partnership (Scotland) Act 2014, s. 36 (2) (3). Bringing into operation various provisions of the 2014 Act on 01.09.2014. - Issued: 14.08.2014. Made: 07.08.2014. Laid before the Scottish Parliament: 11.08.2014. Coming into force: 01.09.2014. Effect: S.S.I. 2014/212 amended. Territorial extent & classification: S. General. - This S.S.I. has been made in consequence of defects in S.S.I. 2014/212 (ISBN 9780111024164, issued 29.07.2014) and is being issued free of charge to all known recipients of that instrument. - 8p.: 30 cm. - 978-0-11-102420-1 £6.00

The Marriage and Civil Partnership (Scotland) Act 2014 (Commencement No. 2 and Saving Provisions) Order 2014 No. 2014/212 (C.18). - Enabling power: Marriage and Civil Partnership (Scotland) Act 2014, s. 36 (2). Bringing into operation various provisions of the 2014 Act on 01.09.2014, in accord. with art. 2. - Issued: 29.07.2014. Made: 22.07.2014. Laid before the Scottish Parliament: 24.07.2014. Coming into force: 01.09.2014. Effect: None. Territorial extent & classification: S. General. - Corrected by SSI 2014/218 (ISBN 9780111024201) which is being sent free of charge to all known recipients of 2012/212. - 8p.: 30 cm. - 978-0-11-102416-4 £4.25

The Marriage and Civil Partnership (Scotland) Act 2014 (Commencement No. 3, Saving, Transitional Provision and Revocation) Order 2014 No. 2014/287 (C.28). - Enabling power: Marriage and Civil Partnership (Scotland) Act 2014, ss. 35, 36 (2) (3). Bringing into operation various provisions of the 2014 Act on 16.12.2014, in accord. with art. 3. - Issued: 05.11.2014. Made: 29.10.2014. Laid before the Scottish Parliament: 31.10.2014. Coming into force: 16.12.2014. Effect: S.S.I. 2002/260; 2005/657; 2006/573 amended. Territorial extent & classification: S. General. - 8p.: 30 cm. - 978-0-11-102477-5 £6.00

The Marriage Between Civil Partners (Procedure for Change and Fees) (Scotland) Regulations 2014 No. 2014/361. - Enabling power: Marriage and Civil Partnership (Scotland) Act 2014, s. 10. - Issued: 19.12.2014. Made: 15.12.2014. Coming into force: 16.12.2014. Effect: 1977 c.15; 2004 c.7 modified. Territorial extent & classification: S. General. - Supersedes draft SI (ISBN 9780111024805) issued 06/11/14. - 8p.: 30 cm. - 978-0-11-102557-4 £6.00

The Marriage Between Persons of Different Sexes (Prescribed Bodies) (Scotland) Regulations 2014 No. 2014/304. - Enabling power: Marriage (Scotland) Act 1977, s. 8 (1) (a) (ii). - Issued: 18.11.2014. Made: 11.11.2014. Laid before the Scottish Parliament: 13.11.2014. Coming into force: 16.12.2014. Effect: S.I. 1977/1670 revoked. Territorial extent & classification: S. General. - 4p.: 30 cm. - 978-0-11-102497-3 £4.25

The Same Sex Marriage (Prescribed Bodies) (Scotland) Regulations 2014 No. 2014/305. - Enabling power: Marriage (Scotland) Act 1977, s. 8 (1B) (a) (i). - Issued: 18.11.2014. Made: 11.11.2014. Laid before the Scottish Parliament: 13.11.2014. Coming into force: 16.12.2014. Effect: None. Territorial extent & classification: S. General. - 4p.: 30 cm. - 978-0-11-102498-0 £4.25

Mental health

The National Confidential Forum (Prescribed Care and Health Services) (Scotland) Order 2014 No. 2014/193. - Enabling power: Mental Health (Care and Treatment) (Scotland) Act 2003, sch. 1A, para. 7 (3). - Issued: 03.07.2014. Made: 26.06.2014. Coming into force: 01.07.2014. Effect: None. Territorial extent & classification: S. General. - Supersedes draft S.S.I. (ISBN 9780111023495) issued 23.05.2014. - 4p.: 30 cm. - 978-0-11-102408-9 £4.25

The Victims and Witnesses (Scotland) Act 2014 (Commencement No. 1) Order 2014 No. 2014/117 (C.7). - Enabling power: Victims and Witnesses (Scotland) Act 2014, s. 34 (2). Bringing into operation various provisions of this 2014 Act on 16.05.2014, 01.07.2014, in accord. with arts 2 & 3. - Issued: 08.05.2014. Made: 30.04.2014. Laid before the Scottish Parliament: 02.05.2014. Coming into force: 16.05.2014. Effect: None. Territorial extent & classification: S. General. - 2p.: 30 cm. - 978-0-11-102334-1 £4.25

National assistance services

The National Assistance (Assessment of Resources) Amendment (Scotland) Regulations 2014 No. 2014/38. - Enabling power: National Assistance Act 1948, s. 22 (5). - Issued: 18.02.2014. Made: 11.02.2014. Laid before the Scottish Parliament: 13.02.2014. Coming into force: 07.04.2014. Effect: S.I. 1992/2977 amended & S.S.I. 2013/41 revoked. Territorial extent & classification: S. General. - Revoked by SSI 2015/64 (ISBN 9780111026496). - 4p.: 30 cm. - 978-0-11-102262-7 £4.00

The National Assistance (Sums for Personal Requirements) (Scotland) Regulations 2014 No. 2014/39. - Enabling power: National Assistance Act 1948, s. 22 (4). - Issued: 18.02.2014. Made: 11.02.2014. Laid before the Scottish Parliament: 13.02.2014. Coming into force: 07.04.2014. Effect: S.S.I. 2013/40 revoked. Territorial extent & classification: S. General. - Revoked by SSI 2015/65 (ISBN 9780111026502). - 4p.: 30 cm. - 978-0-11-102263-4 £4.00

National Health Service

The National Health Service (Charges to Overseas Visitors) (Scotland) (Amendment) Regulations 2014 No. 2014/70. - Enabling power: National Health Service (Scotland) Act 1978, ss. 98, 105. - Issued: 11.03.2014. Made: 05.03.2014. Laid before the Scottish Parliament: 07.03.2014. Coming into force: 01.05.2014. Effect: S.S.I. 1989/364 amended. Territorial extent & classification: S. General. - 4p.: 30 cm. - 978-0-11-102297-9 £4.00

The National Health Service (Free Prescriptions and Charges for Drugs and Appliances) (Scotland) Amendment Regulations 2014 No. 2014/115. - Enabling power: National Health Service (Scotland) Act 1978, ss. 69 (1), 105 (7). - Issued: 07.05.2014. Made: 29.04.2015. Laid before the Scottish Parliament: 01.05.2014. Coming into force: 30.05.2015. Effect: S.S.I. 2011/55 amended & S.S.I. 2012/74; 2013/191; 2014/115 revoked. Territorial extent & classification: S. General. - 4p.: 30 cm. - 978-0-11-102332-7 £4.25

The National Health Service (Functions of the Common Services Agency) (Scotland) Amendment Order 2014 No. 2014/100. - Enabling power: National Health Service (Scotland) Act 1978, ss. 10 (3) (4), 105 (6). - Issued: 08.04.2014. Made: 02.04.2014. Laid before the Scottish Parliament: 04.04.2014. Coming into force: 19.05.2014. Effect: S.S.I. 2008/312 amended. Territorial extent & classification: S. General. - 4p.: 30 cm. - 978-0-11-102319-8 £4.25

The National Health Service (Optical Charges and Payments) (Scotland) Amendment Regulations 2014 No. 2014/61. - Enabling power: National Health Service (Scotland) Act 1978, ss. 70 (1), 73 (a), 74 (a), 105 (7), 108 (1), sch. 11, paras. 2, 2A. - Issued: 05.03.2014. Made: 27.02.2014. Laid before the Scottish Parliament: 03.03.2014. Coming into force: 01.04.2014. Effect: S.I. 1998/642 amended. Territorial extent & classification: S. General. - 4p.: 30 cm. - 978-0-11-102285-6 £4.00

The National Health Service (Pharmaceutical Services) (Scotland) (Miscellaneous Amendments) Regulations 2014 No. 2014/148. - Enabling power: National Health Service (Scotland) Act 1978, ss. 2 (5), 17E (1), 17N (1), 27, 28 (2), 105 (7), 106. - Issued: 04.06.2014. Made: 28.05.2014. Laid before the Scottish Parliament: 30.05.2014. Coming into force: 28.06.2014. Effect: S.S.I. 2004/115, 116; 2009/183 amended. Territorial extent & classification: S. General. - 16p.: 30 cm. - 978-0-11-102366-2 £6.00

The National Health Service (Physiotherapist, Podiatrist or Chiropodist Independent Prescribers) (Miscellaneous Amendments) (Scotland) Regulations 2014 No. 2014/73. - Enabling power: National Health Service (Scotland) Act 1978, ss. 17E (1), 17N (1), 27 (1). - Issued: 18.03.2014. Made: 12.03.2014. Laid before the Scottish Parliament: 14.03.2014. Coming into force: 01.05.2014. Effect: S.S.I. 2004/115, 116; 2009/183 amended. Territorial extent & classification: S. General. - 8p.: 30 cm. - 978-0-11-102301-3 £4.00

The National Health Service (Superannuation Scheme) (Scotland) Amendment Regulations 2014 No. 2014/43. - Enabling power: Superannuation Act 1972, s. 10, sch. 3. - Issued: 26.02.2014. Made: 13.02.2014. Laid before the Scottish Parliament: 24.02.2014. Coming into force: 01.04.2014. Effect: S.S.I. 2011/117; 2013/174 amended. Territorial extent & classification: S. General. - 8p.: 30 cm. - 978-0-11-102271-9 £4.00

The National Health Service Superannuation Scheme (Scotland) (Miscellaneous Amendments) Regulations 2014 No. 2014/154. - Enabling power: Superannuation Act 1972, s. 10, sch. 3. - Issued: 06.06.2014. Made: 16.05.2014. Laid before the Scottish Parliament: 30.05.2014. Coming into force: 28.06.2014. Effect: S.I. 1998/1451, 1594 & S.S.I. 2011/117; 2013/174 amended. Territorial extent & classification: S. General. - 20p.: 30 cm. - 978-0-11-102372-3 £6.00

The Patient Rights (Treatment Time Guarantee) (Scotland) Amendment Regulations 2014 No. 2014/93. - Enabling power: Patient Rights (Scotland) Act 2011, ss. 9 (1) (3), 25 (1). - Issued: 03.04.2014. Made: 27.03.2014. Coming into force: 01.10.2014 for reg. 2 (5) (a); 01.04.2014 for remainder. Effect: S.S.I. 2012/110 amended. Territorial extent & classification: S. General. - Supersedes draft SI (ISBN 9780111022672) issued 25.02.2014. - 4p.: 30 cm. - 978-0-11-102314-3 £4.00

The Personal Injuries (NHS Charges) (Amounts) (Scotland) Amendment Regulations 2014 No. 2014/57. - Enabling power: Health and Social Care (Community Health and Standards) Act 2003, ss. 153 (2) (5), 168, 195 (1) (2). - Issued: 05.03.2014. Made: 26.02.2014. Laid before the Scottish Parliament: 28.02.2014. Coming into force: 01.04.2014. Effect: S.S.I. 2006/588 amended. Territorial extent & classification: S. General. - 4p.: 30 cm. - 978-0-11-102283-2 £4.00

The Public Bodies (Joint Working) (Scotland) Act 2014 (Commencement No. 1) Order 2014 No. 2014/202 (C.16). - Enabling power: Public Bodies (Joint Working) (Scotland) Act 2014, s. 72 (2). Bringing into operation various provisions of the 2014 Act on 25.07.2014, in accord. with art. 1. - Issued: 16.07.2014. Made: 09.07.2014. Laid before the Scottish Parliament: 11.07.2014. Coming into force: 25.07.2014. Effect: None. Territorial extent & classification: S. General. - 2p.: 30 cm. - 978-0-11-102414-0 £4.25

Nature conservation

The Protection of Seals (Designation of Haul-Out Sites) (Scotland) Order 2014 No. 2014/185. - Enabling power: Marine (Scotland) Act 2010, s. 117. - Issued: 01.07.2014. Made: 24.06.2014. Laid before the Scottish Parliament: 26.06.2014. Coming into force: 30.09.2014. Effect: None. Territorial extent & classification: S. General. - 12p.: 30 cm. - 978-0-11-102397-6 £6.00

Pensions

The Firefighters' Compensation Scheme (Scotland) Amendment Order 2014 No. 2014/109. - Enabling power: Fire and Rescue Services Act 2004, ss. 34 (1) to (4), 60 (2). - Issued: 29.04.2014. Made: 22.04.2014. Laid: 24.04.2014. Coming into force: 23.05.2014. Effect: S.S.I. 2006/338 amended. Territorial extent & classification: S. General. - 12p.: 30 cm. - 978-0-11-102326-6 £6.00

The Firefighters' Pension Scheme (Scotland) Amendment (No. 2) Order 2014 No. 2014/110. - Enabling power: Fire and Rescue Services Act 2004, ss. 34 (1) to (4), 60 (2). - Issued: 29.04.2014. Made: 22.04.2014. Laid before the Scottish Parliament: 24.04.2014. Coming into force: 23.05.2014. Effect: S.S.I. 2007/199 amended. Territorial extent & classification: S. General. - Errors in this SSI have been corrected by SSI 2014/149 (ISBN 9780111023679) which is being issued free of charge to all known recipients of 2014/110. - 36p.: 30 cm. - 978-0-11-102327-3 £10.00

The Firefighters' Pension Scheme (Scotland) Amendment (No. 3) Order 2014 No. 2014/149. - Enabling power: Fire and Rescue Services Act 2004, ss. 34 (1) to (4), 60 (2). - Issued: 04.06.2014. Made: 29.05.2014. Laid before the Scottish Parliament: 30.05.2014. Coming into force: 28.06.2014. Effect: S.S.I. 2007/199; 2014/110 amended. Territorial extent & classification: S. General. - This Statutory Instrument has been made in consequence of errors in S.S.I. 2014/110 (9780111023273, issued 29.04.2014) and is being issued free of charge to all known recipients of that Statutory Instrument. - 4p.: 30 cm. - 978-0-11-102367-9 £4.25

The Firefighters' Pension Scheme (Scotland) Amendment Order 2014 No. 2014/60. - Enabling power: Fire and Rescue Services Act 2004, ss. 34, 60. - Issued: 06.03.2014. Made: 27.02.2014. Laid before the Scottish Parliament: 03.03.2014. Coming into force: 01.04.2014. Effect: S.S.I. 2007/199 amended. Territorial extent & classification: S. General. - 4p.: 30 cm. - 978-0-11-102288-7 £4.00

The Firemen's Pension Scheme (Amendment No. 2) (Scotland) Order 2014 No. 2014/108. - Enabling power: Fire and Rescue Services Act 2004, s. 26 (1) to (5). - Issued: 29.04.2014. Made: 22.04.2014. Laid before the Scottish Parliament: 24.04.2014. Coming into force: 23.05.2014. Effect: S.I. 1992/129 amended. Territorial extent & classification: S. General. - 4p.: 30 cm. - 978-0-11-102325-9 £4.25

The Firemen's Pension Scheme (Amendment) (Scotland) Order 2014 No. 2014/59. - Enabling power: Fire Services Act 1947, s. 26 (1) to (5). - Issued: 06.03.2014. Made: 27.02.2014. Laid before the Scottish Parliament: 03.03.2014. Coming into force: 01.04.2014. Effect: S.I. 1992/129 amended in relation to Scotland. Territorial extent & classification: S. General. - 4p.: 30 cm. - 978-0-11-102287-0 £4.00

The Local Government Pension Scheme (Miscellaneous Amendments) (Scotland) Regulations 2014 No. 2014/23. - Enabling power: Superannuation Act 1972, ss. 7, 12, 24, sch. 3. - Issued: 29.01.2014. Made: 22.01.2014. Laid before the Scottish Parliament: 24.01.2014. Coming into force: 03.03.2014. Effect: S.S.I. 2008/228, 230 amended. Territorial extent & classification: S. General. - Revoked by SSI 2014/233 (ISBN 9780111024324). - 4p.: 30 cm. - 978-0-11-102247-4 £4.00

The Local Government Pension Scheme (Scotland) Regulations 2014 No. 2014/164. - Enabling power: Public Services Pensions Act 2013, s. 1. - Issued: 12.06.2014. Made: 05.06.2014. Laid before the Scottish Parliament: 09.06.2014. Coming into force: In accord. with reg. 1. Effect: None. Territorial extent & classification: S. General. - 90p.: 30 cm. - 978-0-11-102381-5 £16.00

The Police Pensions (Contributions) Amendment (Scotland) Regulations 2014 No. 2014/62. - Enabling power: Police Pensions Act 1976, s. 1. - Issued: 06.03.2014. Made: 27.02.2014. Laid before the Scottish Parliament: 03.03.2014. Coming into force: 01.04.2014. Effect: S.I. 1987/257 (in relation to Scotland); S.S.I. 2007/201 amended. Territorial extent & classification: S. General. - 4p.: 30 cm. - 978-0-11-102286-3 £4.00

The Teachers' Superannuation (Scotland) Amendment Regulations 2014 No. 2014/44. - Enabling power: Superannuation Act 1972, s. 9, sch. 3. - Issued: 26.02.2014. Made: 13.02.2014. Laid before the Scottish Parliament: 24.02.2014. Coming into force: 01.04.2014. Effect: S.S.I. 2005/393 amended. Territorial extent & classification: S. General. - 4p.: 30 cm. - 978-0-11-102272-6 £4.00

The Teachers' Superannuation (Scotland) (Miscellaneous Amendments) Regulations 2014 No. 2014/69. - Enabling power: Superannuation Act 1972, s. 9, 12, sch. 3. - Issued: 10.03.2014. Made: 03.03.2014. Laid before the Scottish Parliament: 05.03.2014. Coming into force: 01.05.2014. Effect: S.S.I. 1995/2814, 2005/393 amended. Territorial extent & classification: S. General. - 12p.: 30 cm. - 978-0-11-102295-5 £5.75

Plant health

The Marketing of Vegetable Plant Material Amendment (Scotland) Regulations 2014 No. 2014/111. - Enabling power: European Communities Act 1972, s. 2 (2), sch. 2, para. 1A. - Issued: 29.04.2014. Made: 23.04.2014. Laid before the Scottish Parliament: 25.04.2014. Coming into force: 26.05.2014. Effect: S.I. 1995/2652 amended. Territorial extent & classification: S. General. - 4p.: 30 cm. - 978-0-11-102328-0 £4.25

The Plant Health (Forestry) (Phytophthora ramorum Management Zone) (Scotland) Order 2014 No. 2014/122. - Enabling power: Plant Health Act 1967, ss. 3 (1) (2) (4). - Issued: 12.05.2014. Made: 02.05.2014. Laid before the Scottish Parliament: 07.05.2014. Coming into force: 05.06.2014. Effect: None. Territorial extent & classification: S. General. - 8p., col. map: 30 cm. - 978-0-11-102338-9 £8.50

The Plant Health (Import Inspection Fees) (Scotland) Regulations 2014 No. 2014/338. - Enabling power: European Communities Act 1972, s. 2 (2), sch. 2 para. 1A & Finance Act 1973, s. 56 (1) (2). - Issued: 04.12.2014. Made: 26.11.2014. Laid before the Scottish Parliament: 01.12.2014. Coming into force: 15.01.2015. Effect: S.S.I. 2004/111 partially revoked & 2005/216; 2007/138, 499; 2009/8, 305; 2010/405,; 2011/311 revoked. Territorial extent & classification: S. General. - EC note: These Regulations implement Article 13d of Council Directive 2000/29/EC (OJ L 169, 10.7.2000, p.1) which requires a member State to ensure the collection of fees to cover the costs occasioned by the documentary check, identity checks and plant health checks of certain imports of plants, plant products and other objects from third countries which are required by Article 13a(1) of the Directive. These Regulations revoke and replace the Plant Health (Import Inspection Fees) (Scotland) Regulations 2005 (S.S.I. 2005/216). These Regulations consolidate amendments made to the 2005 Regulations and also increase the level of the applicable fees. They also make provision for additional fees in respect of potatoes originating in Egypt or Lebanon. - 16p.: 30 cm. - 978-0-11-102528-4 £6.00

The Plant Health (Scotland) Amendment Order 2014 No. 2014/140. - Enabling power: Plant Health Act 1967, ss. 2, 3, 4 (1) & Agriculture (Miscellaneous Provisions) Act 1972, s. 20. - Issued: 03.06.2014. Made: 27.05.2014. Laid before the Scottish Parliament: 29.05.2014. Coming into force: 27.06.2014. Effect: S.S.I. 2005/613 amended. Territorial extent & classification: S. General. - 4p.: 30 cm. - 978-0-11-102358-7 £4.25

Police

The Police Service of Scotland (Amendment) Regulations 2014 No. 2014/1. - Enabling power: Police and Fire Reform (Scotland) Act 2012, ss. 48, 125 (1). - Issued: 14.01.2014. Made: 07.01.2014. Laid before the Scottish Parliament: 09.01.2014. Coming into force: 28.02.2014. Effect: S.S.I. 2013/35 amended. Territorial extent & classification: S. General. - 4p.: 30 cm. - 978-0-11-102231-3 £4.00

The Police Service of Scotland (Conduct) Regulations 2014 No. 2014/68. - Enabling power: Police and Fire Reform (Scotland) Act 2012, ss. 48, 125 (1). - Issued: 07.03.2014. Made: 28.02.2014. Laid before the Scottish Parliament: 03.03.2014. Coming into force: 01.04.2014. Effect: S.S.I. 2013/35, 62, 63 modified & S.S.I. 2013/60 revoked with savings. Territorial extent & classification: S. General. - 24p.: 30 cm. - 978-0-11-102294-8 £5.75

The Police Service of Scotland (Performance) Regulations 2014 No. 2014/67. - Enabling power: Police and Fire Reform (Scotland) Act 2012, ss. 48, 125 (1). - Issued: 06.03.2014. Made: 28.02.2014. Laid before the Scottish Parliament: 03.03.2014. Coming into force: 01.04.2014. Effect: S.S.I. 2013/35, 63 amended & S.S.I. 2013/61 revoked with savings. Territorial extent & classification: S. General. - 28p.: 30 cm. - 978-0-11-102293-1 £5.75

Prisons

The Discontinuance of Aberdeen and Peterhead Prisons (Scotland) Order 2014 No. 2014/13. - Enabling power: Prisons (Scotland) Act 1989, s. 37 (1). - Issued: 22.01.2014. Made: 15.01.2014. Laid before the Scottish Parliament: 17.01.2014. Coming into force: 26.02.2014. Effect: None. Territorial extent & classification: S. General. - 2p.: 30 cm. - 978-0-11-102241-2 £4.00

The Prisons and Young Offenders Institutions (Scotland) Amendment Rules 2014 No. 2014/26. - Enabling power: Prisons (Scotland) Act 1989, ss. 8, 39. - Issued: 04.02.2014. Made: 28.01.2014. Laid before the Scottish Parliament: 30.01.2014. Coming into force: 03.03.2014. Effect: S.S.I. 2011/331 amended. Territorial extent & classification: S. General. - 4p.: 30 cm. - 978-0-11-102250-4 £4.00

The Prisons (Interference with Wireless Telegraphy) Act 2012 (Commencement) (Scotland) Order 2014 No. 2014/34 (C.3). - Enabling power: Prisons (Interference with Wireless Telegraphy) Act 2012, s. 5 (3). Bringing into operation various provisions of this Act on 03.03.2014, in accord. with art. 1. - Issued: 12.02.2014. Made: 05.02.2014. Laid before the Scottish Parliament: 07.02.2014. Coming into force: 03.03.2014. Effect: None. Territorial extent & classification: S. General. - 2p.: 30 cm. - 978-0-11-102257-3 £4.00

Proceeds of crime

The Proceeds of Crime Act 2002 (Amendment of Schedule 4) (Scotland) Order 2014 No. 2014/187. - Enabling power: Proceeds of Crime Act 2002, s. 142 (6). - Issued: 02.07.2014. Made: 26.06.2014. Coming into force: 27.06.2014. Effect: 2002 c.29 amended. Territorial extent & classification: S. General. - Supersedes draft SI (ISBN 9780111023464) issued 23/05/14. - 4p.: 30 cm. - 978-0-11-102402-7 £4.25

The Proceeds of Crime Act 2002 (Disclosure of Information to and by Lord Advocate and Scottish Ministers) Amendment Order 2014 No. 2014/49. - Enabling power: Proceeds of Crime Act 2002, s. 441 (9). - Issued: 28.02.2014. Made: 21.02.2014. Coming into force: 22.02.2014. Effect: S.S.I. 2003/93 amended. Territorial extent & classification: S. General. - Supersedes draft SSI (ISBN 9780111022306) issued 13.01.2014. - 4p.: 30 cm. - 978-0-11-102273-3 £4.00

Public bodies

The Public Appointments and Public Bodies etc. (Scotland) Act 2003 (Treatment of Historic Environment Scotland as Specified Authority) Order 2014 No. 2014/239. - Enabling power: Public Appointments and Public Bodies etc. (Scotland) Act 2003, s. 3 (3). - Issued: 08.09.2014. Made: 29.08.2014-. Coming into force: 30.08.2014. Effect: None. Territorial extent & classification: S. General. - Supersedes draft SSI (9780111023983) issued 02.07.2014. - 2p.: 30 cm. - 978-0-11-102437-9 £4.25

The Public Appointments and Public Bodies etc. (Scotland) Act 2003 (Treatment of Revenue Scotland as Specified Authority) Order 2014 No. 2014/191. - Enabling power: Public Appointments and Public Bodies etc. (Scotland) Act 2003, s. 3 (3). - Issued: 03.07.2014. Made: 26.06.2014. Coming into force: 27.06.2014. Effect: None. Territorial extent & classification: S. General. - Supersedes draft S.S.I. (ISBN 9780111023556) issued 28.05.2014. - 2p.: 30 cm. - 978-0-11-102406-5 £4.25

The Public Appointments and Public Bodies etc. (Scotland) Act 2003 (Treatment of the Convener of the School Closure Review Panels as Specified Authority) Order 2014 No. 2014/230. - Enabling power: Public Appointments and Public Bodies etc. (Scotland) Act 2003, s. 3 (3). - Issued: 28.08.2014. Made: 20.08.2014. Coming into force: 21.08.2014. Effect: None. Territorial extent & classification: S. General. - Supersedes draft SI (ISBN 9780111024003) issued 02.07.2014. - 2p.: 30 cm. - 978-0-11-102428-7 £4.25

Public finance and accountability

The Budget (Scotland) Act 2013 Amendment Order 2014 No. 2014/81. - Enabling power: Budget (Scotland) Act 2013, s. 7 (1). - Issued: 27.03.2014. Made: 20.03.2014. Coming into force: 21.03.2014. Effect: 2013 asp 4 amended. Territorial extent & classification: S. - Supersedes draft SSI (ISBN 9780111022580) issued 12.02.2014. - 4p.: 30 cm. - 978-0-11-102305-1 £4.00

The Budget (Scotland) Act 2014 Amendment Order 2014 No. 2014/363. - Enabling power: Budget (Scotland) Act 2014, s. 7 (1). - Issued: 22.12.2014. Made: 15.12.2014. Coming into force: 16.12.2014. Effect: 2014 asp 6 amended. Territorial extent & classification: S. General. - Supersedes draft SI (ISBN 9780111024799) issued 05/11/14 - 4p.: 30 cm. - 978-0-11-102559-8 £4.25

Public health

The HIV Testing Kits and Services Revocation (Scotland) Regulations 2014 No. 2014/42. - Enabling power: Health and Medicines Act 1988, s. 23 (1). - Issued: 25.02.2014. Made: 19.02.2014. Laid before the Scottish Parliament: 21.02.2014. Coming into force: 06.04.2014. Effect: S.I. 1992/460 revoked in relation to Scotland. Territorial extent & classification: S. General. - 2p.: 30 cm. - 978-0-11-102270-2 £4.00

The Public Bodies (Joint Working) (Content of Performance Reports) (Scotland) Regulations 2014 No. 2014/326. - Enabling power: Public Bodies (Joint Working) Scotland Act 2014, ss. 42 (3), 69 (1). - Issued: 26.11.2014. Made: 19.11.2014. Laid before the Scottish Parliament: 21.11.2014. Coming into force: 20.12.2014. Effect: None. Territorial extent & classification: S. General. - 8p.: 30 cm. - 978-0-11-102517-8 £4.25

The Public Bodies (Joint Working) (Health Professionals and Social Care Professionals) (Scotland) Regulations 2014 No. 2014/307. - Enabling power: Public Bodies (Joint Working) (Scotland) Act 2014, s. 68 (1). - Issued: 19.11.2014. Made: 11.11.2014. Laid before the Scottish Parliament: 13.11.2014. Coming into force: 12.12.2014. Effect: None. Territorial extent & classification: S. General. - 4p.: 30 cm. - 978-0-11-102500-0 £4.25

The Public Bodies (Joint Working) (Integration Joint Boards) (Scotland) Order 2014 No. 2014/285. - Enabling power: Public Bodies (Joint Working) (Scotland) Act 2014, ss. 12, 69 (1). - Issued: 04.11.2014. Made: 28.10.2014. Laid before the Scottish Parliament: 30.10.2014. Coming into force: 28.11.2014. Effect: None. Territorial extent & classification: S. General. - 12p.: 30 cm. - 978-0-11-102475-1 £6.00

The Public Bodies (Joint Working) (Integration Joint Monitoring Committees) (Scotland) Order 2014 No. 2014/281. - Enabling power: Public Bodies (Joint Working) (Scotland) Act 2014, ss. 17, 69 (1). - Issued: 04.11.2014. Made: 28.10.2014. Laid before the Scottish Parliament: 30.10.2014. Coming into force: 28.11.2014. Effect: None. Territorial extent & classification: S. General. - 12p.: 30 cm. - 978-0-11-102471-3 £6.00

The Public Bodies (Joint Working) (Integration Scheme) (Scotland) Regulations 2014 No. 2014/341. - Enabling power: Public Bodies (Joint Working) Scotland Act 2014, ss. 1 (3) (f), 1 (15), 20, 69 (1). - Issued: 04.12.2014. Made: 27.11.2014. Coming into force: 28.11.2014. Effect: None. Territorial extent & classification: S. General. - Supersedes draft S.S.I. (ISBN 9780111024539) issued 09.10.2014. - 12p.: 30 cm. - 978-0-11-102530-7 £6.00

The Public Bodies (Joint Working) (Membership of Strategic Planning Group) (Scotland) Regulations 2014 No. 2014/308. - Enabling power: Public Bodies (Joint Working) (Scotland) Act 2014, s. 32 (2). - Issued: 18.11.2014. Made: 11.11.2014. Laid before the Scottish Parliament: 13.11.2014. Coming into force: 12.12.2014. Effect: None. Territorial extent & classification: S. General. - 4p.: 30 cm. - 978-0-11-102501-7 £4.25

The Public Bodies (Joint Working) (National Health and Wellbeing Outcomes) (Scotland) Regulations 2014 No. 2014/343. - Enabling power: Public Bodies (Joint Working) Scotland Act 2014, s. 5 (1). - Issued: 04.12.2014. Made: 27.11.2014. Coming into force: 28.11.2014. Effect: None. Territorial extent & classification: S. General. - Supersedes draft S.S.I. (ISBN 9780111024522) issued 09.10.2014. - 4p.: 30 cm. - 978-0-11-102532-1 £4.25

The Public Bodies (Joint Working) (Prescribed Consultees) (Scotland) Regulations 2014 No. 2014/283. - Enabling power: Public Bodies (Joint Working) (Scotland) Act 2014, ss. 6 (2) (a), 33 (6), 41 (4), 46 (4) (a), 69 (1) (b). - Issued: 04.11.2014. Made: 28.10.2014. Laid before the Scottish Parliament: 30.10.2014. Coming into force: 28.11.2014. Effect: None. Territorial extent & classification: S. General. - 4p.: 30 cm. - 978-0-11-102473-7 £4.25

The Public Bodies (Joint Working) (Prescribed Days) (Scotland) Regulations 2014 No. 2014/284. - Enabling power: Public Bodies (Joint Working) (Scotland) Act 2014, ss. 7 (1) (5), 9 (3), 15 (2), 51 (2) (c)- Issued: 04.11.2014. Made: 28.10.2014. Laid before the Scottish Parliament: 30.10.2014. Coming into force: 28.11.2014. Effect: None. Territorial extent & classification: S. General. - 2p.: 30 cm. - 978-0-11-102474-4 £4.25

The Public Bodies (Joint Working) (Prescribed Health Board Functions) (Scotland) Regulations 2014 No. 2014/344. - Enabling power: Public Bodies (Joint Working) Scotland Act 2014, ss. 1 (6), 1 (8), 69 (1). - Issued: 04.12.2014. Made: 27.11.2014. Coming into force: 28.11.2014. Effect: None. Territorial extent & classification: S. General. - Supersedes draft S.S.I. (ISBN 9780111024652) issued 28.10.2014. - 16p.: 30 cm. - 978-0-11-102533-8 £6.00

The Public Bodies (Joint Working) (Prescribed Local Authority Functions etc.) (Scotland) Regulations 2014 No. 2014/345. - Enabling power: Public Bodies (Joint Working) (Scotland) Act 2014, ss. 1 (7) (12), 69 (1) (b). - Issued: 04.12.2014. Made: 27.11.2014. Laid before the Scottish Parliament: -. Coming into force: 28.11.2014. Effect: 2014 asp 9 amended. Territorial extent & classification: S. General. - Supersedes draft S.S.I. (ISBN 9780111024645) issued 28.10.2014. - 12p.: 30 cm. - 978-0-11-102534-5 £6.00

The Public Bodies (Joint Working) (Scotland) Act 2014 (Commencement No. 2) Order 2014 No. 2014/231 (C.21). - Enabling power: Public Bodies (Joint Working) (Scotland) Act 2014, s. 72 (2). Bringing into operation various provisions of the 2014 Act on 22.09.2014 & 01.04.2015, in accord. with art. 2. - Issued: 28.08.2014. Made: 21.08.2014. Laid before the Scottish Parliament: 22.08.2014. Coming into force: 22.09.2014. Effect: None. Territorial extent & classification: S. General. - 2p.: 30 cm. - 978-0-11-102430-0 £4.25

The Public Bodies (Joint Working) (Scotland) Act 2014 (Modifications) Order 2014 No. 2014/342. - Enabling power: Public Bodies (Joint Working) Scotland Act 2014, s. 70 (1) (a) (2). - Issued: 04.12.2014. Made: 27.11.2014. Coming into force: 28.11.2014. Effect: 2014 asp 9 amended. Territorial extent & classification: S. General. - Supersedes draft S.S.I. (ISBN 9780111024669) issued 28.10.2014. - 4p.: 30 cm. - 978-0-11-102531-4 £4.25

Public service pensions

The Local Government Pension Scheme (Transitional Provisions and Savings) (Scotland) Regulations 2014 No. 2014/233. - Enabling power: Superannuation Act 1972, s. 7. - Issued: 29.08.2014. Made: 21.08.2014. Laid before the Scottish Parliament: 22.08.2014. Coming into force: 01.04.2015. Effect: S.I. 1998/366; S.S.I. 2008/228, 229, 230; 2009/93, 187; 2010/234; 2011/349; 2012/236, 347; 2014/23 revoked. Territorial extent & classification: S. General. - 24p.: 30 cm. - 978-0-11-102432-4 £6.00

The Teachers' Pension Scheme (Scotland) (No. 2) Regulations 2014 No. 2014/292. - Enabling power: Public Service Pensions Act 2013, s. 1 (1) (2) (d), sch. 2, para. 4 (b). - Issued: 12.11.2014. Made: 05.11.2014. Laid before the Scottish Parliament: 07.11.2014. Coming into force: In accord. with reg. 1 (2). Effect: S.S.I. 2014/217 revoked. Territorial extent & classification: S. General. - This Statutory Instrument has been made in consequence of errors in S.S.I. 2014/217 (ISBN 9780111024195) and is being issued free of charge to all known recipients of that Statutory Instrument. - 108p.: 30 cm. - 978-0-11-102485-0 £16.50

The Teachers' Pension Scheme (Scotland) Regulations 2014 No. 2014/217. - Enabling power: Public Service Pensions Act 2013, s. 1 (1) (2) (d), sch. 2, para. 4 (b). - Issued: 12.08.2014. Made: 01.08.2014. Laid before the Scottish Parliament: 07.08.2014. Coming into force: In accord. with reg. 1 (2). Effect: None. Territorial extent & classification: S. General. - Revoked by SSI 2014/292 (ISBN 9780111024850). - 108p.: 30 cm. - 978-0-11-102419-5 £16.50

Rating and valuation

The Non-Domestic Rate (Scotland) Order 2014 No. 2014/28. - Enabling power: Local Government (Scotland) Act 1975, ss. 7B (1), 37 (1). - Issued: 10.02.2014. Made: 04.02.2014. Laid before the Scottish Parliament: 06.02.2014. Coming into force: 01.04.2014. Effect: None. Territorial extent & classification: S. General. - 2p.: 30 cm. - 978-0-11-102251-1 £4.00

The Non-Domestic Rates (Levying) (Scotland) Regulations 2014 No. 2014/30. - Enabling power: Local Government etc. (Scotland) Act 1994, s. 153. - Issued: 11.02.2014. Made: 04.02.2014. Laid before the Scottish Parliament: 06.02.2014. Coming into force: 01.04.2014. Effect: S.S.I. 2012/353; 2013/34 revoked with savings. Territorial extent & classification: S. General. - 8p.: 30 cm. - 978-0-11-102253-5 £4.00

The Non-Domestic Rating (Unoccupied Property) (Scotland) Amendment Regulations 2014 No. 2014/31. - Enabling power: Local Government (Scotland) Act 1966, s. 24B (3). - Issued: 11.02.2014. Made: 04.02.2014. Laid before the Scottish Parliament: 06.02.2014. Coming into force: 01.04.2014. Effect: S.I. 1994/3200 amended. Territorial extent & classification: S. General. - 4p.: 30 cm. - 978-0-11-102254-2 £4.00

The Non-Domestic Rating (Valuation of Utilities) (Scotland) Amendment Order 2014 No. 2014/64. - Enabling power: Valuation and Rating (Scotland) Act 1956, s. 6A (1) (aa) (1B). - Issued: 06.03.2014. Made: 27.02.2014. Laid before the Scottish Parliament: 03.03.2014. Coming into force: 28.04.2014. Effect: S.S.I. 2005/127 amended. Territorial extent & classification: S. General. - 4p.: 30 cm. - 978-0-11-102290-0 £4.00

The Valuation and Rating (Exempted Classes) (Scotland) Order 2014 No. 2014/153. - Enabling power: Valuation and Rating (Exempted Classes) (Scotland) Act 1976, s. 1. - Issued: 05.06.2014. Made: 28.05.2014. Coming into force: 01.06.2014. Effect: None. Territorial extent & classification: S. General. - Supersedes draft SI (ISBN 9780111023075) issued 01/04/14. - 4p.: 30 cm. - 978-0-11-102371-6 £4.25

Registers and records

The Registers of Scotland (Fees) Order 2014 No. 2014/188. - Enabling power: Land Registration etc. (Scotland) Act 2012, ss. 110 (1) (2), 116 (1), 117 (1). - Issued: 03.07.2014. Made: 26.06.2014. Coming into force: In accord. with art. 1 (2) (3). Effect: S.I. 1995/1945; 1999/1085 & S.S.I. 2001/163; 2004/230, 496, 507; 2005/580; 2006/600; 2009/171; 2010/404; 2012/295, 328; 2013/59 revoked & S.S.I. 2011/211 partially revoked. Territorial extent & classification: S. General. - Supersedes draft SI (ISBN 9780111023570) issued 03.06.14. - 16p.: 30 cm. - 978-0-11-102403-4 £6.00

Registration of births, deaths, marriages, etc.

The Marriage and Civil Partnership (Prescribed Forms) (Scotland) Regulations 2014 No. 2014/306. - Enabling power: Marriage and Civil Partnership (Scotland) Act 2014, s. 88 (1) (5), 95ZA & Local Electoral Administration and Registration Services (Scotland) Act 2006, s. 55 (2) & Marriage (Scotland) Act 1977, ss. 3 (1), 6 (1), 7 (2) & Registration of Births, Deaths and Marriages (Scotland) Act 1965, ss. 32 (1), 54 (1) (b). - Issued: 18.11.2014. Made: 11.11.2014. Laid before the Scottish Parliament: 13.11.2014. Coming into force: 16.12.2014. Effect: S.I. 1997/2348, 2349; S.S.I. 2005/458; 2008/386 amended. Territorial extent & classification: S. General. - 16p.: 30 cm. - 978-0-11-102499-7 £6.00

The Registration of Births, Still-births, Deaths and Marriages (Prescription of Forms) (Scotland) Amendment Regulations 2014 No. 2014/141. - Enabling power: Registration of Births, Deaths and Marriages (Scotland) Act 1965, ss. 24 (1), 54 (1) (b). - Issued: 03.06.2014. Made: 27.05.2014. Laid before the Scottish Parliament: 29.05.2014. Coming into force: 06.08.2014. Effect: S.I. 1997/2348 amended. Territorial extent & classification: S. General. - 8p.: 30 cm. - 978-0-11-102359-4 £4.25

Regulatory reform

The Regulatory Reform (Scotland) Act 2014 (Commencement No. 1 and Transitional Provision) Order 2014 No. 2014/160 (C.11). - Enabling power: Regulatory Reform (Scotland) Act 2014, s. 61 (2). Bringing into operation various provisions of the Act on 30.06.2014; 01.04.2015, in accord. with art. 2. - Issued: 10.06.2014. Made: 04.06.2014. Laid before the Scottish Parliament: 06.06.2014. Coming into force: 30.06.2014. Effect: None. Territorial extent & classification: S. General. - 8p.: 30 cm. - 978-0-11-102377-8 £6.00

Representation of the people

The Scottish Independence Referendum (Chief Counting Officer and Counting Officer Charges and Expenses) Order 2014 No. 2014/101. - Enabling power: Scottish Independence Referendum Act 2013, s. 9 (3) (4). - Issued: 08.04.2014. Made: 02.04.2014. Laid before the Scottish Parliament: 04.04.2014. Coming into force: 05.05.2014. Effect: None. Territorial extent & classification: S. General. - 8p.: 30 cm. - 978-0-11-102320-4 £4.25

River

The Conservation of Salmon (Annual Close Time and Catch and Release) (Scotland) (Amendment) Regulations 2014 No. 2014/357. - Enabling power: Salmon and Freshwater Fisheries (Consolidation) (Scotland) Act 2003, s. 38 (1) (5) (c) (6) (c), sch. 1, paras 7 (b), 14 (1). - Issued: 17.12.2014. Made: 10.12.2014. Laid before the Scottish Parliament: 12.12.2014. Coming into force: 09.01.2015. Effect: None. Territorial extent & classification: S. General. - This S.S.I. has been printed to correct an error in S.S.I. 2014/327 (ISBN 9780111025185) and is being issued free of charge to all known recipients of that instrument. - 4p.: 30 cm. - 978-0-11-102553-6 £4.25

The Conservation of Salmon (Annual Close Time and Catch and Release) (Scotland) Regulations 2014 No. 2014/327. - Enabling power: Salmon and Freshwater Fisheries (Consolidation) (Scotland) Act 2003, s. 38 (1) (5) (c) (6) (c), sch. 1, paras 7 (b), 14 (1). - Issued: 28.11.2014. Made: 20.11.2014. Laid before the Scottish Parliament: 24.11.2014. Coming into force: 09.01.2015. Effect: None. Territorial extent & classification: S. General. - 24p.: 30 cm. - 978-0-11-102518-5 £6.00

Roads and bridges

The A9 Trunk Road (Kincraig to Dalraddy) (Side Roads) Order 2014 No. 2014/246. - Enabling power: Roads (Scotland) Act 1984, ss. 12 (1), 70 (1), 145. - Issued: 18.09.2014. Made: 17.09.2014. Coming into force: 23.09.2014. Effect: S.S.I. 2009/366 revoked. Territorial extent & classification: S. Local. - Available at: http://www.legislation.gov.uk/ssi/2014/246/contents/made Non-print

The A82 Trunk Road (Glen Gloy Realignment) (Side Roads) Order 2014 No. 2014/311. - Enabling power: Roads (Scotland) Act 1984, ss. 12 (1) (5), 70 (1)- Issued: 14.11.2014. Made: 12.11.2014. Coming into force: 24.11.2014. Effect: None. Territorial extent & classification: S. Local. - Available at: http://www.legislation.gov.uk/ssi/2014/311/contents/made Non-print

The A82 Trunk Road (Glen Gloy Realignment) (Trunking and Detrunking) Order 2014 No. 2014/309. - Enabling power: Roads (Scotland) Act 1984, s. 5 (2) (6). - Issued: 14.11.2014. Made: 12.11.2014. Coming into force: 24.11.2014. Effect: None. Territorial extent & classification: S. Local. - Available at: http://www.legislation.gov.uk/ssi/2014/309/contents/made Non-print

The Road Works (Inspection Fees) (Scotland) Amendment Regulations 2014 No. 2014/56. - Enabling power: New Roads and Street Works Act 1991, s. 134. - Issued: 05.03.2014. Made: 26.02.2014. Laid before the Scottish Parliament: 28.02.2014. Coming into force: 01.04.2014. Effect: S.S.I. 2003/415 amended. Territorial extent & classification: S. General. - 4p.: 30 cm. - 978-0-11-102282-5 £4.00

The Scottish Road Works Register (Prescribed Fees) Regulations 2014 No. 2014/58. - Enabling power: New Roads and Street Works Act 1991, ss. 112A (4), 163 (1). - Issued: 05.03.2014. Made: 26.02.2014. Laid before the Scottish Parliament: 28.02.2014. Coming into force: 01.04.2014. Effect: S.S.I. 2008/16 amended & S.S.I. 2013/8 revoked. Territorial extent & classification: S. General. - Revoked by SSI 2015/89 (ISBN 9780111026816). - 8p.: 30 cm. - 978-0-11-102284-9 £4.00

Roads and bridges: Special roads

The M8 Special Road (Hillington Footbridge) Order 2014 No. 2014/238. - Enabling power: Roads (Scotland) Act 1984, ss. 9 (1) (c) (d) (f), 143 (1). - Issued: 29.08.2014. Made: 28.08.2014. Coming into force: 11.09.2014. Effect: None. Territorial extent & classification: S. Local. - Available at: http://www.legislation.gov.uk/ssi/2014/238/contents/made Non-print

Road traffic

The Disabled Persons (Badges for Motor Vehicles) (Scotland) Amendment Regulations 2014 No. 2014/145. - Enabling power: Chronically Sick and Disabled Persons Act 1970, s. 21. - Issued: 03.06.2014. Made: 28.05.2014. Laid before the Scottish Parliament: 30.05.2014. Coming into force: 28.06.2014. Effect: S.S.I. 2000/59 amended. Territorial extent & classification: S. General. - 4p.: 30 cm. - 978-0-11-102362-4 £4.25

The Glasgow Commonwealth Games Act 2008 (Duration of Urgent Traffic Regulation Measures) Order 2014 No. 2014/92. - Enabling power: Glasgow Commonwealth Games Act 2008, s. 47. - Issued: 02.04.2014. Made: 27.03.2014. Laid before the Scottish Parliament: 31.03.2014. Coming into force: 02.06.2014. Effect: 1984 c.27 modified. Territorial extent & classification: S. General. - 4p.: 30 cm. - 978-0-11-102313-6 £4.00

The HGV Speed Limit (M9/A9 Trunk Road) Regulations 2014 No. 2014/274. - Enabling power: Road Traffic Regulation Act 1984, s. 86 (2) (3). - Issued: 27.10.2014. Made: 21.10.2014. Coming into force: 28.10.2014. Effect: None. Territorial extent & classification: S. General. - Supersedes draft S.I. (ISBN 9780111023433) issued 22.05.2014. - 4p.: 30 cm. - 978-0-11-102463-8 £4.25

The Parking Attendants (Wearing of Uniforms) (Argyll and Bute Council Parking Area) Regulations 2014 No. 2014/85. - Enabling power: Road Traffic Regulation Act 1984, s. 63A. - Issued: 02.04.2014. Made: 26.03.2014. Laid before the Scottish Parliament: 28.03.2014. Coming into force: 12.05.2014. Effect: None. Territorial extent & classification: S. General. - 4p.: 30 cm. - 978-0-11-102309-9 £4.00

The Parking Attendants (Wearing of Uniforms) (Inverclyde Council Parking Area) Regulations 2014 No. 2014/170. - Enabling power: Road Traffic Regulation Act 1984, s. 63A. - Issued: 18.06.2014. Made: 11.06.2014. Laid before the Scottish Parliament: 13.06.2014. Coming into force: 06.10.2014. Effect: None. Territorial extent & classification: S. General. - 4p.: 30 cm. - 978-0-11-102388-4 £4.25

The Road Traffic Act 1988 (Prescribed Limit) (Scotland) Regulations 2014 No. 2014/328. - Enabling power: Road Traffic Act 1988, ss. 8 (3) (4) (b), 11 (2) (2ZA) (b). - Issued: 27.11.2014. Made: 20.11.2014. Coming into force: 05.12.2014. Effect: None. Territorial extent & classification: S. General. - Supersedes draft S.S.I. (ISBN 9780111024478) issued 02.10.2014. - 4p.: 30 cm. - 978-0-11-102519-2 £4.25

The Road Traffic (Parking Adjudicators) (Argyll and Bute Council) Regulations 2014 No. 2014/86. - Enabling power: Road Traffic Act 1991, s. 73 (11) (12). - Issued: 02.04.2014. Made: 26.03.2014. Laid before the Scottish Parliament: 28.03.2014. Coming into force: 12.05.2014. Effect: None. Territorial extent & classification: S. General. - 12p.: 30 cm. - 978-0-11-102310-5 £5.75

The Road Traffic (Parking Adjudicators) (Inverclyde Council) Regulations 2014 No. 2014/171. - Enabling power: Road Traffic Act 1991, s. 73 (11) (12). - Issued: 18.06.2014. Made: 11.06.2014. Laid before the Scottish Parliament: 13.06.2014. Coming into force: 06.10.2014. Effect: None. Territorial extent & classification: S. General. - 12p.: 30 cm. - 978-0-11-102389-1 £6.00

The Road Traffic (Permitted Parking Area and Special Parking Area) (Argyll and Bute Council) Designation Order 2014 No. 2014/84. - Enabling power: Road Traffic Act 1991, sch. 3, paras 1 (1), 2 (1), 3 (3). - Issued: 02.04.2014. Made: 26.03.2014. Laid before the Scottish Parliament: 28.03.2014. Coming into force: 12.05.2014. Effect: 1984 c.27; 1991 c.40 modified. Territorial extent & classification: S. General. - 12p.: 30 cm. - 978-0-11-102308-2 £5.75

The Road Traffic (Permitted Parking Area and Special Parking Area) (Inverclyde Council) Designation Order 2014 No. 2014/169. - Enabling power: Road Traffic Act 1991, sch. 3, paras 1 (1), 2 (1), 3 (3). - Issued: 18.06.2014. Made: 11.06.2014. Laid before the Scottish Parliament: 13.06.2014. Coming into force: 06.10.2014. Effect: 1984 c.27; 1991 c.40 modified. Territorial extent & classification: S. General. - 12p.: 30 cm. - 978-0-11-102387-7 £6.00

Road traffic: Speed limits

The A7 Trunk Road (Broadhaugh) (50mph Speed Limit) Order 2014 No. 2014/126. - Enabling power: Road Traffic Regulation Act 1984, s. 84 (1) (a). - Issued: 12.05.2014. Made: 09.05.2014. Coming into force: 19.05.2014. Effect: None. Territorial extent & classification: S. Local. - Available at http://www.legislation.gov.uk/ssi/2014/126/contents/made Non-print

The A8 Trunk Road (Bogston to Newark, Port Glasgow) (40mph Speed Limit) Order 2014 No. 2014/97. - Enabling power: Road Traffic Regulation Act 1984, ss. 84 (1) (a), 124 (1) (d), sch. 9, para. 27. - Issued: 02.04.2014. Made: 31.03.2014. Coming into force: 09.04.2014. Effect: None. Territorial extent & classification: S. Local. - Available at http://www.legislation.gov.uk/ssi/2014/97/contents/made Non-print

The A9 and A82 Trunk Roads (Kessock) (50mph Speed Limit) Order 2014 No. 2014/198. - Enabling power: Road Traffic Regulation Act 1984, ss. 2 (1) (2), 4 (1), 14 (1) (a) (4), 84 (1) (a), 124 (1) (d), sch. 9, para. 27. - Issued: 04.07.2014. Made: 03.07.2014. Coming into force: 11.07.2014. Effect: S.I. 2013/28 revoked. Territorial extent & classification: S. Local. - Available at http://www.legislation.gov.uk/ssi/2014/198/contents/made Non-print

The A75 Trunk Road (Crocketford) (Restricted Road) Order 2014 No. 2014/247. - Enabling power: Road Traffic Regulation Act 1984, ss. 82 (2) (b), 83 (1), sch. 9 para. 27 (1). - Issued: 19.09.2014. Made: 18.09.2014. Coming into force: 13.10.2014. Effect: None. Territorial extent & classification: S. Local. - Available at: http://www.legislation.gov.uk/ssi/2014/247/contents/made Non-print

The A96 Trunk Road (Forres Bypass) (40mph Speed Limit) Order 2014 No. 2014/222. - Enabling power: Roads Traffic Regulation Act 1984, ss. 84 (1) (a), 124 (1) (d), sch. 9, para. 27. - Issued: 18.08.2014. Made: 14.08.2014. Coming into force: 25.08.2014. Effect: S.S.I. 1998/1812 revoked. Territorial extent & classification: S. Local. - Available at http://www.legislation.gov.uk/ssi/2014/222/contents/made Non-print

The A99 Trunk Road (Thrumster) (50mph Speed Limit) Order 2014 No. 2014/125. - Enabling power: Road Traffic Regulation Act 1984, s. 84 (1) (a). - Issued: 12.05.2014. Made: 09.05.2014. Coming into force: 19.05.2014. Effect: None. Territorial extent & classification: S. Local. - Available at http://www.legislation.gov.uk/ssi/2014/125/contents/made Non-print

The A887 Trunk Road (Torgoyle) (50mph Speed Limit) Order 2014 No. 2014/96. - Enabling power: Road Traffic Regulation Act 1984, s. 84 (1) (a). - Issued: 02.04.2014. Made: 31.03.2014. Coming into force: 09.04.2014. Effect: None. Territorial extent & classification: S. Local. - Available at http://www.legislation.gov.uk/ssi/2014/96/contents/made Non-print

The M898/A898 and A82 Trunk Roads (Erskine Bridge) (50mph Speed Limit) Order 2014 No. 2014/204. - Enabling power: Road Traffic Regulation Act 1984, ss. 2 (1) (2), 4 (1), 14 (1) (a) (4), 84 (1) (a), 124 (1) (d), sch. 9, para. 27. - Issued: 18.07.2014. Made: 15.07.2014. Coming into force: 23.07.2014. Effect: S.S.I. 2013/248 revoked. Territorial extent & classification: S. Local. - Available at: http://www.legislation.gov.uk/ssi/2014/204/contents/made Non-print

Road traffic: Traffic regulation

The A7 Trunk Road (High Street and Townhead, Langholm) (Temporary Prohibition On Use of Road) Order 2014 No. 2014/203. - Enabling power: Road Traffic Regulation Act 1984, ss. 2 (1) (2), 4 (1), 16A- Issued: 14.07.2014. Made: 11.07.2014. Coming into force: 25.07.2014. Effect: None. Territorial extent & classification: S. Local. - Available at http://www.legislation.gov.uk/ssi/2014/203/contents/made Non-print

The A8 Trunk Road (Chapelhall) (Temporary Prohibition on Use of Road) Order 2014 No. 2014/266. - Enabling power: Roads (Scotland) Act 1984, ss. 2 (1) (2), 14 (1) (a) (4)- Issued: 10.10.2014. Made: 08.10.2014. Coming into force: 20.10.2014. Effect: None. Territorial extent & classification: S. Local. - Available at: http://www.legislation.gov.uk/ssi/2014/266/contents/made Non-print

The A9 and A82 Trunk Roads (Kessock) (50mph Speed Limit) Order 2014 No. 2014/198. - Enabling power: Road Traffic Regulation Act 1984, ss. 2 (1) (2), 4 (1), 14 (1) (a) (4), 84 (1) (a), 124 (1) (d), sch. 9, para. 27. - Issued: 04.07.2014. Made: 03.07.2014. Coming into force: 11.07.2014. Effect: S.I. 2013/28 revoked. Territorial extent & classification: S. Local. - Available at http://www.legislation.gov.uk/ssi/2014/198/contents/made Non-print

The A9 Trunk Road (Blair Atholl Junction) (Temporary Prohibition on Use of Road) Order 2014 No. 2014/11. - Enabling power: Road Traffic Regulation Act 1984, ss. 2 (1) (2), 4 (1), 14 (1) (a) (4). - Issued: 15.01.2014. Made: 10.01.2014. Coming into force: 20.01.2014. Effect: None. Territorial extent & classification: S. Local. - Available at http://www.legislation.gov.uk/ssi/2014/11/contents/made Non-print

The A9 Trunk Road (Kessock Bridge) (Temporary Prohibition of Specified Turns, Width Restriction and Use of Specified Lanes) Order 2014 No. 2014/16. - Enabling power: Road Traffic Regulation Act 1984, ss. 2 (1) (2), 4 (1), 14 (1) (a) (4). - Issued: 22.01.2014. Made: 21.01.2014. Coming into force: 10.02.2014. Effect: None. Territorial extent & classification: S. Local. - Available at: http://www.legislation.gov.uk/ssi/2014/16/contents/made Non-print

The A9 Trunk Road (Munlochy Junction) (Temporary Prohibition of Specified Turns) Order 2014 No. 2014/223. - Enabling power: Road Traffic Regulation Act 1984, ss. 2 (1) (2), 4 (1), 14 (1) (a) (4). - Issued: 19.08.2014. Made: 15.08.2014. Coming into force: 24.08.2014. Effect: None. Territorial extent & classification: S. Local. - Available at: http://www.legislation.gov.uk/ssi/2014/223/contents/made Non-print

The A68 Trunk Road (Bongate and Newcastle Road, Jedburgh) (Temporary Prohibition On Use of Road) Order 2014 No. 2014/199. - Enabling power: Road Traffic Regulation Act 1984, ss. 2 (1) (2), 4 (1), 16A. - Issued: 04.07.2014. Made: 03.07.2014. Coming into force: 11.07.2014. Effect: None. Territorial extent & classification: S. Local. - Available at http://www.legislation.gov.uk/ssi/2014/199/contents/made Non-print

The A68 Trunk Road (Edinburgh Road, Jedburgh) (Temporary Prohibition on Waiting and 30mph Speed Limit) Order 2014 No. 2014/168. - Enabling power: Road Traffic Regulation Act 1984, ss. 2 (1) (2), 4 (1), 14 (1) (a) (4). - Issued: 12.06.2014. Made: 09.06.2014. Coming into force: 21.06.2014. Effect: None. Territorial extent & classification: S. Local. - Available at http://www.legislation.gov.uk/ssi/2014/168/contents/made Non-print

The A78 Trunk Road (Gallowgate Street, Largs) (Prohibition of Waiting, Loading and Unloading) Order 2014 No. 2014/269. - Enabling power: Road Traffic Regulation Act 1984, ss. 1 (1), 2 (1) (2), 124 (1) (d), sch. 9 para. 27. - Issued: 17.10.2014. Made: 16.10.2014. Coming into force: 01.11.2014. Effect: North Ayrshire Council (Largs) (Traffic Management) Order 2010 varied. Territorial extent & classification: S. Local. Available at http://www.legislation.gov.uk/ssi/2014/269/contents/made Non-print

The A82 Trunk Road (Crianlarich Bypass) (Temporary 30mph Speed Restriction) Order 2014 No. 2014/385. - Enabling power: Road Traffic Regulation Act 1984, ss. 2 (1) (2), 4 (1), 14 (1) (a) (4). - Issued: 22.12.2014. Made: 19.12.2014. Coming into force: 08.01.2015. Effect: None. Territorial extent & classification: S. Local. - Available at http://www.legislation.gov.uk/ssi/2014/385/contents/made Non-print

The A82 Trunk Road (Crianlarich Bypass) (Temporary Prohibition of Use and Speed Restriction) Order 2014 No. 2014/276. - Enabling power: Road Traffic Regulation Act 1984, ss. 2 (1) (2), 4 (1), 14 (1) (a) (4). - Issued: 24.10.2014. Made: 22.10.2014. Coming into force: 03.11.2014. Effect: None. Territorial extent & classification: S. Local. - Available at http://www.legislation.gov.uk/ssi/2014/276/contents/made Non-print

ROAD TRAFFIC: TRAFFIC REGULATION

The A82 Trunk Road (Crianlarich Bypass) (Temporary Speed Restriction) Order 2014 No. 2014/216. - Enabling power: Road Traffic Regulation Act 1984, ss. 2 (1) (2), 4 (1), 14 (1) (a) (4). - Issued: 05.08.2014. Made: 04.08.2014. Coming into force: 11.08.2014. Effect: None. Territorial extent & classification: S. Local. - Available at http://www.legislation.gov.uk/ssi/2014/216/contents/made Non-print

The A82 Trunk Road (Drumnadrochit to Fort Augustus) (Temporary Prohibition of Traffic) Order 2014 No. 2014/182. - Enabling power: Road Traffic Regulation Act 1984, ss. 2 (1) (2), 4 (1), 14 (1) (b) (4). - Issued: 20.06.2014. Made: 19.06.2014. Coming into force: 28.06.2014. Effect: None. Territorial extent & classification: S. Local. - Available at http://www.legislation.gov.uk/ssi/2014/182/contents/made Non-print

The A82 Trunk Road (Pulpit Rock Improvement) (Temporary Prohibition of Traffic and Overtaking and Speed Restriction) (No. 2) Order 2014 No. 2014/286. - Enabling power: Road Traffic Regulation Act 1984, ss. 2 (1) (2), 4 (1), 14 (1) (a) (4). - Issued: 30.10.2014. Made: 29.10.2014. Coming into force: 11.11.2014. Effect: None. Territorial extent & classification: S. Local. - Available at http://www.legislation.gov.uk/ssi/2014/286/contents/made Non-print

The A82 Trunk Road (Pulpit Rock Improvement) (Temporary Prohibition of Traffic and Overtaking and Speed Restriction) Order 2014 No. 2014/177. - Enabling power: Road Traffic Regulation Act 1984, ss. 2 (1) (2), 4 (1), 14 (1) (A) (4). - Issued: 20.06.2014. Made: 18.06.2014. Coming into force: 02.07.2014. Effect: None. Territorial extent & classification: S. Local. - Available at http://www.legislation.gov.uk/ssi/2014/177/contents/made Non-print

The A83 (Kennacraig to Campbeltown) (Trunking) Order 2014 No. 2014/215. - Enabling power: Roads (Scotland) Act 1984, s. 5 (2). - Issued: 01.08.2014. Made: 31.07.2014. Coming into force: 04.08.2014. Effect: None. Territorial extent & classification: S. Local. - Available at http://www.legislation.gov.uk/ssi/2014/215/contents/made Non-print

The A83 Trunk Road (Lochgilphead) (Temporary Prohibition On Use of Road) Order 2014 No. 2014/288. - Enabling power: Road Traffic Regulation Act 1984, ss. 2 (1) (2), 4 (1), 16A. - Issued: 03.11.2014. Made: 30.10.2014. Coming into force: 08.11.2014. Effect: None. Territorial extent & classification: S. Local. - Available at: http://www.legislation.gov.uk/ssi/2014/288/contents/made Non-print

The A83 Trunk Road (Poltalloch Street, Lochgilphead) (Temporary Prohibition On Use of Road) Order 2014 No. 2014/175. - Enabling power: Road Traffic Regulation Act 1984, ss. 2 (1) (2), 4 (1), 16A. - Issued: 17.06.2014. Made: 16.06.2014. Coming into force: 21.06.2013. Effect: None. Territorial extent & classification: S. Local. - Available at: http://www.legislation.gov.uk/ssi/2014/175/contents/made Non-print.
We apologise for late appearance on the daily list

The A84 Trunk Road (Callander) (Temporary Prohibition of Pedestrians and Waiting, Loading and Unloading) Order 2014 No. 2014/244. - Enabling power: Road Traffic Regulation Act 1984, ss. 2 (1) (2) (3), 4 (1), 14 (1) (4). - Issued: 15.09.2014. Made: 12.09.2014. Coming into force: 29.09.2014. Effect: None. Territorial extent & classification: S. Local. - Available at: http://www.legislation.gov.uk/ssi/2014/244/contents/made Non-print

The A85 Trunk Road (Comrie) (Temporary Prohibition On Use of Road) Order) Order 2014 No. 2014/380. - Enabling power: Road Traffic Regulation Act 1984, ss. 2 (1) (2), 4 (1), 16A. - Issued: 18.12.2014. Made: 17.12.2014. Coming into force: 31.12.2014. Effect: None. Territorial extent & classification: S. Local. - Available at http://www.legislation.gov.uk/ssi/2014/380/contents/made Non-print

The A85 Trunk Road (Dunollie Road) (Temporary Prohibition on Use of Road) Order 2014 No. 2014/120. - Enabling power: Road Traffic Regulation Act 1984, ss. 2 (1) (2), 4 (1), 14 (1) (a) (4). - Issued: 02.05.2014. Made: 01.05.2014. Coming into force: 14.05.2014. Effect: None. Territorial extent & classification: S. Local. - Available at: http://www.legislation.gov.uk/ssi/2014/120/contents/made Non-print

The A85 Trunk Road (Stafford Street, Oban) (Detrunking) Order 2014 No. 2014/27. - Enabling power: Roads (Scotland) Act 1984, s. 5 (2) (6). - Issued: 03.02.2014. Made: 30.01.2014. Coming into force: 10.02.2014. Effect: None. Territorial extent & classification: S. Local. - Available at: http://www.legislation.gov.uk/ssi/2014/27/contents/made Non-print

The A90 Trunk Road (Cortes) (Prohibition of Waiting) Order 2014 No. 2014/378. - Enabling power: Road Traffic Regulation Act 1984, ss. 1 (1), 2 (1) (2). - Issued: 18.12.2014. Made: 16.12.2014. Coming into force: 30.12.2014. Effect: None. Territorial extent & classification: S. Local. - Available at http://www.legislation.gov.uk/ssi/2014/378/contents/made Non-print

The A90 Trunk Road (Northbound Slip Road from B980 Castlandhill Road) (Temporary Prohibition on Use of Road and Temporary Speed Restrictions) Order 2014 No. 2014/10. - Enabling power: Road Traffic Regulation Act 1984, ss. 2 (1) (2), 4 (1), 14 (1) (a) (4). - Issued: 14.01.2014. Made: 13.01.2014. Coming into force: 20.01.2014. Effect: None. Territorial extent & classification: S. Local. - Available at http://www.legislation.gov.uk/ssi/2014/10/contents/made Non-print

The A90 Trunk Road (Temporary Northbound Slip Road to Ferrytoll Roundabout) (Temporary Prohibition of Overtaking and Temporary Speed Restrictions) Order 2014 No. 2014/156. - Enabling power: Road Traffic Regulation Act 1984, ss. 2 (1) (2), 4 (1), 14 (1) (a) (4). - Issued: 03.06.2014. Made: 30.05.2014. Coming into force: 21.06.2014. Effect: None. Territorial extent & classification: S. Local. - Available at http://www.legislation.gov.uk/ssi/2014/156/contents/made Non-print

The A92/A972 Trunk Road (B969 Western Avenue to the C49 leading to Star) (Temporary Prohibition of Specified Turns) (No. 2) Order 2014 No. 2014/299. - Enabling power: Road Traffic Regulation Act 1984, ss. 2 (1) (2), 4 (1), 14 (1) (a) (4). - Issued: 10.11.2014. Made: 07.11.2014. Coming into force: 17.11.2014. Effect: None. Territorial extent & classification: S. Local. - Available at http://www.legislation.gov.uk/ssi/2014/299/contents/made Non-print

The A92/A972 Trunk Road (B969 Western Avenue to the C49 leading to Star) (Temporary Prohibition of Specified Turns) Order 2014 No. 2014/128. - Enabling power: Road Traffic Regulation Act 1984, ss. 2 (1) (2), 4 (1), 14 (1) (a) (4). - Made: 16.05.2014. Made: 15.05.2014. Coming into force: 26.05.2014. Effect: None. Territorial extent & classification: S. Local. - Available at http://www.legislation.gov.uk/ssi/2014/128/contents/made Non-print

The A96 Trunk Road (Church Road, Keith) (Temporary Prohibition on Use of Road) Order 2014 No. 2014/280. - Enabling power: Road Traffic Regulation Act 1984, ss. 2 (1) (2), 4 (1), 16A. - Issued: 30.10.2014. Made: 28.10.2014. Coming into force: 09.11.2014. Effect: None. Territorial extent & classification: S. Local. - Available at: http://www.legislation.gov.uk/ssi/2014/280/contents/made Non-print

The M8/A8 Trunk Road (Commonwealth Games Time Trial Event) (Temporary Prohibition On Use and Temporary Speed Restriction) Order 2014 No. 2014/211. - Enabling power: Road Traffic Regulation Act 1984, ss. 2 (1) (2), 4 (1), 16A. - Issued: 23.07.2014. Made: 22.07.2014. Coming into force: 31.07.2014. Effect: None. Territorial extent & classification: S. Local. - Available at: http://www.legislation.gov.uk/ssi/2014/211/contents/made Non-print

The M8 and M74 Trunk Roads (Games Lanes) Order 2014 No. 2014/197. - Enabling power: Road Traffic Regulation Act 1984, ss. 2 (1) (2), 4 (1), 14 (1) (4) & Glasgow Commonwealth Games Act 2008, s. 38 (1). - Issued: 04.07.2014. Made: 02.07.2014. Coming into force: 21.07.2014. Effect: None. Territorial extent & classification: S. Local. - Available at: http://www.legislation.gov.uk/ssi/2014/197/contents/made Non-print

The M9/A9 and M90/A90 Trunk Roads (Ryder Cup) (Temporary Prohibition of Waiting and Specified Turns and Temporary 50mph and 30mph Speed Restrictions) Order 2014 No. 2014/240. - Enabling power: Road Traffic Regulation Act 1984, ss. 2 (1) (2), 4 (1), 14 (1) (b) (4). - Issued: 05.09.2014. Made: 03.09.2014. Coming into force: 15.09.2014. Effect: None. Territorial extent & classification: S. Local. - Available at http://www.legislation.gov.uk/ssi/2014/240/contents/made Non-print

The M9/A9 Trunk Road (Aberuthven to Findo Gask) (Temporary Prohibition of Specified Turns) (No 2) Order 2014 No. 2014/138. - Enabling power: Road Traffic Regulation Act 1984, ss. 2 (1) (2), 4 (1), 14 (1) (a) (4). - Issued: 22.05.2014. Made: 19.05.2014. Coming into force: 31.05.2014. Effect: None. Territorial extent & classification: S. Local. - Available at http://www.legislation.gov.uk/ssi/2014/138/contents/made Non-print

The M9/A9 Trunk Road (Aberuthven to Findo Gask) (Temporary Prohibition of Specified Turns) Order 2014 No. 2014/82. - Enabling power: Road Traffic Regulation Act 1984, ss. 2 (1) (2), 4 (1), 14 (1) (a) (4). - Issued: 24.03.2014. Made: 21.03.2014. Coming into force: 31.03.2014. Effect: None. Territorial extent & classification: S. Local. - Available at http://www.legislation.gov.uk/ssi/2014/82/contents/made Non-print

The M9/A9 Trunk Road (Gleneagles Railway Station to Millhill Farm) (Prohibition of Specified Turns) Order 2014 No. 2014/174. - Enabling power: Road Traffic Regulation Act 1984, ss. 1 (1) (a), 2 (1) (2). - Issued: 17.06.2014. Made: 16.06.2014. Coming into force: 25.06.2014. Effect: None. Territorial extent & classification: S. Local. - Available at http://www.legislation.gov.uk/ssi/2014/174/contents/made Non-print

The M9/A9 Trunk Road (Munlochy Junction) (Temporary Prohibition of Specified Turns) Order 2014 No. 2014/340. - Enabling power: Road Traffic Regulation Act 1984, ss. 2 (1) (2), 4 (1), 14 (1) (a) (4). - Issued: 01.12.2014. Made: 28.11.2014. Coming into force: 10.12.2014. Effect: None. Territorial extent & classification: S. Local. - Available at http://www.legislation.gov.uk/ssi/2014/340/contents/made Non-print

The M73, M74 and A725 (Commonwealth Games Triathlon) (Temporary Speed Restriction) Order 2014 No. 2014/205. - Enabling power: Road Traffic Regulation Act 1984, ss. 2 (1) (2), 4 (1), 16A. - Issued: 21.07.2014. Made: 18.07.2014. Coming into force: 24.07.2014. Effect: None. Territorial extent & classification: S. Local. - Available at: http://www.legislation.gov.uk/ssi/2014/205/contents/made Non-print

The M74 Trunk Road (Raith) (Temporary Prohibition of Use) Order 2014 No. 2014/259. - Enabling power: Road Traffic Regulation Act 1984, ss. 2 (1) (2), 4 (1), 14 (1) (a) (4). - Issued: 26.09.2014. Made: 25.09.2014. Coming into force: 06.10.2014. Effect: None. Territorial extent & classification: S. Local. - Available at: http://www.legislation.gov.uk/ssi/2014/259/contents/made Non-print

The M77/A77 Trunk Road (Vicarton Street, Girvan) (Temporary Prohibitions of Traffic and Overtaking and Temporary Speed Restrictions) Order 2014 No. 2014/124. - Enabling power: Road Traffic Regulation Act 1984, ss. 2 (1) (2), 4 (1), 14 (1) (a). - Issued: 09.05.2014. Made: 07.05.2014. Coming into force: 16.05.2014. Effect: None. Territorial extent & classification: S. Local. - Available at http://www.legislation.gov.uk/ssi/2014/124/contents/made Non-print

The M90/A90 and A823(M) Trunk Roads (Inverkeithing to Masterton) (Temporary Prohibitions of Traffic and Pedestrians, Overtaking and Speed Restrictions) Order 2014 No. 2014/228. - Enabling power: Road Traffic Regulation Act 1984, ss. 2 (1) (2), 4 (1), 14 (1) (a) (4), 15 (2), 124 (1) (d), sch. 9, para. 27. - Issued: 22.08.2014. Made: 20.08.2014. Coming into force: 02.09.2014. Effect: None. Territorial extent & classification: S. Local. - Available at http://www.legislation.gov.uk/ssi/2014/228/contents/made Non-print

The M90/A90 Trunk Road (Admiralty to Masterton) (Temporary Prohibitions of Traffic and Overtaking, and Speed Restrictions) Order 2014 No. 2014/245. - Enabling power: Road Traffic Regulation Act 1984, ss. 2 (1) (2) (3), 4 (1), 14 (1) (a) (4), 15 (2). - Issued: 18.09.2014. Made: 17.09.2014. Coming into force: 08.10.2014. Effect: None. Territorial extent & classification: S. Local. - Available at: http://www.legislation.gov.uk/ssi/2014/245/contents/made Non-print

The M90/A90 Trunk Road (Gairneybridge to Milnathort) (Temporary 50mph and 30mph Speed Restrictions) Order 2014 No. 2014/195. - Enabling power: Road Traffic Regulation Act 1984, ss. 2 (1) (2), 4 (1), 14 (1) (b) (4). - Issued: 30.06.2014. Made: 27.06.2014. Coming into force: 09.07.2014. Effect: None. Territorial extent & classification: S. Local. - Available at http://www.legislation.gov.uk/ssi/2014/195/contents/made Non-print

The M90/A90 Trunk Roads (Ferrytoll Junction to Admiralty) (Temporary 50mph Speed Restriction) Order 2014 No. 2014/241. - Enabling power: Road Traffic Regulation Act 1984, ss. 2 (1) (2) (3), 4 (1), 14 (1) (a) (4), 15 (2) (8) (b) (i). - Issued: 05.09.2014. Made: 03.09.2014. Coming into force: 06.09.2014. Effect: None. Territorial extent & classification: S. Local. - Available at: http://www.legislation.gov.uk/ssi/2014/241/contents/made Non-print

The M898/A898 and A82 Trunk Roads (Erskine Bridge) (50mph Speed Limit) Order 2014 No. 2014/204. - Enabling power: Road Traffic Regulation Act 1984, ss. 2 (1) (2), 4 (1), 14 (1) (a) (4), 84 (1) (a), 124 (1) (d), sch. 9, para. 27. - Issued: 18.07.2014. Made: 15.07.2014. Coming into force: 23.07.2014. Effect: S.S.I. 2013/248 revoked. Territorial extent & classification: S. Local. - Available at: http://www.legislation.gov.uk/ssi/2014/204/contents/made Non-print

The North East Scotland Trunk Roads (Temporary Prohibitions of Traffic and Overtaking and Temporary Speed Restrictions) (No. 1) Order 2014 No. 2014/19. - Enabling power: Road Traffic Regulation Act 1984, ss. 2 (1) (2), 4 (1), 14 (1) (a) (4). - Issued: 23.01.2014. Made: 20.01.2014. Coming into force: 01.02.2014. Effect: None. Territorial extent & classification: E. Local. - Available at: http://www.legislation.gov.uk/ssi/2014/19/contents/made Non-print

The North East Scotland Trunk Roads (Temporary Prohibitions of Traffic and Overtaking and Temporary Speed Restrictions) (No. 2) Order 2014 No. 2014/48. - Enabling power: Road Traffic Regulation Act 1984, ss. 2 (1) (2), 4 (1), 14 (1) (a) (4). - Issued: 21.02.2014. Made: 17.02.2014. Coming into force: 01.03.2014. Effect: None. Territorial extent & classification: E. Local. - Available at: http://www.legislation.gov.uk/ssi/2014/48/contents/made Non-print

The North East Scotland Trunk Roads (Temporary Prohibitions of Traffic and Overtaking and Temporary Speed Restrictions) (No. 3) Order 2014 No. 2014/75. - Enabling power: Road Traffic Regulation Act 1984, ss. 2 (1) (2), 4 (1), 14 (1) (a) (4). - Issued: 21.03.2014. Made: 18.03.2014. Coming into force: 01.04.2014. Effect: None. Territorial extent & classification: E. Local. - Available at: http://www.legislation.gov.uk/ssi/2014/75/contents/made Non-print

The North East Scotland Trunk Roads (Temporary Prohibitions of Traffic and Overtaking and Temporary Speed Restrictions) (No. 4) Order 2014 No. 2014/106. - Enabling power: Road Traffic Regulation Act 1984, ss. 2 (1) (2), 4 (1), 14 (1) (a) (4). - Issued: 22.04.2014. Made: 16.04.2014. Coming into force: 01.05.2014. Effect: None. Territorial extent & classification: E. Local. - Available at: http://www.legislation.gov.uk/ssi/2014/106/contents/made Non-print

The North East Scotland Trunk Roads (Temporary Prohibitions of Traffic and Overtaking and Temporary Speed Restrictions) (No. 5) Order 2014 No. 2014/134. - Enabling power: Road Traffic Regulation Act 1984, ss. 2 (1) (2), 4 (1), 14 (1) (a) (4). - Issued: 21.05.2014. Made: 19.05.2014. Coming into force: 01.06.2014. Effect: None. Territorial extent & classification: E. Local. - Available at: http://www.legislation.gov.uk/ssi/2014/134/contents/made Non-print

The North East Scotland Trunk Roads (Temporary Prohibitions of Traffic and Overtaking and Temporary Speed Restrictions) (No. 6) Order 2014 No. 2014/181. - Enabling power: Road Traffic Regulation Act 1984, ss. 2 (1) (2), 4 (1), 14 (1) (a) (4). - Issued: 20.06.2014. Made: 17.06.2014. Coming into force: 01.07.2014. Effect: None. Territorial extent & classification: E. Local. - Available at: http://www.legislation.gov.uk/ssi/2014/181/contents/made Non-print

The North East Scotland Trunk Roads (Temporary Prohibitions of Traffic and Overtaking and Temporary Speed Restrictions) (No. 7) Order 2014 No. 2014/209. - Enabling power: Road Traffic Regulation Act 1984, ss. 2 (1) (2), 4 (1), 14 (1) (a) (4). - Issued: 22.07.2014. Made: 18.07.2014. Coming into force: 01.08.2014. Effect: None. Territorial extent & classification: S. Local. - Available at: http://www.legislation.gov.uk/ssi/2014/209/contents/made Non-print

The North East Scotland Trunk Roads (Temporary Prohibitions of Traffic and Overtaking and Temporary Speed Restrictions) (No. 8) Order 2014 No. 2014/234. - Enabling power: Road Traffic Regulation Act 1984, ss. 2 (1) (2), 4 (1), 14 (1) (a) (4). - Issued: 26.08.2014. Made: 18.08.2014. Coming into force: 01.09.2014. Effect: None. Territorial extent & classification: E. Local. - Available at: http://www.legislation.gov.uk/ssi/2014/234/contents/made Non-print

The North East Scotland Trunk Roads (Temporary Prohibitions of Traffic and Overtaking and Temporary Speed Restrictions) (No. 9) Order 2014 No. 2014/256. - Enabling power: Road Traffic Regulation Act 1984, ss. 2 (1) (2), 4 (1), 14 (1) (a) (4). - Issued: 25.09.2014. Made: 22.09.2014. Coming into force: 01.10.2014. Effect: None. Territorial extent & classification: S. Local. - Available at: http://www.legislation.gov.uk/ssi/2014/256/contents/made Non-print

The North East Scotland Trunk Roads (Temporary Prohibitions of Traffic and Overtaking and Temporary Speed Restrictions) (No. 10) Order 2014 No. 2014/275. - Enabling power: Road Traffic Regulation Act 1984, ss. 2 (1) (2), 4 (1), 14 (1) (a) (4). - Issued: 23.10.2014. Made: 20.10.2014. Coming into force: 01.11.2014. Effect: None. Territorial extent & classification: S. Local. - Available at: http://www.legislation.gov.uk/ssi/2014/275/contents/made Non-print

The North East Scotland Trunk Roads (Temporary Prohibitions of Traffic and Overtaking and Temporary Speed Restrictions) (No. 11) Order 2014 No. 2014/331. - Enabling power: Road Traffic Regulation Act 1984, ss. 2 (1) (2), 4 (1), 14 (1) (a) (4). - Issued: 24.11.2014. Made: 18.11.2014. Coming into force: 01.12.2014. Effect: None. Territorial extent & classification: S. Local. - Available at: http://www.legislation.gov.uk/ssi/2014/331/contents/made Non-print

The North East Scotland Trunk Roads (Temporary Prohibitions of Traffic and Overtaking and Temporary Speed Restrictions) (No. 12) Order 2014 No. 2014/381. - Enabling power: Road Traffic Regulation Act 1984, ss. 2 (1) (2), 4 (1), 14 (1) (a) (4). - Issued: 19.12.2014. Made: 17.12.2014. Coming into force: 01.01.2015. Effect: None. Territorial extent & classification: E. Local. - Available at: http://www.legislation.gov.uk/ssi/2014/381/contents/made Non-print

The North West Scotland Trunk Roads (Temporary Prohibitions of Traffic and Overtaking and Temporary Speed Restrictions) (No. 1) Order 2014 No. 2014/20. - Enabling power: Road Traffic Regulation Act 1984, ss. 2 (1) (2), 4 (1), 14 (1) (a) (4). - Issued: 23.01.2014. Made: 20.01.2014. Coming into force: 01.02.2014. Effect: None. Territorial extent & classification: S. Local. - Available at: http://www.legislation.gov.uk/ssi/2014/20/contents/made Non-print

ROAD TRAFFIC: TRAFFIC REGULATION

The North West Scotland Trunk Roads (Temporary Prohibitions of Traffic and Overtaking and Temporary Speed Restrictions) (No. 2) Order 2014 No. 2014/47. - Enabling power: Road Traffic Regulation Act 1984, ss. 2 (1) (2), 4 (1), 14 (1) (a) (4). - Issued: 21.02.2014. Made: 17.02.2014. Coming into force: 01.03.2014. Effect: None. Territorial extent & classification: S. Local. - Available at: http://www.legislation.gov.uk/ssi/2014/47/contents/made Non-print

The North West Scotland Trunk Roads (Temporary Prohibitions of Traffic and Overtaking and Temporary Speed Restrictions) (No. 3) Order 2014 No. 2014/76. - Enabling power: Road Traffic Regulation Act 1984, ss. 2 (1) (2), 4 (1), 14 (1) (a) (4). - Issued: 21.03.2014. Made: 18.03.2014. Coming into force: 01.04.2014. Effect: None. Territorial extent & classification: S. Local. - Available at: http://www.legislation.gov.uk/ssi/2014/76/contents/made Non-print

The North West Scotland Trunk Roads (Temporary Prohibitions of Traffic and Overtaking and Temporary Speed Restrictions) (No. 4) Order 2014 No. 2014/107. - Enabling power: Road Traffic Regulation Act 1984, ss. 2 (1) (2), 4 (1), 14 (1) (a) (4). - Issued: 22.04.2014. Made: 16.04.2014. Coming into force: 01.05.2014. Effect: None. Territorial extent & classification: S. Local. - Available at: http://www.legislation.gov.uk/ssi/2014/107/contents/made Non-print

The North West Scotland Trunk Roads (Temporary Prohibitions of Traffic and Overtaking and Temporary Speed Restrictions) (No. 5) Order 2014 No. 2014/136. - Enabling power: Road Traffic Regulation Act 1984, ss. 2 (1) (2), 4 (1), 14 (1) (a) (4). - Issued: 21.04.2014. Made: 19.05.2014. Coming into force: 01.06.2014. Effect: None. Territorial extent & classification: S. Local. - Available at: http://www.legislation.gov.uk/ssi/2014/136/contents/made Non-print

The North West Scotland Trunk Roads (Temporary Prohibitions of Traffic and Overtaking and Temporary Speed Restrictions) (No. 6) Order 2014 No. 2014/180. - Enabling power: Road Traffic Regulation Act 1984, ss. 2 (1) (2), 4 (1), 14 (1) (a) (4). - Issued: 20.06.2014. Made: 17.06.2014. Coming into force: 01.07.2014. Effect: None. Territorial extent & classification: S. Local. - Available at: http://www.legislation.gov.uk/ssi/2014/180/contents/made Non-print

The North West Scotland Trunk Roads (Temporary Prohibitions of Traffic and Overtaking and Temporary Speed Restrictions) (No. 7) Order 2014 No. 2014/208. - Enabling power: Road Traffic Regulation Act 1984, ss. 2 (1) (2), 4 (1), 14 (1) (a) (4). - Issued: 22.07.2014. Made: 18.07.2014. Coming into force: 01.08.2014. Effect: None. Territorial extent & classification: S. Local. - Available at: http://www.legislation.gov.uk/ssi/2014/208/contents/made Non-print

The North West Scotland Trunk Roads (Temporary Prohibitions of Traffic and Overtaking and Temporary Speed Restrictions) (No. 8) Order 2014 No. 2014/235. - Enabling power: Road Traffic Regulation Act 1984, ss. 2 (1) (2), 4 (1), 14 (1) (a) (4). - Issued: 26.08.2014. Made: 18.08.2014. Coming into force: 01.09.2014. Effect: None. Territorial extent & classification: S. Local. - Available at: http://www.legislation.gov.uk/ssi/2014/235/contents/made Non-print

The North West Scotland Trunk Roads (Temporary Prohibitions of Traffic and Overtaking and Temporary Speed Restrictions) (No. 9) Order 2014 No. 2014/255. - Enabling power: Road Traffic Regulation Act 1984, ss. 2 (1) (2), 4 (1), 14 (1) (a) (4). - Issued: 25.09.2014. Made: 22.09.2014. Coming into force: 01.10.2014. Effect: None. Territorial extent & classification: S. Local. - Available at: http://www.legislation.gov.uk/ssi/2014/255/contents/made Non-print

The North West Scotland Trunk Roads (Temporary Prohibitions of Traffic and Overtaking and Temporary Speed Restrictions) (No. 10) Order 2014 No. 2014/273. - Enabling power: Road Traffic Regulation Act 1984, ss. 2 (1) (2), 4 (1), 14 (1) (a) (4). - Issued: 22.10.2014. Made: 20.10.2014. Coming into force: 01.11.2014. Effect: None. Territorial extent & classification: S. Local. - Available at: http://www.legislation.gov.uk/ssi/2014/273/contents/made Non-print

The North West Scotland Trunk Roads (Temporary Prohibitions of Traffic and Overtaking and Temporary Speed Restrictions) (No. 11) Order 2014 No. 2014/330. - Enabling power: Road Traffic Act 1984, ss. 2 (1) (2), 4 (1), 14 (1) (a) (4). - Issued: 24.11.2014. Made: 18.11.2014. Coming into force: 01.12.2014. Effect: None. Territorial extent & classification: S. Local. - Available at: http://www.legislation.gov.uk/ssi/2014/330/contents/made Non-print

The North West Scotland Trunk Roads (Temporary Prohibitions of Traffic and Overtaking and Temporary Speed Restrictions) (No. 12) Order 2014 No. 2014/382. - Enabling power: Road Traffic Regulation Act 1984, ss. 2 (1) (2), 4 (1), 14 (1) (a) (4). - Issued: 19.12.2014. Made: 17.12.2014. Coming into force: 01.01.2015. Effect: None. Territorial extent & classification: E. Local. - Available at: http://www.legislation.gov.uk/ssi/2014/382/contents/made Non-print

The South East Scotland Trunk Roads (Temporary Prohibitions of Traffic and Overtaking and Temporary Speed Restrictions) (No. 1) Order 2014 No. 2014/17. - Enabling power: Road Traffic Regulation Act 1984, ss. 2 (1) (2), 4 (1), 14 (1) (a) (4). - Issued: 23.01.2014. Made: 20.01.2014. Coming into force: 01.02.2014. Effect: None. Territorial extent & classification: S. Local. - Available at: http://www.legislation.gov.uk/ssi/2014/17/contents/made Non-print

The South East Scotland Trunk Roads (Temporary Prohibitions of Traffic and Overtaking and Temporary Speed Restrictions) (No. 2) Order 2014 No. 2014/46. - Enabling power: Road Traffic Regulation Act 1984, ss. 2 (1) (2), 4 (1), 14 (1) (a) (4). - Issued: 21.02.2014. Made: 17.02.2014. Coming into force: 01.03.2014. Effect: None. Territorial extent & classification: S. Local. - Available at: http://www.legislation.gov.uk/ssi/2014/46/contents/made Non-print

The South East Scotland Trunk Roads (Temporary Prohibitions of Traffic and Overtaking and Temporary Speed Restrictions) (No. 3) Order 2014 No. 2014/77. - Enabling power: Road Traffic Regulation Act 1984, ss. 2 (1) (2), 4 (1), 14 (1) (a) (4). - Issued: 21.03.2014. Made: 18.03.2014. Coming into force: 01.04.2014. Effect: None. Territorial extent & classification: S. Local. - Available at: http://www.legislation.gov.uk/ssi/2014/77/contents/made Non-print

The South East Scotland Trunk Roads (Temporary Prohibitions of Traffic and Overtaking and Temporary Speed Restrictions) (No. 4) Order 2014 No. 2014/104. - Enabling power: Road Traffic Regulation Act 1984, ss. 2 (1) (2), 4 (1), 14 (1) (a) (4). - Issued: 22.04.2014. Made: 16.04.2014. Coming into force: 01.05.2014. Effect: None. Territorial extent & classification: S. Local. - Available at: http://www.legislation.gov.uk/ssi/2014/104/contents/made Non-print

The South East Scotland Trunk Roads (Temporary Prohibitions of Traffic and Overtaking and Temporary Speed Restrictions) (No. 5) Order 2014 No. 2014/133. - Enabling power: Road Traffic Regulation Act 1984, ss. 2 (1) (2), 4 (1), 14 (1) (a) (4). - Issued: 21.05.2014. Made: 19.05.2014. Coming into force: 01.06.2014. Effect: None. Territorial extent & classification: S. Local. - Available at: http://www.legislation.gov.uk/ssi/2014/133/contents/made Non-print

The South East Scotland Trunk Roads (Temporary Prohibitions of Traffic and Overtaking and Temporary Speed Restrictions) (No. 6) Order 2014 No. 2014/179. - Enabling power: Road Traffic Regulation Act 1984, ss. 2 (1) (2), 4 (1), 14 (1) (a) (4). - Issued: 20.06.2014. Made: 17.06.2014. Coming into force: 01.07.2014. Effect: None. Territorial extent & classification: S. Local. - Available at: http://www.legislation.gov.uk/ssi/2014/179/contents/made Non-print

The South East Scotland Trunk Roads (Temporary Prohibitions of Traffic and Overtaking and Temporary Speed Restrictions) (No. 7) Order 2014 No. 2014/206. - Enabling power: Road Traffic Regulation Act 1984, ss. 2 (1) (2), 4 (1), 14 (1) (a) (4). - Issued: 22.07.2014. Made: 18.07.2014. Coming into force: 01.08.2014. Effect: None. Territorial extent & classification: S. Local. - Available at: http://www.legislation.gov.uk/ssi/2014/206/contents/made Non-print

The South East Scotland Trunk Roads (Temporary Prohibitions of Traffic and Overtaking and Temporary Speed Restrictions) (No. 8) Order 2014 No. 2014/237. - Enabling power: Road Traffic Regulation Act 1984, ss. 2 (1) (2), 4 (1), 14 (1) (a) (4). - Issued: 26.08.2014. Made: 18.08.2014. Coming into force: 01.09.2014. Effect: None. Territorial extent & classification: S. Local. - Available at: http://www.legislation.gov.uk/ssi/2014/237/contents/made Non-print

The South East Scotland Trunk Roads (Temporary Prohibitions of Traffic and Overtaking and Temporary Speed Restrictions) (No. 9) Order 2014 No. 2014/253. - Enabling power: Road Traffic Regulation Act 1984, ss. 2 (1) (2), 4 (1), 14 (1) (a) (4). - Issued: 25.09.2014. Made: 22.09.2014. Coming into force: 01.10.2014. Effect: None. Territorial extent & classification: S. Local. - Available at: http://www.legislation.gov.uk/ssi/2014/253/contents/made Non-print

The South East Scotland Trunk Roads (Temporary Prohibitions of Traffic and Overtaking and Temporary Speed Restrictions) (No. 10) Order 2014 No. 2014/270. - Enabling power: Road Traffic Regulation Act 1984, ss. 2 (1) (2), 4 (1), 14 (1) (a) (4). - Issued: 22.10.2014. Made: 20.10.2014. Coming into force: 01.11.2014. Effect: None. Territorial extent & classification: S. Local. - Available at: http://www.legislation.gov.uk/ssi/2014/270/contents/made Non-print

The South East Scotland Trunk Roads (Temporary Prohibitions of Traffic and Overtaking and Temporary Speed Restrictions) (No. 11) Order 2014 No. 2014/329. - Enabling power: Road Traffic Regulation Act 1984, ss. 2 (1) (2), 4 (1), 14 (1) (a) (4). - Issued: 24.11.2014. Made: 18.11.2014. Coming into force: 01.12.2014. Effect: None. Territorial extent & classification: S. Local. - Available at: http://www.legislation.gov.uk/ssi/2014/329/contents/made Non-print

The South East Scotland Trunk Roads (Temporary Prohibitions of Traffic and Overtaking and Temporary Speed Restrictions) (No. 12) Order 2014 No. 2014/383. - Enabling power: Road Traffic Regulation Act 1984, ss. 2 (1) (2), 4 (1), 14 (1) (a) (4). - Issued: 19.12.2014. Made: 17.12.2014. Coming into force: 01.01.2015. Effect: None. Territorial extent & classification: S. Local. - Available at: http://www.legislation.gov.uk/ssi/2014/383/contents/made Non-print

The South West Scotland Trunk Roads (Temporary Prohibitions of Traffic and Overtaking and Temporary Speed Restrictions) (No. 1) Order 2014 No. 2014/18. - Enabling power: Road Traffic Regulation Act 1984, ss. 2 (1) (2), 4 (1), 14 (1) (a) (4). - Issued: 23.01.2014. Made: 20.01.2014. Coming into force: 01.02.2014. Effect: None. Territorial extent & classification: S. Local. - Available at: http://www.legislation.gov.uk/ssi/2014/18/contents/made Non-print

The South West Scotland Trunk Roads (Temporary Prohibitions of Traffic and Overtaking and Temporary Speed Restrictions) (No. 2) Order 2014 No. 2014/45. - Enabling power: Road Traffic Regulation Act 1984, ss. 2 (1) (2), 4 (1), 14 (1) (a) (4). - Issued: 21.02.2014. Made: 17.02.2014. Coming into force: 01.03.2014. Effect: None. Territorial extent & classification: S. Local. - Available at: http://www.legislation.gov.uk/ssi/2014/45/contents/made Non-print

The South West Scotland Trunk Roads (Temporary Prohibitions of Traffic and Overtaking and Temporary Speed Restrictions) (No. 3) Order 2014 No. 2014/78. - Enabling power: Road Traffic Regulation Act 1984, ss. 2 (1) (2), 4 (1), 14 (1) (a) (4). - Issued: 21.03.2014. Made: 18.03.2014. Coming into force: 01.04.2014. Effect: None. Territorial extent & classification: S. Local. - Available at: http://www.legislation.gov.uk/ssi/2014/78/contents/made Non-print

The South West Scotland Trunk Roads (Temporary Prohibitions of Traffic and Overtaking and Temporary Speed Restrictions) (No. 4) Order 2014 No. 2014/105. - Enabling power: Road Traffic Regulation Act 1984, ss. 2 (1) (2), 4 (1), 14 (1) (a) (4). - Issued: 22.04.2014. Made: 16.04.2014. Coming into force: 01.05.2014. Effect: None. Territorial extent & classification: S. Local. - Available at: http://www.legislation.gov.uk/ssi/2014/105/contents/made Non-print

The South West Scotland Trunk Roads (Temporary Prohibitions of Traffic and Overtaking and Temporary Speed Restrictions) (No. 5) Order 2014 No. 2014/135. - Enabling power: Road Traffic Regulation Act 1984, ss. 2 (1) (2), 4 (1), 14 (1) (a) (4). - Issued: 21.05.2014. Made: 19.05.2014. Coming into force: 01.06.2014. Effect: None. Territorial extent & classification: S. Local. - Available at: http://www.legislation.gov.uk/ssi/2014/135/contents/made Non-print

The South West Scotland Trunk Roads (Temporary Prohibitions of Traffic and Overtaking and Temporary Speed Restrictions) (No. 6) Order 2014 No. 2014/178. - Enabling power: Road Traffic Regulation Act 1984, ss. 2 (1) (2), 4 (1), 14 (1) (a) (4). - Issued: 20.06.2014. Made: 17.06.2014. Coming into force: 01.07.2014. Effect: None. Territorial extent & classification: S. Local. - Available at: http://www.legislation.gov.uk/ssi/2014/178/contents/made Non-print

The South West Scotland Trunk Roads (Temporary Prohibitions of Traffic and Overtaking and Temporary Speed Restrictions) (No. 7) Order 2014 No. 2014/207. - Enabling power: Road Traffic Regulation Act 1984, ss. 2 (1) (2), 4 (1), 14 (1) (a) (4). - Issued: 22.07.2014. Made: 18.07.2014. Coming into force: 01.08.2014. Effect: None. Territorial extent & classification: S. Local. - Available at: http://www.legislation.gov.uk/ssi/2014/207/contents/made Non-print

The South West Scotland Trunk Roads (Temporary Prohibitions of Traffic and Overtaking and Temporary Speed Restrictions) (No. 8) Order 2014 No. 2014/236. - Enabling power: Road Traffic Regulation Act 1984, ss. 2 (1) (2), 4 (1), 14 (1) (a) (4). - Issued: 26.08.2014. Made: 18.08.2014. Coming into force: 01.09.2014. Effect: None. Territorial extent & classification: S. Local. - Available at: http://www.legislation.gov.uk/ssi/2014/236/contents/made Non-print

The South West Scotland Trunk Roads (Temporary Prohibitions of Traffic and Overtaking and Temporary Speed Restrictions) (No. 9) Order 2014 No. 2014/254. - Enabling power: Road Traffic Regulation Act 1984, ss. 2 (1) (2), 4 (1), 14 (1) (a) (4). - Issued: 25.09.2014. Made: 22.09.2014. Coming into force: 01.10.2014. Effect: None. Territorial extent & classification: S. Local. - Available at: http://www.legislation.gov.uk/ssi/2014/254/contents/made Non-print

The South West Scotland Trunk Roads (Temporary Prohibitions of Traffic and Overtaking and Temporary Speed Restrictions) (No. 10) Order 2014 No. 2014/271. - Enabling power: Road Traffic Regulation Act 1984, ss. 2 (1) (2), 4 (1), 14 (1) (a) (4). - Issued: 22.10.2014. Made: 20.10.2014. Coming into force: 01.11.2014. Effect: None. Territorial extent & classification: S. Local. - Available at: http://www.legislation.gov.uk/ssi/2014/271/contents/made Non-print

The South West Scotland Trunk Roads (Temporary Prohibitions of Traffic and Overtaking and Temporary Speed Restrictions) (No. 11) Order 2014 No. 2014/332. - Enabling power: Road Traffic Regulation Act 1984, ss. 2 (1) (2), 4 (1), 14 (1) (a) (4). - Issued: 21.11.2014. Made: 18.11.2014. Coming into force: 01.12.2014. Effect: None. Territorial extent & classification: S. Local. - Available at: http://www.legislation.gov.uk/ssi/2014/332/contents/made Non-print

The South West Scotland Trunk Roads (Temporary Prohibitions of Traffic and Overtaking and Temporary Speed Restrictions) (No. 12) Order 2014 No. 2014/384. - Enabling power: Road Traffic Regulation Act 1984, ss. 2 (1) (2), 4 (1), 14 (1) (a) (4). - Issued: 19.12.2014. Made: 17.12.2014. Coming into force: 01.01.2015. Effect: None. Territorial extent & classification: S. Local. - Available at: http://www.legislation.gov.uk/ssi/2014/384/contents/made Non-print

The A82 Trunk Road (Crianlarich Bypass) (Temporary Prohibition of Use) No. 2014/248. - Enabling power: Roads (Scotland) Act 1984, ss. 2 (1) (2), 14(1) (4)- Issued: 23.09.2014. Made: 22.09.2014. Coming into force: 02.10.2014. Effect: None. Territorial extent & classification: S. Local. - Available at: http://www.legislation.gov.uk/ssi/2014/248/contents/made Non-print

Salmon and freshwater fisheries

The Conservation of Salmon (Annual Close Time and Catch and Release) (Scotland) (Amendment) Regulations 2014 No. 2014/357. - Enabling power: Salmon and Freshwater Fisheries (Consolidation) (Scotland) Act 2003, s. 38 (1) (5) (c) (6) (c), sch. 1, paras 7 (b), 14 (1). - Issued: 17.12.2014. Made: 10.12.2014. Laid before the Scottish Parliament: 12.12.2014. Coming into force: 09.01.2015. Effect: None. Territorial extent & classification: S. General. - This S.S.I. has been printed to correct an error in S.S.I. 2014/327 (ISBN 9780111025185) and is being issued free of charge to all known recipients of that instrument. - 4p.: 30 cm. - 978-0-11-102553-6 £4.25

The Conservation of Salmon (Annual Close Time and Catch and Release) (Scotland) Regulations 2014 No. 2014/327. - Enabling power: Salmon and Freshwater Fisheries (Consolidation) (Scotland) Act 2003, s. 38 (1) (5) (c) (6) (c), sch. 1, paras 7 (b), 14 (1). - Issued: 28.11.2014. Made: 20.11.2014. Laid before the Scottish Parliament: 24.11.2014. Coming into force: 09.01.2015. Effect: None. Territorial extent & classification: S. General. - 24p.: 30 cm. - 978-0-11-102518-5 £6.00

Scottish Land Court

The Rules of the Scottish Land Court Order 2014 No. 2014/229. - Enabling power: Scottish Land Court 1993, sch., para. 12. - Issued: 01.09.2014. Made: 19.08.2014. Laid before the Scottish Parliament: 21.08.2014. Coming into force: 22.09.2014. Effect: S.I. 1992/2656 revoked. Territorial extent & classification: S. General. - 44p.: 30 cm. - 978-0-11-102427-0 £10.00

Sea fisheries

The Sea Fishing (Points for Masters of Fishing Boats) (Scotland) Regulations 2014 No. 2014/379. - Enabling power: European Communities Act 1972, s. 2 (2), sch. 2, para. 1A. - Issued: 29.12.2014. Made: 18.12.2014. Laid before the Scottish Parliament: 22.12.2014. Coming into force: 02.02.2015. Effect: None. Territorial extent & classification: S. General. - 8p.: 30 cm. - 978-0-11-102574-1 £6.00

Sea fisheries: Conservation of sea fish

The Sea Fish (Prohibited Methods of Fishing) (Firth of Clyde) Order 2014 No. 2014/2. - Enabling power: Sea Fish (Conservation) Act 1967, ss. 5 (1) (a) (iii), 15 (3). - Issued: 14.01.2014. Made: 07.01.2014. Laid before the Scottish Parliament: 09.01.2014. Coming into force: 14.02.2014. Effect: S.S.I. 2012/4 revoked. Territorial extent & classification: S. General. - 8p., map: 30 cm. - 978-0-11-102232-0 £5.75

Seeds

The Seeds (Fees) (Scotland) Regulations 2014 No. 2014/167. - Enabling power: Plant Varieties and Seeds Act 1964, ss. 16 (1) (1A) (3) (i) (5) (a), 36. - Issued: 16.06.2014. Made: 10.06.2014. Laid before the Scottish Parliament: 12.06.2014. Coming into force: 18.08.2014. Effect: S.S.I. 2011/413 revoked. Territorial extent and classification: S. General. - 12p.: 30 cm. - 978-0-11-102386-0 £6.00

Shellfish

The Aquaculture and Fisheries (Scotland) Act 2013 (Specification of Commercially Damaging Species) Order 2014 No. 2014/176. - Enabling power: Aquaculture and Fisheries (Scotland) Act 2013, s. 11 (1). - Issued: 23.06.2014. Made: 17.06.2014. Laid before the Scottish Parliament: 18.06.2014. Coming into force: 23.08.2014. Effect: None. Territorial extent & classification: S. General. - 2p.: 30 cm. - 978-0-11-102393-8 £4.25

Sheriff Court

Act of Adjournal (Amendment of the Criminal Procedure (Scotland) Act 1995 and Criminal Procedure Rules 1996) (Miscellaneous) 2014 No. 2014/242. - Enabling power: Criminal Procedure (Scotland) Act 1995, s. 305 & Extradition Act 2003, s. 210. - Issued: 15.09.2014. Made: 09.09.2014. Laid before the Scottish Parliament: 11.09.2014. Coming into force: 10.10.2014. Effect: 1995 c.46 amended. Territorial extent & classification: S. General. - 8p.: 30 cm. - 978-0-11-102439-3 £4.25

Act of Adjournal (Criminal Procedure Rules Amendment No. 2) (Miscellaneous) 2014 No. 2014/349. - Enabling power: Criminal Procedure (Scotland) Act 1995, s. 305. - Issued: 09.12.2014. Made: 03.12.2014. Laid before the Scottish Parliament: 03.12.2014. Coming into force: 04.12.2014. Effect: S.I. 1996/513 amended. Territorial extent & classification: S. General. - 8p.: 30 cm. - 978-0-11-102542-0 £6.00

Act of Adjournal (Criminal Procedure Rules Amendment) (Regulatory Reform (Scotland) Act 2014) 2014 No. 2014/162. - Enabling power: Criminal Procedure (Scotland) Act 1995, s. 305. - Issued: 11.06.2014. Made: 05.06.2014. Laid before the Scottish Parliament: 06.06.2014. Coming into force: 30.06.2014. Effect: S.I. 1996/513 amended. Territorial extent & classification: S. General. - 8p.: 30 cm. - 978-0-11-102379-2 £6.00

Act of Sederunt (Commissary Business) (Amendment) 2014 No. 2014/265. - Enabling power: Sheriff Courts (Scotland) Act 1876, s. 54. - Issued: 15.10.2014. Made: 08.10.2014. Laid before the Scottish Parliament: 10.10.2014. Coming into force: 01.12.2014. Effect: S.S.I. 2013/291 amended. Territorial extent & classification: S. General. - 2p.: 30 cm. - 978-0-11-102458-4 £4.25

Act of Sederunt (Fees of Solicitors in the Sheriff Court) (Amendment) 2014 No. 2014/14. - Enabling power: Sheriff Courts (Scotland) Act 1907, s. 40 (1). - Issued: 24.01.2014. Made: 20.01.2014. Laid before the Scottish Parliament: 21.01.2014. Coming into force: 01.03.2014. Effect: S.I. 1993/3080 amended. Territorial extent & classification: S. General. - 34p.: 30 cm. - 978-0-11-102242-9 £9.75

Act of Sederunt (Fitness for Judicial Office Tribunal Rules) 2014 No. 2014/99. - Enabling power: Sheriff Courts (Scotland) Act 1971, s. 12 C (5) & Judiciary and Courts (Scotland) Act 2008 s. 37 (5). - Issued: 08.04.2014. Made: 02.04.2014. Laid before the Scottish Parliament: 04.04.2014. Coming into force: 20.05.2014. Effect: None. Territorial extent & classification: S. General. - Revoked by SSI 2014/102 (ISBN 9780111023228) which is being issued free of charge to all known recipients of SSI 2014/99. - 8p.: 30 cm. - 978-0-11-102318-1 £6.00

Act of Sederunt (Messengers-at-Arms and Sheriff Officers Rules) (Amendment) 2014 No. 2014/29. - Enabling power: Debtors (Scotland) Act 1987, s. 75. - Issued: 10.02.2014. Made: 04.02.2014. Laid before the Scottish Parliament: 06.02.2014. Coming into force: 17.03.2014. Effect: S.I. 1991/1397 amended. Territorial extent & classification: S. General. - 4p.: 30 cm. - 978-0-11-102252-8 £4.00

Act of Sederunt (Rules of the Court of Session and Sheriff Court Company Insolvency Rules Amendment) (Miscellaneous) 2014 No. 2014/119. - Enabling power: Sheriff Courts (Scotland) Act 1971, s. 32 & Court of Session Act 1988, s. 5. - Issued: 08.05.2014. Made: 01.05.2014. Laid before the Scottish Parliament: 02.05.2014. Coming into force: 30.05.2014. Effect: S.I. 1986/2297; 1994/1443 amended. Territorial extent & classification: S. General. - 4p.: 30 cm. - 978-0-11-102336-5 £4.25

Act of Sederunt (Rules of the Court of Session and Sheriff Court Rules Amendment) (Miscellaneous) 2014 No. 2014/201. - Enabling power: Sheriff Courts (Scotland) Act 1971, s. 32 & Court of Session Act 1988, s. 5. - Issued: 10.07.2014. Made: 04.07.2014. Laid before the Scottish Parliament: 07.07.2014. Coming into force: 01.08.2014. Effect: 1907 c.51; S.I. 1994/1443; 1997/291 amended. Territorial extent & classification: S. General. - 8p.: 30 cm. - 978-0-11-102412-6 £6.00

Act of Sederunt (Rules of the Court of Session and Sheriff Court Rules Amendment No. 2) (Marriage and Civil Partnership (Scotland) Act 2014) 2014 No. 2014/302. - Enabling power: Sheriff Courts (Scotland) Act 1971, s. 32 & & Court of Session Act 1988, s. 5 & Adoption and Children (Scotland) Act 2007, s. 114. - Issued: 18.11.2014. Made: 12.11.2014. Laid before the Scottish Parliament: 14.11.2014. Coming into force: 16.12.2014. Effect: 1907 c.51; S.I. 1994/1443; 1999/929; S.S.I. 2009/284 amended. Territorial extent & classification: S. General. - 12p.: 30 cm. - 978-0-11-102495-9 £6.00

Act of Sederunt (Rules of the Court of Session and Sheriff Court Rules Amendment No.2) (Miscellaneous) 2014 No. 2014/291. - Enabling power: Sheriff Courts (Scotland) Act 1971, s. 32 & Debtors (Scotland) Act 1987, s. 15K (3) (a) & Court of Session Act 1988, s. 5. - Issued: 11.11.2014. Made: 05.11.2014. Laid before the Scottish Parliament: 07.11.2014. Coming into force: 08.12.2014. Effect: 1907 c.51; S.I. 1994/1443; S.S.I. 2002/132, 133 amended. Territorial extent & classification: S. General. - 16p.: 30 cm. - 978-0-11-102483-6 £6.00

Act of Sederunt (Rules of the Court of Session and Sheriff Court Rules Amendment No. 3) (Mutual Recognition of Protection Measures) 2014 No. 2014/371. - Enabling power: Sheriff Courts (Scotland) Act 1971, s. 32 & Court of Session Act 1988, s. 5 & Protection from Abuse (Scotland) Act 2001, ss. 2 (1), 3 (1). - Issued: 23.12.2014. Made: 17.12.2014. Laid before the Scottish Parliament: 19.12.2014. Coming into force: 11.01.2015. Effect: 1907 c.51; S.I. 1994/1443; 1999/929 amended. Territorial extent & classification: S. General. - 36p.: 30 cm. - 978-0-11-102566-6 £10.00

Act of Sederunt (Rules of the Court of Session, Ordinary Cause Rules and Summary Cause Rules Amendment) (Miscellaneous) 2014 No. 2014/152. - Enabling power: Sheriff Courts (Scotland) Act 1971, s. 32 & Court of Session Act 1988, s. 5. - Issued: 04.06.2014. Made: 28.05.2014. Laid before the Scottish Parliament: 30.05.2014. Coming into force: 07.07.2014. Effect: 1907 c.51; S.I. 1994/1443; S.S.I. 2002/132 amended. Territorial extent & classification: S. General. - 16p.: 30 cm. - 978-0-11-102370-9 £6.00

The Judicial Pensions and Retirement Act 1993 (Part-time Sheriff, Stipendiary Magistrate and Justice of the Peace) Order 2014 No. 2014/155. - Enabling power: European Communities Act 1972, s. 2 (2) & Judicial Pensions and Retirement Act 1993, ss. 26 (9), 29 (3). - Issued: 05.06.2014. Made: 29.05.2014. Laid before the Scottish Parliament: 30.05.2014. Coming into force: 30.05.2014. Effect: 1971 c.58; 1993 c.8; 2007 asp 6 amended. Territorial extent & classification: S. General. - Supersedes draft SI (ISBN 9780111023242) issued 24/04/14. - 4p.: 30 cm. - 978-0-11-102373-0 £4.25

Social care

The Carers (Waiving of Charges for Support) (Scotland) Regulations 2014 No. 2014/65. - Enabling power: Social Work (Scotland) Act 1968, s. 87 (5) & Social Care (Self-directed Support) (Scotland) Act 2013, ss. 15 (1) (2) (c) (d), 22 (1) (a). - Issued: 06.03.2014. Made: 27.02.2014. Laid before the Scottish Parliament: 03.03.2014. Coming into force: 01.04.2014. Effect: S.I. 2014/25 amended. Territorial extent & classification: S. General. - 4p.: 30 cm. - 978-0-11-102291-7 £4.00

The Community Care (Joint Working etc.) (Scotland) Amendment Regulations 2014 No. 2014/66. - Enabling power: Community Care and Health (Scotland) Act 2002, ss. 13 (1), 15 (2). - Issued: 06.03.2014. Made: 27.02.2014. Laid before the Scottish Parliament: 03.03.2014. Coming into force: 01.04.2014. Effect: S.S.I. 2002/533 amended. Territorial extent & classification: S. General. - 4p.: 30 cm. - 978-0-11-102292-4 £4.00

SOCIAL CARE

The Community Care (Personal Care and Nursing Care) (Scotland) Amendment Regulations 2014 No. 2014/91. - Enabling power: Community Care and Health (Scotland) Act 2002, ss. 1 (2) (a), 2, 23 (4). - Issued: 02.04.2014. Made: 27.03.2014. Coming into force: 01.04.2014. Effect: S.S.I. 2002/303 amended & S.S.I. 2013/108 revoked. Territorial extent & classification: S. General. - Supersedes draft SI (ISBN 9780111022641) issued 19/02/14; Revoked by SSI 2015/154 (ISBN 9780111027417). - 4p.: 30 cm. - 978-0-11-102312-9 £4.00

The Public Bodies (Joint Working) (Content of Performance Reports) (Scotland) Regulations 2014 No. 2014/326. - Enabling power: Public Bodies (Joint Working) Scotland Act 2014, ss. 42 (3), 69 (1). - Issued: 26.11.2014. Made: 19.11.2014. Laid before the Scottish Parliament: 21.11.2014. Coming into force: 20.12.2014. Effect: None. Territorial extent & classification: S. General. - 8p.: 30 cm. - 978-0-11-102517-8 £4.25

The Public Bodies (Joint Working) (Health Professionals and Social Care Professionals) (Scotland) Regulations 2014 No. 2014/307. - Enabling power: Public Bodies (Joint Working) (Scotland) Act 2014, s. 68 (1). - Issued: 19.11.2014. Made: 11.11.2014. Laid before the Scottish Parliament: 13.11.2014. Coming into force: 12.12.2014. Effect: None. Territorial extent & classification: S. General. - 4p.: 30 cm. - 978-0-11-102500-0 £4.25

The Public Bodies (Joint Working) (Integration Joint Boards) (Scotland) Order 2014 No. 2014/285. - Enabling power: Public Bodies (Joint Working) (Scotland) Act 2014, ss. 12, 69 (1). - Issued: 04.11.2014. Made: 28.10.2014. Laid before the Scottish Parliament: 30.10.2014. Coming into force: 28.11.2014. Effect: None. Territorial extent & classification: S. General. - 12p.: 30 cm. - 978-0-11-102475-1 £6.00

The Public Bodies (Joint Working) (Integration Joint Monitoring Committees) (Scotland) Order 2014 No. 2014/281. - Enabling power: Public Bodies (Joint Working) (Scotland) Act 2014, ss. 17, 69 (1). - Issued: 04.11.2014. Made: 28.10.2014. Laid before the Scottish Parliament: 30.10.2014. Coming into force: 28.11.2014. Effect: None. Territorial extent & classification: S. General. - 12p.: 30 cm. - 978-0-11-102471-3 £6.00

The Public Bodies (Joint Working) (Integration Scheme) (Scotland) Regulations 2014 No. 2014/341. - Enabling power: Public Bodies (Joint Working) Scotland Act 2014, ss. 1 (3) (f), 1 (15), 20, 69 (1). - Issued: 04.12.2014. Made: 27.11.2014. Coming into force: 28.11.2014. Effect: None. Territorial extent & classification: S. General. - Supersedes draft S.S.I. (ISBN 9780111024539) issued 09.10.2014. - 12p.: 30 cm. - 978-0-11-102530-7 £6.00

The Public Bodies (Joint Working) (Local Authority Officers) (Scotland) Regulations 2014 No. 2014/282. - Enabling power: Public Bodies (Joint Working) (Scotland) Act 2014, s. 23 (1). - Issued: 04.11.2014. Made: 28.10.2014. Laid before the Scottish Parliament: 30.10.2014. Coming into force: 28.11.2014. Effect: None. Territorial extent & classification: S. General. - 4p.: 30 cm. - 978-0-11-102472-0 £4.25

The Public Bodies (Joint Working) (Membership of Strategic Planning Group) (Scotland) Regulations 2014 No. 2014/308. - Enabling power: Public Bodies (Joint Working) (Scotland) Act 2014, s. 32 (2). - Issued: 18.11.2014. Made: 11.11.2014. Laid before the Scottish Parliament: 13.11.2014. Coming into force: 12.12.2014. Effect: None. Territorial extent & classification: S. General. - 4p.: 30 cm. - 978-0-11-102501-7 £4.25

The Public Bodies (Joint Working) (National Health and Wellbeing Outcomes) (Scotland) Regulations 2014 No. 2014/343. - Enabling power: Public Bodies (Joint Working) Scotland Act 2014, s. 5 (1). - Issued: 04.12.2014. Made: 27.11.2014. Coming into force: 28.11.2014. Effect: None. Territorial extent & classification: S. General. - Supersedes draft S.S.I. (ISBN 9780111024522) issued 09.10.2014. - 4p.: 30 cm. - 978-0-11-102532-1 £4.25

The Public Bodies (Joint Working) (Prescribed Consultees) (Scotland) Regulations 2014 No. 2014/283. - Enabling power: Public Bodies (Joint Working) (Scotland) Act 2014, ss. 6 (2) (a), 33 (6), 41 (4), 46 (4) (a), 69 (1) (b). - Issued: 04.11.2014. Made: 28.10.2014. Laid before the Scottish Parliament: 30.10.2014. Coming into force: 28.11.2014. Effect: None. Territorial extent & classification: S. General. - 4p.: 30 cm. - 978-0-11-102473-7 £4.25

The Public Bodies (Joint Working) (Prescribed Days) (Scotland) Regulations 2014 No. 2014/284. - Enabling power: Public Bodies (Joint Working) (Scotland) Act 2014, ss. 7 (1) (5), 9 (3), 15 (2), 51 (2) (c)- Issued: 04.11.2014. Made: 28.10.2014. Laid before the Scottish Parliament: 30.10.2014. Coming into force: 28.11.2014. Effect: None. Territorial extent & classification: S. General. - 2p.: 30 cm. - 978-0-11-102474-4 £4.25

The Public Bodies (Joint Working) (Prescribed Health Board Functions) (Scotland) Regulations 2014 No. 2014/344. - Enabling power: Public Bodies (Joint Working) Scotland Act 2014, ss. 1 (6), 1 (8), 69 (1). - Issued: 04.12.2014. Made: 27.11.2014. Coming into force: 28.11.2014. Effect: None. Territorial extent & classification: S. General. - Supersedes draft S.S.I. (ISBN 9780111024652) issued 28.10.2014. - 16p.: 30 cm. - 978-0-11-102533-8 £6.00

The Public Bodies (Joint Working) (Prescribed Local Authority Functions etc.) (Scotland) Regulations 2014 No. 2014/345. - Enabling power: Public Bodies (Joint Working) (Scotland) Act 2014, ss. 1 (7) (12), 69 (1) (b). - Issued: 04.12.2014. Made: 27.11.2014. Laid before the Scottish Parliament: -. Coming into force: 28.11.2014. Effect: 2014 asp 9 amended. Territorial extent & classification: S. General. - Supersedes draft S.S.I. (ISBN 9780111024645) issued 28.10.2014. - 12p.: 30 cm. - 978-0-11-102534-5 £6.00

The Public Bodies (Joint Working) (Scotland) Act 2014 (Commencement No. 2) Order 2014 No. 2014/231 (C.21). - Enabling power: Public Bodies (Joint Working) (Scotland) Act 2014, s. 72 (2). Bringing into operation various provisions of the 2014 Act on 22.09.2014 & 01.04.2015, in accord. with art. 2. - Issued: 28.08.2014. Made: 21.08.2014. Laid before the Scottish Parliament: 22.08.2014. Coming into force: 22.09.2014. Effect: None. Territorial extent & classification: S. General. - 2p.: 30 cm. - 978-0-11-102430-0 £4.25

The Public Bodies (Joint Working) (Scotland) Act 2014 (Modifications) Order 2014 No. 2014/342. - Enabling power: Public Bodies (Joint Working) Scotland Act 2014, s. 70 (1) (a) (2). - Issued: 04.12.2014. Made: 27.11.2014. Coming into force: 28.11.2014. Effect: 2014 asp 9 amended. Territorial extent & classification: S. General. - Supersedes draft S.S.I. (ISBN 9780111024669) issued 28.10.2014. - 4p.: 30 cm. - 978-0-11-102531-4 £4.25

The Registration of Social Workers and Social Service Workers in Care Services (Scotland) Amendment Regulations 2014 No. 2014/192. - Enabling power: Public Services Reform (Scotland) Act 2010, ss. 78 (2), 104 (1). - Issued: 03.07.2014. Made: 26.06.2014. Coming into force: 30.06.2014. Effect: S.S.I. 2013/227 amended. Territorial extent & classification: S. General. - Supersedes draft SSI (ISBN 9780111023471) issued 23.05.2014. - 4p.: 30 cm. - 978-0-11-102407-2 £4.25

The Regulation of Care (Social Service Workers) (Scotland) Amendment Order 2014 No. 2014/129. - Enabling power: Regulation of Care (Scotland) Act 2001, s. 44 (1) (b). - Issued: 22.05.2014. Made: 15.05.2014. Laid before the Scottish Parliament: 19.05.2014. Coming into force: 30.06.2014. Effect: S.S.I. 2005/318 amended. Territorial extent & classification: S. General. - 4p.: 30 cm. - 978-0-11-102341-9 £4.25

The Self-directed Support (Direct Payments) (Scotland) Regulations 2014 No. 2014/25. - Enabling power: Social Care (Self-directed Support) (Scotland) Act 2013, ss. 15, 22 (1). - Issued: 03.02.2014. Made: 27.01.2014. Laid before the Scottish Parliament: 29.01.2014. Coming into force: 01.04.2014. Effect: None. Territorial extent & classification: S. General. - 8p.: 30 cm. - 978-0-11-102249-8 £5.75

The Social Care (Self-directed Support) (Scotland) Act 2013 (Commencement, Transitional and Saving Provisions) Order 2014 No. 2014/32 (C.2). - Enabling power: Social Care (Self-directed Support) (Scotland) Act 2013, ss. 28 (2), (3). Bringing into operation various provisions of the 2013 Act on 17.02.2014, 01.04.2014. - Issued: 11.02.2014. Made: 04.02.2014. Laid before the Scottish Parliament: 06.02.2014. Effect: - Territorial extent & classification: S. General. - 4p.: 30 cm. - 978-0-11-102255-9 £4.00

The Social Care (Self-directed Support) (Scotland) Act 2013 (Consequential and Saving Provisions) Order 2014 No. 2014/90. - Enabling power: Social Care (Self-directed Support) (Scotland) Act 2013, ss. 26 (1) (b), 27 (1). - Issued: 02.04.2014. Made: 27.03.2014. Coming into force: 01.04.2014. Effect: 1968 c.49, 2007 asp 14; S.I. 1992/2997; 1996/2447; SSI 2002/494, 533; 2012/303, 319; 2013/200 amended & 1996 c.30; 2001 asp 8; 2002 asp 5; 2007 asp 10 partially repealed & SSI 2003/243; 2005/114; 2007/458 revoked. Territorial extent & classification: S. General. - Supersedes draft S.S.I. (ISBN 9780111022665) issued 25.02.2014. - 8p.: 30 cm. - 978-0-11-102311-2 £5.75

Social security

The Discretionary Housing Payments (Limit on Total Expenditure) Revocation (Scotland) Order 2014 No. 2014/298. - Enabling power: Child Support, Pensions and Social Security Act 2000, s. 70 (3) (a). - Issued: 13.11.2014. Made: 06.11.2014. Laid before the Scottish Parliament: 10.11.2014. Coming into force: 09.12.2014. Effect: S.I. 2001/2340 partially revoked in relation to Scotland. Territorial extent & classification: S. General. - 2p.: 30 cm. - 978-0-11-102491-1 £4.25

Sports grounds and sporting events

The Glasgow Commonwealth Games Act 2008 (Duration of Urgent Traffic Regulation Measures) Order 2014 No. 2014/92. - Enabling power: Glasgow Commonwealth Games Act 2008, s. 47. - Issued: 02.04.2014. Made: 27.03.2014. Laid before the Scottish Parliament: 31.03.2014. Coming into force: 02.06.2014. Effect: 1984 c.27 modified. Territorial extent & classification: S. General. - 4p.: 30 cm. - 978-0-11-102313-6 £4.00

The Glasgow Commonwealth Games Act 2008 (Repeal Day) Order 2014 No. 2014/356. - Enabling power: Glasgow Commonwealth Games Act 2008, s. 50 (2)- Issued: 17.12.2014. Made: 10.12.2014. Laid before the Scottish Parliament: 12.12.2014. Coming into force: 01.01.2015. Effect: None. Territorial extent & classification: S. General. - 2p.: 30 cm. - 978-0-11-102552-9 £4.25

The M8 and M74 Trunk Roads (Games Lanes) Order 2014 No. 2014/197. - Enabling power: Road Traffic Regulation Act 1984, ss. 2 (1) (2), 4 (1), 14 (1) (4) & Glasgow Commonwealth Games Act 2008, s. 38 (1). - Issued: 04.07.2014. Made: 02.07.2014. Coming into force: 21.07.2014. Effect: None. Territorial extent & classification: S. Local. - Available at: http://www.legislation.gov.uk/ssi/2014/197/contents/made Non-print

The Sports Grounds and Sporting Events (Designation) (Scotland) (Amendment) Order 2014 No. 2014/374. - Enabling power: Criminal Law (Consolidation) (Scotland) Act 1995, s. 18. - Issued: 24.12.2014. Made: 17.12.2014. Laid before the Scottish Parliament: 19.12.2014. Coming into force: 02.02.2015. Effect: S.S.I. 2014/5 amended. Territorial extent & classification: S. General. - 4p.: 30 cm. - 978-0-11-102569-7 £4.25

The Sports Grounds and Sporting Events (Designation) (Scotland) Order 2014 No. 2014/5. - Enabling power: Criminal Law (Consolidation) (Scotland) Act 1995, s. 18. - Issued: 15.01.2014. Made: 08.01.2014. Laid before the Scottish Parliament: 10.01.2014. Coming into force: 08.02.2014. Effect: S.S.I. 2010/199; 2012/164; 2013/4, 229 revoked. Territorial extent & classification: S. General. - 8p.: 30 cm. - 978-0-11-102235-1 £5.75

Taxes

The Revenue Scotland and Tax Powers Act 2014 (Commencement No. 1) Order 2014 No. 2014/278 (C.26). - Enabling power: Revenue Scotland and Tax Powers Act 2014, s. 260 (2). Bringing into operation various provisions of the 2014 Act on 07.11.2014. - Issued: 30.10.2014. Made: 24.10.2014. Laid before the Scottish Parliament: 27.10.2014. Effect: None. Territorial extent & classification: S. General. - 4p.: 30 cm. - 978-0-11-102469-0 £4.25

The Revenue Scotland and Tax Powers Act 2014 (Commencement No. 2) Order 2014 No. 2014/370 (C.35). - Enabling power: Revenue Scotland and Tax Powers Act 2014, s. 260 (2). . Bringing into operation various provisions of the 2014 Act on 01.01.2015. - Issued: 23.12.2014. Made: 16.12.2014. Laid before the Scottish Parliament: 18.12.2014. Effect: None. Territorial extent & classification: S. General. - 8p.: 30 cm. - 978-0-11-102565-9 £4.25

Tenements

The Notice of Potential Liability for Costs (Discharge Notice) (Scotland) Order 2014 No. 2014/313. - Enabling power: Title Conditions (Scotland) Act 2003, s. 10A (3B) (a) & Tenements (Scotland) Act 2004, s. 13 (3B) (a). - Issued: 20.11.2014. Made: 13.11.2014. Laid before the Scottish Parliament: 17.11.2014. Coming into force: 16.12.2014. Effect: None. Territorial extent and classification: S. General. - 8p.: 30 cm. - 978-0-11-102504-8 £4.25

Title conditions

The Notice of Potential Liability for Costs (Discharge Notice) (Scotland) Order 2014 No. 2014/313. - Enabling power: Title Conditions (Scotland) Act 2003, s. 10A (3B) (a) & Tenements (Scotland) Act 2004, s. 13 (3B) (a). - Issued: 20.11.2014. Made: 13.11.2014. Laid before the Scottish Parliament: 17.11.2014. Coming into force: 16.12.2014. Effect: None. Territorial extent and classification: S. General. - 8p.: 30 cm. - 978-0-11-102504-8 £4.25

The Title Conditions (Scotland) Act 2003 (Rural Housing Bodies) Amendment (No. 2) Order 2014 No. 2014/220. - Enabling power: Title Conditions (Scotland) Act 2003, s. 43 (5). - Issued: 19.08.2014. Made: 12.08.2014. Laid before the Scottish Parliament: 14.08.2014. Coming into force: 29.10.2014. Effect: S.S.I. 2004/477 amended. Territorial extent & classification: S. General. - 2p.: 30 cm. - 978-0-11-102422-5 £4.25

The Title Conditions (Scotland) Act 2003 (Rural Housing Bodies) Amendment Order 2014 No. 2014/130. - Enabling power: Title Conditions (Scotland) Act 2003, s. 43 (5). - Issued: 22.05.2014. Made: 15.05.2014. Laid before the Scottish Parliament: 19.05.2014. Coming into force: 17.06.2014. Effect: S.S.I. 2004/477 amended. Territorial extent & classification: S. General. - 2p.: 30 cm. - 978-0-11-102342-6 £4.25

Town and country planning

The Town and Country Planning (Control of Advertisements) (Scotland) Amendment (No. 2) Regulations 2014 No. 2014/249. - Enabling power: Town and Country Planning (Scotland) Act 1997, s. 182. - Issued: 29.09.2014. Made: 23.09.2014. Laid before the Scottish Parliament: 25.09.2014. Coming into force: 10.11.2014. Effect: S.I. 1984/467 amended. Territorial extent & classification: S. General. - 4p.: 30 cm. - 978-0-11-102442-3 £4.25

The Town and Country Planning (Control of Advertisements) (Scotland) Amendment Regulations 2014 No. 2014/139. - Enabling power: Town and Country Planning (Scotland) Act 1997, ss. 182, 186, 275. - Issued: 28.05.2014. Made: 21.05.2014. Laid before the Scottish Parliament: 27.05.2014. Coming into force: 30.06.2014. Effect: S.I. 1984/467 amended. Territorial extent & classification: S. General. - 4p.: 30 cm. - 978-0-11-102356-3 £4.25

The Town and Country Planning (Fees for Applications and Deemed Applications) (Scotland) Amendment (No. 2) Regulations 2014 No. 2014/301. - Enabling power: Town and Country Planning (Scotland) Act 1997, s. 252. - Issued: 18.11.2014. Made: 11.11.2014. Laid before the Scottish Parliament: 13.11.2014. Coming into force: 15.12.2014. Effect: S.S.I. 2004/219 amended. Territorial extent & classification: S. General. - 4p.: 30 cm. - 978-0-11-102494-2 £4.25

The Town and Country Planning (Fees for Applications and Deemed Applications) (Scotland) Amendment Regulations 2014 No. 2014/214. - Enabling power: Town and Country Planning (Scotland) Act 1997, s. 252. - Issued: 06.08.2014. Made: 30.07.2014. Laid before the Scottish Parliament: 01.08.2014. Coming into force: 01.11.2014. Effect: S.S.I. 2004/219 amended. Territorial extent & classification: S. General. - 8p.: 30 cm. - 978-0-11-102418-8 £6.00

The Town and Country Planning (General Permitted Development) (Scotland) Amendment (Amendment) Order 2014 No. 2014/184. - Enabling power: Town and Country Planning (Scotland) Act 1997, ss. 30, 31, 275. - Issued: 27.06.2014. Made: 23.06.2014. Laid before the Scottish Parliament: 25.06.2014. Coming into force: 29.06.2014. Effect: S.S.I. 2014/142 amended. Territorial extent & classification: S. General. - This Statutory Instrument has been made to correct errors in S.S.I. 2014/142 (ISBN 9780111023600) and is being issued free of charge to all known recipients of that Statutory Instrument. - 4p.: 30 cm. - 978-0-11-102396-9 £4.25

The Town and Country Planning (General Permitted Development) (Scotland) Amendment (No. 2) Order 2014 No. 2014/300. - Enabling power: Town and Country Planning (Scotland) Act 1997, ss. 30, 31, 275. - Issued: 18.11.2014. Made: 11.11.2014. Laid before the Scottish Parliament: 13.11.2014. Coming into force: 15.12.2014. Effect: S.I. 1992/223 amended. Territorial extent & classification: S. General. - 4p.: 30 cm. - 978-0-11-102493-5 £4.25

The Town and Country Planning (General Permitted Development) (Scotland) Amendment Order 2014 No. 2014/142. - Enabling power: Town and Country Planning (Scotland) Act 1997, ss. 30, 31, 275. - Issued: 03.06.2014. Made: 28.05.2014. Laid before the Scottish Parliament: 30.05.2014. Coming into force: 30.06.2014. Effect: S.I. 1992/223 amended. Territorial extent & classification: S. General. - Errors in this SSI have been corrected by SSI 2014/184 (ISBN 9780111023969) which is being sent free of charge to all known recipients of SSI 2014/142. - 16p.: 30 cm. - 978-0-11-102360-0 £6.00

The Town and Country Planning (Hazardous Substances) (Scotland) Amendment Regulations 2014 No. 2014/51. - Enabling power: Planning (Hazardous Substances) (Scotland) Act 1997, s. 3. - Issued: 05.03.2014. Made: 25.02.2014. Laid before the Scottish Parliament: 27.02.2014. Coming into force: 29.03.2014. Effect: S.I. 1993/323 amended. Territorial extent & classification: S. General. - 4p.: 30 cm. - 978-0-11-102277-1 £4.00

The Town and Country Planning (Tree Preservation Order and Trees in Conservation Areas) (Scotland) Amendment Regulations 2014 No. 2014/53. - Enabling power: Town and Country Planning (Scotland) Act 1997, s. 173. - Issued: 05.03.2014. Made: 26.02.2014. Laid before the Scottish Parliament: 28.02.2014. Coming into force: 01.04.2014. Effect: S.S.I. 2010/434 amended. Territorial extent & classification: S. General. - 4p.: 30 cm. - 978-0-11-102279-5 £4.00

Tribunals and inquiries

The Scottish Tax Tribunals (Eligibility for Appointment) Regulations 2014 No. 2014/355. - Enabling power: Revenue Scotland and Tax Powers Act 2014, sch. 2 paras 2 (3), 9 (1) (a) (b). - Issued: 16.12.2014. Made: 09.12.2014. Laid before the Scottish Parliament: 11.12.2014. Coming into force: 01.02.2015. Effect: None. Territorial extent & classification: S. General. - 4p.: 30 cm. - 978-0-11-102551-2 £4.25

The Tribunals (Scotland) Act 2014 (Commencement No. 1) Order 2014 No. 2014/183 (C.15). - Enabling power: Tribunals (Scotland) Act 2014, s. 83 (2). Bringing into operation various provisions of the 2014 Act on 14.07.2014. - Issued: 27.06.2014. Made: 19.06.2014. Laid before the Scottish Parliament: 23.06.2014. Coming into force: 14.07.2014. Effect: None. Territorial extent & classification: S. General. - 2p.: 30 cm. - 978-0-11-102395-2 £4.25

Water

The Designation of Nitrate Vulnerable Zones (Scotland) Regulations 2014 No. 2014/373. - Enabling power: European Communities Act 1972, s. 2 (2). - Issued: 23.12.2014. Made: 17.12.2014. Laid before the Scottish Parliament: 19.12.2014. Coming into force: 02.02.2015. Effect: S.I. 1996/1564; S.S.I. 2000/96; 2002/276, 546; 2008/100, 159, 298; 2011/209; amended. Territorial extent & classification: S. General. - EC note: Further implement in Scotland the requirements of Council Directive 91/676/EEC concerning the protection of waters against pollution caused by nitrates from agricultural sources. - 4p.: 30 cm. - 978-0-11-102568-0 £4.25

Water supply

The Public Water Supplies (Scotland) Regulations 2014 No. 2014/364. - Enabling power: Water (Scotland) Act 1980, ss. 76A (3) (b), 76B, 76F (5) (6), 76J, 101 (1) (1A), 109 (1) & Finance Act 1973, s. 56 (1) (2) & European Communities Act 1972, s. 2 (2), sch. 2, para. 1A. - Issued: 24.12.2014. Made: 17.12.2014. Coming into force: 01.01.2015. Effect: 1980 c.45; 2003 asp 8 amended & S.S.I. 2003/331; 2006/209; 2010/95; 2013 177; S.I. 2013/1387 revoked with saving & S.I. 1996/3047; S.S.I. 2001/207, 238 revoked. Territorial extent & classification: S. General. - Supersedes draft SI (ISBN 9780111024782) issued 06/11/14. EC note: Apply measures necessary to deliver the requirements of Council Directive 98/83/EC on the quality of water intended for human consumption. - 48p.: 30 cm. - 978-0-11-102570-3 £10.00

The Reservoirs (Scotland) Act 2011 (Commencement No. 1) Order 2014 No. 2014/348 (C.30). - Enabling power: Reservoirs (Scotland) Act 2011, s. 116 (1). Bringing into operation various provisions of the 2011 Act on 01.01.2015. - Issued: 09.12.2014. Made: 02.12.2014. Laid before the Scottish Parliament: 04.12.2014. Coming into force: 01.01.2015. Effect: None. Territorial extent & classification: S. General. - 4p.: 30 cm. - 978-0-11-102540-6 £4.25

The Water and Sewerage Services to Dwellings (Collection of Unmetered Charges by Local Authority) (Scotland) Order 2014 No. 2014/3. - Enabling power: Water Industry (Scotland) Act 2002, ss. 37, 68 (2). - Issued: 15.01.2014. Made: 08.01.2014. Laid before the Scottish Parliament: 10.01.2014. Coming into force: 08.02.2014. Effect: None. Territorial extent & classification: S. General. - 8p.: 30 cm. - 978-0-11-102233-7 £5.75

Scottish Statutory Instruments 2014

Arranged by Number

1	Police
2	Sea fisheries
3	Water supply
4	Environmental protection
5	Sports grounds and sporting events
6	Agriculture
7	Agriculture
8	Land reform
9	Land reform
10	Road traffic
11	Road traffic
12	Food
13	Prisons
14	Sheriff Court
15	Court of Session
16	Road traffic
17	Road traffic
18	Road traffic
19	Road traffic
20	Road traffic
21 (C.1)	Education
22	Education
23	Pensions
24	Lands Tribunal
25	Social care
26	Prisons
27	Road traffic
28	Rating and valuation
29	Court of Session
	Sheriff Court
30	Rating and valuation
31	Rating and valuation
32 (C.2)	Social care
33	Children and young persons
34 (C.3)	Prisons
35	Council tax
36	Local government
37	Council tax
38	National assistance services
39	National assistance services
40	Energy conservation
41 (C.4)	Land registration
42	Public health
43	National Health Service
44	Pensions
45	Road traffic
46	Road traffic
47	Road traffic
48	Road traffic
49	Proceeds of crime
50	Local government
	Ethical standards
51	Town and country planning
52	Education
53	Town and country planning
54 (C.5)	High hedges
55	High hedges
56	Roads and bridges
57	National Health Service
58	Roads and bridges
59	Fire services
	Pensions
60	Fire services
	Pensions
61	National Health Service
62	Pensions
63	Animals
64	Rating and valuation
65	Social care
66	Social care
67	Police
68	Police
69	Pensions
70	National Health Service
71	Animals
72	Animals
73	National Health Service
74	Local government
75	Road traffic
76	Road traffic
77	Road traffic
78	Road traffic
79 (C.6)	Education
80	Education
81	Public finance and accountability
82	Road traffic
83	Electronic communications
84	Road traffic
85	Road traffic
86	Road traffic
87	Cancelled
88	Cancelled
89	Cancelled
90	Social care
91	Social care
92	Sports grounds and sporting events
	Road traffic
93	National Health Service
94	Electricity
95	Criminal law
96	Road traffic
97	Road traffic
98	Landlord and tenant
99	Sheriff Court
100	National Health Service
101	Representation of the people
102	Judicial appointments and discipline
103	Education
104	Road traffic
105	Road traffic
106	Road traffic
107	Road traffic
108	Fire services
	Pensions
109	Fire services
	Pensions
110	Fire services
	Pensions
111	Plant health
112	Children and young persons
113	Children and young persons

114	Insolvency	169	Road traffic
115	National Health Service	170	Road traffic
116	Education	171	Road traffic
117 (C.7)	Mental health	172 (C.13)	Insolvency
118	Food		Bankruptcy
119	Court of Session		Debt
	Sheriff Court	173 (C.14)	Insolvency
120	Road traffic		Bankruptcy
121 (C.8)	Marriage	174	Road traffic
	Civil partnership	175	Road traffic
122	Plant health	176	Aquaculture
123	Adults with incapacity		Fish farming
124	Road traffic		Shellfish
125	Road traffic	177	Road traffic
126	Road traffic	178	Road traffic
127	Land registration	179	Road traffic
128	Road traffic	180	Road traffic
129	Social care	181	Road traffic
130	Title conditions	182	Road traffic
131 (C.9)	Children and young persons	183 (C.15)	Tribunals and inquiries
	Education	184	Town and country planning
132	Education	185	Nature conservation
133	Road traffic	186	Cancelled
134	Road traffic	187	Proceeds of crime
135	Road traffic	188	Registers and records
136	Road traffic	189	Land registration
137	Children and young persons	190	Land registration
138	Road traffic	191	Public bodies
139	Town and country planning	192	Social care
140	Plant health	193	Mental health
141	Registration of births, deaths, marriages, etc.	194	Land registration
142	Town and country planning	195	Road traffic
143	Education	196	Education
144 (C.10)	Education	197	Sports grounds and sporting events
145	Road traffic		Road traffic
146	Education	198	Road traffic
147	Criminal law		Road traffic
148	National Health Service	199	Road traffic
149	Fire services	200	Local government
	Pensions	201	Court of Session
150	Land registration		Sheriff Court
151	Animals	202 (C.16)	National Health Service
152	Court of Session	203	Road traffic
	Sheriff Court	204	Road traffic
153	Rating and valuation		Road traffic
154	National Health Service	205	Road traffic
155	Justice of the Peace Court	206	Road traffic
	Sheriff Court	207	Road traffic
156	Road traffic	208	Road traffic
157	Adults with incapacity	209	Road traffic
158	Harbours, docks, piers and ferries	210 (C.17)	Criminal law
159	Criminal law	211	Road traffic
160 (C.11)	Regulatory reform	212 (C.18)	Civil partnership
	Environmental protection		Gender recognition
161	Environmental protection		Marriage
162	High Court of Justiciary	213	Food
	Sheriff Court	214	Town and country planning
163	Cancelled	215	Road traffic
164	Pensions	216	Road traffic
165 (C.12)	Education	217	Public service pensions
166	Harbours, docks, piers and ferries	218 (C.19)	Civil partnership
167	Seeds		Gender recognition
168	Road traffic		Marriage
		219	Building and buildings

220	Title conditions	273	Road traffic
221 (C.20)	Criminal law	274	Road traffic
222	Road traffic	275	Road traffic
223	Road traffic	276	Road traffic
224	Harbours, docks, piers and ferries	277 (C.25)	Landfill tax
225	Insolvency Bankruptcy	278 (C.26)	Taxes
		279 (C.27)	Land and buildings transaction tax
226	Insolvency Bankruptcy Debt	280	Road traffic
		281	Public health Social care
227	Insolvency	282	Social care
228	Road traffic	283	Public health Social care
229	Scottish Land Court		
230	Public bodies	284	Social care Public health
231 (C.21)	Public health Social care	285	Public health Social care
232	Legal profession		
233	Public service pensions	286	Road traffic
234	Road traffic	287 (C.28)	Civil partnership Marriage
235	Road traffic		
236	Road traffic	288	Road traffic
237	Road traffic	289	Food
238	Roads and bridges	290	Insolvency Bankruptcy Debt
239	Public bodies		
240	Road traffic		
241	Road traffic	291	Court of Session Sheriff Court
242	High Court of Justiciary Sheriff Court Justice of the Peace Court		
		292	Public service pensions
		293	Bankruptcy
243	Housing	294	Debt
244	Road traffic	295	Charities
245	Road traffic	296	Insolvency Bankruptcy Debt
246	Roads and bridges		
247	Road traffic		
248	Road traffic	297	Environmental protection Marine management
249	Town and country planning		
250	Education	298	Social security
251 (C.22)	Children and young persons Education	299	Road traffic
		300	Town and country planning
252	Cancelled	301	Town and country planning
253	Road traffic	302	Court of Session Sheriff Court
254	Road traffic		
255	Road traffic	303	Marriage
256	Road traffic	304	Marriage
257	Legal aid and advice	305	Marriage
258	Environmental protection	306	Civil partnership Registration of births, deaths, marriages, etc. Marriage
259	Road traffic		
260	Environmental protection Marine management		
		307	Social care Public health
261 (C.23)	Insolvency Bankruptcy Debt	308	Social care Public health
		309	Roads and bridges
262	Education	310	Children and young persons
263	Education	311	Roads and bridges
264 (C.24)	Housing	312	Food
265	Sheriff Court	313	Title conditions Tenements
266	Road traffic		
267	Environmental protection	314 (C.29)	Children and young persons Education
268	Education		
269	Road traffic	315	Children and young persons Local government Education
270	Road traffic		
271	Road traffic		
272	Legal profession	316	Clean air
		317	Clean air

318	Education
319	Environmental protection
320	Environmental protection
321	Environmental protection
322	Criminal procedure
323	Environmental protection
324	Environmental protection
325	Agriculture
326	Public health
	Social care
327	Fisheries
	River
	Salmon and freshwater fisheries
328	Road traffic
329	Road traffic
330	Road traffic
331	Road traffic
332	Road traffic
333	Judgments
334	Cancelled
335	Charities
336	Criminal procedure
337	Criminal procedure
338	Plant health
339	Investigatory powers
340	Road traffic
341	Public health
	Social care
342	Public health
	Social care
343	Public health
	Social care
344	Public health
	Social care
345	Public health
	Social care
346	Land registration
347	Land registration
348 (C.30)	Flood risk management
	Water supply
349	High Court of Justiciary
	Sheriff Court
	Justice of the Peace Court
350	Land and buildings transaction tax
351	Land and buildings transaction tax
352	Charities
	Land and buildings transaction tax
353 (C.31)	Children and young persons
	Education
354	Freedom of information
355	Tribunals and inquiries
356	Sports grounds and sporting events
357	Fisheries
	River
	Salmon and freshwater fisheries
358	Cancelled
359 (C.32)	Criminal law
360	Criminal law
361	Marriage
	Civil partnership
362	Judgments
363	Public finance and accountability
364	Water supply
365 (C.33)	Children and young persons
	Education
366	Legal aid and advice
367	Landfill tax
368 (C.34)	Ancient monuments
369	Building and buildings
370 (C.35)	Taxes
371	Court of Session
	Sheriff Court
372	Children and young persons
373	Water
374	Sports grounds and sporting events
375	Land and buildings transaction tax
376	Land and buildings transaction tax
	Land registration
377	Land and buildings transaction tax
378	Road traffic
379	Sea fisheries
380	Road traffic
381	Road traffic
382	Road traffic
383	Road traffic
384	Road traffic
385	Road traffic

List of Scottish Commencement Orders 2014

21 (C.1)
32 (C.2)
34 (C.3)
41 (C.4)
54 (C.5)
79 (C.6)
117 (C.7)
121 (C.8)
131 (C.9)
144 (C.10)
160 (C.11)
165 (C.12)
172 (C.13)
173 (C.14)
183 (C.15)
202 (C.16)
210 (C.17)
212 (C.18)
218 (C.19)
221 (C.20)
231 (C.21)
251 (C.22)
261 (C.23)
264 (C.24)
277 (C.25)
278 (C.26)
279 (C.27)
287 (C.28)
314 (C.29)
348 (C.30)
353 (C.31)
359 (C.32)
365 (C.33)
368 (C.34)
370 (C.35)

NORTHERN IRELAND LEGISLATION

Acts of the Northern Ireland Assembly

Acts of the Northern Ireland Assembly 2014

Budget Act (Northern Ireland) 2014: Chapter 3. - 48p.: 30 cm. - Royal assent, 19th March 2014. An Act to authorise the issue out of the Consolidated Fund of certain sums for the service of the years ending 31st March 2014 and 2015; to appropriate those sums for specified purposes; to authorise the Department of Finance and Personnel to borrow on the credit of the appropriated sums; to authorise the use for the public service of certain resources for the years ending 31st March 2014 and 2015; and to revise the limits on the use of certain accruing resources in the year ending 31st March 2014. Explanatory notes to the Act are available separately (ISBN 9780105961505). - 978-0-10-595145-2 £9.75

Budget (No. 2) Act (Northern Ireland) 2014: Chapter 10. - [2], 25, [1]p.: 30 cm. - Royal assent, 16 July 2014. An Act to authorise the issue out of the Consolidated Fund of certain sums for the service of the year ending 31st March 2015; to appropriate those sums for specified purposes; to authorise the Department of Finance and Personnel to borrow on the credit of the appropriated sums; to authorise the use for the public service of certain resources (including accruing resources) for the year ending 31st March 2015; and to repeal certain spent provisions. Explanatory notes to the Act are available separately (ISBN 9780105961567). - With correction slip dated October 2014. - 978-0-10-595152-0 £6.00

Carrier Bags Act (Northern Ireland) 2014: Chapter 7. - [12]p.: 30 cm. - Royal assent, 28 April 2014. An Act to amend the Climate Change Act 2008 to confer powers to make provision about charging for carrier bags; to amend the Single Use Carrier Bags Charge Regulations (Northern Ireland) 2013. Explanatory notes to the Act are available separately (ISBN 9780105961543). - 978-0-10-595148-3 £6.00

Education Act (Northern Ireland) 2014: Chapter 12. - 28p.: 30 cm. - Royal assent, 11th December 2014. An Act to provide for the establishment and functions of the Education Authority; to confer power on the Department of Education to make grants to sectoral bodies. Explanatory notes to assist in the understanding of the Act are available separately (ISBN 9780105961598). - 978-0-10-596158-1 £10.00

Financial Provisions Act (Northern Ireland) 2014: Chapter 6. - [12]p.: 30 cm. - Royal assent, 28 April 2014. An Act to repeal the Development Loans Act 1968; to enable the Department of Agriculture and Rural Development to pay grants to certain harbour authorities; to amend the Rates (Northern Ireland) Order 1977; to make provision in relation to the payment of interest on funds in court; to make provision enabling the Northern Ireland Housing Executive to recover certain costs; to make provision for the disclosure of data obtained by the Comptroller and Auditor General for data matching purposes; to enable the Department of Justice to make payments to certain bodies providing services for the police etc. Explanatory notes to the Act are available separately (ISBN 9780105961536). - 978-0-10-595149-0 £6.00

Health and Social Care (Amendment) Act (Northern Ireland) 2014: Chapter 5. - [12]p.: 30 cm. - Royal assent, 11 April 2014. An Act to amend the Health and Social Care (Reform) Act (Northern Ireland) 2009 and to make amendments consequential on that Act. Explanatory notes to the Act are available separately (ISBN 9780105961529). - 978-0-10-595147-6 £6.00

Legal Aid and Coroners' Courts Act (Northern Ireland) 2014: Chapter 11. - [1], ii, 22, [1]p.: 30 cm. - Royal assent, 17 November 2014. An Act to dissolve the Northern Ireland Legal Services Commission and provide for the exercise of functions of the Commission by the Department of Justice or the Director of Legal Aid Casework; to amend the law on legal aid in criminal proceedings, civil legal services and criminal defence services; to provide for the Lord Chief Justice to be president of the coroners' courts and for the appointment of a Presiding coroner. - 978-0-10-595153-7 £6.00

Licensing of Pavement Cafés Act (Northern Ireland) 2014: Chapter 9. - ii, 26p.: 30 cm. - Royal assent, 12 May 2014. An Act to make provision for the regulation by district councils of the placing on public areas of furniture for use for the consumption of food or drink. Explanatory notes to the Act are available separately (ISBN 9780105961550). - 978-0-10-595151-3 £6.00

Local Government Act (Northern Ireland) 2014: Chapter 8. - vii, 94p.: 30 cm. - Royal assent, 12 May 2014. An Act to amend the law relating to local government. Explanatory notes to the Act will be available separately. With correction slip dated June 2014. - 978-0-10-595150-6 £16.50

Public Service Pensions Act (Northern Ireland) 2014: Chapter 2. - ii, 40p.: 30 cm. - Royal Assent, 11 March 2014. An Act to make provision for public service pension schemes. Explanatory notes to the Act are available separately (ISBN 9780105961499). - 978-0-10-595144-5 £9.75

Road Races (Amendment) Act (Northern Ireland) 2014: Chapter 1. - [8]p.: 30 cm. - Royal Assent, 17th January 2014. An Act to amend the Road Races (Northern Ireland) Order 1986 to provide for contingency days to be specified in an order authorising the use of roads in connection with road races and for the substitution of a contingency day for a day specified in such an order. Explanatory notes to the Act are available separately (ISBN 9780105961482). - 978-0-10-595143-8 £4.00

Tobacco Retailers Act (Northern Ireland) 2014: Chapter 4. - ii, 16, [1]p.: 30 cm. - Royal assent, 25th March 2014. An Act to make provision for a register of tobacco retailers; to make provision for dealing with the persistent commission of tobacco offences; to amend the Health and Personal Social Services (Northern Ireland) Order 1978; to confer additional powers of enforcement in relation to offences under that Order and the Children and Young Persons (Protection from Tobacco) (Northern Ireland) Order 1991. Explanatory notes to assist in the understanding of the Act are available separately (ISBN 9780108591512). - 978-0-10-595146-9 £5.75

Acts of the Northern Ireland Assembly - Explanatory and financial memorandum 2014

Budget Act (Northern Ireland) 2014: chapter 3; explanatory notes. - [8]p.: 30 cm. - These Notes refer to the Budget Act (Northern Ireland) 2014 (c.3) (ISBN 9780105951452) which received Royal Assent on 19th March 2014. - 978-0-10-596150-5 £4.00

Budget (No. 2) Act (Northern Ireland) 2014: chapter 10; explanatory notes. - [8]p.: 30 cm. - These Notes refer to the Budget (No. 2) Act (Northern Ireland) 2014 (c.10) (ISBN 9780105951520) which received Royal Assent on 16th July 2014. - 978-0-10-596156-7 £4.25

Carrier Bags Act (Northern Ireland) 2014: chapter 7; explanatory notes. - [12]p.: 30 cm. - These Notes refer to the Carrier Bags Act (Northern Ireland) 2014 (c.7) (ISBN 9780105951483) which received Royal assent on 28 April 2014. - 978-0-10-596154-3 £6.00

Education Act (Northern Ireland) 2014: chapter 12; explanatory notes. - [6]p.: 30 cm. - These notes refer to the Education Act (Northern Ireland) 2014 (c.12) (ISBN 9780105961581) which received Royal Assent on 11 December 2014. - 978-0-10-596159-8 £4.25

Financial Provisions Act (Northern Ireland) 2014: chapter 6; explanatory notes. - [8]p.: 30 cm. - These Notes refer to the Financial Provisions Act (Northern Ireland) 2014 (c.6) (ISBN 9780105951490) which received Royal assent on 28 April 2014. - 978-0-10-596153-6 £6.00

Health and Social Care (Amendment) Act (Northern Ireland) 2014: chapter 5; explanatory notes. - [8]p.: 30 cm. - These notes refer to the Health and Social Care (Amendment) Act (Northern Ireland) 2014 (c.5) (ISBN 9780105951476) which received Royal assent on 11 April 2014. - 978-0-10-596152-9 £4.25

Legal Aid and Coroners' Courts Act (Northern Ireland) 2014: chapter 11; explanatory notes. - [10]p.: 30 cm. - These notes refer to the Legal Aid and Coroners' Courts Act (Northern Ireland) 2014 (c.11) (ISBN 9780105951537) which received Royal Assent on 17 November 2014. - 978-0-10-596157-4 £6.00

Licensing of Pavement Cafés Act (Northern Ireland) 2014: chapter 9; explanatory notes. - [12]p.: 30 cm. - These Notes refer to the Licensing of Pavement Cafés Act (Northern Ireland) 2014 (c.9) (ISBN 9780105951513) which received Royal assent on 12 May 2014. - 978-0-10-596155-0 £6.00

Public Service Pensions Act (Northern Ireland) 2014: chapter 2; explanatory notes. - 36p.: 30 cm. - These Notes refer to the Public Service Pensions Act (Northern Ireland) 2014 (c.2) (ISBN 9780105951445) which received Royal Assent on 11 March 2014. - 978-0-10-596149-9 £9.75

Road Races (Amendment) Act (Northern Ireland) 2014: chapter 1; explanatory notes. - [8]p.: 30 cm. - These Notes refer to the Road Races (Amendment) Act (Northern Ireland) 2014 (c.1) (ISBN 9780105951438) which received Royal assent on 17 January 2014. - 978-0-10-596148-2 £4.00

Tobacco Retailers Act (Northern Ireland) 2014: chapter 4; explanatory notes. - [12]p.: 30 cm. - These Notes refer to the Tobacco Retailers Act (Northern Ireland) 2014 (c.4) (ISBN 9780105951469) which received Royal assent on 25th March 2014. - 978-0-10-596151-2 £5.75

Other statutory publications

Statutory Publications Office.

Chronological table of statutory rules Northern Ireland: covering the legislation to 31 December 2013. - 10th ed. - ca. 962 pages: looseleaf with binder holes: 30 cm. - Supersedes 9th edition (ISBN 9780337098970). - 978-0-337-09936-6 £135.00

Chronological table of the statutes Northern Ireland: covering the legislation to 31 December 2012. - 39th ed. - x, 770p.: looseleaf with binder holes: 30 cm. - 978-0-337-09932-8 £130.00

Chronological table of the statutes Northern Ireland: covering the legislation to 31 December 2013. - 40th ed. - x, 762p.: looseleaf with binder holes: 30 cm. - 978-0-337-09967-0 £132.00

Northern Ireland statutes 2013: [binder]. - 1 binder: 31 cm. - 978-0-337-09908-3 £25.00 + VAT

Northern Ireland statutes 2014: [binder]. - 1 binder: 31 cm. - 978-0-337-09977-9 £25.00 + VAT

The statutes revised: Northern Ireland. - Cumulative supplement vols A-D (1537 - 1920) to 31 December 2013. - 2nd ed. - x, 70p.: looseleaf with binder holes: 30 cm. - The material held in the main updated Statutes revised has been integrated into the UK Statute Law Database, available online at www.statutelaw.gov.uk. However, pre-1921 legislation published in vols A to D and amended since is not currently covered by the Statute Law Database, so printed supplements will continue to be issued for amendments made to that legislation. - 978-0-337-09968-7 £12.30

Title page and index to Northern Ireland statutes volume 2013. - 14p.: looseleaf with binder holes: 30 cm. - A binder for the 2013 statutes is also available (ISBN 9780337099083). - 978-0-337-09930-4 £5.75

Title page and index to Northern Ireland statutes volume 2014. - 14p.: looseleaf with binder holes: 30 cm. - A binder for the 2014 statutes is also available (ISBN 9780337099779). - 978-0-337-09978-6 £5.75

Statutory Rules of Northern Ireland

By Subject Heading

Agriculture

Agriculture (Student fees) (Amendment) Regulations (Northern Ireland) 2014 No. 2014/86. - Enabling power: Agriculture Act (Northern Ireland) 1949, s. 5A (1) (2). - Issued: 20.03.2014. Made: 18.03.2014. Coming into operation: 01.09.2014. Effect: S.R. 2007/54 amended. Territorial extent & classification: NI. General. - 2p: 30 cm. - 978-0-337-99316-9 £4.00

The Common Agricultural Policy Direct Payments and Support Schemes (Cross Compliance) Regulations (Northern Ireland) 2014 No. 2014/291. - Enabling power: European Communities Act 1972, s. 2 (2). - Issued: 01.12.2014. Made: 25.11.2014. Coming into operation: 01.01.2015. Effect: S.R. 2005/6; 2006/459; 2009/316; 2010/174; 2012/452; 2014/1 revoked. Territorial extent & classification: NI. General. - EC note: In Northern Ireland these Regulations supplement and make provision for the administration and enforcement of Regulation (EU) No. 1306/2013 , Commission Delegated Regulation (EU) No 640/2014 and Commission Implementing Regulation (EU) No 809/2014 in relation to cross compliance under the revised system of direct support schemes under the Common Agricultural Policy to come into force on 1st January 2015. - 12p.: 30 cm. - 978-0-337-99525-5 £6.00

The Common Agricultural Policy Single Payment and Support Schemes (Amendment) Regulations (Northern Ireland) 2014 No. 2014/66. - Enabling power: European Communities Act 1972, s. 2 (2). - Issued: 10.03.2014. Made: 05.03.2014. Coming into operation: 01.04.2014. Effect: S.R. 2010/161 amended. Territorial extent & classification: NI. General. - EC note: These Regulations amend S.R. 2010/161 which make provision in Northern Ireland for the administration of Council Regulation (EC) no. 73/2009 and other associated instruments in relation to direct support schemes under the CAP. - 2p.: 30 cm. - 978-0-337-99304-6 £4.00

The Common Agricultural Policy Single Payment and Support Schemes (Cross Compliance) (Amendment) Regulations (Northern Ireland) 2014 No. 2014/1. - Enabling power: European Communities Act 1972, s. 2 (2). - Issued: 09.01.2014. Made: 06.01.2014. Coming into operation: 10.02.2014. Effect: S.R. 2005/6 amended. Territorial extent & classification: NI. General. - Revoked by SR 2014/291 (ISBN 9780337995255); EC note: The Regulations make provision in Northern Ireland for Regulation (EU) No 1310/2013 which amends Regulation (EC) no. 73/2009. - 4p.: 30 cm. - 978-0-337-99248-3 £4.00

The Single Common Market Organisation (Consequential Amendments) Regulations (Northern Ireland) 2014 No. 2014/92. - Enabling power: European Communities Act 1972, s. 2 (2), sch. 2, para. 1A. - Issued: 24.03.2014. Made: 19.03.2014. Coming into operation: 21.03.2014. Effect: S.R. 1989/164; 1996/383; 2008/237, 239, 323; 2010/125, 161, 198; 2011/315 amended. Territorial extent & classification: NI. General. - EC note: These Regulations amend a number of Regulations consequential upon the Regulation (EU) No 1308/2013 establishing a common organisation of the markets in agricultural products and repealing Council Regulations (EEC) No 922/72, (EEC) No 234/79, (EC) No 1037/2001 and (EC) No 1234/2007 ("Regulation (EU) 2013"). Regulation (EU) 2013 repeals (subject to transitional and final provisions) the earlier Single Common Market Organisation - Council Regulation (EU) No 1234/2007 of 22 October 2007 establishing a common organisation of agricultural markets and on specific provisions for certain agricultural products. - Partially revoked by SR 2014/223 (ISBN 9780337994845). - 12p.: 30 cm. - 978-0-337-99378-7 £5.75

The Trade in Animals and Related Products (Amendment) Regulations (Northern Ireland) 2014 No. 2014/196. - Enabling power: European Communities Act 1972, s. 2 (2), sch. 2, para. 1A. - Issued: 03.07.2014. Made: 30.06.2014. Coming into operation: 31.07.2014. Effect: S.R. 2011/438 amended. Territorial extent and classification: NI. General. - 4p.: 30 cm. - 978-0-337-99465-4 £4.25

Animals

The Brucellosis Control (Amendment) Order (Northern Ireland) 2014 No. 2014/266. - Enabling power: S.I. 1981/1115 (NI.22), arts 10 (6), 19, 60 (1). - Issued: 30.10.2014. Made: 24.10.2014. Coming into operation: 03.11.2014. Effect: S.R. 2004/361 amended. Territorial extent & classification: NI. General. - 2p.: 30 cm. - 978-0-337-99510-1 £4.25

The Importation of Animals (Amendment) Order (Northern Ireland) 2014 No. 2014/54. - Enabling power: S.I. 1981/1115 (N.I. 22), arts 5 (1), 19 (e) (i), 20 (1) (2), 21 (a), 24 (1) (1A), 29 (1) (2), 60 (1), sch. 3, part II, para. 2, part III, para. 1. - Issued: 04.03.2014. Made: 27.02.2014. Coming into operation: 01.04.2014. Effect: S.R. 1986/253 amended. Territorial extent & classification: NI. General. - 2p.: 30 cm. - 978-0-337-99288-9 £4.00

The Trade in Animals and Related Products (Amendment) Regulations (Northern Ireland) 2014 No. 2014/196. - Enabling power: European Communities Act 1972, s. 2 (2), sch. 2, para. 1A. - Issued: 03.070.2014. Made: 3.006.2014. Coming into operation: 31.07.2014. Effect: S.R. 2011/438 amended. Territorial extent and classification: NI. General. - 4p.: 30 cm. - 978-0-337-99465-4 £4.25

The Zoonoses (Fees) (Amendment) Regulations (Northern Ireland) 2014 No. 2014/58. - Enabling power: European Communities Act 1972, s. 2 (2) & Finance Act 1973, s. 56 (1) (2) (5). - Issued: 05.03.2014. Made: 26.02.2014. Coming into operation: 01.04.2014. Effect: S.R. 2011/71 amended. Territorial extent & classification: NI. General. - EC note: They make provision for the Department to charge fees for activities required under Commission Regulation (EC) No. 1003/2005, Commission Regulation (EC) No. 1168/2006, Commission Regulation (EC) No. 646/2007, Commission Regulation (EC) No. 584/2008, Regulation (EC) No. 2160/2003 and Commission Regulation (EC) No. 1237/2007. - 4p.: 30 cm. - 978-0-337-99292-6 £4.00

Animals: Animal health

The Animal By-Products (Enforcement) (Amendment) Regulations (Northern Ireland) 2014 No. 2014/184. - Enabling power: European Communities Act 1972, s. 2 (2). - Issued: 30.06.2014. Made: 25.06.2014. Coming into operation: 31.07.2014. Effect: S.R. 2011/124 amended & S.R. 1999/418 revoked. Territorial extent and classification: NI. General. - 4p.: 30 cm. - 978-0-337-99455-5 £4.25

The Foot and Mouth Disease (Amendment) Regulations (Northern Ireland) 2014 No. 2014/151. - Enabling power: European Communities Act 1972, s. 2 (2). - Issued: 04.06.2014. Made: 30.05.2014. Coming into operation: 01.07.2014. Effect: S.R. 2006/42 amended. Territorial extent & classification: NI. General. - 4p.: 30 cm. - 978-0-337-99426-5 £4.25

Animals: Prevention of cruelty

The Welfare of Animals at the Time of Killing Regulations (Northern Ireland) 2014 No. 2014/107. - Enabling power: European Communities Act 1972, s. 2 (2), sch. 2, para. 1A. - Issued: 15.04.2014. Made: 08.04.2014. Coming into operation: 21.05.2014. Effect: S.I. 2004/702 (N.I.3); S.R. 2009/247; 2014/162 amended & S.R. 2000/78; 2001/186 partially revoked & S.R. 1996/558; 2000/76; 2001/66; 2002/304; 2004/209; 2008/277; 2011/407 revoked. Territorial extent & classification: NI. General. - 42p.: 30 cm. - 978-0-337-99394-7 £10.00

Building regulations

The Building (Amendment) Regulations (Northern Ireland) 2014 No. 2014/44. - Enabling power: European Communities Act 1972, s. 2 (2) & S.I. 1979/1709 (N.I. 16), arts 3, 5 (1), sch. 1, paras. 6, 17, 17D, 22. - Issued: 27.02.2014. Made: 24.02.2014. Coming into operation: 25.02.2014. Effect: S.R. 2012/192 amended. Territorial extent and classification: NI. General. - 8p.: 30 cm. - 978-0-337-99279-7 £5.75

Building societies: Insolvency

The Building Society Insolvency Rules (Northern Ireland) 2014 No. 2014/41. - Enabling power: S.I. 1989/2405 (N.I. 19), art. 359 (1C) (2) (2C) (3) (3A). - Issued: 21.02.2014. Made: 13.02.2014. Coming into operation: 13.03.2014. Effect: S.R. 1991/364 applied with modifications. Territorial extent & classification: NI. General. - 52p.: 30 cm. - 978-0-337-99277-3 £9.75

The Building Society Special Administration Rules (Northern Ireland) 2014 No. 2014/40. - Enabling power: S.I. 1989/2405 (N.I. 19), art. 359 (1D) (2) (2D) (3) (3A). - Issued: 21.02.2014. Made: 13.02.2014. Coming into operation: 13.03.2014. Effect: S.R. 1991/364 applied with modifications. Territorial extent & classification: NI. General. - 32p.: 30 cm. - 978-0-337-99276-6 £5.75

Business improvement districts

The Business Improvement Districts (General) Regulations (Northern Ireland) 2014 No. 2014/143. - Enabling power: Business Improvement Districts Act (Northern Ireland) 2013, ss. 2, 10, 14, 15, 16, 17, 18. - Issued: 28.05.2014. Made: 20.05.2014. Coming into operation: 01.07.2014. Effect: None. Territorial extent & classification: NI. General. - 28p.: 30 cm. - 978-0-337-99419-7 £6.00

The Business Improvement Districts (Miscellaneous) Regulations (Northern Ireland) 2014 No. 2014/197. - Enabling power: Business Improvement Districts Act (Northern Ireland) 2013, ss. 5 (2) (f), 6 (3), 9 (3), 17 (2) (b). - Issued: 04.07.2014. Made: 01.07.2014. Coming into operation: 02.07.2014. Effect: None. Territorial extent & classification: NI. General. - Supersedes draft S.R. (ISBN 9780337994203) issued 28.05.2014. - 8p.: 30 cm. - 978-0-337-99468-5 £4.25

Charities

The Charities (2008 Act) (Commencement No. 5) Order (Northern Ireland) 2014 No. 2014/18 (C.1). - Enabling power: Charities Act (Northern Ireland) 2008, s. 185 (1). Bringing into operation various provisions of the 2008 Act on 01.04.2014. - Issued: 30.01.2014. Made: 27.01.2014. Coming into operation: -. Effect: None. Territorial extent & classification: NI. General. - 4p.: 30 cm. - 978-0-337-99259-9 £4.00

Child support

The Child Support, Pensions and Social Security (2000 Act) (Commencement No. 12) Order (Northern Ireland) 2014 No. 2014/138 (C.6). - Enabling power: Child Support, Pensions and Social Security Act (Northern Ireland) 2000, s. 68 (2) (a). Bringing into operation various provisions of the 2000 Act on 16.05.2014, in accord. with art. 2. - Issued: 21.05.2014. Made: 15.05.2014. Effect: None. Territorial extent and classification: NI. General. - 4p.: 30 cm. - 978-0-337-99414-2 £4.25

Civil partnership

The Civil Partnership (Amendment) Regulations (Northern Ireland) 2014 No. 2014/297. - Enabling power: Civil Partnership Act 2004, ss. 139 (2), 159 (1). - Issued: 10.12.2014. Made: 04.12.2014. Coming into operation: 02.03.2015. Effect: S.R. 2005/482 amended. Territorial extent and classification: NI. General. - 2p: 30 cm. - 978-0-337-99535-4 £4.25

Clean air

The Smoke Control Areas (Authorised Fuels) (Amendment) Regulations (Northern Ireland) 2014 No. 2014/249. - Enabling power: S.I. 1981/158 (N.I. 4), art. 2 (2). - Issued: 03.10.2014. Made: 01.10.2014. Coming into operation: 03.11.2014. Effect: S.R. 2013/205 amended. Territorial extent & classification: NI. General. - 4p.: 30 cm. - 978-0-337-99501-9 £4.25

The Smoke Control Areas (Exempted Fireplaces) (Amendment No. 2) Regulations (Northern Ireland) 2014 No. 2014/294. - Enabling power: S.I. 1981/158 (N.I. 4), art. 17 (7). - Issued: 04.12.2014. Made: 01.12.2014. Coming into operation: 31.12.2014. Effect: S.R. 2013/292 amended. Territorial extent & classification: NI. General. - 28p.: 30 cm. - 978-0-337-99531-6 £6.00

The Smoke Control Areas (Exempted Fireplaces) (Amendment) Regulations (Northern Ireland) 2014 No. 2014/166. - Enabling power: S.I. 1981/158 (N.I. 4), art. 17 (7). - Issued: 12.06.2014. Made: 09.06.2014. Coming into operation: 14.007.2014. Effect: S.R. 2013/292 amended. Territorial extent & classification: NI. General. - 20p.: 30 cm. - 978-0-337-99435-7 £6.00

Court of Judicature, Northern Ireland: Procedure

The Criminal Appeal (Amendment) (Northern Ireland) Rules 2014 No. 2014/222. - Enabling power: Judicature (Northern Ireland) Act 1978, ss. 55, 55A. - Issued: 12.08.2014. Made: 04.08.2014. Coming into operation: 05.09.2014. Effect: S.R. 1968/218 amended. Territorial extent & classification: NI. General. - 4p.: 30 cm. - 978-0-337-99483-8 £4.25

The Crown Court (Amendment) Rules (Northern Ireland) 2014 No. 2014/219. - Enabling power: Judicature (Northern Ireland) Act 1978, ss. 52 (1), 53A. - Issued: 11.08.2014. Made: 04.08.2014. Coming into operation: 05.09.2014. Effect: S.R. 1979/90 amended. Territorial extent & classification: NI. General. - EC note: Give effect to Directive 2010/64/EU on the right to interpretation and translation in criminal proceedings. - 4p.: 30 cm. - 978-0-337-99480-7 £4.25

The Rules of the Court of Judicature (Northern Ireland) (Amendment) 2014 No. 2014/220. - Enabling power: Judicature (Northern Ireland) Act 1978, ss. 55, 55A. - Issued: 12.08.2014. Made: 04.08.2014. Coming into operation: 05.09.2014. Effect: S.R. 1980/346 amended. Territorial extent & classification: NI. General. - EC note: Give effect to Directive 2010/64/EU on the right to interpretation and translation in criminal proceedings. - 8p.: 30 cm. - 978-0-337-99481-4 £4.25

Criminal law

The Criminal Justice (European Protection Order) (Northern Ireland) Regulations 2014 No. 2014/320. - Enabling power: European Communities Act 1972. 2 (2). - Issued: 23.12.2014. Made: 18.12.2014. Coming into operation: 11.01.2015. Effect: None. Territorial extent & classification: NI. General. - With correction slip dated February 2015. - 12p.: 30 cm. - 978-0-337-99554-5 £6.00

The Police Act 1997 (Criminal Record Certificates: Relevant Matters) (Amendment No. 2) Order (Northern Ireland) 2014 No. 2014/207. - Enabling power: Police Act 1997, s. 113A (7). - Issued: 08.07.2014. Made: 01.07.2014. Coming into operation: 08.07.2014. Effect: 1997 c.50 amended. Territorial extent & classification: NI. General. - Supersedes draft SI (ISBN 9780337994128) issued 20/05/14. - 2p.: 30 cm. - 978-0-337-99472-2 £4.25

The Police Act 1997 (Criminal Record Certificates: Relevant Matters) (Amendment) Order (Northern Ireland) 2014 No. 2014/100. - Enabling power: Police Act 1997, s. 113A (7). - Issued: 02.04.2014. Made: 26.03.2014. Coming into operation: 14.04.2014. Effect: 1997 c.50 amended. Territorial extent & classification: NI. General. - Supersedes draft S.R. (ISBN 9780337992681) issued 12.02.2014. - 8p.: 30 cm. - 978-0-337-99385-5 £6.00

The Police Act 1997 (Criminal Records) (Amendment No. 2) Regulations (Northern Ireland) 2014 No. 2014/265. - Enabling power: Police Act 1997, ss. 113A (1) (b), 113B (1) (2) (b), 116 (1) (b), 120ZA, 125 (1) (5). - Issued: 28.10.2014. Made: 10.11.2014. Coming into operation: 01.12.2014. Effect: S.I. 2007/3283; 2008/542 amended. Territorial extent & classification: NI. General. - With correction slip dated October 2014. - 4p.: 30 cm. - 978-0-337-99508-8 £4.25

The Police Act 1997 (Criminal Records) (Amendment) Regulations (Northern Ireland) 2014 No. 2014/28. - Enabling power: Police Act 1997, ss. 113A (6), 125 (1) (5). - Issued: 12.02.2014. Made: 05.02.2014. Coming into operation: 14.04.2014. Effect: S.I. 2008/542 amended. Territorial extent & classification: NI. General. - 2p.: 30 cm. - 978-0-337-99270-4 £4.00

The Sexual Offences Act 2003 (Notification Requirements) Regulations (Northern Ireland) 2014 No. 2014/185. - Enabling power: Sexual Offences Act 2003, ss. 83 (5) (5A), 84 (1) (5A), 85 (5), 86, 138 (9). - Issued: 30.06.2014. Made: 23.06.2014. Coming into operation: In accord. with reg. 1 (2). Effect: S.I. 2004/1220 amended. Territorial extent & classification: NI. General. - Supersedes draft SI (ISBN 9780337992643) issued 30.06.14. - 8p.: 30 cm. - 978-0-337-99456-2 £6.00

Dangerous drugs

The Misuse of Drugs (Amendment No.2) and Misuse of Drugs (Safe Custody) (Amendment) Regulations (Northern Ireland) 2014 No. 2014/158. - Enabling power: Misuse of Drugs Act 1971, ss. 7, 10, 22, 31. - Issued: 10.06.2014. Made: 05.06.2014. Coming into operation: 26.06.2014. Effect: S.R. 1973/179; 2002/1 amended. Territorial extent & classification: NI. General. - With correction slip dated June 2014. - 4p.: 30 cm. - 978-0-337-99432-6 £4.25

The Misuse of Drugs (Amendment No.3) Regulations (Northern Ireland) 2014 No. 2014/261. - Enabling power: Misuse of Drugs Act 1971, ss. 7, 10, 22, 31. - Issued: 24.10.2014. Made: 21.10.2014. Coming into operation: 11.11.2014. Effect: S.R. 2002/1 amended. Territorial extent & classification: NI. General. - 2p.: 30 cm. - 978-0-337-99505-7 £4.25

The Misuse of Drugs (Amendment No.4) Regulations (Northern Ireland) 2014 No. 2014/288. - Enabling power: Misuse of Drugs Act 1971, ss. 7, 10, 22, 31. - Issued: 24.11.2014. Made: 20.11.2014. Coming into operation: 11.12.2014. Effect: S.R. 2002/1 amended. Territorial extent & classification: NI. General. - 4p.: 30 cm. - 978-0-337-99524-8 £4.25

The Misuse of Drugs (Amendment) Regulations (Northern Ireland) 2014 No. 2014/21. - Enabling power: Misuse of Drugs Act 1971, ss. 7, 10, 22, 31. - Issued: 05.02.2014. Made: 03.02.2014. Coming into operation: 24.02.2014. Effect: S.R. 2002/1 amended. Territorial extent & classification: NI. General. - With correction slip dated May 2014. - 4p.: 30 cm. - 978-0-337-99263-6 £4.00

The Misuse of Drugs (Designation) (Amendment No.2) Order (Northern Ireland) 2014 No. 2014/159. - Enabling power: Misuse of Drugs Act 1971, ss. 7 (4). - Issued: 10.06.2014. Made: 05.06.2014. Coming into operation: 26.06.2014. Effect: S.R. 2001/431 amended. Territorial extent & classification: NI. General. - 4p.: 30 cm. - 978-0-337-99431-9 £4.25

The Misuse of Drugs (Designation) (Amendment No.3) Order (Northern Ireland) 2014 No. 2014/262. - Enabling power: Misuse of Drugs Act 1971, s. 7 (4). - Issued: 24.10.2014. Made: 21.10.2014. Coming into operation: 11.11.2014. Effect: S.R. 2001/431 amended. Territorial extent & classification: NI. General. - 2p.: 30 cm. - 978-0-337-99506-4 £4.25

The Misuse of Drugs (Designation) (Amendment) Order (Northern Ireland) 2014 No. 2014/20. - Enabling power: Misuse of Drugs Act 1971, s. 7 (4). - Issued: 05.02.2014. Made: 03.02.2014. Coming into operation: 24.02.2014. Effect: S.R. 2001/431 amended. Territorial extent & classification: NI. General. - 4p.: 30 cm. - 978-0-337-99262-9 £4.00

Disabled persons: Transport

The Rail Vehicle Accessibility (Applications for Exemption Orders) Regulations (Northern Ireland) 2014 No. 2014/46. - Enabling power: Disability Discrimination Act 1995, s. 47 (2). - Issued: 28.02.2014. Made: 25.02.2014. Coming into operation: 28.04.2014. Effect: S.R. 2001/265 revoked. Territorial extent & classification: NI. General. - 8p.: 30 cm. - 978-0-337-99281-0 £4.00

The Rail Vehicle Accessibility Regulations (Northern Ireland) 2014 No. 2014/45. - Enabling power: European Communities Act 1972, s. 2 (2) & Disability Discrimination Act 1995, s. 46 (1) (2) (4A) (5), 67 (3) (a). - Issued: 28.02.2014. Made: 25.02.2014. Coming into operation: 28.04.2014. Effect: S.R. 2001/264 revoked with saving. - 40p., figs: 30 cm. - 978-0-337-99280-3 £9.75

Dogs

The Dogs (Licensing and Identification) (Amendment) Regulations (Northern Ireland) 2014 No. 2014/283. - Enabling power: S.I. 1983/764 (N.I. 8), arts 6 (2) (3) (5), 7 (9), 8 (2) (3), 15 (1), 31 (1) (1A). - Issued: 20.11.2014. Made: 17.11.2014. Coming into operation: 01.01.2015. Effect: S.R. 2012/132 amended. Territorial extent and classification: NI. General. - 2p.: 30 cm. - 978-0-337-99519-4 £4.25

Education

The Education (General Teaching Council for Northern Ireland) (Constitution) (Amendment) Regulations (Northern Ireland) 2014 No. 2014/218. - Enabling power: S.I. 1998/1759 (N.I. 13), art. 34, sch. 1, para. 1. - Issued: 08.08.2014. Made: 05.08.2014. Coming into operation: 08.09.2014. Effect: S.R. 2001/288 amended. Territorial extent & classification: NI. General. - 2p.: 30 cm. - 978-0-337-99479-1 £4.25

The Education (Student Loans) (Repayment) (Amendment) Regulations (Northern Ireland) 2014 No. 2014/87. - Enabling power: S.I. 1998/1760 (N.I. 14), arts 3 (2) to (5), 8 (4). - Issued: 21.03.2014. Made: 18.03.2014. Coming into operation: 06.04.2014. Effect: S.R. 2009/128 amended. Territorial extent & classification: NI. General. - 4p.: 30 cm. - 978-0-337-99317-6 £4.00

The Education (Student Support) (No. 2) Regulations (Northern Ireland) 2009 (Amendment) (No.2) Regulations (Northern Ireland) 2014 No. 2014/309. - Enabling power: S.I. 1998/1760 (N.I. 14), arts 3, 8 (4). - Issued: 16.12.2014. Made: 12.12.2014. Coming into operation: 08.01.2015. Effect: S.R. 2009/373 amended. Territorial extent & classification: NI. General. - 6p.: 30 cm. - 978-0-337-99550-7 £4.25

The Education (Student Support) (No. 2) Regulations (Northern Ireland) 2009 (Amendment) Regulations (Northern Ireland) 2013 No. 2014/97. - Enabling power: S.I. 1998/1760 (N.I. 14), arts 3, 8 (4). - Issued: 27.03.2014. Made: 24.03.2014. Coming into operation: 18.04.2014. Effect: S.R. 2009/373 amended. Territorial extent & classification: NI. General. - 2p.: 30 cm. - 978-0-337-99382-4 £4.00

The Student Fees (Amounts) (Amendment) Regulations (Northern Ireland) 2014 No. 2014/116. - Enabling power: S.I. 2005/1116 (N.I. 5), arts 4 (8), 14 (4). - Issued: 17.04.2014. Made: 14.04.2014. Coming into operation: 01.09.2015. Effect: S.R. 2005/290 amended & S.R. 2013/120 revoked. Territorial extent & classification: NI. General. - 2p.: 30 cm. - 978-0-337-99398-5 £4.25

The Teachers' Pension Scheme Regulations (Northern Ireland) 2014 No. 2014/310. - Enabling power: Public Service Pensions Act (Northern Ireland) 2014, ss. 1(1) (2) (d), (3) (4), 2, 3(1), (2), 3 (a) (c) (4), 4 (1) (3), 5 (1), (3) (5), 7 (1) (4), 8 (1) (a) (2) (a), 14, 18 (1) (2) (4) (5) to (10), 34 def. of employer para. (c), sch. 1, para. 4 (c), sch. 1, para. 4, sch. 2, para.3, sch. 3, sch. 5, para. 4, sch. 6 para. 3, & sch. 7, paras. 1 (2) (ii), 2 (2) (ii), 5- Issued: 17.12.2014. Made: 12.12.2014. Coming into operation: 01.04.2015. Effect: None. Territorial extent and classification: NI. General. - 110p.: 30 cm. - 978-0-337-99551-4 £16.50

The Teachers' Superannuation (Amendment) (No. 2) Regulations (Northern Ireland) 2014 No. 2014/70. - Enabling power: S.I. 1972/1073 (N.I. 10), art. 11 (1) (2) (3) (3A), sch. 3, paras 1, 3, 4, 5, 6, 8, 11, 13. - Issued: 10.03.2014. Made: 05.03.2014. Coming into operation: 01.04.2014. Effect: S.R. 1998/333 amended. Territorial extent & classification: NI. General. - Revoked by SR 2015/69 (ISBN 9780337996351). - 4p: 30 cm. - 978-0-337-99305-3 £4.00

The Teachers' Superannuation (Amendment) Regulations (Northern Ireland) 2014 No. 2014/37. - Enabling power: S.I. 1972/1073 (N.I. 10), art. 11 (1) (2) (3) (3A) 14 (1) (2), sch. 3, paras 1, 3, 4, 5, 6, 8, 11, 13. - Issued: 17.02.2014. Made: 12.02.2014. Coming into operation: 10.03.2014. Effect: S.R. 1998/333 amended. Territorial extent & classification: NI. General. - 8p: 30 cm. - 978-0-337-99274-2 £5.75

Electricity

The Guarantees of Origin of Electricity Produced from High-efficiency Cogeneration (Amendment) Regulations (Northern Ireland) 2014 No. 2014/284. - Enabling power: European Communities Act 1972, s. 2 (2). - Issued: 21.11.2014. Made: 18.11.2014. Coming into operation: 10.12.2014. Effect: S.R. 2008/287 amended. - These Regulations transpose art. 14 (10) of, and Annexes II and X to, Directive 2012/27/EU of the European Parliament and of the Council of 25th October 2012 on energy efficiency, amending Directives 2009/125/EC and 2010/30/EU and repealing Directives 2004/8/EC and 2006/32/EC. - 4p: 30 cm. - 978-0-337-99523-1 £4.25

The Renewables Obligation (Amendment) Order (Northern Ireland) 2014 No. 2014/146. - Enabling power: S.I. 2003/419 (N.I. 6), arts. 52 to 55F, 66 (3). - Issued: 28.04.2014. Made: 20.05.2014. Coming into operation: 01.06.2014. Effect: S.R. 2009/154 amended. Territorial extent & classification: NI. General. - 12p.: 30 cm. - 978-0-337-99421-0 £6.00

Employment

The Employment Relations (Northern Ireland) Order 1999 (Blacklists) Regulations (Northern Ireland) 2014 No. 2014/88. - Enabling power: S.I. 1999/2790 (N.I. 9), art. 5. - Issued: 13.06.2014. Made: 19.03.2014. Coming into operation: 06.04.2014-. Effect: S.I. 1996/1921 (N.I. 18) amended. - Approved by resolution of the Assembly on 10th June 2014. Supersedes pre-approved version (ISBN 9780337993794). - 16p.: 30 cm. - 978-0-337-99442-5 £6.00

The Employment Relations (Northern Ireland) Order 1999 (Blacklists) Regulations (Northern Ireland) 2014 No. 2014/88. - Enabling power: S.I. 1999/2790 (N.I. 9), art. 5. - Issued: 24.03.2014. Made: 19.03.2014. Coming into operation: 06.04.2014. Effect: S.I. 1992/807 (N.I. 5); 1996/1919 (N.I. 16), 1921 (N.I. 18); 2003/2902 (N.I. 15) amended. Territorial extent & classification: NI. General. - For the approval of the Assembly before the expiration of six months from the coming into force date. Superseded by the approved version (ISBN 9780337994425). - 16p: 30 cm. - 978-0-337-99379-4 £5.75

The Employment Rights (Increase of Limits) Order (Northern Ireland) 2014 No. 2014/39. - Enabling power: S.I. 1999/2790 (N.I. 9), arts 33 (2) (3), 39 (3). - Issued: 18.02.2014. Made: 12.02.2014. Coming into operation: 16.02.2014. Effect: S.R. 2013/23 revoked. Territorial extent & classification: NI. General. - Revoked by SR 2015/169 (ISBN 9780337997303). - 8p: 30 cm. - 978-0-337-99275-9 £5.75

The Gangmasters Licensing (Exclusions) Regulations (Northern Ireland) 2014 No. 2014/23. - Enabling power: Gangmasters (Licensing) Act 2004, s. 6 (2). - Issued: 10.02.2014. Made: 05.02.2014. Coming into operation: 07.03.2014. Effect: S.R. 2010/162 revoked. Territorial extent & classification: NI. Generals. - With correction slip dated February 2014. - 8p: 30 cm. - 978-0-337-99266-7 £5.75

The Public Interest Disclosure (Prescribed Persons) (Amendment) Order (Northern Ireland) 2014 No. 2014/48. - Enabling power: S.I. 1996/1919 (N.I. 16), art. 67F. - Issued: 03.03.2014. Made: 26.02.2014. Coming into operation: 06.04.2014. Effect: S.R. 1999/401 amended & S.R. 2012/283 revoked. Territorial extent & classification: NI. General. - 12p.: 30 cm. - 978-0-337-99282-7 £5.75

The Social Security Benefits Up-rating Order (Northern Ireland) 2014 No. 2014/78. - Enabling power: Social Security Administration (Northern Ireland) Act 1992, ss. 132, 132A, 165(1) (4) (5). - Issued: 17.03.2014. Made: 13.03.2014. Coming into operation: In accord. with art. 1. Effect: 1966 c.6 (N.I.); 1992 c.7; S.R. 1987/30, 459; 1992/32; 1994/461; 1995/35; 1996/198; 2002/380; 2003/28; 2006/405, 406; 2008/280; 2010/302, 407 amended & S.R. 2013/69 revoked (14.04.2014). Territorial extent & classification: NI. General. - For approval of the Assembly before the expiration of six months from the date of its coming into operation. Superseded by Approved SR 2014/78 (ISBN 9780337993138). - 44p.: 30 cm. - 978-0-337-99313-8 £9.75

The Social Security Benefits Up-rating Order (Northern Ireland) 2014 No. 2014/78. - Enabling power: Social Security Administration (Northern Ireland) Act 1992, ss. 132, 132A, 165(1) (4) (5). - Issued: 13.06.2014. Made: 13.03.2014. Coming into operation: In accord. with art. 1. Effect: 1966 c.6 (N.I.); 1992 c.7; S.R. 1987/30, 459; 1992/32; 1994/461; 1995/35; 1996/198; 2002/380; 2003/28; 2006/405, 406; 2008/280; 2010/302, 407 amended & S.R. 2013/69 revoked (14.04.2014). Territorial extent & classification: NI. General. - Approved by resolution of the Assembly on 9th June 2014; Revoked by SR 2015/124 (ISBN 9780337996634). - 44p.: 30 cm. - 978-0-337-99438-8 £9.75

Energy

The Domestic Renewable Heat Incentive Scheme Regulations (Northern Ireland) 2014 No. 2014/301. - Enabling power: Energy Act 2011, s. 113. - Issued: 12.12.2014. Made: 08.12.2014. Coming into operation: In accord. with reg. 1. Effect: S.R. 2012/396 amended. Territorial extent and classification: NI. General. - 38p.: 30 cm. - 978-0-337-99542-2 £10.00

The Energy Efficiency Regulations (Northern Ireland) 2014 No. 2014/198. - Enabling power: European Communities Act 1972, s. 2 (2). - Issued: 09.07.2014. Made: 04.07.2014. Coming into operation: 25.07.2014. Effect: S.R. 2009/195 amended. Territorial extent and classification: NI. General. - 12p.: 30 cm. - 978-0-337-99475-3 £6.00

Energy conservation

The Domestic Energy Efficiency Grants (Amendment) Regulations (Northern Ireland) 2014 No. 2014/52. - Enabling power: S.I. 1990/1511 (N.I. 15), art. 17. - Issued: 03.03.2014. Made: 07.02.2014. Coming into operation: 21.03.2014. Effect: S.R. 2009/195 amended. Territorial extent and classification: NI. General. - 4p.: 30 cm. - 978-0-337-99287-2 £4.00

Environmental protection

The Controlled Waste and Duty of Care (Amendment) Regulations (Northern Ireland) 2014 No. 2014/117. - Enabling power: S.I. 1997/2870 (N.I. 19), arts 2 (3), 5 (7). - Issued: 23.04.2014. Made: 16.04.2014. Coming into operation: 30.05.2014. Effect: S.R. 2013/255 amended. Territorial extent & classification: NI. General. - 4p.: 30 cm. - 978-0-337-99399-2 £4.25

The Fluorinated Greenhouse Gases (Amendment) Regulations (Northern Ireland) 2014 No. 2014/77. - Enabling power: European Communities Act 1972, s. 2 (2). - Issued: 17.03.2014. Made: 12.03.2014. Coming into operation: 23.03.2014. Effect: S.R. 2009/184 amended. Territorial extent & classification: NI. General. - 4p.: 30 cm. - 978-0-337-99311-4 £4.00

Groundwater (Amendment) Regulations (Northern Ireland) 2014 No. 2014/208. - Enabling power: European Communities Act 1972, s. 2 (2). - Issued: 09.07.2014. Made: 04.07.2014. Coming into operation: 31.07.2014. Effect: S.R. 2009/254 amended. Territorial extent and classification: NI. General. - 8p.: 30 cm. - 978-0-337-99473-9 £6.00

The Nitrates Action Programme Regulations (Northern Ireland) 2014 No. 2014/307. - Enabling power: European Communities Act 1972, s. 2 (2) & S.I. 1997/2778 (N.I. 19), art. 32. - Issued: 16.12.2014. Made: 11.12.2012. Coming into operation: 01.01.2015. Effect: S.R. 2003/319 amended & S.R. 2010/411; 2011/388; 2012/231 revoked. Territorial extent & classification: NI. General. - 36p.: 30 cm. - 978-0-337-99548-4 £10.00

The Phosphorus (Use in Agriculture) Regulations (Northern Ireland) 2014 No. 2014/308. - Enabling power: European Communities Act 1972, s. 2 (2) & S.I. 1997/2778 (N.I. 19), art. 32. - Issued: 16.12.2014. Made: 11.12.2014. Coming into operation: 01.01.2015. Effect: S.R. 2006/488; 2007/273 revoked. Territorial extent & classification: NI. General. - 12p: 30 cm. - 978-0-337-99549-1 £6.00

The Pollution Prevention and Control (Industrial Emissions) (Amendment) Regulations (Northern Ireland) 2014 No. 2014/304. - Enabling power: S.I. 2002/3153 (N.I. 7), sch. 1 art. 4 (1). - Issued: 17.12.2014. Made: 09.12.2014. Coming into operation: in accord. with reg. 1. Effect: S.R. 2013/160 amended. Territorial extent & classification: NI. - Supersedes draft S.R. (ISBN 9780337995033) issued 14/10/14. - 12p.: 30 cm. - 978-0-337-99545-3 £6.00

The Producer Responsibility Obligations (Packaging Waste) (Amendment) Regulations (Northern Ireland) 2014 No. 2014/276. - Enabling power: S.I. 1998/1762 (N.I. 16), arts 3 (1), 4 (1) (b) (c) (d). - Issued: 11.11.2014. Made: 06.11.2014. Coming into operation: 28.11.2014. Effect: S.R. 2007/198 amended. Territorial extent & classification: NI. General. - 2p.: 30 cm. - 978-0-337-99513-2 £4.25

The Sulphur Content of Liquid Fuels (Amendment) Regulations (Northern Ireland) 2014 No. 2014/147. - Enabling power: European Communities Act 1972, s. 2 (2). - Issued: 28.05.2014. Made: 23.05.2014. Coming into operation: 18.06.2014. Effect: S.R. 2007/272 amended. Territorial extent & classification: NI. General. - EC note: The amendments to the 2007 regulations transpose amendments to Council Directive 1999/32/EC made by Directive 2012/33/EU of the European Parliament and of the Council as regards the sulphur content of marine fuels. - 8p: 30 cm. - 978-0-337-99423-4 £6.00

The Waste Electrical and Electronic Equipment (Charges) Regulations (Northern Ireland) 2014 No. 2014/202. - Enabling power: European Communities Act 1972, s. 2 (2) & Finance Act 1973, s. 56 (1) (2). - Issued: 04.07.2014. Made: 02.07.2014. Coming into operation: 25.07.2014. Effect: S.R. 2006/509 revoked. Territorial extent & classification: NI. General. - 4p.: 30 cm. - 978-0-337-99467-8 £4.25

The Waste Management Licensing (Amendment No. 2) Regulations (Northern Ireland) 2014 No. 2014/253. - Enabling power: S.I. 2002/3153 (NI. 7), art. 4 (4). - Issued: 07.10.2014. Made: 02.10.2014. Coming into operation: 24.10.2014. Effect: S.R. 2003/493 amended. Territorial extent and classification: NI. General. - 2p.: 30 cm. - 978-0-337-99502-6 £4.25

The Waste Management Licensing (Amendment) Regulations (Northern Ireland) 2014 No. 2014/137. - Enabling power: European Communities Act 1972, s. 2 (2). - Issued: 19.05.2014. Made: 14.05.2014. Coming into operation: 12.06.2014. Effect: S.R. 2003/493 amended. Territorial extent and classification: NI. General. - 4p.: 30 cm. - 978-0-337-99413-5 £4.25

European Communities

The Energy Performance of Buildings (Certificates and Inspections) (Amendment) Regulations (Northern Ireland) 2014 No. 2014/43. - Enabling power: European Communities Act 1972, s. 2 (2). - Issued: 27.02.2014. Made: 24.02.2014. Coming into operation: 25.02.2014. Effect: S.R. 2008/170 amended. Territorial extent & classification: NI. General. - EC note: These Regulations implement the requirements of Articles 2(9), 11(2)(a), 11(2)(b), 11(3) and 13(2) of the European Parliament of 19 May 2010 on the energy performance of buildings ("the recast Directive"). - 4p.: 30 cm. - 978-0-337-99278-0 £4.00

Groundwater (Amendment) Regulations (Northern Ireland) 2014 No. 2014/208. - Enabling power: European Communities Act 1972, s. 2 (2). - Issued: 09.07.2014. Made: 04.07.2014. Coming into operation: 31.07.2014. Effect: S.R. 2009/254 amended. Territorial extent and classification: NI. General. - 8p.: 30 cm. - 978-0-337-99473-9 £6.00

Family law

The Child Support, Pensions and Social Security (2000 Act) (Commencement No. 12) Order (Northern Ireland) 2014 No. 2014/138 (C.6). - Enabling power: Child Support, Pensions and Social Security Act (Northern Ireland) 2000, s. 68 (2) (a). Bringing into operation various provisions of the 2000 Act on 16.05.2014, in accord. with art. 2. - Issued: 21.05.2014. Made: 15.05.2014. Effect: None. Territorial extent and classification: NI. General. - 4p.: 30 cm. - 978-0-337-99414-2 £4.25

Family law: Child support

The Child Maintenance (2008 Act) (Commencement No. 13) Order (Northern Ireland) 2014 No. 2014/175 (C.10). - Enabling power: Child Maintenance Act (Northern Ireland) 2008, s. 41 (1). Bringing into operation various provisions of the 2008 Act on 18.06.2014 in accord. with art. 2. - Issued: 20.06.2014. Made: 17.06.2014. Coming into operation: -. Effect: None. Territorial extent & classification: NI. General. - 4p.: 30 cm. - 978-0-337-99447-0 £4.25

The Child Maintenance (2008 Act) (Commencement No. 14 and Transitional Provisions) Order (Northern Ireland) 2014 No. 2014/194 (C.13). - Enabling power: Child Maintenance Act (Northern Ireland) 2008, s. 41 (1) (2). Bringing into operation various provisions of the 2008 Act on 30.06.2014 in accord. with art. 2. - Issued: 03.07.2014. Made: 27.06.2014. Coming into operation: -. Effect: S.R. 2012/440 (C.45); 2013/201 (C.13) amended. Territorial extent & classification: NI. General. - 8p.: 30 cm. - 978-0-337-99463-0 £4.25

The Child Support (Ending Liability in Existing Cases and Transition to New Calculation Rules) Regulations (Northern Ireland) 2014 No. 2014/191. - Enabling power: Child Maintenance Act (Northern Ireland) 2008, ss. 11, 36 (1) (2), sch. 2, paras. 2, 3, 5, 6. - Issued: 02.12.2014. Made: 26.06.2014. Coming into operation: 30.06.2014. Effect: None. Territorial extent & classification: NI. General. - Approved by resolution of the Assembly on 24th November 2014. Supersedes pre-approved version (ISBN 9780337994586). - 8p.: 30 cm. - 978-0-337-99528-6 £4.25

The Child Support (Ending Liability in Existing Cases and Transition to New Calculation Rules) Regulations (Northern Ireland) 2014 No. 2014/191. - Enabling power: Child Maintenance Act (Northern Ireland) 2008, ss. 11, 36 (1) (2), sch. 2, paras. 2, 3, 5, 6. - Issued: 01.07.2014. Made: 26.06.2014. Coming into operation: 30.06.2014. Effect: None. Territorial extent & classification: NI. General. - For approval of the Assembly before the expiration of six months from the date of their coming into operation. Superseded by approved version (ISBN 9780337995286) issued 02.12.0214. - 8p.: 30 cm. - 978-0-337-99458-6 £4.25

FINANCIAL ASSISTANCE

The Child Support Fees Regulations (Northern Ireland) 2014 No. 2014/182. - Enabling power: Social Security Administration (Northern Ireland) Act 1992, s. 5 (1) (q), 165 (4) & S.I. 1991/2628 (N.I.23), arts 40 (1), 47 (1) & Child Maintenance Act (Northern Ireland) 2008, ss. 3 (1) to (4), 36 (1) (2). - Issued: 27.06.2014. Made: 24.06.2014. Coming into operation: In accord. with art. 1. Effect: S.R. 1987/465 amended. Territorial extent & classification: NI. General. - For approval of the Assembly before the expiration of six months from the date of their coming into force. Superseded by approved version (ISBN 9780337995293) issued 02.12.2014. - 8p.: 30 cm. - 978-0-337-99452-4 £6.00

The Child Support Fees Regulations (Northern Ireland) 2014 No. 2014/182. - Enabling power: Social Security Administration (Northern Ireland) Act 1992, s. 5 (1) (q), 165 (4) & S.I. 1991/2628 (N.I.23), arts 40 (1), 47 (1) & Child Maintenance Act (Northern Ireland) 2008, ss. 3 (1) to (4), 36 (1) (2). - Issued: 02.12.2014. Made: 24.06.2014. Coming into operation: In accord. with art. 1. Effect: S.R. 1987/465 amended. Territorial extent & classification: NI. General. - Approved by resolution of the Assembly on 24th November 2014. Supersedes pre-approved version (ISBN 9780337994524). - 8p.: 30 cm. - 978-0-337-99529-3 £6.00

The Child Support (Great Britain Reciprocal Arrangements) (Amendment) Regulations (Northern Ireland) 2014 No. 2014/167. - Enabling power: Northern Ireland Act 1998, s. 87 (5) (10). - Issued: 12.06.2014. Made: 09.06.2014. Coming into operation: 30.06.2014. Effect: S.R. 1993/117 amended. Territorial extent & classification: NI. General. - 8p.: 30 cm. - 978-0-337-99436-4 £6.00

The Child Support (Modification, Consequential and Miscellaneous Amendments) Regulations (Northern Ireland) 2014 No. 2014/193. - Enabling power: S.I. 1991/2628 (NI.23), arts 18 (1), 29 (2) (3), 32 (1) (2) (n), 34 (1), 40A, 47 (1) (2) (a) (i), 48 (4), sch. 1, para. 11 & Child Maintenance Act (Northern Ireland) 2008, s. 36 (1) (2), sch. 2, paras. 2, 5. - Issued: 03.07.2014. Made: 27.06.2014. Coming into operation: In accord. with reg. 1. Effect: S.R. 1992/390; 2009/422 modified & S.R. 2012/427 amended. Territorial extent & classification: NI. General. - 8p.: 30 cm. - 978-0-337-99462-3 £6.00

Financial assistance

The Sea Fishing (Financial Assistance to Fishing Boats) Scheme Regulations (Northern Ireland) 2014 No. 2014/96. - Enabling power: Financial Assistance Act (Northern Ireland) 2009, s. 1 (1). - Issued: 26.03.2014. Made: 21.03.2014. Coming into operation: 26.03.2014. Effect: None. Territorial extent & classification: NI. General. - 8p.: 30 cm. - 978-0-337-99381-7 £5.75

Financial provisions

The Financial Provisions (2014 Act) (Commencement No. 1) Order (Northern Ireland) 2014 No. 2014/155 (C.9). - Enabling power: Financial Provisions Act (Northern Ireland) 2014, s. 13 (4). Bringing into operation various provisions of the 2014 Act on 04.06.2014, in accord. with art. 2. - Issued: 09.06.2014. Made: 04.06.2014. Effect: None. Territorial extent and classification: NI. General. - 2p.: 30 cm. - 978-0-337-99430-2 £4.25

The Financial Provisions (2014 Act) (Commencement No. 2) Order (Northern Ireland) 2014 No. 2014/305 (C.17). - Enabling power: Financial Provisions Act (Northern Ireland) 2014, s. 13 (4). Bringing into operation various provisions of the 2014 Act on 01.04.2015, in accord. with art. 2. - Issued: 16.12.2014. Made: 10.12.2014. Effect: None. Territorial extent and classification: NI. General. - 4p.: 30 cm. - 978-0-337-99546-0 £4.25

Fire and rescue services: Pensions

The Firefighters' Pension Scheme (Amendment) (No. 2) Order (Northern Ireland) 2014 No. 2014/169. - Enabling power: S.I. 1984/1821 (N.I. 11), art. 10 (1) (3) (4) (5). - Issued: 13.06.2014. Made: 09.06.2014. Coming into operation: 01.07.2014. Effect: S.R. 2007/144 amended. Territorial extent & classification: NI. General. - 24p.: 30 cm. - 978-0-337-99440-1 £6.00

The Firefighters' Pension Scheme (Amendment) Order (Northern Ireland) 2014 No. 2014/56. - Enabling power: S.I. 1984/1821 (N.I. 11), art. 10 (1) (3) (4) (5). - Issued: 05.03.2014. Made: 27.02.2014. Coming into operation: 01.04.2014. Effect: S.R. 2007/144 amended & S.R. 2013/85 revoked. Territorial extent & classification: NI. General. - 4p.: 30 cm. - 978-0-337-99290-2 £4.00

The New Firefighters' Pension Scheme (Amendment) (No. 2) Order (Northern Ireland) 2014 No. 2014/168. - Enabling power: S.I. 1984/1821 (N.I. 11), art. 10 (1) (3) (4) (5). - Issued: 13.06.2014. Made: 09.06.2014. Coming into operation: 01.07.2014. Effect: S.R. 2007/215 amended. Territorial extent & classification: NI. General. - 8p.: 30 cm. - 978-0-337-99439-5 £6.00

The New Firefighters' Pension Scheme (Amendment) Order (Northern Ireland) 2014 No. 2014/57. - Enabling power: S.I. 1984/1821 (N.I. 11), art. 10 (1) (3) (4) (5). - Issued: 05.03.2014. Made: 27.02.2014. Coming into operation: 01.04.2014. Effect: S.R. 2007/215 amended & S.R. 2013/84 partially revoked. Territorial extent & classification: NI. General. - 4p.: 30 cm. - 978-0-337-99291-9 £4.00

Fisheries

Fisheries Regulations (Northern Ireland) 2014 No. 2014/17. - Enabling power: Fisheries Act (Northern Ireland) 1966, ss. 26 (1), 37, 51 (2), 52 (2), 71 (2) (g), 72 (1), 89, 95, 114 (1) (b) and 115 (1) (b). - Issued: 30.01.2014. Made: 21.01.2014. Coming into operation: 01.03.2014. Effect: S.R. 2003/525; 2004/504; 2005/548; 2006/517; 2007/471; 2008/318, 475; 2010/196; 2011/324; 2012/397 revoked. Territorial extent & classification: NI. General. - 4p.: 30 cm. - 978-0-337-99258-2 £4.00

The Foyle Area (Complimentary Angling Permit) (River Finn and River Foyle) Regulations 2014 No. 2014/299. - Enabling power: Foyle Fisheries Act 1952, ss. 13 (1) (k), 14B (1) (2) & Foyle Fisheries Act (Northern Ireland) 1952, s. 13 (1) (k), 14B (1) (2). - Issued: 12.12.2014. Made: 05.12.2014. Coming into operation: 01.01.2015. Effect: None. - 4p.: 30 cm. - 978-0-337-99538-5 £4.25

Salmon Drift Net Regulations (Northern Ireland) 2014 No. 2014/16. - Enabling power: Fisheries Act (Northern Ireland) 1996, s. 70 (1). - Issued: 30.01.2014. Made: 21.01.2014. Coming into operation: 01.03.2014. Effect: None. Territorial extent & classification: NI. General. - EC Note: Prohibits use of drift nets to catch & kill salmon in tidal water towards fulfillment of obligations under Council Directive 92/43/EEC. - 4p.: 30 cm. - 978-0-337-99257-5 £4.00

Salmon Netting Regulations (Northern Ireland) 2014 No. 2014/15. - Enabling power: Fisheries Act (Northern Ireland) 1996, s. 26 (1) & European Communities Act 1972, s. 2 (2). - Issued: 30.01.2014. Made: 21.01.2014. Coming into operation: 01.03.2014. Effect: None. Territorial extent & classification: NI. General. - EC Note: Prohibits use of bag nets, draft nets & tidal draft nets to catch & kill salmon in tidal water and Lough Neagh towards fulfillment of obligations under Council Directive 92/43/EEC. - 4p.: 30 cm. - 978-0-337-99256-8 £4.00

Food

The Deregulation (Improvement of Enforcement Procedures) (Food Safety) (Revocation) Order (Northern Ireland) 2014 No. 2014/10. - Enabling power: S.I. 1996/1632 (N.I.11), art. 9 (1) (4), sch. 1, para. 3. - Issued: 23.01.2014. Made: 20.01.2014. Coming into operation: 17.02.2014. Effect: S.R. 1996/579 revoked. Territorial extent & classification: NI. General. - 2p.: 30 cm. - 978-0-337-99252-0 £4.00

The Fish Labelling (Amendment) Regulations (Northern Ireland) 2014 No. 2014/287. - Enabling power: S.I. 1991/762 (N.I.7) arts. 15 (1),16 (2), 25 (2), 26 (3), 47 (2) & European Communities Act 1972, sch 2, para. 1A. - Issued: 24.11.2014. Made: 19.11.2014. Coming into operation: 13.12.2014. Effect: S.I. 2013/219 amended. Territorial extent and classification: NI. General. - EC note: These Regulations enforce in Northern Ireland the consumer information requirements in Chapter IV of Reg (EC) no. 1379/2013 on the common organisation of the markets in fishery and aquaculture products. - 4p.: 30 cm. - 978-0-337-99520-0 £4.25

The Food Hygiene (Amendment) Regulations (Northern Ireland) 2014 No. 2014/277. - Enabling power: European Communities Act 1972, s. 2 (2). - Issued: 12.11.2014. Made: 05.11.2014. Coming into operation: 13.12.2014. Effect: S.R. 2006/3 amended. Territorial extent & classification: NI. General. - EC note: These Regulations implement Commission Regulation (EU) No. 216/2014 amending Regulation (EC) No. 2075/2005 laying down specific rules on Trichinella in meat (regulation 2(3)). With correction slip dated November 2014. - 4p: 30 cm. - 978-0-337-99515-6 £4.25

The Food Hygiene and Official Feed and Food Controls (Amendment) Regulations (Northern Ireland) 2014 No. 2014/286. - Enabling power: European Communities Act 1972, s. 2 (2), sch. 2, para. 1A. - Issued: 24.11.2014. Made: 19.11.2014. Coming into operation: 13.12.2014. Effect: S.R. 2006/3, 247 amended. Territorial extent & classification: NI. General. - With correction slip dated December 2014. - 4p: 30 cm. - 978-0-337-99521-7 £4.25

The Food Information Regulations (Northern Ireland) 2014 No. 2014/223. - Enabling power: S.I. 1991/762 (N.I. 7), arts. 15 (1), 16, 17, 25, 26 (3), 44, 47 (2), sch. 1, paras 1, 4 (b) & European Communities Act 1972, s. 2 (2), sch. 2, para. 1A. - Issued: 27.08.2014. Made: 21.08.2014. Coming into operation: In accord. with reg. 1(2) to (5). Effect: 19 SRs amended & 18 SRs partially revoked & 12 SRs revoked. Territorial extent and classification: NI. General. - EC note: These Regulations make provision to enforce certain provisions of Regulation (EU) No 1169/2011 on the provision of food information to consumers, amending Regulations (EC) No 1924/2006 and (EC) No 1925/2006 and repealing Commission Directive 87/250/EEC, Council Directive 90/496/EEC, Commission Directive 1999/10/EC, Directive 2000/13/EC, Commission Directives 2002/67/EC and 2008/5/EC and Commission Regulation (EC) No 608/2004. They also implement certain provisions of Article 6 of Directive 1999/2/EC concerning foods and food ingredients treated with ionising radiation and the second paragraph of subparagraph 1 of Article 3 of Directive 2000/36/EC relating to cocoa and chocolate products intended for human consumption. - 32p: 30 cm. - 978-0-337-99484-5 £10.00

The Infant Formula and Follow-on Formula (Amendment) Regulations (Northern Ireland) 2014 No. 2014/11. - Enabling power: S.I. 1991/762 (N.I. 7), arts. 15 (1) (e), 16 (1), 47 (2) & European Communities Act 1972, s. 2 (2). - Issued: 23.01.2014. Made: 20.01.2014. Coming into force: 28.02.2014. Effect: S.R. 2007/506 amended. Territorial extent & classification: NI. General. - EC note: These regs implement in Northern Ireland, Commission Directive 2013/46/EU. With correction slip dated February 2014. - 4p.: 30 cm. - 978-0-337-99253-7 £4.00

The Products Containing Meat etc. Regulations (Northern Ireland) 2014 No. 2014/285. - Enabling power: S.I. 1991/762 (N.I. 7), arts 15 (1) (a) (e) (f), 25 (1) (a) (2) (a) (2) (e) (3), 26 (3), 47 (2). - Issued: 21.11.2014. Made: 18.11.2014. Coming into operation: 13.12.2014. Effect: S.R. 2004/13; 2008/82; 2009/416 revoked. - 16p: 30 cm. - 978-0-337-99522-4 £6.00

Gas

The Gas (Individual Standards of Performance) Regulations (Northern Ireland) 2014 No. 2014/60. - Enabling power: Energy Act (Northern Ireland) 2011, ss. 1, 2. - Issued: 05.03.2014. Made: 03.03.2014. Coming into operation: 01.04.2014. Effect: None. Territorial extent & classification: NI. General. - 24p.: 30 cm. - 978-0-337-99294-0 £5.75

Government resources and accounts

The Whole of Government Accounts (Designation of Bodies) Order (Northern Ireland) 2014 No. 2014/110. - Enabling power: Government Resources and Accounts Act (Northern Ireland) 2001, s. 15 (1). - Issued: 15.04.2014. Made: 10.04.2014. Coming into operation: 05.05.2014. Effect: None. Territorial extent & classification: NI. General. - 8p.: 30 cm. - 978-0-337-99396-1 £6.00

Health and personal social services

The General Dental Services (Amendment No. 2) Regulations (Northern Ireland) 2014 No. 2014/319. - Enabling power: S.I. 1972/1265 (N.I. 14), arts 55 A (1) (a), 61 (1), (2) (2AA), 106, 107 (6). - Issued: 23.12.2014. Made: 17.12.2014. Coming into operation: 12.01.2015. Effect: S.R. 1993/326 amended. Territorial extent and classification: NI. General. - 4p.: 30 cm. - 978-0-337-99553-8 £4.25

General Dental Services (Amendment) Regulations (Northern Ireland) 2014 No. 2014/3. - Enabling power: S.I. 1972/1265 (N.I. 14), arts 61 (1) (2) (2AA), 106, 107 (6). - Issued: 13.01.2014. Made: 08.01.2014. Coming into operation: 31.03.2014. Effect: S.R. 1993/326 amended. Territorial extent and classification: NI. General. - 4p.: 30 cm. - 978-0-337-99250-6 £4.00

The General Ophthalmic Services (Amendment) Regulations (Northern Ireland) 2014 No. 2014/2. - Enabling power: S.I. 1972/1265 (N.I. 14), arts. 62, 95, 106. - Issued: 13.01.2014. Made: 08.01.2014. Coming into operation: 03.02.2014. Effect: S.R. 2007/436 amended. - 4p.: 30 cm. - 978-0-337-99249-0 £4.00

The Health and Personal Social Services (General Medical Services Contracts) (Prescription of Drugs Etc) (Amendment) Regulations (Northern Ireland) 2014 No. 2014/215. - Enabling power: S.I. 1972/1265 (N.I. 14), arts 57D, 106 (b). - Issued: 28.07.2014. Made: 24.07.2014. Coming into operation: 01.09.2014. Effect: S.R. 2004/142 amended. Territorial extent and classification: NI. General. - 2p.: 30 cm. - 978-0-337-99477-7 £4.25

The Health and Personal Social Services (Superannuation), Health and Social Care (Pension Scheme) (Amendment No. 2) Regulations (Northern Ireland) 2014 No. 2014/225. - Enabling power: S.I. 1972/1073 (N.I. 10), arts 12 (1) (2), 14 (1) (2) (3), sch. 3. - Issued: 22.09.2014. Made: 12.09.2014. Coming into operation: 15.10.2014. Effect: S.R. 1995/95; 2008/256 amended. Territorial extent & classification: NI. General. - 12p.: 30 cm. - 978-0-337-99487-6 £6.00

The Health and Personal Social Services (Superannuation), Health and Social Care (Pension Scheme) (Amendment) Regulations (Northern Ireland) 2014 No. 2014/59. - Enabling power: S.I. 1972/1073 (N.I. 10), arts 12 (1) (2), 14 (1), sch. 3- Issued: 05.13.2014. Made: 03.03.2014. Coming into operation: 01.04.2014. Effect: S.R. 1995/95; 2008/256 amended. Territorial extent & classification: NI. General. - 8p.: 30 cm. - 978-0-337-99293-3 £5.75

Optical Charges and Payments (Amendment) Regulations (Northern Ireland) 2014 No. 2014/154. - Enabling power: S.I 1972/1265 (N.I. 14), arts 62, 98, 106, 107 (6), sch. 15. - Issued: 09.06.2014. Made: 04.06.2014. Coming into operation: 01.07.2014. Effect: S.R. 1997/191 amended. Territorial extent and classification: NI. General. - 8p.: 30 cm. - 978-0-337-99428-9 £4.25

The Pharmaceutical Services (Amendment) Regulations (Northern Ireland) 2014 No. 2014/170. - Enabling power: S.I. 1972/1265 (N.I. 14), arts. 63 (1) (2), 106 (b), 107 (6). - Issued: 13.06.2014. Made: 10.06.2014. Coming into operation: 18.07.2014. Effect: S.R. 1997/381 amended. Territorial extent & classification: NI. General. - With correction slip dated June 2014. - 2p.: 30 cm. - 978-0-337-99441-8 £4.25

Health and safety

The Control of Explosives Precursors etc. Regulations (Northern Ireland) 2014 No. 2014/224. - Enabling power: S.I. 1978/1039 (NI. 9), arts. 3 (1) (c) (2) (4), 17, 40 (2) (3) (4), 54 (1) (2) (b) (3), 55 (2); sch. 3 paras. 1 (1) (4), 2, 3, 5, 14 (1), 15, 22. - Issued: 09.09.2014. Made: 28.08.2014. Laid: 08 .09.2014. Coming into force: 02.09.2014. Effect: 1970 c.10; S.I. 1978/1039 (NI.9) amended & S.R. 1977/128 partially revoked & S.I. 1972/730 (NI.3), S.R. 1972/118, 218; 1973/171, 463; 1974/32; 1976/51; 1981/31; 1996/429 revoked. Territorial extent & classification: NI. General. - EC note: These Regulations implement Regulation (EU) no. 98/2013 on the marketing and use of explosives precursors in Northern Ireland. - With 2 correction slips dated October 2014. - 32p.: 30 cm. - 978-0-337-99485-2 £6.00

The Control of Major Accident Hazards (Amendment) Regulations (Northern Ireland) 2014 No. 2014/74. - Enabling power: European Communities Act 1972, s. 2 (2) & S.I. 1978/1039 (N.I. 9), arts 17(1) to (5), 40 (2) (4), 55(2), sch. 3, paras 1 (1) (2), 14 (1), 15, 19. - Issued: 14.03.2014. Made: 11.03.2014. Coming into operation: 07.04.2014. Effect: S.R. 2000/93 amended. Territorial extent & classification: NI. General. - EC note: These Regulations implement Article 30 of Directive 2012/18/EU of the European Parliament and of the Council on the control of major accident hazards involving dangerous substances. - 4p.: 30 cm. - 978-0-337-99308-4 £4.00

The Explosives (Hazard Information and Packaging for Supply) (Amendment No. 2) Regulations (Northern Ireland) 2014 No. 2014/47. - Enabling power: European Communities Act 1972, s. 2 (2) & S.I. 1978/1039 (N.I.9), arts 17(1) (2) (3) (4) (6), 55 (2). - Issued: 03.03.2014. Made: 25.02.2014. Coming into operation: 28.02.2014. Effect: S.R. 2009/273 amended & S.R. 2014/26 revoked. Territorial extent & classification: NI. General. - EC note: The Explosives (Hazard Information and Packaging for Supply) (Amendment No. 2) Regulations (Northern Ireland) 2014 replaces a reference in the Explosives (Hazard Information and Packaging for Supply) Regulations (Northern Ireland) 2009 to Regulation (EC) No. 689/2008 of the European Parliament and of the Council of 17 June 2008 with references to Regulation (EU) No. 649/2012 of the European Parliament and of the Council of 4 July 2012. - 4p.: 30 cm. - 978-0-337-99283-4 £4.00

The Explosives (Hazard Information and Packaging for Supply) (Amendment) Regulations (Northern Ireland) 2014 No. 2014/26. - Enabling power: European Communities Act 1972, s. 2 (2) & S.I. 1978/1039 (N.I.9), arts 17(1) (2) (3) (4) (6), 54, 55 (2). - Issued: 12.02.2014. Made: 07.02.2014. Coming into operation: 01.03.2014. Effect: S.R. 2009/273 amended. Territorial extent & classification: NI. General. - EC note: These Regulations replace references to Regulation (EC) 689/2008 with references to Regulation (EU) 649/2012121/EC. - Revoked by SR 2014/47 (ISBN 9780337992834). - 4p.: 30 cm. - 978-0-337-99267-4 £4.00

The Health and Safety (Fees) (Amendment) Regulations (Northern Ireland) 2014 No. 2014/280. - Enabling power: S.I. 1978/1039 (N.I. 9), arts. 40 (2) (4), 49, 55 (2). - Issued: 17.11.2014. Made: 13.11.2014. Coming into operation: 12.12.2014. Effect: S.R. 2012/255 amended. Territorial extent & classification: NI. General. - 4p: 30 cm. - 978-0-337-99518-7 £4.25

Health and social care

The Health and Social Care Bodies (Membership) Regulations (Northern Ireland) 2014 No. 2014/318. - Enabling power: Health and Social Care (Reform) Act (Northern Ireland) 2009, ss. 7 (2), 12 (2), 14 (2), sch. 1 para. 3, sch. 2 para. 3, sch. 3, paras. 3, 5. - Issued: 23.12.2014. Made: 16.12.2014. Coming into operation: 06.01.2015. Effect: SR. 2009/93, 95, 97 amended. Territorial extent & classification: NI. General. - 4p.: 30 cm. - 978-0-337-99552-1 £4.25

The Health and Social Care (Disciplinary Procedures) Regulations (Northern Ireland) 2014 No. 2014/267. - Enabling power: S.I. 1972/1265 (N.I. 4), arts 61 (4), 62 (3), 63 (3). - Issued: 29.10.2014. Made: 24.10.2014. Coming into operation: 24.11.2014. Effect: S.R. 1996/137 revoked. - 12p: 30 cm. - 978-0-337-99509-5 £6.00

The Safeguarding Board for Northern Ireland (Membership, Procedure, Functions and Committee) (Amendment No. 2) Regulations (Northern Ireland) 2014 No. 2014/293. - Enabling power: Safeguarding Board Act (Northern Ireland) 2011, ss. 1 (2) (b) (5) (b), 7 (4) (b). - Issued: 03.12.2014. Made: 28.11.2014. Laid before Parliament: -. Coming into operation: 01.01.2015. Effect: S.R. 2012/324 amended. Territorial extent & classification: NI. General. - With correction slip dated December 2014. - 4p.: 30 cm. - 978-0-337-99530-9 £4.25

The Safeguarding Board for Northern Ireland (Membership, Procedure, Functions and Committee) (Amendment) Regulations (Northern Ireland) 2014 No. 2014/111. - Enabling power: Safeguarding Board Act (Northern Ireland) 2011, s. 3 (4). - Issued: 16.04.2014. Made: 11.04.2014. Laid before Parliament: -. Coming into operation: 02.05.2014. Effect: S.R. 2012/324 amended. Territorial extent & classification: NI. General. - 4p.: 30 cm. - 978-0-337-99397-8 £4.25

Health services charges

The Recovery of Health Services Charges (Amounts) (Amendment) Regulations (Northern Ireland) 2014 No. 2014/108. - Enabling power: S.I. 2006/1944 (N.I. 13), arts 5 (2) (5), 19 (3). - Issued: 15.04.2014. Made: 09.04.2014. Coming into operation: 30.04.2014. Effect: S.R. 2006/507 amended. Territorial extent & classification: NI. General. - 4p.: 30 cm. - 978-0-337-99395-4 £4.25

Housing

The Housing Benefit (Habitual Residence) (Amendment) Regulations (Northern Ireland) 2014 No. 2014/98. - Enabling power: Social Security Contributions and Benefits (Northern Ireland) Act 1992, ss. 122 (1) (d), 133 (2) (i), 171 (1) (3) (4). - Issued: 28.03.2014. Made: 26.03.2014. Coming into operation: 01.04.2014. Effect: S.R. 2006/405 amended. Territorial extent & classification: NI. General. - 4p.: 30 cm. - 978-0-337-99383-1 £4.00

The Jobseeker's Allowance (Schemes for Assisting Persons to Obtain Employment) Regulations (Northern Ireland) 2014 No. 2014/150. - Enabling power: Social security Contributions and Benefits (Northern Ireland) Act 1992, ss. 122 (1) (a) (d), 132 (3) (4) (a) (b), 171 (1) (3) (4) & S.I. 1995/2705 (N.I. 15), arts. 14 (1) (4) (a) (b), 19A (1) (2) (5) (a) (b) (d) to (f) (6) to (9), 22, 22A, 22B (4) to (6), 22E (3) (a), 36 (2) & S.I. 1998/1506 (N.I. 10), arts 10, 11, 74 (1) & S.I. 2003/412 (N.I. 2), arts 141, 148 (1) & 2007 c.2 (N.I.), s. 17 (1) (3) (a) (b). - Issued: 04.06.2014. Made: 30.05.2014. Coming into operation: 02.06.2014. Effect: S.R. 1975/113; 1987/459; 1996/198; 1999/162; 2001/216; 2002/79; 2004/8; 2006/405, 406; 2008/280 amended. Territorial extent & classification: NI. General. - 16p.: 30 cm. - 978-0-337-99425-8 £6.00

The Secure Tenancies (Notice) Regulations (Northern Ireland) 2014 No. 2014/103. - Enabling power: S.I. 1983/1118 (N.I. 15), arts. 28 (2) (a), 106 (1). - Issued: 03.04.2014. Made: 27.03.2014. Coming into operation: 05.05.2014. Effect: S.R. 1983/285; 2003/411 revoked. Territorial extent & classification: NI. General. - With correction slip dated May 2014. - 8p.: 30 cm. - 978-0-337-99390-9 £6.00

The Social Security Benefits Up-rating Order (Northern Ireland) 2014 No. 2014/78. - Enabling power: Social Security Administration (Northern Ireland) Act 1992, ss. 132, 132A, 165(1) (4) (5). - Issued: 17.03.2014. Made: 13.03.2014. Coming into operation: In accord. with art. 1. Effect: 1966 c.6 (N.I.); 1992 c.7; S.R. 1987/30, 459; 1992/32; 1994/461; 1995/35; 1996/198; 2002/380; 2003/28; 2006/405, 406; 2008/280; 2010/302, 407 amended & S.R. 2013/69 revoked (14.04.2014). Territorial extent & classification: NI. General. - For approval of the Assembly before the expiration of six months from the date of its coming into operation. Superseded by Approved SR 2014/78 (ISBN 9780337993138). - 44p.: 30 cm. - 978-0-337-99313-8 £9.75

The Social Security Benefits Up-rating Order (Northern Ireland) 2014 No. 2014/78. - Enabling power: Social Security Administration (Northern Ireland) Act 1992, ss. 132, 132A, 165(1) (4) (5). - Issued: 13.06.2014. Made: 13.03.2014. Coming into operation: In accord. with art. 1. Effect: 1966 c.6 (N.I.); 1992 c.7; S.R. 1987/30, 459; 1992/32; 1994/461; 1995/35; 1996/198; 2002/380; 2003/28; 2006/405, 406; 2008/280; 2010/302, 407 amended & S.R. 2013/69 revoked (14.04.2014). Territorial extent & classification: NI. General. - Approved by resolution of the Assembly on 9th June 2014; Revoked by SR 2015/124 (ISBN 9780337996634). - 44p.: 30 cm. - 978-0-337-99438-8 £9.75

The Social Security (Habitual Residence) (Amendment) Regulations (Northern Ireland) 2014 No. 2014/133. - Enabling power: Social Security Contributions and Benefits (Northern Ireland) Act 1992, ss. 122 (1) (a) (d), 131 (1) (2), 171 (1) (3) (4) & S.I. 1995/2705 (N.I. 15), arts 6 (5) (12), 36 (2) & Immigration and Asylum Act 1999, ss. 115 (3) (4) (8) & State Pension Credit Act (Northern Ireland) 2002, ss. 1 (5) (a), 19 (1) (2) (a) (3) & Welfare Reform Act (Northern Ireland) 2007, ss. 4 (3), 25 (2). - Issued: 12.05.2014. Made: 08.05.2014. Coming into operation: 31.05.2014. Effect: S.R. 1987/459; 1996/198; 2003/28; 2006/405, 406; 2008/280 amended & S.R. 2013/167 partially revoked. Territorial extent & classification: NI. General. - 4p.: 30 cm. - 978-0-337-99410-4 £4.25

The Social Security (Miscellaneous Amendments No. 2) Regulations (Northern Ireland) 2014 No. 2014/105. - Enabling power: Social Security Contributions and Benefits (Northern Ireland) Act 1992, ss. 122 (1) (a) (d), 132 (3) (40, 132A, 171 (1) (3) (4) & Social Security Administration (Northern Ireland) Act 1992, ss. 5 (1) (a), 109A (2) (b), 165 (1) (4) to (6) & S.I. 1995/2705 (N.I. 15), arts. 14 (4), 36 (2) (a) & State Pension Credit Act (Northern Ireland) 2002, ss. 15 (3) (6), 19 (1) to (3) & Welfare reform Act (Northern Ireland) 2007, ss. 17 (1), 25 (2). - Issued: 11.04.2014. Made: 07.04.2014. Coming into operation: 28.04.2014. Effect: S.R. 1987/459, 465; 1996/198; 2003/28; 2006/405, 406; 2008/280 amended & S.R. 2009/338 partially revoked. Territorial extent & classification: NI. General. - With correction slip dated April 2014. - 8p.: 30 cm. - 978-0-337-99392-3 £6.00

Human rights

The Attorney General's Human Rights Guidance (Northern Ireland Courts and Tribunals Service - Support for Victims and Witnesses) Order (Northern Ireland) 2014 No. 2014/274. - Enabling power: Justice (Northern Ireland) Act 2004, s. 8 (3) (c). - Issued: 06.11.2014. Made: 31.10.2014. Coming into operation: 15.12.2014. Effect: None. - EC note: This Order brings into operation guidance by the Attorney General for Northern Ireland, pursuant to section 8 of the Justice (Northern Ireland) Act 2004, which was laid before the Assembly on 8th October 2014. - 2p: 30 cm. - 978-0-337-99511-8 £4.25

The Attorney General's Human Rights Guidance (Northern Ireland Prison Service - Conditions of Imprisonment) Order (Northern Ireland) 2014 No. 2014/132. - Enabling power: Justice (Northern Ireland) Act 2004, s. 8 (3) (c). - Issued: 12.05.2012. Made: 06.05.2014. Coming into operation: 09.06.2014. Effect: None. Territorial extent & classification: NI. General. - 2p.: 30 cm. - 978-0-337-99409-8 £4.25

The Attorney General's Human Rights Guidance (Northern Ireland Prison Service - Prison Order and Discipline) Order (Northern Ireland) 2014 No. 2014/152. - Enabling power: Justice (Northern Ireland) Act 2004, s. 8 (3) (c). - Issued: 04.06.2014. Made: 02.06.2014. Coming into operation: 07.07.2014. Effect: None. Territorial extent & classification: NI. General. - 2p.: 30 cm. - 978-0-337-99427-2 £4.25

The Attorney General's Human Rights Guidance (Public Prosecution Service for Northern Ireland) Order (Northern Ireland) 2014 No. 2014/131. - Enabling power: Justice (Northern Ireland) Act 2004, s. 8 (3) (c). - Issued: 12.05.2012. Made: 06.05.2014. Coming into operation: 09.06.2014. Effect: None. Territorial extent & classification: NI. General. - 2p.: 30 cm. - 978-0-337-99408-1 £4.25

Industrial training

The Industrial Training Levy (Construction Industry) Order (Northern Ireland) 2014 No. 2014/173. - Enabling power: S.I. 1984/1159 (N.I. 9), arts 23 (2) (3), 24 (3) (4). - Issued: 16.06.2014. Made: 05.06.2014. Coming into operation: 31.08.2014. Effect: None. Territorial extent & classification: NI. General. - 8p.: 30 cm. - 978-0-337-99444-9 £4.25

Justice

The Criminal Justice (2013 Act) (Commencement No.3) Order (Northern Ireland) 2014 No. 2014/53 (C.2). - Enabling power: Criminal Justice Act (Northern Ireland) 2013, s. 15 (2) (a). Bringing various provisions of the 2013 Act into operation 01.04.2014 in accord. with art. 2. - Issued: 08.04.2014. Made: 03.02.2014. Coming into operation: -. Effect: None. Territorial extent & classification: NI. General. - 2p.: 30 cm. - 978-0-337-99391-6 £4.25

The Criminal Justice (2013 Act) (Commencement No.4) Order (Northern Ireland) 2014 No. 2014/179 (C.11) . - Enabling power: Criminal Justice Act (Northern Ireland) Act 2013, s. 15 (2) (b) (c). Bringing various provisions of the 2013 Act into operation 24.06.2014 in accord. with art. 2. - Issued: 25.06.2014. Made: 19.06.2014. Coming into operation: -. Effect: None. Territorial extent & classification: NI. General. - 2p.: 30 cm. - 978-0-337-99449-4 £4.25

The Justice (Northern Ireland) Act 2002 (Amendment of section 46(1)) Order (Northern Ireland) 2014 No. 2014/322. - Enabling power: Justice (Northern Ireland) Act 2002, s. 46 (6). - Issued: 03.02.2015. Made: 19.12.2014. Coming into operation: In accord. with art. 1 (2). Effect: 2002 c.26 amended. Territorial extent & classification: NI. General. - Laid before Assembly in draft which was withdrawn after publication. - 2p.: 30 cm. - 978-0-337-99588-0 £4.25

Landlord and tenant

The Landlord Registration Scheme Regulations (Northern Ireland) 2014 No. 2014/9. - Enabling power: S.I. 2006/1459 (N.I. 10), arts 65A (1) (2), 73 (1). - Issued: 22.01.2014. Made: 15.01.2014. Coming into operation: 25.02.2014. Effect: None. Territorial extent & classification: NI. General. - 8p.: 30 cm. - 978-0-337-99251-3 £5.75

The Registered Rents (Increase) Order (Northern Ireland) 2014 No. 2014/101. - Enabling power: S.I. 2006/1459 (N.I. 10), art. 55 (5) (6). - Issued: 02.04.2014. Made: 26.03.2014. Coming into operation: 05.05.2014. Effect: None. Territorial extent & classification: NI. General. - 2p.: 30 cm. - 978-0-337-99386-2 £4.25

Land registration

The Land Registry (Fees) Order (Northern Ireland) 2014 No. 2014/139. - Enabling power: Land Registration Act (Northern Ireland) 1970, s. 84 (1) & Ground Rents Act (Northern Ireland) 2001 s. 26 (1). - Issued: 21.05.2014. Made: 16.05.2014. Coming into operation: 08.09.2014. Effect: S.R. 2011/348 revoked. Territorial extent and classification: NI. General. - Subject to affirmative resolution procedure of the Assembly. - 12p: 30 cm. - 978-0-337-99417-3 £6.00

Lands Tribunal

The Lands Tribunal (Salaries) Order (Northern Ireland) 2014 No. 2014/259. - Enabling power: Lands Tribunal and Compensation Act (Northern Ireland) 1964, s. 2 (5) & Administrative and Financial Provisions Act (Northern Ireland) 1962, s. 18. - Issued: 20.10.2014. Made: 15.10.2014. Coming into operation: 16.10.2014. Effect: S.R. 2013/239 revoked. Territorial extent & classification: NI. General. - Supersedes draft S.R. (ISBN 9780337994531) issued 27.06.2014. - 4p.: 30 cm. - 978-0-337-99504-0 £4.25

Legal aid and advice

The Legal Aid (General) (Amendment) Regulations (Northern Ireland) 2014 No. 2014/64. - Enabling power: S.I. 1981/228 (N.I. 8), arts 22, 27. - Issued: 07.03.2014. Made: 03.03.2014. Coming into operation: 01.04.2014. Effect: S.R & O.(NI) 1965/217 amended. Territorial extent & classification: NI. General. - 4p.: 30 cm. - 978-0-337-99298-8 £4.00

The Magistrates' Courts and County Court Appeals (Criminal Legal Aid) (Costs) (Amendment) Rules (Northern Ireland) 2014 No. 2014/178. - Enabling power: S.I. 1981/228 (N.I.8), art. 36 (3). - Issued: 23.06.2014. Made: 17.06.2014. Coming into operation: 26.06.2014. Effect: S.R. 2009/313 amended. Territorial extent and classification: NI. General. - 8p.: 30 cm. - 978-0-337-99448-7 £6.00

Local government

The Local Government (2014 Act) (Commencement No. 1) Order (Northern Ireland) 2014 No. 2014/142 (C.7). - Enabling power: Local Government Act (Northern Ireland) 2014 , s. 129. Bringing into operation various provisions of the 2014 Act on 20.05.2014, in accord. with art. 2. - Issued: 22.05.2014. Made: 20.05.2014. Effect: None. Territorial extent and classification: NI. General. - 2p.: 30 cm. - 978-0-337-99418-0 £4.25

The Local Government (2014 Act) (Commencement No. 2) Order (Northern Ireland) 2014 No. 2014/153 (C.8). - Enabling power: Local Government Act (Northern Ireland) 2014 , s. 129. Bringing into operation various provisions of the 2014 Act on 02.06.2014, in accord. with art. 2. - Issued: 13.06.2014. Made: 02.06.2014. Effect: None. Territorial extent and classification: NI. General. - With correction slip dated June 2014. - 8p.: 30 cm. - 978-0-337-99437-1 £4.25

Local Government (Disqualification) (Prescribed Offices and Employments) Regulations (Northern Ireland) 2014 No. 2014/292. - Enabling power: Local Government Act (Northern Ireland) 1972, s. 4 (1). - Issued: 01.12.2014. Made: 26.11.2014. Coming into operation: 01.02.2015. Effect: None. Territorial extent & classification: NI. General. - 2p.: 30 cm. - 978-0-337-99526-2 £4.25

The Local Government (Indemnities for Members and Officers) (Amendment) Order (Northern Ireland) 2014 No. 2014/264. - Enabling power: Local Government (Northern Ireland) Order 2005, art. 33. - Issued: 27.10.2014. Made: 22.10.2014. Coming into operation: 01.11.2014. Effect: S.R. 2012/422 amended. Territorial extent & classification: NI. General. - Approved. - 4p.: 30 cm. - 978-0-337-99507-1 £4.25

The Local Government Pension Scheme (Amendment and Transitional Provisions) Regulations (Northern Ireland) 2014 No. 2014/189. - Enabling power: S.I. 1972/1073 (N.I. 10), arts 9, 14, sch. 3. - Issued: 03.07.2014. Made: 30.06.2014. Coming into operation: 01.04.2015. Effect: S.R. 2000/177; 2002/352; 2009/32, 33; 2012/183; 2013/71 partially revoked & S.R. 2009/34; 2010/410; 2011/117 revoked. Territorial extent & classification: NI. General. - 36p.: 30 cm. - 978-0-337-99464-7 £10.00

The Local Government Pension Scheme Regulations (Northern Ireland) 2014 No. 2014/188. - Enabling power: S.I. 1972/1073 (N.I. 10), art. 9, sch. 3. - Issued: 03.07.2014. Made: 27.06.2014. Coming into operation: 01.04.2015. Effect: None. Territorial extent & classification: NI. General. - With correction slip dated July 2014. - 92p.: 30 cm. - 978-0-337-99461-6 £16.00

The Local Government (Transitional, Supplementary, Incidental Provisions and Modifications) Regulations (Northern Ireland) 2014 No. 2014/148. - Enabling power: Local Government (Miscellaneous Provisions) Act (Northern Ireland) 2010, s. 20 & Local Government Act (Northern Ireland) 2014, ss. 38, 124. - Issued: 02.06.2014. Made: 28.05.2014. Coming into operation: 28.05.2014. Effect: 1972 c.9 (NI) & 2014 c.8 (NI) modified. Territorial extent & classification: NI. General. - Supersedes draft SI (ISBN 9780337994227) issued 28.05.2014- 12p.: 30 cm. - 978-0-337-99424-1 £6.00

Magistrates' courts

The Magistrates' Courts (Amendment) Rules (Northern Ireland) 2014 No. 2014/12. - Enabling power: S.I. 1981/1675 (N.I. 26), art. 13. - Issued: 24.01.2014. Made: 17.01.2014. Coming into operation: 17.02.2014. Effect: S.R. 1984/225 amended. Territorial extent & classification: NI. General. - 8p.: 30 cm. - 978-0-337-99254-4 £5.75

Magistrates' courts: Procedure

The Magistrates' Courts (Amendment No. 2) Rules (Northern Ireland) 2014 No. 2014/221. - Enabling power: S.I. 1981/1675 (N.I. 26), art. 13. - Issued: 11.08.2014. Made: 04.08.2014. Coming into operation: 05.09.2014. Effect: S.R. 1984/225 amended. Territorial extent & classification: NI. General. - 4p.: 30 cm. - 978-0-337-99482-1 £4.25

Marriage

The Marriage (Amendment) Regulations (Northern Ireland) 2014 No. 2014/296. - Enabling power: S.I. 2003/413 (N.I. 3), arts. 3 (3), 8 (4), 21 (4), 39 (2). - Issued: 10.12.2014. Made: 04.10.2014. Coming into operation: 02.03.2015. Effect: S.R. 2003/468 amended. Territorial extent and classification: NI. General. - 2p.: 30 cm. - 978-0-337-99534-7 £4.25

Medicines

The Human Medicines (Amendment) (No. 2) Regulations 2014 No. 2014/324. - Enabling power: European Communities Act 1972, s. 2 (2) (5). - Issued: 02.03.2015. Made: 16.07.2014. Laid: 18.07.2014. Coming into operation: 01.10.2015 in accord. with art. 1. Effect: S.I. 2012/1916 amended. Territorial extent & classification: NI. General. - 12p.: 30 cm. - 978-0-337-99636-8 £6.00

The Human Medicines (Amendment) Regulations 2014 No. 2014/323. - Enabling power: European Communities Act 1972, s. 2 (2) (5). - Issued: 02.03.2015. Made: 04.03.2015. Laid: 10.03.2014. Coming into operation: 31.03.2015. Effect: S.I. 2012/1916 amended. Territorial extent & classification: NI. General. - 8p.: 30 cm. - 978-0-337-99633-7 £6.00

Pensions

The Automatic Enrolment (Earnings Trigger and Qualifying Earnings Band) Order (Northern Ireland) 2014 No. 2014/81. - Enabling power: Pensions (No. 2) Act (Northern Ireland) 2008, ss. 14, 15A(1). - Issued: 19.03.2014. Made: 14.03.2014. Coming into operation: 06.04.2014. Effect: 2008 c.13 (N.I.) amended & S.R. 2013/79 partially revoked. Territorial extent & classification: NI. General. - Partially revoked by SR 2015/119 (ISBN 9780337996610). - 4p.: 30 cm. - 978-0-337-99314-5 £4.00

The Guaranteed Minimum Pensions Increase Order (Northern Ireland) 2014 No. 2014/75. - Enabling power: Pension Schemes (Northern Ireland) Act 1993, s. 105. - Issued: 17.03.2014. Made: 12.03.2014. Coming into operation: 06.04.2014. Effect: None. Territorial extent & classification: NI. General. - 2p.: 30 cm. - 978-0-337-99309-1 £4.00

The Occupational and Personal Pension Schemes (Automatic Enrolment) (Amendment) Regulations (Northern Ireland) 2014 No. 2014/87. - Enabling power: Pensions (No. 2) Act (Northern Ireland) 2008, ss. 16 (3) (c), 28 (2) (b). - Issued: 21.03.2014. Made: 19.03.2014. Coming into operation: 01.04.2014. Effect: S.R. 2010/122 amended & S.R. 2012/237, 390 partially revoked. Territorial extent & classification: NI. General. - For approval of the Assembly before the expiration of six months from the date of their coming into operation. - 4p.: 30 cm. - 978-0-337-99318-3 £4.00

The Occupational and Personal Pension Schemes (Automatic Enrolment) (Amendment) Regulations (Northern Ireland) 2014 No. 2014/89. - Enabling power: Pensions (No. 2) Act (Northern Ireland) 2008, ss. 16 (3) (c), 28 (2) (b). - Issued: 19.06.2014. Made: 19.03.2014. Coming into operation: 01.04.2014. Effect: S.R. 2010/122 amended & S.R. 2012/237, 390 partially revoked. Territorial extent & classification: NI. General. - Approved by resolution of the Assembly on 16th June 2014. - 4p.: 30 cm. - 978-0-337-99446-3 £4.25

The Occupational and Personal Pension Schemes (Disclosure of Information) Regulations (Northern Ireland) 2014 No. 2014/79. - Enabling power: Pension Schemes (Northern Ireland) Act 1993, ss. 109, 164 (1) (4), 177 (2) to (4), 178 (1) & S.I. 1995/3213 (N.I. 22), arts 10 (3), 41 (1) (5) (5A) (6), 166 (1) to (3) & S.I. 1999/3147 (N.I. 11), arts 3 (1) (b), 21 (1) (a) (b) (i) (c) (i) (2), 31 (1) (b) (ii), 42 (1), 73 (3) (4). - Issued: 18.03.2014. Made: 13.03.2014. Coming into operation: 06.04.2014. Effect: S.R. 1991/37; 1996/493, 619, 621; 1997/40, 159; 2000/142, 146, 262, 349; 2002/74; 2005/169, 171; 2006/48, 161; 2012/120 amended & S.R. 1988/107; 1992/304; 1994/300; 1995/7; 1996/95, 508; 1997/160; 1999/486; 2000/262, 335, 349; 2002/74, 410; 2003/256; 2005/170, 171, 568; 2006/65, 297; 2007/185; 2008/116; 2009/115; 2010/373; 2011/89; 2012/120, 294 partially revoked & S.R. 1987/288; 1997/98; 2012/331 revoked. - 48p.: 30 cm. - 978-0-337-99312-1 £9.75

The Occupational Pension Schemes (Miscellaneous Amendments) Regulations (Northern Ireland) 2014 No. 2014/93. - Enabling power: Pension Schemes (Northern Ireland) Act 1993, ss. 15 (4) (c), 177 (2) (3) & S.I. 1995/3213 (N.I. 22), arts 47 (5) (b), 87 (2), 166 (1) to (3) & S.I. 2005/255 (N.I. 1), art. 235 (7). - Issued: 25.03.2014. Made: 20.03.2014. Coming into operation: 06.04.2014. Effect: S.R. 1997/94, 159; 2005/94, 168 amended Territorial extent and classification: NI. General. - 8p.: 30 cm. - 978-0-337-99380-0 £4.00

The Occupational Pensions (Revaluation) Order (Northern Ireland) 2014 No. 2014/298. - Enabling power: Pension Schemes (Northern Ireland) Act 1993, sch. 2, para. 2 (1). - Issued: 10.12.2014. Made: 05.12.2014. Coming into operation: 01.01.2015. Effect: None. Territorial extent & classification: NI. General. - 4p.: 30 cm. - 978-0-337-99536-1 £4.25

The Pension Protection Fund and Occupational Pension Schemes (Levy Ceiling and Compensation Cap) Order (Northern Ireland) 2014 No. 2014/61. - Enabling power: S.I. 2005/255 (N.I.1), arts 161, 287 (3), sch. 6, paras 26 (7), 27. - Issued: 05.03.2014. Made: 03.03.2014. Coming into operation: In accord. with art. 1 (1). Effect: S.R. 2013/32 revoked. - Partially revoked by SR 2015/79 (ISBN 9780337996375). - 4p.: 30 cm. - 978-0-337-99295-7 £4.00

The Pension Protection Fund (Entry Rules) (Amendment) Regulations (Northern Ireland) 2014 No. 2014/195. - Enabling power: S.I. 2005/255 (N.I.1), arts. 105 (5) (9) (b), 287 (3). - Issued: 02.07.2014. Made: 30.06.2014. Coming into operation: 21.07.2014. Effect: S.R. 2005/126 amended. - 4p.: 30 cm. - 978-0-337-99466-1 £4.25

The Pensions (2005 Order) (Commencement No. 15) Order (Northern Ireland) 2014 No. 2014/183 (C.15). - Enabling power: S.I. 2005/255 (N.I. 1), art. 1 (2). Bringing into operation various provisions of the 2005 Order on 25.06.2014 in accord. with art. 2. - Issued: 27.06.2014. Made: 24.06.2014. Coming into operation: -. Effect: None. Territorial extent & classification: NI. General. - 8p: 30 cm. - 978-0-337-99454-8 £6.00

The Pensions (2008 No. 2 Act) (Commencement No. 11) Order (Northern Ireland) 2014 No. 2014/76 (C.3). - Enabling power: Pensions (No. 2) Act (Northern Ireland) 2008, s. 118 (1). Bringing into operation various provisions of the 2008 Act on 13.03.2014, in accord. with art. 2. - Issued: 17.03.2014. Made: 12.03.2014. Coming into operation: -. Effect: None. Territorial extent & classification: NI. General. - 4p.: 30 cm. - 978-0-337-99310-7 £4.00

The Pensions (2012 Act) (Commencement No. 4) Order (Northern Ireland) 2014 No. 2014/203 (C.14). - Enabling power: Pensions Act (Northern Ireland) 2012, s. 34 (3). Bringing into operation various provisions of the 2012 Act on 24.07.2014, in accord. with art. 2. - Issued: 07.07.2014. Made: 03.07.2014. Coming into operation: -. Effect: None. Territorial extent & classification: NI. General. - 2p.: 30 cm. - 978-0-337-99469-2 £4.25

The Pensions (2012 Act) (Consequential and Supplementary Provisions) Regulations (Northern Ireland) 2014 No. 2014/213. - Enabling power: Pensions Act (Northern Ireland) 2012, s. 28 (1), 31(1) (a), (b) (c). - Issued: 12.12.2014. Made: 23.07.2014. Coming into operation: 24.07.2014. Effect: 1993 c.49 & S.I. 2005/255 (N.I. 1) amended. Territorial extent & classification: NI. General. - Approved by resolution of the Assembly on 17th November 2014. Supersedes pre-approved version (ISBN 9780337994760). - 4p: 30 cm. - 978-0-337-99537-8 £4.25

The Pensions (2012 Act) (Transitional, Consequential and Supplementary Provisions) Regulations (Northern Ireland) 2014 No. 2014/213. - Enabling power: Pension Schemes (Northern Ireland) Act 1993, ss. ss. 29 (1), 31 (1) (a) (b) (c). - Issued: 25.07.2014. Made: 23.07.2014. Coming into operation: 24.07.2014. Effect: 1993 c.49; S.I. 2005/255 (N.I. 1) amended. Territorial extent & classification: NI. General. - For approval of the Assembly before the expiration of 6 months from the date of their coming into operation. An approved version of this instrument was issued using the same isbn (20.11.2014) in error. The approved version has now been re-issued with a separate ISBN (9780337995378) 12.12.2014. That version now supersedes this one (ISBN 9780337994760). - 4p: 30 cm. - 978-0-337-99476-0 £4.25

The Pensions (2012 Act) (Transitional, Consequential and Supplementary Provisions) Regulations (Northern Ireland) 2014 No. 2014/204. - Enabling power: Pension Schemes (Northern Ireland) Act 1993, ss. 70 (5), 93 (1) (2) (b) (3) (c), 97AF (1) (3) (b) (4) (b), 97I, 97L (1) (2) (b), 109, 149 (1) (2) (c), 177 (2) to (4), 178(1) & S.I. 1995/3213 (N.I. 22), arts 10 (3), 37 (4) (a) to (c) (e) (8), 47 (5) (a), 64 (3) (b), 73 (6) (7) (8) (a), 75 (5) (10), 166 (2) (3) & S.I. 1999/3147 (N.I. 11), arts 21(1) (b), 27 (1), 73 (4) & S.I. 2005/255 (N.I. 1), arts 103, 110 (1) (b) (5), 119 (4), 122 (10) (a), 130 (1), 145 (3) (b), 162 (1) (a) (3), 171 (11) (b), 172 (1), 189, 211, 287 (2) (3), sch. 6, pars 12 (3A) (b), 17 (3A) (b), 20 (7), 33 & Pensions Act (Northern Ireland) 2012, s. 28 (1) (2), 29 (1), 31(1) (a), (b) (d)- Issued: 07.07.2014. Made: 03.07.2014. Coming into operation: In accord. with art. 1 (1). Effect: S.R. 1991/37, 38; 1995/482; 1996/619; 1997/94; 2005/ 126, 138, 149, 568; 2006/49, 161; 2014/79 amended. Territorial extent & classification: NI. General. - Partially revoked by SR 2015/154 (ISBN 9780337996948). - 60p: 30 cm. - 978-0-337-99470-8 £10.00

Pensions Increase (Review) Order (Northern Ireland) 2014 No. 2014/99. - Enabling power: S.I. 1975/1503 (N.I. 15), art. 69 (1) (2) (5) (5ZA). - Issued: 02.04.2014. Made: 26.03.2014. Coming into operation: 07.04.2014. Effect: None. Territorial extent and classification: NI. General. - 8p.: 30 cm. - 978-0-337-99384-8 £6.00

The Public Service Pensions (Record Keeping and Miscellaneous Amendments) Regulations (Northern Ireland) 2014 No. 2014/321. - Enabling power: S.I. 1995/3213 (N.I. 22), art. 49 (9) (b), 166 (1) (2) & Public Service Pensions Act (Northern Ireland) 2014, s. 16 (1). - Issued: 30.12.2014. Made: 23.12.2014. Coming into operation: 01.04.2015. Effect: S.R. 1997/94 amended & S.R. 2005/421, 568 revoked. Territorial extent & classification: NI. General. - 6p.: 30 cm. - 978-0-337-99556-9 £6.00

Pharmacy

The Council of the Pharmaceutical Society of Northern Ireland (Indemnity Arrangements) Regulations (Northern Ireland) 2014 No. 2014/126. - Enabling power: S.I. 1976/1213 (N.I. 22), art. 11A (4) to (7), sch. 3, para. 15 (1) (b) (2) (3). - Issued: 07.05.2014. Made: 01.05.2014. Coming into operation: 01.06.2014. Effect: None. Territorial extent & classification: NI. General. - With correction slip dated May 2014. - 4p.: 30 cm. - 978-0-337-99405-0 £4.25

Planning

The Planning (Control of Advertisements) (Amendment) Regulations (Northern Ireland) 2014 No. 2014/118. - Enabling power: S.I. 1991/1220 (N.I. 11), art. 67 (1) (2). - Issued: 23.04.2014. Made: 17.04.2014. Coming into operation: 23.04.2014. Effect: S.R. 1992/448 amended. Territorial extent and classification: NI. General. - 4p.: 30 cm. - 978-0-337-99400-5 £4.25

The Planning (Fees) (Amendment) Regulations (Northern Ireland) 2014 No. 2014/127. - Enabling power: S.I. 1991/1220 (N.I. 11), art. 127. - Issued: 09.05.2014. Made: 02.05.2014. Coming into operation: 28.05.2014. Effect: S.R. 2005/222 amended. Territorial extent & classification: NI. General. - Revoked by SR 2015/73 (ISBN 9780337996412). - 8p.: 30 cm. - 978-0-337-99406-7 £6.00

The Planning (General Development) (Amendment) Order (Northern Ireland) 2014 No. 2014/31. - Enabling power: S.I. 1991/1220 (N.I. 11), art. 13. - Issued: 12.02.2014. Made: 10.02.2014. Coming into operation: 10.03.2014. Effect: S.R. 1993/278 amended. Territorial extent & classification: NI. General. - Revoked by SR 2015/72 (ISBN 9780337996405). - 8p.: 30 cm. - 978-0-337-99271-1 £5.75

The Planning (Hazardous Substances) (Amendment) Regulations (Northern Ireland) 2014 No. 2014/190. - Enabling power: S.I. 1991/1220 (N.I. 11), arts. 53 (3) (4), 60 (3), 129 (1). - Issued: 01.07.2014. Made: 26.06.2014. Coming into operation: 28.07.2014. Effect: S.R. 1993/275 amended. Territorial extent & classification: NI. General. - 4p.: 30 cm. - 978-0-337-99459-3 £4.25

Plant health

The Plant Health (Amendment) Order (Northern Ireland) 2014 No. 2014/172. - Enabling power: Plant Health Act (Northern Ireland) 1967, ss. 2, 3 (1). - Issued: 13.06.2014. Made: 11.06.2014. Coming into operation: 02.07.2014. Effect: S.R. 2006/82 amended. Territorial extent & classification: NI. General. - 2p.: 30 cm. - 978-0-337-99443-2 £4.25

Police

The Police and Criminal Evidence (1989 Order) (Codes of Practice) (Revision of Codes C and H) Order (Northern Ireland) 2014 No. 2014/134. - Enabling power: S.I. 1989/1341 (N.I.12), art. 66 (4). - Issued: 13.05.2014. Made: 08.05.2014. Coming into operation: 02.06.2014. Effect: None. Territorial extent & classification: NI. General. - 2p.: 30 cm. - 978-0-337-99411-1 £4.25

The Police and Criminal Evidence (1989 Order) (Codes of Practice) (Temporary Modification to Code A) Order (Northern Ireland) 2014 No. 2014/181. - Enabling power: S.I. 1989/1341 (N.I.12), art. 66 (6A). - Issued: 27.06.2014. Made: 10.06.2014. Coming into operation: 30.07.2014. Effect: Code of practice A temporarily modified. Territorial extent & classification: NI. General. - 4p.: 30 cm. - 978-0-337-99451-7 £4.25

The Police Rehabilitation and Retraining Trust Regulations (Northern Ireland) 2014 No. 2014/163. - Enabling power: Financial Provisions Act (Northern Ireland) 2014, s. 11 (2). - Issued: 11.06.2014. Made: 04.06.2014. Coming into operation: 10.07.2014. Effect: None. Territorial extent & classification: NI. General. - 4p.: 30 cm. - 978-0-337-99434-0 £4.25

Police Service of Northern Ireland and Police Service of Northern Ireland Reserve Pensions (Amendment) Regulations 2014 No. 2014/19. - Enabling power: Police (Northern Ireland) Act 1998, s. 25 (2) (k), 26 (2) (g). - Issued: 04.02.2014. Made: 27.01.2014. Coming into operation: 01.04.2014. Effect: S.R. 1988/374; 2009/79 amended. Territorial extent & classification: NI. General. - With correction slip dated February 2014. - 4p: 30 cm. - 978-0-337-99260-5 £4.00

Public health

The Tobacco Retailers (2014 Act) (Commencement No. 1) Order (Northern Ireland) 2014 No. 2014/125 (c.5). - Enabling power: Tobacco Retailers Act (Northern Ireland) 2014, s. 25 (2), Bringing into operation various provisions of the 2014 Act on 01.05.2014, in accord. with art. 2. - Issued: 02.05.2014. Made: 29.04.2014. Coming into operation: -. Effect: None. Territorial extent & classification: NI. General. - 2p.: 30 cm. - 978-0-337-99404-3 £4.25

PUBLIC SERVICE PENSIONS

Public service pensions

The Public Service (Civil Servants and Others) Pensions Regulations (Northern Ireland) 2014 No. 2014/290. - Enabling power: Public Service Pensions Act (Northern Ireland) Act 2014, ss. 1 (1) (2) (a), 2 (1), 3 (1) (2) (3) (a) (c), 4 (5) (6), 4 (1), 5 (1) (3) (c), 8 (1) (a), 12 (6) (7), 18 (5) (6) (7) (8), 25 (3), sch. 2, 3 para. 1, & sch. 7 paras 1 (2) (ii), 2 (2) (ii), 5 (1). - Issued: 03.12.2014. Made: 26.11.2014. Coming into operation: in accord. with reg 1 (2) & (3). Effect: None. Territorial extent & classification: NI. General. - 120p.: 30 cm. - 978-0-337-99527-9 £19.00

The Public Service (Civil Servants and Others) Pensions Regulations (Northern Ireland) 2014 No. 2014/290. - Enabling power: Public Service Pensions Act (Northern Ireland) 2014, ss. 1 (1) (2) (a), 2 (1), 3 (1) (2) (3) (a) (c), 4 (5) (6), & 4 (1), 5 (1) (3) (c), 8 (1) (a), 12 (6) (7), 18 (5) (6) (7) (8), 25 (3), sch. 2, 3 para. 1, sch. 7 paras. 1 (2) (ii), 2 (2) (ii), 5 (1). - Issued: 08.12.2014. Made: 26.11.2014. Coming into operation: in accord with reg 1(2) (3). Effect: None. Territorial extent & classification: NI. General. - This S.R. has been printed in substitution of the S.R. of the same number (ISBN 9780337995279) and is being issued free of charge to all known recipients of that S.R. - 118p.: 30 cm. - 978-0-337-99532-3 £19.00

The Public Service Pensions (2014 Act) (Commencement No.1) Order (Northern Ireland) 2014 No. 2014/123 (c.4). - Enabling power: Public Service Pensions Act (Northern Ireland) 2014, s. 37 (2) (3). Bringing into operation various provisions of this Act on 28.04.2014, 01.04.2015 & 01.04.2016 in accord. with arts 2 to 7. - Issued: 01.05.2014. Made: 28.04.2014. Coming into operation: -. Effect: None. Territorial extent and classification: NI. General. - 4p.: 30 cm. - 978-0-337-99402-9 £4.25

The Teachers' Pension Scheme Regulations (Northern Ireland) 2014 No. 2014/310. - Enabling power: Public Service Pensions Act (Northern Ireland) 2014, ss. 1(1) (2) (d), (3) (4), 2, 3(1), (2), 3 (a) (c) (4), 4 (1) (3), 5 (1), (3) (5), 7 (1) (4), 8 (1) (a) (2) (a), 14, 18 (1) (2) (4) (5) to (10), 34 def. of employer para. (c), sch. 1, para. 4 (c), sch. 1, para. 4, sch. 2, para.3, sch. 3, sch. 5, para. 4, sch. 6 para. 3, & sch. 7, paras. 1 (2) (ii), 2 (2) (ii), 5- Issued: 17.12.2014. Made: 12.12.2014. Coming into operation: 01.04.2015. Effect: None. Territorial extent and classification: NI. General. - 110p.: 30 cm. - 978-0-337-99551-4 £16.50

Rates

The Housing Benefit (Habitual Residence) (Amendment) Regulations (Northern Ireland) 2014 No. 2014/98. - Enabling power: Social Security Contributions and Benefits (Northern Ireland) Act 1992, ss. 122 (1) (d), 133 (2) (i), 171 (1) (3) (4). - Issued: 28.03.2014. Made: 26.03.2014. Coming into operation: 01.04.2014. Effect: S.R. 2006/405 amended. Territorial extent & classification: NI. General. - 4p.: 30 cm. - 978-0-337-99383-1 £4.00

The Jobseeker's Allowance (Schemes for Assisting Persons to Obtain Employment) Regulations (Northern Ireland) 2014 No. 2014/150. - Enabling power: Social security Contributions and Benefits (Northern Ireland) Act 1992, ss. 122 (1) (a) (d), 132 (3) (4) (a) (b), 171 (1) (3) (4) & S.I. 1995/2705 (N.I. 15), arts. 14 (1) (4) (a) (b), 19A (1) (2) (5) (a) (b) (d) to (f) (6) to (9), 22, 22A, 22B (4) to (6), 22E (3) (a), 36 (2) & S.I. 1998/1506 (N.I. 10), arts 10, 11, 74 (1) & S.I. 2003/412 (N.I. 2), arts 61, 148 (1) & 2007 c.2 (N.I.), s. 17 (1) (3) (a) (b). - Issued: 04.06.2014. Made: 30.05.2014. Coming into operation: 02.06.2014. Effect: S.R. 1975/113; 1987/459; 1996/198; 1999/162; 2001/216; 2002/79; 2004/8; 2006/405, 406; 2008/280 amended. Territorial extent & classification: NI. General. - 16p.: 30 cm. - 978-0-337-99425-8 £6.00

The Rates (Amendment) (2009 Act) (Commencement No. 3) Order (Northern Ireland) 2014 No. 2014/306 (C.18). - Enabling power: Rates (Amendment) Act 2009, s. 19 (1). Bringing into operation various provisions of the 2009 Act on 01.04.2015. - Issued: 16.12.2014. Made: 10.12.2014. Coming into operation: -. Effect: None. Territorial extent and classification: NI. General. - 4p.: 30 cm. - 978-0-337-99547-7 £4.25

The Rates (Regional Rates) Order (Northern Ireland) 2014 No. 2014/22. - Enabling power: S.I. 1977/2157 (N.I. 28), art. 7 (1) (3). - Issued: 07.02.2014. Made: 05.02.2014. Coming into operation: In accord. with art. 1. Effect: None. Territorial extent and classification: NI. General. - Subject to the affirmative resolution procedure of the Assembly. - 4p.: 30 cm. - 978-0-337-99265-0 £4.00

The Rates (Regional Rates) Order (Northern Ireland) 2014 No. 2014/22. - Enabling power: S.I. 1977/2157 (N.I. 28), art. 7 (1) (3). - Issued: 07.02.2014. Made: 05.02.2014. Coming into operation: In accord. with art. 1. Effect: None. Territorial extent and classification: NI. General. - Affirmed by the Assembly. - 4p.: 30 cm. - 978-0-337-99299-5 £4.00

Rates (Small Business Hereditament Relief) (Amendment) Regulations (Northern Ireland) 2014 No. 2014/68. - Enabling power: S.I. 1977/2157 (N.I. 28), art 31C. - Issued: 10.03.2014. Made: 05.03.2014. Coming into operation: 01.04.2014. Effect: S.R. 2010/4 amended. Territorial extent & classification: NI. General. - 2p: 30 cm. - 978-0-337-99302-2 £4.00

The Social Security Benefits Up-rating Order (Northern Ireland) 2014 No. 2014/78. - Enabling power: Social Security Administration (Northern Ireland) Act 1992, ss. 132, 132A, 165(1) (4) (5). - Issued: 17.03.2014. Made: 13.03.2014. Coming into operation: In accord. with art. 1. Effect: 1966 c.6 (N.I.); 1992 c.7; S.R. 1987/30, 459; 1992/32; 1994/461; 1995/35; 1996/198; 2002/380; 2003/28; 2006/405, 406; 2008/280; 2010/302, 407 amended & S.R. 2013/69 revoked (14.04.2014). Territorial extent & classification: NI. General. - For approval of the Assembly before the expiration of six months from the date of its coming into operation. Superseded by Approved SR 2014/78 (ISBN 9780337993138). - 44p.: 30 cm. - 978-0-337-99313-8 £9.75

The Social Security Benefits Up-rating Order (Northern Ireland) 2014 No. 2014/78. - Enabling power: Social Security Administration (Northern Ireland) Act 1992, ss. 132, 132A, 165(1) (4) (5). - Issued: 13.06.2014. Made: 13.03.2014. Coming into operation: In accord. with art. 1. Effect: 1966 c.6 (N.I.); 1992 c.7; S.R. 1987/30, 459; 1992/32; 1994/461; 1995/35; 1996/198; 2002/380; 2003/28; 2006/405, 406; 2008/280; 2010/302, 407 amended & S.R. 2013/69 revoked (14.04.2014). Territorial extent & classification: NI. General. - Approved by resolution of the Assembly on 9th June 2014; Revoked by SR 2015/124 (ISBN 9780337996634). - 44p.: 30 cm. - 978-0-337-99438-8 £9.75

The Social Security (Habitual Residence) (Amendment) Regulations (Northern Ireland) 2014 No. 2014/133. - Enabling power: Social Security Contributions and Benefits (Northern Ireland) Act 1992, ss. 122 (1) (a) (d), 131 (1) (2), 171 (1) (3) (4) & S.I. 1995/2705 (N.I. 15), arts 6 (5) (12), 36 (2) & Immigration and Asylum Act 1999, ss. 115 (3) (4) (8) & State Pension Credit Act (Northern Ireland) 2002, ss. 1 (5) (a), 19 (1) (2) (a) (3) & Welfare Reform Act (Northern Ireland) 2007, ss. 4 (3), 25 (2). - Issued: 12.05.2014. Made: 08.05.2014. Coming into operation: 31.05.2014. Effect: S.R. 1987/459; 1996/198; 2003/28; 2006/405, 406; 2008/280 amended & S.R. 2013/167 partially revoked. Territorial extent & classification: NI. General. - 4p.: 30 cm. - 978-0-337-99410-4 £4.25

The Social Security (Miscellaneous Amendments No. 2) Regulations (Northern Ireland) 2014 No. 2014/105. - Enabling power: Social Security Contributions and Benefits (Northern Ireland) Act 1992, ss. 122 (1) (a) (d), 132 (3) (40, 132A, 171 (1) (3) (4) & Social Security Administration (Northern Ireland) Act 1992, ss. 5 (1) (a), 109A (2) (b), 165 (1) (4) to (6) & S.I. 1995/2705 (N.I. 15), arts. 14 (4), 36 (2) (a) & State Pension Credit Act (Northern Ireland) 2002, ss. 15 (3) (6), 19 (1) to (3) & Welfare reform Act (Northern Ireland) 2007, ss. 17 (1), 25 (2). - Issued: 11.04.2014. Made: 07.04.2014. Coming into operation: 28.04.2014. Effect: S.R. 1987/459, 465; 1996/198; 2003/28; 2006/405, 406; 2008/280 amended & S.R. 2009/338 partially revoked. Territorial extent & classification: NI. General. - With correction slip dated April 2014. - 8p.: 30 cm. - 978-0-337-99392-3 £6.00

The Valuation (Telecommunications, Natural Gas and Water) (Amendment) Regulations (Northern Ireland) 2014 No. 2014/67. - Enabling power: S.I. 1977/2157 (N.I. 28), art. 37 (4) (5), sch. 12, pt. 1, para. 5. - Issued: 10.03.2014. Made: 05.03.2014. Coming into operation: 01.04.2014. Effect: S.R. 2010/431 amended. Territorial extent & classification: NI. General. - 2p.: 30 cm. - 978-0-337-99301-5 £4.00

Rating

The Rates (Unoccupied Hereditaments) (Amendment) Regulations (Northern Ireland) 2014 No. 2014/69. - Enabling power: S.I. 1977/2157 (N.I. 28), art. 25A(6), sch. 8A, para. 1(1) to (3). - Issued: 10.03.2014. Made: 05.03.2014. Coming into operation: 01.04.2014. Effect: S.R. 2011/36 amended & S.R. 2013/47 revoked Territorial extent & classification: NI. General. - 2p.: 30 cm. - 978-0-337-99303-9 £4.00

Registration of vital events

The General Register Office (Fees) Order (Northern Ireland) 2014 No. 2014/71. - Enabling power: S.I. 1976/1041 (N.I. 14), art. 47 (1) (2) & S.I. 2003/413 (N.I. 3), arts 3 (3) (b), 19 (1) (a), 35 (3), 36 (1) (b) (3), 37 & Civil Partnership Act 2004, s. 157 (1). - Issued: 12.03.2014. Made: 06.03.2014. Coming into operation: 31.03.2014. Effect: S.R. 2012/443 revoked. Territorial extent & classification: NI. General. - Supersedes draft (ISBN 9780337992551) issued 24.02.2014. - 8p.: 30 cm. - 978-0-337-99306-0 £5.75

Rehabilitation of offenders

The Rehabilitation of Offenders (Exceptions) (Amendment) (No. 2) Order (Northern Ireland) 2014 No. 2014/174. - Enabling power: S.I. 1978/1908 (N.I. 27), arts. 5 (4), 8 (4). - Issued: 19.06.2014. Made: 16.06.2014. Coming into operation: 01.08.2014. Effect: S.R. 1979/195 amended. Territorial extent & classification: NI. General. - With correction slip dated June 2014. - 4p.: 30 cm. - 978-0-337-99445-6 £4.25

The Rehabilitation of Offenders (Exceptions) (Amendment) Order (Northern Ireland) 2014 No. 2014/27. - Enabling power: S.I. 1978/1908 (N.I. 27), arts. 5 (4), 8 (4). - Issued: 12.02.2014. Made: 05.02.2014. Coming into operation: 14.04.2014. Effect: S.R. 1979/195 amended. Territorial extent & classification: NI. General. - 8p.: 30 cm. - 978-0-337-99269-8 £5.75

Road and railway transport

Level Crossing (McConaghy's) Order (Northern Ireland) 2014 No. 2014/229. - Enabling power: Transport Act (Northern Ireland) 1967, s. 66 (1) (2). - Issued: 22.09.2014. Made: 18.09.2014. Coming into operation: 20.10.2014. Effect: None. Territorial extent & classification: NI. General. - 8p.: 30 cm. - 978-0-337-99491-3 £6.00

Roads

The A3 Portadown Road, Richhill (Abandonment) Order (Northern Ireland) 2014 No. 2014/268. - Enabling power: S.I. 1993/3160 (N.I. 15), art. 68 (1) (5). - Issued: 29.10.2014. Made: 27.10.2014. Coming into force: 03.12.2014. Effect: None. Territorial extent & classification: NI. Local. - Available at http://www.legislation.gov.uk/nisr/2014/268/contents/made Non-print

The A4 Sligo Road, Belcoo (Abandonment) Order (Northern Ireland) 2014 No. 2014/257. - Enabling power: S.I. 1993/3160 (N.I. 15), art. 68 (1) (5). - Issued: 13.10.2014. Made: 08.10.2014. Coming into operation: 19.11.2014. Effect: None. Territorial extent & classification: NI. Local. - Available at http://www.legislation.gov.uk/nisr/2014/257/contents/made Non-print

The A21 Ballygowan Road, Saintfield (Abandonment) Order (Northern Ireland) 2014 No. 2014/273. - Enabling power: S.I. 1993/3160 (N.I. 15), art. 68 (1) (5). - Issued: 30.10.2014. Made: 28.10.2014. Coming into force: 03.12.2014. Effect: None. Territorial extent & classification: NI. Local. - Available at http://www.legislation.gov.uk/nisr/2014/273/contents/made Non-print

The A29 Armagh Road, Moy (Abandonment) Order (Northern Ireland) 2014 No. 2014/311. - Enabling power: S.I. 1993/3160 (N.I. 15), art. 68 (1) (5). - Issued: 19.12.2014. Made: 15.12.2014. Coming into force: 11.02.2015. Effect: None. Territorial extent & classification: NI. Local. - Available at http://www.legislation.gov.uk/nisr/2014/311/contents/made Non-print

The Annesborough Road, Lurgan (Abandonment) Order (Northern Ireland) 2014 No. 2014/82. - Enabling power: S.I. 1993/3160 (N.I. 15), art. 68 (1) (5). - Issued: 20.03.2014. Made: 18.03.2014. Coming into operation: 07.05.2014. Effect: None. Territorial extent & classification: NI. Local. - Available at http://www.legislation.gov.uk/nisr/2014/82/contents/made Non-print

The Broadway, Larne (Abandonment) Order (Northern Ireland) 2014 No. 2014/312. - Enabling power: S.I. 1993/3160 (N.I. 15), art. 68 (1) (5). - Issued: 19.12.2014. Made: 15.12.2014. Coming into force: 11.02.2015. Effect: None. Territorial extent & classification: NI. Local. - Available at http://www.legislation.gov.uk/nisr/2014/312/contents/made Non-print

The Disert Road, Draperstown (Abandonment) Order (Northern Ireland) 2014 No. 2014/6. - Enabling power: S.I. 1993/3160 (N.I. 15), art. 68 (1) (5). - Issued: 17.01.2014. Made: 15.01.2014. Coming into force: 19.02.2014. Effect: None. Territorial extent & classification: NI. Local. - Available at http://www.legislation.gov.uk/nisr/2014/6/contents/made Non-print

The Drumalla Park, Carnlough (Abandonment) Order (Northern Ireland) 2014 No. 2014/258. - Enabling power: S.I. 1993/3160 (N.I. 15), art. 68 (1) (5). - Issued: 13.10.2014. Made: 08.10.2014. Coming into operation: 19.11.2014. Effect: None. Territorial extent & classification: NI. Local. - Available at http://www.legislation.gov.uk/nisr/2014/258/contents/made Non-print

The Former Glenshane Road at Ranaghan Bridge, Magherafelt (Abandonment) Order (Northern Ireland) 2014 No. 2014/32. - Enabling power: S.I. 1993/3160 (N.I. 15), art. 68 (1). - Issued: 14.02.2014. Made: 11.02.2014. Coming into force: 26.03.2014. Effect: None. Territorial extent & classification: NI. Local. - Available at http://www.legislation.gov.uk/nisr/2014/32/contents/made Non-print

The Green Road, Conlig (Abandonment) Order (Northern Ireland) 2014 No. 2014/8. - Enabling power: S.I. 1993/3160 (N.I. 15), art. 68 (1) (5). - Issued: 20.01.2014. Made: 16.01.2014. Coming into force: 19.02.2014. Effect: None. Territorial extent & classification: NI. Local. - Available at http://www.legislation.gov.uk/nisr/2014/8/contents/made Non-print

The Latt Road, Jerrettspass, Newry (Abandonment) Order (Northern Ireland) 2014 No. 2014/272. - Enabling power: S.I. 1993/3160 (N.I. 15), art. 68 (1) (5). - Issued: 30.10.2014. Made: 28.10.2014. Coming into force: 03.12.2014. Effect: None. Territorial extent & classification: NI. Local. - Available at http://www.legislation.gov.uk/nisr/2014/272/contents/made Non-print

The Lower Galliagh Road, Londonderry (Abandonment) Order (Northern Ireland) 2014 No. 2014/201. - Enabling power: S.I. 1993/3160 (N.I. 15), art. 68 (1) (5). - Issued: 04.07.2014. Made: 02.07.2014. Coming into operation: 08.10.2014. Effect: None. Territorial extent & classification: NI. Local. - Available at http://www.legislation.gov.uk/nisr/2014/201/contents/made Non-print

The M1/Trunk Road T3 and M1-M2 Link (Amendment) Order (Northern Ireland) 2014 No. 2014/36. - Enabling power: S.I. 1993/3160 (N.I.15), arts 14 (1), 15 (1), 16 (1) (2), 68 (6). - Issued: 14.02.2014. Made: 12.02.2014. Coming into operation: 01.04.2014. Effect: S.R. 2003/149 amended & 2004/350 revoked. Territorial extent & classification: NI. General. - 16p.: 30 cm. - 978-0-337-99273-5 £5.75

The Slieveboy Road, Claudy (Abandonment) Order (Northern Ireland) 2014 No. 2014/14. - Enabling power: S.I. 1993/3160 (N.I. 15), art. 68 (1) (5). - Issued: 27.01.2014. Made: 23.01.2014. Coming into force: 26.02.2014. Effect: None. Territorial extent & classification: NI. Local. - Available at http://www.legislation.gov.uk/nisr/2014/14/contents/made Non-print

The Templemore Avenue, Belfast (Footpath) (Abandonment) Order (Northern Ireland) 2014 No. 2014/314. - Enabling power: S.I. 1993/3160 (N.I. 15), art. 68 (1) (5). - Issued: 19.12.2014. Made: 15.12.2014. Coming into force: 11.02.2015. Effect: None. Territorial extent & classification: NI. Local. - Available at http://www.legislation.gov.uk/nisr/2014/314/contents/made Non-print

The Trewmount Close, Killyman, Dungannon (Abandonment) Order (Northern Ireland) 2014 No. 2014/91. - Enabling power: S.I. 1993/3160 (N.I. 15), art. 68 (1). - Issued: 24.03.2014. Made: 20.03.2014. Coming into force: 07.05.2014. Effect: None. Territorial extent & classification: NI. Local. - Available at http://www.legislation.gov.uk/nisr/2014/91/contents/made Non-print

The U232 Aghafad Road (Rubble Road), Newtownstewart (Abandonment) Order (Northern Ireland) 2014 No. 2014/145. - Enabling power: S.I. 1993/3160 (N.I. 15), art. 68 (1). - Issued: 23.05.2014. Made: 21.05.2014. Coming into operation: 01.07.2014. Effect: None. Territorial extent & classification: NI. Local. - Available at http://www.legislation.gov.uk/nisr/2014/145/contents/made Non-print

The U6007 Meadowlands, Downpatrick (Abandonment) Order (Northern Ireland) 2014 No. 2014/199. - Enabling power: S.I. 1993/3160 (N.I. 15), art. 68 (1) (5). - Issued: 04.07.2014. Made: 02.07.2014. Coming into operation: 08.10.2014. Effect: None. Territorial extent & classification: NI. Local. - Available at http://www.legislation.gov.uk/nisr/2014/199/contents/made Non-print

The Westlink (Busways) (Amendment) Regulations (Northern Ireland) 2014 No. 2014/124. - Enabling power: S.I. 1993/3160 (N.I.15), art. 20 (3). - Issued: 02.05.2014. Made: 30.04.2014. Coming into operation: 11.06.2014. Effect: None. - 2p.: 30 cm. - 978-0-337-99403-6 £4.25

Road traffic

The Bus and Coach Passengers Rights and Obligations (Designation and Enforcement) Regulations (Northern Ireland) 2014 No. 2014/180. - Enabling power: European Communities Act 1972, s. 2 (2). - Issued: 27.06.2014. Made: 24.06.2014. Coming into operation: 25.07.2014. Effect: None. Territorial extent & classification: NI. General. - 4p.: 30 cm. - 978-0-337-99450-0 £4.25

Road traffic and vehicles

The B162 Disert Road, Draperstown (Abandonment) Order (Northern Ireland) 2014 No. 2014/141. - Enabling power: S.I. 1993/3160 (N.I. 15), art. 68 (1). - Issued: 22.05.2014. Made: 20.05.2014. Coming into operation: 01.07.2014. Effect: None. Territorial extent & classification: NI. Local. - Available at http://www.legislation.gov.uk/nisr/2014/141/contents/made Non-print

The Bus Lanes (Dublin Road, Antrim) Order (Northern Ireland) 2014 No. 2014/128. - Enabling power: S.I. 1997/276 (N.I. 2), art. 4 (1) (2) (3). - Issued: 09.05.2014. Made: 07.05.2014. Coming into operation: 28.05.2014. Effect: S.R. 1980/370 revoked. Territorial extent & classification: NI. Local. - Available at http://www.legislation.gov.uk/nisr/2014/128/contents/made Non-print

The Control of Traffic (Belfast City Centre) Order (Northern Ireland) 2014 No. 2014/243. - Enabling power: S.I. 1997/276 (N.I. 2), arts 4 (1) (2) (3), 10 (4), 13 (1) (13) (16). - Issued: 03.10.2014. Made: 30.09.2014. Coming into operation: 21.10.2014. Effect: S.R. 2000/383; 2006/327; 2007/270; 2008/180, 317; 2009/49; 2012/197, 198, 199, 201 amended. Territorial extent & classification: NI. Local. - Available at http://www.legislation.gov.uk/nisr/2014/243/contents/made Non-print

The Control of Traffic (Bridge Street, Lisburn) Order (Northern Ireland) 2014 No. 2014/34. - Enabling power: S.I. 1997/276 (N.I. 2), art. 4 (1) (2) (3). - Issued: 14.02.2014. Made: 12.02.2014. Coming into operation: 05.03.2014. Effect: S.R. 1982/158; 2012/362 amended. Territorial extent & classification: NI. Local. - Available at http://www.legislation.gov.uk/nisr/2014/34/contents/made Non-print

The Cycle Routes (Amendment) Order (Northern Ireland) 2014 No. 2014/164. - Enabling power: S.I. 1997/276 (N.I.2), art. 4 (1) (2) (3). - Issued: 11.06.2014. Made: 09.06.2014. Coming into force: 30.06.2014. Effect: S.R. 2008/317 amended. Territorial extent & classification: NI. Local. - Available at http://www.legislation.gov.uk/nisr/2014/164/contents/made Non-print

The Loading Bays and Parking Places on Roads (Amendment) Order (Northern Ireland) 2014 No. 2014/5. - Enabling power: S.I. 1997/276 (N.I. 2), arts 10 (4), 13 (1). - Issued: 17.01.2014. Made: 15.01.2014. Coming into force: 05.02.2014. Effect: S.R. 2008/308 amended. Territorial extent & classification: NI. Local. - Available at http://www.legislation.gov.uk/nisr/2014/5/contents/made Non-print

The Motor Hackney Carriages (Newcastle) Bye-Laws (Amendment) Order (Northern Ireland) 2014 No. 2014/200. - Enabling power: S.I. 1997/276 (N.I. 2), art. 27A (1). - Issued: 04.07.2014. Made: 02.07.2014. Coming into operation: 25.07.2014. Effect: By-laws relating to Motor Hackney Carriages standing or plying for hire made by the Urban District Council of Newcastle on 05.08.1958 amended. Territorial extent & classification: NI. Local. - Available at http://www.legislation.gov.uk/nisr/2014/200/contents/made Non-print

The Motor Hackney Carriages (Newry) By-Laws (Amendment) Order (Northern Ireland) 2014 No. 2014/177. - Enabling power: S.I. 1997/276 (N.I. 2), art. 27A (1). - Issued: 23.06.2014. Made: 18.06.2014. Coming into operation: 08.07.2014. Effect: By-laws relating to Motor Hackney Carriages standing or plying for hire made by the Urban District Council of Newry on 08.04.1968 amended. Territorial extent & classification: NI. Local. - Available at http://www.legislation.gov.uk/nisr/2014/177/contents/made Non-print

The Motor Vehicles (Construction and Use) (Amendment No. 2) Regulations (Northern Ireland) 2014 No. 2014/227. - Enabling power: S.I. 1995/2994 (N.I. 18), arts. 55 (1), 110 (2). - Issued: 18.09.2014. Made: 15.09.2014. Coming into operation: 31.10.2014. Effect: S.R. 1999/454 amended. Territorial extent & classification: NI. General. - 4p.: 30 cm. - 978-0-337-99489-0 £4.25

The Motor Vehicles (Construction and Use) (Amendment) Regulations (Northern Ireland) 2014 No. 2014/216. - Enabling power: S.I. 1995/2994 (N.I. 18), art. 55 (1) (2). - Issued: 29.07.2014. Made: 24.07.2014. Coming into operation: 08.09.2014. Effect: S.R. 1999/454 amended. Territorial extent & classification: NI. General. - 2p.: 30 cm. - 978-0-337-99478-4 £4.25

The Motor Vehicles (Taxi Drivers' Licences) (Amendment) Regulations (Northern Ireland) 2012 No. 2014/303. - Enabling power: Taxis Act (Northern Ireland) 2008, ss. 1 (4), 2 (5), 3 (2) (7), 56 (1). - Issued: 15.12.2014. Made: 09.12.2014. Coming into operation: 29.06.2015. Effect: S.R. 2012/316 amended. Territorial extent & classification: NI. General. - 4p.: 30 cm. - 978-0-337-99544-6 £4.25

The Nicholsons Court, Newry (Abandonment) Order (Northern Ireland) 2014 No. 2014/135. - Enabling power: S.I. 1993/3160 (N.I. 15), art. 68 (1) (5). - Issued: 14.05.2014. Made: 12.05.2014. Coming into operation: 18.06.2014. Effect: None. Territorial extent & classification: NI. Local. - Available at http://www.legislation.gov.uk/nisr/2014/135/contents/made Non-print

The North Circular Road and Tarry Lane, Lurgan (Abandonment) Order (Northern Ireland) 2014 No. 2014/112. - Enabling power: S.I. 1993/3160 (N.I.15), arts 68 (1) (5). - Issued: 16.04.2014. Made: 14.04.2014. Coming into force: 04.06.2014. Effect: None. Territorial extent & classification: NI. Local. - Available at http://www.legislation.gov.uk/nisr/2014/112/contents/made Non-print

The One-Way Traffic (Banbridge) (Amendment) Order (Northern Ireland) 2014 No. 2014/247. - Enabling power: S.I. 1997/276 (N.I. 2), art. 4 (1) (2) (3). - Issued: 03.10.2014. Made: 01.10.2014. Coming into force: 22.10.2014. Effect: S.R. 1980/431 amended. Territorial extent & classification: NI. Local. - Available at http://www.legislation.gov.uk/nisr/2014/247/contents/made Non-print

The One-Way Traffic (Belfast) (Amendment) Order (Northern Ireland) 2014 No. 2014/242. - Enabling power: S.I. 1997/276 (N.I. 2), art. 4 (1) (2) (3). - Issued: 02.10.2014. Made: 30.09.2014. Coming into force: 21.10.2014. Effect: S.R. 2009/49 amended. Territorial extent & classification: NI. Local. - Available at http://www.legislation.gov.uk/nisr/2014/242/contents/made Non-print

The One-Way Traffic (Portrush) (Amendment) Order (Northern Ireland) 2014 No. 2014/84. - Enabling power: S.I. 1997/276 (N.I. 2), art. 4 (1) (2) (3). - Issued: 20.03.2014. Made: 18.03.2014. Coming into force: 08.04.2014. Effect: S.R. 1979/268 amended. Territorial extent & classification: NI. Local. - Available at http://www.legislation.gov.uk/nisr/2014/84/contents/made Non-print

The Parking and Waiting Restrictions (Armagh) Order (Northern Ireland) 2014 No. 2014/313. - Enabling power: S.I. 1997/276 (N.I. 2), art. 4 (1) (2) (3), 10 (4), 13 (1) (13) (16). - Issued: 19.12.2014. Made: 15.12.2014. Coming into force: 05.01.2015. Effect: None. Territorial extent & classification: NI. Local. - Available at http://www.legislation.gov.uk/nisr/2014/313/contents/made Non-print

The Parking and Waiting Restrictions (Ballymoney) (Amendment) Order (Northern Ireland) 2014 No. 2014/241. - Enabling power: S.I. 1997/276 (N.I. 2), art. 10 (4), 13 (1). - Issued: 02.10.2014. Made: 30.09.2014. Coming into force: 21.10.2014. Effect: S.R. 2008/5 amended. Territorial extent & classification: NI. Local. - Available at http://www.legislation.gov.uk/nisr/2014/241/contents/made Non-print

The Parking and Waiting Restrictions (Banbridge) Order (Northern Ireland) 2014 No. 2014/260. - Enabling power: S.I. 1997/276 (N.I.2), arts 4 (1) (2) (3), 10 (4), 13 (1) (13) (16). - Issued: 21.10.2014. Made: 17.10.2014. Coming into force: 07.11.2014. Effect: None. Territorial extent & classification: NI. Local. - Available at http://www.legislation.gov.uk/nisr/2014/260/contents/made Non-print

The Parking and Waiting Restrictions (Belfast) (Amendment) Order (Northern Ireland) 2014 No. 2014/289. - Enabling power: S.I. 1997/276 (N.I. 2), art. 4 (1) (2) (3). - Issued: 26.11.2014. Made: 24.11.2014. Coming into force: 15.12.2014. Effect: S.R. 2008/180 amended. Territorial extent & classification: NI. Local. - Available at http://www.legislation.gov.uk/nisr/2014/289/contents/made Non-print

The Parking and Waiting Restrictions (Cathedral Quarter, Belfast) Order (Northern Ireland) 2014 No. 2014/161. - Enabling power: S.I. 1997/276 (N.I. 2), art. 4 (1) (2) (3), 15 (1). - Issued: 10.06.2014. Made: 06.06.2014. Coming into force: 27.06.2014. Effect: None. Territorial extent & classification: NI. Local. - Available at http://www.legislation.gov.uk/nisr/2014/161/contents/made Non-print

The Parking and Waiting Restrictions (Charlemont Gardens, Armagh) Order (Northern Ireland) 2014 No. 2014/113. - Enabling power: S.I. 1997/276 (N.I. 2), art. 4 (1) (2) (3), 10 (4), 13 (1) (13) (16). - Issued: 16.04.2014. Made: 14.04.2014. Coming into force: 06.05.2014. Effect: None. Territorial extent & classification: NI. Local. - Available at http://www.legislation.gov.uk/nisr/2014/113/contents/made Non-print

The Parking and Waiting Restrictions (Fivemiletown) (Amendment) Order (Northern Ireland) 2014 No. 2014/281. - Enabling power: S.I. 1997/276 (N.I. 2), arts 4 (1) (2) (3), 10 (4), 13 (1) (13) (16). - Issued: 19.11.2014. Made: 17.11.2014. Coming into force: 08.12.2014. Effect: S.R. 2008/309; 2009/23, 24; 2013/11 revoked. Territorial extent & classification: NI. Local. - Available at http://www.legislation.gov.uk/nisr/2014/281/contents/made Non-print

The Parking and Waiting Restrictions (Magherafelt) (Amendment) Order (Northern Ireland) 2014 No. 2014/248. - Enabling power: S.I. 1997/276 (N.I. 2), arts 4 (1) (2) (3), 10 (4), 13 (1). - Issued: 03.10.2014. Made: 01.10.2014. Coming into force: 22.10.2014. Effect: S.R. 2013/242 amended. Territorial extent & classification: NI. Local. - Available at http://www.legislation.gov.uk/nisr/2014/248/contents/made Non-print

The Parking and Waiting Restrictions (Omagh) (Amendment No. 2) Order (Northern Ireland) 2014 No. 2014/245. - Enabling power: S.I. 1997/276 (N.I. 2), art. 4 (1) (2) (3). - Issued: 03.10.2014. Made: 30.09.2014. Coming into force: 21.10.2014. Effect: S.R. 2013/273 amended. Territorial extent & classification: NI. Local. - Available at http://www.legislation.gov.uk/nisr/2014/245/contents/made Non-print

The Parking and Waiting Restrictions (Omagh) (Amendment) Order (Northern Ireland) 2014 No. 2014/211. - Enabling power: S.I. 1997/276 (N.I. 2), art. 4 (1) (2) (3). - Issued: 23.07.2014. Made: 18.07.2014. Coming into force: 08.08.2014. Effect: S.R. 2013/273 amended. Territorial extent & classification: NI. Local. - Available at http://www.legislation.gov.uk/nisr/2014/211/contents/made Non-print

The Parking and Waiting Restrictions (Portrush) (Amendment) Order (Northern Ireland) 2014 No. 2014/30. - Enabling power: S.I. 1997/276 (N.I. 2), arts 4 (1) (2) (3), 10 (4), 13 (1), sch. 1, 4, para. 5. - Issued: 12.02.2014. Made: 10.02.2014. Coming into force: 03.03.2014. Effect: S.R. 2009/199 amended. Territorial extent & classification: NI. Local. - Available at http://www.legislation.gov.uk/nisr/2014/30/contents/made Non-print

The Parking and Waiting Restrictions (Strabane) (Amendment) Order (Northern Ireland) 2014 No. 2014/90. - Enabling power: S.I. 1997/276 (N.I.2), art. 4 (1) (2) (3). - Issued: 24.03.2014. Made: 20.03.2014. Coming into force: 10.04.2014. Effect: S.R. 2011/400 amended. Territorial extent & classification: NI. Local. - Available at http://www.legislation.gov.uk/nisr/2014/90/contents/made Non-print

The Parking Places and Loading Bays on Roads (Glengall Street, Belfast) (Amendment) Order (Northern Ireland) 2014 No. 2014/24. - Enabling power: S.I. 1997/276 (N.I. 2), arts 10 (4), 13 (1). - Issued: 12.02.2014. Made: 07.02.2014. Coming into force: 28.02.2014. Effect: S.R. 2009/281 amended. Territorial extent & classification: NI. Local. - Available at http://www.legislation.gov.uk/nisr/2014/24/contents/made Non-print

The Parking Places (Disabled Persons' Vehicles) (Amendment No. 2) Order (Northern Ireland) 2014 No. 2014/106. - Enabling power: S.I. 1997/276 (N.I.2), arts 10 (4), 13 (1) (16), sch. 4, para. 5. - Issued: 10.04.2014. Made: 08.04.2014. Coming into force: 29.04.2014. Effect: S.R. 2006/327 amended. Territorial extent & classification: NI. Local. - Available at http://www.legislation.gov.uk/nisr/2014/106/contents/made. - Revoked by SR 2015/33 (Non-print) (ISBN 9786666439538) Non-print

The Parking Places (Disabled Persons' Vehicles) (Amendment No. 3) Order (Northern Ireland) 2014 No. 2014/171. - Enabling power: S.I. 1997/276 (N.I.2), arts 10 (4), 13 (1) (16). - Issued: 13.06.2014. Made: 11.06.2014. Coming into force: 01.07.2014. Effect: S.R. 2000/383; 2006/201, 327 amended. Territorial extent & classification: NI. Local. - Available at http://www.legislation.gov.uk/nisr/2014/171/contents/made. - Partially revoked by SR 2015/33 (Non-print) (ISBN 9786666439538) Non-print

The Parking Places (Disabled Persons' Vehicles) (Amendment No. 4) Order (Northern Ireland) 2014 No. 2014/237. - Enabling power: S.I. 1997/276 (N.I.2), arts 10 (4), 13 (1) (16), sch. 4, para. 5. - Issued: 25.09.2014. Made: 23.09.2014. Coming into force: 13.10.2014. Effect: S.R. 2006/327 amended. Territorial extent & classification: NI. Local. - Available at http://www.legislation.gov.uk/nisr/2014/237/contents/made. - Revoked by SR 2015/33 (Non-print) (ISBN 9786666439538) Non-print

The Parking Places (Disabled Persons' Vehicles) (Amendment No. 5) Order (Northern Ireland) 2014 No. 2014/246. - Enabling power: S.I. 1997/276 (N.I.2), arts 10 (4), 13 (1) (16). - Issued: 03.10.2014. Made: 01.10.2014. Coming into force: 22.10.2014. Effect: S.R. 2006/327, 201 amended. Territorial extent & classification: NI. Local. - Available at http://www.legislation.gov.uk/nisr/2014/246/contents/made. - Revoked by SR 2015/33 (Non-print) (ISBN 9786666439538) Non-print

The Parking Places (Disabled Persons' Vehicles) (Amendment No. 6) Order (Northern Ireland) 2014 No. 2014/315. - Enabling power: S.I. 1997/276 (N.I.2), arts 10 (4), 13 (1) (16). - Issued: 19.12.2014. Made: 15.12.2014. Coming into force: 05.01.2015. Effect: S.R. 2006/201, 327 amended. Territorial extent & classification: NI. Local. - Available at http://www.legislation.gov.uk/nisr/2014/315/contents/made. - Revoked by SR 2015/33 (Non-print) (ISBN 9786666439538) Non-print

The Parking Places (Disabled Persons' Vehicles) (Amendment) Order (Northern Ireland) 2014 No. 2014/25. - Enabling power: S.I. 1997/276 (N.I.2), arts 10 (4), 13 (1) (16). - Issued: 12.02.2014. Made: 07.02.2014. Coming into force: 28.02.2014. Effect: S.R. 2006/327 amended. Territorial extent & classification: NI. Local. - Available at http://www.legislation.gov.uk/nisr/2014/25/contents/made. - Revoked by SR 2015/33 (Non-print) (ISBN 9786666439538) Non-print

The Parking Places, Loading Bay and Waiting Restrictions (Newcastle) Order (Northern Ireland) 2014 No. 2014/72. - Enabling power: S.I. 1997/276 (N.I.2), arts 4 (1) (2) (3), 10 (4), 13 (1) (13) (16). - Issued: 12.03.2014. Made: 10.03.2014. Coming into force: 31.03.2014. Effect: None. Territorial extent & classification: NI. Local. - Available at http://www.legislation.gov.uk/nisr/2014/72/contents/made Non-print

The Parking Places on Roads (Bridge Street, Lisburn) Order (Northern Ireland) 2014 No. 2014/35. - Enabling power: S.I. 1997/276 (N.I. 2), arts 10 (4), 13 (1). - Issued: 14.02.2014. Made: 12.02.2014. Coming into force: 05.03.2014. Effect: S.R. 2000/383; 2006/201; 2007/270 amended. Territorial extent & classification: NI. Local. - Available at http://www.legislation.gov.uk/nisr/2014/35/contents/made Non-print

The Parking Places on Roads (Electric Vehicles) (Amendment No. 2) Order (Northern Ireland) 2014 No. 2014/42. - Enabling power: S.I. 1997/276 (N.I.2), arts 10 (4), 13 (1). - Issued: 21.02.2014. Made: 19.02.2014. Coming into force: 11.03.2014. Effect: S.R. 2012/290 amended. Territorial extent & classification: NI. Local. - Available at http://www.legislation.gov.uk/nisr/2014/42/contents/made Non-print

The Parking Places on Roads (Electric Vehicles) (Amendment No. 3) Order (Northern Ireland) 2014 No. 2014/240. - Enabling power: S.I. 1997/276 (N.I.2), arts 10 (4), 13 (1). - Issued: 02.09.2014. Made: 30.09.2014. Coming into force: 21.10.2014. Effect: S.R. 2012/290 amended. Territorial extent & classification: NI. Local. - Available at http://www.legislation.gov.uk/nisr/2014/240/contents/made Non-print

The Parking Places on Roads (Electric Vehicles) (Amendment) Order (Northern Ireland) 2014 No. 2014/7. - Enabling power: S.I. 1997/276 (N.I.2), arts 10 (4), 13 (1) (13) (16), 15 (1) (4). - Issued: 20.01.2014. Made: 16.01.2014. Coming into force: 06.02.2014. Effect: S.R. 2000/383 amended. Territorial extent & classification: NI. Local. - Available at http://www.legislation.gov.uk/nisr/2014/7/contents/made Non-print

The Parking Places on Roads (Londonderry) (Amendment) Order (Northern Ireland) 2014 No. 2014/83. - Enabling power: S.I. 1997/276 (NI 2), arts 10 (4), 13 (1). - Issued: 20.03.2014. Made: 18.03.2014. Coming into operation: 08.04.2014. Effect: S.R. 2011/193 amended. Territorial extent & classification: NI. Local. - Available at http://www.legislation.gov.uk/nisr/2014/83/contents/made Non-print

The Parking Places on Roads (Lurgan) (Amendment) Order (Northern Ireland) 2014 No. 2014/282. - Enabling power: S.I. 1997/276 (N.I. 2), arts 10 (4), 13 (1), sch. 4, para. 5. - Issued: 19.11.2014. Made: 17.11.2014. Coming into operation: 08.12.2014. Effect: S.R. 2013/97 amended. Territorial extent & classification: NI. Local. - Available at http://www.legislation.gov.uk/nisr/2014/282/contents/made Non-print

The Penalty Charges (Additional Contraventions) Regulations (Northern Ireland) 2014 No. 2014/278. - Enabling power: S.I. 2005/1964 (N.I. 14), art. 4 (3). - Issued: 14.11.2014. Made: 12.11.2014. Coming into operation: 14.01.2015. Effect: S.I. 2005/1964 (N.I. 14) amended. Territorial extent & classification: NI. General. - 4p.: 30 cm. - 978-0-337-99516-3 £4.25

The Penalty Charges (Prescribed Devices) Regulations (Northern Ireland) 2014 No. 2014/279. - Enabling power: S.I. 2005/1964 (N.I. 14), art. 8 (1). - Issued: 14.11.2014. Made: 12.11.2014. Coming into operation: 14.01.2015. Effect: None. Territorial extent & classification: NI. General. - 4p.: 30 cm. - 978-0-337-99517-0 £4.25

The Prohibition of Traffic (Giant's Causeway Road) Order (Northern Ireland) 2014 No. 2014/255. - Enabling power: S.I. 1997/276 (N.I. 2), art. 4 (1) (2) (3), sch. 1, para. 5. - Issued: 13.10.2014. Made: 08.10.2014. Coming into operation: 29.10.2014. Effect: S.R. 1984/215 revoked. Territorial extent & classification: NI. Local. - Available at http://www.legislation.gov.uk/nisr/2014/255/contents/made Non-print

ROAD TRAFFIC AND VEHICLES

The Prohibition of Waiting (Amendment) Order (Northern Ireland) 2014 No. 2014/236. - Enabling power: S.I. 1997/276 (N.I. 2), art. 4 (1) (2) (3). - Issued: 25.09.2014. Made: 23.09.2014. Coming into force: 06.10.2014. Effect: S.R. 2001/59 amended. Territorial extent & classification: NI. Local. - Available at http://www.legislation.gov.uk/nisr/2014/236/contents/made Non-print

The Road Passenger Transport (Qualifications of Operators) Regulations (Northern Ireland) 2014 No. 2014/206. - Enabling power: European Communities Act 1972, s. 2 (2). - Issued: 08.07.2014. Made: 03.07.2014. Coming into operation: 18.08.2014. Effect: 1967 c.37 (N.I.) amended. - EC note: Implement Council Regulation (EC) 1071/2009. - 12p.: 30 cm. - 978-0-337-99471-5 £6.00

The Road Races (Armoy Motorcycle Race) Order (Northern Ireland) 2014 No. 2014/205. - Enabling power: S.I. 1986/1887 (N.I. 17), art. 3. - Issued: 07.07.2014. Made: 03.07.2014. Coming into force: 24.07.2014. Effect: None. Territorial extent & classification: NI. Local. - Available at http://www.legislation.gov.uk/nisr/2014/205/contents/made Non-print

The Road Races (Cairncastle Hill Climb) Order (Northern Ireland) 2014 No. 2014/149. - Enabling power: S.I. 1986/1887 (N.I. 17), art. 3. - Issued: 02.06.2014. Made: 29.05.2014. Coming into force: 19.06.2014. Effect: None. Territorial extent & classification: NI. Local. - Available at http://www.legislation.gov.uk/nisr/2014/149/contents/made Non-print

The Road Races (Circuit of Ireland Rally) Order (Northern Ireland) 2014 No. 2014/95. - Enabling power: S.I. 1986/1887 (N.I. 17), art. 3. - Issued: 25.03.2014. Made: 21.03.2014. Coming into force: 16.04.2014. Effect: None. Territorial extent & classification: NI. Local. - Available at http://www.legislation.gov.uk/nisr/2014/95/contents/made Non-print

The Road Races (Cookstown 100) Order (Northern Ireland) 2014 No. 2014/104. - Enabling power: S.I. 1986/1887 (N.I. 17), art. 3. - Issued: 10.04.2014. Made: 04.04.2014. Coming into force: 24.04.2014. Effect: None. Territorial extent & classification: NI. Local. - Available at http://www.legislation.gov.uk/nisr/2014/104/contents/made Non-print

The Road Races (Craigantlet Hill Climb) Order (Northern Ireland) 2014 No. 2014/210. - Enabling power: S.I. 1986/1887 (N.I. 17), art. 3. - Issued: 14.07.2014. Made: 10.07.2014. Coming into force: 01.08.2014. Effect: None. Territorial extent & classification: NI. Local. - Available at http://www.legislation.gov.uk/nisr/2014/210/contents/made Non-print

The Road Races (Croft Hill Climb) Order (Northern Ireland) 2014 No. 2014/94. - Enabling power: S.I. 1986/1887 (N.I. 17), art. 3. - Issued: 25.03.2014. Made: 21.03.2014. Coming into force: 11.04.2014. Effect: None. Territorial extent & classification: NI. Local. - Available at http://www.legislation.gov.uk/nisr/2014/94/contents/made Non-print

The Road Races (Down Rally) Order (Northern Ireland) 2014 No. 2014/254. - Enabling power: S.I. 1986/1887 (N.I. 17), art. 3. - Issued: 06.10.2014. Made: 02.10.2014. Coming into force: 17.10.2014. Effect: None. Territorial extent & classification: NI. Local. - Available at http://www.legislation.gov.uk/nisr/2014/254/contents/made Non-print

The Road Races (Drumhorc Hill Climb) Order (Northern Ireland) 2014 No. 2014/122. - Enabling power: S.I. 1986/1887 (N.I. 17), art. 3. - Issued: 30.04.2014. Made: 25.04.2014. Coming into force: 16.05.2014. Effect: None. Territorial extent & classification: NI. Local. - Available at http://www.legislation.gov.uk/nisr/2014/122/contents/made Non-print

The Road Races (Dungannon Bush Motorcycle Race) Order (Northern Ireland) 2014 No. 2014/157. - Enabling power: S.I. 1986/1887 (N.I. 17), art. 3. - Issued: 09.06.2014. Made: 05.06.2014. Coming into force: 26.06.2014. Effect: None. Territorial extent & classification: NI. Local. - Available at http://www.legislation.gov.uk/nisr/2014/157/contents/made Non-print

The Road Races (Eagles Rock Hill Climb) Order (Northern Ireland) 2014 No. 2014/187. - Enabling power: S.I. 1986/1887 (N.I. 17), art. 3. - Issued: 30.06.2014. Made: 26.06.2014. Coming into force: 18.07.2014. Effect: None. Territorial extent & classification: NI. Local. - Available at http://www.legislation.gov.uk/nisr/2014/187/contents/made Non-print

The Road Races (Garron Point Hill Climb) Order (Northern Ireland) 2014 No. 2014/217. - Enabling power: S.I. 1986/1887 (N.I. 17), art. 3. - Issued: 04.08.2014. Made: 31.07.2014. Coming into force: 22.08.2014. Effect: None. Territorial extent & classification: NI. Local. - Available at http://www.legislation.gov.uk/nisr/2014/217/contents/made Non-print

The Road Races (North West 200) Order (Northern Ireland) 2014 No. 2014/120. - Enabling power: S.I. 1986/1887 (N.I. 17), art. 3. - Issued: 25.04.2014. Made: 23.04.2014. Coming into force: 12.05.2014. Effect: None. Territorial extent & classification: NI. Local. - Available at http://www.legislation.gov.uk/nisr/2014/120/contents/made Non-print

The Road Races (Spamount Hill Climb) Order (Northern Ireland) 2014 No. 2014/130. - Enabling power: S.I. 1986/1887 (N.I. 17), art. 3. - Issued: 09.05.2014. Made: 07.05.2014. Coming into force: 30.05.2014. Effect: None. Territorial extent & classification: NI. Local. - Available at http://www.legislation.gov.uk/nisr/2014/130/contents/made Non-print

The Road Races (Tandragee 100) Order (Northern Ireland) 2014 No. 2014/109. - Enabling power: S.I. 1986/1887 (N.I. 17), art. 3. - Issued: 15.04.2014. Made: 10.04.2014. Coming into force: 01.05.2014. Effect: None. Territorial extent & classification: NI. Local. - Available at http://www.legislation.gov.uk/nisr/2014/109/contents/made Non-print

The Road Races (Tour of the Sperrins Rally) Order (Northern Ireland) 2014 No. 2014/119. - Enabling power: S.I. 1986/1887 (N.I. 17), art. 3. - Issued: 24.04.2014. Made: 18.04.2014. Coming into force: 09.05.2014. Effect: None. Territorial extent & classification: NI. Local. - Available at http://www.legislation.gov.uk/nisr/2014/119/contents/made Non-print

The Road Races (Ulster Grand Prix Bike Week) Order (Northern Ireland) 2014 No. 2014/212. - Enabling power: S.I. 1986/1887 (N.I. 17), art. 3. - Issued: 23.07.2014. Made: 21.07.2014. Coming into force: 12.08.2014. Effect: None. Territorial extent & classification: NI. Local. - Available at http://www.legislation.gov.uk/nisr/2014/212/contents/made Non-print

The Road Races (Ulster Rally) Order (Northern Ireland) 2014 No. 2014/214. - Enabling power: S.I. 1986/1887 (N.I. 17), art. 3. - Issued: 29.07.2014. Made: 24.07.2014. Coming into force: 14.08.2014. Effect: None. Territorial extent & classification: NI. Local. - Available at http://www.legislation.gov.uk/nisr/2014/214/contents/made Non-print

The Roads (Classification) Order (Northern Ireland) 2014 No. 2014/271. - Enabling power: S.I. 1993/3160 (N.I.15), art 13. - Issued: 29.10.2014. Made: 27.10.2014. Coming into force: 17.11.2014. Effect: S.R. 1982/252; 1992/356; 1998/371; 2004/228; 2013/10 revoked. Territorial extent & classification: NI. Local. - Available at http://www.legislation.gov.uk/nisr/2014/271/contents/made Non-print

The Roads (Speed Limit) (No. 2) Order (Northern Ireland) 2014 No. 2014/176. - Enabling power: S.I. 1997/276 (NI. 2), arts 37 (3) (4), 38 (1) (a). - Issued: 24.06.2014. Made: 18.06.2014. Coming into force: 08.07.2014. Effect: S.R. & O 1956/124; S.R. 1976/182; 1979/352; 1987/164; 2000/112; 2012/166 partially revoked. Territorial extent & classification: NI. Local. - Available at http://www.legislation.gov.uk/nisr/2014/176/contents/made Non-print

The Roads (Speed Limit) (No. 3) Order (Northern Ireland) 2014 No. 2014/316. - Enabling power: S.I. 1997/276 (N.I. 2), arts 37 (3) (4), 38 (1) (a). - Issued: 19.12.2014. Made: 15.12.2014. Coming into force: 05.01.2015. Effect: S.R. 1997/348; 1999/458; 2002/13; 2003/82 partially revoked. Territorial extent & classification: NI. Local. - Available at http://www.legislation.gov.uk/nisr/2014/316/contents/made Non-print

The Roads (Speed Limit) Order (Northern Ireland) 2014 No. 2014/85. - Enabling power: S.I. 1997/276 (NI. 2), arts 37 (3) (4), 38 (1) (a). - Issued: 20.03.2014. Made: 18.03.2014. Coming into force: 08.04.2014. Effect: S.R. 1997/348 partially revoked. Territorial extent & classification: NI. Local. - Available at http://www.legislation.gov.uk/nisr/2014/85/contents/made Non-print

The Road Traffic (Financial Penalty Deposit) (Amendment) Order (Northern Ireland) 2014 No. 2014/233. - Enabling power: S.I. 1996/1320 (N.I. 10), art. 91B (2) (b). - Issued: 23.09.2014. Made: 18.09.2014. Coming into operation: 31.10.2014. Effect: S.R. 2012/17 amended. Territorial extent & classification: NI. General. - 4p.: 30 cm. - 978-0-337-99495-1 £4.25

The Road Traffic (Financial Penalty Deposit) (Appropriate Amount) (Amendment) Order (Northern Ireland) 2014 No. 2014/234. - Enabling power: S.I. 1996/1320 (N.I. 10), art. 91C (2). - Issued: 23.09.2014. Made: 18.09.2014. Coming into operation: 31.10.2014. Effect: S.R. 2012/18 amended. Territorial extent & classification: NI. General. - 4p.: 30 cm. - 978-0-337-99496-8 £4.25

The Road Traffic (Fixed Penalty) (Amendment) Order (Northern Ireland) 2014 No. 2014/232. - Enabling power: S.I. 1996/1320 (N.I. 10), art. 59 (1). - Issued: 23.09.2014. Made: 18.09.2014. Coming into operation: 31.10.2014. Effect: S.R. 2007/319 amended. Territorial extent & classification: NI. General. - 2p.: 30 cm. - 978-0-337-99494-4 £4.25

The Road Traffic (Fixed Penalty) (Offences) (Amendment) Order (Northern Ireland) 2014 No. 2014/231. - Enabling power: S.I. 1996/1320 (N.I. 10), art. 57 (2). - Issued: 23.09.2014. Made: 18.09.2014. Coming into operation: 31.10.2014. Effect: S.R. 1997/369 amended. Territorial extent & classification: NI. General. - 4p.: 30 cm. - 978-0-337-99493-7 £4.25

ROAD TRAFFIC AND VEHICLES

The Road Traffic Offenders (Additional Offences) Order (Northern Ireland) 2014 No. 2014/230. - Enabling power: S.I. 1996/1320 (N.I. 10), art. 23 (3). - Issued: 23.09.2014. Made: 18.09.2014. Coming into operation: 31.10.2014. Effect: S.I. 1996/1320 (NI. 10) amended. Territorial extent & classification: NI. General. - 2p.: 30 cm. - 978-0-337-99492-0 £4.25

The Rowantree Road (C355), Dromore (Abandonment) Order (Northern Ireland) 2014 No. 2014/136. - Enabling power: S.I. 1993/3160 (N.I. 15), art. 68 (1) (5). - Issued: 14.05.2014. Made: 12.05.2014. Coming into operation: 18.06.2014. Effect: None. Territorial extent & classification: NI. Local. - Available at http://www.legislation.gov.uk/nisr/2014/136/contents/made Non-print

The Taxi Drivers' Licences Regulations (Northern Ireland) 2014 No. 2014/239. - Enabling power: Taxis Act (Northern Ireland) 2008, ss. 23 (2) to (5), 30 (1) (2), 52, 56 (1). - Issued: 01.10.2014. Made: 26.09.2014. Coming into operation: 31.10.2014. Effect: None. Territorial extent & classification: NI. General. - 16p.: 30 cm. - 978-0-337-99500-2 £6.00

The Taxi Operators Licensing Regulations (Northern Ireland) 2014 No. 2014/302. - Enabling power: Taxis Act (Northern Ireland) 2008, ss. 13 (2), (3) (5), 15 (2), 19 (1), 20, 30 (1) (2), 56 (1), 57 (1). - Issued: 15.12.2014. Made: 09.12.2014. Coming into operation: in accord. with reg. 1. Effect: None. Territorial extent & classification: NI. General. - 24p.: 30 cm. - 978-0-337-99543-9 £6.00

The Taxis (2008 Act) (Commencement No. 3) Order (Northern Ireland) 2014 No. 2014/238 (C.15). - Enabling power: Taxis Act (Northern Ireland) 2008, s. 59. Bringing into operation various provisions of the 2008 Act on 24.09.2014 & 31.10.2014. - Issued: 29.09.2014. Made: 23.09.2014. Coming into operation: -. Effect: None. Territorial extent & classification: NI. General. - 8p.: 30 cm. - 978-0-337-99498-2 £6.00

The Taxis (2008 Act) (Commencement No.4) Order (Northern Ireland) 2014 No. 2014/300 (C.16). - Enabling power: Taxis Act (Northern Ireland) 2008, s. 59. Bringing into operation various provisions of the 2008 Act on 09.12.2014, 01.06.2015 & 29.06.2015. - Issued: 12.12.2014. Made: 05.12.2014. Coming into operation: -. Effect: None. Territorial extent & classification: NI. General. - 8p.: 30 cm. - 978-0-337-99539-2 £6.00

The Waiting Restrictions (Antrim) Order (Northern Ireland) 2014 No. 2014/165. - Enabling power: S.I. 1997/276 (N.I. 2), art. 4 (1) (2) (3). - Issued: 11.06.2014. Made: 09.06.2014. Coming into operation: 30.06.2014. Effect: None. Territorial extent & classification: NI. Local. - Revoked by SR 2015/232 (non-print). - Available at http://www.legislation.gov.uk/nisr/2014/165/contents/made Non-print

The Waiting Restrictions (Ballykelly) Order (Northern Ireland) 2014 No. 2014/4. - Enabling power: S.I. 1997/276 (N.I. 2), art. 4 (1) (2) (3). - Issued: 17.01.2014. Made: 15.01.2014. Coming into force: 05.02.2014. Effect: None. Territorial extent & classification: NI. Local. - Available at http://www.legislation.gov.uk/nisr/2014/4/contents/made Non-print

The Waiting Restrictions (Banbridge) Order (Northern Ireland) 2014 No. 2014/144. - Enabling power: S.I. 1997/276 (N.I. 2), art. 4 (1) (2) (3). - Issued: 23.05.2014. Made: 21.05.2014. Coming into operation: 10.06.2014. Effect: None. Territorial extent & classification: NI. Local. - Available at http://www.legislation.gov.uk/nisr/2014/144/contents/made Non-print

The Waiting Restrictions (Belfast City Centre) (Amendment) Order (Northern Ireland) 2014 No. 2014/251. - Enabling power: S.I. 1997/276 (N.I. 2), art. 4 (1) (2) (3). - Issued: 03.10.2014. Made: 01.10.2014. Coming into operation: 22.10.2014. Effect: S.R. 2012/199 amended. Territorial extent & classification: NI. Local. - Available at http://www.legislation.gov.uk/nisr/2014/251/contents/made Non-print

The Waiting Restrictions (Carrickfergus) (Amendment No. 2) Order (Northern Ireland) 2014 No. 2014/317. - Enabling power: S.I. 1997/276 (N.I. 2), art. 4 (1) (2) (3). - Issued: 19.12.2014. Made: 15.12.2014. Coming into force: 05.01.2015. Effect: S.R. 2013/194 amended. Territorial extent & classification: NI. Local. - Available at http://www.legislation.gov.uk/nisr/2014/317/contents/made Non-print

The Waiting Restrictions (Carrickfergus) (Amendment) Order (Northern Ireland) 2014 No. 2014/129. - Enabling power: S.I. 1997/276 (N.I. 2), art. 4 (1) (2) (3). - Issued: 09.05.2014. Made: 07.05.2014. Coming into force: 28.05.2014. Effect: S.R. 2013/94 amended. Territorial extent & classification: NI. Local. - Available at http://www.legislation.gov.uk/nisr/2014/129/contents/made Non-print

The Waiting Restrictions (Carrickfergus) Order (Northern Ireland) 2014 No. 2014/29. - Enabling power: S.I. 1997/276 (N.I. 2), art. 4 (1) (2) (3). - Issued: 12.02.2014. Made: 10.02.2014. Coming into force: 03.03.2014. Effect: None. Territorial extent & classification: NI. Local. - Available at http://www.legislation.gov.uk/nisr/2014/29/contents/made Non-print

The Waiting Restrictions (Cookstown) (Amendment) Order (Northern Ireland) 2014 No. 2014/250. - Enabling power: S.I. 1997/276 (N.I. 2), art. 4 (1) (2) (3). - Issued: 03.10.2014. Made: 01.10.2014. Coming into operation: 22.10.2014. Effect: S.R. 2007/509 amended. Territorial extent & classification: NI. Local. - Available at http://www.legislation.gov.uk/nisr/2014/250/contents/made Non-print

The Waiting Restrictions (Craigavon) Order (Northern Ireland) 2014 No. 2014/252. - Enabling power: S.I. 1997/276 (N.I. 2), art. 4 (1) (2) (3). - Issued: 03.10.2014. Made: 01.10.2014. Coming into operation: 22.10.2014. Effect: None. Territorial extent & classification: NI. Local. - Available at http://www.legislation.gov.uk/nisr/2014/252/contents/made Non-print

The Waiting Restrictions (Dungannon) (Amendment No. 2) Order (Northern Ireland) 2014 No. 2014/244. - Enabling power: S.I. 1997/276 (N.I. 2), art. 4 (1) (2) (3). - Issued: 03.10.2014. Made: 30.09.2014. Coming into operation: 21.10.2014. Effect: S.R. 2013/230 amended. Territorial extent & classification: NI. Local. - Available at http://www.legislation.gov.uk/nisr/2014/244/contents/made Non-print

The Waiting Restrictions (Dungannon) (Amendment) Order (Northern Ireland) 2014 No. 2014/13. - Enabling power: S.I. 1997/276 (N.I. 2), art. 4 (1) (2) (3). - Issued: 27.01.2013. Made: 23.01.2014. Coming into force: 13.02.2014. Effect: S.R. 2013/230 amended. Territorial extent & classification: NI. Local. - Available at http://www.legislation.gov.uk/nisr/2014/13/contents/made Non-print

The Waiting Restrictions (Larne) (Amendment) Order (Northern Ireland) 2014 No. 2014/269. - Enabling power: S.I. 1997/276 (N.I. 2), art. 4 (1) (2) (3). - Issued: 29.10.2014. Made: 27.10.2014. Coming into operation: 17.11.2014. Effect: S.R. 2011/204 amended. Territorial extent & classification: NI. Local. - Available at http://www.legislation.gov.uk/nisr/2014/269/contents/made Non-print

The Waiting Restrictions (Larne) (Amendment) Order (Northern Ireland) 2014 No. 2014/114. - Enabling power: S.I. 1997/276 (N.I. 2), art. 4 (1) (2) (3). - Issued: 16.04.2014. Made: 14.04.2014. Coming into force: 06.05.2014. Effect: S.R. 2012/220 amended. Territorial extent & classification: NI. Local. - Available at http://www.legislation.gov.uk/nisr/2014/114/contents/made Non-print

The Waiting Restrictions (Londonderry) (Amendment) Order (Northern Ireland) 2014 No. 2014/115. - Enabling power: S.I. 1997/276 (N.I. 2), art. 4 (1) (2) (3). - Issued: 16.04.2014. Made: 14.04.2014. Coming into force: 06.05.2014. Effect: S.R. 2010/256 amended. Territorial extent & classification: NI. Local. - Available at http://www.legislation.gov.uk/nisr/2014/115/contents/made Non-print

The Waiting Restrictions (Lurgan) (No. 2) Order (Amendment No. 2) Order (Northern Ireland) 2014 No. 2014/270. - Enabling power: S.I. 1997/276 (N.I. 2), art. 4 (1) (2) (3). - Issued: 29.10.2014. Made: 27.10.2014. Coming into operation: 17.11.2014. Effect: S.R. 2010/392 amended. Territorial extent & classification: NI. Local. - Available at http://www.legislation.gov.uk/nisr/2014/270/contents/made Non-print

The Waiting Restrictions (Lurgan) (No. 2) Order (Amendment) Order (Northern Ireland) 2014 No. 2014/256. - Enabling power: S.I. 1997/276 (N.I. 2), art. 4 (1) (2) (3). - Issued: 13.10.2014. Made: 08.10.2014. Coming into operation: 29.10.2014. Effect: S.R. 2010/392 amended & S.R. 2010/206 revoked. Territorial extent & classification: NI. Local. - Available at http://www.legislation.gov.uk/nisr/2014/256/contents/made Non-print

The Waiting Restrictions (Markethill) (Revocation) Order (Northern Ireland) 2014 No. 2014/38. - Enabling power: S.I. 1997/276 (N.I. 2), art. 4 (1) (2) (3). - Issued: 17.02.2014. Made: 13.02.2014. Coming into force: 06.03.2014. Effect: S.R. 2011/171 revoked. Territorial extent & classification: NI. Local. - Available at http://www.legislation.gov.uk/nisr/2014/38/contents/made Non-print

The Waiting Restrictions (Randalstown) (Amendment) Order (Northern Ireland) 2014 No. 2014/160. - Enabling power: S.I. 1997/276 (N.I. 2), art. 4 (1) (2) (3). - Issued: 10.06.2014. Made: 06.06.2014. Coming into force: 27.06.2014. Effect: S.R. 2012/433 amended. Territorial extent & classification: NI. Local. - Available at http://www.legislation.gov.uk/nisr/2014/160/contents/made Non-print

The Westlink (Busways) (Amendment) Regulations (Northern Ireland) 2014 No. 2014/124. - Enabling power: S.I. 1993/3160 (N.I.15), art. 20 (3). - Issued: 02.05.2014. Made: 30.04.2014. Coming into operation: 11.06.2014. Effect: None. - 2p.: 30 cm. - 978-0-337-99403-6 £4.25

Salaries

The Salaries (Assembly Ombudsman and Commissioner for Complaints) Order (Northern Ireland) 2014 No. 2014/55. - Enabling power: S.I. 1996/1298 (N.I.8), art. 5 (1) (2) & S.I. 1996/1297 (N.I.7), art. 4 (1) (2). - Issued: 04.03.2014. Made: 27.02.2014. Coming into operation: 21.03.2014. Effect: S.R. 2009/335 revoked. Territorial extent & classification: NI. General. - Revoked by SR 2014/55 (ISBN 9780337995736). - 2p.: 30 cm. - 978-0-337-99289-6 £4.00

Sea fisheries

The Sea Fishing (Licences and Notices) Regulations (Northern Ireland) 2014 No. 2014/209. - Enabling power: Sea Fish (Conservation) Act 1967, s. 4B. - Issued: 09.07.2014. Made: 03.07.2014. Coming into operation: 08.08.2014. Effect: S.R. 1994/2813 revoked. Territorial extent & classification: NI. General. - 8p.: 30 cm. - 978-0-337-99474-6 £4.25

Seeds

The Seeds (Miscellaneous Amendments) Regulations (Northern Ireland) 2014 No. 2014/295. - Enabling power: European Communities Act 1972, s. 2 (2), sch. 2 para. 1A & Seeds Act (Northern Ireland) 1965, ss. 1 (1) (2A), 2. - Issued: 10.12.2014. Made: 04.12.2014. Coming into operation: 31.12.2014. Effect: S.R. 2009/383, 384, 385, 386, 387, 388 amended. Territorial extent and classification: NI. General. - 12p.: 30 cm. - 978-0-337-99533-0 £6.00

Social security

The Child Support Fees Regulations (Northern Ireland) 2014 No. 2014/182. - Enabling power: Social Security Administration (Northern Ireland) Act 1992, s. 5 (1) (q), 165 (4) & S.I. 1991/2628 (N.I.23), arts 40 (1), 47 (1) & Child Maintenance Act (Northern Ireland) 2008, ss. 3 (1) to (4), 36 (1) (2). - Issued: 02.12.2014. Made: 24.06.2014. Coming into operation: In accord. with art. 1. Effect: S.R. 1987/465 amended. Territorial extent & classification: NI. General. - Approved by resolution of the Assembly on 24th November 2014. Supersedes pre-approved version (ISBN 9780337994524). - 8p.: 30 cm. - 978-0-337-99529-3 £6.00

The Jobseeker's Allowance (Habitual Residence) (Amendment) Regulations (Northern Ireland) 2014 No. 2014/263. - Enabling power: S.I. 1995/2705 (N.I. 15), art. 6 (5) (12). - Issued: 10.11.2014. Made: 22.10.2014. Coming into operation: 09.11.2014. Effect: S.R. 1996/198 amended. Territorial extent & classification: NI. General. - 4p.: 30 cm. - 978-0-337-99514-9 £4.25

The Jobseeker's Allowance (Homeless Claimants) (Amendment) Regulations (Northern Ireland) 2014 No. 2014/192. - Enabling power: S.I. 1995/2705 (N.I. 15), arts 8 (4), 36 (2). - Issued: 02.07.2014. Made: 27.06.2014. Coming into operation: 21.07.2014. Effect: S.R. 1996/198 amended. Territorial extent & classification: NI. General. - For approval of the Assembly before the expiration of 6 months from the date of their coming into operation. Superseded by approved version (ISBN 9780337995415) issued 12.12.2014. - 2p.: 30 cm. - 978-0-337-99460-9 £4.25

The Jobseeker's Allowance (Homeless Claimants) (Amendment) Regulations (Northern Ireland) 2014 No. 2014/192. - Enabling power: S.I. 1995/2705 (N.I. 15), arts 8 (4), 36 (2). - Issued: 12.12.2014. Made: 27.06.2014. Coming into operation: 21.07.2014. Effect: S.R. 1996/198 amended. Territorial extent & classification: NI. General. - Approved by resolution of the Assembly on 2nd December 2014. Supersedes pre-approved version (ISBN 9780337994609). - 2p.: 30 cm. - 978-0-337-99541-5 £4.25

The Jobseeker's Allowance (Maternity Allowance) (Amendment) Regulations (Northern Ireland) 2014 No. 2014/226. - Enabling power: S.I. 1995/2705 (N.I. 15), arts. 3 (2C), 8 (4), 36 (2) (a), sch. 1 para. 3. - Issued: 18.09.2014. Made: 15.09.2014. Coming into operation: 16.09.2014. Effect: S.R. 1996/198 amended. Territorial extent & classification: NI. General. - 2p.: 30 cm. - 978-0-337-99488-3 £4.25

The Jobseeker's Allowance (Schemes for Assisting Persons to Obtain Employment) Regulations (Northern Ireland) 2014 No. 2014/150. - Enabling power: Social security Contributions and Benefits (Northern Ireland) Act 1992, ss. 122 (1) (a) (d), 132 (3) (4) (a) (b), 171 (1) (3) (4) & S.I. 1995/2705 (N.I. 15), arts. 14 (1) (4) (a) (b), 19A (1) (2) (5) (a) (b) (d) to (f) (6) to (9), 22, 22A, 22B (4) to (6), 22E (3) (a), 36 (2) & S.I. 1998/1506 (N.I. 10), arts 10, 11, 74 (1) & S.I. 2003/412 (N.I. 2), arts 61, 148 (1) & 2007 c.2 (N.I.), s. 17 (1) (3) (a) (b). - Issued: 04.06.2014. Made: 30.05.2014. Coming into operation: 02.06.2014. Effect: S.R. 1975/113; 1987/459; 1996/198; 1999/162; 2001/216; 2002/79; 2004/8; 2006/405, 406; 2008/280 amended. Territorial extent & classification: NI. General. - 16p.: 30 cm. - 978-0-337-99425-8 £6.00

The Mesothelioma Lump Sum Payments (Conditions and Amounts) (Amendment) Regulations (Northern Ireland) 2014 No. 2014/63. - Enabling power: Mesothelioma, etc., Act (Northern Ireland) 2008, s. 1 (3). - Issued: 03.04.2014. Made: 03.03.2014. Coming into operation: 01.04.2014. Effect: S.R. 2008/354 amended. Territorial extent & classification: NI. General. - Approved by resolution of the Assembly on 31.03.2014. Supersedes version of same number (ISBN 9780337992971), laid before the Assembly for approval, issued on 06.03.2014. - 4p.: 30 cm. - 978-0-337-99389-3 £4.25

The Mesothelioma Lump Sum Payments (Conditions and Amounts) (Amendment) Regulations (Northern Ireland) 2014 No. 2014/63. - Enabling power: Mesothelioma, etc., Act (Northern Ireland) 2008, s. 1 (3). - Issued: 06.03.2014. Made: 03.03.2014. Coming into operation: 01.04.2014. Effect: S.R. 2008/354 amended. Territorial extent & classification: NI. General. - For approval of the Assembly before the expiration of six months from the date of their coming into operation. Superseded by approved version (ISBN 9780337993893). - 8p.: 30 cm. - 978-0-337-99297-1 £4.00

The Pneumoconiosis, etc., (Workers' Compensation) (Payment of Claims) (Amendment) Regulations (Northern Ireland) 2014 No. 2014/62. - Enabling power: S.I. 1979/925 (N.I.9), arts. 3 (3), 4 (3), 11 (1) (4). - Issued: 03.04.2014. Made: 03.03.2014. Coming into operation: In accord. with reg. 1 (1). Effect: S.R. 1988/242 amended. Territorial extent & classification: NI. General. - Affirmed by resolution of the Assembly on 31.03.2014. Supersedes version of same number (ISBN 9780337992964) laid before the Assembly, issued 06.03.2014. - 8p.: 30 cm. - 978-0-337-99388-6 £6.00

The Pneumoconiosis, etc., (Workers' Compensation) (Payment of Claims) (Amendment) Regulations (Northern Ireland) 2014 No. 2014/62. - Enabling power: S.I. 1979/925 (N.I.9), arts. 3 (3), 4 (3), 11 (1) (4). - Issued: 06.03.2014. Made: 03.03.2014. Coming into operation: In accord. with reg. 1 (1). Effect: S.R. 1988/242 amended. Territorial extent & classification: NI. General. - Subject to affirmative resolution of the Assembly. Superseded by approved version (ISBN 9780337993886). - 8p.: 30 cm. - 978-0-337-99296-4 £5.75

The Social Security Benefits Up-rating Order (Northern Ireland) 2014 No. 2014/78. - Enabling power: Social Security Administration (Northern Ireland) Act 1992, ss. 132, 132A, 165(1) (4) (5). - Issued: 17.03.2014. Made: 13.03.2014. Coming into operation: In accord. with art. 1. Effect: 1966 c.6 (N.I.); 1992 c.7; S.R. 1987/30, 459; 1992/32; 1994/461; 1995/35; 1996/198; 2002/380; 2003/28; 2006/405, 406; 2008/280; 2010/302, 407 amended & S.R. 2013/69 revoked (14.04.2014). Territorial extent & classification: NI. General. - For approval of the Assembly before the expiration of six months from the date of its coming into operation. Superseded by Approved SR 2014/78 (ISBN 9780337993138). - 44p.: 30 cm. - 978-0-337-99313-8 £9.75

The Social Security Benefits Up-rating Order (Northern Ireland) 2014 No. 2014/78. - Enabling power: Social Security Administration (Northern Ireland) Act 1992, ss. 132, 132A, 165(1) (4) (5). - Issued: 13.06.2014. Made: 13.03.2014. Coming into operation: In accord. with art. 1. Effect: 1966 c.6 (N.I.); 1992 c.7; S.R. 1987/30, 459; 1992/32; 1994/461; 1995/35; 1996/198; 2002/380; 2003/28; 2006/405, 406; 2008/280; 2010/302, 407 amended & S.R. 2013/69 revoked (14.04.2014). Territorial extent & classification: NI. General. - Approved by resolution of the Assembly on 9th June 2014; Revoked by SR 2015/124 (ISBN 9780337996634). - 44p.: 30 cm. - 978-0-337-99438-8 £9.75

The Social Security Benefits Up-rating Regulations (Northern Ireland) 2014 No. 2014/80. - Enabling power: Social Security Contributions and Benefits (Northern Ireland) Act 1992, ss. 90, 113 (1) (a), 171 (1) (3) & Social Security Administration (Northern Ireland) Act 1992, ss. 5 (1) (q), 135 (3), 165 (1) (4). - Issued: 18.03.2014. Made: 14.03.2014. Coming into operation: 07.04.2014. Effect: S.R. 1977/74; 1987/465 amended & S.R. 2013/70 revoked. Territorial extent & classification: NI. General. - Revoked by SR 2015/139 (ISBN 9780337996764). - 4p.: 30 cm. - 978-0-337-99315-2 £4.00

The Social Security (Claims and Payments) (Amendment) Regulations (Northern Ireland) 2014 No. 2014/73. - Enabling power: Social Security Administration (Northern Ireland) Act 1992, ss. 13A (2) (b), 165 (1) (4). - Issued: 14.03.2014. Made: 11.03.2014. Coming into operation: 01.04.2014. Effect: S.R. 1987/465 amended. Territorial extent & classification: NI. General. - Revoked by SR 2015/109 (9780337996528). - 2p.: 30 cm. - 978-0-337-99307-7 £4.00

The Social Security (Crediting and Treatment of Contributions, and National Insurance Numbers) (Amendment) Regulations (Northern Ireland) 2014 No. 2014/33. - Enabling power: Social Security Contributions and Benefits (Northern Ireland) Act 1992, sch. 1, para. 8 (1) (d) (1A). - Issued: 14.02.2014. Made: 11.02.2014. Coming into operation: 06.04.2014. Effect: S.R. 2001/102 amended. Territorial extent & classification: NI. General. - 4p.: 30 cm. - 978-0-337-99272-8 £4.00

The Social Security (Habitual Residence) (Amendment) Regulations (Northern Ireland) 2014 No. 2014/133. - Enabling power: Social Security Contributions and Benefits (Northern Ireland) Act 1992, ss. 122 (1) (a) (d), 131 (1) (2), 171 (1) (3) (4) & S.I. 1995/2705 (N.I. 15), arts 6 (5) (12), 36 (2) & Immigration and Asylum Act 1999, ss. 115 (3) (4) (8) & State Pension Credit Act (Northern Ireland) 2002, ss. 1 (5) (a), 19 (1) (2) (a) (3) & Welfare Reform Act (Northern Ireland) 2007, ss. 4 (3), 25 (2). - Issued: 12.05.2014. Made: 08.05.2014. Coming into operation: 31.05.2014. Effect: S.R. 1987/459; 1996/198; 2003/28; 2006/405, 406; 2008/280 amended & S.R. 2013/167 partially revoked. Territorial extent & classification: NI. General. - 4p.: 30 cm. - 978-0-337-99410-4 £4.25

The Social Security (Invalid Care Allowance) (Amendment) Regulations (Northern Ireland) 2014 No. 2014/121. - Enabling power: Social Security Contributions and Benefits (Northern Ireland) Act 1992, ss. 70 (8), 171 (1) (3). - Issued: 29.04.2014. Made: 24.04.2014. Coming into operation: 20.05.2014. Effect: S.R. 1976/99 amended & S.R. 2010/81 partially revoked. Territorial extent & classification: NI. General. - Revoked by SR 2015/153 (ISBN 9780337996955). - 2p.: 30 cm. - 978-0-337-99401-2 £4.25

The Social Security (Jobseeker's Allowance and Employment and Support Allowance) (Waiting Days) (Amendment) Regulations (Northern Ireland) 2014 No. 2014/235. - Enabling power: S.I. 1995/2705 (N.I. 15), art 36 (2) (a), sch. 1, paras 4, 10 (1) & Welfare Reform Act (Northern Ireland) 2007 , s.25 (2) (a), sch. 2 para. 2- Issued: 23.09.2014. Made: 18.09.2014. Coming into operation: 27.10.2014. Effect: S.R. 1996/198 amended. Territorial extent & classification: NI. General. - 4p.: 30 cm. - 978-0-337-99497-5 £4.25

The Social Security (Maternity Allowance) (Miscellaneous Amendments) Regulations (Northern Ireland) 2014 No. 2014/140. - Enabling power: S.I 1991/2628 (NI.23), art. 39 (1), sch. 1, para. 4 (1) (b) & Social Security Contributions and Benefits (Northern Ireland) Act 1992, ss. 35 (3), 35B (11), 171 (1) (3) to (5) & Welfare Reform Act (Northern Ireland) 2007, s. 25 (2), sch. 2, para. 1 (a). - Issued: 20.05.2014. Made: 16.05.2014. Coming into operation: 18.05.2014. Effect: S.R. 1987/170; 1992/341; 2001/18; 2008/280 amended & S.R. 1997/156; 2006/361 partially revoked. Territorial extent & classification: NI. General. - 4p.: 30 cm. - 978-0-337-99416-6 £4.25

The Social Security (Maternity Allowance) (Participating Wife or Civil Partner of Self-employed Earner) Regulations (Northern Ireland) 2014 No. 2014/102. - Enabling power: European Communities Act 1972, s. 2 (2). - Issued: 03.04.2014. Made: 31.03.2014. Coming into operation: 01.04.2014. Effect: 1992 c.7 amended. Territorial extent & classification: NI. General. - 4p.: 30 cm. - For approval of the Assembly before the expiration of 6 months from the date of their coming into operation. - 978-0-337-99387-9 £4.25

The Social Security (Maternity Allowance) (Participating Wife or Civil Partner of Self-employed Earner) Regulations (Northern Ireland) 2014 No. 2014/102. - Enabling power: European Communities Act 1972, s. 2 (2). - Issued: 15.04.2014. Made: 31.03.2014. Coming into operation: 01.04.2014. Effect: 1992 c.7 amended. Territorial extent & classification: NI. General. - 4p.: 30 cm. - 978-0-337-99393-0 £4.25

The Social Security (Miscellaneous Amendments) Regulations (Northern Ireland) 2014 No. 2014/105. - Enabling power: Social Security Contributions and Benefits (Northern Ireland) Act 1992, ss. 122 (1) (a) (d), 132 (3) (40, 132A, 171 (1) (3) (4) & Social Security Administration (Northern Ireland) Act 1992, ss. 5 (1) (a), 109A (2) (b), 165 (1) (4) to (6) & S.I. 1995/2705 (N.I. 15), arts. 14 (4), 36 (2) (a) & State Pension Credit Act (Northern Ireland) 2002, ss. 15 (3) (6), 19 (1) to (3) & Welfare reform Act (Northern Ireland) 2007, ss. 17 (1), 25 (2). - Issued: 11.04.2014. Made: 07.04.2014. Coming into operation: 28.04.2014. Effect: S.R. 1987/459, 465; 1996/198; 2003/28; 2006/405, 406; 2008/280 amended & S.R. 2009/338 partially revoked. Territorial extent & classification: NI. General. - With correction slip dated April 2014. - 8p.: 30 cm. - 978-0-337-99392-3 £6.00

The Social Security (Miscellaneous Amendments No. 2) Regulations (Northern Ireland) 2014 No. 2014/275. - Enabling power: Social Security Contributions and Benefits (Northern Ireland) Act 1992, ss. 131 (1) (6), 132 (3), 132A (3), 171 (1) (3) (4) & S.I. 1995/2705, arts 6 (5), 36 (2), & State Pension Credit Act (Northern Ireland) 2002, ss. 2 (3) (b), 15 (3) (6) (b), 19 (1) to (3) & Welfare Reform Act (Northern Ireland) 2007, ss.4 (2) (a), 25 (2). - Issued: 07.11.2014. Made: 05.11.2014. Coming into operation: 26.11.2014. Effect: S.R. 1987/459; 1996/198; 2003/28, 2006/405, 406; 2008/80 amended & S.R. 1996/503 partially revoked. Territorial extent & classification: NI. General. - 8p.: 30 cm. - 978-0-337-99512-5 £6.00

The Social Security Pensions (Flat Rate Accrual Amount) Order (Northern Ireland) 2014 No. 2014/51. - Enabling power: Social Security Administration (Northern Ireland) Act 1992, s. 130AA. - Issued: 03.03.2014. Made: 26.02.2014. Coming into operation: 06.04.2014. Effect: None. Territorial extent & classification: NI. General. - 2p.: 30 cm. - 978-0-337-99286-5 £4.00

The Social Security Pensions (Low Earnings Threshold) Order (Northern Ireland) 2014 No. 2014/50. - Enabling power: Social Security Administration (Northern Ireland) Act 1992, s. 130A. - Issued: 03.03.2014. Made: 26.02.2014. Coming into operation: 06.04.2014. Effect: None. Territorial extent & classification: NI. General. - 2p.: 30 cm. - 978-0-337-99285-8 £4.00

The Social Security (Reciprocal Agreements) Order (Northern Ireland) 2014 No. 2014/156. - Enabling power: Social Security Administration (Northern Ireland) Act 1992, s. 155 (1) (b) (2) (5). - Issued: 09.06.2014. Made: 04.06.2014. Coming into operation: 05.06.2014 in accord. with art. 1. Effect: 1992 c.7, c.8; 2007 c.2 (NI); S.R. & O (NI) 1958/151; 1961/149; S.R. 1984/449; 1992/151; 1994/427; 1997/183 modified. Territorial extent & classification: NI. General. - 4p.: 30 cm. - 978-0-337-99429-6 £4.25

The Social Security (Recovery of Benefits) (Lump Sum Payments) (Amendment) Regulations (Northern Ireland) 2014 No. 2014/162. - Enabling power: Social Security Administration (Northern Ireland) Act 1992, s. 165 (4) & S.I. 1997/ 1183 (N.I. 12), arts 3A (1) to (3), 16 (2) to (4), 21, 23 (3), 25 (1) (2) (6A) (7), sch. 1, para. 4. - Issued: 11.06.2014. Made: 06.06.2014. Coming into operation: 01.07.2014. Effect: S.R. 2008/355 amended. Territorial extent and classification: NI. General. - 8p.: 30 cm. - 978-0-337-99433-3 £6.00

The Social Security Revaluation of Earnings Factors Order (Northern Ireland) 2014 No. 2014/49. - Enabling power: Social Security Administration (Northern Ireland) Act 1992, ss. 130, 165 (1) (4) (5). - Issued: 03.03.2014. Made: 26.02.2014. Coming into operation: 06.04.2014. Effect: None. Territorial extent & classification: NI. General. - 4p.: 30 cm. - 978-0-337-99284-1 £4.00

Statutory maternity pay

The Social Security Benefits Up-rating Order (Northern Ireland) 2014 No. 2014/78. - Enabling power: Social Security Administration (Northern Ireland) Act 1992, ss. 132, 132A, 165(1) (4) (5). - Issued: 17.03.2014. Made: 13.03.2014. Coming into operation: In accord. with art. 1. Effect: 1966 c.6 (N.I.); 1992 c.7; S.R. 1987/30, 459; 1992/32; 1994/461; 1995/35; 1996/198; 2002/380; 2003/28; 2006/405, 406; 2008/280; 2010/302, 407 amended & S.R. 2013/69 revoked (14.04.2014). Territorial extent & classification: NI. General. - For approval of the Assembly before the expiration of six months from the date of its coming into operation. Superseded by Approved SR 2014/78 (ISBN 9780337993138). - 44p.: 30 cm. - 978-0-337-99313-8 £9.75

The Social Security Benefits Up-rating Order (Northern Ireland) 2014 No. 2014/78. - Enabling power: Social Security Administration (Northern Ireland) Act 1992, ss. 132, 132A, 165(1) (4) (5). - Issued: 13.06.2014. Made: 13.03.2014. Coming into operation: In accord. with art. 1. Effect: 1966 c.6 (N.I.); 1992 c.7; S.R. 1987/30, 459; 1992/32; 1994/461; 1995/35; 1996/198; 2002/380; 2003/28; 2006/405, 406; 2008/280; 2010/302, 407 amended & S.R. 2013/69 revoked (14.04.2014). Territorial extent & classification: NI. General. - Approved by resolution of the Assembly on 9th June 2014; Revoked by SR 2015/124 (ISBN 9780337996634). - 44p.: 30 cm. - 978-0-337-99438-8 £9.75

Statutory sick pay

The Social Security Benefits Up-rating Order (Northern Ireland) 2014 No. 2014/78. - Enabling power: Social Security Administration (Northern Ireland) Act 1992, ss. 132, 132A, 165(1) (4) (5). - Issued: 17.03.2014. Made: 13.03.2014. Coming into operation: In accord. with art. 1. Effect: 1966 c.6 (N.I.); 1992 c.7; S.R. 1987/30, 459; 1992/32; 1994/461; 1995/35; 1996/198; 2002/380; 2003/28; 2006/405, 406; 2008/280; 2010/302, 407 amended & S.R. 2013/69 revoked (14.04.2014). Territorial extent & classification: NI. General. - For approval of the Assembly before the expiration of six months from the date of its coming into operation. Superseded by Approved SR 2014/78 (ISBN 9780337993138). - 44p.: 30 cm. - 978-0-337-99313-8 £9.75

The Social Security Benefits Up-rating Order (Northern Ireland) 2014 No. 2014/78. - Enabling power: Social Security Administration (Northern Ireland) Act 1992, ss. 132, 132A, 165(1) (4) (5). - Issued: 13.06.2014. Made: 13.03.2014. Coming into operation: In accord. with art. 1. Effect: 1966 c.6 (N.I.); 1992 c.7; S.R. 1987/30, 459; 1992/32; 1994/461; 1995/35; 1996/198; 2002/380; 2003/28; 2006/405, 406; 2008/280; 2010/302, 407 amended & S.R. 2013/69 revoked (14.04.2014). Territorial extent & classification: NI. General. - Approved by resolution of the Assembly on 9th June 2014; Revoked by SR 2015/124 (ISBN 9780337996634). - 44p.: 30 cm. - 978-0-337-99438-8 £9.75

The Statutory Sick Pay (Maintenance of Records) (Revocation) Regulations (Northern Ireland) 2014 No. 2014/65. - Enabling power: Social Security Administration (Northern Ireland) Act 1992, s. 122 (4). - Issued: 07.03.2014. Made: 05.03.2014. Coming into operation: 06.04.2014. Effect: S.R. 1982/263 partially revoked. - 2p.: 30 cm. - 978-0-337-99300-8 £4.00

Transport

The Bus and Coach Passengers Rights and Obligations (Designation of Terminals, Tour Operators and Enforcement) Regulations (Northern Ireland) 2014 No. 2014/186. - Enabling power: European Communities Act 1972, s. 2 (2). - Issued: 30.06.2014. Made: 26.06.2014. Coming into operation: 28.07.2014. Effect: None. Territorial extent & classification: NI. General. - 4p.: 30 cm. - 978-0-337-99457-9 £4.25

The Private Crossings (Signs and Barriers) Regulations (Northern Ireland) 2014 No. 2014/228. - Enabling power: Railway Safety Act (Northern Ireland) 2002, s. 5, sch. 1. - Issued: 25.09.2014. Made: 18.09.2014. Coming into operation: 20.10.2014. Effect: None. Territorial extent & classification: NI. General- 24p: 30 cm. - 978-0-337-99490-6 £8.50

The Rail Vehicle Accessibility (Applications for Exemption Orders) Regulations (Northern Ireland) 2014 No. 2014/46. - Enabling power: Disability Discrimination Act 1995, s. 47 (2). - Issued: 28.02.2014. Made: 25.02.2014. Coming into operation: 28.04.2014. Effect: S.R. 2001/265 revoked. Territorial extent & classification: NI. General. - 8p.: 30 cm. - 978-0-337-99281-0 £4.00

The Rail Vehicle Accessibility Regulations (Northern Ireland) 2014 No. 2014/45. - Enabling power: European Communities Act 1972, s. 2 (2) & Disability Discrimination Act 1995, s. 46 (1) (2) (4A) (5), 67 (3) (a). - Issued: 28.02.2014. Made: 25.02.2014. Coming into operation: 28.04.2014. Effect: S.R. 2001/264 revoked with saving. - 40p., figs: 30 cm. - 978-0-337-99280-3 £9.75

Statutory Rules of Northern Ireland 2014

Arranged by Number

1	Agriculture
2	Health and personal social services
3	Health and personal social services
4	Road traffic and vehicles
5	Road traffic and vehicles
6	Roads
7	Road traffic and vehicles
8	Roads
9	Landlord and tenant
10	Food
11	Food
12	Magistrates' courts
13	Road traffic and vehicles
14	Roads
15	Fisheries
16	Fisheries
17	Fisheries
18 (C.1)	Charities
19	Police
20	Dangerous drugs
21	Dangerous drugs
22	Rates
23	Employment
24	Road traffic and vehicles
25	Road traffic and vehicles
26	Health and safety
27	Rehabilitation of offenders
28	Criminal law
29	Road traffic and vehicles
30	Road traffic and vehicles
31	Planning
32	Roads
33	Social security
34	Road traffic and vehicles
35	Road traffic and vehicles
36	Roads
37	Education
38	Road traffic and vehicles
39	Employment
40	Building societies
41	Building societies
42	Road traffic and vehicles
43	European Communities
44	Building regulations
45	Disabled persons
	Transport
46	Disabled persons
	Transport
47	Health and safety
48	Employment
49	Social security
50	Social security
51	Social security
52	Energy conservation
53 (C.2)	Justice
54	Animals
55	Salaries
56	Fire and rescue services
57	Fire and rescue services
58	Animals
59	Health and personal social services
60	Gas
61	Pensions
62	Social security
63	Social security
64	Legal aid and advice
65	Statutory sick pay
66	Agriculture
67	Rates
68	Rates
69	Rating
70	Education
71	Registration of vital events
72	Road traffic and vehicles
73	Social security
74	Health and safety
75	Pensions
76 (C.3)	Pensions
77	Environmental protection
78	Social security
	Statutory maternity pay
	Statutory sick pay
	Employment
	Housing
	Rates
79	Pensions
80	Social security
81	Pensions
82	Roads
83	Road traffic and vehicles
84	Road traffic and vehicles
85	Road traffic and vehicles
86	Agriculture
87	Education
88	Employment
89	Pensions
90	Road traffic and vehicles
91	Roads
92	Agriculture
93	Pensions
94	Road traffic and vehicles
95	Road traffic and vehicles
96	Financial assistance
97	Education
98	Housing
	Rates
99	Pensions
100	Criminal law
101	Landlord and tenant
102	Social security
103	Housing
104	Road traffic and vehicles
105	Housing
	Rates
	Social security
106	Road traffic and vehicles
107	Animals
108	Health services charges
109	Road traffic and vehicles
110	Government resources and accounts
111	Health and social care

112	Road traffic and vehicles	169	Fire and rescue services
113	Road traffic and vehicles	170	Health and personal social services
114	Road traffic and vehicles	171	Road traffic and vehicles
115	Road traffic and vehicles	172	Plant health
116	Education	173	Industrial training
117	Environmental protection	174	Rehabilitation of offenders
118	Planning	175 (C.10)	Family law
119	Road traffic and vehicles	176	Road traffic and vehicles
120	Road traffic and vehicles	177	Road traffic and vehicles
121	Social security	178	Legal aid and advice
122	Road traffic and vehicles	179 (C.11)	Justice
123 (C.4)	Public service pensions	180	Road traffic
124	Roads	181	Police
	Road traffic and vehicles	182	Family law
125 (C.5)	Public health		Social security
126	Pharmacy	183 (C.12)	Pensions
127	Planning	184	Animals
128	Road traffic and vehicles	185	Criminal law
129	Road traffic and vehicles	186	Transport
130	Road traffic and vehicles	187	Road traffic and vehicles
131	Human rights	188	Local government
132	Human rights	189	Local government
133	Housing	190	Planning
	Rates	191	Family law
	Social security	192	Social security
134	Police	193	Family law
135	Road traffic and vehicles	194 (C.13)	Family law
136	Road traffic and vehicles	195	Pensions
137	Environmental protection	196	Animals
138 (C.6)	Family law		Agriculture
	Child support	197	Business improvement districts
139	Land registration	198	Energy
140	Social security	199	Roads
141	Road traffic and vehicles	200	Road traffic and vehicles
142 (C.7)	Local government	201	Roads
143	Business improvement districts	202	Environmental protection
144	Road traffic and vehicles	203 (C.14)	Pensions
145	Roads	204	Pensions
146	Electricity	205	Road traffic and vehicles
147	Environmental protection	206	Road traffic and vehicles
148	Local government	207	Criminal law
149	Road traffic and vehicles	208	European Communities
150	Housing		Environmental protection
	Rates	209	Sea fisheries
	Social security	210	Road traffic and vehicles
151	Animals	211	Road traffic and vehicles
152	Human rights	212	Road traffic and vehicles
153 (C.8)	Local government	213	Pensions
154	Health and personal social services	214	Road traffic and vehicles
155 (C.9)	Financial provisions	215	Health and personal social services
156	Social security	216	Road traffic and vehicles
157	Road traffic and vehicles	217	Road traffic and vehicles
158	Dangerous drugs	218	Education
159	Dangerous drugs	219	Court of Judicature, Northern Ireland
160	Road traffic and vehicles	220	Court of Judicature, Northern Ireland
161	Road traffic and vehicles	221	Magistrates' courts
162	Social security	222	Court of Judicature, Northern Ireland
163	Police	223	Food
164	Road traffic and vehicles	224	Health and safety
165	Road traffic and vehicles	225	Health and personal social services
166	Clean air	226	Social security
167	Family law	227	Road traffic and vehicles
168	Fire and rescue services	228	Transport

229	Road and railway transport
230	Road traffic and vehicles
231	Road traffic and vehicles
232	Road traffic and vehicles
233	Road traffic and vehicles
234	Road traffic and vehicles
235	Social security
236	Road traffic and vehicles
237	Road traffic and vehicles
238 (C.15)	Road traffic and vehicles
239	Road traffic and vehicles
240	Road traffic and vehicles
241	Road traffic and vehicles
242	Road traffic and vehicles
243	Road traffic and vehicles
244	Road traffic and vehicles
245	Road traffic and vehicles
246	Road traffic and vehicles
247	Road traffic and vehicles
248	Road traffic and vehicles
249	Clean air
250	Road traffic and vehicles
251	Road traffic and vehicles
252	Road traffic and vehicles
253	Environmental protection
254	Road traffic and vehicles
255	Road traffic and vehicles
256	Road traffic and vehicles
257	Roads
258	Roads
259	Lands Tribunal
260	Road traffic and vehicles
261	Dangerous drugs
262	Dangerous drugs
263	Social security
264	Local government
265	Criminal law
266	Animals
267	Health and social care
268	Roads
269	Road traffic and vehicles
270	Road traffic and vehicles
271	Road traffic and vehicles
272	Roads
273	Roads
274	Human rights
275	Social security
276	Environmental protection
277	Food
278	Road traffic and vehicles
279	Road traffic and vehicles
280	Health and safety
281	Road traffic and vehicles
282	Road traffic and vehicles
283	Dogs
284	Electricity
285	Food
286	Food
287	Food
288	Dangerous drugs
289	Road traffic and vehicles
290	Public service pensions
291	Agriculture
292	Local government
293	Health and social care
294	Clean air
295	Seeds
296	Marriage
297	Civil partnership
298	Pensions
299	Fisheries
300 (C.16)	Road traffic and vehicles
301	Energy
302	Road traffic and vehicles
303	Road traffic and vehicles
304	Environmental protection
305 (C.17)	Financial provisions
306 (C.18)	Rates
307	Environmental protection
308	Environmental protection
309	Education
310	Public service pensions
	Education
311	Roads
312	Roads
313	Road traffic and vehicles
314	Roads
315	Road traffic and vehicles
316	Road traffic and vehicles
317	Road traffic and vehicles
318	Health and social care
319	Health and personal social services
320	Criminal law
321	Pensions
322	Justice
323	Medicines
324	Medicines

List of Commencement Orders 2014

18 (C.1)
53 (C.2)
76 (C.3)
123 (C.4)
125 (C.5)
138 (C.6)
142 (C.7)
153 (C.8)
155 (C.9)
175 (C.10)
179 (C.11)
183 (C.12)
194 (C.13)
203 (C.14)
238 (C.15)
300 (C.16)
305 (C.17)
306 (C.18)

WELSH ASSEMBLY LEGISLATION

Measures of the National Assembly for Wales

Measures of the National Assembly for Wales 2011

Welsh Language (Wales) Measure 2011: 2011 nawm 1. - xi, xi, 138, 138p.: 30 cm. - Corrected reprint replacing original version (2011, ISBN 9780348104943) and being issued free of charge to all known recipients of the original. A Measure of the National Assembly for Wales to make provision about the official status of the Welsh language in Wales; to provide for a Welsh Language Partnership Council; to establish the Office of Welsh Language Commissioner; to provide for an Advisory Panel to the Welsh Language Commissioner; to make provision about promoting and facilitating the use of the Welsh language and treating the Welsh language no less favourably than the English language; to make provision about standards relating to the Welsh language (including duties to comply with those standards, and rights arising from the enforceability of those duties); to make provision about investigation of interference with the freedom to use the Welsh language; to establish a Welsh Language Tribunal; to abolish the Welsh Language Board and Welsh language schemes. Explanatory notes to assist in the understanding of this Measure are available separately (ISBN 9780348105216). - Parallel texts in English and Welsh. Welsh title: Mesur y Gymraeg (Cymru) 2011: 2011 mccc 1. - 978-0-348-10536-0 £31.75

Acts of the National Assembly for Wales

Acts of the National Assembly for Wales 2013

Local Government Democracy (Wales) Act 2013 (correction slip): 2013 anaw 4. - 1 sheet: 30 cm. - Correction slip (to ISBN 9780348105063) dated March 2015. - Parallel texts in English and Welsh. Welsh title: Deddf Llywodraeth Leol (Democratiaeth) (Cymru) 2013: 2013 dccc 4. - Free

Acts of the National Assembly for Wales 2014

Agricultural Sector (Wales) Act 2014: 2014 anaw 6. - ii, ii, 10, 10, [1]p.: 30 cm. - Royal assent, 30 July 2014. An Act of the National Assembly for Wales to make provision in relation to the agricultural sector in Wales. Explanatory notes to the Act are available separately (ISBN 9780348109092). - Parallel texts in English and Welsh. Welsh title: Deddf Sector Amaethyddol (Cymru) 2014 dccc 6. - 978-0-348-10908-5 £6.00

Control of Horses (Wales) Act 2014: 2014 anaw 3. - i, i, 5, 5p.: 30 cm. - Royal assent, 27 January 2014. An Act of the National Assembly for Wales to make provision for and in connection with the taking of action in relation to horses which are in public places without lawful authority or which are on other land without consent. Explanatory notes to assist in the understanding of the Act are available separately (ISBN 9780348109047). - Parallel texts in English and Welsh. Welsh title: Deddf Rheoli Ceffylau (Cymru) 2014 2014 dccc 3. - 978-0-348-10866-8 £5.75

Education (Wales) Act 2014: 2014 anaw 5. - iii, iii, 40, 40p.: 30 cm. - Royal assent, 12 May 2014. An Act of the National Assembly for Wales to make provision about the Education Workforce Council (formerly the General Teaching Council for Wales); to extend the registration, qualification and training requirements of the education workforce; to make provision about the determination of school term and holiday dates in Wales; to make provision in connection with appointments to Her Majesty's Inspectorate of Education and Training in Wales. Explanatory notes to the Act are available separately (ISBN 9780348109078). - Parallel texts in English and Welsh. Welsh title: Deddf Addysg (Cymru) 2014 dccc 5. - 978-0-348-10906-1 £16.00

Further and Higher Education (Governance and Information) (Wales) Act 2014: 2014 anaw 1. - i, i, 11, 11p.: 30 cm. - Royal assent, 27 January 2014. An Act of the National Assembly for Wales to make provision about the governance of institutions within the further education sector and about the supply of information in connection with the provision of support to students in further or higher education. Explanatory notes to assist in the understanding of the Act are available separately (ISBN 9780348109030)- Parallel texts in English and Welsh. Welsh title: Deddf Addysg Bellach ac Uwch (Llywodraethu a Gwybodaeth) (Cymru) 2014 2014 dcc 1. - 978-0-348-10864-4 £5.75

Housing (Wales) Act 2014: 2014 anaw 7. - i - vi, 103; i - vi, 103p.: 30 cm. - Royal assent, 17 September 2014. An Act of the National Assembly to provide for the regulation of private rented housing; to reform the law relating to homelessness; to provide for assessment of the accommodation needs of Gypsies and Travellers and to require local authorities to meet those needs; to make provision about the standards of housing provided by local authorities; to abolish housing revenue account subsidy; to allow fully mutual housing associations to grant assured tenancies; to make provision about council tax payable for empty dwellings. Explanatory notes to assist in the understanding of the Act are available separately (ISBN 9780348109122). - Parallel texts in English and Welsh. Welsh title: Deddf Tay (Cymru) 2014 2014 dccc 7. - 978-0-348-10910-8 £27.50

National Health Service Finance (Wales) Act 2014: 2014 anaw 2. - i, i, 3, 3p.: 30 cm. - Royal assent, 27 January 2014. An Act of the National Assembly for Wales to make provision in relation to the financial duties of Local Health Boards. Explanatory notes to assist in the understanding of the Act are available separately (9780348108675). - Parallel texts in English and Welsh. Welsh title: Deddf Cyllid y Gwasanaeth Iechyd Gwladol (Cymru) 2014 2014 dccc 2. - 978-0-348-10865-1 £5.75

Social Services and Well-being (Wales) Act 2014: 2014 anaw 4. - viii, viii, 182, 182p.: 30 cm. - Royal assent, 1 May 2014. An Act of the National Assembly for Wales to reform social services law; to make provision about improving the well-being outcomes for people who need care and support and carers who need support; to make provision about co-operation and partnership by public authorities with a view to improving the well-being of people; to make provision about complaints relating to social care and palliative care. Explanatory notes to assist in the understanding of the Act are available separately (ISBN 9780348109115). - Parallel texts in English and Welsh. Welsh title: Deddf Gwasanaethau Cymdeithasol a Llesiant (Cymru) 2014 dccc 4. - 978-0-348-10905-4 £39.25

Acts of the National Assembly for Wales - Explanatory Notes 2014

Agricultural Sector (Wales) Act 2014: 2014 anaw 6: explanatory notes. - [1], 9, 9, [1]p.: 30 cm. - These notes refer to the Agricultural Sector (Wales) Act 2014 (anaw 6) which received Royal Assent on 30 July 2014 (ISBN 9780348109085). - Parallel texts in English and Welsh. Welsh title: Deddf Sector Amaethyddol (Cymru) 2014 dccc 6 Nodiadau Esboniadol. - 978-0-348-10909-2 £6.00

Control of Horses (Wales) Act 2014: 2014 anaw 3: explanatory notes. - 4, 4p.: 30 cm. - These notes refer to the Control of Horses (Wales) Act 2014 (anaw 3) which received Royal Assent on 27 January 2014 (ISBN 9780348108668). - Parallel texts in English and Welsh. Welsh title: Deddf Rheoli Ceffylau (Cymru) 2014 dccc 3 Nodiadau Esboniadol. - 978-0-348-10904-7 £5.75

Education (Wales) Act 2014: 2014 anaw 5: explanatory notes. - 11, 11p.: 30 cm. - These notes refer to the Education (Wales) Act 2014 (anaw 5) which received Royal assent on 12 May 2014 (ISBN 9780348109061). - Parallel texts in English and Welsh. Welsh title: Deddf Addysg (Cymru) 2014: 2014 dccc 5: Nodiadau Esboniadol. - 978-0-348-10907-8 £6.00

Further and Higher Education (Governance and Information) (Wales) Act 2014: 2014 anaw 1: explanatory notes. - 5, 5p.: 30 cm. - These notes refer to the Further and Higher Education (Governance and Information) (Wales) Act 2014 (anaw 1) which received Royal Assent on 27 January 2014 (ISBN 9780348108644). - Parallel texts in English and Welsh. Welsh title: Deddf Addysg Bellach Ac Uwch (Llywodraethu a Gwybodaeth) (Cymru) 2014 2014 dccc 1 Nodiadau Esboniadol. - 978-0-348-10903-0 £5.75

Housing (Wales) Act 2014: 2014 anaw 7: explanatory notes. - [1], 43, 43p.: 30 cm. - These notes refer to the Housing (Wales) Act 2014 (anaw 7) which received Royal Assent on 17 September 2014 (ISBN 9780348109108). - Parallel texts in English and Welsh. Welsh title: Deddf Tay (Cymru) 2014 dccc 7 Nodiadau Esboniadol. - 978-0-348-10912-2 £10.00

National Health Service Finance (Wales) Act 2014: 2014 anaw 2: explanatory notes. - 3, 3p.: 30 cm. - These notes refer to the National Health Service Finance (Wales) Act 2014 (anaw 2) which received royal assent on 27 January 2014 (ISBN 9780348108651). - Parallel texts in English and Welsh. Welsh title: Deddf Cyllid Y Gwasanaeth Iechyd Gwladol (Cymru) 2014 2014 dccc 2 Nodiadau Esboniadol. - 978-0-348-10867-5 £5.75

Social Services and Well-being (Wales) Act 2014: 2014 anaw 4: explanatory notes. - 86, 86p.: 30 cm. - These notes refer to the Social Services and Well-being (Wales) Act 2014 (anaw 4) which received Royal assent on 1 May 2014 (ISBN 9780348109054). - Parallel texts in English and Welsh. Welsh title: Deddf Gwasanaethau Cymdeithasol a Llesiant (Cymru) 2014 dccc 4 Nodiadau Esboniadol. - 978-0-348-10911-5 £25.50

ALPHABETICAL INDEX

A

A29 Armagh Road, Moy: Abandonment: Northern Ireland 285
A3 Richhill, Portadown: Abandonment: Northern Ireland 285, 285
A4 Sligo Road, Belcoo: Abandonment: Northern Ireland 285, 285
Aberdeen prison: Discontinuance: Scotland 256
Abernant Church in Wales School: Diocese of St Davids: Educational endowments 37
Able Marine Energy Park Development: Consent 52, 61
Access to Justice Act 1999: Appeals: Destination: Family proceedings: England & Wales 44, 46, 187
Access: Countryside: Coastal margin: Cumbria 26
Access: Countryside: Coastal margin: Durham, Hartlepool & Sunderland 26
Access: Countryside: Coastal margin: Sea Palling to Weybourne 26
Accident hazards: Control: Heavy fuel oil 52, 199
Accounts & audit: Wales 70
Acetylene: Safety 52
Acquisition of land: Home loss payments: Prescribed amounts: England 7, 22
Act of Adjournal: Criminal Procedure (Scotland) Act 1995: Criminal Procedure Rules 1996: Amendments: Scotland 250, 251, 264
Act of Adjournal: Criminal procedure rules: Amendment: Regulatory Reform (Scotland) Act 2014: Scotland 250, 264
Act of Adjournal: Criminal procedure rules: Scotland 250, 251, 264
Act of Sederunt: Commissary business: Scotland 264
Act of Sederunt: Court of Session: Messengers-at-Arms: Sheriff officers: Scotland 245, 264
Act of Sederunt: Court of Session: Rules: Ordinary cause rules & summary cause rules: Scotland 246, 264
Act of Sederunt: Court of Session: Rules: Solicitor's fees: Scotland 245
Act of Sederunt: Court of Session: Sheriff Court: Company insolvency rules: Scotland 245, 264
Act of Sederunt: Court of Session: Sheriff Court: Rules: Marriage & Civil Partnership (Scotland) Act 2014: Scotland 245, 264
Act of Sederunt: Court of Session: Sheriff Court: Rules: Scotland 245, 246, 264
Act of Sederunt: Fitness for Judicial Office Tribunal Rules: Scotland 251, 264
Act of Sederunt: Sheriff Court: Solicitors fees: Scotland 264
Active travel: Wales: Commencements 55
Adoption & care planning: England 13
Adoption & Children Act 2002: Commencements: England & Wales 14
Adoption & Children Act 2007: Compulsory supervision order reports: Permanence orders: Scotland 244
Adoption & Children Act 2002: Register: England 13
Adoption & maternity leave: Curtailment 197
Adoption & paternity leave 197
Adoption agencies 15
Adoption pay: Statutory 198
Adoption pay: Statutory: Curtailment 193
Adoption pay: Statutory: Parental orders & prospective adopters 198
Adoption support services: England 13, 189
Adoption: Information & intermediary services: Pre-commencement adoptions: England 13, 189
Adoption: Overseas: Employment Rights Act 1996: Section 75G & 75H: Application 197
Adoption: Overseas: Social Security Contributions & Benefits Act 1992: Parts 12ZA & 12ZB: Application 198
Adoption: Overseas: Statutory shared parental pay 198
Adults with incapacity: Welfare guardians: Supervision: Local authorities: Scotland 242
Advertisements: Control: Planning: Northern Ireland 283
Advertisements: Control: Town & country planning: Scotland 266
Aerosol dispensers 23
African Development Fund: African Development Bank: Thirteenth replenishment 62
African Development Fund: Multilateral debt relief initiative 62
African Legal Support Facility: Legal capacities 62
Aggregates levy: Registration & miscellaneous provisions 7
Aggregates levy: Revenue & customs: Out of time reviews: Appeal provisions 7, 20, 30, 47, 62, 63, 203
Agricultural employment: Enterprise & Regulatory Reform Act 2013: Commencements 7, 63, 64, 197, 198
Agricultural Holdings (Scotland) Act 2003: Remedial: Scotland 252
Agricultural holdings: Units of production: England 63
Agricultural holdings: Units of production: Wales 64
Agricultural sector: Acts: Explanatory notes: Wales 296
Agricultural sector: Acts: Wales 296
Agricultural subsidies & grants schemes: Wales 8
Agriculture: Agricultural subsidies & grants schemes: Wales 8
Agriculture: Animals & related products: Trade: Northern Ireland 273, 274
Agriculture: Common Agricultural Policy: Basic payment & support schemes: England 8
Agriculture: Common Agricultural Policy: Basic payment scheme: Provisional payment region classification: Wales 8
Agriculture: Common Agricultural Policy: Control & enforcement: Cross-compliance & Scrutiny of transactions & appeals 7
Agriculture: Common Agricultural Policy: Cross-compliance: Scotland 243
Agriculture: Common Agricultural Policy: Direct payments & support schemes: Northern Ireland 273
Agriculture: Common Agricultural Policy: Integrated administration: Control system & enforcement: Wales 8
Agriculture: Common Agricultural Policy: Schemes: Cross-compliance: Scotland 243
Agriculture: Common Agricultural Policy: Single payment & support schemes: Cross-compliance: Northern Ireland 273
Agriculture: Common Agricultural Policy: Single payment & support schemes: Northern Ireland 273
Agriculture: Common Agricultural Policy: Single payment & support schemes: Wales 8

Agriculture: Feed & food: Official controls: England . . . 8, 50
Agriculture: Feed & food: Official controls: Wales . . . 8, 50
Agriculture: Food from Britain: Public bodies: Abolition . . . 7, 85
Agriculture: Less favoured area support schemes: Scotland . . . 243
Agriculture: Phosphorus: Use: Northern Ireland . . . 277
Agriculture: Revocations . . . 7
Agriculture: Rural development programme . . . 8
Agriculture: Single Common Market Organisation: Consequential amendments: Northern Ireland . . . 273
Agriculture: Student fees: Northern Ireland . . . 273
Agriculture: Uplands: Transitional payments . . . 8
Air Force: Disablement & death: Service pensions . . . 79
Air navigation: Amendments . . . 15
Air navigation: Flying restrictions: Abingdon Air & Country Show . . . 15
Air navigation: Flying restrictions: Ascot . . . 15
Air navigation: Flying restrictions: Auchterarder . . . 16
Air navigation: Flying restrictions: Balado . . . 16
Air navigation: Flying restrictions: Bournemouth . . . 16
Air navigation: Flying restrictions: Bristol Channel . . . 16
Air navigation: Flying restrictions: Cheltenham Festival . . . 16
Air navigation: Flying restrictions: Cholmondeley Castle . . . 16
Air navigation: Flying restrictions: Dunsfold . . . 16
Air navigation: Flying restrictions: Duxford Aerodrome . . . 16
Air navigation: Flying restrictions: Eastbourne . . . 16
Air navigation: Flying restrictions: Farnborough Air Show . . . 16
Air navigation: Flying restrictions: Folkestone . . . 16
Air navigation: Flying restrictions: Giro d'Italia stage 1 . . . 16
Air navigation: Flying restrictions: Giro d'Italia stage 2 . . . 16
Air navigation: Flying restrictions: Giro d'Italia stage 3 . . . 16
Air navigation: Flying restrictions: Glasgow 2014 Commonwealth Games . . . 16, 17
Air navigation: Flying restrictions: Glastonbury Festival . . . 17
Air navigation: Flying restrictions: Hylands Park . . . 17
Air navigation: Flying restrictions: Jet Formation Display Team, County Londonderry . . . 17
Air navigation: Flying restrictions: Jet Formation Display Teams . . . 17
Air navigation: Flying restrictions: Jet formation display teams . . . 17
Air navigation: Flying restrictions: Jim Clark Rally . . . 17
Air navigation: Flying restrictions: Newport . . . 17
Air navigation: Flying restrictions: Northampton Sywell . . . 17
Air navigation: Flying restrictions: Northern Ireland International Air Show . . . 17
Air navigation: Flying restrictions: Overton . . . 17
Air navigation: Flying restrictions: Pembrey . . . 17
Air navigation: Flying restrictions: Queen's birthday flypast . . . 17
Air navigation: Flying restrictions: RAF Fairford, Gloucestershire . . . 17
Air navigation: Flying restrictions: Remembrance Sunday . . . 17
Air navigation: Flying restrictions: Rendcomb Aerodrome . . . 18
Air navigation: Flying restrictions: RNAS Culdrose . . . 18
Air navigation: Flying restrictions: RNAS Yeovilton . . . 18
Air navigation: Flying restrictions: Royal Air Force Cosford . . . 18
Air navigation: Flying restrictions: Royal Air Force Topcliffe . . . 18
Air navigation: Flying restrictions: Royal Air Force Waddington . . . 18
Air navigation: Flying restrictions: Royal International Air Tattoo RAF Fairford . . . 18
Air navigation: Flying restrictions: Salthouse, Norfolk . . . 18
Air navigation: Flying restrictions: Shoreham-by-Sea . . . 18
Air navigation: Flying restrictions: Silverstone & Turweston . . . 18
Air navigation: Flying restrictions: Southport . . . 18
Air navigation: Flying restrictions: State opening of Parliament . . . 18
Air navigation: Flying restrictions: Stirling . . . 18
Air navigation: Flying restrictions: Stonehenge . . . 18
Air navigation: Flying restrictions: Sunderland . . . 18
Air navigation: Flying restrictions: Tour de France . . . 18
Air navigation: Flying restrictions: Trooping the Colour . . . 18
Air navigation: Flying restrictions: Wales Rally GB . . . 19
Air navigation: Flying restrictions: Watnall . . . 19
Air navigation: Flying restrictions: Weston Park . . . 19
Air navigation: Flying restrictions: Wimbledon . . . 19
Air navigation: Jersey . . . 15
Air navigation: Overseas territories . . . 15
Air navigation: Overseas territories: Environmental standards . . . 15
Air pollution: Ships: Prevention . . . 72
Air travel: Disabled persons: Access . . . 19, 33
Alcohol: Abstinence & monitoring requirements: Criminal Justice Act 2003 . . . 29
Alcohol: Abstinence & monitoring requirements: Legal Aid, Sentencing & Punishment of Offenders Act 2012: Commencements . . . 29
Ammunition & arms: Firearms: Rules . . . 10
Ancient monuments: Historic Environment Scotland Act 2014: Commencements . . . 243
Angling permit: Foyle area: Northern Ireland . . . 278
Anguilla: International tax: Enforcement . . . 12, 25, 60, 61, 203
Animal by-products: Enforcement: Northern Ireland . . . 274
Animal by-products: Enforcement: Wales . . . 9, 86
Animal health: Animal by-products: Enforcement: Northern Ireland . . . 274

Animal health: Animal by-products: Enforcement: Wales 9, 86
Animal health: Animals: Welfare: Breeding of dogs: Wales. 9
Animal health: Animals: Welfare: Time of killing: Wales 9
Animal health: Brucellosis: Scotland 243
Animal health: Foot & mouth disease: Northern Ireland 274
Animal health: Sheep & goats: Records, identification & movement: England 9
Animal health: Specified diseases: Notification & slaughter: Scotland 243
Animal health: Tuberculosis: Deer & camelid: England. 9
Animal health: Tuberculosis: England 9
Animal health: Tuberculosis: Scotland 243
Animal health: Tuberculosis: Wales 9
Animals & related products: Trade: Northern Ireland 273, 274
Animals: Animal health: Swine: Diseases 8
Animals: Brucellosis: Control: Northern Ireland 274
Animals: Importation: Northern Ireland 274
Animals: Pets: Non commercial movement 9
Animals: Tuberculosis: Deer & camelid: England 9
Animals: Tuberculosis: England 9
Animals: Welfare: Breeding of dogs: Wales 9
Animals: Welfare: Slaughter or killing: England 9
Animals: Welfare: Time of killing: England 9
Animals: Welfare: Time of killing: Northern Ireland 274
Animals: Welfare: Time of killing: Wales 9
Animals: Zoonoses: Fees: Northern Ireland 274
Annesborough Road, Lurgan: Abandonment: Northern Ireland 285
Annual tax on enveloped dwellings: Charities: Definition: Relevant territories 9, 13, 26, 60, 61, 195, 203
Anonymous registration: Northern Ireland 90
Anti-social Behaviour, Crime & Policing Act 2014: Commencements 10, 29, 31, 33, 43, 44, 45, 55, 56, 82, 83, 84
Anti-social Behaviour, Crime & Policing Act 2014: Commencements: Scotland. 246
Anti-social Behaviour, Crime & Policing Act 2014: Commencements: Wales 56
Anti-social Behaviour, Crime & Policing Act 2014: Consequential amendments 10
Anti-social Behaviour, Crime & Policing Act 2014: Publication of Public Spaces Protection Orders: Regulations 43
Anti-social behaviour: Crime & policing: Acts 4
Anti-social behaviour: Crime & policing: Acts: Explanatory notes 5
Antrim: Waiting restrictions: Northern Ireland 289
Aquaculture & Fisheries (Scotland) Act 2013: Commercially damaging species: Specification: Scotland 243, 249, 264
Architects Act 1997: Amendments 10
Argyll & Bute Council: Parking attendants: Wearing of uniforms: Scotland 258
Argyll & Bute Council: Road traffic: Permitted & special parking area: Scotland 259
Armagh, Charlemont Gardens: Parking & waiting restrictions: Northern Ireland 286
Armagh: Parking & waiting restrictions: Northern Ireland 286
Armed Forces Act 2011: Commencements 31
Armed Forces Act: Continuation 31
Armed Forces: Citizenship: Bills 4
Armed Forces: Compensation schemes 79
Armed Forces: Early Departure Payments Scheme 2014: Commencements. 79
Armed Forces: Overseas marriage. 72
Armed Forces: Pension regulations 79
Armed Forces: Pension schemes & early departure schemes 79
Armed Forces: Powers of stop & search, search, seizure & retention 31
Armed Forces: Terms of service 31
Armoy Motorcycle Race: Road races: Northern Ireland 288
Arms & ammunition: Anti-social Behaviour, Crime & Policing Act 2014: Commencements 10, 29, 31, 33, 45, 56, 83, 84
Arms & ammunition: Anti-social Behaviour, Crime & Policing Act 2014: Consequential amendments 10
Arms & ammunition: Firearms: Rules. 10
Army: Disablement & death: Service pensions 79
Assembly Ombudsman: Salaries: Northern Ireland 290
Assisted areas: Industrial development 60
Associated British Ports: Fisher Fleet Quay: Harbour revision 52
Assured tenancies & agricultural occupancies: Forms: Wales 64
Asylum: Immigration Act 2014 57
Asylum: Immigration Act 2014: Transitional & saving provisions 57
Atomic energy & radioactive substances: Nuclear industries: Security 10
Attorney General's Human Rights Guidance: Courts & Tribunal Service: Support for victims & witnesses: Northern Ireland 280
Attorney General's Human Rights Guidance: Northern Ireland Prison Service. 281
Attorney General's Human Rights Guidance: Public Prosecution Service for Northern Ireland. 281
Audible intruder alarms: Noise: Control 86
Audiovisual media services 11, 40
Auditors: Local audit & statutory audit: Delegation of functions. 10, 21, 69
Automatic enrolment: Pensions: Earnings trigger & qualifying earnings band: Northern Ireland 282
Aviation: Civil: Air navigation: Amendments 15
Awdurdod Gwasanaethau Busnes y GIG: NHS Business Services Authority: Transfer of staff: National Health Service Commissioning Board
. . . . 76
Aylesbury Vale: Electoral changes 66

B

Badges: Motor vehicles: Disabled persons: Scotland. 258

Bailiwick of Jersey: International Criminal Court Act 2001 62
Ballygowan Road, Saintfield: Abandonment: Northern Ireland 285
Ballykelly: Waiting restrictions: Northern Ireland 289
Ballymoney: Parking & waiting restrictions: Northern Ireland 286
Banbridge: One-way traffic: Northern Ireland 286
Banbridge: Parking & waiting restrictions: Northern Ireland 286
Banbridge: Waiting restrictions: Northern Ireland 289
Banking Act 2009: Banking group companies 47
Banking Act 2009: Exclusion of investment firms 47
Banking Act 2009: Mandatory Compensation arrangements following bail-in 10
Banking Act 2009: Partial property transfers: Restrictions 47
Banking Act 2009: Partial property transfers: Third party compensation arrangements 47
Banking Act 2009: Restriction of special bail-in provision 10
Banking reform: Financial services: Acts 4
Banking reform: Financial services: Acts: Explanatory notes 5
Banking: Financial Services (Banking Reform) Act 2013: Disclosure & confidential information 48
Banking: Financial Services (Banking Reform) Act 2013: Transitional provisions 48
Bankruptcy & Debt Advice (Scotland) Act 2014: Consequential provisions: Scotland 243
Bankruptcy & Diligence etc. (Scotland) Act 2007: Commencements: Scotland 243, 250
Bankruptcy: Applications & decisions: Scotland 243, 246, 250
Bankruptcy: Bankruptcy & Debt Advice (Scotland) Act 2014: Commencements: Scotland 243, 246, 250
Bankruptcy: Bankruptcy & Debt Advice (Scotland) Act 2014: Consequential provisions: Scotland 243
Bankruptcy: Bankruptcy & Diligence etc. (Scotland) Act 2007: Commencements: Scotland 243, 250
Bankruptcy: Common financial tool: Scotland 244, 246, 251
Bankruptcy: Debt advice: Acts: Scotland 241
Bankruptcy: Fees: Scotland 251
Bankruptcy: Money advice & deduction from income: Scotland 243, 246, 250
Bankruptcy: Scotland 244, 251
Banks & banking: Depositor preference & priorities 10, 12
Banks & banking: Financial Services & Markets Act 2000: Excluded activities & prohibitions 10
Banks & banking: Financial Services & Markets Act 2000: Ring-fenced bodies & core activities 10
Banks & banking: Financial Services (Banking Reform) Act 2013: Commencements 10
Banks & banking: Financial Services Act 2012: Commencements 10
Banks & banking: Recovery & resolution 10, 47
Barnet & Chase Farm Hospitals: National Health Service Trust 74
Barnet, Enfield & Haringey Mental Health NHS Trust: Establishment: National Health Service Trust: Establishment 74
Barnsley, Doncaster, Rotherham & Sheffield Combined Authority 66, 201
Bathing water 204
Belfast City Centre: Traffic control: Northern Ireland 286
Belfast City Centre: Waiting restrictions: Northern Ireland 289
Belfast: One-way traffic: Northern Ireland 286
Belfast: Parking & waiting restrictions: Northern Ireland 286
Belgium: Double taxation: Relief & international enforcement 12, 25, 58, 81
Berry Burn: Electricity: Licence requirement: Exemption 40
Betting duty: General: Excise, general, pool, remote 44
Betting, gaming & lotteries: Courts & tribunals: Fees: England & Wales 11, 27, 46, 51, 70, 72, 188, 195, 202
Betting, gaming & lotteries: Gambling Act (Licensing & Advertising) Act 2014: Commencements 11
Betting, gaming & lotteries: Gambling Act (Licensing & Advertising) Act 2014: Transitional provisions 11
Betting, gaming & lotteries: Gaming machines: Categories 10
Betting, gaming & lotteries: Olympic lotteries: Olympic Lottery Distribution Fund: Payments out 11
Billing authorities: Precepts: Anticipation: Council tax 26
Biofuels & other fuel substitutes: Excise duties: Payment 44
Births, deaths & marriages, etc.: Registration: Fees: Amendments 88
Births, deaths & marriages, etc.: Registration: Overseas registration 88
Births, deaths & marriages, etc.: Registration: Overseas registration: Legislative reform 88, 89
Bolsover: Electoral changes 66
Bonds: Premium savings bonds: Maximum holdings 74
Borders, Citizenship & Immigration Act 2009: Commencements 57
Bovine tuberculosis: Animal health: Scotland 243
Bracknell Forest Borough Council: Permit schemes: Traffic management 54
Braintree: Electoral changes 66
Breckland: Electoral changes 66
Bridge Street, Lisburn: Parking places on road: Northern Ireland 287
Bridge Street, Lisburn: Traffic control: Northern Ireland 286
Bristol Channel: Air navigation: Flying restrictions 16
British nationality 11
British Virgin Islands: International tax: Enforcement 12, 25, 60, 61, 203
Broadcasting: Audiovisual media services 11, 40
Broadcasting: Independent productions 11
Broadcasting: Television 11
Broadway, Larne: Abandonment: Northern Ireland 285
Bromsgrove: Electoral changes 66
Brucellosis: Animal health: Scotland 243
Brucellosis: Control: Animals: Northern Ireland 274
Buckinghamshire County Council: Filming on highways: Local acts 6
Budget (Scotland) Act 2013: Amendments: Scotland 256
Budget (Scotland) Act 2014: Amendments: Scotland 256
Budget: Acts: Explanatory notes: Northern Ireland 272

Budget: Acts: Northern Ireland 272
Budget: Acts: Scotland. 241
Building & buildings: Energy performance: England & Wales 11
Building & buildings: England & Wales 11
Building & buildings: Scotland 244
Building & buildings: Wales 11
Building (Scotland) Act 2003: Charging orders: Scotland 244
Building regulations: England & Wales 11
Building regulations: Northern Ireland 274
Building Societies (Funding) & Mutual Societies (Transfers) Act 2007: Commencements 12, 51, 60
Building societies: Accounts & related provisions 12
Building societies: Bail-in 12, 47
Building societies: Depositor preference & priorities 10, 12
Building societies: Insolvency rules: Northern Ireland 274
Building societies: Insolvency: Special administration rules: Northern Ireland 274
Building: Approved inspectors: Wales 11
Buildings: Energy performance: Certificates & inspections: Northern Ireland 277
Buildings: Listed: Consent orders: Procedure: England 199
Buildings: Listed: Conservation areas: Planning: Heritage partnership agreements: England 199
Buildings: Listed: Lawfulness of proposed works: Certificates: Planning: England 199
Buildings: Recovery of expenses: Acts: Explanatory notes: Scotland 242
Buildings: Recovery of expenses: Acts: Scotland 241
Burbo Bank extension offshore wind farm 61
Burrell Collection: Lending & borrowing: Acts: Explanatory notes: Scotland 242
Burrell Collection: Lending & borrowing: Acts: Scotland 241
Bus & coach passengers: Rights & obligations: Northern Ireland 292
Bus lanes: Dublin Road, Antrim: Northern Ireland 286
Buses & coaches: Passengers rights & obligations: Designation & enforcement: Northern Ireland 286
Business improvement districts: Local government: England 67
Business improvement districts: Local government: Property owners: England 67
Business improvement districts: Northern Ireland 274
Business names: Companies: Sensitive words & expressions 12, 21, 66
Business Rate Supplements Act 2009: Commencements: England 67
Buying Agency Trading Fund 52
BX Swiss AG: Stamp duty & stamp duty reserve tax 195

C

Cafés: Pavement cafés: Licensing: Acts: Explanatory notes: Northern Ireland 273
Cafés: Pavement cafés: Licensing: Acts: Northern Ireland 272
Cairncastle Hill climb: Road races: Northern Ireland 288
Canada: Double taxation: Relief & international tax enforcement 12, 25, 58, 81
Canterbury: Electoral changes 67
Capital allowances: Designated assisted areas 25
Capital allowances: Energy-saving plant & machinery 25, 58
Capital allowances: Environmentally beneficial plant & machinery 25, 58
Capital finance & accounting: Wales 70
Capital gains tax: Chargeable gains: Gilt-edged securities 13, 26
Capital gains tax: Charities: Definition: Relevant territories 9, 13, 26, 60, 61, 195, 203
Capital gains tax: Double taxation: Relief & international enforcement: Belgium 12, 25, 58, 81
Capital gains tax: Double taxation: Relief & international enforcement: Canada 12, 25, 58, 81
Capital gains tax: Double taxation: Relief & international enforcement: Iceland 12, 25, 58
Capital gains tax: Double taxation: Relief & international enforcement: Japan 12, 25, 58
Capital gains tax: Double taxation: Relief & international enforcement: Zambia 12, 25, 59
Capital gains tax: Double taxation: Relief: Germany 12, 25, 59
Capital gains tax: Double taxation: Relief: Tajikistan 12, 25, 59
Capital gains tax: Finance Act 2014: Commencements 12, 59
Capital gains tax: Individual savings accounts 12, 59, 60
Capital gains tax: International tax: Enforcement: Anguilla 12, 25, 60, 61, 203
Capital gains tax: International tax: Enforcement: British Virgin Islands 12, 25, 60, 61, 203
Capital gains tax: International tax: Enforcement: Turks & Caicos Islands 12, 25, 60, 61, 203
Capital gains tax: Lloyd's Underwriters: Conversion of partnerships to underwriting through successor companies 12
Capital gains tax: Offshore funds 12, 26, 60
Capital gains tax: Unit trusts: Unauthorised 13, 26, 60
Capital requirements: Capital buffers: Macro-prudential measures 47
Car & van fuel: Benefit: Income tax 60
Carbon reduction commitment: CRC energy efficiency scheme 20
Carbon reduction commitment: CRC energy efficiency scheme: Allocation of allowances 20
Care & support: After care: Accommodation: England 72, 189
Care & support: Assessment of resources: Charging: England 189
Care & support: Assessment: England 189
Care & support: Continuity of care: England 189
Care & support: Cross-border placements & business failure: Temporary duty: Dispute resolution 189
Care & support: Cross-border placements: Duties of Scottish local authorities: Business failure 189
Care & support: Deferred payment: England 189
Care & support: Direct payments England 189
Care & support: Discharge of Hospital Patients: England 74, 189
Care & support: Disputes between local authorities: England 189

Care & support: Independent advocacy support: England . . . 189
Care & support: Market oversight information: England . . . 189
Care & support: Ordinary residence: Specified accommodation: England . . . 189
Care & support: Personal budget: Exclusion of costs: England . . . 189
Care & support: Preventing needs: Social care: . . . 190
Care & support: Provision of Health Services: England . . . 190
Care & support: Sight-impaired & severely sight-impaired adults: England . . . 190
Care Act 2014: Commencements . . . 74, 76, 86, 190
Care Act 2014: Consequential amendments . . . 53, 190
Care leavers: Care planning: England . . . 13
Care Quality Commission: Reviews & performance assessments . . . 74, 86, 190
Care: Acts . . . 4
Care: Acts: Explanatory notes . . . 5
Carers: Charges for support: Waiving: Scotland . . . 264
Carrickfergus: Waiting restrictions: Northern Ireland . . . 289
Carrier bags: Charging: Acts: Explanatory notes: Northern Ireland . . . 272
Carrier bags: Charging: Acts: Northern Ireland . . . 272
Cars: Motor cars: Driving instruction . . . 92
Cathedral Quarter, Belfast: Parking & waiting restrictions: Northern Ireland . . . 286
Central African Republic: European Union financial sanctions . . . 28
Central African Republic: Overseas territories: Sanctions . . . 78
Channel Tunnel: International arrangements . . . 13
Channel Tunnel: Miscellaneous provisions . . . 57
Channel Tunnel: Planning appeals & assessment of environment effects . . . 200
Channel Tunnel: Rail link: Revocations . . . 200, 201
Charitable deductions: Approved schemes . . . 58
Charities: 2008 Act: Commencements: Northern Ireland . . . 274
Charities: Accounts: Scotland . . . 244
Charities: Definition of charity: Relevant territories . . . 9, 13, 26, 60, 61, 195, 203
Charities: Definition of charity: Relevant territories: Scotland . . . 244, 251
Charities: Registration: Exceptions . . . 13
Chemicals: REACH: Enforcement . . . 23, 42, 52
Chequers & Dorneywood Estates: Transfer of functions: Ministers of the Crown . . . 73
Cheshire East Borough Council: Permit schemes: Traffic management . . . 54
Cheshire West & Chester Borough Council: Permit schemes: Traffic management . . . 54
Child arrangements order . . . 46
Child benefit: Reviews & appeals . . . 194, 196
Child benefit: Tax credits . . . 191, 196
Child benefit: Tax credits: Up-rating . . . 190, 196
Child Maintenance & Other Payments Act 2008: Commencements . . . 45
Child Maintenance Act 2008 Act: Commencements: Northern Ireland . . . 277
Child Poverty Act 2010: Persistent poverty target . . . 13
Child support . . . 45
Child Support, Pensions & Social Security Act 2000: Commencements . . . 45
Child support, pensions & social security: 2000 Act: Commencements: Northern Ireland . . . 274, 277
Child support: Child Maintenance & Other Payments Act 2008: Commencements . . . 45
Child support: Family law: Northern Ireland . . . 277, 278
Child support: Fees . . . 45
Child support: Fees: Northern Ireland . . . 278, 290
Child support: New calculation rules: Transition . . . 45
Child support: Northern Ireland . . . 278
Child support: Reciprocal arrangements: Northern Ireland . . . 45
Child support: Welfare Reform Act 2012: Commencements . . . 45
Child tax credit: Up-rating . . . 196
Child trust funds . . . 15
Childcare Act 2006: Welfare & registration requirements: England . . . 14
Childcare payments: Acts . . . 4
Childcare payments: Acts: Explanatory notes . . . 6
Childcare providers: Information, advice & training: England . . . 14
Childcare: Childminder agencies . . . 13
Childcare: Childminder agencies: Cancellation etc . . . 13
Childcare: Childminder agencies: Registration, inspection etc . . . 14
Childcare: Learning & development requirements: Registration exemption: England . . . 14
Childcare: Payments: Acts . . . 4
Childcare: Payments: Acts: Explanatory notes . . . 6
Childcare: Young children: Information provision: England . . . 14
Childminder agencies . . . 13
Childminder agencies: Cancellation etc . . . 13
Childminder agencies: Registration, inspection etc . . . 14
Children & Families (Wales) Measure: Commencements . . . 15, 76, 190
Children & Families Act 2014: Commencements . . . 13, 46
Children & Families: Acts . . . 4, 6
Children & Young People (Scotland) Act 2014: Ancillary provisions: Scotland . . . 244, 247, 253
Children & Young People (Scotland) Act 2014: Commencements: Scotland . . . 244, 247
Children & young people: Acts: Explanatory notes: Scotland . . . 242
Children & young people: Acts: Scotland . . . 241
Children & Young Persons Act 2008: Relevant care functions . . . 14, 190
Children & young persons: Adoption & care planning: England . . . 13

Children & young persons: Adoption & Children Act 2002: Commencements: England & Wales 14
Children & young persons: Adoption & Children Act 2007: Compulsory supervision order reports: Permanence orders: Scotland 244
Children & young persons: Adoption & Children Act: Register 13
Children & young persons: Adoption agencies 15
Children & young persons: Adoption support services: England 13, 189
Children & young persons: Care leavers: Care planning: England 13
Children & young persons: Child Poverty Act 2010: Persistent poverty target 13
Children & young persons: Childcare Act 2006: Welfare & registration requirements: England 14
Children & young persons: Childcare providers: Information, advice & training: England 14
Children & young persons: Childcare: Childminder agencies 13
Children & young persons: Childcare: Childminder agencies: Cancellation etc 13
Children & young persons: Childcare: Childminder agencies: Registration, inspection etc 14
Children & young persons: Childcare: Learning & development requirements: Registration exemption: England 14
Children & young persons: Childcare: Young children: Information provision: England 14
Children & young persons: Children & Families (Wales) Measure: Commencements 15, 76, 190
Children & young persons: Children & Families Act 2014: Commencements 13, 46
Children & young persons: Children & Young People (Scotland) Act 2014: Commencements: Scotland 244, 247
Children & young persons: Children, Schools & Families Act 2014: Commencements 13, 45
Children & young persons: Children's Hearings (Scotland) Act 2011: Consequential provisions 13, 22, 32
Children & young persons: Children's Hearings (Scotland) Act 2011: Subordinate legislation: Modifications: Scotland 244
Children & young persons: Children's Hearings (Scotland) Act 2011: Supplementary provision: Scotland 244
Children & young persons: Disclosure & Barring Service: Core functions 14
Children & young persons: Her Majesty's Inspector of Education, Children's Services & Skills 14, 35
Children & young persons: Her Majesty's Inspector of Education, Children's Services & Skills: Children's homes: Fees & frequency of
inspections 14
Children & young persons: Information & intermediary services: Pre-commencement adoptions: England 13, 189
Children & young persons: Local authorities: Early years provision: Free: Duty 14
Children & young persons: Looked after children: Scotland 244
Children & young persons: Performances & activities 14
Children & young persons: Performances & activities: Scotland 244
Children & young persons: Protection of Freedoms Act 2012: Commencements 14, 85
Children & young persons: Protection of Vulnerable Groups (Scotland) Act 2007: Miscellaneous provisions: Scotland 245
Children & young persons: Representations procedure 15, 190
Children & young persons: Social services: Complaints procedure: Wales 15, 190
Children, Schools & Families Act 2014: Commencements 13, 34, 45, 46, 196
Children: Early learning & childcare: Specified children: Scotland 248
Children's Hearings (Scotland) Act 2011: Consequential provisions 13, 22, 32
Children's Hearings (Scotland) Act 2011: Subordinate legislation: Modifications: Scotland 244
Children's Hearings (Scotland) Act 2011: Supplementary provision: Scotland 244
Children's homes: Her Majesty's Inspector of Education, Children's Services & Skills 14, 35
Children's homes: Her Majesty's Inspector of Education, Children's Services & Skills: Fees & frequency of inspections 14
Chiropodists: Independent prescribers: Scotland 254
Chiropodists: Independent prescribers: Wales 77
Chronological tables: Statutes 7
Church of England (Miscellaneous Provisions) Measure 2014: Appointed days 33
Church of England: General Synod: Measures 7
Church representation: Rules 33
Churches Conservation Trust: Payments 34
Cinema & films: Films: Co-Production agreements 15
Circuit of Ireland Rally: Road races: Northern Ireland 288
Citizenship: Armed Forces: Acts 4
Citizenship: Borders, Citizenship & Immigration Act 2009: Commencements 57
City of Edinburgh: Portobello Park: Acts: Explanatory notes: Scotland 242
City of Edinburgh: Portobello Park: Acts: Scotland 241
City of London: Various powers: Local acts 6
Civil Aviation Act 2012: Commencements 19
Civil aviation: Air navigation: Amendments 15
Civil aviation: Air navigation: Jersey 15
Civil aviation: Air navigation: Overseas territories 15
Civil aviation: Air travel: Disabled persons: Access 19, 33
Civil aviation: Flying restrictions 15, 16, 17, 18, 19
Civil aviation: Heathrow & Gatwick Airports - London Noise Insulation Grants: Revocations 19
Civil aviation: Overseas territories: Environmental standards 15
Civil aviation: Revocations 19
Civil courts: England & Wales 187
Civil enforcement: Parking contraventions: Designation: England 173
Civil jurisdiction & judgments 63
Civil jurisdiction & judgments: Protection measures 63
Civil jurisdiction & judgments: Protection measures: Scotland 251
Civil legal aid: Financial resources & payment for services: England & Wales 64
Civil legal aid: Merits criteria 64
Civil legal aid: Procedure, remuneration & statutory charge 64
Civil legal aid: Procedure: England & Wales 64
Civil legal aid: Remuneration 64
Civil legal aid: Remuneration: England & Wales 64
Civil legal aid: Remuneration: Financial resources & payment for services 64
Civil partnership & marriage: Acts: Explanatory notes: Scotland 242
Civil partnership & marriage: Acts: Scotland 241

Civil Partnership Act 2004: Consequential provisions	19, 22, 32, 71
Civil Partnership Act 2004: Northern Ireland	274
Civil partnership: Civil Partnership Act 2004: Northern Ireland	274
Civil partnership: Marriage & Civil Partnership (Scotland) Act 2014: Commencements: Scotland	245, 250, 253
Civil partnership: Marriage & Civil Partnership (Scotland) Act 2014: Consequential provisions	19, 32, 71
Civil partnership: Marriage (Same Sex Couples) Act 2013: Consequential & contrary provisions	19, 32, 57, 71
Civil partnership: Marriage (Same Sex Couples) Act 2013: Consequential provisions	19, 32, 71, 72
Civil partnership: Prescribed bodies: Scotland	253
Civil partnership: Prescribed forms: Scotland	245, 253, 257
Civil partnership: Procedures: Scotland	245, 253
Civil partnership: Registration abroad & certificates	19
Civil partnership: Registration: Fees	19
Civil procedure: Rules: England & Wales	27, 187, 188
Civil proceedings: Crime & Courts Act 2013	19, 27, 44, 46
Civil proceedings: Fees: England & Wales	27, 188
Civil servants: Public service pensions: Northern Ireland	284
Civil Service: Public service pensions	87
Civil Service: Public service pensions: Record keeping	80
Claudy, Slieveboy Road: Abandonment: Northern Ireland	285
Clean air: England	20
Clean air: Smoke control areas: Authorised fuels: England	20
Clean air: Smoke control areas: Authorised fuels: Northern Ireland	274
Clean air: Smoke control areas: Authorised fuels: Scotland	245
Clean air: Smoke control areas: Authorised fuels: Wales	20
Clean air: Smoke control areas: Fireplaces: Exempt: England	20
Clean air: Smoke control areas: Fireplaces: Exempt: Northern Ireland	274
Clean air: Smoke control areas: Fireplaces: Exempt: Scotland	245
Clean air: Smoke control areas: Fireplaces: Exempt: Wales	20
Clifton Suspension Bridge: Tolls: Revision	54
Climate change agreements: Administration	20
Climate change agreements: Eligible facilities	20
Climate change levy: Climate change agreements: Administration	20
Climate change levy: Climate change agreements: Eligible facilities	20
Climate change levy: Fuel use & recycling processes	20
Climate change: CRC Energy efficiency scheme	20
Climate change: CRC Energy efficiency scheme: Allocation of allowances	20
Climate change: Greenhouse gas emissions trading scheme	20
Clinical negligence scheme: National Health Service: England	75
Clocaenog Forest wind farm	61
CMA registers of undertakings: Available hours	22
Co-operative & Community Benefit Societies & Credit Unions Act 2010: Commencements	21, 24, 28
Co-operative & Community Benefit Societies & Credit Unions Act 2010: Consequential amendments	21, 24, 28
Co-operative & community benefit societies & credit unions: Arrangements, reconstruction & administration	21, 24, 28
Co-operative & community benefit societies & credit unions: Investigations	21, 24, 28
Co-operative societies: Acts	4
Co-operative societies: Co-operative & community benefit societies & credit unions: Investigations	21, 24, 28
Coal Industry Act 1994: 20	
Coal industry: Superannuation scheme: Winding up	21
Coatbridge College: Transfer & closures: Scotland	247
Cold weather payments: Social fund	192
Colleges: Assigned colleges: Designation: Scotland	247
Colleges: Assigned colleges: University of the Highlands & Islands: Scotland	247
Columbia & Peru Trade Agreement: European Communities: Definition of treaties	43
Combined authorities: Consequential amendments	67, 201
Combined heat & power plants: South Hook	61
Commercial rent arrears recovery: Enforcement agents: Certification	42
Commissary business: Act of Sederunt: Scotland	264
Commissioner for Complaints: Salaries: Northern Ireland	290
Commissioners of Irish Light: Pension schemes: Pensions increase	80
Committee on Agricultural Valuation: Abolition: Public bodies	64, 85
Common Agricultural Policy: Basic payment & support schemes: England	8
Common Agricultural Policy: Basic payment scheme: Provisional payment region classification: Wales	8
Common Agricultural Policy: Competent authority & coordinating body	7
Common Agricultural Policy: Control & enforcement: Cross-compliance & Scrutiny of transactions & appeals	7
Common Agricultural Policy: Cross-compliance: Scotland	243
Common Agricultural Policy: Direct payments & support schemes: Northern Ireland	273
Common Agricultural Policy: Integrated administration: Control system & enforcement: Wales	8
Common Agricultural Policy: Schemes: Cross-compliance: Scotland	243
Common Agricultural Policy: Single payment & support schemes: Cross-compliance: Northern Ireland	273
Common Agricultural Policy: Single payment & support schemes: Northern Ireland	273
Common Agricultural Policy: Single payment & support schemes: Wales	8
Common financial tool: Scotland	244, 246, 251
Commons Act 2006: Commencements	21
Commons registration: England	21
Commons Services Agency: National Health Service: Functions: Scotland	254
Commons: Severance rights: Wales	21
Commons: Town or village greens: Registration: Trigger & terminating events	21
Communications Act 2003: Disclosure of information	40

Community amateur sports clubs: Exemptions	25
Community benefit societies: Acts	4
Community benefit societies: Co-operative & Community Benefit Societies & Credit Unions Act 2010: Commencements	21, 24, 28
Community benefit societies: Co-operative & Community Benefit Societies & Credit Unions Act 2010: Consequential amendments	21, 24, 28
Community benefit societies: Co-operative & community benefit societies & credit unions: Investigations	21, 24, 28
Community care: Joint working: Scotland	264
Community care: Legal Aid, Sentencing & Punishment of Offenders Act 2012	65
Community care: Personal care & nursing care: Scotland	265
Community designs	32
Community infrastructure levy: Amendments	21
Community interest companies	21
Community Legal Service: Funding	65
Community Legal Service: Funding: Counsel: Family proceedings: England & Wales	64
Companies Act 2006: Interconnection registers	21
Companies: Business names: Sensitive words & expressions	12, 21, 66
Companies: Community interest	21
Companies: European public limited-liability companies: Fees	21
Companies: Insolvency: Rules: Scotland	251
Companies: Local audit & statutory audit: Delegation of functions	10, 21, 69
Companies: Payments to governments: Reports	21, 79
Companies: Striking off: Electronic communications	21
Compensation scheme: Firefighters: Wales	49, 81
Compensation: Claims management services: England & Wales	23
Compensation: Home loss payments: Prescribed amounts: England	7, 22
Competition & Markets Authority: Designation: National Competition Authority	22
Competition & Markets Authority: Penalties	22
Competition & Markets Authority: Registers of undertakings: Available hours	22
Competition & Markets Authority: Rules	22
Competition Act 1998: Competition & Markets Authority: Rules	22
Competition Act 1998: Concurrency	22
Competition: Enterprise & Regulatory Reform Act 2013: Commencements	22, 43, 199
Competition: Enterprise & Regulatory Reform Act 2013: Provisions	22
Competition: Enterprise Act 2002: Legitimate interests: Protection	22
Competition: Enterprise Act 2002: Merger fees: Turnover determination	22
Competition: Enterprise Act 2002: Mergers: Interim measures: Financial penalties	22
Competition: Enterprise Act 2002: Part 9: Restrictions on disclosure of information	22, 23, 33
Competition: Financial Services (Banking Reform) Act 2013: Commencements	22, 48
Conlig, Green Road: Abandonment: Northern Ireland	285
Conservation areas: Determination of procedure: Prescribed period: Wales	200
Conservation areas: Listed buildings: Planning: Heritage partnership agreements: England	199
Constitutional law: Children's Hearings (Scotland) Act 2011: Consequential provisions	13, 22, 32
Constitutional law: Civil Partnership Act 2004: Consequential provisions	19, 22, 32, 71
Constitutional law: Marriage & Civil Partnership (Scotland) Act 2014: Consequential provisions	19, 22, 32, 71
Constitutional law: National Assembly for Wales: Remuneration Board: Disqualifications	22
Constitutional law: Revenue Scotland & Tax Powers Act 2014: Provisions & modifications	22, 32, 196
Constitutional law: Scotland Act 1998: Agency arrangements: Specification	22, 32, 40
Constitutional law: Scotland Act 1998: Functions: Modification	7, 22, 32
Constitutional law: Scotland Act 1998: Schedule 5: Modifications	23, 32
Constitutional law: Scotland Act 1998: Transfer of functions	23, 32
Constitutional law: Scotland Act 2012: Commencements	23, 32
Constitutional law: Scottish Parliament: Constituencies & regions	23, 32
Constitutional law: Social Care (Self-Directed Support) (Scotland) Act 2013: Consequential modifications	23, 33, 189
Constitutional Reform & Governance Act 2010: Commencements	86
Construction industry: Industrial training levy: Northern Ireland	281
Consular fees	33
Consultant lobbying: Transparency of Lobbying, Non-Party Campaigning & Trade Union Administration Act 2014: Commencements	23, 90
Consumer Credit Act 1974: Green deal: Amendments	23
Consumer credit: Financial Services & Markets Act 2000	48
Consumer credit: Financial Services & Markets Act 2000: Transitional provisions	48
Consumer credit: Information requirements Licenses & charges: Duration	23
Consumer protection	23
Consumer protection: Aerosol dispensers	23
Consumer protection: Compensation: Claims management services: England & Wales	23
Consumer protection: Enterprise Act 2002: Part 8: EU infringements	23
Consumer protection: Enterprise Act 2002: Part 9: Restrictions on disclosure of information	22, 23, 33
Consumer protection: Financial Services (Banking Reform) Act 2013: Commencements	23, 65
Consumer protection: Gas & electricity: Regulated providers: Redress schemes	23, 40, 51
Consumer protection: REACH: Enforcement	23, 42, 52
Contracting out: Local authorities: Tax billing: Collection & enforcement functions: Wales	24
Contracting out: Social services functions: England	23
Contracting out: Teachers' pensions scheme: Administration: England & Wales	36, 87
Contracts for difference: Eligible generator: Definition	39
Contraventions: Civil enforcement: Bus lanes & moving traffic: Cardiff	174
Contraventions: Parking: Civil enforcement: Cardiff: Wales	174
Convention on International Interests in Mobile Equipment: European Communities: Definition of treaties	43
Cookstown 100: Road races: Northern Ireland	288
Cookstown: Waiting restrictions: Northern Ireland	289

Copyright: Acts	4
Copyright: Acts: Explanatory notes	6
Copyright: Extended collective licensing	24
Copyright: Orphan works: Licensing	24
Copyright: Performances: Disability	24, 91
Copyright: Performances: Duration of rights	24, 91
Copyright: Performances: Orphan works: Permitted uses	24, 91
Copyright: Performances: Personal copies for private use	24, 91
Copyright: Performances: Quotation & parody	24, 91
Copyright: Performances: Research, education, libraries & archives	24, 91
Copyright: Public administration	24
Copyright: Relevant licensing bodies: Regulations	24
Corby: Electoral changes	67
Coroners & Justice Act 2009: Alteration of coroner areas	24
Corporation Tax Act 2010: Real estate investment trusts	26
Corporation tax: Business premises renovation allowances	24, 58
Corporation tax: Capital allowances: Designated assisted areas	25
Corporation tax: Capital allowances: Energy-saving plant & machinery	25, 58
Corporation tax: Capital allowances: Environmentally beneficial plant & machinery	25, 58
Corporation tax: Chargeable gains: Gilt-edged securities	13, 26
Corporation tax: Community amateur sports clubs: Exemptions	25
Corporation tax: Cultural test: Video games	25
Corporation tax: Double taxation: Relief & international enforcement: Belgium	12, 25, 58, 81
Corporation tax: Double taxation: Relief & international enforcement: Canada	12, 25, 58, 81
Corporation tax: Double taxation: Relief & international enforcement: Iceland	12, 25, 58
Corporation tax: Double taxation: Relief & international enforcement: Japan	12, 25, 58
Corporation tax: Double taxation: Relief & international enforcement: Zambia	12, 25, 59
Corporation tax: Double taxation: Relief: Germany	12, 25, 59
Corporation tax: Double taxation: Relief: Tajikistan	12, 25, 59
Corporation tax: Electronic communications	59
Corporation tax: Finance Act 2013: Schedules 17 & 18: Appointed days	25
Corporation tax: Finance Act 2014: Sections 32: Appointed days: Film tax relief	25
Corporation tax: Finance Act 2014: Theatrical production: Tax relief: Appointed day	25
Corporation tax: Instalment payments	25
Corporation tax: International tax: Enforcement: Anguilla	12, 25, 60, 61, 203
Corporation tax: International tax: Enforcement: British Virgin Islands	12, 25, 60, 61, 203
Corporation tax: International tax: Enforcement: Turks & Caicos Islands	12, 25, 60, 61, 203
Corporation tax: Investment transactions: Taxes	25, 60
Corporation tax: Loan relationships & derivative contracts: Accounting practice: Changes	25
Corporation tax: Loan relationships & derivative contracts: Accounting standards: Changes	25
Corporation tax: Loan relationships & derivative contracts: Profits & losses: Disregard & bringing into account	26
Corporation tax: Offshore funds: Amendments	12, 26, 60
Corporation tax: Taxation (International & Other Provisions) Act 2010: Section 371RE: Controlled foreign companies: Amendments	26
Corporation tax: Taxes: Charities: Definition: Relevant territories	9, 13, 26, 60, 61, 195, 203
Corporation tax: Unit trusts: Unauthorised	13, 26, 60
Council of the Pharmaceutical Society of Northern Ireland: Indemnity arrangements	283
Council tax: Administration & enforcement: Wales	26
Council tax: Billing authorities: Precepts: Anticipation	26
Council tax: Chargeable dwellings: Wales	26
Council tax: Demand notices: England	87
Council tax: Demand notices: Wales	26
Council tax: Discounts: Scotland	245
Council tax: Increases: Conduct of referendums: England	68
Council tax: Increases: Referendums: Conduct: England	26
Council tax: Localism Act 2011: Consequential amendments	26, 70
Council tax: Reduction schemes: Prescribed requirements: Default scheme: England	26
Council tax: Reduction schemes: Prescribed requirements: Default scheme: Wales	26
Council tax: Reduction: Amendments: Scotland	245
Council tax: Referendums: Acts	5
Council tax: Referendums: Acts: Explanatory notes	6
Council tax: Wales	26
Countryside: Access: Coastal margin: Cumbria	26
Countryside: Access: Coastal margin: Durham, Hartlepool & Sunderland	26
Countryside: Access: Coastal margin: Sea Palling to Weybourne	26
Countryside: English Coast: Isle of Wight	27
Countryside: National Park Authorities: England	27
County courts: Access to Justice Act 1999: Appeals: Destination: Family proceedings: England & Wales	46, 187
County courts: Appeals: Criminal legal aid: Costs: Northern Ireland	281
County courts: Civil procedure: Rules: England & Wales	27, 187, 188
County courts: Civil proceedings: Fees: England & Wales	27, 188
County courts: Courts & tribunals: Fees: England & Wales	11, 27, 46, 51, 70, 72, 188, 195, 202
County courts: Crime & Courts Act 2013	19, 27, 44, 46
County courts: Crime & Courts Act 2013: Commencements	27, 46, 71, 188
County courts: Crime & Courts Act 2013: Consequential, transitional & saving provisions	27, 188
County courts: Family procedure: Rules	27, 46, 71, 188
County courts: High court & county court: Jurisdiction	27, 189
County courts: Jurisdiction: England & Wales	27
County courts: London Insolvency District: Central London County Court: England & Wales	27

County courts: Remedies: England & Wales 27
Court of Judicature, Northern Ireland: Criminal appeals: Rules 275
Court of Judicature, Northern Ireland: Crown Court: Rules 275
Court of Judicature, Northern Ireland: Rules 275
Court of Session: Messengers-at-Arms: Sheriff officers: Act of Sederunt: Scotland 245, 264
Court of Session: Rules: Scotland. 246, 264
Court of Session: Rules: Solicitor's fees: Scotland 245
Court of Session: Sheriff Court: Company insolvency rules: Scotland 245, 264
Court of Session: Sheriff Court: Rules: Marriage & Civil Partnership (Scotland) Act 2014: Scotland 245, 264
Court of Session: Sheriff Court: Rules: Scotland 245, 246, 264
Courts & tribunals: Fees: England & Wales 11, 27, 46, 51, 70, 72, 188, 195, 202
Courts: County courts: Civil proceedings: Fees: England & Wales 27, 188
Courts: Crime: Acts. 4
Courts: Family court: Constitution of committees: Family panels: England & Wales 44
Courts: Reform: Acts: Scotland 241
Coventry & Warwickshire Partnership: National Health Service Trust: Establishment 74
Coventry City Council: Permit schemes: Traffic management 54
Covert human intelligence sources: Codes of practice: Regulation of investigatory powers 62
Covert surveillance & property interference: Codes of practice: Regulation of investigatory powers 63
Craigantlet Hill Climb: Road races: Northern Ireland 288
Craigavon: Waiting restrictions: Northern Ireland 289
CRC energy efficiency scheme 20
CRC energy efficiency scheme: Allocation of allowances. 20
Credit unions: Arrangements, reconstructions & administration 28, 60
Credit unions: Co-operative & Community Benefit Societies & Credit Unions Act 2010: Commencements. 21, 24, 28
Credit unions: Co-operative & Community Benefit Societies & Credit Unions Act 2010: Consequential amendments 21, 24, 28
Credit unions: Co-operative & community benefit societies & credit unions: Consequential amendments 21, 24, 28
Credit unions: Co-operative & community benefit societies & credit unions: Investigations 21, 24, 28
Credit unions: Electronic communications 28, 60
Crime & Courts Act 2013: Certain enactments: Application & modification. 74
Crime & Courts Act 2013: Commencements 27, 28, 29, 42, 46, 71, 85, 188
Crime & Courts Act 2013: Consequential, transitional & saving provisions 27, 188
Crime & Courts Act 2013: Family court: Consequential provision. 19, 27, 44, 46, 188
Crime & Courts Act 2013: Family court: Transitional & saving provision 44
Crime & Courts: Acts 4
Crime & policing: Anti-social behaviour: Acts 4
Crime & policing: Anti-social behaviour: Acts: Explanatory notes 5
Crime & Security Act 2010: Commencements 83
Crime (International Co-operation) Act 2003: Commencements 28
Crime: Police & Crime Commissioners: Elections 83
Crime: Policing & Crime Act 2009: Commencements 85
Crime: Proceeds of Crime Act 2002: External investigations 85
Crimea: Export control: Sanctions 30
Crimea: Sanctions 78
Criminal appeals: Rules: Court of Judicature, Northern Ireland 275
Criminal cases: Costs: England & Wales 29
Criminal financial penalties: European Union: Scotland 246
Criminal Justice & Police Act 2001: Amendments: England & Wales 29
Criminal Justice Act 1988: Sentencing: Reviews: England & Wales 29
Criminal Justice Act 2003: Alcohol abstinence & monitoring requirements 29
Criminal Justice Act 2003: Commencements: England & Wales 29
Criminal Justice Act 2003: Surcharge 29
Criminal Justice: 2013 Act: Commencements: Northern Ireland 281
Criminal Justice: Data protection: Protocol no. 36 . . . . 28, 31
Criminal justice: Electronic monitoring: Responsible persons. 29
Criminal justice: European protection order 29
Criminal justice: European protection order: Northern Ireland 275
Criminal justice: Victims & witnesses: Acts: Explanatory notes: Scotland 242
Criminal justice: Victims & witnesses: Acts: Scotland 242
Criminal law: Anti-social Behaviour, Crime & Policing Act 2014: Commencements. 10, 29, 31, 33, 45, 56, 83, 84
Criminal law: Anti-social Behaviour, Crime & Policing Act 2014: Commencements: Scotland 246
Criminal law: Central African Republic: European Union financial sanctions 28
Criminal law: Crime & Courts Act 2013: Commencements. 29
Criminal law: Crime (International Co-operation) Act 2003: Commencements 28
Criminal law: Criminal cases: Costs: England & Wales 29
Criminal law: Criminal Justice & Police Act 2001: Amendments: England & Wales 29
Criminal law: Criminal Justice Act 1988: Sentencing: Reviews: England & Wales. 29
Criminal law: Criminal Justice Act 2003: Commencements: England & Wales 29
Criminal law: Criminal Justice Act 2003: Surcharge 29
Criminal law: Criminal Justice: Data protection: Protocol no. 36 . . . . 28, 31
Criminal law: Criminal justice: Electronic monitoring: Responsible persons 29
Criminal law: Criminal justice: European protection order: Northern Ireland 275
Criminal law: Criminal proceedings: Interpretation & translation rights: Scotland 246
Criminal law: Disorderly behaviour: Penalties: Amount: England & Wales. 30
Criminal law: Enterprise Act 2002: Section 188A: Publishing of relevant information 28
Criminal law: European Protection Order. 29
Criminal law: Fixed penalty. 28
Criminal law: Iran: European Communities: Financial sanctions 28

Criminal law: Legal Aid, Sentencing & Punishment of Offenders Act 2012: Commencements 30
Criminal law: Offender Rehabilitation Act 2014: Commencements 30, 32
Criminal law: Police Act 1997: Criminal record certificates: Relevant matters: Northern Ireland 275
Criminal law: Police Act 1997: Criminal records: Northern Ireland 275
Criminal law: Prosecution of Offences Act 1985: Specified proceedings 30
Criminal law: Right to information: Suspects & accused persons: Scotland 246
Criminal law: Serious Organised Crime & Police Act 2005: Designated sites: Section 128: Amendments 30
Criminal law: Sexual Offences Act 2003: Notification requirements: Northern Ireland 275
Criminal law: Sexual Offences Act 2003: Prescribed police stations: Scotland 246
Criminal law: Sudan: European Union financial sanctions 28
Criminal law: Ukraine: European Union financial sanctions 28, 29
Criminal law: Victims & Witnesses (Scotland) Act 2014: Commencements: Scotland 246
Criminal law: Victims & witnesses: Prescribed relatives: Scotland 246
Criminal law: Yemen: European Union financial sanctions 29
Criminal law: Youth detention accommodation: Remand: Recovery of costs 30
Criminal law: Zimbabwe: European Communities: Financial sanctions 29
Criminal legal aid: Costs: Magistrates' courts & county courts: Appeals: Northern Ireland 281
Criminal legal aid: Fixed payments & assistance by way of representation: Scotland 252
Criminal legal aid: Remuneration: England & Wales 64
Criminal Procedure (Scotland) Act 1995: Criminal Procedure Rules 1996: Amendments: Act of Adjournal: Scotland 250, 251, 264
Criminal procedure: Criminal financial penalties: European Union: Scotland 246
Criminal procedure: Rules: Amendment: Act of Adjournal: Scotland 250, 251, 264
Criminal procedure: Rules: Amendment: Regulatory Reform (Scotland) Act 2014: Act of Adjournal: Scotland 250, 264
Criminal procedure: Rules: England & Wales 71, 188
Criminal procedure: Supervision measures: Mutual recognition: European Union: Scotland 246
Criminal proceedings: Interpretation & translation rights: Scotland 246
Criminal records: Police Act 1997 83
Croatia: Accession: Immigration & worker authorisation 57
Croft Hill Climb: Road races: Northern Ireland 288
Crossrail: Insertion of review clauses 199, 201
Crossrail: Paddington Station Bakerloo Line Connection 201
Crown Agents Holding & Realisation Board: Dissolution 62
Crown Court: Rules: Northern Ireland 275
Crown Dependencies: Taxes: International compliance 196
Cultural test: Video games: Corporation tax 25
Curriculum: National: Attainment targets & programmes of study: England 35
Customs & excise: Revenue & customs: Out of time reviews: Appeal provisions 7, 20, 30, 47, 62, 63, 203
Customs & excise: Trade: Statistics 195
Customs: Export control 30
Customs: Export control: Sanctions: Russia, Crimea & Sevastopol 30
Customs: Export control: Sanctions: Sudan & South Sudan & Central African Republic 30
Customs: Export control: Sanctions: Syria 30
Customs: Forest law: Enforcement, governance & trade: Fees 30
Customs: Inspections: HM Inspectors of Constabulary & Scottish Inspectors 91
Cycle racing: Highways: Tour de France 92
Cycle routes: Amendments: Northern Ireland 286

D

Dance & drama: Grants: Education: England 34
Dangerous drugs: Misuse of drugs 31
Dangerous drugs: Misuse of Drugs Act 1971: Amendments 31
Dangerous drugs: Misuse of Drugs Act 1971: Ketamine 31
Dangerous drugs: Misuse of drugs: Designation 31
Dangerous drugs: Misuse of drugs: Designation: Northern Ireland 275
Dangerous drugs: Misuse of drugs: Northern Ireland 275
Dangerous drugs: Misuse of drugs: Safe custody 31
Darlington: Electoral changes 67
Dartford - Thurrock Crossing: Amendments 55
Data protection: Assessment notices: National Health Service bodies: Designation 31
Data protection: Criminal Justice: Protocol no. 36 . . . . 28, 31
Data retention 40
Data retention & investigatory powers: Acts 4
Data retention & investigatory powers: Acts: Explanatory notes 6
Daventry International Rail Freight Interchange Alteration 61
Death & disablement: Navy, Army & Air Force: Service pensions 79
Deaths & births: Registration: Overseas registration 88
Deaths & births: Registration: Overseas registration: Legislative reform 88, 89
Deaths: Presumed deaths: Register: Fees 88
Deaths: Presumed deaths: Register: Prescribed information 88
Debt arrangement schemes: Scotland 246
Debt: Bankruptcy & Debt Advice (Scotland) Act 2014: Commencements: Scotland 243, 246, 250
Debt: Bankruptcy: Applications & decisions: Scotland 243, 246, 250
Debt: Common financial tool: Scotland 244, 246, 251
Debt: Money advice & deduction from income: Scotland 243, 246, 250
Deceased persons: Estates: Inheritance & trustees' powers: Acts 4
Deceased persons: Estates: Inheritance & trustees' powers: Acts: Explanatory notes 6
Deep sea mining: Acts 4

Deep sea mining: Acts: Explanatory notes . . . 6
Deer & camelid: Tuberculosis: England . . . 9
Defence Reform Act 2014: Commencements . . . 32
Defence reform: Acts . . . 4
Defence reform: Acts: Explanatory notes . . . 6
Defence: Anti-social Behaviour, Crime & Policing Act 2014: Commencements . . . 10, 29, 31, 33, 45, 56, 83, 84
Defence: Armed Forces Act 2011: Commencements . . . 31
Defence: Armed Forces Act: Continuation . . . 31
Defence: Armed Forces: Powers of stop & search, search, seizure & retention . . . 31
Defence: Armed Forces: Terms of service . . . 31
Defence: Offender Rehabilitation Act 2014: Commencements . . . 30, 32
Defence: RAF Barford St John . . . 32
Defence: RAF Croughton: Byelaws . . . 32
Defence: Reserve Forces: Payments to employers & partners . . . 32
Dental charges: National Health Service: Wales . . . 77
Dental services: General: Contracts & personal dental services agreements: National Health Service: Wales . . . 77
Dental services: General: Northern Ireland . . . 279
Dental services: Primary: England . . . 76
Dentists Act 1984: Medical authorities . . . 53
Department for Work & Pensions: Employment: Protection: Transfer of undertakings . . . 198
Designs: Acts . . . 4
Designs: Acts: Explanatory notes . . . 6
Designs: Community designs . . . 32
Designs: Registered designs . . . 32
Development corporations: West Northamptonshire Development Corporation: Dissolution . . . 203
Development corporations: West Northamptonshire Development Corporation: Transfer of property etc . . . 203
Devolution, Scotland: Children's Hearings (Scotland) Act 2011: Consequential provisions . . . 13, 22, 32
Devolution, Scotland: Civil Partnership Act 2004: Consequential provisions . . . 19, 22, 32, 71
Devolution, Scotland: Marriage & Civil Partnership (Scotland) Act 2014: Consequential provisions . . . 19, 22, 32, 71
Devolution, Scotland: Marriage (Same Sex Couples) Act 2013: Consequential provisions . . . 19, 32, 71
Devolution, Scotland: Revenue Scotland & Tax Powers Act 2014: Provisions & modifications . . . 22, 32, 196
Devolution, Scotland: Scotland Act 1998: Agency arrangements: Specification . . . 22, 32, 40
Devolution, Scotland: Scotland Act 1998: Functions: Modification . . . 7, 22, 32
Devolution, Scotland: Scotland Act 1998: Schedule 5: Modifications . . . 23, 32
Devolution, Scotland: Scotland Act 1998: Transfer of functions . . . 23, 32
Devolution, Scotland: Scotland Act 2012: Commencements . . . 23, 32
Devolution, Scotland: Scottish Parliament: Constituencies & regions . . . 23, 32
Devolution, Scotland: Social Care (Self-Directed Support) (Scotland) Act 2013: Consequential modifications . . . 23, 33, 189
Devon: South Hams: Electoral changes . . . 68
Diffuse Mesothelioma: Payment scheme . . . 79
Digital Economy Act 2010: Appointed days . . . 65
Diocese of Bangor: Llangristiolus: Educational endowments: Wales . . . 37
Diocese of Bath & Wells: Newbridge St. John's Church of England Infants' School: Educational endowments . . . 34
Diocese of Bradford: St Augustine's Church of England Community School: Educational endowments . . . 34
Diocese of Lichfield: Bereton National School: Educational endowments . . . 34
Diocese of Lichfield: St. John's Infant School: Educational endowments . . . 34
Diocese of Lichfield: St. John's Junior School: Educational endowments . . . 34
Diocese of Lichfield: Wall Church of England School: Educational endowments . . . 34
Diocese of Manchester: Former Scot Lane End Church of England Primary School: Educational endowments . . . 34
Diocese of St Davids: Abernant Church in Wales School: Educational endowments . . . 37
Diocese of St Davids: Llangennech Church in Wales School: Educational endowments . . . 37
Diocese of St Davids: Llangynllo Church in Wales School: Educational endowments . . . 37
Diocese of St Davids: Spittal Church in Wales School: Educational endowments . . . 37
Diocese of York: Ellerton Priory Church of England School: Educational endowments . . . 34
Diplomatic Service: Consular fees . . . 33
Director of Public Prosecutions: Director of Revenue & Customs Prosecutions: Merger . . . 86
Disability Committee: Dissolution: Equality Act 2006 . . . 43
Disabled persons: Air travel: Access . . . 19, 33
Disabled persons: Motor vehicles: Badges . . . 174
Disabled persons: Motor vehicles: Badges: Scotland . . . 258
Disabled persons: Parking badges: Acts: Explanatory notes: Scotland . . . 242
Disabled persons: Parking badges: Acts: Scotland . . . 241
Disabled persons: Rail vehicle accessibility: Northern Ireland . . . 275, 292
Disabled persons: Rail vehicles: Non-interoperable rail-system: Blackpool tramway: Accessibility: Exemptions . . . 33, 201
Disabled persons: Railways: Rail vehicles . . . 33, 201
Disabled persons' vehicles: Parking places: Northern Ireland . . . 287
Disablement & death: Navy, Army & Air Force: Service pensions . . . 79
Disclosure & Barring Service: Core functions . . . 14
Disclosure of information: Enterprise Act 2002: Part 9: Restrictions on disclosure of information . . . 22, 23, 33
Disclosure of information: Serious Crime Act 2007: Anti-fraud organisations . . . 33
Disert Road, Draperstown: Abandonment: Northern Ireland . . . 285, 286
Disorderly behaviour: Penalties: Amount: England & Wales . . . 30
District electoral areas: Northern Ireland . . . 77
Doctors: General Medical Council: Administrative erasure: Restoration . . . 53
Doctors: General Medical Council: Fitness to practise . . . 53
Doctors: General Medical Council: Licence to practise . . . 53
Doctors: General Medical Council: Voluntary erasure & restoration following voluntary erasure . . . 53
Doctors: Medical Act 1983: English: Knowledge . . . 53

Dogs: Anti-social Behaviour, Crime & Policing Act 2014: Commencements 10, 29, 31, 33, 45, 56, 83, 84
Dogs: Licensing & identification: Northern Ireland. 275
Domestic renewable heat incentive scheme: Northern Ireland 276
Donations to candidates: Anonymous registration 89
Dover Harbour: Revision. 52
Down Rally: Road races: Northern Ireland 288
Drama: Dance: Grants: Education: England 34
Drivers: Vehicle drivers: Professional competence: Certificates: Amendments 93
Driving licences: Taxis: Northern Ireland 289
Driving Standards Agency: Vehicle & Operator Services Agency: Merger 62, 85, 92
Driving Standards Agency: Vehicle & Operator Services Agency: Merger: Consequential amendments . . . 92
Driving theory test: Fees 92
Driving: Drug driving: Specified limits 174
Drug driving: Specified limits 174
Drug prescriptions: General medical services: Contracts: National Health Service: England 75
Drugs & appliances: Charges: National Health Service: Scotland 254
Drugs & medicines: Value added tax 203
Drugs: Misuse of drugs 31
Drugs: Misuse of Drugs Act 1971: Amendments. 31
Drugs: Misuse of Drugs Act 1971: Ketamine. 31
Drugs: Misuse of drugs: Designation. 31
Drugs: Misuse of drugs: Designation: Northern Ireland 275
Drugs: Misuse of drugs: Northern Ireland 275
Drugs: Misuse of drugs: Safe custody 31
Drugs: Prescription: General medical services contracts: Northern Ireland 279
Drumalla Park, Carnlough: Abandonment: Northern Ireland 285
Drumhorc hill climb: Road races: Northern Ireland 288
Dungannon Bush Motorcycle Race: Road races: Northern Ireland 288
Dungannon: Waiting restrictions: Road traffic & vehicles: Northern Ireland 289
Durham, Gateshead, Newcastle Upon Tyne, North Tyneside, Northumberland, South Tyneside & Sunderland: Combined authority . 67, 201
Dwellings: Enveloped dwellings: Annual tax & chargeable amounts: Indexation 9

E

Eagles Rock Hill Climb: Road races: Northern Ireland 288
Ealing Hospital: National Health Service 75
East Anglia ONE Offshore Wind Farm 61
East Dorset: Electoral changes 67
East Lindsey: Electoral changes 67
Ecclesiastical law: Church of England (Miscellaneous Provisions) Measure 2014: Appointed days 33
Ecclesiastical law: Church representation: Rules. 33
Ecclesiastical law: Churches Conservation Trust: Payments 34
Ecclesiastical law: Ecclesiastical offices: Terms of service 33
Ecclesiastical law: Judges, legal officers & others: Fees 33
Ecclesiastical law: Legal officers: Annual fees 33
Ecclesiastical law: Parochial fees: Scheduled matters amending 34
Ecclesiastical offices: Terms of service. 33
Ecodesign: Energy-related products & energy information: Amendments 41
Edinburgh Council, City: Leith Links & Surplus Fire Fund: Acts: Explanatory notes: Scotland 242
Edinburgh Council, City: Leith Links & Surplus Fire Fund: Acts: Scotland 241
Education & Inspections Act 2006: Commencements 34
Education & Skills Act 2008: Commencements: England 34
Education & training: Inspectors: Wales 37
Education (Scotland) Act 1980: Section 53B: Dissapplication: Scotland 247
Education (Wales) Act 2014: Commencements: Wales 38
Education (Wales) Measure 2009: Pilot: Revocation 38
Education (Wales) Measure 2011: Commencements: Wales. 38
Education: Acts: Explanatory notes: Northern Ireland. 272
Education: Acts: Explanatory notes: Wales 297
Education: Acts: Northern Ireland 272
Education: Acts: Wales. 296
Education: Aided places: St Mary's Music School: Scotland 248
Education: Assigned colleges: Designation: Scotland. 247
Education: Assigned colleges: University of the Highlands & Islands: Scotland 247
Education: Children & Young People (Scotland) Act 2014: Ancillary provisions: Scotland 244, 247, 253
Education: Children & Young People (Scotland) Act 2014: Commencements: Scotland. 244, 247
Education: Coatbridge College: Transfer & closures: Scotland 247
Education: Diocese of Bangor: Llangristiolus: Educational Endowments 37
Education: Diocese of Bath & Wells: Newbridge St. John's Church of England Infants' School: Educational endowments 34
Education: Diocese of Bradford: St Augustine's Church of England Community School: Educational endowments 34
Education: Diocese of Lichfield: Bereton National School: Educational endowments. 34
Education: Diocese of Lichfield: St. John's Infant School: Educational endowments 34
Education: Diocese of Lichfield: St. John's Junior School: Educational endowments. 34
Education: Diocese of Lichfield: Wall Church of England School: Educational endowments 34
Education: Diocese of Manchester: Former Scot Lane End Church of England Primary School: Educational endowments. 34
Education: Diocese of St Davids: Abernant Church in Wales School: Educational Endowments 37
Education: Diocese of St Davids: Llangennech Church in Wales School: Educational Endowments 37
Education: Diocese of St Davids: Llangynllo Church in Wales School: Educational Endowments. 37

Education: Diocese of St Davids: Spittal Church in Wales School: Educational Endowments 37
Education: Diocese of York: Ellerton Priory Church of England School: Educational endowments 34
Education: Early learning & childcare: Specified children: Scotland 248
Education: European institutions: Student support: Wales 37
Education: European University Institute: Wales 37
Education: Federation of Maintained Schools: Wales 38
Education: Full-time: Excluded pupils: Provisions: Amendments: England 35
Education: Further & Higher Education (Governance & Information) (Wales) Act 2014: Commencements: Wales. 38
Education: Further & higher education: Governance & information: Acts: Explanatory notes: Wales. 297
Education: Further & higher education: Governance & information: Acts: Wales 296
Education: Further & higher: Student support: England 35
Education: Further education corporations: Dissolution: Publication of proposals & prescribed bodies 37
Education: Further: Loans: England 35
Education: General Teaching Council for Northern Ireland 276
Education: Grants: Dance & drama: England 34
Education: Head teachers: Reports to parents & adult pupils: Wales. 38
Education: Her Majesty's Inspector of Education, Children's Services & Skills 14, 35
Education: Her Majesty's Inspector of Education, Children's Services & Skills: Children's homes: Fees & frequency of inspections 14
Education: Higher Education Funding Council for Wales 38
Education: Higher education: Prescribed courses: Information requirements 35
Education: Higher education: Student loans: Living costs liability: Cancellation 37
Education: Independent educational provision: Management participation: Prohibition: England 35
Education: Independent inspectorates: Boarding & accommodation 35
Education: Independent schools: Standards: England 35
Education: Lanarkshire Colleges: Scotland 247
Education: Learning support: Additional: Information: Sources: Scotland 247
Education: Local curriculum: Key stage 4: Wales 37
Education: Maintained Schools: Staffing: Wales 39
Education: National curriculum: Assessment arrangements: Foundation stage, KS2, KS3: Wales 38
Education: National curriculum: Attainment targets & programmes of study: England 35
Education: National curriculum: Foundation phase: Wales 37
Education: National curriculum: Key stage 1, 2, 3, 4: Exceptions: England 35
Education: Plans: School development: Wales. 38
Education: Plymouth College of Art: Transfer to higher education sector 35
Education: Post-16 Education (Scotland) Act 2013: Commencements: Scotland 247
Education: Prospects College of Advanced Technology: Government 35
Education: Prospects College of Advanced Technology: Incorporation 36
Education: Pupil referral units: Management committees: Wales 38
Education: Regional colleges: Designation: Scotland 247
Education: Royal Conservatoire of Scotland 248
Education: Rural primary schools: Designation: England 34
Education: School & early years finance: England 36
Education: School closure review panels: Convener: Scotland 247
Education: School closure review panels: Members: Scotland 247
Education: School companies: England 36
Education: School governance: Constitution & federations: England 36
Education: School Standards & Organisation (Wales) Act 2013: Commencements 39
Education: School teachers: Pay & conditions: England & Wales 36
Education: School term dates: Consultation: Wales 37
Education: Schools: Admissions code: Appointed day: England 36
Education: Schools: Admissions: Co-ordination of arrangements: England 36
Education: Schools: Food: Requirements: England 36
Education: Schools: Independent: Religious character: Designation: England 34
Education: Schools: Maintained schools: Governors: Training requirements: Wales 38
Education: Schools: Religious: Designation: Independent schools: Wales 37
Education: Schools: Staffing: England 36
Education: Schools: Term dates: Notification: Wales 37
Education: Small schools: Wales 38
Education: Special educational needs: Codes of practice: England 36
Education: Special educational needs: Consequential amendments: England 36
Education: Special educational needs: Direct payments: Pilot scheme: England 36
Education: Special educational needs: Disability: England 36
Education: Special educational needs: Personal budgets: England 36
Education: Specified work & registration: Wales 38
Education: Student fees: Amounts: Northern Ireland 276
Education: Student fees: Amounts: Wales 39
Education: Student loans: Repayment 34
Education: Student loans: Repayments: Northern Ireland 276
Education: Student support: Amendments: Northern Ireland 276
Education: Student support: England 35
Education: Student support: Financial: Amendments: Northern Ireland 276
Education: Student support: Wales 38
Education: Teachers: Pensions schemes: Northern Ireland 276, 284
Education: Teachers: Pensions: England & Wales 36
Education: Teachers: Schools: Professional qualifications: England 35, 36
Education: Teachers: Superannuation: Northern Ireland 276
Education: Teachers' discipline 36
Education: Teachers' pensions scheme: England & Wales 36, 87

Education: Training: Inspections: Intervals: Amendments: Wales 37
Education: Young people's involvement in education & training: Provision of information: Scotland 248
Elections: European Parliament: Petitions: England & Wales 89, 195
Elections: European Parliament: Welsh forms 90
Elections: Mayoral: Local authorities: England 68
Elections: Mayoral: Local authorities: England & Wales 69
Elections: Policy development grants scheme 89
Elections: Representation of the people: Candidates' election expenses: Variation 90
Elections: Transfer of functions: Ministers of the Crown 73
Electoral Administration Act 2006: Commencements: Northern Ireland 84
Electoral areas: District: Northern Ireland. 77
Electoral changes: Aylesbury Vale 66
Electoral changes: Bolsover 66
Electoral changes: Braintree 66
Electoral changes: Breckland 66
Electoral changes: Bromsgrove 66
Electoral changes: Canterbury 67
Electoral changes: Corby 67
Electoral changes: Darlington 67
Electoral changes: East Dorset 67
Electoral changes: East Lindsey 67
Electoral changes: Fenland 67
Electoral changes: Gedling 67
Electoral changes: Hambleton 67
Electoral changes: Herefordshire. 67
Electoral changes: Horsham 67
Electoral changes: Kensington & Chelsea 67
Electoral changes: Lancaster 67
Electoral changes: Leicester 67
Electoral changes: Middlesbrough 68
Electoral changes: Milton Keynes 68
Electoral changes: Newark & Sherwood 68
Electoral changes: North Dorset 68
Electoral changes: North Somerset 68
Electoral changes: North West Leicestershire 68
Electoral changes: Selby 68
Electoral changes: Sevenoaks 68
Electoral changes: Shepway 68
Electoral changes: South Hams 68
Electoral changes: South Kesteven 68
Electoral changes: South Oxfordshire 68
Electoral changes: South Ribble 69
Electoral changes: Stratford-on-Avon 69
Electoral changes: Suffolk Coastal 69
Electoral changes: Telford & Wrekin 69
Electoral changes: Three Rivers 69
Electoral changes: Uttlesford 69
Electoral changes: Vale of the White Horse 69
Electoral changes: Warwick 69
Electoral changes: Wellingborough 69
Electoral changes: Wyre 69
Electoral changes: York 69
Electoral Commission: Public awareness: Expenditure: Limit 39
Electoral Registration & Administration Act 2013: Commencements 89
Electoral Registration & Administration Act 2013: Commencements: Northern Ireland 77
Electoral Registration & Administration Act 2013: Transitional provisions 89
Electoral registration: Electoral registers: Disclosure 90
Electoral registration: Pilot schemes 89
Electric cars: Parking places: Northern Ireland 287
Electric vehicles: Amendments: Parking places: Northern Ireland 287
Electrical & electronic equipment: Waste: Charges: Northern Ireland 277
Electrical & electronic equipment: Waste: Hazardous substances: Use: Restriction 42
Electricity Act 1989: Interconnector licence: Requirements: Exemptions 39
Electricity generation: Hydrocarbon oil duties reliefs: Carbon price support 44
Electricity generation: North Killingholme generating station 61
Electricity: Appeals: Designation & exclusion 39, 51
Electricity: Billing 39, 51
Electricity: Capacity 39, 40
Electricity: Contracts for difference: Allocation 39
Electricity: Contracts for difference: Counterparty designation 39
Electricity: Contracts for difference: Electricity supplier obligations 39
Electricity: Contracts for difference: Eligible generator: Definition 39
Electricity: Contracts for difference: Standard terms 39
Electricity: Energy companies obligation 39, 51
Electricity: Energy companies obligation: Determination & savings 39, 51
Electricity: Feed-in tariffs: Amendments 40
Electricity: From high-efficiency cogeneration: Guarantees of origin: Northern Ireland 276
Electricity: Gas: Ownership unbundling 39, 51

Electricity: Generation: Licence requirement: Exemption: Berry Burn 40
Electricity: Internal markets 39, 51
Electricity: Market reform 40
Electricity: Power purchase agreement scheme 40
Electricity: Regulated providers: Redress schemes. 23, 40, 51
Electricity: Renewables obligation 40
Electricity: Renewables obligation: Closure. 40
Electricity: Renewables obligation: Northern Ireland. 276
Electricity: Renewables obligation: Scotland 248
Electricity: Warm home discount. 40, 51
Electronic communications: Audiovisual media services 11, 40
Electronic communications: Communications Act 2003: Disclosure of information 40
Electronic communications: Data retention 40
Electronic communications: Electronic documents: Scotland. 248
Electronic communications: Income & corporation taxes. 59
Electronic communications: Mobile phones: Roaming: European Communities 40
Electronic communications: Wireless telegraphy: Exemption 40
Electronic communications: Wireless telegraphy: Licence charges 40
Electronic communications: Wireless telegraphy: Licences: Limitation of number 40
Electronic communications: Wireless telegraphy: Mobile communication services on aircraft: Exemptions 40
Electronic documents: Scotland 248
Embryology: Human fertilisation & embryology: Quality & safety 57
Emergency Ambulance Services Committee: National Health Service: Wales 76
Emissions trading: CRC energy efficiency scheme: Allocation of allowances 20
Employment & support allowance: Jobseeker's allowance: Social security 193
Employment & training: Industrial training levy: Engineering Construction Industry Training Board 40
Employment agencies & businesses: Conduct: Amendments 40
Employment relations: Blacklists: Northern Ireland 276
Employment Rights Act 1996: Parental order cases 197
Employment Rights Act 1996: Section 75G & 75H: Application: Adoptions from overseas 197
Employment Rights Act 1996: Wages: Deduction: Limitation 197
Employment rights: Limits: Increase 197
Employment rights: Limits: Increase: Northern Ireland 276
Employment Tribunals Act 1996: Conciliation provisions: Applications 197
Employment tribunals: Constitution: Rules of procedure 41
Employment tribunals: Early conciliation: Exemptions & rules of procedure. 41
Employment tribunals: Energy Act 2013: Improvement & prohibition notices appeals 41
Employment: Collective redundancies & transfer of undertakings: Employment protection 197
Employment: Enterprise & Regulatory Reform Act 2013: Commencements 7, 63, 64, 197, 198
Employment: Flexible working: Eligibility, complaints & remedies 197
Employment: Gangmasters: Licensing: Exclusions: Northern Ireland 276
Employment: Protection: Transfer of undertakings: Department for Work & Pensions. 198
Employment: Public interest disclosure: Prescribed persons: Northern Ireland 276
Employment: Social security: Benefits: Up-rating: Northern Ireland. 276, 280, 284, 290, 291, 292
Employment: Terms & conditions: Employment Rights Act 1996: Section 75G & 75H: Application: Adoptions from overseas 197
Employment: Terms & conditions: Maternity & adoption leave: Curtailment 197
Employment: Terms & conditions: Paternity & adoption: Leave 197
Employment: Terms & conditions: Social Security Contributions & Benefits Act 1992: Application: Parts 12ZA &12ZB & 12ZC 198
Employment: Terms & conditions: Social Security Contributions & Benefits Act 1992: Parts 12ZA & 12ZB: Application: Adoptions: Overseas
 198
Employment: Terms & conditions: Welfare benefits: Up-rating. 194, 198
Employment: Work flexibly: Reasonable requests: Code of practice 197
Energy Act 2004: Commencements 41
Energy Act 2004: Publicly owned companies: Designation 41
Energy Act 2008: Commencements 41
Energy Act 2013: Commencements. 41
Energy Act 2013: Improvement & prohibition notices appeals 41
Energy Act 2013: Office for Nuclear Regulation: Consequential amendments 41
Energy companies obligation: Electricity & gas. 39, 51
Energy companies obligation: Electricity & gas: Determination & savings. 39, 51
Energy company obligation: Electricity & gas 39, 51
Energy conservation: Domestic energy: Efficiency grants: Northern Ireland 277
Energy conservation: Ecodesign: Energy-related products & energy information 41
Energy conservation: Green deal: Qualifying energy improvements 41
Energy conservation: Home energy assistance schemes: Amendments: Scotland 248
Energy efficiency: Eligible buildings: Building renovation & reporting 41
Energy efficiency: Encouragement, assessment & information 41
Energy efficiency: Northern Ireland 276
Energy performance: Building & buildings: England & Wales. 11
Energy performance: Buildings: Certificates & inspections: Northern Ireland 277
Energy savings opportunity scheme 41
Energy: Acts: Explanatory notes 5
Energy: Domestic renewable heat incentive scheme: Northern Ireland 276
Energy: Electricity & gas: Appeals: Designation & exclusion 39, 51
Energy: Electricity: Renewables obligation 40
Energy: Electricity: Renewables obligation: Closure 40
Energy: Electricity: Renewables obligation: Northern Ireland 276
Energy: Electricity: Renewables obligation: Scotland 248

Energy: Heat: Network metering & billing 41
Energy: Renewable heat incentives 41
Energy: Renewable heat incentives: Domestic 41
Energy: Renewable: Clocaenog Forest wind farm 61
Energy: Renewable: East Anglia ONE Offshore Wind Farm 61
Energy: Renewable: Hornsea One Offshore Wind Farm 61
Energy: Renewable: Rampion Wind Farm 61
Enforcement agents: Certification 42
Enforcement: Tribunals, Courts & Enforcement Act 2007: Consequential, transitional & saving provisions 42
Engineering Construction Industry Training Board: Industrial training levy 40
English Coast: Isle of Wight 27
Enterprise & Regulatory Reform Act 2013: Commencements 7, 22, 43, 63, 64, 197, 198, 199
Enterprise & Regulatory Reform Act 2013: Competition: Provisions 22
Enterprise & Regulatory Reform Act 2013: Employment 197
Enterprise & Regulatory Reform Act 2013: Lawfulness: Listed building certificate 199
Enterprise & Regulatory Reform Act 2013: Terms & conditions of employment 197
Enterprise Act 2002: Legitimate interests: Protection 22
Enterprise Act 2002: Merger fees: Turnover determination 22
Enterprise Act 2002: Mergers: Interim measures: Financial penalties 22
Enterprise Act 2002: Part 8: EU infringements 23
Enterprise Act 2002: Part 9: Restrictions on disclosure of information 22, 23, 33
Enterprise Act 2002: Section 188A: Publishing of relevant information 28
Entertainment licensing: Legislative reform 66
Enveloped dwellings: Annual tax & chargeable amounts: Indexation 9
Environment: Taxes: Landfill tax 63
Environment: Water industry: Supply: Acts 5
Environment: Water industry: Supply: Acts: Explanatory notes 6
Environmental permitting: England & Wales 42, 43
Environmental protection: Anti-social Behaviour, Crime & Policing Act 2014: Publication of Public Spaces Protection Orders: Regulations 43
Environmental protection: Controlled waste & duty of care: Northern Ireland 277
Environmental protection: Controlled waste: Fixed penalty notices: Scotland 248
Environmental protection: Duty of care: Scotland 248
Environmental protection: Electrical & electronic equipment: Waste: Charges: Northern Ireland 277
Environmental protection: Environmental permitting: England & Wales 42, 43
Environmental protection: Greenhouse gases: Fluorinated: Northern Ireland 277
Environmental protection: Groundwater: Northern Ireland 277
Environmental protection: Liquid fuels: Sulphur content: England & Wales 43
Environmental protection: Liquid fuels: Sulphur content: Scotland 248
Environmental protection: Litter: Fixed penalty notices: Scotland 248
Environmental protection: Marine conservation: South Arran: Scotland 248, 253
Environmental protection: Marine licensing: Application fees 42, 66, 71
Environmental protection: Mobile machinery: Non-road: Gaseous & particulate pollutants: Emissions 42
Environmental protection: Nitrates Action Programme: Northern Ireland 277
Environmental protection: Phosphorus: Agriculture: Use: Northern Ireland 277
Environmental protection: Pollution: Prevention & control: Northern Ireland 277
Environmental protection: Pollution: Prevention & control: Scotland 248
Environmental protection: Producer responsibility & obligations: Packaging waste 42
Environmental protection: Producer responsibility & obligations: Packaging waste: Northern Ireland 277
Environmental protection: REACH: Enforcement 23, 42, 52
Environmental protection: Regulatory Reform (Scotland) Act 2014: Commencements: Scotland 248, 258
Environmental protection: Single use carrier bags: Charge: Scotland 248
Environmental protection: Waste electrical & electronic equipment: Hazardous substances 42
Environmental protection: Waste management: Licensing: Northern Ireland 277
Environmental protection: Waste: England & Wales 43
Environmental protection: Waste: Transfrontier shipments 30, 42
Environmental regulation: Liability: Activity carried by arrangement with another: Scotland 248
Environmental regulation: Relevant offences: Scotland 248
Environmental regulation: Significant environmental harm: Scotland 248
Environmental standards: Civil aviation: Overseas territories 15
Equal opportunities & human rights: Equality Act 2006: Disability Committee: Dissolution 43
Equal Opportunities Commission: Dissolution: Equality Act 2006 43
Equality Act 2006: Disability Committee: Dissolution 43
Equality Act 2010: Equal Pay Audits 43
Equality: Enterprise & Regulatory Reform Act 2013: Commencements 22, 43, 199
Equality: Gender equality: International development: Acts 5
Equality: Gender equality: International development: Acts: Explanatory notes 6
Estates: Deceased persons: Inheritance & trustees' powers: Acts 4
Estates: Deceased persons: Inheritance & trustees' powers: Acts: Explanatory notes 6
Estimates & accounts: Government Resources & Accounts Act 2000 51
Ethical standards: Public life: Registers of interests: Scotland 248, 253
Europe: Economic interest grouping: Fees 21
European Communities: Definition of treaties: Columbia & Peru Trade Agreement 43
European Communities: Definition of treaties: Convention on International Interests in Mobile Equipment 43
European Communities: Definition of treaties: Partnership & Cooperation Agreement: Iraq 43
European Communities: Definition of treaties: Partnership & Cooperation Agreement: Mongolia 43
European Communities: Definition of treaties: Partnership & Cooperation Agreement: Philippines 43
European Communities: Definition of treaties: Partnership & Cooperation Agreement: Vietnam 44
European Communities: Designation 43

European Communities: Energy performance: Buildings: Certificates & inspections: Northern Ireland 277
European Communities: Environmental protection: Groundwater: Northern Ireland 277
European Communities: Iran: Financial sanctions 28
European Communities: Structural Funds: Welsh ministers 43
European Communities: Zimbabwe: Financial sanctions 29
European Economic Area: Immigration 58
European economic interest grouping: Fees 21
European institutions: Student support: Education: Wales 37
European Parliamentary elections 90
European Parliamentary elections: Northern Ireland 91
European Parliamentary elections: Petitions: England & Wales 89, 195
European Parliamentary elections: Returning officers: Charges: Northern Ireland 91
European Parliamentary elections: Returning officers: Local returning officers: Charges: Great Britain & Gibraltar 90
European Parliamentary elections: Welsh forms 90
European public limited-liability companies: Fees 21
European Union: Approvals: Acts 4
European University Institute: Education: Wales 37
Evidence: Police & criminal evidence: Code of practice A: Temporary modification: Northern Ireland 283
Evidence: Police & criminal evidence: Code of practice C & H: Revision: Northern Ireland 283
Excise: Betting duty: General, pool, remote 44
Excise: Biofuels & other fuel substitutes: Excise duties: Payment 44
Excise: Finance Act 2009: Remote gambling taxes 44
Excise: Gaming: Duty 44
Excise: Hydrocarbon oil duties: Electricity generation reliefs: Carbon price support 44
Excise: Machine games: Duty: Types of machine 44
Excise: Other fuel substitutes: Excise duties: Rates 44
Explosives 52
Explosives precursors: Control 52
Explosives precursors: Control: Northern Ireland 279
Explosives: Hazard information & packaging for supply: Northern Ireland 279, 280
Export control 30
Export control: Sanctions: Russia, Crimea & Sevastopol 30
Export control: Sanctions: Sudan & South Sudan & Central African Republic 30
Export control: Sanctions: Syria 30
Extradition: Anti-social Behaviour, Crime & Policing Act 2014: Commencements 44, 82

F

Families: Children: Acts 4, 6
Family court warrants: Specification of orders 44, 46
Family court: Access to Justice Act 1999: Appeals: Destination: Family proceedings: England & Wales 44
Family court: Business: Composition & distribution: England & Wales 44, 46, 188
Family court: Constitution of committees: Family panels: England & Wales 44
Family court: Contempt of court: Powers 44, 46
Family court: Crime & Courts Act 2013 . . . . 19, 27, 44, 46, 188
Family court: Crime & Courts Act 2013: Transitional & saving provision 44
Family court: Family procedure: Rules 45, 46, 188
Family court: Justices' clerks & assistants rules: England & Wales 45
Family law: Anti-social Behaviour, Crime & Policing Act 2014: Commencements 10, 29, 31, 33, 45, 56, 83, 84
Family law: Child Maintenance & Other Payments Act 2008: Commencements 45
Family law: Child support 45
Family law: Child Support, Pensions & Social Security Act 2000: Commencements 45
Family law: Child Support, Pensions & Social Security Act 2000: Commencements: Northern Ireland 274, 277
Family law: Child support: Child Maintenance Act 2008 Act: Commencements: Northern Ireland 277
Family law: Child support: Fees 45
Family law: Child support: Fees: Northern Ireland 278, 290
Family law: Child support: New calculation rules: Transition 45
Family law: Child support: Northern Ireland 277, 278
Family law: Child support: Reciprocal arrangements: Northern Ireland 45
Family law: Marriage: Same sex couples: Jurisdiction & recognition of judgments 45, 63
Family law: Welfare Reform Act 2012: Commencements 45
Family procedure: Rules 27, 45, 46, 71, 188
Family proceedings: Access to Justice Act 1999: Appeals: Destination: England & Wales 44, 46, 187
Family proceedings: Child arrangements order 46
Family proceedings: Children & Families Act 2014: Commencements 13, 46
Family proceedings: Children, Schools & Families Act 2014: Commencements 13, 45
Family proceedings: Children, Schools & Families Act 2014: Transitional and saving provisions 34
Family proceedings: Children, Schools & Families Act 2014: Transitional provisions 46
Family proceedings: Courts & tribunals: Fees: England & Wales 11, 27, 46, 51, 70, 72, 188, 195, 202
Family proceedings: Crime & Courts Act 2013 . . . . 19, 27, 44, 46, 188
Family proceedings: Crime & Courts Act 2013: Commencements 27, 46, 71, 188
Family proceedings: Family court warrants: Specification of orders 44, 46
Family proceedings: Family court: Business: Composition & distribution: England & Wales 44, 46, 188
Family proceedings: Family court: Contempt of court: Powers 44, 46
Family proceedings: Family procedure: Rules 27, 45, 46, 71, 188
Family proceedings: Fees: England & Wales 46, 189
Family provision: Inheritance & Trustees' Powers Act 2014: Commencements 46
Federation of Maintained Schools: Wales 38

Feed: Official controls: England	8, 50
Feed: Official controls: Scotland	249
Feed: Official controls: Wales	8, 50
Fees & charges: European economic interest grouping	21
Fees & charges: Kimberley process: Fees	46
Fees & charges: Measuring instruments: EEC requirements: Fees	47
Felixstowe Branch Line: Land acquisition	201
Felixstowe: Port security: Merchant shipping	73
Fenland: Electoral changes	67
FIFA World Cup: Licensing hours	66
Fife Council: Parking adjudicators: Road traffic: Scotland	258
Films: Co-Production agreements	15
Finance Act 2008: S. 127 & sch. 43, part 1: Appointed days	91
Finance Act 2009: Consequential amendments	59, 191
Finance Act 2009: Remote gambling taxes	44
Finance Act 2009: Schedule 55 & 56: Sections 101 & 102: Stamp duty reserve tax	195
Finance Act 2009: Schedule 55: Penalties for failure to make returns	59
Finance Act 2009: Sections 101, 102: Appointed days	59, 191
Finance Act 2013: Schedules 17 & 18: Appointed days	25
Finance Act 2014	4
Finance Act 2014: Section 12: Appointed days	59
Finance Act 2014: Section 32: Appointed days: Film tax relief	25
Finance Act 2014: Theatrical production: Tax relief: Appointed day	25
Financial assistance schemes: Qualifying pension scheme: Amendments: Pensions	79
Financial assistance: Sea fisheries: Fishing boats: Northern Ireland	278
Financial Provisions (2014) Act: Commencements: Northern Ireland	278
Financial provisions: Acts: Explanatory notes: Northern Ireland	272
Financial provisions: Acts: Northern Ireland	272
Financial Services & Markets Act 2000: Alternative Investment Fund Managers: Regulations	47
Financial Services & Markets Act 2000: Appointed representatives	47
Financial Services & Markets Act 2000: Confidential information: Disclosure	48
Financial Services & Markets Act 2000: Consumer credit	48
Financial Services & Markets Act 2000: Consumer credit: Designated activities	47
Financial Services & Markets Act 2000: Consumer credit: Transitional provisions	48
Financial Services & Markets Act 2000: Excluded activities & prohibitions	10
Financial Services & Markets Act 2000: Market abuse	48
Financial Services & Markets Act 2000: Over the counter derivatives: Central counterparties: Trade repositories	48
Financial Services & Markets Act 2000: Regulated activities: Amendments	48
Financial Services & Markets Act 2000: Regulated activities: Green Deal	48
Financial Services & Markets Act 2000: Ring-fenced bodies & core activities	10
Financial Services & Markets Act 2000: Transparency	48
Financial Services & Markets Act 2000: Way of business: Regulated activities	47
Financial services & markets: Bail-in	12, 47
Financial services & markets: Banking Act 2009: Banking group companies	47
Financial services & markets: Banking Act 2009: Exclusion of investment firms	47
Financial services & markets: Banking Act 2009: Partial property transfers: Third party compensation arrangements	47
Financial services & markets: Banks & banking: Recovery & resolution	10, 47
Financial services & markets: Capital requirements: Capital buffers: Macro-prudential measures	47
Financial services & markets: Central securities depositories	47
Financial services & markets: Financial Services (Banking Reform) Act 2013: Commencements	22, 48
Financial services & markets: Financial Services Act 2012: Complaints scheme: Relevant functions	47
Financial services & markets: Immigration Act 2014: Bank accounts	48, 49, 57
Financial services & markets: Immigration Act 2014: Bank accounts: Prohibition on opening accounts for disqualified persons	49, 57
Financial services & markets: Payments to governments	49
Financial Services (Banking Reform) Act 2013: Commencements	10, 22, 23, 48, 65
Financial Services (Banking Reform) Act 2013: Disclosure & confidential information	48
Financial Services (Banking Reform) Act 2013: Transitional provisions	48
Financial Services Act 2012: Commencements	10, 47
Financial Services Act 2012: Complaints scheme: Relevant functions	47
Financial Services Act 2012: Consequential amendments	47
Financial services: Banking reform: Acts	4
Financial services: Banking reform: Acts: Explanatory notes	5
Financial services: Revenue & customs: Out of time reviews: Appeal provisions	7, 20, 30, 47, 62, 63, 203
Fire & rescue authorities: National framework: Revision England	49
Fire & rescue services: Fire & rescue authorities: National framework: Revision: England	49
Fire & rescue services: Firefighters: Compensation schemes: England	49, 80
Fire & rescue services: Firefighters: Compensation schemes: Scotland	249, 255
Fire & rescue services: Firefighters: Compensation schemes: Wales	49, 81
Fire & rescue services: Firefighters: New: Pension schemes: Northern Ireland	278
Fire & rescue services: Firefighters: Pension schemes: Contributions: Wales	49, 81
Fire & rescue services: Firefighters: Pension schemes: England	49, 81, 87
Fire & rescue services: Firefighters: Pension schemes: Northern Ireland	278
Fire & rescue services: Firefighters: Pension schemes: Scotland	249, 255
Fire & rescue services: Firefighters: Pension schemes: Wales	49, 81
Fire & rescue services: Firemen: Pension schemes: Scotland	249, 255
Fire & rescue services: Pension schemes: Wales	49, 81
Firearms: Rules	10
Firefighters: Compensation schemes: England	49, 80

Firefighters: Compensation schemes: Scotland 249, 255
Firefighters: Compensation schemes: Wales 49, 81
Firefighters: New: Pension schemes: Northern Ireland 278
Firefighters: Pension schemes: Contributions: Wales 49, 81
Firefighters: Pension schemes: England 49, 81, 87
Firefighters: Pension schemes: Northern Ireland 278
Firefighters: Pension schemes: Scotland 249, 255
Firefighters: Pension schemes: Wales 49, 81
Firemen: Pension schemes: Scotland 249, 255
Fireplaces: Exempt: Smoke control areas: England 20
Fireplaces: Exempt: Smoke control areas: Northern Ireland. 274
Fireplaces: Exempt: Smoke control areas: Scotland 245
Fireplaces: Exempt: Smoke control areas: Wales 20
First-tier tribunal: Property chamber: Fees 202
Fish farming: Aquaculture & Fisheries (Scotland) Act 2013: Commercially damaging species: Specification: Scotland 243, 249, 264
Fish: Labelling 49
Fish: Labelling: Northern Ireland 278
Fish: Labelling: Wales 50
Fisher Fleet Quay: Harbour: Revision 52
Fisheries: Foyle area: Angling permit: Northern Ireland 278
Fisheries: Live fish: Keeping or release prohibition 91
Fisheries: Northern Ireland 278
Fisheries: Salmon & freshwater fisheries: Conservation: Annual close time & catch & release: Scotland 249, 258, 263
Fisheries: Salmon drift netting: Northern Ireland 278
Fisheries: Salmon netting: Northern Ireland 278
Fishing boats: Financial assistance: Sea fisheries: Northern Ireland 278
Fishing boats: Points for masters: Scotland 263
Fishing vessels: Satellite-tracking devices: Electronic reporting: Scheme 187
Fishing: Prohibited methods: Firth of Clyde: Scotland. 263
Fivemiletown: Parking & waiting restrictions: Northern Ireland. 287
Fixed penalties: Road traffic & vehicles: Northern Ireland 288
Fixed penalty offences: Road traffic & vehicles: Northern Ireland 288
Fixed penalty: Criminal law. 28
Flexible working: Eligibility, complaints & remedies 197
Flood & Water Management Act 2010: Commencements 204
Flood insurance: Water industry: Supply: Acts 5
Flood insurance: Water industry: Supply: Acts: Explanatory notes 6
Flood risk management: Reservoirs (Scotland) Act 2011: Commencements: Scotland 249, 267
Fluorinated greenhouse gases: Northern Ireland 277
Food from Britain: Public bodies: Abolition 7, 85
Food Hygiene Rating (Wales) Act 2013: Commencements. 50
Food hygiene: Wales 50
Food information: England. 49
Food information: Scotland. 249
Food information: Wales. 50
Food safety: Enforcement procedures: Improvement: Deregulation: Northern Ireland 278
Food: Added phytosterols or phytostanols: Labelling: Wales. 50
Food: Contaminants: Northern Ireland 279
Food: Fish: Labelling. 49
Food: Fish: Labelling: Northern Ireland 278
Food: Fish: Labelling: Wales 50
Food: Hygiene: Northern Ireland 278, 279
Food: Hygiene: Scotland 249
Food: Infant & follow-on formula: Northern Ireland 279
Food: Infant & follow-on formula: Scotland 249
Food: Infant & follow-on formula: Wales 50
Food: Information: Scotland 249
Food: Meat products 50
Food: Meat products: Scotland 249
Food: Meat: Products containing: Northern Ireland 279
Food: Official controls: England 8, 50
Food: Official controls: Scotland 249
Food: Official controls: Wales. 8, 50
Food: Olive oil: Marketing standards 49
Food: Products containing meat: Wales 50
Food: Safety & hygiene 50
Food: Schools: Requirements: England 36
Food: Transfer of functions: Wales. 50
Food: Weights & measures. 204
Foot & mouth disease: Northern Ireland 274
Football spectators: 2014 World Cup control period 195
Forest law: Enforcement, governance & trade: Fees 30
Forestry: Phytophthora ramorum management zone: Scotland 255
Forestry: Plant health: England & Scotland. 82
Forestry: Plant health: Fees: England & Scotland 82
Forests: Reproductive material: Great Britain 187
Former Glenshane Road at Ranaghan Bridge, Magherafelt: Abandonment: Northern Ireland 285
Foundation stage: National curriculum: Wales 37

Foundation stage: National curriculum: Assessment arrangements: Wales. 38
Foyle area: Angling permit: Northern Ireland 278
Freedom of Information (Scotland) Act 2002: Scottish public authorities: Scotland 249
Friendly societies: Building Societies (Funding) & Mutual Societies (Transfers) Act 2007: Commencements 12, 51, 60
Fuel & electricity control: Fuel & electricity: Heating: Control: Revocations 51
Fuel & electricity: Heating: Control: Revocations 51
Fuel poverty: England 42
Fuel: Car & van fuel: Benefit: Income tax. 60
Fuel: Motor fuel: Composition & content: Air pollution: Prevention: Ships 72
Fuel: Use & recycling processes: Climate change levy 20
Fuels: Authorised fuels: Smoke control areas: England 20
Fuels: Authorised fuels: Smoke control areas: Northern Ireland. 274
Fuels: Authorised fuels: Smoke control areas: Scotland 245
Fuels: Authorised fuels: Smoke control areas: Wales. 20
Fuels: Biofuels & other fuel substitutes: Excise duties: Payment 44
Fuels: Exempted fireplaces: Smoke control areas: Wales 20
Fuels: Liquid fuels: Sulphur content: England & Wales 43
Fuels: Liquid: Sulphur content: Northern Ireland 277
Fuels: Other fuel substitutes: Excise duties: Rates 44
Further & Higher Education (Governance & Information) (Wales) Act 2014: Commencements: Wales 38
Further & higher education: Governance & information: Acts: Explanatory notes: Wales 297
Further & higher education: Governance & information: Acts: Wales 296
Further education corporations: Dissolution: Publication of proposals & prescribed bodies. 37
Further education loans: England 35
Further education: Plymouth College of Art: Transfer to higher education sector 35

G

Gambling Act (Licensing & Advertising) Act 2014: Commencements. 11
Gambling Act (Licensing & Advertising) Act 2014: Transitional provisions 11
Gambling: Licensing & advertising: Acts. 4
Gambling: Licensing & advertising: Acts: Explanatory notes 6
Gaming machines: Categories 10
Gaming: Duty 44
Gangmasters: Licensing: Exclusions: Northern Ireland 276
Garron Point Hill Climb: Road races: Northern Ireland 288
Gas Act 1986: Exemptions: Revocations 51, 81
Gas transit: EEC requirements 51
Gas: Appeals: Designation & exclusion 39, 51
Gas: Billing 39, 51
Gas: Electricity: Ownership unbundling 39, 51
Gas: Energy companies obligation. 39, 51
Gas: Energy companies obligation: Determination & savings. 39, 51
Gas: Internal markets 39, 51
Gas: Performance: Individual standards: Northern Ireland 279
Gas: Regulated providers: Redress schemes 23, 40, 51
Gas: Warm home discount 40, 51
Gedling: Electoral changes 67
Gender equality: International development: Acts 5
Gender equality: International development: Acts: Explanatory notes 6
Gender recognition: Courts & tribunals: Fees: England & Wales 11, 27, 46, 51, 70, 72, 188, 195, 202
General Medical Council: Administrative erasure: Restoration 53
General Medical Council: Fitness to practise 53
General Medical Council: Licence to practise 53
General Medical Council: Voluntary erasure & restoration following voluntary erasure 53
General medical services: Contracts: Drug prescriptions: England 75
General medical services: Contracts: England 75
General ophthalmic services: Northern Ireland 279
General Osteopathic Council: Registration & fees: Applications 53
General Register Office: Fees: Northern Ireland. 285
General Synod of the Church of England: Measures 7
General Teaching Council for Northern Ireland 276
Genetically modified organisms: Contained use 52
Germany: Double taxation: Relief 12, 25, 59
Giant's Causeway Road: Northern Ireland 287
Gibraltar: International tax: Enforcement 196
Gibraltar: Taxes: International compliance 196
Gilt-edged securities: Chargeable gains: Capital gains tax 13, 26
Glasgow 2014 Commonwealth Games: Air navigation: Flying restrictions 16, 17
Glasgow Commonwealth Games Act 2008: Repeal day: Scotland 266
Glasgow Commonwealth Games Act 2008: Urgent traffic regulation measures: Scotland. 258, 266
Glengall Road, Belfast: Loading bays & parking places on road: Road traffic & vehicles: Northern Ireland. 287
Gloucester Care Services: National Health Service Trust: Establishment 74
Gloucester Care Services: National Health Service Trust: Originating capital 74
Goats: Records, identification & movement: England 9
Goods & services: Local authorities: Public bodies: England. 68
Goods vehicles: Operators: Licensing: Fees 92
Goods vehicles: Plating & testing: Amendments 92

Goods vehicles: Recording equipment: Tachograph card: Fees 92
Goods: International carriage: Dangerous goods: Road transport: Fees 92
Goods: Taking control: Fees. 42
Government alternative finance arrangements 74
Government Resources & Accounts Act 2000: Estimates & accounts 51
Government resources & accounts: Whole of government accounts: Bodies: Designation. 51
Government resources & accounts: Whole of government accounts: Bodies: Designation: Northern Ireland 279
Government trading funds: Buying Agency Trading Fund 52
Government trading funds: Medicines & Healthcare Products Regulatory Agency Trading Fund: Additional assets & liabilities: Appropriation
 52
Government: Whole of government accounts: Bodies: Designation 51
Government: Whole of government accounts: Bodies: Designation: Northern Ireland. 279
Greater London Authority: Council tax: Requirement procedure 70
Green deal: Qualifying energy improvements. 41
Greenhouse gas emissions trading scheme 20
Greenhouse gases: Fluorinated: Northern Ireland. 277
Groundwater: Environmental protection: Northern Ireland 277
Growth & Infrastructure Act 2013: Commencements. 199
Guardian's allowance: Reviews & appeals 194, 196
Guardian's allowance: Up-rating 191
Guardian's allowance: Up-rating: Northern Ireland 194
Guernsey: Territorial sea: Limits 199

H

Habitual residence: Social security: Northern Ireland. 280, 284, 291
Halton, Knowsley, Liverpool, St Helens, Sefton & Wirral Combined Authority 67, 201
Hambleton: Electoral changes. 67
Harbour authority designation: Scotland 250
Harbours, docks, piers & ferries: Able Marine Energy Park Development: Consent. 52, 61
Harbours, docks, piers & ferries: Dover: Harbour revision 52
Harbours, docks, piers & ferries: Fisher Fleet Quay: Harbour revision 52
Harbours, docks, piers & ferries: Harbour authority designation: Scotland 250
Harbours, docks, piers & ferries: Lymington: Harbour revision 52
Harbours, docks, piers & ferries: Pennan: Harbour revision: Scotland 250
Harbours, docks, piers & ferries: Port of Ardersier: Harbour revision: Scotland 250
Harbours, docks, piers & ferries: Portsmouth Harbour: Portsmouth & Gosport Joint Board: Abolition 52
Harrogate Stray Act 1985: Tour de France. 67
Harwich International: Port security: Merchant shipping 73
Hazardous substances: Planning: Northern Ireland. 283
Hazardous substances: Use: Restriction: Waste electrical & electronic equipment 42
Hazardous waste: Wales. 200
Health & personal social services: General dental services: Northern Ireland 279
Health & personal social services: General medical services contracts: Drug prescriptions: Northern Ireland 279
Health & personal social services: General ophthalmic services: Northern Ireland. 279
Health & personal social services: Optical charges & payments: Northern Ireland. 279
Health & personal social services: Pharmaceutical services: Northern Ireland. 279
Health & personal social services: Superannuation scheme: Northern Ireland. 279
Health & Safety at Work etc Act 1974: Repeals & revocations 52
Health & safety: Accident hazards: Control: Heavy fuel oil 52, 199
Health & safety: Acetylene. 52
Health & safety: Explosives 52
Health & safety: Explosives precursors: Control 52
Health & safety: Explosives precursors: Control: Northern Ireland. 279
Health & safety: Explosives: Hazard information & packaging for supply: Northern Ireland. 279, 280
Health & safety: Fees: Northern Ireland. 280
Health & safety: Genetically modified organisms: Contained use 52
Health & safety: Mines. 52
Health & safety: Offshore installations: Safety zones 78
Health & safety: Petroleum. 52
Health & safety: REACH: Enforcement 23, 42, 52
Health & Social Care (Community Health & Standards) Act 2003: Commencements: Wales 190
Health & Social Care Act 2008: Commencements. 53
Health & Social Care Act 2008: Regulated activities: England 74, 86, 190
Health & Social Care Act 2012: Commencements. 74
Health & social care: Bodies: Membership: Health & social care: Northern Ireland 280
Health & social care: Disciplinary procedures: Northern Ireland. 280
Health & social care: Health & social care bodies: Membership: Northern Ireland 280
Health & social care: Pension schemes: Northern Ireland. 279
Health & social care: Safeguarding Board for Northern Ireland: Membership, procedure, functions & committees 280
Health care & associated professions: Dentists Act 1984: Medical authorities 53
Health care & associated professions: General Medical Council: Administrative erasure: Restoration. 53
Health care & associated professions: General Medical Council: Fitness to practise 53
Health care & associated professions: General Medical Council: Licence to practise. 53
Health care & associated professions: General Medical Council: Voluntary erasure & restoration following voluntary erasure 53
Health care & associated professions: Health & Social Care Act 2008: Commencements 53
Health care & associated professions: Health Professions Council: Registration & fees 53
Health care & associated professions: Indemnity arrangements 53

Health care & associated professions: Medical Act 1983: English: Knowledge 53
Health care & associated professions: Nursing & Midwifery Council: Fees 53
Health Education England 75
Health Education England: Transfer: Staff & Property & liabilities 75
Health education: Acts 4
Health education: Acts: Explanatory notes 5
Health professionals: Public Bodies: Joint working: Health Professionals & Social Care Professionals: Scotland 256, 265
Health Professions Council: Registration & fees 53
Health Research Authority: Transfer of staff, property & liabilities 53, 190
Health Service: King's College Hospital Foundation Trust: Transfer of trust property 75
Health Service: National Trusts 74, 75, 76
Health Service: National Trusts: Establishment 74, 75
Health Service: National Trusts: Originating capital 74
Health Service: National Trusts: Transfer of trust property 76
Health Service: Oxford Health NHS Foundation: Transfer of trust property 76
Health Service: St George's Healthcare: Transfer of trust property 76
Health services: Care Act 2014: Consequential amendments 53, 190
Health services: Charges: Recovery: Amounts: Northern Ireland 280
Health services: Health Research Authority: Transfer of staff, property & liabilities 53, 190
Health: Acts: Explanatory notes: Northern Ireland 272
Health: Acts: Northern Ireland 272
Health: Animals: Brucellosis: Scotland 243
Healthcare & associated professions: General Osteopathic Council: Registration & fees: Applications 53
Healthy Start: Vitamins: Charging 75, 86
Heat: Network metering & billing 41
Heathrow & Gatwick Airports - London Noise Insulation Grants: Revocations 19
Heavy fuel oil 52, 199
Heavy goods vehicles: Exemption of vehicles 92
Heavy goods vehicles: Road user levy: Specified roads 92
Heavy goods vehicles: Trans-European Road Network infrastructure: Charging 53
Her Majesty's Inspector of Education, Children's Services & Skills 14, 35
Her Majesty's Inspector of Education, Children's Services & Skills: Children's homes: Fees & frequency of inspections 14
Hereditaments: Unoccupied: Rating: Amendments: Northern Ireland 284
Herefordshire: Electoral changes 67
Hertfordshire County Council: Filming on highways: Local acts 6
HGV Road User Levy Act 2013: Commencements 92
High court & county court: Jurisdiction 27, 189
High Court of Justiciary: Act of Adjournal: Criminal Procedure (Scotland) Act 1995: Criminal Procedure Rules 1996: Amendments: Scotland
. . . . 250, 251, 264
High Court of Justiciary: Act of Adjournal: Criminal procedure rules: Amendment: Regulatory Reform (Scotland) Act 2014: Scotland . . 250, 264
High Court of Justiciary: Act of Adjournal: Criminal procedure rules: Scotland 250, 251, 264
High court: Business distribution 189
High Hedges (Scotland) Act 2013: Commencements: Scotland 250
High Hedges (Scotland) Act 2013: Supplementary provisions: Scotland 250
Higher Education Funding Council for Wales 38
Higher education: Plymouth College of Art: Transfer to higher education sector 35
Higher education: Prescribed courses: Information requirements 35
Higher education: Student loans: Living costs liability: Cancellation 37
Highways: Active travel: Wales: Commencements 55
Highways: Dartford - Thurrock Crossing: Amendments 55
Highways: England 53, 54, 55
Highways: Heavy goods vehicles: Trans-European Road Network infrastructure: Charging 53
Highways: Motorways: M40: Junction 12 improvements 54
Highways: Reading Borough Council: River Thames Pedestrian/Cycle Bridge Scheme: Confirmation 54
Highways: Severn Bridges: Tolls 54
Highways: Special roads: England 55
Highways: Town or village greens: Registration: Trigger & terminating events 21
Highways: Traffic management: Permit schemes: Bracknell Forest Borough Council 54
Highways: Traffic management: Permit schemes: Cheshire East Borough Council 54
Highways: Traffic management: Permit schemes: Cheshire West & Chester Borough Council 54
Highways: Traffic management: Permit schemes: Coventry City Council 54
Highways: Traffic management: Permit schemes: Norfolk County Council 54
Highways: Traffic management: Permit schemes: North Tyneside Borough Council 54
Highways: Traffic management: Permit schemes: Sefton Metropolitan Borough Council 54
Highways: Traffic management: Permit schemes: Shropshire Council 54
Highways: Traffic management: Permit schemes: Slough Borough Council 54
Highways: Traffic management: Permit schemes: Warrington Borough Council 54
Highways: Traffic management: Permit schemes: Warwickshire County Council 54
Highways: Traffic management: Permit schemes: West Berkshire Council 55
Highways: Traffic management: Permit schemes: Wokingham Borough Council 55
Highways: Wales 55
Historic Environment Scotland Act 2014: Commencements: Scotland 243
Historic environment: Acts: Explanatory notes: Scotland 242
Historic environment: Acts: Scotland 241
HIV testing kits & services: Revocation: England 86
HIV testing kits & services: Revocation: Scotland 256
HIV testing kits & services: Revocation: Wales 86

Home energy assistance schemes: Amendments: Scotland 248
Home loss payments: Prescribed amounts: England 7, 22
Homeless persons: Unsuitable accommodation: Scotland 250
Homelessness: Allocation of housing & homelessness: Eligibility: England 55
Homelessness: Allocation of housing & homelessness: Eligibility: Wales 56
Hornsea One Offshore Wind Farm 61
Horses: Control: Acts: Explanatory notes: Wales 296
Horses: Control: Acts: Wales 296
Horsham: Electoral changes 67
House of Lords: Reform: Acts 4
House of Lords: Reform: Acts: Explanatory notes 6
Housing (Scotland) Act 2014: Commencements: Scotland 250
Housing (Wales) Act 2014: Commencements 56
Housing benefit 191
Housing benefit: Amendments 191
Housing benefit: Functions: Rent officers 55
Housing benefit: Habitual residence: Northern Ireland 280, 284
Housing benefit: Supported accommodation 191
Housing benefit: Transitional provisions 191
Housing payments: Discretionary: Total expenditure: Revocation: Scotland 266
Housing: Absolute ground for possession for anti-social behaviour: Review procedures 55
Housing: Acts: Explanatory notes: Scotland 242
Housing: Acts: Explanatory notes: Wales 297
Housing: Acts: Scotland 241
Housing: Acts: Wales 296
Housing: Allocation of housing & homelessness: Eligibility: England 55
Housing: Allocation of housing & homelessness: Eligibility: Wales 56
Housing: Anti-social Behaviour, Crime & Policing Act 2014: Commencements 10, 29, 31, 33, 45, 56, 83, 84
Housing: Anti-social Behaviour, Crime & Policing Act 2014: Commencements: Wales 56
Housing: Homeless persons: Unsuitable accommodation: Scotland 250
Housing: Jobseeker's allowance: Employment assistance: Northern Ireland 280, 284, 290
Housing: Landlord registration schemes: Northern Ireland 281
Housing: Leasehold: Reform: Acts 5
Housing: Leasehold: Reform: Acts: Explanatory notes 6
Housing: Lettings agency work: Redress schemes 56
Housing: Mobile homes: Written statement: Wales 74
Housing: Prevention of Social Housing Fraud Act 2013: Power to require information 56
Housing: Property management work: Redress schemes 56
Housing: Renewal grants: England 55
Housing: Rent officers: Housing benefits & universal credit functions: Local housing allowance 55
Housing: Residential Property Tribunal: Procedures & fees 64
Housing: Residential Property Tribunal: Procedures & fees: Wales 56
Housing: Right to buy: Discount limits 56
Housing: Right to buy: Maximum percentage discount 56
Housing: Right to buy: Prescribed forms 56
Housing: Secure tenancies: Notices: Northern Ireland 280
Housing: Secure tenancies: Review procedures: Wales 56
Housing: Social housing: Fraud: Detection: Wales 56
Housing: Social security: Benefits: Up-rating: Northern Ireland 276, 280, 284, 290, 291, 292
Housing: Social security: Habitual residence: Northern Ireland 280, 284, 291
Housing: Social security: Northern Ireland 280, 284, 291
Human fertilisation & embryology: Marriage (Same Sex Couples) Act 2013: Consequential & contrary provisions 19, 57, 71
Human fertilisation & embryology: Quality & safety 57
Human medicines: Northern Ireland 282
Human rights: Attorney general: Guidance: Courts & Tribunal Service: Support for victims & witnesses: Northern Ireland 280
Human tissue: Human application: Quality & safety 57
Human tissue: Transplantation: Organs: Quality & safety 57
Humber Bridge: Local acts 6
Huyton: Network Rail 201
Hydrocarbon oil duties: Electricity generation reliefs: Carbon price support 44

I

Iceland: Double taxation: Relief & international enforcement 12, 25, 58
Immigration: Croatia: Accession: Immigration & worker authorisation 57
Immigration & nationality: Cost recovery fees 57, 77
Immigration & nationality: Fees 57
Immigration Act 2014: Bank accounts 48, 49, 57
Immigration Act 2014: Bank accounts: Prohibition on opening accounts for disqualified persons 49, 57
Immigration Act 2014: Commencements 57
Immigration Act 2014: Specified anti-fraud organisations 57
Immigration Act 2014: Transitional & saving provisions 57
Immigration Services Commissioner: Application fees 58
Immigration: Acts 4
Immigration: Acts: Explanatory notes 6
Immigration: Borders, Citizenship & Immigration Act 2009: Commencements 57
Immigration: Channel Tunnel: Miscellaneous provisions 57
Immigration: Control of entry: Through Republic of Ireland 58

Immigration: Employment of adults subject to immigration control: Maximum penalty 58
Immigration: European Economic Area 58
Immigration: Nationality: Fees 57, 77
Immigration: Notices 58
Immigration: Passenger transit: Visas 58
Immigration: Removal of family members 58
Immigration: Residential accommodation: Prescribed cases 58
Immigration: Residential accommodation: Prescribed requirements & codes of practice 58
Immigration: Restrictions on employment: Codes of practice 58
Immigration: Travel bans: Designation 58
Imported goods: Relief: Value added tax 203
Incapacity: Adults with incapacity: Welfare guardians: Supervision: Local authorities: Scotland 242
Income support allowance: Work-related activity 191
Income Tax (Earnings & Pensions) Act 2003: Section 684(3A) 59
Income tax: Business premises renovation allowances 24, 58
Income tax: Capital allowances: Energy-saving plant & machinery 25, 58
Income tax: Capital allowances: Environmentally beneficial plant & machinery 25, 58
Income tax: Car & van fuel: Benefit: Rates 60
Income tax: Charitable deductions: Approved schemes 58
Income tax: Double taxation: Relief & international enforcement: Belgium 12, 25, 58, 81
Income tax: Double taxation: Relief & international enforcement: Canada 12, 25, 58, 81
Income tax: Double taxation: Relief & international enforcement: Iceland 12, 25, 58
Income tax: Double taxation: Relief & international enforcement: Japan 12, 25, 58
Income tax: Double taxation: Relief & international enforcement: Zambia 12, 25, 59
Income tax: Double taxation: Relief: Germany 12, 25, 59
Income tax: Double taxation: Relief: Tajikistan 12, 25, 59
Income tax: Electronic communications 59
Income tax: Extra-statutory concessions: Enactments 59
Income tax: Finance Act 2009: Consequential amendments 59, 191
Income tax: Finance Act 2009: Schedule 55: Penalties for failure to make returns 59
Income tax: Finance Act 2009: Sections 101, 102: Appointed days 59, 191
Income tax: Finance Act 2014: Commencements 12, 59
Income tax: Finance Act 2014: Section 12: Appointed day 59
Income tax: Indexation 59
Income tax: Individual savings accounts 12, 59, 60
Income tax: Interest rates 60
Income tax: International tax: Enforcement: Anguilla 12, 25, 60, 61, 203
Income tax: International tax: Enforcement: British Virgin Islands 12, 25, 60, 61, 203
Income tax: International tax: Enforcement: Turks & Caicos Islands 12, 25, 60, 61, 203
Income tax: Investment transactions: Taxes 25, 60
Income tax: Medical treatment: Recommended 59
Income tax: Offshore funds: Amendments 12, 26, 60
Income tax: Ordinary residence: Removal 59
Income tax: PAYE 59
Income tax: PAYE: Construction industry scheme 59
Income tax: Pension schemes: Registered & relieved non-UK: Lifetime allowance transitional protection: Individual protection: Notification 60
Income tax: Pension schemes: Registered: Provision of information 60
Income tax: Pension schemes: Sums & assets: Transfer 60
Income tax: Professional fees 59
Income tax: Registered pension schemes: Accounting & assessment 60
Income tax: SAYE Option Schemes: Contributions limit 59
Income tax: Tax relief: Social investments: Social impact contractor: Accreditation 60
Income tax: Taxes: Charities: Definition: Relevant territories 9, 13, 26, 60, 61, 195, 203
Income tax: Unit trusts: Unauthorised 13, 26, 60
Income tax: Venture capital trusts 60
Income-related benefits: Subsidy to authorities 191
Independent educational provision: Management participation: Prohibition: Education: England 35
Independent Police Complaints Commission: Investigation of offences 83
Independent prescribers: Physiotherapists: Podiatrists: Chiropodists: Scotland 254
Independent prescribers: Physiotherapists: Podiatrists: Chiropodists: Wales 77
Individual savings accounts 12, 60
Individual savings accounts: Income tax 12, 59
Industrial & provident societies: Arrangements, reconstructions & administration 28, 60
Industrial & provident societies: Building Societies (Funding) & Mutual Societies (Transfers) Act 2007: Commencements 12, 51, 60
Industrial & provident societies: Electronic communications 28, 60
Industrial & provident societies: Shareholding limit: Increase 60
Industrial development: Assisted areas 60
Industrial emissions: Environmental protection: Pollution: Prevention & control: Northern Ireland 277
Industrial training levy: Construction industry: Northern Ireland 281
Industrial training levy: Engineering Construction Industry Training Board 40
Infant & follow-on formula: Northern Ireland 279
Infant & follow-on formula: Scotland 249
Infant & follow-on formula: Wales 50
Infrastructure planning: Able Marine Energy Park Development: Consent 52, 61
Infrastructure planning: Applications: Prescribed forms & procedure 61
Infrastructure planning: Burbo Bank extension offshore wind farm 61
Infrastructure planning: Clocaenog Forest wind farm 61
Infrastructure planning: Combined heat & power plants: South Hook 61

Infrastructure planning: Daventry International Rail Freight Interchange Alteration 61
Infrastructure planning: East Anglia ONE Offshore Wind Farm 61
Infrastructure planning: Hornsea One Offshore Wind Farm 61
Infrastructure planning: National Grid: North London reinforcement project 61
Infrastructure planning: Network Rail: Knutsford to Bowdon improvement 61
Infrastructure planning: Network Rail: Norton Bridge area improvement 61
Infrastructure planning: North Killingholme generating station 61
Infrastructure planning: Rampion Wind Farm. 61
Infrastructure planning: Thames tideway tunnel: Thames Water Utilities Ltd 61
Infrastructure planning: Thames Water Utilities Ltd: Thames tideway tunnel 61
Infrastructure planning: Walney extension offshore wind farm 61
Infrastructure planning: Willington C Gas Pipeline 61
Infrastructure planning: Woodside Link Houghton Regis 61
Inheritance & Trustees' Powers Act 2014: Commencements 46
Inheritance & trustees' powers: Acts 4
Inheritance tax: Accounts: Delivery: Excepted estates 61
Inheritance tax: International tax: Enforcement: Anguilla 12, 25, 60, 61, 203
Inheritance tax: International tax: Enforcement: British Virgin Islands 12, 25, 60, 61, 203
Inheritance tax: International tax: Enforcement: Turks & Caicos Islands 12, 25, 60, 61, 203
Inheritance tax: Taxes: Charity: Definition: Relevant territories. 9, 13, 26, 60, 61, 195, 203
Insolvency: Bankruptcy & Debt Advice (Scotland) Act 2014: Commencements: Scotland 243, 246, 250
Insolvency: Bankruptcy & Diligence etc. (Scotland) Act 2007: Commencements: Scotland 243, 250
Insolvency: Bankruptcy: Applications & decisions: Scotland 243, 246, 250
Insolvency: Bankruptcy: Fees: Scotland 251
Insolvency: Bankruptcy: Scotland. 244, 251
Insolvency: Building societies: Insolvency rules: Northern Ireland 274
Insolvency: Building societies: Special administration rules: Northern Ireland 274
Insolvency: Commencement of proceedings: Insolvency Rules 1986 61
Insolvency: Common financial tool: Scotland 244, 246, 251
Insolvency: Companies: Rules: Scotland 251
Insolvency: Money advice & deduction from income: Scotland. 243, 246, 250
Insolvency: Proceedings: Fees. 62
Insurance premium tax: Financial services: Revenue & customs: Out of time reviews: Appeal provisions 7, 20, 30, 47, 62, 63, 203
Insurance premium tax: Non-taxable insurance contracts 62
Insurance: Flood: Water industry: Supply: Acts 5
Insurance: Flood: Water industry: Supply: Acts: Explanatory notes 6
Intellectual Property Act 2014: Amendments 62
Intellectual Property Act 2014: Commencements 62
Intellectual property: Acts 4
Intellectual property: Acts: Explanatory notes 6
Internal markets: Electricity & gas 39, 51
International carriage: Dangerous goods: Road transport: Fees 92
International Criminal Court Act 2001: Bailiwick of Jersey 62
International Criminal Court Act 2001: Jersey 62
International Development Association: Multilateral debt relief initiative 62
International Development Association: Seventeenth replenishment 62
International development: African Development Fund: African Development Bank: Thirteenth replenishment 62
International development: African Development Fund: Multilateral debt relief initiative 62
International development: Crown Agents Holding & Realisation Board: Dissolution 62
International development: Gender equality: Acts 5
International development: Gender equality: Acts: Explanatory notes 6
International development: International Development Association: Multilateral debt relief initiative 62
International immunities & privileges: African Legal Support Facility: Legal capacities. 62
Invalid care allowance: Northern Ireland 291
Invalid care allowance: Social security 193
Inverclyde Council: Parking adjudicators: Road traffic: Scotland 258
Inverclyde Council: Parking attendants: Wearing of uniforms: Scotland 258
Inverclyde Council: Road traffic: Permitted & special parking area: Scotland 259
Investigatory powers & data retention: Acts 4
Investigatory powers & data retention: Acts: Explanatory notes 6
Investigatory powers: Regulation: Covert human intelligence sources: Authorisation: Scotland 251
Investigatory powers: Regulation: Covert human intelligence sources: Codes of practice 62
Investigatory powers: Regulation: Covert surveillance & property interference: Codes of practice 63
Investment funds: Alternative Investment Fund Managers: Regulations 47
Investment transactions: Taxes 25, 60
Ipswich: Port security: Merchant shipping 73
Iran: European Communities: Financial sanctions 28
Isle of Wight: English Coast 27

J

Japan: Double taxation: Relief & international enforcement. 12, 25, 58
Jersey: Air navigation: Civil aviation 15
Jersey: International Criminal Court Act 2001 62
Jersey: Maritime security. 72
Jobseeker's allowance: Employment & support allowance: Social security 193
Jobseeker's allowance: Employment & support allowance: Waiting days: Northern Ireland 291
Jobseeker's allowance: Employment assistance: Northern Ireland 280, 284, 290

Jobseeker's allowance: Habitual residence 191
Jobseeker's allowance: Habitual residence: Northern Ireland 290
Jobseeker's allowance: Homeless claimants 191
Jobseeker's allowance: Homeless claimants: Northern Ireland 290
Jobseeker's allowance: Jobsearch pilot scheme 191
Jobseeker's allowance: Maternity allowance: Amendment: Northern Ireland 290
Jobseeker's allowance: Work skills pilot scheme 191
Judges, legal officers & others: Fees: Ecclesiastical law 33
Judgments: Civil jurisdiction & judgments 63
Judgments: Civil jurisdiction & judgments: Protection measures 63
Judgments: Civil jurisdiction & judgments: Protection measures: Scotland 251
Judgments: Marriage: Same sex couples: Jurisdiction & recognition of judgments 45, 63
Judgments: Marriage: Same sex couples: Jurisdiction & recognition of judgments: Scotland 251
Judicial appointments & discipline: Addition of office 63
Judicial appointments & discipline: Judicial discipline: Prescribed procedures 63
Judicial appointments: England & Wales 63, 202
Judicial discipline: Prescribed procedures 63
Judicial Office: Fitness for: Tribunal Rules: Scotland 251, 264
Judicial Pensions & Retirement Act 1993: Courts: Scotland 251, 264
Judicial pensions: Contributions: Amendments 79
Judicial pensions: Widows', widowers' & children's benefits 79
Justice (Northern Ireland) Act 2002: Amendments: Northern Ireland 281
Justice of the Peace Court: Act of Adjournal: Criminal Procedure (Scotland) Act 1995: Criminal Procedure Rules 1996: Amendments: Scotland 250, 251, 264
Justice of the Peace Court: Act of Adjournal: Criminal procedure rules: Scotland 250, 251, 264
Justice of the Peace Court: Judicial Pensions & Retirement Act 1993: Scotland 251, 264
Justice: Criminal Justice: 2013 Act: Commencements: Northern Ireland 281
Justices of the Peace: Local justice areas 63
Justices' clerks & assistants rules: England & Wales 45

K

Kensington & Chelsea: Electoral changes 67
Kesteven, South: Electoral changes 68
Ketamine: Misuse of Drugs Act 1971 31
Key stage 2: National curriculum: Assessment arrangements: Wales 38
Key stage 3: National curriculum: Assessment arrangements: Wales 38
Key stage 4: Local curriculum: Wales 37
Kimberley process: Fees 46
King's College Hospital Foundation Trust: Transfer of property 75
Knutsford to Bowdon improvement: Network Rail 61

L

Lanarkshire Colleges: Education: Scotland 247
Lancaster: Electoral changes 67
Land & Buildings Transaction Tax (Scotland) Act 2013: Commencements: Scotland 251
Land & buildings transaction tax: Administration: Scotland 251, 252
Land & buildings transaction tax: Definition of charity: Relevant territories: Scotland 244, 251
Land & buildings transaction tax: Prescribed proportions: Scotland 251
Land & buildings transaction tax: Qualifying public or educational bodies: Scotland 251
Land & buildings transactions: Taxes: Acts: Explanatory notes: Scotland 242
Land drainage: Lower Wye & River Lugg: Boundaries alteration 63
Land drainage: Vale of Pickering Internal Drainage Board 63
Land reform: Long leases: Appeal period: Scotland 252
Land reform: Long leases: Prescribed form of notices: Scotland 252
Land register: Rules: Scotland 252
Land Registration etc. (Scotland) Act 2012: Commencements: Scotland 252
Land Registration etc. (Scotland) Act 2012: Designated day: Scotland 252
Land Registration etc. (Scotland) Act 2012: Incidental, consequential & transitional provisions: Scotland 252
Land Registration etc. (Scotland) Act 2012: Scotland 252
Land registration: Automated: Electronic communications: Scotland 252
Land registration: Compensation: Rate of interest: Scotland 252
Land registration: Land Registration etc. (Scotland) Act 2012: Scotland 252
Land registration: Registers: Information & access: Scotland 252
Land registration: Rules: Scotland 252
Land Registry: Fees: Northern Ireland 281
Land: Acquisition: Home loss payments: Prescribed amounts: England 7, 22
Landfill tax 63
Landfill Tax (Scotland) Act 2014: Commencements: Scotland 252
Landfill tax: Financial services: Revenue & customs: Out of time reviews: Appeal provisions 7, 20, 30, 47, 62, 63, 203
Landfill: Acts: Explanatory notes: Scotland 242
Landfill: Acts: Scotland 241
Landfill: Scottish landfill tax: Prescribed site activities: Scotland 252
Landlord & tenant: Agricultural Holdings (Scotland) Act 2003: Remedial: Scotland 252
Landlord & tenant: Agricultural holdings: Units of production: England 63
Landlord & tenant: Agricultural holdings: Units of production: Wales 64
Landlord & tenant: Assured tenancies & agricultural occupancies: Forms: Wales 64

Landlord & tenant: Enterprise & Regulatory Reform Act 2013: Commencements 7, 63, 64, 197, 198
Landlord & tenant: Landlord registration schemes: Northern Ireland 281
Landlord & tenant: Leasehold Valuation Tribunals: Fees: Wales 64
Landlord & tenant: Registered rents: Increases: Northern Ireland 281
Landlord & tenant: Rent book: Forms of notice: Wales. 64
Landlord & tenant: Residential Property Tribunal: Procedures & fees. 64
Landlord & tenants: Leasehold: Reform: Acts 5
Landlord & tenants: Leasehold: Reform: Acts: Explanatory notes 6
Landlord registration schemes: Northern Ireland 281
Lands Tribunal for Scotland: Fees 252
Lands Tribunal: Salaries: Northern Ireland 281
Larne: Waiting restrictions: Road traffic & vehicles: Northern Ireland 289
Latt Road, Jerrettspass, Newry: Abandonment: Northern Ireland 285
Law: Family law: Child support, pensions & social security: 2000 Act: Commencements: Northern Ireland 274, 277
Law: Forest law: Enforcement, governance & trade: Fees 30
Learning support: Additional: Information: Sources: Scotland. 247
Leasehold Valuation Tribunals: Fees: Wales 64
Leasehold: Reform: Acts 5
Leasehold: Reform: Acts: Explanatory notes 6
Legal aid & advice: Civil legal aid: England & Wales 64
Legal aid & advice: Civil legal aid: Financial resources & payment for services 64
Legal aid & advice: Civil legal aid: Merits criteria 64
Legal aid & advice: Civil legal aid: Procedure, remuneration & statutory charge 64
Legal aid & advice: Civil legal aid: Remuneration 64
Legal aid & advice: Community Legal Service: Funding: Counsel: Family proceedings: England & Wales. 64
Legal aid & advice: Criminal legal aid: Fixed payments & assistance by way of representation: Scotland 252
Legal aid & advice: Criminal legal aid: Remuneration: England & Wales 64
Legal aid & advice: Financial resources: Information: Amendments: England & Wales 65
Legal aid & advice: General: Northern Ireland. 281
Legal aid & advice: Legal aid & assistance: Assistance by way of representation: Time at court & travelling: Fees: Scotland 253
Legal aid & advice: Magistrates' courts & county courts: Appeals: Criminal legal aid: Costs: Northern Ireland. 281
Legal aid & assistance: Assistance by way of representation: Time at court & travelling: Fees: Scotland 253
Legal aid & coroners' courts: Acts: Explanatory notes: Northern Ireland 273
Legal aid & coroners' courts: Acts: Northern Ireland 272
Legal Aid, Sentencing & Punishment of Offenders Act 2012: Alcohol abstinence & monitoring requirements: Commencements 29
Legal Aid, Sentencing & Punishment of Offenders Act 2012: Commencements 30, 89
Legal Aid, Sentencing & Punishment of Offenders Act 2012: Community care 65
Legal Aid, Sentencing & Punishment of Offenders Act 2012: Schedule 1: Amendments 65
Legal officers: Annual fees: Ecclesiastical law 33
Legal Profession & Legal Aid (Scotland) Act 2007: Scottish Legal Complaints Commission: Membership: Scotland 253
Legal profession: Scottish Legal Complaints Commission: Duties & powers: Scotland 253
Legal Services Act 2007: Approved regulator 65
Legal Services Act 2007: Chartered Institute of Institute of Patent Attorneys: Institute of Trade Mark Attorneys: Functions: Modification . . . 65
Legal Services Act 2007: Chartered Institute of Legal Executives: Functions: Modification 65
Legal Services Act 2007: Commencements 65
Legal Services Act 2007: Fees: Claims management complaints: England & Wales 65
Legal Services Act 2007: Institute of Chartered Accounts: Functions: Modification: England & Wales 65
Legal Services Act 2007: Institute of Trade Mark Attorneys: Chartered Institute of Institute of Patent Attorneys: Functions: Modification . . . 65
Legal Services Act 2007: Levy 65
Legal Services Act 2007: Licensing authorities 65
Legal Services Act 2007: Licensing authority decisions: Appeals 65
Legal Services Commission: Community Legal Service: Funding: Amendments 65
Legal services: Financial Services (Banking Reform) Act 2013: Commencements 23, 65
Legal services: Regulators: Referral fees: England & Wales 65
Legislative & regulatory reform: Code of practice: Appointed day 89
Legislative & regulatory reform: Parish & community councils & Charter trustees: Payments 69, 89
Legislative & regulatory reform: Regulatory functions 89
Legislative reform: Clinical commissioning groups 75, 89
Legislative reform: Entertainment licensing 66
Leicester: Electoral changes 67
Leicestershire, North West: Electoral changes 68
Leith Links & Surplus Fire Fund: City of Edinburgh Council: Acts: Explanatory notes: Scotland 242
Leith Links & Surplus Fire Fund: City of Edinburgh Council: Acts: Scotland 241
Lettings agency work: Redress schemes 56
Liabilities: Liabilities to third parties scheme: National Health Service 75
Libraries: Digital Economy Act 2010: Appointed days 65
Libraries: Public Lending Right Scheme 1982: Variation: Commencements 66
Licences & licensing: Legislative reform: Entertainment licensing. 66
Licensing & advertising: Gambling: Acts. 4
Licensing & advertising: Gambling: Acts: Explanatory notes 6
Licensing Act 2003: FIFA World Cup: Licensing hours 66
Licensing Act 2003: Hearings 66
Licensing Act 2003: Mandatory licensing conditions 66
Licensing Act 2003: Permitted temporary activities: Notices 66
Licensing Act 2003: Permitted temporary activities: Notices: Wales 66
Licensing Act 2003: Personal licences 66
Licensing authorities: Legal Services Act 2007 65
Licensing: Marine licensing: Application fees 42, 66, 71

Limited liability partnerships: Sensitive words & expressions	12, 21, 66
Lincolnshire County Council: River Witham Bridge scheme	54
Liquid fuels: Sulphur content: England & Wales	43
Liquid fuels: Sulphur content: Northern Ireland	277
Liquid fuels: Sulphur content: Scotland	248
Listed buildings & conservation areas: Planning: Heritage partnership agreements: England	199
Listed buildings: Consent orders: Procedure: England	199
Listed buildings: Determination of procedure: Prescribed period: Wales	200
Listed buildings: Lawfulness of proposed works: Certificates: Planning: England	199
Litter: Fixed penalty notices: Scotland	248
Live fish: Keeping or release prohibition	91
Llangennech Church in Wales School: Diocese of St Davids: Educational endowments	37
Llangristiolus: Diocese of Bangor: Educational endowments: Wales	37
Llangynllo Church in Wales School: Diocese of St Davids: Educational endowments	37
Lloyd's Underwriters: Conversion of partnerships to underwriting through successor companies	12
Loading bays & parking places on road: Road traffic & vehicles: Northern Ireland	286
Loan relationships & derivative contracts: Accounting practice: Changes	25
Loan relationships & derivative contracts: Accounting standards: Changes	25
Loan relationships & derivative contracts: Profits & losses: Disregard & bringing into account	26
Lobbying: Non-party campaigning: Trade Union administration: Registration: Acts	5
Lobbying: Non-party campaigning: Trade Union administration: Registration: Acts: Explanatory notes	6
Lobbying: Transparency of Lobbying, Non-Party Campaigning & Trade Union Administration Act 2014: Commencements	23, 90
Local Audit & Accountability Act 2014: Auditor panel independence	69
Local Audit & Accountability Act 2014: Auditor resignation & removal	69
Local Audit & Accountability Act 2014: Commencements	67, 68, 69
Local Audit & Accountability Act 2014: Liability limitation agreements	69
Local Audit & Accountability Act 2014: Professional qualifications & major local audit	69
Local audit & accountability: Acts	5
Local audit & accountability: Acts: Explanatory notes	6
Local audit & statutory audit: Delegation of functions	10, 21, 69
Local Audit: Auditor panel	69
Local authorities see also Local government	
Local authorities: Accounts: Scotland	253
Local authorities: Capital finance & accounting: England	68
Local authorities: Capital finance & accounting: Wales	70
Local authorities: Contracting out: Tax billing: Collection & enforcement functions: Wales	24
Local authorities: Council tax: Increases: Conduct of referendums: England	68
Local authorities: Council tax: Increases: Referendums: Conduct: England	26
Local authorities: Disabled persons: Parking badges: Acts: Explanatory notes: Scotland	242
Local authorities: Early years provision: Free: Duty	14
Local authorities: Elected mayors: Elections, terms of office	68
Local authorities: Elections: Wales	70
Local authorities: Goods & services: Public bodies: England	68
Local authorities: Mayoral elections: England & Wales	69
Local authorities: Referendums: Acts	5
Local authorities: Referendums: Acts: Explanatory notes	6
Local authorities: Referendums: Conduct of: England	68
Local authorities: Social services functions: Contracting out: England	23
Local authorities: Standing orders: England	68
Local authorities: Standing orders: Wales	70
Local curriculum: Key stage 4: Wales	37
Local elections: Communities: Welsh forms	90
Local elections: Parishes & communities: England & Wales	90
Local elections: Principal areas: England & Wales	90
Local elections: Principal areas: Welsh forms	90
Local Government (Democracy) (Wales) Act 2013: Commencements	70
Local Government (Wales) Measure 2009: Amendment: Wales	70
Local Government (Wales) Measure 2011: Commencements	70
Local Government Act (Northern Ireland) 2014: Commencements	281
Local government bodies: Openness: England	68
Local Government Byelaws (Wales) Act 2012: Amendment	70
Local Government Byelaws (Wales) Act 2012: Commencements	70
Local Government Finance Act 1988: Non-domestic rating multipliers: England	87
Local Government Finance Act 2012: Transitional provisions	87
Local government see also Local authorities	
Local government: Accounts & audit: Wales	70
Local government: Acts: Northern Ireland	272
Local government: Barnsley, Doncaster, Rotherham & Sheffield Combined Authority	66, 201
Local government: Business improvement districts: England	67
Local government: Business improvement districts: Property owners: England	67
Local government: Business Rate Supplements Act 2009: Commencements: England	67
Local government: Byelaws: Fixed penalties: Wales	70
Local government: Children & Young People (Scotland) Act 2014: Ancillary provisions: Scotland	244, 247, 253
Local government: Combined authorities: Consequential amendments	67, 201
Local government: Committees & political groups	70
Local government: Democracy: Acts: Wales	296
Local government: Disqualification: Prescribed offices & employments: Northern Ireland	281

Local government: Durham, Gateshead, Newcastle-Upon-Tyne, North Tyneside, Northumberland, South Tyneside & Sunderland: Combined authority 67, 201
Local government: Electoral changes: Aylesbury Vale 66
Local government: Electoral changes: Bolsover 66
Local government: Electoral changes: Braintree 66
Local government: Electoral changes: Breckland 66
Local government: Electoral changes: Bromsgrove 66
Local government: Electoral changes: Canterbury 67
Local government: Electoral changes: Corby 67
Local government: Electoral changes: Darlington 67
Local government: Electoral changes: East Dorset 67
Local government: Electoral changes: East Lindsey 67
Local government: Electoral changes: Fenland 67
Local government: Electoral changes: Gedling 67
Local government: Electoral changes: Hambleton 67
Local government: Electoral changes: Herefordshire 67
Local government: Electoral changes: Horsham 67
Local government: Electoral changes: Kensington & Chelsea 67
Local government: Electoral changes: Lancaster 67
Local government: Electoral changes: Leicester 67
Local government: Electoral changes: Middlesbrough 68
Local government: Electoral changes: Milton Keynes 68
Local government: Electoral changes: Newark & Sherwood 68
Local government: Electoral changes: North Dorset 68
Local government: Electoral changes: North Somerset 68
Local government: Electoral changes: North West Leicestershire 68
Local government: Electoral changes: Selby 68
Local government: Electoral changes: Sevenoaks 68
Local government: Electoral changes: Shepway 68
Local government: Electoral changes: South Hams 68
Local government: Electoral changes: South Kesteven 68
Local government: Electoral changes: South Oxfordshire 68
Local government: Electoral changes: South Ribble 69
Local government: Electoral changes: Stratford-on-Avon 69
Local government: Electoral changes: Suffolk Coastal 69
Local government: Electoral changes: Telford & Wrekin 69
Local government: Electoral changes: Three Rivers 69
Local government: Electoral changes: Uttlesford 69
Local government: Electoral changes: Vale of the White Horse 69
Local government: Electoral changes: Warwick 69
Local government: Electoral changes: Wellingborough 69
Local government: Electoral changes: Wyre 69
Local government: Electoral changes: York 69
Local government: Finance: Scotland 253
Local government: Halton, Knowsley, Liverpool, St Helens, Sefton & Wirral Combined Authority 67, 201
Local government: Harrogate Stray Act 1985: Tour de France 67
Local government: Legislative & regulatory reform: Parish & community councils & Charter trustees: Payments 69, 89
Local government: Local Audit & Accountability Act 2014: Auditor panel independence 69
Local government: Local Audit & Accountability Act 2014: Auditor resignation & removal 69
Local government: Local Audit & Accountability Act 2014: Commencements 67, 68, 69
Local government: Local Audit & Accountability Act 2014: Liability limitation agreements 69
Local government: Local Audit & Accountability Act 2014: Professional qualifications & major local audit 69
Local government: Local audit & statutory audit: Delegation of functions 10, 21, 69
Local government: Local Audit: Auditor panel 69
Local government: Local authorities: Capital finance & accounting: England 68
Local government: Local authorities: Capital finance & accounting: Wales 70
Local government: Local authorities: Goods & services: Public bodies: England 68
Local government: Local authorities: Referendums: Conduct of: England 68
Local government: Local authorities: Standing orders: England 68
Local government: Local government bodies: Openness: England 68
Local government: Members & officers: Indemnities: Northern Ireland 281
Local government: Pension schemes 87
Local government: Pension schemes: Northern Ireland 281
Local government: Pension schemes: Offender management 87
Local government: Pension schemes: Scotland 255, 257
Local government: Public interest reports & recommendations: Modification of consideration procedure 70
Local government: Registers of interests: Ethical standards: Scotland 248, 253
Local government: Transitional provisions: Northern Ireland 282
Local government: Transparency requirements 68
Local government: Transparency: Descriptions of information 68
Local government: Valuation Tribunal: Wales 70
Local government: West Yorkshire Combined Authority 69, 202
Local justice areas 63
Local pharmaceutical services: National Health Service: England 75
Localism Act 2011: Consequential amendments 26, 70
London Ambulance Service NHS Trust: National Health Service Trust: Establishment 75
London Government: Localism Act 2011: Consequential amendments 26, 70
London Insolvency District: Central London County Court: England & Wales 27

London local authorities: Transport for London: Local acts . . . 6
London Northwest Healthcare: National Health Service . . . 75
London Underground: Northern Line: Extension . . . 201
London: City of London: Various powers: Local acts . . . 6
Londonderry: Port security: Merchant shipping . . . 73
Londonderry: Roads: Parking places: Northern Ireland . . . 287
Londonderry: Waiting restrictions: Road traffic & vehicles: Northern Ireland . . . 289
Long leases: Appeal period: Scotland . . . 252
Long leases: Prescribed form of notices: Scotland . . . 252
Looked after children: Scotland . . . 244
Lower Galliagh Road, Londonderry: Abandonment: Northern Ireland . . . 285
Lower Wye & River Lugg: Boundaries alteration . . . 63
Lurgan: Roads: Parking places: Northern Ireland . . . 287
Lurgan: Waiting restrictions: Northern Ireland . . . 289
Lymington Harbour: Revision . . . 52

M

Machine games: Duty: Types of machine . . . 44
Magherafelt: Parking & waiting restrictions: Northern Ireland . . . 287
Magistrates' courts: Appeals Criminal legal aid: Costs: Northern Ireland . . . 281
Magistrates' courts: Courts & tribunals: Fees: England & Wales . . . 11, 27, 46, 51, 70, 72, 188, 195, 202
Magistrates' courts: Crime & Courts Act 2013: Commencements . . . 27, 46, 71, 188
Magistrates' courts: Criminal procedure: Rules: England & Wales . . . 71, 188
Magistrates' courts: Family procedure: Rules . . . 27, 46, 71, 188
Magistrates' courts: Fees: England & Wales . . . 71
Magistrates' courts: Rules: Northern Ireland . . . 282
Main estimates: Supply & appropriation: Acts . . . 5
Major accident hazards: Control: Northern Ireland . . . 279
Marine & Coastal Access Act 2009: Commencements: Wales . . . 77
Marine licensing: Application fees . . . 42, 66, 71
Marine Management Organisation: Fees . . . 86
Marine management: Marine conservation: South Arran: Scotland . . . 248, 253
Marine pollution: Marine licensing: Application fees . . . 42, 66, 71
Marine pollution: Prevention: Limits . . . 71
Maritime Labour Convention: Consequential & minor amendments . . . 72
Maritime Labour Convention: Health & safety . . . 72
Maritime Labour Convention: Hours of work . . . 72
Maritime Labour Convention: Seafarers minimum requirements . . . 72
Maritime security: Jersey . . . 72
Market abuse: Financial Services & Markets Act 2000 . . . 48
Markethill: Waiting restrictions: Revocation: Northern Ireland . . . 289
Marriage & Civil Partnership (Scotland) Act 2014: Act of Sederunt: Court of Session: Sheriff court: Rules: Scotland . . . 245, 264
Marriage & Civil Partnership (Scotland) Act 2014: Commencements: Scotland . . . 245, 250, 253
Marriage & Civil Partnership (Scotland) Act 2014: Consequential provisions . . . 19, 22, 32, 71
Marriage & civil partnership: Acts: Explanatory notes: Scotland . . . 242
Marriage & civil partnership: Acts: Scotland . . . 241
Marriage (Same Sex Couples) Act 2013: Commencements . . . 71
Marriage (Same Sex Couples) Act 2013: Consequential & contrary provisions . . . 19, 32, 57, 71
Marriage (Same Sex Couples) Act 2013: Consequential provisions . . . 19, 32, 71, 72
Marriage: Civil partnership: Prescribed bodies: Scotland . . . 253
Marriage: Civil partnership: Prescribed forms: Scotland . . . 245, 253, 257
Marriage: Civil partnership: Procedures: Scotland . . . 245, 253
Marriages: Consular marriages & marriages under foreign law . . . 71
Marriage: Overseas marriage: Armed forces . . . 72
Marriage: Persons of different sexes: Prescribed bodies: Scotland . . . 254
Marriage: Regulations: Northern Ireland . . . 282
Marriage: Same sex couples: Buildings registration: Authorised persons appointment . . . 88
Marriage: Same sex couples: Conversion of Civil Partnership . . . 88
Marriage: Same sex couples: Jurisdiction & recognition of judgments . . . 45, 63
Marriage: Same sex couples: Jurisdiction & recognition of judgments: Scotland . . . 251
Marriage: Same sex couples: Prescribed bodies: Scotland . . . 254
Marriage: Same sex couples: Registration of shared buildings . . . 88
Marriage: Same sex couples: Use of Armed Forces Chapels . . . 88
Marriage: Suspicious marriages: Registration: Reporting . . . 89
Maternity & adoption leave: Curtailment . . . 197
Maternity & parental leave . . . 197
Maternity allowance: Curtailment . . . 191
Maternity allowance: Northern Ireland . . . 291
Maternity allowance: Participating wife or civil partner of self-emplyed earner: Northern Ireland . . . 291
Maternity allowance: Self-employed earner: Wife or civil partner . . . 193
Maternity allowance: Social security . . . 193
Maternity pay: Statutory: Curtailment . . . 193
Measuring instruments: EEC requirements: Fees . . . 47
Meat products: Scotland . . . 249
Meat: Products . . . 50
Meat: Products: Northern Ireland . . . 279
Meat: Products: Wales . . . 50

26 AUGUST 2015 | LONDON GAZETTE | SUPPLEMENT NO.1 329

Medical Act 1983: English: Knowledge 53
Medical services: General & personal: Contracts: England 75
Medical services: General: Contracts: Drug prescriptions: England 75
Medical services: General: Contracts: Drug prescriptions: Northern Ireland 279
Medical services: General: Contracts: Drug prescriptions: Wales 77
Medical services: General: Contracts: England 75
Medicines & Healthcare Products Regulatory Agency Trading Fund: Appropriation of additional assets & liabilities 52
Medicines: Human medicines: Northern Ireland 282
Medicines: Human use 72
Medicines: Human: Northern Ireland 282
Medicines: Value added tax 203
Medicines: Veterinary medicines 72
Medway: Port security: Merchant shipping 73
Mental capacity: Courts & tribunals: Fees: England & Wales 11, 27, 46, 51, 70, 72, 188, 195, 202
Mental health: Care & support: After care: Accommodation: England 72, 189
Mental health: National Confidential Forum: Prescribed care & health services: Scotland 254
Mental health: National Health Service: Commissioning Board & clinical commissioning groups: Responsibilities & standing rules: England 72, 75
Mental health: Victims & Witnesses (Scotland) Act 2014: Commencements: Scotland 254
Merchant shipping: Air pollution: Prevention 72
Merchant shipping: Claims: Liability: Limitation 72
Merchant shipping: International safety management: ISM code 73
Merchant shipping: Light dues 72
Merchant shipping: Maritime Labour Convention: Consequential & minor amendments 72
Merchant shipping: Maritime Labour Convention: Health & safety 72
Merchant shipping: Maritime Labour Convention: Hours of work 72
Merchant shipping: Maritime Labour Convention: Recruitment & placement 73
Merchant shipping: Maritime Labour Convention: Seafarer's minimum requirements 72
Merchant shipping: Maritime security: Jersey 72
Merchant shipping: Oil pollution: Prevention 73
Merchant shipping: Passengers & luggage: Carriage by sea 72
Merchant shipping: Passengers: Carriage by sea 72
Merchant shipping: Pollution: Prevention: Limits 71
Merchant shipping: Port security: Port of Bramble Island Dock etc 73
Merchant shipping: Port security: Port of London 73
Merchant shipping: Port security: Port of Londonderry 73
Merchant shipping: Port security: Port of Medway 73
Merchant shipping: Port security: Port of Plymouth 73
Merchant shipping: Port security: Port of Rosyth 73
Mesothelioma Act 2014: Commencements 79
Mesothelioma: Acts 5
Mesothelioma: Lump sum payments: Conditions & amounts 192
Mesothelioma: Lump sum payments: Conditions & amounts: Northern Ireland 290
Messengers-at-Arms: Sheriff officers: Court of Session: Act of Sederunt: Scotland 245, 264
Mid Staffordshire Foundation: National Health Service Trust: Dissolution & transfer 75
Middlesbrough: Electoral changes 68
Midwives: Nursing & Midwifery Council: Fees 53
Milford Haven: Port security: Merchant shipping 73
Milton Keynes: Electoral changes 68
Mining: Deep sea mining: Acts 4
Mining: Deep sea mining: Acts: Explanatory notes 6
Ministers of the Crown: Transfer of functions: Chequers & Dorneywood Estates 73
Ministers of the Crown: Transfer of functions: Elections 73
Ministers of the Crown: Transfer of functions: Royal Mail pension plan 73
Mistley Quay: Port security: Merchant shipping 73
Misuse of drugs 31
Misuse of Drugs Act 1971: Amendments 31
Misuse of Drugs Act 1971: Ketamine 31
Misuse of drugs: Designation 31
Misuse of drugs: Safe custody 31
Mobile equipment: Convention on International Interests in Mobile Equipment: European Communities: Definition of treaties 43
Mobile Homes (Wales) Act 2013: Commencements 74
Mobile Homes Act 2013: Commencement & saving provision: England 73
Mobile homes: Pitch fees: Prescribed forms: Wales 73
Mobile homes: Selling & gifting: Wales 74
Mobile homes: Site licensing: England 73
Mobile homes: Site rules: England 73
Mobile homes: Site rules: Wales 74
Mobile homes: Written statement: Wales 74
Mobile machinery: Non-road: Gaseous & particulate pollutants: Emissions 42
Mobile phones: Roaming: European Communities 40
Motor cars: Driving instruction 92
Motor fuel: Composition & content: Air pollution: Prevention: Ships 72
Motor hackney carriages: Newcastle: Byelaws: Northern Ireland 286
Motor hackney carriages: Newry: Byelaws: Northern Ireland 286
Motor vehicles: Construction & use: Northern Ireland 286
Motor vehicles: Disabled persons: Badges 174
Motor vehicles: Disabled persons: Badges: Scotland 258

Motor vehicles: Driving licences 92, 93
Motor vehicles: Excise & registration 93
Motor vehicles: Speed limits: Variation 174
Motor vehicles: Taxi drivers: Licences: Northern Ireland 289
Motor vehicles: Tests: Amendments 92
Motorways: A1(M) 94, 95, 96, 97, 98
Motorways: A1(M)/A1 . . . . 94, 95, 97, 98
Motorways: A1(M)/A14 95
Motorways: A1(M)/A194(M) 94, 97
Motorways: A1(M)/A64 94
Motorways: A1(M)/M1 146
Motorways: A1(M)/M62 169
Motorways: A194(M) 135
Motorways: A194(M)/A1(M) 94, 97
Motorways: A194(M)/A184 135
Motorways: A3(M) 103
Motorways: A3(M)/A3 103
Motorways: A404(M) 137
Motorways: A404(M)/A404 137
Motorways: A6(M): Stockport North-South bypass: Connecting roads scheme: Revocation 54
Motorways: A627(M) 141
Motorways: A627(M)/M62 141
Motorways: A66(M) 131
Motorways: A66(M)/A66 131
Motorways: A832(M)/M90/A90: Scotland 261
Motorways: M1 . . . . 143, 144, 145, 146, 147, 173
Motorways: M1/A1(M) 146
Motorways: M1/A42 142
Motorways: M1/A421 143
Motorways: M1/A43 143
Motorways: M1/A46 143
Motorways: M1/A5: Link Dunstable Northern bypass connecting roads 54
Motorways: M1/A5: Link Dunstable Northern bypass detrunking 53
Motorways: M1/A50 127
Motorways: M1/A50/A453 143
Motorways: M1/A52 128
Motorways: M1/A63 143
Motorways: M1/M18 143
Motorways: M1/M25 160
Motorways: M1/M25/A10 160
Motorways: M1/M45 142
Motorways: M1/M6/A14 142
Motorways: M11 . . . . 157, 158
Motorways: M11/A11 158
Motorways: M11/A14/A428 109
Motorways: M11/M25 161
Motorways: M11: Connecting roads 54
Motorways: M18 . . . . 158, 159
Motorways: M18/M1 143
Motorways: M18/M62 158
Motorways: M180 172
Motorways: M180/A180 135
Motorways: M181 172
Motorways: M2 147
Motorways: M2/A2 147
Motorways: M2/M20 102
Motorways: M20 . . . . 159, 160
Motorways: M20/A20 159
Motorways: M20/M2 102
Motorways: M20/M25/A2/A20/A282 102
Motorways: M20/M25/A20 160
Motorways: M23 160
Motorways: M23/A23 112
Motorways: M23/M25/M3 161
Motorways: M25 . . . . 160, 161
Motorways: M25/A13/A1089 108
Motorways: M25/A2/A282 160
Motorways: M25/A21 112
Motorways: M25/A282 . . . . 160, 161
Motorways: M25/A308/A3/A30 103
Motorways: M25/A40 160
Motorways: M25/M1 160
Motorways: M25/M1/A10 160
Motorways: M25/M11 161
Motorways: M25/M20/A20 160
Motorways: M25/M23/M3 161
Motorways: M25/M26 . . . . 160, 161
Motorways: M25/M3 160

Motorways: M25/M4 148
Motorways: M26 161
Motorways: M26/M25 . . . . 160, 161
Motorways: M27 . . . . 161, 162
Motorways: M27/A31 116
Motorways: M27/M271 161
Motorways: M27/M3 147
Motorways: M271 172
Motorways: M271/M27 161
Motorways: M275 & M27 173
Motorways: M3 . . . . 147, 148
Motorways: M3/A316 147
Motorways: M3/M23/M25 161
Motorways: M3/M25 160
Motorways: M3/M27 147
Motorways: M32 162
Motorways: M4 . . . . 148, 149, 185, 186, 187
Motorways: M4/A34 148
Motorways: M4/M25 148
Motorways: M4/M48/A449/A40 185
Motorways: M4/M49 164
Motorways: M40 . . . . 162, 163, 173
Motorways: M40/A34 117
Motorways: M40/A43 121
Motorways: M40/M42 . . . . 162, 163
Motorways: M40: Junction 10 improvements 55
Motorways: M40: Junction 12 improvements 54
Motorways: M42 . . . . 163, 164
Motorways: M42/A45 163
Motorways: M42/A5 . . . . 122, 163
Motorways: M42/M40 . . . . 162, 163
Motorways: M42/M5 . . . . 149, 163
Motorways: M42/M6 . . . . 153, 163
Motorways: M45 164
Motorways: M45/M1 142
Motorways: M48 164
Motorways: M48/M4/A449/A40 185
Motorways: M49 . . . . 164, 165
Motorways: M49/M4 164
Motorways: M5 . . . . 150, 151, 152
Motorways: M5/A38/A30 118
Motorways: M5/A46 150
Motorways: M5/M42 . . . . 149, 163
Motorways: M5/M6 . . . . 149, 152, 153
Motorways: M50 165
Motorways: M50/A40 120
Motorways: M50/A449 138
Motorways: M53 165
Motorways: M53/A494/M56 167
Motorways: M53/M56 166
Motorways: M54 166
Motorways: M54/A449 166
Motorways: M54/M6 153
Motorways: M54/M6/A5/A449 155
Motorways: M55 166
Motorways: M55/M6 173
Motorways: M56 . . . . 166, 167
Motorways: M56/A5103 166
Motorways: M56/A556/A5034/A56 139
Motorways: M56/M53 . . . . 166, 167
Motorways: M56/M53/A494 167
Motorways: M56/M6/M62 155
Motorways: M57 167
Motorways: M57/M62 169
Motorways: M58 167
Motorways: M58/M6 167
Motorways: M6 . . . . 153, 154, 155, 156, 157
Motorways: M6 Toll 157
Motorways: M6 toll motorway 105
Motorways: M6/A30 160
Motorways: M6/A5/A38 104
Motorways: M6/A590 154
Motorways: M6/M1/A14 142
Motorways: M6/M42 . . . . 153, 163
Motorways: M6/M42/M6 Toll 157
Motorways: M6/M5 . . . . 149, 152, 153
Motorways: M6/M54 153
Motorways: M6/M54/A5/A449 155

Motorways: M6/M55 173
Motorways: M6/M58 167
Motorways: M6/M62/M56 155
Motorways: M6/M69 172
Motorways: M60 . . . . 167, 168
Motorways: M60/M61 169
Motorways: M60/M62 168
Motorways: M60/M62/M61/M602 167
Motorways: M60/M67/A57 . . . . 168, 172
Motorways: M602 173
Motorways: M602/M60/M62/M61 167
Motorways: M606 173
Motorways: M61 . . . . 168, 169
Motorways: M61/A666/A580 169
Motorways: M61/M60 169
Motorways: M61/M602/M60/M62 167
Motorways: M62 . . . . 169, 170, 171
Motorways: M62/A1(M) 169
Motorways: M62/A627(M) 141
Motorways: M62/M18 158
Motorways: M62/M56/M62 155
Motorways: M62/M57 169
Motorways: M62/M60 168
Motorways: M62/M61/M602/M60 167
Motorways: M621 173
Motorways: M65 . . . . 171, 172
Motorways: M65/A56 130
Motorways: M66 172
Motorways: M66/A56 . . . . 130, 172
Motorways: M67 172
Motorways: M67/M60/A57 . . . . 168, 172
Motorways: M69 172
Motorways: M69/M6 172
Motorways: M73/M74/A725: Scotland 261
Motorways: M74/M73/A725: Scotland 261
Motorways: M74: Scotland 261
Motorways: M77/A77: Scotland 261
Motorways: M8/A8: Scotland 260
Motorways: M8/M74: Scotland 260, 266
Motorways: M898/A898/A82: Scotland 259, 261
Motorways: M9/A9/M90/A90: Scotland 260
Motorways: M9/A9: HGV speed limit: Scotland 258
Motorways: M9/A9: Scotland 260, 261
Motorways: M90/A90/A832(M): Scotland 260, 261
Motorways: M90/A90/M9/A9: Scotland 260
Motorways: M90/A90: Scotland 261
Museums & galleries: Burrell Collection: Lending & borrowing: Acts: Explanatory notes: Scotland 242
Museums & galleries: Burrell Collection: Lending & borrowing: Acts: Scotland 241
Museums & galleries: Value added tax: Refunds 203

N

National Assembly for Wales: Acts 296
National Assembly for Wales: Acts: Explanatory notes 296, 297
National Assembly for Wales: Measures 296
National Assembly for Wales: Remuneration Board: Disqualifications 22
National assistance services: Personal requirements: Sums: England 74
National assistance services: Personal requirements: Sums: Scotland 254
National assistance services: Resources: Assessment: Scotland 254
National assistance: Social care charges: Wales 190
National Confidential Forum: Prescribed care & health services: Scotland 254
National Consumer Council: Public bodies: Abolition 86
National Crime Agency: Crime & Courts Act 2013: Certain enactments: Application & modification 74
National curriculum: Assessment arrangements: Foundation stage, KS2, KS3: Wales 38
National curriculum: Attainment targets & programmes of study: England 35
National curriculum: Foundation phase: Wales 37
National curriculum: Key stage 1, 2, 3, 4: Exceptions: England 35
National debt: Government alternative finance arrangements 74
National debt: National Savings stock register: Amendments 74
National debt: Premium savings bonds: Maximum holdings 74
National Grid: North London reinforcement project 61
National Health Service bodies: Data protection: Assessment notices: Designation 31
National Health Service Commissioning Board: Awdurdod Gwasanaethau Busnes y GIG: NHS Business Services Authority: Transfer of staff
. . . . 76
National Health Service Trusts: Barnet & Chase Farm Hospitals 74
National Health Service Trusts: Barnet, Enfield & Haringey Mental Health NHS Trust: Establishment 74
National Health Service Trusts: Coventry & Warwickshire Partnership: Establishment 74
National Health Service Trusts: Gloucester Care Services: Establishment 74

National Health Service Trusts: Gloucester Care Services: Originating capital 74
National Health Service Trusts: London Ambulance Service NHS Trust: Establishment 75
National Health Service Trusts: Membership & procedure 76
National Health Service Trusts: Mid Staffordshire Foundation: Dissolution & transfer 75
National Health Service Trusts: North Staffordshire Hospital Centre 76
National Health Service Trusts: Pathfinder 76
National Health Service Trusts: Trust funds: Trustees appointment: England 76
National Health Service: Care & support: Discharge of Hospital Patients: England 74, 189
National Health Service: Care Act 2014 . . . . 74, 76, 86, 190
National Health Service: Care Act 2014: Commencements 76, 86, 190
National Health Service: Care Quality Commission: Reviews & performance assessments 74, 86, 190
National Health Service: Charges, payments & remission of charges: England 75
National Health Service: Charges, payments & remission of charges: Exemptions: England 75
National Health Service: Charges: Overseas visitors: Wales 77
National Health Service: Charges: Personal injuries: Amounts: England & Wales 76
National Health Service: Children & Families (Wales) Measure: Commencements 15, 76, 190
National Health Service: Clinical negligence scheme: England 75
National Health Service: Commissioning Board & clinical commissioning groups: Responsibilities & standing rules: England 72, 75
National Health Service: Common Services Agency: Functions: Scotland 254
National Health Service: Dental charges: Wales 77
National Health Service: Drugs & appliances: Charges: Free prescriptions: Scotland 254
National Health Service: Ealing Hospital 75
National Health Service: Emergency Ambulance Services Committee: Wales 76
National Health Service: Finance: Acts: Wales 296
National Health Service: Finance: Acts: Wales: Explanatory notes 297
National Health Service: General & personal medical services contracts: England 75
National Health Service: General dental services: Contracts, personal dental services agreements: Wales 77
National Health Service: General medical services: Contracts: Drug prescriptions: England 75
National Health Service: General medical services: Contracts: Drug prescriptions: Wales 77
National Health Service: Health & Social Care Act 2008: Regulated activities: England 74, 86, 190
National Health Service: Health & Social Care Act 2012: Commencements 74
National Health Service: Health Education England 75
National Health Service: Health Education England: Transfer: Staff & Property & liabilities 75
National Health Service: Health Professions Council: Registration & fees 53
National Health Service: Healthy Start: Vitamins: Charging 75, 86
National Health Service: Independent prescribers: Physiotherapists: Podiatrists: Chiropodists: Scotland 254
National Health Service: Independent prescribers: Physiotherapists: Podiatrists: Chiropodists: Wales 77
National Health Service: Injury benefits: England & Wales 76
National Health Service: Legislative reform: Clinical commissioning groups 75, 89
National Health Service: Liabilities to third parties scheme 75
National Health Service: Local audit & accountability: Acts 5
National Health Service: Local audit & accountability: Acts: Explanatory notes 6
National Health Service: London Northwest Healthcare 75
National Health Service: Mandate requirements 75
National Health Service: North West London Hospitals 75
National Health Service: Optical charges & payments: Scotland 254
National Health Service: Optical charges & payments: Wales 77
National Health Service: Overseas visitors: Charges 75
National Health Service: Overseas visitors: Charges: Scotland 254
National Health Service: Patient rights: Treatment time guarantee: Scotland 254
National Health Service: Pension scheme: England & Wales 76
National Health Service: Personal injuries: Charges: Amounts: Scotland 254
National Health Service: Pharmaceutical & local pharmaceutical services: England 75
National Health Service: Pharmaceutical services: Scotland 254
National Health Service: Primary dental services: England 76
National Health Service: Primary ophthalmic services & optical payments: England 76
National Health Service: Property expenses scheme 76
National Health Service: Public Bodies (Joint Working) (Scotland) Act 2014: Commencements: Scotland 254
National Health Service: Retirement: Premature: Compensation: England & Wales 76
National Health Service: Superannuation schemes: Scotland 254
National Health Service: Travelling expenses & remission of charges: Wales 77
National Health Service: Welfare reform: Consequential amendments: Wales 77
National insurance contributions: Increases: Acts 5
National insurance contributions: Increases: Acts: Explanatory notes 6
National insurance: Social security: Contributions & national insurance numbers: Crediting & treatment: Northern Ireland 291
National minimum wage: Amendments 197
National Park Authorities: England 27
National Savings Bank: Investment deposits: Limits 187
National Savings stock register: Amendments 74
National Trust for Scotland: Governance: Acts: Explanatory notes 242
Nationality & immigration: Cost recovery fees 57, 77
Nationality & immigration: Fees 57
Nationality: Immigration Act 2014 57
Nationality: Immigration Act 2014: Transitional & saving provisions 57
Nationality: Immigration: Fees 57, 77
Natural gas: Valuation: Northern Ireland 284
Nature conservation: Marine & Coastal Access Act 2009: Commencements: Wales 77
Nature conservation: Seals: Protection: Haul-Out sites: designation: Scotland 254

Navy: Disablement & death: Service pensions 79
Negligence: Clinical negligence scheme: National Health Service: England. 75
Neighbourhood planning: Referendums: England 199
Network Rail: Huyton. 201
Network Rail: Knutsford to Bowdon improvement 61
Network Rail: Norton Bridge area improvement 61
Newark & Sherwood: Electoral changes 68
Newcastle (Northern Ireland): Parking places, loading bay & waiting restrictions: Northern Ireland 287
NHS bodies: Transfer of property 76
NHS Business Services Authority: Awdurdod Gwasanaethau Busnes y GIG: Transfer of staff: National Health Service Commissioning Board
. . . . 76
NHS Direct: National Health Service Trust: Dissolution 76
Nicholsons Court, Newry: Abandonment: Northern Ireland 286
Nitrate vulnerable zones: Designation: Scotland 267
Nitrates Action Programme: Environmental protection: Northern Ireland 277
Noise: Control: Audible intruder alarms: Code of practice 86
Non-contentious probate: Fees 189
Non-domestic rates: Levying: Scotland. 257
Non-domestic rates: Scotland 257
Non-domestic rates: Utilities: Valuation: Scotland. 257
Non-domestic rating multipliers: England 87
Non-domestic rating: Collection & enforcement: England 87
Non-domestic rating: Collection & enforcement: Local lists: Wales 88
Non-domestic rating: Contributions: Wales 88
Non-domestic rating: Demand notices: England 87
Non-domestic rating: Designated areas: England 87
Non-domestic rating: Levy & safety net: England 87
Non-domestic rating: Multiplier: Wales. 88
Non-domestic rating: Rates retention 87
Non-domestic rating: Small business rate relief: England. 88
Non-domestic rating: Small business rate relief: Wales. 88
Non-domestic rating: Unoccupied property: Scotland 257
Non-party campaigning: Lobbying: Trade Union administration: Registration: Acts 5
Non-party campaigning: Lobbying: Trade Union administration: Registration: Acts: Explanatory notes 6
Non-taxable insurance contracts: Insurance premium tax 62
Norfolk County Council: Permit schemes: Traffic management. 54
North Circular Road: Tarry lane, Lurgan: Northern Ireland 286
North Dorset: Electoral changes 68
North Killingholme generating station: Infrastructure planning 61
North London reinforcement project: National Grid 61
North Somerset: Electoral changes 68
North Staffordshire Hospital Centre: National Health Service Trust 76
North Tyneside Council: Permit schemes: Traffic management 54
North West 200: Road races: Northern Ireland 288
North West Leicestershire: Electoral changes 68
North West London Hospitals: National Health Service 75
Northern Ireland (Miscellaneous provisions) Act 2014: Commencements: Northern Ireland. 78
Northern Ireland Assembly: Elections 78
Northern Ireland Prison Service: Attorney General's human rights guidance: Northern Ireland 281
Northern Ireland: European Parliamentary elections 91
Northern Ireland: European Parliamentary elections: Returning officers: Charges. 91
Northern Ireland: Miscellaneous provisions: Acts 5
Northern Ireland: Miscellaneous provisions: Acts: Explanatory notes 6
Northern Ireland: Statutes 273
Northern Ireland: Statutes: Chronological tables 273
Northern Ireland: Statutory rules: Chronological tables 273
Northern Line: London Underground: Extension 201
Norton Bridge area improvement: Network Rail 61
Nuclear industries: Security 10
Nursing & midwifery 53
Nursing & Midwifery Council: Fees. 53

O

Occupational & personal pension schemes: Automatic enrolment 80
Occupational pension schemes 80
Occupational pension schemes: Automatic enrolment: Northern Ireland 282
Occupational pension schemes: Disclosure of information: Northern Ireland 282
Occupational pension schemes: Northern Ireland 282
Occupational pension schemes: Pension Protection Fund 80
Occupational pensions: Revaluation 80
Occupational pensions: Revaluation: Northern Ireland 282
Offender Management Act 2007: Approved premises 84
Offender Management Act 2007: Probation trusts: Dissolution. 84
Offender Rehabilitation Act 2014: Commencements. 30, 32
Offenders: Rehabilitation of Offenders Act 1974: Exceptions: England & Wales 89
Offenders: Rehabilitation of offenders: Exceptions: Northern Ireland 285
Offenders: Rehabilitation: Acts 5

Offenders: Rehabilitation: Acts: Explanatory notes . . . 6
Offenders: Road traffic: Additional offences . . . 93
Offenders: Road traffic: Additional offences: Northern Ireland . . . 289
Office of Fair Trading: Functions in relation to estate agents: Transfer: Public bodies . . . 86
Official food & feed controls: Wales . . . 8, 50
Offshore funds: Tax: Amendments . . . 12, 26, 60
Offshore installations: Safety zones . . . 78
Ofsted: Children's homes etc.: Fees & frequency of inspections . . . 14
Oil pollution: Prevention: Merchant shipping . . . 73
Olive oil: Marketing standards . . . 49
Olympic Delivery Authority: Dissolution . . . 78
Olympic games & paralympic games: Olympic Delivery Authority: Dissolution . . . 78
Olympic Lottery Distribution Fund: Payments out . . . 11
Omagh: Parking & waiting restrictions: Northern Ireland . . . 287
Ophthalmic services: General: Northern Ireland . . . 279
Ophthalmic services: Primary: Optical charges & payments: National Health Service: England . . . 76
Optical charges & payments: Northern Ireland . . . 279
Optical charges & payments: Scotland . . . 254
Ordinary cause: Rules: Scotland . . . 246, 264
Osteopaths: General Osteopathic Council: Registration & fees: Applications . . . 53
Overseas marriages: Armed forces . . . 72
Overseas territories . . . 78
Overseas territories: Central African Republic: Sanctions . . . 78
Overseas territories: Civil aviation: Environmental standards . . . 15
Overseas territories: Russia, Crimea & Sevastopol: Sanctions . . . 78
Overseas territories: South Sudan: Sanctions . . . 78
Overseas territories: Sudan: Sanctions . . . 78
Overseas territories: Syria: Restrictive measures . . . 78
Overseas territories: Ukraine: Sanctions . . . 78
Overseas visitors: Charges: National Health Service: Scotland . . . 254
Oxford Health NHS Foundation: Transfer of property . . . 76

P

PACE: Codes of practice: Revisions to codes C & H . . . 83
Packaging waste: Producer responsibility & obligations . . . 42
Packaging waste: Producer responsibility & obligations: Northern Ireland . . . 277
Paddington Station Bakerloo Line Connection: Crossrail . . . 201
Parental leave: Shared: Terms and conditions of employment . . . 198
Parental order cases: Paternity, adoption & shared parental leave . . . 197
Parental order cases: Social Security Contributions & Benefits Act 1992: Application: Parts 12ZA &12ZB & 12ZC . . . 198
Parental pay: Shared: Terms and conditions of employment . . . 198
Parental pay: Shared: Terms and conditions of employment: Persons abroad & mariners . . . 198
Parking badges: Disabled persons: Acts: Explanatory notes: Scotland . . . 242
Parliament: Lobbying: Non-party campaigning: Trade Union administration: Registration: Acts . . . 5
Parliament: Lobbying: Non-party campaigning: Trade Union administration: Registration: Acts: Explanatory notes . . . 6
Parliamentary elections: European: Returning officers: Local returning officers: Charges: Great Britain & Gibraltar . . . 90
Parochial fees: Scheduled matters amending . . . 34
Parole Board: Amendments: England & Wales . . . 84
Partnership & Cooperation Agreement: Iraq: European Communities: Definition of treaties . . . 43
Partnership & Cooperation Agreement: Mongolia: European Communities: Definition of treaties . . . 43
Partnership & Cooperation Agreement: Philippines: European Communities: Definition of treaties . . . 43
Partnership & Cooperation Agreement: Vietnam: European Communities: Definition of treaties . . . 44
Partnership: Payments to governments: Reports . . . 21, 79
Passenger Transport Executives: Bus operating powers: Exclusions . . . 201
Passenger vehicles: Recording equipment: Tachograph card: Fees . . . 92
Passengers & luggage: Carriage by sea: Merchant shipping . . . 72
Passengers: Carriage by sea: Merchant shipping . . . 72
Patents: Acts . . . 4
Patents: Acts: Explanatory notes . . . 6
Patents: Legislative reform . . . 79
Patents: Rules . . . 79
Patents: Supplementary protection certificates . . . 79
Paternity & adoption: Leave . . . 197
Paternity & maternity leave . . . 197
Paternity leave: Adoption leave . . . 197
Paternity pay: Statutory . . . 198
Paternity pay: Statutory: Parental orders & prospective adopters . . . 198
Pathfinder: National Health Service Trust . . . 76
Patient rights: Treatment time guarantee: Scotland . . . 254
Pay as You Earn see PAYE
PAYE: Construction industry scheme . . . 59
PAYE: Income tax . . . 59
Payment schemes: Diffuse Mesothelioma . . . 79
Payment schemes: Mesothelioma Act 2014: Commencements . . . 79
Payments to governments . . . 49
Penalties: Amount: Disorderly behaviour: England & Wales . . . 30
Penalty charges: Additional contraventions: Northern Ireland . . . 287

Pennan: Harbour revision: Scotland	250
Pension Protection Fund: Entry rules	80
Pension Protection Fund: Entry rules: Northern Ireland	282
Pension Protection Fund: Northern Ireland	282
Pension Protection Fund: Occupational pension schemes	80
Pension schemes: Firefighters: Contributions: Wales	49, 81
Pension schemes: Firefighters: Wales	49, 81
Pension schemes: Health & social care: Northern Ireland	279
Pension schemes: Registered & relieved non-UK: Lifetime allowance transitional protection: Individual protection: Notification	60
Pension schemes: Registered: Provision of information	60
Pension schemes: Registered: Sums & assets: Transfer	60
Pensions Act 2004: Codes of Practice: Funding defined benefits: Appointed Day	80
Pensions Act 2004: Commencements	80
Pensions Act 2008: Commencements	80
Pensions Act 2011: Commencements	80
Pensions Act 2011: Consequential & supplementary provisions	80
Pensions Act 2011: Transitional, consequential & supplementary provisions	80
Pensions Act 2014: Commencements	80, 87, 192
Pensions taxation: Acts	5
Pensions taxation: Acts: Explanatory notes	6
Pensions: 2005 Order: Commencements: Northern Ireland	282
Pensions: 2008 (No.2) Act: Commencements: Northern Ireland	282
Pensions: 2012 Act: Commencements: Northern Ireland	283
Pensions: 2012 Act: Consequential & supplementary provisions: Northern Ireland	283
Pensions: 2012 Act: Transitional, consequential & supplementary provisions: Northern Ireland	283
Pensions: Acts	5
Pensions: Acts: Explanatory notes	6
Pensions: Armed Forces & Reserve Forces: Compensation schemes	79
Pensions: Armed Forces: Pension regulations	79
Pensions: Armed Forces: Pension schemes & early departure schemes	79
Pensions: Automatic enrolment: Earnings trigger	79
Pensions: Automatic enrolment: Earnings trigger & qualifying earnings band: Northern Ireland	282
Pensions: Contributions: Police: Scotland	255
Pensions: Financial assistance schemes: Qualifying pension scheme: Amendments	79
Pensions: Firefighters: Compensation schemes: England	49, 80
Pensions: Firefighters: Compensation schemes: Scotland	249, 255
Pensions: Firefighters: New: Pension schemes: Northern Ireland	278
Pensions: Firefighters: Pension schemes: England	49, 81, 87
Pensions: Firefighters: Pension schemes: Northern Ireland	278
Pensions: Firefighters: Pension schemes: Scotland	249, 255
Pensions: Firefighters: Wales	49, 81
Pensions: Firemen: Pension schemes: Scotland	249, 255
Pensions: Guaranteed minimum increase	79
Pensions: Guaranteed minimum increase: Northern Ireland	282
Pensions: Increase: Commissioners of Irish Light	80
Pensions: Increase: Review	80
Pensions: Increase: Review: Northern Ireland	283
Pensions: Judicial pensions: Contributions: Amendments	79
Pensions: Judicial: Widows', widowers' & children's benefits	79
Pensions: Levies: Past periods: Payment	80
Pensions: Local government: Pension schemes	87
Pensions: Local government: Pension schemes: Northern Ireland	281
Pensions: Local government: Pension schemes: Offender management	87
Pensions: Local government: Pension schemes: Scotland	255
Pensions: National Health Service: Pension scheme: England & Wales	76
Pensions: Navy, army & air force: Disablement & death: Service pensions	79
Pensions: Occupational & personal pension schemes: Automatic enrolment	80
Pensions: Occupational & personal pension schemes: Automatic enrolment: Northern Ireland	282
Pensions: Occupational & personal schemes: Northern Ireland	282
Pensions: Occupational pension schemes	80
Pensions: Occupational pension schemes & Pension Protection Fund	80
Pensions: Occupational pensions: Revaluation	80
Pensions: Occupational pensions: Revaluation: Northern Ireland	282
Pensions: Occupational, personal & stakeholder schemes: Disclosure of information: Northern Ireland	282
Pensions: Pension Protection Fund & occupational pension schemes: Northern Ireland	282
Pensions: Pension Protection Fund: Entry rules: Northern Ireland	282
Pensions: Personal injuries: Civilians	80
Pensions: Police Service: Northern Ireland	283
Pensions: Police: Amendments	81, 83
Pensions: Public Service Pensions Act 2013: Commencements	87
Pensions: Public service pensions: Civil servants & others	87
Pensions: Public Service pensions: Employer cost cap	87
Pensions: Public service pensions: Record keeping	80
Pensions: Public service pensions: Record keeping: Northern Ireland	283
Pensions: Public Service: Acts: Explanatory notes: Northern Ireland	273
Pensions: Public Service: Acts: Northern Ireland	272
Pensions: Public service: Civil servants & others: Northern Ireland	284
Pensions: Registered pension schemes: Accounting & assessment	60

Pensions: Social security: Contributions: Additional units 192
Pensions: Social security: Flat rate accrual amount 193
Pensions: Social security: Flat rate accrual amounts: Northern Ireland 291
Pensions: Social security: Low earnings threshold 193
Pensions: Social security: Low earnings threshold: Northern Ireland 291
Pensions: Superannuation: 1972 Act: Admission to schedule 1 80
Pensions: Teachers: Schemes: Scotland 257
Pensions: Teachers: Superannuation: Scotland 255
Pensions: Teachers' pensions schemes: England & Wales. 36, 87
Pensions: Teachers' pensions schemes: Northern Ireland 276, 284
Pensions: Teachers' pensions: England & Wales 36
Personal care & nursing care: Community care: Scotland 265
Personal injuries: Charges: Amounts: National Health Service: Scotland 254
Personal injuries: Civilians 80
Personal injuries: NHS charges: Amounts: England & Wales 76
Personal medical services: Agreements: National Health Service: England 75
Personal pension schemes: Automatic enrolment: Northern Ireland 282
Personal pension schemes: Disclosure of information: Northern Ireland 282
Personal pension schemes: Northern Ireland 282
Peterhead prison: Discontinuance: Scotland 256
Petroleum revenue tax: Double taxation: Relief & international enforcement: Belgium 12, 25, 58, 81
Petroleum revenue tax: Double taxation: Relief & international enforcement: Canada 12, 25, 58, 81
Petroleum: Health & safety 52
Petroleum: Licensing: Exploration & production: Landward areas 81
Pets: Non commercial movement 9
Pharmaceutical services: England 75
Pharmaceutical services: Northern Ireland 279
Pharmaceutical services: Scotland 254
Pharmaceutical Society of Northern Ireland: Council: Indemnity arrangements 283
Phosphorus: Agriculture: Use: Northern Ireland 277
Physiotherapists: Independent prescribers: Scotland 254
Physiotherapists: Independent prescribers: Wales 77
Phytophthora kernovii management zone: Revocation: England 82
Phytostanols: Food: Labelling: Wales 50
Phytosterols: Food: Labelling: Wales. 50
Pigs: Swine: Diseases. 8
Pipe-lines: Gas Act 1986: Exemptions: Revocations 51, 81
Pipelines: Submarine: Designated owners 81
Pipelines: Submarine: Electricity generating stations 81
Planning Act 2008: Commencements: Wales 200
Planning see also Infrastructure planning
Planning see also Town & country planning
Planning: Advertisements: Control: Northern Ireland 283
Planning: Fees: Northern Ireland 283
Planning: General development: Northern Ireland. 283
Planning: Hazardous substances: Heavy fuel oil 52, 199
Planning: Hazardous substances: Northern Ireland 283
Planning: Hazardous waste: Wales. 200
Planning: Regional transport planning: Wales 202
Plant & machinery: Environmentally beneficial: Capital allowances 25, 58
Plant health: Amendments: Scotland 255
Plant health: England 81
Plant health: Export Certification: Amendments: Wales 82
Plant health: Export certification: England 82
Plant health: Fees: England 82
Plant health: Fees: Forestry: England & Scotland 82
Plant health: Forestry: England & Scotland. 82
Plant health: Forestry: Phytophthora ramorum management zone: Scotland 255
Plant health: Import: Inspection fees: Scotland 255
Plant health: Northern Ireland. 283
Plant health: Phytophthora kernovii management zone: Revocation: England 82
Plant health: Vegetable plant material: Marketing: Scotland. 255
Plant health: Wales 82
Plastic bags: Single use: Charging: Acts: Explanatory notes: Northern Ireland 272
Plastic bags: Single use: Charging: Acts: Northern Ireland 272
Plymouth College of Art: Transfer to higher education sector 35
Plymouth: Port security: Merchant shipping 73
Pneumoconiosis etc.: Workers' compensation: Claims: Payments 192
Pneumoconiosis etc.: Workers' compensation: Claims: Payments: Northern Ireland 290
Podiatrists: Independent prescribers: Scotland 254
Podiatrists: Independent prescribers: Wales 77
Police & Crime Commissioners: Elections 83
Police & Criminal Evidence Act 1984: Codes of practice: Revisions to codes C & H 83
Police & Criminal Evidence Act 1984: Detention: Remote reviews 83
Police & Criminal Evidence Act 1984: Revenue & customs: Applications 91
Police & criminal evidence: Code of practice A: Temporary modification: Northern Ireland 283
Police & criminal evidence: Code of practice C & H: Revision: Northern Ireland 283
Police Act 1996: Equipment 83

Police Act 1997: Commencements 83
Police Act 1997: Criminal record certificates: Relevant matters: Northern Ireland 275
Police Act 1997: Criminal records 83
Police Act 1997: Criminal records: Northern Ireland 275
Police Service of Scotland 255
Police Service of Scotland: Conduct 255
Police Service of Scotland: Performance 255
Police Service: Pensions: Northern Ireland 283
Police: Anti-social Behaviour, Crime & Policing Act 2014: Commencements 10, 29, 31, 33, 44, 45, 56, 82, 83, 84
Police: Complaints & misconduct 83
Police: Conduct 83
Police: Crime & Security Act 2010: Commencements 83
Police: England & Wales 83
Police: Independent Police Complaints Commission: Investigation of offences 83
Police: Misconduct & complaints 83
Police: Overseas Police Forces: Chief Officers appointment: England & Wales 83
Police: Pensions: Amendments 81, 83
Police: Pensions: Contributions: Scotland 255
Police: Performance 83
Police: Protection of Freedoms Act 2012: Commencements 84
Police: Rehabilitation & Retraining Trust: Northern Ireland 283
Policing & Crime Act 2009: Commencements 85
Political donations & regulated transactions: Anonymous electors 84
Political Parties, Elections & Referendums Act 2000: Civil sanctions 90
Political parties: Donations & regulated transactions: Anonymous electors 84
Political parties: Electoral Administration Act 2006: Commencements: Northern Ireland 84
Pollution: Air pollution: Ships: Prevention 72
Pollution: Merchant shipping: Pollution: Prevention: Limits 71
Pollution: Nitrates Action Programme: Northern Ireland 277
Pollution: Oil: Prevention: Merchant shipping 73
Pollution: Prevention & control: Industrial emissions: Northern Ireland 277
Pollution: Prevention & control: Scotland 248
Port of Ardersier: Harbour revision: Scotland 250
Port of Bramble Island Dock: Port security: Merchant shipping 73
Port of London: Port security: Merchant shipping 73
Port of Londonderry: Port security: Merchant shipping 73
Port of Medway: Port security: Merchant shipping 73
Port of Plymouth: Port security: Merchant shipping 73
Port of Rosyth: Port security: Merchant shipping 73
Port security: Merchant shipping 73
Portobello Park: City of Edinburgh: Acts: Explanatory notes: Scotland 242
Portobello Park: City of Edinburgh: Acts: Scotland 241
Portrush: One-way traffic: Northern Ireland 286
Portrush: Parking & waiting restrictions: Northern Ireland 287
Portsmouth Harbour: Portsmouth & Gosport Joint Board: Abolition 52
Post-16 Education (Scotland) Act 2013: Commencements: Scotland 247
Poverty: Fuel: England 42
Premium savings bonds: Maximum holdings 74
Prescriptions: Free: National Health Service: Scotland 254
Presumption of Death Act 2013: Commencements 84
Prevention & suppression of terrorism: Anti-social Behaviour, Crime & Policing Act 2014: Commencements . . 10, 29, 31, 33, 45, 56, 83, 84
Prevention & suppression of terrorism: Protection of Freedoms Act 2012: National security determinations: Renewal & guidance 84
Prevention & suppression of terrorism: Terrorism Act 2000: Examining & Review Officers: Codes of practice 84
Prevention & suppression of terrorism: Terrorism Act 2000: Proscribed organisations 84
Prevention of Social Housing Fraud Act 2013: Power to require information 56
Primary ophthalmic services & optical payments: National Health Service: England 76
Primary schools: Rural: Designation: England 34
Prisons (Interference with Wireless Telegraphy) Act 2012: Commencements: Scotland 256
Prisons: Aberdeen & Peterhead prisons: Discontinuance: Scotland 256
Prisons: Closures: England & Wales 84
Prisons: Parole Board: Amendments: England & Wales 84
Prisons: Young offender institutions 84, 204
Prisons: Young offender institutions: Scotland 256
Private crossings: Signs & barriers: Northern Ireland 292
Probate: Non-contentious: Fees 189
Probation trusts: Dissolution: Offender Management Act 2007 84
Probation: Offender Management Act 2007: Approved premises 84
Proceeds of Crime Act 2002: Amendment: Scotland 256
Proceeds of Crime Act 2002: External investigations 85
Proceeds of Crime Act 2002: Information: Disclosure 85
Proceeds of crime: Crime & Courts Act 2013: Commencements 85
Proceeds of crime: Policing & Crime Act 2009: Commencements 85
Procurement contracts: Defence reform: Acts 4
Procurement contracts: Defence reform: Acts: Explanatory notes 6
Procurement: Reform: Acts: Explanatory notes: Scotland 242
Procurement: Reform: Acts: Scotland 241
Producer responsibility & obligations: Packaging waste 42
Producer responsibility & obligations: Packaging waste: Northern Ireland 277

Property management work: Redress schemes 56
Prosecution of Offences Act 1985: Specified proceedings. 30
Prospects College of Advanced Technology: Government 35
Prospects College of Advanced Technology: Incorporation 36
Protection of Freedoms Act 2012: Commencements 14, 84, 85
Protection of Freedoms Act 2012: National security determinations: Renewal & guidance 84
Protection of vulnerable adults: Protection of Freedoms Act 2012: Commencements 14, 85
Protection of Vulnerable Groups (Scotland) Act 2007: Miscellaneous provisions: Scotland 245
Protection of wrecks: Designation: England 85
Provision of services 85
Public Appointments & Public Bodies etc. (Scotland) Act 2003: Specified authorities: Historic Environment Scotland: Treatment 256
Public Appointments & Public Bodies etc. (Scotland) Act 2003: Specified authorities: Revenue Scotland: Treatment 256
Public Appointments & Public Bodies etc. (Scotland) Act 2003: Treatment as specified authority: Scotland 256
Public Audit (Wales) Act 2013: Approved European body of accountants 85
Public Audit (Wales) Act 2013: Wales 85
Public Bodies (Joint Working) (Scotland) Act 2014: Commencements: Scotland 254, 257, 265
Public bodies: Committee on Agricultural Valuation: Abolition 64, 85
Public bodies: Director of Public Prosecutions: Director of Revenue & Customs Prosecutions: Merger. 86
Public bodies: Food from Britain: Abolition 7, 85
Public bodies: Joint Working (Scotland) Act 2014: Modifications: Scotland 257, 265
Public bodies: Joint working: Acts: Explanatory notes: Scotland 242
Public bodies: Joint working: Acts: Scotland 241
Public Bodies: Joint working: Health Professionals & Social Care Professionals: Scotland. 256, 265
Public Bodies: Joint working: Integration joint boards: Scotland. 256, 265
Public Bodies: Joint working: Integration joint monitoring committees: Scotland 256, 265
Public Bodies: Joint working: Integration scheme: Scotland 256, 265
Public Bodies: Joint working: Local authority officers: Scotland 265
Public Bodies: Joint working: Membership: Strategic planning Group: Scotland. 256, 265
Public bodies: Joint working: National health & wellbeing outcomes: Scotland 256, 265
Public Bodies: Joint working: Performance reports: Content: Scotland 256, 265
Public Bodies: Joint working: Prescribed consultees: Scotland 257, 265
Public Bodies: Joint working: Prescribed days: Scotland 257, 265
Public bodies: Joint working: Prescribed health board functions: Scotland 257, 265
Public bodies: Joint working: Prescribed local authority functions: Scotland. 257, 265
Public bodies: Local authorities: Goods & services: England 68
Public bodies: Marine Management Organisation: Fees 86
Public bodies: National Consumer Council: Abolition 86
Public bodies: Public Appointments & Public Bodies etc. (Scotland) Act 2003: Treatment as specified authority: Scotland 256
Public finance & accountability: Budget (Scotland) Act 2013: Amendments: Scotland 256
Public finance & accountability: Budget (Scotland) Act 2014: Amendments: Scotland 256
Public health: Animal by-products: Enforcement: Wales. 9, 86
Public health: Care Act 2014 . . . . 76, 86, 190
Public health: Care Act 2014: Commencements 76, 86, 190
Public health: Care Quality Commission: Reviews & performance assessments 74, 86, 190
Public health: Health & Social Care Act 2008: Regulated activities: England 74, 86, 190
Public health: Healthy Start: Vitamins: Charging 75, 86
Public health: HIV testing kits & services: Revocation: England. 86
Public health: HIV testing kits & services: Revocation: Scotland 256
Public health: HIV testing kits & services: Revocation: Wales. 86
Public health: Noise: Audible intruder alarms: Code of practice 86
Public health: Public Bodies (Joint Working) (Scotland) Act 2014: Commencements: Scotland 257, 265
Public health: Public bodies (Joint Working) (Scotland) Act 2014: Modifications: Scotland. 257, 265
Public health: Public Bodies: Joint working: Health Professionals & Social Care Professionals: Scotland 256, 265
Public health: Public bodies: Joint working: Integration joint boards: Scotland 256, 265
Public health: Public Bodies: Joint working: Integration joint monitoring committees: Scotland 256, 265
Public health: Public bodies: Joint working: Integration scheme: Scotland 256, 265
Public health: Public Bodies: Joint working: Membership: Strategic planning group: Scotland. 256, 265
Public health: Public bodies: Joint working: National health & wellbeing outcomes: Scotland 256, 265
Public health: Public Bodies: Joint working: Performance reports: Content: Scotland 256, 265
Public health: Public Bodies: Joint working: Prescribed consultees: Scotland 257, 265
Public health: Public Bodies: Joint working: Prescribed days: Scotland 257, 265
Public health: Public bodies: Joint working: Prescribed health board functions: Scotland 257, 265
Public health: Public bodies: Joint working: Prescribed local authority functions: Scotland 257, 265
Public health: Tobacco retailers: 2014 Act: Commencements: Northern Ireland 283
Public interest disclosure: Prescribed persons 197, 198
Public interest disclosure: Prescribed persons: Northern Ireland 276
Public interest reports & recommendations: Modification of consideration procedure 70
Public Lending Right Scheme 1982: Variation: Commencements 66
Public life: Registers of interests: Ethical standards: Scotland 248, 253
Public passenger transport: Public service vehicles: Operators' licences: Fees. 86
Public passenger transport: Public service vehicles: Traffic Commissioners: Publication & inquiries 86
Public procurement: Single source contract 86
Public Prosecution Service for Northern Ireland: Attorney General's Human Rights Guidance. 281
Public Record Office: Provisions 86
Public records: Constitutional Reform & Governance Act 2010: Commencements. 86
Public records: Public Record Office: Provisions 86
Public Service Pensions Act 2013: Commencements 87
Public service pensions: Civil servants & others 87

Public service pensions: Civil servants & others: Northern Ireland 284
Public service pensions: Commencements: Northern Ireland 284
Public Service pensions: Employer cost cap 87
Public service pensions: Firefighters: Pension schemes: England 87
Public service pensions: Local government: Pension schemes 87
Public service pensions: Local government: Pension schemes: Offender management 87
Public service pensions: Local government: Pension schemes: Scotland 257
Public service pensions: Record keeping 80
Public service pensions: Record keeping: Northern Ireland 283
Public service pensions: Teachers' pensions scheme: England & Wales 36, 87
Public service vehicles: Operators' licences: Fees 86
Public service vehicles: Traffic Commissioners: Publication & inquiries 86
Public Service: Pensions: Acts: Explanatory notes: Northern Ireland 273
Public Service: Pensions: Acts: Northern Ireland 272
Public Transport Users' Committee for Wales: Abolition 202
Public water supplies: Scotland 267
Pupils: Excluded: Provisions: Education: Full-time: Amendments: England 35

R

RAF Barford St John: Byelaws 32
RAF Croughton: Byelaws 32
RAF Fairford Gloucestershire: Air navigation: Flying restrictions 17
Rail vehicle accessibility: Disabled persons: Northern Ireland 275, 292
Rail vehicles: Non-interoperable rail-system: Blackpool tramway: Accessibility: Exemptions 33, 201
Railways: Channel Tunnel: International arrangements 13
Railways: Channel Tunnel: Planning appeals & assessment of environment effects 200
Railways: Channel Tunnel: Rail link: Revocations 200, 201
Railways: Felixstowe Branch Line: Land acquisition 201
Railways: Interoperability 201
Railways: Passengers: Rights & obligations: Exemptions 201
Railways: Private crossings: Signs & barriers: Northern Ireland 292
Railways: Rail vehicles 33, 201
Railways: Swanage Railway: England 201, 202
Rampion Wind Farm 61
Randalstown: Waiting restrictions: Northern Ireland 289
Rates (Amendment) Act 2009: Commencements: Northern Ireland 284
Rates: Housing benefit: Habitual residence: Northern Ireland 280, 284
Rates: Jobseeker's allowance: Employment assistance: Northern Ireland 280, 284, 290
Rates: Regional rates: Northern Ireland 284
Rates: Small business hereditament relief: Northern Ireland 284
Rates: Social security: Benefits: Up-rating: Northern Ireland 276, 280, 284, 290, 291, 292
Rates: Social security: Habitual residence: Northern Ireland 280, 284, 291
Rates: Social security: Northern Ireland 280, 284, 291
Rates: Valuation: Telecommunications, natural gas & water: Northern Ireland 284
Rating & valuation: Council tax & non-domestic rating: Demand notices: England 87
Rating & valuation: Exempted classes: Scotland 257
Rating & valuation: Local Government Finance Act 2012: Transitional provisions 87
Rating & valuation: Non-domestic rates: Levying: Scotland 257
Rating & valuation: Non-domestic rates: Scotland 257
Rating & valuation: Non-domestic rates: Utilities: Valuation: Scotland 257
Rating & valuation: Non-domestic rating: Collection & enforcement: England 87
Rating & valuation: Non-domestic rating: Contributions: Wales 88
Rating & valuation: Non-domestic rating: Designated areas: England 87
Rating & valuation: Non-domestic rating: Levy & safety net: England 87
Rating & valuation: Non-domestic rating: Multipliers: England 87
Rating & valuation: Non-domestic rating: Multipliers: Wales 88
Rating & valuation: Non-domestic rating: Rates retention 87
Rating & valuation: Non-domestic rating: Small business rate relief: England 88
Rating & valuation: Non-domestic rating: Small business rate relief: Wales 88
Rating & valuation: Non-domestic rating: Unoccupied property: Scotland 257
Rating & valuation: Rating lists: Valuation date: England 88
Rating lists: Compilation: Postponement: Wales 88
Rating lists: Valuation date: England 88
Rating lists: Valuation date: Wales 88
Rating: Non-domestic rating: Collection & enforcement: Local lists: Wales 88
Rating: Unoccupied hereditaments: Amendments: Northern Ireland 284
REACH: Enforcement 23, 42, 52
Reading Borough Council: River Thames Pedestrian/Cycle Bridge Scheme: Confirmation 54
Real estate investment trusts: Corporation Tax Act 2010 26
Redundancies: Collective redundancies & transfer of undertakings: Employment protection 197
Referendums: Conduct: Council tax: Increases: England 26, 68
Referendums: Conduct: Local authorities: England 68
Regional colleges: Designation: Scotland 247
Regional transport planning: Wales 202
Registered pension schemes: Accounting & assessment 60
Registers of Scotland: Fees 257
Registers: Land registers: Information & access: Scotland 252

Registration of births, deaths, marriages, etc.: Births & deaths: Overseas registration 88
Registration of births, deaths, marriages, etc.: Births & deaths: Overseas registration: Legislative reform. 88, 89
Registration of births, deaths, marriages, etc.: Deaths: Presumed deaths: Fees 88
Registration of births, deaths, marriages, etc.: Fees: Amendments. 88
Registration of births, deaths, marriages, etc.: Forms: Prescription: Scotland. 257
Registration of births, deaths, marriages, etc.: Marriages: Civil partners: Prescribed forms: Scotland. 245, 253, 257
Registration of births, deaths, marriages, etc.: Marriages: Same sex couples: Buildings registration: Authorised persons appointment. . . 88
Registration of births, deaths, marriages, etc.: Marriages: Same sex couples: Conversion of Civil Partnership 88
Registration of births, deaths, marriages, etc.: Marriages: Same sex couples: Jurisdiction & recognition of judgments 45, 63
Registration of births, deaths, marriages, etc.: Marriages: Same sex couples: Jurisdiction & recognition of judgments: Scotland 251
Registration of births, deaths, marriages, etc.: Marriages: Same sex couples: Prescribed bodies: Scotland 254
Registration of births, deaths, marriages, etc.: Marriages: Same sex couples: Registration of shared buildings. 88
Registration of births, deaths, marriages, etc.: Marriages: Same sex couples: Use of Armed Forces Chapels 88
Registration of births, deaths, marriages, etc.: Marriages: Suspicious: Reporting. 89
Registration of births, deaths, marriages, etc.: Presumed deaths: Register: Prescribed information 88
Registration of vital events: General Register Office: Fees: Northern Ireland. 285
Registration, Evaluation, Authorisation & Restriction of Chemicals see REACH. 23, 42, 52
Regulation of care: Social service workers: Amendments: Scotland 265
Regulation of investigatory powers: Authorisation of covert human intelligence sources: Scotland 251
Regulation of investigatory powers: Covert human intelligence sources: Codes of practice 62
Regulation of investigatory powers: Covert surveillance & property interference: Codes of practice 63
Regulators: Referral fees: England & Wales 65
Regulatory enforcement: Co-ordination: Enforcement action. 89
Regulatory Reform (Scotland) Act 2014: Act of Adjournal: Criminal procedure rules: Amendment: Scotland. 250, 264
Regulatory Reform (Scotland) Act 2014: Commencements: Scotland. 248, 258
Regulatory reform: Acts: Scotland 242
Regulatory reform: Births & deaths: Registration: Overseas registration 88, 89
Regulatory reform: Code of practice: Appointed day. 89
Regulatory reform: Legislative & regulatory reform: Parish & community councils & Charter trustees: Payments 69, 89
Regulatory reform: Legislative & regulatory reform: Regulatory functions 89
Regulatory reform: Legislative reform: Clinical commissioning groups 75, 89
Regulatory reform: Regulatory enforcement: Co-ordination: Enforcement action. 89
Rehabilitation & Retraining Trust: Police: Northern Ireland. 283
Rehabilitation of Offenders Act 1974: Exceptions: England & Wales 89
Rehabilitation of offenders: Acts. 5
Rehabilitation of offenders: Acts: Explanatory notes 6
Rehabilitation of offenders: Exceptions: Northern Ireland 285
Rehabilitation of offenders: Legal Aid, Sentencing & Punishment of Offenders Act 2012: Commencements 30, 89
Remand: Youth detention accommodation: Recovery of costs 30
Renewable energy: Clocaenog Forest wind farm. 61
Renewable energy: East Anglia ONE Offshore Wind Farm 61
Renewable energy: Hornsea One Offshore Wind Farm. 61
Renewable energy: Rampion Wind Farm 61
Renewable heat incentives. 41
Renewable heat incentives: Domestic 41
Renewable obligations: Electricity 40
Renewables obligation: Electricity: Closure. 40
Renewables obligation: Electricity: Northern Ireland. 276
Renewables obligation: Electricity: Scotland 248
Rent book: Forms of notice: Wales 64
Rent officers: Housing benefits & universal credit functions: Local housing allowance 55
Rents: Registered rents: Increases: Northern Ireland 281
Commencements 23, 90
Representation of the people: Anonymous registration: Northern Ireland. 90
Representation of the people: Candidates' election expenses: Variation 90
Representation of the people: Combination of polls: England & Wales 90
Representation of the people: Donations to candidates: Anonymous registration 89
Representation of the people: Elections: Policy development grants scheme 89
Representation of the people: Electoral Registration & Administration Act 2013: Commencements 89
Representation of the people: Electoral Registration & Administration Act 2013: Transitional provisions 89
Representation of the people: Electoral registration: Electoral registers: Disclosure. 90
Representation of the people: Electoral registration: Pilot schemes 89
Representation of the people: England & Wales 90
Representation of the people: European Parliamentary elections. 90
Representation of the people: European Parliamentary elections: Northern Ireland. 91
Representation of the people: European Parliamentary elections: Petitions: England & Wales. 89, 195
Representation of the people: European Parliamentary elections: Returning officers: Charges: Northern Ireland 91
Representation of the people: European Parliamentary elections: Returning officers: Local returning officers: Charges: Great Britain & Gibraltar. 90
Representation of the people: European Parliamentary elections: Welsh forms. 90
Representation of the people: Local elections: Communities: Welsh forms 90
Representation of the people: Local elections: Parishes & communities: England & Wales 90
Representation of the people: Local elections: Principal areas: England & Wales. 90
Representation of the people: Local elections: Principal areas: Welsh forms 90
Representation of the people: Northern Ireland 91
Representation of the people: Political Parties, Elections & Referendums Act 2000: Civil sanctions 90
Representation of the people: Scotland 91

Representation of the people: Scottish independence referendum: Chief counting officer & counting officer: Charges & expenses: Scotland 258
Representation of the people: Supply of information 90
Representation of the people: Transparency of Lobbying, Non-Party Campaigning & Trade Union Administration Act 2014: Reserve Forces: Compensation schemes. 79
Reserve Forces: Payments to employers & partners 32
Reservoirs (Scotland) Act 2011: Commencements: Scotland 249, 267
Residential accommodation: Prescribed cases 58
Residential accommodation: Prescribed requirements & codes of practice 58
Residential Property Tribunal: Procedures & fees 64
Retirement benefit: Graduated retirement benefit: Married same sex couples. 194
Revenue & customs: Finance Act 2008: S. 127 & sch. 43, part 1: Appointed days 91
Revenue & customs: HM Inspectors of Constabulary & Scottish Inspectors 91
Revenue & customs: Out of time reviews: Appeal provisions. 7, 20, 30, 47, 62, 63, 203
Revenue & customs: Police & Criminal Evidence Act 1984: Applications. 91
Revenue Scotland & Tax Powers Act 2014: Acts: Scotland 242
Right to information: Suspects & accused persons: Scotland. 246
Rights in performances: Copyright & performances 24, 91
Rights in performances: Copyright & performances: Disability 24, 91
Rights in performances: Copyright & performances: Orphan works: Permitted uses 24, 91
Rights in performances: Copyright & performances: Personal copies for private use 24, 91
Rights in performances: Copyright & performances: Quotation & parody. 24, 91
Rights in performances: Copyright & performances: Research, education, libraries & archives 24, 91
Rights in performances: Extended collective licensing 24
Rights in performances: Orphan works: Licensing 24
River Finn: Angling permit: Northern Ireland. 278
River Foyle: Angling permit: Northern Ireland 278
River Thames Pedestrian/Cycle Bridge Scheme: Reading Borough Council: Confirmation 54
River Witham Bridge scheme 54
River: Fish: Keeping & introduction: Wales 92, 187
River: Live fish: Keeping or release prohibition 91
River: Salmon & freshwater fisheries: Conservation: Annual close time & catch & release: Scotland 249, 258, 263
Road & railway transport: McConaghy's level crossing: Northern Ireland 285
Road passenger transport: Qualifications of operators: Northern Ireland 288
Road races: Amendment: Acts: Explanatory notes: Northern Ireland 273
Road races: Amendment: Acts: Northern Ireland 272
Road safety: Financial penalty: Deposit 92
Road safety: Financial penalty: Deposit: Appropriate amount 92
Road traffic & vehicles: Northern Ireland 286, 287, 288, 289
Road Traffic Act 1988 (Scotland): Prescribed limit: Scotland 258
Road traffic offenders: Additional offences: Northern Ireland 289
Road traffic: Buses & coaches: Passengers rights & obligations: Designation & enforcement: Northern Ireland 286
Road traffic: Civil enforcement: Parking contraventions: Designation: England 173
Road traffic: Commonwealth Games, Glasgow: Time trial event: Scotland 258, 260
Road traffic: Contraventions: Civil enforcement: Bus lanes & moving traffic: Cardiff. 174
Road traffic: Contraventions: Parking: Civil enforcement: Cardiff: Wales 174
Road traffic: Cycle racing: Highways: Tour de France 92
Road traffic: Disabled persons: Motor vehicles: Badges 174
Road traffic: Disabled persons: Motor vehicles: Badges: Scotland 258
Road traffic: Driving Standards Agency: Vehicle & Operator Services Agency: Merger: Consequential amendments 92
Road traffic: Driving theory test: Fees 92
Road traffic: Drug driving: Specified limits 174
Road traffic: England. 54, 173
Road traffic: Financial penalty deposit: Northern Ireland 288
Road traffic: Glasgow Commonwealth Games Act 2008: Urgent traffic regulation measures: Scotland 258, 266
Road traffic: Goods vehicles: Operators: Licensing: Fees 92
Road traffic: Goods vehicles: Plating & testing: Amendments 92
Road traffic: HGV Road User Levy Act 2013: Commencements 92
Road traffic: HGV road user levy: Exemption of vehicles 92
Road traffic: HGV road user levy: Specified roads 92
Road traffic: International carriage: Dangerous goods: Road transport: Fees. 92
Road traffic: Motor cars: Driving instruction 92
Road traffic: Motor vehicles: Driving licences. 92, 93
Road traffic: Motor vehicles: Speed limits: Variation 174
Road traffic: Motor vehicles: Tests: Amendments 92
Road traffic: Offenders: Additional offences 93
Road traffic: Parking adjudicators: Argyll & Bute Council: Scotland 258
Road traffic: Parking adjudicators: Inverclyde Council: Scotland 258
Road traffic: Parking attendants: Wearing of uniforms: Argyll & Bute Council: Scotland 258
Road traffic: Parking attendants: Wearing of uniforms: Inverclyde Council: Scotland 258
Road traffic: Passenger & goods vehicles: Recording equipment: Tachograph card: Fees 92
Road traffic: Permitted & special parking areas: Argyll & Bute Council: Scotland 259
Road traffic: Permitted & special parking areas: Inverclyde Council: Scotland. 259
Road traffic: Road safety: Financial penalty: Deposit 92
Road traffic: Road safety: Financial penalty: Deposit: Appropriate amount 92
Road traffic: Road Traffic Act 1988 (Scotland): Prescribed limit: Scotland 258
Road traffic: Road user charging: Enforcement & adjudication: London. 174
Road traffic: Road user charging: Penalty charges, adjudication & enforcement: England. 174

26 AUGUST 2015 | LONDON GAZETTE | SUPPLEMENT NO.1 343

Road traffic: Road vehicles: Construction & use 93
Road traffic: Road vehicles: Registration & licensing 93
Road traffic: Road vehicles: Registration & licensing: Amendments 93
Road traffic: Scotland 259, 260, 261, 262, 263
Road traffic: Speed limits 93, 94
Road traffic: Speed limits: Scotland 259
Road traffic: Traffic regulation . . 94, 95, 96, 97, 98, 99, 100, 101, 102, 103, 104, 105, 106, 107, 108, 109, 110, 111, 112, 113, 114, 115, 116, 117, 118, 119, 120, 121, 122, 123, 124, 125, 126, 127, 128, 129, 130, 131, 132, 133, 134, 135, 136, 137, 138, 139, 140, 141, 142, 143, 144, 145, 146, 147, 148, 149, 150, 151, 152, 153, 154, 155, 156, 157, 158, 159, 160, 161, 162, 163, 164, 165, 166, 167, 168, 169, 170, 171, 172, 173, 174, 175, 176, 177, 178, 179, 180, 181, 182, 183, 184, 185, 186, 187
Road traffic: Traffic regulation: Scotland. 259, 260, 261, 262, 263
Road traffic: Trunk roads: HGV speed limit: Scotland. 258
Road traffic: Vehicle drivers: Professional competence: Certificates: Amendments 93
Road traffic: Vehicles: Excise & registration 93
Road traffic: Vehicles: Removal & disposal: Wales 174
Road user charging: Penalty charges, adjudication & enforcement: England 174
Road vehicles: Construction & use. 93
Road vehicles: Registration & licensing 93
Road works: Inspection fees: Scotland 258
Roads & bridges: Road works: Inspection fees: Scotland 258
Roads & bridges: Scotland. 258
Roads & bridges: Scottish Road Works Register: Prescribed fees: Scotland 258
Roads & bridges: Special roads: Scotland 258
Roads: Northern Ireland 285, 286
Rowantree Road (C355), Dromore: Abandonment: Northern Ireland 289
Royal Conservatoire of Scotland: Education 248
Royal Mail Pension Plan: Transfer of functions 73
Rural development programmes 8
Rural primary schools: Designation: England. 34
Russia: Export control: Sanctions 30
Russia: Sanctions 78

S

Safeguarding Board for Northern Ireland: Membership, procedure, functions & committees 280
Safety & hygiene: Food 50
Salaries: Assembly Ombudsman & Commissioner for Complaints: Northern Ireland 290
Salaries: Lands Tribunal: Northern Ireland 281
Salmon & freshwater fisheries: Conservation: Annual close time & catch & release: Scotland 249, 258, 263
Salmon & freshwater fisheries: Fish: Keeping & introduction: Wales. 92, 187
Salmon drift netting: Northern Ireland. 278
Salmon netting: Northern Ireland 278
Same sex couples: Marriage: Buildings registration: Authorised persons appointment 88
Same sex couples: Marriage: Conversion of Civil Partnership 88
Same sex couples: Marriage: Jurisdiction & recognition of judgments 45, 63
Same sex couples: Marriage: Jurisdiction & recognition of judgments: Scotland 251
Same sex couples: Marriage: Prescribed bodies: Scotland. 254
Same sex couples: Marriage: Registration of shared buildings 88
Same sex couples: Marriage: Use of Armed Forces Chapels 88
Sanctions: Revocations 203
Savings banks: National Savings Bank: Investment deposits: Limits 187
Savings bonds: Premium: Maximum holdings 74
School & early years finance: England 36
School closure review panel: Members: Scotland 247
School closure review panels: Convener: Scotland. 247
School companies: England 36
School development: Plans: Wales 38
School governance: Constitution: England. 36
School Standards & Organisation (Wales) Act 2013: Commencements 39
School teachers: Pay & conditions: England & Wales 36
School term dates: Consultation: Wales 37
Schools: Admissions code: Appointed day: England. 36
Schools: Admissions: Co-ordination of arrangements: England 36
Schools: Education: Maintained Schools: Staffing: Wales 39
Schools: Federation of Maintained Schools: Wales 38
Schools: Food: Requirements: England 36
Schools: Head teachers: Reports to parents & adult pupils: Wales. 38
Schools: Independent: Religious character: Designation: England 34
Schools: Independent: Standards: Education: England 35
Schools: Maintained schools: Governors: Training requirements: Wales 38
Schools: Religious: Designation: Independent schools: Wales 37
Schools: Rural primary schools: Designation: England 34
Schools: Small schools: Wales. 38
Schools: Staffing: England 36
Schools: Teachers: Schools: Professional qualifications: England 35, 36
Schools: Term dates: Notification: Wales 37
Scotland Act 1998: Agency arrangements: Specification 22, 32, 40
Scotland Act 1998: Functions: Modification 7, 22, 32

Scotland Act 1998: Schedule 5: Modifications . . . 23, 32
Scotland Act 1998: Transfer of functions . . . 23, 32
Scotland Act 2012: Commencements . . . 23, 32
Scottish independence referendum: Acts: Explanatory notes: Scotland . . . 242
Scottish independence referendum: Chief counting officer & counting officer: Charges & expenses: Scotland . . . 258
Scottish Land Court: Rules: Scotland . . . 263
Scottish landfill tax: Prescribed site activities: Scotland . . . 252
Scottish Legal Complaints Commission: Duties & powers: Scotland . . . 253
Scottish Legal Complaints Commission: Membership: Scotland . . . 253
Scottish Parliament: Constituencies & regions . . . 23, 32
Scottish Road Works Register: Prescribed fees: Scotland . . . 258
Scottish tax tribunals: Scotland . . . 267
Sea fisheries: Fishing boats: Points for masters . . . 187
Sea fisheries: Fishing boats: Points for masters: Scotland . . . 263
Sea fisheries: Fishing vessels: Satellite-tracking devices: Electronic reporting: Scheme . . . 187
Sea fisheries: Licences & notices: Northern Ireland . . . 290
Sea fisheries: Prohibited methods of fishing: Firth of Clyde: Scotland . . . 263
Seals: Protection: Haul-Out sites: designation: Scotland . . . 254
Secure tenancies: Notices: Northern Ireland . . . 280
Secure tenancies: Review procedure: Wales . . . 56
Seeds: Fees: Scotland . . . 264
Seeds: Forests: Reproductive material: Great Britain . . . 187
Seeds: Miscellaneous amendments: Northern Ireland . . . 290
Seeds: Nomenclature changes . . . 8, 82, 187
Seeds: Nomenclature changes: Wales . . . 187
Sefton Metropolitan Borough Council: Permit schemes: Traffic management . . . 54
Selby: Electoral changes . . . 68
Self-directed support: Social care: Direct payments: Scotland . . . 265
Self-employed earner: Wife or civil partner: Maternity allowance . . . 193
Senior courts of England & Wales: Access to Justice Act 1999: Appeals: Destination: Family proceedings . . . 44, 46, 187
Senior courts of England & Wales: Civil courts . . . 187
Senior courts of England & Wales: Civil procedure: Rules . . . 27, 187, 188
Senior courts of England & Wales: Civil proceedings: Fees . . . 27, 188
Senior courts of England & Wales: Courts & tribunals: Fees . . . 11, 27, 46, 51, 70, 72, 188, 195, 202
Senior courts of England & Wales: Crime & Courts Act 2013 . . . 44, 46, 188
Senior courts of England & Wales: Crime & Courts Act 2013: Commencements . . . 27, 46, 71, 188
Senior courts of England & Wales: Crime & Courts Act 2013: Consequential, transitional & saving provisions . . . 27, 188
Senior courts of England & Wales: Criminal procedure: Rules . . . 71, 188
Senior courts of England & Wales: European Parliamentary elections: Petitions . . . 89, 195
Senior courts of England & Wales: Family court: Business: Composition & distribution . . . 44, 46, 188
Senior courts of England & Wales: Family procedure: Rules . . . 27, 45, 46, 71, 188
Senior courts of England & Wales: Family proceedings: Fees . . . 46, 189
Senior courts of England & Wales: High court & county court: Jurisdiction . . . 27, 189
Senior courts of England & Wales: High court: Business distribution . . . 189
Senior courts of England & Wales: Probate: Non-contentious: Fees . . . 189
Serious Crime Act 2007: Anti-fraud organisations . . . 33
Serious Organised Crime & Police Act 2005: Designated sites: Section 128: Amendments . . . 30
Services: Provision . . . 85
Sevastopol: Export control: Sanctions . . . 30
Sevastopol: Sanctions . . . 78
Sevenoaks: Electoral changes . . . 68
Severn Bridges: Tolls . . . 54
Sewerage: Water & sewerage services: Dwellings: Unmetered charges: Collection: Local authorities: Scotland . . . 267
Sexual Offences Act 2003: Notification requirements: Northern Ireland . . . 275
Sexual Offences Act 2003: Prescribed police stations: Scotland . . . 246
Sheep: Records, identification & movement: England . . . 9
Shellfish: Aquaculture & Fisheries (Scotland) Act 2013: Commercially damaging species: Specification: Scotland . . . 243, 249, 264
Shepway: Electoral changes . . . 68
Sheriff Court: Act of Adjournal: Criminal Procedure (Scotland) Act 1995: Criminal Procedure Rules 1996: Amendments: Scotland . 250, 251, 264
Sheriff Court: Act of Adjournal: Criminal procedure rules: Amendment: Regulatory Reform (Scotland) Act 2014: Scotland . . . 250, 264
Sheriff Court: Act of Adjournal: Criminal procedure rules: Scotland . . . 250, 251, 264
Sheriff Court: Commissary business: Act of Sederunt: Scotland . . . 264
Sheriff Court: Court of Session: Company insolvency rules: Scotland . . . 245, 264
Sheriff Court: Court of Session: Rules: Marriage & Civil Partnership (Scotland) Act 2014: Scotland . . . 245, 264
Sheriff Court: Court of Session: Rules, Ordinary cause rules & Summary cause rules: Scotland . . . 246, 264
Sheriff Court: Court of Session: Rules: Scotland . . . 245, 246, 264
Sheriff Court: Justice of the Peace Court: Judicial Pensions & Retirement Act 1993: Scotland . . . 251, 264
Sheriff Court: Solicitors fees: Act of Sederunt: Scotland . . . 264
Sheriff officers: Messengers-at-Arms: Court of Session: Act of Sederunt: Scotland . . . 245, 264
Ships: Air pollution: Prevention . . . 72
Shropshire Council: Permit schemes: Traffic management . . . 54
Single Common Market Organisation: Agriculture: Consequential amendments: Northern Ireland . . . 273
Single use carrier bags: Charge: Environmental protection: Scotland . . . 248
Slough Borough Council: Permit schemes: Traffic management . . . 54
Small business hereditament relief: Northern Ireland . . . 284
Smoke control areas: Authorised fuels: England . . . 20
Smoke control areas: Authorised fuels: Northern Ireland . . . 274

Smoke control areas: Authorised fuels: Scotland	245
Smoke control areas: Authorised fuels: Wales	20
Smoke control areas: Fireplaces: Exempt: England	20
Smoke control areas: Fireplaces: Exempt: Northern Ireland	274
Smoke control areas: Fireplaces: Exempt: Scotland	245
Smoke control areas: Fireplaces: Exempt: Wales	20
Social Care (Self-directed Support) (Scotland) Act 2013: Commencements: Scotland	265
Social Care (Self-directed Support) (Scotland) Act 2013: Consequential modifications	23, 33, 189
Social Care (Self-directed Support) (Scotland) Act 2013: Consequential provisions: Scotland	265
Social care charges: Social services: Complaints procedure: Wales	15, 190
Social care: Acts	4
Social care: Acts: Explanatory notes	5
Social care: Acts: Explanatory notes: Northern Ireland	272
Social care: Acts: Northern Ireland	272
Social care: Adoption support services: England	13, 189
Social care: Care & support: After care: Accommodation: England	72, 189
Social care: Care & support: Assessment of resources: Charging: England	189
Social care: Care & support: Assessment: England	189
Social care: Care & support: Continuity of care: England	189
Social care: Care & support: Cross-border placements & business failure: Temporary duty: Dispute resolution	189
Social care: Care & support: Cross-border placements: Duties of Scottish local authorities: Business failure	189
Social care: Care & support: Deferred payment: England	189
Social care: Care & support: Direct payments: England	189
Social care: Care & support: Discharge of Hospital Patients: England	74, 189
Social care: Care & support: Disputes between local authorities: England	189
Social care: Care & support: Independent advocacy support: England	189
Social care: Care & support: Market oversight information: England	189
Social care: Care & support: Ordinary residence: Specified accommodation: England	189
Social care: Care & support: Personal budget: Exclusion of costs: England	189
Social care: Care & support: Preventing needs	190
Social care: Care & support: Provision of Health Services: England	190
Social care: Care & support: Sight-impaired & severely sight-impaired adults: England	190
Social care: Care Act 2014	74, 76, 86, 190
Social care: Care Act 2014: Commencements	76, 86, 190
Social care: Care Act 2014: Consequential amendments	53, 190
Social care: Care Quality Commission: Reviews & performance assessments	74, 86, 190
Social care: Carers: Charges for support: Waiving: Scotland	264
Social care: Charges: National assistance: Wales	190
Social care: Children & Families (Wales) Measure: Commencements	15, 76, 190
Social care: Children & Young Persons Act 2008: Relevant care functions	14, 190
Social care: Community care: Joint working: Scotland	264
Social care: Community care: Personal care & nursing care: Scotland	265
Social care: Health & Social Care (Community Health & Standards) Act 2003: Commencements: Wales	190
Social care: Health & Social Care Act 2008: Commencements	53
Social care: Health & Social Care Act 2008: Regulated activities: England	74, 86, 190
Social care: Health Research Authority: Transfer of staff, property & liabilities	53, 190
Social care: Health: Disciplinary procedures: Northern Ireland	280
Social care: Public Bodies (Joint Working) (Scotland) Act 2014: Commencements: Scotland	257, 265
Social care: Public bodies: Joint Working (Scotland) Act 2014: Modifications: Scotland	257, 265
Social care: Public Bodies: Joint working: Health Professionals & Social Care Professionals: Scotland	256, 265
Social care: Public Bodies: Joint working: Integration joint boards: Scotland	256, 265
Social care: Public Bodies: Joint working: Integration joint monitoring committees: Scotland	256, 265
Social care: Public Bodies: Joint working: Integration scheme: Scotland	256, 265
Social care: Public Bodies: Joint working: Local authority officers: Scotland	265
Social care: Public Bodies: Joint working: Membership: Strategic planning group: Scotland	256, 265
Social care: Public bodies: Joint working: National health & wellbeing outcomes: Scotland	256, 265
Social care: Public Bodies: Joint working: Performance reports: Content: Scotland	256, 265
Social care: Public Bodies: Joint working: Prescribed consultees: Scotland	257, 265
Social care: Public Bodies: Joint working: Prescribed days: Scotland	257, 265
Social care: Public bodies: Joint working: Prescribed health board functions: Scotland	257, 265
Social care: Public bodies: Joint working: Prescribed local authority functions: Scotland	257, 265
Social care: Regulation of care: Social service workers: Amendments: Scotland	265
Social care: Representations procedure	15, 190
Social care: Self-directed support: Direct payments: Scotland	265
Social care: Social Services & Well-being (Wales) Act 2014: Commencements	190
Social care: Social workers: Social service workers: Care services: Registration: Scotland	265
Social fund: Cold weather payments	192
Social fund: Winter fuel payments	192
Social housing: Fraud: Detection: Wales	56
Social investments: Tax relief: Social impact contractor: Accreditation	60
Social Security Contributions & Benefits Act 1992: Application: Parts 12ZA &12ZB & 12ZC: Parental order cases	198
Social Security Contributions & Benefits Act 1992: Parts 12ZA & 12ZB: Application: Adoptions: Overseas	198
Social security: Amendments: Northern Ireland	291
Social security: Benefits: Recovery: Lump sum payments	193
Social security: Benefits: Recovery: Northern Ireland	291
Social security: Benefits: Up-rating	192
Social security: Benefits: Up-rating: Northern Ireland	276, 280, 284, 290, 291, 292
Social security: Categorisation of earners	192

Social security: Child benefit: Reviews & appeals 194, 196
Social security: Child benefit: Tax credits 191, 196
Social security: Child benefit: Tax credits: Up-rating 190, 196
Social security: Child support: Fees: Northern Ireland 278, 290
Social security: Claims & payments: Northern Ireland 291
Social security: Contributions. 192
Social security: Contributions & national insurance numbers: Crediting & treatment: Northern Ireland 291
Social security: Contributions: Limited liability partnership 192
Social security: Contributions: Pensions: Additional units 192
Social security: Contributions: Re-rating & national insurance fund payments 193
Social security: Contributions: Re-rating: Amendments 193
Social security: Earnings factors: Revaluation 193
Social security: Earnings factors: Revaluations: Northern Ireland 291
Social security: Fees payable by qualifying lenders 193
Social security: Finance Act 2009: Consequential amendments 59, 191
Social security: Finance Act 2009: Sections 101, 102: Appointed days 59, 191
Social security: Graduated retirement benefit: Married same sex couples 194
Social security: Guardian's allowance: Reviews & appeals 194, 196
Social security: Guardian's allowance: Up-rating 191
Social security: Guardian's allowance: Up-rating: Northern Ireland 194
Social security: Habitual residence 193
Social security: Habitual residence: Northern Ireland 280, 284, 291
Social security: Housing benefit 191
Social security: Housing benefit: Amendments 191
Social security: Housing benefit: Transitional provisions 191
Social security: Housing payments: Discretionary: Total expenditure: Revocation: Scotland 266
Social security: Income support allowance: Work-related activity 191
Social security: Income-related benefits: Subsidy to authorities 191
Social security: Invalid care allowance 193
Social security: Invalid care allowance: Northern Ireland 291
Social security: Jobseeker's allowance: Employment & support allowance 193
Social security: Jobseeker's allowance: Employment & support allowance: Waiting days: Northern Ireland 291
Social security: Jobseeker's allowance: Employment assistance: Northern Ireland 280, 284, 290
Social security: Jobseeker's allowance: Habitual residence 191
Social security: Jobseeker's allowance: Habitual residence: Northern Ireland 290
Social security: Jobseeker's allowance: Homeless claimants 191
Social security: Jobseeker's allowance: Homeless claimants: Northern Ireland 290
Social security: Jobseeker's allowance: Jobsearch pilot scheme 191
Social security: Jobseeker's allowance: Maternity allowance: Northern Ireland 290
Social security: Jobseeker's allowance: Work skills pilot scheme 191
Social security: Maternity allowance 193
Social security: Maternity allowance: Curtailment 191
Social security: Maternity allowance: Northern Ireland 291
Social security: Maternity allowance: Participating wife or civil partner of self-employed earner: Northern Ireland 291
Social security: Maternity allowance: Self-employed earner: Wife or civil partner 193
Social security: Mesothelioma: Lump sum payments: Conditions & amounts 192
Social security: Mesothelioma: Lump sum payments: Conditions & amounts: Northern Ireland 290
Social security: Miscellaneous amendments 193
Social security: Northern Ireland 280, 284, 291
Social security: Pensions Act 2014: Commencements 192
Social security: Pensions: Flat rate accrual amount 193
Social security: Pensions: Flat rate accrual amounts: Northern Ireland 291
Social security: Pensions: Low earnings threshold 193
Social security: Pensions: Low earnings threshold: Northern Ireland 291
Social security: Pneumoconiosis etc.: Workers' compensation: Claims: Payments 192
Social security: Reciprocal agreements: Northern Ireland 291
Social security: Social fund: Cold weather payments 192
Social security: Social fund: Winter fuel payments 192
Social security: Statutory maternity & adoption pay: Curtailment 193
Social security: Statutory shared parental pay: Administration 193, 198
Social security: Statutory sick pay: Maintenance of records 193
Social security: Statutory sick pay: Maintenance of records: Northern Ireland 292
Social security: Statutory sick pay: Percentage threshold 193
Social security: Supported accommodation 191
Social security: Tax Credits, Child Benefit & Guardian's Allowance Appeals Order: Appointed days 193, 196
Social security: Tax credits: Reviews & appeals 194, 196
Social security: Universal credit: Digital service 194
Social security: Universal credit: Miscellaneous amendments 194
Social security: Universal credit: Transitional provisions 194
Social security: Welfare benefits: Up-rating 194, 198
Social security: Welfare Reform Act 2012: Commencements 194
Social security: Workers' compensation: Pneumoconiosis etc.: Claims: Payments: Northern Ireland 290
Social service workers: Social workers: Care services: Registration: Scotland 265
Social Services & Well-being (Wales) Act 2014: Commencements 190
Social services & well-being: Acts: Explanatory notes: Wales 297
Social services functions: Local authorities: Contracting out: England 23
Social services: Acts: Wales 296
Social workers: Social service workers: Care services: Registration: Scotland 265

South Hams: Electoral changes . . . 68
South Hook: Combined heat & power plant . . . 61
South Kesteven: Electoral changes . . . 68
South Oxfordshire: Electoral changes . . . 68
South Ribble: Electoral changes . . . 69
South Sudan: Sanctions: Overseas territories . . . 78
South West Water Authority: Water industry: Dissolution . . . 204
Spamount hill climb: Road races: Northern Ireland . . . 288
Special educational needs: Codes of practice: England . . . 36
Special educational needs: Consequential amendments: England . . . 36
Special educational needs: Direct payments: Pilot scheme: England . . . 36
Special educational needs: Disability: England . . . 36
Special educational needs: Personal budgets: England . . . 36
Spittal Church in Wales School: Diocese of St Davids: Educational endowments . . . 37
Sport: Value added tax . . . 204
Sports grounds & sporting events: Commonwealth Games, Glasgow: Games lanes: Scotland . . . 260, 266
Sports grounds & sporting events: Designations: Amendments: Scotland . . . 266
Sports grounds & sporting events: Football spectators: 2014 World Cup control period . . . 195
Sports grounds & sporting events: Glasgow Commonwealth Games Act 2008: Repeal day: Scotland . . . 266
Sports grounds & sporting events: Glasgow Commonwealth Games Act 2008: Urgent traffic regulation measures: Scotland . . . 258, 266
Sports grounds: Safety: Designation . . . 195
St George's Healthcare: Transfer of property . . . 76
St Mary's Music School: Aided places: Scotland . . . 248
Stakeholder pension schemes: Disclosure of information: Northern Ireland . . . 282
Stamp duty & stamp duty reserve tax: BX Swiss AG . . . 195
Stamp duty land tax: Taxes: Charities: Definition: Relevant territories . . . 9, 13, 26, 60, 61, 195, 203
Stamp duty reserve tax: Finance Act 1999: Schedule 19: Consequential amendments . . . 195
Stamp duty reserve tax: Finance Act 2009: Schedule 55 & 56: Sections 101 & 102 . . . 195
Stamp duty reserve tax: Taxes: Charities: Definition: Relevant territories . . . 9, 13, 26, 60, 61, 195, 203
Stamp duty: Taxes: Charities: Definition: Relevant territories . . . 9, 13, 26, 60, 61, 195, 203
Statistics of trade: Customs & excise . . . 195
Statutes: Chronological tables . . . 7
Statutes: Chronological tables: Northern Ireland . . . 273
Statutes: Northern Ireland . . . 273
Statutes: Title page & index: Northern Ireland . . . 273
Statutory audit & local audit: Delegation of functions . . . 10, 21, 69
Statutory concessions: Extra-statutory concessions: Enactments . . . 59
Statutory maternity & adoption pay: Curtailment . . . 193
Statutory maternity pay: Social security: Benefits: Up-rating: Northern Ireland . . . 276, 280, 284, 290, 291, 292
Statutory paternity & adoption pay . . . 198
Statutory paternity & adoption pay: Parental orders & prospective adopters . . . 198
Statutory rules (Northern Ireland): Chronological tables: Northern Ireland . . . 273
Statutory shared parental pay: Administration . . . 193, 198
Statutory shared parental pay: Parental order cases . . . 198
Statutory sick pay: Maintenance of records . . . 193
Statutory sick pay: Maintenance of records: Northern Ireland . . . 292
Statutory sick pay: Percentage threshold . . . 193
Statutory sick pay: Social security: Benefits: Up-rating: Northern Ireland . . . 276, 280, 284, 290, 291, 292
Strabane: Parking & waiting restrictions: Northern Ireland . . . 287
Stratford-on-Avon: Electoral changes . . . 69
Structural Funds: Welsh ministers . . . 43
Student fees: Agriculture: Northern Ireland . . . 273
Student fees: Amounts: Northern Ireland . . . 276
Student fees: Amounts: Wales . . . 39
Student loans: Living costs liability: Cancellation . . . 37
Student loans: Repayment . . . 34
Student loans: Repayments: Northern Ireland . . . 276
Student support: Amendments: Education: Northern Ireland . . . 276
Student support: England . . . 35
Student support: Financial: Amendments: Education: Northern Ireland . . . 276
Student support: Further & higher education: England . . . 35
Submarine pipelines: Designated owners . . . 81
Submarine pipelines: Electricity generating stations . . . 81
Sudan & South Sudan & Central African Republic: Export control . . . 30
Sudan: European Union: Financial sanctions . . . 28
Sudan: Sanctions: Overseas territories . . . 78
Suffolk Coastal: Electoral changes . . . 69
Sulphur content: Liquid fuels: England & Wales . . . 43
Sulphur content: Liquid fuels: Northern Ireland . . . 277
Sulphur: Liquid fuels: Scotland . . . 248
Summary cause: Rules: Scotland . . . 246, 264
Superannuation Act 1972: Admission to schedule 1 . . . 80
Superannuation schemes: Health & personal social services: Northern Ireland . . . 279
Superannuation schemes: National Health Service: Scotland . . . 254
Superannuation: Teachers: Northern Ireland . . . 276
Supervision measures: Mutual recognition: European Union: Scotland . . . 246
Supply & appropriation: Main estimates: Acts . . . 5
Support for victims & witnesses: Courts & Tribunal Service: Attorney general: Human rights guidance: Northern Ireland . . . 280

Supported accommodation: Social security: 191
Supreme Court of the United Kingdom: Courts & tribunals: Fees: England & Wales 11, 27, 46, 51, 70, 72, 188, 195, 202
Suspects & accused persons: Right to information: Scotland. 246
Swanage Railway: England 201, 202
Swine: Diseases 8
Syria: Export control: Sanctions 30
Syria: Restrictive measures: Overseas territories 78

T

Tajikistan: Double taxation: Relief 12, 25, 59
Taking control of goods: Enforcement agents: Certification 42
Tandragee 100: Road races: Northern Ireland 288
Tax credits 196
Tax Credits Act 2002: Commencements & transitional provisions 196
Tax Credits, Child Benefit & Guardian's Allowance Appeals Order: Appointed days 193, 196
Tax credits: Child benefit 191, 196
Tax credits: Child benefit: Up-rating 190, 196
Tax credits: Exercise of functions 196
Tax credits: Late appeals 196
Tax credits: Reviews & appeals 194, 196
Tax credits: Settlement of appeals 196
Tax credits: Up-rating 196
Tax relief: Social investments: Social impact contractor: Accreditation 60
Taxation (International & Other Provisions) Act 2010: Section 371RE: Controlled foreign companies: Amendments 26
Taxation: Pensions: Acts 5
Taxation: Pensions: Acts: Explanatory notes 6
Taxes see also Capital gains tax
Taxes see also Corporation tax
Taxes see also Income tax
Taxes see also Inheritance tax
Taxes see also Insurance premium tax
Taxes see also Landfill tax
Taxes see also Petroleum revenue tax
Taxes see also Tonnage tax
Taxes see also Value added tax
Taxes: Business premises renovation allowances 24, 58
Taxes: Chargeable gains: Gilt-edged securities 13, 26
Taxes: Charities: Definition: Relevant territories 9, 13, 26, 60, 61, 195, 203
Taxes: Community amateur sports clubs: Exemptions 25
Taxes: Enveloped dwellings: Annual tax & chargeable amounts: Indexation 9
Taxes: Finance Act 2013: Schedules 17 & 18: Appointed days 25
Taxes: Finance Act 2014: Theatrical production: Tax relief: Appointed day 25
Taxes: International compliance: Crown Dependencies & Gibraltar 196
Taxes: International compliance: USA 196
Taxes: International tax: Enforcement: Gibraltar 196
Taxes: International tax: Enforcement: Uruguay 196
Taxes: Land & buildings transactions: Acts: Explanatory notes: Scotland 242
Taxes: Loan relationships & derivative contracts: Accounting practice: Changes 25
Taxes: Loan relationships & derivative contracts: Accounting standards: Changes 25
Taxes: Loan relationships & derivative contracts: Profits & losses: Disregard & bringing into account 26
Taxes: Offshore funds: Amendments 12, 26, 60
Taxes: Revenue Scotland & Tax Powers Act 2014: Commencements: Scotland 266
Taxes: Revenue Scotland & Tax Powers Act 2014: Provisions & modifications 22, 32, 196
Taxes: Stamp duty & stamp duty reserve tax: BX Swiss AG 195
Taxes: Stamp duty reserve tax: Finance Act 1999: Schedule 19: Consequential amendments 195
Taxes: Tax Credits Act 2002: Commencements & transitional provisions 196
Taxi operators: Licencing: Northern Ireland 286
Taxis: 2008 Act: Commencements: Northern Ireland 289
Taxis: Drivers' licences: Northern Ireland 286, 289
TB see Tuberculosis
Teachers: Head teachers: Reports to parents & adult pupils: Wales 38
Teachers: Pension schemes: England & Wales 36, 87
Teachers: Pension schemes: Northern Ireland 276, 284
Teachers: Pension schemes: Scotland 257
Teachers: Schools: Professional qualifications: England 35, 36
Teachers: Superannuation: Northern Ireland 276
Teachers: Superannuation: Scotland 255
Teachers' discipline 36
Telecommunications: Valuation: Northern Ireland 284
Television: Broadcasting 11
Television: Broadcasting: Independent productions 11
Telford & Wrekin: Electoral changes 69
Templemore Avenue, Belfast (Footpath): Abandonment: Northern Ireland 285
Tenancies: Secure: Review procedures: Wales 56
Tenements: Costs: Potential liability: Discharge notices: Scotland 266
Terms & conditions of employment: Adoption: Overseas: Statutory shared parental pay 198
Terms & conditions of employment: Children, Schools & Families Act 2014: Commencements 196

Terms & conditions of employment: Collective redundancies & transfer of undertakings: Employment protection. 197
Terms & conditions of employment: Employment Rights Act 1996: Parental order cases. 197
Terms & conditions of employment: Employment Rights Act 1996: Section 75G & 75H: Application: Adoptions from overseas 197
Terms & conditions of employment: Employment rights: Limits: Increase 197
Terms & conditions of employment: Enterprise & Regulatory Reform Act 2013 197
Terms & conditions of employment: Enterprise & Regulatory Reform Act 2013: Commencements 7, 63, 64, 197, 198
Terms & conditions of employment: Flexible working: Eligibility, complaints & remedies. 197
Terms & conditions of employment: Maternity & adoption leave: Curtailment 197
Terms & conditions of employment: Maternity & parental leave 197
Terms & conditions of employment: National minimum wage: Amendments 197
Terms & conditions of employment: National minimum wage: Financial penalty: Variation 197
Terms & conditions of employment: Parental order cases: Paternity, adoption & shared parental leave 197
Terms & conditions of employment: Paternity & adoption leave. 197
Terms & conditions of employment: Paternity & adoption: Leave 197
Terms & conditions of employment: Public interest disclosure: Prescribed persons 197, 198
Terms & conditions of employment: Shared parental leave 198
Terms & conditions of employment: Shared parental leave & pay. 198
Terms & conditions of employment: Shared parental leave: Paternity & adoption leave 198
Terms & conditions of employment: Social Security Contributions & Benefits Act 1992: Application: Parts 12ZA &12ZB & 12ZC: Parental order cases 198
Terms & conditions of employment: Social Security Contributions & Benefits Act 1992: Parts 12ZA & 12ZB: Application: Adoptions: Overseas. 198
Terms & conditions of employment: Statutory paternity & adoption pay 198
Terms & conditions of employment: Statutory paternity & adoption pay: Parental orders & prospective adopters 198
Terms & conditions of employment: Statutory shared parental pay 198
Terms & conditions of employment: Statutory shared parental pay: Administration 193, 198
Terms & conditions of employment: Statutory shared parental pay: Parental order cases. 198
Terms & conditions of employment: Statutory shared parental pay: Persons abroad & mariners 198
Terms & conditions of employment: Transfer of undertakings: Protection of employment: Department for Work & Pensions 198
Terms & conditions of employment: Wages: Deduction: Limitation 197
Terms & conditions of employment: Welfare benefits: Up-rating 194, 198
Terms & conditions of employment: Work flexibly: Reasonable requests: Code of practice 197
Territorial sea: Baselines 199
Territorial sea: Limits: Guernsey 199
Terrorism Act 2000: Examining & Review Officers: Codes of practice 84
Terrorism Act 2000: Proscribed organisations 84
Three Rivers: Electoral changes 69
Title Conditions (Scotland) Act 2003: Conservation bodies: Scotland. 266
Title Conditions: Costs: Potential liability: Discharge notices: Scotland 266
Tobacco retailers: 2014 Act: Commencements: Northern Ireland. 283
Tobacco retailers: Acts: Explanatory notes: Northern Ireland 273
Tobacco retailers: Acts: Northern Ireland 272
Tolls: Severn Bridges 54
Tonnage tax: Training requirements 196
Tour de France: Cycle racing: Highways. 92
Tour of Sperrins Rally: Road races: Northern Ireland 288
Town & country planning see also Planning
Town & country planning: Advertisements: Control: Scotland. 266
Town & country planning: Applications & deemed applications: Fees: Scotland 266
Town & country planning: Applications, deemed applications, requests & site visits: Fees: England 199
Town & country planning: Channel Tunnel: Planning appeals & assessment of environment effects. 200
Town & country planning: Compensation: England 199
Town & country planning: Compensation: Wales 200
Town & country planning: Crossrail: Insertion of review clauses 199, 201
Town & country planning: Determination of a procedure: Wales 200
Town & country planning: Determination of procedure: Prescribed period: Wales. 200
Town & country planning: Development management procedure: Section 62A applications: England 199
Town & country planning: Development management procedure: Wales 200
Town & country planning: Enterprise & Regulatory Reform Act 2013: Commencements 22, 43, 199
Town & country planning: Enterprise & Regulatory Reform Act 2013: Lawfulness: Listed building certificate 199
Town & country planning: General permitted development: England 199
Town & country planning: General permitted development: Scotland 266, 267
Town & country planning: General permitted development: Wales 200
Town & country planning: Growth & Infrastructure Act 2013: Commencements: England 199
Town & country planning: Hazardous substances: Heavy fuel oil 52, 199
Town & country planning: Hazardous substances: Wales. 200
Town & country planning: Listed buildings & conservation areas: Determination of procedure: Prescribed period: Wales 200
Town & country planning: Listed buildings & conservation areas: Heritage partnership agreements: England 199
Town & country planning: Listed buildings: Consent orders: Procedure: England. 199
Town & country planning: Listed buildings: Lawfulness of proposed works: Certificates: Planning: England 199
Town & country planning: Neighbourhood planning: Referendums: England 199
Town & country planning: Non-material changes & correction of errors: Wales 200
Town & country planning: Non-material changes: Fees: Wales 200
Town & country planning: Planning Act 2008: Commencements: Wales 200
Town & country planning: Planning: Major accident hazards: Control: Scotland 267
Town & country planning: Revocations 199
Town & country planning: Revocations: England 199
Town & country planning: Tree preservation: Scotland 267

Town or village greens: Registration: Trigger & terminating events	21
Trade Union administration: Non-party campaigning: Lobbying: Registration: Acts	5
Trade Union administration: Non-party campaigning: Lobbying: Registration: Acts: Explanatory notes	6
Trade: Fair trading: CMA registers of undertakings: Available hours	22
Trade: Statistics: Customs & excise	195
Traffic Commissioners: Publication & inquiries	86
Traffic management: Penalty charges: Prescribed devices: Northern Ireland	287
Traffic management: Permit schemes: Bracknell Forest Borough Council	54
Traffic management: Permit schemes: Cheshire East Borough Council	54
Traffic management: Permit schemes: Cheshire West & Chester Borough Council	54
Traffic management: Permit schemes: Coventry City Council	54
Traffic management: Permit schemes: Norfolk County Council	54
Traffic management: Permit schemes: North Tyneside Council	54
Traffic management: Permit schemes: Sefton Metropolitan Borough Council	54
Traffic management: Permit schemes: Shropshire Council	54
Traffic management: Permit schemes: Slough Borough Council	54
Traffic management: Permit schemes: Warrington Borough Council	54
Traffic management: Permit schemes: Warwickshire County Council	54
Traffic management: Permit schemes: West Berkshire Council	55
Traffic management: Permit schemes: Wokingham Borough Council	55
Training: Education: Inspectors: Wales	37
Trans-European Road Network infrastructure: Charging: Heavy goods vehicles	53
Transfer of functions: Royal Mail Pension Plan	73
Transparency of Lobbying, Non-Party Campaigning & Trade Union Administration Act 2014: Commencements	23, 90
Transplantation: Organs: Quality & safety	57
Transport & works: London Underground: Northern Line: Extension	201
Transport & works: Network Rail: Huyton	201
Transport & works: Railways: Felixstowe Branch Line: Land acquisition	201
Transport & works: Railways: Swanage Railway: England	201, 202
Transport for London: London local authorities: Local acts	6
Transport: Barnsley, Doncaster, Rotherham & Sheffield Combined Authority	66, 201
Transport: Bus & coach passengers: Rights & obligations: Northern Ireland	292
Transport: Combined authorities: Consequential amendments	67, 201
Transport: Crossrail: Insertion of review clauses	199, 201
Transport: Crossrail: Paddington Station Bakerloo Line Connection	201
Transport: Durham, Gateshead, Newcastle Upon Tyne, North Tyneside, Northumberland, South Tyneside & Sunderland: Combined authority	67, 201
Transport: Halton, Knowsley, Liverpool, St Helens, Sefton & Wirral Combined Authority	67, 201
Transport: London Underground: Northern Line: Extension	201
Transport: Passenger Transport Executives: Bus operating powers: Exclusions	201
Transport: Public Transport Users' Committee for Wales: Abolition	202
Transport: Rail vehicles: Non-interoperable rail-system: Blackpool tramway: Accessibility: Exemptions	33, 201
Transport: Railways: Interoperability	201
Transport: Railways: McConaghy's level crossing: Northern Ireland	285
Transport: Railways: Passengers: Rights & obligations: Exemptions	201
Transport: Railways: Private crossings: Signs & barriers: Northern Ireland	292
Transport: Railways: Rail vehicles	33, 201
Transport: Regional transport planning: Wales	202
Transport: West Midlands Integrated Transport Authority: Members: Decrease in number	202
Transport: West Yorkshire Combined Authority	69, 202
Travelling expenses & remission of charges: National Health Service: Wales	77
Tree preservation: Town & country planning: Scotland	267
Trewmount Close, Killyman, Dungannon: Abandonment: Northern Ireland	285
Tribunals & inquiries: Courts & tribunals: Fees: England & Wales	11, 27, 46, 51, 70, 72, 188, 195, 202
Tribunals & inquiries: First-tier & Upper tribunals: Chambers	202
Tribunals & inquiries: First-tier tribunal: Immigration & asylum chamber: Rules	202
Tribunals & inquiries: First-tier tribunal: Property chamber: Fees	202
Tribunals & inquiries: Judicial appointments: England & Wales	63, 202
Tribunals & inquiries: Scottish tax tribunals: Scotland	267
Tribunals & inquiries: Security: Rules	202
Tribunals & inquiries: Tribunal procedure: Rules	202
Tribunals & inquiries: Tribunals: Functions: Transfers	202
Tribunals & inquiries: Upper tribunal: Immigration & asylum chamber: Judicial review	203
Tribunals (Scotland) Act 2014: Commencements: Scotland	267
Tribunals, Courts & Enforcement Act 2007: Commencements	202
Tribunals, Courts & Enforcement Act 2007: Consequential, transitional & saving provisions	42
Tribunals: Acts: Scotland	242
Tribunals: Acts: Explanatory notes: Scotland	242
Trunk roads: A1	93, 98, 99, 100, 101, 102, 129
Trunk roads: A1: Scotch Corner to Barton Connecting Roads	53
Trunk roads: A1/A1(M)	94, 95, 97, 98
Trunk roads: A1/A14	93, 99
Trunk roads: A1/A19	98
Trunk roads: A1/A46	94
Trunk roads: A1/A47	125
Trunk roads: A1/A52	94
Trunk roads: A10/A47	125
Trunk roads: A10/M1/M25	160

Trunk roads: A1033. . . . . 141, 142
Trunk roads: A1089 142
Trunk roads: A1089/A13. 108
Trunk roads: A1089/A13/M25 108
Trunk roads: A11. 107
Trunk roads: A11/A14 . . . . 107, 109
Trunk roads: A11/A14/A428 109
Trunk roads: A11/A47 126
Trunk roads: A11/M11. 158
Trunk roads: A12 . . . . 107, 108
Trunk roads: A12/A120 . . . . 107, 108
Trunk roads: A120 . . . . 93, 134
Trunk roads: A120/A12 . . . . 107, 108
Trunk roads: A13 . . . . 93, 108, 109
Trunk roads: A13/A1089 108
Trunk roads: A13/A1089/M25 108
Trunk roads: A138: Replacement Chelmer Viaduct: Trunking 54
Trunk roads: A14 . . . . 93, 109, 110
Trunk roads: A14/A1 . . . . 93, 99
Trunk roads: A14/A1(M) 95
Trunk roads: A14/A11 . . . . 107, 109
Trunk roads: A14/A19 98
Trunk roads: A14/A428/A11 109
Trunk roads: A14/A428/M11 109
Trunk roads: A14/A45 122
Trunk roads: A14/M1/M6 142
Trunk roads: A160 134
Trunk roads: A168 134
Trunk roads: A174 135
Trunk roads: A174/A19 110
Trunk roads: A180 135
Trunk roads: A180/M180. 135
Trunk roads: A184/A194(M) 135
Trunk roads: A19 . . . . 110, 111
Trunk roads: A19/A1 98
Trunk roads: A19/A14 98
Trunk roads: A19/A174 110
Trunk roads: A2 . . . . 102, 103, 173
Trunk roads: A2/A20/A282/M20/M25 102
Trunk roads: A2/A282/M25 160
Trunk roads: A2/M2 147
Trunk roads: A20. 111
Trunk roads: A20/M20 159
Trunk roads: A20/M25/M20 160
Trunk roads: A2070 . . . . 94, 142
Trunk roads: A21. . . . . 55, 112
Trunk roads: A21/M25 112
Trunk roads: A23 . . . . 93, 112, 113
Trunk roads: A23/A27 112
Trunk roads: A23/M23 112
Trunk roads: A249 135
Trunk roads: A259 . . . . 135, 136
Trunk roads: A259/A27 113
Trunk roads: A27 . . . . 113, 114
Trunk roads: A27/A23 112
Trunk roads: A27/A259 113
Trunk roads: A282 . . . . 94, 136
Trunk roads: A282/A2/M25 160
Trunk roads: A282/M25. . . . . 160, 161
Trunk roads: A3. . . . . 103, 104
Trunk roads: A3/A3(M). 103
Trunk roads: A3/A30/M25/A308 103
Trunk roads: A30 . . . . 114, 115, 116
Trunk roads: A30/A38 119
Trunk roads: A30/A38/M5 118
Trunk roads: A30/M25/A308/A3 103
Trunk roads: A30/M6. 160
Trunk roads: A303 . . . . 136, 137
Trunk roads: A308/A3/A30/M25 103
Trunk roads: A31. 116
Trunk roads: A31/M27 116
Trunk roads: A316/M3 147
Trunk roads: A34 . . . . 116, 117
Trunk roads: A34/M4. 148
Trunk roads: A34/M40 117
Trunk roads: A34: Chilton interchange. 54
Trunk roads: A35 . . . . 93, 117, 118
Trunk roads: A36. 118

Trunk roads: A38	93, 118, 119, 120
Trunk roads: A38/A30	119
Trunk roads: A38/A30/M5	118
Trunk roads: A38/A5/M6	104
Trunk roads: A38/A516	118
Trunk roads: A38: Plymouth Parkway slip roads: Trunking & detrunking	54
Trunk roads: A4	186
Trunk roads: A40	120, 121, 175, 176
Trunk roads: A40/A449	175
Trunk roads: A40/A449/M4/M48	185
Trunk roads: A40/A470	174
Trunk roads: A40/A48	177
Trunk roads: A40/M25	160
Trunk roads: A40/M50	120
Trunk roads: A404/A404(M)	137
Trunk roads: A4042	185
Trunk roads: A405	137
Trunk roads: A406	137
Trunk roads: A4076	185
Trunk roads: A417	137
Trunk roads: A417/A419	137
Trunk roads: A419	137
Trunk roads: A419/A417	137
Trunk roads: A42	121
Trunk roads: A42/M1	142
Trunk roads: A421	137, 138
Trunk roads: A421/M1	143
Trunk roads: A423/A45	122
Trunk roads: A428	94, 138
Trunk roads: A428/A11/A14	109
Trunk roads: A428/A14/M11	109
Trunk roads: A43	121, 122
Trunk roads: A43/A5	104, 121
Trunk roads: A43/M1	143
Trunk roads: A43/M40	121
Trunk roads: A44	176, 177
Trunk roads: A446	138
Trunk roads: A446/A452	138
Trunk roads: A449	138, 179
Trunk roads: A449/A40	175
Trunk roads: A449/A40/M4/M48	185
Trunk roads: A449/A5/M6/M54	155
Trunk roads: A449/M50	138
Trunk roads: A449/M54	166
Trunk roads: A45	122, 123
Trunk roads: A45/A14	122
Trunk roads: A45/A423	122
Trunk roads: A45/A452	122
Trunk roads: A45/M42	163
Trunk roads: A4510	142
Trunk roads: A452/A446	138
Trunk roads: A452/A45	122
Trunk roads: A453	138
Trunk roads: A453/A50/M1	143
Trunk roads: A458	138, 179
Trunk roads: A46	93, 123, 124, 125
Trunk roads: A46/A1	94
Trunk roads: A46/M1	143
Trunk roads: A46/M5	150
Trunk roads: A465	55, 179, 180
Trunk roads: A47	125, 126
Trunk roads: A47/A1	125
Trunk roads: A47/A10	125
Trunk roads: A47/A11	126
Trunk roads: A47: Poswick interchange slip roads	54
Trunk roads: A470	138, 174, 180, 181
Trunk roads: A470/A40	174
Trunk roads: A477	181
Trunk roads: A479	181
Trunk roads: A48/A40	177
Trunk roads: A4810	185
Trunk roads: A483	138, 174, 181, 182
Trunk roads: A483/A5	104
Trunk roads: A483/A55	129
Trunk roads: A487	138, 174, 182, 183
Trunk roads: A489	183
Trunk roads: A49	93, 126, 127
Trunk roads: A494	138, 184, 185

Trunk roads: A494/A5	175
Trunk roads: A494/A55	177, 183
Trunk roads: A494/A550	177, 184
Trunk roads: A494/A550/A55	177
Trunk roads: A494/M56/M53	167
Trunk roads: A5	93, 104, 105, 106, 107, 173, 175
Trunk roads: A5/A38/M6	104
Trunk roads: A5/A43	104, 121
Trunk roads: A5/A449/M6/M54	155
Trunk roads: A5/A483	104
Trunk roads: A5/A494	175
Trunk roads: A5/A5148	104
Trunk roads: A5/M1: Link Dunstable Northern bypass connecting roads	54
Trunk roads: A5/M1: Link Dunstable Northern bypass detrunking	53
Trunk roads: A5/M42	122, 163
Trunk roads: A5: A5 - M1 Link Dunstable Northern Bypass	54
Trunk roads: A50	127, 128
Trunk roads: A50/A453/M1	143
Trunk roads: A50/A500	127
Trunk roads: A50/A56/A556	139
Trunk roads: A50/M1	127
Trunk roads: A500	138, 139
Trunk roads: A500/A50	127
Trunk roads: A500/A527	94
Trunk roads: A5034/A56/M56/A556	139
Trunk roads: A5036	142
Trunk roads: A5103	142
Trunk roads: A5103/M56	166
Trunk roads: A5111	142
Trunk roads: A5111/A52	128, 142
Trunk roads: A5111/A6	107
Trunk roads: A5148/A5	104
Trunk roads: A516/A38	118
Trunk roads: A52	128, 129
Trunk roads: A52/A1	94
Trunk roads: A52/A5111	128, 142
Trunk roads: A52/M1	128
Trunk roads: A523: Hazel Grove diversion: Revocation	54
Trunk roads: A527/A500	94
Trunk roads: A55	129, 130, 177, 178, 179
Trunk roads: A55/A483	129
Trunk roads: A55/A494	177, 183
Trunk roads: A55/A494/A550	177
Trunk roads: A550/A494	177, 184
Trunk roads: A550/A55/A494	177
Trunk roads: A556/A5034/A56/M56	139
Trunk roads: A556/A56/A50	139
Trunk roads: A56/A50/A556	139
Trunk roads: A56/M56/ A556/A5034	139
Trunk roads: A56/M65	130
Trunk roads: A56/M66	130, 172
Trunk roads: A57	130
Trunk roads: A57/M60/M67	168, 172
Trunk roads: A580/A666/M61	169
Trunk roads: A585	139
Trunk roads: A590	94, 139, 140
Trunk roads: A590/M6	154
Trunk roads: A595	94, 140, 141
Trunk roads: A6/A5111	107
Trunk roads: A6: Hazel Grove diversion	54
Trunk roads: A6055: A1(M) Junction 51, Leeming Interchange	173
Trunk roads: A616	141
Trunk roads: A627	141
Trunk roads: A628	141
Trunk roads: A63	130, 131
Trunk roads: A63/M1	143
Trunk roads: A638	141
Trunk roads: A64	131
Trunk roads: A64/A1(M)	94
Trunk roads: A66	131, 132, 133, 134
Trunk roads: A66/A66(M)	131
Trunk roads: A66: Scotch Corner Junction to Violet Grange Farm	54
Trunk roads: A666/A580/M61	169
Trunk roads: A68: Scotland	259
Trunk roads: A69	134
Trunk roads: A7: Scotland	259
Trunk roads: A725/M73/M74: Scotland	261
Trunk roads: A75: Scotland	259

Trunk roads: A78: Scotland . . . 259
Trunk roads: A8/M8: Scotland . . . 260
Trunk roads: A8: Scotland . . . 259
Trunk roads: A82/A9: Scotland . . . 259
Trunk roads: A82/M898/A898: Scotland . . . 259, 261
Trunk roads: A82: Scotland . . . 258, 259, 260, 263
Trunk roads: A83: Scotland . . . 260
Trunk roads: A84: Scotland . . . 260
Trunk roads: A85: Scotland . . . 260
Trunk roads: A887: Scotland . . . 259
Trunk roads: A898/A82/M898: Scotland . . . 259, 261
Trunk roads: A9/A82: Scotland . . . 259
Trunk roads: A9/M9: HGV speed limit: Scotland . . . 258
Trunk roads: A9/M9: Scotland . . . 260, 261
Trunk roads: A9/M90/A90/M9: Scotland . . . 260
Trunk roads: A9: Scotland . . . 258, 259
Trunk roads: A90/M9/A9/M90: Scotland . . . 260
Trunk roads: A90/M90/A823(M): Scotland . . . 261
Trunk roads: A90/M90: Scotland . . . 261
Trunk roads: A90: Scotland . . . 260
Trunk roads: A92/A972/B969: Scotland . . . 260
Trunk roads: A92/A972: Scotland . . . 260
Trunk roads: A96: Scotland . . . 259, 260
Trunk roads: A972/A92/B969: Scotland . . . 260
Trunk roads: A99: Scotland . . . 259
Trunk roads: B969/A972/A92: Scotland . . . 260
Trunk roads: M1/T3: M1-M2 link: Northern Ireland . . . 285
Trunk roads: North east trunk roads area: Scotland . . . 261
Trunk roads: North west trunk roads area: Scotland . . . 261, 262
Trunk roads: South east trunk roads area: Scotland . . . 262, 263
Trunk roads: South west trunk roads area: Scotland . . . 263
Trustees powers: Acts . . . 4
Trustees powers: Acts: Explanatory notes . . . 6
Tuberculosis: Animal health: Scotland . . . 243
Tuberculosis: Animal health: Wales . . . 9
Tuberculosis: Deer & camelid: England . . . 9
Tuberculosis: England . . . 9
Turks & Caicos Islands: International tax: Enforcement . . . 12, 25, 60, 61, 203

U

U232 Aghafad Road (Rubble Road), Newtownstewart: Abandonment: Northern Ireland . . . 285
U6007 Meadowlands, Downpatrick: Abandonment: Northern Ireland . . . 285
Ukraine: European Union financial sanctions . . . 28, 29
Ukraine: Sanctions: Overseas territories . . . 78
Ulster Grand Prix Bike Week: Road races: Northern Ireland . . . 288
Ulster Rally: Road races: Northern Ireland . . . 288
Unit trusts: Unauthorised . . . 13, 26, 60
United Nations: Sanctions: Revocations . . . 203
Universal credit: Digital service . . . 194
Universal credit: Functions: Rent officers . . . 55
Universal credit: Miscellaneous amendments . . . 194
Universal credit: Supported accommodation . . . 191
Universal credit: Transitional provisions . . . 194
University of the Highlands & Islands: Assigned colleges: Scotland . . . 247
Uplands: Transitional payments . . . 8
Urban development corporations: Area & constitution: England . . . 203
Uruguay: International tax: Enforcement . . . 196
USA: Taxes: International compliance . . . 196
Uttlesford: Electoral changes . . . 69

V

Vale of Pickering Internal Drainage Board . . . 63
Vale of the White Horse: Electoral changes . . . 69
Valuation & rating: Exempted classes: Scotland . . . 257
Valuation Tribunal: Wales . . . 70
Valuation: Telecommunications, natural gas & water: Northern Ireland . . . 284
Value added tax . . . 203
Value Added Tax Act 1994: Section 55A: Specified goods & excepted supplies . . . 204
Value added tax: Drugs & medicines . . . 203
Value added tax: Financial services: Revenue & customs: Out of time reviews: Appeal provisions . . . 7, 20, 30, 47, 62, 63, 203
Value added tax: Imported goods: Relief . . . 203
Value added tax: International tax: Enforcement: Anguilla . . . 12, 25, 60, 61, 203
Value added tax: International tax: Enforcement: British Virgin Islands . . . 12, 25, 60, 61, 203
Value added tax: International tax: Enforcement: Turks & Caicos Islands . . . 12, 25, 60, 61, 203
Value added tax: Refund . . . 203
Value added tax: Refunds: Museums & galleries . . . 203

Value added tax: Registration limits: Increases 203
Value added tax: Sport 204
Value added tax: Supply of services: Relevant business person: Supplies not made 203
Value added tax: Taxes: Charities: Definition: Relevant territories 9, 13, 26, 60, 61, 195, 203
Vegetable plant material: Marketing: Scotland 255
Vegetable plant material: Nomenclature changes 8, 82, 187
Vegetable plant material: Nomenclature changes: Wales 187
Vehicle & Operator Services Agency: Driving Standards Agency: Merger 62, 85, 92
Vehicle & Operator Services Agency: Driving Standards Agency: Merger: Consequential amendments 92
Vehicle drivers: Professional competence: Certificates: Amendments 93
Vehicles: Driving licences 93
Vehicles: Excise & registration 93
Vehicles: Goods vehicles: Operators: Licensing: Fees 92
Vehicles: Goods vehicles: Plating & testing: Amendments 92
Vehicles: Motor vehicles: Construction & use: Northern Ireland 286
Vehicles: Motor vehicles: Driving licences 92
Vehicles: Motor vehicles: Taxi drivers: Licences: Northern Ireland 289
Vehicles: Motor vehicles: Tests: Amendments 92
Vehicles: Passenger & goods vehicles: Recording equipment: Tachograph card: Fees 92
Vehicles: Public service vehicles: Operators' licences: Fees 86
Vehicles: Public service vehicles: Traffic Commissioners: Publication & inquiries 86
Vehicles: Removal & disposal: Wales 174
Vehicles: Road vehicles: Registration & licensing: Amendments 93
Vehicles: Road: Registration & licensing 93
Venture capital trusts 60
Verne: Prisons: Closures: England & Wales 84
Veterinary medicines 72
Veterinary surgeons & practitioners: Registration: Amendments 204
Victims & Witnesses (Scotland) Act 2014: Commencements: Scotland 246, 254
Victims & witnesses: Acts: Explanatory notes: Scotland 242
Victims & witnesses: Acts: Scotland 242
Victims & witnesses: Prescribed relatives: Scotland 246
Video games: Cultural test: Corporation tax 25
Video Recordings Act 1984: Video works: Exempted 204
Visas: Passenger transit: Immigration 58
Vulnerable persons: Protection of Vulnerable Groups (Scotland) Act 2007: Miscellaneous provisions: Scotland 245

W

Wales Rally GB: Air navigation: Flying restrictions 19
Wales: Acts 5
Wales: Acts: Explanatory notes 6
Wales: European Parliamentary elections: Welsh forms 90
Wales: National Assembly for Wales: Welsh language: Measures 296
Walney extension offshore wind farm 61
Walsall Metropolitan Borough Council: York's Bridge replacement scheme 55
Warm home discount 40, 51
Warrington Borough Council: Permit schemes: Traffic management 54
Warwick: Electoral changes 69
Warwickshire County Council: Permit schemes: Traffic management 54
Waste electrical & electronic equipment: Hazardous substances: Use: Restriction 42
Waste management: Landfill: Acts: Explanatory notes: Scotland 242
Waste management: Landfill: Acts: Scotland 241
Waste management: Licensing: Northern Ireland 277
Waste: Controlled waste & duty of care: Northern Ireland 277
Waste: Controlled waste: Fixed penalty notices: Scotland 248
Waste: Electrical & electronic equipment: Charges: Northern Ireland 277
Waste: England & Wales 43
Waste: Landfill tax 63
Waste: Packaging waste: Producer responsibility & obligations 42
Waste: Transfrontier shipments 30, 42
Water & sewerage services: Dwellings: Unmetered charges: Collection: Local authorities: Scotland 267
Water Act 2003: Commencements 204
Water Act 2014: Commencements 62, 204
Water industry: Non-owner occupiers 204
Water industry: South West Water Authority: Dissolution 204
Water industry: Supply: Acts 5
Water industry: Supply: Acts: Explanatory notes 6
Water resources: Bathing water 204
Water supply: Public water supplies: Scotland 267
Water supply: Reservoirs (Scotland) Act 2011: Commencements: Scotland 249, 267
Water supply: Water & sewerage services: Dwellings: Unmetered charges: Collection: Local authorities: Scotland 267
Water: Nitrate vulnerable zones: Designation: Scotland 267
Water: Valuation: Northern Ireland 284
Weights & measures: Food 204
Welfare benefits: Up-rating 194, 198
Welfare guardians: Adults incapacity: Supervision: Local authorities: Scotland 242
Welfare Reform Act 2012: Commencements 45, 194

Well-being: Acts: Wales 296
Wellingborough: Electoral changes 69
Welsh language: Wales: Measures 296
West Berkshire Council: Permit schemes: Traffic management 55
West Midlands Integrated Transport Authority: Members: Decrease in number 202
West Northamptonshire Development Corporation: Dissolution. 203
West Northamptonshire Development Corporation: Transfer of property etc 203
West Yorkshire Combined Authority 69, 202
Westlink: Busways: Northern Ireland 285, 289
Wildlife & Countryside Act 1981: Invasive non-native plants: Prohibition on sale, etc. 204
Willington C Gas Pipeline 61
Winter fuel payments: Social fund 192
Wireless telegraphy: Exemption 40
Wireless telegraphy: Licence charges 40
Wireless telegraphy: Licences: Limitation of number 40
Wireless telegraphy: Mobile communication services on aircraft: Exemptions 40
Wokingham Borough Council: Permit schemes: Traffic management 55
Work flexibly: Reasonable requests: Code of practice 197
Workers' compensation: Claims: Payments: Pneumoconiosis etc. 192
Workers' compensation: Pneumoconiosis etc.: Claims: Payments: Northern Ireland 290
Working tax credit see also Tax credits 196
Working tax credit: Exercise of functions 196
Working tax credit: Late appeals 196
Working tax credit: Up-rating 196
World Cup: Football spectators: 2014 control period 195
Wrecks: Protection: Designation: England 85
Wyre: Electoral changes 69

Y

Yemen: European Union financial sanctions 29
York: Electoral changes 69
York's Bridge replacement scheme 55
Young offender institutions 84, 204
Young offender institutions: Prisons: Scotland 256
Youth detention accommodation: Remand: Recovery of costs 30

Z

Zambia: Double taxation: Relief & international enforcement 12, 25, 59
Zimbabwe: European Communities: Financial sanctions 29
Zoonoses: Fees: Northern Ireland 274